MW00445185
CENTER
CHICAGO BLACKHAWKS
0
comcast
TOYOTA
OPEN UP A WORLD OF TASTE.
Budweiser
BUD LIGHT
Choose Blue.
$260 MILLION
xfinity
PROGRESSIVE
State Farm
MODELL'S SPORTING GOODS
GEICO
STANLEY CUP FINAL

Jimmy
Merry Christmas.

The PHILADELPHIA FLYERS at...

An official publication of the Philadelphia Flyers hockey club

To Ed,
Your Flyers became big
because
no person was too small.

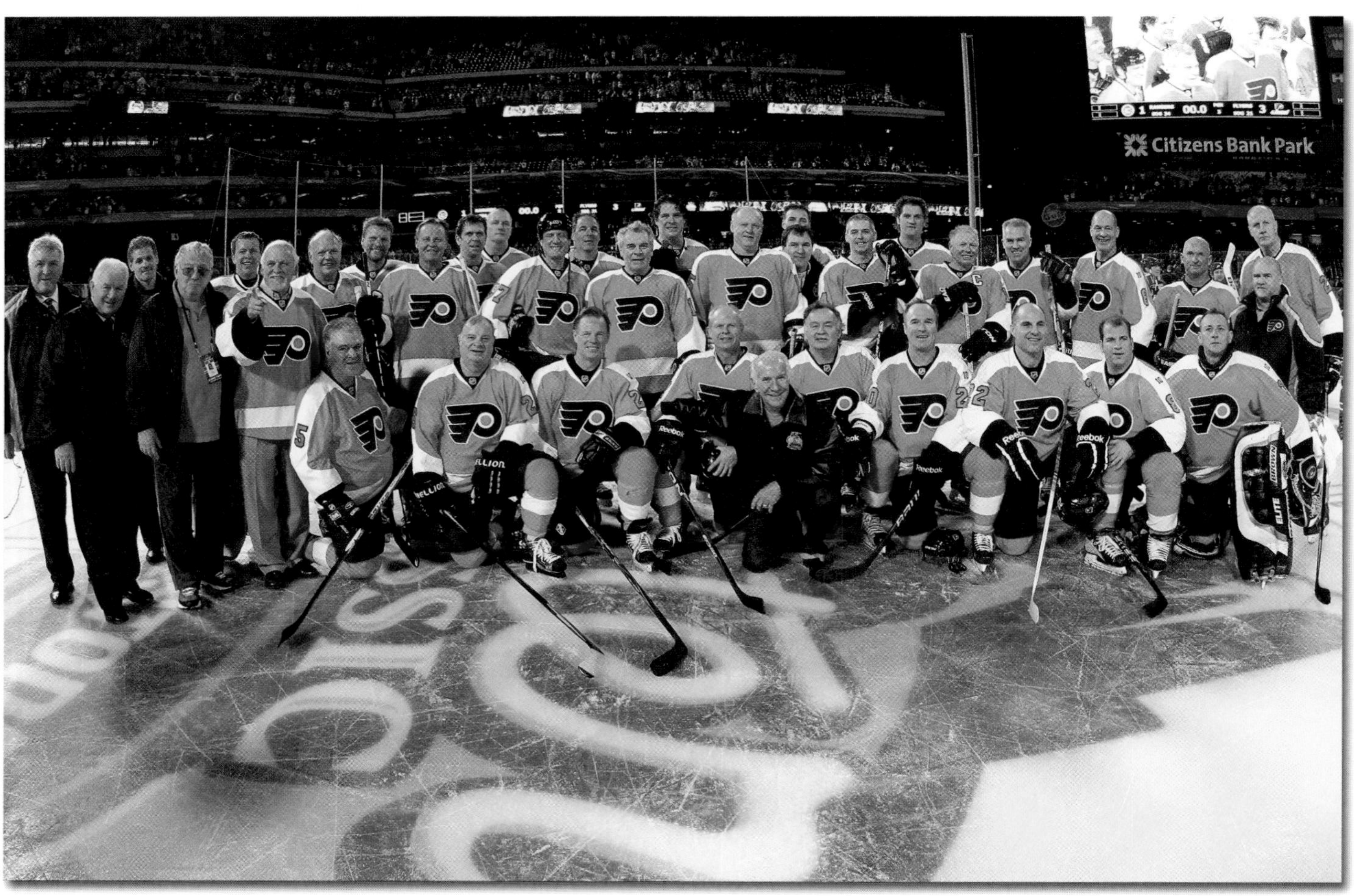

Players from every era of Flyer history wore the orange-and-black for a Legends Game vs. the New York Rangers that was part of the NHL Winter Classic on December 31, 2011. A crowd of 45,808 filled Citizens Bank Park.

Front, center: *Ed Snider.*

Left to right, front row, *Larry Goodenough, Orest Kindrachuk, Brian Propp, Mark Howe, Reggie Leach, Dave Poulin, Rick Tocchet, Mark Recchi, Mark LaForest.*

Middle row: *Terry Crisp, Mike Nykoluk, Bernie Parent, Bill Barber, Jeremy Roenick, Joe Watson, Al Hill, Jim Dowd, Bob Clarke, Dave Settlemyre.*

Back row: *Pat Quinn, Ron Hextall, Neil Little, Bob Kelly, Shjon Podein, Eric Desjardins, Terry Carkner, John LeClair, Chris Therien, Keith Primeau, Eric Lindros, Derian Hatcher, Jim Watson, Brad Marsh, Ken Linseman, Kjell Samuelsson.*

The PHILADELPHIA FLYERS at...

THE STORY OF THE ICONIC HOCKEY CLUB AND ITS TOP 50 HEROES, WINS & EVENTS

JAY GREENBERG

WITH A MESSAGE FROM ED SNIDER

The first installment in the history of the Philadelphia Flyers is described in the book *Full Spectrum*, published in 1996.

Like this book, it is written by Jay Greenberg and celebrates the teams, players and events that made the club's first arena one of the most exciting buildings in hockey.

To obtain a pdf version of *Full Spectrum* please email a request to: FullSpectrum1967@gmail.com

ISBN 978-1-62937-369-0

Trade edition published by: Triumph Books 312-337-0747 www.triumphbooks.com

Staff and Contributors

For the Philadelphia Flyers: Brian McBride, Joe Siville, Brian Smith

Editors: Mona Greenberg and John Moritsugu

Contributing Editors: Alan Bass, Dave Isaac, Bill Meltzer, Jeff Neiburg, Ray Parrillo, Ronnie Shuker, David Strehle

Fact Checking: Bill Meltzer, Alex Samuelsson, Jordan Sprechman

Interview Transcribers: Blake Allen, Gabriella Baldassin, Melissa Bektel-Seidel, Tyler Booker, Gail Cohen, Maddy Cohen, Rick Cohen, Meridith Daniel, Nicki Eisenberg, Joy Epstein, Olivia Gomez, Ell Herbine, Joe Kadlec Jr., Kenny Kang, Evan Kashan, Sara Lamachia, Jenny Marlowe, Nancy Mastrola, Bill Meltzer, Randy Miller, Kristin Moore, Karen Moran, John Morath, Bridget Nolan, Ray Parrillo, Chase Rogers, Judy Romano, Kimberly Sikora, Mary Lou Townsley, Victoria Wilkinson.

Printed in the United States of America by LSC Communications, Kendallville, Indiana

Design and Production Management: Dan Diamond and Associates, Inc. Toronto, Ontario, Canada

Photo Credits: see page 583

Author Jay Greenberg can be reached at Flyersat50@gmail.com.

Table of Contents

Chapter		Season	Page
	A Message from Ed Snider		1
	Ranked List of Top 50 Flyer Heroes		3
1	The Next Great Memory Is Just Around the Corner		4
	Top 50 Flyer Heroes, Part 1		13
2	Shiny, New and Swept	1996-97	66
	Top 50 Flyer Heroes, Part 2		89
3	Coats Off the Rack	1997-99	94
4	"What Else Can Happen?"	1999-2000	128
	Top 50 Flyer Heroes, Part 3		169
5	Czech In, Cech Out	2000-02	178
6	Getting Hitched	2002-03	214
	Top 50 Flyer Heroes, Part 4		245
7	"It Should Have Been Us."	2003-04	250
	Top 50 Flyer Heroes, Part 5		290
8	Peter (Rabbit) Out of a Hat	2004-06	294
9	The Season from Hell	2006-07	326
	Top 50 Flyer Heroes, Part 6		351
10	With a Vengeance	2007-08	354
11	In the Pitts of Their Stomachs	2008-09	388
12	From 3–0 Down	2009-10	404
	Top 50 Flyer Heroes, Part 7		446
13	Glove Triangle	2010-11	454
14	"Watch This First Shift."	2011-13	474
	Top 50 Flyer Heroes, Part 8		504
15	The Guarantee	2013-14	510
	Top 50 Flyer Heroes, Part 9		526
16	The Long-Term Plan	2014-15	532
17	Good Night, Good Hockey, Good Life	2015-16	544
	Top 50 Flyer Heroes, Part 10		566
18	The Next 50 Years – Onward and Upward	2016-	568
	All-Time Top 50 Flyer Wins and Events		572
	In Memorium		580
	Acknowledgements and Photo Credits		582
	Index		584

Flyer Chairman Ed Snider
passed away on April 11, 2016.
He is seen here celebrating a Stanley Cup win
with captain Bobby Clarke

A MESSAGE FROM ED SNIDER

CONSIDERING THAT MANY SKEPTICS DID NOT EXPECT THE FLYERS TO LAST even one year, 50 is quite the milestone. We were the only one of six new franchises placed in a city with no sustained record of support for minor-league hockey. Bank after bank turned us down for financing. We had to pay to get our games on radio. And then, just when we were starting to draw, seven home gates were lost after the roof of the Spectrum was damaged by winds.

But I never required a marketing survey to tell me that the fourth-largest city in the United States needed a modern arena and that people would come to watch an exciting major-league sport. I was young, full of energy, and never doubted we could make this work.

The Flyers won Stanley Cups in our seventh and eighth seasons, which of course, is the franchise's core accomplishment, because once I made Keith Allen the general manager midway through the third year, we were in it to win it. We have put so much effort, money and heartbreak into becoming champions again and so often came up just short, this celebration of the organization's longevity helps sore losers like me to frame all our successes.

Going back to our first winning season, 1972-73, the Flyers are tied with the Canadiens for the most Stanley Cup Final berths (eight) and our 16 trips to the semifinals are the most of any team. Even since the last championship in 1975, only Montreal has a higher regular-season percentage of points won and no team has had more semifinal appearances (13) than ours.

Because there are now 30 clubs—14 more than when we won the first Cup—that are loaded with outstanding executives and coaches, our sustained track record has kept me proud while trying to figure out who has been sticking pins in the Flyer doll. It's been six trips to the Final since last winning. You would think we should have lucked into at least one more title by now.

I believe the 1975-76 team was even better than our Cup winners and that, had we not lost Rick MacLeish and Bernie Parent before the Final against a great Montreal club, we would have won at least one more championship. In November 1985, I remember leaving the Spectrum after a 10th straight win saying "this is the best team we ever have had," and then getting the call the next morning that Pelle Lindbergh had been in a car accident.

In 1980, there was an offside goal and another that should have been waived off for a high stick during a Game Six we lost in overtime. In 1987, outmanned by six eventual Hall of Famers to one, we still took Edmonton to Game Seven. Don't you think having Tim Kerr, our 54-goal scorer, in that final might have made the difference?

So much of our defense was wiped out with injuries when we lost in Game Seven of the conference final in 2004. In 2010, the same goalie who had three shutouts in the conference final against Montreal gave up a Cup-winning goal to Chicago that nobody saw.

We always have made every decision in the context of the question: Will it put us closer to winning the Stanley Cup? So when we don't succeed, it's frustrating. But, that said, some of our proudest moments have been in years we barely missed. And our response to disasters has been inspiring.

We came up with Ron Hextall a year after losing Lindbergh and got back to the Final. We played for the conference title in 2008, the very next season after we suddenly sank to the bottom of the league. We have been a contender in most eras, under two different league economic models, doing it with great stars, most of them fueled by a work ethic so synonymous with the franchise that when you talk about a player being a "Flyer," it is not just an affiliation but a recommendation.

I always have had a great respect for our players. I've watched them break bones, lose teeth, have their eyesight compromised for life and had their careers sacrificed. It's not always glamorous, but they bust their butts for themselves first, but also for the Flyers and Philadelphia. I don't ever forget that.

I also never have taken our fans for granted. With each reluctant ticket price increase, I have worried about our corporate customers eventually outnumbering the diehards who have given us such a home ice advantage. But that hasn't happened, much to my gratitude.

We still have season ticket holders from our first season. The fans came back after three long work stoppages. The loyalty has been overwhelming, and I'd like to believe we have returned it by placing the customer first, starting with putting competitive teams on the ice year after year.

Of course, there are mistakes we've made and regrets I have. But for a fan base that has stuck with us through our few bad times, we have always bounced back by maintaining core values that will outlive me, just like our logo known all over the world. Our sustained success has made us as tradition-bound as franchises that preceded the Flyers by as many as 50 years.

That is why this celebration of our first 50 is such a proud time. They wouldn't have been memorable without your support.

Thank you.

Ed Snider
March 2016

RANKED LIST OF TOP 50 FLYER HEROES

Rank		Page
1	Ed Snider	13
2	Bobby Clarke	17
3	Keith Allen	21
4	Bernie Parent	24
5	Bill Barber	25
6	Fred Shero	26
7	Mark Howe	28
8	Paul Holmgren	351
9	Ron Hextall	526
10	Eric Lindros	89
11	Gene Hart	169
12	Rick MacLeish	31
13	Brian Propp	32
14	Tim Kerr	33
15	John LeClair	171
16	Claude Giroux	566
17	Gary Dornhoefer	35
18	Rick Tocchet	174
19	Dave Poulin	36
20	Mike Keenan	38
21	Eric Desjardins	92
22	Simon Gagne	446
23	Kimmo Timonen	528
24	Joe Watson	41
25	Jimmy Watson	42
26	Ed Van Impe	43
27	Barry Ashbee	44
28	Jerry Melnyk	45
29	Rod Brind'Amour	176
30	Mike Richards	504
31	Reggie Leach	48
32	Mark Recchi	245
33	Danny Briere	448
34	Keith Primeau	290
35	Brad Marsh	49
36	Pelle Lindbergh	51
37	Pat Quinn	52
38	Wayne Simmonds	506
39	Joe Scott	54
40	Terry Murray	56
41	Ken Hitchcock	247
42	Jake Voracek	530
43	Dave Schultz	59
44	Jeremy Roenick	292
45	Chris Pronger	450
46	Andre Dupont	60
47	Peter Laviolette	452
48	Ron Sutter	61
49	Scott Hartnell	508
50	Bob Kelly	64

Game One in The Spectrum

Chapter 1

The Next Great Memory is Just Around the Corner

The first time things looked dark for the Flyers, Ed Snider was at the bank when the lights went out. On June 5, 1967, with the $2 million franchise fee he and his partners desperately had cobbled together over the last few days due in Montreal by 2 p.m., Snider was in the midst of wiring the funds when a massive power outage hit Southeast Pennsylvania.

"I couldn't get through on the phone," recalled Snider. "After all we had been through, I was afraid they were going to give the franchise to somebody else."

He was able to transfer the money to the Canadian bank via one in New York. Team president Bill Putnam and vice president Lou Scheinfeld jumped the divider on Dorchester Street and raced the check to Clarence Campbell, the impatiently waiting NHL president.

In the next day's expansion draft, Bernie Parent became the first Flyer selected, but Snider had already made the franchise's first save. Resilience quickly became the new team's MO.

After dismal early attendance dramatically picked up with sellouts of back-to-back weekend games in February against Chicago and Toronto, winds tore holes in the roof of the Spectrum, putting the team on the road for the final 14 games of its inaugural season. Nevertheless, the Flyers outlasted the five other new clubs for the title of the West Division.

Before Year Three, the organization took a chance drafting a diabetic center, and against great odds, Bobby Clarke lasted 15 years, won three league Most Valuable Player Trophies and became a top-ten all-time player.

In 1971-72, with four seconds remaining in the last game, the Flyers were denied a playoff spot when they suffered a crushing goal from 45-feet out. But they recorded their first winning season the next year and, in 1973-74, overcame the injury absences of three regulars to upset the Boston Bruins in the Final and win the first of two consecutive Stanley Cups.

In 1979-80, one season after the presumably-declining Broad Street Bullies failed to reach the semifinal for the first time in seven years, a blend of old and new players went an astounding 35 games without losing, coming from behind in the third period six times.

During the summer of 1984, Clarke retired to become GM, Bill Barber's career ended with a knee reconstruction, and Darryl Sittler was traded. But the following spring, the youngest team in the league won the Presidents' Trophy and went to the Stanley Cup Final.

When goaltender Pelle Lindbergh died tragically the following fall in a car crash, the Flyers introduced Ron Hextall and went to the Final in 1987 for the second time in three years.

For the Stanley Cup against Edmonton that spring, it was six Oiler Hall of Famers to one—Mark Howe. Philadelphia was also without its 50-goal scorer, Tim Kerr. But after rallying from deficits of three goals (once) and two goals (twice), the Flyers were only one score away from overtime with three minutes remaining in Game Seven before losing 3-1.

"We expected that they weren't going to die," recalls Mark Messier, one of those Oiler greats. "I think that was built into their DNA and had been handed down over time.

"You have to understand that I watched the legendary Flyers all the way through the seventies. I could never get them out of my head. No matter where the Flyers were any year in the standings, I still had a lot of respect for their players because of how much a factor they were when I was growing up.

"They believed they could win (in 1985 and 1987) against a pretty imposing team led by Wayne Gretzky, the greatest player of all time. That says something about the character of those clubs."

Character starts at the top. Most of the hockey world thought team president Jay Snider was being petulant in his insistence that he had a deal with Quebec for Eric Lindros before owner Marcel Aubut took what he thought was a better one with the Rangers. But the Flyers filed a grievance, won a hard-fought arbitration and, with a roster rebuilt around one of the NHL's best prospects ever, surged from a fifth consecutive non-playoff season to the 1995 conference final in one year.

In 2000, coach Roger Neilson had to take a leave of absence for treatment of a deadly cancer before Lindros suffered another in a series of concussions and became alienated from the organization over medical treatment. The team made it to another conference final.

No wonder why, after the orange-and-black battleship capsized in a perfect storm during 2006-07 and shockingly sank to the bottom of the NHL, the Flyers still were able to recruit Kimmo Timonen, Danny Briere and Scott Hartnell that summer, just as if the 56-point season never had happened. "Free agents will come because of you," Peter Luukko, the Comcast-Spectacor CEO, had reassured Snider. They did, knowing the Philadelphia team could not be kept down.

The 2009-10 Flyers won a final-day shootout to sneak into the playoffs, then went to the Final, along the way becoming the third team in Stanley Cup history to come back from a 3-0 deficit to win a series.

In 2013-14, the club started 3-9-3 and made the playoffs, exactly like captain Claude Giroux had vowed during the worst of their struggles.

Last season, while a cancer-stricken Snider outlasted his life expectancy by more than a month, a team that won only five of its first 20 games compiled a .629 winning percentage after mid-November to make the playoffs 30 hours before their founder and Chairman took his last breath.

Flyer fans have learned they jump off the bandwagon at the risk of their eventual shame. From 1972-73, the season of emergence as a contender, the franchise is tied with the Montreal Canadiens for the most Stanley Cup Final berths (eight), and Philadelphia's 16 trips to the semifinals are the most of any team.

Even since the last Cup in 1975, only Montreal has a higher regular season percentage of points won and no team has had more semifinal appearances (13) than the Flyers.

That is an enormous amount of success ending in too much heartbreak. In his later years, Snider lamented, "In six trips to the Final, you would think we would get lucky at least once." Even the greats responsible for denying Snider another title shared his incredulity as injuries, bad bounces, a blatant linesman's mistake, and Montreal, Islander and Detroit dynasties conspired against Philadelphia's return to the throne.

"Game Seven in 1987 might have been the best one the Oilers ever played as a team," recalls Gretzky. "And we needed that kind of an effort because the Flyers were on a high. Those teams we beat [in 1985 and 1987] were good enough to win a Cup, maybe more than one in most eras. They had everything. It just shows you how hard it is to win.

"When the Flyers beat us (the Rangers in the conference final) in 1997, I really thought Mr. Snider was going to get his next one. That was as big and powerful a team as ever had been assembled. I was shocked it got handled (by Detroit) in the Final."

Shock would describe the reaction of many an in-coming Flyer to the level of scrutiny he must endure. Thirty seconds into a stumbling powerplay, you can hear the boos. But they are the same fans who in April 2016 gave the team a standing ovation in the aftermath of its Game Six 1-0 elimination by Washington, not forgetting Philadelphia had been down 3-0 in the series.

"You know the team is not going to win every year," says Shawn Hill, a long-time seat holder in the Wells Fargo Center's Section 219 of the upper deck before he became the third-period Dancin' Shawny and bubbly pregame host on the center-hung scoreboard. "But we can always see from the way the Flyers have gone about it that they are trying.

"The fans kept coming through the [2006-07 collapse] and, before that, the (1990-94) playoff drought because we believe the Flyers are going to make good for us. When they don't win, I truly think they feel bad about it and will try to correct their mistakes."

A resonant history: Preceding page: The Flyers' first home games were played before the clock was finished. Above: Goaltender Pelle Lindbergh won the Vezina Trophy for 1984-85. He died early the following season.

Brian Roberts, the CEO of Comcast, the majority owner of the team since 1995, recognized quickly that his broadcast giant had bought more than just some television programming.

'The Flyers' culture is as good as it gets, and I don't take that for granted," Roberts says. "It's about a lot more than just Ed Snider, but it's been the tone from the top. When we made the partnership, I was very quick to recognize how special this is.

"We're very lucky to be associated, very proud. The Flyers don't tolerate failure. They do the best they can."

Roberts has felt the need to supply only support, a practice he expects to continue under Dave Scott, who has been Comcast-Spectacor CEO since 2014.

"Everything evolves, but there haven't been seismic changes," says Shawn Tilger, the Flyers' chief operating officer. "Comcast has been nothing but the best partner through the whole process."

Such trust and backing enabled Snider to continue to function as he had as the majority owner, keeping the wins and the fans coming, followed by free agents who always have heard through the player grapevine how good it is be a Flyer. Some of the best and the brightest have jumped at opportunities to find out first hand what that is like.

"I came because I wanted to win and there never is a year the Flyers aren't going for it," recalls Luke Richardson, a defenseman from 1998-2002. In his case, as in the majority of Philadelphia signings, it was money well spent. There have been flops, sure, but 39 playoff spots in 48 seasons—and just the one multi-year drought as the Flyers tore up their roster to successfully rebuild around Lindros—testify to how well they have signed and traded through the years.

True, the organization's burning desire to rebound quickly has at

times contradicted the founding principles of patience and development. The salary cap dictates a return to those roots and general manager Ron Hextall, entering his third season, believes in that course. Nevertheless, a franchise that was resented by opponents in pre-cap days for its largess as much as for its fists still spends practically all the league allows because that's what the Flyers do.

"Because of the mindset, they're always in the mix," says Rick Tocchet, the Pittsburgh assistant coach who was an integral part of it in two successful stretches. "When you play for Philadelphia, you are here to win."

From the start, the driving force was the relentlessly ambitious Snider, who in Year Three put his complete trust in a creative and far-sighted first-time NHL general manager, Keith Allen. Their shared dream of championships was shaped by a mutual vision of a happy workplace.

"We were a leader in treating players and employees better than other clubs and all of it goes back to Snider," says Clarke. "Players wanted to play here. We were criticized for being the Bullies, but overall the organization was classy and competitive."

It had class because of Snider and grit largely due to Clarke—one of the most driven athletes in the history of sports before becoming a Flyer GM who produced three finalists and four additional semifinalists.

"Culture is a nebulous concept that I don't think people on the outside truly understand," says Dean Lombardi, who spent three seasons in Philadelphia as part of Clarke's brain trust and has since won two Stanley Cups as GM of the Los Angeles Kings.

"Success is not just about where you are in goals, goals against, and penalty minutes as opposed to a month ago or a year ago. It is not only about roster building in the short term or about the particulars of a certain coach's system. It comes from the mindset that it means something to be a Flyer, whether you are a player, coach, scout, equipment manager, or whatever.

"I don't care whether you like the Flyers or not. It means something to put that jersey on, to represent that organization. When I was fortunate enough to be able to take Ron Hextall with me to Los Angeles to be my assistant, we talked about that constantly. Any comparable sense for being a King, a franchise born the same year as the Flyers, didn't exist when we first got there.

"In Philadelphia, it's all about the team. That was very clear. If you want to see the veins pop out of Clarke's neck, get him talking about a situation where he thought someone was being selfish. Paul Holmgren is an important part of that culture. Hexy is, too. Anything not about the team is beyond intolerable. It is despised.

"Pride is a crucial element and so is tradition. When I came to my first Flyer training camp, all of these ex-players like Don Saleski and Bob Kelly were there. So was Joe Watson, passionate as ever. Seeing that guys who hadn't played in 25-30 years were still part of that identity, all those pictures on the walls, made a big impression on me."

Plenty more disciples of Flyer principles than just Lombardi and Hextall have gone forth and grandly succeeded: Mike Keenan, Terry

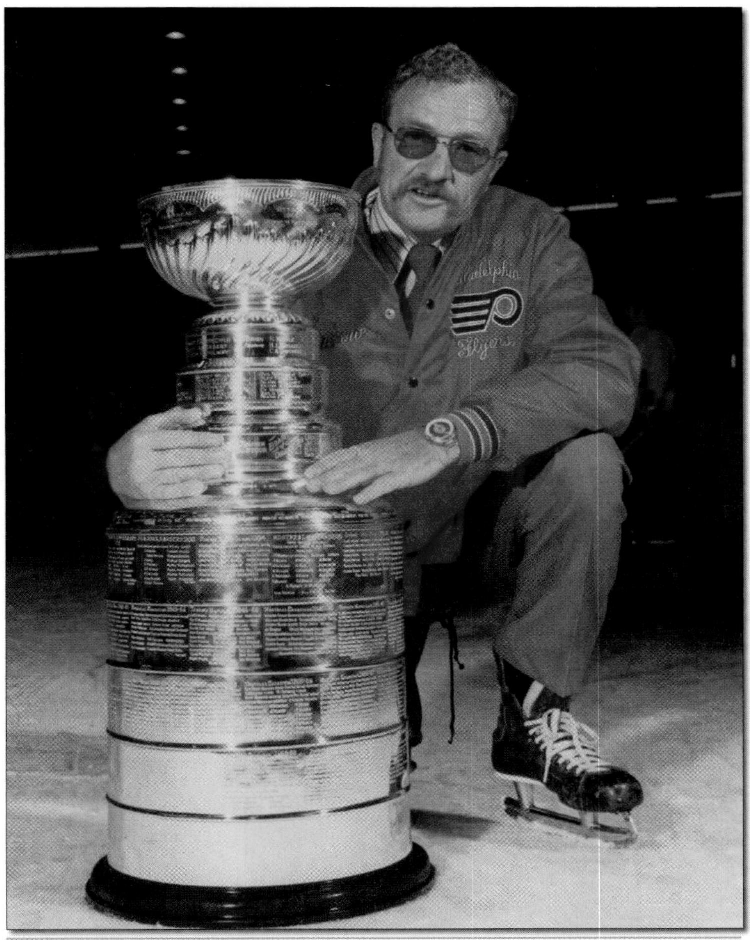

Kate Smith singing "God Bless America" became a Flyer talisman as did the musings of coach Fred Shero, seen here with the Cup his teams won in 1974 and 1975.

Crisp and Ken Hitchcock coached other NHL teams to Cups; Pat Quinn directed Canada to two Olympic gold medals; Ex-Philadelphia players like John Paddock, Dale Hawerchuk, Tocchet and Richardson abound on NHL, junior, and minor-league benches and in front offices.

"Here is the biggest testament I can give about what it meant to be a Flyer," says Robert Esche, the goaltender on the 2004 conference final club and, today, president of the Utica Comets of the American Hockey League: "Every decision that I make running a franchise, I think about in terms of, 'What would the Flyers do?'

"Every bit of success I've had since leaving Philadelphia is shaped by my time there. I'm excited when they do well. I want the best for them. The Flyers, to me, are the best."

That is because some of the all-time best have played and worked for them. Hall of Famers Bill Barber, Clarke, Parent, Howe and Eric Lindros spent either all or their prime years playing in Philadelphia. More Hall inductees—Darryl Sittler, Paul Coffey, Adam Oates, Peter Forsberg, Hawerchuk and the late Allan Stanley—honored the Orange-and-Black by wearing it near the end of their careers. Another Hall of Famer, Joe Mullen, is a current assistant coach.

Fred Shero, coach of the two Cup teams; Snider; and Allen are in the Hall as Builders, as are coaches Quinn and Roger Neilson. The late Gene Hart, the Flyers beloved voice from 1967 to 1995, was the 1997 winner of the Foster Hewitt Award, the Hall's honor for broadcasters.

Great men have brought the organization additional individual honors. The Flyers have won four Hart (NHL Most Valuable Player) Trophies, three by Clarke and one by Lindros; and four Jack Adams Coach of the Year Awards between Shero, Keenan, Quinn and Barber.

Two of Philadelphia's four Conn Smythe (playoff MVP) Trophies, won by Reggie Leach and Hextall, were awarded in years the Flyers did not win the Cup. And the other two, by Parent, came in seasons they couldn't have won without him.

Parent, the winner of two Vezina (best goaltender) Trophies, proudly presented another to his protege, Lindbergh, giving the Flyers that honor for a third time. Frank Selke (best defensive forward) Trophies have gone to Clarke and Dave Poulin and the Bill Masterton Trophy, presented to the NHL player defined by "perseverance, sportsmanship and dedication to the game" has been won by Clarke, Ian Laperriere, and Kerr.

No gleaming trophy was awarded to the Broad Street Bullies for defending the NHL's honor in 1976 by defeating the Soviet Red Army in

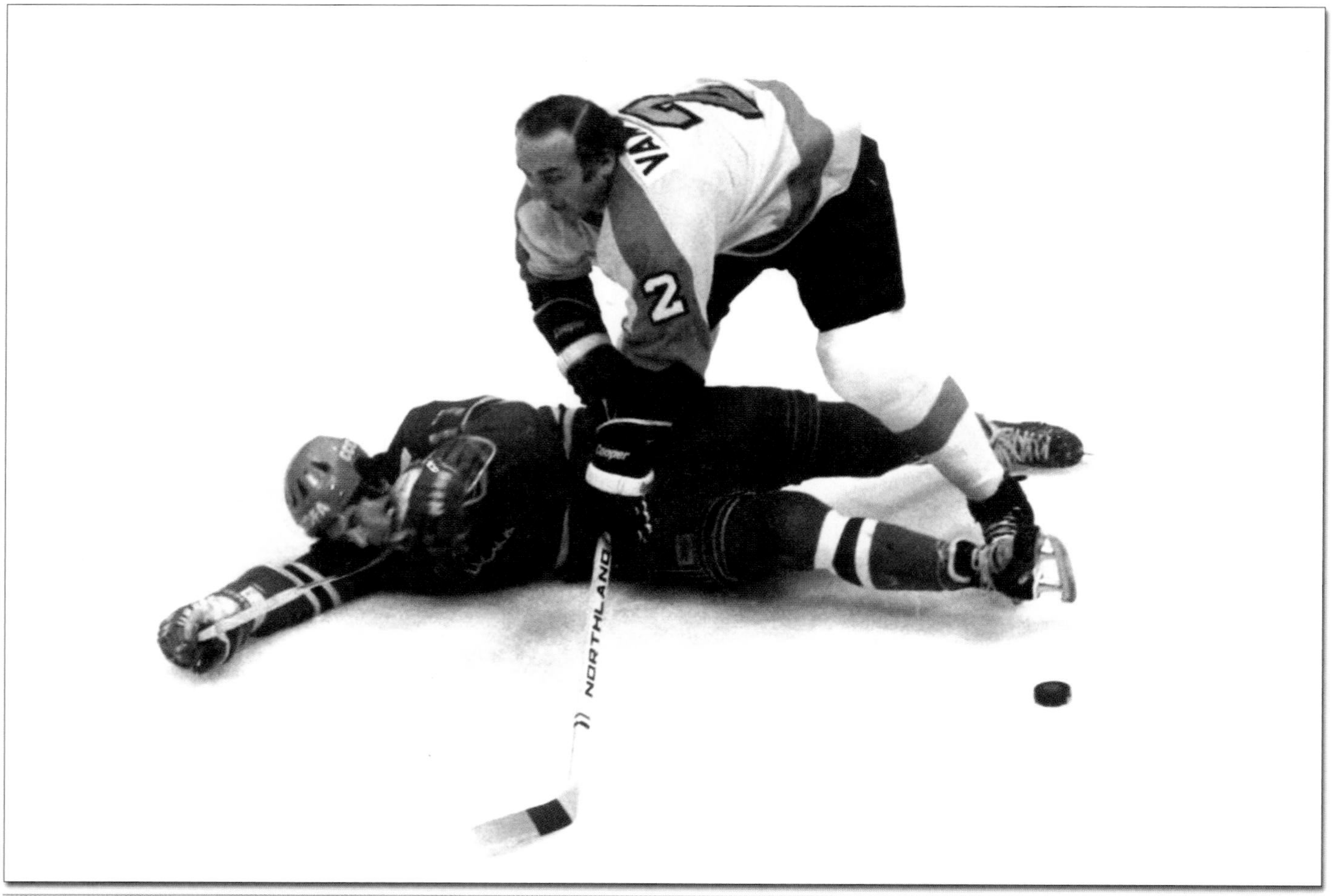

The Flyers were the only NHL club to defeat Soviet superclub Central Red Army in 1975-76.
Rox Hextall, facing page, became the first NHL goaltender to shoot the puck the length of the ice and score.

one of the most compelling and enmity-filled international sporting events in history. But the two-time defending champions honored themselves under searing pressure that January afternoon, winning arguably the biggest game in their history while adding another episode to the legend of the Spectrum as one of the darkest dens—literally and figuratively—in sporting history.

"Would someone please turn on the lights?" Gretzky remembers thinking practically every time he played there. "And we always thought they wanted the ice chippy to slow us down."

In truth, the ice plant was aging. But as 50 years have flown by, stories about the wondrous feats in franchise history never grow old.

The Flyers' 35-game unbeaten streak (25-0-10) in 1979-80 under Quinn is the longest in North American sports history. The 2009-10 club was one of five teams in the history of North American professional sports to have won a series they once trailed 3-0 and, in beating the Bruins, also came back from a 3-0 deficit in the finale.

Keith Primeau's goal in the fifth overtime won for Philadelphia the third-longest game in NHL history during a 2000 playoff against Pittsburgh. Hextall was the first NHL goalie ever to shoot and score a goal, and then became the first to do it in the playoffs.

That's a lot of glory for one franchise and, still, far from the extent of it. Some of the most valiant and painful Flyer losses have been almost as memorable as the team's greatest wins.

Philadelphia lost Stanley Cups in Game Six overtimes following third-period comebacks against the Islanders in 1980 and the Blackhawks in 2010. Arena-shaking Game Six goals by J.J. Daigneault in 1987 and Simon Gagne in 2004 enabled crippled and courageous Flyer teams to take it to Game Sevens.

Wrenching sorrows like the premature passings of Lindbergh, Barry Ashbee, and Dmitri Tertyshny have additionally bonded the club and their fans. Death has put the Flyers through far greater pain than ever can be inflicted on a scoreboard and run the players through tests of character far more challenging than any series deficits. Those teams lost family, but the show had to go on and be performed with courage because, even in hard times, teammates, coaches, management and the customers have had no tolerance for cowardice.

"Being a tough guy in Philly made me tougher than being a tough guy in a place like Florida or wherever," says Todd Fedoruk, a Flyer enforcer for five seasons. "It was because I had that crest on.

"I understood that right away, just because of the way the fans embraced me. They love fighting, love the excitement of it, love the reasoning behind it, and know it is a good part of the game if done right. They see sacrifice and worker mentality in it, just what this city is about.

"It was different when I did it in Anaheim. They liked it because it was entertainment. Here, it is done because something has been done to a teammate and somebody needs to take care of it.

"The fans don't demand everybody fights. But they do demand you put it out there every night because that is just what we do in Philly or you can't play here. Some players just don't understand that. They wonder, 'How can they be yelling at me?'"

They yell because they care. Sure, everybody loves a winner, but it didn't take a Stanley Cup for the Flyers to bond quickly to a city where the sport had repeatedly failed on a minor-league level. The third level of seats at the Spectrum was installed during the summer of 1972, before the first winning season.

Coming off the worst of the playoff disappointments, there have been short periods of a few hundred unsold seats. But since the 1996 opening of what is now the Wells Fargo Center, there has not been a year the Flyers failed to average over the listed capacity—you can always cram a few more into a suite—of the fourth-largest facility in the NHL.

Through cost-of-doing-business ticket price increases, the fans have been made to feel like the Flyers want them to come back.

"Mr. Snider understood that greed will kill you," says Tilger. "He always made sure we put the customer first. We have always asked, 'What is the right and fair thing to do?'

"Everything had been done to make sure we don't price people out. If you look at the way we scale our tickets, it is still affordable for families. We hold out anywhere from 1,000-to-1,500 group tickets a night because we feel it's important to get the casual fan to experience the sport. The Flyer Skate Zones get people to watch and participate in hockey, and have made it available to everyone."

Players necessarily have come and gone to keep the franchise winning. But the continuity goes well beyond the number of ex players—at present they are Clarke, Barber, Parent, Bob Kelly, Dave Schultz, Joe Watson, Danny Briere, Brian Propp, and Brad Marsh—who work for the team.

Lou Nolan began as the public address announcer in 1972. Steve Coates has been in the broadcast booth, the studio, or between the benches since 1980. Television play-by-play voice Jim Jackson is starting his 23rd year, nearing Gene Hart-level longevity. Not far behind is radio voice Tim Saunders, beginning his 19th season.

Lauren Hart became a regular performing "The Star-Spangled Banner" and "God Bless America" on the 1997 night the Flyers recognized her father's Hall of Fame honor.

All the while, the organization not only has taken care of its own, but others. The annual Flyers Wives Fight for Lives Carnival, a much-copied brainstorm of Flyer PR director Ed Golden in 1977, has benefitted charities with more than $28 million, helping some people who don't know a red line from a blueline. The Ed Snider Youth Hockey Foundation, the late Chairman's proudest legacy, has coupled participation in hockey with life skills, curriculum and supplemental educational services for more than 10,000 at-risk boys and girls from Philadelphia, Camden, NJ and Chester, PA.

The Flyers alumni team with Joe Watson still booking dates, recruiting players, and manning the blueline at age 73, has raised $3.5 million for those in need and has entered into an initiative to fund the building of a rink.

Sensitive to the perception of some that they have lived in the past, the Flyers made "God Bless America" go away for a period of years. But the fans are the ultimate judge of what is real and what is contrived, what is worth celebrating and what is not, so the late Kate Smith and Hart are as popular as ever.

The Flyers have a substantial record of firsts—to hire an assistant coach (Mike Nykoluk by Shero), to bring the morning skate to the NHL (Shero again), to develop a star European-born goalie (Lindbergh), to draft a player from behind the Iron Curtain (Viktors Hatulevs), and to give long pants a try. But tradition drives the franchise.

There never has been an alternative jersey that changed the team colors, even if the uniform has undergone some alterations. The black jersey—a third option later used as the regular road sweater, replaced the orange-and-white basic sweaters for parts of six seasons. There have been periodic changes in the shades of orange, and in the striping on the sleeves. But a silver-trimmed variation of the jersey did not go over well with the fans, especially when the logo contained silver.

Yo, don't mess with that logo! The simple and brilliant winged P with the orange puck, drawn by Sam Ciccone of Mel Richman Inc. in 1966, has become recognizable around the world.

"We have stayed consistent with the brand and it all starts with the logo, which I think is the best one in sports," says Tilger. "I've done over 50 town halls (with season ticket holders) and never had one person ask about a logo change. That tells me something.

"If you go to the shore during the summer, people wearing Flyer stuff are everywhere. The fans take pride in saying how long they've been season ticket holders. It's more than a financial investment; they make an emotional one. That logo is like a badge."

The sign high on the home locker room wall—the only one of the four that doesn't hold pictures of Hockey and Flyer Hall of Famers—reads: "The crest on the front is more important than the name on the back."

Some names never go out of style. LeClair and Desjardins are worn on almost as many backs in the stands as Giroux and Voracek. Besides, the logo is what matters, and it has always travelled well.

"It's everywhere the Flyers play, not just in certain places," Coates marvels. "It's almost like being a member of a cult."

According to Shawny Hill, these devotees in uniform believe uniformly that they make a difference.

"Every fan walks through the door of the Wells Fargo Center feeling like they are going to be a factor," he says. "We've seen the negatives of that but, at other times, I've seen players become inspired to

A great draft crop in 1972

pull off incredible things. And if they get to that level just once, they can be heroes in this town forever.

"Primeau was a really solid player, but in 2004, he became a superhero. When he got that puck during that run, you felt this buzz like, 'this is our time!'

"For fans, the biggest difference between the Flyers and other sporting teams in the city is the feeling that we are going to put pressure on the opposing team and have influence. We didn't score the goal or have the assist, but we do believe we are a part of it.

"Even my dancing thing, labeled as a gimmick, was me showing my passion in a weird way, why it wasn't just a novelty sideshow. That's why it has lasted ten years."

While character has been a constant requirement on the ice, the characters in the stands have been enduring and endearing.

Phil (General Schultz) Stein wore a blinking German army helmet during the Bully days.

Dave (Signman) Leonardi, who began to stencil his wit and wisdom because the players couldn't hear him through the glass from his seat in the second row behind the goal, has been telling the visiting team to "Start Your Bus" since 1972, and that even included on the night of his 1982 wedding.

"'Next Goalie' or 'Shake Hands and Leave' are my other favorites," says Signman, who has held up more than 500 of them. "I like the ones that show it's all over."

At age 95, charter season-ticket holder Edgar Weinrott sits with his son Richard in their first-row-of-the-upper-deck seats approximately 13 times a season. It is his Edgar's intention to be there when the Flyers win their third Cup, but he concedes, "It's not entirely in my control."

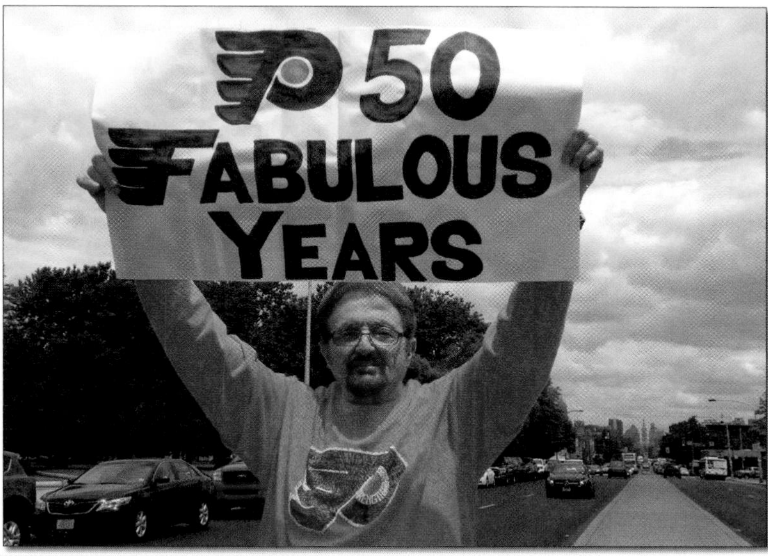

Dave (Signman) Leonardi

Like Weinrott, Jerome Epstein, 81, and his son Gregg were at the first game in 1967. "Walking into the Spectrum that night, feeling the cool of the ice, what a thing that was for an eight-year-old," recalls Gregg. "The 7,000 people felt like 700,000.

"And it was okay for the players to run into and whack each other. I was hooked."

Jerome was checked into the hospital on the Sunday of the Russian game in 1976, scheduled for early morning anesthesia to have three impacted wisdom teeth pulled. He begged to be excused for three hours to go to the Spectrum and the nurse took pity, provided he promise not to eat anything. That was a breeze for him. Jerome once flew 10 hours home from Israel and went straight to a game. Loyalty knows no fatigue.

"I don't think the Flyers owe us a thing," Jerome says. "They have given us more joy and satisfaction than any other Philadelphia team."

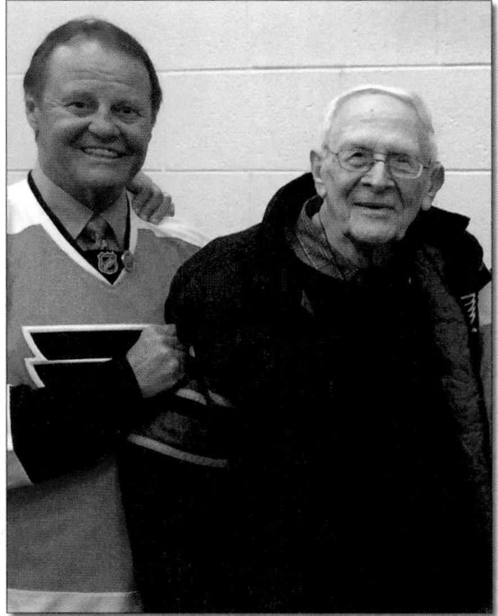

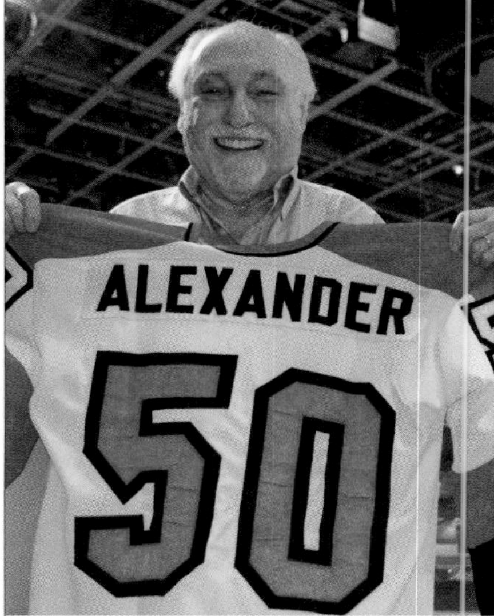

Fifty-year ticket holders Edgar Weinrott (left, with Bill Barber), Jerome and Gregg Epstein (center) and Ben Alexander

The annual Flyers Wives Fight for Life Carnival was first staged in 1977.

the upper deck, feeling obliged to endure that miserable 2006-07 season. Because the Flyers never had let him down quite as much before and likely never would again, Hill figured he owed it to the team to stick it out.

Since that is love, he was a good person to ask, 'What makes the Flyers so lovable?'

"It started with knowing who the owner was," he replied. "But the coaches and general managers have often been familiar guys because we watched them work their way up from being players.

"Everything felt so homegrown and that's what people like in this city. TastyKakes are made in this area, that's why we love them. Cheesesteaks, that's why we love them. You know what I mean? The Flyers truly feel like organic Philadelphia.

"None of the guys on the roster this season, or in most seasons, have Philadelphia as their home town, but we all feel like they become Philadelphians if they're here long enough and play the right way."

There have been years the results indicated that the Flyers were just another decent team. But their body of work over 50 years gives them a status higher than any particular season's standing.

In this history, you will read player after player thankful for the privilege of being a Philadelphia Flyer. Although the team has not won a playoff round since 2012, you can take it from Claude Giroux, the current Flyer star and captain: he feels the same ownership that did Clarke, Barber, Eric Desjardins, Primeau and Mike Richards.

"A lot of good players were here," says Giroux. "It's an honor to wear this logo. The organization is first class. When guys come from other teams, they can see it.

"There is a lot of pressure. Some players respond; some don't like it, and would rather play in a small market. Personally, I don't think I would enjoy that. You want that pressure to win; you want the people to care. There's not a fan in the NHL who cares more than a Flyer fan."

Or as Matt Carle, a Philadelphia defenseman from 2008-2012, says with the deepest reverence and not an ounce of sarcasm: "There is no better city to play for when things are going well, and no scarier place when they aren't."

Yes, but the 1,312 losses since the first one in 1967 have only made the 1,895 Flyer wins that much more exhilarating.

"At low points, I have always thought about the wonderful things that have happened," says Leonardi. "When you look at the body of work, you have to keep going, realizing that just around the corner is the next great memory."

Ben Alexander, 90, who bought season tickets from a Flyer office in Center City while the Spectrum still was a hole in the ground, shares the wisdom of his aged contemporaries. If you live long enough, even Leon Stickle, who blew an obvious off-side call in Game Six in 1980, can be forgiven.

"It still takes me an hour to fall asleep after a loss," Alexander says. "But I am a complete optimist. The Flyers have always been a team that really tried. You can't expect more than that. You just can't."

Before the camera made him a star, Hill was just another diehard in

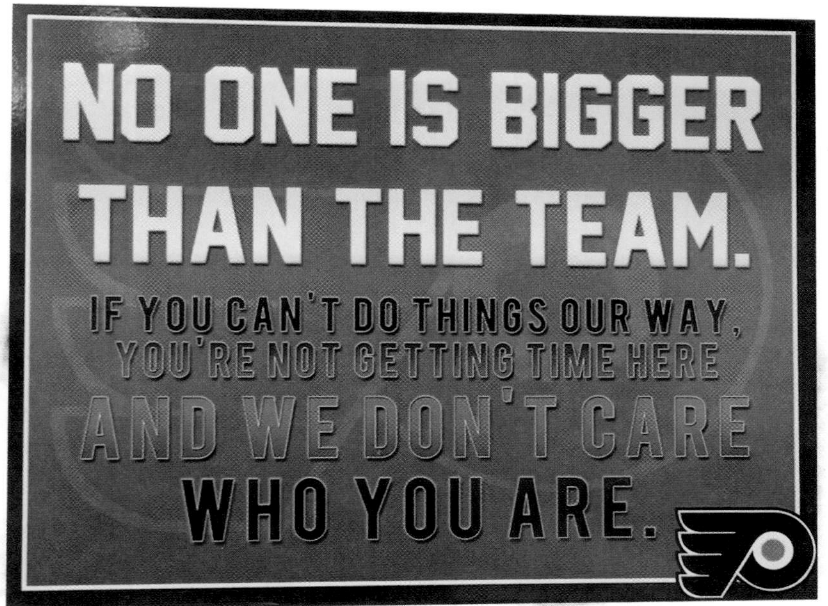

50 Flyer Heroes

On Ice and Off

ED SNIDER

While other NHL owners scoffed at the threat of competition from the World Hockey Association, Ed Snider wasn't taking any chances. In 1972, when two years for a total of $50,000 was a lucrative long-term contract in the sport, the Flyer owner reached agreement with rising star Bobby Clarke on a five-year, $100,000-per-season deal. During July, Clarke flew from his home in Flin Flon, Manitoba to Philadelphia to sign the document.

"I was having a beer at a Center City hotel the night before I was going into (GM) Keith Allen's office to sign the contract," recalls Clarke. "Kevin Johnson, who had been with the Flyers (as a public-address announcer) and was leaving to work for the (WHA Philadelphia) Blazers (as public relations director), happened to be in the bar and asked what I was doing in town in mid-summer.

"I told him I was signing my contract the next day. He excused himself. Ten minutes later, he came back to say that Bernie Brown (the trucking magnate who was co-owner of the Blazers) had told him to offer me $1 million a year for five years.

"I thanked him, but I had no interest in leaving the NHL and the Flyers. Plus, I had given my word to Mr. Snider.

"I never told anybody about this, just signed the deal. John Brogan, (*The Philadelphia Evening Bulletin* beat writer and Flyer employee-to-be) must have found out from the Blazer people. He wrote about it a couple weeks later.

"Mr. Snider called me and asked, 'Is what is in the paper true?' I said, 'Yes.'

"He said, 'thank you. I'll never forget this.' And he never did."

Snider built an organization on loyalty. It won championships because passion radiated from the top.

Recalls Comcast chairman and CEO Brian Roberts: "In 1997, when we played the Rangers in the [Eastern Conference final], I brought the chairman of HBO, Michael Dukes, a life-long New Yorker, to sit in our (visiting owner's) box at Madison Square Garden.

"I think we were up and the Rangers scored. Michael clapped and said, 'Now, let's make this a game!'

"After the Flyers won, as Ed and I were walking out, he put his arm around me and said, 'Don't ever bring a Rangers' fan into my box again.'

"I learned quickly. This wasn't a hobby, a toy, to Ed. He built something from scratch. The losses really hurt, so every time I was on the road with him during the playoffs and we lost, my first instinct was to give [the players] a little privacy, let them have their moment, blow off some steam.

"Ed would say, 'Nonsense, let's go down in the locker room.' He went right into the lion's den, led in the front. That was a great lesson: there's no separation, we're all in this together."

During Rod Brind'Amour's first season with Philadelphia, Snider demanded to know what his player had done to earn a game misconduct, then raced off to berate the referee. "I thought, 'Wow, we're not making the playoffs and he barely knows me,'" recalls Brind'Amour. "I knew this was a guy I wanted to play for.'"

Even before Snider's blood turned orange, entrepreneurship was in his genes. The son of Sol Snider, a mom-and-pop grocery-store owner who built a chain in Washington, DC, Ed sold flowers on corners and banked $100,000 selling Christmas trees while attending the University of Maryland.

When Snider and his friend Gerald Lillienfield learned of a warehouse filled with phonograph records, together they bought and sold them, first out of the trunk of a car, then in supermarkets and drug stores. Snider was 25 when they found a buyer for the business, and the partners split $500,000.

In his youth, Snider collected bubble gum cards and memorized the statistics on their backs, so he was thrilled to gain entre into professional sports. His sister Phyllis married Earl Foreman, an attorney who represented Jerry Wolman, the ambitious DC-area builder who purchased the Philadelphia Eagles in 1964. Wolman brought Snider to Philadelphia to be the team vice president and treasurer with a seven percent ownership stake. Among his responsibilities was spearheading the franchise's efforts toward a new stadium.

In a conversation one day with Bill Putnam, a vice president of the New York bank—Morgan Guaranty Trust Company—that held the Eagles' loan, Putnam mentioned he soon would be leaving to work for Jack Kent Cooke, a Washington Redskins' minority owner who was applying for an NHL franchise in Los Angeles.

"Why, is a franchise available?" asked Snider.

"Maybe as many as six," said Putnam, who soon left the demanding and impulsive Cooke to join with Snider and Wolman in their bid to get one of those teams for Philadelphia.

Wolman had the name and the money, at least on paper, which made him the front man. Snider worked the channels. He met with Bill Jennings of the Rangers, chairman of the expansion committee, proposed to the city an arena on land already purchased by Philadelphia to build a football/baseball stadium at Broad and Pattison Streets, and then toiled through the government bureaucracy at seemingly impossible speed to get the shovels into the ground for the Spectrum.

When the overextended Wolman admitted two weeks before the $2 million franchise fee was due that he did not have the $1 million he had pledged, Snider and Putnam risked almost everything they owned to get the team on the ice.

They secured alternative funding just 48 hours

before the deadline and then brought local beer baron Joe Scott into a reorganized three-man ownership group. After multiple rejections, the partners secured necessary additional operating capital from Girard Bank, making Snider a heavily-mortgaged 60 percent owner of a hockey team in a city that never had shown much interest in the game.

"I didn't need a marketing survey to tell me that the fourth-largest city in the United States needed a modern arena and that people would come to watch an exciting major-league sport," Snider said. "I thought of myself as a regular guy who knew what regular guys would like."

The first season began with crowds consistently under 10,000—and a few even below 5,000—before a wind-damaged Spectrum roof orphaned the Flyers to complete the final month of their home schedule in Toronto, New York and Quebec City.

The ordeal turned out to be a good thing, hastening the fans' bonding to the new team. As attendance gradually grew, so did Snider's knowledge of the sport and his unhappiness with Bud Poile, Putnam's hand-picked GM. Poile was replaced by assistant GM Keith Allen midway through Season Three on the way to Stanley Cups in years Seven and Eight.

Snider had given up his shares in the Spectrum before the first Flyer game in exchange for a majority cut of the hockey team. But in 1971, he entered into a partnership with Foreman that rescued the building from bankruptcy. Every creditor was paid 100 cents on the dollar, and the Spectrum was turned it into one of the busiest and most profitable sports and entertainment centers in the nation. That led to the 1974 genesis of Spectacor, the arena company that has spawned nearly a dozen related businesses. Today, as Spectra, it provides venue management, food services, hospitality and ticketing to more than 300 clients and 400 properties throughout the world.

With Flyer home games as a programming centerpiece, Snider in 1976 pioneered PRISM, one of the first regional sports and entertainment networks in the USA. During the mid-nineties, he built a $210 million arena, now called the Wells Fargo Center, using only $25 million in public funds.

In 1995, Snider sold a 67 percent share of the Flyers and their new building to Comcast, but the Flyers and the Wells Fargo Center remained his show. When Snider died from bladder cancer on April 11, 2016 at age 83, only the late Buffalo Bills' owner, Ralph Wilson, had ever lasted longer as the person in charge of a team in one of the four major North American sports.

"There never was a moment of friction or any chance that we wouldn't try to make the partnership work," recalls Roberts. "As you balance winning, fan loyalty, long-term brand, profits, losses, strikes, lockouts, all the realities that are sports in the modern era, Ed proved to have tremendous integrity.

"The Flyers always think about their fans. Those words are easy to say and hard to do, but particularly in the first 10 years we owned the team together, when we had a lot of meetings getting to know each other, with Ed it was the fan, the fan, the fan. There was a discipline to do the right thing."

The businesses the Flyers spawned made a lot more money than his hockey team ever did, but none came close to exciting him as much. "He liked to build businesses and play tennis, but had no real hobbies," recalls Jay, Ed's son and the Flyer president from 1984-93. "The Flyers were the only thing he was really passionate about."

The amount of time the senior Snider spent at his beloved seaside home in Montecito, CA over his final 30 years periodically fostered a perception that the Chairman's Philadelphia interests were declining. What waned was his tolerance for the pressure of running them. "There never was a time he wasn't watching every game," recalls Martha, Snider's second wife. But things that subsequently came into his life—or almost did—brought him back closer than ever to his team.

Never a control freak, always a believer in trusting people to do their jobs, Snider had come to feel in the mid-eighties that the club might be better off with younger, more energetic, leadership. "He was tired, saying it had been too long since we had won a Cup," recalls Martha. "We were crazy in love and going off to have a good time while Jay was running the team.

"Ed said he had always wanted to make a movie of *Atlas Shrugged* (the pre-eminent work of Snider's Objectivism guru Ayn Rand). I said, 'When have you ever not done what you wanted to do?' We went to California to make a movie, but Leonard Peikoff (heir to the Rand estate) rejected three scripts."

The idea would die, Snider becoming $600,000 poorer for having dreamed it. Meanwhile, another opportunity was knocking. In 1984, bankrupt Eagles owner Leonard Tose thought the only way to save his legacy was to sell the team to Snider, who was about to buy it in partnership with the Pritzker Organization (Hyatt Hotels).

"We would have needed to get into some serious debt relative to what we were worth at that point," recalls Martha. "One morning Ed woke up, wet, pale, and panicked, asking, 'What am I doing?' He said, 'I don't even like football. I'm a hockey guy. This may be a good business [opportunity], but I can't do it.' The deal that he had negotiated with Tose basically was handed to Norman Braman."

From California, it was difficult to referee the disagreements between Jay and Clarke that led to the GM's abrupt firing in 1990, one season into a five-year playoff drought. "A fight between two sons—one blood, one chosen," recalls Martha. "Ed literally was sick, he lost weight."

Jay spearheaded the drive for a new arena to replace the Spectrum and kept the project moving. But ultimately, Ed had to assume the financial burden and make the decision on where to build. During a long and twisted tale that involved Sixer owner Harold Katz and negotiations with governments in Pennsylvania and New Jersey, Snider was required to spend most of his time in Philadelphia.

"Jay was made crazy with Ed's constant second-guessing," recalls Martha. "As a result, Jay was not as well received (in negotiations and with the public) as he should have been."

Eventually, the son resigned to run his own businesses and Clarke was brought back from a five-year exile, while Snider had to decide whether to keep the Flyers at the South Philadelphia Sports Complex or move them across the river.

"[New Jersey] was going to pass bonds for $50 million at least and give it to us," recalls Jay. "It would have been very low interest and we wouldn't have had to guarantee it.

"It was a much better financial deal. But my father just woke up one day and said, 'I'm not going to Jersey.' He could have said it months before, or not at all and continued to use it for leverage. But that ended Camden."

The man who started a team in a sport in which Philadelphians had never shown much interest and who bought a bankrupt arena with the promise to pay the creditors 100 cents on the dollar, was not overtly venturesome. The corner of Broad and Pattison had been good to him. Snider believed there were too many uncertainties about how the Philadelphia Flyers playing in New Jersey might damage the brand.

"He was smart in knowing what he didn't know," recalls Jay. "In my own life, I made mistakes jumping into things I didn't know about and lost money; my father always stuck to his knitting. Great entrepreneurs tend to do things in areas they understand better than other people.

"Being vice president and treasurer of the Eagles, he understood hot dog sales, parking and tickets enough to go into the arena business. Taking control of the building became a cash machine that fueled everything.

"So what was the next move? For PRISM, his concept was sports and entertainment mixed, not all sports. Dad understood the sports side and TV rights; he had the anchor in the Flyers and knew he could get the Phillies and Sixers with more local TV money than they had ever seen.

"My father put money into things only after he had taken most of the risk out. He thought, 'I've managed the Spectrum, why can't I manage other arenas? I don't have to buy or develop them, just hire the right people to run them.' Again, it was a branch off the same tree. Ed Snider didn't make big leaps to other trees.

"He knew himself really well. I must have heard 500 times, 'I'd rather be a big fish in a small pond,' meaning he would rather do it in Philadelphia rather than run all over the country doing business. Dad wanted to sleep in his own bed at night. He didn't even like going to the away playoff games, although he went.

"Of course once he knew something, my father was a very forceful personality. But he could be very indecisive in other areas, an example being [buying] the Eagles. I saw this so many times. He'd investigate and run numbers on things, spend some money, but before he had to spend big, he would say, 'Nah, I'm not going to do it.'"

In the case of the new arena, Snider had no choice and no peace with his decision.

"He had to personally guarantee the construction loan on the new building, which meant leveraging every penny we had," recalls Martha. "There was an imminent big hike in the price of steel so, to meet the budget, he had to order before there was city-council approval. It was a hugely stressful time."

The proposal sailed through the council because Snider's people typically and flawlessly had done their groundwork. "He hired good people and gave them the resources to do their jobs," recalls Flyer COO Shawn Tilger. "When you say somebody 'gets it,' Ed Snider was the epitome of that."

Ron Ryan, the Flyers' chief operating officer from 1998 to 2006, remembers, "Ed never said to me, 'No, you can't do that' or even, 'You shouldn't do that,' but he made sure you thought about whether it was absolutely the right thing to do. In that way, I think he helped everybody."

An ability to see the big picture might have been the Chairman's greatest talent.

"Ed always asked the right questions," recalls Phil Weinberg, Comcast-Spectacor's executive vice president and general counsel. "I've never seen anybody like him. He had an uncanny ability to cut through all the unimportant encumbrances, and really focus on what was at stake."

Recalls Clarke, "He never told me what to do, just asked about things I never had thought about."

Granted, there were times Snider's questions were addressed to the wrong person. While the steam was still coming out of his ears after a referee's decision, GM Allen would get calls from the owner, angrily asking for an explanation.

In signing up to be one of Snider's trusted lieutenants, you volunteered to be his lightning rod. Bulldogs let go of legs faster than Snider let up on things like the temperature in the building or game presentation. And while it is technically true that his GMs fired the coaches, in the cases of Pat Quinn and Mike Keenan, Snider had made his opinion abundantly clear to Allen and Clarke, respectively, before they made their decisions.

That said, it is not true that the Chairman was impulsive. When Clarke went through six coaches between 1997 to 2003, the appearance of instability deeply troubled an owner who employed only six GMs in 48 years.

"For such a dominant man, he was not a bully," insists Clarke. "If you were convinced, he would back you, even if he thought you might be wrong."

In one of Snider's favorite stories, he persuaded Allen to bend when the Hartford Whalers asked for one more prospect than the GM wanted to give up to obtain Mark Howe.

Says Ryan, "When you faced a really serious problem—and we did face serious problems—he was the greatest ally you could have. He would be right there at your side working through it.

"That's what I really admired about him the most. When things got tough, he was the greatest."

Clarke recalls Snider walking into the devastated locker room in Buffalo after a playoff spot slipped away on a 45-foot goal with four seconds remaining in the final game of 1972 and telling the players the future remained bright. "We thought we had died and he probably needed the playoff gates," said Clarke. "But he said, 'this is not going to set us back from being good.'"

One season later, the Flyers had their initial winning season and won a playoff series for the first time. The next year they became the first team from the 1967 expansion to win the Cup. Snider and Allen shared a vision of a good working environment and Myrna Snider, Ed's first wife, added personal touches. Philadelphia had turned into hockey heaven.

"We got anything the team ever wanted," said Clarke. "Every club stays at the best hotels now, but at one point there was a difference between the way we travelled and the way most did.

"Mr. Snider always said he wouldn't put his team on a flight he wouldn't go on himself. Players would get Christmas presents from the teams, but Myrna made sure our wives got presents too. It was family."

To a significant extent, the Flyer way largely became the NHL way. Commissioner Gary Bettman said that rarely did two weeks go by without him calling the Chairman for counsel. "He had a brain that I loved to pick," said Bettman. "He had a passion fueled with an incredible intelligence and a diligence about the way he got things done.

"He's somebody who understood people and how to work with them. Since the creation of the Competition Committee (how the game is played on the ice), he was the only owner on it, and that came from the fact that he was very practical and extraordinarily knowledgeable.

"I doubt there have been many owners who knew more, or as much as he did; that was a respect he commanded from general managers and players.

"He was focused on player equipment and safety and the need to make sure the game is well played. And, at least during my tenure, he always put the league first. (During the lockout) he understood that no matter what (high player salaries) the Flyers could have continued to deal with, in the final analysis he needed to be in a strong NHL.

"Nobody hated revenue sharing more than he did, but Ed went along with it. I've read stories chronicling the disputes he had with my predecessors and the like. We never had anything like that.

"He was a capitalist and believed in a lot of conservative causes. But his values were about putting people first."

And the people who wore the orange-and-black were Snider's first priority, which explains two Cups, eight berths in the Final and 16 in the semifinals, even though Snider died without the third championship he craved.

"If you are in the Final six times (since 1975), you'd think you would luck into one," said Snider. "With all the effort we've put into it, it's very frustrating, but I also understand that as the years have gone by, it's gotten more and more difficult. Things have changed drastically. There are more teams and parity. The quality of the executives and coaching around the league is outstanding.

"But we're second in win percentage (to Montreal) even since the Cups. I think it's a damn good record."

The consistency has stemmed from an unchanging philosophy. In the early years, when it seemed more pragmatic for six new teams competing against each other in the same division to just try to be better than one another, Snider and Allen weighed every move in the context of whether it eventually could help win the Cup. The Chairman's patience wavered at times, but never his resolve to be the best. Snider came to feel he lost a conscience the day he kicked Allen upstairs before he was ready to go.

"Keith was the most underrated general manager ever, so if I regret anything, it is that maybe he retired too soon or should have been kept in," said the Chairman in the last year of his life. "I thought (successor) Clarke would use him more (as an advisor).

"I regret in retrospect the (Eric) Lindros trade, not because of the issues we had (with his family) but because of all the pieces we gave up. If we had kept (Peter) Forsberg, I think we would have won the Cup instead of Colorado.

"I regret passing on (Jaromir) Jagr in the (1991) draft (when Pittsburgh took him fifth, one pick after the Flyers chose Mike Ricci, who went to Quebec in the Lindros trade). Can you imagine Jagr and Forsberg on the same team?"

That is much easier to picture than Philadelphia had Snider never been born. In 1999, readers of *The Philadelphia Daily News* voted him the city's greatest mover and shaker of the millennium.

For his faith and brilliance in making hockey a huge success in the nation's sixth-largest metropolitan area, Snider was elected to the Hockey Hall of Fame (1988) and the United States Hockey Hall of Fame (2011).

In 1980, he received the NHL's Lester Patrick Award for service to the sport in the United States. But a greater contribution than any to a game came in 2005 with the launch of the Ed Snider Youth Hockey Foundation, which has coupled participation in the sport with life skills curriculum and supplemental educational services for more than 10,000 at-risk boys and girls from Philadelphia, Camden, NJ, and Chester, PA.

"He said to many people that Snider Hockey is his legacy, the best thing he ever has done," said the Foundation's CEO and president Scott Tharp. Considering all Snider has built, that remains a considerable statement.

"I grew up in tough neighborhoods and had to be in a gang at one period in my life to survive," Snider recalled. "I was scared in those days and was in lots of fist fights.

"I wanted to do something for the inner-city kids and I thought the best way to help was through hockey. Paul Vallas (CEO of the School District of Philadelphia from 2002 to 2006) worked with me to get it started in schools.

"The city was going to close the rinks. We said we'd remodel (originally four, now five at a cost of $14.5 million that included classrooms and public meeting space) and run them at our expense. Now they're beautiful, like the young men and women we are developing. These kids are doing something they never thought they could do, keeping them off the streets. We're changing attitudes.

"This was the first time I ever put my name on anything. I want it to last forever. For every dollar (mostly from individuals and private foundations, plus some corporate help) that comes in, I put in two. Kids are graduating (at a 90 percent rate) from high school, going onto four-year colleges and trade schools. It's phenomenal."

Snider Hockey is not the only ongoing charitable endeavor with his name on it. The Snider Foundation, run by Jay with the entire family on the board, is set up for 20 years of giving millions to hospitals, schools, and organizations dedicated to preserving free enterprise, American values and Jewish survival.

In April 2015, *The Philadelphia Business Journal* named Snider its Philanthropist of the Year. He also received a Lifetime Achievement Award during the Global Sports Summit in Aspen, CO in 2015.

In addition to honorary degrees from Hahnemann University and Thomas Jefferson University Hospital, Snider received the Greater Philadelphia Chamber of Commerce William Penn Award, the most prestigious business honor in the region; plus the Ellis Island Medal of Honor, awarded to Americans of all ethnic backgrounds who have made significant contributions to society.

His donation in 2014 to the University of Maryland created the Ed Snider Center for Enterprise and Marketing. He also is a benefactor of the Sol C. Snider Entrepreneurial Center of the Wharton School of the University of Pennsylvania, plus vice chairman of the Simon Wiesenthal Center, a Jewish human-rights organization based in Los Angeles.

To Snider, humanity began at home, including his extended family at work.

"He was more sensitive than people understood about him," recalls daughter Lindy. "Dad had an inherent belief in people and would remain loyal to certain persons longer than he should have."

Ann Marie Nasuti, Snider's long-time administrative assistant, says she had to be the bad guy when hard-luck letters asking for money arrived from individuals with no former connection to Snider. The Chairman did pretty well for a Jewish guy who started out selling Christmas trees. He wanted to share the wealth.

"He was a softie," recalls Jay. "There were times when he had to fire someone that he would hire someone to do it.

"He was simple in a lot of ways—in his food taste, in what he loved to do, like playing tennis and watching the Flyers. But he was a complex guy emotionally. He could be as volatile with his children as he was with others. There were times that we were like, 'What's going on? How do you figure this guy out?'

"But if I said, 'Dad, I need you,' he would change his schedule, drop everything, and meet me somewhere.

"In our entire lives, we had one six-month period where we were angry with each other and that was it. After I left the Flyers, anything I did, Dad wanted to invest in. He was a really good father. And his legacy is amazing.

"I believe he had misgivings about not buying the Eagles, and about some of the moves along the way with the Flyers. Personally, I think he got a little impatient with some of the free-agent signings, got away from what he always drilled into me about building a team.

"But whenever he would express some regrets, I'd say, 'Dad, I think you did okay.'"

BOBBY CLARKE

One of the initial unwritten rules Paul Holmgren learned about the Flyers when he joined them in 1976 was that nobody dressed for the morning skates before Bobby Clarke did.

"At first I couldn't figure out what everybody was waiting for, then I realized they were watching him," recalls Holmgren. "Freddie (coach Shero) made it our choice but nobody wanted to be in sweats if Bob was in full equipment.

"That was my first lesson in the silent leadership of Bobby Clarke."

Occasionally he wasn't so quiet.

"Game Five (1974 final in Boston), we were getting killed (in a 5-1 loss)," recalls Bill Clement. "Ricky MacLeish had it in cruise and Clarkie, who was sitting next to me, is muttering under his breath.

"MacLeish came off his shift and sat on the other side of me. Clarkie waited for Ricky to catch his breath, then leaned over in front of me and said, 'Ricky!' MacLeish looked at Bobby, who said 'I sure hope you're saving it for [Game Six], you [bleep].'

"And you know what happened. We won the Cup. MacLeish scored the only goal and was the best player on the ice.

"Bobby used different techniques with different people. I partially tore an MCL against the Rangers that year and missed the first two games of the Bruin series. I got Dr. John Wolf to take off the cast before Game Three, tried to skate on it, and couldn't.

"Before Game Four, Bobby sat down by the whirlpool and asked me, 'How is it?' I said, 'Not very good.' He said, 'I've got to tell you something' and in a calm, level, voice said, "I don't think we can win the Cup without you.' I said, 'What?'

"(Barry) Ashbee, (Bob) Kelly, and (Gary) Dornhoefer were all out with more serious injuries than I had. Bob said, 'I don't want you to do anything to hurt your career, but even if you could just kill penalties, the guys from the minors can't do what you do. I just want you to know that when you're ready to come back, we're ready to have you back.' And he got up and left.

"I took the warmup that night, played sparingly, limped around, and we won. By Game Six I was 80 percent. I ended up playing because Bobby Clarke made me feel I was vital to the outcome."

The Broad Street Bullies, who followed No. 16 twice to hockey nirvana, would have trailed him to hell had they been asked.

Granted, their worst critics thought the Flyers were headed there anyway. Canadiens goalie Ken Dryden once wondered aloud to what limits Clarke would go to win a game. And Soviet star Valeri Kharlamov, who took a wicked two-hander to the ankle from Clarke in the 1972 Summit Series against Team Canada, found out.

Losing is not dying, no matter how often athletes, writers, and commentators have made that exaggeration to illustrate the devastation of defeat. But the way Clarke played suggested he was competing for his very life.

Was it his Type One diabetes? Did he want to get it all in before it was too late? Clarke always denied it. His eyes were good. His cuts healed quickly. He took insulin every day as routinely as he brushed his teeth. No, as a diabetic, he was one of the lucky ones.

BOBBY CLARKE
FLYER HERO #2

"But deep down it had to drive him," said Holmgren, who lost two brothers to complications from the disease, one at age 19. As a result, Clarke and Holmgren bonded.

"When you are stricken with diabetes, you learn right away the seriousness of it," said Holmgren. "Because of my family, I know about that, and I know he did because we talked about it.

"But consciously, he probably never is going to admit a handicap pushed him to what he became."

Clarke loved the game too much to need additional reasons for the ferocity with which he played it. The most-cited reason why Clarke became one of the greatest of the great players in the history of the NHL was his work ethic. But long before he was diagnosed with a killing condition at age 14, hockey never seemed like labor to him.

"Every kid in Flin Flon (Manitoba) played, some three nights a week, some four," he recalls. "I did every night.

"All I ever wanted to do was play hockey. I just played it the way I thought it had to be played."

By age 10, Clarke had a pretty good idea he was good at it. The athletic genes probably came from his mother Yvonne, the daughter of German immigrants turned Saskatchewan farmers. "She was a great (track and field) athlete," Clarke says. "But they were really poor, hungry all the time,"

Her husband to-be, Cliff Clarke, lived on a family farm 50 miles away. Eventually The Great Depression drove the failed farmers to the steady work offered by Hudson Bay Mining and Smelting in Flin Flon, a northern Manitoba town of 5,000 that was 400 miles from Winnipeg, Saskatoon, or just about anywhere.

After his 18th birthday, Cliff took a job in the copper and zinc mines and, for 32 years, held a drill on his shoulder while standing in dirty water.

"Hard [bleeping] job," recalls Clarke.

Dangerous one, too.

"One day, when I was a kid, a rock came down and hit his partner, put him in a wheelchair," remembers Clarke. "We would visit him every Sunday.

"Another time my neighbor, a friend of my dad, was walking way up high on a railing that somebody had moved. He didn't realize it, walked off, and it killed him.

"They made him a boss when he was about 50. He didn't like it. One day, another crew was drilling in an open pit about 10 miles outside of town. While they were up for lunch, the dam broke and hundreds of thousands of tons of ore went down. One guy who had stayed below got killed. But if it hadn't happened at lunchtime, it could have been more.

"Dad quit soon after that, at about 56. He didn't have a bad heart until he was in a car accident. He was in intensive care for four days before I found out. I said, 'You never even let me know!' He said, 'Well, what the [bleep] were you going to do about it in Philadelphia?'

"Dad was physically tough, but pretty easygoing. My Mom was really the tough one. One day when I was about 12, [bleeping] around, my buddy pushed me through a wall at school and we got sent home.

"Mom still was at work at the co-op. It was a sunny day, so I took my skates and went to the outdoor rink, which was down a hill. All of a sudden, I see her marching down towards me. She grabbed the stick and started swinging at my butt.

"She was the disciplinarian of the house. I think that was the usual case. Men worked and the women took care of the kids."

The Clarkes lived in a house that had one bathroom and two bedrooms, one of them shared by Bob and Roxanne, his younger sister by four years, until she got older and Cliff built Bob his own bedroom in the basement.

The teenager was plenty smart enough to get by with minimal effort in school, but didn't want to stay there. When he made the Flin Flon Bombers, the Junior A powerhouse owned by the mining company, coach-GM Patty Ginnell sent Clarke to the company's office.

"I walk in, sit down, and the guy who does the hiring asks, 'What are you doing here?' 'Looking for a job,' I told him. He says, "[Bleeping] diabetic, get out of here, go back to school. Then he calls my dad to make sure he agreed to let me quit.

"Keeping me in school was going to be a losing battle for my dad. We were so far away from the other teams in the league, we went on two-week road trips.

"So I was back at the mine the next day. Reggie Leach was 16 and I was 17. You had to be 18 to work inside, so we shoveled sidewalks outside and cut the lawn and stuff.

"At 18 I went inside and worked the crusher. They would bring in ore on trains and dump it in this huge gyrator to get crushed. That was my job. I never went underground. I was too small.

"If you were on the junior club, you would work from 8-12 in the mine and practice in the afternoon; but they would pay you for eight hours."

It was good work if you could get it, especially when the hockey part was pure play. But it is a myth that Clarke bore down so hard at the rink because he wanted to escape the mine for life.

"I liked working there," he recalls. "All men, chewing tobacco, it was perfect for me; this is what I knew.

"I just wanted to play hockey. It never crossed my mind as a way out of Flin Flon."

As a 17-year-old, Clarke had 183 points in 45 games. Also, 123 penalty minutes. By his draft eligibility year—age 20 at that time—sponsorship of junior teams by NHL franchises was over, making the 1969 draft the first time the best prospects would be selected by clubs in the reverse order of finish the previous season.

Even if the Red Wings, the once-sponsor of the Bombers, were the only team that sent a scout, Danny Summers, all the way to Flin Flon, Clarke was no secret. And, after he scored 168 and 137 points in his final two junior seasons against more than a few players who had graduated to the NHL, the pros were not intimidating to him.

Prior to the draft, Ginnell took Clarke to the Mayo Clinic in Minnesota to get it in writing that diabetes should not preclude a successful professional career. But 11 teams, including the Flyers, passed Clarke over at least once before Philadelphia, at the vehement urging of first-year scout Jerry Melnyk, made Clarke the 17th pick.

Detroit, which was about to take Clarke at No. 21, made an offer as soon as the Flyers selected him. So did Montreal. The Red Wings, who decided on Memorial Cup-winning goalie Jim Rutherford in the first round, knew better than anybody of Clarke's potential.

There had been little hype to this new draft and, to Clarke, not much intrigue as to where he was going to wind up. As long as they had pucks, nets and boards in Philadelphia, this two-year-old franchise was a fine place to land.

Early in camp, Clarke and Lew Morrison, a Flin Flon teammate drafted a year earlier than Clarke, overslept and skipped breakfast. "In the middle of practice, this kid faints," recalls Joe Watson. "What the hell?"

Trainer Frank Lewis, whose wife was a nurse, learned to keep a snack and insulin in his kit, and Clarke, the team's best player from the first day, didn't need much teaching about anything else.

He spoke once about his condition and then not again for many years. "I don't want anyone to think any time I have a bad game, it's because I'm a diabetic," he said. He solved that by practically never having a bad game.

The Flyers turned the corner in his fourth year, won the Cup in his fifth and sixth, and made two more Finals and two more semifinals before Clarke's 1984 retirement, because nothing was more important to their captain than his next shift. He relentlessly blocked everything else out. Once the puck was dropped, big leads, hopeless deficits, January road games in half-empty buildings, exhibition games in junior arenas, illness, injuries, and fatigue were mere excuses to him. His will bordered on the supernatural.

Clarke's body gave no clues as to where the energy came from. As his career progressed, his devotion to conditioning eventually became fanatical, but hour after hour of pumped iron produced little chest definition and modest lumps for biceps. The unremarkable physique, the blond, choir-boy curls, and the easy, gap-toothed grin embellished the legend of his iron resolve but led to his skills becoming underrated, which was absurd.

For his ability to find an open man, Clarke was Wayne Gretzky before Wayne Gretzky. "Probably the closest comparison to Bob before he came long would have been Stan Mikita, because Stan had an edge to him too," said Scotty Bowman, the coach with the most wins in NHL history.

Mikita's .664 assists per game is the highest average by far of any player from an era that preceded Clarke's. Bobby's' was .745, 13th in NHL history.

The statistics have to be weighted for their times, but the beauty of the pass always has been in the eye of the receiver or beholder. Weren't diabetics supposed to be at risk for vision problems? Didn't this kid wear glasses off the ice? Then how could he see everything behind him too, ahead of everyone else?

"I can remember someone who saw Frank Boucher in the '30s, saying Clarke was the best passer since," said Frank Orr, the retired *Toronto Star* writer who began covering the NHL in 1961. "Milt Schmidt, Sid Abel, Mikita and Henri Richard were wonderful passers, but Clarke was as creative as any of them."

That said, 358 goals and 852 assists, which made him the 11th all-time point producer at the time of his retirement, don't come close to defining Clarke's value. Hundreds more points couldn't capture his essence in a hundred years.

Neither did the most clutch score in franchise history, in overtime of Game Two in Boston, changing the course of the 1974 Final, or the spectacular 141 goals scored by the LCB line—Leach, Clarke and Bill Barber—in 1975-76. Even Bowman, whose Canadiens swept the Flyers in the Final that year, calls it the best line he ever saw.

"I was just pretty proud being a member of the Flyers," says Clarke about his place in hockey history or as a Philadelphia icon. "I was just a guy who cared about the team, same as when I managed."

The team was above everything to him, why he was no diplomat whenever he perceived anyone—such as the Lindros family—putting themselves above the greater good.

When asked if any of the individual honors meant much to him, he skips three NHL MVPs and cites the Frank Selke Trophy (best defensive forward), which he was voted in his next-to-last season.

"I had already proven I could score with any of the big scorers," he says, but what he prevented—Clarke was an astounding plus-83 in 1975-76—always was more important to him. By the end of the 2015-16 season, 43 greats of the game had outscored him for their careers. But no player or observer in the know ever has claimed that anyone outplayed Clarke for the full 200 feet of a rink.

"In that era, great offensive players didn't participate as much in the defensive zone; played against other team's top defensive line," recalls Canadiens Hall of Famer Bob Gainey, who coached for Clarke when he was general manager of the Minnesota North Stars. "But Clarke excelled in all areas, including penalty-killing at a time when scorers didn't do that.

"There was not a part of the game where Bob Clarke couldn't be the dominant player and he did it for a long period of time. For me, he's a top-10 all-time player."

And the reasons for that started with how Clarke thought the game.

"His hockey IQ was off the charts," said Clement, Clarke's teammate for five seasons, now one of the game's most respected television analysts. "He understood angles, other players' intentions, what their options were, and closed them, always a step ahead of everybody.

"Because he knew what was going to happen next, he didn't always take a direct path. Very often he could accomplish something defensively by taking a shorter route as opposed to other players taking the obvious route.

"With a wide stance and strong legs, he was more a powerful skater than a fast one. But he would get a jump because he read the play.

"Here's how he thought the game: In backchecking, I would reach for the guy and tug him with my stick, which was allowed then. Clarkie said, 'If you take three more quick strides, you'll be beside him and then you can lift his stick and take the puck before he even knows you're there. I was fast enough to do that, hadn't thought of it like he did."

Faceoff statistics were not kept back far enough to measure Clarke against any center that followed him. The raw percentages wouldn't prove anything regardless. The drop-off in Clarke's success rate between the bluelines as compared to inside the zones suggests he was smart enough to lose some to win more important ones.

There is no argument, statistical or visual, for any other player in the game's history being as dominant a forechecker as was Clarke. "He would eliminate all [opponent] options," recalls Holmgren. "Cut the ice in half and then cut it in half again. "Twelve times a game I would say, 'How did he do that?'"

And only then did the real fun begin.

"He had very underrated lower body strength that enabled him to separate somebody from a puck," recalls Clement. "He would pin their arms against the boards with the bottom part of his body and keep his own hands free so that he could make a play.

"His upper body wasn't impressive to look at—even though he spent more time in the gym than most players did at the time—but he had superb hand strength, why he was so good on faceoffs. You combine that with leg strength, you don't lose the puck."

The greatest goal scorer in history, Gretzky, was not a goal scorer by nature, much more a pass-first guy like Clarke. But the 358 goals scored by No. 16 weren't by accident.

Few were as visually stunning—or reflective of his indomitability—as the one in Detroit, when he was tripped from behind on a breakaway, regained control of the puck as he crawled to the hashmarks and, from his knees, roofed a wrist shot over Eddie Giacomin. On Clarke's patented wrap-arounds, he didn't beat the goalie on every occasion to the far post, just a lot of the times the Flyers needed a goal the most.

Mostly, he scored with accuracy.

"He didn't shoot it hard, but he knew where and when, like how to use screens," said Clement. "And of course he got them by going to the dirty areas."

Those areas got dirtier with him in them. "If he felt he needed to be outside the rules, he would go outside the rules," recalls Gainey. "Once he was locked in, there wasn't anywhere he wouldn't go."

The demands Clarke placed on himself prompted admiration from opponents, but his obsession with victory at practically any cost also drew hatred. Clarke expressed no remorse for what he did to Kharlamov—let the record show that the Russian finished that game and missed only the next one—or for spearing Toronto defenseman Rod Seiling, a good friend from the 1972 series, in the face.

Referee Dave Newell, never the Broad Street Bullies favorite, once crumpled mysteriously in the corner, clutching his midsection, with Clarke in suspicious close proximity.

When an obscure Oakland player named Barry Cummins had suffered enough of Clarke's abuse one 1973 night at the Spectrum and took a full two-hander to open up the star's head, the Flyers attacked Cummins en masse. They protected their captain obsessively, but he hardly escaped from retaliation. By the time Clarke retired, his face, scarred by sticks and pucks, had become a road map of his career.

One enduring impression came from the 1981 game in which he scored a goal for his 1,000th career point. Clarke did it with a jersey stained in blood by a rising Leach shot that had creased his cheek.

In 1983, as he skated off the Chicago Stadium ice with a skate cut on the eyelid that horrifyingly appeared to be in the eye itself, Bobby feared he had lost what was left of his career.

Somehow, the eye never swelled shut. After 10 stitches and seven minutes of the second period, Clarke came back to the bench, and with one minute go in the game and the Flyers down 3-2, he descended upon Blackhawks defenseman Bob Murray just as he was clearing the puck towards an empty net chance

Murray wound up dazed on his back. The puck, fed by Clarke from behind the goal to Miroslav Dvorak, landed in the Chicago net with 54 seconds remaining.

Of course, Clarke was not required to bleed to do a good night's work. And he didn't have to give teammates or trainers a puppy, a gift certificate, or the flannel shirt off his back every time he won something. It only seemed that way during the Cup years.

Too thoughtful to be true when the team was at its peak, Prince Valiant had to turn politician in later seasons and dodge undercurrents of jealousy. He would have played for free, and teammates, frustrated by the low ceiling he set on Ed Snider's payroll, thought Clarke practically did, retarding their earning power. Some Flyers, believing Clarke's bond with Snider gave a player a say in personnel decisions, grew to fear him, but those who shared his hatred for losing only admired and followed him.

"I heard the speech he gave to the Flyers or to the Phantoms many times," recalls Holmgren. He would say, 'It's a [bleeping] game. You've got to love it to be good at it.'

"Watching so many games sitting next to him, listening to things he picks up in watching, I think he would have been a great coach. But maybe not. I can't think of too many people who loved the game like he did. He might have been frustrated by players who didn't."

Between the peak years of Bobby Orr and Guy Lafleur, Clarke, the Hart Trophy winner in 1973, 1975 and 1976, was unquestionably the best player in the game and the record shows he was a good general manager. The teams he played on went 613-360-215 in the regular season and 71-65 in the playoffs. The clubs Clarke managed were 714-443-169-30 in the regular season and 106-93 in the postseason.

"He called me (during the summer of 1984) crying that (Flyer president) Jay Snider was trying to force him out by offering him the GM's job," recalls Holmgren. And yet, when Clarke decided he might never get a better offer, the transformation from rink to office without training was remarkable. So were his first three years as GM, when he supplemented Keith Allen's and Bob McCammon's groundwork and produced two Stanley Cup finalists.

In 17 seasons as general manager, Clarke's teams missed the playoffs twice, if you count 2006-07, when he resigned after eight games and Holmgren inherited the worst team in franchise history.

"I know I apologized to Holmgren a number of times," Clarke said. "It was my fault and I never denied it was my responsibility.

"I knew we had some good young players but I waited too long hoping (Keith) Primeau and (Eric) Desjardins would come back. Then (Peter) Forsberg got hurt and it was just one of those years."

If you stay too long, which Clarke feared doing, you are going to have those seasons eventually. If it has to be "Cup or Bust" in a league that had 12 teams when he debuted and 30 upon his resignation in 2006-07, that standard is too tough for even Mr. Flyer, who was only one of the toughest—as player or negotiator—there ever was.

"We had a lot of success over the years, got deep into the playoffs," said Clarke. "In Philly, you are hired to win the Stanley Cup, but I don't think I was a failure.

"If you compare me to other general managers, I probably was a success. But others won the Cup, so they were more of a success.

"We got criticized for being the Bullies, but overall the organization was extremely competitive and classy. We were a leader in treating players and employees better than other teams, and all of that goes back to Ed Snider. Free agents wanted to play here because it was a given that the team had a chance to win almost every season.

"It is always easy to take four or five years and try to rebuild like Pittsburgh and Chicago have done. But practically everybody who does that loses their jobs. It would have been the death of me to play on a team that was rebuilding.

"You always try to win. If you do [bleep] up, admit the mistake and move on. Trading Davey Poulin (for a fast-aging Ken Linseman) was really dumb. And I would say the same thing about Brad McCrimmon (for a late first-round draft choice). (Michal) Handzus for (Kyle) Calder was horrible.

"The Patrick Sharp (for Matt Ellison) trade turned out bad for us but the circumstances were perfect for Patrick in Chicago. On a team that was trying to lose for a long time, he ended up playing. Had he stayed on a good team, he might not have.

"I look at that a little differently than taking a McCrimmon or a Poulin off a team. It didn't hurt our club to lose Justin Williams (traded for Danny Markov, who proved just a rental). Eight years later I might wish we still had Justin because he is playing so well, but taking Sharp and Williams off those teams at the time didn't hurt us."

Clarke's critics would call the above a grievous list. But in a body of work of 17 seasons, it is not a particularly long one. Clarke made a top-three trade in franchise history in obtaining John LeClair and Eric Desjardins for Mark Recchi and, until the end, still had drafted and traded for enough assets to survive the odd bad deal and maintain a contending. Even when the bottom dropped out in 2006-07, Clarke left Holmgren plenty in talent and cap room for the Flyers to rise from the ashes of 56 points to a conference final the next season.

In the final telling, the major failing of his reign was goaltending.

"That's probably fair enough," Clarke said. "Yet during that time we won some (Jennings) trophies for goals-against (in 2000 with John Vanbiesbrouck and Brian Boucher, and in 2002 with Roman Cechmanek and Robert Esche).

"There are more examples of teams winning the Cup without great goalies than you think. But signing (John) Vanbiesbrouck and not Joseph (in 1998) was a mistake. I don't want to sound like I'm blaming Vanbiesbrouck, but I think we would have won a Cup with Joseph.

"Luck figures into anything you do. The worst was when Pelle Lindbergh [died in an automobile accident]. Detroit offered the first pick in the draft for Ron Hextall. Imagine the assets you would have gotten for trading one of them? We go from having the best two goalies in the league to struggling for 20 years.

"One year (2004), Pittsburgh gets (Evgeni) Malkin with the second pick. (In 2007) We get (James) Van Riemsdyk."

The hockey gods have long memories. Maybe they have been delivering payback for the Flyers passing over Clarke to draft a complete bust, Bob Currier, and still getting a top-10 all-time player a round later.

"I'd put him up with anybody, including Mark Messier, for total value to a team," said Clement. "To this day, I still shake my head at Clarkie's wisdom, his communications skills and sense of when to use which tool.

"When we won our first Stanley Cup, he was 24 and I was 23. I just couldn't believe some of the things he was capable of in a leadership sense. He was amazing."

Philadelphia knew it, too. On Bobby Clarke Night, November 15, 1984, the fans at the Spectrum stood for more than four minutes cheering the greatest Flyer of them all. The team lavished expensive gifts on him and the people bestowed their love, but they owed him still more for what he had given them, which had always been everything he had.

Never once in his playing career did the fans boo him. If they understood that you can't win them all, it was because they watched No. 16 exhaust himself on nights the Flyers fell short.

"In Clarkie's day they didn't know [bleep] about diabetes," said Holmgren. "Now they have these pumps that automatically provide the amount of insulin you need.

"Bob was playing when you had to prick a finger, test your blood once or twice a day, pick a spot in your belly or thigh and give yourself a shot.

"There were times I would be with him when he would have one of those [hypoglycemic] reactions and had no idea where he was. It could happen anytime, anywhere.

"It never did on the ice, but I saw it on planes and in airports. You had to know what to do, get him an orange, candy bar or Coke, and you could get him back quickly.

"Being in good physical condition probably helped him when he didn't take quite as good care of himself as he does now. But the deck was stacked against him in so many ways and he made it 15 years and to a thousand games, two Stanley Cups and three Hart Trophies.

"He was a miracle."

KEITH ALLEN

KEITH ALLEN ONCE TRADED BERNIE PARENT, the Flyers' most beloved player from Day One of the franchise. But it took two years for the GM who put together history's meanest NHL champions to work up the courage to fire a secretary whose demeanor suggested that he worked for her.

Behind that poker face—and after all of Allen's "cogitating," and "exploring of parameters" that led to the deals producing consecutive Stanley Cups—was a bottomless well of good judgment that invariably conquered a heart made of mush.

"Each time we traded one of the Stanley Cup players it tore me apart," Allen said later in his life. "I loved those guys.

"I feel good when I see them now because none of them has expressed any bitterness. And I'm the guy who traded their asses away."

Blake Allen, singer, songwriter and Keith's youngest son, remembers the least popular parental advice in the Allen household as, "Sometimes you have to do things you don't want to do." Joyce Allen, Keith's wife of 65 years, recalls a little sadness—and an extra cocktail or two—following the most gut-wrenching decisions. But she had married the most resolute man in Meota, Saskatchewan, and watched as his coolness under fire carried him all the way to the Hockey Hall of Fame.

"Keith Allen is the only general manager in the NHL with a matching set of pearl-handled revolvers," Bill Torrey, the rival architect of four Islander cup winners, once joked. "He gives you that quiet, dignified look while he's letting you have it right between the eyes."

On the spring 1971 day that Allen fired coach Vic Stasiuk, he kept his afternoon appointment for a physical with Flyers physician Dr. Stanley Spoont.

"I told him I had just fired Vic," Allen recalled. "He said, 'You're a cool customer. Your blood pressure is normal.'"

Actually, Allen's stomach suffered from his job more than did his general good nature. Blake recalls bottles of Maalox continuously being pulled from desk drawers and glove compartments. When it was suggested Allen knock off the caffeine, he took to sipping plain hot water, a habit fully symbolic of both his poker face and the heat that came with his territory.

"I don't think they ever could pay that man enough," said a rival general manager familiar with Allen's particular set of circumstances.

Primarily, the man meant the hotline in front of Allen in the upper row of the Spectrum press box, into which Ed Snider would rail from his box across the arena.

"With my personality, I was seething a lot of times, either about the officiating or about how we were playing," recalls Snider. "I know I drove Keith crazy with my phone calls but he always calmed me down.

"A few years after we had traded Dave Schultz, I was pushing and pushing to bring Davey back until finally Keith exploded and walked out of the hotel suite. 'You want him so goddamn bad, I'll get him for you,' he said.

"To me that said, 'You're the owner, but this is against my better judgment.' Far be it from me to question that so I backed down, like I did the time that I was on my way outside the (Minnesota) Met Center to settle my differences with this fan who had been harassing me and our team. He had big muscles and boy I was getting nervous when Keith jumped in with, 'Now cut that out!' and saved me from myself."

The irony of the architect of the prickliest NHL champions there ever were playing peacemaker to rescue their feisty owner from a back-alley beating is hilarious. But Allen had his breaking point, too.

"He was pretty mellow until pushed to the brink," recalls Traci, his daughter.

One big turnaround whack from Dad in the driver's seat—where he invariably was singing—provided plenty of force to end whatever shenanigans were going on among his three young children in the back seat.

Of course, Allen also didn't believe in sparing the rod on the Flyers' opponents. "Rattle him!!!" Keith would exhort whenever one was lined up for a body check and he insisted Ken Linseman stick those "goddamn drop passes" where the sun doesn't shine. Yet Blake vividly recalls coming down to breakfast on the day after the Flyers were dethroned by the Canadiens to incredulously find his mother and father calmly reading the newspaper.

"Babe, "shrugged Keith, "Into each life, a little rain must fall.'"

"When he got in your face, he was scary," said Blake. "But the other side was a sweetheart.

"He had perfect balance to his life and knew where the switch was, like calling the waiter over to straighten something out and then immediately going back to being the happiest guy."

When new names appeared on the scratch pads Allen left around the house with Flyer lines and defense pairings, a deal was in the works. The closer the trade was to being consummated, the better the

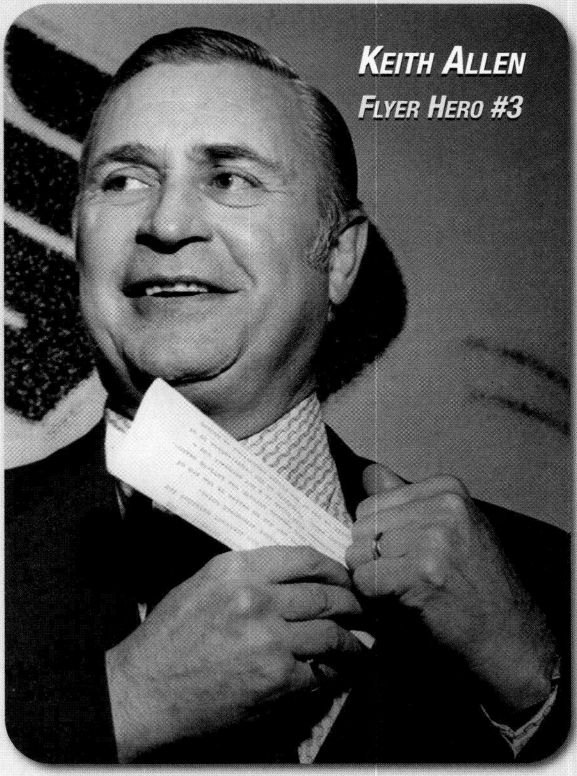
KEITH ALLEN
FLYER HERO #3

mood Keith was in.

"We were sworn to secrecy, of course, but he ran every deal by us," recalls Blake. "He'd say, Would you trade Brent Hughes and Pierre Plante to St. Louis for Moose Dupont and a third-rounder?'"

"Asking me was like telling the dog about your day. I wanted to make every deal as proposed. (Older brother) Brad always wanted another draft choice thrown in."

In 1982, Allen was closing in on a desperately-needed Mark Howe when the Whalers came back with one more thing they wanted in addition to Ken Linseman, a No. 1 pick and an exchange of third rounders—a left wing of some promise named Greg Adams.

"Goddamn it, that's too much, we're not going to do it," Allen told Snider after the Whalers refused substitutes. He was adamant, seemed ready to call the deal off.

Snider always deferred judgment on talent to his GM. The owner's job, he felt, was to ask the big-picture questions.

"How would Mark Howe rank in all the defensemen we've ever had?" he asked Allen.

"He would be twice as good as anybody, potentially one of the top five in the league if we get him into a winning atmosphere," Allen replied.

"And you don't want to do the deal because you want to keep Greg Adams?" asked Snider.

Allen relented. Adams scored 84 goals with seven teams in 10 NHL seasons while Howe became a three-time first-team All-Star and glued together two Stanley Cup Final teams. Still, that deal still represented probably only the third-best one Allen ever made. There was no better example of his vision and patience than the trade of Parent in 1971, when the four-year-old franchise decided to use its only position of depth—goaltending—to address drastic scoring needs.

"This was only the first of many examples of Keith doing what he thought was right and not being paralyzed by the fear of what fans and media would think," recalls Snider. "But what made this deal especially gutsy was that instead of keeping Mike Walton, the established scorer we obtained along with a(first-round) pick for Parent from Toronto, Keith immediately used Walton in another deal with Boston that brought Rick MacLeish.

"Ricky was struggling in the minors at the time. Scoring just three goals in the 43 games he played in Philadelphia over the next season-and-a-half, he floundered for us, too, at first. Philosophically, I had fully endorsed the deal but, man was I nervous, which I probably reminded my GM twice every week or so.

'Don't worry,' Keith would reassure me. 'MacLeish is going to be great.' Then, suddenly he was, exploding to 50 goals in 1972-73, our breakthrough season. That year, when we added Bill Barber with the seventh-overall pick in the draft, the belief I shared in Keith's building philosophy was backed up by my full realization of what an incredible judge of talent he was."

Allen reacquired Parent before the 1973-74 season in a deal for Doug Favell—the goalie who, two years earlier, the Flyers had kept over Bernie—and an exchange of first-round picks. The two best seasons of goaltending (considering Parent's workload) in NHL history followed. Thus the two best trades the Flyers ever made involved the same player, once going, once coming, quite the statement about the relentlessly driven, cool, and reasonable man who made them.

"He let you do your job and he listened," recalls Marcel Pelletier, the Flyers' director of player personnel for 19 years and like Keith, an original employee. "He never held power over you.

"We drafted for toughness for a long time but that was to back up skill and smarts. He traded for MacLeish, drafted Barber, but the talent had to come with courage or he wasn't much interested."

Allen chased Reggie Leach—Bobby Clarke's old Flin Flon right wing taken one pick ahead of MacLeish in the 1970 draft—through underwhelming stays in Boston and Oakland. Refusing to sit tight with a winner, Allen acquired Leach just five days after the first Cup for a package including winger Alan MacAdam, who became a three time 30-plus goal scorer and the most lasting asset Keith ever traded away (Parent being re-obtained).

"Keith wanted talent on the rise and didn't settle for retreads when he picked his coaches either," said Snider. "After firing Stasiuk, Allen told me about the good track record of somebody named Fred Shero, a coach in the Ranger system, and sought permission to talk to him from New York GM Emile Francis.

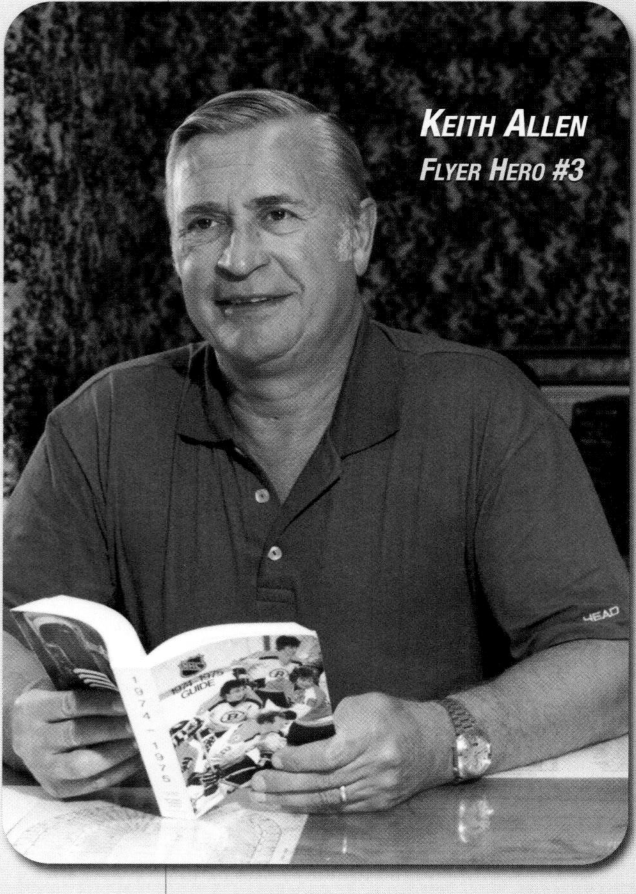

"When I asked him how well he knew Shero, Keith said he didn't know him at all. Think about that. Keith probably knew five guys who had already been NHL head coaches who would have been a safe choice but he wanted to take a chance on someone with a great minor-league record."

While many players were too small or shy for Allen's taste, nobody was too obscure. As he changed knuckles from Dave Schultz to Jack McIlhargey to Paul Holmgren, Keith never thought his teams could have enough of what he euphemistically called "that certain element," even while upgrading the Flyers' skill and speed. While he loved having characters on his team, most of all he valued character. His second-ever acquisition, a career minor-league defenseman named Barry Ashbee, became an NHL All-Star at age 34 and proved probably the Flyers' most courageous player ever.

"Because he so highly valued integrity, our players were attractive to struggling teams, enabling us to make deals for good young talents that were struggling in other organizations," recalls Snider.

"I remember a meeting early in the 1976-77 season where we targeted young defensemen who had gone high in the draft. There were four on our list. By February two of them—Bob Dailey and Rick Lapointe—were Flyers.

"I can't recall one player he traded away in his 14 years as GM that we would come to regret. 'Keith The Thief' (bestowed upon Allen by Bill Fleischman of *The Philadelphia Daily News*), nailed it forever. In our sport, I have not seen a track record like his since. "

Two Stanley Cups, two more appearances in the Final, seven semifinalists and six regular-season divisional titles in 14 years are testament to the vision that resulted in Allen's 1992 election to the Hockey Hall of Fame.

"I always believed our Stanley Cup teams never got all the credit they deserved," said Allen after waiting 17 years after the second title and eight following his retirement as GM for his induction. "A lot of people didn't like us. It made me wonder if this would ever happen."

It would be less of a Hall of Fame without him. Allen was so far ahead of his time that not only were the Flyers the first expansion team to win the Cup but in doing so they were the only one of the six franchises born with them that even had a winning record that season.

Hired a year before the Flyers began play, he

helped scout four expansion-draft picks—Parent, Joe Watson, Gary Dornhoefer and Ed Van Impe – who seven and eight years later were mainstays of the championship teams. In addition, 12 regulars on the 1985 and 1987 Stanley Cup finalists were acquired by Allen before he became a senior advisor in 1983. And Snider insists those hardly were the only gifts that Keith kept on giving beyond his tenure as GM.

"Because of the quality and the color of the Broad Street Bullies team that Keith put together, the Flyers have fans everywhere, a fact reflected by how much orange you see in the stands when our team is on the road," said Snider. "I believe our profile in hockey is comparable to that of the Dallas Cowboys in football and that started with Keith Allen.

"Under this innovator, Mike Nykoluk became the NHL's first assistant coach. And we were an early, if not the first, organization to use computers to quantify and evaluate the opinions of our scouts. I don't specifically remember who came up with those ideas, but it's not important because whatever we did was in consensus. Keith didn't care about credit, only about Stanley Cups.

"We had a phenomenal working relationship."

Snider was a football team treasurer spearheading the building of an indoor sports arena in South Philadelphia for Eagles owner Jerry Wolman when early Flyers figures who knew more about hockey hired Allen as the team's first coach.

Born in Saskatoon, Saskatchewan to two schoolteachers of nearby Blaine Lake in 1923, and wed to Joyce Webster, the secretary at the Canadian Legion 20 miles away in Meota, Allen spent 11 minor-league seasons that bridged his World War II service in the Canadian Navy chasing a precious place on the blueline in the six-team NHL. Finally refusing to be at the mercy of the tyrannical and quirky Springfield owner and coach Eddie Shore, Allen in 1954 quit hockey to go home to sell cars in Saskatoon and arrived to learn he had forced Shore to sell him to the Red Wings.

Four months later, he was a call-up as theWings won their third Cup in five years, then returned to the minors, where the Red Wings top minor-league team in Edmonton was coached by Norman (Bud) Poile. Poile saw coaching and managerial potential in Allen and, when he moved onto the San Francisco Seals of the Western Hockey League, recommended his friend to the ownership of the Seattle Totems.

Allen was coach, GM, and publicist of the Totems for eight years, recording only one losing season. Tired of being the mediator for a fractious ownership group, he was interviewing for a job in the same league with the San Diego Gulls when Poile, the choice of Snider's partner Bill Putnam to be the first Flyers GM, called with the offer to come to Philadelphia to coach, then later move into the front office.

Allen directed the Flyers to first- and third-place finishes in the West division, where all the new teams had been placed, before being made assistant GM in 1970. While Snider learned more about the game—and asked more questions that the blustery, old-school, Poile resented—the majority owner was forging a relationship with Allen.

From the end of the draft table, Snider had watched Allen bend to the pleas of scout Jerry Melnyk to use the second-round pick in the 1969 draft to take a diabetic named Bobby Clarke, and grew to appreciate the measured manner of the assistant GM. When a Poile tirade about Snider on the team bus following a game got back to the owner, he fired the GM and offered Allen the job.

"The Poiles were like family with us," recalls Joyce. Keith asked for time to think about whether taking his friend's job was a betrayal.

"Mom told me Dad disappeared for the weekend while he thought it over," recalls Blake. "On that Sunday, Bud came to the house and told him to take it."

Next to the drafting of Clarke, empowering Allen to construct the team was the best move the Flyers ever made. Philosophically wed to the goal of winning a Stanley Cup, not just beating out the other five new teams for playoff spots, Snider and Allen forged a new-age sports partnership.

"In a different era than today—when GMs work for owners more than they work with them—Keith and I watched games together, ate and drank together," recalls Snider.

"He was one of the nicest, most straightforward and solid persons you ever would meet. I loved him for many more reasons than how instrumental he was in the Flyers' and my personal success."

When Allen was about to hit age 60 and dropped hints about winding down, Snider took him literally. Believing new team president Jay Snider should have his own working relationship with a younger GM—and deciding to keep Bob McCammon after the coach received a coach-GM offer from Pittsburgh, Snider told a shocked Allen he was being moved to a senior advisory position.

Soon after, the Vancouver Canucks came to him with a million-dollar offer but there was little enthusiasm in the family to move. Allen settled in advising McCammon for his one year as GM, and then mentoring Clarke when he went from ice to boss in 1984.

"Keith never ever showed me any frustration or that he thought he should still be the GM, which he should have been because he told me everything about what to do." recalls Clarke. "He was still young, still bright.

"He knew what the other GMs were like, how to talk to them. If other teams lost three or four games, he would know which ones would and would not panic.

"He'd tell me, 'you're wasting your time talking to this guy but say hello from me.'

"One time in a contract negotiation—I forget who the player or the agent was but it was a guy with several clients—Keith said it probably was worth giving a couple thousand more dollars to this player to keep the agent on your side.

"I was just learning and getting into fights over $5,000 for absolutely no [bleeping] reason. Keith was right.

"As tough as he could be about making decisions, he could do it in a gentle way. Everybody he traded away has told me the same story: Keith told them: 'You're really going to like it there. Detroit is a great city, Never mind they haven't made the playoffs in 20 [bleeping] years, you'll love it.'"

Most of the key players on the Stanley Cup teams got sent off with more than just verbal thanks. Allen gave both Andre Dupont (traded home to Quebec, and Simon Nolet (taken in the expansion draft by Kansas City) new three-year contracts before they were moved on. The GM asked Joe Watson for a list of teams where he might want to go and delivered him to one of them, Colorado.

"He shot the straightest arrow," said Bill Barber, probably Keith's favorite of all his beloved Bullies. No wonder that the Allen's summer home on Long Beach Island, NJ—it was destroyed by Hurricane Sandy just four days after Joyce and Keith moved into assisted living in Delaware County, PA—so often was filled with old hockey players.

When Allen died of complications from chronic obstructive pulmonary disease on February 4, 2014 at age 90, the Broad Street Bullies had lost not an old boss but a father figure. They were much more grateful that one of the greatest builders in NHL history thought enough of them to have once made them Flyers than they were bitter at him for eventually sending them away.

BERNIE PARENT

GOALTENDING, THE LAST LINE OF DEFENSE, was not a desperate, sweaty act when Bernie Parent played the position. He made it an art.

His movements were economical and fluid. Parent always seemed to know where the puck had the best chance of hitting him and, in the pre-butterfly days, would patiently stand there waiting for it. He didn't flail at shots but accepted them, cleanly snatching or sticking the puck out of harm's way. Rebounds, the goaltender's quintessential anxiety, were rare when No. 1 was at the top of his game. He reflected a serenity that calmed and inspired his teammates, convincing them that they could beat anybody.

For two years, the Flyers did. Considering Parent's workload, they perhaps were the two greatest any goaltender ever played. In 1973-74, he set NHL records for games (73) and wins (47), compiling 12 shutouts and a goals-against average of 1.89. In the playoffs, Parent went 12-5 with a 2.02 goals-against average. The next season he had another 12 shutouts and a 2.03 average, followed by 10-5, 1.89 in the playoffs. During the consecutive Cup-winning springs, he accumulated six playoff shutouts, including both clinching games.

"He was the best," said Bobby Taylor, then Parent's backup and later the Flyers' radio-television analyst. "The only one who could come close was Glenn Hall.

"Bernie played 65 games a year and there would only be a handful of bad performances. The rest were not just good, but great. He was always there, like the sun rising in the east and setting in the west. He never had to move that much; his anticipation was just phenomenal. His feet were the key. He used them better than anybody."

The defensive-minded Flyers protected their goalie fiercely, at the cost of taking penalties that left him little margin for error. "You get 50 shots against, blow two or three, lose 5-4 but make some spectacular saves and everybody says how great you played," said Taylor. "The 19 or 20-shot shutout or one-goal game is a lot tougher mentally.

"Think about how often we were shorthanded in those years and the pressure Bernie was under. He was incredible."

The youngest of seven children of a financially-challenged Montreal cement-machine operator, Bernie got his start kicking out rubber balls while wearing galoshes but was more serious about baseball until his early teens. Considered too slow by his first organized coach to play forward or defense, Parent was rejected as a goalie, too, by a team the Canadiens sponsored, and settled for a spot on one of the two in the city unaffiliated with the NHL organization.

At 16, Parent signed with the Bruins and went off to their junior team in Niagara Falls. It wasn't just his English that left him poorly equipped to leave Montreal. The team he left behind refused to release his pads, catcher and blocker and because Hap Emms, the Niagara Falls Flyers owner and GM, wouldn't pay for them, Parent sat for two months until his parents dug into their pockets.

Even with the late start, Bernie became a second team All-Star that season and the next year shared the net as his team won the Ontario Hockey Association championship. The following year, the long-suffering Bruins hurried the 20-year-old Parent into their net for 39 games and, for the first time in six seasons, Boston did not finish last. But for an encore in 1966-67, Bernie drank too many beers, stopped too few pucks and heard too many boos before being sent to the minors and left unprotected in the great 1967 expansion draft.

Parent and Doug Favell, with whom Parent had shared the goal in Niagara Falls and Oklahoma City—and the other netminder the Flyers selected in the expansion draft—instantly became the new Philadelphia team's best and most popular players, providing most of the respectability the franchise had.

When the punchless Flyers grew tired of having to play for a tie, they learned Parent, who was a more classically-styled standup netminder than Favell, would have to be the one to go to bring the scoring help they desperately needed. Midway through Philadelphia's fourth season, GM Keith Allen traded Parent in a three-way deal that sent him to Toronto and brought a first-round pick from the Leafs and prospect Rick MacLeish from Boston.

The deal turned fans against Allen and emotionally devastated Parent, but his year and a half with the Maple Leafs allowed him to share a net and thoughts with 41-year-old Jacques Plante, the gray-haired goaltending genius. Plante, aloof, frugal and egotistical, had been essentially a loner at his NHL stops, but took a liking to Parent, was intrigued by his abilities, and set out to refine him.

"He didn't really change my style," Bernie said. "He just taught me how to use my own system." Parent had always stood up well, but didn't challenge or distribute his weight to best facilitate his movements. Plante recommended springing from the right foot to improve balance and structured a mental checklist to help Parent focus more on mechanics and less on his fear of the next goal.

A five-year, $750,000 contract offer—crazy money for a hockey player in 1972—brought Parent to the World Hockey Association Blazers and back to Philadelphia. But the new team that was supposed to steal the town's hockey hearts instead became a cheap substitute for the suddenly-emerging Flyers. When the Blazers' paychecks began arriving late, Parent, under advice of agent Howard Casper, withheld his services for the playoffs. When Casper next

BERNIE PARENT
FLYER HERO #4

insisted that his client would not return to Toronto, the Leafs traded his rights and a second-round pick to the Flyers for a first-round choice and the hot and cold Favell.

On opening night of the 1973-74 NHL season, Bernie shut out the Leafs and Favell at the Spectrum. After that, Parent looked back only to see the cars behind his own in the Stanley Cup parades.

What, Bernie worry? In the final minutes of Game Six in the 1974 Final, with the dreams of any hockey lifetime hanging by one goal, Parent called over teammate Simon Nolet.

"From the bench I see Simon give him an annoyed wave and skate away," said Clarke. "I asked him, 'What did that crazy [bleeper] say?' and Simon told me he was bragging about his new golf clubs."

During the next stoppage, Parent summoned Joe Watson and referee Art Skov to explain the . . . uh, social advantages of winning the Cup, which Parent did with under three minutes to go by coolly kicking out a Ken Hodge bullet labeled for the low far corner. It probably was the biggest save in Flyers history, unless Parent already had made it in Game Two, when he stopped John Bucyk on an overtime breakaway just before Bobby Clarke scored to turn the series.

The bumper stickers said, "Only the Lord saves more than Bernie Parent." In turn, he saved his worst fears only for private expression. During practice, the Flyers barely saw that happy-go-lucky Bernie. Clarke remembers a fiercely competitive Parent throwing his stick at scorers who dared beat him. In times of excruciating tension, however, he left his teammates laughing.

"Take the edge off a little bit, then get back to your concentration," recalls Parent. "It worked."

After the second Cup, he needed the chuckles more than ever. Bernie missed much of the 1975-76 season following neck surgery to repair two discs and then was replaced by Wayne Stephenson both in that spring's playoffs and the next. Though he never again approached a sustained level of excellence, Parent almost was as sharp as ever in the 1978 playoffs, when Philadelphia beat Colorado and Buffalo before losing to Boston in the semifinals.

The following February, he still was making opponents earn their goals when Jimmy Watson, attempting to move a Ranger from in front of the goal, accidently put the blade of his stick through the right eye slit of Parent's mask. He immediately skated up the tunnel, as it turned out forever.

"He can't catch a ball his kids throw to him, let alone stop a puck," said Dr. Edward Viner, the Flyers' physician, when Parent announced his retirement on June 1, 1979.

Suddenly cut off from the life he had known—and more seasons needed to make up the WHA windfall that Casper lost—Bernie sank in a vat of booze before making his biggest save by joining Alcoholics Anonymous. "The Secret", a best-selling self-help book published in 2006, has become the bible of perhaps the most popular athlete Philadelphia ever has known.

The first Flyer elected to the Hockey Hall of Fame (1984), Parent, the father of three, is a game-night greeter at the Wells Fargo Center, living six months a year off his Wildwood, NJ-docked boat named "The French Connection" and hunting from a lodge in Pennsgrove, NJ.

"When you think about it, if I hadn't gone to Toronto, Plante wouldn't have saved my career," said Parent, also inducted along with Bobby Clarke in the first class of the Flyers Hall of Fame (1988). "Then, because I left Toronto (for the WHA), the Leafs didn't want me back after [the Blazers] stopped paying me; otherwise, I never would have come back to Philly.

"The whole path, it's incredible, but it only happens if you want to take the risk and move forward. You get what you see in the mirror."

In time, he could see himself better than ever there. Thanks to the insertion of an intraocular lens, common procedure today for patients with cataracts, Parent's vision in the damaged eye has been restored. Today, the man in the looking glass is distinguished and charming, living a happily-ever-after life.

"He always had to bear the burden of how good he was before the neck injury," said Taylor, "Yet he was one of the most together guys I ever came across.

"Whatever he was going through inside, he was excellent in the locker room before games. He talked about hunting and fishing. He'd laugh, he'd joke, he'd tell stories about his German shepherd Tinker Bell, with whom he always shared a pregame nap in his bed."

Tinker Bell slept not only with her master, but The Master. There was no confusing the Parent who was vulnerable to life with the one who was impregnable in goal. "Bernie always talked about the pressure," said Keith Allen. "But he seemed immune to it."

BILL BARBER

THE HIGHEST COMPLIMENT a player can receive in a team game is the one Bill Barber earned: By dedicating his career to blending in, he clearly stood out.

For 12 seasons, Barber skated up and down left wing so effectively, yet with such modest fanfare, that, even though widely accepted as the best player at his position in the game, he sometimes was taken for granted.

"I'm just happy to be here," No. 7 would joke, usually after insisting team goals came ahead of any of the 420 he scored personally. Ranked 17th on the all-time list when he retired in 1985, Barber's career total of 883 points was far too high to relegate him to anonymity. Yet the "how" to his career still proved more important than the "how many." Barber combined with his artist's skills, a grinder's soul.

BILL BARBER
FLYER HERO #5

"I want to be remembered as being capable of doing my job day in and day out, not just as a goal scorer, but as a good all-around player for every kind of situation," he said. Barber's election to the Hockey Hall of Fame in 1990 indicated that the selection committee had perfect recall of a nearly perfect player.

"He was so intelligent, always in good defensive position," recalls Bob Clarke, Barber's linemate with Reggie Leach in 1975-76, when the LCB line combined for a staggering 141 goals. "It was Scotty Bowman who told me that we were on the ice that year for something like five even-strength goals against the entire year.

"He also told me it was the best line he ever saw."

Clarke, plus-93 that season, is in the top handful of passers who ever lived and probably was the game's greatest-ever forechecker. Leach was a deadly triggerman. Barber, plus-81 that year, did whatever had to be done as the score and clock dictated. He could shoot equally well off the pass or in full stride and was adept from the powerplay point as both a triggerman and feeder.

The strong leg muscles that kept him in the game long after a deteriorating knee should have forced his retirement provided Barber with fine outside speed and a stable base for his underrated corner work. And on defense, No. 7 anticipated so smartly that he scored 31 career shorthanded goals.

"Nothing was as important to me as being on two Stanley Cup winners," recalls Barber, elected to the Flyers Hall of Fame in 1989. Next on his priority list was the completion of his playing career with one team and, afterwards, his continued service to it. After coaching the Flyers' Philadelphia Phantoms farm team for four years—where he won a Calder Cup championship in 1998—Barber was elevated to the Flyer head-coaching job from assistant in December 2000 (upon the firing of Craig Ramsay) and guided the team to a 31-13-7-3 record, and was named the NHL's coach of the year.

It was soon after the injury-compromised 2000-01 Flyers lost in six games to Buffalo that Barber's wife and childhood sweetheart, Jenny, was diagnosed with lung cancer. As her condition rapidly deteriorated, he soldiered on, even, at his children's urging, coaching a game hours after her death on December 8, 2001.

"Brooks and Kerri told me, 'You cannot show weakness to your team, no matter what the cost,'" Barber said. "There is nothing we can do (for Mom) now.'

"It wasn't a shock like a car accident or a massive heart attack. I had been prepared for months. We won (5-1 over Minnesota), then announced Jenny's death after the game was over.

"That year, I told myself never to take any (personal angst) with me to the rink, and I don't believe I did. I hope I have a quarter of the courage that this woman showed."

In March, a Flyer team expected to contend for the Stanley Cup stopped scoring. As it managed only two goals in five postseason games against Ottawa, the players complained publicly and privately before Barber's firing that their coach had no system and no answers to pull them out of their slump.

"They played like I felt," recalls Barber. "Disorganized."

"Even then, I understood that if the roles had been reversed, it might have been me doing the [firing].

"I was disappointed, but on the other hand understanding and relieved. I was tired, really spent, and needed to get away. Kerri's wedding was coming up that summer.

"The Flyers said they would have a job for me but I wasn't interested. I needed to get away."

In August, Barber accepted the position of director of player personnel of the Tampa Bay Lightning, which defeated the Flyers in the 2004 Eastern Conference final on the way to putting a third Stanley Cup ring on Barber's fingers.

"The last thing I would ever do is sit there and say 'how do you like those apples?' when we beat the Flyers. I was just happy Tampa Bay won."

"Business is business."

Indeed, an ownership—and philosophy—change by the Lightning in 2009, caused Barber to leave. At GM Paul Holmgren's urging, he returned to the Flyers in the consultant's position he holds today.

"No grudges," he says. "Clarkie gave me a chance to coach in Hershey and with the Phantoms, then gave me an opportunity to coach in the NHL and it didn't work.

"I love [the Flyers]. These guys have been good to me."

Only 14 players ahead of him on the all-time NHL scoring list played for just one team. "Next to the two Stanley Cups, proudest of that," says Barber. Indeed, the third of five sons of Mary and Harry Barber, farmers from Callander, Ontario in the lake country 200 miles north of Toronto, wanted to be a Flyer long before anyone had good reason to feel that way. With Montreal holding three of the first eight picks in his draft year (1972), the Kitchener center hoped he would be taken seventh by the yet-undistinguished team in Philadelphia and got his wish. "I was afraid I was going to get buried in the Montreal organization," he said.

After nine goals and five assists during an 11-game crash course at left wing in Richmond, Barber was called up and never looked back, except, of course, for the guy he was supposed to check. He scored 30 goals his rookie season and 34 in each of the next two before exploding to 50 in 1975-76.

His astonishing drive from along the boards late in the third period of Game Four of the 1974 final detonated over Boston goalie Gilles Gilbert's shoulder, breaking up a tense 2-2 tie and pushing the Flyers to within one game of their first Cup. "The best wrist shot I've ever seen," Bobby Orr marveled.

Barber career tour de force was the four goals he scored in the 5-3 win in Game Three of the 1980 semifinals five-game victory against Minnesota. While he never had a dramatic series-winner, most of those matchups never would have been won without him. Typical of his career, all of Canada remembers the Darryl Sittler shot that defeated Czechoslovakia for the 1976 Canada Cup and forgets Barber that sent the game into overtime.

The LCB line didn't stay together long enough to again approximate its totals of 1975-76. Barber could do so many things well that three coaches—Fred Shero, Bob McCammon and Pat Quinn—used him as a roving cure for whatever line, or whatever slumping player, ailed the team.

"When they asked me to play a little center, a little defense, in the pinch, I enjoyed that," Barber recalls. "I liked being relied upon."

His troublesome right knee, first injured during the 1976-77 season, gradually eroded his effectiveness and likely cost him membership in the 500-goal club. In August 1985, when Barber surrendered to the pain and drudgery of a fruitless, 10-month, rehabilitation following reconstructive surgery, Clarke was asked what it had been like to play with the best left wing of his time.

"Easy," Clarke smiled.

FRED SHERO

IT TOOK THE HOCKEY HALL OF FAME COMMITTEE 33 years after Fred Shero coached his last NHL game to elect an innovator who won two Stanley Cups, plus reached two other Finals and three more semifinals in nine-plus seasons.

If that delay seems unjustly long, understand that, alongside repetition, patience was 50 percent of the Shero coaching mantra. Besides, to 14 members of the Broad Street Bullies who travelled to his posthumous 2013 induction, there could be no such thing as late, seeing as in 1974, Shero told them they could be linked together forever.

Shero's induction came 23 years after his death, but it was not the first curiously-long delay he ever had suffered. While watching him win four championships in 13 years coaching in the Rangers' minor league system, Flyers GM Keith Allen couldn't figure out why Shero had failed to receive an NHL opportunity.

"It made me wonder why Emile Francis had given other guys a chance and never given one to Freddie," recalled Allen. "His record was so good and I'd never heard anyone say a bad word about him."

Allen met Shero for the first time when he was invited to Philadelphia to interview for the job of replacing the fired Vic Stasiuk. On June 1, 1971, the 45 year-old was hired to coach a four-year-old expansion team coming off a 28-33-7 season and a four-game sweep at the hands of the Chicago Black Hawks.

FRED SHERO
FLYER HERO #6

Next to the Flyers' good judgment to draft a diabetic center named Bobby Clarke and the trade of Bernie Parent that brought Rick MacLeish, Shero probably was the most gutsy and fortuitous decision the franchise ever made. It should be ranked just ahead of Snider and Allen's call not to fire Shero after his first season ended a soul-searing four seconds short of the playoffs because of an unscreened 45-foot goal. Not only were 11 of the eventual Stanley Cup champions already on the roster by the end of that year, but invariably they also were finding each other where they were expected to be on the ice, thanks to Shero.

He drilled Philadelphia's big, strong, essentially plodding team in straight lines, dumping the puck and not taking unnecessary chances. Although the coach sometimes used props like tennis balls and folding chairs at practices, Shero adhered to the fundamental philosophy of doing it again until his players did it right.

"The first and last practice of the year were the same," recalls Clarke. "With a little fun thrown in at the end, yes, but we went over and over the system.

"If you look at the old Montreal teams, they played the 'one-four' that we did, so I don't know if Freddie invented the 'system' for which he has been given credit. His innovation was writing down the rules.

Forty years later, Clarke recites them:

"Never throw a puck out blindly from behind their net. Wings on wings between the bluelines except when able to intercept a stray pass. No forward must ever turn his back on the puck. Never go offsides on a three-on-two or two-on one. The guy going off the ice goes through the gate and the guy coming on goes over the boards"

Clarke laughs. "Except for Eddie Van Impe, who couldn't get over the boards.

"Freddie used to say, 'No rule is too small.' 'these things win games,' he would tell us and we believed him so he got the best out of everybody.

"You think guys like Bob Kelly and Don Saleski would have been as valuable somewhere else? They were real valuable to us because of the positions he put them in, the way he found to make them happy with limited ice time.

"He used to say to Kelly, 'If you have bacon and eggs for breakfast this morning, the chicken made a contribution, but that pig, he made a commitment. Are you going to be a chicken or a pig tonight?'"

Shero philosophized about life, delighted in discussing hockey theory, and rattled on endlessly about his respect for Anatoli Tarasov, the Russian coaching master, even employing some of his training methods. Nevertheless, the Flyers succeeded with a pragmatic system that was the virtual antithesis of that used by the Soviets. Shero beat them soundly with that contrast—trapping in the neutral zone—when the NHL's honor was at stake in the 1976 game between the Flyers and the Soviet Red Army.

Shero was the first NHL coach to talk a management into employing a full-time assistant (Mike Nykoluk), and popularized the morning skate and film study. In the days preceding pre-scouting and Center Ice TV packages, he would listen to Islander and Ranger games on the radio to learn their lines. But Shero's greatest innovations probably were in his dealings with players.

According to his son Ray, 10 years an NHL GM with the Penguins and, currently, the Devils, Shero had "zero" patience for traffic jams, searches for parking, bad restaurant service or waiting in any line. But he almost never raised his voice in the locker room or rink.

"I've hardly ever fined a player," he said at his introductory Philadelphia press conference. "Nowadays, you fine a player and he laughs at you. You sit him on the bench, though, and it's embarrassing."

In a time that coaches motivated mostly by threats and tirades, Shero instead searched libraries for inspirational quotations, dropping notes in his players' lockers.

Some of them were brilliant in their simplicity: "Don't do anything here that hurts your self-respect," was one. "An employee who is willing to steal for me is willing to steal from me."

And: "If you're worth correcting, you're worth keeping. I don't waste time cutting specks off rotten apples."

Some of these messages were ignored, but not one was resented. Almost to a man, the Flyers liked their coach to a greater degree than they comprehended him.

"We understand the fact that everything he does is aimed towards helping us win," Clarke said back in the day. "But we just don't understand some of the things he does."

One time, the Flyers were put through a nonsensical and seemingly endless drill until Clarke challenged its worth. "Now we're getting somewhere," Shero said. "I wanted to see who was thinking."

Non-confrontational by nature, rarely did Shero criticize a player individually, even behind closed doors. "I felt sorry for the fans," Shero once declared to the media after an abysmal loss to the Islanders. "They had to pay. We got in free." But he never embarrassed individuals before their peers and would sometimes go to ridiculous lengths to publicly defend them.

Once when defenseman Tom Bladon, under heavy Black Hawk forechecking, backed up, stumbled and put the puck into his own goal, the coach insisted the defenseman had been wise not to risk a pass.

"If someone made a bad mistake he wouldn't say, 'Saleski, for [bleep's] sake!' like most coaches would," recalls Clarke. "He would go over to the boards and say, 'When you get the puck up here, there is where it is supposed to go.

"Everybody knew who he was talking about but the whole team would get the message.

I played with lots of players over the years who had Freddie in the minors and every one of them could give you his pregame speech: 'Close down wings between the bluelines. Don't throw the puck back over your own blueline.'

"It was the same one every game. It seemed to work."

So deep was the players' trust that Clarke remembers little incredulity when Shero presented the cuckoo plan to throw the puck at Bobby Orr in the 1974 Final. Wouldn't Orr have it enough already?

"He knew the Bruins were undisciplined, that Phil Esposito would take two-minute shifts, that Orr was on the ice all the time," recalls Clarke. "Freddy wanted to make Orr go back hard (to get the puck) and for us to force him with a fresh guy so he couldn't get set up behind the net."

Orr's fatigue mostly manifested itself in arm-weariness and bad aim. Even though the Flyers were depleted by injuries to Gary Dornhoefer, Bob Kelly and Barry Ashbee, Philadelphia proved deeper than Boston. Underdogs only in retrospect, the Flyers had three Hall of Famers—Bill Barber, Bernie Parent and Clarke, the third being also one of the best-ever on-ice coaches and inspirational locker-room influences in sports history. Armed with more stars and superb role players than revisionist historians recall, Shero was set up to succeed. But Van Impe still insists there was not another coach with whom the Flyers could have won.

"I agree," says Clarke. "He won everywhere he went, so I would say he could have won without me.

"I don't think he could have won without Bernie because you have to have a goalie. But maybe the reason we became stars was because of Freddie."

Indeed, the Flyers needed all the elements plus a coach who knew what to do with them. In turn Shero required the autonomy granted him by a brilliant GM who shared his coach's values and tolerated his quirks. Shero never argued internally against any player move Allen wanted to make, yet still made sporadic, generic, public jabs at the front office. They were calculated to convince team members that the coach was on their side.

"I found out a long time ago that players are the only thing that wins for you," Shero said. "Maybe that's why it took me so long to make the majors. I catered to no one but them."

"Judging by the turnout for his Hall of Fame Induction, those players remembered that he was never one to promote himself, never kissed anybody's ass" said Ray Shero. "But he would have been very proud and, to him, [the induction] would have been mostly about his players."

The happiest and most relaxed Ray remembers seeing his father was on a vacation at Parent's Jersey Shore house after the first Stanley Cup. Yet Shero was not a social man. Even after the clinching Stanley Cup games, he came to the locker room only to get the beer he would sip by himself in his office. Smilng was rare for Shero, an introvert who grew up the son of immigrants in a Russian enclave of Winnipeg, boxed in the Royal Canadian Navy, and made it to the NHL for 145 games with the Rangers.

"I want to be miserable," he once said. "That makes me happy.

"I think you can't know joy if you don't know sorrow. If you are happy all the time, there must be something wrong. Evidently you're an idiot. You're doing nothing."

He sat by himself in coffee shops and bars, and often would not acknowledge players when they passed him on streets and in hotel corridors. They nicknamed him "The Fog" because he would materialize in rooms or hallways and then just as quickly disappear.

After coaching his first exhibition game with the Flyers, Shero went out for a postgame smoke and locked himself out of the Flint, MI arena. He woke up the morning of Game Four of the 1974 first-round Atlanta series with facial bruises, lacerations, a broken thumb, and a six-inch gash on his arm and swore he had no idea how they got there.

"I only remember the word 'animal' upset me," Shero said after being put on the next flight back to Philadelphia. "If I was in bar fight, it wouldn't have been the first one."

Summarized Scotty Bowman, the winningest coach of all time: "Sometimes I don't think he knows Wednesday from Thursday. And sometimes I think he's a genius who has us all fooled."

As outrageous as he could be mysterious, Shero took just one exhibition game to declare 17th overall pick Kevin McCarthy the "greatest passer in the history of the NHL" and Paul Holmgren as "the Stanley Cup" after debuting with a memorable dumping of Esposito on his backside.

On some days, one good question from a reporter would prompt a 10-minute soliloquy on hockey and life. "Over a beer he would talk to you for an hour, but he didn't stop to chat with people he didn't know," recalls Ray. "Essentially, he was shy."

Shero learned to embellish "The Fog" persona because it gave him an excuse to avoid confrontations, questions and people. "That was perfect for him because he'd hide behind it," said Clarke. Yet, an essential part of the coaching philosophy of this loner was to bond his team together.

Shero would gather the Flyers in his hotel room at mid-evening for beers. The real purpose of these meetings was to disrupt the players' barhopping and keep consumption at modest levels, but the sessions were far less resented than any strict curfews.

"If my players are hurt, I tell them to go to the hospital," said Shero. "They recover fast in there because it interferes with their night life."

He told his players and the media grossly-embellished stories about events from his minor-league past, but kept the Flyers looking forward by assigning a monthly quota of points. Shero also fed them decades worth of his perspective.

"They can't mean that," he frowned in 1976 after his just-dethroned Flyers declared 118 points and two rounds of success a waste. "They aren't God, they just have to accept it."

Ten months later, Shero so burst with pride after the Flyers recovered from a slow start to hold off the Islanders for a fourth consecutive division title that he declared the playoffs as "meaningless, just there to make money for the owners and players."

Of course, the wilder the quote, the more Shero deflected media criticism from the players. But inevitably, the team that would follow him anywhere aged and its motivation frayed.

"My patience is wearing thin and so are the soles of my shoes," Shero said as he exchanged his skates for street footwear while seated on a folding chair after a 1978 practice in Chicago. "We have tried everything.

"You can lead a horse to water, but you can't make him fish. What else can I do? You want to jump in the river with me?"

After the Flyers were beaten badly that spring by the Bruins for a second consecutive semifinal, Allen and Snider faced a tough call whether to let Shero complete the one year remaining on his contract. He solved the problem for them, dropping off his resignation on Allen's desk in an envelope. Declaring to the media his inability to motivate, Shero vowed he was finished behind the bench before, at the orchestration of his agent, Mark Stewart, signing on as coach-GM of the Rangers.

The genuine sense of betrayal the Flyer players expressed, a reflection of their love for the only NHL coach most of them had ever had, was exacerbated the following spring when the Rangers took out Shero's old team in five games on the way to the Stanley Cup Final. The system clearly travelled well. But Shero, who had never expressed any interest in getting into management nor demonstrated to Allen and Snider much knowledge of the league and its workings, was in over his head as a GM.

One year later, the Flyers had their revenge over the Rangers in five games. After a 4-13-3 start to the following season, Shero resigned under pressure, never to coach in the NHL again.

"It was more corporate with the Rangers than it was in Philly," recalls Ray. "I don't think my dad was good at that.

"The drinking couldn't have helped, but he didn't have the base of support he had with the Flyers."

In 1989, after a year consulting for the Capitals, four seasons in the Devils broadcast booth, and a year coaching in the Netherlands, Shero wrote a letter to Allen, asking to come back. By then, emotional wounds were healed, but Freddy's stomach cancer was too far gone. "I don't think he ever went for a checkup," Ray recalls.

To help with his medical bills, Shero was hired back as a consultant. "Once a Flyer, always a Flyer," he said during the ceremony on March 22, 1990 when he was inducted into the Flyers Hall of Fame.

Only the most cynical chroniclers remembered that when he had returned to New York in 1978, Shero had expressed the same sentiment about his 29 years of playing and coaching in the Rangers' organization. Who cared by that point? The most sustained seven years of success the Flyers ever had still were credited largely to Freddie, when he died on Saturday, November 24, 1990.

"He was a saint," said Clarke, on the day of Shero's passing. "He understood the players and the game better than anyone."

The signature quotation of the many Shero popularized was, of course the one he wrote on the dressing room blackboard with the Flyers two wins away from their first Stanley Cup: "Win and We Will Walk Together Forever."

Indeed, many of them did, carrying their coach's casket out of the Church of St. Mary's in Cherry Hill after Clarke had eulogized the "complex and simple man" who had directed them to nirvana.

"Forever didn't stop on Saturday," said Shero's captain. "Freddie left a piece of himself with every one of us."

MARK HOWE

THERE MAY NOT HAVE BEEN ANOTHER PLAYER in the history of the game, with a skill level as high as Mark Howe's, who suppressed his ego for the greater good of his team. In 594 regular-season games with the Flyers, he failed to score more than 480 points only because they were ahead too often to need more.

Those leads largely were built because Howe was on the defense. He could skate away from pursuers, smother attackers with smart positioning and pinpoint openings in forechecking mazes, every choice based on the clock and the score.

"Being in goal behind Mark, I was in the best position to appreciate his decision-making," said Ron Hextall. "It was impeccable." And if Howe made only 98 out of 100 choices correctly, the two mistakes became a rare treat. In the four pushes it took an opponent to move 30 feet, Howe would take two steps and catch up.

"His glide was almost silent," recalls Mike Keenan, Howe's coach in Philadelphia for four seasons. "It was like he was wearing slippers and everyone else on skates."

The greatest defenseman never to win the Norris Trophy had neither the muscle of Rod Langway nor the heavy shots and relentless scoring drives of Paul Coffey and Ray Bourque. Howe finished second to each of those Hall of Famers in three Norris ballots, proving that while Howe almost always picked the right spots to join the rush, his best seasons—the greatest being 1985-86 when he was an incredible plus-85—weren't as well-timed.

The Flyers, who fell in the 1985 and 1987 final to Edmonton's great offensive machine, shared his problem. Still, the defenseman, even while waiting 16 seasons after his retirement for his 2011 election into the Hockey Hall of Fame, never saw himself as unlucky or unfulfilled.

"Because I've had opportunities no one else ever had or ever will, I take nothing for granted," he said. Indeed, he was one of the three people in the entire world fortunate enough to be a son of Gordie Howe.

"I first realized I had a famous father when he would take me places and everyone would want his autograph," Mark began his 2013 autobiography, *Gordie Howe's Son*. "But I just thought that was normal.

"For as long as I remember, Gordie Howe has been my dad more than he was Mr. Hockey. Interviewers have asked, 'What's it like being Gordie Howe's son?' I've always assumed it was no different than being anybody's son who grew up in a loving, supportive family.

"Of course I felt differently the night he scored his 545th goal to pass Maurice Richard for the all-time lead in the NHL. I was eight years old and the cheering at Detroit's Olympia that night—November 10, 1963—seemed to last forever. I remember

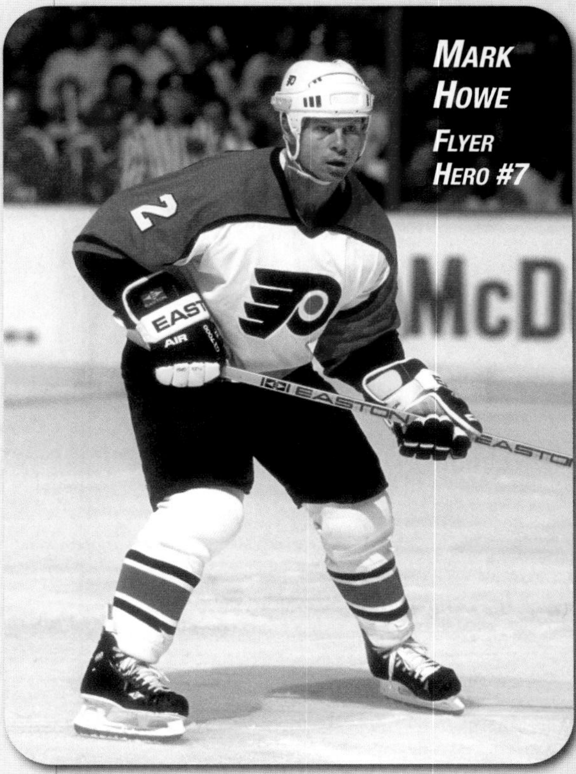

thinking, "Wow, I'm the only person in here who can say, 'That's my dad!

"A wealth of pride, however, was the only wealth into which I was born. When I came into the world on May 28, 1955—14 months after my brother Marty—Gordie, the best player in the NHL, earned a salary of $10,000."

Nevertheless, the middle class had been a big step up for Gordie, born in Saskatchewan during the Great Depression as the sixth of nine children of Kate and Ab Howe. If Mark learned quickly to count his blessings at being a member of the game's most revered—and humble—family, Dad, whose malice on the ice became his legendary as his skill, set the best example by bringing none of his fierceness home to wife Colleen, daughter Cathy, and three sons.

"Maybe my wishes and hopes exceeded my eyesight," Gordie once allowed, "but I think I saw all the boys as NHLers almost at birth. "

Being as level-headed as the haircuts of his day, however, Gordie pressured Murray, Marty and Mark to do only what made them happy. "I guess because he had so much fun playing hockey, he would never make it a chore for any of us," recalled Mark. "He would come to our games and watch, never rant and rave like some of the other fathers.

"There wasn't a lot of unsolicited advice from him or my mom. But when we needed them they were there with the answers, including Mom with the biggest one: How do you deal with being Gordie Howe's son?

"'Maybe there is a negative side with all the attention you get,' she would tell Marty and me. 'But let me make a list of all the positive things, like being able to go anywhere you want at the Olympia and skate there for six to eight hours."

Mark took full advantage of all the perks of being No. 9's kid, including ball hockey on the back steps leading up to the balcony, scalper's rights to the family's four tickets per game, and locker-room visitation after Red Wing victories.

Marty's real passion in his youth was football. Murray, the baby, became a doctor while Mark received an excellent deal in DNA spirals—the skills, instincts and graciousness of his father, plus the brains of his mother.

An A student, he would whiz through his homework in an hour in order to play hockey until bedtime. The youth hockey program in the Detroit area was not adequate for the training of an aspiring professional, so Colleen took charge of upgrading it. The Detroit Junior Red Wings, which she founded, competed against Ontario's best clubs, helping Mark, at 16, become the youngest (still) medal winner in U.S. Olympic hockey history, silver for the 1972 team in Sapporo, Japan.

He had just won the Memorial Cup with Toronto's Junior A Marlboros when Colleen sounded out Bill Dineen, coach-GM of the World Hockey Association Houston Aeros about Mark and Marty—not eligible for the NHL Draft until age 20—turning pro early in the one-year-old rebel league.

Dad, at 45, and two years into a miserable retirement in a do-nothing job with the Red Wings front office, asked Dineen if he would be interested in a third Howe, and Dineen signed the greatest family act since the Flying Wallendas. Gordie, on right wing, averaged 100 points over his first three seasons; Mark, on left wing, scored 79 and was named rookie of the year as the Aeros won the first of consecutive championships.

The Bruins took Mark in the second round of the 1974 draft, but Montreal blocked any family reunion in the NHL by selecting Marty, a defenseman, one round later. With the Houston team under new ownership and financial pressure to rid themselves of the Howes' contracts, Mark turned down Boston's offer—which did not include a role in uniform for his 48-year-old father—and the family moved together to the WHA New England Whalers, who in 1979 were accepted into the NHL.

Mark keyed the renamed Hartford Whalers to an unexpected playoff berth in their premier season. But Gordie had been forced into retirement and another meaningless front-office position and Marty been banished to the minors when in December 1980, the Islanders' John Tonelli barreled into the Whalers' zone with Mark's ticket out of Hartford. Knocked off balance by Tonelli, Howe braced feet first for a collision with the net, and lifted it off its moorings so that a metal flange at the base of the back of the goal pierced his buttocks.

After being rushed off the ice wrapped in bloody towels, Howe remembers his toes being moved by a doctor on the training table.

"I told him the toes weren't the problem," he recalls. "And he told me he was checking my reflexes. An inch one way and [the metal] could have gone into my spinal cord. An inch the other way, it would have pierced my sphincter muscle and I would have been walking around with a colostomy bag. An inch another way and my hamstring would have been severed, ending my career."

When Dad, who had the highest pain tolerance ever, ran down from the press box and talked the doctor into letting him have a look and then almost broke my hand that he was holding, I knew I was in trouble. "

Howe nevertheless returned to the Whalers after just 43 days, 35 pounds lighter and a shadow of himself. Larry Pleau, a recently appointed coach-GM determined to change the culture of the losing team, thought Howe was a whiner and hypochondriac.

Keith Allen, ill from watching his 87-point Flyer team get knocked out in the first round by the Rangers, bore down on Hartford during the summer of 1982, working a deal for Howe that sent center Ken Linseman and first- and third-roundpicks in 1983 to the Whalers. When Ed Snider agreed to take financial obligation for the resale of Mark's new Hartford home, the player gleefully waived a no-trade clause and joined Philadelphia.

Billed as an offensive defenseman who was difficult to motivate, Howe instead provided half the expected offense, twice the defense and three times the motivation. Whereas the Whalers, desperate for leadership, had seen a moaner and malingerer, the Flyers, short on defensive talent but not players who cared, enjoyed a likable kvetch who made leaving their zone painless.

Philadelphia surged to 106 points and a Patrick Division title but was wiped out of the playoffs by the Rangers in three straight first-round games. Howe, who had suffered a bruised spleen in mid-season, played without energy or confidence.

The following spring, the Flyers again were eliminated in the first round in three straight, this time by Washington. But in 1985, when Philadelphia broke a three-year, nine-game playoff schneid, it was Howe's Game One overtime goal against the Rangers that changed the series and his reputation for not coming through in the clutch. Keenan raised Mark's conditioning level and his self-esteem; the defenseman's best years began at age 30.

"I've had a lot of accomplishments with two previous teams, but there was no way my career would have been complete without my time in Philadelphia," Howe said. "Other than winning a Cup, the next best thing would be to play 10 years with the Flyers in the eighties.

"I came to Philadelphia as my father's son and left my own man."

Back problems, which required surgery in 1991, began to take chunks out of Howe's seasons as the Flyers remained tethered to his lifeline. In Mark's final Philadelphia season, 1991-92, the team was 21-18-3 when he was in the line-up and 11-19-8 when he was not. GM Russ Farwell offered Howe a substantial contract to help anchor the Flyers through the rebuild around young Eric Lindros, but with Philadelphia's Cup hopes negligible, Mark took a slightly higher offer from the team of his father to chase Lord Stanley.

He never got it, retiring at age 40 after the Red Wings were swept in the 1995 Final by New Jersey, but the Red Wings' offer of post-playing employment when Howe had signed, turned into a career. Today he is their director of pro scouting.

Following his Hall of Fame induction, Mark's No. 2 went to the rafters of the Wells Fargo Center on March 6, 2012 in front of his three children, a grandchild, Gordie, the appropriately-visiting Red Wings, and 19,892 fans. Many of them were old enough to appreciate that this was the best defenseman the Flyers ever had.

RICK MACLEISH

OF THE 328 GOALS RICK MACLEISH SCORED for the Flyers, only about 327 looked effortless. With his head tilted, the center whom his teammates called "Cutie" would float from blueline to blueline with no idea what he'd do when the puck came to him.

"My style?" he once said. "Freestyle.

"Had my own system. Would go where I wanted to go. Freddie (Shero) didn't bother me about it."

MacLeish didn't say much. Didn't appear to sweat much, either, on the way to 53 Flyer playoff goals, including 10 game-winners. Thanks to hips and arms that swiveled in defiance of the laws of aerodynamics, Cutie moved around the ice with dispassion at best and indifference at worst.

Defensemen knew that most often he would cut right to left. Goalies understood that the puck was headed under the crossbar with far greater velocity than the slight flick of his wrists suggested. Yet, the only one who ever could stop MacLeish was himself. The game came so easily to him that on many nights he forgot to play.

"Normally when the games were important, he played great," recalls Bob Clarke. "Couple times I'd get him in the bathroom before the game and make sure he knew we couldn't win if he didn't play well.

"I was so mad at him during Game Five (in Boston in 1974), I think it was the only time I ever said anything to a player in front of another. I even turned around and yelled at Freddie not to put Ricky on the ice. Then he probably was our best player in the next game."

MacLeish tipped Andre Dupont's four-on-three point drive past Gilles Gilbert for Game Six's only goal and the Stanley Cup, which never could have been won without the 13 times he scored that spring. Almost as casually, MacLeish followed up with 11 as the Flyers repeated in 1975, although Ricky insists today that he never was as oblivious as it appeared.

"Used to puke my guts out before big games," he says.

Whatever, MacLeish marched to a drumbeat that sometimes would frustrate his teammates and coaches.

"Freddie didn't like one-on-one confrontation," recalled the late Ross Lonsberry, MacLeish's linemate with Gary Dornhoefer in the Cup years. "One time when Ricky was floating, Shero called in all three of us to get his point across.

"On the way out, Ricky said to Dorny and me, 'Gee I didn't think you guys were playing that badly.'

Lonsberry, who took the defensive role high in the zone, and Dornhoefer, who relentlessly crashed the corners, backboards, and crease, almost never played badly, allowing MacLeish the base from which to be devastating.

"I needed somebody to push me," he recalls. "That's why Dorny and Ross were so good for me.

"They said, 'Just get open and we'll get you the puck.'"

The consummate river skater indeed had a river running just two blocks from the backyard of his family's home in Cannington, Ontario, 70 miles northeast of Toronto. Each winter, his father Garnet would flood not only a backyard rink but a path to the river with a garden hose. "I could skate from our house to Sunderland, which was eight miles away on the river," recalls MacLeish. "I used to skate there to get a hamburger."

His dad worked nights for General Mills and his mom toiled at the local grocery store. Rick's grandfather, George Nicholson, who raised quarter horses, was hugely supportive towards Ricky's hockey education, driving 40 miles to games after MacLeish was selected in the first-ever Ontario Hockey Association midget draft by Roger Neilson's Peterborough Petes.

"Roger took the captaincy away from me the next day after I got into a bar fight," remembers MacLeish. "Guy hit me, what was I supposed to do?"

He doesn't recall being badgered about checking from Neilson, a systems coach at a time not many teams could tell you what their system was. Neilson largely turned his best weapon loose on left wing for 95 goals in two seasons before MacLeish was selected fourth overall in the 1970 draft by Boston, one pick after Reggie Leach also had been chosen by the Bruins.

That choice Boston used on MacLeish was one Philadelphia had traded three years earlier to obtain Rosaire Paiement. The Flyers realized what they had dealt away before Boston, no longer in the mood for a youth movement while in the midst of winning Stanley Cups in 1970 and 1972, cared to wait for MacLeish to mature.

Having scored only 13 goals in his first 46 games for the Bruins' farm club at Oklahoma City, he became the primary acquisition in probably the boldest trade in Flyers history. On February 1, 1971, Keith Allen dealt the hugely popular Bernie Parent to Toronto for center Mike Walton, a first-round draft choice and goalie Bruce Gamble, then immediately sent Walton to Boston for MacLeish and minor leaguer Danny Schock.

For more than a year Allen heard he should have kept Walton. MacLeish scored only twice in the 26 Flyers games following the deal. "Never gave me a good center," he recalls. Wisely, he was moved to the middle after the Flyers sent him down to Richmond, but upon his call-up to the big club, still had just one goal in 17 contests.

"Zero indication he would score 50," said Clarke. "Zero." Suddenly in 1972-73, the season of the Flyers' emergence, MacLeish did, exploding for 100 points, too.

He never again reached those statistical standards, settling for 49 in 1976-77 when Atlanta goalie Phil Myre stopped him five times in the season finale. But MacLeish's regular-season totals—his 697 points are fourth all time for the Flyers behind Clarke, Bill Barber and Brian Propp—hardly were the truest measure of his value.

RICK MACLEISH
FLYER HERO #12

He pounced on a puck that died in a puddle to stun Ken Dryden with a quick overtime goal in Game One of the 1973 semifinals at Montreal's Forum and had a Game Seven hat trick against the Islanders in 1975 before being successfully matched against Buffalo star Gilbert Perreault in the Final.

Usually an indifferent checker, MacLeish was challenged by the assignment of Perreault, who had gone first overall, three picks earlier than MacLeish in 1970.

"I would angle (Perreault) to the sideboards," says MacLeish. "Could outskate him all day.

"He made a lot of moves and wasn't going anywhere."

Six months later, neither was the Soviet Red Army team, as the patient Flyers bamboozled the fleet Russian robots at center ice, MacLeish breaking away to beat Vladislav Tretiak for the goal that proved to be the winner of the most pressure-packed game the Broad Street Bullies ever played.

Based on his track record, we can only imagine what Ricky might have done in that season's playoffs, when the Flyers had to return to the Final without him, thanks to torn knee ligaments caused by a low hit by Vancouver defenseman Harold Snepsts during February. Minus the player who always was at his best when their plight was most dire, the Flyers lost four straight to the budding Montreal dynasty, by a total of five goals.

In the 1977 quarterfinals vs. Toronto, Philadelphia was down 2-0 in games and 3-2 on the scoreboard when MacLeish intercepted a Borje Salming clear and slapped the puck by Mike Palmateer with 38 seconds remaining, then scored again in overtime, turning around a series the Flyers would win in six games.

"Heavy smoker, didn't train, would just show up and, when we were a good team, carry us," laughs Clarke. "Hard to stay mad at him."

Who cared how little MacLeish did for the first 58 minutes in Game One of the 1980 playoffs, when young Wayne Gretzky and the Edmonton Oilers were about to steal it until MacLeish forced overtime with 1:19 remaining? The Flyers went on to a three-game sweep, keyed by a No. 19 with nine lives.

A van driven by Flyers defenseman Bob Dailey, carrying MacLeish, overturned three times on a rain slickened Black Horse Pike on the way back from a golf tournament in May 1977, landing on its roof. MacLeish climbed out, calmly sat down on the curb, and said, "my neck hurts." It was broken, putting him in a halo brace for the summer.

In April of the next season, he left his feet to knock down a Los Angeles pass and had his throat inadvertently skated over by Marcel Dionne, requiring 80 stitches by Dr. Everett Borghesani, the Flyers oral surgeon, who happened to be on that trip. The blade missed MacLeish's jugular by a quarter-inch. At the bar later that night, MacLeish took a drag of his cigarette and saw smoke coming out of his neck.

For the greatest high-wire act in franchise history there was not always a net however. MacLeish's failure to respond to Bob McCammon was a major reason the coach was fired halfway through his first season. Pat Quinn successfully appealed to the center's pride and his 31 goals the next year helped maintain Philadelphia's NHL record 35-game unbeaten streak. But after Tim Kerr debuted the next year, MacLeish was recycled in the deal with Hartford that brought the Flyers the fourth-overall pick they used to select Ron Sutter.

McCammon, who replaced Quinn, brought Ricky back for 29 games (and 22 points) in 1983-84 before MacLeish went into life insurance, while dabbling in standardbred ownership and training. The father of two married daughters, he lived with his second wife Charlene in Somers Point, NJ, until his death at age 66 on May 31, 2016 from liver and kidney failure, plus meningitis.

Hard living took its toll in the end. But MacLeish had at least quit smoking after a cardiac episode at an alumni game in 2004 resulted in a quadruple bypass. It turned out that the cigarettes put a lot more stress on his heart than any late-game predicament ever had. As long as the Flyers had a minute and a MacLeish, they always had a chance.

BRIAN PROPP

THE SCORING LEFT WING THE FLYERS COVETED in the 1979 draft fell to them like manna from heaven. That always seemed appropriate of a player coming from the Brandon Wheat Kings, particularly one who was passed over by many NHL teams on the half-baked idea that his lifestyle was as bad as his brush cut. Thirteen clubs failed to select a painfully shy sniper with a nose for the net he would hit 425 times in 15 NHL seasons.

Brian Propp, the second of five children of the Reverend Reinhold Propp and his wife Margaret, came to the Flyers from Neudorf, Saskatchewan, a farming community of 300 where everybody knew everybody, eliminating much need to be outgoing. Arriving at his first NHL camp as quiet as a mouse that might have lived in his father's house of worship, Propp was as good at dodging eye contact as body contact. "When I have something to say, I'll say it," he said in a voice as low as his shot.

When he got the winning goal in his first NHL game, it was not such a big deal to someone who had scored 94 times the previous season. The Flyers extraordinarily lost only one of the first 37 contests in which Propp played for them, but that wasn't out of the ordinary either for the 20-year-old gunner. The Wheat Kings, anchored on defense by Flyer teammate-to-be Brad McCrimmon, had been defeated only five times during Propp's final—and Memorial Cup—season there

"I was young and used to winning," Propp recalls. "I figured we would be winning for a long time."

He figured correctly, at least in the sense that the Flyers never recorded a losing season in the 10 full ones Propp played for them. With a drive to score so relentless that he kept count of his goals during warm-ups, Propp scored 40 or more in four seasons, amassing more than 90 points each time.

The Flyers third all-time point-getter (849) behind Bobby Clarke and Bill Barber, Propp reached 97 in both 1984-85 and 1985-86, years in which he missed four and eight games, respectively, with injuries. Thus, the player as quick to pounce on a loose puck as any in franchise history left a loose end of never recording a 100-point season. This was symbolic of a bittersweet career in which Propp repeatedly fell just short. He is one of five players in NHL history to play in five Finals—one each with Boston and Minnesota after the rebuilding Flyers traded him to the Bruins for a second-round pick in 1990—and never win the Stanley Cup.

In helping Philadelphia to the brink of the title three times, Propp had 112 points in 116 postseason matches, second all-time behind Clarke—more than satisfactory production for a slightly undersized forward (5-10, 195) in the heavier going of the postseason. But when he scored only three playoff goals over three springs in the early 1980s and the Flyers went out in the first round each time, their best point producer became an easy and not completely undeserving target. Propp also went goalless when the Flyers were shocked by the Rangers in the 1986 first round.

"I think it was a matter of learning what it takes to succeed in the playoffs," recalls Mike Keenan, whose mental gymnastics lifted the levels of all the veteran Flyers when he became coach in 1984. "He was a competitor, but he probably felt he couldn't stretch himself beyond a certain point and since he was our most talented all-around forward we needed that."

"To be fair, he wasn't a big man. "

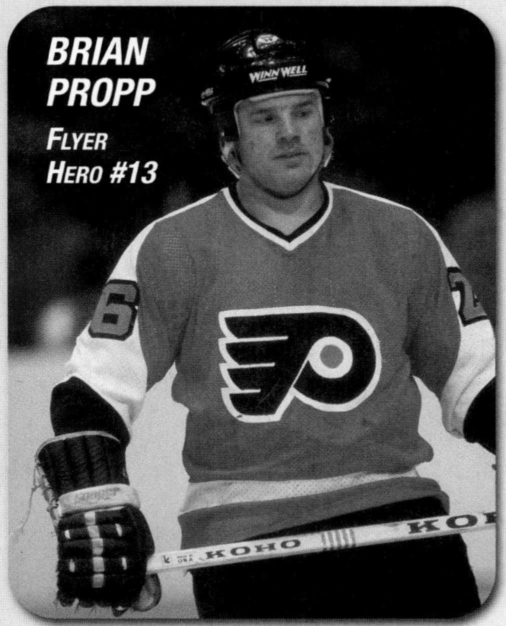

Propp had a skin thick enough to keep his confidence through Keenan's relentless badgering, and the conscience to re-invent himself as a clutch playoff performer.

"I took some heat," he recalls. "I realized we wouldn't win in the first round unless I was one of the reasons.

"I finally put more pressure on myself to score every game in the playoffs. Dr. Steve Rosenberg was our sports psychologist and I worked a lot with him on visual and mental relaxation and positive thinking. A lot of the first rounds were harder than the second and third rounds (in 1980, 1985 and 1987)."

He fully shot down the reputation for choking with a brilliant second-round Game Seven against the Islanders in 1987. "Played like he was possessed," said Mark Howe after Philadelphia, faced with blowing a series it had led 3-1, dominated the contest 5-1 with Propp scoring shorthanded. "It probably was the best I've ever seen him."

Propp scored 28 points in 26 playoff games that season and was also excellent in the 1989 semifinal run, right up until his head was rammed against the Montreal Forum glass by Chris Chelios in Game One of the conference final.

When Propp regained consciousness, he believed he was still playing in the previous round against Pittsburgh. It was probably the only time the winger ever lost his bearings on a rink. Propp almost always was where he was expected to be, both offensively and defensively. His speed and sense of anticipation made him an excellent penalty killer and, when paired with Dave Poulin, a devastating shorthanded threat.

Careless at best and mean-spirited at worst with the use of his stick through much of his career, Propp eventually underwent changes in both his on and off-ice personalities. He matured into an engaging conversationalist and even a showman, celebrating his goals with a "guffaw" hand motion popularized in the 1980s by comedian Howie Mandel.

"Timmy Kerr wouldn't even raise his stick when he scored," Propp laughed. "I saw Mandel in Atlantic City and thought I could use the personality.

"When I came back to the bench, Keenan said, 'What the [bleep] was that? Don't do it again.' I kept doing it anyway."

In 1979, a deed to the Walt Whitman Bridge, purchased on a street corner, would have been a better investment than a wager on Propp ever becoming a radio color analyst, which he was for the Flyers for nine seasons. Currently a sales representative for Wolf Commercial Real Estate, Propp in 2016 joined Dave Schultz and Bernie Parent as game-night ambassadors for the Flyers.

In September 2015, atrial fibrillation caused a stroke and compromised some of the movement in his right arm. But Propp's speech has improved greatly—one could say for the second time in his life.

"When Bob Clarke retired, it gave me and a few other players the chance to mature as leaders," recalls Propp. "I developed media skills and participated in community charity events.

"My (second) wife Kris was a broadcast major and also helped me tremendously."

He came a long way, although No. 26 never played on an NHL team that went all the way.

"It's disappointing because the Stanley Cup is your ultimate goal," said Propp. "But all you can do is give it your best. Fortunately, I was able to win a Canada Cup (in 1987).

"Awards are nice and I have a ton of them. I was named the all-time greatest left wing in Canadian junior history, which to me is like getting into the Hockey Hall of Fame.

"The Flyers put me in their Hall of Fame (in 1999). The Saskatchewan Hockey Hall of Fame inducted me. And I'm 35th all-time in career plus-minus, which I'm pretty proud of because I played both ends of the ice.

"Some of the greatest players never had the experience of the playoff games we did for 10 years. It was a given we always were going to be a good team. Except for winning the Cup, you can't ask for anything more than that."

TIM KERR

SINCE DEFENSEMEN THOUGHT IT UNFAIR for someone with a huge body to have such quick hands, most showed no mercy in their futile methods to stop Tim Kerr. Opponents chopped at his legs and clung to his shoulders but 225 pounds of defiance stood willing to take whatever abuse was necessary for that next goal.

Kerr flipped pucks into nets like they were coins into the basket at a toll booth, scoring at a goals-per-game pace that only eight NHL players have bettered. The tolls Tim paid were on the surgeon's table for shoulder and knee problems that prevented Hockey Hall of Fame level career totals. But the big guy never complained about any of his setbacks.

"Listen, if you're looking for real trouble, you don't have to look too far in this world," Kerr had said after a 1987 shoulder surgery went bad, costing him all but eight games of the 1987-88 season. Indeed something far worse found him two years later. His wife, Kathy, who was scheduled to go home that day after being treated for what was considered a routine post-partum infection, was found dead in her hospital bed for reasons never fully explainable, leaving Tim a widower with three young daughters.

Two days after the funeral, Kerr went to the gym. He returned to the lineup in two weeks before twice more being forced out with injuries. From rehab after rehab, from suffocating personal loss, from a business setback—the failure of a restaurant in Avalon, NJ—Kerr continued to rise.

"Everybody has periods in their life they look back upon as not an easy time," he says. "I am certainly not one to dwell on what-if."

It was the Flyers' incredible fortune to have Kerr fall through the cracks of a six-round 1979 draft (the age limit was lowered that season from 20 to 19, creating two draft classes in one), enabling scout Eric Coville to sign for just $10,000 a 19-year-old free-agent center from Tecumseh, Ontario whom many talent evaluators laughably felt had questionable drive.

That was the extent of the team's and Kerr's good luck for the next three years, however. A trio of knee injuries and a broken leg held him to a total of 54 goals in four years until, finally healthy in 1983-84, Kerr put up 54 in just one season, prelude to 54, 58 and 58 over the next three years.

During the Flyers' 1985 drive to the Final, Kerr had 10 goals in 12 games before damage to his knee knocked him from the playoffs. Two years later, when the team made it all the way to Game Seven, again against Edmonton, he scored eight times in 12 contests, most of which were spent in agony from a gradually-separating left shoulder that ultimately stopped him from continuing past the second round.

After a two-stage operation that summer, a surgical pin came loose and was replaced by another that became infected. Those setbacks robbed him of a season, yet by gulping aspirin in a regimen that desensitized his allergies for anti-inflammatory medication, he rebounded the following year to score 48 times, despite missing 12 games, and win the Bill Masterton Memorial Trophy for "perseverance, sportsmanship and dedication to hockey."

TIM KERR

FLYER HERO #14

"He was as dedicated an athlete as I ever have worked with," said Mike Keenan, who coached 20 years in the NHL and won 672 games.

Finally feeling robust for the 1989 playoffs, Kerr scored 14 goals in 19 games before his thumb was broken by a Penguin slash that rendered him effectively useless during the Flyers' semifinal loss to Montreal.

Between all these setbacks, he had 17 career regular-season hat tricks and made his still-NHL record for most powerplay goals in a season (34 in 1985-86) appear perfunctory.

"I wasn't excited when I scored because I expected to score," he recalls. In the quintessential Kerr goal, he would sweep in a passout in the blink of an eye, but this horse was no one-trick pony. He could beat goalies with wrist shots from 35 feet, step outside a defenseman and pick the far corner with backhanders, and even scored from his knees or chest.

In the signature game of his career—and of the Flyers' run to the Final in 1985—Kerr stunned Madison Square Garden by scoring on two close-in forehands, a backhand and on a one-timer up the slot, four goals all within 8:16, to turn a 3-2 deficit into a 6-3 lead. The Flyers, who had not won a series the previous three springs, withstood a Ranger comeback to complete a 6-5 win and 3-0 sweep.

"We were feeling that pressure, needed some confidence," recalls Keenan. "And that mountain of a man gave it to us."

So what would Kerr be capable of today, in an NHL where defensemen have been disarmed of most weapons but the pokecheck?

"Actually, I wanted teams to put their biggest defenseman on me because chances are I would be quicker than that guy," he recalls. "I could use my body off of his and have a field day.

"The guys who defended me better were smaller guys who closed off the angles. Once I got the puck, bigger or smaller than me wasn't going to make a difference.

"The guys on the powerplay unit laughed about 'the Pelle Eklund option.' It meant that if I wasn't one of the best three options for Pelle (Kerr's primary setup man) then, and only then, could Pelle do something else.

"Hey, if I was going to take a beating, I wanted the puck."

In just 27 games in 1990-91, Kerr still had 24 points. The Flyers needed a rebuild though, so new GM Russ Farwell let Kerr go in the expansion draft to San Jose, which, by pre-arrangement, traded him to the Rangers. A year-and-a-half later, Tim was out of the game at the too-young age of 32. Nevertheless, today he thanks fate for never giving him more than he could bear.

"I had some crazy things with injuries that certainly hurt my time playing and numbers, but I enjoyed the challenge of all those rehabs," recalls Kerr, elected to the Flyers Hall of Fame in 1994. "The games were a lot of fun, so I kept getting up until I couldn't get back up again.

"I had a great run, a lot of fun with a great group of guys. It was unfortunate we didn't win the Cup. That was hard because we sacrificed so much and wanted it so badly. But I guess I would be more disappointed if we had a team that didn't give everything it had.

"I look back on guys taking shots between games to freeze up, remember playing that (1987) Islander series with a strap-on when I couldn't get my hand out of my pocket without using my other arm. We had some warriors who would do anything to win."

Today, Kerr, his second wife Midge and their five children are equally dedicated on behalf of Tim Kerr Charities, whose efforts became intensified in 2005 when Wesley, the middle of their three boys, was treated at Children's Hospital of Philadelphia for a rare bone infection.

"We went home with a well child while others were still there facing life-threatening illnesses," said Midge. "We had to do more." Wesley recovered to star in basketball at Philadelphia's University of the Arts, as have brothers Garrett and Tanner. And the charity has raised more than $2 million over two-plus decades staging participatory athletic events at the shore.

The proprietor of Tim Kerr Power Play Realty in Avalon, NJ—and the owner of the Pensacola (FL) Ice Flyers of the Southern Professional Hockey League—has a Jersey Shore home, plus places in the Cayman Islands and Vermont. And thanks to a successful 2012 knee replacement, Kerr is having the happily-ever-after he has earned.

"Knee replacement worked, shoulders are amazingly good considering," he said. "Neck is a little bit of an issue, but I can't complain."

Griping never was his style.

"One thing I learned from Kathy's death is that there are no [guarantees]," he said. "There are only privileges and life is one of them.

"You have to enjoy it because you can have it taken away from you at any time.

"I was blessed to meet another woman and be able to grow my family. A lot of people have said to me that they could never have gone through what I have. But people underestimate themselves. When they have to, they handle things."

Of the 363 goals Kerr scored for the Flyers, many came on his own rebounds. It is easy to understand why.

GARY DORNHOEFER

THE COLLECTION OF SKELETAL REMAINS that made up Gary Dornhoefer was good at rattling goaltenders. This thin-as-a-ghost right wing would climb into the crease and haunt the net-keepers' attic.

"If I were a goalie and had to battle someone like me, I would be frustrated as hell," Dornhoefer once said. "I'd end up being thrown out of the game because I'd blow my cool.

"They try not to let it bother them, but some guys get so occupied trying to move me out of their way, they forget about the game."

If it was any consolation to them, at the same time Dornhoefer was indulging in sadism, he was practicing masochism. There never has been a Flyer who willed more out an unimposing body, to the greater detriment of it.

"He was such a maniac that, when I had played against him, I thought he had to be a drinker and carouser off the ice," recalled the late Ross Lonsberry, Dornhoefer's linemate through the Stanley Cup years. "Turned out, he was the opposite.

"He wanted to play golf, didn't go out with us much, but at the rink he was the greatest teammate you could have. He spent himself at practice, looked like death warmed over after games. But he had a huge pain threshold.

"When I went on the line with he and Ricky (MacLeish), Dorny told me, 'You chase them behind the net and then get the hell out of the way. If you are at the net when I get there, I'm not responsible for your safety'"

Of course that meant his own, too. Before the Flyers selected the Hershey winger late in the expansion draft, the 145-pound Dornhoefer had failed to stick with the Bruins in three different trials.

Because his first loves growing up in Kitchener, Ontario were golf and baseball, he didn't skate for the first time until he followed his friends to the rink at age 11. Once the kid was smitten, Otto Dornhoefer, a German immigrant who worked as a mechanic at the local candy factory, built his son a back-yard rink. But it wasn't only Dornhoefer's interest that bloomed late. So did his body.

"I had no stamina," he recalls. "I'd go up and down the ice and I was exhausted. I'd get hit once and be out for three or four shifts. The Flyers once ordered me to drink Stout beer over the summer to put on weight. I couldn't stand the stuff, think I gained like three pounds."

By the time of Dornhoefer's retirement after the 1977-78 season, he was a veritable hulk at 210 pounds, although that figure probably included the weight of all the casts ever worn on his body. Sadly, he paid a price that can't be easily rationalized, even having won two Stanley Cups.

The Broad Street Bullies walk together forever, as Fred Shero prophesied on the locker room blackboard during the 1974 Final, but that was little consolation to Dornhoefer who, just a few years after retirement, couldn't walk more than a few holes on a golf course.

The successful left knee replacement he received in 2012 after "nine years of hell" from a previous replacement was the seventh orthopedic procedure of a post-hockey life that put him in the broadcast booth for *Hockey Night in Canada* and the Flyers, for whom he worked as a greeter in the Wells Fargo Center concourse on game nights. The sport has been good to him. But Dornhoefer still regrets what he went through.

"I retired at 35 and am now 71, so I've experienced these physical problems for half of my life," he said. "If I had to do it all over again, I wouldn't.

"But I'm alright. Thank God there are golf carts. You walk with a little limp, you are hunched over a little and sometimes you are a little short of breath. But you keep trucking."

Emotional pain lingers, too. Dornhoefer lost his daughter Stephanie to breast cancer at 35 and for years had no contact with a troubled son, Stephen. But Stephanie left him a granddaughter, Sydney. And though arthritis may be keeping him from a completely happily-ever-after, not so for the multiple rescued greyhounds enjoying their golden years at the Port Republic, NJ, home of Gary and his second wife Jackie.

Dornhoefer's voice still cackles with self-deprecation, and he remains as thin as was the goalies' patience with him. Looking back, the only thickness to him was in his skull. "MacLeish hit his head on my cheekbone, knocked me cold for two, three minutes, and I didn't miss a game," he said. "I had severe headaches for months, took a couple of aspirin and played.

"I think players are a little smarter today. We didn't think about it at the time. I made the choice and was able to be on a team that won a couple Cups. I think your game is what it is. I couldn't dance around and try to avoid injuries."

He suffered enough of them in the Flyers' first two years for the organization to expose him to waiver claim following an eight-goal 1968-69 season. "I got a call from the Rangers asking me if I planned to keep playing and I said 'yes', but they never picked me up," he recalled. "Nobody wanted me, the Flyers kept me, and I started to put the puck in the net."

Lonsberry arrived in a mid-season trade in 1971-72. MacLeish, acquired in a three-way deal that sent Bernie Parent to Toronto, came up for good at the start 1972-73. One of the best No. 2 lines of the seventies anchored the Flyers for six straight seasons in which they never failed to reach the semifinals.

The first time they got there, Dornhoefer had the pivotal goal. With the series and game tied 2-2 with the Minnesota North Stars, he broke down his off wing, took a step inside defenseman Barry Gibbs, pushed the puck ahead and switched to his backhand. Tom Reid grabbed Dornhoefer as he lifted his shot, which flew waist-high past Cesare Maniago, before the right wing could avoid the goalie, not that Dorny had ever been known to step aside. Before he hit the ice, his stick was in the air and so were 16,066 delirious fans who had waited six years, just like Dornhoefer, for the franchise's first big home playoff moment.

Its impact was such that sculptor Gilman B. Whitman created a statue, "Score!" in commemoration of the goal. Dedicated in 1976 at the south entrance to the Spectrum, the art was relocated outside XFINITY Live! when the arena was rázed.

"It was near the end of the shift and I was so tired, I didn't want to go out there anymore," recalls Dornhoefer of the goal. "One mistake and the game is over, you have to force the issue.

"The first time I saw a replay of it was when I was inducted into the Flyers Hall of Fame (in 1991)," said Dornhoefer. "Didn't know I had that move, works maybe one time out of a thousand."

The North Stars were finished off 4-1, two days later in Bloomington. The Flyers, who then got a split in the first two semifinal games in Montreal, came home to a six-minute standing ovation when they hit the ice for Game Three. He doesn't recall scoring a goal on Gary Dornhoefer Night, his final regular-season game in 1978, but that ovation in the middle of a 1-1 series still replays in Dorny's mind.

"You could not talk over it," he said. "It's probably the most memorable moment of my years as a Flyer."

The Canadiens didn't lose another game and went on to win the Stanley Cup. But the upstart Flyers went home for the summer utterly convinced of their destiny to become champions and played like it from the 1973-74 opener.

"Every time you think you're gaining ground on those guys, they just kick the skates out from under you," said New York goalie Ed Giacomin, after the Flyers outlasted the Rangers in Game Seven in the semifinals of the next spring.

Primarily he meant Dornhoefer. During the third period that day, Dornhoefer had lost Steve Vickers on a goal that cut the Flyers third-period lead to a nervous 3-2. "I wanted to crawl in a hole," Dornhoefer recalled. Instead, he went to the net and 12 seconds later, scored what proved to be the winner in the 4-3 triumph.

Seven days later, he suffered a shoulder separation in Game Three against the Bruins that precluded him from playing in the Final, making Dornhoefer all the more appreciative of being able to triumphantly follow Clarke and Parent around the Buffalo Memorial Auditorium surface 12 months later.

Dornhoefer had scored one of the biggest goals of that second Cup drive, after the Islanders, down, 3-0 in the semifinals, forced a Game Seven at the Spectrum. On the first shift after Kate Smith left the ice, No. 12 blasted a perfectly-placed 40-footer past Chico Resch that almost took the Spectrum roof off for a second time.

Dornhoefer's second ring, the one he understandably most cherished, sadly was stolen years later from clothes he left in a golf locker room. But his proudest possession remains the respect he had earned.

"Give me 15 Dornhoefers and I don't have a care in the world," Fred Shero once said. "He doesn't make excuses."

Dornhoefer didn't buy them from teammates either, not that they had the temerity to offer them after watching him practically kill himself for the cause.

"There wasn't that much toughness around him when I got here (for the 1969-70 season)," recalls Bobby Clarke. "But that didn't seem to matter to him.

"And when Holmgren got here, Dorny was a big influence on Paul."

Holmgren most remembers Dornhoefer during the 1976 Cup Final, when he was hit so hard by Larry Robinson during Game Two that the Forum sideboards cracked.

"While they were fixing them, Dorny stood on the bench yelling at Robinson, "That's the hardest you can hit?"" laughed Holmgren.

The scorer of 20-plus goals five times, and of 30 once (in 1972-73). Dornhoefer was down to only seven goals in 1978 when he declined Keith Allen's offer to play another year.

"What are you watching?" he told the GM. "When the puck is in their end, I'm still in our end.

"Problem is, when you hit somebody bigger than you, over time you get the worst of it," he says. "Must be the [stubborn] German in me.

"That's the way I played; I wasn't going to change. I loved the contact and I played in an era that was perfect for me. So even though I look back and feel it wasn't worth it, I can't say I would change a thing."

DAVE POULIN

A GUY WHO SKATED AS QUICKLY AS ANYBODY in Flyer history came even more rapidly out of nowhere to become their leader. Dave Poulin, who wasn't big enough or fast enough to be chosen for major junior, captained Philadelphia clubs that twice reached Stanley Cup Final.

Poulin's is a remarkable tale of both destiny and dedication. In 1977, a teammate on the Jr. B Dixie Beehives in the Toronto suburb of Mississauga received a questionnaire from Notre Dame University. Already committed to Michigan State, he gave it to Poulin, who filled it out.

"Recruiting pretty much was word of mouth in those days," he recalls. "If you had one offer from a good program, you would have 10.

"I think I ended up talking to 20 schools. I visited Notre Dame first, fell in love, and canceled five other visits I had scheduled."

As his body filled out from 165 pounds, he thrived in a developing Irish program. But whatever chance Poulin had to attract NHL interest essentially was wiped out when he came down with spinal meningitis and missed a third of his draft-eligibility season. By his senior year, when he captained the Irish to one of only six winning records in a 25-year period, Poulin had put on 25 pounds and become stronger and quicker. But his 1.42 points per-game average was attracting a lot fewer recruiters than his 3.24 grade point average.

Poulin had been accepted into Procter and Gamble's prestigious management-training program when he received a call from Ted Sator, a former player at rival Bowling Green State University who coached Rogle, a Swedish minor-league team. As the rules allowed two American imports per club, Sator had phoned his friend, Ron Mason, coach at Michigan State, for recommendations of college players with the wheels to thrive on the larger European ice.

"I had never been to Europe, so it was an opportunity to do something different," recalls Poulin. "Procter and Gamble said it would defer my offer for a year."

With Rogle, Poulin scored 35 goals and 27 assists in the short Swedish season of 32 games. When Sator, who had impressed Bob McCammon as a guest power-skating instructor for the Flyers, got a call from the Philadelphia coach asking for recommendations of stretch drive help for the farm team at Maine, Sator dropped the name of Poulin.

"It was just for the rest of the year," he recalls. "I had nothing to lose." Neither did the Flyers after

Poulin scored a point a game in 16 contests for the Mariners. He was summoned to Maple Leaf Gardens, the arena of his childhood dreams, for the next-to-last game of the 1982-83 regular season.

For Poulin, playing there turned out to be easier than it had ever been to get tickets. He was set up by Darryl Sittler for his first goal and scored on his first two NHL shots.

A week later, Poulin was taking a regular shift on left wing, recording four points and—no exaggeration—being the Flyers' best player as the Patrick Division champions collapsed in three straight losses to the fourth-place Rangers.

"I fought Ron Duguay in Game Three," Poulin recalls. "Thought I had to get that first one over with.

"I had no idea he was a tough kid, and he cut me badly over the eye. I can remember while I was getting stitches the yelling in our locker room, somebody saying 'we're getting swept and only the college kid wants to fight!'"

Soon after, Poulin received a letter from his boss-to-be at Procter and Gamble. It included a newspaper clipping of his debut in Toronto. "Obviously our paths are going different ways," he wrote. "I'm happy for you."

The road less travelled suddenly didn't have a speed limit. A flabbergasted and flattered Poulin received an invitation from Bobby Clarke to become his workout partner for the summer.

"I'm just back from Europe and had to have a car," Poulin recalls. "I was told to call Clarke, who had a tie-in with a dealership.

"He hadn't said 10 words to me at that point. Does he even know who I am? He told me to meet him at the dealership, where he set me up. Then he asked what I was doing for the summer.

"'No idea' I said. He should I should sublet a place for the summer and work out with him. And it changed my life.

"I think he was looking for someone to push him through his final years, someone who would get up at 7 in the morning six times a week. We ran five miles a day and eight on Saturday, did stuff way ahead of what hockey players did in the off-seasons in that era, with constant conversation about what it took. Essentially, I became a 24-year old version of him.

"That was a long summer, waiting to prove the whirlwind previous year wasn't a fairy tale. I read a book by Roger Angell about a kid who came up to the majors and was player of the month and led his team in RBIs, then gradually faded away. Angell wrote about him, 'to some, the best comes first, a miserable arrangement.'

"I cut that quote out and carried it in my wallet for years."

Poulin, trained by Clarke, essentially took his spot on the first line the next season, scoring 76 points between Brian Propp and Tim Kerr. After another first-round loss, this one to Washington, Clarke left the ice to become Flyer GM and then, in his first trade, moved Sittler, the heir apparent captain, to Detroit on the eve of the season. On advice of Clarke, new coach Mike Keenan bypassed seemingly more qualified young veterans to make Poulin the official Flyer leader in only his second NHL season.

"Brad Marsh had been a captain (with the Flames) and really worked hard at the rink, but he liked to party and wasn't quite as serious as Davey," recalls Clarke. "Mark Howe wasn't shy but was almost too humble, staying behind the scenes. Tim Kerr was quiet and I think just wanted to play the game.

"Davey was mature, bright, worked his ass off. When he came into the gym that summer before, he was twice as strong as I was in everything you could do. His work ethic was as good as anybody's we ever had here. And he wasn't shy, either. He would speak out."

Nevertheless, "Why me?' was a question Poulin decided not to vocalize.

"Off one year of pro experience, it made no sense to me," he recalls.

"I didn't start that season well but there was mentorship from Clarkie and Brad McCrimmon was tremendous in support. Mike's MO was us-against-him, intended to make the guys rally around me. A big part of my job was to convince guys that what he said wasn't personal, that there was a method to it.

"But basically, I tried to lead the Flyers by playing. Just keep going no matter what happened. Arguably, that's one my strengths, to just keep going."

He went quickly. An exceptional penalty killer with Howe, McCrimmon and Propp on one of the great units in NHL history, Poulin, an average passer at best, mostly created offensive opportunities with his speed. But he had enormous peripheral vision for the locker room and bench, where his intelligence, command of the language and courage earned him the pulpit.

"Dave was the best leader I ever played with," Howe recalls. "I never played with anyone I respected more."

After sustaining cracked ribs early in the 1985 Eastern Conference final against Quebec, the captain sat out two games, then returned in Game Six to step between the points, pick off a pass by Mario Marois, and solo for a three-on-five goal on goalie Mario Gosselin. The most electrifying turn-around goal in Spectrum history put the Flyers up 2-0 and essentially finished the Nordiques.

"They were compressed so low on the power play, I was surprised (Marois) tried (the pass)," recalls Poulin. "It wasn't like I had to cheat high."

In 1987, Poulin's ribs again were broken, this time in the first round. But when his team, which had led the Islanders 3-1, faced a quarterfinal Game Seven, he donned a flak jacket, submitted to a nerve block, and, playing for the first time in the series, set up two goals that sparked Philadelphia's 5-1 victory.

"I vividly still picture him sitting there while the doctors gave him the medicine, sweat pouring off his head," recalls Keenan. "I was afraid if he got hurt, he wouldn't know it. It took an unbelievable amount of courage and set the tone."

"When it wore off, I couldn't get off the couch the next day," recalls Poulin.

In 1989 against Washington, a shot chipped the bone on the ring finger of Poulin's left hand, but he played the next night, scoring once to help the Flyers even a series they went on to win in six games. Two rounds later against Montreal, Poulin suffered two broken toes that had to be frozen before Game Five, yet he pushed in the game-winner in overtime.

None of these injuries caused him—or the Flyers organization—as much agony as when coach Paul Holmgren, citing the need to transfer leadership to younger players, yanked No. 20's captaincy in December 1990.

"It hurt tremendously," Poulin said. "I hadn't seen any change in the team's leadership. I think they did it because they thought I was breaking down and were getting ready to trade me. "

Indeed, frustration with Poulin's recurring lower abdominal pulls, plus the Flyers' desperation for offense, led to his trade to Boston a month later for Ken Linseman. After the Flyers missed the playoffs for the first time in 18 seasons, Linseman was gone. Poulin, soon joined by Propp, keyed the Bruins to the Stanley Cup Final.

The pulls that had plagued Poulin because of his bowlegged skating style were corrected in surgery. Before he retired to become Notre Dame's coach for 10 seasons, director of hockey operations of the Maple Leafs for five, and, currently, commentator for The Sports Network (TSN) in Canada, Poulin gave the Bruins and Capitals five more strong years on the ice.

Philadelphia got the best ones though, thanks to some of the greatest strokes of serendipity in the franchise's storied history. "The roads don't have to be perfect to get you to the same place," said Poulin. "If you tried to map out a route like mine, there would be no chance."

MIKE KEENAN

REVERSING NINE STRAIGHT PLAYOFF LOSSES over three springs was the essential dilemma Flyer president Jay Snider made into a lengthy questionnaire for head-coaching candidates in 1984. Mike Keenan turned it into his thesis.

"Personally, I have experienced a contagious phenomenon whereby the more I win, the more I want to win," Keenan wrote. "Nothing short of this objective is acceptable.

"Winning is perhaps the single most significant solution for every problem your team can encounter. Therefore, the challenge, as I see it, is to teach the team to expect to win."

In his previous five seasons, Keenan had directed Oshawa to consecutive Ontario Junior B championships, Peterborough to an Ontario Hockey League (Junior A) title, Rochester to a Calder (AHL) Cup and the University of Toronto to a Canadian college crown.

Having never failed to meet his own highest expectations, Keenan was the best choice, even at the young age of 34, to rekindle the hopes of an NHL franchise that had become frustrated enough to have diverted its eyes from the ultimate prize.

Not only were the Flyers nearly a decade removed from the pinnacle, but the first round had become a mountain unto itself. And there were ample reasons to fear things were going to become worse before they could get better.

Bobby Clarke had just left the ice to become general manager. Bill Barber was about to begin rehab from a knee reconstruction that, as it turned out, ended his career. Owner Ed Snider, who even in the early years had set an eventual Stanley Cup, not just postseason berths, as the goal for his run-of-the-mill expansion team, had expectations so low going into that 1984-85 season that he told Keenan; "If you can get this team to the playoffs, I'll kiss your butt at center ice."

Keenan, cards close to the vest, announced his ambition for the Flyers as only "some form of excellence," and then, in that first year, performed arguably the greatest single-season coaching job in NHL history. As it turned out, there was a lot more talent on the youngest roster in the league than the hockey world had understood, and, more importantly, than the players themselves had believed.

The careers of holdovers Brad Marsh, Brad McCrimmon, Mark Howe, and Pelle Lindbergh had gone stale in the final year under Bob McCammon. None of those players, all heading into prime seasons, grasped how much more they had to give until Keenan proved it to them, oftentimes the hard way.

In four tumultuous and sparkling seasons, he took the Flyers to two Stanley Cup Finals, three division championships, and a .638 regular-season winning percentage, just barely below Fred Shero's franchise-high .642.

The window to a Stanley Cup was closed in 1985 and 1987 by the Edmonton dynasty and, in 1986—the season of Lindbergh's death—by a shocking first-round upset at the hands of the Rangers. But Keenan's Flyers teams were better than a lot of history's one-time NHL champions. And the path to those two close calls was littered with so much guts and glory that nobody remembers his era as a failure.

Those four years produced 12 of the all-time top 50 games listed in this book. And the heroes of those contests account for 10 of our top 50 figures in the team's history.

"I didn't have stellar years before Keenan got here," recalls one of them, Marsh. "I mean, I was OK, but I wasn't a standout in anything.

"It was a new start and I ate it up as much as anyone. I remember the first practices we had under him. It was like nothing I'd been a part of up to that time. There had always been a lot of standing around; these were short, fast, crisp, and right in my wheelhouse.

"I was in the best shape I ever had been in. I liked the whole atmosphere he created. Mike put the carrots out there, pushed the buttons. You were going to play if you did what he wanted, so I made sure I did that."

Keenan threw 30-plus minutes a game at Howe, convinced he could handle it. The coach got McCrimmon, just like Marsh, into superior condition, and told Lindbergh, whose promise Keenan had witnessed coaching against him in the AHL playoffs, that, never mind how much the little Swede had struggled in goal since the fine start to his rookie season of two years earlier, the Flyers' net belonged to him.

Lindbergh keyed an astonishing 16-4-4 start before seeming to tire in December. Keenan, instead of cutting back on the goalie's starts, increased his workload during practice and, in improved physical condition, Lindbergh began to play better than ever.

The Keenan system was to chase the puck and force the opposition with a relentlessness demanded by a coach relentlessly in his players' heads. They had no escape from this former Toronto gym teacher out of St. Lawrence University, whose ambitions burned much brighter than had his brief career on defense in the low minors.

"He is capable of everything," described the Flyers' new captain, Dave Poulin three months into Year One. "And he has figured each of us out very quickly."

The coach used words like "intrinsic," and "synergistic" with the media, deployed unrepeatable and sometimes unconscionable utterings with his players, impulsively juggled lines and made position changes all the way to 53 victories that first season, the most in franchise history.

To a man, the players Keenan inherited say they became 20 percent better under him. Almost every button he pushed uncannily worked. Three rookies from an astoundingly successful 1983 draft without a No. 1 pick—Rick Tocchet, Peter Zezel, and Derrick Smith—gave Keenan more pieces and not one player received any mental peace, especially Poulin, who in only his second NHL season, became the demanding and demeaning new coach's lightning rod and buffer.

"A lot of it was directed at me because he thought I could handle it," recalls Poulin. "He also wanted the group to rally around me."

Ego repairs largely were left to assistants E.J. McGuire, the sweetest of men and brainiest of assistants Keenan brought with him from his Rochester days, and Paul Holmgren, who joined the staff in 1985-86 after Ted Sator left to become head coach of the Rangers. The boss applied the pressure on players who subsequently pushed it onto the opposition with energy fueled by conditioning techniques Ron Hextall, who joined the Flyers in 1986, describes as "cutting edge."

"Mike's coaching was aggressive motivation; it wasn't technical," recalls Poulin. "E.J. had the color-coded folder systems and all the stuff that made Mike look organized."

McGuire and Holmgren were more than buffers, actually more like Bufferin for the pounded brains of easy-going personalities like Brian Propp and Ilkka Sinisalo.

"E.J. cleaned up my messes," recalls Keenan.

Together, they were a perfect balance.

"E.J. was one of the best people I have ever met," recalls Marsh. "He'd come around after Keenan gave you [bleep] and give you a pep talk that wasn't bull; you knew he was being sincere and that's why it worked.

"E,J. was sharp, too, as were Homer and Ted, who was really big in improving my skating. You need a coaching staff that's not just going to fall in line but also contributes its own knowledge and ideas."

The Flyers started that 1984-85 season with a surprising three points out of four against the Washington team that had swept them the preceding April. During their next game, a 5-2 loss in Montreal, they pretty much looked like seven sophomores, three rookies and veterans who had been losing in the playoffs for too long. Pity the Flyer who nevertheless thought 1-1-1 was a decent beginning. The next day at practice, Keenan tortured his team with 45 minutes of starts and stops, their first lesson that expectations had been raised. The Flyers beat Vancouver, 13-2, in the following game.

After Philadelphia lost five out of six and fell to 18-9-5 for the season, the players wished themselves a Merry Christmas with a December 23 victory over Washington. Keenan seemed to be in the holiday spirit.

"I went to Mike maybe two days before that game and asked if we could skate at 8:30 a.m. on the 24th so the guys who lived close enough could fly home for Christmas, then come back on the 25th for our game on the 26th in Washington," recalls Poulin. "He said, 'Absolutely, just make sure you win the game on the 23rd.'

"So we did. That morning, he brought a boom box and was playing Christmas carols during the practice. We were going to do our Pollyanna gift exchange afterwards and have a little Christmas cheer together. We had the usual, probably 35-minute, practice with the aerobic, end-to-end drills at the end. Guys were in a great mood; We're flying.

"He then lines us up on the goal line and skated us for another 45 minutes. Guys were cramping, seizing, throwing up, cursing and I remember he had a smirk on his face the whole time. Finally, he called us together and said, 'Expect the unexpected. Have a Merry Christmas' and went off the ice. Guys were scrambling to catch their flights. I wanted to kill him.

"We lost the game in Washington 6-0 because he killed our legs. Afterwards, he said we had no leadership, a swipe at me. And then we [won six of the next seven] including one in Edmonton (against the Stanley Cup champions)."

The Flyers lost Howe for a time to torn cartilage near his clavicle, fell 11 points behind Washington, then beat the Capitals in Landover on Brian Propp's goal with two seconds remaining. They reeled off eight straight wins, then had another streak of 11 to blow past Washington. And even when that run ended in Chicago, Keenan ripped their effort.

Philadelphia had stunned the hockey world in winning the division and conference going away. But, with two weeks to go, Keenan pulled out the remaining schedules of the Flyers and defending champion Oilers and said, "We're only four points back and have a game in hand. If we're close, I'd like to go for it."

They won 16 of the final 17 to catch the Oilers, too. With Keenan's shoes in their rears, the players grinded their way through a nervous first-round sweep (margin of victory four goals) of the Rangers and beat an Islander team—"Who the hell is Mike Bossy? Who the hell is Bryan Trottier?" Iron Mike asked his team—just one season removed from four straight Cups.

Against Quebec, when the Flyers were tied 2-2 in the Eastern Conference final—and thanks to Lindbergh, were behind only 1-0 after two periods of Game Five at Le Colisée—Keenan climbed the table in the middle of the dressing room with a stick, knocked off all the water bottles, and accused his players of quitting just six wins short of the Stanley Cup.

The Flyers rallied for a 2-1 win, were the best they had been all year in closing out the Nordiques 3-0, in Game Six, then may have been even better in smoking the Oilers, 4-1 in Game One of the Final.

Reality, and six future Hall of Famers to just one for Philadelphia (Howe) set in as the Oilers won the series and the Cup in five, but merely being named NHL Coach of the Year didn't do Keenan justice. He probably had been the coach of any year.

A locker room of terrific guys, half the time thanking him, half the time cursing him, had learned through "Mike Fright" what it took to win. Still, the next season began with Keenan overwhelmed with anxiety that success would spoil the Flyers. When, during the second week, they outshot the Nordiques 43-14 and lost 2-1, Howe remembers a 75-minute punishment skate without pucks followed by a warning that the next time the Flyers ran into a hot goalie, "somebody had better run him over."

"The bottom line with Mike was if you didn't win, you didn't work hard enough," recalls Howe. "'You think it's okay to outshoot a team and lose? It's not okay.'"

The Flyers won their next 10 before Lindbergh's car hit the wall and the players saw a different Keenan. "From that first morning when he and I went to the hospital to identify the body, he was unbelievable," recalls Poulin.

"Most of us had never been through a death of anybody we knew. He kept us all together, made us talk to each other. It was the best I ever saw him."

The worst of him was coming. Keenan's fear of complacency was replaced by a fear of his team using Lindbergh's death as an excuse. So he pushed even harder, to another 53 victories behind backup Bob Froese, until emotional fatigue and a near-perfect Ranger Game Five sent the Flyers down in a stunning upset.

The next season, when the hockey gods sent Philadelphia Hextall as compensation for the loss of Lindbergh, the Flyers started 25-7-2 until the year became one long wait for the return of injured players. The team had learned how to win despite anything, taught by a teacher who, in turn, hadn't learned to trust his pupils.

"We were probably needing [mind games] less and getting them more," recalls Poulin. The joy of winning that had driven the 1984-85 team had morphed into a fear of losing. The Flyers became a grim team whose leaders doused brushfires with reminders that the end—winning—justified the means.

"Things like that Christmas skate worked the first year," recalls Marsh. "It hardened us as a team and helped our young guys mature as hockey players because they had to be prepared every single day.

"We weren't supposed to win because we lacked experience just about everywhere: the GM, the coach, the roster. In my mind, I think we all just focused on how we kept winning and winning. Whatever he did, and we did, worked.

"But as time went on, that sort of stuff didn't while the abuse grew. It touched everybody in some way. I had my times with him, too, but probably it wasn't as bad for me as other players. When Keenan started to lose his grip, he got out of control."

Off of all those championships and a near Stanley Cup as a rookie NHL coach, Keenan believed he could will just about anything and took offense when he couldn't. There always had been a method to the madness, but increasingly, there was just madness.

During one game, Keenan put his foot into the back of Thomas Eriksson, who had suffered a broken kneecap on a previous shift, and shoved. He ordered Ron Sutter, above reproach in his efforts, off the bench for losing a faceoff; and another time tried to get more out of him by threatening to bench his twin brother, Rich.

After Hextall's right arm had been virtually paralyzed by a shot in a 1988 game against the Rangers, he was left in the game to surrender four goals. The whipping boy Zezel was made to dress in an anteroom, away from his teammates, during the Stanley Cup Final.

"Mike was really good for some guys," recalls Bob Clarke. "Had it not been for him, Zezel and Smith wouldn't have made the NHL.

"McCrimmon was overweight and drinking too much; he was almost untradeable before Keenan got him.

"Unfortunately, Mike destroyed guys like Tommy Eriksson, who had made the All-Rookie team the year before. Mike wasn't here for a month when Tommy was in my office crying, 'Why does Mike hate me?'

"I understand scaring guys, but Mike didn't have to be so cruel. Eriksson went back to Sweden, costing us a really good player. And he wasn't the only one. Mike was cruel to Sinisalo and Scott Mellanby, although Scott was tough."

In the 1987 playoffs, the Flyers shut down the Rangers, Islanders and Canadiens in part to shut up their coach, then rallied from a three-goal deficit, plus two more two-goal deficits, to take to the limit the most loaded offensive team the game ever has known. Kerr, a four-time 50-plus goal scorer, had been done with a shoulder separation before the second round was over, but Hextall played his heart out and the Oilers couldn't kill off the Flyers until there were fewer than three minutes to go in Game Seven.

A Stanley Cup for that team would have been perhaps the supreme triumph of will in the history of the sport.

"I make this comment with all due respect to our team but when I went to the Canada Cup (that August) and I'm coaching (Wayne) Gretzky, (Mark) Messier, (Paul) Coffey and (Grant) Fuhr and could more fully [comprehend] the skill they had, I came to realize even more that our team did an unbelievable job to take it to seven games," recalls Keenan.

"We scared the Oilers. They were a better team, but it took them six-and-a half friggin' games to figure it out. With a break or two, we might have gotten out of Game Seven (a 3-1 loss) with a win."

The next year, the trade of McCrimmon and a severe concussion suffered by Marsh thinned the defense—and Keenan's patience—even farther. With the arm of Kerr, who missed most of the season with complications from shoulder surgery, hanging limply by his side, Philadelphia ignominiously blew a 3-1 lead to Washington and lost in the first round. Ed Snider wanted a better work environment and a torn Clarke decided reluctantly there wasn't enough left between coach and players to give Keenan another year.

"I think you would have had to change three or four players, not anyone specific, to bring him back," believes Poulin, not that everybody, including Howe, agrees today. But after four seasons, few Flyers were sorry to see Keenan gone.

"They had no reason to fire me," recalls Keenan. "It caught me by surprise and I cried like crazy.

"Haven't cried at a firing since."

Perhaps that was because Keenan never again received the level of support he had in Philadelphia.

"I wanted to scout Quebec before we played them in 1985," recalls Keenan. "I remember Ed Snider getting (the coaches) a jet to fly up to see the game and bring us back for practice the next day.

"In that era, I don't think there were many owners who were that assertive in supporting a coach.

"Because of Snider's vision, we were much more advanced than most teams. We had Mike Finocchiaro doing the video, Pat Croce doing fitness. Clarkie was completely on board with all the video equipment E.J. and I wanted, before every team had that stuff."

Keenan went on to take the Blackhawks to a Final and a semifinal, the Rangers to their first Stanley Cup in 54 years, and Magnitogorsk to a KHL championship. Stints in St Louis, Vancouver, Boston, Florida and Calgary were shortened more because the bosses who had hired him were quickly gone than any failure of Keenan to get along with his superiors and players.

He mellowed. Some.

While many of the stars Keenan coached in eight NHL stops—and in winning two Canada Cups—loved him and a few hated him, the first ones he coached in Philadelphia are, today, almost universally grateful to him. Winning solves every problem, Keenan wrote in 1984. That includes grudge-holding.

As Philadelphia started to rebuild, and Keenan, the GM for a time in Chicago, was rumored to be interested in trading for many of his nucleus Philadelphia players, virtually all of the same Flyers who had suffered too much Iron Mike said, without hesitation, they would welcome the opportunity to play for him again.

When Zezel, whom Keenan brought to play for him in Vancouver and St Louis, died of organ failure caused by hemolytic anemia in 2009, the meanest coach Peter ever had was asked by his parents to speak at the funeral. Even Snider, so convinced the Flyers needed a softer hand in 1988, put a big contract in front of Keenan in 1993 asking him to please return, before the coach accepted the Ranger job instead.

Memories are short; that is a good thing sometimes. But the winners from the second-winningest era in Flyers history have not forgotten what Keenan did for them.

"You know, I never viewed myself as a scorer, but Mike pushed and prodded and, like with everybody, never let you be comfortable with where you were," recalls Poulin. "While you're going through that, it's very, very difficult, but when you're done, there's a sense of reward.

"You realize that you couldn't have done it on your own. There's no way I could have gotten to where I was without Mike Keenan."

JOE WATSON

IT CUT THROUGH CLOSED LOCKER-ROOM DOORS, carried clearly over the hiss of spraying showers, pierced the roar of 17,077 fans and occasionally even dented the cement in some of his teammates' heads. One time, the voice of an injured Joe Watson even called an offsides from the press box, bellowing so loudly that linesman Neil Armstrong, apparently about to ignore the infraction, blew his whistle.

Joe "Thundermouth" Watson never scored more than six goals or recorded more than 30 points in any of his 14 NHL seasons. But he broke every existing record for decibels.

His style of play was not nearly as loud as his voice. Still, there was more than just a whisper around the NHL that Watson was as reliable in his own zone as any defenseman of his day. Teammates asked only that Watson keep it down, which he did. The score we mean, not his voice.

It is unclear why a kid who came from a northern British Columbia town with a population of 2,400 had a sound louder than the Canadian Brass. Later, of course, the citizens of Smithers shouted to whoever was in earshot—two moose, three elk and a couple of bears—how proud they were of Joe. When his little brother Jimmy joined Watson on two Flyers Stanley Cup teams, the sun stayed up all night through the entire summer to celebrate.

Granted, the guy who put Smithers on the map also was appreciated in the big city. "If you want to measure a guy in every way, not just what he's done today on the ice, but for everything he's done for a franchise and a city, Joe would come out near the top," said Pat Quinn, the late Flyer coach.

Watson was a throwback, not only to Year One of the franchise, but the youth of every player when he would skate all day and then talk about it all night. "If you can't enjoy it, you can't do it," Watson said. He adored being in the NHL and respected the privilege of being a Flyer.

"A lot of guys mellow and play out the string," said Keith Allen. "Joe's not that kind. It's amazing how he never lost his enthusiasm."

Woe unto any teammate who did. "I guess you've got to know the right thing to say at the right time, but I hope they all realize it's constructive criticism," Watson, who played in two NHL All-Star Games and was elected to the Flyers Hall of Fame in 1996, allowed. "It all stays in the locker room and these guys know how I am."

His words had all the subtlety of a bludgeon, and on scoring chances his stick wasn't exactly a precision instrument. When Joe scored in the epic 1976 game against the Soviet Red Army, and Fred Shero said the goal set Russian hockey back 15 years, Watson laughed harder than anyone. His good humor was interrupted only by the thoughts of anyone laughing at the Flyers.

"The word I think of is 'sincere,'" said teammate Terry Crisp. "He never embellished the truth.

"It was just there, good and bad. You never got it from him unless you deserved it, and Joe was there with the right words when you needed it."

In Boston, where Watson broke into the NHL a year before the 1967 expansion, he was a roommate and best buddy of fellow rookie Bobby Orr. With the long-bedraggled Bruins ready to climb on Orr's coattails, Watson's ego was blown to smithereens when he was taken in the expansion draft by the new Philadelphia team.

"A Tuesday, I'm working for the public works department in Smithers, flagging traffic," said Watson. "You know, there wasn't a lot of traffic in Smithers.

"About 10 after seven, a guy comes by and says, 'I just heard your name on the radio. You just got drafted by Philadelphia.

"Whatttt???? I went to my boss, Vern Flockhart, (future Flyer) Ron's father, and said I had to take the rest of the day off. I was in shock.

"Teams could only protect 11 (and one goalie). (Bruins coach) Harry Sinden told me they thought they would lose Bob Woytowich, then protect me, but I got taken.

"Oh, was I mad. And other than starting a family, it turned out to be the best thing that ever happened to me."

The Flyers started their family when, with their second pick (of forwards and defensemen) they selected Watson. Eleven years later, the woebegone Colorado Rockies were looking for that same kind of influence when the 35-year-old, given the option by Allen of staying on as a Flyers' spare, decided to accept a new challenge.

One month into that season, Joe was checked from behind, fell awkwardly against the end boards at the St. Louis Arena, and suffered a leg broken in 13 places.

"We had tied the Flyers 2-2 the night before in Denver," recalled Watson. "Wayne Babych pushed me in my lower back as we went to the boards.

"Sure, it was a dirty play. I was in shock, I guess, because I tried to get up. (Linesman) John D'Amico said, 'Better lay there," I didn't know the bone had pierced my sock. Then oh God, I was in such pain in the ambulance, every bump was just terrible. They had to wait until 1:30 a.m. to operate because the doctor had been out and had to sober up."

The Rockies got a room for Marianne, Joe's then-wife, and their two-year-old son Ryan at a hotel up the street from the hospital where Watson underwent six operations over six weeks.

"A lot of Blues came up to see me," he recalled. "Steve Durbano brought beers and Marianne yelled, 'Get that outta here, I'm trying to get my husband better!"

"Steve came back after she left and we had a couple. He came to see me about five times. What bothered me more than anything else, Babych never did.

"He wrote me a letter about six months later, said, 'I understand you think it was dirty.' He left a number so I called back and said, 'Yeah, I think it was, and if you had come to visit me, it would have made me feel better.'

"A couple years later, when I was scouting for the Flyers, I told Behn Wilson before a game, 'If you ever get a chance...' He hit Babych so hard it broke his nose and cheekbone.

"I shook Behn's hand after the game. I walked on the right toe of a leg two inches shorter than the other for 24 years."

While providing services to the Flyers over practically 50 years as an assistant coach, scout, ambassador and—to this day—salesman of signage in the Wells Fargo Center, Watson, who has been the driving force of Flyer alumni teams for decades, played in pain. Finally, Dr. Art Bartolozzi sawed the leg in two areas, attached a 12-inch titanium rod in his thigh, and screwed the cuts into the rod, leaving a three-quarter-inch gap so calcification could lengthen the leg.

"It worked, yup," said Joe. "Very little pain now, so I can play.

"Holy [bleep], (the recovery and rehab) was brutal! But I'm not complaining. When I turned pro, I wanted to play in the NHL and win a Stanley Cup and I won two of them.

"Hey, I'm lucky. I know a lot of guys who broke their legs and never got out of Smithers."

JIM WATSON

Flyers fans never came to the Spectrum for the express purpose of watching Jimmy Watson play hockey. But once inside, they were happy he was there.

For nine seasons, Joe Watson's little brother did big, important, things. He moved the puck and erased scoring chances, always staying calm and purposeful amidst the chaos of the defensive zone. The enthusiasm with which the five-time midseason All-Star played made obvious how much he cared.

Writers on the Flyer beat were amused to find it virtually impossible to ask the affable Watson any question without getting this answer: "You know, this team has a lot of pride." But it was true because players like Jimmy Watson looked at their jobs as a trust.

"He gave everything," Paul Holmgren said when Watson retired with back issues just before the 1982-83 season, "and everything to him was the team.

"If there ever was anyone complaining in the locker room, he'd be the first guy to shut it up."

Watson liked being a Flyer too much to allow teammates to take the privilege for granted. "I was very proud to be a loyal soldier," he says today. "I had a lot of respect for what that uniform stood for."

That began with Joe wearing one for five years before Jimmy did.

Mary and Joe Watson Sr. produced six sons, all of whom grew up in Smithers, British Columbia, sharing passions for the outdoors, hockey and the Detroit Tigers. Joe Watson Jr., always the pitcher, burned the palms of his designated catcher, Jimmy, with fastballs and carved out a career path for him to follow. When Jimmy struggled during his first junior season with the Calgary Centennials and pondered quitting, Joe had his kid brother come to Philadelphia to see for himself what life was like at the end of the rainbow.

Jimmy stuck it out in Calgary, but not without further disappointments. Despite being named best defenseman in the Western Canada Hockey League during his final season, Watson was the 39th player taken in the 1972 NHL Draft. "Never knew why," he said. "Maybe because I left that first year to get my head together."

Teams that passed over him two and three times needed their heads examined. After Watson spent a season on the Flyer farm team in Richmond, he became the final piece of the Stanley Cup defense and by Cup Two, Philadelphia's most important blueliner.

"In a day of a more up-and-down game, his lateral movement was exceptional," recalls Bob Clarke. "He anticipated the play and was hugely competitive, just a really good player.

"After Mark Howe, either Eric Desjardins or Jimmy was the second-best defenseman the Flyers ever had. Kimmo Timonen was close, better offensively than Jimmy, but Watson's offense was diminished by injuries."

First came the broken cheekbone he suffered playing for Team Canada in the 1976 Canada Cup, on a slapshot from Team USA's Gary Sargent. Watson was back with the Flyers for opening night of the season, but during a December game Blues' Jerry Butler—"Never got along with that guy, sort of a dirty player," recalls Watson—tried to lift Jimmy's stick, missed and left half of his hard contact lens in the eye and the other half on the St. Louis Arena ice.

"Creased the retina, created a fuzziness in my one eye," recalls Jimmy. "Eventually, after I quit, had to have a cataract removed.

"But the eye didn't keep me from playing. It was more my back that caused my early retirement. The problem started as early as the second Cup year. We kept it hidden, but I was getting treatment in Buffalo during the Final."

As his disk problem worsened and his peripheral vision was compromised, the Flyers settled for an almost strictly defensive defenseman. But they never had reason to feel cheated.

After his clavicle had been broken on a check by the Rangers' Barry Beck during the second round of the 1980 playoffs, Watson reached the Final on painkillers. A couple of hard hits in Game Six at Uniondale left him in the locker room for the third period and overtime, when Bob Nystrom scored to give the Islanders the championship.

"We almost won a third Cup," said Watson. "Leon Stickle, jeez."

With surgery, the shoulder healed. But in 1980-81, Watson played only 18 games before undergoing spinal fusion surgery. Watson participated in 76 games in 1981-82 but clearly was diminished. The following September, after a fruitless try in an exhibition game at the Meadowlands Arena, he sat sobbing on the locker room bench, knowing it was over.

"Told Joe (then an assistant coach) I just couldn't go any more," Jimmy recalls. "A bad back just wears you down emotionally.

"It was stiffening up all the time. Didn't have the range of motion, couldn't be as active and the Flyers could see that."

Anticipating the inevitable, Keith Allen had rebuilt the defense that summer around the acquisitions of Mark Howe, Brad McCrimmon and Miro Dvorak. Watson retired on the eve of the season, taking a scouting job with the team until his contract expired.

"I got nine years in, should have had five or six more, maybe even longer," says Watson, elected to the Flyers Hall of Fame in 2016. "I always was in great shape. But injuries eventually get almost everybody in the game; got Joe, got me.

"Turns out, Dr. Ian McNabb at Wellesley Hospital in Toronto, world-renowned back guy, did a great job. I feel great today, work out, have no back problems at all.

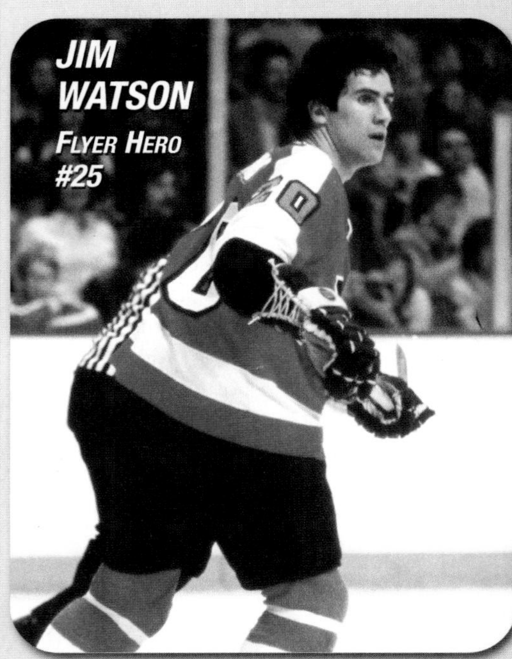
JIM WATSON
FLYER HERO #25

"I don't feel cheated at all, no sir. I feel very, very fortunate and grateful for everything I got."

Fuzzy as Jimmy's eyesight became, he retained a 20-20 look at a world of two distinct categories: 1) Good for hockey 2) Bad for hockey. After 15 years as a Delaware County housing contractor, it is not surprising to find Watson's life is focused on something enormously positive for the game.

At IceWorks, an arena he and five partners built in Aston, PA, he runs The Jim Watson Academy, which has helped more than 30 players to NCAA or major junior hockey programs.

"When we built the rink in 1997, I had to be here in the summertime to work my camps and keep the cash flow going," he said "That's your busy time for building.

"Frankly, it was a blessing in disguise. The contracting business hit the skids with everything else. I got the hell out at the right time.

"We built this rink in eight months, just a wonderful accomplishment. I won two Stanley Cups and I'm more proud of my work with these kids than of anything I've done in my life. It's about more than just the ones we get to the next hockey level. It's life lessons.

"You can't say enough about fully-involved, do-it-yourself endeavors and that's what we have here."

Jimmy Watson's sleeves always were rolled up, revealing no tricks. He not only was one of the best Flyers ever, but one of the most sincere.

ED VAN IMPE

HE SPOKE SOFTLY AND MADE HIS STICK USEFUL in the way Teddy Roosevelt once implied. Ed Van Impe played with such enormous heart that he would have rather cut yours out than let you go around him.

Van Impe epitomized the Flyers even before there became much about them that anyone cared to epitomize. Earlier than the franchise turned the corner, no winger ever turned Van Impe without getting a stick in the gut as a warning never to do it again. It was a dirty job, night after night holding the opposition to one or two goals so that the expansion team might have a chance to tie, but this defenseman bloodied his hands willingly.

He was uncompromising, unflinching, unselfish, a smart and tough cookie whom the Flyers wisely pulled from the expansion jar with their first pick from forwards and defensemen in 1967. When Philadelphia selected Van Impe from Chicago, he was a 27-year-old rookie of the year runner-up to Bobby Orr.

"There might have been six rookies in the league that year before the expansion," he recalls. "Any similarity between myself and Orr was nonexistent.

"I had played five years in Buffalo (in the AHL) before I finally cracked the lineup in Chicago. But then they traded for Gilles Marotte (in the Phil Esposito deal) and I became expendable.

"At that age, I wasn't sure I wanted to start over again. But it turned out getting drafted by the Flyers was the best thing that ever happened to me."

It proved fortuitous for the Philadelphia franchise, too, even if the Spectrum fans needed a few years to become convinced. Van Impe, particularly embarrassed on the November 1968 night that Red Berenson of St. Louis scored six goals at the Spectrum to set an NHL record for a road game, was the subject of boos in his early Flyer seasons.

"I didn't handle the puck that well, couldn't shoot very hard, and wasn't a big body checker, so I didn't have the one thing that convinced the fans that I should be out there," Van Impe recalls. "But they weren't any more frustrated than I was. We weren't winning."

Even the harshest of critics never questioned his toughness, though. In 1968, a drive by Oakland's Wayne Muloin tore Van Impe's lip for 35 stitches, his tongue for another17, and broke seven teeth off at the gums. He returned to the game in the third period.

"It is the popular belief that you can't swallow the puck, but I tried," Van Impe recalls. "I felt like I had gone 10 rounds with Joe Frazier.

"I got a letter from (Vice President) Hubert Humphrey, who said he read about it and personally wanted to congratulate me."

Even when Van Impe's mouth was intact, he never was one to flap his jaws. As Bobby Clarke ascended to superstardom in 1972-73, Fred Shero knew the kid's emerging leadership skills demanded the Flyer captaincy that Van Impe had held since Year Two of the franchise. For the good of the team, he gave it up with no kicking and screaming.

"I would be lying to say it didn't bother me a bit," said Van Impe. "But at the same time I knew it was the right thing to do if the team was going anywhere."

After suffering a humiliating physical pounding by St. Louis in the 1968 sweep and two playoff misses in three years by long-distance goals in the final regular-season game, Van Impe was ready to follow wherever Clarke would lead the Flyers.

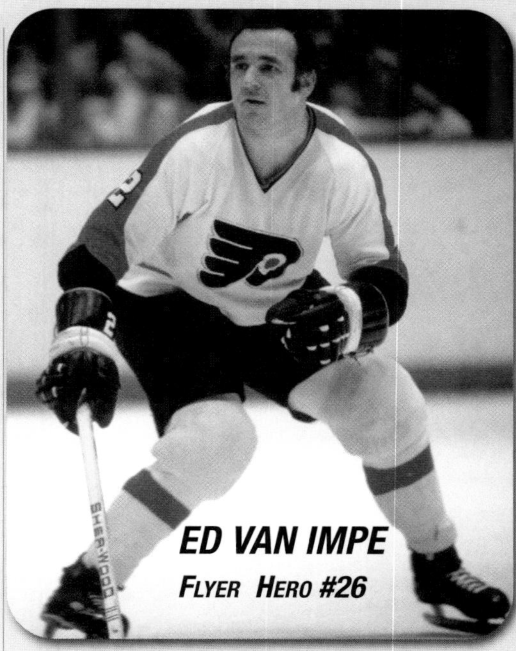
ED VAN IMPE
FLYER HERO #26

"Oh God, we had a lot of heartbreak," Van Impe recalls. He reveled as the Flyers went from the bullied to the Bullies and, with the help of Shero's incessantly drilled system, became a more efficient defender than ever. Van Impe was a master of both the sweep and hip checks, and was an unerringly effective short passer.

In 1974, after Barry Ashbee suffered a career-ending eye injury in the semifinal series against the Rangers, Shero went with four defensemen. At age 34, Van Impe paired with rookie Jimmy Watson in outstanding shutdown work in the Final against Boston's Phil Esposito, Eddie's old apartment neighbor in Chicago.

By then, Flyers fans were long since won over, even if opponents remained understandably less warm.

"Pitchfork in his hand," laughed Joe Watson, Van Impe's original Flyer partner. "If Eddie don't getcha here, he'd getcha there."

Van Impe certainly got his share.

The elbow thrown to the head of star Valeri Kharlamov that prompted the Soviets to leave the ice during their epic game with the Flyers in 1976 actually may have been below the mean on Van Impe's long list of mean, even if Kharlamov took a while to rise.

"[Kharlamov] had his head down as I came out of the penalty box," recalls Van Impe. "I got him in the shoulder and the head.

"I have taken a lot worse and given a lot worse. I think [the Russians] could sense things weren't going well and they needed an excuse to regroup. I never thought they weren't coming back. There was too much attention to that game for them to quit.

"We were fired up. Practicing the day before the game at the Spectrum with the Russians in the stands watching, Freddie calls us into the corner to tell us, 'they're laughing at you!" Probably they were just goofing about something like we would do, but boy, by then we were ready to swallow the Kool Aid.

"Freddie had been preparing us for the game for two weeks, even as we played our league schedule. We were the Stanley Cup champions, [Montreal, Boston and the Rangers] had not beaten the [Soviet Red Army on their tour]. We had to win."

The Flyers did with astonishing efficiency, 4-1. For the record, Reggie Leach, Joe Watson, Rick MacLeish and Larry Goodenough scored the goals. Mostly what people remember about the game was the Van Impe elbow to Kharlamov.

"I played 17 years, won a couple of Stanley Cups," he said. "So it surprises me a little bit to be remembered mostly for that one thing.

'If that's how it is, I'll take it. Better than not being remembered at all. My skills weren't polished so I had to make up for it in other areas. I had to play that way to be effective. Whatever happened, I didn't feel remorse.

"Later in my career there were certain situations I regretted that told me my career was winding down. You hear cliches about mellowing when you get older. I guess it's true."

After undergoing hernia surgery in October 1975, he struggled in his return. While laying out Kharlamov, Van Impe was already losing his regular job to rookie Jack Mcllhargey. At the March 1976 trading deadline, one month before the Flyers began their quest for a third straight championship, Keith Allen dealt Van Impe to Pittsburgh for goaltender Gary Inness.

Van Impe was crushed. "I couldn't understand the reasoning," he recalls. "I think I could have helped the way things wound up against Montreal (a four-game Canadiens' sweep of the Final)."

Instead of giving Van Impe a new lease on life, the trade to the Penguins sounded the death knell for his career. He suffered a shoulder injury at training camp and had to file suit to eventually reach a settlement on his contract. Van Impe was shocked by the attitude of his new teammates and their adversarial relationship with the team's management.

"We weren't winning," he said. "It wasn't what I was used to."

During his years selling commercial real estate in Chester County, PA, he learned there were far bigger losses than games. One of Ed's and Diane's three children, daughter Melanie, was killed at age 17 in a car/truck accident.

"You never get over it," Van Impe said. But retirement in Nanaimo, British Columbia—"all our family was in Canada, we always planned to move back,"—is fulfilling and so is almost every second reflecting upon hockey days that were the best the Flyers ever had.

"A Flyer always gave more than he had, did what he had to do to win, and would do it game in and game out, not just every fourth or fifth time he played," said Van Impe.

He not only fit those criteria, but helped establish them.

BARRY ASHBEE

IT BROKE THE FLYERS' HEARTS when Barry Ashbee died but he never was into flowers. So much of his life could have been set to violins that his funeral warranted the Hollywood Strings, yet Ashbee would rather have taken a puck in the eye, which he did, than accept your pity.

Tough? You could extinguish cigarette butts on Ol' Ashcan's hardened hide and he wouldn't have flinched. "Look, I don't want this written up as a 'Win One for the Gipper' story," Ashbee told reporters gathered around his hospital bed the day after his April 1977 diagnosis with leukemia. "The players know I'm sick and I'm going to get better, that's all."

Thirty days later, he was gone, a reality incomprehensible to anyone who had ever known his strength. "He never complained, never batted an eye," said Dr. Isadore Brodsky, who treated Ashbee at Hahnemann Hospital. "All he asked was that we be straight with him."

It was the only way Ashbee knew through a career avalanche of bad breaks, cancer of the blood proving to be the only adversity he could not overcome.

Because Ashbee had missed the entire 1966-67 season at the Bruins' AHL club in Hershey following back surgery, he went unselected in the 1967 expansion draft that stocked six new NHL teams. "I'm sure he was disappointed; he just didn't talk about those things," recalls his wife Donna. "Very occasionally, he would grumble about some people with the Bruins who he thought had kept him from the NHL.

"But at that time he was determined to come back from that surgery and they did win a championship [in 1968-69] at Hershey."

It would be three more years before Keith Allen, in his second deal as Flyers' GM, traded Darryl Edestrand and Larry McKillop to Pittsburgh (it had become Hershey's parent team) to obtain the rights to Ashbee, an unheralded laborer who immediately improved both the skill level and mindset of the Flyers defense.

After teammates had broken a training-camp curfew in 1972, the principled and stubborn Ashbee, also angered by Allen's contract offer, asked for a trade. Barry proved to have more tolerance of pain than for lackadaisical teammates. The following year, a chipped neck vertebra sent searing pain from his shoulder to his hand, but Ashbee taped the arm snug to his body, jammed the stick into his glove, and earned a place on the end-of-season second All-Star team, a remarkable accomplishment for someone who did not make the NHL until age 31.

"The strongest guy mentally I've ever seen," Bobby Clarke recalls. Probably the unluckiest, too.

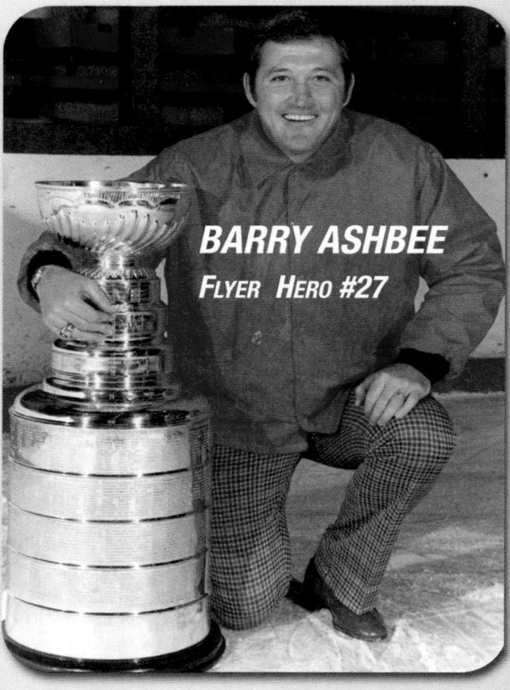
BARRY ASHBEE
FLYER HERO #27

During Game Four overtime of the 1974 semifinals at Madison Square Garden, a slapshot by Ranger Dale Rolfe caught Ashbee flush in the right eye, knocking him out of the Flyers' drive to their first Stanley Cup, ruining his peripheral vision and ending his career.

"He laid in the hospital for almost two weeks with both eyes covered to save the one," recalls Donna. "He had been out of the hospital about a week when the Flyers won the Stanley Cup. Barry watched it with me from Ed Snider's box.

"I still remember Mr. Snider leading Barry down the stairs to the locker room after the game to make sure he wasn't jostled. Then he just stood there against the wall in his dark glasses, taking in the scene.

"Barry was a black and white guy, no shades of grey to him. You couldn't change what had happened and he knew he was a main part of why they won. Again, Barry didn't talk about these things, but in my opinion, he was very proud."

"Don't write me up as the great tragic figure." Ashbee lectured reporters when he was forced to announce his retirement 15 days after the Cup clinching. "One thing I've learned is that the world isn't such a bad place; can't tell you how many people have written, offering their eyes to me.

"I'm just happy I was able to get my name on the Stanley Cup. These things happen and you have to accept them."

The Flyers instituted an annual award in Ashbee's name to be presented to their best defenseman. Having two seasons earlier hired Mike Nykoluk, the NHL's first fulltime assistant coach, they decided to add another coach for the defensemen.

Ashbee took the job reluctantly, feeling work was being created for him out of pity. But real embarrassment would have been his former defense mates not understanding what he had to offer as an instructor. Ashbee commanded such a presence that three years later, he was emerging as coach Fred Shero's heir apparent.

Then the bruises began appearing.

"I saw one on his thigh when he was cutting the lawn one day," recalls Donna. "He told me he had been hit with a slapshot by Moose (Dupont)."

The evening of the Flyers' first playoff game in 1977, Ashbee showed assistant coach Terry Crisp, who had succeeded Nykoluk, the rapidly-multiplying marks, and said from the reading he had done, it probably meant leukemia. "Get out of here," said Crisp, but when Dr. Edward Viner, the Flyers' chief physician, visually examined Ashbee that night, his heart sunk. Viner ordered Barry to come for blood work the next day and delivered the devastating diagnosis of acute leukemia to the family that evening.

The Flyers, reeling from the news, lost to Toronto the next night and fell behind 2-0 in the quarterfinals. They fought back to win the series and would have also bet on Ashbee but two massive doses of chemotherapy, which would were to be followed by a still-experimental bone marrow transplant, failed. Within two weeks his condition had deteriorated to the point, Barry didn't want his 15-year-old daughter Heather and 12-year-old son Danny visiting until "I get better."

"It was a month in a fog for me," recalls Donna. "He went so fast, all these years later, I still find it hard to believe."

The Flyers delivered a VCR to Ashbee's room so he could coach from there, but by the time the Boston series began, his ability to focus had disappeared. When his kidneys failed it was clear the end was coming faster than anyone would have imagined. He never got out of the hospital.

"I'm tired now, but I'll whip this thing in the morning," Barry told Donna before going to sleep for the final time.

"The bravest man facing death I've ever seen," recalled Allen. And, despite Ashbee's sometimes intractability, he not only was the best friend anyone could ever have but the greatest of fathers, too.

"Wherever we lived, when people would knock on our door and this strong, supposedly no-nonsense, man would always speak to every kid, and sign autographs in restaurants," recalls Heather. "He was just a really nice guy. Around home he wasn't stern, we always had fun.

"So much of his illness is a blur to me, but I remember the funeral. People everywhere. It was just overwhelming. "

When Ashbee was laid to rest in Glendale Memorial Gardens Cemetery outside his native Toronto at age 37, the Broad Street Bullies finally were in a fight they couldn't win, unable to hold back their tears.

"The essential thing in life is not to have conquered, but to have fought well," a quivering Bobby Clarke eulogized. "Barry never gave into the luxury of exhaustion or pain."

Danny Ashbee took over the annual presentation of his father's award. "It makes me so proud, like everything the Flyers did then and do now to continue his legacy," said Danny.

It survives through generations of Flyers who not only have skated under the No. 4 hanging in the Spectrum and Wells Fargo Center rafters but have manned booths, as did Barry and Donna on February 1, 1977 at the first Flyers Wives Carnival, an event that, in tragic coincidence, had been instituted to fund leukemia research and treatment.

"This disease can get any of us," Bernie Parent said that night.

Turned out, it got the strongest of them. So powerful was Ashbee's will that even though he had not played a game in three years, the Flyers' golden era died with him.

JERRY MELNYK

JERRY MELNYK DROVE A TAURUS, NOT A MERCEDES, all over Western Canada, searching for the players who put the Flyers on the map. Nevertheless, he died the world's richest man in the only things we take with us—love and respect.

"Never met a man in any walk of life better liked," said Keith Allen, Melnyk's boss of 15 years, after leukemia claimed him on June 14, 2001. He left a wife, two children, two grandsons and a franchise which never would have been what it is today had a rookie scout not been a broken record about the diabetic who had smashed all those records for the Flin Flon Bombers.

In the hockey version of *It's a Wonderful Life*, the Flyers might have wound up as Pottersville had Melnyk not become apoplectic as they were about to pass over Bobby Clarke for the second time in the 1969 draft.

"Our second pick (17th) comes up and still nobody has taken Clarke and holy [bleep], I can't believe it," Melnyk recalled. "I'm saying 'We have to take him', and they're all saying 'No, we already took a center (Bob Currier with the sixth pick) and 'No, he has diabetes.' And I'm saying, 'I don't care what he has; I played pro for 14 years and this kid already is a better player than I ever was.'

"(GM Bud) Poile wasn't going to listen to me. It was (assistant GM) Keith Allen who said, 'Wait a minute, maybe we'd better listen to Jerry.' And I remember Ed Snider agreed."

Six years later, the Flyers had consecutive Stanley Cups and Melnyk a job for life if he never hit on another player. Of course, he identified many others in 30 years on the job to help produce 13 additional Philadelphia teams that got at least as far as the semifinals. But to fully appreciate his significance, a person had to be close to the inside of the operation. And one of the purest pleasures in being there was the opportunity to relish Melnyk's hearty laugh and his disdain for fancy stickhandlers, both on the ice and in front offices.

"You had to know what you were talking about or he didn't have any patience for you," recalls Judy Twardowski, his daughter. "You had to be authentic."

He told Allen and later Clarke, his phenom-turned boss, not what Melnyk thought they might want to hear, but what they needed to know. Granted, Melnyk never had to be reminded they liked players big and a little bit mean because Jerry did, too, although he knew scouting always started—

and usually ended—with a prospect's skating stride.

The evaluation forms the Flyers used later in Melnyk's time asked for ratings on a scale of 1-9 in every category, including the bottom line, "What are his chances of playing in the NHL?" The only nine Melnyk could ever remember giving was to Paul Coffey, perhaps the smoothest skater there ever was.

Had the scout been asked to grade himself, he probably would have received only about a six, not just because he was a tough grader, but due to the fact there was not a pretentious bone in his body.

"I went scouting more than other GMs because I liked being with him," recalls Clarke. "Every day there was a new joke. When you were in his company you always felt good about yourself.

"One time we stopped in Vienna after being at a World Junior Championship. Went for a hotel steam and first, we got on the scale. We both had put on almost 10 pounds on the trip. I said, 'Holy Christ, Jerry, what are we going to do?' He looked at the attendant and said, 'Can you get us a couple of beers?'

"That trip we went into the back streets, found a bar with a wood stove and about eight guys sitting there. Jerry knows enough Ukrainian to get by and within five minutes, we're all drinking like old buddies.

"That was Jerry. He could get information without working at it because people liked talking to him."

That included the other Flyer scouts. "Some guys are good scouts but a little tough to be around for a long period of time," said Dennis Patterson, the organization's long-time man in Ontario. "In the old days you might be out 20 days at a time, but it was always a pleasure to be around Jerry. You would never get upset once."

That time well spent included both meetings and the drafting table. Except for a dry period in the late eighties—when Clarke admits he didn't referee the disdain Melnyk had for assistant GM Gary Darling—the Flyers have had a harmonious, industrious and successful evaluation staff, largely due to the lessons learned from their head scout (1984-95).

"I remember going with him to see (defenseman) Kevin Hatcher in North Bay (Ontario)" recalls Patterson. "They had a terrible game, something like 9-0, and Hatcher had a bad night.

"I was almost apologetic to Jerry. 'He really is a much better player than this.' I told him. And I always will remember what Jerry said in that calm voice of his: 'Don't worry about it. If I like a player, I stay with him.'

"That was a good lesson I've always taken with me. Like when I went to see Simon Gagne the first time and told (Quebec scout) Simon Nolet, 'this guy didn't get off the bus tonight. 'simon said, 'I'm telling you, Dennis, he can play. He's one of the best guys we could get this year.' So we came back and saw what we needed to see."

If this were a 60th anniversary book, with 60, rather than 50, profiles of the most important persons in Flyers history, Patterson and Nolet would be two of them. And a good reason for the organization's success has been the time they spent with Melnyk. Although he was retired by the time the Flyers used two 22nd overall selections for Gagne (1998), and Claude Giroux (2006), "What would Jerry think about this kid?" still was a guiding principle.

"Jerry told me that when it comes right down to it, there's no substitute for talent," said Patterson. "A few years ago there was a lot of focus on bigger kids and that could create some situations where you hope the talent level of the bigger guy would catch up to that of the smaller guy. But size isn't nearly as much a factor as it used to be.

"I mean, if the talent is close and one guy is big and the other small, it's pretty obvious what you should do. For a long time the identity of the Flyers was big, tough, strong and hard to play against. But especially with the game changing, you can't overlook those 5-foot-10 guys who can really play. And Jerry was right about that all along."

Clarke was 5-10. Peter Forsberg was a skinny Swede eligible for the 1991 draft, at a time Europeans rarely were considered blue chippers. He was rated No. 18, sleeper territory, by NHL Central Scouting but, at Melnyk's urging, GM Russ Farwell took Forsberg sixth, before his stock shot way up the following season. Melnyk had no North American or Canadian biases.

"Taking a European goalie (Pelle Lindbergh) that high (second round) in what was a very deep draft (in 1979) was bold," recalls Patterson. "But Pelle was a prototype then—stand up and play the angles, of course in his case, with very quick reflexes.

"Hexy (three years later in the sixth round) stood up, too, but had a different, combative personality and he added the puck handling when not many goalies were doing it. Some coaches didn't see the value in it. So these were two different goalies and I think it's a testament to Jerry that he liked both of them."

Melnyk said what he liked about Hextall was what many others hated. He seemed crazy. To this scout, that meant competitive, albeit with some rough edges. Without character, talent ultimately would prove worthless. And neither of those attributes would take a top prospect anywhere if he didn't have a brain for the game.

"A smart hockey player can recognize another smart player," said Jerry's son, Bruce.

"From what I read, from what people tell me, Dad was a real smart hockey player himself."

Indeed, Michael Gerald Melnyk—as he learned to write, the J was easier for him to form than the G, so he went with it and stayed with it—once was the Edmonton Oil Kings junior setup man for John Bucyk and Norm Ullman.

When there were six NHL teams, each with exclusive rights to the players on their sponsored junior development teams, a kid signed the C form as early as age 14, binding him to an organization until he was traded. Ullman and Bucyk went to the NHL and the Hockey Hall of Fame, Melnyk only to the Edmonton Flyers, Detroit's farm club, where he led the team in scoring four of the five years it took to convince the Red Wings to give him a chance.

When it came, it was as a checker. He played two full seasons with Detroit, even scoring three playoff goals during a first-round elimination in 1960, then stuck for a third NHL year after being traded to Chicago.

For the next five seasons, Melnyk barely got a sniff at the NHL. To keep extra guys around for the playoffs, the Black Hawks would call him up from their Buffalo farm team every year, paying $100 for any game he played, $75 for those he didn't. Thanks to injuries, he got into all six postseason games in 1964-65, but most years he went up for not enough money to make it worthwhile to leave Judy and Bruce and wife Jeannette back in Fort Erie, Ontario, just across the Peace Bridge from Buffalo.

"If the Black Hawks didn't know what I could do by then, they would never know," Melnyk recalled. He asked for $150 and $100, which was refused, along with the privilege of keeping his family settled for a fifth-straight season in Buffalo. Apparently annoyed, the Black Hawks shipped Melnyk to their Central Hockey League team in St. Louis but that turned out to be the long-overdue break he needed. A year later, the city got one of the six new NHL franchises and the Blues took Melnyk in the expansion draft.

He had 50 points (and another eight during the 1968 playoffs, including the only Blues goal in Philadelphia's double overtime Game Six victory) before Poile, who had once run the Edmonton team, acquired him for the Flyers in exchange for their unhappy first captain, Lou Angotti.

On his 34th birthday, Melnyk was skating up and down at his first Flyer training camp in Quebec City when he suddenly became a scout.

"I get this real weird feeling," he recalled. "My breath got short and I got a ringing in my ears.

"I went two more times and now the lights are starting to flicker. Holy [bleep], what's this?

"I went over to (coach) Keith (Allen) and said, 'I don't feel too good.' He said, 'You don't look too good either, go in and sit down.' After 20 minutes I was back to normal but the doctor suggested I get an EKG the next day.

"I did the stress test. I'm sitting in the office, waiting for the results. This [attendant] walks in with a wheelchair and I'm the only one in the room.

"We had a history of heart problems in the family. My grandfather died at 53, my dad at 51. So all this starts me to thinking, 'How are they going to get the body back to Edmonton?'

"After nine days they sent me back to Philly, to Lankenau. A specialist there and another in New York agreed with the doctor in Quebec. I had had a heart attack. They said I might be able to play a long time with no problem or I could be scraped off the ice after 20 minutes. My daughter was 11 and my son 9. I couldn't take the chance.

"The most money I ever made as a player was that year in St. Louis—$16,500. I had been negotiating with Poile for $20,000. Bud said I could go out west and scout and that was fine. But then he told me they would have to split the $16,500 over two years. I almost had another heart attack. But what could I do?"

Melnyk lined up a summer job with the gas company in Edmonton and hit the road for prospects. It occurred to him early that nobody had told him exactly what he was supposed to look for, but the first time he saw Flin Flon play, he knew he had found it.

"Bobby Clarke is still the best all-around junior prospect I have ever seen," Melnyk said 20 years after that draft. "The skills, the drive, the leadership, jumped out at you.

"He was no secret. They had a great team. Not that many guys bothered to make the trip to Flin Flon (an eight-hour drive from the closest league city, Winnipeg) like I did, but everybody saw him."

Bruce can recall his father shouting into the phone during that season to someone on the other end of the line in Philadelphia, "I don't care if he is purple and has three eyes, we have to take him!"

Snider vividly remembers the sour look on Melnyk's face when the Flyers passed on Clarke in the first round. The neophyte owner appealed to Allen, with whom he had a much better relationship than with Poile, that the scout who would know this kid the best was being ignored. Poile and Bill Putnam, the Flyers' first president, had different recollections of the events at that table. But there is no denial that Melnyk's passion forced that franchise-making decision.

"I didn't go east that year so I had never seen this Currier," Melnyk recalled. "I go to camp and said 'Holy [bleep]!'

"I mean he could skate like the wind, but he had no hands and was dumb like a stone. Clarke was the best player on the team from Day One so, for a scout, it was like hitting a home run. Some guys scout their whole lives and never latch onto something like that."

JERRY MELNYK
FLYER HERO #28

Melnyk didn't need to keep that summer job at the gas company for long. Allen, whom Snider promoted from assistant GM to GM when he fired Poile halfway through the next season, brought Melnyk to Philadelphia for two years in the early seventies to learn the front office, but mostly what he learned was that his heart was in the field. So he returned to Edmonton and the road—Waylon Jennings and the Travelling Wilburys on the cassette player, and a shovel, bag of sand, flares, candles and extra clothes in the trunk in case of a sudden blizzard and impassable roads.

The lifestyle had to be difficult on a family, but Dad was so easy to get along with that his kids cherished the time he was there a lot more than they resented the time he wasn't. "He was like a brother to me more than a father," says Bruce.

"Sometimes it was hard because you'd want to share something with him and it had to wait, but you did," recalls Judy. "But I can't think of a single time when I was devastated by the fact that he wasn't there.

"I knew he would be coming home. If he had had to miss my birthday, he would be making a big deal about it as soon as he walked in the door.

"Between all the places he played and then two different jobs with the Flyers, I was in 20 different schools before high school, but that was okay. I had a great relationship with my dad. He liked to have fun. Somebody told a joke, oh my gosh, it would get him rolling."

Melnyk believed the best place to scout a game was from the corners, where you could get the best visual confirmation of how much wobble there was in a player's stride. That corner also happened to be the best place to be in any arena on any night Melnyk was in the house, especially if he was with his best buddies Tex Ehman from the Islanders and Lorne Davis from the Oilers, sharing laugh after laugh but never any information.

Making evaluations on 18 year-olds is so hard, Clarke once wondered to Melnyk how he did it.

"We can project whether a kid can skate well enough to play in the NHL and how his skill might measure up," Melnyk said. "But except in the obvious cases, we can't measure the desire of the kid.

"That's the mystery of the thing. But I still find the best way to judge a player's character is by the way they conduct themselves on the ice.

"You do learn to trust certain people around the league. But [coaches, GMs, trainers] tell you what they want you to hear. And I don't want to sound old-fashioned, but I don't buy a lot of this psychological (testing) stuff. The game is still played on the ice."

Melnyk never was tempted by offers from other organizations, not even after Clarke was fired in 1990. Clarke was followed by Patterson to Minnesota, Florida and then back to Philadelphia, but Melnyk and Nolet stayed with the Flyers throughout the exile, There were two reasons for this: Jerry had known Clarke's replacement, Russ Farwell for years as a Western Canada junior team operator. Also, because the Sniders never had done Jerry wrong.

"The Flyers were first class all the way, even at the beginning, when I know there wasn't much money," Melnyk said. "When we would have our mid-season meetings someplace warm to go over our lists, the wives were included. It made us all feel appreciated."

Melnyk's last draft was in 1995 and Brian Boucher his final No. 1 pick. Despite an offer from Clarke for Jerry to work at his own pace in a semi-retirement, he decided he had had enough. "He didn't like the new rinks, the constant noise, music, commotion," recalls Patterson. "Just didn't want to be there anymore."

In December 1999, the Flyers flew him to Philadelphia for confirmation of the leukemia diagnosis that had been made in Edmonton. When the doctors here said they could consult with the ones in Edmonton, Jerry wanted to go home.

The chemo got him into remission for a good five months that included a visit for the 2000 Eastern Conference final against the Devils. "We ought to be able to win one more out of three," he said before flying home with the Flyers up 3-1. But they faded and soon, so did Jerry, although towards the end only the morphine dulled his sense of humor. "The nurses cried when he went," recalls Bruce.

"He was very brave through the whole thing," said Judy. "Near the end, when I thought it only was going to prolong suffering, I was trying to advise him not to do the last round of chemo and radiation. But he said, 'I have to do what I can to stay in your boys' lives.'

"He felt loyalty to the Flyers early on and it carried through to the end. If you were his friend, you knew that you were his friend for life. He would do anything for you."

REGGIE LEACH

When Reggie Leach had one step on the defenseman and could see a few inches of net, the puck was as good as in.

"He gets his shot off so quickly and with so little body movement," Bernie Parent, Leach's practice foil, once said. "He can change in mid-shot, aiming for a different area entirely, and still pinpoint it."

If only the right wing then could have managed the same control of his life that he exhibited with a puck, the 306 regular-season goals he scored for the Flyers would have represented perhaps as little as half of his career total. As it was, he accomplished much and overcame even more.

Leach's father drifted off to work in the mines before Reggie was born, and his mother, an unmarried young Indigenous Canadian, soon left Riverton, Manitoba, for a new life in Edmonton. Leach lived with his paternal grandparents who raised him with 12 of their own children and never discouraged any of the kids from drinking. One of Leach's siblings perished in an automobile accident, another froze to death, drunk in a snowbank. Two sisters died young, one of asphyxiation in the front seat of a car, the other in a mental hospital.

"I was at Reggie's home when I was 17 and he was 16," said Bob Clarke, Leach's junior linemate, friend and often caretaker. "There was no running water, a grandmother raising the whole bunch of them.

"I never would have thought he would make it this far."

Kate McKay-Leach took odd jobs, but money for skates was nonexistent, so Reggie would borrow from older friends and fill the space around his feet with crumpled newspaper. The water to freeze a rink came from an outdoor pump, in buckets carried by Leach, so he could shoot a puck for up to eight hours a day.

Never serious about school, he lived for hockey. "I knew that was all there was for me," Leach said. By age 13, he played on the town's adult team, was spotted by a Red Wings scout and signed to a contract with their junior club in Flin Flon, Manitoba.

Leach struck up a friendship with the team's best player and the town's favorite son, Clarke. Fortunate enough to be his right wing for two years, Reggie scored 123 goals with him (despite missing two-thirds of the second season with an injury) then 65 without him in 1969-70, after Bobby had gone to Philadelphia.

With NHL sponsorship of entire junior teams ended, the Bruins made Leach the third overall pick in the 1970 draft, then used him to fill a hole towards a second Stanley Cup in three years by trading him to Oakland in a deal that brought defenseman Carol Vadnais.

In California, Leach floundered like the franchise until, on Clarke's recommendation, Reggie came to Philadelphia in exchange for center Larry Wright, winger Al MacAdam and a first-round pick. Acquired one week after the Flyers' first Cup, the winger, on a line with Clarke and Bill Barber, contributed 45 regular season and eight playoff goals towards the second title.

The next year, Leach scored 61 times, followed by 19 in 16 playoff games, and seemed just a trailing pass behind Clarke on the way to the Hockey Hall of Fame.

"He makes the bombs and I drop them," Leach said. But Reggie's speed also created his opportunities. Of the five goals (on seven shots) he recorded against Boston to close out a five-game victory in the 1976 semifinals, three were on backhands after he had carried the puck to his off-wing.

In the Final, Scotty Bowman, the winningest coach in hockey history, checked the "best line I ever saw" with five players who gained election to the Hall of Fame for their defensive abilities—goalie Ken Dryden, defensemen Larry Robinson, Guy Lapointe and Serge Savard, plus left wing Bob Gainey. Leach still stuck four darts behind Dryden during the four tight games (total margin five goals) that ended Philadelphia's reign and began Montreal's dynasty. The Riverton Rifle became only the third player from the losing team to win the Conn Smythe Trophy as playoff MVP.

"When he wound up, Dryden shrunk before your eyes," laughed Clarke. "He started the series 6-foot-4 and was 5-8 by the time Reggie was done."

"Reggie was way more accurate than Bobby Hull. And he was such a good skater that he could check too, just most of the time didn't want to. He loved to score goals, just lit up when he did it. All his career, all he wanted to do was shoot."

Leach maintains that from 30 feet out in practice, 10 times out of 10 he could nail the crossbar. In games, he would hit just under the bar more often than he got under the skin of three Flyers coaches.

He drank too much and at times cared too little. The afternoon of that five-goal playoff game with Boston, teammates alarmed by his failure to show up for the morning skate found Leach passed out drunk in his basement and had to revive him with coffee, a shower and even a few more beers.

More than once, Shero—no tee-totaler himself—relied on Clarke's judgment to get Reggie ready to play and looked the other way when he wasn't. The coach demanded that Leach check, however, and the pouting winger resented the badgering and benchings. By 1978, he had slumped to 24 goals.

After Bob McCammon replaced Shero, Clarke suggested that Leach's 115-mile-an-hour shot could be refueled with sugar rather than vinegar. McCammon, who was fired after only three-plus months, never benefited from the vote of confidence he gave Leach, but successor Pat Quinn continued the stroking and Reggie bounced back to a 50-goal season in 1979-80, when the Flyers ran off a 35-game unbeaten streak and went to the Stanley Cup Final.

"He would tell me sometimes how he didn't feel Freddie (Shero) showed any confidence in him by taking him off the line late in games when we had the lead," said Clarke. "Pat got him going again by using him to kill penalties.

"Reggie trusted Pat, at least for a while, and Reggie didn't really trust too many people."

Inevitably, Quinn's high opinion of Leach ebbed, as did Reggie's enthusiasm, and the coach's failure to discipline Flyer underachievers eventually prompted his firing. McCammon, brought back with six games to play in the 1981-82 season on a mandate to get tough, had an instant example at his disposal when Reggie got onto the ice a few minutes late for practice on the first full day of the coach's second reign. Leach was waived and released.

He scored 15 goals with a bad Detroit team in 1982-83, the season before he left the game, virtually broke and with a failed marriage. In 1985, he began 31 years—and counting—of sobriety, counseling the youth of Aundeck Omni First Nation on "Life Choices."

"A lot of these kids don't have role models or someone to guide them or someone to believe in them," Leach says. "A lot of them don't have anybody at all."

"I was lucky. I had hockey. But I came from that same background and made a lot of bad choices, too, so I can relate. The hockey part and the Stanley Cups and all that is exciting to them. But just spending time with them and giving them a hug can mean a lot.

"If you help one or two people, it's all worthwhile."

For 20 years the owner and operator of a successful landscaping service in South Jersey, Leach met his third wife, Dawn, a lawyer who works for a financial company that makes loans primarily towards First Nations economic development, during an appearance at a Native hockey tournament. Nine years ago, he moved with her to a Northern Ontario reservation, 90 minutes from Sudbury, Ontario.

Reggie and son Jamie Leach conduct 30 hockey camps a year (Shoot to Score Hockey Schools). Jamie is a winger who played 81 games in the NHL over six seasons, won two Stanley Cups with the Penguins, and is a golf pro in Winnipeg.

"Best thing I ever did was move to the reservation," Leach said. "Don't miss the Philly traffic; do miss being able to have a pizza delivered at 10 pm.

"In life, when you have your great moments, the bad are all gone, making you a better, happier person.

"Ï was one of the best at getting into scoring position and I knew I could score from anywhere. I worked hard on my shot; I would take about 200 after practice. Shooting probably was the only thing I worked on, though.

"Once I had that big year they expected me to do it every [season] and that was hard. I know I had as many bad years as good ones, but I still averaged almost 32 goals (in 12 seasons) and I don't think that's bad.

"I never had a DUI. Some of the coaches who got down on me had their own (alcohol) problems. I could go on, but I don't. I'm happy with what I did. Now, I'm happy to make it to age 66."

Indeed, a Stanley Cup, a Conn Smythe Trophy, 47 playoff goals, and a place on the 1976 Canada Cup squad was a significant set of achievements. When the Flyers were feeling as good about Leach as he was about himself, The Rifle was a devastating weapon.

BRAD MARSH

Bobby Clarke always said that Brad Marsh's basic problem was his feet were as big as his heart. For seven largely happy and successful seasons in black and orange, Marsh used every ounce of strength from his helmetless head to his webbed toes to throw himself in front of shots, maul forwards, and make you care about his teams almost as much as he did.

"The ultimate Flyer," Mark Howe, Marsh's teammate on two Stanley Cup finalists, called him without contradiction, even if none of the seemingly eight arms or 16 hands Marsh would place upon opponents proved useful on the rare occasions when he would get into scoring position. But this ugly duckling of a player's apparent lack of skill for the game only made his passion for it that much more endearing.

"When [the fans] see me out there, they see themselves playing on Sunday afternoon for their company team," Marsh once said. More than that, they observed a guy who turned on only 23 red bulbs over 15 NHL seasons unfailingly light up the Spectrum with his enthusiasm.

The last Flyer to encouragingly tap the pads of the goalie before the opening face-off, Marsh would also be the first to congratulate him at the final buzzer—moving faster, it seemed, than at any point during the game. Of course, he couldn't have lasted a decade and a half in the NHL by consistently losing sprints to pucks. But in races to support teammates, Marsh went undefeated.

When Miroslav Dvorak, the first player from the Soviet bloc countries to become a Flyer, arrived at training camp in 1982, Marsh put one of his ever-clutching-and-grabbing paws around the veteran Czech star's shoulder. For his three years in North America, Cookie Dvorak never was alone.

"We would ride together to practice and the families would eat at each other's homes," recalls Marsh. "He couldn't speak English and I couldn't speak Czech and we still would talk on the phone. Patti (Marsh's wife) would ask, 'What are you possibly talking about?'

"Everybody would say I was a good guy for taking him everywhere. But it wasn't just something I did to be a good teammate. I really liked the guy."

The friendship thrived through multiple Marsh visits to the Czech Republic, including a final one to Dvorak's 2008 funeral. "Throat cancer," said Marsh. "Lifelong smoker. Sad."

Sad didn't begin to characterize the Flyers' pain

at the death of Per-Erik (Pelle) Lindbergh, the reigning Vezina Trophy winner, in a 1985 automobile accident. Six weeks later, Patti and Brad named their newborn son Erik. "It just seemed right," said Marsh.

Patti came from a family of 11 kids, most of them musicians, many of whom joined their father in the Quaker City String Band. In Philadelphia, that is about as down-home as one can get, so it wasn't surprising when Patti picked a husband without pretense. Ten years into his NHL career, Marsh was driving a truck with 185,000 miles on its odometer and wearing his old London Knights jacket that had been chewed around the collar by Ernie, his Rottweiler.

The Atlanta Flames, who chose Marsh in the first-round of the 1978 draft on his size and intangibles, made him the captain at age 22. "I still had no idea how to be a pro until I got to Philadelphia," he recalls.

Regardless, after Marsh neutralized Paul Holmgren in a stunning Game Seven win at the Spectrum for the Flames in their first year in Calgary, the Flyers coveted the defenseman's size and character. Early the next season, Keith Allen traded center Mel Bridgman for Marsh, never mind that the Flames had come to feel he was a basset hound in a game increasingly dominated by greyhounds.

"If [my speed] was that bad, I would have been beaten to a lot more icings," he insists today. "I just looked clumsy, like a big oaf, but from Point A I knew what I was supposed to do when I got to Point B.

"Whether I ran or slid on my skates, I had to be quick only from the front of the net to the corner, then outmuscle and outfight my opponent. Thanks to (assistant coach) Ted Sator, to whom I owe so much for working with me on my skating, and Mike (Flyers coach Keenan), who would play me for 25 minutes, I adapted."

A general speed shortfall on the backline had been blamed for the Flyers going 1-9 in Marsh's first three Flyer playoff series, but upon Keenan's arrival, Marsh improved his fitness and off-ice habits, thrived in partnership with Doug Crossman as second-pair defensemen behind Howe and Brad McCrimmon and reveled in two runs to the Final, the second all the way to Game Seven in Edmonton in 1987.

BRAD MARSH
FLYER HERO #35

The Oilers had six eventual Hall of Famers to the one—Howe—and the Flyers, who played without 50-goal scorer Tim Kerr, are fondly remembered for having done it on guts and the goaltending of Ron Hextall. But the Flyers one edge on Edmonton was four defensemen who could log huge minutes, forcing the most talented team ever to crank it all the way up to finally put Philadelphia away with less than three minutes to go in the final game.

"The Cup was in our hands," Marsh said. "A great memory, also a bitter memory because the next chance for me never came.

"I follow every sport, but I always turn off the TV prior to any trophy awarding or Champagne locker room. I never got to do it and it [bleeps] me off."

After the NHL grandfathered a helmet requirement one year after Marsh's rookie year, he became determined to be the last bareheaded player in the league. The cost for his stubbornness was a December 1987 Ray Bourque-Cam Neely double-team check that inadvertently smacked Marsh's skull against a Spectrum glass support, leaving him frighteningly still on the ice.

"I thought he was dead," recalls Keenan, but Marsh returned just nine days later. His reflexes slowed, the coach cut the defenseman's ice time drastically.

"In those days, they didn't understand concussions like they do now," Marsh recalls. "I didn't have the extra drive and determination I normally had.

"Perhaps I didn't realize how bad I was playing. I got into '[bleep] you' matches with Keenan when he stopped using me."

When the Flyers went down in the first round, Keenan was out. So was March the following fall as GM Clarke, determined to make the defense younger, exposed Marsh in the waiver draft to the claim of the Maple Leafs.

"I felt awful," recalls Clarke. "You represent an organization where loyalty and character always have been stressed and you have to make a miserable decision like that."

Marsh played four more seasons in Toronto, Detroit, and Ottawa—where the father of three owned a restaurant in the Corel Centre and worked as a sales representative in the health nutrition industry before returning to the Flyers in 2015 as director of community development and alumni president.

"Patti and I were visiting here a lot with her family so it was no big deal for me to just go over the Skate Zone and say hi to [Paul Holmgren]." Marsh said. "I had written a blog for *Hockey Buzz* about making the transition from player to working in the business world and (*Hockey Buzz* columnist) Bill Meltzer made sure Paul saw it. He loved it.

"One day Paul asked if maybe I'd want to come back and work here. He also asked me, "What do you think of the alumni?" and I said it was like was five different small groups and that they needed to be brought together so that the guy who retired yesterday can be comfortable with the guy who retired 30 years ago.

"He said to put a resume together, which I did that night. Obviously I'm very happy to be back here and to work with the Flyers. I played in five different organizations, but this was where I put my stamp on my career."

So he came home. But wherever he played, Marsh was loved, fans recognizing that what made him so real was exactly what made him so good.

PELLE LINDBERGH

The official notice of Pelle Lindbergh's death in Stockholm newspapers filled the space usually reserved for a biblical passage or inspirational quotation with only one word:

"Why?

The loss of one of the most endearing personalities and brilliant talents ever to wear the orange-and-black was irreconcilable; the waste of talent impossible to rationalize, even if the compulsion with speed that killed the 26-year-old goaltender was a tragic extension of his passion for life.

"He was a terrific competitor with an unmatched will to win," Dave Poulin, the Flyer captain, eulogized at a memorial service three days after Lindbergh's red Porsche hit the wall of an elementary school following an all-night team party. "Anything he did, he had to be the best at, and through his exuberance and personality, he transmitted that to us. He wasn't happy unless there was something on the line."

The Flyers' first European star possessed a grin wider than the Atlantic Ocean and an affability that preceded—and transcended—the status he gained in winning the 1985 Vezina Trophy.

After his first start for the Flyers in 1982, Lindbergh suffered dehydration, became nauseated and was forced to excuse himself twice from the postgame media crowd around his locker. Most of the writers showed mercy and moved on. One, however, hovered even after the chalk-white goalie returned for the third time. Lindbergh stacked up his pads as pillows, lay down on the locker room floor and, holding his hands over his forehead, continued to answer questions.

Utterly without pretense and loyal to old friends, Per-Erik Lindbergh's desire to savor everything in life included sincere interest in anyone who came into it. He attacked the nuances of his second language without embarrassment.

"Although he was not good with English at first, he still was always very curious about meeting people, " recalls Kerstin Somnell, nee Pietzsch, Lindbergh's fiancee at the time of his death. "He wasn't shy in any way."

When, following a slump-ending victory, the goalie was asked if he had the "monkey off his back," he looked over his shoulder quizzically. Told it was just an expression for a release of pressure, Pelle used the cliche for a month, declaring an absence of monkeys after every win.

The third child, and first son, of Sigge and Anna-Lisa Lindbergh was told at age 12 by Curt Lindstrom, the coach of the Hammarby athletic club on the working-class south side of Stockholm, that he had a chance to be the greatest goaltender on earth. Later, Lindstrom, who doubled as the Swedish national team coach, brought a film of the 1975 Stanley Cup Final to Hammarby. Watching Bernie Parent—then emulating him by adopting his style of white mask (complete with Flyer logo) and mannerisms—Lindbergh determined that playing for his country would not be the end unto itself it was for most Europeans at that time, but a means to the National Hockey League.

"This is meaningless to me, I am going to be the goaltender for the Philadelphia Flyers some day," he once wrote on a test paper at school, before Anna-Lisa made him apologize to the teacher.

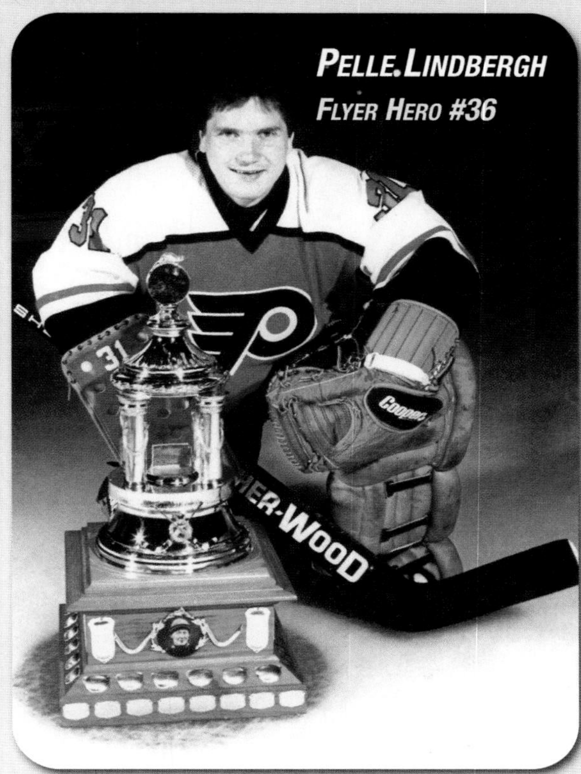

Performing in Sweden's First Division by age 16, Lindbergh was a backup for the national team at 19, and the starter at 20. Flyer scout Jerry Melnyk spotted the short goalie with lengthy aspirations in Moscow at the 1979 World Championships.

"The Flyers! The Flyers! Mom and Dad, I can't believe it, the Flyers," Pelle screamed when Melnyk called two months later with the news Lindbergh had been drafted by the team of his dreams in the second round. "And Thomas Eriksson (national team buddy whom the Flyers' selected in the fifth round), too!'"

Following a 2-2 tie in the opener against the eventual gold-medal winning Americans, Lindbergh backstopped the Swedish Olympic team to a bronze medal in the 1980 Olympics at Lake Placid. That fall, with Eriksson, he joined the Flyer farm team in Maine.

Lindbergh learned quickly that in North America a goalie had to move towards the shot, not wait on the goalline for that one last pass. In his first American Hockey League season, he was the regular season MVP and took his team to Calder Cup final, then chafed through a second minor-league season before Philadelphia traded Pete Peeters to open up the No. 1 job.

Lindbergh carried the Flyers into the Patrick Division lead until suffering a broken wrist bone during a Spectrum exhibition match against the Soviet national team, followed by a rookie-hazing haircut from teammates just before the All-Star Game. His embarrassment at the event's banquet turned to mortification the following night when Lindbergh was lit up for four goals by Wayne Gretzky. He largely struggled the rest of the season and through a first-round sweep by the Rangers.

The next year, his self assurance bottomed out in a grotesque performance during a February 6-5 Spectrum loss against Vancouver. Lindbergh kicked a puck that had caromed off the end boards into the net to tie the game, and then lost his balance as the winner trickled by him.

When he read in a newspaper the next day a beat writer's lament how stunning it was to see such a natural talent's confidence erode to the point where "he would have trouble tying his shoelaces," Lindbergh walked to a bench where the author was seated and, with a sadly endearing smile on his face, put his foot up and tied his shoe.

"I remember it was a depressing time," said Kerstin. "But I never met a person, before or since, with the self-confidence Pelle had.

"He knew always that he was going to be on the top."

Rushing to get there, in 1983-84 Lindbergh stopped fewer pucks than free-agent signee Bob Froese, who gained the starting job. As a born approval seeker, Pelle listened to too much contradictory advice but, when the next season began, new coach Mike Keenan's opinion was the only one that mattered. Having coached Rochester in the AHL, the rookie Flyer coach had seen enough Lindbergh to believe the only thing holding him back was the lack of another extended opportunity.

"My very first meeting with him, in July, I told him 'regardless of what anyone says about you in the media or what anyone tells you, you are our No. 1 goalie,'" recalls Keenan. "I don't want you to forget that."

"Pelle asked, 'Really?' I told him, 'Absolutely.' That was all he had to hear."

Lindbergh performed a marathon—83 games, counting regular season and playoffs—at sprint pace. He won 40 times as Philadelphia accumulated a league-leading 113 points, and, in the playoffs, ended a nine-game Flyers losing streak over three springs with a sweep of the Rangers.

He next finished off the Islanders, one season removed from four consecutive Stanley Cups, in five games with a brilliant 1-0 shutout. After his one subpar game during that 1985 run, a 5-3 loss to Quebec in Game Four that squared the series, Lindbergh read *Mad Magazine* on the way to Quebec City. What, did Pelle worry, when the Flyers came out flat in Game Five? In his signature game as a Flyer, he almost singlehandedly held them in the match until they rallied for two third-period goals and a 2-1 victory.

In that game, he was great as he had been almost all season, which earned him a Vezina presented by his idol and mentor, Parent.

"The man I really want to thank is standing next to me," said Lindbergh at the ceremony in Toronto. "He taught me everything I know to play hockey in North America."

Parent, gifted with a needed project after his career ended prematurely because of an eye injury, had much to work with. Lindbergh might have enjoyed the best set of reflexes on any goalie in history. Shooters who assumed there was room between his bowed legs found out otherwise when the pads closed as quickly as a blinking eyelid. Lindbergh's balance was excellent, and his glove hand as soft as his personality.

"Unbelieeeeevable," he repeatedly called that 1985 playoff run with the NHL's youngest team.

Incomprehensible was saved for the morning of November 10, 1985, when his sports car, which he had sent back to the factory to increase its power, failed to make a bend on Somerdale Road in Somerdale, NJ, leaving Lindbergh, who had been drinking, brain dead. A contract making him the highest paid Swedish NHL player—and Flyer—was to be announced two days later.

Two passengers who were going with him to breakfast when he crashed were seriously injured but largely recovered. The 1985-86 Flyers did not, getting upset by the heavily underdog Rangers in the first round. Sent the gift of Ron Hextall the following season, the Flyers made another run to the Final, considerable consolation to them, but, of course, none to Kerstin and the Lindbergh family.

"Some occasions I get sad, but on many I think about the positive things we did together," said Kerstin, who returned to Stockholm in 1988, married aircraft engineer Kurt Somnell in 1990, and began a family (three children) and career as a physical education teacher.

"On all levels, hockey was the most important thing in Pelle's life, that is the honest thing to say, and he was at the top when the accident happened," she said. "I think he felt nothing could happen to him.

"That car scared me. He wasn't mature enough to handle it, although I don't know who would have been."

Lindbergh's sister, Ann-Christine, diagnosed with cancer while Pelle was a Flyer, died two years after he did. Sigge Lindbergh, the father who signed Pelle up at Hammarby on the day of his birth, was unalterably saddened by the death of two children before he passed in 2002.

"Pelle's mother, Anna-Lisa (who was visiting Lindbergh at the time of his death) was a very social person who had enjoyment in her life, even if, of course, she never forgot," said Kerstin. "I always said to her that if Pelle had gotten old, he would have turned out like her. She had a lot of body aches that limited her before she died in 2012."

On Lindbergh's birthday and the anniversary of his death, Kerstin and Ann-Louise—Pelle's oldest sister—go to Skogkyrkogarden and the grave with the Flyers' logo on the stone, accompanied sometimes by the surviving fan club of the defunct Hammarby club's forever young star. The first European goalie to make it big in the NHL, Lindbergh's loss was not only Philadelphia's.

"Much too young," said Kerstin. "But it always feels good to know that Pelle never understood what happened to him."

His devastated teammates and fans, left to make sense of it, fail to this day. The day the best goalie in the NHL died was the worst one in Flyer history.

PAT QUINN

While playing nine seasons with three NHL teams, Pat Quinn had thought little about becoming a coach. A man's man with a big body and a bigger heart, he only knew he didn't want to be treated like a child.

Long before Quinn started reading up on coaching methodology, it was his personal theory that the kind of coach he always had wanted to play for could effectively motivate through trust rather than fear.

"I think what the players would see at the rink was what we saw at home," said Quinn's daughter Kalli. "Very patient, very supportive.

"He wanted to teach and include you rather than just tell you what to do. He knew if he gave the players on the ice too much it would be counter-productive, so he sometimes took them to do things like play flag football, creating a bond.

"He was very patient because he always saw something in people that others didn't."

No NHL team besides Quinn's 1979-80 Flyers ever has had 35 straight unbeaten games, or even come close. Quinn looked at the picture of that club years later and wondered how it had reached even 10 in a row.

So it must have been the pinball machine that he and his wife Sandra had hidden in their basement to surprise Kalli and her sister Valerie on Christmas Day that produced the longest unbeaten streak in North American team sports history.

"Dad was a little superstitious," recalls Kalli. Late in the afternoon on game days, while she and Valerie were at swim practice, he went to the storage area and played until reaching the score he had determined was required to keep the Flyers immune from defeat.

That would be the only logical explanation for going 25-0-10 from game three through game 37 of a season. Quinn had a defense containing three recycled minor leaguers that would not last four more years in the league, two journeymen goalies, and a powerplay that was operating under 10 percent efficiency during most of the streak.

That team had seven holdovers from their Cup teams, plus a new nucleus of high picks, although only one, Brian Propp, became a stalwart of the franchise through the eighties, "We were sort of a dog's breakfast," recalls Paul Holmgren. But the Flyers had some speed up front and a young coach heading into his first full NHL season with the vision and determination to use it.

Quinn turned his forwards loose to chase the

puck, to crisscross both on the attack and leaving the defensive zone, while urging a defense that would have been in trouble in its own end to get up into the play like Flyer defensemen never had done before.

The undermotivated Reggie Leach and Rick MacLeish had become reasons why Ed Snider and Keith Allen believed it was just as well that Fred Shero had left for the Rangers. Quinn got both going again while transforming organizational depth defensemen such as Frank Bathe, Norm Barnes and Mike Busniuk into rocks on a team that finished with the best record in the NHL.

"My God, it's Christmas and they've lost one game," said Boston coach Fred Creighton after the Flyer' 29th straight contest without a loss, a 5-2 win at Boston Garden, broke the Canadiens' NHL record. "It's hard to comprehend."

That day, the Flyers had played as good a game as they ever have, while probably under the most pressure. After having downplayed the meaning of the streak almost since it began attracting attention, Quinn finally admitted, "You know that's a crock" when the Flyers were two games away.

"You might play 100 years and never get another chance at something like this," he said. In Boston, after appearing nervous in the two preceding ties, the Flyers seized the once-in-a-lifetime opportunity ravenously. In the most hostile and claustrophobic rink of the era, the Flyers attacked their strongest rival of that decade as if convinced of their destiny.

They still had Bobby Clarke, five seasons removed from the last of his three MVP awards; Bill Barber, who remained a perennial All-Star; a 30-goal Holmgren in the best season of his hard rock career, and the great expectations that had become the organizational trademark. But that team didn't do it on talent, experience or muscle as much as on enthusiasm. Over 35 games a relentless four-line attack rallied the Flyers from one three-goal deficit, seven two-goal disadvantages, and six come-from behind efforts in third periods.

"It was a magical ride," recalled Quinn, And after it finally ended with a 7-1 defeat at Minnesota, two games later the Flyers started another unbeaten streak of 11 (8-0-3).

In the playoffs, they swept the young Oilers of Wayne Gretzky, Mark Messier, Jari Kurri and Glenn Anderson; avenged their defeat by Shero's Rangers of the previous spring in five; smoked the North Stars in five, and remain convinced to this day that, but for two non-calls on Islander goals that shouldn't have counted during a Game Six overtime loss in Uniondale, would have gone home for Game Seven to win the Stanley Cup.

PAT QUINN
FLYER HERO #37

Despite a two-goal third-period rally to tie Game Six, the Flyers were awfully beat up by then, so we will never know. But they had a guy behind the bench who believed in them as much as they did in him.

"Pat could motivate, he could change things tactically, he had every asset of a coach," recalls Holmgren. And Quinn, who was hired to work with the Flyer defensemen after the death of Barry Ashbee in 1977, had been an NHL head coach for not even a full season when he made all this happen.

"He wasn't long in experience but he didn't come in unprepared," Bob Clarke recalls. "So much of the coaching in hockey at that time was play good or get [bleep] from the coach. When Pat came in, he was interested in helping each player individually.

"He and Herb Brooks changed the game tactically. Brooks' (University of Minnesota, 1980 Olympic and Ranger) teams circled back some to form the attack while ours was more straight line, but both introduced more motion to the old wings-on-wings style of play.

"Our players left over from the Cup years needed that change. We went to the Final with a team that probably was middle of the road."

When a badly broken leg from a fall off Valerie's skateboard in 1977 ended Quinn's playing career in Atlanta at age 34, there weren't hordes of ambitious young technocrats breaking down video, waiting for their next assistant gig. In fact, there were few assistant jobs at all, the Flyers having recently started that trend with the addition of Mike Nykoluk in 1972.

Quinn had no experience—only a reputation around the game and the players' association for being a bright and well-spoken guy—when approached by GM Keith Allen to replace an irreplaceable person in the late Barry Ashbee.

The big, cigar-smoking, Irishman had been toying with the idea of law school, but had his eyes opened by a year under Shero, and not just because Freddie came to work with a briefcase that the fledgling coach decided he should have too.

So his wife Sandra got Pat one and, while deciding what to put in it, he watched Shero open his one day and take out only his lunch.

Whether or not the valise contained anything else, there was plenty more about the game in Shero's head and no reluctance by the architect of a two-time Cup winner to share it.

"Dad told us that Freddie said to him, 'You can play the game but if you also learn it, you can teach it,'" recalls Kalli. "Freddie really gave my dad the opportunity to find something he loved—teaching."

When Shero left at the end of that season, Allen chose as the replacement the guy in the organization with head coaching experience—Bob McCammon—and sent Quinn to take McCammon's place with the Flyer AHL team in Maine. Fifty games later, Allen believed he had made a mistake and had Quinn and McCammon change places.

A big guy with a big presence—in 1969 the rookie Quinn had announced himself to the NHL by knocking Bobby Orr unconscious during a Leafs-Bruins playoff game in Boston, starting a bench-clearing brawl—the coaching neophyte calmed the choppy waters left under two-thirds of a season by the excitable McCammon.

Philadelphia went 18-8-4 the rest of the way, a running start to Quinn going 141-73-48 and winning five playoff series in three-plus seasons before a second-half slide in 1981-82 and the perceived failure to come down on headstrong building blocks like Ken Linseman and Behn Wilson cost the coach his job.

By then, the Flyers had become the defenseless, undisciplined and aging team that they had been predicted to be in 1979-80. Rather than being thanked for holding off the inevitable for two seasons, Quinn was fired for being unable to fix it.

"The players should have handled the problems we had within the locker room," recalls Holmgren. "We let Pat down; it wasn't his fault."

Recalls Clarke, "I doubt if Keith was the only one involved. But it was one of the worst decisions he ever made and he made very few."

Snider had made clear to Quinn at a meeting in early March his dissatisfaction with the team's direction. But the coach nevertheless was blindsided by a firing just eight games before the playoffs.

When Quinn met with reporters three days later about the "biggest disappointment of his life," he said that if he could no longer reach players with the same motivational skills that had worked so well two years earlier, then it was up to management to move those players.

The Flyers lost in the first round to the Rangers regardless, three months before including Linseman in a trade for Mark Howe, who would have fixed a lot of Quinn's problems.

"But Dad never held onto stuff," recalls Kalli. Burned by unreasonable expectations, however, Quinn was determined that his second bench would give him more longevity than the first.

Having hit the books throughout his five years of riding the busses in the minors before breaking into the NHL, Quinn decided to put his B.A. to use for two years at the Widener University School of Law before finishing up his degree at the University of San Diego while coaching the Kings.

During his first season in Los Angeles, he improved a moribund franchise by 23 points. Later, as GM-coach of the Canucks, Quinn got them to Game Seven of the 1994 Final against the Rangers, then, in Toronto, fulfilled a prophesy made by Snider on firing day. "I wouldn't be surprised if someday Pat Quinn came back to haunt us" had said the Flyers Chairman, and indeed, Quinn's Leafs beat Philadelphia in six games in the first round in 1999.

The Flyers eliminated two more of Quinn's good Toronto teams in 2003 and 2004. He never won a Stanley Cup, only 684 NHL games, sixth most of all time, plus Canada's first gold medal in 50 years at the 2002 Salt Lake City Olympics. It was a body of work more than good enough to warrant his election to the Hockey Hall of Fame in 2016.

At NHL general manager meetings, at 13 years of Hockey Hall of Fame selection committee sessions (he chaired for two), before his death on November 23, 2014 from a variety of intestinal issues, hockey people came to know that the smoke coming out of Quinn's cigar never was intended to hide his purposes.

"Everyone in those meetings knew the intelligence factor was high and that he wasn't self-serving," recalls Holmgren. "When he spoke, people listened. His motivation always was for the good of the game.

"There were a lot of times in my life that he showed up. I ran into him at the Minneapolis airport when my mom passed away in 2000. I was devastated and he had strong words of encouragement for me.

"He was awesome for me as a coach, tuned me loose to be the first forechecker, put me on a line with skilled players like Linseman and Propp that enabled me to score. But he also was a strong influence on my life.

"I cried the day the Flyers let him go."

JOE SCOTT

Before anyone in Philadelphia had a clue who Bernie Parent was, the new Flyers franchise needed a name.

Having barely been able to pay the $2 million NHL franchise fee with a last-minute $500,000 advance from ARA Services, the Spectrum's concessionaire-to be, the fledgling team was in need of operating capital. Joe Scott, having recently sold Scott and Grauer, the world's largest beer distributorship, not only was liquid but also had time on his hands that had pressed much of the flesh in the Philadelphia business community.

A star pitcher on scholarship at Penn Charter in his youth, whose brief time in the Phillies organization ended with a bad knee, Scott had morphed from athlete to supporter as he had gotten into sales in the liquor industry and then grown his Ballantine Beer business. He was an investor in Cloverlay, the syndicate that financed heavyweight champion Joe Frazier's career, and became a member of a group that attempted to purchase an American Football League expansion franchise for Miami that went instead to Joe Robbie.

During a time when athletes needed jobs in the off-season, a number of Philadelphia's bigger sporting names had gone to work for Scott. His favorite day had been payday, when, in the days before automatic deposit, he could hand out the checks and chat.

Scott hadn't grown a beer empire only by being a nice guy. "He once pulled a teamster boss into his office, locked the door and said, 'Either we are going to come to an agreement or only one of us is going to walk out of this room alive.'" says Greg Scott, Joe's son.

Foreseeing that regional brands would face a tough fight for a share of the market against the behemoths, Scott sold the distributorship at age 58. A self-made guy knew what to do with his money, but not his time.

"My wife Pat had just had another child and I had turned into a big pain in the butt around the house," was the way Scott used to tell it. So when Pat answered the telephone one morning and Ed Snider said he wanted to offer her husband not only stock in his NHL franchise but critical responsibility for its success, the joke continues to this day that she found an excuse to kick Joe out.

"He was a very vital person who needed something to do," Pat recalls. "So I told him, 'Ed Snider has a proposal and you are going to say yes.'"

Actually, this was not the first time Scott had heard from Snider, who as an Eagles vice president had engaged in promotions with Ballantine. Previously, Snider had offered Scott a share of a partnership with 12 or 13 owners. "You don't want me," he told Snider. "I'd be the oldest guy and the biggest pain in the butt in the group."

Nevertheless, he had attended the Spectrum ground-breaking and the party that followed at Old Original Bookbinders. And after Eagles owner Jerry Wolman, the front man of the Philadelphia NHL bid, had exchanged his stock in the team for shares in the under-construction Spectrum, Snider was proposing a three-man Flyers ownership group of himself at 60 percent, team president Bill Putnam at 25 percent and Scott at 15 percent.

"Then, I got serious," Scott said. "I told Ed that my wife wouldn't just want me to invest, she wanted me to work."

"Great," said Snider. "You can have a job."

Actually, what Snider had for Scott was a thankless task—drumming up interest in a team widely predicted to fail. But he was just the guy for that kind of work. In Philadelphia, where Snider was the recently transplanted Washingtonian and Putnam was the former New York bank executive, Scott was the person who knew the *Who's Who* of the Delaware Valley business community.

Snider, still in need of operating capital, was confident that there was a bank somewhere in Philadelphia that would not turn Scott down. He maintained that belief all the way through the sixth rejection. "The guy from the Industrial Valley Bank fell asleep while we were talking to him," Scott said in *Full Spectrum, the Complete History of the Philadelphia Flyers*.

Girard Bank, the last one Scott and Snider tried because it had the reputation for being the most conservative, was the longest shot that came in, mostly because president Steve Gardiner and vice president Bob Baer had been exposed to hockey at Harvard. Girard loaned the Flyers $1.5 million in operating capital, which, combined with $375,000 of television-rights fees from Kaiser Broadcasting (Channel 48), assured the team would be on the ice in the fall.

Scott tried to sell additional Flyer stock. "But not one of the five richest guys in town was interested," he recalled. "They said, 'You're tossing your money out the window.'

"Myself, I didn't have any doubts because I thought with national television, we'd be riding clear within three years."

When 7,812 people showed up for the Flyers' first home game, 5,783 attended the second, and 4,708 the fourth, he rolled up his sleeves. Actually, that's just an expression, because the camel sports coat, essentially Scott's uniform, stayed on. "It had stains, I thought it was the same jacket he wore every day," laughs Joe Watson, an original Flyer. "No, Joe said he had five of them, all of them stained."

Scott didn't have to be from *Gentleman's Quarterly*. He had sold beer to Philadelphia, so he could pitch tickets to another major-league team playing the fastest sport in the world in a state-of-the-art arena.

JOE SCOTT
FLYER HERO #39

"Whether it was the trash man or the guy fixing the roof, he would talk up the Flyers to anybody," recalls Greg. "He knew that if people saw the product, they would like it."

But of course, there was a deeper strategy than just word of mouth. Scott wrote schools, offering free tickets to deserving students. "We thought that adults already knew what they liked but kids might try something new," he recalled in *Full Spectrum*. "So I brainwashed thousands of them.

"At first I had to make a lot of calls to get even one school to go along with me. But then it started to pick up. If I saw a school had won a championship in something, I'd offer it tickets, figuring they'd be appreciative of the opportunity to treat the kids. The idea was that if the adults came along, they would have to buy a ticket. That was the way to expose the game to the parent.

"We sat them in the upper deck, sometimes with the school band, so they wouldn't disturb what customers we had. There was lot of room at the Spectrum for bands in those days."

Indeed, there were far more empty seats than hours in a Scott day, but the bulldog was determined to fill the house. "I was a lot younger and he literally wore me out, running from place to place," recalls Lou Scheinfeld, Ed Snider's first front-office hire, as a marketing vice president. "To Johnny Taxin at Bookbinders to (get him to) buy a block of season tickets or consider a sponsorship; to radio stations; to TV stations; to car dealers. I'm telling you, each time I went out with him; I was worn out by the end of a day.

"Joe was a great force for good. Inside that camel hair coat were Flyer brochures, Flyer tickets, and Flyer souvenirs to hand out. He had an office next to Ed Snider's and it was filled with all kinds of Flyer paraphernalia. It looked like a pewter factory with mugs, clocks and ashtrays embedded with the logo.

"He had piles and piles of pink slip messages from people who would call because he would never throw them away. You went into his office, it was like going back into time, but he knew where everything was.

"He worked it at two different levels—among executives and officials he knew all over Philadelphia—and then the schools. He wanted to get the suburban people to buy season tickets, so he felt the obvious demographic was private schools. That was a great marketing scheme by Joe and he brought in a bunch of young guys, on commission, to man telephone banks in what they called the boiler room.

"I was lucky, he liked me so I could do no wrong in his eyes. If Joe liked you, he liked you forever, but if he didn't, you never stood a chance. Allen Flexer, who followed me as president of the Spectrum, for some reason rubbed Joe the wrong way. Joe wouldn't give him the time of day. Chuck Bednarik once commented to Joe, 'Hey, you put on a couple pounds, huh?' so that was it for Bednarik. Joe wouldn't talk to him.

"He was funny that way. But Joe loved Ed Snider. Coming out of retirement, or semi-retirement, he really wasn't looking to create his own dynasty or run a business and he had such respect for Ed that they worked seamlessly. Ed was a super smart guy and a very sharp businessman and Joe recognized that and respected it. I never ever saw them have a cross word. They made a hell of a team."

When Snider bristled at the Philadelphia media's initial apathy or skepticism toward the Flyers, Scott would remind the boss that he needed the newspapers and stations on his side.

"Although Dad always said if you're going to buy a business, buy 51 percent," recalls Joe's son Jeff, "he and Mr. Snider worked so well together that I saw nothing, but admiration and trust.

"They balanced and pushed each other, too. Somebody told me a story that Dad would come in and say, 'Hey I just sold X amount of tickets and Mr. Snider would say, I sold one more.'"

The box-office reports from the team's first four games were framed on Scott's wall to remind him of the team's humble beginnings. For year six, even before the Flyers turned the corner to contention, they needed a third level of seats installed at the Spectrum to meet demand. Scott's work essentially was done, but his passion for the team continued.

Even after, for estate-planning purposes, he sold his shares to Fran and Sylvan Tobin in 1984, Scott became Chairman Emeritus of the Board, still attending virtually every game with the Flyer pin on his lapel. At Snider's insistence, Scott remained in the team picture every year and he was inducted into the Flyers Hall of Fame in 1993. In good health and even in the decline leading to his death at 93 on June 24, 2002, Scott was at luncheons, his beloved Union League, wherever he could be the self-described "jolly fellow, well-met."

"Eddie had always wanted him in the (owner's box) with him," recalls Pat. "Joe preferred to sit in the stands with the people."

To the players, too, Scott was one of the guys.

"Got him with the mongoose," recalls Watson.

"I put this squirrel's tail in a box with some carrots in it, said it was a mongoose and that they liked carrots. I told people the story about the cobra and the mongoose and how the mongoose was so vicious and cunning it would get the cobra every time.

"When guys would get curious and lean over the box to see the mongoose, I'd activate this spring, and the tail would fly up and hit them in the face, and they would think they were being attacked.

"I got some guys with it one day, and then Joe walked in, so thought I'd get him, too. He leans in, and I sprung the trap and the tail flies up into his throat. He thinks the mongoose has got him by the throat and he's running around yelling.

"Omigawd was it funny. Joe said, 'You almost killed me.' And Ed said, "You could have scared my partner to death.'

"When I came here in 1967, a young single guy, Joe would take me out to meet all these people, have a good time, laugh our butts off. Everybody knew Joe Scott."

Which is why, 14 years after his death, everybody should know all he tirelessly did to make the Flyers what they are today.

TERRY MURRAY

When Bob Clarke returned from the Florida Panthers to begin his second reign as Flyers GM in 1994, a team that had missed the playoffs five consecutive years needed size on the wings, defense and goaltending. But first it required structure.

"There wasn't accountability, respect for a workplace," said Clarke. "Our trainers were sitting for players' kids and dogs in the training room during practice.

"We needed stability."

He knew where to get it. Terry Murray, fired midway through the previous season by the Capitals, had completed the year coaching the Panthers' International Hockey League team in Cincinnati.

"I always thought Murph's Washington teams were organized," recalls Clarke. "He took control for me in Cincinnati so I knew he would do the same with the Flyers."

Fate must have recognized that Murray, a responsible third-pair defenseman through two stints and parts of four seasons with the Flyers, someday would return to the organization that twice had rescued him from the minors. Even after the Flyers had let him go to the Capitals in the 1981 waiver draft, he had kept his home in South Jersey.

Clarke was offering Murray the head-coaching position of a Flyer team stripped of depth by the huge Lindros trade and hiring its fourth coach in four seasons. But for reasons that went much deeper than their talent at that time, Murray thought this was the opportunity of his lifetime.

"I had a lot of great feelings about how things were when I was there," he recalls. "I knew the ownership and the culture, which had been established, so it wouldn't be that hard to bring it back, unlike a place where they never had it.

"Every team needs rules and regulations, so I put them in place right away. There were people walking around in areas where they never should have been, space that belongs to the players. Players came in with soda and fast-food items that I never allowed with the Capitals.

"People are going to fight it, sneak things in, butt heads, but you have to hold the line. Most players want authority, direction.

"The good ones bought in quickly. I give them the credit."

Ten contests (3-6-1) into that strike-shortened, 48-game, 1995 season, Clarke's trade of Mark Recchi obtained left wing John LeClair, about to become a three-time 50-goal scorer, and defenseman Eric Desjardins, who would be named a seven-time Barry Ashbee Trophy winner. Ron Hextall was brought back for character as much as goaltending, while Murray provided leadership that sent the Flyers to a Stanley Cup semifinal in his first season and a Final in his third.

Under him, they were 118-64-30 (.556), the fourth-best winning percentage of a Flyer coach after Fred Shero, Pat Quinn, and Mike Keenan. Over three seasons Murray won six playoff series—tied with Keenan for second to Shero's franchise-best 11—while Clarke was changing everybody on the team besides Lindros, Rod Brind'Amour and Mikael Renberg.

"Murph brought a style that forced a commitment to play properly so you could trade for guys and put them into the system," said Clarke.

After the Flyers ran over smaller Pittsburgh, Buffalo and Ranger teams in five games on the way to the 1997 Final, a deeper and more mature Detroit club made Murray's team break down. By then, so had relationships between players and coach, whose aloofness, perceived or otherwise, wore on more team members than just Lindros.

The captain had refused to defend Murray amidst almost season-long speculation that his contract was not going to be renewed. Clarke had been reluctant to make a larger commitment to a troublesome dynamic where players sometimes were offended by Murray's bluntness, but mostly put off by his detachment. Murray has always felt his job was to supply direction, leaving the passion up to the players.

"If you play strictly on the emotional side, there's

going to be a time in a big game where you're going to have a lull and not know what to do," he said in 1996. "As a player, I never wanted a coach to come in and lose it, embarrassing and destroying people.

"If you indulge yourself like that, you might have won the battle but you're going to lose the war. You're going to have some of those emotions come back at you at a time when you need that player to make an extra effort."

They came back at him regardless, even before Murray characterized his team to the media as being in "a choking situation" after a 6-1 humiliation in Game Three of the Red Wing sweep. Some Flyers understood his reference point—Detroit's hard-earned experience edge from having been swept by the Devils two years earlier. Others thought they were being called chokers, the ultimate athletic insult.

Murray's incredulity at the resultant furor reflected a stunning naivety by a lifer in the sport. He eventually apologized to the team for his choice of language. But the GM already had determined the relationship with the players irreparable.

"This is the worst thing I ever had to do as a manager," said Clarke in announcing the firing one week after the Final. "I just felt the problems we had were not going to go away."

Murray did not go away for long. After being let go as coach of the Florida Panthers in 2000, less than a year after directing them to 98 points, he was brought back to Philadelphia by Clarke, first as a pro scout and then as an assistant coach under Ken Hitchcock and John Stevens.

The Kings had not made the playoffs in five years when they named Murray head coach in 2008, but he got them there in back-to-back seasons before being fired after 29 games (13-12-4) of the 2011-12 season, when they won the 2012 Stanley Cup under Darryl Sutter.

History had repeated itself. A franchise Murray directed to the cusp of a championship again wanted more emotion from a coach to get it over the top. But King president Tim Leiweke gave Murray a championship ring regardless, recognizing him for his groundwork.

"What it often comes down to is timing and fit for your needs as those needs change," says King general manager Dean Lombardi. "I didn't coin this phrase—I heard someone say it in another context—that sometimes the reason you need to fire a coach is the same reason you needed to hire him.

"You come to need a different M.O. But that in no way is a reflection on someone necessarily being better at what you do.

"Murph was a huge part in the process of creating [the two Stanley Cup championships] we have here today, as much as, if not even more so, than any one player we had or still have. When you build the way we did—getting a lot younger and working to get a little better every year—a huge piece of it is obtaining structure and learning to play the right way.

"He was an unbelievable teacher. His temperament and his know-how were perfect for it. Those guys who are still here today that played under Murph owe him a debt of gratitude.

"He knows what the characteristics are of a consistently good team and drums it in. He doesn't soft-pedal things. He's honest but also fair and is in his players' corner to the hilt. There's no ego with Murph. If he has an assessment of a player and the guy proves him wrong in a positive way, no one is happier for the guy than Terry. All he wants is for his players to succeed and for the team to be better for it in the end."

Still craving for the Flyers what Murray has spent a career demanding, GM Paul Holmgren didn't need the recommendation of Ron Hextall, who was with the Kings alongside Murray, to hire him to coach the Phantoms from 2013 to 2015. Wanting to return to the NHL, he then became an assistant coach for the Sabres in Buffalo.

Today Lindros calls Murray "one of the best teaching coaches I ever had", a consensus viewpoint from the players of that era.

"Murph wasn't going to sit there with pom-poms," recalls Chris Therien, the defenseman-turned-Flyer television commentator. "There was a time I didn't like Terry Murray either, didn't like sitting in the stands for nine games (in 1996-97), but he made me play (harder) and I'm grateful for it."

In turn, Murray considers every day he worked for the organization to have been a gift.

"The Flyers," he said, "gave me my big playing break."

The seventh child—and youngest boy—of 10 children of Rhoda and Clarence Murray of the English-speaking Ottawa Valley enclave of Shawville, Quebec, went off 40 miles to Ottawa at age 16 to pursue his dream in major junior hockey.

Dad, who once owned a farm but had moved the family into town when Terry still was young, found work in Ottawa as an installer for the gas department. As if Mom, a real life lady in a shoe, didn't have enough to do, she brought in money by prepar-

TERRY MURRAY
FLYER HERO #40

ing lunches at the school and taking night cleaning jobs at the church and bank.

"As a kid, do you really recognize how much of a struggle it is for your parents?" said Murray. "I knew there always was plenty of food on the table."

Brother Bryan, seven years Terry's senior, played Tier II hockey in nearby Pembroke and at McGill University before returning to the town of seven churches and 1,800 people to teach physical education, start a sporting goods store with the oldest Murray brother, Bill, then own and operate The Pontiac House, the town's inn. Bill, a star at Pembroke, showed enough to be invited to NHL camps before a wrist injury, marriage, and the desire to run a business kept him rooted to Shawville.

"Terry was one of the few guys in our town at that time that had an ambition to go see where he fit in the hockey world," recalls Bryan. "In high school, I coached him in hockey, basketball, volleyball, and he always listened well, wanted to get better."

When Bill Long, the Ottawa coach, told Terry to move the puck up, not carry it, he listened. Paired at age 16 with a 14-year-old wunderkind named Denis Potvin, Terry wasn't certain he moved it well enough, however, to make a living at it. It will not surprise any player ever corrected by Murray to learn that when a team questionnaire asked the Ottawa players for their future occupations, he filled in: Royal Canadian Mounted Police officer.

"In those days, we were all just kids playing hockey, not talking of the draft," said Murray. "The owner of the team put his three prospects—Bill Clement, Pete Laframboise and me—into a car and we went to the (1970) draft in Montreal to see what would happen."

Clement was taken 18th by the Flyers. Laframboise and Murray went 19th and 88th, respectively, both to Oakland.

"There are a lot of bad stories about the Seals but it was a good thing to get drafted there, especially after (owner) Charlie Finley refused to match some of the World Hockey Association Offers and the better players were leaving for $4-5,000 more," recalls Murray. "That opened up a lot of spots and one went to me."

Murray played 58 games in 1973-74 for an Oakland team that won 13 games. He spent most of the next season in the minors at Salt Lake City.

"Then came an ownership change when the NHL took over operations and a lot of us got letters two weeks before camp saying that we were not going to be renewed," Murray said. "Larry Wilson (the Flyer coach at their then-Richmond affiliate) had been my coach in Providence, where the Seals sent me my first year of pro.

"My understanding is that Larry and (Flyers GM) Keith Allen went through a list and my name was there. The Kings called me the same day the Flyers did but because of Larry, I signed with the Flyers.

"I went from a team that was very disorganized to a Stanley Cup champion that had a culture, including a management and coaching staff that would talk to you.

"I meet Ed Snider and, the next time he sees me, he knows my name. Are you [bleeping] kidding me? I'm certain to be going to the minors but Bobby Clarke still asks me to go to lunch and have a beer. Before I go down,

"Barry Ashbee spends time with me after practice, showing me what a defenseman does in Freddie Shero's system and it was like a light bulb came on. In the exhibition games, the people were in the right place at the right time, as opposed to where I had come from. The game suddenly became clear.

"Not only did I get called up for three games during the regular season, but I was around for the playoffs, even dressed for a couple games in the Stanley Cup Final."

Midway through the next season, Murray was part of the package the Flyers used to obtain defensemen Rick Lapointe, a former high first-round pick, from the Red Wings. "Detroit at that time was the Seals again," said Murray but the Flyers rescued him again the next season to play for their new AHL team in Maine. When injuries struck, Murray was up for 71 games with the big club in 1980-81 under Pat Quinn.

"Pat was a real good coach, an instructor and teacher like Ashbee had been, explaining the purposes of the drills," said Murray. "That was the time it started to click in that I might like to coach sometime."

Washington claimed him in the 1981 waiver draft. Bryan, who had built a reputation moonlighting as a coach in Pembroke, got his first major junior offer in Regina, then was hired by the Caps to coach their Hershey farm club. When he was moved up to head coach of the Capitals for the 1981-82 season, David Poile, who had become general manager, offered Bryan's little brother an assistant-coaching job. At age 32, with two years left on his playing contract, he hung up his skates to follow his career calling.

"People don't remember that after the Rangers fired Fred Shero, David brought him in to evaluate our team," said Murray. "Just as I was getting into coaching, I could talk with Freddy for two hours after practice and have a beer with him on the road. How great was that?"

Murray coached with his brother for five years. "Very knowledgeable, very technical," recalls Bryan. "You know Terry—he has lots of opinions if asked, just doesn't volunteer to be the talker.

"I was the mouthy one, he was the quiet one, really respected by the players."

After a year-and-a-half as head coach of the farm team in Baltimore, Terry replaced Bryan as head coach. The Caps, to that point perennial playoff flops, went to the 1990 semifinals before he was fired 47 games into the 1993-94 season, only to be hired by Clarke in Florida.

Though a hit with the instantly competitive Panthers, he couldn't stay away in 1994 after being asked home by Ed Snider. Three times Murray has felt the same way.

"I can remember baiting Clarke from the bench, 'Why don't you retire, you old bugger' and Terry getting really mad at me for saying that," said Bryan. "He's a loyal son-of-a-gun to the people who have given him a chance."

Once thrown under the bus after getting Philadelphia to within four games of the Stanley Cup, he jumped back on it 16 years later to develop their players with the Phantoms.

"I took a couple weeks to think about (Holmgren's offer), then, 45 minutes after I called him to accept, I got a call from Mike Babcock, asking me to be an assistant coach in Detroit," recalls Murray. "I was flattered, but I already had given my word.

"At that stage of my career, I never would have coached in the minors for another team. That's what the Flyers have meant to me."

DAVE SCHULTZ

HARD TO BELIEVE IT LASTED ONLY FOUR YEARS. Most games Dave Schultz played for the Flyers seemed to take four years. From the Hammer's first glare to the final shove up the tunnel by the linesman, Schultz's ritual was as symbolic of the Broad Street Bullies as Bobby Clarke goals and Bernie Parent saves.

"There is no way we win the Stanley Cups without him," insisted Keith Allen, the architect of those teams. The people who hated those clubs agreed, insisting that the Flyers were champions only of brawn and intimidation. To them, Schultz was the ultimate hockey thug, but to Philadelphia he was a liberator from years of losing. Coach Fred Shero always said Schultz gave the team courage on the road. And at home he could do no wrong.

Schultz hardly invented the role of enforcer. But no one ever has raised tha role to such a grandiose level. His arms windmilled not only at competitors' faces but also in continuing exasperation with the referees. Hair pulling and head butting were not punishable with gross misconduct penalties until the summer of 1974. Schultz exercised both during notorious 1974 playoff poundings of Atlanta's Bryan Hextall and the Rangers' Dale Rolfe.

No. 8 memorably exited the Maple Leaf Gardens ice during the wild 1976 quarterfinals, holding his nose to signal his disdain for the officiating and the crowd. A wrestling villain on ice, he dodged air horns, bottles, right and left hands, plus the disdain of do-gooders who thought he was the worst thing that ever happened to the game.

Forever turning over the moral dilemma of the role in his mind, Schultz could be as introspective as he was hair-triggered. Always a competent defensive player, The Hammer's unpredictability created a buffer that helped him earn 20 goals in 1973-74. Still, there was never any misunderstanding of his primary role.

As a Junior B player who fancied himself a goal scorer, he surprised himself one day with a right-handed punch that staggered Butch Deadmarsh, later an adversary with the Flames. As Dave grew into one of the bigger players at Swift Current and Sorel, he gradually became those teams' protector.

The most penalty minutes he had in a junior season was 138, but his aggression and 30-goal ability made him a fifth-round selection by Philadelphia in the 1969 draft, the first after the team's philosophy-changing four-game annihilation by the big, bad St. Louis Blues.

In his initial game with Roanoke Valley of the Eastern Hockey League, Schultz destroyed a player named Denis Romaneski and found the process exhilarating. An appetite for blood whetted, he fought his way up the ladder, arriving at the right time—and to the bench of the right coach—to become a phenomenon in Philadelphia.

"My whole life changed in Roanoke Valley," Schultz said. "But away from the ice I never became a different person.

"I never had a fight in the playground as a kid and to this day haven't had a fight on the street or in an establishment. But I came to enjoy people thinking I was tough.

"That was the only fun part, though. Preparing for it was no fun whatsoever. When I think about how I used to psych myself up to play that role, I don't know how I did it. I would sit there the afternoon of every game, thinking about who I was going to fight and visualizing it.

"It was nerve-wracking. I was always afraid of that one punch, the one that would knock me out of my career. Fortunately, it never happened. I had some well-publicized losses but I never really got the whipping that would destroy my confidence and value.

"It was different then, the rules were such that you could really help your team if you scared the right [opponent]. I knew what the Flyers expected and I just totally got caught up in it. I was this kid from Rosetown, Saskatchewan, suddenly a hero, making all this money and being afraid of losing everything. I knew it was a special time and how lucky I was to be part of it. So I did what I had to do to keep it going."

It wasn't a lonely vigil. Flyers who had not been particularly courageous before Schultz's arrival dropped their gloves and followed him to glory and ignominy.

Schultz had a relatively subdued playoff in 1976, when Philadelphia surrendered the Cup to Montreal, and the arrivals of Paul Holmgren and Jack McIlhargey made the Hammer expendable to Los Angeles for second- and fourth-round draft choices. He was never the same after that. Subsequently moved to Pittsburgh and finally to Buffalo, Schultz's disillusionment grew. In a book with Stan Fischler, written soon after Schultz's retirement, he said he resented having to fight Bobby Clarke's battles and criticized the pack mentality that had fueled the Flyers' success.

Four decades later, he no longer has any problem with what he did, just can't believe he was that person who did it. "Despite all the anxiety, I guess I loved it," he said.

After throwing his last punch and temper tantrum in 1980, Schultz coached several teams in the low minors, owned a car service, managed a skating rink, has done public speaking and even a little bit of stand-up comedy. Alas, he was a one-hit wonder with his record "The Penalty Box."

"Baby, you got me charging, holding and hooking and then you blow the whistle on me," sang The Hammer, to mixed reviews in 1975. So today, in addition to his role as a game-night greeter for Flyers games at the Wells Fargo Center, Schultz works as a salesman of energy—and of energy-conservation systems—to commercial concerns.

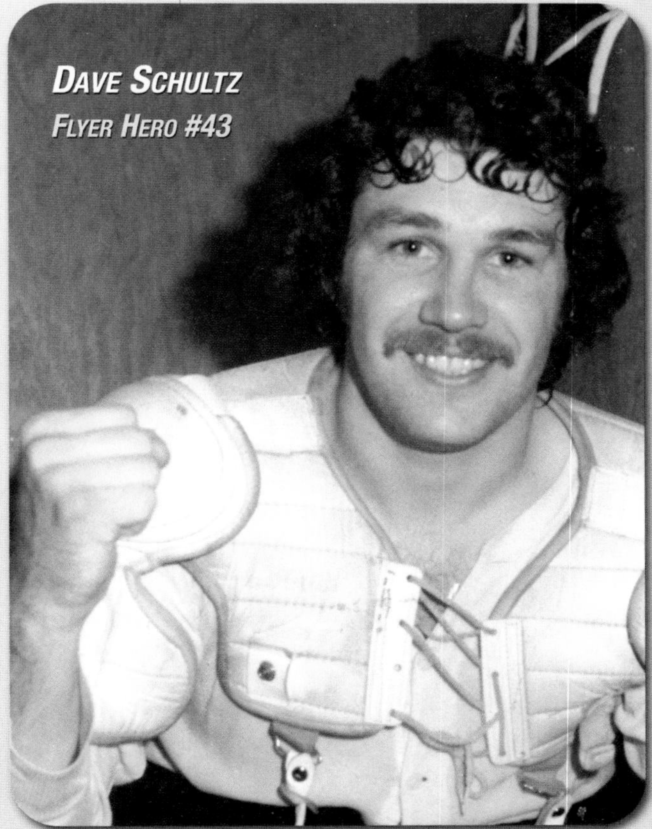
DAVE SCHULTZ
FLYER HERO #43

This is a great irony: A guy whose job was to turn out your lights now works to turn them on. But because Schultz only loved the glory, not really the gory, while breaking new ground and multiple faces with his role during the seventies, the Hammer also was part actor, part salesman, and with two career hat tricks and a 20-goal season, part hockey player, too.

"Once you get into that [role], you can't get out, he said. "Or, I didn't think I could.

"Sure I wanted out, why wouldn't I want to play hockey? I did play some hockey."

Schultz picked off a pass by Terry O'Reilly, forced by Clarke, that led to Clarke's Game Two overtime goal in Boston that turned the 1974 Final. Two rounds earlier, The Hammer had kept his gloves on long enough to score the winning goal in overtime to complete a sweep of Atlanta. He also scored twice in the pivotal Game Five against the Sabres in the 1975 Final after the Sabres had won both games in Buffalo to even the series.

Until somebody messed with Clarke—who usually had started the messing himself—Schultz was a disciplined checker with linemates Orest Kindrachuk and Don Saleski on a reliable third unit. He may never have been the baddest guy in the league, only the most willing. And as hard as that got for him, he doesn't believe it was nearly as difficult as it became for the muscle-bound enforcers of later times.

"Guys are getting hurt in fights now, getting concussions; that never used to happen," said the most reflective man today in Somers Point, NJ, and no longer the toughest. "I can't hit hard; I played at 195-7 pounds.

"When I played, the injuries that came from a hockey fights were that one of the two guys had his feelings hurt. That was it. It wasn't always two tough guys going at it all the time, like it is now, when it doesn't have much to do with the game."

In the mid-seventies, Schultz had so much to do with the Flyer games that in 2009 he was elected to their Hall of Fame. He conducted his press conference from the penalty box, of course. Schultz had his feelings hurt a few times, sure. But at age 66, The Hammer retains his original body parts, all of his faculties and, four decades later, his reputation.

ANDRE DUPONT

When Andre Dupont scored a goal, his knees pumped up near his chest as emphatically as blood flowed through his oversized heart. Fred Shero witnessed the birth of the Moose Shuffle coaching him in Omaha in 1969 and hated it almost as much as he loved the man who performed it.

"Why does he have to do that?" the coach would ask, rolling his eyes. The defenseman may have celebrated his occasional goals like a hot dog, but his relish for the game was beyond reproach. "I didn't score that many," recalls Andre, "I would get excited."

That enthusiasm never diminished, even after the chips on the Broad Street Bullies' shoulders were shaved down to sawdust.

In late December 1978 at Boston Garden, the Flyers were losing 3-0 when Dupont stuck his stick into the gut of Stan Jonathan, perhaps the best fighter of the era. Because Moose's abilities in the fistic arts never matched his ardor, the result was predictable. Dupont needed stitches to close the cut near an eye that was rapidly swelling shut as he returned to a hopelessly lost game.

With the Bruins shoving the score and their gloves into Flyer faces during the third period, Dupont nevertheless pushed Wayne Cashman. Then, while Andre's teammates stood frozen, he yelled at Terry O'Reilly and John Wensink, two more of the toughest customers in the game. "You're next!"

Wensink took Dupont up on it, delivering one more beating.

"I had to assure everybody that the Flyers were not dead," recalls Dupont. "You don't want anyone to make fun of the Flyers."

The Bruins could have severed each of Moose's arms and legs that night, just like the defiant knight in *Monty Python and the Holy Grail*, and Dupont still would have defiantly asked whether they had already taken their best shot. Prone to the spectacular giveaway, there were times he played like his head also had been lopped off, but Shero never believed even the worst-timed Moose minuses could cancel out his plusses.

ANDRE DUPONT
FLYER HERO #46

"He'll [bleeping] die for you," the Flyer coach once said. "He'll kill himself.

"He'll try to beat five guys and then come back and ask you if he did the right thing. He'll drive you crazy because he can't see the forest for the trees sometimes, but he never has to be told to work."

Shero, a long-time minor-league coach in the Rangers' system, received early insight into the makeup of their once seriously overweight first-round choice (eighth-overall, nine picks ahead of Bobby Clarke) in the 1969 draft, but before Dupont could graduate from Omaha to New York, the Rangers had moved him as part of a six-player trade to St. Louis.

The Blues, losing grip on their early dominance of the six new teams, always were a few losses away from a panic-stricken purge when Shero, who had been hired by the Flyers in 1971, urged GM Keith Allen to make a spot in the Flyers' growing menagerie for a Moose.

Most of the muscle being flexed by the emerging Broad Street Bullies was on the forward lines; Shero wanted a beast of prey to protect the goalie, too. So in December 1972, Dupont showed up with St. Louis for a game at the Spectrum only to be informed by the Blues trainer he would instead be playing for the home team.

Traded to the Flyers for defenseman Brent Hughes and right wing Pierre Plante, Dupont changed uniforms more quickly than loyalties.

'I had fought a lot of [Flyers]," recalls Dupont, "When I walked in they asked, 'What the hell are you doing here?'

"Brent Hughes was really well liked, a nice guy apparently. I passed Plante in the hallway as we went to our new locker rooms. I didn't have time to call my wife until after the game. Crazy night. Hard game to play."

The Flyers initially found Dupont distant, but soon learned that they never had to place a long distance call for his help. The Moose gave the franchise courage, color, humor and one of the most vital goals in team history.

Philadelphia had lost Game One of the 1974 Final to the heavily favored Bruins, on a goal by Bobby Orr with just 22 seconds remaining. The Flyers were about to fall just short again in Game Two when Dupont jumped up to the hash marks, took a blind backhand pass from Rick MacLeish, and slapped in the tying goal with 52 seconds on the clock.

"I shot it as hard as I could and the thing went in," Dupont recalls. "I was just as amazed as anyone in the building."

After Clarke scored in overtime to turn the series, Dupont's offensive contributions to Cup One were not over. After the Flyers dominated Game Three and Bill Barber's astonishing wrist shot from the boards put the Flyers ahead late in Game Four, Dupont took a drop pass from Clarke, went by a feebly waving Phil Esposito, and put the contest away to Gilles Gilbert's stick side.

The "Mooooooooose," calls that would accompany his forays up ice were never louder than they were for that goal. If Dupont's sense of when and when not to attack seemed less than opportune, he nevertheless was an impressive plus-269 for his eight Flyer seasons. Thus, forgiven were his excesses. Besides, anytime the Moose got caught up ice it was never because he got caught up in himself, only in his team.

"As long as they think I'm doing the job, that's all that matters," said Dupont, today a consultant for Group Baraphe, a Quebec-based player agency for which he schools clients much like he once was taught by Shero. Sensitive to the public image that he was not very bright, Dupont, on the contrary, was an apt student who knew a good teacher when he had one.

"Everything I know about hockey I learned from Freddie," said Dupont. "If you made a mistake, he explained it to you, and always put you back on the ice to build up your confidence. "

Wounded when Shero left for the Rangers following the 1978 playoffs, Dupont responded strongly when Pat Quinn replaced Bob McCammon and was a mainstay on the 1979-80 defense that produced a 35-game unbeaten streak and took the Flyers to within two victories of the Stanley Cup.

Less than four months later, Allen, anxious to make room for a Swedish prospect named Thomas Eriksson, traded Dupont to his native Quebec for a seventh-round draft choice, but not before giving him a three-year contract, an example of the organization taking care of one of its most passionate and loyal servants.

"I was going to where I was from, but my real home by then was New Jersey," recalls Dupont. "My son and daughter wondered, 'Why are we coming back here? Even Ginette (his Francophone wife) didn't want to go."

"But Keith and Mr. Snider wanted to take care of me with that (last) contract. I can never say enough good things about the Flyers. They gave me a chance to be part of history."

RON SUTTER

THE FLYERS WERE THE BAD GUYS trying to deny Ron Sutter's older brother, Duane, his first Stanley Cup. But as Ron watched the 1980 Final against the New York Islanders, he thought to himself that Philadelphia wouldn't be a bad club to play for.

"I thought it would be awesome to be on that kind of a team in that type of a game," Sutter remembers thinking.

Just because there eventually were going to be enough Sutters in the NHL—six—to ice an entire team, he knew they wouldn't all get to play on the same one.

Two years later, the Flyers made Ron the fourth player taken in the 1982 draft, assuring him of years of divisional battles against Duane and Brent, the Isles' first-round pick in 1980. And Ron Sutter couldn't think of a better place to land.

What had mom, Grace, always told her seven sons? "If you can't do anything all the way, then don't bother doing it at all." Brian, the second oldest brother, remembers there used to be fist fights among the brothers on the way to the school bus. So bring on those Islanders.

"Honestly, I thought it was perfect—the chance to play against the best team in the league and against your older brothers," Sutter recalls. "If you want to beat the best, you have to play the best."

GM Keith Allen's sentiments, too. Brian Bellows, the target of that pick when Philadelphia had acquired it from Hartford for Rick MacLeish the previous summer, went second to Minnesota. Two big defensemen, Gord Kluzak and Gary Nylund, were taken first and third. It left the Flyers with a choice of Scott Stevens, a heavy-hitting defenseman with developing puck skills; Phil Housley, a smallish, offense-oriented defenseman; or Ron Sutter, a center of grit and skill with the best credential in the draft—his last name.

Allen saw it as an opportunity to combat Sutters with more Sutters. In the NHL of that time, one could never have enough Sutters. In fact, as soon as the Penguins used the 10th pick to draft Ron's twin brother Rich, Allen made Pittsburgh an offer. In October 1983, Flyer GM Bob McCammon reunited the two in a trade.

There have been many good days on that Viking, Alberta farm since Brian made the Blues in 1976, but none better than when Allen rejoined the "Magpies"—the nickname given to the twins in their junior days at Lethbridge, Alberta.

For Flyer purposes, they became the "Coyotes," so named by defenseman Brad McCrimmon after a predatory species that travels in packs. Perhaps if you've seen one coyote, you've seen them all, sort of like identical twins. Ron was a little more stoic in personality, had a mole on his left shoulder, and wrote with his right hand; Rich was slightly more excitable, and used his left. Otherwise, they had to be in uniform No. 14 (Ron) and 15 (Rich) or around the goal with a scoring chance for anyone to tell the difference.

On a team in transition, there were a lot of new faces, even if two of them were the same. Among the arrivals the following year (1984) was Rick Tocchet, who relegated Rich to fourth-line duty or, on some nights, no duty at all, much to Ron's discomfort. Two seasons later, Rich was dealt by Bob Clarke to Vancouver in a deal for defenseman J.J.Daigneault.

"I think subconsciously Ronnie had put too much pressure on himself, trying to play for both of them," recalls teammate Dave Poulin.

Indeed, Ron had grown weary of trying to be his brother's keeper, with no control of the situation.

"I got tired of being compared to Richie, having Richie being compared to me, and those mind games (coach) Mike (Keenan) played. He'd say, 'If you don't score tonight or have a good game, Richie won't be dressing,'" Ron recalls. "He did that more than once.

"I had been excited when we traded for Richie because I knew he was struggling so badly [in Pittsburgh] and wanted to get on a good team. But we had not gone into our draft wanting to play together. We always wanted to be our own individuals, to forge our own ways.

"Mom and Dad were upset when the Flyers traded Richie, but it was way more emotional for them than it was for me. I felt bad mostly because he was going to an awful team at the time."

Clarke knew he didn't have to worry about breaking Ron's heart. He continued to be everything the Flyers believed they had drafted—a relentless worker, defensive blanket, contributing scorer and a big winner on two Stanley Cup finalists and a semifinalist.

"Ronnie brought that energy and passion the Flyers were all about," recalls Paul Holmgren, who became the head coach for Sutter's final three seasons in Philadelphia. "He cared about his team and probably was an underrated player.

"He could kill penalties and check, but could also play the powerplay if you needed him."

And, just as Allen had projected, the Flyers even benefitted with two series wins over the Islanders during Philadelphia's 1985 and 1987 drives to the Stanley Cup Final. The first of those victories was climaxed by Ron winning a final-seconds faceoff from Brent and jamming the puck out to center to wrap up Game Five, 1-0, and the series.

No bragging rights were attached. As fiercely as the brothers competed against each other, trying to find a gloat during summer get-togethers was like searching for a needle in the haystack in the loft of the family barn.

That said, Brent wasn't just another good center, and certainly the four-time champion Islanders hardly were another opponent.

"The joy of winning those series wasn't in the handshakes as much as getting back to the dressing room, and realizing you just beat a dynasty," Ron recalls. "The Islanders still had the majority of their key players. If anything, it was exciting because it made me realize [the Flyers] were a good team now.

"Hockey always came up in conversations because we lived and breathed it, but we never did any (needling), even good-naturedly. I knew those Islander players. I was in the dressing room with them when they won their third Cup in Vancouver.

"Because of the age and respect factors, Brian (Ron's senior by 7 years) was a little harder for me to play against. But Brent and I were [18 months] apart, so we always were competitive against each other. I can remember Brian barking at us at different times about being [too nasty] to each other.

"There was so many of us playing—Brian in St. Louis, Darryl in Chicago, Duane and Brent on the Island, there were a lot of games to look forward to. And I approached them like, 'You know what? I can be as good as you.' There was always going to be pressure trying to live up to expectations, but seeing what my brothers had done [while developing] gave us all confidence.

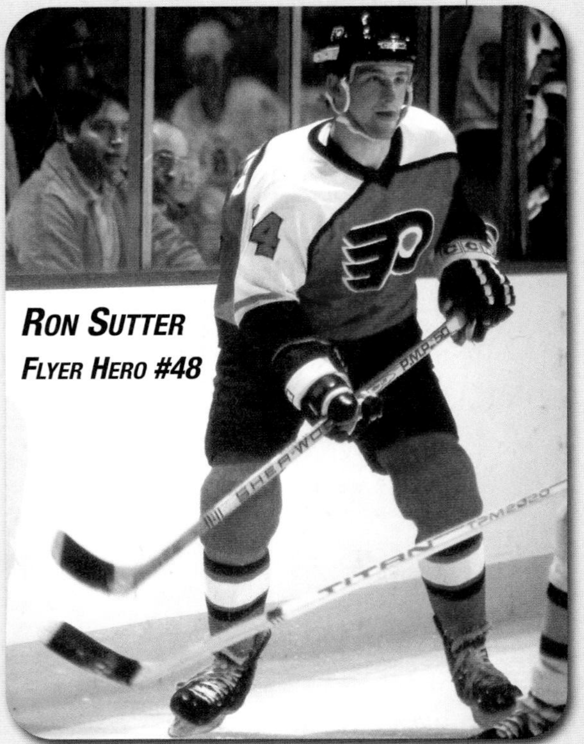

RON SUTTER
FLYER HERO #48

"Brian opened up all our eyes that we could make it, but also opened them up to how much work we had to do. The biggest thing I learned from my older brothers, what I've told my son Riley (a junior A player), is, 'Never take anything for granted. Don't think because you had one good shift, you can take the next shift off.'"

Grace and Louis Sutter produced sons who played more than 5,000 NHL games and won six Cups. Left wing Brian scored 303 goals in 12 seasons, and was the Blues captain and coach. Right wing Duane had 342 points in 11 seasons with the Islanders and Blackhawks.

Darryl enjoyed 40- and 31-goal seasons among his eight on left wing with the Blackhawks, and has coached the Los Angeles Kings to two Cups. Center Brent averaged more than one point per playoff game during the fourth Islander championship run (of four), and had 829 points during a 17-season career that concluded with the Blackhawks. Turned out, there were plenty of hockey genes left for right wing Rich, who played for seven teams over 13 seasons and scored 149 goals. A second generation has yielded Brent's son, Brandon, who is in his ninth NHL season.

At the time of his draft, Ron was believed to have the best hands of all the brothers, including the eldest, Gary—a good junior who never pursued a pro hockey career. With seasons of 26 and 22 goals while totaling 137 as a Flyer, Ron surely would have done better had he been used in more offensive situations.

"Mike Keenan pulled me in one of the first days of camp my second year and told me, '[Third line] is what your role's going to be,'" Sutter recalls. "Was I happy about it? Not necessarily, but I knew the importance of it because I saw the success the Islanders had with Brent and Duane doing it.

"From a longevity standpoint, it probably helped my career. But more often than not, it kept me from playing with skilled guys.

"After putting me on the third line, Mike then would throw shots at me, using Brent's [better production] as an example. I would always say, 'Brent is playing with John Tonelli, Mike Bossy, Clark Gillies.' I had to tell Mike a couple times, 'I'm not Brent. I don't play every powerplay.'

"Mike was hard on you, but he was hard on everybody. He also was one that would pull you aside and compliment you. But one time on the Island, I had just lost a faceoff to Brent and was sitting down on the bench when Mike said, 'Get the [bleep] in the dressing room!' and pointed to where you go off the ice. I'm like, 'Are you serious?' I didn't know what to do, so I just sat down and he didn't make (any further) issue of it.

"What can you say? Mike's a proven winner. Different players will answer differently about him, but whether it was through his hockey intuition or the fear he put into you, he always seemed to be able to get the best out of players. I can't say today he was my favorite coach, but I certainly can say he made me understand the game a lot better and realize how to make better use of the players around me.

"The mind games he played were with the guys he knew could handle it."

In Game Three of the 1985 best-of-five first round, with the Flyers up 2-0 in the series and what had been a 6-3 lead over the Rangers suddenly down to 6-5 early in the third period and Madison Square Garden howling, Keenan put out Sutter because he could handle it.

He and linemates Tocchet and Lindsay Carson jammed the puck into the New York zone, produced two scoring chances and totally reversed the momentum of the game. The Rangers didn't get another opportunity until three minutes remained. After Sutter won three defensive-zone draws with the goalie pulled, the Flyers had their first series win in four years.

"Ron was a very reliable player for us, important in terms of his ability to be used against the better players from the other team," recalls Keenan.

Only partially can Sutter's impact be measured in his 359 Flyer points, but in Game One of that same 1985 series, he had one of the biggest assists in team history. Having blown 3-0 and 4-3 leads, Philadelphia was in overtime when Sutter pounced on long-time Flyer killer Reijo Ruotsalainen behind the goal, swiped the puck, and set up Mark Howe's overtime winner, breaking a nine-game playoff losing streak for the franchise.

The Flyers, under huge pressure to end that misery after stunning the league with a first-overall finish, played nervously through much of that series, but Sutter always proved to be as unintimidated by situations as he was by close relatives. "Against his brothers or anybody, he played the same," recalls teammate Brad Marsh. "That's the identity of the Flyers brand, right? Ronnie was vital to that."

After being forced from the lineup in early March 1987 with a stress fracture in his back, Sutter returned after two games of the second-round series against the Islanders and played remarkably. It was a huge advantage for Keenan to have two excellent defensive centers—Sutter and Poulin—to share duties against Peter Stastny in 1985, Bobby Smith in 1987, Wayne Gretzky in two Finals and Mario Lemieux in a Game Seven triumph over Pittsburgh in 1989.

"If Dave was tired or in the penalty box, or if we were on the road and couldn't dictate the matchup, there was a trust factor that if he couldn't do the job, I was going to do it, and vice versa," remembers Sutter. "There was always communication between the two of us."

Recalls Poulin, "It allowed each of us think that within our role, we could be an offensive player as well. When you're told you're just a defensive specialist, it's easy to escape into that area and not put pressure on yourself. Having each other was enormous."

Poulin and Sutter, rookies together in 1983-84, made it to Philadelphia in time for the final playing season of Bobby Clarke, Bill Barber and Darryl Sittler, experience invaluable to the two kids when, one year later, it became their show.

"I had a good feel for what that logo meant before I got there," recalls Sutter. "But in terms of how to carry myself, I was very fortunate to have time around those guys.

"You wanted to prove to them you were worthy. I remember Paul Holmgren taking me aside after a scrimmage my second camp and telling me I was showing Clarkie too much respect; to compete harder against him. That was a wake-up call for me.

"When they—and Homer, too—were gone the next year, I knew the importance of having to carry on for what they had done for the franchise."

The transition was astonishingly smooth. Around Mark Howe, Pelle Lindbergh, Tim Kerr, Marsh, McCrimmon and the two sophomore centers, the Flyers compiled the best record in the league in 1984-85 on the way to two Finals against Edmonton in three seasons.

A huge opportunity slipped away in 1985-86, when Edmonton was upset by Calgary after the Rangers shocked Philadelphia in the first round. "Absolutely, that was our best chance, as it turned out," recalls Sutter, who finished second to Chicago's Troy Murray for the Frank Selke Trophy that season.

The Flyers took their last, best shot the next spring, when they avenged their loss to the Rangers in six, squashed an Islander attempt to come back from 3-1 in seven, and dethroned Montreal in six on the way to another Edmonton Final. No team ever went down harder. After rallying from three two-goal deficits to force Game Seven, Philadelphia lost, 3-1.

"At the funeral for my dad, my daughters said it was the only time they had ever seen me cry," Sutter recalls. "I told them they hadn't seen me after Game Seven."

"They said 'Over a hockey game?' I said, 'It wasn't just another hockey game.'"

After Holmgren succeeded Keenan, the Flyers had one more run in 1989. Sutter got a chance to play with Brian Propp and set up his critical first goal in the 4-1 Game Seven win in Pittsburgh.

The conference final ended badly with a 4-2 defeat in Game Six, climaxed with Ron Hextall leaving the net to attack Montreal's Chris Chelios in retaliation for the elbow that had concussed Propp in Game One. But Hextall hadn't gotten the idea until Sutter had left his feet in the final two minutes to drill Chelios.

"To this day, what Chelios did to Proppie [bleeps] me off," says Sutter.

The era ended with that game, even if the Flyers didn't know it. When groin problems increasingly forced Poulin out of the lineup, coach Paul Holmgren took the captaincy from him and gave it to Sutter a month before Poulin was traded to Boston in January 1990.

Sutter tried to lead as he always had—by example. But Poulin was missed and the team was deteriorating. Ron was among the players forced into offensive roles greater than their capabilities. "We were rebuilding and it was hard to go through," recalls Sutter.

With a March collapse in 1991, the Flyers missed the playoffs for a second consecutive year and change was accelerated. Through GM Russ Farwell's trade of Sutter to St. Louis in a package for center Rod Brind'Amour, the team became eight years younger and better offensively.

Even though he was leaving a shadow of the Flyer teams he knew and was going to play for his brother Brian, Ron still was not happy to leave.

"We agreed (with Farwell) on a new contract during camp, and then, bang, a few days later I got traded," he recalls. "I didn't see it coming at all.

"Emotionally it was hard. I was ingrained in the community and felt like I was a good fit going forward. But the Flyers made a good trade. It was the best thing in the long run for me and for Rod, just like Richie getting traded from the Flyers was the best thing for both of us."

Ron soldiered on for 10 more seasons playing with the Blues, Bruins, Sharks, Nordiques, Islanders and Flames. He now works for Calgary as director of player development but, having won a lot of games with Philadelphia, has unending loyalty.

"I don't know how many times I've heard (wife) Margo say that the thing she remembers most about Philly was how close the guys and the wives were," he recalls. "When we couldn't get home from Quebec because of bad weather, she drove Diane Hextall to the hospital to have (son) Brett.

"The loss of Pelle (Lindbergh) strengthened that much more how we cared for each other, and I think that was something you saw on the ice."

BOB KELLY

BATS OUT OF HELL LOOKED BOTH WAYS if Bob Kelly was coming. Seemingly propelled by an industrial-strength rubber band that Fred Shero had pulled all the way back to Camden, the Hound catapulted over the boards and, with choppy strides shorter than his shifts or his attention to Shero's system, hurled himself into the offensive zone.

The Broad Street Bullies were Goliaths armed with the slingshot, too, not what you would call a fair fight. Adrenaline surging, knees pumping, Kelly bounced from body to body with enough energy to power all of South Philadelphia. "He would go for 40 seconds and hit eight guys," recalls defenseman Joe Watson. "Sometimes our guys, sometimes their guys."

Coaches didn't roll four lines in those days; instead played their best players until they dropped, often from a body check by a well-rested No. 9.

The Flyers picked up their second Stanley Cup on one of those Kelly pick-me-ups. On a steamy late May night, in a Buffalo Memorial Auditorium minus air conditioning, with Game Six scoreless headed into the third period, assistant coach Mike Nykoluk reminded Shero that he had not been utilizing Kelly enough. So the winger was started on a line with Bobby Clarke and Reggie Leach.

The Hound, unleashed, arrived at the backboards first to reach a Leach dump-in, took a hit from 220-pound Jerry Korab, kept those legs churning, used a screen from Clarke, and walked out without resistance to slide the puck past goalie Roger Crozier to the far side of the net at 11 seconds.

Kelly recognized immediately the enormity of what he had done.

"You owe me five bucks," was the first thing he said at the bench to Shero.

Nineteen minutes from the title, his name just a few Bernie Parent saves away from joining Gordie Howe, Jean Beliveau, Bobby Orr and Andy Bathgate as Stanley Cup-winning goal scorers, Kelly's first thought was not immortality, but the five dollars Shero offered Flyers for wraparound goals in games and during practice.

"Yep, five bucks," Kelly confirms today. "Hey, that could buy a tank of gas in those days.'

"Besides, there was a long way to go in that game. It's never over until it's over."

Bill Clement, the Flyers' fourth line center, put away the 2-0 win. The team's stars thought it was the coolest thing that, in the end, the grunts had earned some glory. But if Kelly really were in it for the notoriety instead of the five bucks, he would have rebelled earlier at being used as a bowling ball. He had a 22-goal season in 1977 and netted 26 in finishing up his career in Washington.

In fact, during his first Flyer season, 1970-71, Kelly had been Clarke's regular left wing. He not only scored 14 goals, he didn't put the franchise star-to-be in the hospital.

"Clarkie, me and Lew Morrison, it worked well until we got some people with more talent, as in Billy Barber," recalls Kelly. "I'm going to complain about it?

"I never put myself ahead of anybody. If I was dressed, I would do whatever you needed me to do. If I played every other shift, I was happy. If I got one shift, I was happy.

"People said, 'You're good enough to get out and go play second line somewhere.' I said, 'Why would I do that? I've got an owner who gives us everything, a general manager I love, good players all around me, and was in a great city with great fans. We went deep into the playoffs every year. Why would you want to change that, just for more ice time?

"It wasn't about me, it was about the team."

Four decades later, as the Flyers' Ambassador of Hockey, it still is. "Bob might be the hardest-working guy in the organization," says president Paul Holmgren, a statement Kelly shrugs off. Fitting servicemen with Flyer jerseys, visiting schools, hospitals, and doing clinics is not work, he insists, while pinballing from event to event as though Freddie still was manning the flippers.

Kelly may be the only guy of our 50 we have profiled who once went offside on a two-on-zero, and who Gene Hart needled should have his name written on the Cup in crayon. But The Hound still rounds out our list ahead of lots of guys who scored many more points. He has been a Flyer fixture even longer than the lights or kitchen sinks they took out of the Spectrum for auction before the place was torn down.

In fact, when the old building fittingly refused to crumble from the first few swings of the iron ball, one had to wonder why they didn't just mount The Hound on the hook and pound away with him. Hey, it worked on a lot more defensemen than just Korab.

Kelly wasn't the first of the big, tough guys to be drafted after the 'Never Again' front-office decree that followed the Flyers manhandling by the bad Blues in the 1969 playoffs. Dave Schultz was selected two months later. But Kelly was the first to make the team, right after he was taken in the third round in 1970. And because he hit, The Hound became an instant hit.

Although two years away from becoming the Broad Street Bullies, the Flyers, who had also just added Barry Ashbee to Clarke, Ed Van Impe, and Gary Dornhoefer, were beginning to stick up for themselves. The barrel-chested rookie left wing didn't have to be taught anything about marking one's territory.

His hometown of Port Credit, Ontario, on the Lake Ontario shore west of Toronto, was its own municipality before it was absorbed in 1974 by the massive suburb of Mississauga. When the kids from the next town over, Lakeview, were dumped into the Port Credit schools during the 1960s, it didn't go as graciously as handshakes following a hard fought seven-game series.

There were rumbles Friday and Saturday nights, the winners licking their wounds proudly at the movie theatres, losers going away to plot for the next time.

"We had some, uh, interesting, people," laughs Kelly. Hockey kept him busy enough through the winter to avoid deeper troubles than fist fights, plus an uncle's farm 110 miles away in Trenton, Ontario, got Bob in with a better crowd—of cows and pigs—at the time of year hockey couldn't occupy his time.

His dad, Jim, who worked at the Gulf refinery, was not pleased to learn at the breakfast table that his 16-year-old son was on his way that day not to school, but to a job with an electrical company. But when, as a Junior B player, he was part of a five-player package going to Junior A Oshawa for Dale Tallon, that team required its players to attend school, and Kelly completed Grade 12.

Tallon would become the second player taken in the 1970 draft. Kelly went 32nd to a Philadelphia organization loading up on 200-pounders. He was sent the first plane ticket of his life for Quebec City and training camp, where he looked instantly useful to a three-year-old franchise that had never before had a Tasmanian devil.

"We're having a scrimmage and here comes this kid down the ice," recalls Watson. "His head is down, so I go to hit him, and he ran over me without ever breaking stride.

"I said, 'Keith (GM Allen), who the hell is this guy?' He laughed his butt off."

Watson and the other flattened veterans had the last laugh. They set him up better even than Bobby Clarke could in front of an open net, talking for a month in front of the rookie about their upcoming hunting expedition for "snipe", a pigeon-kind of prey who, according to Van Impe, was quite the delicacy when cooked in his wife's wine sauce.

"They knew I loved to hunt and I begged them to come along," recalls Kelly. So it was quite the honor when he was included in three carloads to a park in Media, PA, on a November evening with rifles, plus flashlights and poles to root out the snipes from the bushes.

"There's one!" somebody yelled and Kelly fired, only to hear Flyer center Earl Heiskala cry out in the dark, "I've been shot." A carload of cops in on the joke soon arrived at the scene, and Kelly was handcuffed and taken before a local magistrate, where, as additional teammates hid behind one-way glass busting a gut—and Heiskala limped in with a leg bandage soaked in ketchup—Kelly was fined $1,500 for hunting snipe out of season.

When he couldn't produce ID, the judge—authentic and a friend of Van Impe's like the policemen—threatened the Canadian with deportation. "But I just got here," said Kelly.

He was afraid to dial Allen with the allotted one phone call, instead used it on his Mom back in Port Credit. Unable to make bond, Kelly was convinced he was going to jail for the night—if not longer—when the judge told him to turn around and face the music. "Welcome to the NHL," said his teammates standing in the back.

The perfect caper. Kelly wasn't mad, just relieved. A real team picks only on the guys who can take it.

"The culture was there from my start with the Flyers, we just needed some more talent," Kelly recalls. As good players arrived, The Hound's ice time shrunk but, with him, less proved to be more.

"Whatever, you do, don't pass it to Hound in our zone," was Van Impe's strict advice when Jimmy Watson came up from the minors. But a guy without a clue ended up playing more games than all but five players in franchise history. He must have been doing something right.

"In addition to having character, Hound was a character," said Clarke. As the latter, Kelly was about as subtle as a Stanley Cup parade attended by 2.3 million. After the Flyers won Game Five of the Buffalo series, he came out of the shower to see sitting on his locker bench a gentleman in a suit. "Hey buddy, get the [bleep] out of my seat," said the Hound. But Clarke graciously moved over and offered his place to Pennsylvania Governor Milton Shapp.

"When I saw Clarkie do that, then noticed two guys in top coats standing right there, I thought, 'Uh-oh, who is this guy?'" recalls Kelly. He apologized to Shapp after the next game, although in doing so, mentioned he wouldn't think of coming to Harrisburg and sitting in the governor's chair.

Hearing that, citizens of Pennsylvania heaved a sigh of relief. Shapp laughed and agreed. Kelly might not have said anything in the first place if he didn't believe he had the most exclusive throne in sports, in the locker room of the Stanley Cup champions. Having suffered torn knee ligaments in Game Six of the semifinals against the Rangers during the spring of 1974 and missing the Final against Boston, the first championship hadn't quite sat right with him, so the second Cup really felt like his first.

"If you are there through all the ups and downs, start to finish, it means more," he recalls. "If you're not bleeding with the guys, you just don't feel a part of it.

"There were a lot of people in that tiny (visiting) locker room in Buffalo. I remember flying home, just us and the Cup. Special time."

The Canadiens dethroned the Flyers the following spring. When the Flyers lost to Boston in the 1977 semifinal, the band of brothers, as he calls it, started to be broken up, but the Hound had shelf life remaining. In 1978, he scored two goals and an assist in a five-game second-round series against—who else?—the Sabres. "No wonder I got a speeding ticket going through Buffalo," he says.

In 1979-80, under coach Pat Quinn, Kelly played with regular linemates Mel Bridgman and Tom Gorence on the team that went 35 games without losing. The Hound had a goal in game No. 29 that broke the NHL record in Boston.

At the end of that season, Allen got a third-round pick for Kelly from Washington, where he scored 26 goals the next year on the top line. "Proved I could still be a goal scorer if I wanted to be," he recalls. But a new Capital regime brought in the next season didn't value Kelly and his career was over after just 16 games.

He owned and operated a liquor store in Deptford, got into the construction and management of roller hockey rinks at The Coliseum, the Flyers' former training site in Voorhees, and in Delaware. In 2003, Ed Snider asked Kelly if he wanted to represent the team in the community. Now in his 14th year, the ultimate role player is enjoying this one as much as ever.

"We have such an opportunity to touch so many current and potential fans," he said. "We are around the military and the police everywhere you can be; go to 80 to 100 schools a year, plus banquets, golf outings, and Snider Hockey events.

"It's pretty cool to reach out. From the day Keith Allen brought me here, it's been nothing but first class."

That included when Shero paid off on the five bucks. Quite the bargain for a championship.

"I would imagine a lot of guys who scored Cup-winning goals turned over in their graves when I got one, but everybody gets a day and that was mine," said Bob Kelly, still making those days for multitudes of Flyer fans.

Bob Kelly
Flyer Hero #50

John LeClair

Chapter 2 • 1996-97

Shiny, New and Swept

On *August 31, 1996*—only 717 days after groundbreaking, but more than seven years since Philadelphia Mayor Wilson Goode had told Ed Snider there would be a deal for a new arena on the site of JFK Stadium "in five days"—the Flyer founder and Chairman dropped the CoreStates Center's ceremonial first puck.

To 19,511 first-nighters attending a World Cup of Hockey match between Canada and the USA, the sight of two Flyers—Eric Lindros (for Canada) and Joel Otto (for the USA)—flanking Snider for the ceremonial draw was a grand display of the franchise's progress.

The Flyers had come a lot farther in 29 years than just 751 feet across the parking lot to their $215 million new home. The initial game in 1967 at the $12 million Spectrum had been attended by 7,812. The Broad Street Bullies had won two Stanley Cups (1974, 1975), and the team reached four more Finals (1976, 1980, 1985, 1987) and five additional semifinals (1977, 1978, 1989, 1995), in a cozy arena that became notorious for the level of discomfort inflicted upon the opposition.

Thus the new building, which stood 30 feet taller, was 300,000 square feet larger, and seated an additional 2,434 people, needed a housewarming. When Lindros, the enemy for one night, instantly threw a log on the fire by knocking off Otto's helmet during the first shift, creature comfort was delivered to Flyer loyalists that trumped even the wondrous amenities of the new palace, designed by Ellerbe Becket and built by Philadelphia's L.F. Driscoll Company.

From two concourses, as opposed to one at the Spectrum, fans could access 8,500 seats on both the first and second levels, priced for game-day sales from $20 to $62.50. When the Spectrum opened, empty seats had been attributed to their $2 to $5 price.

At CoreStates Center, a club level featuring Victors Restaurant had 18 suites going for $140,000 a season; two super boxes held 94 seats, each one priced at $12,500 per season; and club box seats sold for $4,750 to $6,000 per person. Above that were mid-level suites going for $125,000 to $155,000 per season. And ringing the top (accessed via elevators the Spectrum never had) were 26 balcony suites priced at $75,000 each.

In addition to a brewpub on the main concourse, three "action stations" featured more upscale cuisine choices than could be had at the 115 standard concession stands, 25 more than at the Spectrum.

"If you pay $12 for a sandwich, you are going to be totally happy with what you are getting," promised Chef Bennett Fass, the director of food service at both the CoreStates Center and renamed CoreStates Spectrum, which was becoming home to the Flyers' new American Hockey League farm team, the Phantoms, as well as being a venue for smaller shows.

The biggest stars were booked for the new arena. Fourteen concerts, including Neil Diamond and Oasis, were scheduled in the first 42 days. Performers no longer were getting ready in the Flyer and Sixer locker rooms, but in a suite with four dressing rooms, private showers, plus reception and food-preparation areas.

There were 621 television sets in the arena. The hot tub in the Flyer dressing room could seat 12. Everything was grander, and not only when one looked up at a 16-ton octagonal scoreboard with four 9x12-foot color video screens, or at the Martha Madigan sculpture hanging in the main atrium with 4x9-foot glass panels containing digitized images, each representing a sport to be played in the building. Even the dinner plates in Victors were larger, 13 inches in diameter, as compared to the 10-inch versions at Ovations in the Spectrum.

Fans walked into the "Disneyland of Arenas," as it was called by Bob Schwartz, vice president for marketing and sales at the CoreStates Complex, over a sidewalk of 19,620 pavers, each available for personalized inscription at only $75 each. But no value could be placed on the sweat and anxiety from Snider and his wife Martha that went into every brick in the walls, 7,000 tons of steel, 19,000 cubic feet of concrete, and 32,000 square feet of glass.

"We had to put up almost everything we had for collateral," recalls Martha, who designed and purchased the uniforms for the building personnel and furnished the suites on a budget slashed from $5 million to $1.5 million because the cost of the building's steel had increased sharply.

The Sniders had mortgaged $140 million of the construction costs (the public share in loans and grants had been $25 million and Spectacor equity put up the rest) before Comcast bought 66 percent of both buildings, the Flyers, and the 76ers for $500 million in March 1995.

Ed Snider, by contract still in managing control of the teams and the arenas, retained a one-third financial stake but 100 percent sense of ownership of the project, from its frustrating beginnings to its proud finish.

The 12,000 workers who had completed the project on time and on budget were thanked with invitations to a private Ray Charles concert staged 18 days before the arena's opening to the public. But Philadelphia had mostly Snider to thank for its largely privately-financed showplace.

"The new building wouldn't have happened without me, I know that," Snider told Phil Jasner of *The Philadelphia Daily News*. "I am very proud. I put my butt on the line when no one thought it could get done."

The same had held true 30 years earlier, with the building of the Spectrum in only 15 months. But that had not made the stress—or risk—any easier for the Chairman to handle three decades later.

"The first time, Ed had a passion and a dream. He didn't really know he was doing the impossible," recalls Martha. "He did it on the force of his personality.

"The thing that made it harder the second time was he was at a point of his career where everybody could watch him fail.

"He had a lot of pride, that man. To build in Camden, we had been offered $60 million that we wouldn't have had to finance. He used it for leverage, but never seriously considered it.

"The Philadelphia Flyers in Camden? He couldn't stand the thought; he believed he would get crucified."

Snider received nothing but appreciation as he walked through the concourse on opening night, greeting season-ticket holders who had been given first opportunity to buy strips for the three World Cup games—including a semifinal and the first of a three-game final—to be played in Philadelphia.

In five tournaments from 1976 through 1991, the six-entry Canada Cup had staged some of the most breathtaking hockey ever played. This eight-nation sequel featured six Flyers—Lindros, Rod Brind'Amour and Eric Desjardins for Canada; Otto and LeClair for the USA, and Patrik Juhlin for Sweden—plus prospect Janne Niinimaa for Finland. Two other Flyers, Mikael Renberg of Sweden and Petr Svoboda of the Czech Republic, declined invitations as they were rehabbing as a result of health issues before Philadelphia's training camp.

Lindros, pictured on the opening night tickets alongside LeClair in Flyer uniforms with Canadian and U.S. flags behind them, was the first player introduced and drew probably the biggest cheer an opposition player ever received from Philadelphia fans. LeClair received a larger one on behalf of the Red, White and Blue.

"The only thing left to say," announced Gene Hart, the Flyer broadcaster from their inception until 1995, as he closed the pregame festivities, "is 'Let's play hockey!'"

This wasn't particularly easy on predictably chippy ice barely broken in during two Team USA practices that preceded the first game.

"Brutal," reviewed LeClair after the game. "The puck wouldn't sit down." Nevertheless, he one-timed a feed from Bryan Smolinski past Canada goaltender Martin Brodeur for the first goal in the building.

"I didn't get the puck; I should have," LeClair lamented after Brett Hull, with his second goal, put the USA up 4-3 in the third period. Although one of the escalators failed, but there was no breakdown by a U.S. defense under siege from a world hockey power. The Americans beat Canada for the first time in any Canada or World Cup, 5-3, then followed up with a 5-2 victory over the Russians and a 9-3 win over Slovakia, both at Madison Square Garden. The U.S. went into the semifinal with a 3-0 record.

"Now is the time for the U.S. team," declared center Pat LaFontaine. "This is a measuring point to see just how far we've come in hockey."

Canada, 2-1, in the round robin, returned to the CoreStates Center for a semifinal match with Sweden and won when Theo Fleury's goal at 19:47 of the second overtime ended the longest international hockey game ever played. Thus, on only Night Two, the building already had staged a classic, and when the Americans beat the Russians again, 5-2 in the other semifinal in Ottawa, the matchup everyone wanted to see—USA vs. Canada—came back to the new building for Game One of the final.

By this time there was little sentiment left in Philadelphia for any Canadian, including Lindros. The crowd cheered hits on the Flyer captain by Derian Hatcher and even Chris Chelios, who seven years earlier had been pelted with debris at the Spectrum at the conclusion of a Flyers-Canadiens conference final for having concussed Philadelphia's Brian Propp with a vicious Game One elbow into the glass.

"This is not about the Philadelphia Flyers, this is about your country," said Brind'Amour. "The crowd here obviously is going to root for the Americans. I wouldn't expect anything else."

Lindros, played on the wing by Team Canada coach Glen Sather in deference to a loaded center ice of Wayne Gretzky, Mark Messier, Steve Yzerman and Joe Sakic, deflected in Team Canada's first goal. The U.S. trailed 3-2 until Otto won a faceoff from Adam Graves and Desjardins, trying to shove the puck under goalie Brodeur, may have helped along LeClair's tying rebound with 6.3 seconds remaining. But in overtime, Canada got the break when an apparent offside by Brind'Amour was ignored and Yzerman's shot went in awkwardly off goalie Mike Richter's glove.

The 4-3 loss, which sent the Americans to Montreal's Molson Centre for the final two contests, was painful but hardly discouraging to LeClair. In Game Two, he put in a rebound of a Gary Suter point drive to open the scoring, then tipped in a Smolinski shot to make it 2-0.

Lindros successfully screened Richter after dropping the puck to Brendan Shanahan, who cut the lead in half. Although Hull scored on a breakaway, Sakic successfully deflected Lindros's drive to again pull Canada within one. But the U.S. twice hit the empty net to put away a 5-2 victory.

Going into the deciding contest, LeClair led the tournament with 10 points. "He has played unbelievable," said U.S. coach Ron Wilson. "I think he wants to prove to everybody he doesn't need Eric Lindros to be a great hockey player."

"I don't really think about anything like that," said LeClair, with a big shrug that suggested his shoulders felt a lot less weight than there was on the Canadian players.

"Enormous," said Lindros about the pressure of retaining the country's birthright. "That's a motivator all right.

"I think it's good; the fear of losing can really inspire."

The Americans had attacked the tournament with no lack of mission—"Ron Wilson and (GM) Lou (Lamoriello) had been pounding it (as a potential watershed event) since the first day of training camp," recalls Paul Holmgren, then the Flyer director of pro scouting, serving as an assistant coach for Team USA. Still, the load on the red, white and blue team was lighter.

"Two hundred and 25 million Americans don't care about this tournament, but that's not what this is all about," said Wilson. "We're just playing for ourselves, a lot less of a burden."

LeClair had told the media, "We aren't going to be scrutinized as much as Team Canada if we lose," and he was hoping that tight would beat uptight. "We were having so much fun winning, we were really together," he recalls.

For two periods of Game Three it looked like the Americans, not the Canadians, had the anvil strapped to their backs. But Richter was so good that Canada needed Lindros's wrist shot from the top of the circle with 5.5 seconds remaining in the second period to tie the game, 1-1.

In the third period, the U.S. found so much energy that when Adam Foote's goal off Kevin Hatcher gave Canada a 2-1 lead with just 7:10 to play, LeClair stood up on the bench along with teammate Tony Amonte and insisted things still were under control.

"I thought we were taking it to them," LeClair said later. Turned out, he hadn't seen anything yet. Hull, reaching behind his back, deflected Brian Leetch's shot past Curtis Joseph with 3:18 remaining to tie the game and Amonte, climaxing a long shift in the Canada end, put in a rebound just 43 seconds later.

Video reviews were needed to uphold both goals. Even better, Wilson reasoned, because "we got to celebrate twice." Hatcher scored into the empty net, Adam Deadmash added a fifth goal and the U.S. stunningly won 5-2.

"You could hear a pin drop everywhere," said Amonte, meaning not just in the Molson Centre but across Canada.

"Unbelievable, we're world champions," said winger Keith Tkachuk. But this was no American hockey miracle, as in the 1980 Winter Games, when college kids almost incomprehensibly upset the same Soviets who had dominated decisive games against the best Canadian professionals in the 1979 Challenge Cup and 1981 Canada Cup. The 1996 U.S. World Cup triumph was the next generation of American pros, inspired to play the sport by Lake Placid, winning a two-out of-three series against the once-and-again best hockey-playing country on earth. USA hockey had fully grown up.

"It was like your lifetime in three hours," said Wilson.

And to Lindros and the Canadians, their lives had passed before their eyes in three minutes and 18 seconds. "This [locker] room is crushed," said Gretzky. "The whole country probably is crushed."

"This is not a fun spot to be in right now," said Lindros, who carried home from the tournament three goals, three assists and praise for his performance and sacrifices in making a position switch.

"When you look at Eric, you want to put pressure on his shoulders, but every game he's been a major force," Shanahan had said before the final match. "This isn't baseball where you look at the stat sheet and decide who is playing well. Eric does a lot for our bench."

For his efforts, Lindros came home with not only a disappointing second place but an inflamed elbow that had been drained during the Canada Cup without the knowledge of the Flyers, much to the annoyance of general manager Bob Clarke.

Lindros had not thought it to be a big deal. "This has been happening to me since I was 14 years old," he said. "It's like what Gordie Howe once said: An elbow is to hockey what fenders are to cars; they are going to take some abuse."

Actually, Clarke felt that not only Lindros, but the Flyers as a whole, had accepted too much maltreatment at the hands of the Florida Panthers when going down in six games in the second round the previous spring. In June, the GM added two crashers—forwards Eric Lacroix and Scott Daniels. At Hartford, Daniels had totaled 254 penalty minutes, 50 more than Flyer leader Shawn Antoski, who had signed with Pittsburgh when he wasn't retained by Philadelphia.

"[The upset by Florida] showed us all that hockey has not changed," said Clarke. "If you get into a war, you need people to absorb and give it back.

"We'd like to be the ones who initiate."

Murray, who said early in the previous year that he didn't want Lindros fighting anymore, had changed his mind by the end of the season. With the instigator penalty reduced from a game misconduct to just 10 minutes for the 1996-97 season, there was even less reason for restraint.

"I think this new rule will keep everybody a little more honest," said Murray. "Guys who wouldn't go anywhere near him if they thought he might take the gloves off were suddenly challenging him, so I withdrew that statement in a meeting with him in the middle of the year.

"He's the best judge of what he needs to do in various situations."

The Flyers dismissed trainer David (Sudsy) Settlemyre, who had first worked for them in 1981 and had come back to the organization with Clarke when the GM returned in 1994 from birthing the Panthers. Dave Brown, who had done two stints totaling 11 years as the Flyer enforcer, retired from the San Jose Sharks to take an assistant coaching position in Philadelphia, replacing Tom Webster who, as a former NHL head coach, wanted a larger role.

"I didn't think long about it," said Brown. "This is a team with a lot of potential, a pretty exciting way to start a new career."

In the search to add more talent to his young, skilled nucleus, Clarke had called the 1996 draft the "most confusing I've ever seen."

"Usually you can predict at least the names of 12 of the first 14 players taken, if not the order, but we weren't even close this year," he said.

Still on the board at No. 15—a pick the Flyers had acquired from Toronto the previous August for defenseman Dmitri Yushkevich and a second-rounder—was Dainius Zubrus, a Lithuanian center who had been playing Tier II in Pembroke, Ontario rather than for Laval, the Quebec league team that owned his Junior A rights.

Zubrus, who spoke four languages, had left Lithuania at age 11 to play in a higher level of hockey than existed in his home country.

While travelling with Druzhba '78, a barnstorming team, he had stayed in Great Neck, NY with former Cornell hockey star John Hughes, whose daughter Sarah would win the 2002 Olympic figure skating gold medal. Hughes had connections with the Pembroke owner, where Zubrus had billeted that season. "It was most comfortable for Dainius there," recalls his agent, Jay Grossman.

Clarke was less at ease with making Zubrus the first Tier II player taken in the top round of the draft since Rod Brind'Amour was selected ninth overall eight years earlier by St. Louis. Quebec scout Simon Nolet thought Zubrus had an advanced defensive game for his age, but had not been a consistent scorer.

"Listening to the scouts, Zubrus was a huge gamble," Clarke recalls. "One night he would get five points, the next he would get nothing, usually a bad sign about a player.

"But he already was over 200 pounds with all this skill and hockey smarts, so we took him."

Goalie Ron Hextall was hours from taking the Flyers to a contract arbitration hearing when his agent, Steve Mountain, and Clarke met in the middle at three years and $7 million. "I was under a lot of pressure from the players' association to sign for just one year (for higher dollars), but I did what was right for me," recalls Hextall. "I had a wife, kids and strong ties here and the Flyers had a chance to win."

Trent Klatt, who had played well on a checking line with fellow Minnesotans Otto and Shjon Podein through the 1996 playoffs, was signed for two years and $962,000. Defenseman Karl Dykhuis struck a multi-year deal that started at $262,000 per. After balking originally, Clarke acceded to defenseman Svoboda's wishes for security by giving him a three-year, $5 million contract.

Niinimaa, the organization's best defensive prospect, came to camp bulked up 24 pounds from when he had been drafted 36th overall in 1993. The Flyers expected him to reduce the offensive workload on Eric Desjardins, their cornerstone defenseman who had appeared worn down during the playoffs.

"I was not feeling my best; the whole playoffs I felt sick with the flu or something," Desjardins told reporters at camp. "It was a tough first series (against Tampa Bay) and it never got better, a big disappointment for me."

Like all other Flyer participants in the World Cup, he was given a week to rest up. Lindros, it turned out, needed more. On the first day his elbow allowed him to be on the ice, the captain's skate got tangled in Hextall's pads, causing a groin injury.

"I'm sitting around here like a fifth wheel, dying to get back on the ice," Lindros said as the team's disjointed camp continued. A cortisone shot taken before the opener didn't solve his problem, and the Flyers, 18-28-7 in games without The Big E over his first four seasons, would have to suck it up again.

"We should be used to this," said Murray. "That's the way it goes."

The coach also challenged his players to create a new home ice-advantage in their pristine and spacious new digs. "It's never going to be the Spectrum or have the same emotions, adrenaline and energy no matter what we want," said the coach before the opener with Florida. "What it becomes, I don't know, but we have a chance to go in and make it our building."

Fittingly, Zubrus, the youngest player ever to wear the orange-and-black at 18 years and 109 days, scored Philadelphia's first goal in the new palace. Just 13 seconds after the Panthers' Brad Smyth had christened the new nets with a backhander past Hextall, Zubrus—his place in the lineup created by a strong camp and the waiver-draft losses of Rob DiMaio and Bob Corkum—chased down a dump-in by Podein, fought off Ed Jovanovski with one arm, and put a shot in off goalie John Vanbiesbrouck's skate.

But Vanbiesbrouck, who had made the Flyers one of his victims during the Panthers climb to the 1996 Final, was sharp and Scott Mellanby broke a 1-1 tie in the second period. Florida, which had won the last Flyer game at the Spectrum, also spoiled the first one in their new home, with a 3-1 win before 19,137 fans.

"Everything was so nice and the locker room and arena so much bigger that even the ice seemed bigger too," recalls Podein. "The fans weren't on top of us anymore and a little bit of the coziness was gone.

"There had been nowhere to hide at the Spectrum, not for us or the visitors. The new building lost that neighborhood feel."

Two nights later, the Flyers trailed the Devils 1-0 into the third period when Brind'Amour scored shorthanded, then set up Dykhuis for the winning goal in a 3-1 victory. Brind'Amour's talents not only had created the first Flyer win in the CoreStates Center, but justified Clarke's reluctance in making the longest-serving Flyer part of a deal for Shanahan, who had asked out of Hartford soon after his trade there for Chris Pronger.

"Think about it, you can't trade Eric, Hexy, Rennie (Renberg) or Johnny, so who else are you going to talk about?" said Brind'Amour. "I understand."

Ed Snider didn't. "Those idiots on (sports radio station) WIP got people whipped into a frenzy talking about Shanahan like he's a free agent," ranted the Flyer Chairman. "They want a king's ransom for him."

Two days later, Shanahan was traded to Detroit in a multi-player deal that included Keith Primeau. Relieved or not, the next night Brind'Amour saved the Flyers, who had blown a 3-0 lead, with an overtime goal that beat Los Angeles, 4-3, before a CoreStates crowd 1,363 short of capacity. About 1,000 upper deck fans had to be moved down, some into premium seating, when a lighting overhang that was blocking their view couldn't be raised to its proper level.

The sight lines at the Spectrum still looked good to 9,161 who sat in the old arena watching the new Philadelphia Phantoms debut with a purple splash added to the traditional black, orange and white uniforms of their parent team. After the Phantoms mascot, Phlex, was lowered from the ceiling on a cable, coach Bill Barber's team beat Rochester, 3-1, in the first American Hockey League (AHL) game played in the city since 1979, when the Philadelphia Firebirds flew the coop.

"We have to be major-minor, we can't do it minor," said Phantoms' CEO John Wenzell.

At the rate the Flyers were becoming injured, the major team was having to do it minor. The season road debut was a 5-1 shellacking at the Nassau Coliseum. Otto and Svoboda were lost to injuries and then so was Dale Hawerchuk, who, despite an arthritic hip, had taken Lindros's place on the first line.

Lindros, rehabbing at home in Toronto, took a trip to Duke University to be reassured by specialist Dr. William Garrett that his groin problem would heal with rest. But the wait for No. 88 got even longer as all four centers went out at some point during the first month and Renberg struggled to come back from surgery to repair a complete tear of the abdominal muscles from the pubic bone. Murray juggled 14 line combinations, including moving the rookie Zubrus onto the first unit between Renberg and LeClair.

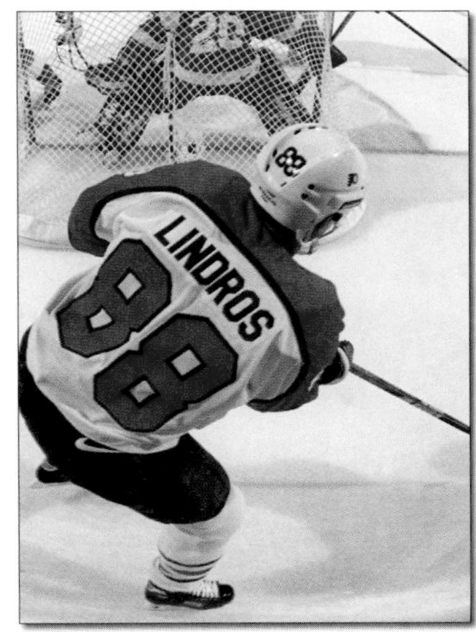

Eric Lindros was one of four centers injured early in 1996-97.

The lack of cohesion started to catch up with the defensive effort. Philadelphia gave up all three goals on odd-man rushes as Florida won again at CoreStates, 3-2.

Complaints about the new building's ice were ongoing. "It's been awful," said Clarke. But that was no excuse for rampant defensive breakdowns. LeClair, off to a slow start, scored on the powerplay early in the third period to tie a game 2-2 against the Capitals in Landover, MD, but the Flyers promptly gave up a breakaway to Steve Konowalchuk and, worse, had several players chase the rebound, leaving Jason Allison in front for the winning goal in a 4-2 loss.

The bright spot was the Minnesota Line. "Actually, the guys started to call us the 'Sorry Line' because when we came off the ice, one of us would apologize to the other for not doing better," recalls Podein. "We pushed ourselves every shift."

Klatt, whose tying and winning goals capped a comeback from a 3-0 deficit to a 4-3 win at Tampa, started another rally from a 2-0 hole in Miami as the Flyers beat their Panther nemeses, 3-2. Clarke was so impressed with Podein, he tore up a contract that had a year to go and raised him to $550,000, $600,000 and $650,000 over the next three seasons. "It's something they didn't have to do," said Podein. "Nice to know they give you a little positive incentive."

The Flyers again rallied from 2-0 to win their first-ever game at Buffalo's new Marine Midland Arena, 5-2. But they came home to have backup goalie Garth Snow chased in a 4-1 loss to the Blackhawks that dropped them back under .500. They were 3-5 in their new arena.

"All the history was at the Spectrum," recalls Desjardins. "This was different. At first I think everybody hated it."

Or they were getting too caught up in trying to be fancy. "Your road game is to be patient and work," Podein told the media. "Here, we're trying to make it exciting, but nothing is happening and we can't relax."

Hextall jacked the home crowd by going the length of the ice to fight Toronto goalie Felix Potvin, who had slashed Dan Lacroix in response to Lacroix crosschecking Larry Murphy. "I was so damn tired when I got to the other end," said Hextall, but he engaged Potvin regardless. Though bloodied by a head butt, Hexy retained enough strength to exit the ice pointing to the scoreboard before revealing he had left the house with strict orders from daughter Rebecca not to fight.

"Oops," Hextall grinned.

Before the goaltender drove off to face a stern rebuke from a five-year-old, Murray stepped up on the bench to lecture Leaf coach Mike Murphy for putting out tough guy Tie Domi to fight Daniels on the final shift. "Sometimes a little get-together is good for the hockey club," smiled Murray after the 3-1 victory.

The Flyers' new house already had a doghouse. Pat Falloon, the intensity-challenged right wing, was scratched for two games before returning to score in consecutive contests, the latter to beat the Rangers, 2-1, at Madison Square Garden. Win or lose, it already had been a good day though. Lindros had joined the Flyers for the morning skate.

"I feel like a kid in the candy store right now," he said. "No one wears a cape around this team, but there might be a spark (upon my return)."

As the Flyers counted the days until the big center's comeback, they went home to stink up their Taj Mahal in a 5-2 loss to Washington, and then squandered a 2-0 lead into a 2-2 tie with San Jose. LeClair, who scored both goals against the Sharks, was heating up, but other Flyers were trying too hard to score in Lindros's absence. Even the new scoreboard malfunctioned for a second time in the young season.

While the building's sound system was working fine, there seemed little enhancement by the fans, and not only because the Flyers were giving them so little to cheer about. "All the new rinks are quiet," said Hawerchuk. "The fan is afraid that if he watches the game, he'll miss something on the video scoreboard."

Thanks to the work of independent therapist John D'Amico, Hawerchuk produced some replays worth watching. The future Hall of Famer scored four goals for his first hat trick in five years in a 7-3 blowout of Pittsburgh.

The 12-10-1 Flyers were 4-1-1 in their last six when Lindros returned to the lineup on November 26 in Boston. After just 14 seconds, the Big E repaid a check from Sandy Moger, then laid crunching hits on several Bruins, including old teammate DiMaio. But Lindros gave the puck away on the second Boston goal, which was one more than their goalie Bill Ranford needed to stone Philadelphia 2-0.

"[Ranford] was out of this world," said Renberg, who was coming off sports hernia surgery and understood best what Lindros had gone through to get back on the ice.

"If you weren't on a bike or in a pool or having needles stuck in your leg, there wasn't much to do," conceded Eric. His rust was evident. So was a shortage of chemistry on the once-more reshuffled lines.

The new second unit of Brind'Amour, Hawerchuk and Zubrus was on for three goals against as the Flyers lost 4-1 on the road to the Islanders. But in Ottawa, Lindros's shot was converted on the rebound by a heretofore pressing Brind'Amour (minus-13 for the year) to tie the game. Zubrus, who had missed an earlier game in Montreal while returning to Lithuania to get papers, used his new Canadian visa to add his first goal since opening night as Philadelphia beat the Senators, 4-3.

Daniels, sparking a fourth line of three Dans—alongside Dan Lacroix and Dan Kordic—scored in the third period for the 4-3 win over Vancouver. This not only was becoming one of the most effective fourth lines in the NHL, but probably the most artistic, thanks to the cartoons of Lacroix, who had studied art at a college in Granby, Quebec, while playing junior there.

"I can do most any medium, but I'm not very good at any of them," said Lacroix. "By hockey-player standards, I might be decent, but at any college there's a lot more talent. I would much rather have a knack for accounting or something like that."

Renberg didn't need a CPA to inform him he had scored only three goals through the first 28 games. "I come [to the rink] a little tense," he told Tim Panaccio of *The Philadelphia Inquirer*. "You have to have scoring confidence to shoot, and when you don't, you're hesitant and give (the puck) off."

Yanick Dupre's battle with leukemia would claim him at age 24. An award in his memory is given each year to the Flyer who best illustrates character, dignity and respect for the game on and off the ice

He was yanked from the big line in favor of Hawerchuk, a move that immediately paid off when the veteran won a third-period draw and fed Lindros for his first goal of the season in a 1-1 tie at Madison Square Garden.

Four days later, while stretching on the ice after practice, Lindros reached for a water bottle just as Hextall rolled over and caught the goalie's skate blade in the forehead. Lindros immediately covered it with a towel, but blood began to spurt from a two-inch long cut. He had to be helped to the locker room by equipment manager Turk Evers and the few teammates who still were on the ice.

"I told him stay away from me," said Hextall the next day, "a long ways away from me." After receiving stitches, Lindros nevertheless skated that afternoon with his teammates' children at the team Christmas party.

The mood was improving. A 5-4 win over Florida—with Falloon, reinserted after another five consecutive scratches, contributing two assists—ended an 0-4-3 home winless streak against the Eastern Conference leaders. After being excused for four games while his wife suffered complications following the birth of their second child, defenseman Kevin Haller was reunited in a pairing with his old Montreal partner, Desjardins.

Any of the Flyers' travails no longer seemed so troubling during a pre-Christmas visit by Yanick Dupre.

Late the previous season, four months after scoring his first NHL goal in San Jose during one of three call-ups with the Flyers, the swift left-wing prospect—taken 50th in the 1990 draft—had begun playing sluggishly. "Bill Barber (the interim Hershey Bears coach) called me and said, 'You have to talk to Yanick, he's not hustling,'" recalls Dupre's former agent, Ron Weiss.

It progressively became clear that the problem was not attitudinal. "Yanick told me if he didn't set an alarm before dinner, he could sleep through an entire day," recalls then-Hershey GM Jay Feaster.

Dupre told his father Jacques that he was exhausted by the second half of his shifts and was being caught by even the slowest Bears during practice drills. Believing he might have mononucleosis, Dupre asked for a blood test. He was sent by the team physician, Dr. Kevin Black at the Hershey Medical Center, for a workup that yielded a shocking diagnosis—Dupre had acute myelogenous leukemia, a cancer of the blood that only 50 percent of diagnosed adults under age 45 survive for five or more years.

"The doctor called to tell me what it was," recalls Feaster. "I called (team president) Doug Yingst and we tracked down Billy and Yanick. We called Yanick into the office and told him."

"He was devastated. We were trying very hard not to be emotional for him and told him he would have the best doctors and the best of medical science. "But I don't know how much he heard."

The Bears, for whom Dupre had scored 70 goals and 99 assists over parts of four seasons, staged a bone marrow drive at Hershey Park Arena. Doctors at Hahnemann Hospital in Philadelphia, where the diagnosis was confirmed, recommended he undergo treatment at Hôpital Maisonneuve-Rosemont in Montreal, near his native Laval, Quebec, where, as part of the chemotherapy, Dupre was induced into a 16-day coma in order to slow a heart beating so fast that doctors compared it to the effects of running a marathon for a week.

"They told us every minute he was alive was a miracle," recalls Yanick's sister Nancy.

When Desjardins, who had taken the French-Canadian kid under his wing during call-ups totaling 36 games, visited Dupre after the Flyers' playoff elimination, there was a tube in his throat and only one eye functioned. The treatments had so devastated his once-sculpted body that Yanick's father Jacques ordered the mirrors removed or covered in the hospital room so as not to discourage his son.

But the chemo was successful. After September, when many Flyers had visited while the team was in Montreal for an exhibition game, Dupre's progress became astounding. Released from the hospital on Halloween, he had put on 40 pounds and was doing light workouts.

"I never thought I would get back to this," said Dupre, Desjardins' houseguest for a holiday visit to Philadelphia. "In May, I weighed 148 pounds and my body was refusing everything my mind was telling it to do.

"I was pretty much a vegetable. I feel great right now."

Desjardins told Bowen that when the Flyers had visited Allegheny University of the Health Sciences in Center City Philadelphia on a recent publicity tour for the Flyers' Wives Carnival, the defenseman saw a patient who had "looked so much like Yanick when he was in bad shape that I had to stop looking at the guy and walk away.

"Last night we were talking and suddenly I realized that we were finally just able to talk about normal things instead of Yanick's health. That was a great thing."

So great, it made all other things inconsequential. "Things don't bother me," Dupre said. "Life is simple."

Even the idea of returning to the game didn't seem overly complicated. At an upcoming January appointment, Dupre hoped to be cleared to work out more strenuously. "When you have been through something like that," said Desjardins, "I think you can accomplish a lot."

Indeed, a scoring slump was just a scoring slump. Renberg broke a 12-game goalless streak with two in a 6-3 win over Dallas. "The pressure is gone now," he declared. The Flyers increasingly were getting out of their own way. But Clarke still worried about them getting out of their own end, so he bought one of the best tickets ever.

On December 15, Philadelphia obtained Paul Coffey, the most prolific scoring defenseman in the game's history, from Hartford.

"A player who's played as long as he has will help and he'll be good in the locker room," said Clarke, specifically citing the mentoring the 35-year-old three-time Norris Trophy winner could do for Niinimaa. "Everybody I've talked to says Coffey is a real good team player."

The GM, who gave Hartford first and seventh-round picks in 1997 and also was receiving a third-round pick in 1997, was taking on a contract that had two-plus years and more than $7 million remaining. The top pick was expendable, Clarke felt, because the Flyers, who would be picking near the end of the first round, had a probable high No. 2 pocketed as part of the 1995 deal that had sent Dmitry Yushkevich to Toronto. And because Coffey had produced 74 points the previous season at Detroit, the GM prepared to tolerate his latest star's defensive indifference.

"Why would you want a guy that good on offense to play defense?" Clarke says today.

Haller, an Albertan whose wife badly wanted for him to play in Western Canada, was not happy to go to Hartford, even though the Whalers were unexpectedly holding first place in the Northeast Division. Coffey, skeptical of their progress during the two months since his acquisition in a trade for Shanahan, had made it clear he wanted out.

"Hartford was tough," he told Philadelphia reporters upon his arrival at the CoreStates Center between periods of a 6-0 blowout of Boston, the Flyers' eighth consecutive game without a loss. "Some of the guys couldn't figure out why I didn't want to play there when they were doing so well and a lot of times I couldn't explain it.

"They have good ownership, good people running it. But they didn't have the background or the hockey tradition for me to end my career there. I've had a chance to play with Wayne (Gretzky in Edmonton) and Mario (Lemieux in Pittsburgh) and now I consider myself a lucky guy (to play with Lindros)."

It saved Coffey a hotel bill or apartment rental, too. Having gotten friendly with Lindros as a World Cup teammate, No. 77 moved into No. 88's house.

"I'm ecstatic," said the gracious host. And Niinimaa--"He was my idol," said the rookie—wasn't the only Flyer joyous at the prospect of coming from behind the play as defenses backed up in fear of one of the fastest skaters the game ever had known. Desjardins, playing almost 30 minutes a game, could take a lesser role on the team's disappointing, 24th-ranked, powerplay. Coffey's setups figured to be more exacting than what Lindros and LeClair had been receiving from the points.

Two nights later, against the Islanders, Coffey fanned on his first attempt. But Lindros took a pass from the new Flyer to set up a goal by Niinimaa, and then worked a give-and-go that enabled the Big E to put in a Coffey rebound. "That's why he's here," said Lindros after Coffey's three assists enabled a two-goal, two-assist game from Lindros, one of the most dominant performances of his five-season career.

The Big E was the poster boy for the NHL's largest team, averaging 6-foot-2 and 210 pounds.

"That's where the new (Three Dan) line has made a difference," said Murray. "They are like a loaded gun.

"Last year, teams went right at Lindros and his line to wear them down. As an opposing player, you notice [the opposition's size] in the warmup. "

At 6-3, Hextall filled enough of the net to never have felt he needed extra coverage from equipment. With that 5-0 win over the Islanders, No. 250 in his career, the goalie met the December 15 deadline for using the NHL's newly-mandated 12-inch pads.

"Pads are pads," shrugged Hextall, who was losing only ¾ of an inch off his previous version, less than most goalies, including Snow. But Hextall's back-up seemed unfazed, too, in a 4-0 win over St. Louis that stretched the Flyer shutout streak to four games.

"Crazy, I've never experienced anything like this," said LeClair. The next night, the streak—it wasn't verifiable in minutes as one of the longest in league history because records weren't keep during the low-scoring 1920s—ended in Chicago at 265:08 on a goal by Jeff Shantz. But Lindros's two scores forged a 2-2 tie that extended Philadelphia's unbeaten streak to 11 and moved the team into first place ahead of the Panthers.

High scoring defenseman Paul Coffey joined the Flyers in a trade from Hartford of December 15, 1996. He would record nine points in 17 playoff games in 1997.

"I told [Lindros] the other day, this is the best I've seen him since I've been here," Murray said. "And it has nothing to do with scoring points."

Hawerchuk, who had accumulated more points than all but 10 players in NHL history, passed Gilbert Perreault with goal No. 513, one of four straight the Flyers scored to overcome a 4-2 deficit for a 6-4 win in Edmonton. LeClair had two of them, then two more two nights later in a 4-2 victory at Calgary that stretched the streak to 13, the Flyers' longest since a 14-gamer (12-0-2) in 1987.

"It hasn't been one or two guys," said Hawerchuk, playing with a hot Klatt and Brind'Amour while a third line of Podein, Otto, and Falloon was scoring consistently, too. "I played so many years in a frustrating situation (in Winnipeg) and this is a genuine opportunity.

"We're starting to really believe in ourselves."

Through Snow (a 5-3 win while a blizzard raged outside in Vancouver), torrential rain (during Hextall's 4-1 win in San Jose) and, finally, the gloom of a 4-2 third-period deficit in Denver, the Flyers rallied for a 4-4 tie against the Stanley Cup champion Avalanche to complete their six-game holiday journey undefeated.

"It would have been so easy to sit back and say, 'We've had a great trip,'" praised Murray. "Our character is coming out.

"You are going to have to call on something more than talent later in the season."

Fog in Philadelphia caused the Flyer charter home to make a stop in the wee hours in Pittsburgh. Many of the players stretched their legs in the airport concourse, then two nights later stretched the streak to 17 by scoring four times in the first 14:13 of a 7-3 CoreStates Center blasting of Boston.

"It was so easy to play the game, you almost had the feeling that you couldn't lose," recalls Desjardins of the hottest stretch one of his teams ever enjoyed.

Not just figuratively, but literally, the Flyers were feeling no pain. In that Boston win, Chris Therien, who had been scratched for 11 of 14 games, had gotten back into the lineup when Kjell Samuelsson suffered a neck injury in Calgary. Therien was jostling with the Bruins' Rick Tocchet when he accidentally put his stick though the eye slit of Hextall's mask. Nine stitches and 5:53 later, Hextall came back to finish up the game. "A little blood never hurt anybody," he said.

The streak was ended at 17 (14-0-3) in a 3-1 home ice loss to Tampa Bay, which in the process also stopped Lindros from recording a point in his 18th straight game, one short of Clarke's team record. But Philadelphia started another five-game run with a comeback 3-3 tie against the Capitals, then downed Montreal, 3-2, when Coffey, returning to the lineup for the first time since becoming concussed in a collision with Lindros at Vancouver, scored with 45 seconds remaining.

Samuelsson wasn't as fortunate. He underwent surgery for a herniated neck disk that increasingly robbed him of strength in his left arm. So the Flyers became the ninth NHL team of Michel Petit, a defenseman Clarke 10 years earlier had tried to obtain for Brad McCrimmon, now available on a waiver claim from Edmonton.

Gary Bettman made Hawerchuk, who had not been an All-Star since 1988, the Commissioner's Selection for the All-Star Game at San Jose. Mario Lemieux's acknowledgement that this probably was his last classic forced Lindros to answer questions about replacing Mario as the league's new standard bearer. "Everybody keeps talking about this torch," smiled Eric. "I've never, ever seen this torch."

LeClair had a chance to take one from legendary 100-mph-plus blaster Al MacInnis in the hardest shot contest but instead became the only person in the competition to miss the net. "The net moved and the ice was bad," LeClair joked before admitting, "Pathetic, just pathetic."

Lacroix agreed. When LeClair returned from the weekend, the artist-winger parodied LeClair's aim with a cartoon of him toppling a cameraman in the corner and posted the art on the way to the shower.

Renberg, a caricature of his old, confident, self as he struggled to recover his old skating burst, was dropped from the line with Lindros and LeClair by Murray. "To me Mikael seems more relaxed playing with Otto and Podein right now," said the coach. "He'll calm down, get a couple of things going and be back on the regular line soon."

Hextall's heroics enabled the Flyers to pull out a come-from-behind 2-2 tie in Detroit. But Philadelphia lost not only the second game of the home-and-home with the Red Wings, 4-1, but Svoboda to an injury. Still looking for a shutdown pairing, Murray, impressed with the play of the thinned-down, rededicated Therien, put him with Desjardins in the following game, the same night the coach experimented with new forward lines. Voila! Renberg fed Podein for one goal and Zubrus set up Lindros for another as the Flyers outshot Phoenix 55-18 in a 4-1 victory.

"Sometimes change is good," Renberg rationalized. Indeed, it appeared this new Therien-Desjardins pairing was a master stroke, but one good thing that never varied was a Philadelphia lineup containing the remarkable Brind'Amour. In the win over the Coyotes, he broke Rick MacLeish's Flyer franchise record by playing in his 288th straight game, bringing Iron Rod's participation to 581 games out of a possible 587 since being acquired in 1991 from the Blues.

The person least impressed was Brind'Amour. "Those ironman streaks don't mean that much to me," he said. "If you're healthy, you are supposed to play.

"If I get up around 500 or 600, that would be amazing."

His shot off Otto's skate with 1:55 to play gave Philadelphia a 1-1 tie with Buffalo, rewarding Snow for a grand duel against Dominik Hasek. "He's the best in the world as far as I'm concerned," said Lindros, meaning Hasek as a goalie, not a fighter. When Snow went after Michael Peca for having thrown Coffey into the net, Hasek tried to help, only to have his mask torn off by the feisty Flyer backup goaltender.

Ultimately unable to disguise his sense of displacement, Renberg was put back with Lindros and LeClair as the latter had four goals and two assists in a 9-5 win over Montreal, Renberg and Lindros each contributing a goal and four assists. "They were happy to be reunited, I guess," said the coach.

The 16 points by the threesome were the most a Flyer line had ever

scored in a game, breaking the mark of 14 set by Bill Barber, Darryl Sittler and Ilkka Sinisalo in January 1983 at Hartford. LeClair stretched his goal total against the Canadiens to 14 in 10 games since they traded him to Philadelphia.

"It's nice if a big moment can happen against a team you played for," said LeClair. "Montreal isn't forgotten but isn't the first thing on my mind. It's been two years; a lot has changed."

At least one thing had not. The Devils, against whom the Flyers had won just two of the last nine season series, took advantage of Lindros being tossed from the faceoff circle and LeClair losing the draw. The ensuing goal by Valeri Zelepukin started New Jersey's comeback from a 2-1 deficit to a 4-2 victory, the first time all season Philadelphia dropped a game it had led in the third period.

Hawerchuk caught a skate in a rut during a 4-2 win over Ottawa, reinjuring his hip. In Pittsburgh, where the Flyers had not won in 14 games (0-10-4), they spotted the Penguins two goals, then roared back to a 6-2 victory without Lindros, who was sidelined with a back strain, not that his reason for absence was believed by Craig Carton, a talk show host on WIP.

When Carton reported two weeks later that Lindros had been held out with a hangover, both the team and their captain did more than just heatedly deny the report. The Flyers filed a document declaring their intention to sue the station in Common Pleas Court and Snider said he would look into buying out the remaining one year-plus of WIP's contract to broadcast Flyer games.

"If management and ownership won't support their players, then you don't really have a team, just a bunch of people playing hockey," said Clarke. "It happened to be Eric this time but if it was any other player we would do the same."

Lindros said he appreciated the support. After being called a drunk on the radio, he then was accused of "showboating" by the Sabres' Peca after a tough Flyer loss in Buffalo. Retreating behind the Philadelphia net instead of clearing the puck while killing an overtime penalty, Lindros had handed Peca the winning goal.

Lindros had no comment about the insult. But Brind'Amour had been so upset that he was not on the penalty kill that he exchanged angry words with Murray on the bench at the game's end.

"I killed every penalty," Brind'Amour recalls. "That was my job, and taking that faceoff was not what Eric did at the time.

"He lost and it wound up in our net. I was so mad. I said something to the effect of, 'What the [bleep] was that?' and [Murray] got in my face. I hadn't done that before or after to a coach."

Murray had a talk with Brind'Amour in the morning. "It's sorted out," the coach said. "I want players like that who want to be on the ice at key times of the game."

Brind'Amour, too, said he had no hard feelings. But with the trade deadline approaching and his versatility making him an ongoing much-desired commodity, he admitted to being frustrated by more than just one failure to be used on an overtime penalty kill.

"Two years ago in the playoffs, my line played really well," he said. "Ever since then they always seem to be moving in centers.

"It would be nice to have a line and just play. I have been through a lot here, would like to see it through."

Certainly Klatt, his current linemate, had no desire to see Brind'Amour move on. He had a hat trick in a 5-5 tie in Boston, while Harry Sinden, the Bruin boss, was turning down the advances of Clarke to reacquire Tocchet. Boston instead traded the former Flyer to Washington in a six-player deal.

Trade rumors also swirled about Philadelphia's interest in goalie Felix Potvin, but Hextall, who had given up 10 goals in his last two starts, bounced back with a shutout of Washington. The deadline passed with Clarke not making any changes in his goaltending. "Our team has to play better defense," he said.

When Lindros missed a March 8 game in Pittsburgh with a hip bruise, the Flyers called up Vaclav Prospal, the AHL's No. 3 scorer. The third-round pick in the 1993 draft scored twice in a 3-2 loss and moved in as center on an improved second line with Brind'Amour and Falloon.

Meanwhile, the first line exploded at Maple Leaf Gardens. Lindros scored four times, including the tying and go-ahead goals 1:12 apart, as Philadelphia overcame three one-goal deficits in a 6-3 victory. "Won the game all by himself," said LeClair. "He was head and shoulders above anybody else on the ice."

As unlucky as he was dominant, Lindros limped out of the lineup again with a knee tweak due to a clip by the Islanders' Rich Pilon. Nevertheless the Flyers shut out the defending champion Avalanche 2-0 and the revived Renberg recorded his 31st point in his last 24 games the game-winner in a 5-4 match at New Jersey. But his star, too, remained crossed. Four games later, Renberg fell in the course of interfering with Randy Cunneyworth off the opening faceoff and had his face kicked by the Ottawa winger's skate.

Oral surgeon John Burke administered 200 mostly internal stitches to Renberg's chin, cheek and jaw, the majority of which were performed at Cooper University Hospital following an ambulance ride. "Like a surgeon's scalpel," Flyer physician Dr. Gary Dorshimer described the cut. "It's as bad as I have seen and I have been with the team since 1984."

The next day Renberg conceded the outcome could have been far worse. "My helmet got knocked backwards and I think my visor might have kept the skate from going up into my eye," he told reporters. "I'm glad I'm a guy with a wife and kid who doesn't have to worry about how he looks."

No reporter asked Stina, Renberg's wife of less than a year, if she shared that opinion. But looking better, finally, after repeated benchings was Falloon, who had scored his second game winner in the 2-1 win while Renberg was being repaired. "I've said this before, we need a hot stick from Pat Falloon," said Murray. "We've got to get scoring from our second line."

After the Flyers had lost in the second playoff round despite winning the division championship the previous year, their coach had insisted all season that winning the Atlantic was a low priority. But as his team went into April neck and neck with the hot Devils, Murray said he wanted to go for it.

Philadelphia's chances took a hit when Lindros retaliated for a shove by the Rangers' Alexander Karpovtsev by crosschecking the defenseman into the crossbar. The captain then used the shaft of his stick to break Shane Churla's nose, taking a double minor during which the Rangers scored twice in rallying from a 2-0 deficit to a 3-2 win at Madison Square Garden. At the buzzer, the steaming Lindros crosschecked the infernally aggravating Ulf Samuelsson in the face.

"We completely lost our composure, showed no maturity as a team," said Brind'Amour.

The next day, Murray called a meeting where he made clear the Flyers had to be initiators, not retaliators. Although he pleaded through the media for more calls of fouls committed against Lindros, the coach also decried publicly his captain's loss of discipline.

"That shove (into the goal frame) is something you're going to see 40 times maybe in an 82-game season," said Murray. "It's nothing that requires that level of reaction."

For the crosscheck to Churla, the league required Lindros to sit for two games and lose $100,000 in pay. Having expressed remorse after the game—"That's not a position I want to put the rest of the team in,"—Eric had no comment on the suspension. "It doesn't do a lot of good to express bad feelings," he said. But Hextall summed up the Flyers' sentiments.

"I don't think there is a player on our team who doesn't want to stick up for Eric Lindros, but he's 6-4, 230 pounds," said the goalie. "He hits people and he's going to be hit.

"For a guy to knock Eric over, it's a feather in his cap. You get your whole bench going by doing that. The big thing is that it's the retaliators who sit in the box. In the playoffs, we'll be in trouble if we think like that."

Without Lindros, Renberg and Hawerchuk, the latter struggling again with his hip after coming back from a 14-game recuperation, Philadelphia also lost the second game of the home-and-home to the Rangers, 6-3. But the bigger problem in that contest was five softies allowed by a slumping Hextall.

Murray turned to Snow, who was sharp in a 3-3 tie in Game 81 in Montreal that made New Jersey the division titlist. But for the following night's season finale against the Devils, the coach went back to Hextall, who was beaten on the first two shots and four of his first 11 before being yanked.

LeClair joined Tim Kerr as the only Flyer to score 50 goals in back-to-back seasons, helping the team rally for a 5-4 victory. But as LeClair was presented his first Bobby Clarke Trophy as Flyer MVP and Desjardins his third consecutive Barry Ashbee Trophy as the team's best defenseman, the honor of Game One goalie for a three vs. six matchup against Pittsburgh had to be determined.

"I'm not going to discount all of the play from Ron Hextall over the year," said Murray. "One game or one period is not going to make a difference in my decision."

But the coach admits today it really did. "It had been Hexy up until that game," recalls Murray. "He had won a Conn Smythe Trophy and that was always on my mind.

"Hexy had some physical issues by the time he came back to the Flyers; his game was a little sideways and a lot of work had to be done to get some of the basics back again. Still, he was so competitive, would do anything for the team, and was so unbelievable handling the puck that he relieved the pressure, calming down the pretty young defense we had then.

"But he was fighting the puck late in the season."

Murray promised to inform both goalies at a Tuesday team dinner preceding Thursday's Game One, until Hextall pressed for a decision after that day's practice. Murray said Snow, 9-0 in his last nine starts, was the pick for Game One.

"You want to be playing well going into the playoffs, but if you look at the history, you don't have to," Hextall says today. "In 1987, I gave up nine goals in the regular season's last game and we played after that for two months."

In going 33-12-12 from late November on to finish with 103 points, one fewer than New Jersey, the Flyer goaltending had been adequate to good. Despite winning only two of its last six contests, the team was heading into the playoffs with a sense of destiny.

"People were expecting Eric to be what Lemieux had been and Gretzky had been before him," recalls Therien. "We all felt Eric had arrived and that we were fortunate to be in Philadelphia playing with him.

"The big disappointment losing to Florida (in 1996) had led to even higher expectations. We had good players everywhere."

Renberg dressed for Game One at the CoreStates Center wearing a wraparound mask that made it difficult to find the puck in his feet. Lindros had no such problem. Early in the contest, when he had the stick knocked from his hands by Pittsburgh's Ian Moran along the backboards, the captain controlled the puck in his skates for 38 seconds. When LeClair brought his linemate another stick, Lindros kept the puck some more, an ominous sequence for the much smaller Penguins.

His team up 1-0 on a goal by Falloon, Lindros crashed into Darius Kasparaitis and fed LeClair, who scored 39 seconds into the second. Brind'Amour put his own rebound past Ken Wregget and, when the Penguins surged following a goal by Petr Nedved, Snow made a sliding save on Mario Lemieux to preserve a 3-1 lead. Lindros added a power-play goal as the Flyers rolled 5-1, to christen the CoreStates Center's first playoff game with a performance that wasn't missing anything except perhaps more decibels from a crowd the loyalists accused of having become corporate and dispassionate.

"Ninety-six to 97 percent of the fans came from the Spectrum with us," said Spectacor CEO Peter Luukko. "The building doesn't hold the noise as well."

To Murray, there was too much clamor from the media about his goaltending choices. "I'm not going to talk about starting goaltenders again—ever," he huffed, forming a policy that he carried forward for much of his coaching career.

"I always thought pre-scouting was so important at that position," Murray recalls. "But now, you can get the last 100 shots at any goalie within 15 seconds on a computer so I don't see reason any more for secrecy."

Hextall, who in good health had previously been denied only one playoff start in his career—for the Islanders in 1994—made no waves in the locker room. "It's difficult for me, I'm not going to lie," said the veteran. "But it's pretty darn hard to argue. Garth played great."

He did again in Game Two. Lemieux's goal held up as the only one through two periods. Then, after Otto tipped home a Niinimaa drive, the retiring Penguin star fed Jaromir Jagr, who dragged Desjardins 30 feet to put Pittsburgh up again, 2-1 in the third period. LeClair quickly tied the game, however, and Klatt fought through traffic to bloop one off Wregett's stick and in off the crossbar with 6:20 remaining. Snow preserved the 3-2 victory with a good stick save on Jason Woolley.

Pittsburgh coach Craig Patrick had put his Grade A Jumbo eggs—Jagr, Lemieux and Ron Francis—all in one basket. But the defensive pair assigned to them, Desjardins and Therien, was not cracking. As for the other matchups, men were dominating boys. "I don't think we're going to grow overnight," said Pittsburgh coach Craig Patrick resignedly.

The Penguins were going home to an arena where the Flyers had been 1-11-4 going back six-plus seasons. But Philadelphia made itself at home quickly in Game Three, firing a record—for regular-season or playoffs—28 shots at Wregget in the first period. Because of two goals by Jagr, all that work nevertheless left the Flyers behind 2-1. Still, they lost no sense of their inevitability.

"You can't get frustrated when you're doing pretty much what the game plan says you should do," said Lindros. "Sooner or later, something was going to happen."

Indeed, Falloon pounced on a broken-down Dykhuis shot to tie the game and Lindros scored off a steal by Renberg to put Philadelphia ahead, 3-2. LeClair pounded the fourth goal past Wregget just before the winger was pounded into the goal by Craig Muni. With a team playoff record 53 shots on goal, the Flyers went on to a 5-3 victory and a 3-0 lead in the series.

"In the third period, they were a lot stronger than we are," said Jagr, who had four of the six Pittsburgh goals in the series. Meanwhile, there were only two Flyers—Coffey and Svoboda—who had not scored a point.

"Lemieux could barely bend over to tie his skates so we really went after him," recalls Podein. "We were pretty methodical in keeping Lemieux and Jagr out of the middle."

Mario, indeed, sounded weary. "We have to be realistic, we're down 3-0 to one of the biggest, strongest, teams in the league, "said Lemieux, sounding like he had one foot out the door.

But not two. In Game Four, Eddie Olczyk made Snow pay for the goalie's giveaway up the slot, and a Dykhuis turnover on the powerplay led to a Nedved breakaway shorthanded goal. But though the Penguins, leading 3-1 deep into the third period, appeared on their way to a Game Five, the Pittsburgh fans were not going to take a chance on a Game Six to say goodbye to *le Magnifique*.

No sooner had they risen to say thank you, when Lemieux got behind Therien. "I am unfortunately hinged to that video clip for the remainder of time," smiles Therien today. Lemieux took a pass from Moran and went in alone on Snow.

"Did you think, 'Oh my God?'" the goalie was asked afterward.

"Every time he comes down, it's 'Oh my God!'" said Snow, who had forced Lemieux to shoot wide on a second-period breakaway. Not this time. Mario put away the 4-1 Pittsburgh win through the goalie's legs.

"It was perfect," said Patrick after the organ had serenaded Lemieux with "Simply the Best" and headwear thrown on the ice celebrated the first-ever one-goal hat trick. "Simply perfect."

The ovation went on for five minutes. "When I came off I started crying, the only time in my career I did that," Lemieux said afterwards. "I was struggling a little tonight but to get a great opportunity like that one-on-one with the goaltender, I'll take that any day.

"Maybe we can come back [for Game Six]. This gives us a little confidence."

The Flyers could appreciate their role in one of the great farewells in NHL history. But disappointed that their level of play had dropped a notch from the first three games, they thought the theatrics needed to end.

At least Lindros did. He won the opening draw of Game Five, raced into the Pittsburgh zone and put in his own rebound after just 14 seconds, the second-fastest opening goal in Flyer playoff history (Terry Murray scored on a misplay of a dump-in off the opening faceoff at Quebec in 1981).

On just three first-period Pittsburgh shots, Lemieux and Kevin Hatcher gave the Penguins a 2-1 lead. When Svoboda went off for slashing, Pittsburgh had a chance for more before Brind'Amour broke out twice, scoring electrifying shorthanded goals 54 seconds apart by victimizing Woolley, then Fredrik Olausson. No longer was anything disappointing about the sound level of the CoreStates Center.

Klatt, LeClair and Prospal added goals as the Philadelphia cruised, 6-3, reaching the second round for the third-straight spring while their fans reached an unprecedented level of magnanimity. They chanted "Mario! Mario!" in standing tribute as he was named the only star of the game.

In the handshake line, Lemieux, one of the two most anticipated No. 1 draft picks in NHL history, told, Lindros, the other: "Now is the time to go out and win this year."

"It's hard in 15 or 20 seconds to say exactly how you feel," Lindros told the media. He meant about Lemieux, not about Eric's chances to make Mario a prophet.

The Flyers' depth and size had made Pittsburgh a relatively easy mark. "We got overpowered," said Lemieux. But while preparing for the second-round series with a better-balanced Sabre team that had six 20-goal scorers, an important piece of Philadelphia's scoring machine was lost.

Prospal, who had centered a line with Brind'Amour and Falloon to 11 goals in the 12 games they had been together (regular season and playoffs), tried during a scrimmage to squeeze past Therien and Niinimaa along the boards but caught his hand between the two defenders' sticks and suffered a broken wrist that would leave him out for the duration of the playoffs.

"Prospal makes the people around him better," said a dejected Clarke. "He's very competitive, very enthusiastic, will be important to this organization for a long time."

"This is why you have depth; I'll be ready," said Hawerchuk who had played sparingly against Pittsburgh after being limited to 51 games during the regular season. "The last week I have been able to get it to another level."

Despite ending the season 11 points superior to Buffalo, the Flyers, second-place Atlantic Division finishers, would not have home-ice advantage against the Northeast Division champions. Still, that disadvantage was more than erased by the absence of Hasek, the Sabres' all-world goalie. He was suspended for Game One by the NHL for tearing the shirt of Buffalo writer Jim Kelley, who had questioned the veracity of a Hasek knee injury.

In his absence, Steve Shields had brought the Sabres back from a 3-2 series deficit against Ottawa. But the Flyers, of course, were happy to take their chances with the backup. And Snow figured Buffalo wasn't too sorry to see him, either. He had scuffled with three Sabres goalies, enforcer Robert Ray and pest Matthew Barnaby over the last two seasons.

"I'm sure they are going to try and get me going," predicted Snow.

Sure enough, with Philadelphia trailing 2-1 in Game One, Snow was assessed an extra two minutes as the aggressor in a punch-out with Shields. Donald Audette cashed in on the powerplay. But after Buffalo's Garry Galley was called for interfering with Otto just 10 seconds before the end of the second period, Coffey knocked down a clearing attempt and fed Renberg, whose shot went off the rear end of Richard Smehlik as the buzzer sounded.

Renberg went to the locker room assuming the goal did not count, until the replay proved there were 4/10 of a second on the clock when the puck crossed the line. Thus, the Flyers trailed only 3-2.

Ten minutes into the third period, Falloon stole the puck from Ray in the neutral zone and Brind'Amour put a Hawerchuk setup through Shields' pads. It stayed tied after an apparent go-ahead goal by Ray was disallowed because of a man in the crease. With under a minute on the clock, Klatt worked the puck free behind the net, fought off Alexei Zhitnik, and, with Shields expecting a walkout on the short side, instead fed Podein.

Podein came out the other side, scored easily on a wraparound, and leaped a full foot in the air. Brind'Amour hit the empty net and Philadelphia, though largely outplayed, escaped with a 5-3 win.

"Personnel-wise, we're pretty close to what we were last year," said Brind'Amour. "But being there before is the difference that helps in every situation.

"If you look at the teams that are left, will people be surprised if we end up winning? I don't think so. And that's all you can really ask for."

In a figurative sense, the favored role was putting a lot on the Flyers' shoulders. The Sabres complained about what else might be up there under Snow's jersey, never mind that the NHL's only pad restrictions were on what goalies strapped to their legs.

"I wasn't so sure if they brought up a goalie from Philadelphia's lacrosse team or something," said coach Ted Nolan on the off day before Game Two. "I was kind of glad that Shields made sure it was Snow under there (during the fight)."

He complained that the Sabres had been denied two goals because of "pieces of wood" in Snow's jersey. When reporters were allowed into the Flyers' room, the pads were not hanging in the goalie's locker.

"They are down in the wood shop," Snow deadpanned. "We have two-by-fours inside them."

He enjoyed the joke smug in the knowledge of being inside the Sabres' heads. "I assumed they couldn't see the net," Snow recalls. "It just gave me that much more confidence."

So he told ESPN tales about the family's roofing-supply company in Wrentham, MA. "Shingles," Snow said, letting the Sabres use their own imaginations before he flexed his biceps for the cameras. "That's just muscle," the goalie added. "We have a better strength program than they do."

Less heat, however, in the locker room. Murray complained that the visitor's room at Marine Midland Arena was being kept too cool to dry his team's sweat-soaked gear.

"It started before the series, when we had forgotten a piece of equipment (for call-up Colin Forbes)," said Turk Evers, then the Flyer equipment manager. "I had gone down to the Sabres locker room to use the phone to have the stuff sent—this was in the days before cell phones—and was told that I was not allowed in there on orders of the coach.

"Teams always had co-operated before over stuff like that."

Rip Simonick, the Buffalo equipment manager, recalls that the

Buffalo's Darryl Shannon and Flyer left wing Shjon Podein both scramble to get back into the play

Sabres produced building records proving the heat was on overnight in the visiting locker room. "After they complained, I felt their stuff and it was damp, but not completely soaked," Simonick remembers. "I don't know, did they forget to turn up the thermostat and blame us?"

Clarke believes it was a scheme of Nolan's orchestration. "Not my idea," recalls Nolan, although he believes it was a good one.

"I didn't have anything to do with it," he insists with a smile. "I wish I would have, though. I loved it."

The morning after Game One, which ended close to 11 p.m., the Flyers were given earlier-than-usual practice times at Marine Midland Arena. "It's a stupid game their coach or GM (John Muckler) wants to play," said Murray. "They'll get the same skating time in our arena."

Peca, a premier defensive center drawing Lindros duty, would get no skating time at all in Game Two, thanks to a bad back. Replacement Wayne Primeau promptly gave up the puck to LeClair, and Renberg put in a second rebound to give Philadelphia a 1-0 lead. Soon after, Therien walked out and beat Shields with another stuffer. Buffalo's Jason Dawe was alone at the post to cut the lead in half, but Snow preserved the 2-1 win by sliding across to stop Derek Plante.

The best save by Snow had been against Brind'Amour, who had been bumped trying to make a clear and instead put the puck on his own goal. But the Flyers had been much sharper than in Game One, including in the discipline department, as Lindros skated away from provocations by Ray and Barnaby.

"I wish I could wear No. 88, I could run around and do everything I want," said Barnaby. "Now, whether that is preferential treatment, I can't say."

Coffey had no special pass to put a foot on the other side of the red line during the warmup for Game Three at CoreStates. For that transgression, he was given a warning whack by Barnaby. Coffey responded by setting up Lindros from the left boards, and then Hawerchuk up the middle, to put the Philadelphia ahead 2-0.

The Sabres' Darryl Shannon cashed an Otto giveaway on the powerplay before Brind'Amour, crisscrossing with Falloon, beat Shields late in the second period to make it 3-1. Desjardins hit the empty net to give the Flyers, 4-1 winners, a commanding 3-0 series lead.

"I felt pretty young until I came in and looked in the mirror," said Coffey, nearly 36, following his three-assist effort.

Just a little senior humor, but the last laugh was on Barnaby, who took three minors amidst mocking chanting of his name. Asked if these same haters would love him as a Flyer, Barnaby agreed. "They are a big team, I'd be pretty good," he said. "I could say some pretty mean things."

The morning of Game Four, when a few of the Buffalo players tried to skate at the CoreStates Center, the magnets to hold the nets in place had been removed and the lights suddenly went out. Jay McKee taped a flashlight to his helmet and skated in the semi-darkness.

With just one more Philadelphia win, the Sabres would be out of both gamesmanship and games. Hasek wasn't going to be there to save them. He quit the pregame warmup after just eight minutes, saying his knee didn't feel right.

Buffalo handed the Flyers 9:19 of powerplay time in the final 13:01 of the first period. Nevertheless, going to the third period, Philadelphia, with a goal by LeClair disallowed on a charge of crease interference even though the replay showed he had touched the puck before it entered the net, led only 2-1.

The Sabres started to play, requiring the Flyers to score rebound goals by Klatt and Renberg to twice fight back for a 4-4 tie. In overtime, Galley, who had taken consecutive penalties with the game tied, intercepted a clear after the Legion of Doom line—Lindros, LeClair and Renberg—had prematurely left the zone and Snow pushed a rebound right onto the stick of Ed Ronan. In 18 games that season, he had scored only once, but Ronan banked the winner off the struggling Snow 6:24 into overtime.

"I remember being really pissed off," recalls Podein. "We hadn't tried our hardest."

Two series out of two, Philadelphia had failed to put away a sweep.

"We lacked the killer instinct all that year, stepped back and let the other team push back," recalls Murray. The Flyers, outshooting the Sabres 43-20 and having a good goal disallowed, had been as unlucky as they had been sloppy. Still, they had to go back to Buffalo, where Larry Quinn, CEO of the Sabres, was waiting to help the Flyer equipment staff hang their gear.

Hextall had been hanging for 28 days when Murray took him down and put him in goal for Game Five.

"After a long layoff or injury, I have tended to be anxious in the past," the goalie said. "But I've really learned to tell myself to just go out there and play."

The Sabres' inability to get the puck to him during a scoreless first period didn't help sand off his rust. Meanwhile, Shields wound up beneath Lindros, who had been taken down by Zhitnik. It took five minutes for the dazed Sabres goalie to wobble to his feet and practically no time after that for the Flyers to pounce.

Brind'Amour relayed a Coffey feed to LeClair, who opened the scoring, then sprung Lindros for a breakaway goal. With Coffey caught up ice, Michal Grosek jammed in a rebound off a two-on-one to cut the Philadelphia lead in half. But Lindros, taken down by Shannon on another solo, was awarded a penalty shot.

"Fake and go high," advised Hextall, but Lindros pushed the puck ahead a little too far, catching up just in time to throw off Shields, who had to turn again and was beaten between the legs. The first-ever successful Flyer playoff penalty shot (in four tries) put them up 3-1.

After Brind'Amour took a retaliatory penalty, Niinimaa got caught with an illegal stick and Randy Burridge cashed the two-man advantage. Just 32 seconds later, Zubrus scored the Flyers' fourth goal in their last 10 shots, but Hextall cleared the puck right into Plante, enabling Burridge to cut the lead to 4-3 just one second before the second-period break.

Lindros, who had been double shifting with Brind'Amour because a cut on Otto's face wouldn't clot, needed an IV between periods, but then pulled the tube on Buffalo's season by forcing the play into the offensive end, and shooting the puck into the net off the leg of Podein, restoring a two-goal lead. Zubrus hit the empty net to seal Philadelphia's 6-3 series-clinching victory.

Asked how he felt about one of the best playoff performances of his career, Lindros said, "Tired."

"He was a real leader today and we needed him to be," said Hextall, whose win was a franchise-high 42nd in the playoffs.

"The Flyers were just too big, too strong for us," conceded Barnaby. "We would hit them and just bounce off."

The Devils would not likely have had that problem. So as the Flyers waited outside the Marine Midland Arena to board the bus to the airport, they were not disappointed at the news that the Rangers, thanks to Adam Graves's overtime goal in Game Five, had finished off an upset of New Jersey.

"Guys were saying this was a best-case scenario for us, to avoid Brodeur and the Devils who had been a real thorn in our side," recalls Therien. "The Rangers were older and we had swept them two years earlier, when Lindros had been a huge matchup problem for them."

No Flyer follower had to be told that New York presented plenty of issues too, including the ghosts of Stanley Cup Final losses to Edmonton in 1985 and 1987—Wayne Gretzky and Mark Messier—now both in the uniforms of the hated Rangers. And they still weren't the threats that concerned the Flyer coaches the most.

"It was all Brian Leetch," recalls Murray. "He was flying under the radar compared to the other guys, but he was playing huge minutes and was the key to making that team work.

"When I was coaching Washington and Freddy (Shero) was working there as a consultant, I remember having a long conversation with him about how the Flyers threw the puck to Bobby Orr's side (during the 1974 finals) to try to tire him out.

"If you put the puck to other side of a player with the skating ability of an Orr or Leetch, you are letting him jump in and get it at full speed, putting everything at risk. We wanted to get pucks to Leetch then make him rush a pass or two."

The plan left the 1997 Flyers just as incredulous as the 1974 Flyers had been.

"When Terry presented that to us, I thought, 'Are you crazy?'" recalls Podein. "You can't let Leetch have the puck."

Indeed, he wanted it. Never mind the Rangers had just found the patience to work their way through the Devils' neutral-zone trap that so often had confounded Philadelphia. Leetch couldn't wait for the Flyers to bring it on, so he could bring it right back at them.

"I knew it would be dump it in my corner and go get me," Leetch recalls. "Even though we had success against New Jersey, I liked that straight-ahead, forecheck pressure, up and down, kind of game.

"We knew their big line was a big problem for us. But if you moved it quick, you could catch them and go the other way. Even if you beat them once, they still would keep coming. We thought it was one of our strengths that we could afford to give up more opportunities than the Flyers could."

That was because of Richter, the Flourtown, PA native and World Cup hero who entered the Eastern Conference final with a 1.31 goals-against average, a .978 save percentage, and three shutouts during five-game stonings of Florida and New Jersey. He had beaten Philadelphia three times during the season.

After four off-days of answering questions about the hot Richter, LeClair finally let off some of his own steam.

"You guys make him out to be invincible," LeClair said. "He's going to make mistakes like anybody else and we've got to be there to capitalize."

As for his own goalie, Murray again wanted the opposition guessing about Game One. But he had an additional motive for his secrecy. "Everybody wanted to know about the goalie, so I wasn't asked one Lindros question in four days," the coach recalls.

Meanwhile, Ranger coach Colin Campbell used much of his media time grinding an ax against the Flyers' Paul Bunyan.

"The way [Lindros] wields his stick, he's a mean player, maybe the meanest in the league," said Campbell. "If they called everything he did, he wouldn't be on the ice very much. We'll have to see how the officials handle it."

Of course the better question was whether the Ranger defense could handle the Big E. Early in Game One at the CoreStates Center, Lindros dropped the puck to LeClair and took Bruce Driver and Doug Lidster to the net, enabling Zubrus to put in a rebound. After Alexander Karpovtsev took down Falloon, Brind'Amour forced Jeff Beukeboom to the goal and Lindros walked out to feed a wide-open Niinimaa for a roofer and a 2-0 lead after just 4:39.

When Driver couldn't hold off LeClair to avoid his tip-in of a Desjardins drive, Lindros had his third assist, and Snow, beaten only on a late goal from the slot by Luc Robitaille, had plenty of margin to win Game One, 3-1.

But the Flyer goalie resumed his struggles in Game Two. Less than a minute after LeClair bunted in a Desjardins powerplay drive, Snow gave the goal back on an unscreened shot by Lidster. When Niinimaa was called for closing his hand on the puck, Gretzky took advantage of a cordial bounce off the glass support, then an even friendlier give-away by Snow, firing in a goal off of Dykhuis.

After a goal by Coffey, Brind'Amour stole the puck from Beukeboom and soloed to beat Richter cleanly. But Gretzky, who had been switched to a line with Messier in a Campbell attempt to avoid a No. 99 matchup against Lindros, drifted in from the high slot and put a softie off Snow's glove to restore a 4-3 New York lead.

When Messier scored four minutes later, Snow was yanked for Hextall. Podein's goal less than two minutes later was too late to save the day, but not for Klatt to alter the series. With six minutes remaining and Leetch attempting to move the puck out of the corner, Klatt banged the defenseman's right arm against the glass. He left the ice with no feeling in his wrist.

It returned and so did he, helping Richter hold off the Flyers for a series-evening 5-4 victory. But Leetch's ligaments were torn and the Ranger chances frayed, even though he recalls the damage could have been worse.

"Being a lefthanded shot, my left (bottom) hand was my workhorse. It was perfectly healthy, so I could pass fine as long as I had

both hands on the stick. My shot was never that strong anyway and I could still get it to the net. If it had been the other wrist, it would have been a significant detriment."

Klatt, whose intention was only to throw a body check, had missed the bullseye. "I came off the ice not even knowing he was hurt," he recalls. But essentially reduced to one hand, Leetch was compromised in his ability to pokecheck and get any steam on his shots.

Lindros, meanwhile, was taking more than just body blows. To finish off a nasty afternoon in which he was hammered in the back by Tikkanen—to which Lindros responded by crosschecking Samuelsson—Beukeboom and Samuelsson both jumped on No. 88 at the buzzer.

Brian Burke, the league's disciplinarian as director of hockey operations, called it "a man's game out there," but Snider wondered in what sport.

"That wasn't hockey out there, that was football," he steamed. "The third period was as violent as it gets in hockey but without anyone serving time in the box. It was a disgrace.

"Eric is the biggest guy in the league. There is no way they can stop him unless he's tackled or grabbed and then he gets penalized for his size and strength."

"The Ranger coach got what he wanted from the official," added Clarke. "It was smart."

Murray, being no fool, decided to go back to Hextall for Game Three at Madison Square Garden. Though mocked in that building for a decade, the Flyer goalie had won two of his three career series against the Rangers and also had a 2.10 goals-against average in seven games at MSG since being traded back to Philadelphia two years earlier.

"They chant my name, I get all warm and fuzzy up there," Hextall told the media. And he still does today.

"If you ask me what was my favorite building to play in, it's probably Madison Square Garden," he recalls. "If you weren't ready to play, people hanging over the boards yelling everything in the book at you was, to me, like a 'Let's get ready to go here.'

"The fans were out of their minds. It was awesome."

Even if names never would hurt Hextall, sticks and stones were breaking bones in this series. "It was like a Tom and Jerry cartoon," Driver characterized Game Two. "You know, with the cat taking a sledgehammer and hitting every character over the head with it?"

Even family could not be neutral. Two minutes into Game Three, Klatt knocked the Rangers' Ken Gernander, his brother-in-law, into the boards, putting him out for the series with a shoulder separation and concussion. Their twin wives, Kelly and Kirby, were sitting together at the game.

"He always has been understanding that I was just doing my job, but I still feel terrible about it," recalls Klatt, who the next day explained his remorse to Kirby in an awkward phone call.

There were no apologies forthcoming from anybody on the ice. When Richter, trailing 1-0 on a wraparound goal by Lindros, dropped his stick in a collision with teammate Mike Eastwood, Zubrus kicked it out of reach, enabling Svoboda to move down from the left point and score on the semi-helpless, and suitably enraged, goalie.

The Flyers nursed the two-goal lead until early in the third, when Petit, a seventh defenseman dressing for the first time in the playoffs (replacing forward John Druce), took a double minor for high sticking, enabling a Russ Courtnall powerplay goal. Courtnall scored again on a one-timer to tie the game 2-2, before Zubrus, who was playing in place of Renberg (ankle spurs), chipped the puck loose from Churla and Lindros restored the lead.

When Niinimaa lost the puck while trying to kick into his stick a handoff from Hextall, Gretzky pounced to tie the game once more. But only for 38 seconds, until Podein beat two Rangers through center and Klatt finished off a two-on-one at the goalmouth.

Brind'Amour scored an insurance goal on a breakaway, then Lindros overpowered Messier to the empty net to finish off a hat trick and a 6-3 victory that gave Philadelphia a 2-1 series lead.

"I think the biggest difference from last year is that Eric isn't trying to do it all himself," said Klatt. Indeed most of the work making Messier look 36 years old was being done by Otto, a veteran of Calgary-Edmonton wars who had chosen the Flyers over the Rangers in signing as a free agent in 1995.

"Joel had a hard, dirty, [bleep] you, attitude," recalls Murray. "He showed no fear, the attitude we needed to show against that premier team.

"We had talked in team meetings about the atmosphere we would face at Madison Square Garden (in the playoffs), new for a lot of our guys. That's where Coffey's leadership came in, too. He said, 'Forget those guys, just play our game,' important reinforcement from a player who had been a champion."

Of course, so had most of the Ranger stars, but Father Time was centering a fresh, fifth line for the Flyers. "Injuries (the Rangers had seven regulars out, mostly role players) have affected us so much, we're now expecting too much of a guy like Mark," said Campbell, who had played Messier 26 minutes. "And that was not Brian Leetch tonight."

Leetch, who had taken just one shot on goal, had played only because Karpovtsev had been called away that morning at the news of his mother's death in Russia. "I didn't even know that until right before warmup," recalls Gretzky. "I said in the locker room, 'Potsy, you're doing good, keep playing the same way,' and somebody had to say to me, 'Uh Gretz, he's not here.'

"He had been playing as well as he ever played, so we went from having a solid defense to having one guy at a funeral and one playing with [torn wrist ligaments]. It became tough to stop the onslaught, but honestly I don't know if it would have mattered if we had had the entire squad together. The Flyers were among the biggest, most powerful teams hockey had ever seen.

"We were counting most on our experience."

Also on Richter, who had given up four goals on just eight Philadelphia third-period shots. Nevertheless, Campbell, trying to stay in the series by playing two-and-a-half lines, insisted his edge in goal still existed.

"If they were that confident in [Hextall], he would have started the first game of the playoffs," said the coach. "We believe we can get him to blow up."

But it was Richter who again gave up the first goal in Game Four—on a second whack by Renberg with Graves in the penalty box for roughing Klatt. The hard-nosed—and obviously targeted—Flyer winger also took an unpenalized whack over the head from Beukeboom, who got away with a crosscheck on Lindros to the kidneys. Desjardins retaliated during a Ranger powerplay by slashing Gretzky on the wrist, numbing the greatest set of hands the game ever has known, helping Philadelphia kill the five-on-three.

They nursed the 1-0 lead until early in the third period, when Tikkanen burst between Coffey and Dykhuis and caught Hextall leaning the wrong way. At 1-1, the game opened up wide, the teams trading chances until Otto went to the box. Druce, a penalty killer who had scored just eight goals for the Flyers all season, slapped the puck from the left circle, then went to the net and roofed his own rebound with 3:13 to go.

Druce escaped from obscurity for just 1:05, until he was beaten up the slot by Leetch, who scored to tie the game again, 2-2, just as the penalty to Otto expired.

The pace was breathtaking. And blood-letting. Beukeboom hooked LeClair by the arm along the backboard and when the he spun, the Rangers' stick rose into the Flyer winger's face. He was cut in four places above his left eye and on the bridge of the nose.

"Hope they caught it," LeClair thought. He peeked to see referee Kerry Fraser's arm in the air to call a double minor with 1:35 to play.

Trainer John Worley quickly got the bleeding under control with petroleum jelly, enabling LeClair to join the second shift of the powerplay. He took a pass from a barely onside Brind'Amour and drew out Richter before backhanding the puck through the slot past Samuelsson.

"I didn't see anybody, just figured somebody would be going to the net," LeClair said. A good guess was that it would be Lindros, who lifted a backhander from near the edge of the circle over the sliding Graves. The overcommitted Richter dove headfirst through the goalmouth and crumpled against the post, getting a piece of the puck only after it had crossed the goal line.

"I just fired it at the net, you don't really get too fine," said Lindros. But the red light, glowing with just 6.8 seconds remaining, was the finest sight yet of Philadelphia's playoff run. Exhilarating 3-2 winners, the team had a 3-1 chokehold on the series.

New York defenseman Lidster had undergone a root canal that morning. Novocaine could not numb the pain of the valiant Rangers from an excruciating loss. But even with 10 regulars hurt, they fought back in Game Five at CoreStates from an early Lindros powerplay goal. Karpovtsev returned from his mother's funeral to score five-on-three and Tikkanen cashed the five-on-four to put New York up 2-1.

Nevertheless LeClair, with Driver draped all over him, quickly tied the game. Then Brind'Amour, fed by Therien on a three-on-two rush led by Lindros, made Richter open up on a forehand-to-backhand move and slid the puck between the goalie's legs.

Almost seven minutes into the third period, Brind'Amour, again fed by Therien, scored his 10th goal of the playoffs on another backhander to extend the Flyer lead to two. When Hextall, prone after having just stopped Driver, flung his stick up to foil Gretzky, the crescendo built through the end of Philadelphia's series-clinching 4-2 victory at a sterile-no-more CoreStates Center.

"It was kind of deafening out there," said Lindros. "You're going over who is covering who for a faceoff, and you had to yell.

"That was fun. If that was a hint of it, I want to see more."

In the handshake line Gretzky, on the losing end 10 years after outlasting Hextall in Game Seven in Edmonton, told the goalie, "Go get it."

"I thought Mr. Snider was going to get his (long-awaited next) Cup," Gretzky recalls thinking. To emphasize that there still was work remaining to be done, Lindros left the Prince of Wales Trophy untouched on its table. "We haven't really done anything yet," he told the media.

In retrospect, Lindros says, "Maybe we should have appreciated more where we were, but I just thought, 'Keep your foot on the gas.'"

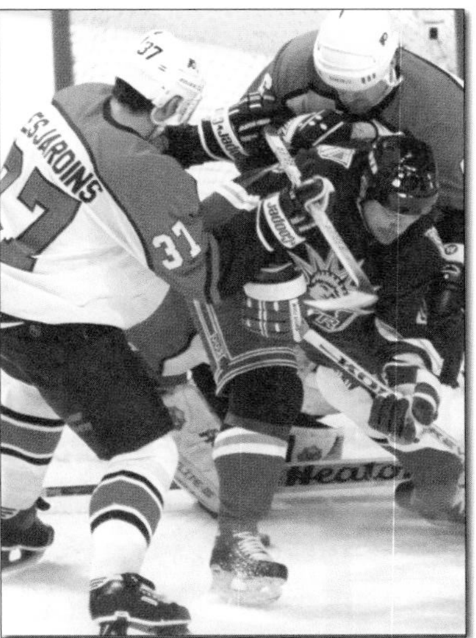

Defensemen Eric Desjardins and Chris Therien put the squeeze on the Rangers.

Indeed, Campbell praised Lindros, who had five goals and nine points during the five-game series, for having already floored it. "I think he has stepped up," said the Ranger coach. "It seems like he never wanted to come off the ice."

The Flyers felt like they never wanted to leave the Big E's side, either.

"We had a great player in Pittsburgh who wanted just one thing and we've got the same thing with Eric," said Coffey. "I feel like a kid all over again, which is just how I felt with that Pittsburgh team."

Hextall, 10 years older and wiser as the sole survivor—albeit once removed—from the last Flyer Stanley Cup finalist, had turned back the clock, too. "Been awhile, feels pretty special," he said. "Only two teams get there."

The other was the Detroit Red Wings, whose sweep by the Devils in 1995 had been the franchise's sixth loss in a final since its last Stanley Cup in 1955. (The Flyers had lost four since winning in 1975). Having had a 131-point regular season ruined in the 1996 Western Conference final by the eventual champion Avalanche, the Red Wings were just off a sweet vengeance defeat of Colorado in six games.

Their addition of right wing Brendan Shanahan had added size and clutch scoring, and the talented third-year defensive pair of Nicklas Lidstrom and Vladimir Konstantinov had grown up. The Flyers had proven they were bigger and deeper than the thin Penguins, the smallish and starless Sabres, and the aging, crippled, Rangers. But Scotty Bowman's Red Wings had skill and moxie that went four lines deep.

"[Detroit's] games had been mostly on our off nights and I had been watching them through the whole playoff," recalls Podein. "In Game Two, they turned that Colorado series around by outshooting them [40-17] and won, 4-2.

"Watching it, I remember crying. My wife asked why and I said, 'We can't beat Detroit; we make too many mistakes that they don't make, like carrying the puck instead of chipping it in.' Their transition game was much better than ours. They attacked very fast."

Murray, too, wasn't naïve to what his team would be up against.

"I knew coming in they were better than us," he recalls. "They had superstars who, through repeated playoff failures, had learned how to win through losing, which usually you have to do.

"You can get hot and win a Cup. But most of the time you have to go through disappointments. One year before the Devils won, they had a 3-2 lead and a 2-0 lead in Game Six on the Rangers.

"The Red Wings' hearts had been questioned. When they had lost to the Devils, Scotty said some things that weren't very kind. Their attitude had become that they were not going to be denied."

As a city, Philadelphia didn't share any of the insiders' apprehension. Atop City Hall, William Penn was dressed in a Flyer jersey (No. 1 on the back, of course) created by Doug Verb of Action Sports America, a Lafayette Hills, PA sports-marketing firm representing Modell's Sporting Goods. The idea had been hatched by Mayor Ed Rendell two years earlier, when the jersey had been signed by 13,000 fans but wasn't used because the Flyers had been eliminated by New Jersey two wins short of the Final.

But with six days off before Game One at the CoreStates Center—the Red Wings had only four—not only did the anticipation build, but the tension, too. "Fewer days off would have helped us a ton," recalls LeClair, meaning mostly to knock off the rust. But Murray also thought the media presence bordered on suffocating.

"The only thing I wished I had done (differently) was get us the [bleep] out of Philadelphia for a week," the coach recalls. "After every practice, the dressing room was filled; I think that really distracted us."

It probably was hardest on Murray, who had to endure at least one of those days taking questions about his murky future. "If he wants to be back, yeah, he'll be back," said Clarke. "We've talked about it and we have an understanding."

That understanding was a secret, one-year, extension that had been agreed to during the season. It went only through 1997-98, but the coach felt that was enough for him. "Maybe if I hadn't known Clarke so long I would have [sought a longer extension]," Murray, the 13th highest-paid of 26 NHL coaches at $335,000, told reporters. "It doesn't bother me."

Coffey, LeClair, Desjardins, Samuelsson, Svoboda and Otto were the only Flyers who had won Stanley Cups. Of those who had not, probably Hawerchuk, the Hall of Fame shoe-in who in 14 years before coming to the Flyers the previous season had won one series, appreciated this opportunity the most.

"I get up in the morning now and it's warm and sunny, then I realize we're still playing," he said. "I never had that opportunity before. We're so close to winning the Cup, what you play for.

"So many times this season I thought my career was over. Age wasn't the problem. I'm only 34. It was my left hip. When it feels good, it's great, but arthritis is not a predictable thing. This might be it for me. I hope not."

Detroit goalie Mike Vernon, also 34, was no spring chicken either, but he had won a Cup with the Flames. "We thought we had an advantage in goal," recalls Bowman, but as Game One broke at the CoreStates Center, the Red Wings' greatest apparent edges were their poise and structure.

Six minutes in, Kurt Maltby poke-checked Lindros and converted a give-and-go feed from Kris Draper over Hextall's shoulder. Brind'Amour, crashing the net, lifted the stick of Red Wing star Steve Yzerman and tied the game but Kjell Samuelsson, dressing for the first time since a herniated disk had forced him out of the lineup in December, made a play too similar to the ones that had gotten Dykhuis scratched. The rusty vet threw the puck off the half-boards into the path of Joe Kocur, who skated in and flipped a backhander over Hextall.

"We have to show early that we are going to hit as hard and as often as they are," Kocur had said during a pre-series buildup that questioned whether Detroit could handle Philadelphia's size and strength. Indeed Darren McCarty, who had nailed Coffey on the first shift, hit him a second time, sending Murphy and Sergei Fedorov on a two-on-one that Fedorov converted past Hextall's glove for a 3-1 lead.

Even though LeClair cut it to one with a late second-period goal, the Red Wings had possessed the puck seemingly the entire 40 minutes. Early in the third period, LeClair gave it away to Murphy, who fed Yzerman, who fired from just one step over the blueline to beat Hextall.

"A long way out, I need to make that save," said Hextall, who faced constant odd-man rushes as Detroit countered off the Flyers' confusion through center ice, leading to their 4-2 victory. Bowman had surprised Philadephia by not using the big and combative Konstantinov against the Legion of Doom, instead going with a quicker pair of Lidstrom and Murphy, plus two checking lines. "Look, we can't match up against that line, so I throw different lines at them trying to keep our guys as fresh as possible," said the Detroit coach.

The newly found composure the Flyers supposedly had demonstrated in the first three rounds suddenly had vanished on the biggest hockey stage of all. "I'd like to lie to you and say I didn't get all caught up in the whole thing but . . . " said Klatt.

Murray, like everyone, had thought a long series could be turned into a Philadelphia advantage. But his forecheckers already were getting mentally worn down by their failure to turn the key to Detroit's left wing lock. With an extra day to practice before Game Two, Murray drilled his team in reversing the puck through center ice and restored Zubrus to the Lindros line. But neither move would make a difference should the Flyers be unable to get saves.

Citing the long Yzerman goal on Hextall as the reason, the coach told Snow he was going to get another shot in Game Two.

Just 90 seconds into it, Shanahan scored from another Samuelsson giveaway, off the skate of Coffey. "It was a bad decision," Samuelsson says today about trying to come in cold to the Stanley Cup Final, but with Svoboda lost for the series in Game One with a broken foot, options were dwindling. Not wanting to break up his best pair—Desjardins and Therien—or put the turnover-prone Dykhuis with the rookie Niinimaa, Murray formed a Coffey-Dykhuis unit.

Fedorov revealed to reporters that part of the Red Wing plan was to go after Coffey, a player whom Bowman had trashed for his lax effort in Detroit. "All that talent, why can't he play defense?" Bowman had asked. "And he's not as good on the powerplay as people think."

Coffey was in the box when Yzerman converted a bad rebound off a shot from the boards to make it 2-0. But thanks to a Fedorov penalty, the Flyers got life. Brind'Amour deflected a Niinimaa powerplay drive past Vernon, then Niinimaa scored again at even strength to tie the game. The building rocked until Brind'Amour, set up by Lindros on a two-on-one, fired through the crease into the corner and Murphy beat Snow from 56 feet.

Shanahan put a second consecutive 4-2 Red Wing victory away off a two-on-one through Coffey's futile dive. "It didn't feel that close," recalls LeClair, in part because the Detroit shooters had not been required to get very close to beat the Flyer goalies.

"Not getting the big stops is our worst nightmare in the Final," said Murray. So he was going back to Hextall, the fourth goaltending change the coach had made in four rounds.

"I don't like playing musical chairs. I was going on a hunch and it didn't work out," Murray told reporters. "We're going into a building that demands a lot of experience and Hexy will get the call."

At least the Red Wings wouldn't have Coffey to exploit anymore. Concussed by a hit to the jaw by McCarty, Coffey joined Svoboda as out for the rest of the series. Like their defense, hope was thinning. The discombobulated Flyers put their hopes in Game Three at Joe Louis Arena on their 6-1-road record during the first three rounds.

LeClair braved a "we're going to win," then promptly did something about it, putting in a Desjardins rebound on a powerplay for a 1-0 Philadelphia lead. It lasted two minutes, until Yzerman converted a Dykhuis giveaway with a screened shot from the point.

Dykhuis then gave it away to Fedorov, who chipped the puck ahead of Otto and put a savable shot past Hextall. Not only did a two-man Flyer advantage for 1:20 not result in a shot on goal, Martin Lapointe came out the penalty box to make the score 3-1.

"They saw our blood in the water," recalls Podein. When Fedorov put in a rebound on a second-period powerplay, the rout was on.

"A debauchery," Podein called the 6-1 Philadelphia defeat. "An embarrassment," said Murray, whose Flyers were down 3-0 in the series almost before they knew what had hit them. Or before they realized they weren't hitting enough.

"I think Eric and John were waiting for the big hits from their defensemen and never got them," recalls Desjardins. "They got Lidstrom and Murphy instead. I think we had gotten surprised."

Desjardins also believes the change in the system to deal with the left wing lock hastened the Game Three collapse. "We started doubting what we had done for 100 games," he recalls. "It was stupid; I don't know why we did that.

"But the big thing was the way they were coming at us with speed and waves from the third and fourth lines, which we hadn't seen against Pittsburgh and the Rangers."

Murray cited Therien, oft criticized as a reluctant hitter, as "the only one taking the body." Trying shock treatments to rouse anger, he was pointed in his criticism towards many individuals at a meeting before an optional practice the next day, although those interviewed for this book were either unwilling to disclose, or couldn't remember, who was singled out.

"There is no incident I can point to, but we just weren't sticking together during that series, became individuals instead," recalls Hextall. "We had been tight all year and suddenly we were fractured."

Murray then went to the media availability. "Many teams have been through these problems before," he said. "Basically, it is a choking situation for our team right now.

"We're still developing, still trying to figure out what it takes to win a championship. This time of year the spotlight becomes a heat lamp. Sometimes competition brings out the best in you and sometimes it brings out the worst. [Choking] is what the state is called. There is no hiding that fact, it's how we have played."

The coach added he had only meant to say that a team this young had to know adversity before it could triumph. Philadelphia, he believed, still could turn the series around.

Lindros had taken the coach's offer to skip practice. "I had answered every question the night before, done everything they had asked me to do from a media standpoint," he recalls. "I just wanted to take the day off and regroup."

Thus the team captain was not in the locker room when the media asked the Flyers how they liked being called chokers by their coach in the middle of the Stanley Cup Final.

"Ai-yi-yi-yi-yi," said a stricken Desjardins. "I don't want to start a big war in the paper, but of course it hurts to hear that.

"[Reporters] would have the right to say that to us (for) going into the Final and playing like that. But [Murray] didn't say that to us. And it is always worse to hear from somebody else."

Not all the Flyers took offense. "[Murray's] right," said Brind'Amour. "You see a basketball player miss a free throw, his confidence is shot, he's tentative, he's choking, not playing his game. Isn't that what we've been doing?"

Clarke told the media, "It's not the word you want to use," but otherwise withheld comment. Wondering about the context, he asked Murray if it had been a motivational ploy. When Murray said it was not, the GM suggested the coach explain himself to the team. But in talking to reporters before the pregame skate the next morning, Murray, 26 years in the NHL as both a player and coach, seemed bewildered by the furor created by his use of the C-word.

He called choking "a real sports-psychology term that is used all the time. That's not detrimental; you identify it and work through it," he said.

Still, Murray sought Hextall's advice on addressing the club about the comment. The goalie said not to bother. "It was minuscule," Hextall says today. "A comment, big deal, we had a game to win."

"I never thought he was throwing us under the bus, never doubted he had our backs," recalls LeClair. "I never thought it was that big a deal as people made it out to be."

Today, Desjardins concedes the Flyers were doing exactly what Murray said they were doing. "Yeah, we were choking," he recalls. "We get to the Final and can't execute, can't play the right way and he saw it, but at the same time you don't need that from the coach at that time."

In his pregame talk, Murray didn't haul out the standard "one shift at time" that coaches had relied upon for decades to keep their players from being overwhelmed by an 0-3 deficit. Instead, he suggested each Flyer think of someone who inspired them on the way to the NHL and play Game Four for them.

"I remember thinking 'That's pretty good motivation,'" recalls Therien.

However many Flyers wanted to choke their coach, they didn't quit on him in Game Four. They killed off three first-period powerplays and for the first time in the series established a semblance of a forecheck. But Hextall did not look confident and Yzerman, set up in the high slot when Maltby beat Lindros off the boards, scored between the goalie's legs.

In the second period, Tomas Sandstrom got away from LeClair along the wall and fed McCarty, one-on-one against Niinimaa. One of the Philadelphia's least experienced players, Niinimaa may have been their best in the Final. But McCarty put the puck between the defenseman's stick and body, beat him on the backhand, avoided Hextall's poke check, and scored.

Hextall got stronger, stopping an Yzerman breakaway, but as the Red Wings, leading 2-0, were content to sit on the lead, the Flyers,

Garth Snow turns away Brendan Shanahan in Game Two of the Stanley Cup Final. The Red Wings would go on to win this game 4-2.

who had not scored at even strength since Game One, produced minimal chances as the season drained away.

With Hextall pulled, Lidstrom threw the puck away but, thanks to Brind'Amour's deflection, it came right to Lindros at the opposite post. The captain scored his first goal of the series into a half-empty net with 14.8 seconds left.

It was too little and, when Brind'Amour was offside as Lindros desperately dumped the puck in off the center-ice faceoff, way too late. The Flyers politely watched as the Red Wings, 2-1 winners, celebrated the franchise's first championship in 42 years. LeClair consoled Hextall; Niinimaa wiped away tears. A dominant run by Philadelphia had ended in their own domination, difficult for them to quickly rationalize as a learning experience.

"I hope we have nightmares all summer long," said Desjardins in the locker room. "I hope we buy the tape and look at it and see how we took ourselves out of it."

Clearly, the Flyers had not believed this was possible.

"I didn't think we could be beaten four games in a seven-game series, let alone four straight," Lindros told the media, after the game. "We got the chance and, boom, the chance was gone. We didn't adjust well.

"I'll be the first to admit I didn't have a great series. I'll get back in the saddle but I'm not looking at the big picture now. I'm still in shock."

The finished product that the organization believed it had put together in the three seasons since ending the five-year playoff drought had turned out to be—as described by Bowen of the *Daily News*—nothing but "a rough draft."

"I didn't think Detroit should have been a sweep better, but I thought they were better," recalls Clarke. "We had to get real good goaltending and a huge series out of Lindros and LeClair, and didn't.

"I didn't think either goalie was good enough at that stage to be No. 1. Until the end, [Murray] got the right goalie in at the right time. But against Detroit, our big players didn't compete.

"I remember at the start of the Ranger series, Eric plowed through Messier like he was determined to show he was better. But he never did that with Yzerman. LeClair didn't either. Detroit had some toughness—Konstantinov was as good as any defensemen in the game, and mean. But we had to go after their smaller players and didn't.

"I think Scotty, brilliant in analyzing those things, saw Eric wasn't going to get physically involved and put out those quick puck movers. Murphy could see the ice so well if he knew he wasn't going to get hit."

The Flyers had fallen four games short of the Cup that, a year earlier, Snider had predicted for them in the first season at their new home. But in the devastated locker room, the team Chairman reiterated, "We have a great future ahead of us," and denied he was any more humiliated by the sweep.

"It would have been just as disappointing to lose in seven games," Snider said. "It took the Red Wings 40 years to do it, now we want to win it.

"Maybe it's going to take us longer than we hoped. Maybe everybody overrated us."

As the Flyers took the next day off before their season break-up meeting on Monday, Lindros admitted that he had become passive, just as he had in the elimination losses to New Jersey and Florida the previous two years.

"I do that, I know I do it," he told Tim Dwyer of the *Inquirer* in a Sunday phone conversation. "I think the whole team does it.

"I'm not going to sit here today and say I'm the best at [leadership] but I'm better at it than I was last year and will be better next year than I was this year. You go through things and learn.

"We lost every shred of confidence after the two losses at home. Then we went to Detroit and had an awful game and this was hard enough to get through . . .I don't see any reason to say anything like (Murray) did."

Headed into the final season of the six-year deal he had signed before his rookie year, Lindros said, "I love what we have ahead of us," but again refused to say he wanted Murray to be part of that future. "It doesn't matter what a person thinks," he said while Murray expressed incredulity that there was any problem between him and his star.

"I think my relationship has been very good with Eric over the time I've been here," the coach said. "I don't see that changing. My relationship with players in here is really good."

He included the goaltenders.

"In the 1972 Summit Series (matching Team Canada for the first time against the Soviet National Team), the greatest series that ever will be played, (coach) Harry Sinden without hesitation used both Ken Dryden and Tony Esposito," Murray says today.

"Everybody talks about a Stanley Cup run being a marathon, but I don't agree with that. I think it's a long relay. There are injuries. There is fatigue. Players get overwhelmed by the situation and sometimes a change is better for the team. In my judgment, that was going to be the best thing to win that night."

Murray believed the changes would not destroy the confidence of Hextall or Snow because he trusted their resiliency.

"That's probably good thinking," Hextall says today. "I think Snowy and I for the most part handled it professionally.

"We were really good for each other, joked about all the media questions and supported each other to the hilt. We are good friends to this day.

"It doesn't mean it was easy. I think you're always best to go with one guy, better for the team's stability. But it worked pretty well until the Final and I don't think what happened there was because of the flip-flopping. I just needed to play better."

On the day of the breakup meeting, Clarke refused comment about Murray's future. Feeling he had already gathered enough sense of the players' unhappiness, over the next three days the GM did not ask their opinions, only met with Murray twice, the second time for two hours, before deciding that the relationship was irreparable. Six days after the Flyers' elimination, Murray was in his office when Clarke walked in.

"I have to make a change," the GM said.

Having tuned out the speculation for months, Murray was shocked.

"When Dave Hodge had asked me (about the coach's job status) after Game Four (on *Hockey Night in Canada*), I was angry," he recalls.

"I thought, 'What the [bleep] are you talking about? We had been in the Stanley Cup Final and that was the first thing I hear about, 10 minutes after the game?' But I never spent a lot of time thinking about it. So when Clarkie walked in, I was blindsided."

Murray did not argue. "What's the point? It was over," he recalls. "I grabbed my family and went away on vacation to Alberta."

Clarke informed the media of the firing in the locker room of the training facility at the Coliseum. "He has a right to hate me for what I've done," said the GM. "This is the worst thing I have ever had to do as a manager, but I just felt the problems we had weren't going to go away.

"These didn't just surface. They have been basically there over the last couple years. We solved some and haven't been able to solve some others."

Asked about the bogus vote of confidence he had given on the eve of the Final, Clarke said the timing of the questions left him no choice.

Five-game victories in three series were not going to save Murray because the GM did not believe they required a superior coaching job. "This was one of those seasons where teams we got matched up against were the right matchups for us," Clarke said.

Anonymous players trashed Murray in the media. "He had no respect for us and as a result we had no respect for him," one said to Dwyer.

Coffey remembers it quite differently. "Real good coach, understood the psyche of the game, prepared the team, then left it in the players' hands; never over-coached or under-coached," he recalls. Even on the day of the firing, Podein told Bowen he was upset by characterizations of season-long turmoil.

"Because it seemed like everything went haywire in the final seven days, the conclusion was that the whole season was like that," said the winger. "It wasn't."

But Podein also said there had been an ongoing struggle to get key players to buy into the defensive sacrifices that inevitably the Detroit series made painfully clear were needed. Their coach had realized that all along.

"Terry was really a technician, very good in video meetings and at making the guys understand what he wanted," recalls Desjardins. "He never went right after guys in front of everybody. And I always thought I could go in and talk to him."

Not every Flyer felt that way, but none questioned their coach's knowledge. "During the Red Wing series, he had us working on reversing the puck through the center zone, exactly what we needed," recalls Brind'Amour. "So he did the right things, just said the wrong ones.

"As long as you respected him for what he was doing, you could still hate him. Actually, that solidifies your team. He wasn't a prick, just distant, didn't talk to players. So to say we liked him or didn't like him, I don't think we gave a crap to be honest with you. We were worried about what we had to do."

In the immediate aftermath of the firing, Snider said Lindros had not been asked for his opinion, but conceded the captain and coach "did not have a good relationship."

"I think that probably one of the areas Terry needs to work on is his communication skills," said Snider. But the low-maintenance Hextall believes to this day that the atmosphere was fine.

"I think a lot of guys liked Murph and I think most guys respected him. I think the respect thing always is a hell of a lot more important than the liking," Hextall recalls.

"I think there was a time early where Eric and Murph got along very well. Towards the end, I heard about [a problem between them], but I didn't really see Eric not liking Murph. Maybe I just didn't see it."

Neither did Murray. Called today by Lindros "a really good teaching coach," Murray remains baffled by the characterization of a poor relationship between him and key players on the team.

"I thought my relationship with Eric was good," Murray says. "When early in the '94-95 season he came back out of shape before we made the trade for Desjardins and LeClair (in 1995), I told him he was a much better player than that, and he responded. I thought we had a good relationship from that point on.

"He was MVP of the league (in 1995). We went to the Stanley Cup Final (in 1997). If you're a top player not on the same page with the coach, you're not going to get there if your top guy doesn't take the whole thing on his shoulders. And he did that.

"Ice time, overstaying shifts, that never was an issue for me. I wanted my best players on the ice, felt that three lines in those days could get the job done. If [Eric] played his whole career like he did his three years for me, he's a Hall of Fame shoe-in. I just have a lot of respect for how he played."

Though the choking comment was down the list of reasons for his firing, it tops Murray's reasons for regret. "I underestimated [the impact]," he says today. "I regret it and I apologized (at the team exit meeting preceding his dismissal), but I know it never will go away. "

With all the NHL head positions filled by the time of his dismissal, Murray stayed to take a job he had been promised by Clarke on firing day. A coach who had won 62.7 percent of his games with Philadelphia and had been 6-2 in playoff series was going to scout while he awaited his next bench.

"It's probably typical of coaching that there is a timeline," says Hextall today. "Whether that is right or wrong, I don't know. Murph did a good job."

So did a team that seemed to have every component to win a championship until it ran into one that was deeper and more experienced.

"Of all the playoff runs I ever have been on, that was the easiest," recalls Brind'Amour. "We didn't break a sweat so we didn't know how tough it was to win.

"Had we got [to a Final] again, we would have been more prepared to go through the wall. I swear, if we had kept that group together, we would have won the Stanley Cup."

ERIC LINDROS

Eric Lindros's eight polarizing seasons with the Flyers have become too much about what he didn't deliver and not enough about what he did.

In 486 regular-season games with Philadelphia, Lindros totalled 659 points, a 1.36 points-per-game average, better than all but four players in NHL history. In an era in which scoring was starting to decline, he was the fifth-fastest player to achieve 500 points, the sixth-quickest to 200 goals and his 57 points in 53 playoff games helped Philadelphia realize six wins in the 10 series in which he fully played.

With Bobby Clarke, Lindros is one of only two Hart Trophy (MVP) winners in Flyers history and easily was the franchise's greatest presence since the Cup years. If No. 88 wasn't the best combination of brute force and skill in NHL history, he was well on his way to becoming it when injuries intervened.

"Teams were drafting to play against him," says John LeClair, who combined with Lindros to give the Flyers their most lethal one-two combination since Clarke and Bill Barber. "He was dominant for five years."

The Big E broke down, as did his relationship with the Flyer organization. But Clarke, whose falling out with Lindros and his family helped make No. 88's position in Philadelphia untenable, nevertheless argued annually as a member of the Hockey Hall of Fame selection committee that Lindros did enough to be worthy of induction. He was elected in 2016.

Lindros scored 85 goals in 126 games in his first two seasons for sub-.500 Flyer teams stripped by the trade to acquire him. The next year, by which time LeClair and Eric Desjardins arrived and the winning resumed after a five-year drought, Lindros joined Wayne Gretzky as only the second player since 1927 to win a Hart Trophy by the third year of his career. That spring, he carried the Flyers to the Eastern Conference final and two years later to the Stanley Cup Final.

The transplanted Quebec Nordiques won two Stanley Cups in Colorado around Peter Forsberg, the best player among the six—plus two first-round draft choices and $15 million—the Flyers gave up in 1992 to obtain Lindros. So hindsight will cause the wisdom of arguably the biggest deal in NHL history—two more players than were exchanged in the Wayne Gretzky trade to Los Angeles, albeit one less pick and the same amount of money—to forever be debated.

But if the results are arguable, the organization's logic in making the trade remains unassailable. Having won two Cups with a three-time MVP, Clarke, then losing their next four Finals to teams led by Guy Lafleur, Bryan Trottier and Gretzky, the Flyers wanted the best player in the league again.

And they had it, only too briefly.

Lindros was a 6-foot-4, 229-pound steamroller—he once memorably picked up Florida's Stu Barnes and threw him aside on the way to a goal—who could press beautiful designs. He used his long reach to shield a puck that he would deliver off either the forehand or the backhand with a touch that belied his brute force. One of the best wrist shots in the game rose from one of its quickest releases, and his vision and sense of anticipation became more refined by the season.

"The guy is just an absolute hockey machine," said teammate Craig MacTavish.

Nobody questioned Lindros's leadership skills the 1997 night he took a pass from LeClair and beat Mike Richter on the backhand with only six seconds remaining to give the Flyers a 3-2 win and 3-1 series lead over the Rangers. No one argued Lindros was overstaying his shifts when he scored twice and set up the putaway goal to clinch that year's Buffalo series, or suggested he was being selfish when, stickless, Lindros controlled the puck for 38 seconds in his skates while the CoreStates Center crescendo built early in Game One of a Round One rout that same year against Pittsburgh.

The most hyped prospect since at least Mario Lemieux and maybe ever, Lindros delivered goals in both his NHL and Spectrum debuts, then scored twice in his fourth game while Quebec fans wearing mocking diapers chanted organ-accompanied obscenities at him. Projected by body type to be the next Mark Messier, Lindros memorably shrugged off that great, if aging, bull to get to the empty net and complete a 1997 playoff hat trick.

"At the end of a nasty series with Tampa Bay (1996), Eric grabbed (Igor) Ulanov, a pain in the butt, and beat him to a pulp," recalls teammate Chris Therien. "Guys feared him.

"When (Sami) Kapanen came to us he said that it had been like playing again Darth Vader. One night Eric grabbed Stu Grimson, the toughest enforcer in the league, and just pounded him into the ice. Those two or three years, before all the other [stuff] came into it, he was as dominant a player as I have seen. He turned men into boys very quickly and was a good teammate, too.

"I wish he didn't think someone was out to get him all the time, because that never was the case. Everyone wanted Eric to succeed."

The relationship grew complicated by resentments between the family and the organization, problems that existed with GM Russ Farwell before Clarke's 1994 return. Terry Murray, who coached the Flyers to the 1997 Final, has said it was a different, less relaxed, Lindros when his parents were visiting, and there also were also expectations, internally and externally, put upon Lindros to live up to the standards of Clarke's Camelot captaincy.

"When things didn't go good, Eric didn't go good," recalls Therien. "When things weren't rosy, Eric had a hard time coming in and painting them rosy.

"He couldn't take a rough road and smooth it over quickly enough while some captains in the NHL could. Sometimes you need someone to help you with that."

Ron Hextall thought Lindros had plenty of that help to go along with the overabundance of blame he absorbed: "I don't think it's fair to saddle Eric with the whole burden of the leadership when he was 23 or 24 years old; leadership comes from a group of four, five, six, eight players," said Hextall. "I think he probably took too much criticism for that."

And probably took too much of it to heart, also.

"It's not personal, it's professional, you gotta separate," added Hextall. " Sometimes Eric took things too personally.

"I think criticism from fans and media hurt him and I think that affected his game. "

Then, too, there was the ongoing debate about what Lindros's game should be. Was it best he fight his own battles or keep himself on the ice? Defer his offense and ice time for the greater good of the team or win contests all by himself because sometimes he could?

"I think Eric worked hard in practice, trained hard; I thought he cared about the team," recalls Craig Berube. "I thought he was a good teammate.

"But I think he probably worried about scoring too much rather than just playing the game. I think he thought he had to lead the league in scoring. If he didn't have that mindset, he would have been a better player and the team would have been better.

"Sometimes the captain has to make sure the team is playing the right way and that's not just about scoring."

Lindros took his leadership responsibilities seriously, despite evidence that they didn't come naturally to him.

"I thought I got better as I went along," he recalls. "I don't think I need to defend myself—not at all.

"Did we win the Cup? No. That's the end-all, be-all of it; we didn't win the Cup. But does that make me a bad leader? Does Ray Bourque win the Cup unless he gets traded to Colorado? Would you call him a bad leader?"

Bourque, an eighth-overall pick, had years to become Bourque. Lindros was expected to be the complete package, on ice and in the locker room, almost as long as he remembered and before he had a clue about how to rally a team around him.

"He had an interesting teenage life," recalls Therien. "He never really got to be a kid and was misunderstood in a lot of ways, but he was a pretty decent guy that I just think probably needed a little more to believe in himself as a normal person. I don't think he ever had a chance to do that. "

Lindros sat up when he was four months old. He walked at seven-and-a half months, skated at 18 months, rode a two-wheeler at three years and water-skied at age five. His parents enrolled him in hockey for the first time because they needed to tire out a busy baby.

At age nine, father Carl's accounting firm relocated from London, Ontario, to Toronto, where the pool of the house the Lindroses purchased was removed in favor of a backyard rink where Eric, his younger brother Brett and sister Robin could skate.

That same year, mother Bonnie says she woke up in the middle of the night in a Buffalo hotel room trembling at the revelation that her son, who had dominated a minor atom tournament that day, was extraordinary. "He wasn't even bigger than the other kids at that age," she recalled. "Just better."

When Eric grew seven inches between age 13 and 14, the movers of the hockey world began shaking just like Mom. He leaped to national attention on the celebrated Junior B team at St. Michael's College School, becoming one of Canada's best-known athletes even before he had performed in his first major junior contest.

The family's determination to plan his development caused him to twice reject drafts and become labeled as arrogant and selfish. The resulting pressures and jealousies took away much of the innocence of his teenage years.

Citing education concerns because of travel to the Ontario Hockey League's most distant outpost, the Lindroses warned the Sault Ste. Marie Greyhounds, possessors of the first pick, not to draft their son. When they did anyway, Eric was boarded with a family in suburban Detroit, where he played in the top U.S. developmental league while completing high school and awaiting the trading of his OHL rights.

They were acquired by Oshawa, 45 minutes from Lindros's home, for three players, two draft picks and the unparalleled junior sum of $80,000. In one full season there, Lindros scored 149 points in 57 games, added another 38 in 16 playoff matches, and led the Generals to the championship.

When Quebec made Lindros the first pick in the 1991 NHL Draft, he turned down a $50 million offer and spent the next year with Oshawa and three Canadian national teams, including the Canada Cup competition amongst NHL stars. Lindros sparkled and Canada won the tournament, driving his desirability to an unprecedented level in the history of the game.

At the 1992 draft, Nordiques' president Marcel Aubut conducted a frantic auction of Lindros's rights that led both the Flyers and Rangers to believe they had acquired the future megastar. On the basis of a thumbs-up sign from Aubut to Jay Snider while on the phone in a hotel suite the morning of the draft, league-appointed arbitrator Larry Bertuzzi validated Philadelphia's claim that it had made its deal first.

Before he even played one NHL game, a 19 year-old who liked to hang out with his friends and play video games became the league's highest-paid player in addition to being the sudden savior of a proud franchise that had fallen upon hard times. It got lonely fast.

"There weren't many single guys," Lindros recalled. "Everybody would go home to their wives and girlfriends and I would hang at the rink by myself.

"I had a condo in a ghost town. I cooked meals for myself and had no one to talk to. My phone bills were thousands a month. I would talk my friends into driving down 10-12 hours because I had nobody else. It was horrible. I hated it."

Having come to a franchise that, by his very acquisition, had proven its determination to succeed at the highest level, Lindros had landed well, nevertheless. In Year Three, LeClair, who would become a six-time first- or second-team NHL All-Star, arrived. And with a Stanley Cup window opened, the organization was determined to keep it from closing.

"Money was generally not a large concern," recalls Lindros. "On July 1, or at the trade deadline, sometimes it happened, sometimes it didn't, but at least there was an effort. Many teams weren't in the Bourque or Chris Chelios talks. The Flyers always made the effort.

"I was happy to be traded to Philadelphia. Some guys avoid playing in Toronto or Montreal because it's so intense. Philadelphia is the closest thing to a Canadian city in that regard—very loyal fans there. They're great, they really are.

"Philly is a big part of my life. There was a new development that went up (in Voorhees, NJ) and there were seven or eight of us within a seven-minute bike ride from the others. So it was good that eventually there were a lot of close teammates.

"You know what, I got a chance to play some good hockey—a lot of good hockey. I'm proud of that. I just wish I would have been a lot healthier but I'm not the only guy who that ever happened to. That's the way it was for me so I'm not going to look back and be upset or disappointed or frustrated because there's nothing to be gained by that, there really isn't.

"If I had it to do over again, I would have dialed

back the hitting about 25 percent. But I don't care to go into the what-ifs. I'm just going to look at it overall and think of positive times, some real good teams that had chances to win. I'm grateful for that. Some guys go through their careers and don't have a chance at it ever. So I'm not going to look back and think of anything other than good times. There's no point."

The best of those times—he had never been happier than under coach Roger Neilson, more comfortable in his own skin, nor more determined to be a Flyer for life—evaporated after Lindros suffered a collapsed lung and five concussions in a two-year period.

Tensions fueled by Clarke's belief that Eric's parents were meddling in organization affairs and putting their son ahead of the team, intensified, as did the family's concern that Eric was not fully supported by the organization. Brother Brett, an Islander first-round pick, lost his career to concussions. And when Eric began to suffer them repeatedly, his criticism of the Flyer training and medical staff caused him to lose his captaincy and, subsequently, his desire to remain in Philadelphia.

"If there was the protocol (on clearance to return following concussions) then that there is now and if everything had been handled according to that protocol, it would have been taken out of everybody's hands," says Keith Primeau, founder of stopconcussions.com, which advocates to diminish the risk of the head traumas that prematurely ended his career. "A lot of what happened would have been moot."

"I can't honestly say that everything between Eric and the Flyers would have been sunshine and roses, because it was deeper than [just the handling of the concussions] issue but it definitely would have alleviated a lot of the tension."

The Flyers' subsequent run to the 2000 Stanley Cup amidst all that controversy was made despite the absence of the team's best player, not to spite him. There are plenty of stories—from Lauren Hart about her phone calls from Lindros as she battled non-Hodgkin's lymphoma, from Polina Tertyshny about the captain making rookie defenseman Dmitri and his wife with virtually no English skills feel at home, from a rookie Lithuanian named Dainius Zubrus being invited home to Toronto with Eric for Christmas break—to belie the perception of a selfish, haughty and entitled star.

"'Eric cares about people; Eric cares about kids," says Hextall. "To this day, one of my son Brett's favorite people is Eric because he treated Brett very well. He would defend Eric all the time in school.

"I use that as a small example, but he has a good heart. Sometimes we all could have done a better job of handling things and I don't think Eric's any different."

A thaw in his decade-plus alienation from the Flyers began when Lindros put on the orange-and-black again at the Legends Game at the 2012 Winter Classic at Citizens Bank Park. He has been welcomed back in little ways—to the annual alumni golf tournament and for a morning game day skate in Toronto—and in large ones, like his induction together with LeClair on November 19, 2014 into the Flyers Hall of Fame.

"I really worked hard to rid my mind of anything negative, I really have," said Lindros. "Things take time.

"There were different points along the way that I really disliked playing but that was never from the pressure. The pressure was fine. Just go play."

After 72 days of recuperation and recrimination, that's all Lindros wanted to do when cleared by doctors for his final acts as a Flyer—Games Six and Seven of the 2000 Eastern Conference Final. He performed remarkably, probably being the team's best player in a limited Game Six role that begged for a bigger one for Game Seven. Ten minutes into it, he was driven to the ice and from the game by a shoulder to the head from New Jersey's Scott Stevens. Lindros didn't resume his career for a year, until after he was traded to the Rangers for Kim Johnsson, Jan Hlavac and Pavel Brendl.

"It was not a penalty then; it would be a penalty today (for targeting the head)," Lindros says. "I'm not saying it was right or wrong, just that it was a time when the rules were different. The better question is for all we've [learned] about concussions, what real strides are we taking?

"I wasn't the same player after I left Philadelphia. I had a huge fear of cutting through the middle and you can't play with fear. You can still have some decent years but you can't be close to the level you want to play at.

"I couldn't shake it. There were times I hated the game, really did. I'm looking for doctors to give me a clean bill of health while there are little birds (of doubt) chirping in your ear. So where do you draw the line? I tried to play a safer game and you can't change the stripes. You can still get by because you're good, but you're never going to be what you were."

He got out with his health regardless, no small triumph.

"Despite not being able to remember some of these things you are asking me about, I feel good, I feel strong, so I'm quite blessed with that," he said. "I wish I would have had [sports hernia] surgery my last year (2006-07), not to play another season, but to be able to push off laterally in tennis now.

"I still play hockey, 20 of us, every Thursday morning, same arena, same manager, same Zamboni driver, some of the same players as when I was 10. It's fun."

Again, Lindros can be the little boy that he was not allowed to be for long.

"I always remember thinking, 'I'm glad I'm not him,'" said Shjon Podein, Lindros's Flyer teammate for four-plus seasons. "Every day it was like someone was trying to knock him off a pedestal or trying to point out something he was not doing right.

"He would do something great and it was cool, but as soon as there was a little mistake . . . I think it would get tiring getting poked in an open wound with a stick almost daily. When I dumped the puck in everyone was standing and cheering, but Eric had to run over a few guys and get five points a night."

And that took its toll.

"People talked about me as someone who put pressure on himself," recalls Rod Brind'Amour. "But Eric was one who went to the whole other end.

"I had so many conversations with him about, 'Just go play. You're an absolute train wreck out there, you're like a monster, so you're a leader by the way you play. You don't have to say a word. Everyone will follow that lead to kingdom come.'

"I think there was so much pressure here to follow in Clarke's image that he tried to do more than he had to. So when we didn't win, he would say, 'What else do I have to do?'

"I don't think that was his thing, to get up in front of guys and speak. That wasn't what he was comfortable doing. I think it just put way too much on him."

The only real freedom Lindros felt was on the ice. Ultimately, it wasn't any failure in his playing that caused his departure from the Flyers. It was all about not playing.

"I think it really hurt him emotionally, as well as physically, the fact that this dominant-sized man was getting hurt and couldn't play the way he wanted to play," recalls former Flyer coach Craig Ramsay.

The rest remains in the eye of the beholder, a reflection of the level of scrutiny that unavoidably impacts Lindros's legacy.

"I think Eric had to answer to a lot of other things that weren't always taken into account," says LeClair. "Like being the next face of the league. He was still the best player in it.

"I thought he did a fine job. I really did."

ERIC DESJARDINS

On a chartered jet from Montreal to Philadelphia, John LeClair, Gilbert Dionne and Eric Desjardins sat opposite one another, trying to read their futures in each other's faces.

"It was intense," recalls Desjardins of February 9, 1995, the day the trio was traded from the Canadiens to the Flyers. "We were all pretty nervous and John said, 'Hey guys, it's going to be alright.'

"We got there and lost the first game (3-0 to Florida). The next day in the Montreal paper said, 'this is why Desjardins is going down.'"

Eric Desjardins did go down: as one of the best defensemen in Flyers' history. Take the word of the organization's ultimate company man.

"After Mark Howe, between either Eric Desjardins or Jimmy Watson would be awfully close," said Bob Clarke, who played with a lot of guys and traded for just as many. "Kimmo Timonen would be up there, too.

"Jimmy had such great lateral mobility. Eric was a better defensive guy than Kimmo, who was the better offensive guy. But Desjardins was a defensive defenseman who also could score, just didn't try to rush the offense, similar to Mark that way.

"Eric was extremely smart as far as seeing the ice and who to give it to. No forcing anything, he always knew who was open and wouldn't try to score until he felt the team needed a goal. He was one of the most complete players that have come through this organization. Everything was about helping the team to win. And you could count on one hand the amount of poor outings he would have in a year."

Desjardins suffered his one-and-only of 1995 on that February day he got off the plane. Born in Rouyn, Quebec, plus drafted by the Canadiens (38th overall, 1987), the "hockey-English only" that Desjardins spoke upon his arrival to Philadelphia at age 25 initially was of little help to him at South Jersey supermarkets. No translation was needed for the booing, however, as the defenseman went minus-1 in his Flyer debut for a 3-7-1 team that was five seasons removed from its most recent playoff spot.

Two days later at the Meadowlands, Eric Lindros chased down a Desjardins rebound and wheeled the puck to LeClair, whose goal staked the Flyers to a first-period lead in a 3-1 victory, their first at New Jersey in five years. As the Legion of Doom, so named by Philadelphia center Jim Montgomery, was born that afternoon, Desjardins was plus-three for a team what would go 25-9-3 the rest of the season and reach the Eastern Conference final.

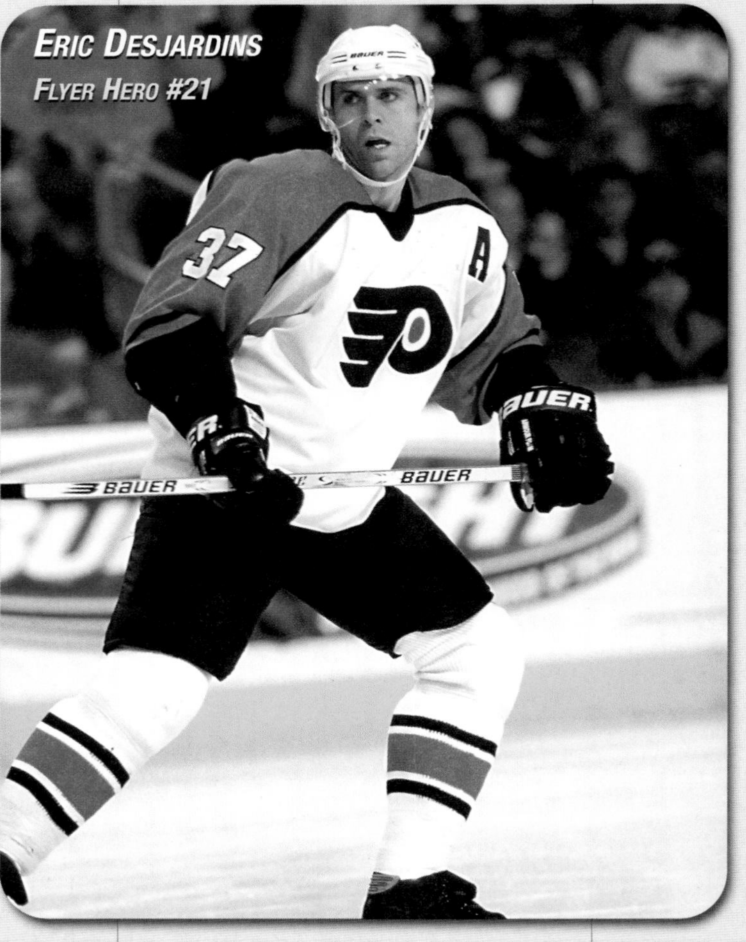

ERIC DESJARDINS
FLYER HERO #21

Except for the Game 82 shootout that put the Flyers into the playoffs over the Rangers in 2010, and the record-breaking win in Boston—No. 29 without a loss on the way to 35 straight unbeaten during 1979-80—there has not been a more memorable or pivotal regular-season win in Flyer history than that one at the Meadowlands. And after Keith Allen's trades for Bernie Parent, Rick MacLeish and Howe, there hasn't been a better deal in the 50 years since the franchise's birth than the one in which Clarke sent one star, Mark Recchi, to Montreal, for what turned out to be two.

LeClair became a three-time 50-goal scorer. Desjardins was a consummate presence on the Flyer defense for 11 seasons.

"A great lateral skater and one of those guys that could load up minutes on the powerplay, kill penalties, and get his body and stick in front of people one-on-one," said Lindros. "Everything he did was at 90 percent or better."

One hundred percent of it was for the team, too.

"There are guys that can rush the puck and stuff like that, but they give up things at the other end," said LeClair. "Combine his offensive ability with how (little) he gave up on the back end and there have not been too many like him.

"As good as Big E was, Rico was the backbone of why we had so much success. He was the constant guy. He had a stick that was unbelievable, in the right place all the time."

So was his heart, a testament to why Desjardins could speak softly yet still effectively. One of the quietest guys in the room, he still was the obvious choice to captain the 2000 run to the Eastern Conference final through the absence of the injured Lindros and cancer-stricken coach Roger Neilson.

"A pro," recalls Rick Tocchet. "If you asked him, he would give an honest opinion.

"He was an open book. There was no gimmick, no hidden agenda."

The honest man was taught an honest game by Jacques Laperriere, who, despite never bettering 40 points, won a Norris Trophy and six Stanley Cups in 12 seasons with the Canadiens. Through another 16 years in Montreal as an assistant coach, Laperriere never steered any kid wrong.

"I was lucky I had him there," recalls Desjardins. "That's how I became really sound defensively, without which I couldn't have survived. I was not a guy to excel physically or with the big shot. I tried to be consistent, to always work at everything."

Twice, Desjardins was an end-of-season NHL second-team All-Star and seven times a Barry Ashbee Trophy winner as the best Flyer defenseman. He was the defensive anchor of one team that reached the Final (1997) and one more that reached Game Seven of the conference final (2000).

Without him in 2004, the Flyers again got to within five wins of the Cup, leaving all its members believing Desjardins would have keyed them to the championship if not for an incorrectly-set broken arm that snapped just as he was about to return for the beginning of the playoffs.

Philadelphia also had its share of early round postseason flops in the Desjardins years. And when that happens, it seems a team's best players never can do enough. "They wanted Eric to be a superstar and he wasn't," says Clarke. "So when you're not winning, the expectations usually are put upon your top guys.

"But he was key to the team. I never was going to trade him unless he asked."

Recalls Chris Therien, Desjardins' usual partner, "If either of the Erics was out with an injury and we had our choice of who was the most important guy we wanted back, Desjardins would have been pretty unanimous. Lindros was a special type of player and a big difference, but Desjardins was the calming influence that grouped us together."

In bad times, fans couldn't always understand. But Desjardins had far too much class and good sense to ever pick a fight with them. "I never felt they didn't appreciate me," he recalls. "I really thought that they were fair."

But he forgets, or ignores, not being treated well while struggling through the 2001-02 season with a shoulder in need of surgery. Ron Hextall questions whether Desjardins, who only twice made the top five in Norris Trophy balloting, got his due outside the stands, too.

"I don't think you knew how good he was until you played with him," said Hextall. "He had all the intangibles, the unselfishness, playing in all situations, always thinking of the team before himself and rarely making a mistake.

"I mean how many defensemen rarely make a mistake? The more you saw him, the more you liked him. He had some traits similar to Mark Howe that way."

Desjardins did not have a four-point night for the Flyers, never broke 15 goals or 55 assists. His only NHL hat trick was in Game Two of the 1993 Final for the Stanley Cup winning Canadiens, a contest and series remembered more for the Kings' Marty McSorley getting caught with an illegal stick in the final minutes.

Desjardins' most dramatic individual feat in Philadelphia was burying a Game One overtime winner under the crossbar behind Mike Richter, starting the Flyers to a 1995 sweep of the defending champion Rangers. But the contest for which he most appropriately should be remembered was Game Four in 2000 at Pittsburgh, when his point drive went in off LeClair to tie the game 1-1 in the third period. Before Keith Primeau scored in the fifth overtime, Desjardins had logged 73 shifts and 56:08 of ice time.

Dehydrated after what he calls "the worst experience of my life," he suffered the dry heaves on the flight home. Nevertheless, nobody had scored on Desjardins that longest of nights and mornings. And the sleep of coaches was uninterrupted, knowing they had him on their side.

"I've had two players in my life who are zero maintenance," recalls Ken Hitchcock. "Desjardins and Jere Lehtonen (in Dallas).

"Never told Eric how to play, never told him what to do. No . . .once I told him he could be better offensively, not to be afraid to join the rush because his reads were perfect.

"Never had to worry about whether he was coming to play. Never worried about him in the summer. He was just a given. And every time he went out with an injury, it took us two weeks to reorganize ourselves because of every situation in which he played—a minute-and-a-half of every powerplay, point shot, penalty killing, and against the best players."

If Desjardins wasn't quite a superstar, nevertheless, he was assigned the ultimate definition of one by Craig Ramsay, coach of the Flyers on the 2000 run: "He made everybody around him a better player."

"He wasn't a big man," said Ramsay, "but was willing to get in and battle. In Philly, there was always the perception that if you're not fighting or banging, you're not tough enough. He was tough enough.

"He was a special person and everybody knew that. I can't imagine anyone who didn't like him, who didn't feel good if they got to play with him. He and Therien were a great match."

More efficient than flashy, more enduring that dominating, Desjardins' near-perfect sense on the ice extended to locker rooms and press conferences.

"He had a terrific feel, knew when the team was in trouble or when it was really going good," said Clarke. "I think he should have gone into coaching."

Desjardins actually did following his 2006 retirement, taking a player-development job that sent him on the road to mentor Flyer draftees. "I did that for four months," he recalls. "It was one thing to travel with the team, another to travel by yourself all the time. I just didn't think it was my thing.

"I wanted to coach my son. And then, once you get out of the game, you find other things to do. I don't feel like coming back."

Living in Montreal, he invests, hunts, plays in a recreational league three nights a week and lives the life he loves out of the limelight. Desjardins' nickname, Rico, inspired by the rap song "Rico Suave," was a compliment to his good looks, but he never spent time admiring himself in the mirror.

"I'm not the kind of guy that would read a lot of papers, listen to a radio show or stuff like that," he said. "For me, what was important was that my teammates, the coaching staff, and the organization appreciated me.

"That was my only concern really. It's not that I didn't appreciate the Philadelphia fans. They were good fans. But I wasn't waiting for a big article in the paper about me, or a big ovation from the fans."

He could evaluate himself. Unhappy with his play following the lockout, and still on the fence about giving it another year, Desjardins waited for a contract offer from Clarke that finally came after the defenseman, weary of the process of preparing a 36-year-old body to play, had made up his mind to retire. In between, he had calls from contenders including Detroit, plus the chance to wrap it up where it all began, in Montreal. He didn't consider any of them.

"I was a Flyer for 12 years," Desjardins says. "I'm still a Flyer today.

"I didn't want to play anywhere else. To be part of a great organization like Philadelphia was a privilege. To become part of that Hall of Fame group (in 2015) made it even more special."

The elite group became even more impressive when Desjardins joined it. The smooth Rico Suave did not have an ounce of slick. No 37 conducted himself with as much sincerity and dignity as anyone in franchise history.

Therien will tell you how much better a player he became because of his friend Rico's company, but off the ice, any Flyer was smart to study him in the pursuit of becoming a better person.

"Desjardins is the kind of guy we all should be," said Clarke. "Terrific man."

Rod Brind'Amour

Chapter 3 • 1997-99

Coats Off the Rack

Bob Clarke did not fire Terry Murray for the purpose of conducting an open search for a new coach. "When you make a move like we made, you need to have an idea of what you are going to do next or there is no sense doing it," Clarke would explain later.

His interest in Wayne Cashman, an assistant coach for 10 years with the Rangers, Lightning and Sharks, surprised Ed Snider but the Flyer Chairman entrusted the selection to his GM. Clarke thought Cashman, a hard-nosed player on two Bruin Stanley Cup winners who had earned praise in all three assistant stops as a strong shoulder for players to lean on, was what the Flyers needed after Murray.

"Wayne had a tremendous reputation," recalls Clarke, who, because Cashman had just been passed over for the San Jose head job in favor of former Blackhawks coach Darryl Sutter, received permission to interview from Sharks' GM Dean Lombardi. Clarke called Cashman and asked that they get together during the weekend of the June 21 Entry Draft in Pittsburgh.

Cashman arrived too late on Friday to make a scheduled meeting with Clarke before Saturday's draft but, while awaiting his interview, was open about the job's appeal. "They are the team I am interested in," Cashman told Philadelphia reporters. "I am looking forward to seeing Bob again."

The two had seen plenty of each other during the seventies. Cashman, who was the cornerman for Phil Esposito and Ken Hodge on a breakthrough scoring line in Boston, had played with Clarke for Team Canada in the epic 1972 Summit Series against the Soviet National Team and had captained the Bruins' during four series Boston had split with the Flyers.

During a 1977 exhibition game, Cashman and Paul Holmgren had extended a brouhaha into the corridor between the two Spectrum locker rooms, necessitating the installation of an iron gate. While this hardly recommended Cashman for a job with the enemy 20 years later, certainly Clarke, tasked with replacing the aloof Murray, was not in the market for dispassion.

After the Flyers, who had traded their first-round choice to Hartford for Paul Coffey, used pick No. 30—obtained from Toronto in the Dmitry Yushkevich trade—to take Cornell goaltender Jean-Marc Pelletier, Clarke and the personable Cashman met for four hours in two sessions. "Both his interviews knocked your socks off," recalls Clarke.

Leaving for six days to attend a reunion of his junior team in Flin Flon, Manitoba, Clarke returned and interviewed Flyer assistant Keith Acton. Most of the media speculation was that Acton—a Flyer for five years and their assistant coach for three—had the job. But he was interviewed largely as a courtesy befitting a loyal servant of the organization.

"We wanted a man who was experienced in the National Hockey League and in dealing with NHL players," said Clarke when Cashman was introduced as the Flyers' 11th coach at the CoreStates Center on July 7. "We wanted a man we felt was tough but fair; more importantly, a man the players could trust and a man who could trust the players."

When Cashman took the podium, his pledge for communication even extended to seeking more input from assistant coaches Acton and Dave Brown, both of whom were retained.

"Players ask questions nowadays," said Cashman. "They like answers. You have to keep an open line."

The new coach immediately moved to end the ambiguity about Eric Lindros's responsibility to fight his own battles when physical liberties were taken against him. "If someone goes after our best player, I am not going to send my tough guy after that guy; I am going to send him after the best player on the other team," said Cashman, who then called his best player to explain the new policy.

"That's the clearest I ever heard it made out," Lindros, who had not been asked for his input into Cashman's selection, told Tim Dwyer of *The Philadelphia Inquirer*. "Obviously, there were some communication problems, or [Murray] would have been back."

Cashman refused to directly offer his perception of anything that had gone wrong under Murray, but was not reluctant to portray himself as the antithesis of his predecessor, a coach who had said his job was to supply direction, not emotion. "It's the coach's responsibility to make sure players are motivated," Cashman said.

The players felt inspiration would come more easily if their roles were clear. "Everybody needs to know where they stand," said goalie Ron Hextall, who also received a call from the new coach. "I believe he is the type of guy who will listen.

"We have a lot of guys who have had problems in the past and they need to be addressed."

Cashman agreed with Murray on at least one point—that the Red Wings' biggest advantage in sweeping Philadelphia had been their failure to win a game against New Jersey two years earlier. "A great learning experience for the Flyers," Cashman called it, adding that he was not intimidated by taking over a team that had just fired a coach off a berth in the Stanley Cup Final.

"I'm fortunate to get a team I feel is capable of winning the Stanley Cup," he said. "I think pressure is being in an organization where you have to make the playoffs with a hockey team that isn't good enough."

The Flyer defense had not been good enough during the Final, providing Clarke with a clear priority but a limited pool of unrestricted free agents to target. Edmonton's Luke Richardson, who was permitted by the Collective Bargaining Agreement to shop himself because he had played 10 NHL seasons while earning less than the NHL average of $981,000—had multiple suitors, including Atlantic Division rivals Rangers and Panthers. But the 28-year-old defenseman, once a seventh-overall pick, had pretty much targeted the Flyers.

"Donnie (Meehan, his agent) didn't want to upset anyone that we were just using an offer to get a better one from somebody else," recalls Richardson. "So he just [solicited] interest and brought it to me to decide.

"I had already been (four seasons) in Toronto. For a young guy from (Ottawa) Ontario, playing in Toronto on Saturday night is pretty neat, but I wanted a better chance to win. (Florida GM) Bryan Murray had been a family friend—my dad had played hockey with him—and [Murray] wanted me to come there.

"But as Donnie did his due diligence, I think it was Philly all the way. They had just come off a Cup Final and Mr. Snider always was driven to provide the best means for his team to win. That's what I was looking for."

Indeed, after Clarke agreed to pay Richardson $12.6 million over five years, big money for a defensive defenseman, Richardson told the Philadelphia media he had not had a difficult choice. "I wanted to look at all the teams because this was the biggest decision of my life," he said. "But I never heard anything negative about the Flyers."

Having added Richardson's six-foot-three inches, 208 pounds and badly-needed physicality to the defense, Clarke also wanted more size up front—either on the next shift following Lindros or in his place should the Flyers, heading into the final year of his six-season deal, be unable to sign a long-term contract with a market-setting player.

After unsuccessfully attempting the acquisition of 6-5 Keith Primeau from Hartford the previous season, Clarke remained intrigued by a flying wedge of huge centers, hoping to create no good choice for an opposing coach to play his biggest, most physical, man in the middle.

Clarke asked Phil Esposito, GM of the struggling Lightning, shopping 22-year old Chris Gratton, a 6-4 center who was the third player taken in the 1993 draft, what it would take to make him a Flyer.

"Rod Brind'Amour and $5 million," Esposito said.

Wishing to give up neither, Clarke instead on August 12 signed Gratton, a restricted free agent, to a 5-year, $16.5 million offer sheet, then poisoned the pill for the cash-poor Lightning—who had the right to match—with a $9.5 million signing bonus that would pay more than half the value of the total deal during its first season. Tampa Bay's owner, Takashi Okubo, who had put the team up for sale almost nine months earlier, now would have seven days to sign Gratton at the Flyers' terms or take the CBA-mandated five No. 1 draft choices as compensation.

Clarke thought Gratton—with Keith Tkachuk one of only two players to have bettered both 30 goals and 200 penalty minutes in 1996-97—merited five picks that figured to come late in the first round. Not only was Gratton, who had played well against Philadelphia during the 1996 playoffs, deemed worth the money and the picks, but also the risk of the Flyers being called hypocrites. A week earlier, Clarke had publicly condemned a $21 million offer sheet by the Rangers to Colorado star Joe Sakic, saying that writing a check didn't require a lot of managerial talent by New York GM Neil Smith.

"Once the Rangers did it, it looked like the reins were off," Clarke rationalized to reporters. "It's similar to what the Rangers did in that [Gratton] is a Group II (right to match), but Tampa was trying to trade him."

Indeed Esposito appealed to the NHL that he had completed a deal with Chicago 38 minutes before the Flyer offer sheet was faxed to the league and the Lightning at 10:10 p.m. The league knew the trade, which would have sent Ethan Moreau, Steve Dubinsky, Keith Carney and cash to Tampa Bay, was agreed upon because Commissioner Gary Bettman, feeling too much money was going the Lightning's way, had asked the two teams to restructure it. Esposito and Chicago GM Bob Murray were in the process of doing so when the Flyers' offer was faxed.

Esposito argued that the league had not been informed of the trade's consummation only because he was having trouble reaching NHL Deputy Commissioner Bill Daly. But Bettman ruled the Chicago-Tampa Bay deal had not been completed with the required conference call between the teams until 1:30 a.m. The conference call had been a procedure implemented by the league after arbitrator Larry Bertuzzi had awarded Lindros to the Flyers over the Rangers in 1992 on the basis of a hand gesture by Quebec owner Marcel Aubut.

Esposito also claimed that the offer sheet was invalid because a smear mark had made the $1.5 million salary for the middle year look like $1.8 million. But he lost that one, too, leaving the Tampa boss smearing Clarke as a "backstabber" for having signed Gratton to an offer sheet while Esposito thought the Flyers still were negotiating a trade for the player. Esposito didn't mention that he was talking to at least two teams at the same time.

Snider wasn't offended by the insults hurled at his GM by Esposito.

"Mr. Snider called me, told me to make a deal for Gratton instead, and get the draft choices back," recalls Clarke. "He said, 'You can't leave Tampa without any players and a ruined team.'

"He likes Phil, didn't want him embarrassed."

As the seven-day signing period expired, Esposito agreed to trade the four first-round picks back to the Flyers in exchange for winger Mikael Renberg and defenseman Karl Dykhuis. "I think Phil panicked a little, should have kept the draft choices and traded them for better players," recalls Clarke.

Dykhuis, who had scored two game-winning goals among eight points during Philadelphia's 1995 semifinal run, had frustrated the Flyers with repeated gold-plated giveaways. Renberg had debuted with 38 goals in 1993-94 and appeared set for a long run on the Legion of Doom line with Lindros and John LeClair until a sports hernia and prolonged bouts with confidence had halved his normal production during the 1996-97 season.

"I kind of figured something might happen eventually," Renberg told Tampa Bay writers in a conference call. "Maybe this is a new start for me."

Clarke felt the 62 points Gratton had scored the previous season, his fourth in the NHL, were just a start on the way to stardom. "We think he is one of the premier young power forwards in the game," the GM said at Gratton's introductory press conference, where Clarke was much less complimentary about himself.

"We're like vultures," he said. "I think it's wrong that the rule is there to be used, but I also think that if you allow your opponent to use it, you're wrong."

Certainly cancer had not played fairly with Yanick Dupre. While the Flyers were winning their fight with Tampa Bay, their left wing prospect lost a war that trivialized all else. On August 16, the 24-year-old Dupre died of complications from leukemia at Hôpital Maisoneuve Rosemont in Montreal.

"He was doing so much better," recalls Hextall. "Then the next we heard he was gone." Dupre, who had put on 75 pounds after successful chemotherapy in the spring of 1996, had told Flyers during their trip to Montreal during the final weekend of the regular season that even though his Philadelphia contract had expired, he was going to be trying out at training camp. Just a few days later, the results of follow-up blood work floored him in a more lasting way than had the initial diagnosis a year earlier.

"The first time Yanick said, "I'm going to fight this," recalls his sister Nancy. "Because of his experience visiting kids with cancer in the hospital even before he was diagnosed, my brother knew there was a good [cure] rate.

"I remember asking him, 'How can you be so positive?' He said 'I'll take you to where kids two years old have leukemia. I'm 24, but they're just beginning. It's not fair.'

"But the second time he wasn't as positive. He said, 'Hockey is all I know and it's obvious the Flyers are not going to take me back now. I will always have a black cloud over my head.'"

Dupre underwent a bone marrow transplant from an unidentified Vancouver donor on June 5, but his weakened immune system couldn't fight an infection that settled into his lungs. In his last four months, he left the hospital only for a few days to go to his cottage in the Laurentian Valley with just his beloved chocolate lab Ruby.

"I had an expression of interest from a team in Germany and called to tell him," recalls Dupre's agent Ron Weiss. But he was at the cottage and there was no phone, so Yanick never knew."

He was too sick regardless. During the first week of August, a biopsy showed the infection had gone to his brain, paralyzing Dupre from the neck down. Having organized a golf tournament for leukemia research from his hospital bed—it raised $27,000—he was unable to attend.

"In his last few days, he woke up and saw that instead of all the bags of medication, the only thing that was there anymore was the white one with fluids and nutrition," recalls Nancy. "He must have known that meant the doctors couldn't do anything more for him. He looked at it and started to cry."

Yanick weighed 130 pounds when he passed away. "He fought hard," said Clarke. "It's a tough deal."

But a lesson, too. "Live your life, enjoy it, appreciate friends and family," recalls Eric Desjardins, Dupre's best friend on the Flyers during his three callups. "Yanick's death and my father's death (also from cancer) taught me that.

"I don't wait until bad things happen."

Desjardins, Dykhuis, Devils' goaltender Martin Brodeur and Ian Laperriere (Dupre's junior teammate at Drummondville, Quebec) were among those attending the service at Paroisse Saint Sylvain in Laval, Quebec. "Never a happy place," Desjardins says about funerals. "But to see so many young people there, and his girlfriend (Christina), you really felt the pain."

The printed program contained a poem composed by Yanick. "All I wish…is to leave this world of morphine and nightmares unknown to me," he wrote. "My heart of stone and strength keeps me alive and rising, rising to be the man I used to be."

With four more NHL teams to be born between 1998 and 2000, that man could have won one of those new jobs, believes Bill Barber, Dupre's coach at Hershey. "He had the wheels for it," said Barber.

Also, the determination. "He was hardly older than me as a junior and he was one of the veterans who was professional already, coming to the rink early, doing the right things," recalls Laperriere. "He always was really focused on his future.

"Yanick put up numbers in junior, but he was more a good checker, responsible on both sides of the platform. He would have played for a long time. Such a smooth skater."

That effortless stride had gotten Dupre selected with the 50th pick in 1991. Seated in the stands of Buffalo's Memorial Auditorium at the draft, he jumped up when Toronto announced "Yanic" at No. 47 and, when it turned out to be Yanic Perreault, had to sit down and wait three more picks, but Dupre had made it into the Flyer lineup for opening day in Pittsburgh that fall.

The first of his two NHL goals, scored at San Jose during the 1995-96 season, is framed alongside his picture in the home of Yanick's mother Huguette, inspiration that she says helped her survive breast cancer.

"There is nothing worse than losing a child," says Dupre's father, Jacques. "But I could not have been more fortunate in having Yanick for a son."

The American Hockey League instituted a Yanick Dupre Memorial Award, given to its man of the year for service to the local community. The Philadelphia chapter of the Professional Hockey Writers Associa-

tion put its Class Guy Award, which had been given for 21 years to a Flyer exemplifying co-operation with the media, into Dupre's name. At the proposal of Rob Parent of the *Delaware County Times*, the criteria were re-worded to "the Flyer who best illustrates character, dignity and respect for the sport both on and off the ice."

"I thought the award should represent something better than just the guy who is nicest to the writers," Parent recalls. Laperriere says they got it right, too.

"When somebody dies, you read, 'Oh, he was a good guy,' and we know sometimes that's bull," he said. "For this guy, it wasn't."

Jacques Dupre has not had contact with the Flyers in years. "They had done enough after he got sick; I didn't want to bother them," said the father. But he annually checks to see the Dupre award winners, noting so many of them in the early years were Yanick's friends.

"You can't describe the feeling when we were told these awards were going to be given in my brother's memory," said Nancy. "Especially because they both are given for unselfishness.

"My brother thought of other people first and himself second. But one time he said to me, 'I didn't do enough for the Flyers. Who is going to remember me?'

"I just know he is glowing, saying, 'I did something.'"

Long before coming to the Flyers in March 1996, Dale Hawerchuk had accomplished so much that his place in the Hockey Hall of Fame was assured. But after adding 54 regular season and 11 playoff points during his season-plus in Philadelphia to his NHL total of 1409, he knew an arthritic hip had used up his remaining time on the ice. At age 34, he decided to retire.

"I ripped it again during the season, but then came back and played on the fourth line during the Pittsburgh series," recalls Hawerchuk.

"I started coming on against Buffalo but then I had a little hiccup in the Ranger series. As close as we were, I wanted to push it as hard as I could but, by the time we got to Detroit, I didn't have my game anymore. It's frustrating when your mind is telling you one thing and your body is saying another.

"I had tried everything for two seasons to make it work. Bob Clarke let me bring in a guy to stretch and work me hard, but it was degenerative and getting worse. I couldn't be the difference maker I had been.

"There were a couple teams interested that summer. But I had to decide whether I was going to walk away from the game or crawl.

"I wish I could have got to Philly earlier. I loved the atmosphere. It was all business—and business together as a team, too—something I came to appreciate more later in my career. Being on the coaching side now (the Barrie Colts of the Ontario Hockey League), I brought a lot of the things here I learned from Mr. Snider, Bobby Clarke, Mr. Murray and a good group of Flyers. I can't say enough about playing with Eric Lindros."

Hawerchuk's presence honored an iconic franchise as well, despite his limited availability.

"It was in the days when the only medical check you did before a trade was to ask the other GM, 'Is he healthy?'" recalls Clarke. "Mike Keenan traded [Hawerchuk] here (from St. Louis for Craig MacTavish) with that really bad hip. We ended up having to pay the rest of the contract, but we got a year out of Dale that was pretty good.

"He helped Lindros and LeClair a lot because he could think the game so well, could really see things. He was a great player."

Coming off eight playoff victories, goalie Garth Snow wanted a salary commensurate with being a good player. Having asked for $900,000—the Flyers countered with an offer of $550,000—he was awarded $675,000 in arbitration. Dan Kordic also was re-signed for two years at a total of $950,000.

Radio play-by play man John Wiedeman resigned after just one season and was replaced by Tim Saunders, a Grosse Pointe, MI native who for the previous two seasons had done the games of the IHL's Cleveland Lumberjacks.

"Larry Gordon, the owner of the Cleveland team, who knew (Flyer president) Ron Ryan from the [World Hockey Association] made a call to him on my behalf," recalls Saunders. "I flew in, spent the morning with Ron, then in the afternoon he took me around to all the people who were going to weigh in on the decision—Jim Jackson, Bob Clarke, Steve Coates—and Ron offered me the job before I got back on the plane."

It wasn't the recommendation, remembers Ryan, but the auditioning tape. "I don't think Larry's [plug] was insignificant, but I picked Tim out of about 20 I listened to because I thought he had a good delivery and knowledge of the game," says Ryan.

Saunders, who two months earlier had rooted his Red Wings home against the Flyers, had to do a quick allegiance switch. Meanwhile, year one Flyer PR director Joe Kadlec stayed in the family, becoming director of fan services when they raided Tampa Bay again to hire away Barry Hanrahan to become director of team services. The Gloucester, MA native, who had been an original Lightning employee, was being given the opportunity to also perform contract preparation in Philadelphia's hockey operation.

Hanrahan's duties did not include wheeling barrels of cash to Gratton who, thanks to his front-loaded contract, would earn $10.15 million his first year with the Flyers. That amount wouldn't make satisfying Philadelphia's two established stars any easier.

In order to appease the Lindroses with the six-year deal negotiated for Eric before his rookie year, Snider had verbally promised a new contract before the old one's final season, 1997-98. Thus, the family headed into it hoping to make Eric, scheduled to bank $3.82 million, the highest-paid player in the game.

Thanks to the $21 million offer sheet Sakic had signed with the Rangers, the Lindroses had one static target, plus a moving one—Anaheim's Paul Kariya, the Hart Trophy runner-up to Dominik Hasek. Like Eric, Kariya was a year away from restricted free agency.

An exchange of five-year proposals between the Flyers and the Lindroses on the eve of camp failed to produce an agreement.

"Although the Flyers' most recent offer to Eric Lindros would make him the highest-paid player in the National Hockey League, we have not been able to reach an agreement," Clarke said in a statement. "As long as he honors his existing contractual commitments, we will continue to work towards negotiating a new contract."

Indeed, Lindros was on the ice as camp opened the next day. "I want to win here; I love it here," he said. LeClair, however, did not report, even though a five-year-old deal that paid the left wing a far-below market $1.2 million in 1996-97 (only $10,000 had been collected in performance bonuses despite scoring 50 goals) still had three years to run.

A five-hour-and-thirty-minute meeting between Snider, Clarke, LeClair and his agent, Lewis Gross, resulted only in LeClair and Gross hurrying angrily away from the team practice facility at the Coliseum in Voorhees, NJ.

"The most ridiculous evening I have spent in 10 years in this business," Gross called it. "They say they don't have the money to pay John what he is worth."

"A lot of pressure is being put on a lot of players by the players' association, which could care less about the health of the game," Snider replied.

While Chris Therien, who also did not have a contract for the upcoming season, agreed to three years and $3.7 million, Lindros continued to practice and LeClair remained out.

But one week into camp, while the Flyers were in Montreal opening their exhibition season, LeClair and Snider spoke. "John came to see me on Sunday night and we had a great discussion," the team Chairman said. "I clarified a few issues that made him a lot more comfortable that we'd be able to negotiate a deal."

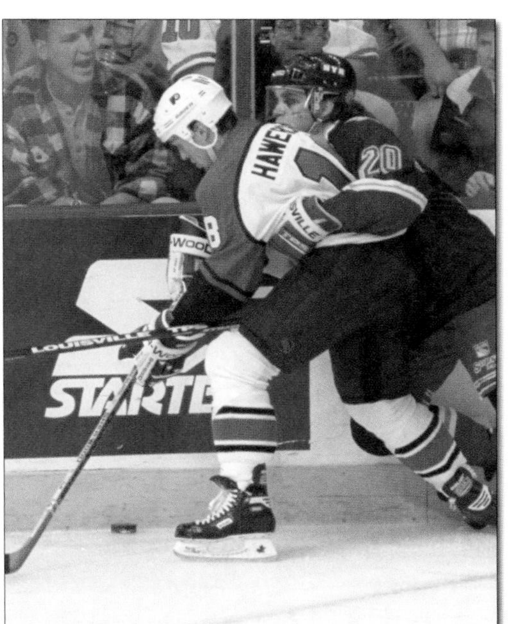

Future Hall of Famers: Dale Hawerchuk and Luc Robitaille.

Lindros skipped the game in Montreal while disability insurance was being arranged but continued to express patience with the process.

"I've been through this before; I sat out a whole year," he said, remembering his refusal to sign with Quebec. "This, too, will come to a stop at some time and hopefully we'll all be smiling when it does."

The captain said he no longer was running during summers at his Muskoka, Ontario cottage and rode a stationary bicycle instead. "I don't exactly have a runner's body," he explained, expressing concern for the pounding to his knees. "Plus, there are bears; they're quick up there.

"You think you're going to run for 50 minutes, but you could be gone for a couple days."

Gone from the Flyers forever was fourth-liner Scott Daniels, taken in the waiver draft by the Devils. His No. 22 was claimed by Richardson, who had worn it in Edmonton.

Cashman, who needed an endoscopic procedure to correct a swallowing problem, deferred his address to the troops on opening day of camp to assistant GM John Blackwell. But figuratively, too, the new coach looked forward to opening night with a lump in his throat.

"The first exhibition game I walked out behind the bench in the new arena, I felt like I was back in the big time, in the NHL, that this was really serious," he said. "Since I left New York (five years earlier), I'd kind of lost that.

"The last few places I was in (Tampa and San Jose), it was sort of entertainment."

Having been swept in the Final, the Flyers opened the 1997-98 season on a serious mission, but Lindros nevertheless felt that wouldn't preclude them from having more fun. "[Cashman] wants to get on the horse and go," said the Big E. "Why not go in and forecheck as hard as you can?

"It might take some time to get things in place, but we have guys who can really skate and have great size."

The newest of them, Gratton, came into opening night with just one point in seven exhibitions. But he converted Therien's drive that had hit the crossbar and added an assist while Zubrus, playing in the traded Renberg's spot with LeClair and Lindros, scored on a rebound.

Pat Falloon, who had been told at the beginning of camp to take some points off of his 16 percent body fat, also scored during Hextall's 3-1 win over Florida in the first game televised by the new Comcast SportsNet, the inspiration for the burgeoning cable and internet giant's 1995 purchase of the Flyers, Sixers and their arena.

For openers, the summer retooling of the Flyers appeared seamless.

"There is so much size and talent in this dressing room, I am very fortunate," said Gratton, feeling just as much in the right place at the right time as his coach, even if the players had to remind Cashman to put out an extra center before one defensive zone draw.

"I really think I was more excited than nervous," said the new bench boss. "I do have to admit that when they started singing the national anthem, it got to me a little, but there isn't any real nervousness when you know the team is ready."

Not everybody was, even if the members of the new Legion of Doom combined for eight points in a 5-3 win over Ottawa. Desjardins, the bone chips in his elbow having been removed over the summer, was not ready to begin the season because of a groin issue, and Petr Svoboda had suffered a broken bone in his right hand during an exhibition game.

Also not quite prepared in the early going was Snow to accept the NHL's new regulations on shoulder pads.

"What if they start regulating the size of these or these?" he complained, pointing into his locker at other pieces of equipment before losing 2-1 to Phoenix.

"It's old news, the Beatles broke up!" said Snow after the defeat, seemingly sorry he had even mentioned it, but a 4-1 defeat to the Flyers' nemeses, the Devils, seemed so much like the same-old, same-old that Cashman barked at his players during practice the next day to pick up the tempo. "If guys [want ice time] this will get turned around quickly," said the coach, ending a short honeymoon.

Desjardins returned in time for a 6-2 victory in his favorite place to win, Montreal. Snow, his shoulders lowered, shouldered the load nevertheless in San Jose, stopping 43 shots as Brind'Amour, subbing for the injured Zubrus on the Doom line, tied the game in the final three minutes before Lindros won it on an assist from Gratton, 3-2, in overtime.

In Anaheim, Paul Coffey assisted on both goals in a 2-2 tie but admitted to still feeling the effects of the concussion he suffered in a collision with Lindros in Vancouver nine months earlier.

"Even now when people are talking to me, if I don't really pay attention, my mind wanders," Coffey said. "If they write something out, I can glance at that and get it, but with (verbal) words, it's not that easy.

"I don't know, maybe it has nothing to do with concussions. Hell, maybe I'm just losing it."

Coffey was definitely losing ice time, too, at least in part because he was not a member of the penalty killing units of a team spending excessive time in the box. In a 5-1 loss at Los Angeles, Lindros, who was caught up ice on one goal and penalized during another, was benched for much of the third period. "I tried to get some people on the ice that were working," said Cashman, who went with a line of Eric Lacroix, John Druce and Kordic instead.

"It's embarrassing," said Lindros. "I didn't deserve to play."

LeClair got his raise, from $1.3 million per year to $3.6 million and $3.9 million, respectively, for the 1998-99 and 1999-2000 seasons. Vinny Prospal raised Doom's level of play with four points in a 7-1 win over Tampa, when Lindros scored goal No. 200 in his 207th game, fifth fastest in league history. Then Prospal set up LeClair's winner in a sloppy 4-3 win over Calgary.

Svoboda was welcomed back in a 5-0 loss to the Devils, during which the Flyers gave up three goals in just 69 seconds. Clarke, fast becoming concerned with his team's helter-skelter play, recommended to Cashman that he coach the neutral-zone trap.

"Not my style to get too involved," recalls Clarke. "I was more a devil's advocate than a dictator, but we weren't making any adjustments at all, just changing the lines."

So much for the offensive freedom Cashman had promised. The Flyers had only two third-period shots during a 3-2 loss to St. Louis, Pavol Demitra bouncing in the winning goal just 23 seconds after LeClair had tied the game late in the third period. The Flyers then blew a 2-0 lead into a 2-2 tie in their final game at the Capital Centre.

Coffey with just four points in 12 games, was not helping a power play on an 0-for-17 schneid, so he took a seat. "I wouldn't call it a benching," said Cashman. "Sometimes it's a game or two just to refocus."

Asked if he had learned anything by watching, Coffey said, "What was I supposed to be looking for?"

He went back into the lineup at the expense of the struggling Niinimaa. Told he would not be dressing for a game against Ottawa, the sophomore defenseman asked Cashman for permission to attend a pregame Metallica concert in the Sports Complex parking lot.

When Niinimaa, who had just wanted to unobtrusively watch backstage, obliged a photo opportunity by autographing a jersey for his favorite band, he got rocked and rolled in the media for his outing on a game day.

"People thought I got benched that night because I went to the concert," recalls Niinimaa. "But I was already benched and had permission.

"People still ask me about that."

Coffey, his mentor role with the young Finn minimized by the veteran's own struggles, survived a collision with Hextall that put the goalie out of the lineup with neck and back strain and then scored to score the only goal of the 1-0 win over the Senators.

As was the case with Hawerchuk, the Hockey Hall of Fame would eventually welcome Coffey without any late Philadelphia decorations to his resume. But on November 17, 1997, a Flyer original received his due. Gene Hart was presented the Foster Hewitt Memorial Award, the broadcasting honor by the Hall, at a Toronto luncheon.

He remembered his debut in the first Flyer game on radio, November 4, 1967 at Montreal, nine games into their initial season. "I thought at the time maybe I was just penciled in as an expediency," recalled Hart, who, indeed, was a budget hire when the Flyers paid $35,000 to radio station WCAU-1210 to get on the air. "I thought, 'I hope I stick around and we win something.'

"I guess I really stuck around and we won a lot of things."

Originally, only the Flyer third periods were sent over the airwaves. If that still had been the format in November 1997, their fans wouldn't have missed much. Down 2-1 after the second intermission, Philadelphia rallied on two Brind'Amour goals to beat Tampa Bay, 3-2, then stunk out Maple Leaf Gardens for the full 60 minutes, losing 3-1. "We had no right to win [against the Lightning] and we carried it right over into tonight," said Cashman.

He juggled to make Gratton, who had four goals and 10 assists in 24 games, a key for a productive second line. "He's trying to figure out what he has to do to fit in," said Cashman, who was pounding square pegs—left handed shooters—into the round hole on right wing created by Renberg's trade.

"We need to get some lines together and leave them," said Clarke. Cashman vowed to do that and let the chemistry grow on its own, again with Zubrus accompanying LeClair and Lindros. Brind'Amour, displaced to left wing by the addition of Gratton, scored twice in a 3-1 win at Buffalo.

"The way the season started with all the moves we made, I thought that everything I did last season was forgotten," Brind'Amour admitted. "I was ticked off, wanted to play center but I have learned to accept my role.

"I'm still looking to play center and figure before it's over, I'll be back there."

He wasn't the only Flyer wondering how the team had improved itself with the big player move of the summer. "I don't know if we needed drastic changes, just some tweaks," recalls LeClair.

Indeed, there was plenty of tweaking, too. Druce was demoted and Colin Forbes and Paul Healey brought up from the Phantoms in time to wear new duds, a third, all-black, Flyer uniform that debuted in a 4-1 win over the Islanders on November 28. "Better to be men in black than pumpkins," approved Lindros. But only cosmetically were the Flyers looking sharp.

Against Buffalo, Lindros scored for the first time in 10 games, then wrongly assumed Falloon was coming off, drawing a too-many-men penalty that the Flyers had to kill in the final minutes to preserve a 1-1 tie. "Our flow isn't there," said the captain. "One line will perform, then the next line won't follow the lead. We're dropping the baton."

The heretofore-struggling Bruins beat the Flyers over the head with it, 3-0, at an increasingly unsettled CoreStates Center. "The wake-up call was a while ago, this was just salt on a wound," said Lindros.

Clarke didn't take himself off the hook for having shuffled the deck into a bad hand.

"We thought Gratton would score as much if not more than Renberg and that Vinny (Prospal) would take over for Dale Hawerchuk," said the GM. "We thought Pat Falloon would come around. [Zubrus] has been inconsistent, he's got to work harder.

"Every night we're playing against that dead trap, that has to be a concern for the league. But I think this team should be more mature than it has been. We play one game with emotion, then one game without."

It wavered from period to period, too. When the Flyers jumped to a 4-1 lead against the Rangers, then settled for a 4-4 tie, it was the third time in four games they had blown a third-period advantage. "When a team gets a goal on us at a bad time we kind of come unraveled," said Shjon Podein.

Cashman was trying to get the Flyers to trap while lamenting the tactic at the same time. "That Rangers game was the best up-and-down game of the season, really entertaining," said the coach. He split up LeClair and the slumping Lindros, who had one goal in 13 games.

In search of a laugh, The Big E did *The Late Show with David Letterman*. "You're Zorro, let's face it!" said the host. But Lindros came back from New York to confess that the ongoing fencing over his contract was getting to him. "The last 10 games I haven't played real well," he said.

"I came to camp, I've done everything they've asked me to do. I don't want to sit here and sound like I'm whining, I just want closure. Ask Johnny, it gives you a little security, a good feeling about what's ahead."

Carl Lindros pushed for a pre-Christmas resolution. But amidst speculation that Eric was being pressured by the players' association to do a precedent-setting deal, the father-agent wondered aloud whether Snider, with his arena already built, still needed an expensive superstar.

Snider bristled as always at the suggestion that Lindros had been required to get the CoreStates Center built. "Winning has always been our No. 1 goal," reiterated the Chairman. "We want Eric here for his entire career. We're looking for a creative way to solve this problem."

The Ducks came up with one, signing the holdout Kariya for two years and $14 million, effectively setting a market for Lindros. "Yes, it has a bearing," said Eric. His anxiety apparently relieved, he scored his 10th career regular-season hat trick as Philadelphia—with Hextall returning to the net—broke a four-game losing streak with a 4-3 win over the Islanders.

On the morning of December 17, the Flyers and the Lindros camp exchanged proposals. When they could not agree, Carl called Eric to say it looked like he would be playing out his contract and becoming a restricted free agent at the end of the year.

The son ordered the father back to the table. "Eric made it very clear to me that we were to do whatever it took to make him a Flyer," Carl said. So he did, agreeing to a two-year deal that would raise Lindros from $3.746 million to $7.5 million for the current season, then pay him $8.5 for 1998-99, what Kariya was scheduled to earn.

"It's not exhilarating to pay $16 million for a hockey player," said Snider who, minus Clarke and Lindros, held a one-man press conference after the two sides reached agreement late that afternoon. "(But) I'm relieved that Eric has got this behind him. He can relax and have fun this year and play hockey at the highest level in the league.

"I fully expect Disney (the Ducks' owners) will sit down and extend the (Kariya) contract and when they do that will again set some guidelines for us. We're letting Disney run the Flyers now."

Snider said a longer-term deal for Lindros would "depend on the results of Eric's performance and also the performance of the team, whether or not we've reached the promised land."

That seemed like a fine promise to Lindros. "I think everybody's happy this has been put to bed for a while," he said in a message recorded for reporters. And Carl and Clarke expressed satisfaction, too.

"We're all back on the same page, how we got there is irrelevant," said the elder Lindros.

Added the GM, "Eric has said it's been bothering him. If it has been affecting his play, it shouldn't now."

The next day, Lindros was buoyant both before and after he bounced in a goal off Boston's Dave Ellett in a 2-2 tie that enabled Philadelphia to stretch an unbeaten streak to six (4-0-2). He seemed not at all put off by the organization's insistence that there would be no precedent-setting, long-term contract without a Stanley Cup.

"Somebody (in the dressing room) was saying, 'Now the heat's on,'" Lindros said. "Well, the heat's always been on; that never changes."

Even before the piano came off their captain's back, the Flyers had begun to make some sweet music. "Earlier we were waiting to see how teams would come out against [us]," Cashman said after his players won their first-ever contest against the Carolina Hurricanes, nee Hartford Whalers, 4-2. "Lately, we have decided we are the Philadelphia Flyers and here's how we play."

Ultimately however, that was determined pretty much by how Lindros and LeClair played. Eric had four-point nights during 8-0 and 7-2 wins in Vancouver and Ottawa, respectively, but the luckless Prospal went down for the second occasion in two seasons, this time with a broken leg.

Gratton was put in the middle of LeClair and Zubrus in the endless search for consistent second-line scoring. But with the Hurricanes' Keith Primeau holding Lindros to just one shot, backup finally arrived. Gratton hammered a drive from just inside the red line for his 10th point in six games to produce a 3-3 tie in Greensboro, NC, where the Hurricanes were playing for two seasons while awaiting the completion of their arena in Raleigh.

Another first visit, the next night at Washington's new downtown MCI Center, did not go as well, the Flyers losing, 4-1. But Trent Klatt's three points enabled them to close a seven-game holiday trip with a 5-2 win at Tampa. Philadelphia was 14-4-3 in its last 21 games.

The first game back from a long trip usually is mental trap. Sure enough, just after an obvious Montreal trip of Zubrus was ignored, the Flyers screamed for a call instead of hustling back up ice. Brian Savage made them pay with the knotting goal in a 3-3 tie.

On January 17, in an effort to make the Flyers faster, not smarter, Clarke moved the injured Prospal, Falloon, and a second rounder to Ottawa for winger Alexandre Daigle.

Best on best: Eric Lindros and Dominik Hasek

"We needed more scoring," recalls Clarke. "And we had enough guys down the middle that we didn't feel losing Vinny was going to hurt us."

Falloon, the second player taken in the 1991 draft, had scored 38 goals in 144 games for Philadelphia since being acquired from San Jose in November 1995 for a No. 1 pick and prospect Martin Spanhel. "Bad trade," Clarke recalls. "[Falloon] never was in shape."

"I didn't think he was soft," recalls Hextall. "I think he was an enormously talented guy who liked to play hockey but just didn't have the commitment, conditioning-wise, to make him as successful as he could have been."

Out went one bust and in came another. Daigle, the first player taken in the 1993 draft—and, according to the tabloids, the boy toy of Pamela Anderson—had neither broken 51 points nor the league-wide belief that starring some day on the silver screen was more important to him than headlining at hockey. But hoping the Senators and GM Pierre Gauthier had been too fast to condemn Daigle's character, Clarke thought his team could use Alexandre The Great's legs.

"He'll be a guy who can back off the other team's defense," said Clarke. Sure enough, in his debut, Daigle assisted on Lindros's power-play goal in a 3-0 win over Buffalo. One of the NHL's great underachievers was put on a line with a slacking Gratton while the disappointing Zubrus was bumped down to the third line, centering Podein and Colin Forbes.

"A few weeks of riding buses might bring the edge back to his game," Clarke had said of Zubrus during the All-Star break. Properly warned, the center scored the winning goal as Philadelphia held on to beat the Rangers, 4-3, in New York.

"I think Zubie sees the ice so well that when you put him in the middle, he has a lot more options," said LeClair hopefully. While Cashman lamented that the Flyers, who had reached the Final the previous year on talent, had to become a team that won on effort, Daigle, not exactly brought in for his character, remained goalless in the 15 games since his trade.

In their first meeting with Detroit since being defeated in the Final, the Flyer effort was beyond reproach until the last three minutes, when Brendan Shanahan tipped home a Nicklas Lidstrom drive for a 1-0 Red Wings win. But a 6-1 loss in Uniondale prompted a 35-minute closed-door postgame meeting. In Montreal, two late Philadelphia scores also failed to save a listless effort—and two bad goals allowed by Hextall—in a 3-2 loss.

"There's a gap between our top guys and our bottom guys that doesn't seem to be filling in too well," Clarke told reporters. The problem wasn't just up front, but on the back end, where Niinimaa, who had been the best Flyer defenseman in the Final, was not turning into the offensive catalyst they expected him to become. Still, Clarke hoped he could fix the problem with more speed up front. On February 5, the GM sent a fifth-round pick to Mike Keenan's Canucks for another former first-round choice, center-winger Mike Sillinger.

"We've got to get more goals in our lineup and we think Mike can do that for us," said Clarke. Meanwhile, goaltending remained an issue. When Hextall was beaten between the legs by Eric Lacroix for the winner in a 3-2 loss in Denver, Philadelphia dropped to a combined 0-6-1 against the leading four teams in the standings—New Jersey, Colorado, Detroit and Dallas.

Underscoring the top-heavy nature of their roster, the Flyers had seven players going to Nagano, Japan as the NHL participated in the Winter Olympic Games for the first time. Three—Lindros, Brind'Amour and Desjardins—were going to play for Canada and its GM, Clarke.

"Pretty high up as an individual honor for me," recalls Clarke, who was chosen by Bob Nicholson of Hockey Canada. With so much depth of Canadian talent and therefore so many options, the roster Clarke picked naturally was open to criticism. But perhaps his most controversial call was Lindros as the captain over Mark Messier and Wayne Gretzky.

"There are a lot of players from [Lindros's] age group now," Clarke told reporters. "It's time for a new group to take some responsibility."

The Canadians and Americans were placed together in Group C for a three-game round-robin to determine seeding for the elimination rounds. The Americans—counting the Flyers' LeClair and Joel Otto among 18 players from the 1996 World Cup championship team—got off to a bad start with a 4-2 loss to Sweden. They managed only a win over Belarus before losing to Canada, 4-1, and then went down in the elimination round to the Czech Republic, 4-1.

Team Canada won close over Sweden, 3-2, then convincingly beat the Americans and Belarusians and rolled into the semifinals with a 4-1 defeat of Kazakhstan. In a semifinal against the Czech Republic that glowed with the very purpose of the NHL shutting down for 20 days to put its best players on the Olympic stage, it appeared Jiri Sleger's third-period goal on Patrick Roy would hold up for a 1-0 Czech victory until Lindros's passout set up Trevor Linden to tie the game with only 1:03 remaining in regulation.

But after Robert Reichel scored for the Czechs on their first attempt in a five-round shootout, the Canadians couldn't beat Dominik Hasek at all. After Lindros, their fourth shooter, put a backhand off the post, Canada coach Marc Crawford never called on Gretzky. Hasek stopped the last shooter, Shanahan, with his left pad and the Czechs won, 2-1.

"We had a good team," recalls Clarke. "We lost a [bleeping] shootout." The crushing disappointment showed in just 15 shots—one of them Brind'Amour's only goal of the tournament—as Niinimaa's far more motivated Finnish club beat the Canadians 3-2 for the bronze medal. "This is a big deal for us," Niinimaa explained.

Time-zone differences of up to 14 hours for television purposes in North America, the failure of the U.S. and Canada to medal, and some damaged chairs left behind in the Olympic village by the Americans cast doubts upon the value of the NHL's participation, but certainly not to Flyer defenseman Svoboda. He slapped in the gold-medal-winning goal off a third-period faceoff as Hasek and the Czechs stoned the Russians, 1-0.

To make it additionally meaningful, Svoboda was playing for his country for the first time since defecting at age 18 during a 1984 tournament in Germany. "All of a sudden I'm back and I'm with those guys talking in my own language," he said. "The first game, I had shivers going through my body."

And it got even better than that when the Russians, only seven years earlier the occupiers of a forced marriage by the Czech and Slovak communists, were beaten in that gold medal game. "I didn't hear that [anthem] for many years," said Svoboda, then 32. "My feeling then, I can't put into words."

He is a little better at it today. "When I defected, I never even thought I would get to go back, let alone play for my country," he recalls. "And when you get older, you understand much more the meaning of country; especially then, under the circumstances.

"When democracy took its place, there was a struggle in the transition from Communism. That (gold medal) really uplifted the Czech Republic for a while. Everybody says it was the biggest sports moment in its history. Our top 10 guys were great players, but our next ten were not [NHL caliber] guys. So no one really thought we could do anything like that."

Having played probably the best hockey of his career, even with an elbow injured in the Canada game, Svoboda passed on the midnight charter to Prague for a celebration with his countrymen and President Vaclav Havel. "It is one of the greatest feelings I ever have gone through, but we have a schedule to resume here," he said upon arriving back in Voorhees.

And he would resume it without Hasek as a teammate. Back to reality with a Flyer club for which goaltending was an issue once more, even though Hextall had a goals-against average of 1.99. "How can you get any better than that?" asked Clarke before two clunkers got by Hextall in a 4-3 loss at New Jersey.

Snow's 2.52 save percentage looked decent on paper, but his work habits annoyed Clarke. So on March 5, two days after losing 3-1 at the Islanders, Snow was dealt to Vancouver in a one-on-one swap for goaltender Sean Burke.

"When we had Garth, he never worked in practice, just goofed around all the time," recalls Clarke. "I really liked him personally and I'm sure his teammates did, too, but that's one position that can mess up practice."

Burke, considered a franchise goalie in the making when he came up with the Devils, had a weak 3.51 goals-against average for the struggling Canucks, who had acquired him just two months earlier from the just-relocated Hurricanes.

Snow, who felt rescued when the Flyers had acquired him from Colorado—which had been relocated from Quebec in the summer of 1995—was unhappy with his second career deal. "It was the first time I went through the lows of a trade," he recalls. "Went from a Stanley Cup finalist to a team close to last place."

But Burke kissed the ground where a bucking merry-go-round horse had thrown him.

"It was a fresh start going to a team that was always trying to win the Cup," he recalls. "And the Broad Street Bullies was the team I had gravitated to as a kid, even when surrounded by Leaf fans growing up in downtown Toronto.

"But I wasn't confident in my game. And it was a hard way to [build it] near the end of a season."

Welcome to the club. On the night of the Burke deal, after saying goodbye to Snow, probably Ron's best friend in hockey, Hextall beat Washington 3-2. It was only the Flyers' third win in 10 games.

"We felt disorganized," recalls Desjardins. And Clarke, who began fearing he had made a poor coaching choice when Cashman did not address the team on the first day of camp, had become convinced his concerns were justified.

"He wasn't making any adjustments at all, just changing the lines," recalls Clarke.

Virtually all the Flyers agreed. "Outstanding man and a good guy, he [earned] a lot of respect," recalls Hextall. "But he didn't have the "it" factor to do what he had to do as a head coach."

Having made his reputation as a confidant of players, Cashman increasingly was confiding to himself that he was best suited for a subsidiary role.

"I just don't think he wanted to be the guy that sometimes has to deliver the tough message," recalls Richardson. "He wanted to be the guy to console the guy that got the tough message."

At Nagano, where he served as an assistant coach for Team Canada, Cashman had appeared more animated and happier than at any time since the Flyers hired him. He had admitted to Clarke that patting players on the back again was much more enjoyable than benching and admonishing them.

"I loved talking with Wayne," recalls Brind'Amour. "He had the stories; I could sit all day and listen.

"But he had no idea what he was doing. Absolutely no business being a head coach."

The most experienced man not currently holding that position was someone Clarke knew well. He called St. Louis GM Larry Pleau and asked for permission to talk to Roger Neilson, who was working as a Blues assistant under coach Joel Quenneville.

"We had worked well together (in Florida, where Neilson had been Clarke's first coach with the Panthers). "I wouldn't say we were friends because I don't know if Roger had too many 'friend' friends.

"But I always felt that with limited talent, he was a great coach, able to get players to play the game properly. Ours was a more talented team, but we'd lost our organization.

"I don't know what I would have done had we not been able to get Roger. [Pleau] wanted a draft choice. It took a couple of weeks."

During that time, the Flyers lost Lindros, who had missed only one game in his healthiest-ever season, on a second-period shoulder hit to the head by Darius Kasparaitis during a 6-4 loss at Pittsburgh. Burke, suffering from back spasms, had to come out of the same game.

"We're giving ourselves too many chances to lose," said Clarke before the home-and-home with the Penguins concluded the next night. "We go good for 30-35-40 minutes, then all of a sudden, we just seem to fall apart."

A few hours later, Podein scored with 45 seconds left in regulation to give the Flyers an apparent 3-2 victory, only until Brind'Amour missed the empty net and Ron Francis's passout enabled Jaromir Jagr to tie the game again. Hextall, who had flopped badly on an earlier Jagr walkout goal, was saved—and Lindros, who would be out for a minimum of two weeks with a concussion, was avenged—when Daigle's first Flyer goal won the game, 4-3, with 56.5 seconds remaining in overtime.

Therien remembers hearing the Neilson rumors even before the contest. Cashman hardly was stunned when he walked into his office after the game to find Clarke waiting for him.

"I told [Wayne] we wanted him to stay on as an assistant and he accepted right away," said Clarke, who then met Neilson—released from the Blues in exchange for a seventh-round draft choice and signed for a pro-rated three years at $650,000 per—at Philadelphia International Airport.

Both denied comment to reporters, as had Cashman about his status at the postgame press conference. But the next day, when the 63-year-old Neilson was introduced as the Flyers' 12th head coach—their third in nine months—Cashman looked relieved.

"I think I was doing a good job of separating myself from the players, but I felt it was hard," he told the media. "It's a good bunch of guys here and I like them.

"I was wanting to be patting them on the back and talking to them in some situations where maybe I should have been tough on them. Not that I don't think I'm capable again of being a (head) coach. But for this time, I think it's perfect. I'm working with a man I've got the utmost respect for in hockey."

That guy, whom Cashman had served as an assistant with the Rangers, was going to get just 21 games to organize the 32-20-9 Flyers for the postseason competition. "I knew it wasn't much time," recalls Clarke. "I just wanted to get to the playoffs and maybe get through a round or two."

Neilson's first six head-coaching jobs in the NHL had ended on charges that he put his teams—and their fans—to sleep by obsessively coaching defense at the expense of the attack. Much like Terry Murray, Neilson did not particularly breathe fire.

He had engineered a huge Maple Leaf upset of the Islanders in 1978, coached the Canucks to the Final in 1982, won a Presidents' Trophy with the Rangers, and directed the Panthers to within one game of .500 in their expansion season. Yet Neilson had lost three of those four jobs within the next year.

"It's always been a little annoying," he said to Philadelphia reporters questioning his dismissals. But everywhere Neilson had been there was praise for the rumpled, professorial, Captain Video's knowledge of the game and his ability to teach it in a calm, concise, and positive manner.

"Coaching is certainly motivation but there won't be any mind games here," Neilson said in his introduction to the Philadelphia media. "We'll have our system, the way we want the team to play."

Contrary to his stereotyping, he insisted that style would not demand Lindros and LeClair wait for the opposition at center ice. "We want to be a hard fore-checking team," Neilson said. "But there are some times you can't get in, and then you have to have a contain system.

"I don't think many people understand what a trap is. It's based on a counter attack."

With the Flyers having played both days on the weekend and scheduled to face New Jersey on the day after Neilson's coronation, he elected not to hold a full-scale practice before his first game. After just a 30-minute morning skate, the team's energy level rose enough for them to get a late 2-2 tie with the Devils on Daigle's second clutch goal in two games, but they were outshot 35-19.

"You've got to keep it simple to start," said the coach. "You make a list of eight things to do and you've got to cut it to four."

The next day he cued up a recording of the Flyer failings, then huddled with them between drills. "There wasn't a lot of uncertainty about what your job is position-wise," said LeClair after the practice.

There also wasn't much question that Cashman, joking with the players on the ice, was entirely comfortable with the new arrangement. "You feel like you failed a little bit, but that's personal," he said. "You shove that in the back closet and go on. I'm not mad at anybody." Suddenly third wheel among the assistants, Dave Brown was furious about being reassigned to a scouting position. "Less than two years ago, I quit playing to take a coaching job," Brown told the media. "I didn't expect it to turn into a scouting job; it's very disappointing."

So had been LeClair's production until he put the winner off the post and the backside of goalie Arturs Irbe for Neilson's first Flyer win, 3-2, over the Canucks. "I felt a little bit more comfortable," the coach said. "I know most of their names now."

Lindros, the team's biggest name, was on the stationary bike, pedaling toward a late April return. His scans matched the baseline established during camp, but the diagnosed grade two concussion had left him lightheaded. "I cannot say this will clear in a week or two weeks," said Dr. Jeff Hartzell, not good news because Lindros, LeClair and Brind'Amour had contributed 49 percent of Philadelphia's goals.

So it seemed a step forward when the Flyers scored on four powerplays to blast Detroit, 6-1, their first victory of the season against one of the top four clubs in points.

"If you are not beating good teams, people are going to want to read a lot into it, as well they should," said Neilson, whose club went to 3-0-1 since he became coach by beating struggling Toronto, 4-1. Daigle, who had scored five goals in five games, helped the equally speedy Sillinger record a three-point night on a line with rookie Forbes, an improved act by Alexandre The Great, the self-described future thespian.

"[Pursuing a second career] is something I could not have done (in Ottawa)," said Daigle. "Hockey is so big there, you are only allowed to sleep and play hockey, but I never have thought that way.

"Why not be interested in other things? [In the U.S.,] you are expected to have other things in your life."

Only when you are winning, however. The only Philadelphia victory in the next six contests was 5-4 over the Rangers on Podein's goal with 20 seconds left in overtime. It came after the Flyers had blown two leads, the last when Gretzky beat Burke with only 1:42 to play.

To finish the season, Clarke already had made the only goaltending move he planned. "Why would we give up something when we can sign one of those guys as a free agent," said Clarke, referring to three accomplished goalies—Edmonton's Curtis Joseph, the Rangers' Mike Richter, and Florida's John Vanbiesbrouck, all of whom would become unrestricted on July 1.

But the GM thought the Flyers still needed immediate help on defense. On the afternoon of March 24, with his team in North Jersey to play the Devils, Clarke stunningly traded Niinimaa to Edmonton for defenseman Dan McGillis and a second rounder.

"There were rumors, but Clarkie had told me a few days earlier that I was going nowhere," recalls Niinimaa. "The phone rang in my room on a game day and Colin Forbes and I looked at each other.

"He answered and said, 'Roger asked to speak to you.' I thought, 'Oh [bleep], here we go.'"

Clarke told Niinimaa later in the day that he was being traded because the Flyers needed to get bigger and stronger, exactly what the GM told the media.

"We gave up a young, talented player," said Clarke, who, in another deal, got back from the Canucks the fifth-round pick he had traded for Sillinger plus 36-year-old defenseman Dave Babych, while picking up a third-rounder. "McGillis is a lot bigger (actually one inch and five pounds), a lot more physical, and a lot better defensively."

Richardson vouched for McGillis, an Edmonton teammate the Oilers thought would be too expensive to sign when his $525,000-a-year contract expired at the end of the 1998-99 season. "He was our best defenseman," said Luke. But Niinimaa had been a presumed blueline catalyst in training, a kid who a year earlier Clarke had refused to put in any trade packages for a veteran difference-maker.

"Janne was such a good skater, but he went backwards all the time," recalls Clarke. "He used to drive me crazy; I would think it was going to come, but it never did. And that's what I would see from him in Edmonton after we traded him."

Niinimaa recalls victimizing himself with expectations that matched those of the Flyers'. "I wanted so badly to be better in every way, I was thinking too much," says Niinimaa, who today runs a concert and festival business near his hometown in Oulu, Finland. "I pressed, was playing just average, and then I pressed a little more.

"If Clarkie remembers me [taking the puck backwards too much], I'm pretty sure it's accurate. I really wanted to grow into someone who was in control of the game. I do remember them telling me I needed to get more pucks to the net.

"I was sad to leave."

There hardly has been a player in the game's history who didn't feel that way about the team that brought him into the NHL. The first trade always hurts the most.

"My happiest Flyer memory?" Niinimaa recalls. "Walking into the locker room for the first time and seeing 'Niinimaa' hanging with 'Lindros, LeClair and Desjardins.' My worst? Seeing Steve Yzerman pick up the puck at the end of Game Four and watching the Red Wings celebrating. It was horrible, still don't like to talk about it."

The Oilers turned down a bigger deal that would have included Zubrus and brought back Edmonton winger Ryan Smith. Despite Clarke's efforts, there were no takers for Coffey, who was on the ice for three goals against while McGillis was debuting in a 4-2 loss to Boston.

After Hextall was beaten 4-2 by Carolina, Burke defeated his exmates in the second half of the home-and-home, 3-1. Philadelphia's 3-2 win against the Blackhawks clinched a playoff spot even though Zubrus delivered a two-hander that struck Chris Chelios above the eye, earning a two-game suspension.

A five-goal burst in 11:04 of the third period produced a 6-1 win in Tampa Bay, although a sucker punch by the Lightning's Andrei

Nazarov to Dan Lacroix's left eye didn't put the Flyers in a celebrating mood. Lindros, on the trip and waiting with teammates by the bus after the game, had words for Nazarov as he left the Ice Palace.

"It would have been six (Flyers) to one," Nazarov said. "I told them to save it for the ice." With some help from the cooler head of Kjell Samuelsson, Lindros did. But he shared his opinion on Nazarov with reporters. "Gutless," said Lindros.

Clearly the Big E, who had just donated to the Childrens' Miracle Network an unspecified settlement from the Flyers' suit against WIP Radio—the station also issued an apology for talk show host Craig Carton reporting Lindros missed a February 1997 game with a hangover—was feeling better about his concussion, too. He was deemed ready to return five days later in Buffalo.

"I've seen it so many times on tape," Lindros said about the Kasparaitis hit that had put the captain out for 18 games. "I've been hit harder before and I'll probably be hit harder in the future."

The Flyers, who had been 34-40-9 during past Lindros absences, had not struggled as much this time, having gone 10-6-2. His re-entry was eased when Neilson used him on wing and on the point of the power play. But during 20 chippy minutes, the captain knocked off Michael Peca's helmet and was stopped on a breakaway by Hasek.

Lindros wasn't the only Flyer frustrated by the Sabres goaltender. Thanks in part to four minor penalties in the third period, the only scorer who solved Hasek in the 2-1 loss was LeClair, who reached 50 goals for the third consecutive season.

"Hasek does this every night, it's not like it was a fluke," said Klatt who, facing a half-empty net behind the stickless goalie, was stopped by Hasek's blocker. "I won't be sad if we don't have to come back here (for the playoffs)."

Like most tourists, Lindros would rather have been in Florida. With two goals and an assist during a 7-3 rout in the last hockey game ever at the Miami Arena, he ran his record there to 7-0 since the Flyers' crushing 1996 playoff loss.

"I think he was fired up for this one," said Neilson. "The thing I didn't know about him was that he was very vocal on the bench.

"Glad to see that, I had an impression of him as a quiet guy."

The Rangers, about to miss the playoffs, had not enjoyed much of a season to speak of, but Mike Richter beat the Flyers 2-1 at CoreStates in Game 81, ending Philadelphia's chance to move past the Penguins into second place behind runaway Eastern Conference champion New Jersey.

Dreading a three-versus-six matchup with Hasek, the Flyers had an opportunity to avoid him by winning in Boston in the season finale. Burke, 6-3 since his acquisition and looking more and more like Neilson's choice over Hextall (winless in his last five starts), stopped 37 Bruin shots. But Gratton had the only goal in an otherwise weak effort that helped Boston solidify the fifth spot with a 2-1 victory.

"[The Sabres] are the hottest team in the league the second half (21-10-10)," warned Neilson. Essentially Buffalo was as starless up front as a year earlier, when run over in five games by the Flyers. But the Sabres had a new coach in Lindy Ruff and most importantly, a healthy Hasek.

"There's going to be a lot of goals that might get past another guy that are not going to get past him," said Lindros. "We have to keep at it, accept the challenge."

The challenge became to pretend this was just another goalie, an idea presented to the Flyers by their own netminder, Burke, whose choice over Hextall was confirmed by Neilson at the end of Monday's practice. "Boston doesn't even talk about him before they play him," said Burke. "I think that's something we should do.

"He's human, like the rest of us. I'm not going to worry about him."

But Burke remembers that his new teammates would rather have been playing almost anyone else, even though they had won the season series 2-1-1.

"Hasek had been so good that year, we were almost psyched out before we went into the playoffs," Burke recalls. "I played fairly well down the stretch and was starting to get things back, but when your team has a block mentally with the other team's goaltender, it puts a little pressure on you.

"It just didn't set up very well for us, a tough environment to win that first round."

The Flyers had gone 10-9-2 since the coaching change, actually a lower winning percentage than they had under Cashman.

"At times we looked very strong," Neilson told the media. "But we were more up and down than we would have really liked."

In part that may have been because some players didn't much enjoy each other. "We were in disarray, not a very happy team," recalls Lindros without elaboration. "Our chemistry just wasn't the same (as the previous season)."

Zubrus, facing a half-empty net, hit the post on the first shift of Game One at the CoreStates Center. When Babych flopped to the ice, enabling Matthew Barnaby to go in alone, Michael Grosek's rebound gave Buffalo a 1-0 lead, but the scoreboard was the least of the adversity facing the Flyers. Just after Sillinger was concussed on a clean hit by Alexei Zhitnik, Svoboda dove for a puck at center and hit his head on Dixon Ward's knee.

Prone on the ice, Svoboda threw off his glove and helmet and, legs thrashing, motioned to the bench for medical help. "My left arm was dead and I felt burning in my body like I was lying in a fire," he recalls.

He was administered oxygen and wheeled off to a standing ovation. When the game resumed, the crowd had lost enthusiasm and so had the Flyers. Nevertheless, they were 1:42 away from getting out of the second period down just a goal when Wayne Primeau beat Klatt's check off an odd-man rush and made it 2-0.

Midway through the third, the Flyers rallied furiously. First, Brind'Amour put a left circle shot past a Lindros screen. Just 19 seconds later, Gratton, alone in the slot, beat Hasek under the crossbar to create a 2-2 tie.

It lasted only 2:55 until Therien's clear was intercepted by Bob Boughner at the point. His rebound was converted by Donald Audette with 7:13 left in the game and Philadelphia didn't have another good chance in the remainder of its 3-2 defeat.

The Sabres matched the Flyers hit for hit while blocking 16 shots.

"They're small but that doesn't seem to bother them," noted Neilson, whose powerplay had gone 0-for-6 in the ongoing absence of Coffey, a regular scratch down the stretch.

"It must be hard to get to the point where the coach doesn't want to give you much ice time when you've been a star," sympathized Neilson, but Svoboda, released from the hospital after a diagnosis of two compressed nerves, was the greater object of compassion.

"I thought I broke my neck," the defenseman told *The Philadelphia Daily News*'s Ed Moran. "I consider myself very fortunate. A little left or right and you're going home paralyzed."

Svoboda said he would be ready by Game Three. In the meantime, Neilson, trusting Richardson no more than Coffey, dug in for Game Two with Desjardins and Therien as one workhorse pair and McGillis and Babych as another.

Lindros eased the pressure 5:24 into the first period, powering in a backhander off a McGillis rebound. Early in the second, Gratton picked off a weak Hasek clear and made it 2-0, but a dubious too-many-men-on-the ice call—"We watched the video and did not have too many men on the ice," Neilson later insisted—got Buffalo back into the game.

On the powerplay, Grosek high-sticked McGillis in the face without penalty, then put in a Barnaby rebound. With Brian Holzinger off for roughing, Ward stole the puck from Otto and, just after the penalty expired, beat Burke to tie the game.

Neilson kept going to his best players. Zhitnik, first ducking a Lindros check at the Sabres' bench, bumped the Flyer captain through the open door, where he fell among sticks and skates. The defenseman took a look around before giving Lindros a gratuitous push down, but didn't get away with it, giving Philadelphia a four-on-three. On their 14th powerplay of the series, the Flyers finally cashed one when Lindros set up LeClair's tap-in at the post with 3:32 remaining.

With 1:16 to go, Grosek butt-ended McGillis in the face, took a swing at the protective awning over the opening to the visitor's tunnel, smashed two sticks over equipment-drying fans, and high-sticked the locker room door.

"I used to have tantrums like that when I was in kindergarten," said Burke, but the Sabres, while certainly instruments of their own demise in losing Game Two, 3-2, had made it clear they were not surrendering as easily as they had a year earlier.

"They lost it there in the end, but they are not going to go away," said Neilson. "They're small but that doesn't seem to bother them."

His own club, with seven players having played 20 or more minutes—including Desjardins at 31 and Lindros at 30—was tired, welcoming an extra day off before Game Three in Buffalo.

But the Sabres, their team treasury lightened by a $2,500 bill for the locker-room damage and bolstered by the first appearance in the series of Lindros antidote Michael Peca, came out with quicker feet, too. Svoboda, back in the lineup as promised, and Therien took back-to-back penalties. On the second, Miroslav Satan converted a carom off the backboard.

"We knew we were fortunate after the first period; we had played terrible and it was only 1-0," said LeClair later, but the Flyers' brains were even slower than their legs. They survived a five-on-three due to consecutive penalties on LeClair and Lindros, but 12 seconds after the second one expired, three Flyers chased the puck to the corner, leaving Grosek alone to take a feed from Barnaby and make it 2-0.

LeClair next took the second of his three second-period penalties, which Satan cashed, before Philadelphia gave up shorthanded goals to Darryl Shannon and Holzinger in a four-goal period.

"We've got to face adversity a whole lot better than we did tonight," said Lindros after the Sabres, helped by repetitive giveaways by himself and LeClair, seemingly had won every race during the 6-1 victory.

"I don't think they're quicker, just working harder," scoffed Desjardins. But between games Clarke admitted that a season-long NHL obstruction crackdown had left him caught with a bigger, slower team.

"We took a gamble that once the playoffs started the players would have a little more freedom to determine the outcome of the game," the GM told reporters. "But in every series you're seeing a lot of penalties.

"A guy 170 or 180 pounds (once) could be put on his butt by a guy 220 or 230. That's the way [the larger player] was taught to play, but now he gets penalized for it."

Neilson, too, complained it was difficult for the Flyers to get a hitting game going. They were receiving powerplay opportunities but had scored only twice in 22 advantages. When Sillinger, back in the lineup for Game Four, was stoned by Hasek midway through the first period,

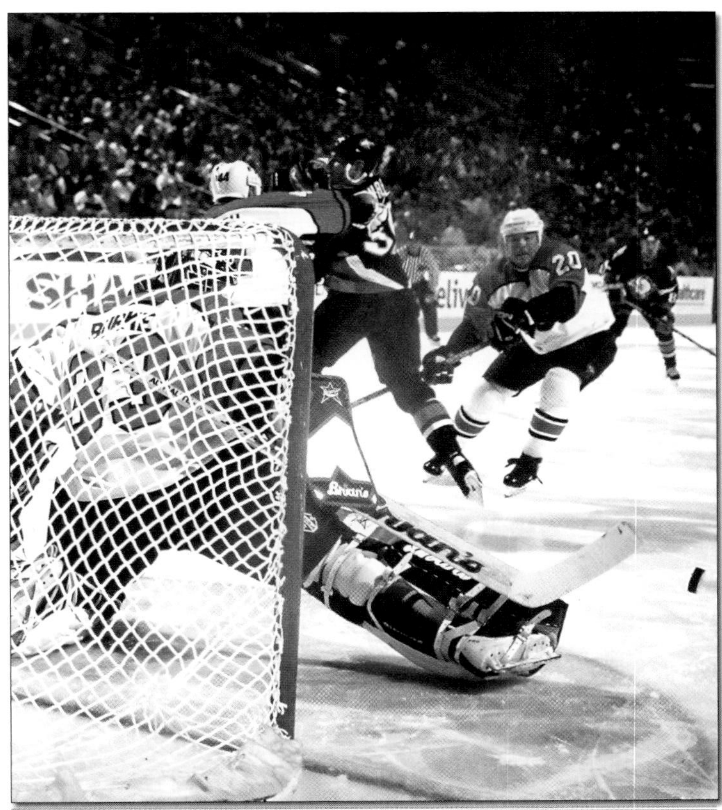

The Sabres would prove to be a much tougher oppnent in the 1998 playoffs.

Philadelphia's determination seemed to die.

"That year, Buffalo was starting to play Hasek hockey, keeping things to the outside," recalls Podein. "If you didn't get it under the crossbar or move him from side to side, you weren't going to score, so you missed the net more and stopped doing the little things you needed to do to have success."

"Richter had been playing great before we faced him the year before," recalls LeClair. "But I don't think he had that reputation that gets into guys' heads like Hasek did. If you got a goal, it was like you snuck one by him. He was stopping everything."

Peca beat Klatt to the puck and Ward went by Desjardins and LeClair to break a scoreless tie late in the first period of Game Four. With Forbes in the box, Satan was all alone to convert a Holzinger pass in the final minute of the period and the Flyers crumbled again. Barnaby scored through a crowd and the Sabres went on to a 4-1 win and a 3-1 series lead. Lindros and LeClair managed only one shot on goal combined, 25 of the misleading total of 45 Flyer shots on goal were taken by defensemen, and the failing power play was two-for-28.

"When you hit the playoffs, emotion shouldn't be a problem," said Neilson. "This is when you find out about a team, when the chips are down.

"As a new coach, that's what I'm trying to assess now. They had to get used to a new coach, then another one. However tough that is for the players, I don't know. We felt like 21 games was enough time."

Snider insisted there still was time. "I don't think it's as bad as it looks," he told the media before Game Five. "We don't think the season is over yet."

Jason Woolley's powerplay drive, with Lindros in the box for a retaliation penalty on Barnaby, went through traffic, then ticked off Burke and in, putting Philadelphia behind the eight-ball again just 2:29 into the contest. But Daigle, invisible until now, stole the puck at center and hit Sillinger all the way from the left boards to the right wing. Sillinger put the puck between Hasek's blocker and body for an energizing, game-tying goal.

The Flyers outshot the Sabres 16-4 through the first 16 minutes of the second period. They went to the locker room tied 1-1 and feeling good about themselves for the first time in three contests.

But with McGillis and Woolley off for roughing penalties 29 seconds apart, Therien arm-hooked Holzinger and, on the four-on-three, Audette put in his own rebound on the backhand.

Buffalo, no more disciplined than Philadelphia, gave the Flyers two more chances 1:40 apart when Ward roughed Desjardins and Holzinger slashed LeClair across the arm. After LeClair's jam kept Ward from clearing the puck, Lindros knocked the Sabre player's stick out of his hand, helping Babych, off a saucer pass by Brind'Amour, score on the power play with 6:52 to go, tying the game at 2-2.

McGillis retaliated on Audette for taking down Gratton, costing Philadelphia a powerplay, but Burke kept the Flyers alive by stopping Barnaby on a breakaway backhander.

In overtime, LeClair almost won the game from his butt before Gratton, trying to lift Barnaby's stick, missed and raised his helmet. Barnaby pretended he had been hit in the face and referee Paul Devorski called Buffalo's 10th man advantage of the game.

On the kill, Babych tipped the puck past two pinching Sabres, sending away Podein on a semi-breakaway, but Hasek got a piece of the left-circle drive and the puck rolled barely wide. At the other end, after a McGillis wind-around was held in by Shannon, Grosek worked a give-and-go with Richard Smehlik that suckered Babych, leaving Grosek alone in the slot for the return pass.

Thwarted by Burke on two previous breakaways, this time Grosek hit the post. But the rebound came right back to him and he ended the Flyers' season into a half-empty net at 5:40. The Sabres, 3-2 winners, had beaten Philadelphia in five games.

"Hasek was the only goalie I've ever played against that I could honestly say was the difference," recalls Brind'Amour. "It was like a brick wall we were shooting at and our own goaltending was terrible.

"When you have confidence in your back end, you play different, you just do."

For all the other reasons that the Sabres had beaten the Flyers in the playoffs for the first time in five tries, the fulcrum of the series had been the mindsets created by the goaltending.

"I don't know about any goals in particular, but at the end of the day I didn't deliver the goaltending that I was capable of giving," recalls Burke. "I wish I would have done better."

He didn't do any worse than Philadelphia's special teams. Eight of Buffalo's last 13 goals in the series had come on powerplays, while the Flyers had gone 3-for-35 for the series with the man advantage. Lindros and LeClair had each scored just one goal.

"Expectations were high, a lot of changes were made, and things just snowballed," recalls Svoboda. "I think a lot of guys thought [management] should have stayed the course."

After losing badly in the first round, that course now was required to change again. Like a chastised dog, the Flyers' ears were back. But they also were open.

"I think the whole team knows we're going to need a more controlled style next year," said LeClair as the players cleaned out their lockers. "I think this team has played a go-go style for the last four years. I don't think it's the way to win in the playoffs.

"One thing Eric said today was, 'The guys will really be ready, whatever system [Neilson] is ready to put in next year.' Maybe now that we've had this early exit, it'll be a character builder."

The builder, Clarke, had hired a reluctant coach who had lasted only three-quarters of the season, altered the team's chemistry for the worse with the Gratton signing, and compromised some character in his mid-season push to add speed.

"I screwed up," Clarke told the media after taking a week to gather his thoughts. "More than anybody on the team, I screwed up."

But of course Lindros took most of the heat for the collapses in the two games in Buffalo. "You don't have to be a rah-rah guy to be captain," defended Neilson. "You can have quiet guys be very effective.

"Eric is our top player. He can control a game. There's no better leader than that. He wants to win very badly and everybody knows that."

Lindros admitted to some growing pains. "As a captain, I enjoy it but sometimes what's good isn't always easy," he said. "Everyone in the world wants to be liked; at times you can't be. Sometimes, saying what's on your mind is hard to do."

Snider reiterated his desire to sign Lindros, who was committed only through the following season at $8.5 million, to a long-term contract. "Your actions speak louder than your words and when Eric is banging people on the ice, that's fire," said the Flyer Chairman to Rich Hofmann of the *Daily News*. "Eric is not the primary issue here; it was a team breakdown."

"I'm sure John (LeClair) will tell you he was disappointed in his play. Maybe one reason our stars didn't do so well is that the rest of the players didn't pick it up."

For a badly needed organizational pick-me-up, the Phantoms defeated the Saint John Flames, 6-1, at a sold-out Spectrum to win the American Hockey League's Calder Cup. The fourth AHL title won by a Flyer farm team—following the 1977 and 1978 Maine Mariners, and 1988 Hershey Bears—was the first professional sports championship in Philadelphia since the Sixers had won the NBA crown 15 years earlier.

"It's been so long that I forgot some things about winning," said a teary Bill Barber, the coach of the two-year-old franchise anchored on defense by veterans John Stevens and Jamie Heward, and goaltender Neil Little.

Perhaps right wing Mike Maneluk, who added three assists in the clinching game to total 34 points in 19 playoff games, could upgrade the speed of the big club. With NHL Board of Governors' decisions to move the goal line out two feet, add a second referee (in as many games as the supply would allow) and extend the goal creases a foot past the posts, Clarke saw the trend.

"I think the league has made a concerted effort to open up the game for speed," he said on June 27, after using the 22nd pick in the 1998 draft to choose the skinny, fleet Simon Gagne, a center from the Quebec Remparts.

"You would watch him and think, "Oh, [bleep], he's smart," recalls Simon Nolet, then the Flyers' Quebec scout. "A lot of guys are skilled; Simon was skilled and smart.

"He was about six feet tall, but not very strong or [muscular], probably why he drifted back (in the draft) a little bit. But we were scared Montreal was going to take him at 16."

That had been Gagne's expectation, too. "Now they don't care if you only weigh 170 like I did; if you are quick and good, they are going to draft you," he recalls. "At that time my size [was going to be a negative factor] so I knew I wasn't going to go near the top.

"The night before the draft, the general manager of the Remparts told my dad that he had spoken with a couple of scouts from Montreal and that 'Simon is going to get drafted by the Canadiens tomorrow.' When I was driving home from a family dinner that night, that same thing was on all the channels.

"The Nordiques had been my team (before moving to Colorado three years earlier), so I hated the Canadiens. But I became a Canadiens' fan for that night. And when Montreal went to the stage and said, 'From the Quebec Remparts. . .Eric Chouinard,' it was like somebody put a needle in my bubble."

Chouinard had shared a powerplay with Gagne and comparable first-round ambitions. "He could score, we liked him," recalls Nolet. "Just liked Simon better because he was more complete."

The Flyers never had told that to Gagne, though. "With most of the teams, I had one-on-meetings with managements," he recalls. "Not the Flyers.

"So (picks) 17, 18 then 20 go by—my old team, Colorado, had three of those picks—and then the Kings, who had told me they would take me, didn't either. When the Flyers drafted me and I went to the stage, I still was upset. I didn't know until afterwards about Simon Nolet knowing my dad."

Pierre Gagne, a police officer, had been friends with Nolet since they attended 1967 and 1968 Flyer training camps at Quebec City together—Nolet winning a spot on the Philadelphia farm team located there, Gagne being cut. "You had better draft my kid," Nolet remembers Gagne telling him, but Ontario scout Dennis Patterson and western scout John Chapman didn't need a blood connection or an old friendship to endorse the idea.

"I saw Simon the most of course," said Nolet, "But one scout doesn't make the decision for the Flyers; it just doesn't work that way.

"When Chappie came through mid-year, Simon was a good prospect but not the top. When he came back for the playoffs he said, 'Good player, fine with me if we draft him.'"

At No. 22, the Flyers took the player Clarke told reporters was "10th to 12th on their list," even without an interview. "We didn't do much of that in those days," recalls Clarke. "You could find out more talking to the trainer and the coach.

"You bring a player in, 10 teams already have interviewed him and his agent has already told him how to answer each question. Every time we interviewed, every kid that left the room sounded like the greatest kid in the world."

Although this one was not pleased to have dropped so far in the first round, Nolet figured Gagne would get over it. "He was the best player available there, without a doubt," the scout told the media. "He can execute at a very high speed."

Perhaps nobody in the NHL ever executed at a higher speed than Paul Coffey. But lingering effects of the concussion suffered when he collided with Lindros had dulled his reflexes during the Flyer run of 1997, and issues of age and fit had made him an extra player, unused by Neilson during the playoffs.

By late June, Clarke called Coffey in and spoke about the difficulty of trading him with another $4.1 million left on his contract. "I listened for awhile respectfully, then said, 'I don't know where this is going,'" Coffey recalls. "I said, 'You might think I make too much money, but somewhere along the line I earned that money and you guys are going to pay me.'

"He gave me a look and kind of threatened me. Said something about sending me to Cincinnati (an independent IHL team). I said,

'That's your decision to make. I'm under contract.'

"Maybe a week later, they traded me."

After agreeing to pay $1 million of the money left on the deal, Clarke found a taker in the Blackhawks, dealing Coffey on June 29 for a fifth-round pick. "I think he had a bad concussion and never recovered," recalls Clarke.

Teammates remember an unhappy Coffey as his usage declined during his second Philadelphia season. But he has gotten past any bitterness. "I came back too soon (from the concussion)," he recalls. "Things were so good for the Flyers, I wanted to be part of it. Plus I knew my career was winding down and wanted to play in one more All-Star Game.

"The worst defeat of my career was losing the way we did to the Red Wings. Not being able to provide anything to the team felt pretty bad. We were a lot better than we showed.

"How much of my game did I have left? I don't know. But you have to play too, and my ice time got cut down. I'm not blaming anybody, that's just how it went. After the trade, I got a really nice note from Roger that I have kept.

"It had been really exciting to feel the pride, history and tradition around that logo. I respect the heck out of the Philadelphia Flyers and Mr. Snider, and I thank Clarkie for getting me out of Hartford.

"I still sign a lot of Flyers stuff. It wasn't my easiest year, but that's how it goes."

Coffey wasn't the only old warrior moving on that summer. With Otto's effectiveness reduced, the club didn't pick up its option for the fourth year of the free-agent deal signed by the defensive center before the 1995-96 season.

"As soon as Grosek's goal went in, I remember sitting there thinking 'I just played my last game,'" Otto recalls. The Flyers had receive their money's worth, though, and he had gotten everything possible out of his Philadelphia experience.

"My wife and I still talk about how cool it was there, how passionate the fans were after how polite they had been in Calgary," Otto says." I got to play a year at the Spectrum; that meant a lot to me."

To replace Otto, Clarke moved quickly after free agency began on July 1 to sign away from Montreal center Marc Bureau (three years, $3.3 million), never mind bad feelings that lingered from Bureau's February 1, 1996 elbow of Svoboda that put the victim on a stretcher and the perpetrator in the press box for a five-game suspension.

"My wife was giving birth to my little boy, we were playing two games in two nights, and it was like three days without sleeping," Bureau explained. "I hope he understands a few things happened to me and that you've got to get over it."

That would be up to Svoboda, who had accepted Bureau's telephoned apology from his hospital bed, only to become enraged at its viciousness when viewing it for the first time on video during an NHL officiating presentation at training camp the next fall. Now that they were teammates, Svoboda couldn't bring himself to promise to talk things out with Bureau.

"We'll see how it goes," Svoboda told Les Bowen of the *Daily News*. "I've played with guys before where there are things. What are you going to do?"

Be as professional as possible was what Svoboda did. "It was not easy," he recalls. "That was one of the dirtiest hits I ever received.

"He apologized; I took it with a grain of salt, but at the end of the day he was a teammate. Basically, you have to be professional. But have I forgotten it? No."

Burke, a free agent-to-be, understood he could forget about remaining a Flyer, during his postseason meeting with Neilson.

"I didn't get the feeling I would be back and I don't blame him," he recalls. "If I could have come back another year, things would have turned around, no question, but I just didn't deliver."

"He looked better in the net than how he played," recalls Clarke, who was prepared to fish in a more exclusive pond since the contracts of Richter, Joseph and Vanbiesbrouck also were up.

When Vanbiesbrouck had been rumored headed to the Flyers at the previous trading deadline, Clarke scoffed and said, "He hasn't exactly done a lot for [Florida] this season."

But as July 1 approached and agents Don Meehan (for Joseph), Herb Pinder (for Richter), and Lloyd Friedland (for Vanbiesbrouck) prepared to solicit offers, Clarke sounded much more interested in-Vanbiesbrouck, his former Panther goalie, even though he was coming off the worst season—18-29-11, .899 save percentage—of his 14 in the NHL.

Two years older than Joseph, 32, and three years Richter's senior, Vanbiesbrouck was coming to market with reduced bargaining power.

"If you go long term and pay the huge dollars that are being asked (by Richter and Joseph), you're tying up your organization for a long time," Clarke told the media. "You've got to make sure about what you are doing."

Pinder, whose client had turned down an initial offer of three years and $15 million from the Rangers, called Clarke on July 1, the first day of free agency, soliciting an offer. The GM, convinced he was being used, did not make one. "I didn't think Richter was ever leaving the Rangers," recalls Clarke.

Indeed, remaining a Ranger was Richter's first choice. "There was a very, very short list and of course it started and in some ways ended with New York," the goalie recalls. "That's my home. I spent my adult life there; it's an amazing place."

But he waited nervously with a potentially overplayed hand. "I kept saying (to Pinder), 'Find out what the Rangers are doing; they are too quiet.' In my opinion, there was a wait-and-see attitude that my camp was having that I didn't like."

Richter hadn't heard back from the Rangers because GM Neil Smith was negotiating with Meehan for Joseph.

On Monday morning, July 7, Friedland asked Clarke for $10.7 million over three years—the last unguaranteed at $3.5 million but with a $1.3 million buyout—for Vanbiesbrouck. Clarke took those numbers to Meehan, asking if Joseph would take less than the four years and $24 million he was seeking. After Meehan talked it over with his client and declined, Clarke called back Friedland and quickly reached an agreement for Vanbiesbrouck, who had been relieved to get an offer from the strongest team of those in the market for a goalie.

"It was that simple," he recalls. "The Flyers had the best player in the league and the reputation for trying to win every year."

Neilson, who had coached Vanbiesbrouck in Florida, hadn't complicated things for Clarke, either. "They are all good goalies," he had told his GM. "I would be happy with any of them."

"So I was happy to save about $4 million," recalls Clarke.

Of course, Meehan and Pinder were not nearly as pleased that the Flyers left the market so quickly.

"I really thought [they] were going to take a little more time," recalls Meehan. "It was disappointing for Curtis, too.

"When I went to see him to tell him the Flyers were out of the picture, he was wearing a Philly jersey. "He thought I was coming to tell him we had moved ahead with the Flyers. They were his preference, the best team in the market that summer."

Meehan turned to the Rangers. Successfully, too, the agent at first thought. "In essence we had a deal," recalls Meehan. "There were just a few minor things.

"And then Neil called me and said, 'We had to change what we have on hand.' I said, 'What are you talking about? We had a deal.'

"He told me that when (Madison Square Garden chairman) Marc Lustgarten became aware of the contract, he wanted Neil to renegotiate with me."

When Smith came back to Meehan with new terms, the agent already had begun discussion with Leafs' GM Ken Dryden. Richter, without an offer from either the Rangers or Flyers, agreed to a deal Pinder negotiated with Florida and booked an evening flight there for a press conference. But that afternoon he fired Pinder, called MSG president Dave Checketts and successfully negotiated a contract, saving the Rangers from being shut out.

The dust settled with Joseph signing a four-year, $24.2 million deal with the Leafs; Sean Burke a two-year, $4.1 million contract with Florida; and Richter going back to New York (for four years and $21 million) where he was headed all along, in Clarke's belief. But had the Flyer window still been open while Joseph was all but delivered to the Rangers, Richter, his first choice apparently gone, could have been signed by Philadelphia.

"I was getting that [news of the tentative Ranger deal with Joseph] from a distance," Richter recalls. "So I don't know for sure.

"But I know there were more goalies out there than there were teams. Nobody wants to be holding the bag when the music stops. So sure, Philly would have been exciting.

"I grew up there. The Flyers meant everything to me growing up, and they weren't just good, but unique. New York (having missed the 1997-98 playoffs) was going through the reset button and Philly still had a damn good team.

"No question they were my second choice, but when Beez signed with the Flyers that option was out for me. So of course at that point I am going to do what I can to sign with New York."

On July 13, Vanbiesbrouck was introduced to a Philadelphia media that naturally wondered how he felt about being the bargain goalie. "I don't consider myself a coat off the rack," he said, getting a huge laugh.

John Vanbiesbrouck would finish the 1999-2000 season with a 27-17-15 record and a GAA of 2.18.

"It wasn't rehearsed," the goaltender recalls. "I was just frustrated at the tone of the questions that weren't giving the Flyers any credit for making [a good decision]."

Vanbiesbrouck tailored his remarks to emphasize the Flyers did not need serious alterations to be a contender, a larger priority to him than getting the last dollar. "I looked at free agency a little different than most people looked at it," he told reporters. "I didn't look at it like I was going to win the lottery. I was trying to get myself to a position where I wanted to be.

"You have to live in reality, rather than a fairy-tale land. I had a poor, poor season. Our team had a poor season."

Those struggles had obliterated Philadelphia's memory of Vanbiesbrouck stoning the heavily favored Flyers out of the 1986 and 1996 playoffs, and left Clarke explaining a budget decision.

"All three are terrific goaltenders, but the numbers that were thrown at us and the years involved were really going to handcuff us," he reiterated.

Clarke had no plans to sign any other free agents but still had to re-up Lindros, who very much wanted to remain in Philadelphia.

"Winning a Stanley Cup is the only thing left for me," said the six-year veteran, second behind Gretzky in points per game among active players with 1.41. "I was brought here to win championships.

"Guys are going to get paid fairly in the market but that's secondary to winning."

Still, with just one year remaining at $8.5 million on the extension he had agreed to during the previous season, money had to come first.

"If he wants to be the best-paid player, he should play like the best player," said Clarke on July 30 in his first public criticism of his star. He said it was time for Lindros to earn the $8.5 million he was due for the coming season and that the Flyers needed "more games" and "better games" from their captain, who needed to play with "real passion."

Having not heard this face to face from either Clarke or Neilson in exit meetings following the playoffs, Lindros was taken aback.

"I'm confused by what he said," Lindros told the media. "But I'm not going to have an open forum about it. I've always had a lot of respect for Clarkie."

In an August 13 meeting, the GM submitted to Lindros and family attorney Gordon Kirke a 100-page proposal on a five-year, incentive-laden deal that could top out at $50 million. It gave Lindros, going into the 1998-99 season essentially tied with Anaheim's Kariya as the game's highest-paid player, no immediate raise but the opportunity to earn more with performance bonuses.

If Lindros played out the upcoming season without a new contract, he would become a restricted free agent eligible to receive an offer sheet; Philadelphia could match the offer or receive five No. 1 picks as compensation. The Flyers likely would get better value than those picks in a trade, which was a Lindros family concern in their approach to contract talks, especially since Clarke had gone public with his unhappiness about Eric's inconsistency.

Clarke told Carl Lindros his remarks were intended to challenge Eric, then told the media the family was now "comfortable" with his remarks.

"Carl accepted Bob's explanation but I'm not sure he was pleased," Kirke replied. Nevertheless, the goal for both sides was to keep Lindros in Philadelphia, which the family remained convinced would become more problematic if it agreed to a five-year deal.

"You wonder if a long-term deal sets him up for a trade," Kirke speculated aloud.

The family was taking every rumor—and Snider's non-involvement in the contract talks—seriously. "Before I was even offered a deal, I was shopped around," Eric told the *Inquirer*'s Bill Lyon. "I need [Snider's] assurances on this deal."

In a prepared statement, Snider said the Collective Bargaining Agreement, which prohibited no-trade clauses for players under age 31, made a contractual guarantee impossible. But the Chairman strongly reiterated his desire to have Lindros go forward as a Flyer.

"There has been a lot of speculation about our motives in offering Eric a long-term contract," Snider said. "Our motive is really simple: we want Eric here for a long time.

"We don't want to be negotiating every year because it's a big distraction. We'd just like for it to end and to know we're going to have him for a while."

Three days before the Flyer-imposed deadline of a deal by the September 11 start of camp—Clarke, Snider, Kirke, Eric, Carl, and Comcast-Spectacor general counsel Phil Weinberg met for two hours. They shook hands on a verbal one-year extension that would pay Lindros $8.5 million for the 1999-2000 season, a rate equal to the second year in the Flyers' five-year offer of $45 million. This would leave Lindros even with Kariya as the game's highest-paid player.

"A gesture of good faith," Lindros said at a press conference in a meeting room at the Airport Marriott, not attended by Clarke or Snider. "There is no guarantee I won't be traded, but the other end of it is they have my word I will play in 1999-2000.

"They talked about wanting to keep me and this gets it done. Both sides walked out of there really happy." Clarke and Snider issued statements in agreement. "We're thrilled with Eric's pledge and attitude," said Snider. "It shows tremendous leadership on his part.

"This is very generous of Eric and helps give us stability for a couple years for our hockey club," said Clarke.

The GM went one year further—for three years and $11.25 million—to re-sign Brind'Amour—an offer extended and quickly accepted by agent Ron Perrick just as the parties sat down for a hearing before NHL-appointed arbitrator Rolf Valtin.

Philadelphia had revised their offer after the Canadiens' Mark Recchi had received the highest arbitration settlement in NHL history—$4.5 million—just two days earlier. Klatt, meanwhile, took the Flyers to arbitration and won $900,000, then agreed to an extension that would pay him $3.2 million over three years. Clarke threatened Hextall, who had become a 34-year-old backup following the Vanbiesbrouck signing, with being waived if he didn't convert the one-season remaining at $2.4 million into a two-year deal at less per season.

"[Clarke] was off my Christmas card list for a while," said Hextall, who ended up deferring $900,000 and agreeing to play the 1998-99 season for $1.2 million. He figured that wasn't bad for approximately 20 nights a year of work.

"[Backing up] was going to be an adjustment, but I realized I still had the best job in the world, goaltending in the NHL," he recalls. "I was going to play as long as I could, so I just took what came my way. I wasn't going to whine, just play when I was told."

Assistant coach Keith Acton left for a similar position with the Rangers. "He was hard-working and enthusiastic, but he had been [Murray's] guy and had gotten a little too vocal in his criticism of what was going on around here," recalls Clarke. "It was time for him to go somewhere else."

For a replacement, Neilson went with someone he knew, calling Craig Ramsay, the former Sabre stalwart who had played junior for Roger in Peterborough, Ontario, plus coached on his staffs in Buffalo and Florida.

"The Senators (where he had been an assistant for three seasons) had told me they wanted me back but had to take care of (head coach) Jacques (Martin) first," recalls Ramsay. "My contract was expiring on July 1; they told me I couldn't talk to anybody before then.

"So I'm cutting my grass in July, when one of my boys tells me Roger Neilson is on the line. I ran in. He said, 'Got a spot in Philly, let me know if you want it,' and then bang, he hung up.

"I had to call him back. I said, 'Yeah, I'd be interested.' He said 'talk to Clarkie.' It went from there pretty easily.

"Rick Dudley, who had just taken over (as GM) in Ottawa, soon called. I said 'I've got an offer from Philly.' He was upset and I was disappointed, too, because I liked Ottawa, an up-and-coming team. But I'd already worked with Clarkie in Florida and was comfortable with him, too, besides just Roger."

One year after the birth of Comcast SportsNet, the Flyers still weren't comfortable deserting non-cable households, so they did a deal with WPSG, Channel 57 to do at least 20 games. A kid who had grown up watching Flyer telecasts, defenseman Mark Eaton of Wilmington, DE and Notre Dame University, signed with Philadelphia as a free agent, becoming their first-ever acquisition of a Delaware Valley born-and-bred player.

Another Philly guy, Jim McCrossin—a protege of original Flyer strength and conditioning director Pat Croce plus the holder of a similar position in Hartford during Holmgren's head-coaching days there—was promoted from the Phantoms to the big club. Unfortunately, Daigle was out of McCrossin's daily control over the summer. Camp opened in Neilson's Peterborough with Daigle taking a highly unsatisfactory 54 minutes to finish the six-mile conditioning test.

"The majority of the guys trained real hard," said an irritated Clarke. "Somebody doesn't do real well, I think it's going to have to be addressed by us. "The GM, outspoken during negotiations with Lindros, Hextall and Klatt, had been doing a lot of addressing over the summer. "I'll be a lot more strict than I was," said Clarke. "Usually you leave that up to the coaches, but sometimes that doesn't work.

"I don't really see myself as being more critical. I want to address things quicker than in the past."

Lindros waved the olive branch. "When you go through what we went through last spring, there are obvious issues he has to address," said the captain. "Whether you agree with people's perceptions or not, that's the way it is.

"You've always got to respect the way he was as a player, that's a given."

Echoed Brind'Amour, "If there's ever been a player's GM in the league, it's him. He played with his heart on his sleeve.

"I've watched a lot of old tapes and he was just non-stop out there. It's just natural that he expects that from everyone else."

It was practically guaranteed that nobody on the 1998-99 Flyers would expect more of himself than Iron Rod. But one player reported to camp with less body fat than Brind'Amour, defenseman Dmitri Tertyshny, a rail-thin 1995 sixth-round pick. "He has a real good stick," noted Neilson. "He's going to be a player."

It quickly was clear the Russian could read the play better than the English language, beating out veteran signee Chris Joseph and replacing the non-tendered, 39-year-old, Samuelsson—who had signed with Tampa Bay—in the six-man defensive rotation.

Valeri Zelepukin, the veteran Russian winger acquired from Edmonton on October 5 for Lacroix, would be able to keep Tertyshny in the loop. "That wasn't a real high priority but certainly is a benefit," said Clarke, who in the Zelepukin deal sacrificed more size for speed and skill, even though his production had markedly slipped since taking an inadvertent stick in the eye during a Devils practice in 1996.

"He probably hasn't been that good since," conceded Clarke. "But he is a physical player, a good team player, a skater and a passer."

Having talked through the summer about a need for another right wing, the GM also signed free agent Jody Hull, a Neilson favorite from the Rangers and Panthers.

"Checking player; he knew how Roger wanted him to play," recalls Clarke.

Mike Maneluk, purchased a year earlier at a price of a single dollar from Ottawa for organizational depth, followed up the 13 goals he had scored in the AHL playoffs for the champion Phantoms with five goals in nine exhibition games. The rookie earned the opportunity to start the season on right wing with LeClair and a recharged Lindros, who won the most-fit player award at camp. "He has been great since the first day, seems really fired up," said Neilson.

"There has to be some anger on some players' parts after what happened last year and into the playoffs," said Clarke as camp ended. "I think we'll be a real good team this year because of it."

Brind'Amour, bumped to the third line as Neilson reached for some magic in a Daigle-Gratton-Zubrus combination, was willing to take one for the team, as always. "Whatever we have to do to win, we have to accept," he said. 'It's not a perfect world.

"It bothered me more when I was younger."

The head coach had to miss an exhibition game to put out a fire in his back caused by lifting boxes during the move into his South Jersey apartment. Having forgotten to pay his electric bill, Neilson suffered in the dark, too, but was enlightened by Ramsay about the way the Flyers could best play.

"Roger didn't need me to come in and help him coach defense," recalls the assistant. "He had always been happy to win 1-0.

"I wanted to play a more aggressive trap. More important, I wanted to alter our back-checking principles to take away the middle. But most important to me, I wanted the defense to get up in the rush.

"Desjardins was capable of doing that. Chris Therien could skate. Overall, we needed to get quicker, which was Clarkie's job, but in the meantime, Roger was not averse to playing a more up-tempo game.

"To do that, we had to develop more continuity between our offense and defense, have all guys up and all guys back. Eric and John were dominant in the offensive end. Participation would be more enthusiastic if players accustomed to doing good things with the puck still felt that was permissible.

"I think Wayne Cashman's rapport with our higher-end guys really helped with that. He once was on the best line in the league and could speak to them as an equal, tell them, 'They don't want you to be only checkers, just to do more.'"

Neilson acknowledged the change during camp.

"The difference between my trap in Florida and what we are doing here is that we're sending them after the puck," he said. "It's a little risk and reward; you need to have some speed, but we've got that."

The renewed commitment by the 1998-99 Flyers seemed obvious on Day One, when they held the Rangers to 20 shots in Vanbiesbrouck's 1-0 shutout at Madison Square Garden, the goal coming from Daigle on a second-period powerplay.

Behind Lindros's two goals, they beat Anaheim 4-1 in their home opener at the renamed First Union Center—the buyout of CoreStates had been the biggest banking deal in U.S. history—and LeClair then pumped in a hat trick for a 5-2 victory at Tampa Bay.

The addition of Hull had made Klatt a third-line luxury—too expensive for any team to have taken in the waiver draft—so in sending him to the Canucks on October 19 for a sixth-round pick, Clarke agreed to pay Vancouver $1 million of the $3 million the Flyers owed the winger over the next three seasons.

"I could be wrong, but I went to arbitration that summer and think that had to do with why I was shipped," recalls Klatt, whose goal production had dropped by 10 goals to 14 the previous year, but with 42 points still had come close to his high watermark of 45. "I don't know how I could have the two years like I did and get put on the waiver wire."

Clarke insists today the move was not made out of spite. "I don't think we ever had a bitter arbitration; absolutely not," he recalls. Klatt, praised by Lindros on the day of the trade as "a really good guy in the room," didn't stay bitter, either.

"The chance to play on a team in the Final was the highlight of my career," says Klatt, now director of scouting for the Islanders. "Philadelphia was incredible. I won't say anything bad about that organization."

The Flyers had extra bodies and, seemingly, extra motivation for a bounce-back year until the Devils ended the unbeaten start at four games with a 4-3 win at the First Union Center, a game interrupted for 17 minutes because of a light failure. "You didn't have anything to do with paying the electric bill here, did you?" LeClair asked Neilson.

He had not, but the Flyers' best intentions suddenly got turned off regardless. Neilson juggled combinations of the same underachievers who had disappeared in the playoffs against Buffalo. "I've always believed you play like you practice," said Desjardins, annoyed with the work ethic.

Lindros and Neilson insisted they didn't see anything wrong with the practices. But when Vanbiesbrouck's 2-1 win over the Blues was the Flyers' only victory in the next six contests, Clarke saw problems,

"Some players take shortcuts," he said. "We should demand more from them."

Despite the fact that Daigle hadn't scored since opening night, he didn't exactly sneak into Ottawa in plain clothes for his first game there since being acquired from the Senators.

"Whether they boo me or applaud me, it's a good sign because it means they didn't forget me," he announced. By now, Clarke's memory had lapsed as to why he ever had made that deal.

"Ridiculous for a player of his caliber to be out of shape," he said to *The Ottawa Citizen*, in which it was rumored the Flyers were offering Daigle to Tampa Bay to get Renberg back. "Who would want [Daigle]?" pooh-pooed the GM before Philadelphia, minus Desjardins with a groin pull, lost its fourth straight, 5-4.

Multiple teams had coveted Zubrus in deals Clarke explored for veteran upgrades over the last season-plus. But as the third-year center and winger zigged and zagged instead of playing in the straight lines the Flyers wanted, their patience wore thin. Then again, so had their scorers. Lindros, LeClair and Brind'Amour had accounted for twenty-three of the team's 33 goals.

Maneluk fizzled on the Big Line, as did Zubrus, so Maneluk got another shot. "I know Eric likes him up there," said Neilson. A microcosm of the Flyers' start was outplaying the Sabres, yet giving up goals on a breakaway and a two-on-one to settle for a 2-2 tie.

"That was a huge problem in the playoffs," said Neilson. "We would have the puck in the Buffalo zone forever, then give up a great chance." When Daigle finally scored his first goal in 13 games to cut a deficit in Montreal to 2-1, Vanbiesbrouck gave up a bad angle goal off his pad to Turner Stevenson and the Flyers faded into a 5-1 loss.

Alexandre Daigle played parts of two seasons with the Flyers.

"We didn't get the save, didn't get the defensive play to give your team hope," said Vanbiesbrouck. "It's tough to accept reality. You don't get out of slumps with efforts like this."

Clarke, who had changed so much of the roster, thought part of the problem was Neilson so often altering the combinations. "I think we've been out of sync since we started messing around with the Lindros line and moved Daigle from center," the GM said. "It's okay to experiment if we're winning, but if we're going through a stretch like this, we've got to let the lines stay together to accomplish something."

Neilson was being more aggressive than many of the players. Clarke thought his team lacked attitude so, on November 12, the GM traded Podein, the last remaining member of the Minnesota Line that had been key to the 1997 final run, to Colorado for one of the bigger mouths in the game, winger Keith Jones.

"We think he'll be able to stir up crap and score more goals," said Clarke.

Jones had played in only 23 games the previous season because of knee problems. "I was never quite right," he recalls. "I knew the Avalanche was looking to trade me and I knew the Flyers were one of the teams interested.

"Paul Holmgren was scouting a game I played in Phoenix, where I suddenly had an A on my sweater, which I had never worn before. Colorado wanted to [advertise] I was a leader. I pointed it out to (Phoenix's) Rick Tocchet during the warmup and we laughed about this being it for me with the Avalanche.

"Flew home and the next morning I read I had been traded for Shjon Podein. I walked into the practice rink without hearing anything from the team and nobody in the locker room knew anything.

"Finally, the PR guy came down and said 'Jonesey, they want to talk to you upstairs,' and I got the official word.

"I was going to get to play with Lindros and LeClair, so how bad could it be? I had been lucky to get traded from Washington to the Avalanche the year after they had won the Cup. Maybe it was my style of play that good teams wanted me. Or, I'll pretend that anyway.

"I called Bob Clarke. He said, 'We play Florida tonight but I just want you here and ready to go for New Jersey (two nights hence).' I told him that if he saw my numbers against Marty Brodeur, something like no goals in 20 games, he might re-think that. He kind of laughed and said, 'Just get here.'"

Podein was in no hurry to leave but reluctantly agreed it was for the best.

"Shjon turned out to be a better player than we had thought when we signed him," recalls Clarke. "Terrific man, everything was upbeat and hard work.

"Colorado called us about him. They had wanted to do a bigger deal for a defenseman but we couldn't work that out, don't remember why, but they still wanted to do the one-for-one of Podein for Jones. They didn't think he could skate anymore, but that was never the most important part of his game anyway.

"I remember calling Shjon in and telling him we'd make the deal if he said okay. I think he's the only guy I ever did that with, that's how much I liked him."

Clarke liked Podein even more when he said to do what was best for the Flyers.

"Mr. Clarke told me what the deal was," Podein recalls. "I knew Keith Jones and what he brought to the offensive end.

"I told Mr. Clarke, 'I don't want to go anywhere else but I understand what you have to do for the team.'

"I went home, got a call. 'Shjon, it's Clarkie.' I said, ['Bleep!'] And he goes, 'Yeah.'

"I told him I would give my left [arm] to be here again and he said, 'I know you would.' My time in Philadelphia was one of the best experiences of my life."

Minus the en-route Jones, the winless streak stretched to seven (0-5-2) with a 2-1 loss to coach Murray's Panthers. "I don't know how to explain outshooting a team 40-15 and losing," said Lindros, although the jilted ex-Flyer coach had no trouble articulating his satisfaction. "I would be lying if I didn't say it was emotional for me," Murray said.

Jones reported for duty and just as he had hoped, immediately was put on the line with LeClair and Lindros. "Roger said to me, 'Maybe it will work and maybe it won't,'" recalls Jones. "I told him, 'Everything will be fine.'"

With the Flyers and Devils tied 1-1 in the third period of Jones' debut, he appeared to fit right in, flubbing his first scoring chance. But he swung again on his backhand and scored his first goal ever on Brodeur, which seemed to be a spell-breaker for more than just the newcomer. Lindros scored twice as Philadelphia blew the game open, 6-1, the team's first victory over New Jersey in two seasons.

"I wasn't there for the struggles at the beginning of the season," recalls Jones. "I just came in thinking, 'This is a great team on paper, so let's go!'"

He set up Lindros for the first goal in Vanbiesbrouck's 4-1 win against the Penguins, only the Flyers' second in their last 30 regular-season games in Pittsburgh. Perhaps this human shot in the arm could even inoculate the struggling Gratton from his paralyzing self-doubt.

"He was from my hometown (Brantford, Ontario), so Mr. Snider asked me, 'Can you fix this kid for us?'" recalls Jones. "I said, 'I'll do what I can.'"

He wasn't the only one trying. "Chris wasn't a natural center, although he wanted to play center," recalls Ramsay. "He was a shooter who, with his size, could have been dominant off the wing if he wanted to be.

"But he also was put in a tough spot in a city that can be hard. He wasn't someone who could slough it off and just go about his business."

Recalls LeClair, "I know Clarkie was trying but [Gratton] just never fit. He was a good kid, but it was like he had been given a winning lottery ticket."

Clarke wanted to keep the tailing-off Maneluk—not a good fit anywhere besides on a first line with superstars—as an organizational depth player. But when agent Neil Sheehy refused to extend the contract of his client, who was scheduled to become a free agent at the end of the season, Maneluk was moved to Chicago for grinder Roman Vopat.

It was the third time Vopat had been traded in three weeks. "Am I that bad a player that this keeps happening?" he asked.

Hextall kept the Flyer resurgence going and passed Bernie Parent as the franchise's all-time winningest regular-season goalie with victory No. 233, a 3-1 win over Carolina in Greensboro. It was Hextall's 471st Flyer appearance, nine fewer than Parent had needed to get to 232.

"Wins or losses are not a goalie's stats, those are team stats," said Hextall. But after flashing out his left pad while falling to the right and stopping Martin Gelinas to preserve a 2-1 lead, Hextall pocketed the puck at the buzzer regardless. "It might mean something to my four kids someday," he said.

Vanbiesbrouck felt like a big kid watching. "I'm just glad to have been here to witness it," he said. "These are things that nobody will be able to take away from you."

Vanbiesbrouck enjoyed one of those moments of his own two nights later, when Jones' goal in overtime gave the Philadelphia goalie a 2-1 victory in his and the Flyers' first game at the Panthers' new National Car Rental Center in Sunrise, FL.

"That had been a very special time for me in Florida," Vanbiesbrouck recalls. "You really think you built something there and then all of a sudden you are on the other side of the fence.

"I stuck one of the first shovels in the ground to build that building and still have the hard hat to prove it. I just tried to take the emotion out of it and focus on all the details."

After having scored just five goals in 35 games with the Avalanche, that was Jones' third goal in his four games with the Flyers. "He's an irritating person, but he's hilarious," said Lindros after the line had dominated in a 4-3 win in Toronto and Vanbiesbrouck had outplayed Joseph. Not that opponents necessarily appreciated Keith's brand of humor.

"Going back to junior, I was a guy who got in and out fast," recalls Jones. "Fortunately, bigger guys on the team liked me and would fight for me.

"In Washington, in fact, Craig Berube would thank me for setting up fights for him. When I got traded to Colorado, Ken Baumgartner chased me around yelling, 'Berube isn't here!'

"The distraction I brought enabled me to play on two top lines—with Peter Forsberg and (Valeri) Kamensky, and then with Lindros and LeClair. They appreciated having another target besides them."

Under such cover of darkness, LeClair pumped four goals past Snow in a 6-2 win over Vancouver and moved into a tie for the league goal-scoring lead. Nevertheless, a late, window-dressing goal by the struggling Gratton received just as much attention. Playing the wing since Neilson wanted Brind'Amour back at center, Gratton's efforts along the boards seemed to be earning him more support from teammates than a year earlier.

But given the opportunity to undo a mistake, Clarke seized it on December 15, returning Gratton to Tampa Bay in a four-player deal that brought back Renberg. The Flyers also obtained center Daymond Langkow, the fifth player taken in the 1995 draft, while sending Sillinger to the struggling Lightning.

"I thought Gratton was intimidated by the salary, like it was too big a load for him to carry," recalls Clarke. "Langkow had been a great junior, not very big (listed at 5-10, 181), but a really good faceoff guy, playmaker and checker.

"Mikael was a good person with no baggage, a guy who could score 15 to 18 for us, that's the way we looked at him at that stage."

A center ice of Lindros, Langkow and Brind'Amour made improved logic, particularly to Brind'Amour.

"I had played against Gratton and knew I was better than him," he recalls. "Why would you move me to a position where I'm not as comfortable and move in someone who was not as productive? It made no sense to me."

Neither did a trade that reversed transactions of 16 months earlier, at least to those not yet aware of Langkow's capabilities.

Renberg, who had been told by Clarke in Nagano that he was wanted back and that the GM was working on it, was thrilled. "I was coming home," he recalls.

"We were better in Tampa that second year than the first, but we weren't as good as the Flyers. The only really good thing about my time in Tampa was getting to go to the World Championships because we didn't make the playoffs."

Clarke's admission of error with Gratton didn't prevent his players from continuing to make too many of them. Late goals by Lindros and Brind'Amour gave them a 5-5 tie at the Meadowlands that seemed inspiring until two nights later, when the Devils came from three goals down to win 5-4 in overtime at the First Union Center.

Desjardins scored with just 23.9 seconds remaining for an apparent win over Edmonton, but the Flyers gave a goal right back to Boris Mironov with 6.5 seconds to go and settled for a maddening 2-2 tie. They then blew two-goal leads into deadlocks with Calgary and Tampa Bay, the latter in Gratton's return.

These repeated third-period collapses didn't put the fans in the mood to be magnanimous. They booed Gratton throughout the game.

"It's a little hurtful and disappointing," he said afterwards. "You go through everything we went through last year and all of a sudden you're playing against them.

"It was very emotional. It's been a tough week."

After Jones cooled off, Renberg went back on the Legion of Doom line until being checked into the seamless glass in Boston by Kyle McLaren, unfortunately suffering a shoulder separation during Vanbiesbrouck's 2-1 victory. Things were no easier for Svoboda. Having undergone nine hours of off-season shoulder surgery, he was hit hard by Tampa Bay's Wendel Clark and went to the locker room with a burner that still didn't hurt the proud 32-year-old defenseman as much as finding himself increasingly scratched.

"We just thought he could be playing with more intensity," Neilson had explained. "He's a competitive guy and I'm sure he will respond."

But after he was benched in favor of Tertyshny and/or Babych for four games in a nine-contest stretch, Svoboda was traded to Tampa Bay on December 28 for yet another Clarke reacquisition—Karl Dykhuis.

"I'm shocked," said Svoboda. "I don't know what to say.

"I have no idea why I'm being traded. I think I was playing all right."

Clarke simply felt he was moving an increasingly broken-down defenseman for a more durable one with an upside.

"We were looking to add more speed back there," he explained. "Petr played hard, but he's not very big and he's going to get hurt.

"Dykhuis never gets hurt. He's a little faster, bigger. With Petr, age was becoming a factor."

So was being able to shift Richardson, who appeared to be gaining Neilson's hard-earned trust, back to the left side and to provide a spot on the right for the talented-but-turnover prone Dykhuis. "You can't find these types of guys," said Clarke. "We think in our environment, he can be fine."

The trade was not fine with the players, who wondered why a "mean little guy," in the words of Ramsay, was gone. "Every night you knew you were going to get Petr's best," recalls Desjardins. "Lively, funny, made sure everyone would be awake.

"He would take some hits and you wondered how he got up."

Svoboda repeatedly rose, setting such a memorable example for younger players and earning such respect that Neilson felt the need to call a meeting in San Jose to tell the players to move on. "Nobody likes to lose a friend," said the coach. "You have to be mentally tough and put these things behind you."

Svoboda eventually did, feeling he got a lot more out of his Philadelphia years than a burning sensation on his left side that lingers to this day. "I was coming back from a pretty big surgery," Svoboda, today a player agent, recalls. "They felt I wasn't the healthiest guy so they rather would have had somebody else.

"The thing that I'm sorry about was we couldn't break that Cup drought. I was feeling so good through the ('97) playoffs and then that stupid little dump-in broke my foot in Game One. That was very hard."

Dykhuis, who allegedly never got hurt, took a stick in the face in Calgary during his first game back and left a trail of blood off the Olympic Saddledome ice. But he wasn't the greatest loss for the team that night. Lindros, hit three times by Jason Weimer, came out of the game early.

"I feel like I've got a little concussion," he told reporters. "Where I stand in terms of severity, we'll deal with it tomorrow."

Without him, the Flyers, who had not arrived until 5:30 a.m. after a 1-1 tie in San Jose because of a U.S. Customs delay, rallied from a 3-1 deficit to a 4-3 overtime victory on Zelepukin's goal.

They then blasted Vancouver 5-2 before the team closed the trip by blowing a 3-1 lead into a 3-3 tie in Edmonton. "We might have been running out of gas," said Neilson, meaning more players than just Dykhuis, who had rejoined the team after being told by Flyers' physician Guy Lanzi in Philadelphia that there was no cheekbone fracture after all. Dykhuis had flown six straight days, three times virtually across the continent, a small price to pay for his team closing their six-game holiday trip unbeaten.

Lindros, challenged by Clarke over the summer to stay healthy, yet making appearances to build concussion awareness after they had ended his brother Brett's career with the Islanders, downplayed his own symptoms. "Don't make a big deal out of this injury, it's not a real severe concussion," he assured reporters. Indeed, No. 88 was back when the Flyers returned home for a Vanbiesbrouck 5-0 shutout of the Islanders.

When Hextall pulled a groin two nights later against Carolina, he was relieved by the Beezer during a 2-0 shutout, the first by two goalies in Flyer history, then Vanbiesbrouck followed up with whitewashes of Nashville (8-0) and Washington (3-0). The team's goalless streak was at 212 minutes and its unbeaten streak at 10-0-5, the fifth longest in franchise history. "John is so cool and calm back there," praised Lindros.

Clarke appeared to have solved Philadelphia's multi-year goaltending riddle, and, in ending the Gratton agony, had picked up Langkow, the 5-10 center who had eight points in his first 15 Flyer games and was a plus-10. "He can play on the power play, kill penalties, he's decent on the draw, has a nice quick shot and makes good plays," raved Neilson.

"I went back to the scouting reports before he was drafted and (since-retired Flyer head scout) Jerry Melnyk said, 'This guy can be a star,'" recalls Clarke, who on January 12 called up his son-in-law, center Peter White, the AHL's two time scoring champion. The move displayed the same defiance of potential criticism with which the GM cut his losses in reversing the Gratton-Renberg deal.

"Bob knew the razzing he would get," Snider told reporters. "He didn't care and I want a guy like that.

"A lot of people don't admit their mistakes, they get stubborn about it. With [Cashman], Bob realized it wasn't right and he made the change. Right now I wouldn't trade Dan McGillis back to Edmonton for Niinimaa, and I don't think anybody else would either.

"We have the nucleus of players to win the Cup .We have probably the best player in hockey in Eric Lindros; if not the best, then in the top two or three. Lindros and LeClair, these guys don't last forever. This is the time for us. That's all we're trying to do, win the Cup."

Clarke had changed 10 players from the team that lost to Buffalo eight months earlier, and apparently, his mind about Lindros, too. "Eric's been unbelievable," said the GM.

Six months before, he had publicly demanded more from his star and now was getting it at both ends of the rink. But that wasn't happening because Big E's feet had been held to the fire. Lindros had warmed to a Flyer coach for the first time since probably his rookie year under Bill Dineen.

Asked by *Daily News* columnist Sam Donnellon what he had learned about dealing with scrutiny since his early teens, the 25-year-old Lindros replied, "Don't fight fights you can't win."

But No. 88's most contented days as a Flyer probably had the most to do with Neilson.

"He made Eric believe he cared about Eric Lindros the person, not the player," recalls Ramsay. "Eric had this thing that he was disliked, which I think was a fallacy, but there was no question he grew to understand that Roger cared about him personally."

"Roger didn't take a motivational position, but an educational position," adds Vanbiesbrouck. "Eric has a high intellect; I think he respected Roger for giving him information and not just trying to play on his heartstrings."

Indeed, it wasn't just Neilson's compassion that impressed Lindros, but the coach's brain.

"Roger was the best coach I ever played for," Lindros recalls. "He didn't just do a drill; there was a reason for it, and they would change all the time depending upon who you were playing.

"A large portion of his ability was reading what was going on in guys' lives, dig a little deeper that way. He would converse with players more than any coach I'd ever seen. He had a good feel for the pulse of the team.

"And he was goofy, funny, quirky. We were once in a video session upstairs—going over what we had to do against so-and-so, and this is exactly how we are going to do it—and all of a sudden there are geese flying across the screen. Roger says, 'If geese are flying and one has to land, another one will join him, so there always are two.' That was Roger's way of teaching us we had to have each other's backs."

And he did it with more humor than fire. "Even when he got upset, he would joke," recalls Desjardins.

After Vanbiesbrouck let in a couple softies in a 4-3 loss to Toronto that ended the unbeaten streak on January 16, Neilson cancelled the morning skate for the next game in Ottawa. Instead, Captain Video cued up the bit from *Monty Python and the Holy Grail* where the spit-and-vinegar knight continues to threaten his opponent even while being dismembered limb by limb.

Vanbiesbrouck's 5-0 shutout that night, his fourth in five games, was Neilson's 400th NHL win, cause for the presentation of a cake after practice the next day in Voorhees, Lindros holding it.

"In New York, they gave me donuts (for No. 300)," Neilson said. 'This is a lot better." Actually the Rangers had given him 300 biscuits and 300 ties, the latter being the gift that to Roger, always kept on giving.

"His only show was his ties. He loved his ties, and they became a wonderful thing, another way he could poke fun at himself," recalls Ramsay. "He enjoyed being quirky and made you feel comfortable laughing with him."

Even Richardson, who had not gained the coach's trust, could appreciate the utter lack of pretension of the rumpled 64 year old in the ball cap, nylon workout pants, and t-shirt advertising a Key West bar.

"One game I wasn't going to dress and was steaming about it," Richardson recalls. "After the morning skate, I decided to let my roommate have his nap.

"I packed my bag—we were leaving after the game—and headed down to watch a sports event in (massage therapist) Tom D'Anconna's room, which was on the same hotel floor as the coaches' rooms.

"Suddenly, here's Roger coming my way, seeing me, then having that look on his face like there was no other place to go. He looked at my bags and wondered what the hell was going on. I hadn't been traded.

"'Gee, where ya' goin?' he asked.

"I said, 'I don't want to disturb my roommate's sleep, so I'm going to the trainer's room to watch golf.'

"He said, 'Oh, I thought maybe you were leaving the team.'

"'Day's not over yet,' I said, and stormed by him. A little sarcasm and hostility there, but he caught the wit and laughed."

Accused of coaching defensively to a fault in previous stops—in fact fired in New York because of a clash in philosophy with Captain Mark Messier—the Flyer millionaires embraced Neilson's philosophy and idiosyncrasies almost totally.

"There were some chuckles because he was a forgetful guy at times, but never about hockey," recalls Vanbiesbrouck. "He was more dedicated to the sport than anybody I've ever known." A narcoleptic who never slept more than four hours a night—as a 16-year-old, Ramsay remembers the coach falling asleep during a one-on-one talk in his Peterborough office—Neilson would awaken at 2 a.m., pedal his bicycle to a diner near the Coliseum for breakfast and be in his office before 4 a.m. looking at video.

"He's the most knowledgeable of any of the (six) coaches I've had here," Brind'Amour told reporters. "And I think he's very professional in the way he deals with people.

"It's fun to come to the rink. Even when you're not playing well, he has a subtle way of letting you know. He treats us like men. We're in it together and I think that's why we feel like he's one of us."

The sentiment was mutual.

"I've been around a long time and I've been in a lot of different places," said Neilson. "I really enjoy this team.

"When a coach is really under pressure, I think it's hard for him to be a likable guy. I don't feel pressure in this job. I'll work as hard as anybody, maybe harder than most, but it's not like I'm worried about my job."

Neither, apparently, was Daigle. For his $1.9 million, he was spending most of his games in the press box or, as Clarke remembers, in limousines to Atlantic City.

"Great wheels, happy-go-lucky kid," Neilson told the media when asked about Daigle's status. "There are other guys we want to give ice time to who deserve it."

Recalls Ramsay, who had coached Daigle in Ottawa, too, "He just wanted to skate and shoot and have some fun. The Senators drafted him first overall, gave him an unprecedented contract, and then asked him to be the poster child for an NHL star.

"His defense mechanism was to find something else outside the game that helped him survive and would take away from his (poor) performance."

Edmonton's Glen Sather had expressed some interest, but was unwilling to give the Flyers any assets in return unless Daigle, a restricted free-agent-to-be come July, agreed to a year's extension at $1 million.

"Alexandre understands he's going to make less next year, but he wants to go to Edmonton, prove himself, and make sure that's the right place for him before agreeing to an extension," said his agent, Craig Levin.

In fact, Daigle wanted to go to Hollywood and the Kings—in order of priority—and refused the deal with the Oilers.

"Spoiled little girl," Clarke said. "Sooner or later the player has to realize that playing is more important than money."

He banned Daigle from practice and assigned him to skate by himself at Voorhees.

"It's a distraction for everyone," Daigle agreed. "If they don't want one, they did the right thing.

"You can't be happy to be thrown off the team, but I don't think I did anything wrong."

With or without him, the Flyers remained capable of blowing two-goal leads. For the eighth time in their first 45 games, one got away on a hat trick by Florida's newly-arrived Pavel Bure as Philadelphia settled for a 3-3 tie, Vanbiesbrouck being unable to finish the game after getting hit in the rear end with a puck with just 23 seconds remaining.

"Humiliating," the goalie said. "When people ask what's wrong, I have to say, 'Geez, I've got a sore butt.'"

On a team with Brind'Amour, there was shame attached to missing a game with any kind of injury. "I couldn't breathe, thought I was in trouble," said Iron Rod after his ribs crashed the boards in a 4-2 win over Phoenix. But x-rays taken at Pennsylvania Hospital were negative for a fracture, showing only a dislocated joint.

"You just pop it back in and you're fine," said Brind'Amour, who scored the first of his two goals on the first shift of a 6-2 win over Tampa Bay that stretched his consecutive game streak to 449.

It only seemed like it took Daigle that long to accept his trade to Edmonton for right wing Andrei Kovalenko. But on January 29, Alexandre did, bringing the "Russian Tank"—as Kovalenko had been called while a Quebec teammate of Hextall's—to Philadelphia with his own reputation to live down.

Kovalenko once had missed an Oiler flight after a night of alleged

John LeClair led the Flyers with 51 goals in 1997-98 and 43 in 1998-99.

carousing. But after being informed of his trade and having a connection to Philadelphia cancelled, he flew to San Francisco, caught a flight to Philly that landed at 6 a.m. and was at the Flyer morning practice.

"I don't think he is going to be a problem," said Neilson. And if Kovalenko was, Hextall thought the Flyers could handle it. "This room is as stable as I have seen it in a long time," the goalie said.

So, hopefully, was the defense, even though Cashman, who had been changing the D from behind the bench, had to take a leave of absence to have two back discs fused. Mike Stothers, Barber's right-hand man with the Phantoms, was promoted. Dykhuis, who had been minus-21 in 33 games with Tampa Bay, was plus-6 in his first 13 games back in Philly. Nevertheless, Clarke was looking for a cornerstone defenseman and asked Chicago GM Bob Murray about the availability of Chris Chelios. Murray acknowledged the inquiry publicly, much to Chelios's displeasure.

"I know I'm not going to be traded to Philadelphia because they're just offering Zubrus and that's it," the future Hall of Famer told reporters. "Tell Clarke to leave me alone and shut up."

Clearly, Chelios didn't want to go. Neither did Vanbiesbrouck to the All-Star Game in Tampa, after an injury to Joseph opened up a spot at the last minute.

"I was in the car when I got the call from Clarkie," recalls Vanbiesbrouck. "My wife (Rosalind) and I had been looking forward to some special time in New York, and I would have had to get on a plane quickly.

"I had to make a hasty decision. It wasn't the right one, in part because I put Clarkie in a bad position. He totally got it, though and, had I wanted to go, my wife would have too. She was shocked I turned it down."

At the All-Star break, the Flyers had completed a seven-game homestand (5-0-2) with a 28-10-12 record. They were not just hot on the ice, but burning up from cabin fever.

"We had a team that liked to have a good time together," recalls Jones. "We went out two days early to LA, and while it was not like we did anything embarrassing, we enjoyed ourselves and lost concentration, a mistake.

The party ended when a late Lindros-LeClair inspired rally fell short in a 5-4 loss at Anaheim. The following night, the Flyers last visit to The Forum—where they went 34-19-7 in 31 seasons—ended horribly, a 4-3 loss in which Hextall gave up three goals in the final 3:08, the last through the five-hole from the blueline with just one second remaining.

In Denver, Neilson's players blew yet another two-goal lead only to save a 4-4 tie on LeClair's 35th goal of the season. But they appeared to get their mojo back with a trip-closing 4-1 domination of Phoenix, highlighted when Tertyshny's shot caromed off the right post and goalie Nikolai Khabibulin's rear for the defenseman's first NHL goal. "It feels very good," said Tertyshny. "I hope it's not my last."

Soon enough the Flyers, managing just one score apiece in listless losses to Montreal and the Senators, en masse began to wonder where their next score was coming from. A 15-minute postgame player meeting in Ottawa seemed to draw the proper response—Hextall's 2-1 win at Pittsburgh. But a 5-3 loss in Florida morphed into a 4-1 defeat in Tampa. "There are no excuses," said Lindros.

Clarke had a good one—the 2-6-2 record in the last 10 games—to cancel a pre-playoff R&R trip to New Orleans. "Rumor has it that we have the biggest party team in the NHL," said Neilson to the boys in breaking the hard news. But the coach took no joy in it.

"I think he was as disappointed as we were," recalls Richardson. "He was talking about riding a bike to all these museums and we were thinking we were going to be there for St. Patrick's Day. Instead, we stayed home to practice."

At least in a couple of years, they would have a state-of-the-art facility in which to do so. Nevertheless, Neilson begged off attending the February 22 ground-breaking for the new $20 million practice facility on Laurel Oak Road in Voorhees, joking, sort of, that this job wouldn't last long enough for him to run practices there upon the building's completion.

When an accident on the Walt Whitman Bridge delayed officials coming from Philadelphia, Clarke was among those who took refuge from the frigid weather at Voorhees Senior Living, next to the construction site. Thus, the GM found one more reason for relocation from the decrepit Coliseum than just promised state-of-the-art facilities and separate practice rinks for the Flyers and Phantoms. "Roger, there's an assisted-living center right next door; you can live there," Clarke told his coach.

The way the Flyers were playing was getting old fast. Lindros and Brind'Amour were scoring but LeClair, playing with a hip bruise, was not; Langkow's production also had tailed off. Increasingly frozen in fear of getting caught up ice, Philadelphia's hitters had stopped hitting and, not surprisingly, scoring.

"Last year we had too many guys hanging around, so they couldn't play good; this year we didn't keep extra guys," said Clarke. "Now, maybe we need some competition."

When Vanbiesbrouck, leading 1-0 into the third period at Mon-

treal, let in four goals in his final 11 shots of a 4-1 loss, Neilson and Clarke went to the shock treatments, calling up Jean-Marc Pelletier, the Flyers' second-round pick in the 1997 draft, to play two nights later at Ottawa.

"This is not about my confidence, it's about us getting a win," said Vanbiesbrouck. Neilson said it was only about giving his beleaguered veteran goalies some practice days to sharpen up. But if the general purpose was to catch the team's attention, it didn't work. Pelletier gave up a goal on the second shot he faced in the NHL, one minute in, then played well until the Senators broke open their 5-0 win in the third period. Unable to part the waters, the kid was sent back to the Phantoms.

"I felt disrespected, sure," recalls Vanbiesbrouck. "But it was Philly, which always struggles with confidence in its goalies, so I tried to look at it that way."

The only thing worth looking at on the night of March 4, when Philadelphia lost 5-0 to Ottawa, was Brian Propp's pregame induction into the Flyers Hall of Fame. Just two months earlier, its 16th member had become the team's radio color broadcaster, replacing Steve Coates, who was joining Jim Jackson and Gary Dornhoefer on the television side.

Two nights later, Brind'Amour set up two of the three Flyer goals in the final 3:06 to get a comeback 3-3 tie against the Islanders, seemingly a rousing step in the right direction. Kovalenko, with just one assist in 13 games, was not being used enough by Neilson to make an impact, so Clarke quickly dealt the Russian Tank to Carolina for a serviceable sedan with 11 NHL years on it, defenseman Adam Burt. But the GM continued to look for scoring help.

Fat chance, Clarke had told suitors wanting Zubrus during his promising rookie season. But with the kid's waistline expanding, so was the GM's willingness to part with a 21-year-old former first-round pick. "Push yourself away from the table, man," Zubrus had been told by Clarke as he ballooned to a less-than-chiseled 225 pounds; no wonder he had scored just three goals in 63 games. "Hell, I could still score three goals in this league," Clarke said.

Nevertheless, there was interest in Zubrus from the rebuilding Canadiens, who were anxious to recycle the 31-year-old Mark Recchi before he cost them huge money in free agency. So on March 10, the Flyers' single-season scoring leader (123 points in 1992-93) and bait in the three-for-one deal that had brought Desjardins and LeClair (plus Gilbert Dionne, who lasted only 22 games) to Philadelphia, was returned in exchange for Zubrus, a second-round pick and another conditional pick.

"Now it's four-for-one," said a smiling Desjardins. "[Recchi] brings speed to the wing, sure."

Whether or not Recchi sped himself out of Montreal shouting to reporters during a hard practice that the Habs, who had lost to Florida 5-2 the previous game, were being punished to satisfy the media, he happily caught the next flight out of St. Louis, where the Canadiens were playing the following night.

"I wanted a five year-contract and [Montreal] didn't want to give me five," Recchi recalls. "I was pretty sure they were going to trade me.

"I don't remember hearing that the Flyers wanted me. But I was excited. I was coming back to a team that was a contender, more than Montreal was at that time, and I knew a lot of the guys."

Clarke believes rushing Zubrus to the NHL at age 18 ultimately set him back. "He was teasing us, but that was our own fault; the expectations were too great," the GM recalls. "He had size and skating ability but no interest in being great, just wanted to play hockey at his own level."

Remembers Ramsay, "Dainius was huge, skated 100 miles an hour, shot rockets but didn't know the game even a little bit. He just didn't understand the value of playing without the puck."

Today, Zubrus, who turned out to be a solid complementary player in Montreal, Washington and New Jersey, agrees he was given too much responsibility too soon.

"The Flyers gave me a great opportunity to play with great players and I don't know if I handled that as well as I should have," he recalls.

"Rod Brind'Amour was always in the gym when players didn't go workout after games. Maybe I should have talked to him.

"The first year I played a lot, so I was learning. Second year, not so much. I would have been better off in the minors.

"I remember Keith Jones telling me that getting traded would be a fresh start for me. He was right. First game in Montreal I scored a goal, we won a couple more games and I played with more responsibility. But I don't blame anybody in Philly. There is nothing bad I can say about the way I was treated. When I got traded, I called Clarke and thanked him for drafting me.

"I scored the first (Flyer) goal in the new building. It's something I can tell my kids."

Clarke re-acquired Recchi without asking agent Rick Curran whether the winger was open to making a long contractual commitment to Philadelphia. But the GM had the money and was certain of Recchi's value. "He can play the point or in front of the net on the power play, score five-against-five, kill penalties and, if absolutely necessary, he can play center," said Clarke.

"We needed a shot in the arm. A player like this can really help our playoff drive."

That is, if the player was healthy enough to do so. Until contracting pneumonia earlier that season, Recchi had been among the league scoring leaders.

"[The Canadiens] had two or three other guys hurt and they needed me to play," he recalls. "I lost about 15 pounds—down to 172 at one point—before I told them I just couldn't do it anymore. I sat out four games and came back, but never regained my strength."

Traded back to the Flyers while on a one-game trip, Recchi first had to gain a wardrobe. "I didn't have time to go home for clothes," he remembers. "Had to buy some suits in Philly."

Neilson, meanwhile, didn't have enough bodies to put into orange and black suits. LeClair, his hip not responding well to treatment, couldn't answer the ball, ending his consecutive game streak at 317, so Recchi's Philadelphia return was made on a line with Lindros and Jones. After Big E and Zelepukin giveaways staked the Avalanche to a

4-1 lead, Recchi's goal started Philadelphia back to within 4-3. But Colorado hit the empty net in a 5-3 victory that pushed the Flyer winless streak to 0-6-3.

"Obviously, I'm very comfortable here," Recchi told the media after the game. Not so Snider with his manic-depressive squad. "I think this team has had a complete mental collapse," he said. "To see a team play so well and then play so poorly for such long stretches, I've never seen this happen."

While Clarke tried to get Matthew Barnaby, who was traded instead to Pittsburgh, the players, not beating on opponents, beat themselves up at another team meeting. "We've got to get back to taking the body," said Langkow. In doing so, they seemed to quickly exhaust themselves during a 4-0 loss in Pittsburgh, making the Flyers the first team in NHL history to have both 10-game unbeaten and 10-game winless streaks in the same season.

"We tried everything short of human sacrifice," recalls LeClair. Neilson, angered that Hull's stick was held while Pavol Demitra's powerplay goal had put the Blues up 3-1 in St. Louis, tried to get the attention of his team—and the refs—by grabbing Recchi's stick and throwing it on the ice, almost hitting linesman Lonnie Cameron.

"When there was trouble, Roger did things to make sure the focus came back on him," recalls Ramsay. "Even things that seemed spur of the moment, there was a thought to them.

"He had a unique ability to not care what was said about him because it meant it was not being said about other people."

And besides, Recchi could get another stick. "I thought it was awesome," he recalls. "Anything to spark the team.

"Everything was going wrong when I got there. Even if we played a good game, we would lose."

With a more-frustrating-than-ever 5-2 loss in St. Louis—the Flyers had two goals disallowed—their winless streak went to 12 games and Neilson to the penalty box; he was suspended for two games by NHL disciplinarian Colin Campbell.

"One game for throwing his stick and one for making such a poor throw," smiled Clarke. Neilson's long-time companion, Nancy Nichols, chimed in from Dallas that he "threw like a girl." But by missing the linesman (no intent to hit, ruled Campbell), the coach avoided having the book thrown at him.

"Probably a reasonable suspension," said the sheepish Neilson. He rationalized that perhaps a different voice behind the bench—Ramsay—for two games might help. But watching from upstairs as the Flyers gave up two shorthanded goals and fell behind the Red Wings 4-1, things only looked worse to Neilson.

"We're having trouble making three-foot passes," he said between periods. "You can see the team is not playing with any confidence at all. And you can't coach confidence."

Nor leadership, which rises under bad circumstances. Lindros fed Recchi for a proximity goal, then, after a Renberg stuffer tied it, the captain stole a pass, took a return feed from LeClair and, with 1:53 left, won the game, 5-4. "We haven't had a lot of things go our way," said Lindros. "[Today] it took everything."

Unfortunately, that included Desjardins. After tying a personal mark with his 47th assist, the ace defenseman collided with Tomas Holmstrom and was diagnosed with a slight tear to his ACL that would leave him out for 7-10 days.

That didn't cause Clarke to cave on Chicago's asking price for Chelios—Langkow and prospect Simon Gagne. "Way out of our range," said the GM after the Blackhawks traded the future Hall of Famer to Detroit for Anders Eriksson and two first-round picks.

The next guy on the Flyer GM's list—the Rangers' Ulf Samuelsson—would have cost the team Tertyshny, who had been an object of New York's desire going back to the 1995 draft. Confusion about the Russian's birth date had made the Rangers unaware of his eligibility, causing them to file an unsuccessful protest.

Samuelsson went to Detroit right behind Chelios for second- and third-round draft choices. So Clarke moved Babych, who had been scratched for 25 of 58 games, to Los Angeles to bring back defenseman Steve Duchesne, but not until the Kings bought out the remaining two years, plus an option, of his contract, making him a free agent at the end of the 1998-99 season.

"He's the kind of player we need," said Neilson, who had coached Duchesne in St. Louis, one of the defenseman's three stops since the Flyers had included him in the Lindros trade with Quebec almost seven years earlier.

Having just picked up tough guy Sandy McCarthy in a two-for-one deal with Tampa Bay that also brought winger Mikael Andersson for the turnover-prone Forbes and a fourth-round pick, Clarke still wasn't satisfied he had enough muscle or character. Before the trading deadline, he re-acquired Craig Berube from Washington for future considerations.

"George [McPhee, the Washington GM] asked Dale (Hunter) and me if we wanted to go to a team with a chance to win," recalls Berube. "We said, 'Sure.' Dale went to Colorado."

Berube had never scored more than eight goals in any of his 12 years in the NHL. But just as he had been in Philadelphia, which had traded him in 1991 in the three-way deal that brought Duchesne the first time, The Chief had been a respected locker-room voice everywhere he had played.

Twelve Clarke deals in 11 months left only eight players from the team that had lost to Buffalo in the preceding playoffs. "Guess I liked what I was doing, so I kept going," he laughs today, but newcomers and survivors alike no longer were accusing him of an itchy finger.

"I thought every trade that year was for the better," Vanbiesbrouck recalls. "The chemistry was good.

"This was part of the mystique of Philadelphia, too, trying to win every year. That's why I jumped to sign there."

But no one was under any illusion that Andersson, Berube or McCarthy could replace Recchi, who, six games after his return, missed a check, slammed into the boards and suffered a concussion during a 3-1 win at Toronto.

"Went to the bench, thought I was fine; then, sitting there, I got this tingling in my ears that went down my arms," he recalls. "I couldn't put my gloves on, and the next thing I knew, I woke up in the locker room."

Still in the process of saying hello, Recchi had to say goodbye for four games. With all these newcomers, Neilson thought a little bonding would be a good idea. During a two-day break, the strangers—actually wearing nametags—boarded buses for the New Jersey Pinelands for team-building problem-solving exercises like getting each other through a fence and calculating how many Flyers could stand on one board.

Incoming, amidst all the playing acquisitions, was skating coach David Roy, and—naturally for Neilson—video coach Rob Cookson, who had worked with Clarke for the Canadian Olympic team.

But through all the newness—Berube became a record 43rd person to don the orange-and-black in one season—there had at least been one constant in the lineup. That was Lindros, who had missed just one game until he was hooked on the arm by Ranger Petr Nedved late in the Flyers' third straight victory, 3-1, over New York. Lindros's stick spun back and hit Nedved in the face.

"Sooner or later, somebody's eyeball will be lying on the ice and Lindros will be saying, 'Geez, I didn't mean it,'" said Ranger GM Smith, vowing he would call the league like "Snider would do."

"We don't send in films to get players suspended; we refuse to do that," responded Clarke. "Neil has enough problems with his own team (about to miss the playoffs for a second straight year) than to worry about ours.

"It's not a very bright move on his part to criticize our owner. It's not like Neil is Sam Pollock."

Lindros was suspended for two games. "I didn't know where the player was," he protested. "Why would I take a penalty with three-and-a-half minutes to go on purpose?

"There goes the Lady Byng."

And there went another critical player to the sideline, just as the Flyers had a chance to build momentum in the final 10 regular-season games. Without Lindros, Recchi and Desjardins, Philadelphia put up a good fight in Detroit but, after an apparent winner by Brind'Amour was disallowed due to a LeClair foot in the crease, lost 3-2 on Wendel Clark's overtime goal.

"Hopefully the rule will come out soon," said Neilson, who counted three critical goals—and games—the Flyers had lost because of tippy toes in the crease.

"It's killing us," said Lindros. But so were lapses of energy. The compromised lineup had Philadelphia up 3-1 against Carolina until Gelinas turned Tertyshny on the tying goal and the Flyers barely hung on for a 3-3 tie.

The team announced a $16 million deal for Desjardins for four more seasons, but would they have him for the upcoming playoffs? That "slight tear" had turned out to be an 80 percent severed ACL.

"Hockey is a sport than can be played with a partial ACL injury," said Dr. Art Bartolozzi, the team orthopedist. "[Desjardins] has regained motion and doesn't have much swelling. He's right on track."

As April began, the Flyers were only 3-2 since the end of their losing streak, but at least they had Lindros back.

Until they didn't.

After Philadelphia had squeaked out a 2-1 win in its first-ever visit to Tennessee, the captain complained about pain in his ribs, even though he could not remember a specific hit that would have caused it. "The Nashville doctor checked his lungs, ribs, everything," recalls strength and conditioning coach Jim McCrossin. "Everything was fine."

So Lindros joined his roommate, Jones, for a beer and a chicken sandwich, with plans to go hear some live country music until Eric said his side hurt. He cancelled the entertainment portion of the evening and returned to their room at Loew's Vanderbilt Hotel.

"When I went back there, he still was in pain, moaning a little bit," recalls Jones. "I thought it was just a rib issue and gave him some Advil.

"I went to bed and slept through the night."

It was a long time until dawn for Lindros, who took refuge in a hot bath to no relief. At around 8 a.m. a concerned Jones called trainer John Worley. Having been at Baptist Hospital most of the night with Recchi—who also was feeling poorly during a postgame meal and soon was suffering a return of the tingling down his arms—Worley was in the shower, so Jones called McCrossin.

"He's really having trouble breathing." Jones said. McCrossin found Lindros in the bathtub, "pale as white paper" and sweating profusely. When Worley quickly arrived, he called Dr. Rick Garman, the Predators' physician.

"Get him to the hospital right now," Garman told Worley. Fast-arriving paramedics lifted Lindros from the tub, rushed him to Baptist

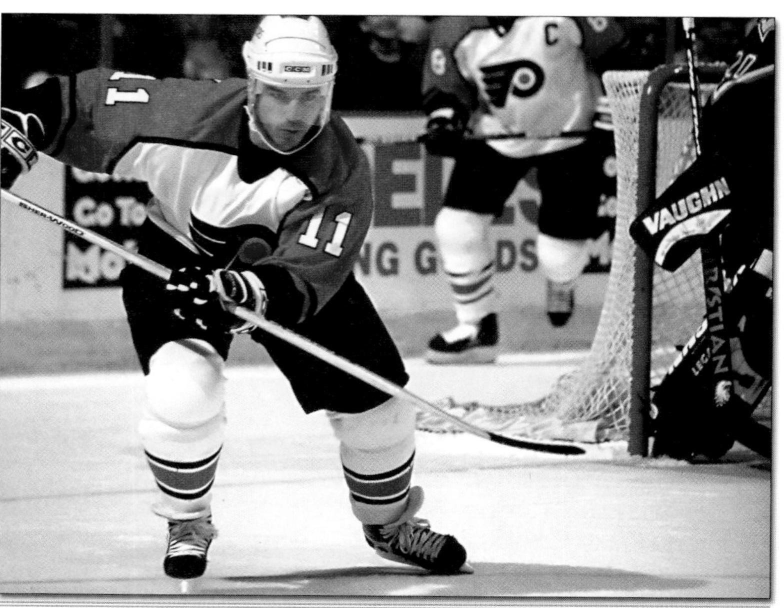

Mark Recchi came to the Flyers from Montreal with a big contract and matching expectations.

Hospital just minutes away, where they arrived at 9:44 a.m. "Even when he was sitting up, he was feeling lightheaded," the doctor would tell reporters. "I couldn't hear much in the way of chest sounds on the right side."

Told he would have to stand for a chest x-ray, Lindros buckled on the way to the machine and quickly was returned to a table. The emergency room doctor rapidly diagnosed a hemothorax. The accumulation of three liters of blood—half of that contained in a human body—from an apparently punctured artery had caused one of Lindros's lungs to collapse.

"I've got to [drain] this now," said the summoned pulmonologlist, not wanting to wait to get Lindros to an operating room upstairs. A female nurse was asked to hold down an agonized 6-4, 240-pound hockey player.

"The shunt is like [the funnel] that a gas attendant sticks in an oil can to pour it," recalls McCrossin, who was called in for reinforcement after Lindros sent the nurse flying.

"Eric gave an 'Oh!' and then all of a sudden an 'Ahhhhhhhh' and you could see the blood pouring out," recalls McCrossin. "I looked down and my feet were soaked in it.

"So much came out, it looked like I'd been shot," Lindros would say later. But, able to breathe, he felt better even as the blood drained.

McCrossin stayed with Lindros. Recchi was sent home with therapist Tom D'Anconna.

The Flyers boarded the bus to the airport that morning and learned their captain was in the hospital.

"I was like, 'What?' But that was what you would say every day," recalls Brind'Amour. "It was a circus around here. You got to the point where it was like normal.

"So it didn't affect the team the way people probably think. It affected Eric a lot, of course. But I don't think it affected the team."

Lindros had Jones to thank for being alive. "No question," recalls McCrossin. "He was not in good shape when he arrived at the hospital.

"I don't have anything but good things to say about the medical treatment there. The doctor at the arena had checked everything; it must have been a very slow bleed at that point."

Lindros's teammates learned of his collapsed-lung diagnosis after landing in Boston later in the day. Following a decent start the next afternoon, the Flyers faded and lost 3-0, then weren't much better two days later against the Rangers, as the struggling Hextall allowed four questionable goals, the first off his glove on a backhanded dump-in from the red line by Chris Tamer. "Probably the worst goal I ever let in," Hextall said.

A few days later, Neilson told him that Vanbiesbrouck would be playing the rest of the games to prepare for the playoffs.

From the Nashville hospital, Lindros stayed on the doctor-ordered liquid diet, watched movies with McCrossin, and vowed to return for the postseason. But his father, noting that Eric could not leave his bed for more than a minute and a half without becoming exhausted, hardly shared that optimism.

"It probably will take more than a couple of doctors to convince me," Carl said. "But in the end, the decision will be Eric's to make."

Asked about his son's atrocious injury luck, Dad said, "The good luck this time is he is still alive."

Snider shared Carl's caution. "This is a very scary thing," said the team Chairman. "Until doctors are unanimous in the opinion that he can play, he won't play."

A pale Lindros, still suffering temperatures spiking to 102 degrees, returned to Philadelphia on Snider's private jet after six days in the Nashville medical facility, only to be readmitted to Pennsylvania Hospital for the insertion of another tube to drain clotted and infected blood in his chest. It was more clear than ever that the Flyers would be starting the playoffs in two weeks without him.

Dr. Larry Kaiser, a thoracic specialist at the University of Pennsylvania—and the eventual husband of Snider's daughter Lindy—said Lindros would need three to four weeks just to recover to full health. "From the start, we thought we were going to have to deal without having Eric for the rest of the year," Clarke told reporters.

The remainder of the cavalry tried to limp back.

Recchi, diagnosed with stress headaches that he said were exacerbated by the separation from his family during the birth of his first child, returned to the lineup against Pittsburgh after missing three games and scored a goal. Also back were LeClair and Desjardins, the latter fitted with a brace. "A few times I felt my leg going a bit, but I felt the brace doing its job, preventing it from going too far," the defenseman reported after the Flyers clinched a playoff spot with a 3-1 victory.

Desjardins remained in the lineup. Recchi did not. Hit once in the first period of a 2-2 tie with Buffalo, then again in the second, a return of the same symptoms drove him from the lineup. "I don't believe I came back too soon," he said the next day. "I felt good.

"I'll play in the playoffs. I don't know whether I'll start or exactly when I'll be there, but I'll play."

Neilson had gone as far as he wanted to with Richardson, benching him in favor of Burt. But LeClair, who scored twice in the Buffalo tie, seemed better, and Renberg's third-period goal brought Philadelphia back from a 2-0 deficit at New Jersey, even though the Flyers lost in overtime, 3-2.

To avoid a matchup with either the Atlantic Division champion Devils or the 103-point Senators, Philadelphia needed a point in Game 82 against Boston. They got two, holding the Bruins to just 11 shots in a 3-1 home win that set up a first-round match with the third-seeded Leafs.

For the first time since 1989, the Flyers, who finished with 93 points, would start the playoffs on the road. But having a 3-0-1-season record against Toronto, the task hardly seemed daunting, even without Lindros. "Brind'Amour got a lot of minutes; he could handle it," recalls Jones. "I don't think there ever was a moment where we felt we couldn't get past the Leafs."

The matchup, however, was not especially kind to Vanbiesbrouck, the "bargain" goaltender Philadelphia had signed before Joseph had taken double the money from Toronto. The Flyers, Joseph told reporters, had been his preference. So the obvious choice of story angles during the series would be the goaltenders.

"Toronto made a decision and Philadelphia made a decision," Vanbiesbrouck, who was 3-1 versus Joseph during the season, told the media. "This doesn't enter into this playoff, even though it might make a good story. I don't shoot on Cujo (Joseph)."

If Pat Quinn, whose speedy Leafs had improved by 32 points in his first season behind the bench, felt Toronto had better goaltending, he wanted to make certain his team could take advantage of it. Having complained about the crease-crashing of the bigger and stronger Flyers during their win at the Air Canada Center three weeks earlier, he didn't back off in pre-series interviews.

"You watch, they back up there all the time," he said. "It's not a mean thing, but they get away with it."

Jones considered that quote a highway into Joseph's head. "He's a very active goalie and he does a good job of acting," said the Philadelphia winger. "He's fooled his own coach, obviously, into thinking he's getting hit.

"[Annoying goaltenders] is a skill I have and this is the time for it."

Neilson, the once-Leaf coach, accused Quinn, the ex-Flyer coach who had earned a degree at Widener Law School after his Philadelphia dismissal in 1982, of jury tampering. "Pat's an old lawyer, he's smart with the press," said Neilson. "We assume the referees are too smart for that."

So was Lindros to even think about playing after losing 18 pounds. "I rode the bike and lasted only 1:40 because my pulse went up to 150," he said. "I've got a lot of work ahead of me."

Recchi, who had never made the playoffs in his first run with the Flyers, was determined to participate. A headache specialist, Dr. Peter Sheptak, a Pittsburgh neurosurgeon, still saw no evidence of a concussion, just migraines.

"That's what we always said in those days," smiles Recchi today. Expedience was the winger's only concern, and Toronto's quickness was the theme for much of the pre-series analysis, memories lingering from the previous spring when Philadelphia had been made to look ponderous by the Sabres.

"I don't think speed had anything to do with why we lost that series," Brind'Amour told Rich Hofmann of the *Daily News*. "We lost because of our special teams.

"Because we're big doesn't mean we are slow."

Certainly the 5-8 Vanbiesbrouck made himself look huge in the net in Game One. After Therien and Jones were called for simultaneous cross-checking penalties nine minutes into the contest, the goalie made two stops on the five-on-three.

Langkow forced a giveaway and fed Zelepukin, who top-shelved a backhander to give the Flyers a 1-0 lead before twisting his knee in a second-period entanglement with Toronto's Garry Valk. It became 2-0 in the second when LeClair cashed a five-on-three.

Eleven Leafs making their playoff debuts seemed to be belatedly acclimating themselves to the level of the competition in the third period, when a dubious penalty-shot call—Duchesne used his glove to sweep a puck out of the crease but did not close his hand—gave Toronto a chance to get back into the game. But in classic Vanbiesbrouck style, he stood his ground on Leaf star Mats Sundin and batted out of the air the first penalty shot against the Flyers in their playoff history. Desjardins hit the empty net to seal the 3-0 win.

"I was so upset about the [call on Duchesne] I didn't see the first 10 minutes of the third," said Neilson, not taking advantage of a vintage Beezer. "He looked like he did when they went to the Final in Florida," said LeClair.

Asked if he ever had seen better goaltending, Brind'Amour thought for a moment. "I've seen a lot of good ones," he said. "Against us more than for us."

Lindros, feeling well enough to travel in support of his teammates, chipped in with a restaurant suggestion for the boys on the off night before Game Two. He chose a chain pasta place that received bad reviews. "We've been through a lot together this year," said Neilson. "Including this meal."

"Roger doesn't like my offensive suggestions and doesn't like my restaurants either," smiled Lindros.

He offered no touts to the coach about his defensive pairs. Having alternated for much of the season five-six combinations of Richardson-Dykhuis and Tertyshny-Burt, the coach decided to stay with Burt and Tertyshny for Game Two, leaving Richardson, the expensive free agent, in the press box.

No reason to change what was working, though. Eleven minutes into the game, Mark Greig, a veteran callup from the Phantoms playing in place of the injured Zelepukin, made a pretty backhand pass to feed Jones, who fired over Joseph's glove for a 1-0 lead.

The Flyers protected it confidently, killing seven Leaf powerplays. After two periods, they had only 11 shots and Neilson counted just three Toronto chances. "We were playing a perfect game," recalls Recchi. "It wasn't even a contest."

But their bids for insurance all had been foiled by Joseph when, with a little more than two minutes to go, Brind'Amour tried again, centering the puck off the sideboards towards Recchi in the middle. "Roddy always made the right choice," recalls Jones. "I'm thinking, 'Oh no, that's not the right choice.'"

Bryan Berard picked off the puck and fed Steve Thomas, who gained the zone when Therien stumbled. The defenseman recovered enough to keep Thomas wide, but his shot still sneaked between Vanbiesbrouck's legs.

So complete had been Philadelphia's control that the Air Canada Centre could hardly believe the game was tied with 1:59 to go. But the Leafs were empowered. When Sundin blocked LeClair's shot, Therien had to dive to foil Sundin's breakaway.

The fans, wanting a penalty, littered the ice, forcing the faceoff back outside the blueline and giving the Flyers plenty of time to compose themselves during the cleanup. But Toronto controlled the draw and threw the puck in. Sergei Berezin circled the net dogged by Therien, but still was able to get a shot away.

Vanbiesbrouck stopped the attempt, which rebounded just past Desjardins, who got his stick on Sundin's shot just enough to accidentally deflect it up over Vanbiesbrouck's shoulder before he could square himself.

Suddenly losing 2-1, the stunned Flyers still had 52 seconds to come back, but LeClair's stick broke as he slapped the puck from 45 feet out. He threw it away disgustedly, the perfect metaphor for his team's discarded opportunity to gain complete control of what was now a 1-1 series.

"I felt terrible," recalls Therien. "I thought I was to blame, but Roger came up to me the next day said the goal wasn't my fault, that the goalie has to make that save."

Philadelphia had been so superior for 58 minutes, the players told themselves one loss easily could be shrugged off. "I never thought that game would be our swan song," recalls Therien. "We were going home and were much better than that Toronto team."

But, of course, they could only turn the series back around with better goaltending. Just 10 seconds after Dykhuis's drive through a LeClair screen gave the Flyers a 1-0 lead late in the first period of Game Three, Mike Johnson beat Vanbiesbrouck, who had failed to set his feet, from the lower edge of the left circle.

When Thomas, harassed continually by Jones, dramatized a post-whistle bump by Berube in the final minute of the period and drew a penalty, the Leaf winger drove a powerplay slapshot from high in the left circle over Vanbiesbrouck's shoulder to put Toronto ahead 2-1 40 seconds after the first intermission.

The Flyers outshot the Leafs 26-9 over the second and third periods, but with a minimum of rebounds and traffic to the net, couldn't solve Joseph, even after a Sundin high stick of LeClair enabled Philadelphia to play six-on-four for the final 65 seconds. Toronto had made minimal chances hold up for a 2-1 victory and a 2-1 series edge.

"It slipped through, somehow, someway," Vanbiesbrouck told reporters about the Johnson goal. "[Thomas] made a good shot but there was probably more room there than there should have been.

"It certain affects your sleeping patterns."

While the goaltender searched for words to reflect his disappointment in himself, McCarthy, who had an African-American father and a mother of mixed races, claimed that Leaf tough guy Tie Domi had racially defamed the Flyer winger during the second period.

"By no means did I use that word," insisted Domi, who, in turn, claimed he had been spat on by McCarthy. Because no one else on the ice heard any such comment, a league investigation found nothing, much like the Flyers in search of the net behind Joseph.

"I think we know we're playing very well," said Recchi. "Eventually we're going to break out."

And they did in Game Four. McCarthy held the puck in at the point, and Berube scored on a tip to put Philadelphia ahead 1-0. After Berezin tied the contest on the power play, Desjardins, practically playing on one leg with his badly damaged ACL, made a good hold at the point to set up a LeClair score, then the gutsy defenseman broke a 2-2 tie with a powerplay goal early in the second period.

LeClair added a cushion before the intermission and the Leafs managed only four third-period shots before Brind'Amour's empty netter sealed a 5-2 win and a 2-2 tie in a series the Flyers continued to dominate territorially.

"They had a couple (good) players, maybe one or two defensemen," recalls Desjardins. "We were stronger than them."

When, only 1:52 into Game Five at the Air Canada Centre, Jones gave Philadelphia the first goal of the game for the fifth straight contest, the Flyers appeared in better shape than ever to establish control. But the Leafs were hitting more and, at Quinn's urging, supporting their defense better. Even before Yushkevich evened the game at 1-1 while Duchesne was in the penalty box, Toronto was playing evenly with Philadelphia for the first time in the series.

Believing his depth would make the difference, Neilson rolled four lines to Quinn's three, but as the logjam held through the third period, the Leafs were carrying the play. The Flyers, just 2-3-11 during the season in overtime, dodged one bullet in sudden death—Sundin hit the cross bar—but Neilson, settling in for the long haul, didn't shorten his bench. He had his checking line—Renberg, Andersson and McCarthy—out in the overtime when Renberg, who was playing the series with cracked ribs, circled the net, attempted to feed the slot and flubbed the puck, trapping himself up ice.

Valk's back pass found Yanic Perreault, who was deep inside the circle when his weak backhand ticked off Vanbiesbrouck's glove, went over his pad and in at 11:51, giving Toronto the 2-1 win and 3-2 series advantage.

Of the eight goals the Philadelphia goalie had given up in five games, three had been backhands from bad angles.

"A backhand can fool you anyway because you never know the release point," he recalls. "It came off [Perreault's] stick awkwardly; he actually flubbed it.

"But if you are playing well. . ."

The Flyers' seventh-consecutive postseason overtime defeat (going back four springs) left them going home to face elimination. When Joseph, pressured by Brind'Amour on Philadelphia's penalty kill, slipped behind his net, the Flyers had an excellent opportunity to get in front for a sixth straight game. But the goalie got his stick down to prevent Brind'Amour from getting to the post.

Referees Terry Gregson and Rob Shick awarded Toronto four consecutive powerplays, then gave five straight to Philadelphia.. But having scored only 13 goals in the seven regular-season games once Lindros had gone out, beating Joseph only 11 times in the five playoff games, then missing the net 18 times during Game Six, the Flyers couldn't break a scoreless deadlock that continued deep into the third period.

After a Philadelphia push, the Leafs' Kris King got in the way of Brind'Amour as he skated back trying to prevent a three-on-two. Schick, the trailing referee, ignored the infraction. Gregson was not so inclined when, with 2:54 to go, LeClair elbowed Johnson in the head along the backboards.

"Back then you could grab people, but I don't even think that's a penalty today," recalls LeClair. "Rod got absolutely raped a shift earlier; it was ridiculous."

The furious Flyers buckled down. Therien blocked a drive by

Bryan Berard, and the penalty killers cleared the puck three times. They were six seconds away from escaping when Berard fired while being shoved by Jones. The puck hit Burt in the backside and ricocheted to Berezin, who put it through Vanbiesbrouck's pads with 59.2 seconds left.

With the goalie pulled, Recchi was blockered away by Joseph and Desjardins, off a Recchi passout, was blocked by King just before the buzzer of the Leafs' series-clinching 1-0 victory.

LeClair and McGillis chased Gregson to the tunnel as the referee was hit by thrown debris. He heard it even worse than did Jones from Thomas in the handshake line.

"I swear on my kids' heads I am going to kill you next year," said the Leaf, hardly in the intended spirit of traditional post-series sportsmanship.

But the hottest guy in a seething First Union Center was Snider. Told by the NHL security appointees Anthony Esposito and John Malandra at the officials' dressing room door that the NHL prohibited any postgame conversations between club officials and referees, Snider took Malandra's walkie-talkie, threw it against the door, and went to the locker room to unload to the media.

"It's a disgrace to the league what [Gregson] did tonight," said the Flyer boss. "I don't know what I can do about it, but I'll tell you one thing, everybody in the stands knows what this guy did.

"We had a guy tripped on the way back and that gave them the three-on-two and they didn't call it. Jody Hull, just a few minutes before, nearly had his head taken off and they didn't call it. Then they call this chicken-you-know-what penalty on John LeClair, one of the cleanest players in the league.

"LeClair was mugged the whole night; they didn't call a thing. Gregson, I hope he can sleep well tonight because you know what he did."

Turned away a second time at the official's door, Snider went back to the locker room again to call Gregson a coward. "This guy has an attitude, thinks he's greater than God," said Snider. "And he stinks as an official."

Neilson, who called it an "awful end," was not as loud but just as angry. "To lose on a call like that is unbelievable, a disgrace to the game," said the coach. "Right from the start of the series, we had no idea how games were going to be called."

"He blew it," said LeClair in the locker room. "Maybe he didn't know what the score was or how much time was left. That's all I'm going to say."

Leaf GM Ken Dryden had an opposing view, of course. "We got called (Johnson for tripping) not too long before that last one," he said. "The replay [showed] a pretty dramatic elbow and right in front of the referee."

Indeed, that's what Gregson saw.

"Maybe calling penalties late in the game wasn't quite as acceptable as it is now," the referee recalls. "I felt the blow made contact with the head.

"It wasn't safe. I had to call it. And that was the end of it."

Gregson remembers being made aware only that Philadelphia personnel—Clarke was there too, although he remained silent—were at the door of the officials' dressing room. Responsibility for dealing with their anger fell to the late John D'Amico, the NHL-appointed officiating supervisor for the series, and responsibility for getting the officials safely out of the building came back upon Esposito and Malandra.

They waited, by Malanadra's recollection, "a good hour" to get Gregson and Schick down a largely-deserted hallway and outside to a police vehicle without harassment.

For the purposes of keeping the officials together for the night, those staying downtown were rebooked to the Airport Marriott, where Gregson, who had used his real name when checking in, returned to his room to find threatening phone messages. He called Malandra and Esposito, who still were at the arena. Linesmen Pat Dapuzzo, who had served as a backup that evening, suggested the officials share a rental car immediately to a hotel at Newark Airport, and the security people agreed.

On the New Jersey Turnpike, Dapuzzo's car hit a deer, smashing a headlight, but they continued to the hotel, where a message was waiting for Gregson from director of officiating Bryan Lewis to fly out in the morning for Game Seven of the Blues-Coyotes series in Phoenix two nights hence. Gregson called a 1-0 St. Louis overtime victory without incident.

"It was the craziest 36 hours or so after game that I ever had," Gregson recalls. "But I understand the emotion.

"Years later at a meeting (Gregson was NHL director of officiating from 2009-2013), Mr. Snider said something to me like, 'I said some things quite a while ago,' and I said, 'Geez' I don't remember,' and we just left it at that.

"It's history. I worked games after that in Philly without any incident that I can recall, maybe got booed, but you get booed most places. I never felt like I had to sneak back into Dodge, never remember hearing comments on the ice from Flyer players about that call."

Winning two of the four games in which they were badly outplayed, then getting opportunities in the end of the two even contests, the Leafs had taken advantage of their breaks.

"A goal off [Hull's] butt into the slot; I'm not saying Toronto is a lucky team, but by the same token, it is what it is," Vanbiesbrouck reflected to reporters.

But so had been three goals to his short side that had put the Flyers at the mercy of a controversial call. Vanbiesbrouck had allowed just nine goals in six games, yet the series had disappeared through the cracks in the previously flawless positioning and unbending calm that had made him a Vezina winner and two-time All-Star.

"At that position, when you are off, it's a mental breakdown more than anything," recalls Vanbiesbrouck. "Look, I'm more critical of myself about those moments than anybody could ever be. It was a really painful end of the season. It hurt.

"I felt it was the Thomas goal (to win Game Three) that changed the momentum of the series. "He kind of cut in, something Thomas did well, and beat me on the stick side.

"I remember the pressure I felt from Eric staring at me in the locker room before games in that series, almost like he was trying to will me to win because he wanted to play in the next round so badly.

"But you put a lot of pressure on yourself, too. I never felt myself getting into the same mind-set in Philadelphia that I had in Florida.

"Maybe it was physical—my back was a periodic problem those two years—and maybe it was mental. But in that series, it wasn't Curtis Joseph. I respected him a lot and he played well, but did he really play great? I mean he had a couple good moments and did what he had to do, but I didn't look at it like him against me anymore than I did all those times against Patrick Roy."

Naturally, the conclusion that the Flyers had made the wrong goaltending choice the previous summer was inescapable.

"When your team is dominating a playoff series and you lose, and your team could have signed the goalie at the other end, you are going to feel the pressure," recalls Berube about Vanbiesbrouck. But the short-side goals allowed by a goalie who had made a career of near-perfect stand-up positioning were almost unfathomable.

Eric Desjardins played much of the Toronto series with a dmamged knee.

"I think John was so technically strong that if he got beaten by one, he couldn't quite understand it," theorizes Ramsay.

"You didn't give up those kinds of goals so now maybe you think, 'I have to change something.' The answer is probably no, but if you are worried about it you freeze a little bit.

"I think John was shocked by those goals, couldn't believe it and got kind of stuck. But I also think that ever since the Flyers won consecutive Stanley Cups with Bernie (Parent) shutouts, it had been a Philly thing to want to blame the goalie. All John could do in that sixth game was keep it scoreless. If we had scored two goals, we still win.

"It was devastating, as hard a loss as I ever have suffered. We had convinced them to play a certain way, they were doing it and we still didn't win when we were better than the other team."

However much of the 1999 series slipped through the short side, it produced long memories. "That was not a penalty," LeClair insists today. "Terry Gregson owes me one. I'm still pissed about it."

Post-series, Clarke tried to deflect the blame from Vanbiesbrouck. "Zero fault," claimed the GM.

An exhausted Recchi, who had one point in the six games, was willing to take some of it, had told reporters, "I got lots of scoring chances and couldn't finish them off, which was what this team needed. That was the way my whole year went from the time I got [pneumonia], when I was second in the league in scoring.

"I need to take a month off and get healthy."

The free-agent-to-be said he would not require an entire 30 days to accept an offer to remain a Flyer. "This is one of the best work-ethic teams I ever played on," he said.

Lindros felt the same way. "We've got a real good room in here now," he said. "If we'd gotten by the first round, you never know what would have happened.

"I agreed to a one-year deal and I'm going to stand by it, absolutely. I don't want to leave Philadelphia. For us to go through a [2-12-5] month like we did and stay together, that says something. I really like playing for Roger."

Despite the wild swings in a season of drastic personnel changes and a devastating end, Neilson, too, liked the team Clarke had re-created on the fly. "We probably need at least one more natural scorer, some guy like Berezin," said the coach. "When he shoots, it goes in. We had too many guys who shot and it never went in.

"But it feels like a team, as good a spirit as any team I've been with, and I've been with a few. I think we have become sound defensively, that's the basis you have to have."

Clarke pronounced his makeover largely completed. "When Freddie Shero came here, I think it took at least a year to get all the players playing the way he wanted to play," said the GM. "I told Roger I thought it would take a year and it did."

The NHL made Snider $50,000 poorer for his Gregson rant, a drop in the bucket for the "millions" he said his expensive team, budgeted to go deep into the playoffs, had lost. But even as he had railed in the aftermath of the Gregson call, the team Chairman said he felt much better about his club than when the year had begun.

"You can't go on forever with the same mix, but we've had a lot of changes," he said. "There comes a time when you have to stick with what you have and let it grow."

Simon Gagne made his NHL debut in 1999-2000.

Chapter 4 • 1999-2000

"What Else Can Happen?"

Gene Hart died of complications from diabetes and liver cancer on July 14, 1999 at Our Lady of Lourdes Hospital in Camden, NJ. He was 68 years old.

"I am sure we do not grieve alone," said his daughter Lauren that evening in a family statement that proved understated as the affection poured in during the days following.

"You're talking about a legendary figure in hockey," said Ranger play-by-play announcer Sam Rosen. "Gene was The Guy, the elder statesman."

That reverence from Hart's peers, who in 1997 had voted him the Foster Hewitt Award, the broadcast honor of the Hockey Hall of Fame, was dwarfed by expressions of what the Flyer franchise's play-by-play broadcaster of 28 years meant to the Delaware Valley, even four seasons after he had called his final Flyer game.

"Gene Hart and the Flyers were one and the same," said general manager Bob Clarke about the first voice a Philadelphia hockey fan-to-be ever heard on a radio broadcast.

Hart had instructed Philadelphia in a Canadian sport with such joy that the city had gotten caught up in his enthusiasm. Long before he shouted "The Flyers Win the Stanley Cup! The Flyers win the Stanley Cup!" on May 19, 1974, people had fallen for the roly-poly opera aficionado, whose voice ranged from tenor to basso profundo as he made each broadcast sing.

"He was largely responsible for making hockey popular in Philadelphia," said Ed Snider as "Good night and good hockey" was said during a two-and-a-half-hour service at the First Union Center on a hot Sunday, July 18. "He had the unique ability to explain and teach without offending those who already understood."

Snider borrowed the words Hart had used as the master of ceremonies for the pregame memorial service four days after Pelle Lindbergh's death in 1985. "Rather than mourn, we are here to celebrate the life that enriched all of us," the Flyer Chairman told the nearly 2,000 in attendance. Broad Street Bullies, current Flyers, and fans heard the former high school history instructor recalled by an array of family members, hockey people, broadcast figures, and patrons of the arts as a Renaissance man, mentor, and humanitarian.

"Gene Hart took his gifts and he nurtured them, developed them, used them, but most important, shared those gifts with humanity," said the Reverend Ed Casey, the Delaware County priest and hockey devotee since Day One of the franchise. "His words, his voice, his wisdom, and his knowledge brought joy and passion to so many."

His impact on the city best was summarized by Mayor Ed Rendell: "Philadelphia is truly blessed to have four wonderful professional sports franchises," said Rendell. "But if you look back over the last 32 years, only one of those organizations has had stability, consistency.

"Only one has had the same major players and actors through three decades and that is the Flyers. And the thing that tied all those 32 years together was Gene Hart. He was there in the glory days, in the tougher days, and was there in the resurgence."

Hart, a local South Jersey high school and minor league announcer who was not taken seriously by Philadelphia's teams and stations until he was 37 years old, treasured the opportunity to utter every word, said his son Brian.

"He knew every step of the way how lucky he was to be doing what he did," Brian told the audience. "He felt he was a regular guy living extraordinary circumstances."

Among those was the first Stanley Cup parade in 1974, which Hart told his son was for his upcoming fourth birthday. "Birthdays really haven't been the same since," said Brian.

Joe Watson recalled being told by Gene that his goal in the Flyer victory over the Soviet Red Army in 1976 had "set Russian hockey back 20 years." Wayne Fish of the *Bucks County Courier Times* recalled Hart telling Bob Kelly, with whom he enjoyed an ongoing jab fest, that his name was easy to find on the Cup because it was "written in crayon."

Master of Ceremonies Steve Coates recalled 30-minute phone conversations where all he was able to get in was "Hello Gene" and "Goodbye Gene." And Bobby Taylor, Hart's broadcast partner from 1977 to 1993, remembered a conversation between them being interrupted by a "Hang on a minute," then next hearing Gene calling a race at Brandywine Raceway before picking up the conversation again immediately after the wire.

Solo performances by Lauren, members of the Opera Company of Philadelphia, and the Philadelphia Orchestra of "Adagio for Strings," "An Die Musik," and "Abide with Me" were interspersed throughout a program that concluded with a single flute accompanying some of Hart's most famous calls.

"In Gene's mind, hockey and opera were very similar," said Craig

Hamilton, director of marketing and production for The Opera Company of Philadelphia. "He would always say that both have violence, bloodshed and where would either be without a score?"

Hart's death was followed two days later by the passing of Bill Flett, a right wing on the Flyers' first Stanley Cup team, at age 55 in Edmonton. Flett had recently undergone a liver transplant after a sobriety of eight years that had earned him an increasingly-respected stature in the oil-drilling business.

Flett, who scored 43 times as Clarke's right wing during the Flyer breakthrough season of 1972-73, came off the boards to set up arguably the most important goal in team history—Clarke's overtime winner of Game Two in Boston that turned the 1974 Final.

A rodeo rider in his youth and, to anyone's recollection, the first NHL player to sport a full beard, Flett's career seemed to be on the rise with his team's following his 1972 acquisition (along with Ross Lonsberry) in a then-largest-ever eight-player trade with the Kings. But his production during the first Cup season had declined to 17 goals and zero in the playoffs, so he was moved to Toronto by GM Keith Allen to make room for Reggie Leach in a separate deal with Oakland.

"Cowboy and I were a good pair," remembered Clarke. "He wasn't creative, but he could power to the net and really shoot hard and I could get him the puck.

"He was a good guy, a gentle person, big and strong but without a mean bone in his body. Things were pretty uncomplicated in those days. We played, drank beer and didn't worry about tomorrow. It became the norm to have a dozen after practice, then after a game the same thing. Some guys recognized a problem and overcame it. Others, it was their downfall."

A summer of difficult goodbyes was continuing painfully. Goaltender Ron Hextall had not been the starter for a year or a star for most of the last 10 when he went unclaimed by the Atlanta Thrashers in the expansion draft, was waived, and the remaining $1.2 million of his contract bought out on July 1. Clarke echoed the fan base's sadness.

"I don't feel very good about it," said the Flyer GM. "Here's a guy who wants to play here and we're telling him he can't. In some ways, it's not right. But I feel it has to be done for our team."

Believing goalie Brian Boucher, the 1995 No. 1 pick (22nd overall), was worthy of advancement from the AHL Phantoms, Clarke considered exposing John Vanbiesbrouck for claim by Atlanta and making a trade for Dallas goaltender Roman Turek. But knowing there would be another NHL expansion draft in a year to stock new teams in Columbus and Minnesota, the Flyer GM strategized to use the nearly 36-year-old Vanbiesbrouck at that time to satisfy the Flyers' obligation.

"If we expose Vanbiesbrouck now, who do we expose next year?" Clarke said. "The water was too muddy every way we thought about it."

Besides, there was hope the veteran goaltender would bounce back from the bad 1999 playoff while serving as a mentor to Boucher. There could not have been a better role model for Vanbiesbrouck than Hextall, who had lost his starting job the previous season.

"He was fantastic beyond anything I could say," recalls Vanbiesbrouck. "The opposite of the ax-chopping, hard charging, hard-to-deal-with Hextall that was the outside perception around the league. He was cooperative, smart, friendly, supportive and, off the ice, a great family guy."

Uprooting that family potentially was a tough decision for Hextall, desired in the front office by Clarke, but waiting to see if he received an offer to extend his playing career. "I had wanted to retire a Flyer, but I wanted to play another year, another five years, another 10 years," he recalls. "Goaltending in the NHL, I had the best job in the world."

That is, unless Eric Lindros had it. As pledged during the previous season, the Flyer star mailed back a signed, $8.5 million, one-year contract with no attempt having been made by either his representatives or the Flyer management to extend it.

"We're not interested in a long-term deal at this time," said Lindros's father Carl to Snider in a phone call. The elder Lindros told the media he had "no comment" on rumors that their condition for a longer deal was the removal of Clarke as GM.

"I don't know (why the family didn't want a multi-year contract) and I don't have the energy to figure it out," said a weary Flyer Chairman after Clarke had not participated in the negotiations. "I haven't got a clue. It's to our advantage to keep doing it year-to-year."

Mark Recchi, on the other hand, wanted to remain a Flyer for a long time. After the simplest of negotiations, the winger acquired the previous March signed a five-year, $25 million deal. Winger Keith Jones also was re-upped for three years and $5.1 million. "The Flyers showed a tremendous amount of loyalty to me offering me three years," said Jones when the deal was announced on July 20. "At this point in my career, a chance to win the Cup is very important to me."

Hextall received an offer from Calgary to continue playing, which he was mulling while attending John LeClair's annual charity golf outing in St. Albans, VT. The goalie and several Flyers were at the Burlington airport, preparing to fly home, when his cell phone rang.

"Hexy turned white," recalls Chris Therien. "He got off and said, 'You aren't going to believe this. Dmitri Tertyshny was killed in a boating accident.'

"He was right. I couldn't believe it."

Tertyshny, a pencil-thin sixth-round pick in 1995, whose quick stick and ability to read the play had gotten him into 62 games as a rookie in 1998-99, had joined Sandy McCarthy as Flyers attending a two-week camp run annually by Flyer skating instructor David Roy in Kelowna, B.C.

Phantoms Francis Belanger, Mikhail Chernov, Ryan Bast, Brian Wesenberg and Jesse Boulerice, plus recent free-agent signee Mark Eaton, also had been campers as part of a 13-person Flyer travelling party that also included director of team services Barry Hanrahan, his wife Lisa, and strength and conditioning instructor Jim McCrossin and his wife Robyn.

The camp ended on the morning of Friday, July 23, with a beach volleyball game on the shore of Lake Okanagan. Tertyshny, Chernov and the McCrossins had eaten McDonalds takeout for lunch, with Dmitri, who at a previous meal during the two weeks had accidently dropped marinara sauce on Robyn's leg while eating calamari for the first time, joking about not dripping the ketchup from his French fries.

The players went their own ways for the afternoon. McCarthy made arrangements to hire a houseboat with a driver to go out on the lake but, upon arriving at the dock, learned that Belanger, Chernov and Tertyshny had decided to rent a 17-foot runabout with Michelle Munro, a 22-year old Kelowna woman they had met at the beach during the volleyball game.

After dinner, Robyn wanted to take Jim on a drive for a view of the lake that she had seen earlier in the morning.

When they arrived, Jim didn't want to get out of the car and take the short walk through the trees. "You ever have a sixth sense?" he recalls. "I don't know why, but I didn't want to look at the lake, couldn't put my finger on it."

He ultimately agreed, until his annoyed wife, seeing his heart was not in it, suggested they return to the Holiday Inn where the Flyer party was based.

"When we got there, Canadian police officers were at the top of the lobby stairs," recalls McCrossin. "As I walked up, one of them came down to me and asked, 'Are you Jim McCrossin?' as Mikhail Chernov, crying and shaking, ran up to me and said, 'Dmitri's dead, Dmitri's dead.'

"I thought, 'He can't be. This is some kind of a sick joke.'" Solemnly, the police said otherwise, but McCrossin nevertheless pounded on the rooms of players, demanding, 'Where is he? Where is he?'

His body was at Kelowna General Hospital, waiting for formal identification.

Chernov told McCrossin that he and Tertyshny were seated properly in the cutout seats of the boat with Belanger and Monroe in the back by the motor. The vessel was returning to the dock when Belanger accelerated, creating a wave that knocked Tertyshny out of the boat and into the path of the propeller in the rear.

The carotid artery and jugular vein were among six major blood passageways severed, along with one of Tertyshny's hands. The horrified Chernov and Belanger got their friend into the boat, where Chernov cradled Tertyshny, the life draining from him, while Belanger gunned the boat five minutes back to the shore.

"From what I saw of the body, it was not likely he still was conscious when they got him into the boat," recalls McCrossin.

Rick Ito, a marina employee who had rented the craft to the players four hours earlier, saw it approaching and heard passengers shouting about a cut arm. He grabbed towels and ran out the door. The horrifying sight he would witness was about more than just a cut arm. There was nothing anybody could do.

"They all were in shock," Ito would tell Les Bowen of *The Philadelphia Daily News*.

The 911 call went out at 7:32 PDT. The ambulance arrived three minutes later and transported Tertyshny to the hospital, where he was pronounced dead.

The police took Belanger in for questioning. While there had been alcohol consumed on the boat, he was not above the legal limit and was not charged with being impaired.

McCrossin went to his room and began the grim task of calling an incredulous Paul Holmgren, then Bob Clarke. Holmgren phoned Evgeny Zimin, the Flyer Moscow-based scout, to ask his wife Natasha, who spoke English, to inform Tertyshny's wife, Polina, and his parents, Tatyana and Valeri, in Chelyabinsk, Russia.

McCrossin headed for the police station to get Belanger.

"Don't blame yourself," McCrossin said. "The police said it was nobody's fault."

"But I was driving the boat," Belanger said.

Over the lake that evening was a rainbow—one that Robyn believes was a message of peace from Dmitri—as McCrossin went to Tertyshny's room to gather his belongings. On the nightstand were books of baby names. "I think his wife is pregnant," he told Robyn.

In Chelyabinsk, Polina Tertyshny, four months expectant with what she had learned two days earlier was a boy, had been shaken awake that Saturday morning by a dream. "Somebody was in the center, dying, with people around him. I couldn't tell who it was," she recalls. "I woke up crying.

"My mom (Lidia) said, 'It's just the pregnancy hormones.' But I said, "No, something really bad happened. I just don't know to who."

Dmitri had told some members of the travelling party that he was going to become a father, and would be finding out the gender of his child when he called home at the time he had pre-arranged with Polina on Friday night. "It was harder to make international calls then," recalls Polina. "I don't know why he didn't call that night."

She assumed she would hear from him Saturday. Polina was staring at a picture of Dmitri in his Flyer uniform, "thinking about how lucky I am, how happy we are," when Dmitri's father called. "My Mom picked up the phone, then came out of the room in tears," Polina recalls. "She told me Dmitri was gone.

"I said, 'No, no, that can't be.'"

The next morning McCrossin drove everybody to the airport in the van he had rented for the week. "Mikhail and Francis told me every time they closed their eyes, they saw it," McCrossin would tell Bowen, but there was little conversation otherwise.

McCrossin was staying behind with Robyn to make arrangements to get the body back to Russia.

The rest of the Flyer entourage landed in Philadelphia late Saturday night. The next day, seven team members met with psychologist Dr. Joel Fish at the Coliseum in Voorhees, NJ.

"I'm scared to death for those kids," said Clarke, who only a few weeks earlier had lost his father Cliff to a sudden heart attack, ironically, while playing golf at a Kelowna resort.

Clarke and Holmgren relayed their devastation from the losses of Barry Ashbee in 1977 and Pelle Lindbergh in 1985, an important step, according to Dr. Fish, towards helping the players, particularly the ones who had been in the boat, not internalize their feelings.

"Typically, after shock there is denial, sadness, anger, then hopefully acceptance," Dr. Fish told the media. "Sometimes mysterious and tragic things happen. There are no right or wrong feelings."

Back in Kelowna, there was no counseling for McCrossin with his grim task. "The police and coroner were really kind and the funeral parlor did a wonderful job," recalls Robyn. "Dmitri looked peaceful. His dignity was important to Jim.

"I told him it was okay to break down, but he never did. He said he was afraid he wouldn't be able to do what he had to do."

And that was negotiating a bureaucratic labyrinth.

"Dmitri was going to Toronto, to England, and to Russia, and each country had its own [regulations] for preparing the body and what kind of casket," recalls McCrossin. "Thank goodness for Natasha Zimin. She was the go-between to tell me exactly what the Russians wanted.

"I was told to pick out only a wooden casket, not an elaborate one because thieves would take the body out and steal the casket. He had to be wearing just a plain suit because if the clothes were too nice, they'd take them right off his back. Dmitri had to undergo an orifice check by the Russian consulate in Toronto to make sure we were not smuggling drugs.

"I mean, it was nuts. Thankfully, Natasha and Evgeny would meet Dimitri in Moscow so that he would be in good hands from there."

When the body arrived in Chelyabinsk 12 days later, Polina identified it." My family said, 'You have to see him so you don't keep wondering if he's alive or something," she recalls. "The doctors gave me medicine to stay calm."

She went to the viewing but, on doctor's advice, not to the service at the Chelyabinsk arena, attended by 1,000 people, including Valeri Zelepukin, Tertyshny's Flyer teammate who flew in from his home two-and-a-half hours away in Moscow to represent the team. Flowers sent by several Russian clubs surrounded the casket, watched over throughout the service by a standing Sergei Tertyshny, Dmitri's brother, a defenseman for Mettalurg Magnitogorsk.

For most of the next two months, Polina was on doctor-ordered bed rest. The baby was what remained of their dream life together. "When Jim told me he had found the books with the baby names, I thought, 'Could this be any worse?'" recalls Robyn. "Then I came to realize what a blessing it was."

Not long after her first look at the tall, skinny guy with the collar-length, jet-black hair, Polina had decided to put off her fine arts studies for a life of adventure with a professional athlete.

"He was with some other hockey players at the (Ural Mountains) lake where my family went every summer," Polina recalls. "Even though Chelyabinsk is a big hockey town, I didn't know anything about hockey back then.

"I thought he looked like an athlete, but I didn't know. He wouldn't tell me his last name for like a week, was shy about that, did not want to brag. After he told me, he would make fun of me not knowing anything about hockey.

"There was one hockey player—Valeri Zelepukin—my mother told me that she knew. And then, just after we got to Philadelphia, Dmitri said, "Guess who is coming to play for the Flyers?"

Dimitri, drafted on the recommendation of Zimin, had signed with New York-based agent Jay Grossman. Another client, Sergei Zubov, had a brother who had played with Tertyshny's brother. Then, not too different from now, skepticism about Russian prospects' willingness to leave home for the NHL, plus the vastness of their country, made the search for raw talent and late bloomers less than cost-effective. But while Tertyshny didn't have first-round speed or a shot, he had quick hands and a brain for the game that matched his passion for it.

A growth spurt between ninth and tenth grades made him the biggest and easiest to notice among the 500 who had started at age six in the youth program run by Traktor, the team owned by the main employer of the industrial city. Dmitri became the only one who eventually made it to Traktor's Russian Super League team. But there were even bigger opportunities in North America, and three years after being drafted by the Flyers, it was time to try.

"I remember Zimin being adamant he could play here, that he was worth signing," recalls Holmgren.

Ten months after their marriage, Polina and Dmitri boarded a flight to North America with no knowledge of English and, as it turned out, no money. Their savings had disappeared in a Russian bank collapse. "We heard the news; tried our bank cards and they didn't work," recalls Polina.

They had to borrow cash from Chernov, a defenseman the Flyers drafted in the fourth round out of Yaroslavl two years after taking Tertyshny, until Dmitri would receive his first regular-season check, probably at the rate of $50,000 a year from the Phantoms.

"It wasn't about the money," recalls Polina, never minding that they didn't have any. "It was about the dream.

"Did you know Dmitri played in the World Junior Championships with a broken foot? That's how determined he was."

On the first day of Flyer training camp in Peterborough, Ontario, Dmitri was awakened with the rest of the players. Wearing flip-flops, he followed them to the start of a six-mile race course before it was made clear to him they were going for a run. He borrowed shoes, but not socks, and took off having no idea about the course's length.

"Hill after hill, he said he was thinking, 'When is it going to be over?'" Polina laughs. "His sneakers were all in blood, what a mess."

On the ice, however, there was tidiness to Tertyshny's game that caught coach Roger Neilson's eye from Day One. Even if he didn't have the bulk to keep the puck when hit, Dmitri had the hands and brains to move it.

"Young Tertyshny," as he invariably was called by Clarke, beat out a 10-year veteran, Chris Joseph, and made the team at a salary of $425,000. "Without knowing the language, without any time in the minor leagues, for a coach to show that much confidence in you, that was impressive," said Grossman.

Dmitri's time on the road was hard on Polina, who was so homesick she went back to Russia at Christmas and returned with her mother. But the Flyers, Eric Lindros in particular, didn't make the Tertyshnys feel like tourists.

"Eric always sat with us when the team ate together," Polina recalls. "Eric Desjardins, John LeClair, Mark Recchi were so nice, too, but really everybody was."

The Flyers quickly nicknamed him "Tree," not because he had the sturdiest trunk but really good branches. "Good, quick, stick," recalls

Recchi. It produced only two goals and eight assists in 62 games, stats even lighter than his 180 pounds, no matter how much food the training staff tried to stuff into him.

"He just couldn't put on weight," smiles McCrossin, but failing that, at least Tertyshny could gain respect.

"He wanted to be coached," recalls Craig Ramsay. "There are a lot of young players who don't; the Russians of that day seeming even less interested. They were going to play the way they already played. Dmitri didn't."

He thought the game well. "Made good decisions, the hardest part for a young player," remembers fellow blueliner Luke Richardson. "He would have been a No. 4 or No. 5 defenseman on an NHL team for a long time."

Recalls Desjardins, "Smooth skater, moved the puck really well, had good vision. A good kid, didn't speak much."

Most of the reason for that was because of the language, making Zelepukin and Dainius Zubrus the primary means of communication for Tertyshny. "When the Flyers were on their (12-game) winless streak, the team decided to meet at a restaurant to talk," recalls Polina. "Dmitri didn't know where it was, said he would follow Zubrus.

Dmitri Tertyshny, 1976-1999

"Dainius just flew and Dmitri got lost behind him and never made it. He came home very upset. 'They are going to think I don't care,' he said. I said, 'Maybe they will not even realize you weren't there,' but he couldn't sleep all night, worrying. The next day at practice, he said, 'Dainius, why did you lose me?' and Dainius said, 'You weren't there?'"

Dmitri was there for his friends, always. When former Traktor teammate, Mikhail Okhotnikov, who had become paralyzed in a diving accident during a lake swim that ended a summer camp, asked to see the watch the Flyers had given their players for Christmas, Dmitri told Mikhail to keep it. There would be plenty more jewelry, maybe a Stanley Cup ring someday. But now all those hopes had disappeared senselessly.

"I live with it every day," said McCrossin, who didn't speak about the tragedy for 16 years, until interviewed for this book. "What if we would have gone to the gym and worked out instead of playing volleyball, then just had a meal and stayed together for the day?

"Or, what it we had brought David Roy to Voorhees and done the camp here? We thought Kelowna would be a breath of fresh air.

"I've tried to just keep the fondness in my heart for Dmitri and block out everything else. But I haven't been really good at it. I had to get help. My thumb twitched for six months. Joel (Fish) said it was stress."

On August 26, the Flyers announced they were adding an exhibition game on September 21 at the Spectrum—the First Union Center was booked that night for a Bruce Springsteen concert—the proceeds to benefit the education of Dmitri's unborn child.

"Eric (Lindros) reached out to me several times," recalls Grossman. "I think he was really instrumental, as were (Flyer president) Ron Ryan and Bob Clarke in organizing that event."

As distance and bureaucracy had made it difficult for members of the organization besides Zelepukin to attend the funeral, the Flyers held a memorial service for players and staff on September 8, their reporting date for physicals.

Clarke tearfully spoke about closure and young men pushing forward with their careers and lives. Lindros remembered an earnest and fearless young man who had managed to endear himself to teammates despite his struggles to communicate with them.

"The first thing I noticed about [Dmitri] was how hard he worked," Zelpukin told reporters afterwards. "But I remember many things. He is with me forever."

That same day, the team, which would wear a memorial No. 5 patch on their jerseys during the 1999-2000 season, boarded a charter for Peterborough, Ontario, where, on the first day of camp, Neilson was asked what he wanted most from the preseason.

The Flyer coach said it would be for an unheralded prospect to surprise him. "Like Tertyshny did last year," he said.

Thus did a 1999-2000 season of promise begin with the Flyers trying to move on from a withering tragedy. Defenseman Steve Duchesne, offered $800,000 for a year from Philadelphia, turned it down for $1 million with Detroit, but Daymond Langkow, Zelepukin, Karl Dykhuis and Mikael Renberg re-signed as did both policemen—McCarthy and Craig Berube.

"I thought it was weird they wanted both Sandy and me," recalls Berube, who took a one-year deal at $700,000. "But Roger told me he wanted me on the checking line, so I signed."

Wayne Cashman, who had missed much of the previous season because his disc surgery was followed by a ruptured colon, came back for another year to coach the defensemen. Mike Stothers, who had been promoted from the Phantoms to coach the defensemen during Cashman's absence, returned to work on the minor league club's staff with head coach Bill Barber and assistant John Stevens, who had retired after 14 seasons as an AHL defender because of an eye injury.

Holmgren was promoted to assistant general manager, replacing John Blackwell, a Russ Farwell hire who had survived five years under Clarke. The GM felt more need to beef up personnel evaluation than administration, which was Blackwell's strength.

And, after a month of soul searching, Hextall decided to retire and scout.

"Calgary offered me, I think, a two-year deal," recalls Hextall. "I would have made more money playing two years there than I would have in forever as a scout, but I told them, 'I just don't know, let me start working out and see.'

"I started doing two-a-days while they were calling every second day to see how I was doing. My body was breaking down; I wasn't sure how much I had left—a hard thing to admit when you're a pro athlete—but I didn't want to go out there and just take the money.

"I kept thinking back to that last game (against the Rangers, six games from the end of the season) and that goal (from the red line) by Chris Tamer, and it gave me some distance.

"I held off Calgary for three-and-a-half weeks. Finally (GM) Al Coates called and said, 'We just traded for Grant Fuhr; we're going to pull the offer.' I told him, 'I'm relieved because I don't know how much I have left.' My hip was pretty bad.

"Clarkie had asked if I wanted to coach. But because I knew everybody on the team, I knew I would have been just like a player. I thought I needed distance from my teammates and always wanted to get into management. He said, 'Ok, start out scouting.' I said, 'Perfect.'"

Clarke's announcement stated, "He is so competitive and smart and humble; everything was about the team. Why would I go outside the organization when I've got guys just as good inside?"

The GM went outside regardless to fill two other spots. Al Hill, a former Flyer who had asked Holmgren about a position a year earlier, quit coaching in the minor leagues and became a pro scout. Chris Pryor, who had scouted for Islanders, was added, at Holmgren's recommendation, to become the organization's first full-time scout of U.S. amateurs.

"Because of the (austere) budget (under owners Howard Milstein and Steven Gluckstern), Mike Milbury (Isles' GM) had told our scouts he could only keep us on from year-to-year," recalls Pryor. "Mike was good enough to give us permission to look elsewhere.

"I knew Paul, a St. Paul (MN) guy like me, a little bit and I knew their scouts, Chappy (John Chapman) and Dennis (Patterson) from the road. But I think everybody wants to work for Philly because they do things the right way."

Pryor brought with him a strong recommendation to sign Ruslan Fedotenko, a Ukrainian-born winger, hockey-educated in Finland, who had completed his junior career with Sioux City of the USHL. Twice, Fedotenko had gone untaken in the NHL Entry Draft, the last time as Pryor was finishing up his duties with the Islanders just before joining the Flyers on July 1.

"It was hard not to like [Fedotenko] if you saw him," recalls Pryor. "From a numbers standpoint, he obviously had some offense in his game and he played it the right way.

"You scratch your head. 'How could this guy go through the draft?' I said to Homer, 'If you get a chance, this guy's still available.' I'm sure other scouts liked him, but Clarkie and Homer listened to me and did something about it."

Fedotenko, signed to a contract, soon was sent to Trenton of the East Coast Hockey League. Expectations were considerably higher for center Simon Gagne, the 22nd overall choice in 1998 who, in his final junior year, practically had doubled his pre-draft season point total from 69 to 120 points. Those numbers and a superb performance in the World Junior Championships had helped Gagne get a three-year deal for the rookie maximum total of $975,000, should he make the Flyers.

"Certainly going back to junior is probably what is going to happen," said Clarke, until the center combined with Renberg and Recchi for 10 points in the Tertyshny benefit game against the Phantoms.

"He's a great person, fun to play with," said Recchi. And Neilson was seeing what he liked best in a young player. "Smart in his own end," endorsed the coach.

Granted, Gagne had shined only against the organization's minor leaguers. Then again, the evening, attended by 15,462, was about the Flyers taking care of their own.

"Of course, it was sad and painful," recalls Polina. "But we were so happy that the Flyers would do that for him after he played only one year."

Tertyshny's parents had decided on a trip to Philadelphia even before the game was arranged. "We wanted to see where he was playing, where he was living," said Valeri, who, through Zelepukin's translation, said his son had had nothing but good things to say about how welcoming and helpful the Flyers had been. "And we also came here to say thank you."

Dmitri's father was taken to the locker room at the First Union Center, where he touched the gold-trimmed plate that once held his son's name.

"It's very hard to be here right now, but it's hard everywhere," he said.

The following night, in pregame ceremonies, Polina and Dmitri's mother were each presented (by Zelepukin and Chernov) one of Tertyshny's helmets signed by all the Flyers.

"After going to the funeral, I felt like I got over it already," said Zelepukin afterwards. "But today I look at 15,000 people cheering, and his parents, and it's very hard."

A crowd that large for a late-announced intrasquad scrimmage seemed to satisfy Lindros's expressed wish that, "It gets through to everybody what a loss this is."

The Flyers themselves already fully understood. "The more we get together and play like this, the more we miss him," said LeClair.

Polina believed the medical care was better in the U.S. and that there would be more opportunities here for a single parent. So she and her mother stayed in Philadelphia on a visa that the Flyers helped her obtain and started a new life with the support of Desjardins' wife, Manon, and Zelepukin's wife, Stella.

Alexander Tertyshny was born January 3, 2000 at Hahnemann University Hospital, destined to look much like his father and match his passion for the game.

When her son was five months old, Polina returned to Russia, but then, eligible for a one-year education stipend through the NHL Players' Association, came back to Philadelphia to study interior design at the Arts Institute in Center City.

She received a green card, then U.S. citizenship, finished school, and, as motherhood and her immigration status permitted, worked at an architectural firm. Polina eventually married a health insurance executive, moved to the Chestnut Hill area of the city and had two more children, Lydia and Lev.

Separated from her second husband, Polina says, "I've never felt the same way with anybody else but Dmitri.

"I ask God all the time, 'Why him, why him?' So early, the whole life open to us.

"I'm Russian Orthodox. It helps. Yeah, I believe he is somewhere in a better place, but I still have a hard time. It hurts.

"I saw three therapists. All they did was take (emotions) out of me and then give me no help. Until recently, I still had dreams that he was alive somewhere. They have stopped now, but I don't think anybody will ever help me recover. The grief just changes its form; I don't believe it will ever go away. So through the years, I've tried to concentrate on Alexander and hockey.

Sasha, as he is nicknamed, has the same dream his father lived too briefly. He played for the Little Flyers, the Valley Forge Minutemen, and Comcast, and is on an athletic scholarship at Choate Rosemary Hall in Wallingford, CT.

"His room at home is all Flyers," said Polina. "Big poster of his father. I still have a VHS player so Sasha can watch him play. He has a chest with pucks, newspapers, and pictures.

"The essay he wrote applying to (prep) schools was about his father. He is always on the internet finding things about him and has cried that he never had a chance to meet him.

"He is the same hardworking kid his father was. He thinks about everything he could have done better in the game, never is satisfied, even when he is good."

The $70,000 the Flyers cleared with the exhibition game was invested in a trust, which Sasha can access on his 18th birthday. "I've always wanted to be a defenseman, just like he was," says Alexander. "When I watch his games, he was a very smart player; one of those guys calm with the puck and good without it.

"I try to be more creative, but I watch him and pick up playing better defense as well."

Polina received a death benefit from the NHLPA, but because she took a fight for workers' compensation to court, her attorney's advice was to no longer ask the Flyers for tickets. For years, she did not, but has resumed after being reassured she is welcome to them. In addition to some games, she and Alexander have occasionally gone to practices at the Skate Zone to watch the team his father made against long odds.

"All the things I have in my treasure chest are very important to me, but I think the most important one is his jersey," Alexander said. "It tells me that his dream came true, that all his work had paid off."

Twelve months after Tertyshny had succeeded, confidence and diligence were helping another Flyer prospect, Gagne, make the team a year ahead of projections.

"We had finished the last season talking about the need to play faster," recalls Ramsay. "Well, this kid could play fast.

"We were fighting over whether we should use him as a center or a winger."

Gagne didn't care, only wanted to prove he didn't need another year of junior. "I'd never played with NHL players, had no feeling for the level, but the more camp went better and better, I felt like I could stick around maybe a little bit," he recalls. "Roger liked me, put me with good players—Recchi and Renberg—and on the power play, so that helped.

"It was almost easier than junior because the defensemen don't put you in trouble. They make the pass on the tape and you don't have to worry about someone killing you."

Those major-league passes didn't save Keith Jones from colliding with Desjardins and undergoing arthroscopic surgery on a left knee that appeared to quickly be running out of NHL life. This became another reason—in addition to making room at center for Gagne—for a Flyer coach to shift Rod Brind'Amour to the wing again.

"I could name 15 players they brought in and kind of pushed me over and it ends up with me going back (to center)," Brind'Amour shrugged. "Now it is easier to accept because it has happened so many times."

When Gagne was held out of an exhibition game against the Devils with the slightest of groin pulls, Brind'Amour stepped in to play for a third straight night. No good deed ever going unpunished, he took a Brian Rafalski shot in the foot, causing a hairline fracture that put his consecutive game streak of 484 in jeopardy.

Neilson, another tough guy, couldn't coach an exhibition game because of a bad head cold. But Therien, in the shape of his life after a summer of morning workouts with Brind'Amour and McCrossin, was down to 229 pounds from 241. "I was mad at myself for letting my weight get up that high," said the six-year veteran.

There had never been any question about the dedication of Richardson, who on the first day of camp had the fastest time in the 23.4-mile bike race players were offered as an alternative to the run. The greater surprise was that the defenseman, a healthy scratch during the playoffs, was in attendance at all.

"I blame Roger; he didn't like Luke (as a player) at all," recalls Clarke. "He wasn't great with the puck so there would be nights with bad passes, but Luke was what Luke was—a big body, who played nasty and brought a lot to the team by taking forwards out and making them hesitate a little. You always need that kind of defenseman."

It puzzled all that such a defensive-oriented coach had little use for an earnest, veteran defender.

"I needed an ear to vent," recalls Richardson. "Bob Clarke told me during the playoffs, 'It's our fault; we brought you here, but I don't get involved in the coach's decisions.'

"I totally respected that. At the end of the season I said, 'If I don't fit in here, maybe you should move to another team.' Bob agreed and told Donnie (Meehan, Richardson's agent) that, too. I sold my (Voorhees, NJ) house in about two weeks and moved the family back to Ottawa to wait it out.

"The Flyers left me exposed for the (Atlanta) expansion draft. I remember listening to it while working out at the lake, not that I expected to be taken because of my contract ($7.6 million remaining over three years), but it wouldn't have totally surprised me either.

"Then Dmitri passed away and they couldn't re-sign Steve Duchesne, so all of a sudden we were down to five defensemen not including me. My wife said, 'I thought we were getting traded?' I said, 'I don't know now.' So she and the kids stayed in Ottawa and I went to training camp, where Bob told me, 'We need you. I want you here. I promise if you don't fit into Roger's lineup at the beginning of the year, I'll move you."

Another expensive contract was Vanbiesbrouck's—$4.3 million for the 1999-2000 season—especially in light of his 30th-best .902 save percentage in 1998-99. Still, the plan not only was to break in Boucher slowly but for Vanbiesbrouck to make adjustments to both his 36 years and the demands of playing for the Flyers.

"We averaged about 22 shots (against) last year," he said after a summer of work with goaltender coach Reggie Lemelin. "There are big lulls where we don't get shots for long periods of time and that has been an adjustment for me.

Rookie Brian Boucher would play 35 games in 1999-2000, finishing with a goals-against average of 1.91.

"I have to make myself more proactive this year during down times."

Neilson made clear the Flyers needed better goaltending. "[Vanbiesbrouck] had a great first half, but if you are going to be a factor, you've got to win some games for your team," said the coach. "We didn't get that in the second half."

It wasn't only in the nets that Neilson expected more in 1999-2000. "Last year I didn't like all the talk about the Cup at the beginning of the year, but yes, I think it's justified this year," he said as camp wound down.

The team had gotten older through the massive turnover of the preceding two disappointing seasons and a window was closing on an era of great expectations. The Flyers had 10 players whose contracts would expire at the end of the upcoming season. During training camp, Ed Snider said the organization was "overpaying" and that he expected Clarke to get rid of "high-priced players who maybe aren't worth it."

"Our revenues are in the top two or three in the league every year so we can afford to be more stupid than anyone else," said the Chairman. "But that doesn't mean we will continue to be stupid."

Snider didn't name any names, but LeClair didn't believe it necessary.

"Everyone on this team understands that there is a certain point where if things aren't working, then it's time to move on," he said. "It could be the last year Eric and I are together."

Lindros didn't want to hear it. "I haven't even thought about that possibility," he said, although headed into the season on just the one-year deal that his family had wanted. "(But) because of the situations with so many guys (with expiring contracts), there is going to be an extra push this year."

The newly-dedicated Gene Hart Memorial Press Box—an unveiling of the memorabilia-filled wall in tribute to the broadcaster had been held before the first exhibition game—was where Brind'Amour and Desjardins watched the season opener, a 3-0 win for Ottawa. Desjardins, who took a puck to the mouth during the preseason on top of an off-season knee cleanup, was back two nights later when Dykhuis giveaways led to both Carolina goals in a 2-0 defeat. It was the first time Philadelphia had been shut out successively to start a season.

Brind'Amour's league-high consecutive playing streak was over but at least he was expected to return for the road opener at Boston. His foot still was killing him, however, so he was told to get another x-ray. "Went on my own to a local hospital in Cherry Hill, NJ, to get it done quickly and they found the bone was in like 10 different pieces, probably because I had been skating on it," he recalls.

Indeed, Brind'Amour had been cleared to play after just 10 days. "He was getting better," said Dr. Art Bartolozzi, the Flyer orthopedist. "We based our timeline on what we saw on the first film and the fracture pattern he now has is completely different than in the first x-ray. We don't really know how that occurred.

"If we had known Rod had two displaced fractures, we never would have allowed him to skate. He was getting better.

Two pins were inserted and a cast put on, the plaster being almost as hard as the lesson learned. Brind'Amour had been warned to stay off the foot by Ramsay, the benefit of his own experience from having foolishly rushed back in 1983 to keep a 776-game streak alive.

"Bad mistake. I just should have stayed off it like the emergency-room doctor had told me to do," said a glum Brind'Amour. "I would have missed the opener and ended my streak, but now I'm going to be out until Christmas."

He dragged a Gatorade bucket into the workout room, rested his cast on it, and pedaled with one leg.

"With hindsight you could say there should have been more caution," Clarke told the media. "But Rod has a high pain threshold."

Snider's pain tolerance was being tested, too. Recchi scored to get the Flyers a 1-1 tie in Boston, but despite Gagne's first NHL goal just 51 seconds into a contest at Washington, they dropped to 0-3-1 when two goals by Petr Bondra in the final four minutes beat Vanbiesbrouck, 5-4.

"I don't think anybody is ready to jump off the Walt Whitman Bridge," said Neilson after the Chairman spent time after practice with the coach, who was on the final year of his contract. "He often drops by," said Neilson.

Echoed Snider, "I happen to be a member of the organization. I like to talk to the people who work for it."

Boucher, who wanted to work for it for a long time, was no more relaxed than the fan base. In his NHL debut, he surrendered the game-tying third-period goal to Montreal's Brian Savage and then, following a giveaway by Desjardins, was beaten by Savage again, sending the Flyers down to defeat, 5-4, in their first test of the NHL's new four-on-four overtime.

"That's not the way I want to play," said Boucher after surrendering five goals on only 22 shots to the favorite team of his youth. He was anything but proud to have earned the first standings point for a loss in Flyer history, another innovation by the league.

There was some comfort in being guaranteed a point for a hard-earned 60-minute standoff, perhaps even as much as Neilson found in having the defensively-conscious Jody Hull on his roster. Lost in the expansion draft to Atlanta, Hull was reacquired for cash. "Roger always had to have Jody," recalls Clarke with a smile.

Neilson could take or leave the Therien who got caught on a three-on-two for Detroit's 3-2 winning goal at Joe Louis Arena, leaving the Flyers winless (0-4-1) in their opening five games for the first time in history. It was time for a talk and Lindros delivered it, admitting to his teammates before a home game with Buffalo that he had been allowing his personal problems with Clarke to interfere with his captain responsibilities.

"He just stood there and didn't blame anyone else, just blamed himself," reported Zelepukin when Big E's address became public almost two months later. "I was surprised at the emotion.

"The message was to look inside ourselves and not point at someone or something else as the reason."

When the story eventually broke, Lindros was public with his relief. "It felt good to get it off my chest; I could finally talk openly about it," he said.

Richardson recalls it as, "The most heartfelt I ever saw Eric in the dressing room.

"He didn't talk a lot of personal stuff, so I think the release was probably good for him. If he doesn't talk about something, how can we joke about it? I think it broke some ice."

"He had been under pressure for a long time and guys understood that," remembers Recchi, who assisted on three goals as the unburdened Flyers beat the Sabres for their first win of the season, 5-2. "He was trying to do the right thing.

"Everybody knew there were issues going on with him and Clarkie. But Clarkie treated us good and Eric was our captain so I don't think there was anybody choosing sides."

The Flyers had never had a Delaware Valley born-and-bred player on their side until Wilmington's Mark Eaton, the free agent signed out of Notre Dame University, made his debut during the Buffalo win. He replaced the slow-starting Therien, but Clarke still was looking to add a nasty dimension when he signed a veteran who had spent his career playing with an edge, an indication he was born to be a Flyer. Ulf Samuelsson lowered contract demands that had left him on the market all summer and, on October 19, was signed to a two-year deal worth $3.8 million.

"He was pretty beat up but I thought he had a little bit left," recalls Clarke. "He had always been a good team player and nobody wanted to play against him."

Added Snider, "He gives us a physical element we don't have right now and he's got a lot of experience."

Most of it with Lindros had been unpleasant. "He's a broken shoulder and broken nose ahead of me," said the new Flyer about his captain. "I still owe him a few things, but I guess I can't pay him back now."

Lindros faked amnesia. "They are all a blur," he said. "He's always been a consistent, gritty player."

With Brind'Amour and Jones out, antagonism had practically vanished from the Flyer act, a concern to their GM. "Someone, I assume it's Lindros, got them fired up for the Buffalo game, but you can't look at one person to do it all the time," said Clarke. "You have to play physically, have to play with emotion."

Because the Flyers couldn't play with eight defensemen, Clarke sold one of them—Dykhuis—to Montreal, despite having given him a three-year, $3 million deal just that summer.

"Really bright, but zero consistency even within a game," recalls Clarke, who in 1995 believed he had salvaged a top-four defenseman languishing in the Blackhawk system after having been a first-round draft choice. Though scoring eight points during Philadelphia's 1995 semifinal run, Dykhuis had ticketed himself into the Chris Gratton deal two years later by turning the puck over, but Clarke had refused to give up, reacquiring the defenseman for the fragile and aging Petr Svoboda 16 months later.

The earnest-to-a-fault Dykhuis, so happy to have had a second chance as a Flyer, was at home when he took the call from Clarke telling him that his opportunities had run out in Philadelphia.

"I knew there wasn't going to be a third time," Dykhuis recalls. "I wasn't playing well, but I guess I was surprised because this was so early in the season.

"I probably was trying too hard because I loved it there so much. That hurt me at times. We could go into a long discussion about different things I went through, but to sum it up, yeah, I was trying too hard. That's who I am, very passionate, always going to the extreme. I was my own worst enemy.

"But all I could think of to say that day (to Clarke) was, 'Thank you.' I was playing in the minors and suddenly I'm on a Flyer team that was running teams out of the building, scoring two goals in Madison Square Garden in the game we eliminated the Rangers, playing two years at the Spectrum, where the crowd, on top of you, would go crazy if you hit somebody. I wish I could have done it for 15 years, but I feel fortunate to have gotten the time I did."

His teammates and coaches remember Dykhuis's intensity as his curse. Looking back, Ramsay says the defenseman endlessly and unnecessarily taped his ankles. "A nervous wreck, an awful way to play," he recalls.

Teammates were unable to get a talented player to relax. "I really like Karl, he was good teammate," recalls Therien. "He had all the tools in the world to become a long-time player and at the end of the day, he did have a [644-game] career, but I just think he was one of those guys who thought too much about things he didn't have to."

Even with Dykhuis gone, Philadelphia still had to pass a defenseman through waivers to make room for Samuelsson. It was Richardson, who in the 36 hours he was subject to claim played 15 good minutes of a 5-0 win over the Rangers. As the Flyers won four out of five, Eaton went from first pair with Desjardins to the minors, replaced in the rotation by another rookie defenseman, Andy Delmore, an undrafted free agent who had played two seasons with the Phantoms. Vanbiesbrouck had followed that shutout of the Rangers, his first NHL team, with a 2-0 blanking of Florida, his second team, extending a shutout stretch to 214 minutes, 27 seconds.

Asked if, deep inside, he didn't take a little joy in beating teams that had not kept him, the compulsive truth teller said, "Somewhere not so deep inside."

The Flyer surge had put to the back burner speculation on the future of Neilson. "I believe in stability," Snider said on the *Comcast SportsNet*'s *Daily News Live* telecast. "I have been very distressed that we have had so many coaches in recent years. I don't think that's good for our organization."

Thus Neilson could shake speculation that he had become a placeholder for Phantom coach Bill Barber, but not the month-long cough for which he was given a steroid inhaler from Dr. Michael Casey, a pulmonary specialist.

"It was tough for him to get through a game," recalls Ramsay. "But like always, he was there when I got to the rink, still putting the game reports under my door at 6 a.m. and still there when I went home at night."

Clarke suggested Neilson go to Dallas during a three-day break to visit his long-time girlfriend Nancy Nichols. "Roger doesn't have anybody to cook for him or anything like that. I think it would be good for him to get away, rest up and get healthy," said the GM.

"It's not a bad idea," said Roger, who then laughed. "But sending me away?"

That was no longer a consideration for Gagne who, after scoring four goals and two assists in his first 11 games, not only was told to check out of the Voorhees Hampton Inn and into a suite hotel but to move over to left wing.

"If you want to play more, we can put you on left wing for the first two lines," Neilson said. That was fine by the 19-year-old, who had been assigned Desjardins as a road roommate and defenseman Dan McGillis as a chauffeur to practices, while Lindros provided tips on protecting oneself on the ice, an art that he had learned the hard way.

Coming off a collapsed lung, Lindros—who like LeClair was on the ice for four goals against in a 5-2 pasting by Vancouver—was reassured by doctors that his ongoing chest and head congestion was viral in nature. "It was good to hear that," said the captain. "I was obviously a little nervous."

So was the entire First Union Center when the Flyers blew a 4-0 lead to Colorado, even though recall Mark Grieg had scored a goal in Lindros's place on the first line. But all was well that ended well. Zelepukin's pass to the reinstated Therien caromed off a skate and went between goalie Marc Denis's legs with just 8.2 seconds remaining for the 5-4 victory.

After going eight straight times to Vanbiesbrouck, Neilson finally gave Boucher the second start of his NHL career. Though the Devils beat the kid twice in the third period to go ahead, Philadelphia scored the last three goals of the game to win 5-3 and go over .500. In Anaheim, Lindros returned to assist on all three goals in a comeback 3-3 tie, and the Flyers began to fly, even if getting from city to city became a sudden problem.

Star Charter, their private air service, went out of business during the western swing. Thanks to a plane loan from the Phoenix Suns, the team got from San Jose to Los Angeles in time to play the Kings and won its first game ever at the new Staples Center, 5-3, to make their record 8-1-1 in the last 10.

"You can tell how well we played by looking at the shot totals (16 by San Jose, 18 to LA)," said Lindros. "We're playing the system."

It only got them close at New Jersey, where they suffered their standard Meadowlands loss, 2-1. But the Flyers held Carolina to just 11 shots in Boucher's 4-1 win over a Hurricane team playing without the estranged Keith Primeau who, seeking a four year, $20 million deal, had turned down owner Peter Karmanos' offer of three years and $12 million.

Clarke, obsessed with getting a second huge center behind Lindros—or a first-line replacement if the captain and mothership couldn't live happily ever after—had made an unsuccessful run at the 6-5 Primeau during the 1996-97 season. When Plan B—Chris Gratton—disappointed, Clarke stayed on the prowl as Primeau's holdout continued, even negotiating a five-year, $23.5 million contract with his agent, Don Reynolds, before the deal fell through on the day of the Hurricane loss in Philadelphia.

"There was a proposal on the table that we rejected," Clarke told the media. According to Reynolds, Clarke had never told the agent the players involved, only that "they were big ones."

Karmanos, wanting Primeau to continue to squirm, was in no hurry to deal. Neither were the Flyers, as their defense settled in. Therien's game had picked up; Samuelsson, paired with McGillis, was making an impact; and Richardson, playing with the steadier Adam Burt rather than Dykhuis, was winning over Neilson finally.

"He would throw a good clip of me on the video he loved to show every day and that would boost my confidence." Richardson recalls. "Roger didn't talk to players (individually) a lot, but he taught the game well in practice and in video, so I tried to learn something new every day."

Remembers Ramsay, "I think initially Roger wanted something from Luke that he didn't have. I told him, 'We don't need you to carry the puck; we need you to play defense and shoot the puck out off the glass.'

"I just think we simplified things for Luke. He is such an honest, caring, hardworking guy that I couldn't have been happier for him."

Gagne had cooled off, but the Flyers kept rolling. Recchi already had 15 points just on the powerplay. Langkow, playing with Zelepukin and McCarthy, was averaging a point a game, and even the struggling Renberg scored unassisted on the power play in a 3-2 victory over the Sharks on November 13.

Just about the only downer during the surge was Mike Modano's goal with 31 seconds remaining that gave Dallas a 1-1 tie as Terry Gregson worked a Flyer game for the first time since his late Game Six penalty call that had doomed Philadelphia the previous season. "I don't think there were any controversial calls," deadpanned Snider, even if Derek Plante had gotten away with a haul down of Lindros.

"What's the point of getting into that?" said Lindros. "We're going to see Terry Gregson again."

When McGillis suffered a non-displaced foot fracture, Delmore was re-called for a second time, only to give the puck away to Ottawa's Vinnie Prospal for Shawn McEachern's goal with 23 seconds remaining in a 3-3 tie at Ottawa. It was the second time in a week that a point had gotten away in the final minute, but Clarke was moving to minimize the frustrations. With reports swirling of a Lindros-for-Primeau trade, the GM told his team that the rumors should have been put to rest a long time ago and that Lindros was not on the market.

"It was great for me to hear him say that," said Eric, who had been informed by Clarke just before he told the team. "I'm taking him at his word."

So was the rest of the team. "I think we needed to hear it," Recchi told reporters. "There is nothing out there to replace Eric.

Added Jones, "This has to relax him. No player wants to be traded and he very much wants to be here."

It showed in a 4-2 victory at Buffalo as Lindros contributed a goal, an assist, five hits and three takeaways.

Gagne, playing with Renberg and Recchi since the return of Jones, set up Recchi's winner in the Quebec native's first game in Montreal, a 3-2 winner. The next night at the First Union Center, LeClair went around behemoth Chris Pronger for the late winner in a 3-2 victory over the Blues.

"No question about it, balance is why we're doing better," said Neilson. "And the goals against show a real team effort."

When that energy lagged—the Leafs, once down 3-0, were buzzing for the tying goal in the third period—Lindros finished off a hat trick and a 4-2 victory on December 9 that produced a building-record 263 pieces of headwear on the ice and put Philadelphia past Toronto into first place overall.

The Flyers, 17-7-4, had spent three seasons getting back to the point where they felt this good about themselves. The next day, Neilson showed them a Rob Cookson-prepared video of an off-balance Therien trying to fight Leaf Kris King, spliced with Roger's favorite scene from Monty Python and the Holy Grail where the knight continues to threaten an opponent even while having his limb after limb severed.

The laughter barely had subsided when the coach said,

"I have cancer."

Tests to explain the persistent flu-like symptoms that had bothered Nielson for more than three months had turned up a diagnosis of multiple myeloma, a disease in which plasma cells in the marrow multiply uncontrollably, causing blood chemistry changes that damage organs and the body's ability to fight infection. Multiple myeloma had taken the life of Neilson's 67-year-old sister Joan just one year earlier. The five-year survival rate is 45 percent.

Neilson had been given the news of the diagnosis—made by Dr. David Mintzer, Chief of Hematology Oncology at Pennsylvania Hospital—after the Toronto win, by Flyer physician Dr. Jeff Hartzell. Regardless, Roger beat Ramsay into the office in the morning.

"He said, 'Come in, I've got something to tell you,'" recalls Ramsay. "Then he did. "I said 'Oh no' or 'Oh God,' or whatever is the first thing you would say when you hear sudden horrible news about someone so close to you. Roger had come into my life at age 16.

"He said, 'Oh no, don't worry about that. I am going to have to go for treatment (a bone marrow transplant) sometime and we need to have a plan here for when the time comes.'

"I was devastated. And he thought his job was to make it okay for me."

Neilson told Ramsay that he and Cashman would become co-coaches. Ramsay replied that shared responsibilities would not work; the coach should make a choice.

Clarke, who had been informed by Dr. Hartzell the previous evening, wasn't yet in the mood to offer any input on that decision when Neilson walked into the GM's office that morning and said, 'I guess you know,' then started enthusing about practice and the gag video.

"He's crazy," Clarke told reporters with tears in his eyes.

Indeed, the players were almost as flabbergasted by Neilson's offhandedness as they were by the terrible news. "I couldn't believe how positive and upbeat he was," said Lindros.

Recalls LeClair, "The guy was so happy to be alive. We felt so bad for him. I took it personally."

Only in retrospect did some Flyers realize Neilson's pallor since training camp had been an ominous sign. Certainly Nichols, with whom Neilson had enjoyed a relationship—often a long-distance one—since they had worked together for the Central Hockey League's Dallas Black Hawks, suspected something seriously was wrong.

"He never went to a doctor," she recalls. "Roger grew up in a really religious family so it was sort of like a cold or a flu or a temperature was no big deal, just part of life; God's plan.

"Most of the time we came to blows, it was over his health. When you would ask him to see a doctor, he would pretend to joke. 'I'm way too tough for that.' But he was serious."

It was only at the persistent urging of Flyer trainer John Worley that Neilson finally had gone to see Dr. Hartzell. The coach was told there was no evidence heredity had played any part in his contracting the same disease that had killed his sister. It was just coincidental, terrible luck.

"She was my only family left in the world," said Roger, but Clarke assured Neilson that the Flyers were extended kin.

"We're all part of a team and the strength of the team is drawing from each other," Clarke said. "We were going to let Gagne go to the World Junior Championships, but he is part of the team and we're going to stick together.

"My instinct says you do that. As far as we're concerned, over the next three months (the estimated time until Neilson completed the transplant), we won't trade anybody.

"This is part of life; you have to deal with it and the team still needs to win. We're a pretty strong franchise. If you couldn't handle the challenge, you probably wouldn't get them."

It had been an especially difficult morning for Clarke. The day before, he had learned that Jerry Melnyk, the Flyer scout of 27 years living in retirement in Edmonton, had been diagnosed with leukemia.

Neilson met with Dr. Isadore Brodsky at Hahnemann Hospital that afternoon. Dr. Brodsky had spearheaded Barry Ashbee's treatment for the same disease 21 years earlier. The coach then joined the team in Toronto for a return match with the Leafs. Or was it for his comedy tour?

"I'm a really strong Christian and if this treatment doesn't work out, well, wherever I go, it's got to be better than Philadelphia," Roger said.

He also cracked, "(Hall of Fame football coach) George Allen said he would give up a year of his life for a win. I don't know if I am that committed."

Actually, he probably was.

The next night, the Leafs wished their former coach well on the Air Canada Centre scoreboard during the first television timeout. Neilson bit his lip as the ovation swelled. "It's one of the nicest things that has happened to me in hockey," he said.

Business being business, Neilson pulled Vanbiesbrouck after five goals on 18 shots, then angered Toronto coach Pat Quinn by adding McCarthy to a line with Berube during the second period, helping to incite fisticuffs that resulted in penalty time for 15 players. "He thinks he's still coaching in the seventies," said Quinn after a late Flyer rally fell short in the 6-4 defeat.

Philadelphia lost again three nights later in Buffalo when Boucher, rather than leaving the puck for Desjardins, shot it off Miroslav Satan, enabling Michael Grosek to score on a tip-in during a 3-1 defeat. "My fault," said the rookie goalie as the Flyers dropped consecutive games for the first time since mid-October.

They continued to struggle though the first two periods against Phoenix. So did Neilson with his emotions when his image was posted on the First Union Center's center-hung scoreboard for the first time since his diagnosis. As the ovation swelled, the coach both acknowledged and tried to end it by putting his fist in the air. The Flyers, trailing 3-2 in the third period, had to kill off a four-minute minor to Zelepukin, then broke a 3-3 tie on Recchi's goal with 1:05 remaining, and won 5-3.

"It will take a while for this to die down," Neilson said. "Eventually, I hope it will. But it's nice knowing you've got friends and support. The cards and letters have been amazing."

Even better for his spirits than flowers and chocolates was the return of Lindros for Boucher's first NHL shutout, 4-0, over Tampa Bay, followed by a Desjardins goal with 54 seconds remaining to save a 1-1 tie with Nashville.

Through the chemo, Neilson continued to put the game reports under Ramsay's door before 6 a.m. and ran practices like nothing was wrong. Flyer staffer Joe Kadlec, who drove Neilson to Hahnemann for treatments, said he only once commented on how fatiguing they were.

"It was taking its toll," recalls Ramsay, "but he pushed and pushed."

A sense of normalcy was hugely important. And nothing seemed more normal than having Brind'Amour back after a 34-game absence, even if in his return he took a third-period penalty that was converted by Patrik Elias for a 3-2 Devil victory at the Meadowlands.

"People have gone through worse, but it still was tough on me," said Iron Rod. "I haven't had anything like this; it took forever to heal."

On the slim chance that worldwide computers would fail to turn over at the start of the new millennium, the NHL had told its teams not to be in the air at midnight on December 31. As a result, Philadelphia was making just two stops on its annual holiday western swing.

The 20th century, which had been good to the Flyers, remained true to its end. The team scored four times in the third to win in Calgary, 5-1; then, Gagne's game-tying goal and Burt's overtime winner against Garth Snow defeated Vancouver, 3-2, on December 29.

The 21st century started promisingly, too. A pair of LeClair goals broke an eight-game winless streak (0-6-2) at the Nassau Coliseum as the Flyers won 4-1. "This is the first time we haven't had a 45-minute meeting after the game here," said Jones. "Means we finally got a win, huh?"

Recchi had three assists as Philadelphia completed a home-and-home sweep of the struggling Isles, 3-2, bringing his mid-season goal and point totals to 18 and 55, respectively, a huge boost to an offense that was suffering less-than-usual production from Lindros and LeClair. Gagne's goal with just 1:19 remaining was the first game winner of his career as the Flyers outlasted Carolina, which still was playing without Primeau.

Not only were LeClair, Recchi, Desjardins and Lindros added to the North American team for the All-Star Game in Toronto, Neilson was named an assistant to Quinn. "I'm honored, but I have to watch he doesn't wing any sticks at me," smiled Roger, as Quinn joked to be on good behavior "as long as Roger doesn't send out any goons."

Neilson's health wasn't the only intrusion upon a team that was 25-10-6. Six months after the death of her father, Gene, Flyer anthem singer Lauren Hart was diagnosed with non-Hodgkin's lymphoma. And worse than being embarrassed 1-0, by the expansion Thrashers in the Flyers' first visit to Atlanta since the Flames left for Calgary in 1980, Lindros suffered collisions on the same shift with Chris Tamer and Darryl Shannon and reported mild concussion symptoms.

"I hit Tamer pretty hard and felt woozy afterwards," Lindros said. "Then I never saw Shannon. I don't think that (seamless) glass helps."

With Gagne centering the first line, LeClair could save his team only from being shut out for the second time in two nights, a 4-1 defeat by the Devils at the First Union Center. In Sunrise, FL, Langkow was called for holding a stick, allowing Robert Svehla to score on the power play, breaking a late tie in a 3-1 loss.

The winless streak then went to four with a 1-1 tie against the Senators, even as Boucher was extending belief that the Flyers were a better team with him in the nets. He had given up just 10 goals in his last six starts.

On Friday, January 21, despite Clarke's pledge not to make any deals until Neilson's transplant was completed, the GM called Primeau's agent, Reynolds, to inquire if the five-year, $22.75 million terms negotiated in November, before a deal had fallen through, still would be acceptable. They were.

Clarke asked Neilson if the players would understand his breaking of the trade moratorium in order to improve the team. The coach met with Lindros, LeClair, Recchi and Brind'Amour to find out. "They said they understood completely," Neilson would tell the media.

Brind'Amour said so even through his fear that he was the guy likely to go. It hadn't been just good fortune and a sense of duty that had driven him to have played 484 consecutive games coming into the season. Despite his two-plus-month absence, the Flyers had stayed in the race for the best record in the league.

"Out of sight, out of mind," Brind'Amour recalls. "The team is thinking, 'We don't really need him.' If I'd been there, maybe they wouldn't have thought that way.

"So the trade rumors start. On December 7—I remember the date because Homer (Holmgren) started the conversation with a joke about it being Pearl Harbor Day—he called me in [for advice] about guys (under consideration for trade) from other organizations. I remember telling him, 'I thought you were calling me in to trade me.' He goes, 'No, we wouldn't do that, we love you.'

"I had never been told that here in eight years. I went home and told my wife, 'Pack our bags.'"

On January 23, at the morning skate in Pittsburgh, Brind'Amour was asked about reports that said he was on his way to Carolina for Primeau. "I've heard a lot of rumors and it would be nice to know if any of them are true," he said. "After all these years, you feel a bond with an organization and that makes it tough."

At about 2 that afternoon, Brind'Amour got a call from Carolina coach Paul Maurice. "Welcome to the Hurricanes," he said. "There's a flight to Raleigh in an hour."

Before Clarke could reach Brind'Amour at the hotel, he was in the cab. "Ed Snider called in the taxi," Brind'Amour recalls. "I never heard from Clarkie, but Ed Snider is the top of the chain and that was more than enough. He said, 'You've been great.' That meant a lot to me."

The Flyers had given up Brind'Amour, goaltending prospect Jean-Marc Pelletier, and a second-round pick in 2000 for a fifth rounder and Primeau, who was working out in a gym in North Carolina with a personal trainer when his wife Lisa phoned.

"She told me Bobby Clarke had telephoned," remembers Primeau. "I went home, called the number he left, and was told he had made the deal.

"I was excited and relieved that I could move past the business part of the game to the playing part. It had taken a long time.

"I felt I was dealing with a 30-team market and the Hurricanes were valuing me on just theirs. It quickly spiraled out of control when the owner kind of attacked me in the paper.

"Then I had some teammates attack me for not being there. The owner (Karmanos) squashed the deal in November because he didn't want me getting my way.

"I knew the Rangers and Phoenix were interested, but I always felt I was closer to coming to Philadelphia. As early as the '98 Olympics in Nagano, I knew Clarkie had liked me as a player. I always thought that I played a Flyer style of game."

Karmanos finally approved the trade because Philadelphia would not be paying Primeau more money for the coming season—$3.5 million pro-rated for the 33 remaining games—than he had offered prior to the player's holdout.

The Flyers had gained one year of age—Primeau was 28, Brind'Amour 29—four inches, 10 pounds, and some speed. Clarke also believed they had upgraded their scoring ability, even if over the last four seasons Brind'Amour had averaged 28.25 goals to Primeau's 27.25.

"In some respects, they are the same player," LeClair told the media, but to Clarke, who had been bed-ridden with the flu as he made the deal, it was mostly about Primeau's body and wingspan.

"Rod has been a real warrior for us, but this gives us a better team," Clarke told reporters. "We felt with the competition in our division, we needed a little more size."

Many players wondered if the deal meant that the biggest Flyer of all was in his final days in Philadelphia. "I think most of us thought this had to be precursor for a Lindros trade," recalls Vanbiesbrouck.

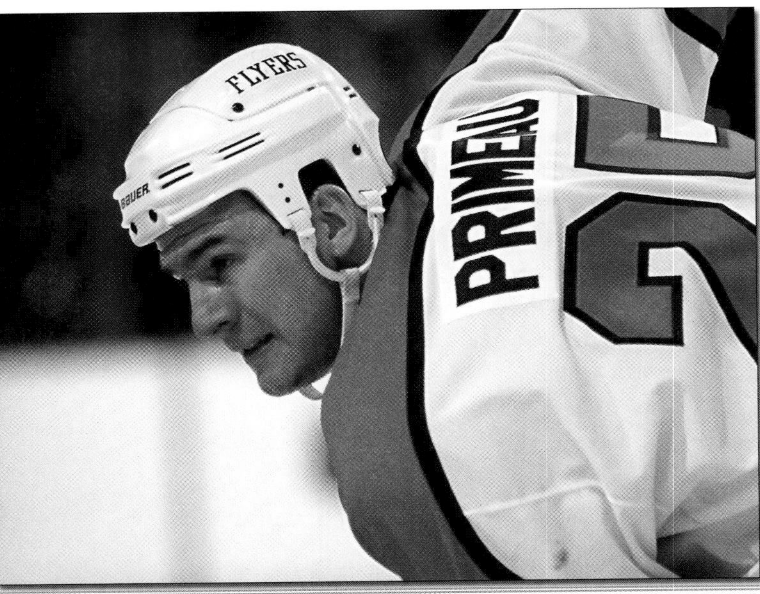

Keith Primeau joined the Flyers from Carolina in a trade for Rod Brind'Amour.

Recchi recalls being stunned. "I thought Brindy was a centerpiece for the team. It was tough to see him go."

But the players generally felt that, at worst, Clarke had made a lateral move.

"I knew Primeau was a force, I had hated to play against him," recalls Desjardins. "He did the same things Roddy did, kill penalties, play on the power play, take faceoffs, but he was maybe a little more physical than Rod."

Primeau had no trepidation about following an extremely popular Flyer of nine seasons. "I knew Roddy and me were different types of players," he recalls.

"He was a post-up guy, good from a standing position, a distributor. I was harder on the forecheck, wanted to rumble around in corners, a little rougher around the edges.

"I was quite content to take a secondary role behind Eric, looked at it as a great opportunity. Having him and me down the middle could be pretty dynamic. Nobody else had that. You would have to pick your poison."

On the night of the trade, the Penguins did not have to swallow either the injured Lindros or Primeau, who, after a three-month self-imposed exile, needed at least one practice before he could play a game. Regardless, LeClair was present and didn't go down easily. His last-minute goal enabled the Flyers to scramble to a 4-4 tie after Boucher had let in goals by German Titov on two of the first three shots he faced.

Back in Voorhees the next day, Clarke, a public critic of inflationary contracts, defended the five-year deal he was giving Primeau, predicting Brind'Amour, whose contract was up in two seasons, would become a $5 million-a-year player at that point, too.

"We should lower our payroll to be a lousy team so that we don't fill our building and don't draw on the road?" argued Clarke. "How does that help the NHL?"

It still was a lot of money to play a second-line center, but Neilson bristled at those semantics. "I hate that second-line-center stuff," the coach said. "We don't like to think of our players as first, second, third or fourth."

Whatever. The Flyers now had a 1A and 1B big enough to blot out the sun on the opposition's hopes. The following night, Lindros returned to drill Florida's Robert Svehla, win a fight with Todd Simpson, and watch Primeau play 13:41 and win 65 percent of his draws as Philadelphia snapped an 0-3-2 skid with a 4-2 victory.

"Playing a game felt good," said Primeau.

Not so for Brind'Amour, still working off his rust and feeling displaced more than 400 miles away.

"Probably the worst game of my life," he told Bob Ford of *The Philadelphia Inquirer* after taking three penalties in a 3-2 Hurricane overtime victory over Montreal before just 8,552 fans in Raleigh, NC.

"In Philadelphia, you talk about being the best team in the league, finishing first. Here, it's a battle to make it to the playoffs. At this point, it's just about winning for me.

"I made Philadelphia my home. People there were great to me. I don't have any ill will. Trades happen. I was just surprised they traded me for another centerman. Disappointed is a good word for it."

Actually, it was a grossly-understated word for it.

"I was crushed," Brind'Amour looks back. "Crushed."

"I was a Flyer. To me, it meant something to be a Flyer. When you get traded for somebody at your same position, that tells you they think he is better. And that shocked me.

"I knew Preems from playing with him at the Olympics and obviously from playing against him. He's a good player. But I didn't see how they were upgrading. I understand size if that's what you're trying to do, but I don't think I played small. I think I was tough to play against.

"That did bother me. It wasn't like I was a bad apple. I think I could have brought every bit of the same thing he did."

Having missed 47 games, Primeau wasn't likely to immediately bring much, although in his second game, he scored in a 2-2 tie on January 29 in Montreal, not that it received much attention. When the Canadiens Trent McCleary dropped down 10 feet in front of Therien to block his shot, the right wing took a puck in the throat.

"It had been one of those shots you dream of, coming off the boards slower than molasses in the winter, and I teed up the hardest one I took all year," recalls Therien. "And then I see this guy sliding out, like, 'What is he doing?' And it hits him.

"I lean over him and heard this horrible noise, this long, loud, gurgling in his throat and see this absolute fear in his eyes like 'I can't breathe.'"

Trainers and teammates got McCleary to his feet quickly, but a fractured larynx had caused bleeding that collapsed one of his lungs. Medical personnel on duty at the Molson Centre had to work in the hallway to partially open up McCleary's airway, critical to getting him to Montreal General Hospital in time for a tracheotomy so urgent that it had to be performed while he was wearing his full equipment, including skates.

"I knew when they took him off he was seriously hurt," recalls Therien. "That made for a long game for me, not knowing whether he was going to be alright.

"After I showered and went out the tunnel (to the team bus), I'm hearing there is a possibility he may die, it was that dire. I knew I did nothing wrong, knew that immediately, but we don't sign up to kill somebody. It was really a terrible day to be in hockey.

"I got on the plane (for Washington, DC) not knowing whether Trent McCleary was going to survive. I remember Bob Clarke on the plane being as compassionate as Bob Clarke can be, saying, 'I know how you feel, but you gotta move on from it.'

"I was LeClair's roommate that night. He felt for me. The next day almost the whole Washington team came over and gave me taps (on the pads) during the warmup, to say, 'This could have happened to any of us,' which I thought was pretty classy."

After McCleary stabilized, his surgeon told him he had "come as close as you could come" to dying at the arena. He was unable to talk for six weeks and, after several surgeries, had to retire at the following training camp because of a permanent 15 percent narrowing of his air passage.

"Soon after it happened, I left a message for him but never heard back," recalls Therien. "In a documentary done years later, Trent and his wife said it never occurred to them that I did anything wrong, but nobody wants to be remembered for almost killing someone and ending his career.

"It bothered me for some time, but I eventually moved on."

The Flyers were shut out, 2-0, by the Capitals the next day. Their secondary scoring had almost entirely disappeared, sending them to the All-Star break only 2-4-4 in their last 10 contests. "Every goalie is playing well these days against us," said a frustrated Neilson after 48 shots on Anaheim's Guy Hebert got Philadelphia only a 3-3 tie.

Lindros, now on a line with Gagne and Recchi, pumped in two goals in a 5-2 win at Toronto. "It's a treat backing up Eric," said Primeau, but he was struggling with the flu as well as rust while back issues forced Lindros again from the lineup for five games. Samuelsson also had to leave for 10 with a shoulder that had been bothering him ever since a December hit by the Blues' Jamal Mayers.

Vanbiesbrouck was an issue, too. "There is no excuse for that," said the self-flagellating goalie after a short-side goal by Edmonton's Bill Guerin caused a 3-2 defeat. Vanbiesbrouck had just one win in his last eight starts.

"Lately Boosh has played well enough to earn a good crack at it," said Nielson. "So he's got to play a few more games."

Just like the young goalie, Neilson—his hemoglobin count pleasing doctors as his bone-marrow transplant approached—was in the market for a vote of confidence. "They seem very keen on bringing him back," said Neilson's agent, Rob Campbell, who added his client was insisting on a clause that he would not get paid for any games missed because of his health. The two sides agreed to put negotiations off until after the season.

The slumping LeClair's work with skating coach Roy seemed to pay off when he walked out and tucked an overtime backhander past Buffalo goalie Martin Biron, climaxing a rally from a 2-0 deficit to a 3-2 Flyer win. But that good news was muted when Primeau tucked his elbow too tight while throwing a check and tore his own rib cartilage, putting him out for an expected three weeks.

"It was frustrating, but with everything I'd faced the last five months, I had been hardened," recalls Primeau. "I just had to get better, that's all."

In case Samuelsson didn't, Clarke picked up defenseman Zarley Zalapski, a nine-year veteran who hadn't played in the NHL in more than a year. The GM also traded winger Mikael Anderson, who had dressed in only five of the most recent 13 games, to Vancouver for Gino Odjick, a 10-year NHL player. Odjick gave Philadelphia three of the NHL's top-20 all-time penalty-minutes leaders—with Berube and Samuelsson—plus, as Berube pointed out, an "All-Native line" with he, Odjick and McCarthy.

"To add a 6-foot-three, 227-pound winger who has some aggression and nastiness favors our club," said Clarke. "There will be less reason for other teams to want to mix it up with us."

He hoped the conference-leading Devils, whose edge on the Flyers was 13 points when they went to the Meadowlands on February 15, would be one of those clubs. "Pretty much impossible," said Jones, when asked about the likelihood of catching up to them. "They've won games in January and February, when a lot of teams tend to slide like we did."

Nothing changed. Sergei Brylin chopped the stick out of Langkow's hands during a delayed New Jersey penalty, sending the puck into the vacated net and Philadelphia to a 4-2 defeat. "It leaves you with a sick feeling in your stomach," said Langkow about the goal, credited to Marty Brodeur, the second of his career, tying him with Hextall for the all-time lead among goalies.

But that hardly was the Flyers' biggest disappointment in what they had considered a statement game against the runaway division leader and Philadelphia nemesis. "We're having a hard time scoring," said Lindros. "And last night we had a hard time doing anything."

Vanbiesbrouck got another chance against the Islanders but let a shot by Mark Lawrence dribble through, then couldn't get back to the far post before Lawrence circled the net to tuck in a tying goal midway through the third period. After Lindros slashed Zdeno Chara, cutting short a late powerplay opportunity, the Flyers settled for a 2-2 tie and had won only four of their last 14 games.

With their coach scheduled to have stem cells withdrawn from his body during the last week of February—Stothers would be coming up from the Phantoms again to join Cashman as an assistant under interim coach Ramsay—Neilson cancelled practice on his next-to-last day on the job in favor of a team lunch. "We didn't talk hockey," Berube reported. "We're really pressing right now."

For inspiration, they looked to Neilson. "I think it was Mark Recchi who said in the locker room before we went out, 'Win this one for Roger,'" said Boucher after Therien scored to open a two-goal lead in a 4-2 First Union Center victory over the Capitals. "It'll be his last game for a long time and I think we were really inspired by that."

Scoring depth had been a Clarke pursuit throughout his second run as Flyer GM. Ramsay took charge determined to increase the Philadelphia offense by building the ice time and confidence of third and fourth liners.

The interim coach, who had played with Don Luce and Danny Gare on one of the NHL's best two-way lines for Buffalo against the Flyers in the 1975 Stanley Cup Final, had been an eight-time 20-plus goal scorer, and a seven-time top five vote-getter for the Selke Trophy, winning it in his final season. He also was one of hockey's legendary survivors, having undergone surgery in 1993 for bleeding ulcers that required 32 units of transfused blood and necessitated feeding through a tube for two months.

Literally without a stomach, Ramsay figuratively found one before his first game to call in Lindros and LeClair and explain they had to be leaders that night at Madison Square Garden by not overstaying shifts.

After Vanbiesbrouck allowed another wide-angle score (by Mike York), Renberg's first goal in 14 games tied the game and Jones, back

on the big line, set up LeClair's winner with a pretty diagonal pass. "This is the type of character win we need," said Jones after the 3-2 victory, the Flyers' first in consecutive games in six weeks.

Two nights later, Lindros had to leave the warmup with a recurrence of back pain and McGillis, who had been playing for a month with a groin pull, couldn't make it through the second period. But Boucher was outstanding in a 3-1 win over Chicago on February 22, the fans chanting "Boosh! Booosh!" following a spectacular save on Anders Eriksson. "Something like that doesn't happen very often," said the appreciative goalie. "This town can be very hard on you."

Ramsay, who wanted scoring from everybody, even got it from Richardson, who tallied with nine seconds remaining in overtime to beat Pittsburgh 5-4, before a sprained collarbone caused him to join McGillis on the injured list.

No Lindros, no Primeau, no problem. Todd White joined Peter White as call-ups from the Phantoms to center the top two Flyer lines in a 5-1 rout at Uniondale, with LeClair scoring two of Philadelphia's four powerplay goals, three of those on opportunities drawn by Jones.

"Guys were very alert; we've got more mental energy," said Ramsay, who received permission from Clarke to do a dinner to establish his authority and team unity. "We had a great night out in St. Louis, but then we lost the game the next night, (when Vanbiesbrouck let in another short-sider in a 3-2 loss)," recalls Ramsay. "I was pretty upset because we played well, and I didn't want them [to stray] from the plan because we lost.

"To play at the pace we wanted, we needed to play short shifts and four lines. [The players] didn't overtly not want to do it, but habits had to be changed. I'd say, 'I'll be coming back to you,' 'Get on,' 'Get off,' and 'You're right back on,' plus 'You will get away from a matchup.'

"Big John said, "We like what you're doing, it's going to be fine."

Recchi added a public endorsement, saying he expected Lindros and Primeau to "do the same things" when they came back. And LeClair doesn't remember thinking it was a sacrifice. "I could see guys felt more important to the team, so it was easy to follow through with what we were doing," he recalls.

While Neilson hardly had been a screamer, Ramsay was even more soft spoken. "I'm never going to yell at you guys," Gagne remembers the new coach saying. "We're all adults and professionals here."

Indeed, Ramsay had inherited a veteran team of strong leaders equipped to police themselves. "We didn't need a coach to kick our ass, just to run the bench," recalls Berube. "He communicated a lot with individuals; with our team, he was a good fit."

By keeping both wingers along the boards instead of coming across at the blueline, Ramsay changed the breakout, but other than eliminating morning skates, he altered little else. Contributions were coming from everywhere.

"I can't say enough about the coaching at the Phantoms," said Ramsay. "Everybody we've called up has done a great job."

Included were kid defensemen Delmore and Eaton, even if the latter was sent down when Samuelsson returned to the lineup on March 4 in Boston. All this depth didn't deter Clarke, however, from a vigorous pursuit of Ray Bourque, who at age 39 had determined he wanted to leave the struggling Bruins to pursue a Stanley Cup before retirement.

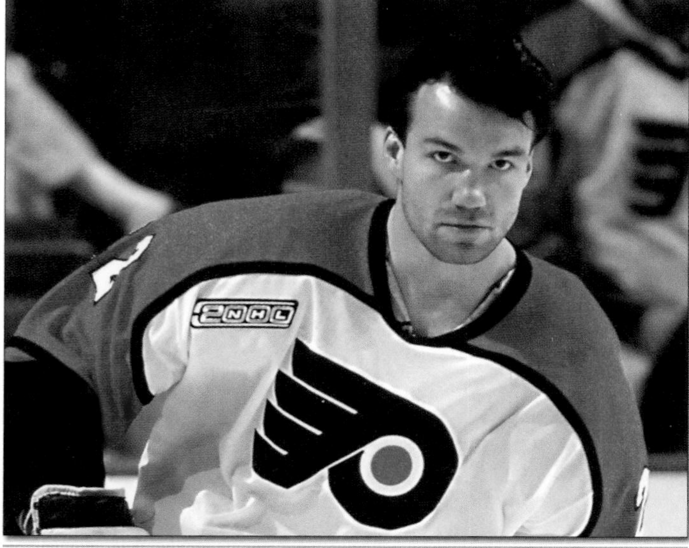
Big-bodied Luke Richardson played five seasons on the blueline for the Flyers.

As the trading deadline approached, the Hall of Famer-to-be was telling confidants that the presence of Cashman, Lemelin (a former Bruins goalie), and Desjardins, a best buddy from Nagano, plus Philadelphia's proximity to his family in Boston, made the Flyer organization his destination of choice.

Bourque also could have been impressed with Boucher, the Rhode Island native who, as a sideshow to the Bourque speculation, shut out the Bruins 3-0 to lower his goals-against average to 1.60. The kid was taking ownership without any resentment from Vanbiesbrouck.

"I wasn't surprised at Brian's success because he was smart, engaged, and respectful," recalls Vanbiesbrouck. "I thought he was the real deal and we built a good relationship.

"[The team] had a good vibe. People were able to put their own personal situations aside and I knew that's what I had to do. I didn't want to detract away from anything."

When the Flyers returned home and blew a 3-1 third-period lead to the Islanders, losing on Mariusz Czerkawski's goal in overtime, Boucher smashed his stick over the net. "The guys worked like that and I let them down," said the goalie, never acknowledging that only one of the four New York scores was stoppable.

Clarke believed no more multi-goal leads would get away with both Desjardins and Bourque on the same defense. "If he is available to us, we'll get him," said Clarke with rare candor, but the Red Wings and Avalanche also were in the hunt.

The Flyers dangled Langkow, a first-round pick, a choice of either Delmore or Eaton, plus McCarthy. But when Boston GM Harry Sinden chose the Colorado offer of a first rounder, Brian Rolston, Martin Grenier and Samuel Pahlsson, Bourque waived his no-trade clause and agreed to go west.

"Ray was kind of disappointed," Lemelin told Philadelphia reporters following a conversation with his friend. "But he knows so many people [in Colorado] and the GM (Pierre Lacroix), so he decided to go. Harry had told Ray he would try to accommodate [his Philadelphia preference] but also said he was not going to give him away."

Indeed, at Logan Airport on his way to Denver, Bourque confirmed to Boston reporters that he wanted most to be a Flyer. "Philly was my first pick in terms of location and I like the makeup of the team," he said. "From the beginning, [Sinden] told me the Philly deal wasn't as good as some of the other deals out there. But it could have been nice."

He didn't seem as bitter as the Flyers.

"[Sinden] didn't care about Raymond, where he wanted to go, or anything else," said Desjardins. "I don't think that's right."

Recchi echoed, "The guy's been 21 years in that organization. That's Harry, what are you going to do?"

What the Flyers could do was get their act together from the meltdown loss to the Islanders. Clarke stayed busy, trading the increasingly unused Marc Bureau to Calgary for AHL player Travis Brigley and a sixth rounder. Bureau bitterly told the media he had never been made to feel like a good fit in his 21 months in Philadelphia.

"I knew I wasn't going to play 20 minutes a game like I did (in Montreal)," Bureau said. "But not even getting a handshake (from management) welcoming me to the team, I don't know what happened. It was hard to take."

To Renberg, so had been his first trade away from the Flyers during the summer of 1997. But two-plus seasons later, when he walked into the visiting room in Tampa for the morning skate on March 8 to see the gear removed from his stall, he wasn't surprised when Clarke walked up to him just minutes later with the news that Renberg had been traded to Phoenix for Rick Tocchet.

"I was disappointed the first time, not very disappointed the second time," Renberg recalls. "I kind of expected it then.

"I didn't play well and it was different hockey for a more defensive-minded coach (Neilson). I was all about offensive; I kind of had the feeling they didn't want me to stay."

There had been nothing vague about the desire of Tocchet, the one-time Flyer captain and two-time Stanley Cup finalist, to return.

"I had been with Clarkie in a few settings, down at the shore or wherever, and I had mentioned to him, 'If you ever get a chance, I'd like to come back,'" recalls Tocchet. So the call he took from Coyote GM Bobby Smith that morning was one of the better ones of the right winger's life. "I'm letting you go back to Philly," Smith said.

This return had a chance to be the Flyers' most celebrated since Bernie Parent's in 1973.

"The players knew Rick, the veterans liked him, and because he had had success, they were fired up to bring him back," recalls Ramsay.

"He could be a dominant personality, but he does it in a positive way. He has that edge to him and you know you can trust him; he'll have your back. I wanted us to be physical but wasn't looking to fight. And I felt he was a guy who could get that message across."

Renberg had played himself off the Legion of Doom line with Lindros and LeClair through a combination of injuries—the worst being a sports hernia suffered at his peak in 1995—personal issues, and self-doubt.

"I think hockey had kind of changed," recalls Renberg, a massage therapist in Stockholm. "When I got [to Philadelphia], the game was really open and then it became more defensive.

"The first two years (38 goals as a rookie, 26 goals in his lockout-shortened sophomore season) set the standard for me. I thought if I didn't score, I was bad. Even though I always did my best, worked out hard, practiced hard, if I didn't perform well in games, I almost punched myself mentally. I was too tough on myself at times.

"Sometimes life from the side affects the way you perform in any kind of job. I don't want to talk about my private life, but I got divorced.

"I know my career was up and down. But I got a chance to play in the NHL—the best league in the world—for 10 years and in the Swedish Elite League for 10 years; that's a long career.

"There were just [four] guys (Mattias Öhlund, Thomas Holmstrom, Lars Lindgren) born in my hometown (Pitea) that made it to the NHL, which shows how hard it is to reach that level. I was in a Stanley Cup Final, got a chance to play with John and Eric on a first line in the NHL, and made it to the Swedish National Team."

Clarke felt the 27-year-old Renberg, who would go on to play only three more NHL seasons (in Phoenix and Toronto), was as far past his prime as the 35-year-old Tocchet. Hugely earnest and likable, the Swede had frustrated management and teammates as much as himself.

"I'd want to go over and shake him, say, 'Forget about it; it's only one game,' but he wasn't the type," recalls Richardson. "You had to handle him with delicate hands.

"He was really hard on himself and the harder he worked, the more things bounced off his stick. We were trading him for a guy who was the total opposite, would go through a brick wall to get something done, would never take no for an answer, on or off the ice. It was a huge move for our team."

The Flyers played a right wing short that night at Tampa, where ghosts of their trading pasts—Gratton and Mike Sillinger—staked the Lightning to a 2-0 lead on Vanbiesbrouck before Recchi set up Lindros, LeClair, and then, in overtime, Desjardins for a 3-2 victory.

Tocchet flew to Philadelphia the next day with no intention of playing that night against Washington. "I didn't get in until mid-afternoon, didn't want to come in tired and looking like an old goat," he recalls. "(Steve) Mountain (Tocchet's agent) was like, 'Who cares? Sleep on the plane, suck it up.'"

During the afternoon, a famished Tocchet and his representative went to South Philly in a car, searching for some Italian fuel. Over spaghetti, Mountain told him, "You're nuts if you don't play."

Agents are hired to give such good advice. Wearing No. 92 (his old No. 22 was taken by Richardson), Tocchet was put on a line with Langkow and Zelepukin and rose from a knockdown by Caps' defenseman Ken Klee to jam a rebound past Olaf Kolzig, tying the game 1-1 late in the second period.

"I had goose bumps," Tocchet would say after Odjick scored on a breakaway, Desjardins followed on a five-on-three, and the Flyers had cooled off the red-hot Caps, 3-1, to pull within four points of slumping New Jersey. "If you were sleepwalking at the Spectrum, the fans got you out of your coma. You had the same feeling here.

"You're nervous. You want to fit in. I don't want to come back and have people think, 'Sentimental reasons, too old.' I want to contribute."

So did an antsy Primeau, who had played in only eight of 20 games since being acquired. He returned two games earlier than projected to join the team in Colorado. "If I waited another week, there would be only 10 games left," he said. "It would be a real scramble.

"I'm probably guilty of coming back too soon last time. I feel more confident about it now."

Playing between Recchi and Gagne, Primeau struggled all night. So did Lindros and it was not only because he was matched against Adam Foote and Bourque, the latter making his Colorado home debut during the 3-1 Flyer defeat. After the game, Lindros, easily shrugged off by Dave Reid on the clinching goal, told Jones that he had felt dizzy since being hit by Hal Gill four games earlier in Boston and was having trouble remembering his shifts.

Following the wee hours flight from Denver to a game the next night in Phoenix, Lindros slept most of the day, then mentioned his symptoms to athletic trainer John Worley. Worley called team doctors in Philadelphia and was told that Lindros shouldn't play until he underwent neurological testing.

While media relations director Zack Hill walked Lindros to a taxi outside America West Arena one hour before game time, the Flyer captain did not speak to beat reporters. Carl Lindros told media callers he believed his son, who was "under stress for a variety of reasons" was suffering a migraine just as Recchi had late in the previous season.

Ramsay and some teammates told reporters they were aware of the headaches, just not of their severity. "He's been having headaches all week," said Primeau. "He's hesitant because when he makes a hit, he gets jolted.

"He's not playing his game, just trying to get through it without getting a headache."

Primeau's rust melted off quickly with two goals and an assist in a 4-1 win over the Coyotes. "We needed a big game and he really stepped up," said Ramsay. "Our whole team stepped up." That included Tocchet who, in his return to Phoenix, forced a turnover that Zelepukin converted for the lead goal.

Tests supervised over the next two days in Philadelphia by headache specialist Dr. Stephen Silberstein indicated Lindros had suffered a mild, grade one, concussion. Dr. Hartzell said Big E, who remained at Thomas Jefferson University Hospital taking medication intravenously, could be back in the lineup in 10 days.

The next morning, the *Inquirer* published a piece by Tim Panaccio in which an anonymous person inside the Flyer organization criticized their medical staff for ignoring Lindros's symptoms.

The source said Lindros had suffered yellow vision in the aftermath of the Gill hit in Boston, then vomited between the second and third periods. Lindros also regurgitated on the training table the next day while being given head and neck massages before the home game against the Islanders. The sources said that the training staff had sent him to a dentist, suggesting the headaches might be caused by jaw problems.

Snider and Clarke reacted angrily to the story. "Eric is more familiar with the aspects of a concussion than most players," the Chairman said from his home in California. "If Eric got hit, he has to say something. We can't read minds.

"If you talk to most players, they think our organization is one of the best in sports. It pains me to see this stuff written."

Clarke called the story, "Lies."

"We're very confident that our trainers did the right thing," he said. "We think our doctors are the best and our trainers are the best. If Eric has a problem, he can bring it up. We don't need all this hanging over our hockey club heading into the playoffs."

Clarke added he felt Lindros had played well until the contest in Denver. "I'm quite sure he didn't think he had a concussion," said the GM, who suggested a joint press conference with Lindros, the trainers, and team doctors so reporters could decipher the various accounts.

Primeau said teammates were concerned about the Gill hit by the way Lindros got up from it, but that he had downplayed it. "The guys closest to him might know there is something wrong, but they're not medical doctors," said Primeau. "If he doesn't say exactly what the problem is, we're not going to push it."

Tocchet scored to get the Flyers and a sharp Vanbiesbrouck a 1-1 tie in Montreal. When Lindros was released from the hospital, Dr. Silberstein stated his belief ibuprofen had exacerbated the patient's symptoms.

"Overuse of over-the-counter medication can result in the conversion of an intermittent headache to a daily headache," said Dr. Silberstein at a press conference. "When he came to see me, he was taking between 14 and 18 over-the-counter ibuprofen a day. He developed an analgesic rebound headache."

Silberstein said the cycle had been broken by giving Lindros high doses of corticosteroids.

Lindros, speaking publicly for the first time since after the game in Denver, said it was more like eight-to-ten pills a day. But he praised Dr. Silberstein and Thomas Jefferson Headache Center for their thoroughness, even though he was going to get a second opinion from Northwestern University's Dr. James Kelly, a sports concussion specialist.

While undergoing that evaluation in Chicago, Drs. Silberstein, Kelly, and Hartzell participated with Lindros and his father in a media conference call.

"[Eric] had just missed five games with a back injury; (Boston) was his first game back, and he acknowledged he was not totally forthcoming," said Hartzell. "Perhaps we didn't fully recognize that he might be doing this and press him.

"In retrospect, we could have been more sensitive to the fact that he didn't want to miss more games."

Hartzell said the Bruin doctor who had examined Lindros—the Boston organization had refused to provide his name—might not have been aware he was suffering yellow vision. Hartzell added that the next night, before the Islander game, Flyer internist Dr. Gary Dorshimer had asked Lindros if he "got his bell rung" and had been told, "No, I'm fine."

According to Dorshimer, Lindros appeared "vigorous and energetic," so the matter was not pursued. When Lindros subsequently complained of headaches and jaw pain, Hartzell said another team physician, Dr. Guy Lanzi, felt Lindros had a temporomandibular joint problem with his jaw.

It was clear that Lindros, who for three previous concussions had been required by the Flyer medical staff to undergo neurological testing, should have received the same following the game in Boston.

"Had the game occurred in Philadelphia, we probably would have done that," Hartzell said. "We try to do the right thing for the players and all of us from time to time would like to have a second chance.

"One of us should have taken Eric aside and asked him, 'How do you feel?' Maybe that would have prevented this. But there is no one I have more admiration for as a man, a person, and trainer than John Worley. And he has been hung out there the most."

Dr. Kelly's tests subsequently—and surprisingly—revealed "sensory abnormality on one side of [Lindros's] body and one abnormal reflex." The concussion was upgraded from grade one to two, and the timetable for the captain's return was set for no sooner than six weeks, into the second round of the playoffs.

The next day, Lindros asked for time with the Philadelphia hockey writers. He acknowledged brushing off the Bruin team doctor but told reporters that, "John Worley knew what I had.

"I was not concealing it. John Worley knew everything went to a yellow tinge, that I'd come in after the period and vomited, that I was having heat packs on my head.

"I wasn't pounding down the notion that I was experiencing real bad headaches. I wanted to keep playing. As the week went on, I was hoping that the team would take me out.

"The other reason I kept playing was that the environment here is interesting. The last time I got a concussion (January 14), I didn't talk to Clarke for three weeks. I knew that if I told my dad or my agent what went on, I would not be playing. You know what happens when my dad gets involved around here. It's just a big headache.

"I'm very unhappy about what's gone on here. It's a whacky situation."

Asked why, despite all the distrust between he and Clarke, he wanted to remain a Flyer, Lindros said, "A lot of it has to do with Roger."

Dr. Kelly, who said the scan had not indicated to him Lindros should retire, only rest, told reporters that in light of athletes being reluctant to report all symptoms and their severity, the Flyers should reexamine the way they evaluate possible concussions. But Kelly held Lindros partially at fault for the same reasons. "I'm disappointed," said the doctor, "and he's disappointed in himself."

Worley said the accusations of his negligence made him, "sick to my stomach."

"This hits me hard," he told Ed Moran of *The Philadelphia Daily News*. "I feel confident in the decisions that were made with the information we were all presented."

Worley said the vomiting in Boston occurred as a gag reflex while a therapist had his fingers in Lindros's mouth trying to lessen the tension in his jaw, a suspected reason for the headache. The trainer added that the player had been feeling better at times through the week and had said before the game in Colorado that he was not suffering a headache. It was only the next day in Phoenix, Worley said, that Lindros for the first time all week reported to him nausea and forgetfulness.

The team issued an "organizational statement" that read: "Based on Eric's comments today, it is obvious that he and the Philadelphia Flyers have different perspectives concerning the medical judgments that were made following his most recent injury. However, this is no way impacts upon the high level of confidence we have in the integrity and skill of our training staff.

"In light of Dr. Kelly's conclusions, we are moving forward under his guidelines and are looking forward to Eric's complete recovery."

The players almost universally felt Worley had been scapegoated by Lindros.

"I remember guys asking, 'Are you really going to blame Worley?'" recalls Primeau. "There's no way.

"I had a concussion and never told Worley. You make the decision, that isn't Worley's fault. It's not the trainer's job to jump inside your head and tell you how you are. I thought it was idiocy and ignorance to blame it on the trainer. Eric was a member of the Flyer family; we'd had his back. And now you're going after the trainer?"

Berube was equally disgusted: "The trainers work hard for you," he says today. "They want to take care of you.

"In this organization, it's about the team, so you feel like you should play. So guys play hurt, but you need to have the balls to make that decision yourself. No trainer is going to tell me how I feel or if I'm going to play."

Desjardins points out today that it was another time, with reduced sensibilities about concussions than there are currently. "It's different now because of the protocols you go through," he says. "But I just think that if you say you're alright to play, who is better to tell you not to?"

Lindros had not made himself a pariah in all corners of the locker room. "He was a good player, everyone knew that," recalls Therien. "At some point, we would have to welcome him and make him comfortable."

The Flyers were weary of the circus and determined to move on. "It's not a one-man team," Berube told the media. "It's too much emphasis on one guy around here and I think that's a problem."

But as Lindros went back to Toronto to heal, he was out of sight and largely out of mind, so the players agreed with Clarke that leadership needed to be formalized in Big E's absence. Four days after Lindros had criticized the handling of his concussion and two after the Flyers crept within two points of the plummeting Devils with a 3-1 win over Pittsburgh, Ramsay, Desjardins, Recchi and LeClair met with the GM about choosing a new captain.

Clarke suggested Desjardins, who wanted the team to vote on it, but Recchi and LeClair insisted that wasn't necessary. "It was a feeling everybody had," LeClair told reporters. "I think Rico's a real strong quality leader who definitely has the respect of everyone in this room.

"He doesn't say much. But when he does, guys really listen because he is right-on."

That was quite the tribute to the growth in personality and language skills of a player who barely had spoken English upon his arrival in Philadelphia from Montreal five years earlier.

"I would never have dreamed of this," Desjardins said. "But they gave me this job because they like the way I am.

"The worst thing I could do is change myself. I think I will be up to it. I welcome this challenge."

Acknowledging the circumstances, Desjardins said, "We all know what happened. We felt we needed a change in that area.

"You have to understand you can't have your captain, or anybody on your team, criticizing any member of your organization. (But) as far as I know, Big E's still a big part of our team."

Desjardins looks back at the transition as an awkward one for himself.

"He had been my captain for so many years and such a presence in the league and on our team that I felt strange," he recalls. "But I took it because I wanted to do more since he wasn't there. I thought that when he came back, I would give the captaincy back.

"There were a few situations, but I didn't have a problem with Eric. He was a normal guy, a normal person. There are guys in the locker room who demand the attention, but I never felt that way about him. He would get attention just by what he was doing on the ice."

Clarke was not as forgiving. "I think it's fair to say that when a guy like Lindros comes out and criticizes the doctors, trainers, the organization and everything else, he's thinking of himself and not the team," said the GM.

Asked if he was concerned about Lindros's reaction to the loss of his C, Clarke said, "No. Wouldn't have done it if we were."

Lindros issued a written statement: "Although I haven't talked to management, I'm aware of the change in the captaincy of the team. It was a role I felt honored to have and wished to continue in it.

"I'd like to wish Rico the best. I look forward to the day I'm healthy and able to come back to contribute to our team's upcoming challenge of this year's playoffs."

Lindros had spoken to some players, but the principal link between he and the Flyers remained Neilson. While not consulted about the captaincy change, he nevertheless called Eric to explain it.

"It's a shame, but he understood why it was done," said Neilson, who returned to the Coliseum four days after being released from the hospital looking gaunt and grimacing about the 60 ounces of water that doctors wanted him to drink every day. Nevertheless, he reiterated his desire to coach the team at some point in the playoffs.

"My blood counts are good and they're still going up," Neilson said.

Clarke had jammed in one more trade at the deadline, moving McCarthy to Carolina for winger-center Kent Manderville. And Zalapski had been sent back to Utah of the IHL because Samuelsson's shoulder was healed.

The shoulder was doing better than his psyche, though. For what he said was the first time in his 18-season career, Samuelsson was a healthy scratch as Boucher beat the Bruins, 6-2 on Gagne's 18th goal of his rookie season.

Afterward the game, Samuelsson complained to the writers that his bashing style was being changed to increase his availability for passes. "We're not allowed to come up and make big hits in the neutral zone," said the defenseman, but a day later he recanted his protest. "It's a good system made for the playoffs," he said. "My personal agenda should not enter it."

Replied Ramsay, "We have a team style of play, that's all I can say."

Egos were being checked at the locker room and bench doors. The Flyers, 9-6-3 with Lindros out of the lineup for the season (57-57-17 for the absences during his career) were becoming accustomed to not having him.

"We never used '[bleep] Eric' as a rallying point at all, and I would challenge anybody who says differently," recalls Primeau. "It wasn't us against Eric, us against management, us against the world, just a good bunch of guys with a job to do, trying to go deep into the playoffs.

"I had only been there a few months and maybe I was naïve, but I didn't feel as though Eric's issues with management infiltrated the locker room. We had too many veteran guys that just weren't going to let it happen. If it came up in conversation it was like, 'What's going on now? What's going on next?' But it didn't preoccupy our time: it wasn't a topic that we took seriously."

Then again, the Flyers didn't take themselves very seriously, either.

"I'd be lying if I said there wasn't some personal stuff with some guys," recalls Tocchet. "Yeah, some players said, 'Forget about it. We don't need him,' that type of thing.

"But really, he was like a vapor—gone to Toronto. No one really talked about him. You read about how he was doing in the paper, but in the room it was business as usual and our character came out even more.

"From what I was told, it became a funnier, looser locker room. I don't know the full story, so to say him leaving the dressing room made the room better, that's an unfair statement. But we had a great room. Eight to 15 guys would go to dinner together.

"While Berube was getting a massage before the game, Therien or Jonsey would get Chief's stick and tie a pail to it, like that was what he needed to pick up a pick. One day we taped a whole wheelbarrow to it.

"Therien came in with lobster claws one day to make fun of Berube's hands and Manderville's hands. Luke used to sneak things on your back bumper, like a poster or a sign that said "Rick Tocchet." I would drive around Voorhees wondering why people were waving at me.

"Therien did something to me once, I forget what. But I got him back by jamming my kid's dirty diaper under his driver's seat. After three days in the hot sun during playoff time, his car didn't smell too good.

"A lot of teams don't do that stuff. We did. It was enjoyable to come to the rink. You jumped out of bed and said, 'Practice today, cool!'"

Philadelphia was nine minutes away from its fifth win in eight games minus Lindros when Vanbiesbrouck allowed a 58-foot goal by Igor Kravchuk, prompting a collapse into a 5-2 loss in Ottawa. "For two periods, [the Senators] weren't even there," lamented Desjardins.

Neither had been Samuelsson much since he had complained about the physicality being removed from his game by Ramsay. Repeatedly a scratch since returning from his shoulder issue, the aged warrior limped off from a practice two days after the Ottawa loss with a knee problem.

Ramsay was committed to going with the kids Eaton and Delmore regardless. Delmore played 21 minutes as the Flyers and Boucher nursed a one-goal lead for 27-plus minutes to a 3-2 victory in Pittsburgh on April 11.

The next night in Raleigh, Primeau put on the black hat for his Carolina return before 17,075 haters, the Hurricanes' second-largest crowd of the season. One fan held up a Primeau jersey with all the letters blacked out except for the m and e.

"The guys had a good laugh at some of the signs," he said after Arturs Irbe bested Boucher, 1-0, and McGillis needed 31 stitches after taking a knee in the head. "The only disappointment," said Primeau, "is that they got a full building."

Brind'Amour, whose Hurricanes unexpectedly were going to the wire in the playoff race, of course, was asked for his view from afar of the Lindros controversy. "I like the stance [the Flyers] made," Brind'Amour said. "They're saying they are going to treat everybody equally.

"I always thought Eric took a bad rap because he always came to play. But I've known Worley and McCrossin for years and they're top notch. That bothered me."

Sandy McCarthy played parts of two seasons for the Orange-and-Black, recording 136 penalty minutes in 71 games.

Bothersome probably had understated the Flyer failure to beat the expansion Thrashers in their first two meetings ever. But the third was the charm. Gagne's 20th goal put away a 5-3 win at Philips Arena. "I lost a couple pounds on my shoulder," said the kid, very much wanting the milestone.

Clarke still felt the need to weigh in on Lindros, telling Wayne Fish of the *Bucks County Courier Times* that an apology to the medical and training staff and a "make peace" with his teammates would be required before any return.

"What Eric did was so foreign to any team," said Clarke. "He was wrong in what he did and the players felt strongly about it."

Certainly Berube did. "We're going to have to sit down and talk," he said. "Things aren't right, they have to be made right, somehow. You can't just do what he did and walk away from it."

Clarke subsequently softened, suggesting that he wouldn't demand an apology but wanted a sit-down between himself, Snider and Lindros. "We want to make sure he understands where we come from," said the GM. "And maybe he'll tell us where he's coming from."

Ramsay told Boucher where he was going—into the nets for Game One of the playoffs scheduled to begin the following week. That night, the kid responded to the vote of confidence with a 3-1 victory that completed a sweep of the home-and-home with Atlanta and left Philadelphia three points away from the conference title going into their final two games.

Three goals in the third snapped a scoreless tie in Boucher's 3-0 First Union Center shutout of the Bruins. Recchi then broke another 0-0 deadlock in the first minute of the second period to launch a 4-1 win at Madison Square Garden.

In a season that started with a promising player's funeral, which proceeded with a diagnosis of their coach's deadly cancer and then the injury and alienation of their captain, the Flyers 105 points—their highest total since 1985-86—had won the franchise's ninth regular-season conference championship by two points over the Devils.

"We fall 15 points behind and you say 'Holy [bleep], let's just get this to the playoffs,'" said Clarke. "I think this was pretty impressive.

"They got stronger as a group. They got that, 'We'll show you,' attitude."

Ramsay, under whom the team had gone 16-8-1, glowed with the accomplishment. "A lot of people tried to write us off," he said. "It's been a really great ride."

The driver had been Boucher, whose 1.91 goals-against average made him the first rookie since 1950-51 (Detroit's Terry Sawchuk and Toronto's Al Rollins) to play 25 games and record a goals-against average under 2.00. "I don't think any player in our organization has done anything bigger than that since we started," praised Clarke.

A 23-year-old kid wouldn't know about that. But the guy who had presided over the entire team history had the best perspective.

"This reminds me of teams past with the Flyers, where everybody was pulling together," said Snider. "I'm very proud of this organization."

With Lindros hoping to get the okay from Dr. Kelly to begin working out within a week, the Chairman endorsed Clarke's contention that an apology would be necessary before No. 88 returned. "Everybody in our organization feels that way, unanimously," said Snider.

The exception would have been Neilson, who told the *Daily News*'s Bowen that Philadelphia couldn't win the required four rounds without No. 88. In the meantime, Roger didn't want the team to proceed for even one round without him behind the bench.

"Dr. Brodsky kept telling Roger, 'We're going to have you back by the first round of the playoffs,'" recalls Nichols. "And Roger would just [nod] yes.

"I would go to Brodsky and say, 'I know what you're doing, I appreciate that. But please don't tell him that, because if you tell him that, he will do it. That's just the kind of person he is. Tell him the second round, lie on that side of it.'

"He said, 'No, I think he can be around for the first round.'

"I don't remember whether [Brodsky] meant as a head coach, but head coach was the way Roger was going to take it. You give him that carrot, there would be no ifs, ands, or buts about it, he was going to be standing behind the bench on that day despite everything.

"I was there the day that, as they did the tranplant, his pulse went to zero. Flatlined for a few seconds. They take you down as far as they can without killing you, then hope to bring you back fast. I mean, it went according to their projections, but when you are there watching it, you never forget it.

"He was a sick man and didn't want to accept it. When he was rehabbing, it was, 'Get me this videotape, get me the stats on that.' He was going for this operation and he was going to be fine, and that was all."

The day after the regular-season ended, Neilson, just back from a week at Clarke's condominium in Sarasota, FL, walked back into the GM's office. "Here's what we're doing in practice today," he said to Clarke.

"Rog, you're not the coach anymore," Clarke told Neilson.

Shouting ensued.

"He was fuming angry," recalls Clarke. "He had done everything the doctor had told him to do, so he thought he could coach. We knew otherwise. Nancy had told me more than once, 'There is no way he can do it.'

"It was so sad. Coaching was his whole life and he wasn't healthy enough."

That day, the GM told reporters that even if the doctors declared Neilson good to go at some point during the spring, he would be reluctant to reduce Ramsay's role. "You can't make a change if the team is going really good," Clarke said. "Roger understands that; he's said that before.

"If the decision is what we think would be the right one for the team, we all have to accept it."

Neilson made it clear acceptance by him was going to be difficult. "If the doctors say you're OK, then you're the coach of the team," he told Bowen. "I would expect to be back then."

Neilson added that his agent, Rob Campbell, would be calling Clarke later in the week to finalize a new two-year contract that would replace the one expiring on July 1. Clarke shot that down, too.

"We're not going to initiate contract talks until after the season," said the GM, who added Neilson was "trying to put us in a position like, 'You promised me I'd be back as soon as I'm ready,' when that was not the case."

Neilson was the only person who thought he was capable of immediately resuming as the head coach.

"My God, did he look awful," recalls Ramsay. "There wasn't a chance in hell that he could have coached, but that was Roger.

"Clarkie said, 'I'll take the heat; I won't let him.' Nancy was a true champion of this whole thing. She backed us a hundred percent."

The players, whom Desjardins recalls wanted to change nothing, felt terrible for Neilson nevertheless. "Actually, to see him in that state of health wanting to be out there was one more rallying point," recalls Primeau.

The Flyers were preparing for the defending Eastern Conference champion Sabres, who, with 16 points in their final 20 games, had closed the season even more impressively than Philadelphia. Buffalo had humiliated the Flyers in five games two seasons earlier. But after a barrage of reporters' questions about Neilson and Lindros, Desjardins had to plead for one about the Sabres.

When it finally came, the subject naturally was Dominik Hasek, who having stoned Philadelphia in 1998, hardly seemed like a reward for earning the top seed. "Hasek is there in the first series, but he could have been there in the second series anyway," said Desjardins, captain of a team eliminated in the first round the last two years.

Primeau said he was happy that Buffalo, for which Hasek only had been physically able to play 35 games during the season, had edged out the Hurricanes for the last playoff spot. "I didn't like the idea of [Carolina] getting playoff gates," he told reporters.

That was a stronger grudge than most Flyers held against the Sabres, despite this being the fourth series between the two teams in six years. There were only five holdovers—Desjardins, Therien, McGillis, Richardson and LeClair—who had played in the 1998 series, a fresh start conceivably to Philadelphia's advantage, even if the Flyers were throwing a rookie in goal against a five-time Vezina Trophy holder and two-time Hart Trophy winner.

"I try not to even look at the other end, who I'm playing," said Boucher.

Basically, Ramsay told his shooters to take the same approach. "Just shoot, look for rebounds," he instructed. "Don't try to be perfect; don't worry about keeping dump-ins away from him.

"We would send one guy at him and two to the wall, where the puck was going. He's a goalie. How great can he be with the puck?"

Buffalo was a bottom-third team in the NHL in scoring, so Boucher wasn't exactly facing Murderer's Row for his postseason debut. "Actually, it kind of scared me that I was too relaxed," he would say later.

A big early save is always comforting, such as the one the Flyer goalie made in Game One at the First Union Center on a Curtis Brown breakaway. Also useful is a first-period lead, which Jones provided with a powerplay goal. When Langkow, backhanded and shorthanded, successfully went up top just 7.5 seconds before the end of the first period, Philadelphia had beaten Hasek on two of its first six shots.

The Flyers pounded a 16-9 shot advantage in the second period, only to wind up 2-2 when Stu Barnes cashed a McGillis elbowing penalty and Miro Satan, Buffalo's leading scorer, tied the game.

But five minutes into the third period, Gagne pounced on a powerplay rebound and scored his first playoff goal, between Hasek's legs. So complete was Philadelphia's control as they checked away a 3-2 victory that Buffalo never got set up in the Flyer zone with Hasek pulled.

"The support among the players for each other is wonderful," said

Ramsay. "We were as vocal tonight as we have been for a long time."

In Game Two, Satan was lost by Eaton during a turn-up move by Jason Wooley, enabling Buffalo to jump up 1-0. But with Recchi having successfully embellished an Alexei Zhitnik trip early in the second period, McGillis fed LeClair, who wound up from the top of the right circle and apparently beat Hasek just inside the near post, even though his skate was against it.

"It didn't look right but the light went on, so I just raised my hands," recalls LeClair. "I thought it must have gone in."

So at first did Hasek, who took swigs from his water bottle while shaking his head. "I thought maybe I left a hole," he said, but the Sabres' Dixon Ward, who was on the ice when the red light went on, wasn't as convinced.

"His pad was right against the post, and I'm thinking, 'How did that puck go in?'" Ward said later. "We found [a hole], tried to get somebody's attention, but . . ."

The two videos of the goal available to replay official Mike Condon and series' official supervisor, John D'Amico, were from overhead cameras. But an ESPN camera located inside the net revealed the puck had gone through the mesh from outside the post.

Only after the puck had been dropped at center ice of a now 1-1 game did D'Amico and Condon get a knock on the door of the officiating box telling them of the ESPN replay. There was no procedure to disallow the goal once the game had resumed. "We can't review what we can't see," D'Amico would say apologetically later.

It was unclear whether the net had been ripped by LeClair's shot or the puck had gone through an existing hole. Linesman Brad Lazarowich stitched it up, too late to save the Sabres a goal or the NHL from embarrassment.

Of course, LeClair didn't feel that badly.

"When I saw what had really happened, I got a kick out of it," he recalls. "Hasek stole enough goals from other people, he might as well lose one."

Obviously, that logic wasn't going to appease Buffalo's netminder. Six minutes later, still irked by a goal that wasn't, Hasek drew a roughing penalty by jumping Primeau.

Early in the third period, with Vladimir Tsyplakov in the box for interfering with Zelepukin on the faceoff, Desjardins, set up by an impressive Recchi keep and saucer pass, kicked the puck onto his stick and closed to the top of the circle. Desjardins beat Hasek high through a LeClair screen to put Philadelphia ahead.

Boucher, much busier than in Game One, made a blocker save on Barnes with Hasek pulled, and the Flyers had been gifted Game Two, 2-1, to take a 2-0 series lead.

"It's a nightmare, is what it is," said Buffalo coach Lindy Ruff. A recurring one, too, since 10 months earlier, the Dallas Stars had eliminated the Sabres in Game Six of the Stanley Cup Final when Brett Hull's overtime goal was allowed to stand despite video evidence of his foot being in the crease.

"What a great hockey game it was, but regardless of the outcome, it has to be marred by something stupid like that," said Ward before adding, "It was 1-1 at that time and we still had a chance to win the game.

"That team is as good as they've been in a long time. Give them all the credit in the world. They got their opportunity and they got it done. Certainly, we'll get a break like that sometime and it'll even out. Hopefully, it'll happen on Sunday (in Game Three)."

The Sabres, scored upon in four of the 11 powerplay opportunities they had given Philadelphia in Games One and Two, had to first start helping themselves. Within two minutes of Game Three at Marine Midland Arena, Gratton took a slashing penalty.

"Grats, you're finally paying off for the Flyers," taunted Jones, cracking up the Philadelphia bench but earning the silent treatment from Gratton that Jones recalls lasted two years.

Peter White, taken down by Zhitnik as Hasek snapped his pads together on a first-period breakaway, was awarded a penalty shot, but having hit his head on the ice, was too woozy to take it. Rules required the replacement had to have been on the ice at time of the foul. This didn't completely answer Desjardins' question—"Why me?"—when chosen by Ramsay.

No good reason, it turned out. Hasek closed his pads, made the save and juiced the crowd. But with Vaclav Varada off for charging LeClair, Big John got payback by converting a Gagne passout to put Philadelphia ahead 1-0 late in the first period.

With the huge help of five more Sabre penalties, the Flyers roped the Buffalo dopes with a magnificently disciplined checking effort. Berube skated away from Jean-Luc Grand-Pierre's big hit and Manderville absorbed a hard body blow from Michael Peca before getting the puck out in the final minute.

Philadelphia, outhit 38-17 by the desperate Sabres, nursed LeClair's goal all the way until Recchi hit the empty net, finishing off a 2-0 road masterpiece. It was the win—and control of the series—that had gotten away in a stunning final two minutes a year earlier in Game Two at Toronto.

"They played harder than us and smarter than us," conceded Ruff. "Philly has added some mobility, that's the difference."

Rookie defensemen Delmore and Eaton had played 18 and 14 minutes, respectively, to back up Desjardins' dominant 25. The Flyers, who had not been able to buy a goal against Hasek in 1998, had only six on him in three games this time, but were up 3-0.

"Two years ago, we were on the other side of this," remembered LeClair, an irony applauded even by the Sabres. "Defensively, that's as good as I ever have seen them," said Ward. "There's not a guy out there that's not committed to the system that's been put in place by the coaching staff."

LeClair had been Exhibit A. "He played an outstanding defensive game, drew penalties and scored the game-winning goal as well," said Jones.

One win from a probable week's rest, the Flyers still were at least three from getting Lindros back, according to testing conducted by Dr. Gerri McGinnis, a neuropsychologist retained by the team in the aftermath of the diagnosis controversy.

Time was much closer to running out for the Sabres. They came at

Philadelphia even harder in Game Four. Referee Dan Marouelli waved off what should have been a first-minute goal by Tsyplakov—Boucher had not frozen the puck. Buffalo, accustomed to bad goal calls, was not letting up. Boucher made superior stops on Doug Gilmour and Peca, but with five seconds remaining in a five-on-three created by Therien and Delmore penalties, Brown's deflection put the Sabres ahead.

Satan one-timed a feed from Ward early in the second to make the score 2-0, but Zhitnik's high stick of Langkow got the Flyers back into the game. Tocchet tipped in a Recchi feed on the powerplay and Primeau blooped the first Philadelphia even-strength goal of the series over Hasek with 1:35 left in the second period for a 2-2 tie.

Boucher dueled evenly with Hasek through the third period, which ended on a powerplay after Zhitnik drove Primeau's head into the glass. But the Sabres survived into the overtime, when Eaton's attempted clear up the boards was cut off by Geoff Sanderson.

Mark Recchi on Dominik Hasek in the first round of the 2000 playoffs.

Barnes fumbled the puck but had time to kick it onto his stick. McGillis, arriving late because his stick was being held by Gratton in the corner, was unable to keep Barnes from successfully roofing the puck at 4:42. The 3-2 loss was the Flyers' eighth-straight in playoff overtime, an NHL record.

"Too bad, tonight was probably Bouch's best game," said Desjardins in a locker room that still emanated the confidence of a team up 3-1. Buffalo, shorthanded 12 more times than Philadelphia through four games, had enjoyed most of its best chances on the penalty kill.

"Every game, [Boucher] has made unbelievable key shorthanded stops that have changed the game," raved Vanbiesbrouck on the off day as the Flyers, happy to see Zhitnik suspended for Game Five for his high stick of Langkow, again prepared their knockout punch. "Everyone knows how tough on a team shorthanded goals are."

Veteran Flyers understood how difficult any bad goals were on a team.

"It was the first time in a long time that I didn't think about our goalie," Therien recalls.

Thus, when Delmore unnecessarily iced the puck, Peca won the draw, and Smehlik scored 8:44 into the first period to give Buffalo a 1-0 lead in Game Five at the First Union Center, the Flyers didn't waste anxiety about momentum changing.

In the final 10 seconds of the period, Langkow beat Gratton on an offensive zone draw. McGillis, who had replaced Recchi on the point earlier in the series despite having scored only four goals all season, didn't wait to settle down the puck off its edge before blowing it by Hasek.

"When we came into the locker room after that, they couldn't flood the ice fast enough," said McGillis.

Midway through the second period, with Varada off for roughing a refusing-to-retaliate Tocchet, LeClair tipped in another drive by McGillis to put Philadelphia ahead, 2-1.

Langkow, taking a mid-body pass from Tocchet, swung at the puck before it could hit the ice and remarkably batted it between Hasek's legs to make it 3-1.

In the third period, the Flyers lost a goal off the lead when Barnes, set up at the left post by Satan while Zelepukin was off for high sticking, scored at 3:34 into the third period. But again the Sabres couldn't stay out of the box. With Chris Taylor serving time for holding, Gagne, set up by Desjardins, calmly waited for Hasek to sprawl and backhanded in an insurance goal at 9:55 that started a long and sustained celebration.

"With two or three minutes to go, we've got a two-goal lead and the building is going crazy and it hit me," Primeau said after Langkow's empty-netter put a bow on a 5-2 victory that clinched the series in five games. "I just began thinking back to eight or 10 months ago—where I was to where I am now.

"It's great. I'm just trying to let it sink in."

The Flyers had struggled so much against expectations and adversity since their final run of 1997 that getting out of the first round for the first time in three years was hugely satisfying, especially the way they had done it. "We supported each other in every area of the ice," said Desjardins. "Everyone felt they could make a difference, shift after shift, working the corners, working the boards. It's no magic trick."

"When you work that hard, you are going to get the bounces," Buffalo's Peca praised. "My hat's off to them."

The Flyers had made themselves better without their best player.

"I'm proud, not surprised," said Snider. "We have more spirit; we're more upbeat in that locker room than we have been in a long, long time.

"Some of that obviously is the result of winning, but when these guys had the run that won the conference, it wasn't a fluke. When people call us a dysfunctional franchise, it makes me mad. I believe we're one of the best organizations in sports.

"One player is unhappy with the organization. I don't know any other player that is. The rest of them seem pretty damn happy to me. I think Craig Ramsay has done an incredible job.

"We're concerned about Roger's health. We've talked to an awful lot of doctors. Normal people who have desk jobs don't come back from this in three-to-six months.

"I looked at Roger after our first playoff game. He was pale. He has been though a hell of a lot. He's a strong, fabulous man, but I'd hate to see him under the pressures he's going to be under if he coaches. It would be surprising to me if [the doctors] said he could be the head coach."

Neilson, claiming he didn't want to be a distraction, had worn a head set in the press box for only one game of the Buffalo series before returning to his home in Dallas. But four days after the elimination of the Sabres, while the Flyers awaited their series with Pittsburgh, he showed up in Clarke's office, announcing for a second time that he was ready to coach.

Clarke again told Neilson no. He pedaled away on his bicycle without comment to reporters.

"It was just a very emotional and complicated time, and to see Roger so crushed was heartbreaking," recalls Nichols.

The team issued a statement quoting two of Neilson's doctors—Brodsky and oncologist Pamela Crilley—saying it was inadvisable for their patient to return to the bench at this stage of his recovery.

"I regret if there was a misunderstanding that arose from my previous comments," said Brodsky. "I was referring to the time when Roger might be able to assume a limited role and not to the point when he could realistically take on the stress and pressure of a head coach in playoff hockey."

The statement quoted Roger as saying, "I am very disappointed. Although I had hoped to come back as head coach, I am completely respectful of the doctors' opinions and I look forward to helping out Craig and the coaching staff in any way I can."

But the next morning, in a radio interview with Toronto's Fan 590, Neilson said, "I don't think they want a cancer patient who is a friend with Eric Lindros behind the bench right now."

Talking to reporters later in the day at the Coliseum, Neilson said he didn't remember saying that, but if he had, he was "just trying to be light." But Neilson added that, "The Lindros situation certainly has come up and it could be tied in, in some way."

Neilson also said that a day earlier he had been on a conference call with his agent Campbell, Clarke, and Flyer president Ron Ryan, and that when the subject of a contract extension came up, "We didn't get any encouragement."

Clarke denied that the Lindros situation impacted Neilson. "His relationship with Eric Lindros has nothing to do with him having cancer or not being the head coach," the GM said. "The doctors told us Roger is not allowed to coach right now.

"There is nothing complicated about it. We wish Eric were healthy. [Neilson] said (his radio) comments were just lighthearted, so I believe that."

Ramsay accepted it, too. His relationship with Neilson was undamaged, contradicting some pieces of media speculation that Ramsay recalls as being hurtful. In an attempt to set the record straight, Neilson made calls to media members who had reported a rift. "Roger was not angry with him at all," recalls Nichols. "It wasn't Craig's decision, and besides, who could ever be mad at Craig Ramsay?"

That week, Roger was a guest of Susan and Craig Ramsay for dinner. Meanwhile, far from ready to break bread with Bob Clarke was Lindros, who could finally ride the bike without a seriously-elevated heart rate.

Cleared by Dr. Kelly for solo skating, Big E took to the ice ahead of a Flyer practice two days before Game One against the Penguins. Lindros was about to hold his first press conference since leaving the team when reporters were summoned to meet with Neilson in front of his office.

"We all say things in the media that sometimes don't come out the right way," Neilson said. "In this case, it was entirely my fault; I take the complete blame for it.

"It was a really a poor decision on my part to crack the joke I did. Certainly I've always made light of the cancer. And the reference to Eric Lindros was just an attempt to poke fun at the common idea that, because we're friends, it has some effect on my coaching here, which is ridiculous.

"The other comment that resulted in a poor choice of words by me was about whether Bobby Clarke was responsible for the distractions we've had. I know when I came back from Florida, I was kind of on my own agenda and kind of surprised everybody. I haven't communicated enough. I think that's been a problem.

"I've been devastated by the publicity this has received. We should be talking about the team and Pittsburgh. Certainly I've never been a guy that criticizes his players publicly and I don't want to be perceived as a guy that criticizes management publicly.

"Bobby Clarke and I go back quite a ways. He's given me my last two jobs. I used his condo in Florida. We argue and fight all the time and the next day it's all over. I wouldn't want anything to hurt that friendship. Mr. Snider flew me down (to Sarasota) on his private jet. I've been treated like a king here."

Lindros, in the press conference that followed, said that he was agreeable to the proposed meeting with Snider and Clarke, provided Gordon Kirke, the family attorney, was present.

No. 88 dismissed any personal concerns about his acceptance by teammates and refused to issue an opinion about Neilson's treatment by the team. "I'm sure he's very disappointed, but that's not my area and I'm not getting into it," Lindros said.

Really, all Big E wanted to talk about was how good it had felt to be back on the ice. "It's a little frustrating that it's not going quicker," said Lindros. "At least I'm making headway.

Meanwhile, back at the conference semifinal series, Boucher, seeming immune from pressure in his head while winning his first playoff round, was about to take on the Penguins with pressure in his head from a sinus infection. This was just about the only secret left unhung on the line by Team Dirty Laundry as Game One began at the First

Union Center.

Jaromir Jagr, the three-time defending NHL scoring champion, banked one in off his old antagonist Therien before Martin Straka beat Delmore on a bad Flyer line change.

The Penguins had been coached since December by 62-year-old Herb Brooks, who had masterminded not only the Lake Placid 1980 Olympic miracle for the USA, but a devastating Ranger sweep of a 106-point Flyer team in the 1983 playoffs. Seventeen years later, Philadelphia was again playing into Brooks' hands.

"I don't think our mindset was the same as it had been against Buffalo," recalls Tocchet. "I think we were like, 'Let's play real aggressive and they'll roll over,' but they fell down and acted like they got shot and were beating us with their skill."

Indeed, Matthew Barnaby and Darius Kasparaitis had gotten to the Flyers like nobody had gotten to them in months. Barnaby, who had his hand under Zelepukin's shield, crumbled when the Philadelphia winger swung to knock the pest away, but referee Don Koharski called only the retaliation.

The exasperated Flyers left themselves shorthanded two more times in the third period. When Tocchet cross-checked Kasparaitis to the ice at the end of the game, the Penguin defenseman jumped to his feet, chest-bumped the glass in front of angry Flyer fans, then high-fived his teammates.

"When you get a penalty and you didn't deserve it, then get another one, you get frustrated," said Tocchet. Ron Tugnutt stopped 28 shots in Pittsburgh's 2-0 shutout—the team's first win in 16 trips to Philadelphia.

"Tonight was a game of Academy Award performances," said Tocchet. "We're going to have to throw a couple of supporting actors at them."

But there was another bad screenplay for Game Two. Robert Lang cashed in the third of three straight Flyer first-period penalties—a roughing call on Langkow—to give the Penguins a 1-0 lead.

Philadelphia continued to carry the play until Jagr scored from the edge of the circle through Boucher's legs to make it 2-0 and frustration set in again. Desjardins, up ice trying to make something happen, was caught as Lang moved to within 25 feet to blow one by Boucher's short side.

After Gagne flipped Langkow's rebound over a prone Tugnutt to break the Flyers' five-period scoring drought, Tyler Wright was penalized for chopping Langkow on the hand. But Tugnutt stopped a Primeau powerplay attempt and Therien's giveaway enabled Jagr's second goal, to create a 4-1 Pittsburgh advantage.

Three goals down deep in the third period once was the Broad Street Bullies' automatic signal to announce they were not going to lose without collecting their pound of flesh. Now the team had to ask permission.

"[Assistant coach Mike Stothers] came to me to me and said, "The boys have had enough with Tyler Wright," recalls Ramsay. "I said 'Stutsy, I don't like that, you know that,' but the boys were looking at me, so I said 'Alright.'

"Toch said, 'Okay, I got this one.'"

Recalls Tocchet: "I remember Wright telling me, 'You suck old man, you suck.' Look, I've been called worse and he's probably a great kid. But I grew up in an era when you send a message.

"I jumped the boards and took the draw. In fairness to Craig Ramsay, he did not send everybody out; this was my thing."

Tocchet shoved Wright during a scrum as Tugnutt was freezing the puck. "I'm an old man? Let's see if I'm an old man," Tocchet said, then snapped Wright's head back with a right hand and began throwing uppercuts.

"He turtled. Then I see Bob Boughner beating on Daymond," recalls Tocchet. "So I run over to him and start beating Boughner up. The linesmen grabbed me to take me to the box and then a five-on-five ensued."

Berube and Barnaby tied each other up. Rene Corbet tried the same with Richardson, who got his right arm free to pound away. Tocchet drew roughing, fighting, instigating, misconduct and game misconduct penalties. Five players on each side went to the box and the Flyers had to kill a five-on-three.

"Typical Philadelphia goon tactics," groused Brooks and the Flyers were ripped in the media for their lack of discipline.

"You have your detractors that say, 'That's [bullbleep],'" says Tocchet. "But selfishly for what he had called me and for the team, I thought it sent a message.

"It's not like Pittsburgh was scared all of a sudden, but they knew we were going down swinging. I didn't hear Wright or anybody say anything to me the next game or the rest of the series. So maybe it did resonate, I don't know."

It certainly did. Richardson remembers players in the locker room after Game Two saying they would win the next one. Rookie Gagne was one of those inspired.

"We lost the game but we won the fight, you know, and it wasn't even close," he recalls. "It was part of our blood, in our culture; it sent the message that we wouldn't lose."

But the Flyers never intended to goon their way back into the series. "When you are trying to run guys, your positioning is off," recalls Tocchet. "We had to get back to being methodical."

Though they had more than doubled Pittsburgh's shots in the first two games, Tugnutt had stopped 72 of 73. "I've seen Ronnie play for a long time," Primeau told reporters. "Who would have thought we would have an easier time with Dominik than Ronnie?"

Ramsay noted how rebounds were flying out past players trying too hard to crowd the net—LeClair in particular. The coach thought his team mostly was stopping itself. After having killed Buffalo on the powerplay, Philadelphia was 0-for-10 in two games against the Penguins.

"We have to calm down," said the placid coach, ordering the Flyers away from the rink for the first of the two days off before Game Three in Pittsburgh. "I think they have to understand that this is supposed to be fun.

"They should do something with family and friends, enjoy the day. We are good enough to win. We have to believe that and not press quite so much."

Richardson tried some reverse psychology. "When we get a couple that sneak in on [Tugnutt] like we did in Pittsburgh (a 3-2 Philadelphia victory on April 1), he gets down on himself. He's talking to himself, you can see it in his body action."

Meanwhile, Boucher already had had a conversation with himself, his mask hiding his nerves. "The extra few days off after Buffalo had not helped," he recalls. "All my good feelings were gone.

"I didn't particularly like playing in Pittsburgh. Old rink. Hated the locker room—it smelled. They had good players like (Alexei) Kovalev, (Martin) Straka and Jagr. I just had a bad feeling."

It helped the kid that the media had found another scapegoat for Games One and Two. Primeau, who had been on for all four even-strength Pittsburgh goals in the series and had only six goals and 14 assists in 64 career playoff games, decided to have a talk with reporters, in addition to himself, about his dismal postseason track record.

"Does it play in your mind?" Primeau said. "I think in the back of your mind, it has to.

"The criticism is just but it doesn't change the fact that I want to be out there. I want to try and be the guy. I felt really good in Game Two, too good. I took more chances than I should have and ended up getting caught a few times.

"We have worked hard, but we haven't worked smart. Now we get to find out what we're made of. The adversities we faced off the ice all season long were going to make us a better club, a closer-knit group. But that adversity was off the ice. Now it's on the ice and we get to see how we respond."

Primeau was removed from the first line with Recchi and LeClair and put between Tocchet and Gagne. Ramsay also scratched Eaton in favor of Burt who, in 10 years with Hartford/Carolina, never had made the second round.

The Flyers got the good start in Game Three that was badly needed.

Delmore, who had the team's best chances in the first two contests, slammed in a rebound low to Tugnutt's glove side just after a Zelepukin penalty expired. Therien poke-checked Kovalev at the Flyer line, and Jones rang one off Tugnutt's blocker and the post to make it 2-0 after a period.

But it didn't last. After Boucher had to shrug off Jiri Hrdina's shot at the shoulders, neither Desjardins nor Therien could find the puck, allowing Jagr to sneak in and, on the second whack, cut the lead in half at 0:40 of the second period.

If that goal was all scramble, the game-tying one almost 10 minutes later was a thing of beauty. Desjardins and Zelepukin chased Jagr out at the blueline and Straka got behind White to take a brilliant feed from the boards by Boughner for a tap-in.

Nevertheless, the Flyers were carrying the play, as they had been since the series started. LeClair put them back ahead with a stunning effort, fighting his way out front for a spinning backhander, retrieving the rebound, then finishing off a short give-and-go with Recchi while being taken down by Pat Falloon. But there was still 12:33 remaining in his duel with Jagr, who tackled LeClair to save one chance before Big John lifted the Pittsburgh star's stick on a dangerous chance while Primeau was in the penalty box.

Jagr was not going to be denied, though. He beat Desjardins at the Philadelphia line, took a drop from Straka via Hrdina, closed to the hash marks and wristed the puck past Boucher's blocker with 5:32 remaining.

"It's only tied, we're still in this," Berube shouted on the bench. The Flyers also were a goal away from going down 3-0 in the series. But after Therien rode off Jagr as he tried to cut in and Tugnutt made a kick save on Langkow to get the game to overtime, LeClair, who had been a Flyer for all eight of their consecutive sudden death losses declared, "This is great, one shot wins it.

The shots were 33-13 Philadelphia as overtime began, and, after good chances by LeClair, Recchi and Manderville, 10-to-1 for the Flyers in the extra session when Josef Beranek tried to move wide on Delmore on a rush and lost the puck.

Manderville picked it up and fed ahead to Hull while Jones took defenseman Janne Laukkenen wide, opening up the middle for Delmore, who was yelling for the puck practically all the way up ice. "You couldn't miss hearing him," said Jones, who relayed the puck from Hull onto Delmore's backhand as he reached the top of the circle.

The rookie put the puck on his forehand and fired. "I didn't even look where I was shooting and it went right where it was supposed to," recalls Delmore. The puck glanced off Tugnutt's catching arm and into the net at 11:01.

In the Flyers' ninth try over four playoff years, sudden death was their Grim Reaper no more. "We were drowning, now we have life jackets on," said Jones after the 4-3 victory forged with two goals by an undrafted rookie defenseman who had been sent back to the Phantoms five times during the season.

"It's hard for anyone to handle a defenseman that jumps up that quickly," said Ramsay. No faster than Bonnie and Carl Delmore did off their couch back in Windsor, Ontario. After attending both losses in Philadelphia, they had been discouraged by their son from going to Pittsburgh.

"When you get a chance to call your parents after doing something like that, that's really what it's about," recalls Delmore. "I've never heard them so happy, even if my dad couldn't think of anything better to say than, 'Great game!'"

Delmore had gone through two entry drafts—475 total selections—without being taken, one more reason for the Flyers to believe that this was becoming a special spring. There seemed no ceiling to their confidence until equipment manager Turk Evers nailed the shoes of Vanbiesbrouck, Langkow, Therien and Eaton to the locker room roof during the off-day practice.

That practice was necessary to figure out a way to stop Jagr, who had five goals in the first three games. "That was the best I've ever seen him play against us," said Desjardins, twice beaten on Jagr goals during Game Three. "I can do a better job on him for sure."

"You could throw a blanket on him and he's going to get chances; he's that good right now," said Manderville who, along with Jones and Hull, had been used successfully against Jagr in the overtime.

Jones, Tocchet and Berube didn't want to spend time after practice at their hotel. They went to the movies only to emerge from a cinema complex in Bridgeville, PA to discover they had locked the keys into the rental car and left the motor running. "I remember Jonesy sitting on the ground without a care in the world," recalls Tocchet. "I was like, 'What are you doing? We gotta get out of here!'

"What a [bleep] show that was, calling the car rental place. I don't even remember how we got back."

Time also was hanging heavy on the hands of Lindros, who received permission from Dr. Kelly to join the Black Aces (callups from the Phantoms staying in shape in case of an emergency) for a no-contact scrimmage.

Lindros, trying to follow instructions, stepped aside as Francis Lessard attempted to put the puck between the Big E's skates. But Lessard raised his head and struck Lindros on the mouth, opening a 20-stitch cut and giving No. 88, whose headaches had not full subsided, another one.

"It was innocent, they just collided," recalls McCrossin. "But Francis was devastated and I was shaking when I called Clarkie and said, 'Bad news. Francis collided with Eric and I'm taking him to the doctors.'

"In all my years, I never met a man who was better to deal with than Clarkie. He just said, 'Okay.' I drove Eric, bleeding into a towel, to (Dr. Gary) Dorshimer's office (near Pennsylvania Hospital).

"He had this little office in an alleyway. I was going to drop Big E and go find a place to park. Eric says, 'No just pull up here and I'll wrap the towel on top of my windshield. No cop will come near it. He'll think somebody was seriously hurt.'

Dorshimer reported Big E had suffered a contusion of the lower lip, a laceration of the upper lip, and a superficial headache, postponing his upcoming check-up with Kelly and extending a run of bad luck that had streaked well beyond eerie.

"Bizarre, totally bizarre," said Snider in Pittsburgh after Dorshimer briefed reporters there while the puck was being dropped to start Game Four. But the Chairman hadn't seen anything yet.

Kovalev beat Boucher along the ice to the glove side with the first shot of the game at 2:27. Gagne, playing with a hand frozen because of a slash he had taken in Game Three, was hit by Boughner at center ice, fell on his wrist, and one attempted shift later, couldn't get a grip.

"I think they put in too much medicine; I couldn't feel anything," Gagne recalls. Fortunately Zelepukin, cross-checked by Wright into the net without a call, was able to return after missing a few shifts.

The Penguins were losing the battle of the zone time and again but, having been outshot in 18 straight games going back to the regular season, were not uncomfortable playing for a break. Boucher kept the deficit at just one by winning a race with Jagr to a loose puck—and getting a complimentary tap of the pads from the Pittsburgh star—then stopping Kasparaitis point blank after he got a step on Manderville.

Into the third period, the Flyers still were getting only sporadic clean looks at Tugnutt when Straka, beaten by a step in the high slot, slashed McGillis on the wrist and was called by referee Rob Shick.

Langkow won the resultant offensive zone draw cleanly from Hrdina and Desjardins one-timed a shot from the point. The puck glanced off the helmet of LeClair, who was tied up in the slot by Boughner, and broke down into the bottom of the net.

"I didn't even know I scored; I was just checking to see if I was bleeding," recalls LeClair.

The Penguins argued that his stick, above crossbar height and parallel to the ice as he jostled with Boughner, had touched the puck. Replays studied upstairs by Denis Morel, the series' supervisor of officials, were inconclusive, so he left the decision up to referees Schick and Marouelli, who let their call on the ice stand. At 4:47, the Flyers' first powerplay goal of the series in 17 attempts had tied the game 1-1.

Jagr got wide on Therien and fed Straka, who missed the net on a golden opportunity. Boucher then made a stop on Wright though traffic to get the game to overtime. LeClair, swiping the puck on an attempted Tugnutt handoff to Peter Popovic, could have won the game just 31 seconds into sudden death. There was time and space as he walked out at the opposite post, but instead he fed Langkow, who shot off the crossbar.

Almost six minutes later, the Penguins had a chance just as good when Jagr, with the help of a Straka pick, got away from Jones and hit Michal Rozsival coming in from the point. Boucher knocked away the 20-foot drive with his stick.

When LeClair fumbled a setup in the slot from Recchi, Burt picked up the puck and, with Tugnutt still on the other side of the net, missed. After a Tocchet steal, Langkow shot though Tugnutt's pads and wide.

Gagne, who had played just 6:54 through three periods, felt sensation returning to his hand as the freezing wore off and told Ramsay he could go, exactly what a coach hoping to roll four lines wanted to hear.

Eleven minutes and 38 seconds into the second overtime, the game became the longest in Flyer history, surpassing Game Six in Year One (1968), when Don Blackburn's tipped shot from center ice beat Blues goaltender Glenn Hall to tie the series.

It was beginning to look like a stroke of luck would be necessary this time, too. Philadelphia, getting significant offensive-zone time from the fourth line of Berube, Manderville and Hull, carried the play, but the Penguins had the better opportunities. Kovalev hit the post off a drop by Jagr before Boucher stopped Laukkenen with the knob of his stick.

With Boucher pulled after Tugnutt froze the puck for a faceoff 2.2 seconds before the buzzer, Jagr, nursing a hip-groin issue that had limited him to 63 regular-season games, didn't bother to hang on the bench, going to the locker room to steal an extra minute of rest.

"Jagr was playing hurt, I could tell," recalls Boucher. "I gave him a whack at one point and he really grimaced, part of the reason I felt we could win."

In the third overtime, the Flyers killed a Langkow high-sticking penalty for clipping Kovalev in the helmet, not allowing a Pittsburgh shot. Philadelphia then survived a too-many-men-on-the ice penalty when Jagr one-timed a perfect seam pass from Kovalev off the side of the net.

The Flyers were fortunate again when Robbie Brown's tip through traffic hit a spread-out Boucher on the right pad. But with Kasparaitis off for holding Primeau in the slot, Philadelphia cranked seven shots at Tugnutt, the best of which, by Recchi, ticked off the inside of the goalie's pads and went just wide behind him.

The supply of energy bars and gels in the locker room was exhausted before the break preceding the third overtime. "Juice, waters, Pedialyte and Powerade, popcorn in the coach's office, we'd gone through everything," recalls Worley.

This was no time or place for the weak of heart. The longer it went, the more devastating the defeat would be. And the exhausted Flyers were one mistake away from a 3-1 series' deficit.

"I think we settled into a mindset of staying patient," recalls Tocchet. "When you do that, you don't think of the bad outcome, only what you have to do as an individual. That's big for an athlete."

The Penguins still had the best one on the ice in Jagr, but as fatigue leveled the playing field, he wasn't much more effective than a Manderville.

"Jagr and Kovalev could kill you with one play," said Therien, an old Jagr-killer going back to their matchup in the series in 1997.

"My attitude was to keep the middle.

"They were shooting from the outside, never even tried to go one-on-one with us. If they knew how tired we were, I wonder if they would have tried to do something different, but we sure weren't going to tell them. They may not have been able to do it either."

Matchups went by the wayside as double-shifting became impossible. Relieving an exhausted teammate after just 20 seconds was the only priority. With little strength left to climb the boards, players almost all were using the gate. Forechecking was minimal as players dumped the puck and went off, fearful that cramps would seize their legs at the worst possible time.

Every inch of ice was contested vs. Ron Tugnutt and the Penguins.

"I'm so tired, I can't even yap anymore," Barnaby told Delmore, who on the contrary, remembers being a rookie in the Stanley Cup quarterfinals and, damn the fatigue, having the time of his life. It helped to be young, or to have played fewer minutes in regulation, or both, but some of the most dynamic players still found energy in bursts.

"At different points during the game, you'd go out, feel good, have that second wind," recalls LeClair. "And then there would be a shift where you thought you were going to pass out from exhaustion.

Primeau saw some opportunity in that, though. "There was less clutching, grabbing and hooking because guys were getting tired," he recalls. "So there actually ended up being more room out there.

"You could only go 20 seconds because the lactic acid in your l egs builds up, but I felt like I was using less energy, so for those 20 seconds, I felt good.

Not so Desjardins. "It was the worst experience of my life," he recalls. "I would go on the ice and my legs would cramp.

"It became the only time I can ever remember being scared to go out there, not be able to move and getting beat one on one."

Jones, accustomed to playing just 13 minutes a game, might as well have been attached to a retractable line. "I kept busy laughing at Jonesy," recalls Berube. "His knee was so bad that he would go over the boards, skate out 20 feet and come back. He knew it was too much for him."

"Get me a coffin, I am [bleeping] dead," Jones said one time as he reached a bench that, in the absence of sports drinks, was trying to gas up on laughs. "It was jovial," recalls Primeau. "All my years, all the playoff series I've played in, this probably was the most calm of any team I played on.

Jones asked Jagr, a reputed day-trader, for stock market reports, and even tried to talk him out of winning the game so he could avoid facing Scott Stevens and the Devils in the next round.

"He had a really good sense of humor," recalls Jones. "One time, when Craig sent me out on the powerplay early in the game, he looked at me and said, "There must be some mistake."

The pizza that had been ordered for the bus ride to the airport had arrived before the fourth overtime, so several players dove in. A few of them, Gagne remembers, munching while hooked up to IVs.

A joke Jones made with his shirt off and pizza sauce on his face rang true:

"All you fitness freaks, you got no more fat; you guys are done," he said, pinching his spare tire. "I'm like a bear. I hibernated for this the whole year; this is where I come to shine.

"We laughed our butts off," recalls Therien, but it occurred to him their butts just might fall off from fatigue. "Nobody has enough energy to score," he thought. "What if it doesn't end? What if we're here

all night?"

The participants lost track of the number of overtimes and the time of the morning.

"What period are we in?" Cashman asked Ramsay on the bench at one point.

"I don't know," said Ramsay, who ran out of sage advice to Jones, one urinal over at a period break. "Just keeping going, Jonsey," said the coach. "Just keep going."

"The 15-minute intermissions seemed to get shorter and shorter," Tugnutt would say later. "You walked in, changed shorts and by that time you were throwing equipment back on saying, 'OK, which end do I go to now?' or other things like, 'What time is it? What day is it?'

"Or 'Who are we? And 'What are we doing here?'"

The trainers and equipment managers didn't have any time to ponder such big-picture questions.

"It was like Groundhog Day," said Evers. "It just kept happening over and over and over again.

"We went through five or six dozen t-shirts. Some guys wore two or three jerseys and some went through three pairs of gloves. We had hair dryers and fans going all over the place."

As the length of the game began to challenge that of NHL marathons dating back to the 1930s and 1940s, the broadcasters dutifully marked each milestone as it was passed. Tim Saunders, who reported to work with a cold, had the tea and honey ready, but his voice was holding up fine.

"This game could be on ESPN Classic before it is over," said ESPN's play-by-play voice Steve Levy as overtime period four began and Boucher made a superior pad save on Beranek, set up by Brown.

Indeed, Boucher felt his job actually was getting easier as it went. "The shots were slowing down, you could better read them," he recalls.

It became the fourth-longest game in NHL history—passing a 1943 Toronto win over Detroit, midway through the fourth overtime. In the final minute of that period, it went to No. 3—passing a Pittsburgh 1996 victory in Washington as the longest game of the expansion era.

There were about 9,000 fans remaining in the 16,958-seat Mellon Arena. Whatever was left of the pizza in the Flyer locker room was cold, some famished players just nibbling on the crust, figuring it safer to digest than the cheese. "If they had let me, I would have gone to the concession stands to buy food for us," said Vanbiesbrouck.

Jones was out of jokes. "He said, 'The good thing about this is that the next goal, the game is over,'" recalls Desjardins. "He didn't say anything about us scoring it."

Worley, his IV bags exhausted, went to the paramedics stationed in the arena to borrow more. "We didn't have enough for everybody, so we used them for guys who already were having issues," he recalls. "Some guys did more than one bag."

Before the fifth overtime, both LeClair, who had been cramping on the bench, and Recchi took IVs. Boucher, cramping as he tried to stretch in his crease, suddenly wished he had taken one too, and stopped out of fear of bringing on pain that would finish him for the night. But he found the strength to get his catcher up on Ian Moran after the Penguin prevented a chip-out by Desjardins.

After an extended Penguin cycle, Desjardins made a block on Laukkenen's drive, then Boucher stopped Jagr up the slot, after, seemingly with his last ounce of strength, he spun off Delmore.

White pounced on the puck after Boughner lost his stick and fed Jones, who missed high and just wide. But Primeau, who had fanned on a golden Recchi setup during the third overtime, felt a surge when he jumped on for the next shift.

"I had kept telling myself I had played [just 23] games that season, I should have more energy left than guys who played 80," he recalls.

The Penguins dumped the puck out and were changing when Richardson went halfway back in the Philadelphia zone to retrieve. He passed up the boards to McGillis, who fed ahead to a streaking Primeau, who took the pass barely onside, just before it got to the red line.

The next shift of Pittsburgh forwards was not back in the play, but Kasparaitis was in solid one-on-one defending position as Primeau barely saved a skittish puck from rolling off his stick, then pulled up at the right faceoff dot.

"Two other times in the game I was one-on one with Kasparaitis," Primeau would say. "One time I went around the net, one time he kind of met me at the post. So this was the third time.

"I opened up like I was going to drive wide and as soon as he crossed over, I brought the puck back."

Kasparaitis couldn't stop in time. "I was kind of surprised," he would say. The puck was a foot to the right of the dot when Primeau let go a wrister just before being whacked on the right arm by the desperate Kasparaitis. Tugnutt barely had time to twitch as the puck flew over his shoulder into the top of the net.

Primeau had plenty of strength left to lift both his arms. "It's over," he thought. "And I finally scored in the playoffs."

The Flyers came off the bench faster than some of them had moved for two periods, almost trampling Richardson and Jones, who were coming back to the bench for their change.

"We were making the only noise I heard in the building," said Primeau. At 2:35 a.m., after 92:01 of overtime, the Flyers were 2-1 winners of the third-longest game in NHL history—and the longest in 64 years—to even the series, 2-2.

They mobbed each other enthusiastically, at least for zombies. In going to the locker room quickly, they were not too preoccupied with their relief and joy to notice the faces of some Penguins as they left the ice.

"Even though we knew we had done something special, in our locker room, we didn't have music on and guys weren't dancing around like sometimes when you win," recalls Tocchet. "It was a really happy locker room but we could imagine theirs.

"I wasn't feeling sorry for them—I would never feel sorry for another team—but I thought, 'Those guys must be devastated right now. This is the time to put the foot on the gas pedal.'"

Indeed, the Penguins were feeling like road kill.

"I tried to do my best and somebody did something a little better," said Kasparaitis. "I'm going to see that play a lot for the rest of my life."

Tugnutt wasn't likely to remember any of the 71 shots he had stopped, 14 more than Boucher, only the one that won the game. "I was thinking hopefully that it just hit the post," the Penguin goalie said. "When I looked back, I just got numb.

"It's the wildest thing I've ever been through. What period was it, the sixth? The eighth? Your mind is in a daze."

To achieve the sublime, the Flyers had gone through the surreal. "It was a weird feeling, like you're going through the motions out there," said Langkow, who had taken 59 faceoffs, as he ate a cold piece of pineapple pizza.

McGillis had played a game-high 61:05. "I'm glad I didn't know that," he told reporters while Boucher, who had played 151:48 admitted he had been worried about having to say, '*No mas!*'

"That last period, there, that was enough, that was plenty," said the goalie. "You start cramping when you're just stretching, you know you're in trouble."

Desjardins spent much of the short plane ride home in the lavatory dry heaving. "I had been drinking just water, lots of water, but it was just making me go to the restroom all the time and not giving me the electrolytes I needed," he recalls. "It was just a horrible feeling."

Thus, he was not among the Flyers—and their Chairman, Snider—who remained so exhilarated even after landing well past daybreak that they went to the Penrose Diner for breakfast. What the hell, it was a bleary-eyed, but happy morning regardless in Philly, where 166,000 households, 43 percent of the audience that had started the overtime, were still tuned in at the finish.

"I went right home, but only slept about three-four hours," recalls Primeau.

"My parents were in town. I remember going to Atlantic City with them for the day, walking the boardwalk, trying to figure out how to re-reenergize."

The extra day off before Game Five was critical. But the First Union Center crowd helped, too, with a rocking warm-up, then exploded when Langkow beat Tugnutt between the pads just 23 seconds in. With Hans Jonsson off for hooking, Delmore fired past Tugnutt's glove to make it 2-0 after a period.

"The [Penguins] had come so far to get nothing (in Game Four)," recalls Boucher. "I think they were totally demoralized."

Another opening-shift goal in the second period—this one by McGillis—boosted the lead to 3-0. After Recchi connected on the powerplay, Jagr stayed on the bench to fight another day.

There was another star on this one. Delmore, set up by LeClair, smoked a one-timer for his second goal, chasing Tugnutt in favor of Peter Skudra.

"No, I wasn't thinking hat trick," Delmore recalls. "This already was crazy." But with the help of a spinning backhanded pass from Primeau, the rookie defenseman completed only the 10th three-goal game by a defenseman in Stanley Cup history.

"Even when I dream at night, I don't dream that," Delmore told the media after 225 hats—plus four orange wigs—were thrown onto the ice. The Flyers took a 3-2 lead in the series with a 6-3 victory.

"The extra day (of rest) was very important; I don't know what they would have been like without it," said Worley. "But to look as good as they did today is really a testament to all the work they did leading up to this."

Given more distance from the Game Four crusher and a home crowd for Game Six, the Penguins didn't figure to go away easily. Sure enough, with only 48 seconds played, Boughner, who had sworn vengeance against Richardson when hit in the chest with a puck during Game Five, sent a message instead through Primeau. Seconds after an errant pass had gone by the Flyer center in the neutral zone, a shoulder to the jaw leveled him.

Primeau appeared to be out even before his head bounced off the ice. He had regained consciousness before being wheeled off on a stretcher, telling LeClair on his way to UMPC Presbyterian Hospital of his intention to be back before the game was over.

Ramsay summoned his Flyers to the bench. "You got a choice, boys," he said. "You can get your revenge right now, we can get this over with, or you can try to win the game for him.

"I think it was Toch who said, 'Let's win this game.'"

Ramsay moved Gagne, who had not played in Game Five because of his hand problem, to center in Primeau's place. With Boucher making a big blocker save on Jagr, the Flyers survived penalties to Therien and Berube, the latter ending a jabbing contest with Kovalev by breaking a stick over him.

Philadelphia was being outplayed until Jiri Slegr got called for interfering with Tocchet. On the powerplay, LeClair kicked the puck to Recchi while being taken down by Boughner, and Recchi flipped the first goal of the game into a half-empty net at 11:04.

In the opening minute of the second period, Desjardins made a save at the point and Recchi smartly reversed behind the net to feed LeClair, whose tap-in at the right post was his fourth point in three games.

When Jagr hit the crossbar just a minute later, the Flyers, up 2-0 after taking just six shots, were fortunate again, but they had a sense of their own inevitability. "You got the feeling somehow, someway, we were going to win the game," recalls Therien.

They nursed that two-goal lead until Manderville fell during a faceoff, Richardson turned too late, and Corbet roofed one from just 10 feet out, pulling Pittsburgh to within 2-1 with 9:14 remaining.

Boucher made a pad save on Jagr from the top of the circle. Therien deflected away a Hrdina pass for a wide-open Jagr, and Lang missed a good chance from near the faceoff dot. Down the stretch Boucher got to the post to stop Corbet's wraparound, then Jagr had the puck cleanly whisked from him by LeClair, who took it the other way in the final minute.

Desjardins stopped Corbet and Boucher blockered the Penguins' last prayer, by Laukkenen, from center ice. Richardson was keeping the puck in the corner when the clock ran out, yet he still was the first Flyer to reach a jumping-up-and-down Boucher.

"It seemed like an eternity," the goalie said about the final nine minutes, this coming from a kid who had played into seeming infinity two games earlier. Philadelphia's series-clinching 2-1 victory was the most evenly played of the six games and also probably Boucher's best.

"His composure surprised me," said Barnaby. "I tried to talk to him a little bit, but that didn't work. He never unraveled."

Boucher had worked at keeping the pressure off himself. "I said coming into these playoffs that no matter what happened, this would be good for my career," he told reporters. "Not many 23-year-olds have an opportunity like this one. And when you win, it's irreplaceable."

LeClair, trusted on the ice for the final 1:30 with the Flyers hanging by a goal, had outlasted Jagr's hot start to become the most dominant forward in the series.

"It really started toward the end of the season," Ramsay said to the media. "Johnny found out what it was like when you play in every situation and he realized he had to elevate his game if we were going to survive.

"He won battles, chased pucks, and did anything there was to do. He wanted to be the man."

So had the worn-down Jagr, who didn't have a point in the final three contests. "Every time I skated hard, I would feel the pain," he said.

But it didn't hurt as much as the loss.

"We're not a perfect team, don't get me wrong, but we blew it," said Jagr. "Maybe we didn't have enough experience. Maybe when we were up 2-0, we thought it would be easy."

Brooks announced he had coached his last game. To express his regrets for the hit, Boughner sought out Ramsay after the handshake line and also called Primeau. "I played with Keith in the minors (at Adirondack). I know him well off the ice," Boughner said. "It is not my intent to see someone carried off on a stretcher, but it was a clean hit."

Primeau disagreed, but accepted the apology regardless. The only payback that mattered now would have to be delivered against a New Jersey team that was 11-2-2 against Philadelphia over the last three seasons. The Devils, who had swept Florida and beaten the Leafs in six—holding Toronto to just six shots in the clincher—had scored the most goals in the league, making New Jersey a favorite for more reasons than its patience and Marty Brodeur.

"They have had our number the last couple years, but everything is totally different now," said Therien.

The experts, noting the difficulty of the hard-forechecking Flyers over the years to negotiate the Devil neutral-zone trap, didn't buy it. Thus, the more brainpower Philadelphia could bring, the better. Neilson returned to the ice for practice. "It's a little strange, but we have to accept it," he said. "I've been a head coach and an assistant coach several times."

The Flyers weren't the only Eastern Conference finalist that had made a change on their bench in mid-season. For the Devils, Larry Robinson had replaced Robbie Ftorek with just eight games left before the playoffs. Only seven Devils and three Flyers—Therien, LeClair and Desjardins—remained from their last playoff meeting—the 1995 conference championship series New Jersey had won in six games on the way to the Stanley Cup. And one player, Zelepukin, had changed sides.

"Now the Flyers start to do some good things, protect the middle, play more defensively," Zelepukin said. "We don't leave the zone without the puck, there's nobody cruising around. Everybody protects their spot."

Safeguarding something even more critical—his future health—barely was a passing thought to Primeau when he decided to play Game One at the First Union Center.

"The neuropsychologist (Dr. Gerri McGinnis) said, 'You passed the baseline; I can't keep you from playing, so just do me a favor and be careful,'" Primeau recalls. "I kind of chuckled and said, 'I'm okay, I know what I'm doing,' then walked down the street with a cutting headache from concentrating so hard during my baseline exam."

He told reporters that his wife Lisa had not offered an opinion. "She knows I'll probably ignore it," Primeau said. "She explained that sometimes you're so focused by a goal that it clouds the rest of the picture. That may be the case.

"Yeah, I'm a father and a husband, but I'm also a hockey player and I want to be out there."

He would play 17:05, deliver four hits, and win 15 of 20 faceoffs. But when McGillis tried to nail Jason Arnott and collided instead with Gagne, Scott Niedermayer one-timed a Randy McKay pass just 55 seconds into the game. Recchi tied it at 8:20 on a rebound, but Petr Sykora put a softie between Boucher's legs and, just 26 seconds later, Bobby Holik converted with the over-aggressive McGillis being out of position again for a 3-1 lead.

"We tried to throw the body, maybe too much," said McGillis, but when the Flyers settled down, Philadelphia outshot the Devils 20-8, surrendering only Holik's powerplay goal through the remainder of New Jersey's 4-1 victory.

"This is not a typical Flyers team of the past," warned Holik. "They have more speed and depth.

"Marty made some big saves for us, otherwise this would have been a different game."

Tocchet agreed. "I really believe we think we can win," he said.

To back that up, he outmuscled Brian Rafalski and scored just 1:38 into Game Two. But after Scott Gomez tied it off a puck that hit a discarded stick, Lindros, the discarded captain who had just been cleared by Dr. Kelly to resume workouts with McCrossin, met with the media.

"As a hockey player, you're given a career of about 10 years," Lindros said. "To miss one playoff is 10 percent, that's a big chunk.

"I wasn't able to play last year. This is what you work for all year and why we are really bearing down."

Dr. Kelly had described the recovery process to Lindros as a cerebral gas tank filling up. "Feeling right, feeling sharp, feeling clear," said Eric. "I've got to believe the gas station is open."

The Flyers, who had been forced to floor it to beat Pittsburgh, looked like they were on fumes in the second period. Primeau unwisely fought McKay before Arnott bounced one in off Therien to give New Jersey the lead. Patrik Elias, with Delmore badly caught up ice trying to join a rush, finished off a three-on-one to make the score 3-1.

"We thought it was going to be a walk in the park," recalls Elias.

With Holik off for interfering with Boucher, the Flyers fed that belief with an aimless and shotless powerplay until Tocchet, given an inordinate amount of time to hold the puck along the left wing boards, saw Desjardins breaking for the net past a flat-footed Sergei Brylin. Tocchet hit the defenseman perfectly at the post for a tap-in with 39 seconds left in the period and everything changed.

"We were in complete control and they got that backdoor goal," recalls Brodeur. "The crowd got going and then next thing we knew, we couldn't figure out how to play them anymore. It was just weird how that goal messed us up big time."

Barely more than minute into the third period, Zelepukin beat Ken Daneyko along the back wall and Tocchet one-timed his 50th career playoff goal through Brodeur's legs to tie the score. Just 52 seconds after that, Jones forced a Niedermayer giveaway, enabling a Tocchet-Langkow two-on-one. Tocchet shoved defenseman Colin White just as Langkow's rebound caromed off White and Brodeur, into the net.

The ice was littered with 643 hats in the belief that Tocchet had scored three straight times to bring the Flyers into the lead. Langkow, the last guy to touch the puck, instead got the goal, but after Primeau had won three defensive-zone draws in the final minute and Philadelphia had hung on for a series-tying 4-3 victory, Tocchet received most of the credit.

"He just drove through people," said Ramsay. "Our whole team played like that, especially late. It was a really desperate effort."

The 36-year-old Tocchet had turned back the clock to 1987. Actually, in the minds of the fans who had witnessed that remarkable drive by Mike Keenan's club to within one game of the Stanley Cup, so had this entire 2000 team.

"I've only been here three months," Tocchet told reporters. "But teams don't go through in five years some of the stuff that this one has in one.

"Every day there's something new; you could shock this team now with something else and guys wouldn't even care. It's amazing. I could be in Phoenix playing golf right now. I don't know how many chances I have left.

"This game really gets us back in the ballgame but it also makes New Jersey think. They know it's going to be a series now. I think Jersey respected us, but I think we respected Jersey too much.

"It's a great hockey club, a great organization, but they haven't done much the last four or five years (just one series victory from 1996-1999). I don't mean to sound disrespectful, but they're struggling to make a name for themselves and go to the Stanley Cup Final just like we are."

Not only was the series tied but, in Tocchet's view, the playing field evened. "I was just trying to put a little pressure on them," he recalls. "I don't know if it worked or not."

Regardless of whether the Flyers were getting into the Devils' heads, their opponents complained about being hit there. Robinson said he was tired of being "elbowed in the head and punched in the face.. The Flyers feed off that stuff and that's not our style."

Such tactics had left Philadelphia 0-7-1 at the Meadowlands since their last win, 6-23-2 in the regular season and playoffs combined since 1990-91. What's more, Langkow had been concussed by a third-period Stevens hit in Game Two, causing Ramsay to scramble the lines once more. He summoned Mark Grieg from the Black Aces, put Primeau with Jones and Tocchet, and moved Recchi into the middle between Gagne and LeClair, who would be playing right wing for the first time as a Flyer.

Claude Lemieux clashes with John LeClair.

"I actually like it," claimed LeClair. "It's easier to protect the puck."

Three minutes into Game Three, he moved it perfectly to Recchi, who finished off a two-on-one that had been created by Vladimir Malakhov's fumble at the point. Claude Lemieux split Richardson and McGillis to tie it just 1:27 later, but Jones put in a Tocchet rebound to restore the lead, 2-1.

Boucher held it with the save of the series, flinging his blocker up on Elias after missing a poke check on his shorthanded breakaway. "Desperation," the goalie would say. "I got lucky." But good fortune builds confidence. Tocchet shot a puck off its edge through Brodeur's legs from the top of the circle to make it 3-1.

Philadelphia was playing like a team and LeClair took one for it—a 36-stitch cut on the side of the nose caused by a Brodeur follow-through. Niedermayer put a shot through Arnott's legs and past a screened Boucher with 4:01 to go to cut the lead to one. But McGillis blocked a drive with his face—"At least I used my head for something," he smiled, referring to his pinching misadventures in Game Two—and Gagne went around Brodeur for a putaway goal with 1:49 remaining.

"Right before the series, you read and heard it was going to be a cakewalk," said Tocchet after the Flyers had taken a 2-1 series lead with their 4-2 victory. "Guys take it personal, sure."

Desjardins knew better than to take seriously the perpetually trash-talking Claude Lemieux, who, noting the C on the Philadelphia captain's chest, said, "What does the C stand for? Selfish?" Tocchet was only too happy to share his irascible opponent's spelling skills with the public, annoying Lemieux, who felt he should be allowed to be mean in private.

Whether or not the Devils had been caught reading their own press clippings, the difference in Game Three was black and white to Robinson. "They played our game better," said the coach, while Brodeur added, "It was my worst game of the playoffs."

Game Four didn't start any better for him. His soft attempt to shovel the puck to Rafalski went to Gagne, who threw it up from the corner for a Recchi redirection that went through Brodeur's armpit, off his hip, and into the net. Primeau turned it over for a Holik goal, sending the game into the third period tied 1-1 until Ramsay put out the Manderville-White-Berube checking line with eight minutes remaining.

Manderville forced Gomez's giveaway just inside the line and Berube, on his backhand, chopped down a wobbly McGillis drive past Brodeur with 7:02 remaining.

"What was he doing out there?" Jones turned around to ask Ramsay, all due respect to a coach on a roll while steam was pouring out the ears of his counterpart. Robinson demonstratively waved his arms in utter disgust.

LeClair was clipped on the face by a Brodeur follow-through for the second consecutive game—"Starting to wonder if the first wasn't intentional," he later would half-joke—but the puck bounced to Desjardins, who fed Gagne. He went around Brodeur for a deposit with 3:10 remaining and the 3-1 victory gave Philadelphia a stunning 3-1 series lead.

"After Chief got that goal, we thought, "Man, everything is going our way, we're destined to win this," recalls Therien.

Berube, scoring for just the third time in 86 career playoff games, had been the ninth Flyer with a game-winning goal during a run that had brought the team to within one game of the Stanley Cup Final. The least expected of the nine probably was the most appreciated.

"I've seen Chief with broken knuckles," recalls Tocchet. "Tough guys work the hardest, stay the longest after practice, don't get the glory.

"He kept everybody together, was a very respected guy in that locker room, whether he played one shift or 30. He always was cheering on guys when they scored, so that's the guy you're really happy for. It's his stage, his moment, you're excited for him to have it."

Philadelphia had turned New Jersey upside down with some classic role-reversal. Berube, the grinder suddenly turned scorer, today credits LeClair, the star who was goalless for the series, for his relentless work.

"On right wing, LeClair was going against Stevens every shift, and Stevens couldn't handle him," recalls Berube.

During the bus ride headed south on the NJ Turnpike, Big John's rapidly closing eye watered throughout the card game, while back at Exit 16W, tears of a different cause were being shed.

A red-eyed Robinson, exasperated mostly by the Devils' willingness to play into the Flyers' hands by refusing to dump the puck, kicked a trashcan in the locker room and yelled so loudly he could be heard by reporters waiting to be let in.

"I wish I could give you three words or 10 words he said, but the words weren't as important as the emotion," recalls Ken Daneyko. "Larry wasn't a rah-rah guy normally; that's why it was real.

"The Flyers had a really good team and had us dead to rights, foot on the throat. We were as demoralized as any team I ever have been on. But we could see he cared so much and that he wanted to make sure we cared as much as he did."

Recalls Brodeur, "It was just so emotional, begging us to trust him to do the things he would say. It was one of the best speeches I ever heard a coach give."

In order to become the first team ever to rally from a 3-1 deficit to win a conference final, the Devils would need patience as much as emotion to win twice in Philadelphia. But the Flyers had done a better job maintaining their composure away from home, where they were 6-1 during the playoffs, as opposed to 5-3 at the First Union Center.

"We have to come out controlled," said Boucher before Game Five. "Maybe that's why we've played so darn well on the road, doing the little things to take the crowd out of it. Maybe at home at times it gets a little crazy."

Richardson remembers being concerned with his team's demeanor. "We were loose and I worried about it," he recalls. "But we had gotten there by being loose."

There was another challenge to the Flyers staying in the moment. "The talk that Eric is coming back, it's strong now," recalls Tocchet. "And not everybody on the team felt good about it."

But there were no such mixed feelings about a significant contributor like Langkow, who, after becoming concussed in Game Two, became available again for Game Five. In the short term, like Lindros in the long, Philadelphia had thrived during Langkow's absence. But disruption of the lines was much less Ramsay's concern than getting back a top-two center.

The coach moved the emergency centerman, Recchi, back to the right wing and LeClair to the left, never mind his success on the right side.

Three minutes into Game Five at a First Union Center wired for the kill, Brodeur had to make a stick save on Burt off the faceoff, then a glove on a Langkow drive following a Recchi steal. Boucher then made a pad save on Gomez off a Lemieux passout, but the first big breakdown was the Devils', when Tocchet fought through a White stick check at center, trapping him and two forwards, sending the Flyers into the New Jersey end four-on-one with only Malakhov back.

When Primeau's pass was too close to Desjardins' body for him to get his stick on it, the golden opportunity was squandered and the adrenaline in the building drained away.

While Manderville was off for interfering with Niedermayer at the point, a release was being passed out to the media.

"Eric Lindros was examined and cleared today in Chicago by Dr. James Kelly to participate in full-team practices," was all it read.

Philadelphia was two seconds away from killing the penalty when Arnott shot a puck end-over-end from above the left circle that beat Boucher on the short side to give the Devils a 1-0 lead.

"I didn't pick it up right away," Boucher said later. "But he shoots it pretty good and he blew it past me."

Less than five minutes later, after Brodeur had made a good kick save on a Primeau one-timer and Boucher had countered with a big left pad save on Alexander Mogilny, Malakhov picked off a Jones lob out of the Flyer zone towards Primeau. While Primeau, struggling with a skate problem, was unable to get back into the play, Boucher made a shoulder save on Jay Pandolfo, but was off balance when McGillis couldn't find the rebound. Holik pounced to made it 2-0.

Primeau immediately went up the tunnel to get his skate sharpened, but the damage was done. Relief blew through the Devil bench.

"That killer punch, an early goal would have really hurt them," recalls Desjardins. "But if we didn't get it, we had to not give them anything and make them believe it was going to be too hard to come back.

"Stuff it in their face all the time is what I sensed we didn't do."

New Jersey outshot Philadelphia 14-6 in the first period, then added a third goal early in the second, when Elias got inside McGillis and finished off a two-on-one with Sykora. The Devils' control remained complete even after a funky bounce behind the net enabled Primeau to feed a Zelepukin powerplay goal.

The arena half emptied during the third period, as the New Jersey tank of confidence half-filled with a 4-1 victory made the Flyer series lead 3-2.

"I think because we had faced some adversities and calmly worked through them, we started to build a sense of invincibility," recalls Primeau. "We just thought we were going to finish this off.

"We had gotten ahead of ourselves, no question."

LeClair wholeheartedly—and publicly—agreed.

"We were thinking it was just going to happen," he said disgustedly. "You earn your bounces and I don't think we earned too much. It's incredibly disappointing."

A win would have given Philadelphia up to a week to rest for the Final and time to re-integrate Lindros into the lineup. But now they had a quandary and a potentially divided locker room.

"[Lindros] had a press conference during the (second) game," recalls Recchi. "That bothered me. What's the focal point—Eric or the team?"

Clarke thought it would be a mistake to bring Lindros back, but told Ramsay it was his call. The coach didn't feel it wise to make the decision in a vacuum.

"I think Rammer called about seven or eight of us in after the game and said 'Eric wants to come back,'" recalls Tocchet. "I could feel a little bit of discomfort with Rammer, like, 'What do I do?' A couple guys spoke up."

"It was a discussion of an hour," recalls Therien. "I personally did not want him to come back. I just felt that things were going so good. The guys loved the team, loved the coaches, it was as good as it ever was here. The majority thought, 'No.'"

According to those at the meeting, Desjardins seemed the player most against Lindros returning.

"I think we all felt we were better with Eric in the lineup," Desjardins recalls. "But what we felt was that we didn't want him to come back and have it change everything that we had worked so hard to put together.

"We had a strong feeling as a team. We were going to war together. We didn't want Big E to come back and do the things the way Big E wanted things to be done. We wanted to make sure he came back and did things we were doing as a team.

"I knew if he came in and played the way we wanted to play, we were a lot better with him. But the other thing is, he hadn't played in a long time. Was he really ready to come in and play that kind of intense hockey?

"I felt some guys didn't want him to play, but I never said that."

Tocchet, being the relative newcomer, was asked for his opinion last.

"I said I couldn't speak to what had happened in Eric's mind or anybody's mind," recalls Tocchet. "But at that moment, I wanted to win. I had visions of the parade that the Broad Street Bullies had told me about.

"So I said, 'It's between playing Eric or Peter White. And, no offense to White, I want Eric Lindros in the lineup.'"

His concerns, however, were the same as those of Desjardins. The players thought they had to know what Lindros was thinking. They called upon his biggest supporter at the meeting, Tocchet, to find out.

"I said, 'Okay, give me the phone,'" recalls Tocchet.

"If Eric tells me, 'I'm ready to play, I want back in,' then let's go.

"But if he is hemming and hawing and pulls the old, 'Well, this happened and that happened,' then I would say, 'That's it. You're out,' and relayed that to the guys.

"I had to know, 'Are you all in? Are you with us?'"

"I relayed that message to Eric on the phone. The call was very short. There was a little bit of tension there like, 'Of course I want to play, why are you even asking me?'

"He was kind of hemming and hawing about whether he would be accepted in the room, trivial kind of stuff. I said, 'At this point, I don't give a [bleep] whose fault it was, or if it was anybody's fault at all. We got a chance to do something special.'

"It wasn't a warm and fuzzy phone call, but it wasn't malicious either. He said, basically, 'I want to play,' and that's all I wanted to hear."

Tocchet told Lindros—who in a lengthy interview for this book said he did not wish to talk about any of the events that caused him to become estranged from the Flyers—that the team leaders all felt that he should not wait until Game Seven, which was believed to be his preference.

John LeClair, Mark Recchi and Daymond Langkow jam Martin's Brodeur's crease.

"If he is ready to play, then he plays in Game Six," Richardson said.

Vanbiesbrouck, still wondering if Lindros should play at all, called him after Tocchet did.

"Toc is pretty straightforward," Vanbiesbrouck recalls. "I was more sensitive to Eric getting hurt again, so that's kind of the angle I took.

"I was like, 'What if you sustain another blow to your head?' He was like, 'Well, that's a good point.'

"I wasn't on the ice, paying the high price, so I didn't want to get too deep into it. I was going with what the guys wanted to do. But if I had been the coach, I don't know how much I would have brought the team into it to answer the question.

"You make all the other decisions and then you're asking everybody's opinion on this one? I just would have said, 'This is a tough decision and the one I made has to be supported.' In my opinion, part of the job as a coach and as manager is to take the drama and emotion out of the game, not put it in."

Ramsay recalls draining practically every beer from his office refrigerator over the course of two hours, "wondering if I was doing the right thing and what to do next."

But to the media the next day, he expressed not a doubt in the world. Asked if inserting Lindros at the expense of another player would alter the chemistry, Ramsay said, "If we thought that, it wouldn't happen.

"This was a tough decision because I wanted to be fair to everybody. Eric said the right things and he seemed, as I suspected, very sincere about his desire to come back and be part of the team.

"He's been a big part of it for a long time and I felt he deserved that opportunity."

Asked if the attention towards the decision was a distraction to a team one win from the Stanley Cup Final, Ramsay smiled at 100 reporters and said a mocking, "Nooooooooooo."

The coach announced his players would not be answering any questions about Lindros. "It's a team decision," Ramsay said. "Everybody supported it and we've said what has to be said.

"We're not going to deal with this. Otherwise, it's just going to drive us crazy."

Of course, reporters asked anyway. Desjardins at least conceded the distraction.

"It's going to be tough," he said. "But it doesn't matter how hard it is as long as you find a way to deal with it.

"We are 60 minutes from being in the Stanley Cup Final."

The Lindros apology Clarke had insisted was in order never happened. Neither had the meeting between Eric, Snider and Clarke.

"We just forgot about that," Clarke told reporters. "There's no point now.

"It's been so long ago, it's hard to know what it was all about even."

Of course that wasn't true, but the GM was determined to maintain solidarity. "It's been a long time, but it's not as if he hasn't been training," Clarke said. "If he's ready, he's got to play. It's the end of the year. You don't have much time to wait.

"A lot of times guys come back from injuries and they're all fired up the first two or three games—you get a lot out of them. Sometimes they fall off a little bit after that, but I think it will be fine."

He laughed. "We seem to play better when it's all [bleeped] up. It's only been like that for three months."

White, a solid contributor during that time, was coming out of the lineup regardless. "I've had a chance to be here," Clarke's son-in-law told reporters. "Even if I don't get to play anymore, as long as we raise that Stanley Cup, I'll know I was part of it; it's not like I didn't play any games at all.

"If we get one of the best players in the world back in the lineup, it definitely helps the team."

Lindros did his part to sound instead like just another Peter White coming back from another injury.

"Obviously we're not given [much] time, but I feel right now that I can help out," he said.

Meanwhile, Daneyko remembers the Devils wisely being determined to have no opinion. "You want to add a player like that to your lineup. But does it disrupt what you've got going?" he recalls thinking. "That wasn't for me to judge and we didn't want to get caught up in it."

But the opponents never dismissed Lindros's potential impact. "We knew he was a key player who could change the tide regardless of how they were doing without him," Brodeur recalls.

"We knew he wasn't going to play at center on the top line because at center he had to look on both sides of the ice and that's difficult for a guy trying not to get hit, especially when you have a guy like Scotty Stevens out there."

The Flyers' focus on the road during their run had been extraordinary. It was disturbed now, the only question being how much.

"I was a kid, they tried to shield all this from me," recalls Boucher. "I had done as well as I had done by worrying about myself only.

"But I couldn't understand why guys would get so rattled about him coming back."

Recalls Tocchet, "I don't know if there was as much (pregame goofiness) as there usually was. Maybe that was all because it was Game Six, but we had shown some of that in crucial moments up to that point.

"I was watching him from the bench, wondering what he is was going to do, how he was going to play. Would he take the puck and try to go the length of the ice? He could do that."

Ramsay went back to what had worked so well for his team in Games Three and Four, putting Recchi back at center and LeClair on the right wing. Lindros, wearing a new type mouth guard that protruded the lower jaw—hopefully cushioning the TMJ joint—was going to play the right side of the third line with Langkow and Zelepukin.

"Ramsay did it right, didn't disrupt anything," recalls LeClair. "It's not easy to jump back out there, so playing Eric on the wing was smart, really smart."

Just 2:05 in, the Big E took his first shift in 73 days, dropping Steve Kelly with a body check, then doing it again the next time out. On his fourth shift, Lindros nailed Lemieux.

Tocchet had the best opportunity of a cautious first period but couldn't control a bouncing Primeau feed. With two minutes to go before the intermission, Gomez, off a drop pass by Mogilny, fired a riser that Boucher couldn't duck.

The second time the goalie had been hit in the mask during the series was many times more frightening than the first. The puck had lodged in his cage mask, but blinded, Boucher thought the puck was in his right eye.

"I could smell the rubber," he recalls. "It was scary."

He whipped off his mask. The puck stayed lodged, a much better place for it than the alternative.

"You're telling me, there is nothing in my eye?" Boucher said to John Worley.

"No," said the trainer.

"My cheekbone was just very slightly bruised and that was all," recalls Boucher. "I just couldn't believe I wasn't cut.

"After that, I became fanatical about changing my cage if it was bent."

When a screwdriver couldn't pry out the puck, Boucher finished the period in his old Phantom mask. His good one was ready for the second 20 minutes, as had to be its wearer. The Devils so controlled the play that LeClair didn't record Philadelphia's first shot in the second period until there was 2:24 remaining. But thanks to a big Boucher stop on Holik, whose pairing with Lemieux since an injury to Sergei Nemchinov in Game Four was starting to make a difference for New Jersey, the game remained scoreless.

Ramsay pulled Boucher for a faceoff in the Devil end with 2.7 seconds remaining before the intermission. Lindros, taking only his third shift of the period and first with LeClair, won the draw, and from the goal line, fired a Desjardins' rebound into Brodeur, then a second one over him and under the crossbar.

The green light, not the red one, was on, however. Replays showed the clock at 0.0 before the puck had left Lindros's stick on the second shot. The game still was scoreless.

"Obviously, it would have helped," Lindros would say afterwards. "But at the same time, we were headed into the third period on the road tied up."

The Devils, however, seemed to relish the opportunity more. "They were becoming the Jersey we knew," recalls Tocchet. "Smart dump-ins, suffocating you defensively."

In the third, Boucher slid across with stacked pads to make a glove save on Holik, then, after Arnott knocked down a Desjardins clear and Sykora faked LeClair, the goalie was saved by the post. The Flyers continued to generate little. Lindros, who was stopped on a walkout by Brodeur, became just about the team's best player besides Boucher.

Eleven minutes into the period, Delmore couldn't get the puck up the boards past Lemieux. Burt blocked a shot by Jay Pandolfo, but with Boucher committed, Lemieux followed and put his second try past the off-balance goaltender to give New Jersey the 1-0 lead.

With 4:50 to go, after Kelly got away with a punch at Lindros's jaw during a shoving match with Daneyko, Brylin sneaked up behind the struggling Desjardins, dug the puck out of his skates, and put it between Big E's legs to Mogilny, who went up top to make it 2-0.

With 30 seconds remaining, Lindros won another faceoff and roofed the puck again, this time the goal counting. But in practicality, this one was just as late as his first had been. As the Flyers huddled at their bench, Lindros did most of the talking. But Holik tied up Primeau on one last faceoff in the New Jersey end and the Devils, who had dominated the game, 26 shots to 13, had forced Game Seven with a 2-1 victory.

In 13:47 of ice time, Lindros had scored Philadelphia's only goal, won six of nine faceoffs, and recorded three of their 13 shots.

"As it went on, I felt better and better," he reported. "I get another practice now. I would like to think that every day, I will keep improving."

Of course, those precious days would expire if the Flyers didn't play a lot better in their first Game Seven since emergency goalie Ken Wregget had beaten the Penguins in Pittsburgh 11 seasons earlier.

"[The Devils] made some adjustments and they're playing solid," said Boucher. "When teams get momentum, it's tough to get it back.

"We're going to have to play one of our best games of the year."

The movie of choice on the bus ride home was *Analyze This*. The team spent the night at the Philadelphia Westin and dined together the next evening at The Saloon, then rented out a theatre to see *Mission Impossible II*. Like the magician they had hired for entertainment during dinner, the movie titles were not meant as statements on their predicament.

Ramsay, again Mr. Positive after being subdued in the Game Six aftermath, tried to ease the pressure of the situation.

"To have a chance to play in Game Seven in any playoff series, but in this case to go to the Stanley Cup Final, is one of the greatest experiences they will ever have," said the coach. "What is the worst that can happen?

"There's nobody with machine guns waiting to shoot you."

Indeed, it wasn't life or death. Five months earlier, Lauren Hart had found bumps all over her body and been diagnosed with non-Hodgkin's lymphoma. After grueling chemotherapy, she was in remission and, in a sense, so had been "God Bless America," which had not been sung in Philadelphia's new arena in the four seasons since it had opened.

"I thought the Kate thing had gotten old," recalls Ron Ryan, then the Flyer president. "We were getting some comments like, 'How long are you going to live in the past?'

"People from the Cup years still loved it, but I don't think everybody did."

Even in escrow, Kate Smith's record remained a glittering 64-15-3, the majority of her victories accrued in must-win situations like the one now facing the team. In the usual game-day presentation meeting at mid-afternoon, it was decided to revive the song, this time with Hart singing it.

"Why not?" said Snider, when it was suggested to him. In the face of having nothing to lose and seemingly everything to lose, the roaring First Union Center crowd agreed.

"Absolutely electric," Hart would say later. In the dressing room, the Flyers had drawn from team history too, if only for laughs.

"We took a picture of Fred Shero and pasted Jonesey's head on it, because he was always the one with the (inspirational) lines," recalls Tocchet. "I remember a very loose locker room."

Ramsay had seen enough good things from Lindros in Game Six to put him back at center between LeClair and Jones as Game Seven began.

When Jones was stood up on an early rush, Delmore followed and put a good chance over the net. After LeClair stole the puck behind the goal from Stevens, a promising Tocchet feed was just out of the reach of Recchi. Boucher didn't glove the first Devil shot, taken by Mogilny, until 5:28 in.

The Flyers had the start they wanted until Jones, trying to force Rafalski at center, shoved his helmet back and Marouelli called roughing.

Philadelphia never got the puck out on the penalty kill. Holik knocked down an attempted Tocchet clear, Hull fell down, Holik beat Desjardins with a move off the boards, and Arnott's pass got past Therien to Elias at the right post. With both defensemen trapped on one side, Elias put the Devils ahead, 1-0.

A little more than a minute later, Lindros picked up a LeClair tip at center and carried it back into the New Jersey end. "Johnny is on my right," Lindros recalls. "If I could get that puck behind [Stevens], we've got a chance at a breakaway or at least a one-on-one with the defenseman skating backwards against Johnny going top speed.

"That was my plan, anyway."

Lindros effectively deked Niedermayer at the blueline, cut inside, and put his head down for an instant to dump the puck. Stevens, coming across with his elbow tucked, put his shoulder into Lindros's chin, snapping back his head, which bounced off the ice when he went down.

Lindros lay motionless on his side, his helmet jammed down over his eyes, as the arena fell almost utterly silent.

"Can you believe this?" said Berube to Therien on the bench about a scene both incredible and predictable at the same time.

A few Flyers started after Stevens, but several Devils got between them and the protest died with barely a shove. The hit, delivered with the shoulder in the days when the head could be targeted without penalty, was as clean as it was devastating.

"We just saw that kid's career end," Primeau recalls as the first thought through his mind.

"The second was, 'What is the situation we've created? What is the predicament we are in now?'

"We're 10 minutes into Game Seven, down a goal, down to 11 forwards and their best player has come determined to win at any cost. Are we prepared to do the same?"

Within a minute, Lindros was up on his knees, Worley holding a towel to a cut on his nose caused by his helmet pushing forward. "Had a job to do," Worley recalls, personal feelings no consideration. Burt and LeClair draped Lindros over their shoulders and helped him off the ice.

"It was sickening," recalls LeClair. "I was just trying to encourage Eric and tell him everything was going to be ok."

"I'm praying for you," said Vanbiesbrouck, gently squeezing Lindros's legs as he was carried by.

Gagne, a rookie who had not understood why his older teammates would have any problem taking Lindros back—and who thought, off his Game Six performance, No. 88 would make the difference in Game Seven—was shaken.

"A 6-5, 230-pound guy goes down like that, it was almost like seeing Godzilla knocked out," recalls Gagne.

A stone-faced Stevens only glanced at the video replay of the hit on the scoreboard. "With him it was all business," recalls Daneyko. "I've never seen him rattled that much; but he was really quiet on the bench.

"Having said that, once it happened, we knew we were going to win."

But, from a season's worth of practice with adversity, the Flyers also knew they were going to respond.

"We did most of that playoff run without Eric, so the kind of thinking that we couldn't do it without him was gone," remembers LeClair.

Recalls Tocchet, "It's like the old gladiator days. You take one off and its back into the mode again."

On the first shift after the hit, Tocchet bumped Colin White off the puck behind the net and Sykora had to take down Recchi with a cross-check, putting Philadelphia on the powerplay. An undeterred Stevens hip-checked Primeau behind the net and the Flyers did not get a shot during that advantage. But when Lemieux was given a phantom penalty for high sticking, Brodeur went down on all fours to make a save on Gagne off a Langkow passout.

Just as Philadelphia gained momentum, McGillis left his feet to board Madden and was penalized. But the Devils were no more disciplined. Elias's stick clipped Manderville on the side of the face, knocking out teeth and earning another New Jersey penalty in the final minute of the first period.

During the break, a few of the Flyers went to the training room to see the dazed Lindros, who was with his father. Big E was able to walk to his ride to Pennsylvania Hospital as the team, still down only a goal, resumed their work.

After White got caught holding Recchi's stick 4:44 into the second period, LeClair stopped a Brodeur wind-around and Delmore fired. LeClair stopped the shot before it got to the Devil goaltender, just before a Stevens cross-check knocked LeClair into the netminder. Brodeur had no chance as Tocchet followed to tie the game, 1-1, 6:01 into the period.

On the next shift after the powerplay, he went to the net again. "Primeau won a battle in the corner," Tocchet recalls. "[Malakhov] was in front of me.

"Keith is gonna pass me that puck. It was a flip of the coin—do I go right or to my backhand? I went to my forehand and the puck came across and through where my stick had been. Had I been on my backhand, it's a tap-in. We go up 2-1 and win the game.

"That haunts me. Anybody could have scored that goal and I went the wrong way."

Tocchet sat on the bench shaking his head. But Philadelphia suffered no let-up. Only a Richardson slashing penalty on Mogilny slowed their effort in the second period, when they outshot the Devils 15-8, and spent most of the last five minutes in the New Jersey end. When Jones jammed the boards and threw the puck on goal, LeClair's tip went off the inside of Brodeur's pads and just wide.

Scott Stevens' hard open ice hit knocked Eric Lindros out of Game Seven.

The two teams pounded away at each other for six shotless minutes of the third period. McGillis sent Lemieux's stick flying into the Flyer bench. Malakhov, bloodied by a Langkow follow-through, had to go to the locker room for repairs. Boucher stopped a one-timer by Sykora, who had found a seam in the slot.

Brodeur had to stop a Langkow turnaround. Then, Colin White tied up Tocchet as Primeau cut in. Berube, going to the net for a LeClair feed, fanned on an opportunity with 7:35 remaining.

The clock was under three minutes when Stevens stopped McGillis's pressured wrap-around. The defenseman's shot deflected to the sideboards to Mogilny, who had been unable to get off at the end of his shift. He circled out of the corner and tried to feed Arnott, who was knocked down by Primeau. The puck came through to McGillis, but before he could clear it, Elias snuck up behind the defenseman, lifted his stick and cleanly beat Boucher before

he could reset himself.

The Devils led, 2-1, with just 2:35 left in the game. "Plays happen, didn't see him," recalls McGillis. "Not my best memory."

With Boucher on the bench, his teammates gained the zone and held the puck in for most of the last minute. But Lemieux pinned Recchi along the backboards with 25 seconds to go and Niedermayer tipped away a Primeau pass intended for LeClair.

Lemieux dove to get the puck out just before the buzzer went off on the most alternately heartbreaking and inspiring season in Flyer history. It had ended with a devastating hit and a crushing 2-1 Game Seven loss.

"In the end, fate was the only difference," recalls Brodeur.

"I didn't see one of those shots I stopped just before Patrik scored."

Daneyko recalls it as the most satisfying series victory of an era that would produce three Devil Stanley Cups in nine years. But Stevens wasn't smiling as he and his teammates were congratulated.

"I found it a little tough playing after [the Lindros hit]," he said. "I know it was clean and this was a big game for our team, but I just don't like to see people get hurt."

Down the hall, the Flyers were trying to find a way to celebrate their effort in the most disappointing loss most of them ever would know.

"We played a hell of a hockey game," Ramsay said. "I'm as proud as I can be of this group of men and the battle we put up tonight.

"You don't want to see this young man get hurt again. Your heart is in your mouth. But we had to focus and get back to work, same as in the Pittsburgh game (and hit on Primeau).

"This was a never-ending saga for us and our guys pulled it together again. They pushed themselves, they policed themselves, they gave me absolutely everything I could possibly have asked, and I didn't even have to ask.

"This has been a great accomplishment. We won three in a row, they won three in a row. They just happened to win the last three."

But, of course, that was what hurt.

"It comes down to two minutes, somebody scored a goal and somebody goes home a loser," said Boucher. "I'm not going to remember losing Game Seven; I'll be more mad during the summer thinking back that we had three cracks at it.

That wasn't just a rookie's perspective. "I thought we played better than New Jersey tonight," said Tocchet. "But I think Game Five we let them back in the series. I don't think we were ready to play that game."

Mostly for that reason, those Flyers still beat themselves up today.

"The Devils were a real good team but we blew it, that's the way I see it," recalls Gagne. "We had control of that series."

Did they lose it—and their soul—by taking back Lindros? There is no consensus.

"Toc swung [the decision] but I had a chance to shut it down," Ramsay recalls. "I should have just said, 'No,' for that series or, 'No' period, and I didn't.

"I don't have many regrets. But that is one of them."

Ramsay shouldn't, LeClair insists. "Tocchet had the respect of everyone and he brought up a great point," recalls LeClair. "It wasn't even close between [Lindros and White] so it was tough to argue that it would break the chemistry."

Lindros played well in a limited role in Game Six and was injured early in Game Seven. Any disruption was not on the ice. But having opinion split within the team, did the Flyers give themselves a scapegoat?

Tocchet says he always asks himself, "If Eric had been there the whole time, around the practice rink and travelling with the team when he was feeling better, would it have been an easier transition instead of just coming out of the blue again, showing up in the dressing room when we hadn't seen him for more than two months?

"I don't know."

Recalls Berube, "If we had played well in Game Five and lost it, we still would have felt good about everything going into Game Six. Lindros comes back and now we're watching him, and I think that affected everything. I don't think we looked at it like we were up 3-2.

"I think it really bothered Desjardins. He didn't play well the last two games. I think Langkow getting injured and the (lineup) changes around that really hurt us, too."

The pain was exacerbated by the Devils going on to beat Dallas in a six-game Final.

"I knew in my heart that the winner of our conference was going to win the Stanley Cup," recalls Primeau. "I think we both were bigger, stronger, faster than Dallas, even if they were the defending champions. I was actually surprised at the fight they gave the Devils."

When the Flyers gathered to clean out their lockers three days after their loss, the players were as proud as they were disappointed.

"After a while, it was like, 'What else can happen?'" LeClair told the media. "It became comical, really, easier and easier to block things out.

"With everything that occurred, it was enjoyable coming to the rink because we had such a good group of guys.

"That's the biggest thing I'm going to take from this season, that feeling. I have respect for every single guy in that room."

In his files, Neilson had found several copies of 1998-99 game programs signed by Dmitri Tertyshny. He said he was giving them to Clarke to present to Tertyshny's widow, Polina.

Thus, the last poignant act of the 1999-2000 Flyers was a reminder of how they had begun—with a memorial service for a teammate. If death and life-threatening disease had not devastated them, how could defeat?

"I could sleep," recalls Tocchet. "I was pissed off about a blown opportunity, yeah, but I could sleep.

"It was a damn good team that overcame a lot of stuff. You could go away saying, 'It was a helluva run.'

"It was a close, funny, misfit kind-of-a-team and when I see guys from it, we talk about it as a fun time more than as a disappointment. I won a Cup (in Pittsburgh), went to two finals with the Flyers and that year was right with those as my most enjoyable one.

"But one more bounce, or if we had played better in Game Five, it's a different conversation."

GENE HART

THE SMALLER THE CLASS SIZE, the more effective the teachers, many believe. But Gene Hart masterfully took on an education project more colossal than anything he ever performed in his high-school classrooms.

He taught hockey to Philadelphia.

"Gene gave the line in his speeches that, 'Hockey is my fun, but teaching is my nourishment'" said Sarah Hart, his wife of 36 years. "It was a perfect marriage."

Everybody fell in love with the Stanley Cup champions the Flyers became, but an increasing demand for tickets built the third level of the Spectrum before the team had its first winning season. Even prior to the arrival of Bobby Clarke for Year Three, there was one recognizable person in Philadelphia hockey—the voice initially heard on the public address system, explaining icing and offsides to 7,812 first-nighters.

It wasn't until the Flyers' ninth game that they bought their way onto WCAU-1210 for $35,000, a princely sum that didn't leave much budget for anybody big to do the play-by-play. Instead, they picked somebody literally big, a 300-pound South Jersey high school broadcaster and master of ceremonies at Aquarama, a water circus just across Broad Street from the Spectrum. But after banging his head against the wall for years in a bid to be taken seriously by Philadelphia's stations and teams, Hart had been part of enough animal acts at Aquarama and Atlantic City's Steel Pier to be willing to work for peanuts.

"He had to fight for everything because of his size and because he wasn't the typical broadcaster with the hair and the teeth," said Bobby Taylor, Hart's partner in the Flyers booth from 1977 to 1993. "He ended up doing 20 years on television, when he really was the anti-broadcaster in looks."

Hart was a living metaphor for the persistence shown by Ed Snider and fellow Flyer founders to get the team on the ice. An audition tape of a Rangers-Black Hawks game done from a corner of the Madison Square Garden press box had not gotten him the Flyers' first television play-by-play job, which went to Stu Nahan, Captain Philadelphia on a UHF children's show, a Canadian by birth and even a former goaltender.

Hart's experience doing third periods of the Eastern Hockey League Jersey Devils, who played at the Cherry Hill Arena, did, however, put him in the company of Bill Putnam, the first Flyer president. It got Gene at least the initial Flyer PA job and entre to Nahan, who pushed to get Hart the radio gig.

The station announced that it would do the third periods of the games—on tape delay if the Sixers were playing—without naming its play-by-play man. Hart heard the news believing he had been passed over again until Nahan reached him late that night.

Gene covered the phone. "I'm a star," he said to Sarah. Indeed the former water clown of his athletic days was on his way to becoming one of the most compelling voices in the sport, if not all of sport.

GENE HART
FLYER HERO #11

"He had a way of building drama with just the tone of his voice," said Jim Jackson, who largely succeeded Hart in 1993. "The call that springs to mind was the Dave Poulin shorthanded goal (three-on-five in Game Six against Quebec in 1985), Gene's voice rising with "Going on in. . . . . Score!!!!

"He could capture the moment, sensed what it needed, and that's an art. Some guys are basically off the charts for the entire game and they've got nowhere to go for the big moment. Others are sort of monotone. Gene was calm when he had to be and exciting when needed.

"I don't think he minded being called a homer. I think he thought that was basically what he was supposed to do, broadcasting to fans that rooted for the Flyers, but he didn't take it to the point of rooting right on the air. When guys were doing extraordinary things against the Flyers he would certainly acknowledge it with his call, not with the same enthusiasm as when Bobby Clarke or Eric Lindros or Tim Kerr did them, but he had respect for players' craft and for the game."

Hart's love for it came, perfectly enough, through the radio, listening to his hometown Rangers for years before he ever got to The Garden to see them. Born in 1931 in Manhattan to a former Viennese immigrant opera singer Fredrica (Fritzie) Matilda Fischer and orphaned Hungarian acrobat Eugen Hochsander—"Hock" is Hungarian for heart, hence the showbiz surname Hart that his parents took to the vaudeville circuit—the stage was in Gene's genes.

During summers, Eugen ran the water show on Steel Pier. Fritzie rode the world famous high-diving horse that concluded the show. Offered a year-round job by Steel Pier impresario George Hamid to book European acts, the elder Hart moved the family to the Jersey shore, where Gene became an All-State baseball player at Pleasantville High School while working summers at the Pier as a stage hand and clown diver for an act named Binswanger's Bathing Beauties.

Hart received his teaching degree from Trenton State College, then, thanks to the start given him by his father's command of Eastern European languages, served in the Russian Linguistic unit for US Army Intelligence before becoming a car salesman, repo man, night-shift disc jockey, high school and minor-league hockey play-by-play man, basketball official, racetrack announcer, history teacher and lifelong patron of the arts.

Gene's mother's opera background notwithstanding, he had become an aficionado pretty much on his own. Sarah, a student at the University of Florida hired for the summer to swim in Hamid's water ballet—and, later, following her future mother-in-law as a rider of the diving horse—could hear the opera recordings being played one dressing room over.

Perhaps on an airborne equine—"The horse didn't mind or I wouldn't have been on him," she insists—was the one place Sarah could escape her relentless suitor.

"Gene chased me around for five years," she said. "I mean, he was an interesting person but I was going back to school to pursue a medical career. I lived in Florida, he lived here. I didn't see marriage in my life."

Gene was a persuasive guy, in addition to being a renaissance man, such a maestro of crossword puzzles that he did them in ink just to show off; plus a history teacher of such skill, dedication and compassion that he would bring learning-challenged students with him on Flyers trips.

"He was the most interesting guy I ever met," said Taylor. Also one of the most prepared—hours of statistical work and backgrounding went into Hart's broadcasts—and adaptable, too.

When Gene didn't have enough tenure at Audubon High School to survive cutbacks, he taught at Leesburg Prison for a year—"captive audience," Hart always joked—until being hired at Lenape High School in Marlton, NJ, where he stayed until 1975. Hart was so good at what he did, and so dedicated to catching pre-dawn flights home on the morning after Flyer road games, that the school administration gladly tolerated his absences for longer trips. Only when the district split into two high schools in 1975 did Hart, who would be working for new administrators, decide to give up teaching.

The Flyers were paying him better money by then. Besides, this gave him time for more charity work, speaking engagements, and taking daughters Lauren and Sharon to the theatre, opera and rock shows and son Brian on Flyer trips. Brian was four when Dad told him the first Stanley Cup parade was for his birthday. None since, Brian smiles, have been as much fun.

Actually, that parade was as much for Gene as it was for Clarke or Fred Shero.

"In addition to the performing, it was how he related to people," said Sarah. "They just loved him so much, like they loved a player, but it was on an even different level because he was their guy. He wasn't out of reach, was right in there with people, talking and teaching."

He became one of them, talking about their guys—the Flyers.

"Being a teacher, he had a good command of the English language," said Taylor. "But for me, what made him so good was the passion.

"He really cared if the Flyers won and was really upset when they lost. That's what made him such a fan favorite."

Two years after the Flyers determined Hart's eyes and health were betraying him, the birth of the Phantoms gave him his old Spectrum booth again for two years before his July 14, 1999 death. It was no comedown at all for this man of the people, but another podium. "One summer when we were first married, he was a cashier at Garwood Mills, nothing was beneath him," recalls Sarah. Truth was, her husband loved radio more anyway, because he hated television production meetings.

Though hugely disappointed to be off the big stage for the final four years of his life, Hart still was in huge demand as a toastmaster and hardly out of mind of the peers whom could best judge his work. Hart's election by his fellow broadcasters to the Foster Hewitt Award—the Hockey Hall of Fame's broadcast honor—two years before his death made Gene the happiest Sarah says she ever saw him, unless it was when together they got to hear Wagner's "The Ring Cycle" in Bayreuth, Germany (typically a 20-30-year wait for a ticket), or when Gene got to perform Frosh, the drunken jailer in "Die Fledermaus", with the Opera Company of Philadelphia.

Hart's good friend, violinist Herb Light, was Gene's pass backstage at the Philadelphia Symphony, just as Hart was the ticket for Herb, a huge Flyer fan, into their locker room. For a guy who in his mid-thirties was still doing games on stations with a five-mile broadcasting radius, Gene eventually went places, the most important being where people would light up at his presence.

"There are not many games that go by now that someone doesn't come up to me and say, 'Your dad spoke at my high school' or 'your dad visited me in the hospital when I was a kid," said Lauren.

The man could take over a room instantly and switch topics seamlessly.

"I used to watch him speak on something, anything and think, 'How does he do that?' said Lauren. "How does he go on TV and be fluent and engaging and exciting?

"I watched him a lot growing up. When it came my turn to do it, I just knew how."

Gene got his first-born onto the Spectrum floor to sing the National Anthem for the first time when she was 15. Lauren's career has taken her to Monte Carlo, where she warmed up for Frank Sinatra, Harry Belafonte and Stan Getz. She sang onstage at Bill Clinton's Inauguration and in Los Angeles began recording deals with Columbia and Red Ant/BMG Records and produced six albums. Lauren has written and performed songs for the movie "Miracle", television shows "One Life to Live", "Joan of Arcadia", and "Party of Five", in addition to co-hosting "NBC 10!" and "All Hart" on WMCN Network out of Philadelphia.

On opening night of the 1997-98 season, when the Flyers staged pregame ceremonies recognizing Gene's election to the Hockey Hall of Fame, she walked Dad out onto the red carpet, sang "The Star-Spangled Banner," and came off practically into the arms of Flyer president Ron Ryan, who asked her to do the job permanently.

He had no idea how permanently. When Lauren was diagnosed with non-Hodgkin's lymphoma in January 2000, she missed just one game, damn the hair loss from the chemotherapy, damn the fact that most nights she was too exhausted to stay through the second period.

"I was in such a weird state of mind that it didn't occur to me other people out there had cancer, too," she said. "In later years, people have said they remember when I had it and me being out there regardless helped them. At the time, I didn't know I was doing that.

"I wasn't responding to the treatment at first; they were ready to discuss alternatives when it started to work. After six months, you feel better in some ways and worse in some ways, but in order to get better you have to get to the breaking point. At the end, it is a train wreck, but you're still standing."

How is this for karma? She turned the corner from her illness during the Flyers glorious semifinal run that spring. Also received her five-year, cancer-free, all clear on the day, on her Channel 10 show, she interviewed Todd Carmichael, who owns a Philadelphia chain of La Colombe coffee houses, about his expedition to the South Pole.

They fell in love, married and adopted four Ethiopian children. The trips to Africa to bring them home have caused her to miss just three games and that's all since 1997. She has sung "The Star-Spangled Banner", "O Canada" and "God Bless America" by herself and with The Hooters, Jeffrey Gaines and two gospel choirs, Voices of Praise and Philadelphia NARAS. And, of course, when the Flyers need a victory in the worst way, she is at her best singing the most traditional and goosebumps-raising pregame number in sports with the late, great Kate Smith on the video screen.

"I have no say in it, but when they want [the "God Bless America" duet], I gladly do it," Lauren says.

Whatever the theatrics, whatever the occasion, she is there, just like Dad, who never missed a game in person, even the ones when doctors wouldn't let him go on the air immediately after undergoing heart bypass surgery in 1985. He came to watch regardless.

"It's a unique transition," Lauren says. "Players

would come and go but he would still be there and now that's me.

"I'm still standing, still singing every night in front of different players, different faces, which makes you understand even more what the Flyers represent to the fans, something bigger than any one person.

"Only a few people in that organization have been around long enough to have that sense. I do, and I'm just so fortunate."

JOHN LECLAIR

DECEPTIVE WAS NOT A WORD used to describe 700 pounds of bulldozing Doom that the Flyers unleashed on the NHL with their top line of the mid-to-late nineties. Take it from the goalies, though, John LeClair could turn his back to the net on the power play and never give away his intentions.

"John had a twist to his stick, so you wouldn't think he could get much on his backhand," said netminder John Vanbiesbrouck, who, near the end of his 19-season career, was blessed to enjoy two years in Philadelphia where he only had to worry about LeClair during practice. "But he could, that's how strong he was. The goalie never knew which way the puck was coming,"

Whether playing facing out towards the points, or with his back to the boards powering down left wing, Big John could either flip the puck up high or keep it as low as the profile he preferred to keep.

An essentially shy guy, except around the net, LeClair scored 333 Flyer goals in 10 seasons, including years of 51, 50, 51, 43 and 40. Left to your imagination is what he could have done with a full campaign in 1995, when LeClair scored 25 in 37 post-lockout games after his acquisition in the transforming deal of Bob Clarke's second run as general manager.

But it is a strong guess that the franchise's five consecutive losing seasons would have turned into more had Clarke not taken the risk of trading one of the league's premier scorers, Mark Recchi, in the February 9, 1995 trade with Montreal that brought LeClair, Eric Desjardins and throw-in Gilbert Dionne to Philadelphia.

Clarke, being as honest as a LeClair day of work, insists he had no idea of the monster talent he was obtaining, but that's not to say he wasn't thinking big all the way.

"Eric Lindros was playing with (190-pound) Brent Fedyk," recalls Clarke. "Every huge defenseman was going after Lindros. Common sense said we had to get some big guys."

The Flyers had stripped their talent down to practically Rod Brind'Amour and Mark Recchi in the massive 1992 trade for Lindros. After two more years of losing, Recchi, a three-time 100-point scorer, became the card to play for, well, as much as the GM could get.

"We needed a big winger and a defenseman who would work the power play, do a lot of penalty killing, and take the first and last shift of the period," Clarke recalls.

Montreal felt it had a surplus of both. Desjardins was falling short of the great expectations he had raised during the Canadiens' 1993 Stanley Cup season. As for LeClair, since scoring two overtime goals in that Final, he simply kept falling down. Curiously shaky on his skates for his 6-3, 225-pounds, LeClair had not broken 20 goals in three seasons.

Desjardins, who instantly became a glue defenseman in Philadelphia, proved value alone for Recchi, who, as a significant bonus, was re-obtained by Clarke four years later to help key semifinal playoff runs in 2000 and 2004. But LeClair turned out to be the jackpot.

"We thought we would try him on wing with Lindros and if that didn't work out, we would make John a checking center," recalls Clarke. Plan B was gleefully tossed into the wastebasket in the second game after the trade, Playing with the 6-2 rookie Mikael Renberg, the 6-4 Lindros chased down a Desjardins rebound and fed the 6-3 LeClair in the slot for the initial goal of the Flyers' first win in 13 games at the Meadowlands.

"They looked like the Legion of Doom out there," said Philadelphia center Jim Montgomery.

Renberg would fade in subsequent years due to injuries and anxiety. But power on top of power, Lindros and LeClair instantly boosted each other; Lindros to the Hart Trophy and LeClair to superstardom. He never needed a skating instructor to correct that balance problem, just the confidence boost from playing alongside the best player in the NHL.

"When John came to town he told me, 'I'll take myself out of the play to allow you to come out in front of the net,'" recalls Lindros. "He created a lot of space.

"Johnny was very good at digging out pucks and finding a place to shoot. In front of the net he was so strong that many times one person wasn't enough to keep him from getting his stick open.

"The rules were different. Size and strength were a big deal. New Jersey had (Scott) Stevens and (Ken) Daneyko. The Devils also had a nimble guy like (Scott) Niedermayer back there who could really skate, so speed was important. But primarily it was a holdup game and being able to get through it was vital. Fifty-five percent of John's goals were scored from within eight feet of the net. He was that powerful.

"But don't get me wrong. John had a wonderful shot and could score from anywhere."

As the goalies became quicker and their equipment larger, the unscreened 40-foot goal was vanishing from the game but LeClair's 100 mph slapshot continued to find the mark. Defensemen aligned to put him down wound up on their derrieres following Big John shoulder dips. Dexterity completed the package that made LeClair the first American to put together three consecutive 50-goal seasons, getting him elected to the United States Hockey Hall of Fame in 2009, and the Flyers Hall of Fame as an appropriate co-inductee with Lindros in 2014.

"Eric threw the hardest passes I've ever seen and John and Dale Hawerchuk were the only persons I saw who could handle them," said former Flyers coach Terry Murray, who especially remembers LeClair climbing out of a hyperbaric chamber for Game Four in Tampa Bay with Philadelphia down 2-1 in games. On a bad ankle he scored a game-opening goal that swung the momentum in this 1996 series the Flyers would go on to win in six games.

The only soft part of Big John was his hands. That said, bullish resolve was the greatest factor in making LeClair the best pure goal scorer the organization ever had, in the opinion of Clarke.

"Bill Barber scored 50 goals (once) and played the point on the power play," said Clarke in 1999, when LeClair was finishing up a four-year period when he had the most goals of any player in the NHL. "But to score 50 with the tight defenses today, playing against the other teams' best checkers every night, is unbelievable to me."

It's hard to compare performances in different eras, not so difficult to contrast the abilities of the best scorers the Flyers ever had.

Barber had a near-perfect combination of skills and brain for the game. Clarke, like Wayne Gretzky, was a pass-first guy with such uncanny hockey sense that the puck came to him in places where he couldn't miss.

Tim Kerr, who broke 50 goals four times to LeClair's three, possessed incredibly fast hands, a body like LeClair's, and a matched willingness to take abuse in the eternal quest for the loose goalmouth puck. Brian Propp had quickness, superior instincts and insatiable hunger by the posts and in the slot.

Reggie Leach had speed, a short backswing, and was a marksman, ringing up shots just under the crossbar. Rick MacLeish was fast, shifty, and gifted with one of the most explosive wrist shots in NHL history.

Who was the deadliest? It's apples versus oranges, sweet bushel after bushel.

"In practice, John wasn't a real hard guy to stop, but in the game he would push himself to the net and just bang away," recalls Ron Hextall. "Timmy knew how to get open and had the real quick release, but he was more stationary. Johnny was more the driving, nose-down, big horse."

As long as Doom's salad years lasted, no NHL team ever had bigger, more powerful, horses pulling their loads. Lindros, already fearing his time on top would prove even shorter than the ponies he had to carry, was grateful for the company.

JOHN LECLAIR
FLYER HERO #15

"My body can't go through the abuse I was giving it in the first year or two," Eric said in 1996. "You can't just charge into the opponent's zone like a bull in a china shop, trying to cause havoc for 15 years.

"The acquisition of John saved my career. I got a winger with speed in addition to size, so I didn't have to be physical. I think I have the best job in hockey right now."

Either he did or LeClair did. In six seasons together, they were too busy combining for 465 goals, 519 assists, a trip to a Final plus another semifinal, and earning 10 end-of-season first- or second-team All-Star berths between them to waste time figuring out who was the meat and who was the gravy.

LeClair scored 53 goals and 45 assists during the 95 games Lindros was absent from 1995-2000, so time would be better spent looking up the definition of "synergy" than arguing who was the lead guy. Much more interesting is how two players who came to the Spectrum at opposite ends of the spectrum in career expectations created the anticipation of a goal every time they stepped on the ice together.

Lindros weighed 240 pounds, not counting the anvil he carried on his shoulders from being projected as the next great player from the time he had barely turned a teen. LeClair, drafted 33rd overall by the Canadiens in 1987, was surprised they thought enough of him to coax his exit from the University of Vermont before his eligibility was up.

"Maybe this means I'll get in a couple years in the minors before I go to work for a living," LeClair recalls thinking.

Who would have guessed he would turn out to be the third most famous person ever to come out of St. Albans, VT—albeit a distant third after Ben and Jerry?

One of five children of a nurse and a paint-store manager, LeClair also played soccer and baseball while growing up in the community of 13,000 just 20 minutes from the Canadian border. Geography made hockey the town's and LeClair's first passion and he played it on a volleyball court flooded by the father of his good friend, Jeremy Benoit, boards and lights later added so the kids could play until midnight.

LeClair didn't make the team at Bellows Free Academy as a freshman, but was plenty good enough as a junior to stand out at Hockey Night in Boston, a meat market for college players, and to lead Bellows to the state championship his senior year.

He could have gone to most of New England's high-powered NCAA programs. Instead, the Vermont high school player of the year decided to attend the state university 30 miles away—never mind its relative shortage of hockey tradition, LeClair changed that, helping the Catamounts to the NCAA Sweet 16 in his freshman year. A torn ACL and a bout with meningitis limited him to 18 and 10 games, respectively, during his sophomore and junior seasons, keeping his personal professional expectations low and his desire to stay in school high.

The Canadiens always saw more, though. Those two overtime winners in the 1993 Stanley Cup Final had prompted coach Jacques Demers to pronounce LeClair the "next Kevin Stevens," high praise since the Pittsburgh star was the quintessential power forward of the day.

"If you know Jacques, he says a lot of things," said LeClair. Indeed, Demers was almost as colorful as the multitude of swatches found at Butch LeClair's paint store, but his son's career had gone gray and his mood was turning increasingly black before being rejuvenated by the 1995 trade to Philadelphia. John arrived in fear he would soon be out of hockey.

"They expected me to score more than 20 in Montreal, but I really was doing the best I had in me," recalls LeClair. "I got to know what it was like to be out of the lineup, to be struggling.

"You don't want to be a failure. So when I started to have success, I was thinking that the higher you get up, the farther you can fall."

The difference between putting the puck into the net rather than into the goalie's pads is as much a matter of will as it is skill, which is why some guys with hands capable of annually scoring 40 average only 20. But it probably helped that LeClair had taken his knocks before opportunities came knocking in Philadelphia.

"In Montreal, the style we played was so defensive, I didn't get many open chances," he said. "We won a Cup, so that's not a complaint; I'm just saying that's why I didn't score much there.

"But never did I think I would score 50 goals. I'm just glad to know that all those people who always said I had potential were right."

They were right as rain. Too soon, however, storms gathered over the chances of Lindros and LeClair staying together. Lindros, oft-concussed and alienated from the organization about medical treatment, decided to insist on a trade following the 1999-2000 season, which put more pressure on the team to pay and keep LeClair.

The Flyers lavished him with a five-year, $45 million contract just as his body started to break down. After playing only 16 games in 2002-03, LeClair enjoyed a solid 55-point 2003-04 season, but the pay grade was well above his role. With the post-lockout Collective Bargaining Agreement granting teams the right to buy out remaining years for two-thirds value, the organization exercised that option to terminate LeClair's deal with two seasons remaining.

"I was underpaid for a long time, then I would wind up overpaid, so it kind of evened out," he recalls. With offers from the Devils, Bruins and Penguins, LeClair signed a two-year contract with Pittsburgh and, in his first season, produced a respectable 22 goals and 29 assists.

"Sid (Crosby) was coming in, Rex (Recchi) was there," recalls LeClair. "We had (Sergei) Gonchar and Ziggy Palffy, older players but pretty good ones, which is why I went.

"It didn't pan out. I was living in Pittsburgh and my family was in Philly. During the second year, [the Penguins] were going to send me down, but I wasn't going to go. I had enough. I just came home."

It was a humbling end, but LeClair, was always, in Clarke's words, "a humble guy." John wouldn't admit to holding a grudge against the Canadiens after scoring any of his uncanny 30 goals in 34 games—including two four-goal explosions—against Montreal as a Flyer. "It was amazing to me, too," he recalls. "It wasn't like I wanted to beat them more than the Rangers, who were our biggest rivals."

Nothing personal, LeClair insisted after killing the Canadiens time and again. What player doesn't get up for playing hockey in an iconic place, he would ask, never mind half those games against Montreal were in Philadelphia.

He sounded mostly like a guy refusing to call attention to himself, which is what LeClair essentially was, never putting himself above his team. Paying him appropriately became an organizational priority—and a distracting media preoccupation—from the time he was sold short with his first big deal, but LeClair kept coming to work, figuring all that stuff would eventually work itself out. The organization's problems with his good friend Lindros never became LeClair's issue, either.

"He and his wife (Christina) used to throw team parties," recalls Rick Tocchet. "He was real generous with the trainers. Just a good guy, a pleasure to play with.

"He liked to keep to himself but he also liked to be with us. Not a loner, but not the guy leading the charge either."

Likewise, LeClair was neither the team spokesperson nor the guy ducking out on the media, either, in spite of his loathing of the limelight.

"I don't find myself newsworthy," he once said. "I get bored listening to myself so I don't know why other people would want to."

They did, in part, because LeClair was, and remains, a compulsive truth teller.

"I can't be disappointed, but you always wish you could've done more," said LeClair who, continues to live in Haverford, PA, and serves as a consultant for his long-time agent, Lewis Gross.

"I was (33) games short of 1,000. Obviously, for goal scorers, 500 is a big number (LeClair finished with 406). I got a Cup in Montreal but I don't have one from [Philadelphia], disappointing because we had much better teams here and I look back at myself as a Flyer.

"Detroit (which swept the Flyers in the 1997 Final) was not ready to win in 1995 (when the Red Wings lost four straight to the Devils). Had we not lost Game Five to Jersey (in 1995 on Claude Lemieux's late goal), I think we would have won the Stanley Cup.

"The 2000 team that lost to New Jersey (in a conference final Game Seven), was one where everybody felt they were doing something important, and that's why that run was so much fun. But I'm not so sure we would have beaten Dallas, which would have been a tough matchup for us.

"I am sure our 2004 team would have beaten Calgary if we had gotten by Tampa Bay, but it just didn't work out.

"Timing is everything. But realistically, my career went far beyond what I ever imagined it would be."

RICK TOCCHET'S NOSE MAPS THE PLAYER he was for nine-plus seasons in Philadelphia. There seems to be a bump on it for each time he

RICK TOCCHET

pushed the Flyers over the hump during four valiant Stanley Cup chases to two Finals and two other semifinals. Just like Tocchet, a right wing upon whom the organization gambled in the sixth round of the 1983 draft, those teams usually got farther than expected.

"I've always asked myself, 'If I went to a different team, would I still be a good player?" Tocchet says. "Yeah, I think I would have, but the Flyers really helped me identify myself as the player I became.

"That's why Philadelphia really was the perfect marriage for me, because I wasn't the most talented guy. I got the most out of what I had and I owe that to the Flyers and their fans.

"I never had a problem in Philadelphia. Yeah, if you play bad, the press says, 'You stink,' and with the fans, it's, 'Hey, you gotta play better.' But I always understood that and it made me feel at home."

He liked it so much here the first time that, eight years after being traded to Pittsburgh for Mark Recchi, Tocchet was thrilled to receive the opportunity to do Philadelphia again. His reacquisition in March 2000 brought him full circle to key one more Orange-and-Black semifinal run before his body gave out two years later at age 38, following 440 NHL goals, 952 points, and 2,972 penalty minutes, 10th all time.

Between Flyer gigs, Tocchet won a Stanley Cup with the Penguins, and in 2016, did it again as a Pittsburgh assistant. Both team president Mario Lemieux, a teammate on the 1992 champions, and Wayne Gretzky, a 1987 Canada Cup buddy and later, coach of the Phoenix Coyotes, have put Tocchet on their staffs, which might represent the finest one-two character reference in NHL history. But Flyer fans didn't need to read a resume to see Tocchet's return in a trade for Mikael Renberg as one of the most joyous in the team's history, right behind Bernie Parent's and Ron Hextall's.

The clock wound back more than a decade when Tocchet, scoring two goals and an assist, brought the Flyers back from a 3-1 second-period deficit to a 4-3 victory that squared the 2000 Eastern Conference final against the Devils at a game apiece.

After taking a 3-1 lead in the series, Philadelphia fell short in seven contests, turning into one more long run by a Tocchet Flyer team that ended in heartbreak. The franchise probably never has had a worse loser, so he feels the organization's pain that the third Flyers championship has yet to happen, never mind he won two rings with a blood rival.

RICK TOCCHET
FLYER HERO #18

"The franchise has gotta win another Cup," Tocchet says. "Mr. (Ed) Snider gave the tools; money's not an issue, so I'm surprised they haven't.

"They made some mistakes that I'm sure they'll admit. But they are always in the mix because of the mindset.

"The Flyers were always ahead of their time for the way they treated their players, providing a comfort level that wasn't instilled other places during the eighties. The doctors were great; when you needed something, boom, somebody always was there to help you so there were no excuses when you hit the ice.

"If you play for the Flyers, you are here to win, not just to pass the time, and the city makes you feel that way, too. Who would want to play in Philadelphia for a crappy team in front of these fans? They scare the hell out of you. Everybody says the same thing: 'In Philadelphia, you gotta play.'"

In his case, it wasn't behavior learned the hard way. From his first shift as a 20-year-old, Tocchet showed up as a pre-made Philly-kind-of-a-guy.

The third son of first-generation northern Italian immigrants who settled in the working class east end of Toronto was a nice kid with a passion for all games and an ambition especially suited for a sport where the rules allow the participants to knock each other down.

When Mom, Norma, wasn't busy preoccupied with her son saying over and over again how he was going to make it in the NHL, she created spaghetti sauce so spectacular that he had to learn the recipe to avoid having to eat that bogus stuff served in restaurants.

Nat Tocchet, Rick's dad, worked in an auto body

shop and made the best wine Terry Crisp, his son's junior coach at Sault Ste. Marie, (Ontario), ever tasted. "Mr. Tocchet always had some for me, too," laughs Crisp, who won two Cups as a Flyer center. "It helped put Rick on the powerplay, no secret to that."

Crisp mentioned nothing about those Tocchet veal sandwiches. Nevertheless, only a knee injury suffered by a young Tocchet stopped Crisp from committing the epicurean and coaching mistakes of his life by cutting Tocchet from his first camp.

"I was on the bubble," recalls Tocchet, who was a fifth-round choice in the Ontario Hockey League's midget draft. "Then I got a partial MCL tear and because I didn't play or practice enough, they decided to wait for me to heal to get a better look.

"The clock was ticking, so first game back, I fought the toughest guy and played pretty well."

A career was born in forging opportunities. In his second junior season at Sault Ste. Marie, Tocchet began to bring pucks out of the corners where he left defensemen crumpled, every play he made getting him closer to his dream.

"I always wanted one chance to play one game in the NHL, just to prove I belonged," Tocchet recalls. But that didn't look too promising in 1982, when 12 rounds passed without his being selected.

At the next draft, Flyer GM Bob McCammon, having recently fired long-time eastern scout Eric Coville, invited Sam McMaster, the Sault Ste. Marie GM, to sit at Philadelphia's table to impart his knowledge of the OHL.

"Rick wasn't a great skater, but I knew his heart and that he would score," recalls McMaster. Minus a first-round pick because of the trade to obtain Mark Howe, the Flyers took three OHL touts of McMaster—Peter Zezel in the second round, Derrick Smith in the third, and Tocchet in the sixth.

Under the instruction of power-skating instructor Cindy Bower (daughter of Hall of Fame goaltender Johnny), Tocchet pressed himself from coal into a diamond. He improved 42 points, all the way to 108, in his final junior season, plenty to convince McCammon that the kid would play more than just that one NHL game. The 1984 training camp was still six months away when Paul Holmgren was traded to Minnesota to make room for Tocchet.

The transition of Flyer bedrock right wings—Gary Dornhoefer to Holmgren to Tocchet—was seamless. Zezel and Smith made huge first-year contributions, too, as the youngest team in the NHL, whipped by rookie slave-driving coach Mike Keenan, stunningly compiled the league's best regular-season record and went to the Stanley Cup Final.

"Sometime you look at players and they are less than the sum of their parts," says Flyers' GM Ron Hextall, Tocchet's teammate for six seasons. "With Rick it was the opposite.

"He wasn't a great skater, didn't have great vision. He had real quick hands and knew how to get open. But in the end it was his willingness to go to the hard areas and back up every word he ever said by playing and practicing the right way that separated him."

Inside the checker's body that had scored 14 goals on the third line during each of his first two seasons had been a scorer's soul, screaming to be released. "I accepted the role they wanted me to fill," recalls Tocchet, "But I told Keenan that I thought I could do more."

Already blessed with plenty of right-wing scoring from Tim Kerr and Ilkka Sinisalo, the coach filed Tocchet's confidence away for a rainy day. It came as Kerr's shoulder gradually separated during the 1987 run to another Final. Tocchet stepped up with five goals in the first-round Ranger series and the series winner against Montreal in the semifinals. He then added three more goals and four assists in the Final versus Edmonton, when the Flyers came within one win of stealing the Cup from probably the best offensive team of all time.

That fall, as a selection for the Canadian team coached by Keenan in the Canada Cup tournament, Tocchet thrived in competition with and against the best players in the world. After a knee issue kept him from the second contest of the three-game final against the Soviets, he begged Flyer orthopedist Dr. John Gregg to allow him to dress for the finale, then scored to start his team out of a 3-0 hole towards a 6-5 victory and the championship.

Tocchet's confidence surged. In 1987-88, he scored 31 goals and established himself among the best right wings in the game, not merely among the toughest.

"He's a self-made player who deserves everything he's gotten," Keenan praised, and Tocchet had still more skill to show under coach Paul Holmgren, increasing his goal total to 45 in 1988-89.

'We used to joke with him early on in his career that his backswing was like (golfer) John Daly's," recalls Holmgren, who had been assistant coach under Keenan. "As soon as [Tocchet] learned to tone it down, he developed a knack for getting his shot off quicker.

"He had good hands, strong wrists, and a willingness to go into the dirty areas to make himself a scorer. I don't think anyone envisioned 45 goals but we always thought he would be a 30-goal-plus guy."

Tocchet became the Flyers' best player. As they aged and broke down around him, he also became their most burdened. Holmgren gave Tocchet the captaincy for the 1991-92 season but when he got off to a bad scoring start, the additional duties became his albatross.

"The way things were going got to him," recalls Holmgren. "I think he had good leadership skills, but in that position you have to know what to say to your teammates. When he was younger, Rick didn't always have that filter."

Predictably, he was revitalized by his trade to a contender. Tocchet had 19 points in Pittsburgh's championship playoff drive and, the following year as Lemieux's right wing, scored a career-high 48 goals and 109 points.

Dealt to Los Angeles for All-Star left wing Luc Robitaille, then to Boston for another, Kevin Stevens, Tocchet had again become an unhappy player with a mediocre Bruins team when he mentioned to golfing partner Bob Clarke, "If you ever get a chance to bring me back. . ."

It came three years later, after Tocchet had signed with Phoenix as a free agent. Coyotes GM Bobby Smith switched courses, deciding to get younger and cheaper, enabling Clarke to bring a gleeful Tocchet home.

"It was a huge move for our team," recalls Flyer teammate Luke Richardson. "Rick would go through a brick wall to get something done, would never take no for an answer, on or off the ice."

Despite the injury and alienation of Eric Lindros, and the absence of coach Roger Neilson as he underwent cancer treatment, Philadelphia caught fire down the stretch, rallied from a 2-0 deficit to beat Pittsburgh, and almost pulled an upset of eventual champion New Jersey. Tocchet, a straight-ahead player, got to come full circle, tying his Flyer experience into a neat bow.

"That (1999-2000) season was something I needed," Tocchet recalls. "It was a big moment in my career, being back in Philly, reacquainting with people, seeing my old friends again.

"As a kid with the Flyers, I had lived the Stanley Cup years through the stories told to me by the Broad Street Bullies. They kind of made me feel like I was there."

Bill Barber, one of those storytellers—and later Tocchet's coach—came up with the simplest, most perfect, characterization of what this player was, even if Tocchet spent only 11 of his 17 playing seasons with his first and last team.

"A Flyer," said Barber.

ROD BRIND'AMOUR

Sixteen years since the end of Rod Brind'Amour's team-record 484 consecutive game streak, no Flyer has gotten within two seasons (164 games) of it, yet still he believes his endurance deserves no commendation. If Brind'Amour didn't play in those contests, somebody else would have.

"Why would I give that guy an opportunity?" he asks. "I think never feeling my spot was guaranteed helped keep me on my toes.

"Obviously, if you are too hurt to play you can't. But if there's a way, you do. It's your job to play, what was the accomplishment?

"That kind of mentality doesn't exist anymore. Right or wrong, it's just different. I come from the older school where if you had to take a Toradol shot to get through the pain, you did."

In an era when teammates were likely to go to the bar after a game, Iron Rod went back to the weight room, a routine practically as unprecedented as Rod's father Bob designing a lifting program for a scrawny, 10-year old, two-time hockey dropout. Those 10-minute workouts became a habit that grew into an obsession.

"I always thought the way I'm going to be better than the kids I'm playing against is to do something different to get ahead," Rod said. "When it started to kick in at a younger age, I saw the results.

"I think the only reason I made it to the NHL at 18 was that I was physically mature enough. It was working for me, so why would I change it? I would try to be the hardest-working guy wherever I was."

When a charter carrying the Flyers back from the West would land around daybreak and his teammates went to bed, Brind'Amour instead would go to the training facility in Voorhees to work for two or three more hours. "Tired like the rest of us, one time he skipped and went home," recalls Mark Howe. "When Rod didn't score for something like the next four games, he swore 'I'll never do that again.'

"He was the best-conditioned athlete I ever played with."

Statues for which Rod Brind'Amour apparently posed are mounted throughout Athens. Every coach he ever had mounted No. 17's work ethic on a pedestal.

"Even if we didn't always see eye to eye about some (usage) situations, I loved Rod," said Terry Murray, who directed the Flyers to the 1997 Final. "Very low maintenance, you spent zero time telling him to work."

The first big piece of the Flyer rebuild during the only sustained losing period in their history (missed playoffs from 1990-94) set an example for toil that built a bridge back to contention.

"When I first got here (during 1991 training camp) I remember Bill Barber took me under his wing and told me how they had these expectations built," Brind'Amour said. "It came to mean something to me to live up to."

But did anyone really have to tell this kid?

Born in Ottawa and raised in Campbell River, British Columbia, Brind'Amour left home at age 15 to attend the noted Athol Murray College of Notre Dame in Wilcox, Saskatchewan, where he helped the Hounds to a national midget championship. At 17, he earned a place on Canada's team competing for the Spengler Cup in Davos, Switzerland. When Canada took first place, a Swiss businessman bought the players a $1,000 bottle of Champagne. Rod quietly sat drinking milk.

"He was the most mature fresh-

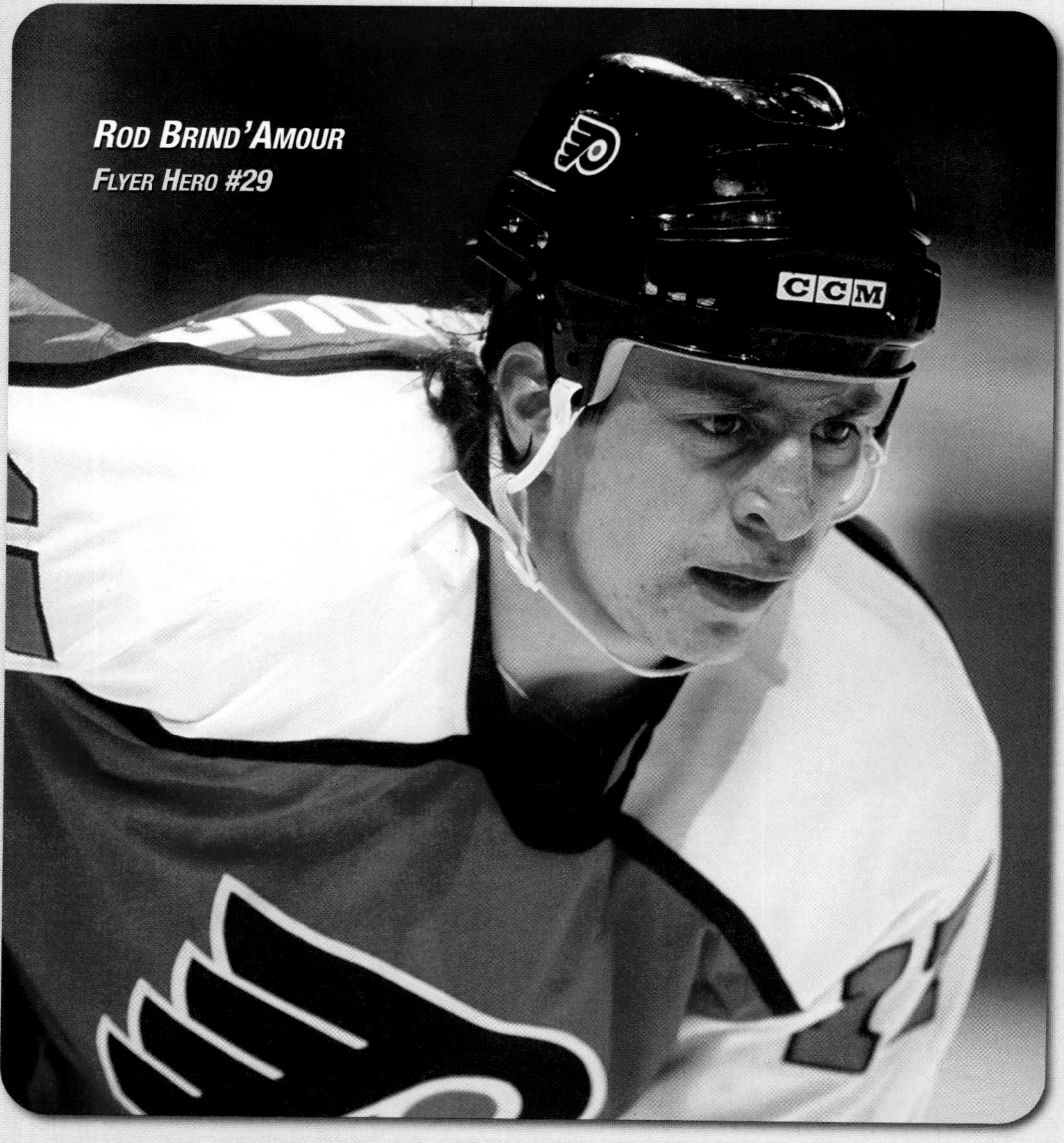

ROD BRIND'AMOUR
FLYER HERO #29

man I ever had," said Ron Mason, who coached 23 seasons at Michigan State, where Brind'Amour played for a year after St. Louis made him the ninth-overall choice in the 1988 Entry Draft.

During a 61-point rookie year, the Blues also adored the kid for his dedication. But when he regressed by 12 points the following season, they began to see his devotion as self-defeating. Watching Brind'Amour fight long slumps in the workout room, even the tightly-wound St. Louis coach, Brian Sutter, began to believe Brind'Amour was getting muscle-bound in the head.

When the Blues signed free agent Brendan Shanahan away from New Jersey, Rod and goaltender Curtis Joseph were offered as the compensation required by the Collective Bargaining Agreement. The Devils instead argued for Scott Stevens and Judge Edward Houston, the NHL-appointed arbitrator, agreed, leaving a big hole in the St. Louis defense as well as in the egos of Joseph and Brind'Amour.

Flyer GM Russ Farwell, who had been told by the Blues in 1990 that Brind'Amour was untouchable, tried again after the arbitration ruling and GM Ron Caron accepted Ron Sutter—the coach's brother—and defenseman Murray Baron in a trade.

"Sutter was a top-end third-line center whose best days were behind him," recalls Farwell. "Rod was another level of player." Arguably Farwell's greatest return in a deal for the lowest cost—not to overlook his acquisition of Mark Recchi in a multi-player swap for Rick Tocchet—gained the rebuilding franchise eight years at the center position and their foothold on becoming, well, the Flyers again.

"I was a 20-year old kid, out of a bad situation in St. Louis, and it felt like a breath of fresh air," recalls Brind'Amour. "I was lucky in the sense that I went from Brian Sutter, who was a hard ass, to Paul Holmgren, who was a tough ass to play for, so all I knew to start my career was that there's no cheating of the game.

"I'd played [44] games as a Flyer when I learned how it was special here. We [hosted] the All-Star Game and I'm in it only because every club has to be represented.

"I realized all that, sure. But they announced me last and, of all the players, I got the loudest ovation. Wayne Gretzky and Mario Lemieux are in the game and the place goes (off) like I'm the best player to ever play because I'm wearing the Flyer jersey. And the fans barely knew me.

"I'm like, 'Wow, you don't get that everywhere.' I once scored two shorthanded goals to finish off a playoff series (against Pittsburgh in 1997) and that All-Star Game is still my most memorable moment here. I don't know if players think like that now, but it meant a lot to me."

The appreciation proved reciprocal, When the Flyers, who were making some progress back toward contention, decided to tear up their foundation to start a new one around Eric Lindros in 1992, Farwell made negotiable every piece he had except for Brind'Amour and Recchi.

Recchi ended up being the big chip in Bobby Clarke's spectacular 1995 haul—John LeClair and Eric Desjardins—that propelled the Flyers back into the playoffs, Brind'Amour providing far more than just secondary scoring support in a one-two, up-the-middle, combination with Lindros.

"Rod did everything second-line centers should do—win draws, kill penalties and play the power-play," recalls Chris Therien, a teammate for five-plus seasons. "That they moved him around (with multiple linemates and to left wing) was a tribute to how good he was. Rod had offensive skill he didn't use because he played the game the right way."

The skill would desert Brind'Amour during scoring droughts when his hands became as tight as his abs. Repeatedly told to relax, Rod didn't do relaxed.

"Even though you're doing the exact same things when you are scoring, no one ever says you are trying too hard, right?" he says. "When things are going badly, [fans and media] are gonna find things.

"What makes successful teams are guys who care and compete. Yeah, looking back, it would have been easier not putting so much pressure on myself, but if you're going to err on one side I want to be the guy who is trying too hard."

Even with all this periodic paralysis-by-overanalysis, Brind'Amour, inducted into the Flyers Hall of Fame in 2015, scored 601 points in 633 Philadelphia games and 24 goals (including 13 in the '97 drive to the Final) in 57 playoff contests. Those were strong numbers for a guy who never kept count, signing contracts that had no bonuses for points.

"I don't want to worry about stuff like that," he said. "If the team wins, I'll sleep at night."

And if his intensity cost him a few winks, he's convinced all that work off the ice kept him on it during the consecutive-game streak that began on February 24, 1993 and ended on opening night 1999, after Brind'Amour's foot was fractured in an exhibition game. He missed 33 games and had been back for only 12 when he, goalie Jean-Marc Pelletier and a second-round choice were dealt to Carolina for Keith Primeau and a fifth-rounder.

Bob Clarke was obsessed with getting a second oversized center behind Lindros—or eventually to replace him. Indeed, after Lindros moved on, Primeau played heroically during Philadelphia's 2004 run to within one game of the Final. But Rod doesn't believe the deal ever would have happened had the Flyers not gone 19-9-5 in his absence.

"Goes back to what I was saying about not wanting to miss games," he said. "Out of sight, out of mind. Their thinking, I'm sure, was they didn't need me anymore.

"I was crushed. Crushed. I was a Flyer. To me, it meant something to be a Flyer."

Nine years after his first trade to a team starting over, he was on his way to another. But six years later, when Brind'Amour captained Carolina to the Stanley Cup that the guys he left behind in Philadelphia never won, not a one begrudged him that championship.

"I think the ending for Rod Brind'Amour was well-scripted," said Therien. "The guy deserved to captain a Stanley Cup winning team. I wish I would have won one with him."

That feeling went all the way to the top of the Flyers organization.

"Ed Snider was one of the first calls I got when we won," said Brind'Amour who retired in 2010 after 20 NHL seasons, and has become a Hurricanes' assistant coach. "Six years later, he still remembered. That meant a lot to me.

So did busloads of Flyer fans coming to Raleigh to root Brind'Amour to his Cup and attending his retirement ceremony there in 2010. Of all the beloved players the Flyers ever traded away, he might be the best remembered.

"This place is special," Brind'Amour says. "I walked around the [Wells Fargo Center] when I was there scouting the [2014 Frozen Four] and I got mobbed, what, 14 years after I played here?

"If there's a fan group that deserves [another] championship, it's the Flyers, and it's so disappointing that it hasn't happened. I think after the '97 Final, which we lost because we weren't mature enough yet to win, we tore it up too early. I would have loved to stick it out and see whether we could have won one, and I'm sure we would have if I had stayed my whole career here.

"I mean, there aren't too many years that start off with people saying 'the Flyers can't win.' They deserve to do it finally."

Roman Cechmanek

CHAPTER 5 • 2000-02

Czech In, Cech Out

WITH BRIAN BOUCHER coming off the best goals-against average (1.91) by a rookie NHL goalie in 50 years, agent Tom Laidlaw wanted double the $1 million a year Bob Clarke was offering the restricted free agent to play the 2000-01 season.

"There's a lot of young goalies who have come into the league and had a great first year then died on the vine," said the GM. "I don't think Bouch is going to do that, but it could happen.

"No player can afford to miss training camp, especially a young goaltender just getting started. He might never get caught up."

Clarke had some leverage. He had just used a sixth-round pick—although only the Flyers' third choice—on Roman Cechmanek, a five-time champion for HC Vsetin of the Czech Extra League and the backup to Dominik Hasek at the Nagano Olympics.

"We needed a backup goalie and our scout (Vaclav Slansky) said he had a guy in the Czech Republic who wanted to come over, " recalls the GM, who already had a taker for John Vanbiesbrouck and $1.5 million of the $3.5 million due on the remaining contract year of the about-to-turn 37-year-old veteran.

"I was at the players' association meetings in Whistler (B.C.) when I got a call from my wife telling me (Islander GM) Mike Milbury wanted to speak to me," recalls Vanbiesbrouck. "What in the world would Mike Milbury want with me?

"Clarke called first and said, 'We traded you to the Islanders.'

"I was surprised. I thought I could still play and was doing a good job helping the young goalie."

Milbury, who had just used the first overall pick on netminder Rick DiPietro, wanted Vanbiesbrouck exactly for that role, ending his much second-guessed and ultimately bittersweet two-year free-agent term in Philadelphia.

"I wasn't the answer to the Flyer goalie woes over the years that I had felt I could be, and that pressure maybe was the reason I never completely got comfortable in goal there," recalls Vanbiesbrouck, now a junior hockey general manager with the Muskegon Lumberjacks of the United States Hockey League. "I gave up weak goals against Toronto that cost us the (1999) series, unfinished business I would love to have back.

"But I wouldn't change my decision to come there for the world. I had a lot of good moments on the ice, like going into Madison Square Garden in my first game with the Flyers and shutting out the Rangers. And there were a couple shutout streaks where I really played well.

"Most of all, I always respected the Flyers for never failing to take care of our families and wives. I have a lot of respect for Bob Clarke and that organization."

At age 29, it was NHL or bust for Cechmanek, who had no interest in taking a great North American adventure just to play in the American Hockey League. He was lured with a one-year, $1 million deal that did not call for a reduced minor league salary, but obligated the Flyers to pay him only a $300,000 signing bonus if he failed to impress at camp.

Seeking further leverage with Boucher, Clarke looked into 35-year-old Daren Puppa, whose back issues had limited him to 18 games the previous two seasons with Tampa Bay.

"I was getting anxious," recalls Boucher. On August 31, with Ed Snider playing mediator, Boucher met the Flyers near the middle, reaching a two-year deal for a total of $3 million, plus $500,000 in makeable incentives. "I still have a lot to prove," Boucher told the media.

That generally was not the case for the veteran-laden team that he had backstopped to within one game of the Stanley Cup Final despite the absence of injured and alienated star Eric Lindros.

Ten days after Philadelphia's elimination, Clarke had unloaded to a group of beat reporters, saying in a one-hour interview that Lindros's parents, Bonnie and Carl, had pushed for trades and insisted that coaches and trainers be fired. Clarke revealed that he had been accused by Bonnie of trying "to kill my son" by seeking to put him on an airplane, rather than in the hospital, on the night of Eric's 1999 lung collapse following a game in Nashville.

"It's pretty hard to believe that (trainer) John Worley wouldn't treat Eric properly [or that] I would put him on a plane and try to kill him," said Clarke. "This is the kind of stuff that just never ends.

"It's disruptive. And as hard as it's been on all of us on this team, it's been a lot harder on Eric.

"We want to retain his rights. We want him back; we don't want his mom and dad back. The majority of the players will tell you that he's a good team player until his dad gets involved. And then, [Eric] gets all confused and nobody knows what the hell is going to happen. "

Clarke said he had never told Lindros to fire Carl as his agent.

"No, it's not my business," said the GM. "But I've had to listen to the conversations with, 'You shouldn't trade for this guy because Eric

doesn't like this guy's agent,' and 'This guy shouldn't be playing with Eric because he doesn't pass him the puck enough.' Or 'Get Mike Peca because Mike Peca is taking runs at Eric.' If you were coaching a 12-year-old Little League team and a parent said that, that parent would be considered the biggest jerk in the world.

"I like Eric. Well, I did at one time. But I pity him now. Who wants to be 27 years old and have their mom and dad run their life?"

Three weeks later, at the July 1 deadline to make a qualifying offer that would retain the Flyer rights to Lindros for another season, Carl was faxed a one-year, $8.4 million contract, accompanied by an olive branch from Clarke.

"Eric Lindros is one of the top players in the game and an integral part of our organization," the GM said in a statement. "We're hopeful that he will enjoy a complete recovery and return to play hockey at the high level to which we have been accustomed.

"On a personal level, I greatly regret the extent to which the relationship between myself and Eric and his family has deteriorated. I intend to do what I can to try to move this relationship on a better course."

Recalls Clarke, "I said that just in case he changed his mind. His dad had (privately) made clear Eric wasn't coming back."

A clause that would pay Lindros $85,000 to play for the Phantoms—the Flyers said NHL Commissioner Gary Bettman was pushing teams to use that Collective Bargaining Agreement right in cases of restricted free agency—only became one more reason the Lindroses considered the rift irreparable. In reality, the only purpose the organization could serve by sending Lindros to the minors would be to make itself appear punitive and vindictive.

"The league wanted us to make use of that clause," said Clarke. "Carl is his agent; he's supposed to know the rules."

Clarke already had invited teams to bid, offering them a five-year window to exercise any draft choices obtained in a deal should Lindros, expected to sit out at least half of the upcoming season after suffering five concussions in a two-year period, have setbacks in his recovery.

When the Lindros family attorney, Gordon Kirke, called Flyer counsel Phil Weinberg just before the midnight August 1 deadline and turned down the offer, Kirke cited concerns that Clarke would have been empowered to force Lindros back onto the ice ahead of his mid-season timetable.

"This is what gives him the best shot at a full recovery," Kirke said, terming it a "well-being decision, not a business one."

Removing an $8.5 million price tag from Lindros actually made him able to shop for an incentive-laden deal more likely to bring about the trade he wanted. But since the contract offer enabled Philadelphia to retain his equalization rights until he became eligible for unrestricted free agency at age 31, the team was in the driver seat.

The virtually unavoidable trade made it equally crucial that the Flyers reach a multi-year deal with the other face of their franchise, left wing John LeClair. But with the sides far apart, LeClair, a restricted free agent subject to compensation, and agent Lewis Gross decided on the Collective Bargaining Agreement mandated option of a one-year contract through arbitration.

Following an August 11 hearing, during which the team offered a $1 million raise to $5 million and LeClair asked for $8 million, arbitrator Michel Picher decided on a salary of $7 million, the largest arbitration reward in NHL history by a whopping $2.25 million margin.

"As soon as a player files for arbitration, he is essentially signed," says Clarke. "So I always told the lawyers we hired for the hearings, 'I don't want him cut up. Use stats to make our argument.' We never let it get personal."

LeClair attended with the mindset that it wouldn't. "They compare you to one player and you compare yourself to another," he recalls. "I didn't leave thinking Clarke was a bad guy or anything. He is doing what he's got to do."

In the aftermath of the decision, Clarke first needed to be conciliatory. "The decision was pretty much in the middle of both sides, which was fine," said the GM in a statement. "We will continue in our effort to sign John to a long-term contract."

LeClair, who had been trying to get a deal worthy of a 50-plus goal scorer since reaching that mark for the first of three times in 1995-96, set a deadline of the beginning of camp. "It's been ample time and I don't want to be a distraction," he said. "We've had enough distractions around here."

That was fine by Clarke. "We respect his wishes," said the GM. "I really have a hard time believing John will not be here for a long time."

For $1.5 million, Clarke signed defenseman Michal Sykora, a five-year NHL veteran with San Jose and Chicago, who had returned to play the 1999-2000 season in his native Czech Republic. "Best defenseman in Europe," said Clarke, who meanwhile bought out the remaining $2.1 million of Ulf Samuelsson's contract at the CBA-mandated two-thirds value. Shoulder issues had ended the warrior's career after 15 seasons.

Valeri Zelepukin left for a one-year offer from Chicago. Clarke re-upped playoff hero Andy Delmore for two years, signed center Derek Plante, a six-season NHL veteran, for depth, and traded an eighth-round pick to Carolina for 13-year veteran winger Paul Ranheim, reuniting him with his former Hurricane penalty-killing partner, Kent Manderville.

Far less under the radar than those moves was the signing of 35-year-old winger Kevin Stevens, twice a first-team All-Star with Pittsburgh, to a one year, $600,000 deal despite his arrest seven months earlier at a suburban St. Louis motel for possession of several grams of crack cocaine.

Stevens still faced charges of possession of drugs and drug paraphernalia, plus solicitation of a prostitute, but had gone though a two-month substance abuse program mandated by the CBA. "I learned a lot about myself," he said. "I don't feel good about it, but I feel good about myself right now."

Said Clarke, "He had some personal problems we feel he has overcome.

"Kevin is a pretty interesting player. He brings some size on the wing. He can score, can play second line or third line, and he allows us to move (Simon) Gagne to the middle if Lindros doesn't play."

At age 36, Rick Tocchet signed what he expected to be his final contract for two years and $4.4 million. "I probably could have gotten a little bit more with somebody else, but I wanted to come back," he recalls.

That also would have been the preference of Craig Berube, 34, another influential personality in the locker room, but the Flyers allowed themselves to be outbid by the Capitals on a one-year $700,000 deal.

Roger Neilson, who following the Philadelphia playoff success was not going to be reinstated as head coach over Craig Ramsay, had cleaned out his office after midnight on one of the first nights following the Flyer elimination. He returned to his home in Peterborough, Ontario without a conversation about staying on as Ramsay's assistant.

"Somewhere along the line, he thought I promised him a long-term contract," recalls Clarke. "I wouldn't make that promise and not fulfill it.

"He could have stayed as an assistant, of course."

Ramsay does not recall ever discussing a position with Neilson. "I don't think he had any interest in coming back as anything but a head coach," recalls Ramsay, which also is the recollection of Neilson's long-time companion, Nancy Nichols.

"Roger had an ego and there were a lot of flash points of emotions," she says. "He had worked so hard to get back (from stem cell treatments) and felt really devastated when the Flyers [refused to give him the bench.]

"I don't know if there ever was an offer and a 'screw off,' which would have been the strongest word Roger would have used. Regardless, he wasn't going back there."

Neilson, who conceded"there aren't many head-coaching jobs for a 66-year-old with cancer," took an assistant job with Ottawa under Jacques Martin.

After four years as head coach of the Phantoms—one of them, 1997-98, bringing a Calder Cup championship—Bill Barber joined Mike Stothers as an assistant to Ramsay, who had received a two-year deal for $400,000 and $450,000 on top of an $80,000 bonus the Flyers gave him for directing the team to the conference regular season championship and two series victories.

Barber, who had interviewed for the head-coach position with Columbus that spring, just as he had with Atlanta the previous one, had told Clarke that he did not want to return to the Phantoms. "Clarkie really looked after me," recalls Barber. "I think I was the highest-paid coach in the minors. But the long rides home on the bus with a bad neck made me want to move on.

"I had been branded as a Flyer and wanted it that way. To stay with one organization is rare. And even an (NHL) assistant job was a step up."

Clarke brought in former Flyers Kjell Samuelsson and Don Nachbaur to assist new Phantom head coach John Stevens, who had been an assistant under Barber.

Chris Therien, captain Eric Desjardins' long-time defensive partner, agreed to a new four-year, $9 million, deal on the first day of training camp.

"At 10 the night before, Bob barked out, 'This is our final offer,'" recalls Therien. "It was something like (one year at) $1.63 million. Then he said, 'We will deduct 3 percent every single day until it's signed.'

"I said to (agent) Pat (Morris), 'What do we do here? I'm getting nervous.'

"Pat said, 'He wants you to be nervous. At the end we're going to be happy.'

"The next morning I'm in the car headed to the Flyers Skate Zone (the new Flyer practice facility, to be dedicated that day) when Pat calls and says, 'We got them at four years, $8 million.' I said, 'You're kidding me,' and he said, 'But we're not done yet. I can get more out of them.'

"What I didn't realize was that Bob's daughter Jody had just had her second child, so he was in a great mood. He had called Pat and said, 'I've had a change of heart; we're going to give Chris a long-term contract.'

"Pat says, 'Go to Clarkie's office. I'll call in and we'll finalize it while you are there.' I get into his office at 9:30 a.m. and Pat doesn't call. It's me and Clarkie in there alone for half an hour and I'm [really nervous]. Pat called and we ended up getting another million. I was going to take eight.

"We shook, and Bob said, 'This is a good deal for both sides. I'm happy we could reach it.'"

Clarke's recollection was that when negotiations for a longer-term deal stalled, he made the one-year offer as a restarting point before raising it over multiple years. "It was great to become a grandfather again, but I don't know if I was so happy that I gave away a million dollars," he laughs.

"Maybe, though. Chris was a good player at that stage for us."

Not every Flyer had such a literally lucrative first day of training camp. But following a ribbon cutting, all of them walked into the Skate Zone that morning feeling like a million dollars. The club's new $20 million training facility on Laurel Oak Road in Voorhees, NJ was the first ever built for an NHL team with two separate rinks (one for the Phantoms). It featured nine locker rooms for community and youth hockey players and figure skaters, party rooms, a dining area, pro shop, and interactive computers in the lobby.

"We went to everybody, person by person, and asked them what they wanted," said Pat Ferrill, Comcast-Spectacor's president of rink management and development. "We didn't build this rink to be the nicest rink in the country this year. We built it to be the nicest rink in the country for years to come."

Unlike at the Coliseum, the Flyer practice facility since the 1982-83 season, this one had an ice surface without bumps, an eating lounge for team members and enough space in the hot and cold tubs for multiple teammates.

"There's a nice atmosphere; players are excited," said Ramsay.

So was LeClair about reporting for camp, even if his long-term deal wasn't done. "Considerably," he said when asked if the sides had gotten closer. "As long as they keep talking, a lot can happen."

He called the talent at camp, the "the best we've had in a long time." Opening eyes was 18-year-old Justin Williams, a right wing from the Plymouth Whalers of the Ontario Hockey League, whose 170-pound frame had caused him to fall to the 28th overall pick just three months earlier.

Justin Williams and Petr Hubacek scored their first NHL goals in the Flyers' season opener, a 6-3 win vs. Vancouver.

"We had zeroed in on either Justin or Niklas Kronwall (a defenseman who went to Detroit 29th)," recalls Ontario scout Dennis Patterson. "We didn't know Kronwall would turn out to be such a competitor.

"Williams' worth ethic and hockey sense stood out. He was a late birthday (had just missed being eligible for the preceding draft) and I think a little more mature as a result."

Though convinced that the development of departed No. 1 pick, Dainius Zubrus had been set back by rushing him to the big team at age 18, the Flyers believed Williams' brain for the game would make him a different case. "He didn't panic with the puck," recalls Ramsay.

Therien had to put some of his newly found wealth to almost immediate good use. Skating back to play a dump-in during an exhibition game in Trenton, he twisted himself into two herniated disks and was in so much pain on the bus ride home that his only comfort was to lay on the floor in his suit. "It got so dirty; I threw it out," he recalls.

For depth, Clarke picked up Chris McAllister, the biggest defenseman in Philadelphia history at 6-foot-7, 238 pounds, from Toronto for minor-leaguer Regan Kelly. "He struggled some last year, but two years ago he looked like he was on the upswing," said the GM, who made room by sending Mark Eaton, the first-ever Delaware Valley born-and-bred Flyer, to Nashville on September 29 for a third-round pick in the 2001 draft.

Meanwhile, the Flyer organization sadly noted the passing in Villanova, PA of the Reverend John Casey, 88, an original season ticket holder and sweetest of men who performed team chaplain duties on repeated occasions—including on-ice services after the passing of Pelle Lindbergh and Tim Kerr's wife, Kathy.

Cechmanek had a good camp, but not superior to that of Maxime Ouellet, Philadelphia's first round pick in 1999, so the Flyers informed the Czech he was being sent to the Phantoms. He called his wife Dagmar and said he was coming home. She told him to stick it out.

The No. 1 goaltending job was Boucher's to lose.

"I didn't really think over the summer about how well I did (the previous season," he told Rich Hofmann of *The Philadelphia Daily News*. "I just kept thinking we were up 3-1 against the Devils and we spoiled it; I never had a chance to enjoy it.

"Then they started negotiating and shoot you down a little bit by talking about bringing in a goalie. I'm at home thinking, 'They must not think very highly of me,' but it worked out and there are no hard feelings. I know how important this season is for me."

Despite how grandly the Flyers had achieved through the turbulence of 1999-2000, they looked forward to a more tranquil 2000-01. Clarke, who had received only preliminary inquiries, no firm offers, from the Kings, Leafs and Rangers for Lindros, predicted a "long, slow process" before Philadelphia received players for him, but that was not an issue in a locker room where it already was accepted Lindros would not return.

"For the guys who had been through the tumultuous relationship, they were ready to close the chapter and move on," recalls Keith Primeau. "I had come here the year before thinking it was going to be the two of us the next 10 years, having a real chance to win some championships, so personally I was a little disappointed.

"I got it—I had wanted to move on myself (from Carolina)—but not having [Lindros] was going to change my role. I hadn't found the chemistry with John (LeClair) that Eric had, and it wasn't as simple as me being a left-handed shot and Eric a right-handed shot. So trying to recreate that Eric-John combination was not going to transpire. I was only going to be what I was."

Rookies Petr Hubacek (a ninth-round pick in 1999), Ouellet and Williams made it to opening night. Ouellet and Williams were on 10-game deadlines to be sent back to their junior teams should the Flyers—who thereafter would be obligated to pay them an NHL salary for the entire season—decide they weren't ready to contribute.

Williams made a fast case for himself by scoring his first NHL goal on only his second shift, then added two assists while Hubacek was one-timing a pass from Tocchet in the second period for a goal in his initial game, too. "They looked a lot less nervous than all the older guys," said Mark Recchi after the team had played loosely in a 6-3 victory over Vancouver.

Two nights later, the Flyers were no tighter in a 5-1 loss to Boston. And their participation in the NHL's return to Minnesota after seven seasons was nothing to get Wild about. The Flyers' Peter White christened the St. Paul Xcel Energy Center with its first goal, but the expansion team earned a 3-3 tie with Philadelphia, a game LeClair missed with back spasms.

When LeClair's pain was not eased by steroid injections, he went to Los Angeles, where Dr. Robert Watkins repaired herniations in two disks, leaving the Flyers without their best player for an expected six weeks. Recchi, who was hit on the head by Ed Jovanovski on opening night, also came out of the lineup for Ouellet's first NHL start, a 4-2 loss in Dallas that left Ramsay's team 1-3-1 when Roger Neilson's

Senators came to town.

"I suppose [returning to Philadelphia] is a little bittersweet, but it was a business decision that is all over and behind me," Neilson said.

The normally mild-mannered Ramsay tried to awaken the Flyers with some strong words when they fell behind 3-0 after a period. Following Philadelphia's 6-1 loss, captain Desjardins and the players took their turns speaking behind closed doors for 27 minutes.

"We have gotten away from the simple, hard-working, grinding team that was successful last year," said Ramsay.

That wasn't aiding the struggling Boucher, who, on reflection, wasn't helping himself. "There were expectations I wasn't ready for emotionally," he recalls. "A lot of pressure. I think I had too much success too soon."

The Flyers thought Boucher needed some head-clearing time on the bench. Thus, Cechmanek, who had given up three goals in three games with the Phantoms, became the oldest-ever debuting Flyer rookie netminder (29 years, seven months and 17 days) in the same week Ouellet (19 years, three months, 24 days) had become the youngest. The Czech backstopped Philadelphia to a 3-3 tie with Montreal and then spoke to the media through translator-defenseman Sykora. "He said if you like the way he played, he'll stay here," Sykora reported. "If you don't like it, he'll go home."

While Keith Jones, slashed by Anaheim's Vitaly Vishnevsky, was suffering a concussion, the Flyers continued to hit themselves over the head. A 2-0 lead against the Ducks fizzled with the help of two Stevens third-period penalties, the latter cashed in by Teemu Selanne for the game winner with 2:38 to play. "It's not like we don't have faith in Ramsay's system," Desjardins said. "We're not doing any system at all."

That's what it seemed like to Clarke, who told Ramsay it didn't appear the team was being coached. Whether or not the cause was a to-be-expected hangover from a long, hard, and ultimately disappointing spring, panic already was setting in. "We're thinking too far ahead, [fearing] we're going to lose another game, and soon we'll be something like 1-10-2," said Luke Richardson.

As Hubacek faded to the fourth line and then to the Phantoms, Recchi returned. But on the afternoon of the October 24 game in New York, Mark admitted ongoing concussion symptoms to roommate Stevens. Stevens told Recchi it wasn't smart to play, then ratted him out to Ramsay before the team left the hotel for Madison Square Garden.

Ruslan Fedotenko, who had been dressing for a Phantom game, was sped to the 5:45 Metroliner by equipment manager Anthony "Rock" Oratario and the rookie reached the Flyer bench for his NHL debut 4:19 after the puck had been dropped.

"[The train] was really crowded; I had to stand for about 10 minutes," Fedotenko reported. Up 3-0, Philadelphia started standing around, too, and almost blew an early lead for a third straight game, but behind third-period goals by Williams and White, survived a late, long-distance, score by Valeri Kamensky for a 5-4 victory.

Asked about that last goal, Boucher told reporters, "You guys want to make it a headline, then do what you want. A win is a win."

He didn't feel that way the next day, smashing his stick over the goal after letting in a softie. "Did you watch me in practice?" he told inquiring minds about his tantrum. "I stunk."

After shutting out the Rangers 3-0 in the return match, Boucher next complained about media coverage of his practice outburst. "Must be a real slow news day," he said. "To make that the story upsets me. People think I'm a mental case."

Ouellet stayed sane, somehow, when, at the 10-game deadline, he was sent back for a fourth year in junior, dropping his salary to $50 a week. But Williams was told his days of free continental breakfasts at the Hampton Inn by the Skate Zone were over. He had made the team and should get his own place.

"I was a little tired of Alpha-Bits and bagels," he said. For certain, the menu was more varied at the Primeau home. "Not only did we room together on the road, but he basically grew up at my house," recalls Keith. "My kids were 12 and 13 at the time and Justin was only 18, so he'd be there playing mini-hockey with them.

"One time, he called (wife) Lisa and asked, 'What are you having for dinner?' She told him, and he said, 'Okay, I'll be right in.' He was already in the driveway.

"Justin had said he could make the team—that just doesn't happen for late first-rounders—and his confidence rubbed some of the older guys the wrong way. But he reminded me of a younger me when I first went to Detroit. I wanted the opportunity and it was perceived as arrogance when it was just the burning desire to play. That's what I loved about Justin."

Bumped by Tocchet late in a 1-1 tie with Washington, Primeau suffered concussion symptoms and, three nights later at the Meadowlands, was talked out of playing by Ramsay. The Flyers called up Todd Fedoruk, a 1997 seventh-round pick and, minus LeClair, Recchi, Primeau, Jones, Therien and Tocchet (ankle), managed a 1-1 tie against the Stanley Cup champs on fourth-liner Ranheim's conversion of a Desjardins rebound off the post with only 1:26 remaining.

Ramsay was wary of the apparently unsystematic style of the flopping, 6-2 Cechmanek, who also was learning on the fly the different angles of shots coming on the smaller rink, as well as the shoot-first mentality of the NHL. But the coach played a hunch and started Cechmanek against Buffalo's Dominik Hasek. Czechmate! Helped by the returns of Tocchet, Primeau and Therien and the first NHL goal by Fedotenko, the Flyers won 3-0.

"I'm sure it was in [Cechmanek's] mind in coming over here to get that chance (vs. his iconic countryman) and I thought he responded well," said Ramsay. "He was more in control, although he did some interesting things."

Thus Cechmanek won over Ramsay while Fedoruk, who had his last name tattooed on his back—"Family is big for me and hockey players have their names on their back," the hulking rookie nicknamed The Refrigerator explained—won over the crowd by fighting veteran Sabre enforcer Rob Ray.

"I lined up against him; he saw my number and asked, 'Who the [bleep] are you?'" recalls Fedoruk. "I asked him if he wanted to fight.

"I didn't have a reputation, so Robert said, 'Are you sure?' And I said,

'Look, man, I want to stay here, and fighting you is my best chance.'

"He was a league leader in fighting majors, so I could make my name right here, at home in Philly, where they love it. But that only happens if somebody gives you the chance. He was in his thirties. I was 20. He didn't have to do it, but he did.

"It was just glancing blows until I switched hands and hit him with a good right to the side of the head. It must have hurt him because he grabbed on and said, 'That's enough.' And I just said, 'Thanks, man, for the opportunity.'"

The next game, in Pittsburgh, Fedoruk took on long-time pest Matthew Barnaby.

"Matthew's coach was on him to be more aggressive," recalls Fedoruk. "He saw Ray had fought me and called him and asked, 'Who is this guy?'

"Ray said, 'He's tough, be ready.' So Barnaby asked me to fight him and I obliged and did really well, cut him, put him down. Then I scored my first NHL goal."

It didn't keep Boucher from being bombed 5-2. Ramsay went back to Cechmanek, who pitched another shutout, 2-0 over Edmonton, then beat Ottawa, 4-3, when Simon Gagne scored the winning goal on Patrick Lalime early in the third period on a shot from nearly the red line.

Jones' head had healed, but when he returned to practice in early November, his twice-repaired left knee failed to cooperate, worsening by the day. In the meantime, Williams and Fedotenko had given the Flyers better options, while the team's surge gave Clarke more license to wait and maximize his return for Lindros.

"If no one wants to give us what we think he's worth, he might have to play for us," said the GM.

Clarke requested a meeting with the Lindroses during an upcoming Flyer visit to Toronto. By the count of family attorney Kirke, Holmgren phoned "seven times" asking if Lindros would come back.

"I made it clear when I turned down $8.5 million that I would not play for them again," Lindros told reporters during a visit to Toronto's Hospital for Sick Children. "I have talked to Paul Holmgren several times and explained to him any meeting about coming back would be pointless.

"I tried for a number of years to work with the situation and it just goes to show you what we've ended up with. I will have nothing more to say on this. And I don't want to get into slinging mud back and forth."

Asked why he would want Lindros back, Clarke slung some more shovelfuls.

"Because he can play hockey," said the GM. "It's not like the rest of the league doesn't know about his family. They're not going to want to put up with the same things.

"We put up with all that thinking Eric would grow up, and he never did. They have tried to bully their way through from kids' hockey. They bullied people around in the OHL. They forced Quebec's hand. They always got their way."

Though the Flyers did not get their meeting in Toronto, they did get a victory as Recchi returned after missing nine games to take a cross-crease feed from Primeau for the 2-1 win in overtime.

Improved health appeared to be lifting Philadelphia from its early-season funk. So was an increasingly healthy attitude about Cechmanek's eccentricities. He occasionally deflected high shots away with his mask. "First time I saw it, I said, 'Did I just see that?'" recalls Clarke. "What the [bleep] is the matter with him?"

Not much, it appeared. "When I looked at him, I said, 'Holy cripes, how can this guy play for anybody?'" marveled the GM after Cechmanek beat Atlanta, 3-2 in overtime, for his fourth win in four starts. "But he's improved a lot around the net. He looks like a good goalie to me."

As the Flyers' patience bore fruit, it ran out for Phantoms left wing Francis Belanger, the driver of the boat from which defenseman Dmitri Tertyshny fell to his death into the propeller blade in July 1999. Belanger was released after a repeat positive test for prescription painkillers.

"It's hard to imagine seeing something like that and it not affecting you for a long time afterwards," recalls Therien. "There was a lot of reaching out to him."

Said Holmgren in making the announcement, "We tried to work a number of different angles with Francis and couldn't reach him. In the end, you can only help people who want to help themselves."

Jones, his patellar tendon (a portion of which had been used to repair his ACL while in Colorado), unhealed, went to Dr. John Faulkner, a joint specialist in Hartford, CT whose diagnosis was grim.

"Something like five percent of the persons who have that operation have that problem," recalls Jones. "I had been managing it for a number of years, hoping it would hold up, but losing a step each season."

After scoring 117 goals in 491 NHL games that a seventh-round pick never expected to play, Jones retired on November 21 at age 32. "I took it pretty hard," he said at a press conference packed not only with media but teammates. "At the same time I recognize I was in a tremendous amount of pain and whatever was wrong was going to get worse."

So would the jokes in a locker room without him. "This is like attending your own funeral, except you get to shake the guy's hand," Jones said. "The hardest part is leaving friends."

LeClair, out 20 games, kidded about his friends forgetting who he was. On a bet with Richardson, the winger wore an Afro wig during the warmup for his return game on November 26 against Phoenix. "We always joked about John's bad hair anyway," recalls Therien.

"I didn't think he had the guts to do it," said Richardson. But after many yuks, the last laugh was had by Phoenix's Sean Burke who, with a 2-1 win, followed Pittsburgh's Garth Snow as the second rejected Flyer goalie to beat them in two games.

Cechmanek had given up just five goals in his last three starts and lost them all. Next, the Senators got to him for three early ones in a 5-3 loss, two of the scores having come on Ottawa man advantages. After being in the top three in the NHL the previous season in both powerplay and penalty killing, the Flyers now had the worst penalty killing and were in the bottom half in powerplay success.

Ramsay called his veterans to a meeting, where Therien recalls the coach saying 'I heard some stuff (from Clarke) a little bit difficult to hear. You need to start playing better or I'm going to be released.'"

Clarke's primary complaint was a shortage of energy, so Ramsay asked his players to pick it up in that day's drills. They did, Delmore shoving Gagne after a play, Gino Odjick hot-dogging after scoring a goal on Boucher, and Tocchet ripping a stick from McGillis.

"There has been no intensity in our practices and it's carried over into games where we're playing safe," said Tocchet. "I'm a guy who has to lay down low, get into scrums, rush the net, and I haven't been doing that.

"I'm going back to my style, not this you-high stuff."

Ramsay's system—centers forecheck, wingers seal the walls—had succeeded grandly during the preceding playoffs. So generally the players were not questioning the strategy, wondering more about the methods.

"Craig is one of the nicest men in the game I've ever met," recalls Primeau. "Always positive.

"He had a definite idea of how the game was to be played that wasn't necessarily the norm. Because he believed in rest and days off, we weren't in condition to play 60 full minutes."

Recalls Tocchet, "I'm a Craig Ramsay fan. I would love to coach for him, loved to play for him, just thought maybe if he skated us a little harder, we would have gotten into the mindset we should have had."

Although LeClair scored his 10th regular season hat trick in a 6-3 win over Tampa, it didn't seem to energize the team, nor did Clarke's trade of one fourth-liner, Odjick, to Montreal for another, P.J. Stock. Acquired for his toughness, Odjick had only two fights in his 30 games in a Philadelphia uniform.

When Steve Yzerman weaved through the offensive zone absolutely unchallenged for a goal during a 5-1 loss in Detroit, the fifth Flyer defeat in seven games, their record dropped to 12-12-4.

"It was a really poor effort," said Ramsay. "Unacceptable."

Clarke thought players were not upset enough about losses and saw nothing changing. "I'd hoped it would, but it didn't," he recalls. The GM invited assistant coach Barber to the Phantom game the following night to discuss Flyer issues.

"The team was blah; I was seeing what everybody was seeing," recalls Barber. "I hadn't said anything about it to Craig, didn't want to go in and be forceful. His knowledge of the game was phenomenal.

"I wasn't going behind his back. Clarkie wanted to know how I felt. I wasn't sure if it was a job interview or just him asking for input."

Clarke went home and thought some more. Sometime after 2 a.m., he decided to fire Ramsay. "Like Wayne Cashman, I thought he was a great assistant coach, just wasn't a commanding enough presence as a head coach to hold players accountable," the GM recalls. "I had made a mistake, had to admit it and move on."

In the morning, with Philadelphia scheduled to play the Islanders at First Union Center that night, Clarke called Ed Snider at an NHL Board of Governors meeting in Florida to tell him his plans, then went to the Skate Zone and to Ramsay's office.

"I think I have to make a change," he said. Neither man recalls there being a discussion. Clarke then went to the locker room and invited Barber upstairs to the GM's office. Barber wondered if he had done something wrong but was then told he was the new head coach.

"I could only see it getting worse," Clarke explained to reporters at a noon press conference, never mind the Flyers had just gotten back LeClair and Recchi, their two best scorers. The GM, who had first raised his eyebrows on Day One of camp when Ramsay had watched from the balcony rather than run drills on the ice, said he had "several" meetings with the coach about his team's lack of physical play, shortage of emotion, and poor practice habits.

"Right from the start of training camp I thought we lacked the drive and emotion we had last year through the playoffs," said Clarke. "We won some games because at times our goaltending has been outstanding.

"To lose as many games as we have without the proper response from our players is not acceptable to any organization. Our [team was] not in the type of skating condition you need to play hard for 60 minutes."

Of course there had been no such complaints about passivity while Ramsay was directing Philadelphia to within one game of the Stanley Cup Final as a fill-in for Neilson.

"Players compete their hardest in the playoffs without the necessity of being pushed," said Clarke. "In an 82-game schedule, it's a constant battle to do it on a daily basis through hard work, confronting your problems, and addressing them."

Some of the team's members immediately agreed, including Boucher, who had played for the Phantoms under Barber. "I like Rammer," the goalie told the media. "He did great handling a job that was not very easy, but there's been some games this year that we have not really competed in for whatever reason.

"I'm not saying it was accepted, but nothing was really done about it. I can tell you right now that Billy will not let that happen."

Said Recchi, "We haven't played with a lot of emotion and grit. "We've played a little bit of a different system where it's not as physical as before. Last year, when he came in late, we'd been pushed one way all year; he just basically changed lines and things like that. We'd already been coached a lot."

And by several men. Barber was the fifth Flyer coach in three and one-half years. "I don't think we're unstable at all," argued Clarke. "I think when there's hard decisions that have had to be made, we haven't been afraid to make them.

"I was afraid we could be out of the hunt by Christmas. Billy is a fiery guy who will put the emotion and direction back in our team. He'll hold players accountable for poor performances."

Ramsay took calls from reporters at his home that same afternoon. "I don't care what anybody says, they played hard," he said. "I'm proud of who I am and what I've done, and of how this team has played.

"Look at these five losses (in the eight preceding games). You don't get 35 to 40 shots a night (in nine of his last 10 games, the Flyers totaled 30-plus) if you're not playing hard, and we were playing hard. This team battled through a lot of different things. Maybe if we had been healthy all along, it would have been different."

He remains convinced of that today. "We started three goalies in the first five games," he recalls. "When Keith got hurt, Peter White was our best centerman. I love Peter, but that's probably not ideal. We had a compromised lineup.

"I always wanted to forecheck, always wanted to attack; that was an excuse, just not true.

"I took a contract (two years at $450,000 and $475,000), the minimum for an NHL coach at that time, like they weren't sold on my ability to be a head coach. I took it because I loved the team and wanted the chance.

"I had my battles through the years against the Flyers, including when they beat [Buffalo] out (for the Stanley Cup) in 1975. Never would I have expected to coach there. I enjoyed so much the atmosphere that, of course, it increased the disappointment when it didn't last. My wife (Susan) took it really hard because we liked it there so much."

In turn, the players liked Ramsay so intensely that many believed had he remained coach, the team would have picked up their pace. It wasn't only injuries that plagued Philadelphia's mediocre play in the first two months.

"When you go that far in the playoffs and have a short summer, you're always going to have that slow start," recalls Gagne. "It's hard on the body and harder to get motivated after you were just in the biggest games of the year.

"As a young guy, I felt I could just go, go. But we had an older team and I think it's tough for the older guys to come back and be motivated right away.

"It's sad because Craig was a really good person and coach. To me, as [Neilson's] assistant, Rammer was one of the best in the league. As a head coach, we never found out."

Primeau is not sure the Flyers needed a different coach as much as an altered Ramsay. "I don't know if [the players] thought we had to have a coaching change as much as we had to have a philosophical change," recalls the center. "He could have been the right guy in charge and just needed to demand more, but that just may not have been his personality.

Therien remembers, "He told the (team) leadership that management didn't think we forechecked hard enough. But Rammer's attitude was if there is a hit, go get it, but don't run out of the way.

"I think Craig was a great hockey mind, years ahead of the curve to where the game's at now. He did want to pursue the puck. He knew what he was doing. You rarely see a big hit today.

"He was fair, honest, and understood that mistakes happen. He wasn't going to bring you in for six hours showing you the same mistake over and over again. It was like, 'Hey, you guys know better.' To me, we were going to turn the corner no matter who was coach."

LeClair knew the organizational mindset though. "There's a little bit of history where they are not patient around here, so I wasn't shocked but, yes, a little surprised," he recalls. "I hadn't been around the whole season, but I didn't feel there was any lack of respect for Craig, who was a great listener.

"That's the way the coaching cycle goes. From a guy who is kind of a players' guy to a guy who does it his way."

The latter was going to be Barber, who, having stayed in the face of the minor leaguers all the way to a championship, thought major leaguers needed the same approach.

"We have to play with some urgency and feeling," the coach said at the press conference. "There were games that concerned me, games when we were the same all the way through.

"We weren't an excited team when we should have been excited. We weren't strong in areas when we had to be a little more physical. We need to be a team that controls the puck and doesn't give it up offensively."

Barber fought back tears as he was introduced as the 14th head coach of the only NHL team for which he had ever served as a player and in whatever capacity asked.

"My goal was to become a head coach in the NHL and if the opportunity ever presented itself with the Philadelphia Flyers, it would be a dream come true," he said. "I don't think you ever lose your dreams. If you give that up, you lose living; you become stagnant."

That night, Andy Delmore, living his own dream after going unselected in two drafts, took Barber's words to heart just six seconds into the game, high-sticking Islander Roman Hamrlik and drawing a double minor.

Islander Brad Isbister opened the scoring late in the period, but Primeau, breaking a four-game drought, responded quickly to tie the game, then added another goal. Stevens, dressing for only the second time in eight games, had a goal and two assists while the Flyers outshot New York 40-18 in making Barber's debut a 5-2 success.

"At times a hockey club takes on the personality of its coach," said Primeau. "I felt the energy Billy had all day.

"There was more room to create. He loosened the reins. We did a better job of forechecking."

Barber praised his players for becoming exhausted "like they should be after the game," and added he would be more of an attitudinal coach than a tactical one. "I expect players to play desperate," he said. "It's what we stand for."

To some in the media, desperation was starting to stand for the front office, too. Twice in four years, Clarke had fired a coach before he had completed a season. When, during a segment on Canada's TSN, interviewer Gord Miller said to Clarke, "Never a dull moment in Philadelphia," Clarke blurted out, "We didn't tell Roger to get cancer. It's too bad that he did and we feel sorry for him, but then he went goofy on us."

Recalls, Clarke, "It was a little bit crude but I don't regret it. Roger blamed us."

Snider, meanwhile, shot at the messengers in the media suggesting impatience was getting the Flyers nowhere.

"The Devils fired their coach last season with eight games to go and won the Stanley Cup," he told *The Philadelphia Inquirer*'s Claire Smith. "They have a very outstanding general manager, Lou Lamoriello, and he did what he thought was best.

"I read all this crap—Bob did this, Bob did that. If Bob feels like there's something wrong, he moves to correct it. He has us competing in the playoffs every year, a hard thing to do these days, and all everybody can do is bitch and moan.

"Nobody is mistake-free. And there aren't many people out there who can admit when they made a mistake.

"We want the team playing Flyers hockey. Now the definition has changed over the years and we all understand that. But I just don't know that Flyers hockey entails being the least penalized team in the league. It's not the kind of hockey that the fans here were brought up on and have grown to love. And that was [the reason for the change] more than anything.

"I'd hate to knock Craig Ramsay. To be 12-12 with all the injuries and everything, it wasn't horrible. But there was just a lackadaisical feeling on the team."

At his first practice the day following the Islander win, Barber upped the tempo and shortened the duration. "I played long enough to know that if you are standing around out there, you stand around during the game," said the coach. He then talked about managing risk on the two-man forecheck he was employing and predicted unpredictability with his line combinations. "I will do that," he explained. "It's not panic."

He was going to navigate by gut a team ready to feel better about itself. Even though the Flyers gave up a shorthanded goal, then a third period score, during a 2-2 tie at Nashville in their new coach's second game behind the bench, Barber said, "I was pleased with the way we played."

Following a flight delay, a 4 a.m. arrival, and a seesaw battle, he was even happier the next night in Denver. With eight seconds remaining, Gagne converted the final of three last-minute faceoffs that Primeau won from Joe Sakic to give Philadelphia a 3-3 tie.

"You can start to feel it," said Recchi. "The energy we're playing with, everyone getting back to help out.

"For most of the night, we really outplayed them. We're making good D-to-D passes instead of flipping the puck around the boards. Colorado is the best team in the league and the air is thinner up here, yet we seemed to have more stamina at the end. We're attacking the puck and driving the net. Obviously, the players like this style."

On Clarke's recommendation, E.J. McGuire—Mike Keenan's right-hand man during his Flyer years—joined Mike Stothers as Barber's assistant coaches. McGuire had followed Keenan to Chicago, been an assistant coach in Ottawa, and then an AHL head coach in Portland and Hartford.

"When E.J.'s name came up, I said, 'Absolutely,'" recalls Barber. "Great technical guy, dedicated, always had your back."

In the meantime, LeClair, not wishing his bad back on anyone, returned to Dr. Watkins in Los Angeles for therapy. Primeau had spasms, too, but even without two first-line players, the Flyers were on a honeymoon. They smoked the Devils, 6-3 behind Cechmanek and, despite a shaky Boucher, bounced back from a 2-0 deficit to get a 4-4 tie in Boston.

The moribund powerplay clicked to life with three goals in a 4-3 win over the Pacific Division-leading Sharks, when the winning goal came on a McGillis wrister that went in off Tocchet's skate as he was being taken down in front.

"Tocchet is everything the Flyers stand for," said Barber including taking more than one for the team. When his cheekbone was fractured by Dan McGillis's slapshot—"I wasn't even in front of the goal; I was so [bleeped] at him," Tocchet recalls—during a 2-1 win over Carolina, it was the second time in a month he had been hit in the face by a Flyer defenseman's errant aim. "The way our defense shoots, I'm thinking about wearing a welding mask," said Tocchet.

Danger lurked everywhere and could strike at any time. McGillis suffered a cut at the base of his thumb unloading the dishwasher on Christmas Day. "That's why I always tell my wife I can't help with the dishes—I might get hurt," said Primeau.

McGillis didn't miss a game and neither did Tocchet, who scored in a 5-2 victory at Florida to bring his line with Daymond Langkow and Gagne to a whopping 30 points in six games.

But after getting hit in the hand, Tocchet finally couldn't go the next night in Tampa. Because Boucher had allowed three first-period goals against the Lightning, Philadelphia's 35-18 shot advantage still wound up as a 4-3 defeat, Barber's first in nine games as the coach.

When Cechmanek, suffering from the flu, had to turn over a 3-2 lead in Washington to Boucher, the Flyers lost again 6-3. "That puck's got to be stopped, that's the bottom line," said Barber.

With Tocchet, LeClair and Primeau (shoulder sprain) all out, Cechmanek blocked 22 in a 1-1 tie at New Jersey that Barber declared a "very big point" for

Bill Barber was hired partway into 2000-01 to up the Flyers' intensity level.

Philadelphia, especially so since LeClair's healing had stalled. The winger confessed to not being nearly as close to returning as the team had been suggesting.

"The last two weeks have been probably the most frustrating times I've ever had in hockey," said Big John, who was told he was enduring a scar tissue issue.

Primeau missed only three games before returning with two goals in Atlanta, where Recchi hit the empty net after a 5-0 third-period lead had dwindled to 5-4. "Good for fans, high score," said Cechmanek, who then was much stronger as Primeau's third period redirection saved a 2-2 tie in a rematch with the Thrashers. The Czech's 1.99 goals-against average and .922 save percentage were both fifth in the league.

"There is no question he has been our rock back there," said Recchi. "You can't say enough about his composure."

Meanwhile, the news from Ottawa was painful. Roger Neilson suffered his second cancer diagnosis in 13 months, this time melanoma. A mole of a dozen years that had turned malignant was removed, but the cancer had spread to his lymph nodes, leaving a prognosis more immediately threatening than the multiple myeloma that had ended his time behind the bench in Philadelphia.

"I think we're still good friends and my concern for him is sincere," said Clarke.

He wouldn't say the same about Lindros, who had been medically cleared to return during December. Eric was awaiting a trade the Flyers were willing to make, but the GM said it would not be any of those so far proposed by the Maple Leafs.

"Rest for Eric is not a bad thing," said Kirke. "He is so intent on a deal with the Leafs, it makes him more patient. No other teams are even on the radar screen."

Snider, not happy with the Leaf offer—reportedly either right wing Jonas Hoglund or center Yanic Perreault, plus conditional draft choices based on Lindros's availability and performance—went on Toronto's Fan 590 radio to announce that he had told Clarke to cut off negotiations.

"[The Leafs] feel we should make a totally contingent deal and we don't feel that way," said Snider. "A lot of other clubs in the league don't feel that way either.

"I believe that Toronto feels they have us over the barrel. Who they have over a barrel is Eric. I believe that they feel they're going to wear us down or we're going to panic. But they're not offering us anything that would help our team this year. There are other teams that would satisfy us."

Kevin Stevens had reached a deal with Illinois authorities, donating $5000 to the drug program in (Madison) county where he had been arrested for cocaine possession in a hotel room the previous January. But after being scratched from 16 of 44 Flyer games, the winger was traded to Pittsburgh on January 14 for defenseman John Slaney, who was assigned to the Phantoms.

"[Stevens] has gone through some tough things and he's getting his life in order," said Barber. "But our young kids (Williams and Fedoruk) have stepped up."

So did some veterans, including Primeau, who had 10 goals and four assists in 13 games under Barber. "[The coaching change] came at a time where my game was starting to come around," said the center. "But I've always felt I played the way I practiced and there's a lot more tempo, a lot more energy."

Philadelphia also was getting a lot of goaltending from Cechmanek, earning him a spot backing up his rival Hasek for the World team in the NHL All-Star Game.

"He thinks it came too fast," said Sykora, Cechmanek's translator. "He doesn't want to be considered the star because he might not be."

With a dynamic rookie season under his belt, Gagne had no such compunctions, having come to camp with the intention of "being the guy."

"Obviously, he's a star player at this age," said Barber when Gagne was picked for the North American team.

"None of us will ever know why some players have sophomore jinxes, but a lot of them seem to have it," said Clarke. "With [Gagne], it's like he's been here forever."

Having enjoyed perfect attendance in five of his first six Flyer seasons, LeClair had seemed eternal, too. But his back's redness, soreness, and pain were being caused by an infection in the same (herniated) disk repaired on October 21 by Dr. Watkins. It would take eight weeks of intravenous antibiotics, followed by a dose of oral ones, to clear up the problem.

Clarke said it remained the club's objective to sign LeClair to a multi-year deal. It also was the team's intention to continue to surge without him. "It's no different than last year when we pulled up our socks without Eric Lindros," said Tocchet.

Indeed, the Flyers were getting so much scoring it even appeared for fleeting seconds that Manderville had broken his 116-game goalless streak during Cechmanek's 3-0 shutout of Los Angeles. Problem was, Manderville had scored after hooking Lubomir Visnovsky off the puck. "When it has been that long you expect the worst," Manderville said. "And sure enough, when I turned around the official had his arm up."

After sitting for 11 consecutive games, Boucher got a start in Chicago. "It's his turn," Barber deadpanned, referencing Fred Shero's classic answer as to why he had chosen a national television game to give Bobby Taylor one of his eight starts in 1973-74 in relief of Bernie Parent. Boucher responded as though he deserved another turn, winning 5-1. "It's been a long time since I had a good game," he said.

Not true for the red-hot Gagne who, having scored the winning goal in three of the team's last four victories, went to a line with Recchi and Primeau against Mario Lemieux, who was facing the Flyers for the first time since coming out of retirement. In a 5-1 Philadelphia victory at Mellon Arena, the line combined for four goals.

The next night, Luke Richardson became the 159th player to reach 1,000 NHL games and only the fifth to reach the milestone (Clarke, Ron Hextall, Darryl Sittler, and Craig MacTavish) while wearing a Flyer uniform. "The games pile up; you don't realize how many years (14) you've been plugging away at this," said one of the sport's most earnest pluggers, presented with a Tiffany crystal prism (from the NHL), a wine refrigerator (from teammates), an engraved Patek

Philippe watch (from the Flyer organization), and a Harley Davidson Road King (via wife Stephanie).

With Desjardins' hamstring issue limiting his mobility, Richardson probably had been the Flyers' best defenseman. Desjardins became the luckiest, though, as his 70-footer on Rick DiPietro early in the third period broke a scoreless tie, giving Richardson the best gift of all on his night—a 2-0 victory over the Islanders.

All the crystal prisms and motorcycles in the world still may not have been a treasure to match Gagne's first trip to an All-Star Game. "Lemieux sitting next to me, I will get a chance to talk to him," said the kid, presuming alphabetical seating. "I'm a little nervous. It's kind of tough to believe this."

Even better than the conversation, as it turned out, were the two goals Gagne scored playing with Lemieux and Brett Hull in the third period after having been stopped by Cechmanek on a good chance in the second. That was just about the only thing the Flyer goalie, bombed for six in 20 minutes of work, stopped during the North American team's 14-12 win over the World club.

"Second period no fun," said Cechmanek. "After game, yeah, we had fun."

For the Flyers, the good times didn't last. They sat on a Philadelphia International Airport runway for 4½ hours during a snowstorm before being told their charter to Boston was not allowed to take off, forcing them to bus back to the Skate Zone, dig out their cars, then return the next morning to fly on game day.

They lost 4-3 to the Bruins when P.J. Axelsson put a softie between Boucher's legs in the third period. "It stinks; this is home for me," said the Woonsocket, RI native. But he wasn't the only holdover hero of 2000 to be struggling. The next night in Pittsburgh, Delmore was benched for a fourth straight game in favor of Sykora, who was performing more steadily after a struggling start.

"[Delmore] is playing with way too much risk for us," said Barber, who also had benched the defenseman during their time with the Phantoms. "We have met with him more than a couple times. He's got to sit down and watch what is going on, absorb what we are saying."

Unfortunately, in Pittsburgh, the view was no better from the press box. Cechmanek was yanked after giving up six in a 9-4 bombing. "Like All-Star Game," said Roman. But at least Manderville, in his 122nd game and on the181st shot since his last goal, scored—and shorthanded, too. "When my son (Ethan, seven months) gets older," said Manderville, "I am going to tell him, 'Don't get down or angry, just put a bright face on it and keep plugging away.'"

That was the tack of the Flyers and Cechmanek. They bounced back for a 5-2 win at Uniondale when a Langkow score that gave Philadelphia a 3-1 lead was first disallowed by the upstairs goal judge, who called down with a changed mind just before the faceoff.

The only thing more off and on than that goal was the negotiation between the Flyers and the Leafs, who could not satisfy Clarke with an offer of winger Sergei Berezin and a first rounder for Lindros. Names of other players being discussed continued to leak in Toronto papers, much to the distress of their distracted and struggling club.

Said Leaf coach and GM Pat Quinn, "When we see the type of errors we're making, they are errors of pre-occupation and poor concentration. We're answering the same question, I don't know the answer and I'm feeding the monkey."

Clarke wanted forward Nik Antropov and either defenseman Danny Markov or defenseman Tomas Kaberle. On the night of Thursday February 15, Quinn agreed to give Philadelphia Antropov and Markov and, by Sunday, had satisfied the Lindros clan with a contract offer. But Flyer doctors, examining medical records the Leafs provided upon request, learned Markov had a herniated disk.

Clarke asked for Kaberle instead. Quinn not only refused, but publicly accused the Flyers of being "a moving target" of "irresponsibility" and "a breach of good business manners."

Snider reacted angrily. "I heard all his [bullbleep] and it made me sick to my stomach," he said. "We never had a deal. The proposal fell through as we obtained more facts.

"They knew damn well we had to review [the medical reports]. You don't have a deal until two teams say they have a deal."

Added Clarke during a conference call as the Flyers rode a charter train for a game at Uniondale, "We never exchanged faxes, he's just covering his butt.

"He wanted to send us a centerman (Antropov) with a major knee surgery (out for the remainder of the season) and we were willing to accept that. But we were not going to take a defenseman with a herniated disk in his back who might not play for four to six weeks.

"'[Quinn] said Markov and Kaberle were equal players in his mind. So we said, 'We'll take the healthy guy.' We told him if he wanted to substitute one defenseman, we would take the deal back to Mr. Snider. It never happened."

The next night, Tocchet celebrated his 500th game as a Flyer by scoring on John Vanbiesbrouck, producing the team's second win on Long Island in five days, 3-1. Philadelphia wrapped up a stretch where 17 of 21 games were on the road with a 13-6-2 record. "It could have made or broken our season," said Recchi. "The guys did a good job of playing smart."

As the trading deadline approached, Clarke recalls Islander Mike Milbury inquiring about Lindros. The Flyer GM remembers requesting 23-year-old defenseman Zdeno Chara and being rebuffed, even though Milbury insists he never pursued Lindros, even to use him in a trade.

Unrelated to any Lindros deal, Clarke had conversations with the Kings about star defenseman Rob Blake, who instead was traded to Colorado for four players and two first-round choices. Another object of Philadelphia's desire, defenseman Eric Weinrich, went to Boston from Montreal (for Patrick Traverse) after the Canadiens had asked for Williams.

Clarke had been willing to wait for Antropov to rehab because the Flyers were not having any immediate trouble scoring goals. "Rex is playing out of his mind," said Primeau, who had 20 points in his last 12 games, while Gagne had 16 in 12 and Recchi 14 in 14.

Philadelphia was 18-6-5 since its coaching change despite the absence of LeClair, who, because the IV port immobilized his arm, had to deny a report that the staph infection had left him with limited range of motion.

"Are you sure that it was a medical doctor and not a witch doctor who said that?" said the rehabbing winger, lifting his arm in demonstration to reporters. "I'm not paralyzed."

However, as the Flyers began a run of 15 out of 18 games at home, they were fast becoming debilitated. During Cechmanek's sixth shutout, 4-0 over Carolina, Williams was pinned against the boards, then hit by David Tanabe, and lost for two to four weeks with a broken hand.

Next, Gagne got into an altercation with Andrei Zyuzin during a scoreless tie with Tampa Bay. "I was in a lot of pain and said something to Zyuzin, and he stopped (punching)," recalls Gagne, who had suffered a partial dislocation of his left shoulder that was expected to keep him out of the lineup for at least a month. Barber moved Langkow to the left side to play with Primeau and Recchi.

Cechmanek kept his finger in the dike by beating Hasek again, 2-0, for his eighth shutout of the year, second to Parent's team record 13, although Cechmanek admitted he never had heard the name.

Recchi's late powerplay goal saved the game after Philadelphia had blown three one-goal leads to Boston, and Primeau secured the 6-4 win into the empty net. The big center became the 60th player in NHL history—and only the sixth Flyer—to reach 1,000 career points in a 5-2 win over the Blues, but the depth behind him unfortunately diminished. Langkow's streak of 227 consecutive games ended because of stress fractures in both feet.

Langkow was replaced on the top line by 31-year old call-up Michel Picard, who had five points in six games. Philadelphia, still shorthanded, had reason to want to get a deal done by the March 13 trading deadline. And so did Lindros, who had been healthy enough to participate in just seven playoff games the previous three springs. The center finally expanded the list of teams to which he would accept a trade.

St. Louis appeared to be a serious suitor, but when GM Larry Pleau called Clarke 90 minutes before the 3 p.m. deadline to say he couldn't do a deal, a subsequent announcement that the Blues had consummated a trade with Phoenix for Keith Tkachuk made it clear to the Flyers that Lindros had been Plan B.

When the Rangers, who were not on Lindros's list, called to kick the tires, Clarke told GM Glen Sather that he would be interested in winger Jan Hlavac, defensemen Kim Johnsson and either of two prospects the Rangers had selected in the top nine of the 1999 draft—center Jamie Lundmark or right wing Pavel Brendl.

Sather never got back to the Flyers before the deadline. The Leafs, however, did, offering to substitute Dmitri Yushkevich, the former Philadelphia defenseman, for the still-sidelined Markov, but Clarke was holding out for Kaberle.

"There was never a chance to make a deal we thought would be beneficial for our club," said Clarke after the deadline passed. "We made a sincere attempt."

Lindros was skeptical, of course. "I don't know if Bob Clarke went into this with the intent of trading me," he said. "A lot goes on behind closed doors and the truth never comes out. Hopefully I'm not sitting on the end of this phone again next year."

The trading deadline passed with the Flyers picking up only center Dean McAmmond from Chicago for a third-round pick in 2001. "He has a lot of speed, he's good with the puck, and he's a hard worker," said Clarke.

McAmmond debuted uneventfully in the Philadelphia 3-0 win over the Wild. "Very easy shutout; I could sleep," said Cechmanek, called upon to stop just 15 shots after the only excitement of the night had been Mark Howe becoming the 17th member of the Flyer Hall of Fame during pregame ceremonies.

"I came here as Gordie Howe's son and left as my own man," said Howe, who nevertheless hardly objected to his father's presence on the red carpet. "You didn't realize [Mark's] talent; he was such a quiet man," said Gordie.

Manderville scored again as Cechmanek made two sterling, prone, pads-up saves on Hlavac and Kamensky in a 2-1 win over the Rangers, then Boucher beat the hot Oilers 4-2 to start a Canadian trip that quickly veered with a 3-1 loss in Calgary. "Unacceptable the way we played," said Barber, but even the arrival of the cavalry in Toronto—LeClair and Gagne returned after missing 46 and 12 games respectively—didn't stop the Flyers from going down 5-3.

When Gagne, playing with a harness, scored two nights later in Ottawa to tie the score in the second period, all seemed well again for the big line and big-time team that expected to go on a second long postseason run in two springs. But that only was until Primeau, pushed by Senator Chris Phillips, caught a rut and went into the boards left knee first.

"Not dirty, but I knew it was bad right away," Primeau said as the partial MCL tear was expected to keep him out for three weeks with only two remaining until the playoffs. "I'm going to push the envelope and force them to let me play," he vowed.

With Langkow expected to be out until the final week of the regular season and Gagne unable to take faceoffs, Recchi became the best option to move to a middle where McAmmond suddenly was the Flyers' No. 2 center. LeClair was being sent to right wing. "I haven't played much on left wing either, so what's the difference?" he asked.

The team recalled Plante from the Phantoms. Like the rest of the Flyers, he skated unobtrusively during a 2-1 First Union Center loss to Toronto in which the big event was a fight between Toronto's Tie Domi and a fan who tumbled along with the protective glass into the visitor's penalty box.

Domi, who said he had been hit by thrown debris, had been playfully retaliating by squirting fans with a water bottle. "Here, you need to cool off" he said. When Chris Falcone of Havertown climbed over three rows to hurl insults, Domi said, "Here, you need to cool off, too," and took the lid off the squeeze bottle and threw the rest of its contents over the glass onto Falcone who, enraged, lunged and shattered the glass. Domi granted the fan full NHL pugilist privileges, pulling Falcone's shirt over his head and whaling on him.

"If he wants to come in here, he will have to pay the price, "said

Domi. "I wasn't going to let anyone take a swing at me; I don't care who it was. He hit (linesman) Kevin (Collins, who went in to try to restore order) with a pretty big one. I was trying to stick up for Kevin."

Falcone, a cement worker, suffered a cut on his head. He was subdued and ejected from the building but, because no one pressed charges, never faced legal action. Domi, considered by the police and

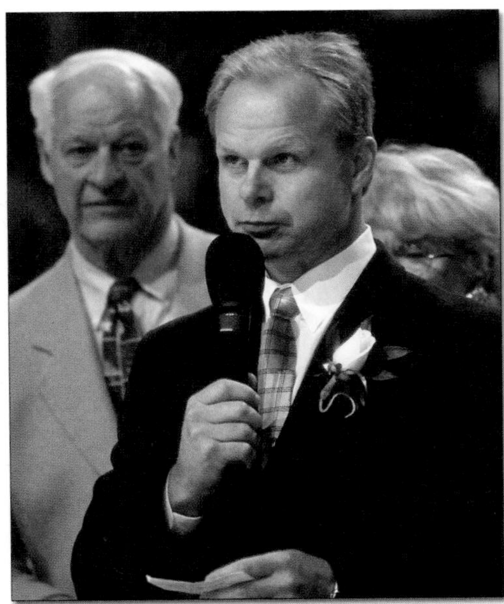

Mark Howe, flanked by his father, Gordie, became the 17th member of the Flyers Hall of Fame.

the NHL to have been acting in self-defense—never mind his geysers that provoked the incident—was not removed from the game. He would receive a $1,000 fine, but no suspension.

"Never seen anything like that," said Tocchet. "It was kind of comical."

Not so funny was the Flyer depleted center corps losing 63 percent of the draws during the dismal loss. "We have to make the best of what we have," said Barber, and what Philadelphia had wasn't feeling so great either. Tocchet was receiving acupuncture on his back, groin and left knee.

To the rescue rode Cechmanek with his 10th shutout of the season, plus Manderville, who not only successfully performed shutdown duties against Steve Yzerman but also became the unlikeliest goal scorer in a 1-0 Flyer home victory over Detroit.

"That line (Manderville, Hull and Ranheim) has been great all year neutralizing top lines," said Barber. "I'm standing behind the bench and it's 0-0 in the third period and I can honestly say I didn't feel uncomfortable."

Neither did Langkow as he returned to practice, at least until afterwards when he saw a miniature chair made of hockey sticks in front of his locker, placed there by Fedoruk to poke fun at his idleness. Langkow flipped it across the room in anger.

"It's funny the first couple of times, but not anymore," said the center. He was back on the ice the following night with Tocchet on the right side and LeClair on the left, but a 40-shot effort produced only Sykora's goal in a 2-1 loss to Florida.

Before the game, Cechmanek won the Bobby Clarke Trophy (Flyer MVP). Dan McGillis, whose point total jumped from 18 in 1999-2000 to 49 through his increased usage on the powerplay, was presented the Barry Ashbee Trophy (Best Flyer Defenseman), ending a six-year run by Desjardins.

Philadelphia still had home-ice advantage in the first round to clinch and, with three games remaining, Barber was running out of patience with some of his recently-returned players trying to get up to speed.

"I'm scared to shoot, scared to pass," the hesitant Gagne admitted, but Barber didn't want to hear it.

"I can go with the confidence argument for a short period of time, but don't stick with it," warned the coach. "It's your job to go to the net.

"What defines confidence is work ethic and commitment. We need more from Gags and LeClair. The guys who (recently) got back need to find ways to be a factor now, not a freakin' week from now.

"I'm not going after one player, but as a collective group, they have to push themselves."

With Primeau out, Barber moved White between Gagne and Recchi, who had gone four games without a point. "I don't change things up because we're panicking," said the coach. "But we're sorting things out here a little bit."

Tocchet had to miss a 3-2 overtime loss in Montreal. But LeClair scored twice in Pittsburgh, including the four-on-three winner in overtime past Snow, as Philadelphia rallied from 3-0 to beat the Penguins 4-3, clinching the fourth seed and a fifth matchup in seven springs against the Sabres.

First, however, the Flyers had to play Buffalo in Game 82 the next afternoon at HSBC Arena. Plante broke a third-period scoreless deadlock and Fedotenko's goal, with 7:34 to play, helped Cechmanek (36 saves) to beat Hasek for the fourth time in four tries, 2-1, giving Philadelphia its 14th 100-point season. Barber's team finished two ahead of their first-round opponents.

"Roman is the reason we're here, we can't fool ourselves about that," said the Flyer coach after the goalie stopped three breakaways. He completed the season with a 35-15-6 record, 2.01 goals-against average, a .921 save percentage, and 10 shutouts.

"The Czech newspapers write, 'Who's really better, Dominik or me?'" said Cechmanek to reporters. "Same thing you write, everything the same."

To a large degree, that included the Sabres, with 14 players who had gone down in five games to Philadelphia the previous spring. Despite the Flyer season sweep and home ice advantage, LeClair tried to make his team the underdog. "Not many people give us a chance to do much," he said. "That's good for us. The way Roman's playing, we feel we can win every night."

Of course, Buffalo had the same confidence in Hasek, a good book on Cechmanek from the regular season's four meetings, statistically the better powerplay and penalty killing, plus a score to settle with

Philadelphia from 12 months earlier. "We know how to beat them but sometimes that's the way it goes during the regular season," said Sabre center Doug Gilmour. "If they want to allow us 35 shots a game, we'll take that and beat them."

With Plante, a call-up, centering the Flyer first line, there no longer was much to choose between the teams offensively. Nor did there figure to be many corners to be picked on Hasek. "If we get up in the series and Checko continues to do it, then we might see them get frustrated," said Recchi before adding, "Remember, Hasek does the same thing to you."

Sure enough, after Cechmanek opened up the five-hole for Chris Gratton's goal 4:09 into Game One, Hasek refused to buy Recchi's head feint and gloved aside his penalty shot attempt. Desjardins tied the game, 1-1, by following up on a Ranheim fumble of a two-on-one opportunity, but Gilmour was stronger than McGillis in front of the net and jammed Donald Audette's rebound through the Philadelphia goalie's legs to restore the Buffalo lead.

The Sabres, pinching frequently, controlled the boards and kept the offensively compromised Flyers bottled up the rest of the way in a 2-1 victory.

"I think the coaching staff did a good job of building up our confidence," said Sabre Dave Andreychuk. "Once we got that first goal, that was the key because we were going into a series against a guy who had played well against us."

In Game Two, a cross-crease powerplay feed by LeClair set up a Langkow tap-in to give Philadelphia a 1-0 lead. But Langkow took a roughing penalty in the final minute of the period, allowing Miro Satan to convert 47 seconds after the intermission.

Alexei Zhitnik's shot off the skate of McGillis put Buffalo ahead for four minutes, until LeClair blasted one past Hasek's short side. Recchi next pounced on a Sykora shot that caromed off Richard Smehlik to put the Flyers ahead 3-2 going into the third period.

Sykora ominously missed a half-empty net with a chance to make it 4-2 and, sure enough, Philadelphia paid. Plante won a defensive zone draw from Curtis Brown, but Gagne's stick jammed against a Buffalo skate in an attempt to reach the puck. Vaclav Varada leaned off Desjardins, enabling Brown to quickly fire from the lower edge of the circle and beat Cechmanek once more between the legs to tie the score 3-3.

With the Sabres sealing off the boards and winning 77 percent of the draws, Cechmanek had to be much sharper than he had been in Game One, stopping Erik Rasmussen with the shaft of his stick in overtime following a Desjardins giveaway.

Hasek made one of his patented rolling saves on Fedotenko, who had been sprung by McAmmond on a semi-breakaway, then the netminder got lucky as Gagne couldn't lift a backhand.

The Flyers largely pressed the attack in the overtime until LeClair couldn't control a short pass off a Therien keep-in. With the help of Recchi making a premature change, Rasmussen broke out the other way, did a turn-up on Therien at the half-wall, and hit the late-arriving Jay McKee, who thanks to LeClair's indecision, was 20 feet from the closest Flyer. The defenseman closed in and beat Cechmanek under his glove through a Brown screen at 18:02 to give Buffalo a 4-3 win and sweep of the two games in Philadelphia.

"We had a great overtime, with lots of chances to score and finish the game," said Gagne. "And now we are back to nothing."

Cechmanek felt he had done his job well enough to complain of "too many open men and too many breakaways." While essentially this was true, zone time had been seriously compromised without Primeau. "You are taking out one of the best faceoff men in the league," said Buffalo coach Lindy Ruff.

Primeau announced after the contest he was putting himself back in for Game Three. "I'm probable, if you ask me," he said. "Obviously there is a possibility you can tear it (fully) before that ligament heals, but there is no guarantee it will (heal) anyway if I wait until the end of the first round."

He gave the knee a test with a full practice, and after a pregame examination by Dr. Art Bartolozzi was declared to have full range of motion, plus no inflammation. After the warmup, Barber played a hunch and took out McAllister, reinserting Delmore, who had been a healthy scratch for seven of the final 11 regular-season and first two playoff matches.

Gratton had once owned the keys to the Flyer doghouse—as he had been reminded every time he touched the puck during Games One and Two. But he suffered no ghosts in Buffalo and cashed in on Richardson's holding penalty at just 3:53 of Game Three.

After Manderville tied the score on a silver-plated gift from Audette, McAmmond took a penalty. Gratton fought off Desjardins, and Steve Heinze took Satan's relay, going between Cechmanek's legs for the fourth time in Buffalo's eight series goals.

But Barber's team rallied. With Brown in the box for hooking, Gagne put back a Primeau drive off the post to knot the game at two and, after Cechmanek foiled Gratton on a breakaway, the Flyer coach proved prescient. Delmore went to the net following a Langkow steal from Rhett Warrener and redirected the puck past Hasek with 8:54 remaining. Cechmanek made it hold up for a 3-2 Flyer victory that cut Buffalo's series lead to 2-1.

"Call it lucky or whatever, but having Dilly in tonight rewarded our team with a win," said Barber.

Primeau, assisting on the tying goal and winning 56 percent of his faceoffs—including one against Gratton with Hasek pulled—had made an impact during his 19:42 of ice time. The Flyers, who a year earlier had turned around a Pittsburgh series that opened with two losses at home, had visions of doing it again.

Their brains locked early in Game Four, however. McGillis was caught badly in the neutral zone, resulting in an odd man rush on the second shift, and when Richardson's weak clearing attempt was stopped at the point, Satan had all day to convert a J.P. Dumont rebound. Delmore, under pressure in the slot, turned it over and fell, Heinze swept in, and Audette followed to roof a backhander. The Flyers were down 2-0 after just 2:18.

For a second straight game they fought back. Before the period was over, Langkow poked in a puck Tocchet and LeClair had forced to the net with extended pressure. Just 48 seconds after the intermission, Recchi pinched on a James Patrick wraparound and fed Gagne for a redirection that tied the game, 2-2.

The Flyers had opportunities to seize control, but referee Don Koharski prematurely blew the whistle with Primeau on the doorstep for a Recchi rebound and both Gagne and Fedotenko put good chances over the net. A cross-checking penalty by the seriously-struggling Delmore had been over for just six seconds—and Primeau was playing without his broken stick—when Satan took a passout past McGillis, and Recchi didn't close on Gratton, who put his third goal of the series past Cechmanek's glove to restore Buffalo's lead at 3-2.

Brown, who had become the Sabres' top defensive center with Peca sitting out the season in a contract dispute, was fighting his own war against Primeau. "I think Primeau must have broken seven or eight of Brown's sticks on faceoffs alone," said Ruff.

Gagne, who had been refused permission by Dr. Bartolozzi to take off a harness that was inhibiting his shooting, was one-on-one with Hasek again in the third period, but the often down, but never out goalie flung his glove up to save a tying goal.

Therien took a cross-checking penalty while the Flyers were on 3-2 rush, leaving them shorthanded with 10:25 to go. Opportunity seemingly was running short until Ranheim stole the puck, shot, and Hasek lost his stick in the process of making the save. Ranheim quickly retrieved the puck and hit McGillis, who fired a one-timer from the high slot between Hasek's legs for a stunning, shorthanded, tying goal.

Philadelphia was now only one goal away from going home with an even series. Tocchet tried but his tip went wide, and a two-on-one opportunity rolled off LeClair's stick with 2:40 to go. The team had another chance in the overtime when LeClair strong-armed the puck out front, but Gilmour got away with a high stick in Langkow's face before the Flyer could shoot.

The Sabres, who iced the puck three times in the first five minutes, were being booed until Primeau, trying to one-arm the puck up the boards, was unable to get it past Varada. The Sabre winger jammed it back down to Brown, a step up on Desjardins, who peeled off for the near post thinking that's where the puck carrier was headed.

Instead, Brown continued behind the net towards the far post. When Sykora flopped and Gagne looked to defend the point, Brown had so much time he could circle all the way out past the hashmark. He fired over Cechmanek's glove at 6:13 to win the game, 4-3.

The Flyers' third one-goal loss of the series, and second in overtime, left them down 3-1 and in no mood to pat themselves on the back for twice coming from behind in Game Four. "Obviously, we have to get better right off the bat," said Recchi. "Mental mistakes led to those first two goals."

In a desperate hole going home for Game Five, Barber asked his team for more desperation. "[Primeau] leaped through two [defensemen] to give himself a scoring chance," the coach said. "If we had everybody doing that, I don't think we'd be in the situation we're in right now."

If somebody had to leap a tall building in a single bound, Recchi decided it could be him. "I'm not ready," he told his wife Alexa as he left his house for Game Five. "I'm going to be miserable if our season ends tonight.

"I want to play my best game of the series."

Fourteen minutes into the first period, he went to the net hard and was tripped by Warrener. On the powerplay, Gagne accepted a passout that Primeau put between McKee's legs and, with a second jab, beat Hasek. When Recchi didn't get the puck deep enough on a change, Maxim Afinogenov blew past Sykora at the blueline and beat the charging Cechmanek to the short side to tie the game 1-1.

But the Flyers, hitting relentlessly, carried the play through the second period. Brown was called for high sticking Langkow and, on the resultant four-on-three powerplay, nobody closed on Recchi as he moved in from the point. He fired a dart over Hasek's glove at 16:02 of the second period to restore the Philadelphia lead at 2-1.

It appeared to go to 3-1 when a centering pass for Recchi went off Dmitri Kalinin's skate, necessitating quick glovework by Hasek after the puck had crossed the plane of the goalline. The replays were inconclusive, however, leaving the evidence circumstantial and then, fortunately, irrelevant after Langkow beat Gratton on a faceoff and Therien's drive hit a skate and rocketed up in the net, putting the Flyers up two.

After Primeau got knocked into the goalie, Hasek threw his glove, admitting later he was trying to get a response from his team. Whatever the Sabres mustered, it didn't match the Philadelphia's determination to survive an elimination game for the first time in 12 springs—since the Pittsburgh series in 1989.

"Every time everyone starts to look at us in a different light, [Primeau, Recchi and Gagne] keep coming up big," said Barber after his team's 3-1 victory—the only one by either team during the series that was not by a one-goal margin—had cut Buffalo's series lead to 3-2, "Is it a big mountain?" asked the coach. "You betcha, but I'm not going to rule this team out."

"We played our best game," said Recchi. "If we can go in there and play that same type of game, it will come down to Game Seven."

Barber had benched Delmore in favor of an extra energy forward, P.J. Stock, in Game Five, and decided to double up on that route by dressing Fedoruk instead of McAmmond for Game Six. "I remember a lot of the guys wondered why we would dress two fourth-liners in a game like that," remembers Therien.

Perhaps it was a reflection of the way Primeau, struggling to push off, felt physically, but he doesn't remember believing that the series had turned. "Unlike other times we were down in my Flyer years, I didn't have a strong sense of us fighting our way back into it," he recalls.

Indeed, the bad start they had suffered in Game Four turned out not to be their worst nightmare, not even close. Gratton won a faceoff from Plante and deflected in Andreychuk's shot off Cechmanek's arm for a 1-0 lead after only 2:23. Therien tackled Varada and went to the box, and when Andreychuk's shot went off Richardson's skate, Gilmour had an easy-tip at the other side of the crease to make it 2-0.

Sykora tried too hard to get one of the goals back but had his shot

Paul Ranheim runs over Jay McKee en route to the Buffalo net. The Sabres routed the Flyers 8-0 to clinich the series four games to two.

blocked by James Patrick. Audette then broke out past the vacated point and beat Cechmanek with what appeared to be a savable shot from the right circle. When a frustrated Richardson got penalized for throwing an elbow, Andreychuk made it 4-0 on only the eighth Buffalo shot of the first period.

"I think the score was indicative of our mind state going in," recalls Primeau.

"After the first period, Bill came in and said, 'I know we're not going to win this game, but I'll tell you one thing, I'm going to be able to use it to separate the men from the boys. I'm going to have my own people next year.'"

In the second period, Therien tried to come off the boards and had the puck lifted by Dumont, who drove the middle and scored. The slimmest of comeback hopes were all-but gone and so was Cechmanek for Boucher, not that it mattered. "We kept taking penalties," recalls Tocchet. "And the snowball turned into an avalanche."

Primeau went to the box twice in the third period and Fedoruk, cruising for trouble, went into the Buffalo bench. "I remember [Gilmour] hitting me and being [bleeped] off, and Luke is like, 'Go get 'em, Fridgie,'" recalls Fedoruk. "If you're going to beat us, we are going to take something with us."

All that LeClair took with him was the sound of the foghorn going off after each goal as the Sabres poured it on. "I still hear it," he says.

Boucher gave up three more scores in mopping up the greatest defeat in Flyer playoff history, 8-0, worse than the 9-3 drubbing by which the Rangers completed a sweep at Madison Square Garden in 1983.

"There is no explanation for this," said Desjardins. "We were a solid team all year. We never played like this."

Every other game in Buffalo's six-game triumph could have gone either way. But in the end, the Flyers collapsed from the accumulation of their cracks.

"We got outplayed in every facet of the game," said Snider. "I'm still in a state of shock.

"We can't blame one player and certainly can't look at [Cechmanek] because he's the guy that got us here. I think we just lacked cohesiveness all around."

The Flyers also suffered without an up-to-speed LeClair, Primeau and Gagne, but the latter two had gotten the team back into the series and Big John was given amnesty by the coach. "God bless his heart, he did the best he could," said Barber.

"The guys didn't quit, there is no way in hell they quit."

Tocchet, doing what his knee allowed, had one point in the series. Like Cechmanek, McGillis had struggled during the playoffs after having the most effective season of his career.

Desjardins' subpar season ended with him being on the ice for five of the first six Sabre goals in Game Six. Barber had constantly tried to fix whichever defenseman was struggling the most at any given time by putting him with the captain, which may have succeeded only in dragging down Desjardins. Asked if the constant shuffling of his partners had been a factor, Desjardins said, "Maybe. I don't know. If it did, it's too late now."

Ultimately, that had proven to be the case when a sub-par Primeau returned to a team in a 2-0 hole.

"He was our best player this year," said Clarke in the corridor outside the dressing room. "You take that big centerman out of your lineup, there's a big hole that nothing could camouflage.

"I think our fans are knowledgeable enough to know they really got a good effort out of our team this year—lots of grit, lots of aggression, great goaltending. We're short in some areas of talent."

Since the GM wasn't pointing any fingers at his players, they returned the favor by not complaining about Clarke's inability to fix the team's shortages before the playoffs.

"Amazingly, never once after a loss in the playoffs did anyone say, "Gee, I wish we had another body' or 'Gee, I wish they would have moved Eric (Lindros) to give us a better chance,'" said Primeau. "That was never said once around me or to me."

Barber, too, indicated no impatience with awaiting the bundle the Flyers would receive in the inevitable Lindros deal. "You have to think about what's best for your hockey team, not for 2000-01," said the coach. "You don't win a championship in one year, there are no shortcuts to the Stanley Cup.

"Everybody knows we need another center and a defenseman, but my job is to make sure the club is playing to its ability until that is addressed."

Clarke promised to make those fixes in free agency. And he still believed the first place to put Comcast's money was in keeping LeClair, the truncated season the 32-year old had suffered notwithstanding.

"A big factor is how I feel about my chances of winning," the winger told reporters on breakup day. "Philadelphia's always going to have a chance of winning; obviously they'd be high on my list.

"All good things have got to end sooner or later, but you also can feel that there's unfinished business."

LeClair's goals would be a lot for the Flyers to replace. And, with the Lindroses alleging persecution by the organization of a star player, LeClair's comfort level in remaining would provide other important free agents a read upon Philadelphia as a still-desirable destination.

"I think more players than not around the league thought that the Flyers had been the bad guys," Primeau recalls. But, with three seasons and $15 million to go on his contract, it behooved him to do what he could to change that perception. "There's no question that this is a place that's spoken of highly by players around the league," Primeau said on breakup day. "We knew some guys around the trade deadline who would have been quite pleased to come."

Having never taken personally contract frustrations that went back almost to his first 50-goal season, LeClair proved willing to stay and not just for lunch with Snider at The Palm during the second week of June. Next day, same restaurant, this time with LeClair's representative, Lewis Gross, the Chairman offered LeClair a five-year, $45 million deal that was accepted and announced on June 14. It had a no-trade clause for the first three years and gave LeClair the right to pick his trade destination in the final season.

"It's not easy for me to spend $9 million of another man's money," recalls Clarke. "Snider really closed the deal.

"We didn't want to lose both star players. John was a good man and, at that stage, I don't think he wanted to go anywhere else. We may have ended up paying a bit more, but we paid a little less for a few years, too."

Recalls LeClair, "It wasn't so much being underpaid for years and wanting to make it up as it was going by the recent market value.

"I had been a little curious (to wait until July 1) to see who else wanted me. Not every team would. But I also didn't want to get paid a bunch of money and then lose 50-60 games a year. So when the Flyers came up to where we were asking, I didn't feel that I would find a better place.

"Clarkie didn't tell me who he was going after (in signings or trades) or anything like that. But he did say they were going to try to be active, which they had done in the past, always improving the team whenever they could.

"I didn't have the same experience that Eric had. I thought his was an isolated incident. He was my friend and we still talked often, but you have to move on. I felt young, healthy, and confident I could get back to where I was."

Free agents usually are attracted by the money and opportunity to win, the coach being down the list of considerations. But anxious to rid the organization of the perception of instability, Snider and Clarke awarded Barber and assistants Stothers and McGuire three-year deals, the head coach receiving a total of $2.5 million for having produced a 31-13-7 record after he replaced Ramsay. This was a financial package befitting the NHL's Coach of the Year, which Barber was named on June 14 at the league award ceremony in Toronto.

"When you look at the great coaches that are out there, the names that are on this Jack Adams Trophy, I couldn't be any more honored," said Barber.

Among them were Fred Shero, Mike Keenan and Pat Quinn. And the players influential in making those Flyer coaches huge successes were drafted at the recommendation of Jerry Melnyk, who, on the same day Barber was honored, died of leukemia in his native Edmonton at age 66, four years after giving up his chief scout position for an advisory role.

There are conflicting versions of the discussions that took place at the Flyer table in 1969 that led to the drafting of Bobby Clarke during the second round. But in all of those, Melnyk is credited for having the largest influence in convincing assistant GM Keith Allen—and ultimately GM Bud Poile—to take a diabetic who had been passed over for 16 selections.

The reputation built by that franchise-defining pick was augmented by other choices such as Jimmy Watson, Pelle Lindbergh, Ron Hextall, Peter Forsberg and Dave Schultz, out-of-the-box selections for which Melnyk summoned the courage of deep convictions built over 30 years of beating the bushes.

"He knew tough guys from bluff guys," said Clarke as he mourned the passing of his once-deliverer and, later, confidant and friend. "He had a unique ability to pick players who weren't highly rated, but extremely competitive and mentally tough."

Nine days after his death, the Flyer brain trust went to the table—this year in Sunrise, Florida—minus Melnyk's fine judgment and good humor for the first time in 32 drafts. Clarke picked up an extra second-round pick in 2002 from Ottawa to move down four places to 27th and take the player his scouts rated 12th—defenseman Jeff Woywitka of Red Deer (Philadelphia's fallback was defenseman Fedor Tyutin, chosen 40th by the Rangers).

Clarke then traded his second-round 2001 selection (56th overall) to Florida for the rights to Jiri Dopita, an already twice-drafted 32-year old Czech center considered by many the world's best player not in the NHL. He previously had turned down the Bruins (1992) and Islanders (1998), the latter trading his rights to the Panthers, who also had failed to sign him.

With Vsetin—Dopita's Czech team—in bankruptcy, he figured that as long as he had to make a change, it might as well be a big one. Agent Petr Svoboda (not the ex-defenseman who also had become a player representative) had told the Flyers that his client had been tempted finally by the presence of his good friend Cechmanek in Philadelphia. "I'll fly over there and shoot you if you don't come," Svoboda said he told Dopita, who was receiving a two-year, $3.5 million contract.

Clarke thought Dopita would be an upgrade on the reliable and versatile Langkow, but the GM, wanting to create a dynamic one-two center-ice punch with Primeau, had bigger fish to fry. Presuming that center Joe Sakic and defensemen Rob Blake were re-signing with Colorado, which both did along with goalie Patrick Roy before the July 1 start of free agency, Philadelphia zeroed in on center Jeremy Roenick.

Resigned to losing Roenick, the cash poor Phoenix Coyotes gave the primary bidders—Dallas, Detroit, Boston and Philadelphia—permission to woo him prior to July 1.

"We would need a centerman and we liked Langkow," recalls then-Arizona GM Cliff Fletcher. "Nothing was contingent; I didn't expect Bob to play Santa Claus. But if he was able to sign Roenick, who we were going to lose anyway, perhaps he would give us a chance to make a deal for Langkow."

In mid-June, ex-Coyote teammate Tocchet had invited Roenick to Philly, where he had received a full court press that included seats for Game Four of the NBA final between the Sixers and Lakers. Imploring Flyer fans followed Roenick and Tocchet from concourse to car, where they beat on the hood telling the recruit he had no business signing elsewhere. "A respectful mauling," Roenick later would call it.

The team of Roenick's youth, Boston, offered the most money, but had missed the playoffs in consecutive seasons. Compared to Philadelphia, Detroit presented a seemingly equal opportunity at a Stanley Cup over the next few seasons. But on the recruiting visit, Roenick's equestrian wife, Tracy, had not been convinced that the Michigan suburbs had places equal to South Jersey for stabling the horses she and daughter Brandi trained and rode.

"It was a big part of our life and their lives when I was on the road," recalls Roenick. "Rick and I were really good friends in Phoenix and being able to play again with him was huge, but I also had a good relationship with Chelli (former Chicago teammate, now Red Wing, Chris Chelios) and he tried to convince me to come to Detroit.

"I thought the Flyers were closer to winning than Detroit. But ultimately it was life away from the rink that made the decision."

After dinner on June 30 with Wing GM Ken Holland, Tracy and Jeremy were in their Detroit hotel room talking about their options when Clarke called with a five year, $37.5 million, offer, pushing for a quick decision that would enable Philadelphia to move on if necessary, to another free agent. Through his representative, Neil Abbott, Roenick asked for a restructuring of the offer that would give him $8.5 million his first season, and $8 million and $7.5 million in years two and three. Clarke quickly agreed, making one of the game's most grandiose personalities a Flyer.

On July 2, the 31-year-old, two-time 50-goal scorer (with Chicago), and two-time 30-goal scorer (with Phoenix) was presented to the Philadelphia media at the First Union Center, not that the player instantly recognized around hockey as simply "J.R." needed any introduction.

"I'll try to get John (LeClair) back up to 50 goals if I can," said Roenick about his presumed new left wing partner. Roenick talked about the fear engendered in teams visiting Philadelphia, but showed none for the array of microphones in front of him, embracing as many as he could get in his hands for symbolic purposes.

He turned to Clarke, then Snider, from the dais and emphatically announced, "You will not be disappointed," and then finished the press conference by giving the Flyer Chairman, whom he had met just that morning, a hug.

"Hey, if someone gave you $40 million, you would hug them too," says Roenick today. "Besides, I'm a hugger by nature—hug every Flyer fan I meet, even today."

Clarke told the media he had no problem investing in hockey's greatest hambone, and he even thought some personality was what the team needed. "It's a plus," said the GM. "We have a fairly reserved team and this guy is good. People are really going to like him."

Clarke, clearly enjoyed the day and within 24 hours moved Langkow, a top-six forward on the 2000 conference final team, to Phoenix for a first-round pick in either 2002 or 2003, the year being Philadelphia's option.

Though still targeting a defenseman in a deal for Lindros, the GM wasn't going to wait. He won the bid for 34-year-old free agent Eric Weinrich with an offer of $8.7 million over three years and the promise of what the reloaded Flyers could be.

"I never thought it would be possible to be on a team like Philly," said Weinrich, a defenseman who had been traded at the previous deadline to Boston after turning down an extension from Montreal. He chose Philadelphia over a comparable money offer from Vancouver. "I got the call from my agent (Steve Bartlett), and my wife (Tracy) and I were jumping up and down on my boat.

"They got Johnny LeClair back and added Jeremy Roenick. I don't know how much time I have left to play, but I want to get the Cup."

Clarke thought the Flyers had become that much closer to it with the addition of a steady defender of 13 NHL seasons who had consistently scored 20-30 points a year.

During the 2000 playoffs, that level of production had seemed like the low end of Andy Delmore's promise. But a failure to manage risk on the ice had led to excessive giveaways and unproductive rushes, so he was traded to Nashville in July for a third-round pick in 2002.

"He made himself expendable," recalls Clarke. "Andy struggled with hockey sense.

"He probably was the best skater on the club and could shoot the puck, but even as an American Leaguer had been average."

Delmore today thinks he was not ready to continue what apparently had started with five goals in that Pittsburgh series. "It was a short summer and I just didn't come as prepared as I probably should have," he recalls. "I wouldn't say it was a sophomore slump, just the full grind of an NHL season.

"I wasn't scoring and wasn't really playing great D; I lost confidence."

Nevertheless, after having gone untaken in two drafts, he departed Philadelphia with memories for a lifetime.

"If I would have just played one game in the NHL, I would have met my childhood goal," says Delmore today. "Of course everybody wants 1,000 games, but the day my agent called and said that the Philadelphia Flyers, one of the great organizations in hockey, wanted to sign me was just amazing.

"Those playoffs didn't pass in a blur for me, not at all. I cherished every game because I was not supposed to be there."

Clarke received an offer for Lindros that the GM found acceptable—defenseman Tom Poti and center Jochen Hecht from the Oilers—but the Lindroses, citing their presupposition that the Oilers wouldn't have the money to sign Eric for the long term, had little interest in Edmonton. While in Toronto to testify on the Coyotes' behalf in a Langkow arbitration hearing, Clarke had breakfast with Carl.

"He still had it in his mind that Eric was going to wind up with Toronto," Clarke told the media. "I had to tell him that wasn't going to happen, that the talks with the Leafs are over. He wasn't too happy with it."

For the first time, Eric conceded that maybe he would like it in New York.

"Bob wanted me to open it up to new teams, so I opened it up to the Rangers," Lindros had told the *Inquirer*'s Tim Panaccio in early July, around the time of the failed Ranger attempt to make a trade with Pittsburgh for the disgruntled Jaromir Jagr. Jagr went to Washington for a package of prospects on July 9, increasing New York GM Glen Sather's sense of urgency to obtain a marquee player.

A rich team facing a fifth consecutive year without playoffs and a player looking at a second straight season out of the game had become bedfellows. On Saturday, August 11, Clarke and Sather essentially agreed to a trade of Jan Hlavac, Kim Johnsson and Pavel Brendl, principals they had talked about just before the trading deadline, pending, of course, the Rangers reaching a satisfactory contract deal with Lindros.

New York would receive the Flyers' 2003 first-round choice if Lindros sustained a head injury before playing 50 games in 2001-02, then didn't play again for the next 12 months. The Flyers also were getting a third-round draft choice in 2003 that was not contingent on Lindros's health.

"We always had big guys that couldn't move the puck well," recalls Clarke. "We were looking for a puck-moving defenseman and Johnsson was really intelligent.

"In Hlavac, we thought we were getting a scorer. Brendl could really shoot and handle it in junior but he was just a gamble. If [the Rangers] had said they weren't putting him in, we probably would have done the deal anyway."

The Flyers had accused Carl Lindros of asking for more money from the teams he and Eric had found undesirable. But this time, the Lindroses agreed to take a four-year deal similar to the one worked out with the Leafs—bases of $1.1 million, $2.7 million, $3.3 million and $4 million a year, plus $80,000 for each game played.

Eric flew to Chicago to be examined one more time by Dr. James Kelly, who had okayed Lindros's return in November, then went to New York for an examination by the Ranger doctors. In the meantime, King CEO Tim Leiweke called Snider and wanted to make an offer for Lindros, but the Flyer Chairman replied they would listen to Los Angeles only if the Rangers backed out.

Sather called back his acceptance on Friday August 17, asking that Philadelphia delay the announcement until Monday, when the Rangers could include Mark Messier, who had a family wedding over the weekend, as part of their welcoming press conference.

It was done, finally, confirmed by Snider to reporters on Sunday, August 19. Nine years earlier, the Flyers had won an arbitration case over their most bitter rivals for the rights to the game's next great player. Now, they were trading him to them.

"From our point of view, that was the only negative," said Snider. "From Eric's point of view, from the rivalry point of view, this is positive.

"We know from time to time he is going to come back to haunt us. There will be a game when he comes into our building and scores four goals and everybody will go nuts. The [Philadelphia Flyers] could be undefeated in December and Keith Primeau could have 50 goals and it's still only going to be about Lindros.

"It's okay. We're in the entertainment business. We decided whomever came up with the best offer, we were going to take it. I think the [family] got to a point where they realized this was his best shot at continuing his career this season. For maybe the first time in their lives, they didn't get what they wanted.

"I don't look back (at Lindros's eight Flyer seasons) and think we could have done anything differently. We constantly tried to accommodate Eric and his parents, and they were never satisfied."

The next day it became official. Messier handed a Ranger jersey to Lindros at a press conference at Madison Square Garden while Clarke, looking more weary than relieved, answered questions from the Philadelphia media at the Flyers Skate Zone.

"We strayed from what we've always believed, what we've been taught since we got here—that the important thing is the team," he said. "We won't lose our focus on the team again."

Asked what he wished for Lindros, Clarke said, "He hurt this organization. I could care less about him."

McGuire, who had both coached the Ranger farm team at Hartford and served as their pro scout, said Hlavac, 24, a 28-goal scorer for New York the previous season, was "shifty and skilled," and that Johnsson, 25, the last player taken in the 1994 draft and had been a two-season regular with the struggling Rangers, was a "player with offensive upside." Brendl, said McGuire, had been "out of shape," but was "a tremendous talent."

Barber said he would try Hlavac with countryman Dopita, and pair Johnsson with the other newcomer on defense, Weinrich. "We have a whole new bag of tricks here," said the coach.

Lindros, returning to the ice for the first time in 14 months at the August orientation camp in Calgary for Canada's 2002 Olympic team, mixed with Primeau and Desjardins without apparent tension. "We shook hands and talked about the equipment," said Desjardins. "I don't feel I have to clear (up) anything."

One of the happier persons to see Lindros on the ice again was Scott Stevens, the deliverer of the devastating hit in Game Seven of the 2000 Eastern Conference final. "I don't want him to not be able to finish his career because of me," he said. "You really don't need those things hanging over your head."

With the Lindros saga behind them, Philadelphia's laundry finally seemed washed and neatly folded as the players reported for camp. Sykora had returned to the Czech Republic, McAmmond had been traded to Calgary for a fourth-round pick, and Jody Hull, not offered a contract, had found work under Neilson again in Ottawa. The Flyers' other support players were intact and in roles that better fit their abilities amidst all the fresh talent that had been brought in over the summer.

The only hole was in Barber's heart. Jenny, his teenage sweetheart going back to Kitchener, Ontario, and wife of 28 years, had been diagnosed in May with lung cancer.

Soon after Philadelphia's first-round elimination, she had gone to a family doctor about a cough that had persisted for a few weeks. "I thought maybe it was a touch of pneumonia," recalls Bill, but an MRI showed a tumor of significant size. Dr. Larry Kaiser, a thoracic surgeon at the University of Pennsylvania Hospital—and the husband of Ed Snider's daughter Lindy—operated on Jenny in May in hopes of extracting the malignancy.

"Lindy was with me in the waiting room," recalls Bill. "To remove it would be a five to six-hour operation. If they found out they couldn't do anything, I would know sooner.

"Just an hour later, they paged me. I looked at Lindy and said, 'Bleep.' Larry told me the cancer was in Jenny's lymph nodes.

"I hope I have a quarter of the courage that this woman had. Deep down inside, I felt she knew she was going to die, but you would never know it. She never expressed hate or 'Why did this happen to me?'

"She smoked a long time, but never expressed any regrets about that and I wasn't mad at her either. It was her life. I see people die from lung cancer who never touched a cigarette."

Jenny began chemotherapy with the hope that it might extend her life long enough to attend her daughter Kerri's wedding the following summer. Kerri asked her father about postponing the affair until Jenny had completed chemo and radiation. "We're talking months, not years," he told his daughter. "I don't think your mother is going to be in any condition to attend."

While she had felt well enough—and perhaps even if she didn't—Jenny had insisted on attending the June ceremony in Toronto where Bill was named Coach of the Year. "She was already weak and getting thin, so I was against it," recalls Barber. "I thought it was too much for her and I didn't want it to be known publicly. But she came."

There seemed no end to the heartbreak that within a five-year period had taken Yanick Dupre, Dmitri Tertyshny and left a terrible prognosis for Roger Neilson and Jenny Barber. Soon the world joined the Flyers in disbelief and sorrow.

Players were doing their off-ice work on the first day of training camp when, on the televisions mounted in the workout room, there was video footage of a plane flying into one of the towers of New York's World Trade Center. When another commercial airliner followed into the second tower 17 minutes later, the horrific was now also sinister.

"Almost a Third World War situation," said Desjardins. "Hockey is nothing."

The players' attention on the ice was so skewed that morning, Barber sent them home. Some instead went back to the workout room to watch people jumping out of the burning towers before the buildings collapsed, and to learn of a third hijacked plane crashing into the Pentagon in Washington while a fourth, apparently targeted for another government landmark before passengers heroically interceded, dove into a field in Western Pennsylvania.

"It seems like we're watching a movie," said Roenick. "The most precious parts of America going down like toothpick buildings."

The next day, Boucher learned that one of the flight attendants on the second plane to hit the WTC was the sister of a close friend, Matt Jarret. Two scouts for the Kings—Ace Bailey and Mark Bavis—also had been on that plane, headed for training camp in Los Angeles.

Philadelphia's first exhibition game, scheduled four days hence in Washington, was moved back 72 hours. Before the skate that morning, Therien asked the bus driver to go past the Pentagon. "It's not what you think it is when you see it on TV," he reported. "The destruction is big."

The MCI Center in Washington was only one-third filled that night. The subdued fans waved flag placards given out at the doors only when encouraged by the public address announcer.

The Flyers, like the nation, had wrestled with issues of propriety and safety in going back to work, in their case particularly so at a venue close to where one of the terrorist attacks had occurred. "But I think everybody [knows] that we have to go on with the rest of our lives," LeClair said after a lineup comprised largely of Phantoms got two goals from Brendl and two assists from Roenick in a 7-1 win.

Two nights later, for their home exhibition opener, Lauren Hart performed "God Bless America" *a cappella* so that the 14,000 in attendance could more easily sing along. The Flyers and Rangers wore flag decals on their helmets, and Philadelphia police and firefighters unfurled two large flags at center ice between the two teams.

As the players returned to the ice for the third period, President Bush's live address to the nation was taken off the video scoreboard—it was announced he would still be shown in the Broad Street Atrium. But there was so much booing that Snider and COO Ron Ryan quickly ordered the President back on the screen and cancelled the rest of the 2-2 game, enabling both teams to sit on their benches and watch.

"How can you play hockey after that?" said Roenick. The Flyers, who handed out flags at the door, tripled donations collected from the fans for the Twin Towers Civil Servants Emergency Fund benefitting the families of police officers and firefighters who died in rescue attempts. Raised was $120,000.

The nation would remain somber for months, if not years, so the exhibition games seemed even less relevant than usual. Barber had informed the beat writers of Jenny's illness at the beginning of training camp, asking them to respect the family's privacy. Then, once the opening night roster was all-but set at the conclusion of camp, the coach emotionally informed the team that his wife was dealing with a health issue. "I hated the word cancer," he recalls. "But I think some of the players knew."

Recalls Fedoruk, "He told us he wanted to be around the team and that she wanted him to be around the team, and he let it go at that."

Indeed, prognosticators were suggesting that working with this team would be hugely rewarding. Both *The Hockey News* and *ESPN, The Magazine* picked the Flyers to win the Stanley Cup, while *Sports Illustrated* and *The Sporting News* predicted they would reach the Final.

"You look to your ownership to give you the opportunity to be one of the top teams," said Primeau. "We have been given that."

Certainly Roenick was hot to get started. Even before the Flyer rock star acquisition had been completely introduced by public address announcer Lou Nolan on opening night at the First Union Center, Roenick jumped the gun, skating out to a thunderous ovation.

"That was three months of waiting there," J.R. explained later. He embellished his goal, two assists and election as the game's first star by throwing his stick into the seats, practically begging for the fight over the souvenir that ensued.

"A guy ripped it away from a woman and I went back and said, 'Hey, that's hers, give it back,'" reported Roenick. "And he did."

Weinrich scored in his debut, too as Philadelphia beat Florida, 5-2, the only downers on the evening being the absence of a still-recovering Tocchet following May 22 arthroscopic knee surgery and the loss of Dopita, who limped off with a strained MCL after getting low-bridged by Dan Boyle.

"Sore and angry," Dopita was described by translator Cechmanek. Two days later, as the Flyers fought to the first of consecutive ties with Columbus, they announced Dopita would be out six weeks and recalled Marty Murray, a former Flame who had been signed in July for exactly such depth purposes.

Brendl, who had surprisingly played his way onto the team at age 20, suffered a sprained ankle and Barber, not happy with a 2-1 loss in Buffalo, came down with a serious case of frustration. "Marty Murray is one of our better forwards," said the coach after Murray had set up Gagne for the only Philadelphia goal. "We have to have more than that obviously."

The next day, the coach skated the 1-2-2 Flyers without pucks for 36 minutes and left the ice denying he was angry. "We had a workday, that's all" he said. "We needed it and all our guys felt good about it."

Apparently the coach didn't poll the entire team. "If we needed to pick up our conditioning level, I wouldn't have had a problem with it," recalls LeClair. "Punish 30-year old men though? I don't know."

Big John wasn't alone with his doubts. "There were a lot of guys who weren't happy about it, but we weren't working hard," said captain Desjardins. "That was the message."

Apparently, it was received. Two nights later Philadelphia threw a franchise road-record-tying 53 shots at Florida in a 5-2 victory, Justin Williams scoring his fourth goal in five games.

Primeau, who sprained an ankle and was unavailable as the Flyers rallied on a LeClair goal with 3:15 to play for a 3-3 tie in Atlanta, tried to come back two nights later in Detroit, but had to pull himself during the warm-up.

"It seemed like the right decision until about 40 seconds left in the game," said Primeau after Sergei Fedorov's one-timer tied the contest in the last minute, before Red Wing Brett Hull scored the winner off a Richardson giveaway with 18 seconds remaining. Reporters told Roenick it would have been Philadelphia's first win at Joe Louis Arena in 13 years. "Now I'm even more sick to my stomach," Roenick said.

Barber told reporters the team had worked hard to "overcome the last-minute lineup change." Asked what had happened with Primeau, the coach said, "I don't know," waved his hand dismissively, and walked away.

Recalls Barber, "He tried to play; I wasn't mad."

Primeau still wasn't ready to go two nights later against Washington. Regardless, Recchi, who scored a hat trick in a 6-3 victory, went back to the wing because the Flyers were just as short along the wall.

Tocchet, who had yet to play a game, received another opinion from former Flyer orthopedist Dr. John Gregg and was diagnosed with a ruptured patella tendon. Since that problem is uncorrectable by surgery, the only hope for Tocchet—56 minutes away from joining Dale Hunter as the NHL's second-ever 1,000 point, 3,000 penalty-minute player—would be to strengthen his quadriceps. "He's a warrior, he's a Flyer," said Barber, predicting Tocchet, 37, could do it.

Without him in the lineup, an important voice was missing in the locker room. And, the following day, a more official transfer of leadership was made when the Flyers surprisingly announced Desjardins

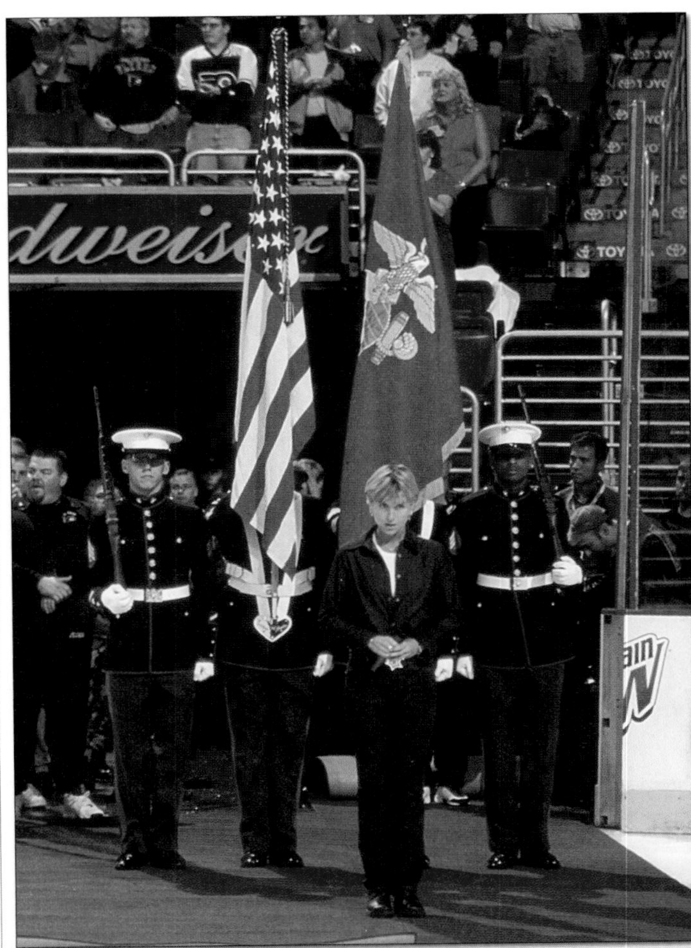

"God Bless America" and the trooping of the colors had extra meaning in the first games that followed the attacks on 9-11.

was giving up his captaincy to Primeau.

"I never felt like I was doing everything right," explained Desjardins, who had gone to Barber a week earlier in Atlanta and asked to be relieved of his duties. "It was affecting my play.

"You don't want to put more pressure on yourself, but it's there. I was never comfortable with it."

Clarke said that was news to him.

"We weren't aware how that was affecting him," said the GM, who didn't try to talk Desjardins out of a decision he called "courageous."

Today, Desjardins insists his personal discomfort with the role was the sole reason. He never has disclosed otherwise to anyone interviewed for this book, but many believe he had grown tired of bridging a disconnection between Barber and the players.

"He didn't believe in what Bill was doing," recalls Recchi, and Clarke, today, feels similarly. "I'm guessing the problems were getting so big, Desjardins didn't think there was anything he could do to help," says Clarke.

LeClair remembers, "Rico was quiet, but he was good at being captain. My feeling is he didn't have the same message Billy wanted to portray and felt uncomfortable. But you don't need to wear the C to be the guy people look up to. I don't think anybody earned more respect than Eric."

After consulting with Barber and his coaching staff, Clarke called in Primeau, Recchi and LeClair, and offered Primeau the job. "I was surprised," he recalls. "It was only was my second full year there.

"I said, 'I'm honored and okay with it as long as John and Mark are.' Both said they were and I accepted right there.

"There is truth in what Rico said about it being a burden. It takes a certain type of personality. I believe that by worrying about more than just preparing himself to play, his game was affected.

"I saw the same thing when I got to Carolina and Kevin Dineen gave it up near the end of his career. It takes a big person to be able to do that."

The rules governing on-ice conversation with the officials allowed only two assistants per team. Desjardins was not assigned an A since neither Recchi nor LeClair had demonstrated any reason they should lose theirs.

The Flyers felt they had plenty of leadership, officially designated and otherwise. But two days after the announcement of the captaincy change, the team was routed by the Senators, 7-2.

"I'm as frustrated as I can get right now," said Barber. "I'm tired of shuffling, trying to find answers.

"Why our emotion level is not higher, I don't understand. I want to see our team be mad, upset after the [loss]. I did not see enough of that."

Thus, the coach decided to take the rehabbing Tocchet with the team to Montreal. "Maybe he'll send some messages about what he is seeing from the press box," Barber said.

Boucher, at the moment seeing the puck better from the crease than was Cechmanek, beat the Canadiens 5-1, then became the first Flyer goalie ever to record shutouts on consecutive nights, by 3-0 at Washington and Pittsburgh. "I'm not putting as much pressure on myself," said the third-year goaltender.

At the other end of the spectrum was the struggling LeClair. "The back was pretty close to good as new," he recalls. "But I put a lot of pressure on myself that year after signing that big contract.

Barber was doling out enough stress for everybody. After the powerplay failed on a five-on-three for 1:40 in a 2-1 loss to the improved Islanders, and then the Flyers went down again by that score two nights later in Chicago, the coach wasn't sticking any stars on foreheads just for effort.

"We've got to find a way to win these kinds of games," he said. "Somebody needs to score a big goal for us, tie the game, or at least make that stop.

"We had some good chances and all that tonight, but it's still not good enough. The battles along the wall and our faceoffs have to improve. Our key guys have to be our key guys."

Said a terse Recchi, "We're trying. We won three in a row, now we've lost two 2-1 games to good hockey teams. We did not play a bad road game. I'm not going to let anyone tear us apart because we lost two 2-1 games."

Next time out, Philadelphia won a 2-1 game in Tampa, hanging on even after Pavel Kubina's goal went through the webbing of Boucher's glove midway through the third period. After the team swept the Florida trip, winning 3-2 in Sunrise on LeClair's overtime goal, Barber glowed. "You couldn't ask for any more than we got today from our players," he said.

Richardson suffered a fractured foot against the Panthers on November 10 that would leave him out for 10 games. But at least Dopita was ready one game later in New York, when the Flyers, 12 of them never having played with Lindros, faced the Big E in a Ranger uniform for the first time.

"The media made a much bigger deal of it than I did," said Lindros, who nevertheless appeared nervous enough to give the puck away four times early before converting a pass off his chest from Theo Fleury to open the scoring. As Philadelphia was outshooting the Rangers 42-27 and piling up five more minutes of offensive zone time, the only hit Lindros delivered was to Roenick. No grudge there, just a good, competitive, divisional game, won by New York, 4-2, despite a goal by Hlavac.

Dopita, who had returned in New York from a 15-game absence, demonstrated everything the Flyers had found so intriguing, scoring a goal in a 5-0 win over Washington. "He was a dominant factor in the game," said Barber. "Great player when he has the puck and when he doesn't have it."

Cechmanek, feeling more confident in his English, decided that serving as Dopita's translator with the media would be good practice. But he also resumed his real job—goaltender—after Boucher, caught in a goalmouth sandwich between Johnsson and Cap Peter Bondra, suffered a grade two hamstring strain. "It stinks," said Boucher. "Things were starting to look good. But I've rehabbed injuries before."

Jenny Barber was setting a supreme example of resiliency for everyone. "A warrior," recalls Bill. But just after the Flyers had concluded practice the day following the Washington victory, she called her husband saying a scan had shown lesions on her brain.

"Like one becoming five, and five soon to become 25," recalls Bill. "Wildfire.

"She never called me at the rink, just this time. I told Mike and E.J. that I had to run. I met her at a Subway (restaurant) in Voorhees and it was the first time I saw her rattled. She had thought she would have more time."

The quintessential hockey wife, Jenny insisted her hockey husband keep going to the rink, so he did.

"I left it up to Billy, of course, if he wanted to keep working," recalls Clarke. "I think sitting at home with his wife probably wouldn't have helped him or her. She would feel guilty and he'd be crawling up the wall."

Recalls Barber, "I had two smart kids (Kerri and Brooks) old enough to take some of the load off me. And I needed the team."

Stothers recalls Barber vented a little sometimes to the coaches, but never to the players, who were mindful and respectful.

"Some guys were saying maybe coaching was good for him," remembers Gagne. "He didn't let it affect him with us as far as I could see.

Recalls Captain Primeau, "We wanted to support whatever decision he made."

The best way they could do that was to win, of course. Cechmanek, playing with a mild flu, backstopped a 3-1 win at the Meadowlands, Philadelphia's first victory there in 11 regular season visits. The rematch with the Devils two days later took place without the farmed-out Brendl—"He needs to go down and show some hunger," said Barber—and didn't go so well. The Flyers gave up 45 shots and blew a 3-1 lead into a 3-3 tie forged by Bobby Holik's goal with 3:22 remaining.

Three nights later in Dallas, Clarke came down from the press box between periods to tell Barber that Kerri had called. She had found her mother on the floor of the bedroom, the victim of an apparent stroke. Likely the chemo had weakened Jenny's heart. She was taken to University of Pennsylvania Hospital.

"I think things happen for a reason," recalls Bill. "[God] kept her out of a lot of pain. Not having that heart attack and stroke would have prolonged it another six-to-seven months."

Barber coached the final two periods as his team surrendered three one-goal leads in a 3-3 tie with the Stars. He thought the effort, particularly from Murray, whose seventh point since joining the team set up Ranheim for the lead goal, was much improved. But then the Flyers came home to stink out the Wachovia Center in a 4-1 loss to the Canucks.

"It's about time the players find a way to make things work so we don't have to search to find a spark," said the coach, again juggling the lines. "It gets a little annoying."

The struggling Desjardins, who had missed four games with back and elbow issues, was being booed. "They have a right to ask for a lot," he said, but in light of his resigned captaincy, Clarke had to deny trying to trade the 32-year-old. "He isn't going anywhere, it's ridiculous," the GM said. "And his family reads that [bleep]."

A noble effort by the flu-ridden Recchi and linemates LeClair and Primeau brought the team back from a 2-0 deficit to Boston until Cechmanek fumbled away a puck in overtime leading to Josef Stumpel's 3-2 winner.

Roenick had tailed off after a fast start but wasn't the only big gun firing blanks. "I don't think they're riding very high as far as confidence goes, but you have to find a way to battle through it," said Barber. "Change [the] routine, change [the] thinking process; find ways."

The players had noticed their coach leaving the Skate Zone soon after practices, but no real change in his demeanor. Nor was there any in his up-and-down club, which beat the Islanders 3-2 in Uniondale only to come home to lose to them, 2-0, before a jittery, booing crowd. "We've got to find a way to relax," said Recchi.

Barber was getting the hardest practice at positive thinking in his Hall of Fame career. "Jenny was begging me, 'I want to go home, I want to go home,'" recalls Bill. "The doctors convinced me that the best thing was to get hospice involved.

"We got her home. It made her happy."

At 5:30 a.m. on Saturday December 8, Barber was awakened by the night nurse. "I think we're almost there," she said and told him to come downstairs to Jenny's bed.

"Her vital signs had all but stopped," Bill recalls. "But we got downstairs and the kids started talking to her and all of a sudden the vital signs improved again briefly."

Jenny took her last breath at 12:05 p.m., a little less than three hours before the Flyer home game with Minnesota. Bill called Stothers with the news and said he would not be coming in, but when Kerri and Brooks insisted that their father change his mind, he decided to go.

"We'd had time to prepare," recalls Barber. "There wasn't much left for me to do. God bless my kids. Jenny would have wanted me to go to work."

Barber informed just a few veteran players before the game. Only after the Flyers, staked to a 2-0 lead on goals by Recchi and Richardson (in his return after missing 10 games), won 5-1 did the coach inform the rest of the team, breaking down as he did so. Some of the players followed.

"I was good friends with Billy and Jenny before he became the coach," recalls Richardson.

"I had gone motor biking with Bill and, even that summer she got sick, we were at their pool with our kids. Except for the wig, which she joked about, and the weight loss, which she really couldn't afford, you wouldn't have known she was ill. She was laughing, enjoying the day.

"She had always done everything for Bill, had the (pregame) meal ready, kept the kids quiet during his nap so he could concentrate on the game. She always put him and his job first. So when Billy said she would have wanted him to coach that day, he absolutely was right."

Primeau recalls being shocked to see Barber. "People deal with tragedies in different ways," he said, and the players seemed to understand that.

"Some guys were like, 'What is he doing here?' and others said they were glad he was; it would be good for him," recalls Fedoruk.

So was the Flyer victory, as small a thing as that seemed.

"Fighting for your life, fighting for your family, she did all that," Barber told the media after practice the following day, before flying to Atlanta with the team. "You talk about courage."

Snider and Clarke had told the coach to take as much time off as he needed, but Barber insisted that he wanted to keep going.

Philadelphia beat the Thrashers the next night 3-1, Roenick and Primeau breaking a tie with the kind of clutch third-period goals the team had gone close to a half-season without. "We played with some patience tonight, which we haven't seen for a while," said Barber.

In the morning, 600 persons—including Barber's old teammates, current players and caring ex-Flyers like Rod Brind'Amour—overflowed the Hope United Methodist Church in Voorhees to say goodbye to a woman who didn't know how to put herself first.

"She would spend all day catering to everyone else's needs," said Brooks. "She dedicated her life to family and friends, never once looking for anything in return. Being kind and caring was so easy for her because all she had to be was herself."

Jenny had been one of the organizers of the first Flyers Wives Fight for Lives Carnival in 1977, as well as a den mother to the wives and girlfriends of the Phantoms during her husband's years coaching that team. Mary Ann Saleski told Bill Fleischman of the *Daily News* following the service that Jenny had been practically a sister to her, Carolyn MacLeish and Cathy Schultz.

"Always organizing things," Saleski said. "She kept everybody in touch."

That role had even brought her together with Bill during his junior days in Kitchener, Ontario, where he was trying to organize a gathering for his teammates to meet girls and knew just the person in town who could help. Jenny was pleased to do it and even happier to ignore the advice of girlfriends to not date the son of the gas station owner whose "socks didn't match his v-neck sweaters."

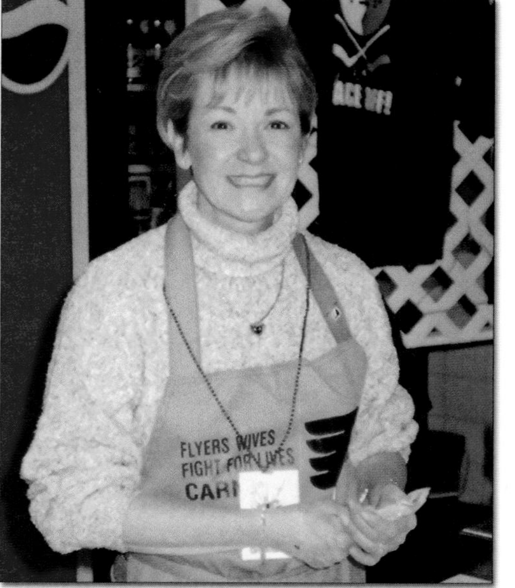

Jenny Barber's passing was felt throughout the Flyer family. She had been a close friend to many of the players' wives and girlfriends.

"I went out with him on a bet," Jenny had once told the *Daily News*'s Dana Pennett-O'Neil. "Four months later, I told my mother I would marry him."

They tied the knot at the end of his first season with the Flyers, went on a ride together through two children ("Well-spoken, well-educated, she's totally responsible for that," said Bill), two Stanley Cups and a ravaged knee that prematurely ended his time on the ice after 11 seasons. It meant practically everything to Barber to have played his entire career with one team and serve it afterwards in whatever capacity was needed. And Jenny became an almost equal-part organizational fixture.

"We have our own alumni wives [group]," Mary Ann told Fleischman. "Jenny always made sure everybody was involved, the young with the old.

"Somebody called me a few weeks ago and asked, 'What are we going to do about our Christmas dinner that Jenny always arranged?'

"I said, 'We're not going to have it.'"

Barber spoke to reporters after the service. "I need my kids and I want to be around the guys," he said. "I want to be in my environment."

The First Union Center hardly was an uplifting place, though. During a 3-2 loss to Montreal, only a third-period goal by Johnsson interrupted the booing of a 14-9-5 team. "Our fans don't have any tolerance for us being behind," noted newcomer Roenick. "We start hearing the boos, it deflates you. I'm not going to lie. We have to battle through stuff like that."

After having found no chemistry with LeClair, Roenick began to cook with Gagne, leaving Big John to go goalless in nine games, his longest drought as a Flyer. "I don't have the confidence to challenge a guy one-on-one right now," he admitted. "I wouldn't care so much about scoring if I were playing better."

Barber recalled he had stayed on the fans' good side during slumps by making his effort obvious. Certainly they found a lot to like in Johnsson, who had been the Flyers' best defenseman since Day One of the season. "He's added a (puck-moving) dimension we haven't had in a long, long time," praised the coach.

Hlavac had nine goals playing on the third line, most of them scored during Dopita's absence. Nevertheless, the Czech became bait to fill the void of grit and leadership in the absence of Tocchet. On December 17, Hlavac and a third-round pick were traded to Vancouver for Donald Brashear plus a sixth rounder.

"He is tougher than boiled owl," said Canucks GM Brian Burke describing Brashear, one of the NHL's premier pugilists, who had pleaded guilty to an assault charge at his condominium in Vancouver and also paid $415,000 to two Philadelphia residents as a settlement for a June 1997 altercation at the Jersey shore.

"We didn't think [the court record] was a problem," said assistant GM Holmgren. "Based on our team's needs, we felt this was a trade we had to make. Hlavac wasn't getting ice time behind Gagne and LeClair."

Added Barber, "I think [Brashear] will add some space. I don't have to worry about liberties being taken on our talent."

Brashear, who had been in Montreal with the Canucks, got to Philadelphia in time to play the next night against St. Louis, but thanks to an unloading snafu, his equipment did not. The stuff he borrowed for the warm-up, including LeClair's skates, were a half size too small, so Brashear was scratched. Without either Hlavac or the player obtained for him, Philadelphia scored six goals for only the second time in the season and defeated the Blues, 6-3.

Asked what his thoughts had been on the Flyers when Vancouver had beaten them 4-1, 23 days earlier at the First Union Center, Brashear said, "We thought if we took the body we would win. That's probably one of the reasons I'm here."

In his first game, Brashear's only contribution was a penalty that led to the lone Dallas score. But thanks to Boucher and a winning goal by the heretofore struggling Primeau, Philadelphia prevailed regardless, 2-1, to complete the team's first back-to-back home wins of the season. "Brian is much more mature now," said Flyer goalie coach Reggie Lemelin about the third-year netminder. "He controls rebounds so much better."

When Recchi scored in overtime to beat Carolina, 4-3, a victory largely made possible by the seventh and eighth goals of the season by Murray, Philadelphia had three straight victories to its credit. Aiding the cause was Brashear's three shots, seven hits and two takeaways.

"Obviously Janny (Hlavac) is a good player, but you see the difference [with] a guy that can skate and add a physical presence," said Recchi.

As they headed West—first stop Phoenix—the Flyers had wiped their feet on seven of their last nine opponents, good practice for when they were invited to Roenick's home near Camelback Mountain. "I've never seen a house like that in my life," reported Therien the next day. It was like *Lifestyles of the Rich and Famous* and Robin Leach gave us a tour."

Primeau was particularly impressed with the wine cellar. No mention was made of any doghouse, but the next night, after Boucher allowed goals on four of the first nine shots, Barber gave the netminder a rare pass. "I don't think he had his A-game, but as well as he's played for us this year, I'm not going to put this on his shoulders," he said after the 4-2 defeat. "We didn't get many breaks."

The Phoenix fans didn't appear to be holding any grudges against Roenick, even if he had left for more money. He was cheered in assisting on both Philadelphia goals. J.R. added another the following evening as the Flyers, despite a wee hours arrival, beat the powerful Avalanche with surprising ease, 5-2. He then set up the Gagne winner with just three seconds remaining in Cechmanek's 2-1 win on a happy New Year's Eve in Vancouver.

Gagne had scored with a bruised shoulder that forced him and his team-leading 17 goals from the lineup. In his absence, Philadelphia and Cechmanek were overrun by the Sharks' three third period goals in a 5-2 defeat, but Barber's team wrapped up the five-game trip at 3-2-0 when Murray, playing the wing in Gagne's place, scored twice in Boucher's 4-3 victory in Raleigh. "This has been a huge road trip for us and we finished it with a bang," said Roenick.

The Flyers also wrapped it up with a share of first place, despite having trailed the Rangers by nine points five weeks earlier. "We were a pretty good team on paper but it has taken this amount of time to understand each other and our coaching staff," said the coach.

Dopita still barely comprehended a word the coaches said, which didn't stop him from being the 15th Flyer ever with a four-goal game as they thrashed the Thrashers, 7-4, in Gagne's and Desjardins' return. The Czech center also needed a translation about all the hats that hit the ice when goal No. 3 went in during the second period, that not being the custom where he came from. "Lucky game for me," Dopita said through Cechmanek's loose translation.

Maybe some of the good fortune had even rubbed off on the struggling LeClair, who had a goal and two assists. "I think I have a lot of catching up to do," said the marquee Flyer player as Lindros, their erstwhile star, came to town for the first time wearing the uniform of the hated Rangers.

His 19 goals and 20 assists had keyed New York to a surprising 21-14-3 start before he suffered the seventh concussion of his career, the result of a stick in the face by San Jose's Mark Smith. No. 88 was out only four games, but the Rangers had won just one of six since the accident.

"You wouldn't believe me anyway if I said it was just another game," said Big E. "I remember a lot of good things about playing in Philadelphia.

Whatever cheers there were for Lindros were drowned out by thunderous boos as he took three shots, recorded no hits, suffered one cross-check in the slot (by Weinrich), and lost 13 of the 24 draws he took against Primeau during a 4-2 Flyer victory.

"You step into a building you played in for many years and you've got a lot of things going through your mind," said Lindros. "It was very hard; I didn't feel real comfortable until about halfway through the second period."

His tiptoeing had been a jarring sight.

"I think Eric has to be careful," said Recchi. "I don't know the situation with his last concussion, but if he's going to start hitting, that's when people are going to start taking runs at him to respond.

"If he stays to the perimeter, he's going to stay out of those situations."

Cechmanek, who had asked to be traded while Boucher was getting the lion's share of the starts, nevertheless was given a three-year, $10 million, contract extension, then came in cold to pitch a third-period shutout as the Flyers rallied from a 3-2 deficit to a 5-3 victory in Montreal. The contract, he told a Czech newspaper, "assured me that the Philadelphia media pushing Brian into the goal every way possible won't sweep the floor with me anymore."

He added, "And I don't care whether I'll stay with the Flyers or whether they'll ship me somewhere else."

Boucher could only hope.

"Roman was always telling me, 'Be ready,' like he wasn't feeling right," Boucher recalls. "I'd be like, 'Of course,' and then he would go out and get a shutout.

"It would rattle me. 'Stop telling me to be ready.'"

Roenick, who had been minus-five when the Flyers were routed in Ottawa in October, scored a goal and two assists in their first victory against the Senators in three seasons, 4-1. He was now plus-24 for the season. "The coaches keep stressing Mike Modano to me, how he gave up some offense in order to become a better two-way player and won a Stanley Cup," said J.R.

The win streak went to seven when Justin Williams scored the tying goal and then set up LeClair as Philadelphia surged past lowly Atlanta, 6-3. "It's a mental battle," said Barber about the compressed schedule to accommodate the NHL's upcoming hiatus to participate in the Olympic Winter Games in Salt Lake City. "We need those young legs."

Boucher stumbled during a 5-2 loss in Pittsburgh and the Flyers, after leading 1-0 into the third period, lost to Nashville 3-2 in overtime. But for once, the players were more critical of themselves than was their coach. "They are showing as much concern as the staff; I love every minute of it," said Barber.

Murray, given a three-year deal for $1.95 million—"as good a utility player as there is in the game today," insisted Clarke—scored to beat the Penguins in overtime after Primeau's goal with just 17 seconds remaining was set up by Roenick's steal from Kovalev, who had been trying to stickhandle out of the Pittsburgh zone. "A dangler shouldn't try to beat a dangler because they know the moves," said Primeau.

Roenick had displayed enough of those over 14 seasons to become the 63rd NHL player—and both the fourth Flyer and fourth American—to reach 1,000 points with his opening goal in Ottawa. But Philadelphia, playing its 13th game in 23 days, faded late in a 3-1 loss that preceded the All-Star Game being staged in Los Angeles. "Fatigue probably had something to do with it," said Barber.

Although Clarke thought it highly inappropriate that Johnsson was overlooked—"It's pretty hard not to know what kind of a year he is having," said the GM—Roenick was an appropriate selection for the celebrity-filled game in Hollywood. Gifted a disco ball and microphone stand at the team's annual, anonymous, pollyanna Christmas exchange, the center/entertainer had brought *Saturday Night Fever* to Philadelphia's pregame locker room.

"We would have the lights going all around and I would get out my air hockey stick and do a little disco," recalls Roenick. "Pretty funny."

One wouldn't expect that J.R. would visit L.A. just to be content to play a little no-check hockey. The Flyer did a shoot for the HBO series *Arli$$*, participated in a street hockey event, was miked for the skills competition, and interviewed players—including Williams, a participant in the YoungStars Game—with JRCam. "Not too many people get to do what I do, and I don't want to waste it," Roenick said.

Accomodatingly for the tired All-Star, Philadelphia resumed its schedule in Los Angeles. Beneficially for Barber, the team won 3-1 behind Weinrich's goal and assist, the coach lauding his players' attention in their first game back from vacation.

Two nights later in Anaheim, Boucher gave up three goals in the final 14 minutes—including Oleg Tverdovsky's score with 13 seconds remaining—and stunningly lost 5-4 to the Ducks, but Philadelphia finished the trip with Cechmanek's 5-0 shutout in St. Louis.

The Flyers were 18-9-3 on the road and 16-5-1 overall since Brashear had joined their lineup. "In addition to getting people' s attention on the ice, he could skate and play," recalls LeClair. "He was a real asset."

In the locker room, too. "He scared people into playing harder," recalls Roenick. '"He would stand up and yell and scream, tell you to get going or he would fight you."

After J.R.'s giveway allowed Islander Peca to painfully beat Cechmanek, 1-0, with 6.7 seconds remaining, Roenick was not challenged by Brashear to put up the dukes. But like the rest of the Flyers, frustrated by the failure to score on eight powerplay opportunities in the game, he went to the 14-day Olympic break with a bad taste in his mouth.

The Islander loss was especially hard on Fedotenko, who, bad ankle regardless, had flown back to Philadelphia that morning from Salt Lake City, UT, where he had scored a goal to help his Ukraine team beat Switzerland in its opener of the play-in competition for one of two open spots in the main Olympic draw. While he was playing at the First Union Center, Fedotenko's country was eliminated by France.

Roenick and LeClair (USA), Gagne (Canada), Dopita and Cechmanek (Czech Republic) plus Johnsson (Sweden) all got to skate for teams with medal hopes. The Czechs were defending the gold they had won four years earlier while Gagne was trying to help Canada to its first gold medal in 50 years (Canada had not entered a team in 1972 and 1976; 1998 had been the first Olympic participation by NHL players.)

The Americans were being coached by Herb Brooks, the mastermind of the 1980 gold medal team, and were represented by eight 30-plus-year-old members of the generation that had been inspired to play hockey by that Lake Placid miracle.

"I remember when Herbie was putting the team together, he called and asked how my back was," recalls LeClair. "His exact words were, 'Don't [bullbleep] me. If it turns out you did and I've given you a spot, I'll kill you.'

"In the Olympics, there can't be much preparation; you show up and play. There's some strategy, but mostly it's a matter of the coach getting guys in the right frame of mind. Herbie was really good at that. The Herbie-isms were awesome."

Brooks had once told a 1980 team member, "You are getting worse every day, and today you are playing like next Tuesday." He took a more positive approach with the NHL millionaires. At their first meeting, he told them never to underestimate their influence on the growth of the sport in the USA, and to not allow their 1-3 showing in Nagano and the $1,000 in damages left behind in the athlete's village to be their legacy.

"Herbie was part of the greatest event in the history of hockey in the USA," recalls Roenick. "Because of that, all of us waited for almost every word that came out of his mouth."

Though the first three games were just for medal-round seeding, the Americans had found out the hard way in Nagano that they had to hit the ground running. Twelve members of the 2002 team that had played in 1998, learned from their sour experience, on and off the ice.

"We were coming off the World Cup (USA's spectacular two-out-of-three final round upset of Canada) feeling good about it. We thought it would be similar and it wasn't," recalled LeClair.

"The damage in Nagano was completely overblown. The place was put together real quick, and chairs were breaking just as you sat on them.

"Was there some stuff that shouldn't have been done? Absolutely.

(Two fire extinguishers were taken off the wall and used for prank sprayings before one was thrown to the courtyard below.) And we did not do ourselves any favors by not playing well. It wasn't a good experience, the whole thing. I think after what happened in Nagano, guys were a little more focused when we went to Salt Lake."

Recalls Roenick, another veteran of Nagano, "When it is in your home country, there's obviously a bigger sense of pride to play well," he said. "To go in half-assed would have been probably a bigger catastrophe than '98."

LeClair had a hat trick as the USA opened the Group D round robin with a 6-0 win over Finland, the defending bronze medalist. He followed up with two more goals in an 8-1 clobbering of Belarus.

The only problem the American team seemed to be having was Roenick's producing a urine sample for drug testing. He told Les Bowen in a diary for the *Daily News* that it required an hour and forty-five minutes for him to void the required 75 millimeters.

"It took six Gatorades and three bottles of water; I thought I was going to throw up," reported J.R. "Someone follows you around the whole time; stage fright could have been a factor, too.

"Then once I got going, I couldn't stop. It was quite an evening with lots of interruptions."

Canada started out like its efforts were going to be a big waste, losing to Sweden 5-2, struggling to get past Germany 2-1, and tying 3-3 with the Czechs, drawing so much criticism that general manager Wayne Gretzky decided to create a distraction, calling for suspensions of Czech players for stick fouls and declaring "the whole world wants us to lose except Canadians."

But Gagne's team got a huge break during the single-elimination quarterfinal when Swedish goalie Tommy Salo dropped an 80-foot Belarusian shot over the line for a late third-period winner. The Canadians, who had barely gotten by the Finns 2-1 in their quarterfinal, blasted overmatched Belarus, 7-1 in the semifinal. That set up a gold medal game with the Americans who, in their semi match, had dominated the Russians for two periods in jumping up 3-0, and then survived a 19-shot third-period onslaught to win, 3-2.

Roenick and Gagne caught one another's attention during the gold medal game warm-up and had a rapport-sharing laugh at both their good fortune to be part of the first-ever Canada-USA Olympic final and the irony of playing on opposing teams.

"He was my centerman, almost like a big brother to me," recalls Gagne. "It's special, playing against your teammate."

"I was so nervous; I couldn't feel my legs. Fortunately for us, Joe Sakic was unbelievable. He took a lot of pressure off guys."

Brian Rafalski's goal at 15:30 of the second period pulled the USA into a 2-2 tie. But with Roenick in the box for tripping Paul Kariya, Sakic put Canada back ahead before the 40-minute period break.

With the Canada line of Mario Lemieux, Steve Yzerman and Kariya badly outplaying the American unit of LeClair, Modano and Brett Hull, the Americans generated little pressure until Jarome Iginla's second goal of the game dropped out of Mike Richter's glove and over the line with 3:59 to go.

The Canadian players rose from their bench as if 30 million persons had jumped off their backs, and celebrated the country's first gold in five decades with a 5-2 victory.

"The gold medal is right there and you're one game away from it, so it's disappointing," recalls LeClair. "We felt we could have beaten that team."

But there was no question the superior—and more driven—club on that day had won.

"Reporters asked me afterwards whether the U.S. wanted to win but Canada needed to win, and I think that's probably true," said Roenick. "Canada was just better.

"I wish I had played better. But I'm proud to have a silver medal around my neck. Was it worth it? Ten times over."

Playing the tournament with Sakic and Iginla, Gagne had scored a goal and six assists. "To be in an Olympics, you have to be one of the best 22 guys in your country," Gagne recalls. "And then to win a gold medal—especially the first one in 50 years—with all that pressure, wow!"

The next day, the conquering hero spent five hours in a security line at the airport, missed his flight and had to catch another one. But the following night, there were no hard feelings towards Roenick. The Flyer teammates assisted on each other's goals as Philadelphia began a stretch of 35-games-in-48 days with a sluggish 5-4 victory over the Blackhawks at the First Union Center.

That schedule would not be Tocchet's friend as he tried to find out whether his knee and sore back, rehabbed in the pool, would hold up. "I don't know if I can play hockey any more but I sure can swim," he joked. "I'm excited because my legs feel really good."

Tocchet set up Gagne for the only goal in a 1-0 win over the Devils at the Meadowlands, beating John Vanbiesbrouck in an effort highlighted by the presumed-to-be-ponderous Brashear racing to catch and foil Patrik Elias after having given the puck away to the New Jersey star.

In New York, Cechmanek suffered an ankle sprain during the first period, gave up an early goal to Lindros, and then got tossed after taking unsportsmanlike conduct and slashing penalties. So this time Boucher really had to be ready. He wasn't though, as Lindros got a hat trick and the Rangers held off a three-goal effort by Gagne for the 6-5 win.

"Roman apologized to me afterwards," recalls Boucher, who was much better in Boston as Dopita scored two, and Gagne's sixth goal since the Olympic break became the game winner in a 4-1 triumph. Philadelphia, up five points on the Bruins and Leafs, led the conference.

The Flyers lost not only two one-goal leads, but Recchi. The winger received a two-game suspension for elbowing Jean Gauthier in a 4-2 defeat by Calgary, Philadelphia's first home regulation loss in 13 games. But with Cechmanek expected to miss a month and Primeau out with strained ribs, Roenick took a Ben Clymer shot in the mouth at Tampa for 29 stitches and returned to the game. It was won 4-2 after Therien tapped in the mid-third period winner after every Flyer on the ice had touched the puck.

"We're fortunate to have the depth to stay in the game," said Barber.

"Other teams can't really say the same. "

Philadelphia was 37-17-6 despite a 13 percent powerplay. The players had converted on only five of their last 45 opportunities when, following a 3-1 First Union Center loss to Toronto, members of the unit went to Barber before practice the next day and asked him to stop altering the personnel so much. "If you want to change some guys fine, but keep the (basic) group together, " Primeau told reporters was the message.

Barber said he agreed and would, but pointed out that he had done so earlier in the year and, when there was no improvement, was forced to make further changes. "I'm trying to find stability in our lines in the sense that I'm not shuffling the deck as much as we have," he said. "Hopefully, the players will jump on board with that and play hard together.

A 1-1 tie in Toronto made possible by LeClair's second goal in 10 games didn't satisfy anybody, not after a bad change had led to Gary Roberts' tying goal with 2:05 to go, and a snow mound around goalie Cory Schwab had foiled Recchi on a breakaway in overtime.

Powerplay problems became an overall scoring problem as Roenick managed the sole goal in a 3-1 home loss to Buffalo. When the Flyers doubled the shots on Colorado but were stoned 2-1 by Patrick Roy, they had lost four straight at the First Union Center, scoring once in each game.

"It was a circus out there and [Roy] was the acrobat," said Roenick. "They have the best goalie in the world and that's why they won."

But it wasn't the only reason. "We practiced the powerplay 10 days in a row at one time," said Barber as the players, asking to work on it more, voluntarily stayed longer to do so. "You can have set plays, but if you can't even do the basics . . .

"It takes courage to shoot the puck. Clarke would rip the hell out of me if he would pass it to me and I wouldn't shoot."

Added Clarke, "Our theory was that if the point got the puck, one pass and then a shot. The rest of us knew that shot was coming and went to the net. Right now our players don't know when that shot is coming. Everyone is standing around waiting."

Rather than go to the net, key players went instead to Clarke's office, where they aired their concerns about the coaching. "We had a bunch of guys wanting to do the right things," recalls Recchi. "We had had Roger, we had Rammer, we had been very structured. If you're not having structure, it's hard to win hockey games."

The structure the GM found most important was one where coaches coach and players play. "I thought it was weak coming to me instead of trying to find a way to help each other," recalls Clarke. "I told them they had better try taking some responsibility.

"Billy had done a pretty good job the year before. There was nothing a new coach could do [that late in a season]. Still, when important players come to you to complain, you basically know it is over for a coach. But it [bleeped] me off. When I played, players never would have done something like that."

Gagne, the team's burgeoning star, was not among the posse.

"For the most part, things with me and Billy were very good," he recalls. "Even if I wasn't playing well, he was positive, hadn't put extra pressure on me. As long as you worked hard, he let you be creative a little.

"I was still just in my third year and, offensively, I had fun playing that type of system. It was always forward, forward, forward. But near the end of his second year, Billy started to feel pressure, so he started to talk to me a little differently than he had before.

"There were veterans—some who had even won the Cup—who said you can't win like this in the playoffs. Looking back, with my experience and some playoff success, I can see why guys got a little [bleeped] off."

Recalls LeClair, "There are different ways to go about it and Billy's way always was the same, even if it didn't work. Everybody's different, you know; what pushes your button might not be what pushes my button.

"The team really took off when he came in. That fresh voice helped, but I think it was a voice that didn't last long. After a while, instead of being helpful, it became detrimental.

"It's not like you don't know what to do. But not everything is going to work against every team. Some work the powerplay low; some want to get point shots and crash the net. (For Barber), it all came back to, 'You guys have played enough hockey, just go do it.' Ok, but we need some help with what we're going to do.

"E.J. was the guy everybody wanted to talk to. Besides being a terrific human being, he was just easier to [deal with]. He listened, did what he could, tried to explain Billy's message differently, without yelling, 'Do it my way.'"

Recalls Roenick, who also had played under McGuire in Chicago, "He would talk to you with such a calming tone that even if he was being critical, he did it in a way that made you enjoy it. Not just good cop versus bad cop, but kind of sneaky cop in that way. He was just a wonderful, wonderful man."

In light of all the talent additions, Barber had gone into the season worrying about egos. He thought Roenick was "out there" but likable, and making an effort to do the right thing.

Dopita's role, as third center behind Primeau and Roenick, was not what the Czech had in mind, however. "He was slow footed, but had size and could make plays," recalls Barber. "I thought he was a good fit but, in his mind, he wasn't."

Primeau said it was more than just role dooming Dopita's chance to be successful with the Flyers. "I was so excited about that signing because I had seen him in Europe," the captain recalls. "I believe he wanted to see if he could be a good player here as well, but on that big ice he had been a tactician.

"It was a chess match to him; you win with your brain, not by 'Go harder, work harder.' He was the guy who didn't like Billy at all. And I think that was the beginning of the end for Cechmanek, too."

Recalls Barber, "So I'm battling [Dopita's unhappiness with his role] and then I hear from both him and Roman that we had a bad dressing room. When Desjardins says he doesn't want to be captain, it's a red flag. He knew he couldn't handle the room."

The teacher, Barber, was from an old school.

"I like Billy," recalls Therien. "I thought he was a pretty good guy, but there was frustration both ways between he and the players.

"My father told me, 'Never talk back to a coach,' but at times I did with Billy out of sheer frustration. He had a marriage to what once was the Philadelphia Flyers, and it just wasn't the seventies anymore."

Barber had his supporters, too.

"He was in your face, trying to make you play hard," recalls Fedoruk. "I liked it because I could take it, and because I had him in the minors, he was kind of all I knew.

"It bugged some guys because they didn't want to hear it. I think there were just a couple of guys who wanted something different and the rest of us really didn't care either way.

"Sometimes, 'Just play, just go [bleepin'] play,' isn't good enough for people. Decisions are going to be made that you are not going to like, but you don't have to like them. If the way we had the lines was not working, who cares if we switch the lines up?

"I took it personal because I liked Billy."

At one point, according to Tocchet, he was asked by Barber to become a coach and help convey his message. "I said it wouldn't be a good idea," recalls Tocchet. "I wasn't ready to relinquish playing and, if I were doing both, I couldn't be part of the staff and still gain the trust of the players."

Future Hall of Famer Adam Oates was added at the 2002 trade deadline.

On March 14, Clarke dealt Manderville—a scratch in 17 of the previous 27 games because of the effectiveness of Murray—to Pittsburgh for Billy Tibbetts, a 27-year-old winger who had scored a goal and an assist while up for 33 games with the Penguins, having spent the rest of his season with their Wilkes-Barre/Scranton farm team.

Ten years earlier, at 17, Tibbetts had been convicted of raping a 15-year-old girl. Because of his age, his sentence had been suspended. But subsequent convictions for assaults in 1994 and 1995 had put him in prison for 39 months, in part for violation of the probation from the rape charge. There also was a recent citation on his record for driving 120 miles an hour on an interstate near Scranton.

"I always felt that a player getting a second chance would probably take advantage of it," recalls Clarke. "Billy (Barber) loved Tibbetts from the AHL; we liked the fire in him."

Clarke meant on the ice, of course, but Tibbetts' track record off it, created a media firestorm.

"I didn't always think about the other person before I acted, but I do now," Tibbetts said after the morning skate on his first full day as a Flyer. "It was a selfish act, something I have to live with and something that probably will never go away unless maybe you really get to know me. And that's what I am hoping for."

The winger was minus-two that night in 13:28 of ice time as Philadelphia blew a 3-0 lead into a 3-3 tie with Tampa Bay. He played longer than Roenick, low-bridged by Clymer, and Primeau, hit in the ribs by Shane Willis. Fortunately, Brashear scored twice, enabling the Flyers, only 6-7-2 in their last 15 games, to get the point.

"I'm glad we're in the position we're in (tied for second place in the East with Toronto)," said Barber. "I wouldn't want all this happening while we were fighting at the bottom of the pack."

It was with the belief that the Flyers still could be what preseason prognosticators had said that, one hour before the trading deadline, Clarke dealt first, second and third-round choices in the 2001 draft, plus 1999 first-round pick Ouellet to Washington for center Adam Oates, at 39 still the league's leading assist maker.

"When you believe you have a legitimate shot at going a long way in the playoffs, you've got to take that chance," said the GM.

It seemed like a ton to give up for an about-to-be 40-year-old three months from becoming an unrestricted free agent. But Clarke felt he had other goaltending prospects as talented as Ouelett (16-13-8, .911 save percentage with the Phantoms). The late first-round choice Philadelphia was trading was practically a second rounder, and besides, Clarke had banked 11 extra picks for the next two drafts.

"[Oates] is a brilliant playmaker," said Clarke. "He's got great vision and great ice hockey knowledge.

"Even at his age, he still is one of the top players in the league. He should give us a better powerplay, a real top faceoff man, and that should help some of our players who are struggling to score."

Indeed, Oates—who had the fourth-highest assists per game average (.853) in NHL history behind Bobby Orr, Gretzky and Lemieux—set up LeClair with 7:34 to go to get the Flyers their first home win in six games, 2-1, over Anaheim.

"I've played with [the Caps] for [five seasons] and I've got a lot of buddies there," said the Hall of Famer-to-be. "But when you hear it's Philly, one of those teams that you always hope you get a chance to play for, you're kind of excited."

Cechmanek, believed to be prepared to go against Anaheim, had begged off during the morning skate and wasn't ready the following night in Pittsburgh when Boucher gave up two soft goals in a 4-4 tie. It dampened Recchi's 1,000th NHL game, fittingly being played in the city were he won back-to-back Cups.

"I think this ranks No. 1 for milestones for sure," he said. "I was a [fourth-round pick] who wasn't supposed to make it in the league."

Tocchet, once a sixth-round pick, had been an even longer shot, but turned the opportunity into a 19-year career. But now that it was nearing its end, he asked to be benched in favor of little-used swingman McAllister.

"I've never been in a situation where I only played five minutes every night and I don't want to start now," said Tocchet. "I respect guys who do it, but it's young players.

"If a couple guys are injured down the line, hopefully I can step in. But I'd rather stay on the sideline and work hard there."

Oates' arrival bumped Primeau, returned after only two games, to a checking unit with Fedotenko and Brashear. The captain still scored twice in a 4-1 win over Toronto on March 25, the Flyers' most complete game in weeks.

"I really like it, it's a tremendous challenge," said Primeau, endorsing both his role and the acquisition of Oates. "Teams were not respecting us along the half-wall, would force us against it and ultimately steal the puck.

"Adam has great vision and presence. If you press him, he's going to find the open guy."

With Cechmanek's ankle still not healed, Boucher surrendered Lindros's fifth goal in four games against Philadelphia. It wasn't enough for the Big E's fading team as Recchi scored for the first time in 19 games and Primeau hit the empty net in the 4-2 Flyer victory at Madison Square Garden..

Rather than play Boucher back to back the following night in Raleigh, Barber asked Clarke to call up Neil Little, a once 11th-round pick who had played 379 minor league games and sat on the bench for 43 more for Philadelphia without ever getting into an NHL game. "He was a big factor in us winning a (Phantom) championship in '98," said Barber. "He's been here a long time and has paid his dues,"

Little's reward for his perseverance was a miserable effort in front of him and a 4-1 loss. "I felt privileged I could represent the Flyers and did the best I possibly could," he said after giving up a 40-footer to Sami Kapanen that hit the post and went in off the goalie's back. Another Carolina goal was scored when Kevyn Adams was thrown into Little by Tibbetts, who also drew a two-game suspension for his third instigator penalty of the season. "Bummed out, let the team down," Tibbetts said.

Little was returned to the Phantoms when Cechmanek came back after 14 games. The Czech allowed three goals on 17 shots as the Sabres, enabled by a collision between Oates and Weinrich on Dumont's winning goal, completed a sweep of a home-and-home by identical 3-1 scores.

As the Bruins, neck and neck with Philadelphia for the conference lead, came to town, Barber insisted the more important showdown was between his players and their images in the mirror. "This is not a first place issue," he said. "The most important thing is how this team is playing."

Again, it was not well. The return of Roenick, only 15 days after suffering a partial ACL tear, seemed to help inspire Oates and Primeau goals in the first eight minutes, but the emotional effort seemed to exhaust the Flyers. Boston came back to win 4-2, prompting a closed-door meeting. "You don't win 40 games by chance," said Recchi afterward. "Something good is bound to happen."

It didn't against Montreal, when Barber's lines remained unaltered in a 3-1 loss, Philadelphia's fifth straight. "If I start shuffling now, it will only hurt us," said the coach sounding more understanding about his team's ebbing belief in itself. "No matter how much experience you have, you can start pushing too hard. We have to try to get the confidence level raised."

Recchi had three goals in 29 games; LeClair six in 32. "I'm playing in between, making bad decisions when to jump and when not to," said Big John, the six goals he scored in the Olympics seeming to have had no carryover once the NHL season had resumed.

The Flyers were feeding off each other's anxieties. "For the first time in my three years here, I am at a loss for words," said Primeau. "I don't know what to say, how to make this better."

The panic crept into the stands. Or was it from the stands onto the ice? During the Montreal loss, Roenick engaged a heckling fan.

"I told him to zip it," said J.R. "I'd heard enough. Yes, we want to do it for them, but we want to win for ourselves. If we win for each other, the fans will follow and enjoy it.

"Everybody can yell and boo all they want; it's not going to do any good. They pay a lot of money but have to understand it's not for our lack of effort."

Desjardins couldn't play against division bottom dweller Pittsburgh because of back spasms suffered against Montreal, but Williams and Roenick staked the team to a 2-0 lead and Oates put away the first Flyer victory in six contests, 3-1 over Pittsburgh, into the empty net.

The next day, the Tibbetts experiment ended after nine games, one assist, and 69 penalty minutes, his pleas for another chance falling on deaf ears when he engaged Clarke in the lobby of the Skate Zone. Fedoruk had been asked by Holmgren to hang around in case there was trouble.

Recalls Clarke, "Messed up kid, couldn't trust him. We had been grasping for straws. A very short fuse and when he snapped it was like, 'Everybody duck.' He was taking stupid penalties and just didn't fit into an NHL locker room.

"We deserved all the criticism we got for signing him."

Roenick adds, "I knew him since I was eight years old, went to high school with him. Always a problem child; always getting in fights and trouble in school."

The Flyers didn't need a loose cannon on their fourth line. They already had one in goal. After a second period go-ahead score by Panther Sandis Ozolinsh at Sunrise, Cechmanek skated to the blueline and looked at the bench.

"I think we was stretching, that's how I looked at it," said Barber. "I've seen him do that before.

"Whether he was just trying to collect his thoughts or not, he was going to play. He wasn't coming out."

A goal by Johnsson, then Gagne's 33rd of the season, had brought the team to within 17 seconds of a buoying second consecutive victory when Ozolinsh shot the puck through Cechmanek and Pierre Dagenais shoved it into the empty net. After Philadelphia settled for a 4-4 tie, the goalie denied he had asked to be removed. Sort of.

"I was a long time injured and I know I didn't play good," Cechmanek said. "I'm doing everything to play good, but I felt that I didn't help my teammates."

Barber said the Flyer effort showed "some steps in the right direction." They pretended to take more in losing to the Devils 1-0 on John Madden's third-period rebound goal at the Meadowlands. "Defensively, we couldn't have played much better than we did, " said Primeau, but the team needed goals and a goalie who was in the right state of mind.

"I know there is short time to playoffs, but I feel day-by-day better," reported Cechmanek. "I know we need confidence; maybe next game."

It would have to come without his compatriot, Dopita, who, having missed seven of nine games with knee inflammation, required arthroscopic surgery that would leave him out of a first round that was too quickly approaching.

Barber's team needed 45 shots to squeeze a goal each from Oates and Recchi and beat the moribund Rangers 2-1, assuring a first-round meeting with Ottawa—a seventh seed that had finished with only three fewer points than the Flyers. An Atlantic Division title by one point over the Islanders and two over the Devils had given Philadelphia the second seed with 97 points.

Roenick was excused from the meaningless season finale at Uniondale to be with his wife Tracy and her terminally ill mother, Dorothy Vazza. But a number of big-ticket players remained missing in action since practically the Olympic break.

In scoring only 37 goals in their last 19 games, the Flyers had gone 5-10-4. Ottawa hadn't been much better, finishing up 8-12-22. Though it seemed like sputtering Philadelphia might have lucked out to draw a franchise that had enjoyed just one series victory in its 10-year existence, the Flyers hardly had playoff success to fall back upon, having advanced only once in the last four springs.

"If they lost this year, it would be a disaster for them," said Ottawa assistant coach Roger Neilson. "They spent so much money and, with the Oates trade, everything is for now."

The Flyers hardly were in denial about that. "Looking at this team on paper, I don't think the expectations were overblown," said McGillis. But Richardson pointed out those expectations had been a problem as things had started to go bad.

"Sometimes we take for granted that we have a lot of talent and a lot of depth here," said the defenseman. "I think at times we figure that things will just happen for us and, when they don't after a game or two, we start trying too hard, getting off our game and chasing.

"We have to be patient. We have to understand that you can't win a playoff series on the first shift."

There was nothing about the first shift—or the second, or the 20th—in Game One at the First Union Center to suggest the Flyers, 3-9-4 against the Senators in their last 16 meetings, were going to win anything, either immediately or later. They didn't even take their first shot for 11 minutes and were badly outplayed for the first 40.

Cechmanek, however, was strong and kept the game scoreless.

Barber juggled the lines and his team haltingly began to pick up the pace. Nevertheless, the Flyer chances remained minimal into overtime until Murray—his versatility being Barber's wildcard—moved into Brashear's spot with Primeau and Fedotenko, and tried to spin away along the wall in the Senators' zone.

Murray fell as he shoved the puck to the middle, but it deflected off a skate to Fedotenko, who spun and beat goalie Patrick Lalime cleanly with a backhander at 7:47 to give Philadelphia a 1-0 victory.

It had taken five years for Philadelphia to win a playoff game in overtime in their new home. And it was an epic struggle to get one goal past Lalime, who had never won a playoff series in junior, minor pro or the NHL.

"I thought the win would wake us up," says Barber, but no member of the team interviewed for this book remembers being so encouraged. "I knew we were in trouble," recalls Recchi.

If anything, Game One had re-confirmed to Ottawa—a team with six core players who had lost nine straight road playoff games—that the Flyers could cure the Senators' frustration.

"After the first game, we knew we could hang with this team," said Daniel Alfredsson, Ottawa's best player.

Cechmanek, who had made 35 saves, kept reporters waiting 40 minutes after Game One while he got treatment for his knee, which had been re-sprained while making a second-period save. He made 15 more in the first period of Game Two, when again it took the Flyers a period before they began to assert a semblance of pressure. But this time, the Senators broke through, Alfredsson banging in his own deep rebound through a screen at 7:19 of the second period.

In the third period, Mike Fisher soloed after blocking a Therien shot and put the puck over a flopping Cechmanek. Philadelphia had more chances than in Game One, but couldn't beat Lalime as the booing intensified until Jody Hull put the game away and the First Union Center became as empty as the bullet chambers of the Flyer gun.

"We're trying," said Recchi. "They have to understand that it's not from lack of effort.

It's like this in every playoff series. It's going to be 1-0, 2-1; we understand that."

Hit in the head by the 6-9 Zdeno Chara on the first shift of Game Three at the Corel Center, Recchi was woozy thereafter while his teammates merely were befuddled by the trap of the Senators. Ottawa was content to wait for the anxiety-ridden Flyers, one and done on their chances, to make mistakes.

With Gagne in the box for tripping Tommy Salo as the winger tried to come out of the corner early in a scoreless third period, Philadelphia broke down terribly off a faceoff just outside its blueline. Murray lost the draw and neither Desjardins nor Therien took Radek Bonk as he burst up the middle to accept Martin Havlat's relay of a smart Alfredsson feed. Cechmanek went into a slide and Bonk went up top easily to give Ottawa a 1-0 lead.

The Flyers, not reaching any of their dump-ins, allowed the Senators to clear the zone without difficulty, Philadelphia reaping just a few chances on scant faceoffs following Ottawa icings. Cechmanek had a big glove save on Alfredsson that enabled Barber to pull his goalie while the team was down by only one, but Recchi decided not to take an open shot and tried to go to the opposite point to Primeau, only to have the pass picked off by Marian Hossa, who soloed to the empty net. Alfredsson hit it again off a center ice turnover and Philadelphia, shut out 3-0 for the second consecutive game, trailed the series, 2-1.

"We're just not making the right decisions," said Primeau. "We end up standing still in the neutral zone and in the corner.

"We try to beat a guy out of the corner instead of cycling it and hitting someone in front of the net like Ottawa is doing."

Barber admitted his bewilderment. "I can't remember ever being involved with anything like this," he said. "I don't want to change everything up; I'm just trying to find answers, something that is going to work for us.

"What else can I do? We've got to find some ways to turn it around and we've got to find them real soon."

Nine of the 26 Flyer shots had been taken by defensemen. Dating back to the Buffalo series of the previous spring, Philadelphia had become the first NHL team since 1936 to go four consecutive playoff games without scoring a regulation goal.

"I think (coach Jacques) Martin had a better system for his team than we had for ours," recalls Gagne. "Ottawa skated well, liked to control the puck, and had good back pressure, almost like skating into a storm.

"It wasn't a good matchup for us, maybe the worst team we could have played in the first round."

But there wasn't any playoff team that the Flyers could beat playing the way they were. "We had no cohesion, no confidence, no compete," recalls Primeau. "We were losing battles and didn't know how to fix it."

The frustrated players were questioning their coach in off-the-record conversations with reporters. Even the quotes begged for permission to take more offensive chances.

"We're always taught to be on the defensive side of the puck," said Roenick. "I know you don't like to talk like this, but maybe we (should) cheat to the offensive side of things and hope that the puck squirts loose.

"We need to find a way to create odd-number situations—maybe guys flying into the zone a little earlier or getting the long pass from one side to the other."

Barber defended the strategy and questioned the commitment. "Yes, we can take some kinds of risks at periods during the game," he said. "But if you think you can win a series by Hail Mary-ing it—lobbing it as hard as you can into the end zone and guys going up and catching it—that's not going to work.

"I have played on winning teams and coached winning teams. I think players should play and coaches should coach. We're doing the best possible presentation of what's going to work to beat this hockey team. Are you willing to pay the price and do the right things?"

Clarke seemed to agree with the players that caution was getting the team nowhere. "If you open it up too much you are going to give up scoring chances, but if you don't score, you don't win anything," said the GM. "Even when we were a poor team, we still could score the odd goal. We don't even get the odd one now."

He smiled and added, "Maybe we'll get a couple in practice."

At the skate the next morning, Snider made it clear that the things he was reading—and read between the lines—troubled him.

"We're in the middle of a fight here, how could you not be bothered by it?" he said. "It's a shame that stuff is out there; everybody should be working together behind closed doors to resolve whatever issues there are.

"I think a lot of the stuff is there because every single human being in our organization is frustrated. We're just totally baffled by it. The worst teams score goals by accident. Four games without scoring in regulation, it's mind-boggling. It's like a nightmare.

"But I'm not ready to focus on it one way or the other because, even as we speak right now, we're still in the series. I haven't thrown in the towel. It looks bad, but two of the last three games are in our building."

Before Game Four, Barber changed the system to a barely-practiced left wing lock, hoping that freeing up the center and right wing would free up their minds.

"It just added confusion," recalls LeClair. "Before a game we were changing from something we had done all year to something nobody had done."

The gonged Recchi reported a "floating feeling" two hours before faceoff and was yanked from the lineup. "It doesn't feel like any concussion I've ever had," he said, but it likely was the fourth of his career regardless. Barber dressed call-ups Brendl and defenseman John Slaney plus, in Recchi's absence, moved Brashear to right wing with Gagne and Roenick.

At the start, the Flyers appeared to be playing with more passion. But passing up shots and missing the net, they managed no chances while Chara was in the box for four minutes for drawing blood from Williams.

In the final minute of the period, Weinrich lost clear possession and Philadelphia had to jam the puck over the line. Ranheim and

Murray both ran at Alfredsson as he emerged from a crowd, leaving Wade Redden open to take the pass, burst in alone, and beat Cechmanek for a 1-0 Senator lead.

Fifty seconds into the second period, Roenick gratuitously hooked Redden during a line change. The Flyers killed the penalty and, thanks to good work by Cechmanek, appeared to have gotten through another one—on Therien for coming up high on Hull. But before they could get fresh bodies on the ice, a McGillis giveaway up the boards helped result in Sami Salo being left so alone in front that he had time to put in his own rebound over the sprawled Philadelphia goalie.

Two minutes later, Williams, who should have dumped the puck, lost it instead just inside the Ottawa line and the Senators countered quickly. On the two-on-one, Cechmanek came way out to challenge Shawn McEachern, leaving the goalie no chance when the puck was relayed to Hossa, who easily made it 3-0 from the edge of the circle.

Cechmanek skated immediately to center ice, said something to apparently no one in particular, and then made another circle while shaking his head. When Desjardins undemonstratively urged the goalie back into the net, he went quickly, Weinrich following to hear Cechmanek say into the back glass, "C'mon, we have to score a goal."

He had not approached the bench, never made his intentions clear, but the Flyers had become convinced their goalie had made a plea to come out of the game.

"Most key position of all, I wasn't going to allow that to happen," recalls Barber.

"I think the whole bench was in shock."

Recalls Roenick, "I think he was saying, '[Bleep] you guys, you aren't going to score any goals, I'm going to stop playing.'"

Cechmanek didn't though, making a good save on Chara before Barber went to Boucher for a third period in which Roenick took his fourth minor of the game, Brashear incurred an instigator penalty for jumping Chris Phillips and the Flyers, on a 2-man advantage, missed the net four times.

Weinrich smashed his stick as they went up the tunnel as 3-0 losers for the third straight game. Philadelphia's 316 minutes and 43 seconds without a regulation playoff goal was an NHL record.

Cechmanek denied that he had asked to come out, but not that he was exasperated by his teammates' lack of support. "We play a little easy and they play too tough, too hard," he told reporters. "They had lots of scoring chances off breakaways and I said after the third goal, 'We need to play better in neutral zone.'"

Asked by the media what his goaltender had been doing, Barber joked, "My Czech is not that good," then covered for Cechmanek.

"It doesn't matter what I think," said the coach. "He probably is a little upset. If you look at what's been going on, I think I would be a little angry, too.

"There are a lot of negatives flying around. It gets to players. It gets to everybody in his own way but, as a group, we have to put that behind us.

"I thought we were better than in the first three or four games. We got some quality scoring chances and the puck didn't go in. I'm still a firm believer that with the personnel and experience we have, we can focus on just one game (as a start to get back in the series)."

The next day at the Skate Zone, Desjardins shot pucks at Cechmanek's head, inviting teammates to do the same.

"I gladly obliged," recalls Roenick.

Remembers Therien, "Roman skated out and looked over at us like, 'What the [bleep] are you guys doing?'

"Well, if you don't know, then you should go the [bleep] back to Europe, buddy. This is the NHL. We're not going to pull your dress up and tie it for you. Be a big boy."

LeClair recalls there being malice in every one of those shots.

"Most guys when they shoot like that on a goalie will say stuff like, 'Hey, smarten up.' Nobody was saying a word. [Desjardins] wanted to kill him, didn't care if he hurt him at all.

"Roman didn't get it. You're responsible for 20 other guys."

Though no one can recall the proof, many Flyers remember having reason to believe that Cechmanek and the injured Dopita, who had already sent their families home for the summer, had booked flights to be able to play for their country in the World Championships in late April.

"It had crossed the line from quirky to not committed," recalls Primeau. "He wasn't the most engaging person, never engaged with anybody except the Czech guys."

With Dopita not dressed, Hlavac traded, and the taciturn Brendl the only countryman remaining, Cechmanek was with all his friends at the end of the Philadelphia bench when Game Five began at the First Union Center with Boucher in goal and Recchi back on the wing.

Late in the first minute, Gagne stole the puck from Todd White and forced Lalime to make a save, apparently energizing the Flyers. When Chris Neil got caught cross-checking Ranheim in the back, a powerplay that was 0-for-27 going back to the regular season, tried yet again.

Oates stole the puck out of the corner from Chara, fed a backhander past Hull to Desjardins, who relayed to the opposite point for a McGillis one timer. It sailed through traffic and the screened Lalime into the net, ending the drought at 183:53. The Philadelphia bench jumped up and down with joy.

Boucher made a good paddledown save on Bonk, then got an arm up on Havlat after a steal from Weinrich. Recchi and McGillis sandwiched Marcus Arvedson, who got up shakily. The Flyers were hitting and alive. But Fedotenko, Philadelphia's most active forward in the series, boarded Shane Hnidy after the defenseman got rid of the puck and, on the powerplay, Alfredsson's one-timer through traffic beat Boucher high to the glove side to tie the score, 1-1.

As the Flyer adrenaline dissipated, the pace became slow and whistle-laden, very much to the liking of the visiting, trapping Senators. Unable to get a second forechecker to the puck, most of Philadelphia's shots were coming from the defense. Richardson—Barber's best player in the game—almost got lucky when he beat a screened Lalime, but the puck hit the post, as did Bonk's drive with 1:14 to go. Boucher's pad save on Alfredsson in the final minute got the game into overtime.

As it began, the Flyers had gotten 25 shots on goal and missed it another 17 times. And they didn't get another good chance. The Senators had Philadelphia pinned in its own end up for a full minute in the overtime when the brilliant Alfredsson spun away from Richardson to get the puck towards the net. Primeau decided the only way to relieve the pressure was to cross-check Fisher in the slot.

On the powerplay, the Flyers got the puck out just once before Bonk smartly faked a shot and instead fed Hossa at the side of the net. With Johnsson caught high by the pass, Boucher came to the post and Hossa threw the puck by him to Havlat who, despite Desjardins' hold, had position on him for a tap-in that ended both the game, 2-1, and series in five.

Martin Havlat's overtime goal gave the Senators a 2-1 win, eliminating the Flyers in five games.

Philadelphia had been picked by knowledgeable analysts to win the Stanley Cup. The team had seemingly filled all its holes and everyone thought the angst of the Lindros years was done. Instead, the Flyers suffered their most complete first-round collapse since a 106-point club that had been shockingly swept by the Rangers in 1983. And while a late season swoon had predicted trouble for the 2001-02 team, nobody could have foreseen an inept total of two goals during a five-game series.

"I don't have any answers at all why we didn't put pucks in the net and how it got to the point where it just snowballed,"
said Barber. "Maybe in time, but I don't have any for you right now. I really don't.

"The expectations were so high. It's been a devastating year for me, period."

Two days later, Barber met with reporters in his office. The coach said it was his organizational obligation to take the anonymous hits in the media from players without retaliating. But he defended his system as the one that had righted the Flyers to a 26-9-2 surge at mid-season. "It worked from December through the Olympic break and it got us out of trouble," said Barber.

The next day, as the players cleared their lockers, Boucher was among many who were asked what had gone wrong. He became the first not to pull punches.

"There were a lot of problems, not only in the playoffs but in the last two, two-and-a-half months," said the goalie. "There were meetings upon meetings, and it seemed like nothing ever got solved.

"Everybody made suggestions about what was needed and I think, for the most part, we felt we didn't get it. I know that people are saying the players are crybabies. But we're players and wanted to be led . . . were talking about making adjustments when a team [was] smothering us. We needed a game plan to counter what they were doing."

When Boucher's comments were relayed to Primeau, the captain decided not to allow the goalie to stand-alone.

"I had just finished having my meeting with Mr. Snider, who wanted to understand what had happened," Primeau recalls. "He met with four or five guys—Eric, Mark, me, I don't remember who else. He said he was information gathering. He literally said, 'I don't know if I'm getting rid of the coach or I'm getting rid of the players.'

"I came down the stairs from that meeting and the media attacks me that Brian Boucher is the problem. In that moment, I made a conscious decision to support my goaltender."

To do that, Primeau didn't see any other choice but to excoriate Barber.

"I'm sticking up on behalf of my teammates because I want to walk out of here with my pride intact," the captain told reporters.

"We know when we are making mistakes. We're getting yelled at when we come back to the bench. [Barber] wants the players to make the adjustment. Well, our job is to play. I felt like I was having to make the adjustments on the bench, and I don't feel that is part of my job description.

"I know I had an off year. I accept blame for that and full responsibility. I'll accept that I was terrible in the playoffs. (But) explain to me why every one of our good players had an off year.

"We had the worst powerplay in the league, so why weren't we practicing it? [People] can say, 'We have the guys to get it done,' but when you are being forced on the half-wall, you need to be able to make a pass to an open guy. You want repetition at practice day-in and day-out so you know.

"We'd say, 'Look, we'll do whatever is asked; we just want to be led in the right direction.'"

Primeau added that, out of his desire not to cause controversy, he had not gone to Clarke with his concerns until later in the regular season. And that he had done so only after his efforts with Barber were met with, "Don't make suggestions; work harder."

On break-up day, Recchi acknowledged that Jenny Barber's illness and death had made the problem more difficult to address. "It's been a tough year for him," he said. "I know that; we all know that. That's probably why we left it as long as we did.

"You have to respect the man for what he went through and how he handled it. I think we all like Billy, I don't think that was ever a question. But ultimately, things didn't get done."

LeClair remembers being surprised to learn what Primeau and Boucher said. "We tended to keep that stuff in-house," he recalls. "And I think that upstairs knew what was going on without having to read about it."

As Tocchet told reporters: "I understand where the players are coming from. They wanted to be coached and taught certain things, and they felt that they didn't get that. Is that Billy's fault? That's not for me to decide. It's for Bobby Clarke and Ed Snider to decide."

Of course, everyone knew what the outcome would be. "Billy was emotional and it worked for a while, but players have to be told how to work properly," recalls Clarke. "They'll work hard if they know what they are doing."

Barber said both players and coaches have to put work into what he called a marriage, adding that he wished to continue behind the bench, but would "stand tall with whatever decision was made."

After four coaching changes—albeit one caused by illness—and four first-round losses in five years, the last thing Clarke and Snider wanted was to further foster the image of instability by letting Barber go. He was a franchise icon who had won far more in a Flyer uniform than the players now denigrating him. Instead, *Daily News* columnist Sam Donnellon called for the dismissal of Clarke.

But in announcing the firing of Barber and assistant coaches McGuire and Stothers at a grim press conference four days after the Flyer elimination, Snider said Clarke would continue to be the general manager, even as the Chairman's fact-finding would continue.

Snider pointed to Primeau's comments about all the top players going bad at once. "Is that Billy's fault totally?" asked Snider rhetorically. "Probably not. But is it the general manager's fault that the group of outstanding players he put together all had bad years?

"I love Billy Barber. He's been in this organization since he was a kid. Nobody wanted him to succeed more than me. No one. And if I felt in any way, shape or form that he was being rail-roaded by players who had gone behind his back, I would have taken another tack.

"I hope that Bill decides to remain in the organization, and I think that what's happened is unfortunate. But I have to tell you, there was unanimity among the players and that's very unusual. It's not a clique of guys, not one power player. Unfortunately, Bill lost the team."

Snider added, "There's a lot of fault to go around this organization, starting with me. Maybe we (Clarke and he) are the next to go."

From the same dais, Clarke could not duck. "It's not a lot of fun to sit here and have people talking about you getting fired," he said. "But I certainly acquired the players and hired Billy. If a change has to be made and it's good for the organization, they should make it."

Barber had two years and $1.5 million remaining on his contract, but all the money in the world wasn't going to bring back either his wife or job. Reached at home by reporters, he still refused to rebut the players.

"I just think that some of the things that were said were not very accurate and I would rather not get into it right now," he said.

"I'm hurting, to be up-front and honest. It's been tough, real tough, and now is just not the time. I need to get away for a little while and get a clearer head than I have right now."

Time has caused Barber to concede that he could have better-communicated "what we were trying to get across as a staff." But he admits that the worst year of his life had wrung the energy from him and perhaps from the Flyers.

"I was tired, really spent," he recalls. "The team had played like I felt.

"I think a coach has to be understanding and listen. I wasn't that bad, screaming in the players' faces; I told the truth. If you can't accept that, I'm sorry. If I am a bad guy for that, trying to make players accountable, so be it.

"I knew when I got fired that I was done with coaching. The way the game was changing, I am not a good fit.

"I was disappointed but, on the other hand, understanding and relieved. I didn't have any grudges. The Flyers have been good to me, why I never fired back. But I didn't have any interest in staying in the organization. I appreciated the offer but it was time to move on."

Today, Boucher has deep misgivings about what he said on breakup day and the firestorm it lit. "One of my biggest regrets as a pro," he recalls. "They asked if Barber lost the team, and I said he did.

"I answered truthfully when I shouldn't have. It put Keith in a bad spot and he stood up for me. Billy is a Hall of Famer who had a tough family situation. What I said was uncalled for."

Primeau, too, says he didn't think it all the way through.

"As my dad pointed out to me, 'Billy Barber, the Flyer Hall of Fame player and Billy Barber, the Flyer coach, are two separate things,'" recalls Primeau. "I was thinking of Bill Barber, the coach, and what was going on in our locker room that we could play like that.

"I got crucified for it and rightly so. I could have found a way to support Brian without saying what I did about the coach."

Both his convictions and lack of diplomacy had presented Primeau publicly as the captain of a choking team blaming a boss for its horrendous performance. Portrayed as self-serving coach-killers, the only place the Flyers could live it down would be the ice.

"We are not what people perceive us to be," said Primeau. "And I truly believe we will all be better for what we're going through right now."

Keith Primeau

Chapter 6 • 2002-03

Getting Hitched

There was no *Plan B* for a coach to replace Bill Barber, only one candidate with a Type A personality and a Stanley Cup ring, even if Ken Hitchcock claimed not to know in which of his socks it was stored.

Regardless, the gleam from that jewelry would catch the eyes of Philadelphia players stymied by four first-round exits in the last five seasons.

Hitchcock's Flyer experience as an assistant under Paul Holmgren and Bill Dineen from 1990-93 was down the list of reasons for his desirability to general manager Bob Clarke, who had been exiled in Florida and Minnesota during all but the last of those years. While running the North Stars, Clarke had developed a deep relationship with his coach, Bob Gainey, who later became GM, hired Hitchcock and, after the franchise moved to Dallas, won the 1999 Stanley Cup.

Through Gainey, Clarke had a first-hand book on Hitchcock's pluses and minuses. Dwarfing everything on both sides of that list was the fact that, unlike any of the accomplished coaches available to Philadelphia, Hitchcock had taken a team, the Stars, all the way.

"I liked Pat Burns (who had been let go by Boston in 2000) a lot," recalls Clarke. "I'm sure he would have been my second choice.

"Lots of good coaches haven't won Cups. But if they have, players see that and for us, it was important. We were in a shambles. We needed a veteran with credibility."

The Rangers, having gone five seasons without even making the playoffs, were in the market for street cred, too. Hitchcock, who had been fired in January 2002 by the declining Stars, during March had met with Ranger GM Glen Sather at his Manhattan condo and toured the team's new training facility under construction in Greenburgh, NY.

Sather, who would dismiss coach Ron Low at the conclusion of the 2001-02 season, made it clear to Hitchcock other candidates were under consideration. At the top of Sather's list was Herb Brooks, the mastermind of the 1980 USA Olympic miracle and a former Ranger head coach, who had retired after coaching the 1999-2000 Penguins on an interim basis.

Hitchcock, serving as an assistant to coach Wayne Fleming of Canada at the April World Championships, was in Karlstad, Sweden when he got a call in his hotel room from Flyer assistant GM Paul Holmgren, who was in the restaurant across the street with director of professional player personnel Ron Hextall. They met for several hours with Hitchcock and promised to be in touch after the tournament.

"The Rangers got wind of it and said, 'Don't do anything until you talk to us,'" recalls Hitchcock. On May 12, the day he landed back in North America, Hitchcock received a call from Clarke inviting him to interview in Voorhees the next day, which he did with the GM and Chairman Ed Snider. Hearing what he expected, Clarke had determined not to let Hitchcock out of the building without a deal. So Hitchcock, in no hurry to go anywhere else regardless, went to the workout room while his representative, Rob Campbell of Toronto, negotiated with Clarke on the phone.

"I was on the elliptical when Clarke came in and said, 'I don't know if this is going to get done, Hitch.'

"And I said, 'Don't worry, at the end of the day it will.'"

While those negotiations continued, Ranger scout Gilles Leger reached Hitchcock on his cell. Brooks had changed his mind about returning to the NHL and the Rangers were back in the market, but Hitchcock had decided on Philadelphia.

"I'm an Edmonton (born) guy; Glen (who built and coached the Oiler dynasty) had been my hero," recalls Hitchcock. "But when I sat down with Clarkie, I felt like, 'This is (Dallas GM) Bob Gainey. Same sense of loyalty, same sense of right and wrong, same quiet confidence.'

"I was in the locker room where the coach's office was and Clarkie came back down and said, 'I think we've got a deal.' I went upstairs."

Four years and $4.6 million had obtained the guy the Flyers most wanted, and who most wanted them, too.

"When we were done with some background work and checking on candidates, Ken was by far the person we wanted to coach us," said Clarke when Hitchcock, the 15th man to stand behind the Flyer bench, was introduced to the media as their coach for four years, guaranteed.

"We've had so much instability in our coaching situation (six in six years) that it's personally embarrassing to me," said Snider. "I can assure you that Ken is here for the duration of his contract.

"If he is not successful, we'll change the players."

A former sporting-goods clerk whose tireless efforts as a moonlighting local amateur coach had earned him a chance to become a tremendous success (.693 winning percentage) with the major junior Kamloops Blazers of the Western Hockey League, Hitchcock's compulsions had once included an eating disorder that caused him to balloon to 476 pounds.

Having begun a diet in his final season at Kamloops (1989-90), 12 years later he was taking over the Flyer bench weighing 240. Such evi-

dence of self-discipline, combined with that 1999 Stanley Cup, would enable Hitchcock to, in his words, "get players to do the things they don't want to do and be comfortable doing them."

"We frustrated teams (in Dallas) because we never gave up anything easy," he said. "They didn't get two-on-ones, didn't get clear-cut breakaways because we were very smart with the puck. We placed it in proper forechecking areas and that's what I want to put in place. The part that's not negotiable is how we play without the puck.

"I'm technically sound, but that's not my strength. I think my strength is building the team and that means discipline, structure, firm direction and strong leadership from the veteran players.

"Am I demanding? Yes. Do I make players accountable? Yes. But I try to give ownership back to the players. I don't feel like me going into the locker room every day or between periods is necessary."

Hitchcock, who also had reached the 2000 final and won five division titles in seven years in Dallas, said he expected little resistance from a Flyer team perceived as headstrong and selfish. "Players have to reach a certain stage when they are willing to enjoy doing things that are difficult," he said. "I feel this group is there right now."

But teaching the Flyers how to channel their endeavors was the greater challenge. "Coaching against them, I thought maybe they overworked, trying to win games too quickly," he said.

Hitchcock called Keith Primeau a player "against whom the other team's players don't get a lick," compared John LeClair to a Brett Hull who needed to realize there could be more to his game than just scoring, and labeled Jeremy Roenick as a "player you can build a strong emotional base around." Another goal, said Hitchcock, was to help Eric Desjardins get back his "passion."

Yes, he had watched the Flyer meltdown to just two goals in their five-game loss to Ottawa. "When you're not sure, when you're not 100 percent committed and trusting, there's indecision on the ice and a loss of energy," Hitchcock said. "One guy is going north and the other south and then it looks like you've got 15 guys out of the 20 that cannot play.

"There are productive players here. We need to refocus and re-energize them in the right direction."

The members of the Dallas team Hitchcock had pushed to a Stanley Cup may have become burned out by his obsessions, but they had no doubts that with a fresh audience, he again would be successful.

Said defenseman Richard Matvichuk to Jennifer Floyd of *The Dallas Morning News*: "Sure, winning with him wasn't always a picnic, but losing with him was worse. Philly hasn't had a lot of success in the playoffs, but I can almost guarantee that will change under Hitch. He somehow finds a way to get the best out of people.

"He is going to lay down the law and the law is simple. Nothing, and he means nothing, is as important as winning the Cup. Not personal stats, not excuses, nothing."

Despite the prevailing impression of a mutiny against Barber, the players insisted they didn't want their way, only to be shown a better one.

"As far as his job security, that's great," said Primeau, the Fletcher Christian of this HMS Bounty, when reached by reporters on the day of Hitchcock's hiring. "This way, there are no question marks.

"Does this make us more accountable? Maybe, but that's all we ever wanted, that and reciprocal communication. We don't care if we have a tough coach. We just want direction."

Added Mark Recchi, who had played for Hitchcock at Kamloops: "What happened in the end of the season puts the onus on the player. We know that and it's no problem."

Simon Gagne recalls, "The team probably was going to make a change even if Preems or [Brian Boucher] or some other guys hadn't [complained publicly]. But Bill Barber was like the Mark Messier or Wayne Gretzky of the Flyers, so personally, I felt really guilty that we pushed away a guy like that. The Flyers were sending us a message that this coach was going to be there for a while."

Hitchcock settled in the next day by meeting with Primeau, John LeClair, Justin Williams and Chris Therien, all of whom were working out at the Skate Zone. "We went over systems and that was great," Primeau told the media. "And we told him we've got a great bunch of guys who are willing to listen."

Hitchcock not only had these players' instant attention but carte blanche from Clarke to choose the coaching staff. Craig Hartsburg, a Flyer assistant from 1990-1994—two of those years on the staff alongside Hitchcock—and later an NHL head coach in Chicago and Anaheim, had committed to following him wherever he landed. To handle the X's and O's, Hitchcock hired Wayne Fleming, with whom he had been impressed during their time together on Team Canada staffs at the Salt Lake City Olympics and the recent World Championships.

On the market once again were two veteran free-agent goaltenders—Curtis Joseph and Ed Belfour. Either would have provided the credibility in the nets that the Flyers had coveted, yet Clarke was going again with Roman Cechmanek.

Instead of a new starter, the GM prioritized a better dynamic between the Czech and his backup. When Phoenix expressed interest in Brian Boucher, it enabled Clarke to upgrade his center-ice position as well.

On June 12, he traded Boucher and a third-round choice to the Coyotes for another young netminder, Robert Esche, and center Michal Handzus.

"Handzus was the priority in that trade for us," recalls Clarke. "He was big and competitive and I thought he would turn out to be a terrific third-line centerman."

The Flyers had first sought Handzus—6-foot-5 and, at age 25, already a Frank Selke Trophy (best defensive forward) finalist—two seasons earlier, when he played in St. Louis and the Blues had inquired about what it would take to get Eric Lindros. When they instead traded with Phoenix for all-star Keith Tkachuk, Handzus was part of the package.

Despite scoring 44 points playing behind Danny Briere and Daymond Langkow during his one full season in Phoenix, Handzus didn't believe the Coyotes were happy with him or that the franchise had the wherewithal to build on a 95-point season. "I didn't play well, so I wasn't surprised about the trade (to Philadelphia) and was really happy," he recalls. "Every player's dream is to play for an organization that pays the money and wants to win right away.

"It was really exciting for me."

Esche was putting a roof on the home he was building near his native Whitesboro, NY when he got the call from Hitchcock welcoming him to the Flyers. The goalie had no urge to jump.

"Going to any big market would have been exciting, but the Flyers—that was awesome," Esche recalls. "There was a lot of stuff going on in Phoenix with ownership changes and I don't think I hit it off with Mike Barnett, the general manager they brought in."

Boucher, seemingly set up for a long Philadelphia run off his work during the 1999-2000 season and playoffs, had become a victim of his own insecurities and Cechmanek's gaudy stats (59-20-12, 2.02 GAA, .921 save percentage) over two regular seasons.

"We understood that Brian wants to be a No. 1 goalie and Cechmanek feels the right to be No. 1," said Clarke in announcing the deal.

"I don't think either of our goaltenders was happy with his role on the team.

"Right now Cechmanek is our No. 1. We did Brian a favor."

Boucher, who got the news in his driveway via a call from Clarke, was trying to look at it that way.

"I was surprised because there were no rumors," recalls Boucher. "I had even seen Clarkie that morning and there were no clues.

"I don't remember wondering why they wanted Esche over me. I knew [the Coyotes] had Sean Burke, but thought it might be an opportunity to repeat my rookie year. But I was disappointed, yeah, even though I didn't realize until a year at Phoenix just how much I liked Philadelphia.

"I went through a bad time in Philly, had growing pains as a professional, and wasn't the person the team wanted me to be. I think I was traded in part because of what I said (about Barber on breakup day). I spoke truthfully and I could have been more mature, more professional about a Hall of Famer who did a lot of things for this hockey club. I was out of line, wish I could take that back."

His teammates would have taken him back in a second over Cechmanek. "I was surprised that the Flyers didn't work with Brian for a longer period of time," recalls John Vanbiesbrouck, who had been traded a year earlier to make room for the Czech. "In other organizations, when you have a guy that takes a team one game away from the Stanley Cup Final, you get the benefit of the doubt.

"Boosh was a great kid, he'd do anything for the organization. They never came to me and said, 'Hey, in your final year, would you work with him?' Then he had to deal with Roman, whom I believe hurt Boosh more than helped him.

"That is a part of the game; you have to be professional and put your nose to the grindstone. But another part of the game is that you've got to bring guys along. That's just my viewpoint; not saying I was right."

Roenick believes Vanbiesbrouck was correct about Boucher as a competitor and a teammate. "I love Boosh," Roenick recalls. "He was a proud guy and one of fiercest I remember playing with.

"Unfortunately, he seemed to not have the luck or the talent on a nightly basis to be that goaltender that you needed to win a Cup. But it wasn't for a lack of fight."

In Esche, a former sixth-round choice who had backed up Burke for 47 games over the previous two seasons and performed well for the USA team at the 2000 World Championships, Clarke saw a 24-year-old with No. 1 potential.

The Flyers felt the same about Antero Niittymaki, their sixth-round choice out of Finland four years earlier, whom they signed to a two-year, $1.4 million, contract with the intention of breaking him in with the Phantoms. But for the upcoming season, Philadelphia was going with Cechmanek, who had stirred such enmity from his teammates for apparently trying to pull himself from a playoff game that they fired pucks at his head in practice the next day.

"I'm not worried about how his teammates feel," said Clarke. "He probably had the right to be unhappy.

"We expressed to him that [leaving the net] was not acceptable to North American players. But we have seen this before over in Europe when (goalies) get frustrated. Who caused more trouble in Buffalo than (Dominik) Hasek year after year?

"Goaltending is one position where you can get away with a lot of stuff. As long as you stop the puck, players don't care what you say or do."

The Flyer frustrations with their incumbent lead goaltender went deeper than his performance, but this was one more reason management was paying Hitchcock the big bucks.

"There are issues with Roman that need to be worked out and we will all work them out," said the new coach. "I had a good talk with him and am convinced he wants to be among the elite in the league."

Cechmanek had done most of the talking for countryman Jiri Dopita, who, in any language, including body language, had not been happy being a third-line center enjoying little powerplay time behind Primeau and Roenick. With Handzus being a younger, better fit, Dopita was traded to Edmonton for a 2003 third-round pick.

Described 12 months earlier by Clarke and other hockey people as "the best player outside the NHL," Dopita had scored 11 goals and 16 assists in an injury-interrupted, 52-game season in Philadelphia.

"One year was enough," recalls LeClair. "I never felt any heart from him."

Clarke felt it was because that heart was in the Czech Republic.

"We had chased him before and he had never wanted to come over here," recalls the GM. "Finally, I think he just wanted to see what the NHL was like, but he had no fire. If he had showed anything offensively, he would have been moved up (to a scoring line). He was slow and non-competitive, just a mistake."

Recalls Todd Fedoruk, "[Dopita] looked the part, but I think it was just too rich of a league for him and he could sense that. It was like 'Holy [bleep], these guys are nuts!'"

Not everybody on the team thought so little of the import, however. "He wasn't the hyped player we thought we were getting, but he was a good player; there was nothing wrong with him," recalls Chris

Therien. "I don't remember him ever dogging it.

"He wasn't comfortable with the language and didn't speak much, but I thought he competed hard in the corners and went out to win faceoffs."

Handzus also was good on draws, giving Clarke one more reason not to re-sign Adam Oates, despite the seemingly enormous cost to acquire him—first, second and third-round draft choices, plus prime goaltending prospect Maxime Ouellett. With Oates expected to attract bidding on the free-agent market, even at age 40, Clarke called the future Hall of Famer with the news that the Flyers would spend their money elsewhere.

"That was classy for him to call because he didn't have to do that," said Oates, who, after managing 10 points in 14 regular-season contests while Philadelphia was going into shock, had assisted on the team's only two scores in five playoff games. "I had hoped to talk to Ken Hitchcock to see if he liked me as a player, but that never happened.

"I'm kind of bummed. I really enjoyed being with those guys. But if I had played better and helped the team, maybe they would not have felt the need to go out and make a deal. That's what I told Bob. I feel I let people down."

Actually, the fracturing team Oates had been unable to singlehandedly rescue had let him down, more than the other way around. "He might have been able to help a solid, secure team, but ours was a mess," Clarke recalls. "But we gave up way too much for him when he was basically finished."

Clarke broke the news about Oates at a pre-draft media briefing, when the GM also announced he would not exercise the option on the No.1 pick Philadelphia had received a year earlier from Phoenix for Daymond Langkow until 2003, a draft Clarke's scouts advised would contain a deeper pool of excellent talent.

That said, the Flyers still liked the players available at the top of the 2002 draft. Clarke made offers to trade up for one of the top four picks and found an interested party in Tampa Bay, which was selecting fourth.

"We had checked with (Lightning GM Jay) Feaster like every team had, I guess," recalls Clarke. "We had all the scouts out for dinner (the night preceding the draft in Toronto) when Jay called and asked for Ruslan Fedotenko and two (2002) second-round picks (Philadelphia had traded its No. 1 in the Oates deal)."

Feaster, the former Hershey GM who had developed a relationship with Barber when he coached the Bears, had offered him a player personnel evaluation job in Tampa almost immediately following his firing from the Flyers. Barber had asked for more time to get over his April dismissal, to further grieve the December death of his wife Jenny, and to enjoy the June 29 wedding of his daughter Kerri.

But Feaster sought Barber's advice in negotiating with Philadelphia.

"Jay asked me, 'If you had a choice of any young player from the Flyers, who would you take?'" recalls Barber. "I said 'Ruslan Fedotenko' with no hesitation.

"I said, 'He's a good, all-around player, he competes, and you can put him anywhere—right side, left side. I don't think the team here accepted Fedotenko, who had come up from the minors with me."

Today, Fedotenko doesn't feel he was shunted, only grateful that Philadelphia had given an undrafted player a chance.

"I was younger than the majority of players, didn't have a family like the older guys, and I was never much into partying and drinking, so I didn't hang with the guys too much," Fedotenko recalls. "But at the rink, I didn't feel like an outsider, not at all.

"I always say Bill Barber probably had the biggest impact in my hockey career as a coach and a person. If you played well, he was the first guy to pat you on the back; if you did not, he was the first to give you an earful. He was the key to me developing as a player."

Fedotenko might have been the Flyers' best performer during the Ottawa playoff debacle. But given the opportunity to obtain a potential star for a gritty player plus two less-than-prime picks in a shallow draft, Clarke recalls he closed the deal in just 20 minutes.

The next day, after Columbus led the draft with winger Rick Nash, Atlanta selected goalie Kari Lehtonen and Florida chose defenseman Jay Bouwmeester. The Flyers took Finnish defenseman Joni Pitkanen.

"We had five kids on our list," recalls Clarke. "The three that were taken (before the Philadelphia pick) were in a little different order than we had them, but we would have been happy with any of the four, including the goaltender."

Pitkanen became the highest Flyer pick since 1990 (Mike Ricci, also fourth overall). The Finn needed some bulk and probably at least another year of development, but Clarke thought they had obtained a cornerstone defenseman.

"He can play physical, but he's not going to run around and hit people," said Philadelphia's European scout Inge Hammarstrom. "He's very smart with the puck. He makes the right decisions most of the time and is a good skater."

Recalls Clarke: "Jerry Melnyk (the Flyers' late head scout) had seen [Pitkanen] when he was 14 or 15 and said I should see him. All our guys loved him. I believe we may have had him ranked No. 1."

The club did not anticipate this projected treasure making their 2002-03 team. But there was belief they did have an NHL-ready defenseman in Bruno St. Jacques, a ninth-round pick in 1998 chosen at the urging of former Flyer Andre Dupont, a consultant for Group Baraphe, a Quebec-based player agency.

"Take Bruno St. Jacques!" Dupont had shouted at Clarke from the stands that day in Buffalo. Clarke only promised he would talk over the kid with Quebec scout Simon Nolet, but Dupont told Nolet, "Clarke said to draft St. Jacques." With their last pick of the day, the Flyers did.

After playing a total of 13 games in Philadelphia during two call-ups the previous two seasons, St. Jacques had turned into a prospect that made 33-year-old Luke Richardson, an unessential re-signing.

"It was something like mid-November (2001) when (agent) Donnie Meehan said, 'The Flyers want to extend your [expiring five-year deal],'" recalls Richardson. "I said, 'Perfect, easy, would love it.'

"I was always the guy who didn't care about that stuff, thought if you played your hardest, things would look after themselves. So time went by and it wasn't until the end of the season that I asked Donnie whatever happened about the new contract. He called Clarkie and got back to me with, 'They don't know if they are going to be able to sign you or not.'

Paul Holmgren with Joni Pitkanen, taken fourth overall at the 2002 NHL Draft

"So July 1 comes, and Columbus flies me there, gives me the tour, shows me areas to live. While I'm there, the phone rings with a 609 area code. It's Clarkie, asking, 'What are you doing?'

"I told him I was in Columbus. Clarkie said he had a two-year deal for me at the same [$2.6 million per] I had gotten the previous year. I told him I'd been offered four years here for more money (starting at $2.75 million). He said, 'We can go three years, but not four.'

"Since everybody suspected a lockout was coming (after two more seasons), that third year meant nothing. But the fourth year was huge. Clarkie was telling me, 'We want you here,' but when I had seen Hitch at [the Skate Zone] while working out, he never said that. Clarkie also had said in the papers he wanted to go with young guys. So I said to Donnie, 'I just don't get a good vibe.'"

Richardson signed with the Blue Jackets, ending five years as one of the most successful veteran free-agent acquisitions in Flyer history, even after struggling for ice time for a season following Roger Neilson's hiring as coach. Finally winning Neilson's trust, Richardson, today coach of the AHL's Binghamton Senators, gave the Flyers toughness and resiliency, plus a locker-room presence as strong as any of the great character players who wore black and orange.

"I liked to play with guys with common sense, not only in terms of understanding the game, but everything that surrounded it," recalls Primeau. "Luke was a guy that everybody liked because he sifted through anything that was fake and never got caught up in the drama."

Adds Therien, "He would do anything for his teammates and was an unbelievably great friend off the ice, in addition to being a very effective defenseman."

Another of the franchise's great locker room voices—that of Rick Tocchet—had been largely muted the previous season due to his unavailability because of injuries. At 38, Tocchet's body was scolding him to quit, even though he put off a retirement announcement.

"I was just tired of coming to the rink three-four hours before the game to get my back worked on," Tocchet recalls. "I had been a workout freak, but I was just done with it.

"That's a hard thing for me to say because I was a guy who would never give up. But I just didn't want to do it anymore. Part of me still thinks that if I would have given myself four months in L.A. training with my guy, TR Goodman, who worked with Chris Chelios and Rob Blake, I might have rejuvenated myself, but who knows?

"I was talking to Anaheim, which ended up going to the (2003) final with Adam Oates and other older guys. That could have been fun. But I was married with a kid and would have had to drop everything to do it, so I kind of gave up. Part of me regrets that I succumbed to that; it's not my style."

Whatever the Ducks might have put on the table would have been the only thing Tocchet left there over 18 NHL seasons, 11 of them in Philadelphia. He produced 232 goals and was key in two Flyer runs to the Final and two more to the semifinals. Though Tocchet won his only Stanley Cup in Pittsburgh and works for the Penguins today as an assistant coach, he played his last games in the place most appropriate to his career and fulfilled his contract with class.

"At the end, you either go left or right with the young guys," he recalls. "You can be that grizzled, veteran guy that is hard on the rookies or you can ask yourself, 'Did I make Justin Williams a better player? Did I make Simon Gagne a better player?'

"That made the end of my career enjoyable instead of going out as a bitter guy."

Even before Philadelphia ever put a player on the ice, Ed Snider had his own relentless cornerman setting examples for future generations of Tocchets. Joe Scott, who tirelessly had Snider's back when the Flyers had little liquidity and practically no identity, died on June 24, 2002 at the age of 93 at St Joseph's Manor in Meadowbrook, PA.

Snider, who had barely raised the $2 million franchise fee after partner Jerry Wolman admitted he could no longer produce his pledged $1 million, needed capital when he called Scott, the prematurely-retired baron of Ballantine Beer, asking him to buy an ownership share of the hockey team. Scott decided to also invest his time, and tirelessly spearheaded campaigns to get tickets to school groups, the target audience for the city's new sport.

Snider, the recently-transplanted Eagle executive born in Washington, DC, was without entree into the Philadelphia business community enjoyed by Scott, the tireless promoter and self-described "jolly fellow well-met."

"He was a terrific guy and always was 100 percent behind me," said Snider at Scott's passing. The Chairman had made sure Scott remained in every team picture even after he sold his Flyer minority share to Fran and Sylvan Tobin in 1984.

Philadelphia had long been recognized among NHL players as one of the best places to play because they saw how Snider took care of his own. A young Bob Clarke also had a guardian angel in Frank Lewis, a Flyer trainer from 1967 to 1981 and the head trainer from 1969 to 1977.

Lewis died of lung cancer at age 83 on July 4, 2002 in Broomall, PA.

"A few days into my first training camp, I overslept, skipped breakfast and passed out during practice," recalls Clarke. "Frank's wife, Helen, was a nurse with knowledge about diabetes, and Frank took charge of my care.

"He had a Coke for me before the game, orange juice between periods, and carried insulin in his bag for an emergency. He always was watching over me and it was more than him doing his job. We really liked each other. I was at his house for dinner many times. He and I had a special relationship."

Lewis, an accomplished saxophone and clarinet player who had performed with the Tommy Dorsey Orchestra among other big bands, had gained his entry into hockey as trainer—and backup goalie—for the Philadelphia Ramblers of the Eastern Hockey League. "He was a really good man to me in particular, but also to all the players," said Clarke.

A hockey player's best friend is the trainer, unless it happens to be the team's enforcer. Clarke re-upped Donald Brashear for four years at a total near $8 million, a deal the tough guy negotiated himself. "I don't remember anyone else ever doing that before," recalls Clarke.

Todd Fedoruk, who had agent representation, was signed for two seasons at a total of $1.1 million. But Snider challenged his players on bigger tickets to give him bang for his $56 million payroll.

"If this team can't win under Ken Hitchcock, then I am convinced it can't win under anyone," said Snider from his Montecito, CA home to *The Philadelphia Inquirer*'s Tim Panaccio.

Of course, a healthier relationship with the coach needed to be supplemented with some wellness for veteran players coming off sub-par seasons. During the summer, Desjardins underwent an arthroscopic shoulder cleanup and L.A.'s Dr. Robert Watkins performed the second back operation in two years on LeClair to relieve a herniation.

Primeau had spent the summer in Los Angeles, working out with Goodman, slavedriver to the athletic stars. "It's a lot of [focus on] posture, deep core muscles, rotators, hip protractors, shoulder protractors to help them avoid injury," Primeau recalls. "It's about getting right to the core and for me, it was transforming. I wish I would have found him when I was 18."

Primeau fully realized that his image needed more rehabilitation than his body. Hitchcock recalls the captain returning from LA in August owning not only muscles, but resentment.

"There was so much anger in him at getting blamed with the playoff loss that he walked by my office for two weeks," remembers Hitchcock. "I let it go because I felt like he needed to get it out—feel comfortable looking at another new coach, you know? I felt he would come around.

"And one day, he just walked into my office and sat on the couch. We talked for about three hours and he did a lot of venting. He just said, 'We've got problems. We don't function as a team. We've got too many people blaming each other, too many people blaming me. People above me are mad at me.' He said, 'I get that comes with losing, but this is unnatural.'

"He had a unique situation. [He was] a captain of a team with a lot of ex-captains and older players, and the transfer of power was not gonna be smooth. Eventually he had to make a decision whether he was going to be either the captain or the most popular guy on the team.

"I gave him reading [material about leadership]; I wanted to build up his confidence so he could make the right decisions. And we worked really hard at it."

Recalls Primeau, "I was just trying to fly under the radar, come in and do my work. I probably was walking by his office waiting for him to grab me. He was the coach. At that point of my career I certainly did not lack confidence, but I don't disagree with his version of me reinventing myself.

"I knew there was hostility towards me, probably didn't know its extent. But I certainly knew I had to back up what I had said. I had gotten sidetracked making excuses. I think instead of accepting responsibility and taking onus, I made excuses for it. I'm not diminishing that the issues were reality, but there was a different way to deal with it."

The coach said to start on the ice. "Part of it was convincing him to go out on the island and play a certain way, which was to check," recalls Hitchcock. "He was always out there to score but he needed to lead by example and let the points take care of themselves.

"Then I needed to build the support around him, which is where guys like Recchi, with whom I'd had a relationship for years, really helped me allow Keith to feel people had his back."

After taking a few months to become certain he was ready to return to work, Barber accepted the player personnel position with Tampa Bay and, for the first time as a professional, became employed by a team other than the Flyers. To those who had questioned why Barber was gone and Clarke still had his job, the GM returned fire.

"I know we've had a couple of bad years in the playoffs recently, but do you think the people criticizing me could do this job?" Clarke told *Philadelphia Daily News* Flyer beat reporter Ed Moran. "Let's face it, you guys judge people without ever having sat in this chair.

"Fire me, Sam Donnellon (of the *Daily News*) writes. So give him the job and let me write an article about Donnellon, so that his kids and family can see it. See how he likes it. I criticized Tim Panaccio once and was criticized for six months in the newspapers for it. You would think I was criticizing God. The anger I feel is only because I'm not allowed to fight back.

"If the writers judged themselves the way they judge me, they would all be fired. The papers are losing readers, advertisers, money, everything. But you never judge yourselves; you judge me.

"I've always felt that criticism is necessary and part of the business. But it doesn't have to be vicious. You would hate it if your son or daughter came home crying about what someone wrote about you. You don't have to agree with a trade I made or agree who is on the powerplay. But it doesn't make the coach bad or the players bad or me bad.

"The last time I was fired (in 1990), I had no problem with that. I did a [horsebleep] job. If I'm messing up, then I shouldn't be here. But I don't think that I am. Every year we're well over 90 points. The last couple of years we haven't been successful in the playoffs, but we've won a lot more playoff games than we've lost in the last seven or eight years. We've got all kinds of extra draft picks. We're developing more kids than any team in the NHL. I don't know what else you can do but win a Stanley Cup. And we're all trying to do that.

"It's hard. So are you going to fire 29 coaches and 29 managers every year? When was the last time you guys got prizes for writing?"

Indeed, it was not the easiest of times for the Flyers. Players came to camp fully invested in living down their reputations as self-absorbed coach killers. But on the day when Hitchcock, their anointed savior, was invited to ring the closing bell at the Philadelphia exchange, the market dropped 330 points.

Still, a blue chipper like Gagne didn't suffer. With the three- or four-year deal he sought unlikely to come to fruition because the owners were vowing salary reductions when the Collective Bargaining Agreement ended after the 2003-04 season, the star winger took a two-year, $4.7 million, deal on the eve of training camp. "I'm happy we got it done," he said. "It was on my mind to not miss camp."

Hitchcock, through assistant Hartsburg, immediately set out to fix the broken powerplay and to help the Flyers navigate yet another crackdown on obstruction being promised by the NHL. Primeau wasn't thinking about either when defenseman Chris McAllister got his stick up in the captain's throat on the first day of scrimmages. Primeau retaliated with an elbow, setting off a fight that both combatants laughed off afterwards.

"Dan McGillis, a puppy dog, was whacking me in the scrimmage, so I smacked him. Then McAllister, who was on the same team with him, comes after me," recalls Primeau. "I said, 'What are you doing?' and he did it again.

"Afterwards I said to him, 'Yeah, Dan was on your team in the scrimmage, but I'm your captain.' I just thought it was disrespectful. He understood; we were fine."

The fight that mattered more was the one by Cechmanek to prove himself trustworthy again after his apparent mid-game attempted bailout during the Ottawa series.

"It came out different than what I meant and what it means in Europe," said the goalie, suggesting that such demonstrations by goalies and team leaders in Europe were not considered blasphemous. "I want to win every time."

"I think he can find a way to forget what happened last year," said Gagne, but his olive branch was extended mostly on its own while the goalie was stopping only .847 of the shots he faced during the exhibition season. "Roman is our starting quarterback; we just need him sharper," said Hitchcock.

Said the goalie, "I must wake up because I'm sleeping on the ice."

So was Pavel Brendl, the right wing acquired a year earlier in the Lindros deal, which promised opportunity for Patrick Sharp, a third-round pick in 2001 from the University of Vermont who had been moved from center to right wing because of an overflow in the middle.

Concerned that fans were dozing off like Cechmanek, the NHL had mandated that its linesmen drop the puck within 18 seconds of the whistle—and just five seconds after the home team's change of personnel—cutting the average length of exhibition games to 2:17 from the NHL's regular-season average of 2:33 in 2001-02.

In the aftermath of the first fan fatality in the NHL's 85-year-history—13-year old Brittanie Cecil, struck by a deflected puck in the temple during a game in Columbus during March of the previous season—the league had made another fast decision, mandating the installation of safety nets above the end glass.

"I don't take it lightly that people get hurt, and I feel kind of crass in saying this, but the injuries were few and I thought it was an overreaction," recalls Ron Ryan, the Flyer president in 2002.

"I never could really figure out why. It wasn't as if the insurance companies said they were going to stop insuring us, or anything like that. There just was a decision made and we were all forced to do it."

The nets had been in use in Europe for years without complaint by the fans, the NHL insisted. "In less than three minutes, they won't even know they are there," had said Commissioner Gary Bettman. But customers in the lower bowl just above the glass discovered during the first exhibition game that they could barely see at all.

"The first nets were just awful," recalls Ryan. "We had fans who loved those seats who all of a sudden wanted to move and we didn't have a lot of room to move them.

"We brought in groups of about 30 to talk. It was a very uncomfortable time because the people were unhappy and I didn't blame them. So I called everybody in the world that made netting and had them send samples. I think we probably tried three or four different ones before finding a lighter color more tolerable than the black.

"Every time we wanted to change the netting the league would send in these people with a machine that fired pucks at 100 mph. They wouldn't just put it inside the blueline and shoot; they'd get it like six feet from the netting and blast these pucks to make sure it would hold.

"Pucks don't go into the netting like that. They're on an upward trajectory, flipping, you know. So I thought that was overboard because we had a couple we liked that the league wouldn't approve. They were very serious about this."

The net testers were even tougher than the reputation of the new coach on rookies. But right wing Radovan Somik, a fourth-round pick in 1995 out of Slovakia, had demonstrated an almost instant chemistry with his countryman Handzus.

Dennis Seidenberg, a sixth-round choice in 2001 from Germany, had never thought about the NHL until receiving a call telling him he was picked by Philadelphia. The defenseman had caught the eyes of Holmgren and Hextall while playing for the national team as an 18-year-old. In Flyer camp, he was outplaying St. Jacques.

"[Seidenberg] does a lot of things naturally that a coach would like," praised Hitchcock. "We are all looking at this guy like a rookie, but he's played at a much higher level than the AHL. Can he do it at another level when it gets turned up in the next little while?"

Recchi, the junior-hockey disciple of Hitchcock, knew it wasn't only the first-year Flyers who would have to turn the crank. "You will see the structure and accountability being very high on this team under Hitch," Recchi said as camp wound down. "He is in-depth in everything he does.

"If this team can't win under Ken Hitchcock, then I am convinced it can't win under anyone," said Ed Snider.

"It's pressure hockey. The forwards really have to skate. We won't be enjoyable to play against, I can tell you that."

LeClair said his back felt as good as his vibes about the team chemistry. "Guys will buy in," he predicted. "Just watch us, you'll see.

"It's not like [Hitchcock] won a Cup 10 years ago when the game was played more open. He has won recently, under our (current) conditions."

Hitchcock, however, thought this team needed a lot more than just his resume to come together.

"Every day you could feel the debris from the season before," he recalls. "Twice I tried to load the lineup just to win a game in exhibitions, so we had a good feeling coming in, and we got our butts kicked. Dead. The whole game.

"I thought, 'Man, this is gonna be a (squad) teardown if we can't correct this problem.'"

Gagne recalls feeling surprised at the offensive freedom afforded by Hitchcock's system, so the coach was not suffering from player resistance, mostly just searching for confidence. Hitchcock noted that when the Flyers had stopped scoring late the previous season, a lack of structure had left them with nothing to cling to. "You reach a stage where you start to get desperate," said Hitchcock before the team flew to Edmonton to begin the 2002-03 season. "This group is ready to sacrifice."

The Ken Hitchcock era, guaranteed to last the length of his four-year contract by Snider, opened with the Flyers blowing a 2-0 third-period lead into a 2-2 tie with the Oilers. LeClair got both of the Philadelphia goals. But 23 minutes of penalties, most of them having nothing to do with the crackdown on obstruction, cost the Flyers a point.

Instead of taking them to the woodshed, the new taskmaster gathered them to the woods in the foothills of the Canadian Rockies at Canmore, Alberta where, for a day and a half, the players fell backwards off a picnic table into each other's arms, led blindfolded teammates, and crawled through a wire fence without touching it during "Science of Team Building" exercises.

"A bunch of burly hockey players running around in the woods at first seems weird, but it was fun," said Roenick. "Even Pavel said he liked it. And he doesn't like much."

Two nights later, when the Flames picnicked with three consecutive two-man advantages leading to three powerplay goals and a 4-2 lead going into the third period, the Flyers indeed were falling off a table in slow motion. But they caught themselves. Recchi scored twice to complete a hat trick and Roenick tallied with 1:10 remaining to pull out a 5-4 win.

"We were pretty much put on ultimatum (by Hitchcock) in that third period," reported Roenick. "Now that was team building."

Recalls Hitchcock, "You make the comeback and it's like, 'Whoa!' All of a sudden it seemed like a lot of the issues just went 'pfft.' We started to really build something from there."

LeClair had traveled many miles of bad road over the previous two seasons, but the streets of Montreal remained paved in gold for him. He scored four goals, bringing his total to a staggering 28 in 29 games vs. the Canadiens since they had traded him, as Philadelphia closed the trip with a 6-2 victory.

"I can't explain it," said LeClair, who was playing with Roenick and Recchi. "But there is something about playing in a city like Montreal with all the hockey tradition.

"I had a chance to taste it and win a Cup here. It's just one those cities you get a big charge when you come into."

That had not been the case for the Islanders in Philadelphia since their dynasty years in the eighties. But despite being outshot 41-18, they spoiled the Flyers' first home game with a 3-3 tie, Brad Isbister easily converting a Cechmanek dropped save with under three minutes remaining.

"Disappointing, because we should have been up 10-1," said Hitchcock. Also because there were empty seats (365 of them) at a home opener for the first time since the franchise's earliest years.

In his Philadelphia debut, Esche tried to drum up more interest by using his blocker to punch Capital Peter Bondra. It enabled a Washington five-on-three goal, but the Flyers rallied to win 3-1.

After just four games, LeClair already had seven goals. "He is knocking people out of their space," said Hitchcock. But all that room disappeared against the Sabres when Philadelphia visited unsuccessfully for a fifth straight time, losing 2-1, after Miro Satan converted a bad Eric Weinrich pass midway through the third period.

"It's more how you lose, not so much losing," lamented Hitchcock after his club's first defeat. "You don't want the other team to control the tempo."

Somik suffered a groin injury and Sharp was sent to the Phantoms, but Handzus was a newcomer making a splash, scoring twice during a second 6-2 win over Montreal in nine days, then adding two more in a 6-2 victory at Uniondale. "With his size and strength, he can be a 20-

minute player," said Hitchcock.

It would take a lot longer than that for the Flyers and Primeau to live down the Ottawa debacle and its aftermath, but the captain brought his goal total for the young season to five by scoring both Philadelphia tallies during a 2-1 win over the Senators at the Corel Centre. "I think he is on mission," said Roenick, who seemingly was on one, too, only his was to push the buttons of the relentlessly button-pushing Hitchcock.

J.R. had shown up at camp weighing 211 pounds, but he quickly realized they weren't going to help him, even if the additional 10 pounds were all muscle. "I was hoping it would help me around the net so I could take more of a pounding, but I wasn't as nimble," he recalls.

"We talked to him about realizing he's 32, not 22," said Hitchcock. Among the options was to dance off the weight—Hitchcock hated the disco ball Roenick brought to the locker room for pregame entertainment, but it stayed—or to laugh it off. With the help of equipment manager Rock Oratario, who found an old pair of Clarke's long pants from the Flyer uniforms of the early eighties, Roenick dressed up as No. 16, complete with blackened teeth and a curly wig, for the warm-up when Phoenix came to town on Halloween.

"Apparently hockey players had grown a lot since then," recalls Roenick. "In my pads, I couldn't even get the pants past my knees, so I went out in warm-ups without any shin pads or girdle.

"It was awesome. I'll always remember the way [Clarke] laughed in the press box."

Even Hitchcock thought it was "really funny." Much more seriously inclined that afternoon, however, were the two goaltenders. Esche and Boucher had been traded for each other just four months earlier.

"You don't want the guys you didn't like (as teammates) to score on you," said Esche. "Even more, you don't want to be scored on by the guys you like."

Boucher, who was playing regularly in the injury absence of Sean Burke, thought he could prove in one game that Philadelphia had made a mistake. "I wanted to shove it up there so bad," he recalls, but instead the equally inspired Handzus shoved one through the Coyote goalie's five hole to break a 2-2 second-period tie as the 7-1-2 Flyers and Esche went on to defeat the Coyotes (4-7-0) 6-2.

"I'm happy it's over with," Boucher said. "It's a game I circled on my calendar and maybe I put too much emphasis on it from a personal standpoint. It's time to move on and focus on winning."

Said Esche, "Those people who say the grass isn't greener on the other side, they're full of it. It's pretty nice over here. They've got nice, rolling hills."

It was uphill all the way for veteran Dan McGillis to become an integral part of the new sheriff's posse. Struggling in a more defensive role with the rookie Seidenberg than with old partner Richardson, McGillis was a healthy scratch for the Phoenix game. "We want our defensemen to stay underneath the play, not drift above it," Hitchcock explained.

It was going to be his way or the highway. Recchi knew the transition could not come off without a Hitch.

"I knew it was going to be tough, so I told players, 'Don't listen to the bark, listen to the message,'" recalls Recchi. "Eventually he will want players to have ownership of the room. He is very good at that."

It was inevitable than Hitchcock and Roenick would butt heads. "No coach ever has scared or intimidated me," recalls J.R. "I heard rumors he was very particular, very defensive-oriented, thorough in everything he did to the point of almost being neurotic. And neurotic is what I got."

The players were almost as afraid of failure as the coach, which made for an attentive locker room. "I remember getting there and thinking, 'You could put a C on about 80 percent of the team,'" recalls Esche.

Primeau was used primarily to check the opposition's top center, but his sixth score in the first 11 Flyer games produced a 2-1 win over the Capitals. Then LeClair's goal in overtime against Carolina—Philadelphia being an appropriate opponent for Rod Brind'Amour's 1,000th NHL game—produced the team's sixth straight victory, 2-1.

The only loss in a two-week stretch was in court. Former Flyer Dave Babych was awarded $1.37 million for lost wages plus pain and suffering, by a jury deciding that former Flyer physician Dr. Art Bartolozzi had committed malpractice by injecting the defenseman with painkillers so he could participate in the 1998 playoffs with a broken foot.

It also had been Babych's claim that pressure to play in that series (a five-game loss to Buffalo) by (coach) Neilson ultimately cut short an 18-year career, which ended after eight games with the Kings the following season. But a judge had dismissed Comcast-Spectacor as a co-defendant, citing a lack of evidence that the Flyers committed fraud or misrepresentation.

Many members of the Philadelphia hockey jury remained out during the early 2002-03 season. It took seven matches to produce a sell-out.

"Everybody is having trouble because of the economy," said Ryan. The team president had ended the worst of the complaints about the safety nets behind the goal by installing a clear, monofilament material, but still not everybody liked what they saw, booing a 9-2-2 team during a 1-0 shutout by New Jersey. "[The Devils] have a different coach and different players, but they still know how to play these kinds of games," said Desjardins.

While coaching the Flyers, as well as six other NHL teams, Neilson had successfully concocted enough of such shutdown efforts to earn induction into the Hockey Hall of Fame on November 4.

"He hated dinners and functions; was just miserable at them because he didn't want the attention focused on him," recalls Nancy Nichols, the long-time companion of the cancer-stricken Ottawa assistant. "I don't think Roger was feeling that well either; he didn't go to all the festivities (around the induction).

"But when it got down to the actual night with just a smaller group of (friends surrounding him), and it hit Roger that he actually was in the Hall, he was like, 'Yeah, this is pretty neat.'"

Said Neilson to the media, "You think of all the names that are in there and the ones that aren't and you wonder what you're doing there.

"Right now, the doctors are pretty happy. They feel both cancers are under control. I feel like I may live forever."

Roenick had not been around quite that long. But having broken in at age 18, he was able to reach 1,000 NHL games by age 33, just one game after Brind'Amour, a neat twist since Roenick, the eighth pick in the 1988 draft, went one choice ahead of the ex-Flyer.

Regardless of the fact that only 169 of Roenick's contests had been spent in a Philadelphia uniform, he received a standing ovation at the First Union Center during a 2-2 tie with the Bruins on November 16. "A lot of friends and family in Boston got to watch it," said Roenick, the 82nd player to reach the milestone and the eighth to do so in a Flyer uniform.

In the same game, Therien reached No. 600—all with Philadelphia—an achievement LeClair laughed was more impressive than many higher figures. "With a body like that to be able to play 600 games in the NHL, it's really amazing, isn't it?" LeClair teased. "He's been here forever. What a mess!"

"Big defensemen with Chris's mobility are valuable people," Hitchcock praised, but he was making Therien crazy, too. "Hitch was what we had asked for—organization," Therien recalls. "But he would attack his veterans in a way that wore them out. It never stopped."

Despite just six points in 17 games, Desjardins wasn't hearing it from Hitchcock, only from the fans while the Flyers were going eight contests without scoring more than two goals.

"I don't think people see what I see, a [wiry, 6-1] defenseman who plays around the NHL's big forwards," said Hitchcock, who had learned to appreciate Desjardins far faster than fans who foolishly expected more from a player who always gave everything. "He has a big impact playing against the top lines, when all you're looking for is drawing even."

Hitchcock's team was drawing even a lot. The Boston tie was their third straight until Gagne broke a 12-game scoreless streak, then assisted on LeClair's winner over Southeast Division-leading Tampa Bay, 3-2.

With Cechmanek warming from a slow start—"I need a long time," he said—and Esche saving a 2-2 tie with San Jose, the Flyers had the lowest goals-against in the league, not a huge surprise considering their coach's track record. It also was assumed by the media that obsessive defensive coaching had much to do with the struggling offense, even as the scorers swore they didn't feel fettered. "I see it as aggressive because we attack and have the puck quite a bit more," said Weinrich.

As long as Philadelphia maintained possession, the goals would come, Hitchcock maintained.

"My experience in Dallas helped me a lot because I knew if you became a really good counterattack team, you could be really successful," he recalls. "I always use the phrase 'checking for chances.'

"If you want to create offense, you've got to be willing to check a puck back. It wasn't going to be as freewheeling as it had been five-six-seven years before. From Day One of training camp, we just started working to get people to be on the right side (defensively) of the puck. We needed structure because we weren't quick, but we could play with our smarts.

"Actually, playing without the puck is the easiest thing in this league to teach because the players are so smart, but protecting the puck is hard. So I found the buy-in defensively easy and the buy-in offensively more challenging.

"There was a little bit of a pushback. In the offensive zone, we had no structure. One line was cycling with three, one was cycling with two, one wanted to play spread out. We were all over the map offensively.

"Structure was really coming into the game. Educated coaches were coming into the game. Systematic play was prevalent and you needed to get on board with that stuff. But the only real resistance I got was from J.R. about the powerplay. He wanted to play on the half-wall like he always had and I didn't think it worked."

Primeau understood he had much to live down and embraced Hitchcock as an enabler.

"I saw they had struggled in Dallas with [Hitchcock] for three months and then they were lights out for three years," Primeau recalls. "But I guess I didn't understand just how aggressive and forceful he was.

"When he first showed up, we had a powerplay meeting at, let's say 5:30. I rolled in at 5:30 and 10 seconds and he absolutely went off on me. I look at the clock and to me it said 5:30. I felt demeaned in front of my teammates, but he was 100 percent right. I was late. Ten minutes or ten seconds late, it doesn't matter, you're still late.

"So I understood the message. After that, if we would go through tough times, I'd be like, 'Hitch go at me.' If you hold me accountable, everybody else has to be held accountable.

"Another Hitch message was, 'Don't worry about who you're playing with; your responsibility is to elevate the play of those around you.' So that's what I tried to do. I wanted to be hard to play against, wanted to lead by example.

"There were days at the back of the bus where J.R. would be having like a meltdown about Hitch. I would be like 'J.R., listen to the message, not the delivery. If you get past how he delivers it, 98 percent of the time, he's right.

"I liked his system. He wanted possession. I mean, if you held onto the puck going across the blueline 100 percent of the time, there was a pretty good chance he was going to come down your throat. That said, he hated defensemen who ran pucks around the boards. He wanted defensemen to work to get to the net, forwards to work down low. You don't just give up the puck. You make the other team work hard to take it away."

But to win, at some point, you have to put the puck in the net. Philadelphia's powerplay had started the season well, but went to 3-for-61 in a 6-0 loss at Toronto. A 7-2 defeat on November 27 at Pittsburgh left the Flyers 1-4-4 in their last nine.

"Winning begets losing," recalls Hitchcock. "The more we won, the more full of ourselves we had been getting, the more bad habits—careless play, cheating, bad line changes—were coming into our game.

"We had tried to kind of massage it, you know, 'We're gonna be okay.' But in Pittsburgh, we cheated from the opening faceoff to the end of the game and paid for it. We couldn't put the brakes on it."

In part, Philadelphia's drive for redemption was fading because the opposition was redeeming too many undisciplined penalties. The Penguins popped in four powerplay goals, the 17th time in 21 games the Flyers had been burned for at least one. To complete a disastrous night, LeClair, trying to hit a ducking Marc Bergevin, crashed the boards and suffered a dislocated right shoulder that projected him being out four-six weeks.

"I've played a long time without ever having any (injury)," said LeClair, who, with 11 goals and 17 assists, was the only member of the team ahead of his scoring pace in the previous season. "And now it's one thing after the other. It's frustrating and disappointing."

Philadelphia's problems were not camouflaged by a new, third, jersey—burnt orange and silver with white piping—that was debuted November 29 in a home game against Toronto. The 3-0 loss left them 1-5-4 in the last 10 games, outscored by 29-12.

"I think we're panicking, especially on the offensive cycle," Hitchcock told reporters. "We're trying to force everything."

It wasn't even December, but the Flyers felt they were on the clock to save their season. When Justin Williams blocked a shot by Canadien Patrice Brisebois in the final seconds of overtime on November 30 at the Molson Centre, he glanced up at the time while soloing the length of the ice, then beat goaltender Jeff Hackett with seven seconds to spare. The Flyers, 2-1 winners, poured off the bench in relief.

Their feel-good time proved limited. LeClair would need surgery on a fracture discovered in his humerus bone, extending his expected absence to 10-12 weeks. And the magic experienced in Montreal refused to travel to the Meadowlands. Just after Gagne failed to lift a backhander over Marty Brodeur in overtime, Brian Gionta put the winner between Cechmanek's legs to decide the fourth consecutive 1-0 game Philadelphia and New Jersey had played, an NHL record for opponents.

"We should be angry," said Hitchcock, who certainly was. "We had them pushed in the third period and didn't squeeze."

Every game was like putting toothpaste back in the tube. Thanks to two clunker goals allowed by Cechmanek, the Flyers needed their first-ever overtime penalty-shot winner, by Handzus, to beat goalie Dan Blackburn and the Rangers 3-2, before about 13,000 fans at the First Union Center on a bad weather night. Nevertheless, Hitchcock still wasn't pressuring his scorers to score, but rather to be better all-around players.

"Listen, we wanted to win, wanted to get better, so we had to go along with it," recalls Gagne. "But at the same time, he broke some of the guys. There were guys who just couldn't play for Hitch under all that constant pressure."

Dan McGillis had been scratched for four of the previous six games when he was traded to San Jose on December 6 for defenseman Marcus Ragnarsson.

"Danny was big and strong and could really shoot it, but had always been just okay, never had the real drive," recalls Clarke. And after a 24-game sampling, Hitchcock agreed.

"I liked Danny as a person; he was a really good guy, but I thought he'd lost his edge," recalls Hitchcock. "He was losing battles that he had won before, not getting pins and seals. People were getting the puck off the wall on him."

McGillis does not remember this ever being communicated to him directly.

"I tried to play the same way I always played," he recalls. "If I wasn't playing right, I expected feedback from the coaches, not a stonewall and a 'Watch this video, watch that video and think about what you did wrong.'

"Hitchcock would ask me how I thought I played. You were damned if you do, damned if you don't.

"I would have liked a better shot. I would have liked to have finished my career as a Flyer. We really loved it there; my wife still keeps in contact with a lot of people and it feels like home when I go back.

"Those were the best years of my career, for sure. We really did something special in that [five-period overtime win in 2000], and I was really fortunate to play with an organization that gave us a chance to win every year."

McGillis, 30, had twice broken 45 points in his four full Flyer seasons. Ragnarsson, 31, had never scored more than 25 playing his entire, seven-season, NHL career to that point as a Shark. But on the recommendation of Hitchcock, who had coached in the Western Conference, Clarke was confident he was upgrading the Flyer defense.

"We have six [defensemen] who can come up hard now; know when to get in and when to get out," said Hitchcock, who, in Ragnarsson's debut, paired him with Johnsson during a 5-2 victory in Florida. It was the first time in 16 games that Philadelphia had managed more than three goals, two being scored by Gagne, who had been stuck at just two for the year. He next one-timed a feed from Weinrich to give his team its first goal in three games against Toronto, and the first win, 2-1.

The Flyers would just have to get used to making a few goals go a long way, as they again did in Buffalo, when Brashear managed only his second of the season in a 2-0 win by Esche, who ran his record to 5-1-2 with .915 save percentage.

"Reggie (goaltending coach Lemelin) really challenged Robert to make adjustments," said Hitchcock.

Apparently the goalie adapted quickly, unlike the head coach who, 28 games into his Flyer run, still would write "Dallas" at the top of his lineup forms. "You never want to give up your post and I had," said Hitchcock when the Stars came to town on December 17.

"To tell you the truth, I'm dreading it a little bit. When you have that kind of attachment to a group of people, it does get a little emotional."

And even if any tears shed by his Dallas players at Hitchcock's dismissal were tears of joy, they all appreciated that there would have been no Stanley Cup without him.

"If you wanted to line up every player who ever played for Hitch, I'm sure he'd have some kind of negative story," said Craig Ludwig, who was a defenseman and later a coach under Hitchcock with the Stars. "But the bottom line for a lot of us is that whether he was right or wrong, he got us to the end of the rainbow."

Mike Modano credited Hitchcock for helping to "push some right buttons." Then, in the first period against Philadelphia, the Dallas star was pushed face-first into the boards by Roenick and became concussed. The Flyers rallied on third-period powerplay goals by Primeau and Recchi 59 seconds apart to pull out a 2-2 tie on their coach's emotional 51st birthday. "Getting through this day was good for me," Hitchcock said. "I would like to move on now."

After apologizing to Modano, Roenick had the same sentiment, but was nonetheless suspended by league disciplinarian Colin Campbell for two games.

"They can kiss my behind," said Roenick. "The game is like touch football. Guys are afraid to hit somebody. You just don't know what to do out there."

He missed Desjardins' 1,000th game—a 3-1 win at Atlanta—and a 3-1 home loss to Ottawa. But in a home-and-home rematch at the Canadian capital, Roenick returned with a vengeance, feeding a third-period goal by Gagne that saved a 2-2 tie. Then, at Colorado, Roenick tapped in the tying goal with 4:17 to go and set up a Desjardins' overtime backhand winner in a thrilling 2-1 victory.

Paul Ranheim, who had lost his regular penalty-killing job, was traded to Phoenix for a conditional pick in the 2004 draft, but the unit wasn't doing any better without him. The Coyotes scored three powerplay goals in Burke's 4-0 victory. "Special teams, we keep absorbing it," said a steamed Hitchcock.

He moved the laconic Brendl up on a line with Roenick and Recchi. But that neither stirred the offense nor prevented a 2-1 loss in San Jose when Ragnarsson was lost to a pinched nerve in his neck and Jonathan Cheechoo's apparent pass through the crease early in the third period went in off Cechmanek's skate. "We scored one goal, that's the bottom line," said Hitchcock.

The Flyers picked up right wing Tomi Kallio off waivers from Columbus. The right winger got credit for a goal on a carom off his skate during a 4-1 victory in Los Angeles, and helped Philadelphia survive six man disadvantages. The following night, the penalty killers went seven-for-seven and Primeau's powerplay goal was the only score in Esche's 1-0 shutout in Anaheim.

"The powerplay is getting a little better," said Hitchcock. "The penalty kill is a lot better."

The Flyers completed a 4-2-1 holiday trip and moved ahead of New Jersey into first place in the Atlantic Division with a seesaw 5-4 victory in Atlanta, marked by Somik's first NHL goal. "He's the best checking winger on our team right now," said Hitchcock. "That's why he plays [15 minutes a game] even though he doesn't score."

Philadelphia had the second-best defensive record in the NHL, the primary reason its division title chances survived the offensive struggles during that 1-5-4 November slump. The Handzus-Brashear-Somik line pitched in two goals and took over from Roenick, Gagne and Williams the checking of Detroit's Brett Hull and Henrik Zetterberg in the Flyers' sixth consecutive victory, a 3-2 win over the Red Wings before a First Union Center sellout.

Despite being third on the club in scoring with 23 points, Williams was bounced to the fourth line with Murray and Fedoruk as Philadelphia called up 13-year NHL veteran Joe Sacco from the Phantoms to replace the quickly waived Kallio.

"You never like it when the coach is on you, but I take it as a positive," said Williams. Soon enough there was a negative—he suffered a knee-on-knee hit with Tampa Bay's Brad Lukowich during a 3-2 home victory over the Lightning.

At first Williams was given some hope he might be able to keep playing with a brace. But team orthopedist Dr. Peter Deluca determined there was a 90 percent tear in the ACL that would take four-to-eight months to heal.

"It didn't even seem like it was serious [when it happened]," Williams said. "I can't voice how utterly frustrated I am right now."

Sacco and defenseman Jim Vandermeer, an undrafted free-agent signee summoned from the Phantoms to fill in for Ragnarsson, both scored goals in a 4-1 win over Montreal before Handzus's sixth game-winning goal of the season brought the Flyers back from a 2-0 deficit to beat the Rangers, 4-2, at Madison Square Garden. "I thought Todd Fedoruk was a huge factor tonight," said Hitchcock after moving the fourth-liner up to a play with Primeau, who scored to tie the game, and Recchi.

Recchi's 200th goal as a Flyer helped them to their sixth-straight road win—and 10th in 11 games overall—3-1 in Toronto. But Hitchcock still found things to be unhappy about. He bristled at suggestions in the Toronto papers that his team played boring, defensive hockey, then railed at the officials when two goals were taken off the scoreboard—one by a penalty on Recchi, who appeared to have been pushed into goaltender Garth Snow, and the other on a quick whistle—as the Islanders beat Philadelphia 3-1 at the First Union Center.

"[Referee Don VanMassenhoven] put himself in a bad spot where he could see only half the goal," chimed in Roenick. "Good refs like Paul Stewart make sure they get directly behind the net so that they can see that stuff.

"[VanMasenhoven] messed up. He knew it. He was swearing at himself."

When Snow read that quote, he, in turn, was swearing about Roenick.

"He should be worried about his game, not innovating it," said Snow. "He thinks he's Brett Hull or something.

"You should remind him that he didn't go to college. He's a junior guy, so he's not that bright."

Snow was a graduate of the University of Maine, while Roenick had gone directly to the NHL from Thayer Academy in Braintree, MA.

Replied Roenick, "If going to college gets you a career backup goaltender job and my route gets you a thousand points and a thousand games, compare the two contracts. It doesn't take a rocket scientist to figure out whose decision was better."

J.R. remained convinced he had made a learned decision to sign with the Flyers, even if, like most of his teammates, he chafed under the constant soul-searching meetings and nagging from Hitchcock.

"One day I was fighting for the puck right in front of the bench and he was yelling at me," recalls J.R. "I literally stopped and looked up and said, 'Shut the [bleep] up; I'm trying to play a game here.'

"All the boys started laughing."

Hitchcock, Roenick's straight man, was happy to continue to be unhappy. After Philadelphia lost in Boston, 1-0 on Brian Rolston's overtime goal, then laid an egg in a 3-0 home loss to Tampa Bay, the coach complained of "far too many passengers" and said the "people who usually carry the mail were not ready."

With Gagne (groin pull), joining LeClair and Williams on the injured list, all hands had to be on deck. Clarke kept picking up new ones, though. On January 26, the GM traded a second-round choice to Montreal for Eric Chouinard, the former Quebec Remparts teammate of Gagne who had been taken six picks ahead of the Flyer star in the 1998 draft.

"The pressures of being a first-round pick and being compared to Simon Gagne were unbearable," Canadien GM Andre Savard told Quebec newspaper *le Solei*. But Clarke figured if the kid couldn't beat Gagne, perhaps there would be some benefit in joining him.

"He hasn't proven ready for the NHL yet, but we think he'll be a scorer in the league," said the GM.

Indeed, Chouinard became the team's third acquisition since the season started to tally in his first Philadelphia game, but it was the only score in a 5-1 annihilation at the Meadowlands. The Flyers played the second and third periods with only 17 skaters after Hitchcock, having a late change of heart to dress Brendl, put his name on the lineup card to be submitted to the game officials but accidentally handed over the original without the winger's name. The Devils brought the omission to the attention of referee Bill McCreary after a period and Brendl was disqualified.

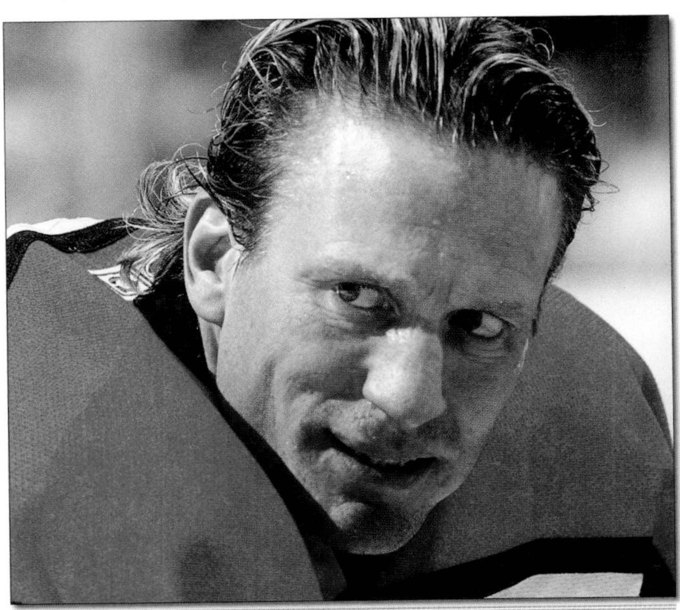

Jeremy Roenick scored 27 goals and played his typical tough and flashy two-way game in 2002-03.

A number of Philadelphia players legally dressed still were absent mentally. "We're missing so many people and key performers, we have to win with enthusiasm and energy," said Hitchcock. "In the last four games, we've had a lot of people way below the bar. That's troublesome."

The Flyers split for the All-Star break with what Roenick called the need to "let it stew." As the team's lone representative in the festivities in Sunrise, FL, perhaps he took his frustration out on the targets during the shooting accuracy segment of the skills competition—Roenick was the winner.

The team came back to the grind seemingly ready to grind, winning 2-1 at Uniondale on a goal midway through the second period by Recchi. "These are the type of games we're going to have to get used to for the rest of the year," said Hitchcock, who, already annoyed at having spent 10 contests during the season without Gagne, lost him again due to a re-aggravated groin pull.

Clarke picked up journeyman Todd Warriner from Vancouver for future considerations. Thanks to a 43-save effort by Cechmanek, Philadelphia gritted out a 2-2 tie in Ottawa with Seidenberg playing on the wing with Roenick and Chouinard, the latter scoring his second goal as a Flyer. "It was a rich game for those kids to play in and they did fine," said the coach.

Nevertheless, the GM continued to look for winger upgrades. Clarke asked Primeau his opinion of ex-teammate Sami Kapanen, a five-time 20 goal scorer who had managed to find the net just once during the Hurricane's 23-game drive to the Stanley Cup Final the previous spring.

"I said, 'You guys will absolutely love the way this kid plays,'" recalls Primeau. 'He is fearless.'

"I used to say to him, 'Just once go around [the checker]' because he never would. He always would go right through him or try. Sami never hesitated once. There wouldn't be much room between the defenseman and the boards, and he still wasn't going around. Ever.

"He was as competitive as they come. He wanted to fight. Literally. I'd come back to the bench after a fight and he would be like, 'I wish I was 6-3.'"

Even at 5-9, Kapanen sounded like a Flyer kind-of-a-guy, which Brendl never would be.

"Not only the laziest hockey player I ever encountered, but the laziest human being," recalls Roenick. Nevertheless, as a former fourth-overall pick, Brendl still intrigued Carolina, which also wanted a young defenseman.

Clarke had plenty of those—Seidenberg, Vandermeer, St. Jacques, Pitkanen and Jeff Woywitka—either already on his roster or arriving in the next year or two. So the GM put St. Jacques, 22, in a deal with Brendl, 21, for the 29-year-old Kapanen and former Flyer farmhand Ryan Bast.

"We didn't like the idea of having to give up a young defenseman like St. Jacques, but we felt Vandermeer had passed him and you've got probably the best young defensemen outside the NHL coming next year in Pitkanen and Woywitka," said Clarke.

Brendl had scored six goals and seven assists in 50 Flyer games.

"We nicknamed him 'Heartbeat' because he didn't seem to have one," recalls Fedoruk.

It was a gross waste of hugely talented hands. "My first thinking, watching him in drills was, "Big, strong, world-class skill, world-class vision," recalls Hitchcock.

"You'd say, 'Man, if that ever comes into games, this guy's going to be incredible.' You'd give him a two-on-one or a breakaway, it was in the net. Three on two, he's going to make a good play. But you can't play the game if you're intimidated. The physicality of the National Hockey League really troubled him.

"I think he just didn't like hockey at that level. The body language showed that this was just too hard."

Remembers Therien, "One time, when we're down a goal or two at the end of the first period, getting ready to go back out, Johnny LeClair says 'Come on boys, let's feed off Pavel's energy and we'll get back in it.'

"I turn around and see Brendl just sitting there with this big, droopy look. Jezzuz. Cracked us up."

The prospect's work-ethic deficit was not unknown to Clarke when he had made the Lindros deal, but the GM took a flier in the hope that getting Brendl to a winning team might change him. There had been no sign of it. "Once I asked him if he was going to play for the Czechs in the World Tournament and he said, 'Not even the Czechs like me,'" recalls Clarke. "Didn't seem to bother him.

"His skating was off and his competitiveness was way off."

There were no effort issues about Kapanen. But he seemed to have lost his hands in Carolina.

"[The Hurricanes and I had] come to [an agreement] the night before arbitration, but things had gotten a little uncomfortable on both sides, so I thought I might be traded over the summer (of 2002)," he recalls. "I had a tough start to the season because it seemed a lot of my focus was on a trade.

"For whatever reason, it didn't go that well. The issue seemed to be that I didn't score enough five-on-five. I was working hard, but at some point I lost confidence a bit and started passing more than shooting. There was hesitation in my game.

"When it got to December I thought, 'Maybe they're not trading me.' But then my name kept coming up. So I waited, and when nothing was happening, I thought I was going to finish the season there.

"They finally pulled the trigger when we were in L.A.; I was excited right away. I got a flight and the next day was in Philly for an afternoon game against the Rangers.

"I thought that was the best way to come in—play a game, no practice, no time to think and get nervous."

Kapanen became the fourth player the Flyers had obtained since the beginning of the season to debut with a goal—in this case the winning one on the powerplay—as Cechmanek beat the Rangers, 2-1. "I felt lucky I was able to do something right away," Kapanen recalls. "It gave me good feelings."

Instantly, Hitchcock had them, too, about this acquisition. "He does a lot of things well that add up at the end of the night," the coach told the media. "He is on the right side of the puck, has quickness and courage."

Philadelphia still needed goals, though. The Wild shut out the team back-to-back, bringing the total number of blankings on the season to nine, so Hitchcock got grief in the media for teaching a too-defensive system.

"If that were the case, why are we third or fourth in shots on goal in the league?" asked Clarke. "Maybe we don't hang in there for second chances, though. Sometimes I think we leave the scoring areas too quickly.

"When LeClair and Gagne get back, there's the potential for more goals. And it also changes the way your opponent plays against you. For the longest time, we did not have two lines that were really threats. So teams bring good lines against Roenick and Recchi."

Hitchcock remained convinced that defense would lead to offense, perhaps why his team didn't panic in the face of a 3-0 deficit on February 13 in St. Louis. "My job is to be positive," said the often Mr. Negative. He switched Kapanen off Primeau's line to play with Recchi and Roenick, the latter's goal getting the team back to within one midway through the third period. Johnsson tied the game and Handzus put in a Somik rebound in overtime for a buoying 4-3 victory.

"It was amazing to me how quickly Sami fit in," recalls Hitchcock. "Talk about instant impressions. It took like one week, as if he were made to be a Flyer.

"Not that he had an overwhelming personality, but he was just one of those guys that everybody loved, you know? You loved the way he played; you loved his fearlessness for a little guy. And I loved him because I could play him in any position in any situation."

Philadelphia overcame another deficit, 2-0, in gaining a 2-2 tie with Carolina on third-period goals by Brashear and Primeau. 'Working hard, clawing and scratching," said Hitchcock.

Also, digging. When 19 inches of snow hit South Jersey during the week of Presidents' Day, every player made it to practice on time. "It would be very disappointing if hockey players could not get around during the winter," smiled Hitchcock.

A checking unit of Sacco, Brashear and Primeau wasn't throwing any snow during a 2-2 First Union Center tie with the Devils. It was the Flyers' first point against New Jersey in four cracks, and the frost that had encased their scorers' hands since early in the season was beginning to melt, thanks to the continuing efforts of the third and fourth lines.

Chouinard scored twice as Philadelphia gave Cechmanek rare breathing room in a 5-0 rout of the Kings, and then followed up with another shutout, 2-0, in Chicago. Then, with the help of powerplay goals by Johnsson and Recchi, the Flyers beat the Blackhawks again, 5-2, at home.

Roenick's second goal of the game defeated Boston, 3-2 in overtime at the Fleet Center, then Cechmanek, who had a league-best goals-against average of 1.89, cooled down hot Vancouver, 3-0, to record his third shutout in 13 days.

"Roman was a little unnerving, bizarre at times," recalls Hitchcock. "But having talked to the people in Buffalo that had Hasek, I could see some of those things in Cechmanek.

"Paddle down, taking away the low part of the net, he played a game where the shot never came from the angle that started into the zone. In Europe, there always was a next pass. It was all about closing off doors in and around the crease so [the style] didn't bother me as much as it bothered others because there was a method to the madness. Those [Czech goalies] actually practiced those things.

"He played some of the best games I've ever seen a goalie play. When he was aggressive and out on top of the crease, I thought, 'They're never going to score on him.' There were some weeks when he was connected and weeks he was disconnected, when it looked like he was just going to stand on the goal line and hope the puck hit him."

Like all goalies, this one was best when closer to the shooters. Hitchcock had also tried to bring Cechmanek closer to his teammates by inviting him into the leadership meetings the coach held with key players. In his third Flyer season, Cechmanek said he felt much better about what was going on in front of him.

"Last year I was very upset," said the goalie. "I wondered if we were serious. Now we are trying to build a team."

The boss of the team, Clarke, didn't yet think it was as good as it could be. Having regularly tried to obtain defenseman Mathieu Schneider since 1995, when Clarke "settled" for Desjardins in a deal with Montreal, the GM pitched the Kings and again was willing to go with Plan B. Instead of the 33-year-old Schneider, Philadelphia re-obtained 31-year-old Dmitri Yushkevich, eight years after trading him to Toronto in a deal that primarily brought the No. 1 draft choice the Flyers used to select Dainius Zubrus.

This time, Clarke gave up fourth and seventh-round picks for essentially a $600,000 rental of Yushkevich, whose contract was expiring at the end of the season. "It's nice to come back to the team that opened the door for me," he said. "I was so sad to get traded."

It was even nicer to get a defenseman who wasn't so nice. "He gives us an edge back there," agreed Roenick, and the experience level was upgraded, too, for an immediate Cup run. Armed now with a veteran defense of Desjardins, Johnsson, Weinrich, Yushkevich, Ragnarsson and Therien, the Flyers returned Seidenberg and Vandermeer to the Phantoms.

"In some ways they should be angry about it; they played well enough to be in the NHL," said Clarke. "They will be up here when we need them."

Gagne, meanwhile, needed either more patience from Hitchcock or better luck with a groin problem that had left the sniper out of the lineup in two different stretches.

"Hitch said I had to push myself harder and play through pain," recalls Gagne. "He said it to me but also in the paper, and I remember my agent (Bob Sauve) called me and was really angry.

"He flew in to talk to Clarkie. I mean, Hitch was questioning my character, almost saying I was faking. That hurt.

"I did the rehab, played, and hurt it again (when cross-checked by Ranger Ronald Petrovicky in a 5-1 loss on March 2 at Madison Square Garden). [The groin] always was giving out. So finally I went to Clarkie. He said, 'Shut it down for the season and come back for the playoffs.'

"Doing the rehab at a smart pace finally helped. But Hitch got pissed about it. So things between us got pretty bad for a while."

Cechmanek allowed three goals on nine shots during that Ranger defeat before being yanked. He was much sharper in losing 2-1 on a breakaway overtime goal by Colorado's Peter Forsberg. "For 60 minutes, that was our best effort," maintained Hitchcock.

And the general manager was working even harder.

After making his seventh deal since the season began—picking up center Claude Lapointe from the Islanders for a fifth-round pick—Clarke called Roenick the next day to get his input on one more proposed trade.

"He asked me about Tony Amonte," recalls Roenick. Questions like, 'How do you guys get along, how do you think you'd play together?'"

"I said, 'I can play with Tony with my eyes closed. I've known him since I was nine. I played with him for the North Shore Raiders, played with him at Thayer Academy, and for the Blackhawks. I'd never played better with anybody at any level than with Tony.'

"So I said (to Clarke), 'Get him as fast as you can.'

"I called Tony and said, 'We have a chance to get you, would you want to come here?' He says, 'Make the call to Clarkie.' So it was Clarkie to me, me to Tony, me back to Clarkie, and then the deal was done."

Well, not quite. LeClair, a USA Olympic buddy of Amonte's at Nagano and Salt Like City, also had called him, only to be told to save his pitch. "Hey, I'm already coming," Amonte told LeClair. "I'm excited to get to Philly and start over."

The Coyotes, coming off a 95-point season, had signed Amonte the previous summer for four years and $24 million, but were struggling both on the ice and in the coffers. Quickly, they were back in cost-cutting mode. For second- and third-round picks, plus fringe left-wing Guillaume Lefebvre, Phoenix traded a player who had reached 30-plus goals eight times in 12 NHL seasons.

Amonte delightedly waived his no-trade clause, and even more happily waived the No. 10 he had always worn, it having been on LeClair's back in Philadelphia for nine years. Amonte took No. 11.

The team's most glaring need was filled. But Clarke counted on there being more than just one dimension to Amonte.

"He is not just a scorer," said the GM. "He has great speed and great hands, and he can kill penalties and be used in the last minute of games."

The deal was announced after a 2-1 loss at Washington in which Lapointe, obtained the previous day, became the fifth Flyer that season to score in his debut game. Amonte, playing with Roenick and Marty Murray, uncannily became the sixth in a 5-3 home win over Carolina. LeClair, returning to the ice for the first time in 47 games, received a standing ovation before his shift began, and was able to score on a wraparound.

That was a South Philly, 'Yo Tony!' said a reporter.

"Yeah, fugetaboutit," laughed Amonte who next assisted on two Roenick goals in a 4-1 triumph at Pittsburgh. Each of the childhood best buds then had a point as the Flyers, who had been down eight points to the Devils in mid-February, moved into a first-place tie on March 17 with a rare and highly satisfying 4-2 win at the Meadowlands.

"Getting Johnny back was a long time waiting, but getting Tony in here has dramatically improved my energy level," Roenick said after Philadelphia had outplayed New Jersey from start to finish in what Hitchcock looks back upon as a watershed triumph.

"It was the way we lost to the Devils all the time, always the last 10 minutes," he recalls. "It was always them grinding us down and us breaking down.

"We finally got them to crack (albeit early, as the Flyers jumped to a 4-1 lead after two periods), and it felt good, like the cycle was broken a little bit. We could stay with it as long as they could."

The following night in Buffalo, when the little-used Esche gave up a softie to Maxim Afinogenov just 1:02 after Philadelphia had erased a
2-0 deficit on goals by LeClair and Amonte, Hitchcock told Cechmanek to go in. The goalie said, "No, no, groin sore!"

"Kind of found out about it through osmosis," Hitchcock said the next day, having been too steamed about his team's play to meet with the media following the 5-2 defeat.

"He wouldn't go in, so I finished," recalls Esche. "Hated those Buffalo games.

"I always had 150 people coming from (hometown) Utica (NY). Had to get 'em all tickets, and I wanted to play well in front of them.

"After the game Hitch told me, 'It's not your first time playing bad and it won't be your last,' so I kind of tried to laugh it off. But the next day, I don't know why, he went up one side of me and down the other.

"After that, though, things were okay between us."

That was because there were no firearms within reach of Hitchcock when Esche surrendered two goals in the first 4:06 two nights later against Pittsburgh. He lived to bounce back with a 4-2 victory while Amonte was scoring for the fourth time in five contests and LeClair was staying hot with two more goals, bringing him to five in five games since his return.

Since the principal stars of the win over the Penguins—Esche, LeClair, Amonte and Roenick—were all U.S. born, it made a Flyer fan proud to be an American. And with the invasion of Iraq to topple Saddam Hussein just underway, the organization decided to do some pregame flag-waving on March 22 with "God Bless America."

"Generally, we would discuss whether or not it was a right occasion during our game presentation meeting for the week," recalls Brian Mantai, the Flyer director of game presentation from 1996-2003. "Ultimately, Ron Ryan would sign off on it, but a lot of times he let us do our thing.

"We all kind of knew the history of it and not to overdo it. So, we really picked our spots. "

Robert Esche, above, and Roman Cechmanek would combine to share the William Jennings Trophy for fewest goals against with New Jersey's Martin Brodeur.

This time, however, instead of playing the video of the late Kate Smith or Lauren Hart performing live, Ryan wanted them together.

"I actually got the idea from the "Unforgettable" duet Natalie Cole did with her (late) father Nat (King Cole in 1991)," recalls Ryan. "I brought it up at a production meeting."

It became a project for Vinny D'Aprile, the husband of Lisa D'Aprile, Ed Snider's then-administrative assistant, and Mantai.

"Essentially, we first needed to remove Kate Smith's vocals from (parts of) the video but still have seamless organ music underneath Lauren," recalls Mantai. "The tricky part was to combine the original recording of Kate and those transition pieces to where we would go live with Lauren. It had to be smooth.

"Ron brought back the music from Vinny asking, 'Is there anything we can do to make that possibly work?' I took a listen and thought, 'Yeah, we could definitely pull this off.' So I grabbed the video of Kate Smith from the Stanley Cup Game Six in 1974 and started to piece together where these transitions would be.

"We put it together in two or three days and brought Lauren in to look at it for the first time. She said, 'Yeah, I think this could be a great thing.' With her in the control room upstairs, we stepped through it a few times; then she went down to ice level using her ear monitor.

"We ran through it two to three times and she did a fabulous job as always. The transitions were very smooth. I said to myself, 'This is going to be extraordinary.'

"That night it looked like it was going to be the normal "God Bless America" with Lauren, like we saved for big games and special events. Lauren goes through the first verse and then we hit them with Kate Smith on the screen and there was this roar."

It didn't shake Ranger backup Don Blackburn, who relieved the injured Mike Dunham after a period and stoned the Flyers 2-1. The winning goal, by Petr Nedved, ticked off the knob of Esche's stick with 3:12 remaining.

"Over the course of the season these things happen," said Hitchcock, "But you (must) beat the goaltender in the playoffs."

It took 41 shots before Handzus got one past Nashville's Tomas Vokoun. And all that effort left Philadelphia with only a point when Mark Eaton tallied with 1:34 remaining to give the Predators a 1-1 tie. "We scored, then stopped playing," seethed Hitchcock, who, with just six games remaining before the postseason, said it was high time Cechmanek started playing.

"Everybody this time of year is sore," said the coach, who had dealt with another goaltending kvetch in Dallas—Ed Belfour. "It's general soreness; if there is a risk of injury, there is no way we would ever put [Cechmanek] in goal.

"It will get better as we go on. He is not injured, just complains all the time. "

Said Cechmanek, "In practice, one save and I feel it is still sore. But it is not time to take off. I must be ready for the playoffs."

He appeared to have trouble getting to his feet a few times before Amonte's second goal of the game, shorthanded with 6:49 remaining, saved a 2-2 tie with Boston. But the netminder looked supple in a 3-0 triumph over the last-place Penguins, a good thing, according to Hitchcock, who saw problems in his team's game even after a shutout.

"If he couldn't bitch, he wouldn't be Hitch," said Roenick, who, after the laughter died, added, "Look, we won 3-0 tonight and I thought we were in control all the way. But if that's what Hitch thinks will motivate us to go into their building (two nights later), he's going to talk about how we played like [bleep] tonight."

It wasn't a terrible idea. The Flyers celebrated Weinrich's 1,000th NHL game with a 6-1 triumph in the rematch. Then, as Gagne returned, Cechmanek needed to stop only 10 shots in recording a remarkable 20th shutout in just three Philadelphia seasons, 4-0, over Columbus.

Nevertheless, the goalie was worried about rust. "Ten shots is not nice for me," he said. "I want more."

Recalls Hitchcock, "A couple of times when we had outplayed and outshot the team badly, he let in these sleepy, dozy goals and said, 'I can't play like this. I fall asleep in the net.'

"It was a little bit like Hasek. Forty, forty-five shots, he didn't care; the more action, the better. But Roman would wander mentally. When we dominated a game, he'd do some of the most bizarre stuff you'd ever seen outside of the net. It used to drive me crazy. 'What the [bleep] are you doing? Where are you going?'

"He got bored, just flat got bored."

It had been 13 games since the Flyers had given up 30 shots and, in six of them, they had held opponents under 20. Ragnarsson was proving an upgrade, Johnsson had suffered no dropoff in his second year, and Desjardins, playing with two good shoulders to a bounce-back plus-30 season, became the Barry Ashbee Trophy winner for a seventh time, in the final year of his contract.

"I always thought your job was to do your best with what you have," he told the *Daily News*'s Rich Hofmann about his 2001-02 season's struggles. "I was trying, it just didn't work.

"It's hard to be where you feel you're not appreciated. Hopefully people will forgive me and give me a chance to play here for a few more years. That's all I ask."

As Philadelphia was defeating the Southeast Division champion Lightning 4-1 in Game No. 81, the Devils were wrapping up the conference's best record with a 2-1 victory that not only eliminated the Rangers but also dropped the Flyers to a fourth seeding behind the three division winners. Fifth-place Toronto would be Philadelphia's opponent in the first round, not that it mattered much.

"I don't see us afraid to play anyone right now," Hitchcock said. The Flyers had gotten Gagne back in the lineup during the final week and, with a 6-2 win at Florida to close the season, had finished 6-0-2 to enter the playoffs in their best physical and mental condition since their 2000 semifinal run.

Philadelphia's 107 points, the most for the franchise since 1985-86, seemed remarkable in light of the extended absences of Gagne, LeClair and Williams. But as evidenced by Cechmanek and Esche sharing the Jennings trophy with the Devils' Brodeur, the Flyers ultimately had gone 45-20-13, a 10-point improvement on the preceding season, on defense and organization.

"I could really tell from the first day I came here that this team wants to win real bad," Amonte told the media. "Hitchcock is upset when the team doesn't win the right way and guys are devastated after losses.

"Every day at practice, the team tries to get better at everything. It's refreshing to be part of something like this."

It was especially so for key holdovers who had been accused of having their own agenda, and then became vindicated by their acceptance of Hitchcock's teachings. "We didn't have a system at this point last year," said Recchi. "Well, we had one, but we weren't very good at it."

Said Roenick, "Just the opposite of last year—we're winning, scoring goals and getting guys back instead of losing them."

The timing wasn't quite as good for coach Pat Quinn's Leafs, who had 14 returnees from the team that had gotten to within one game of the Final the previous spring. Although Toronto added Owen Nolan, Doug Gilmour, Phil Housley and Glen Wesley before the trading deadline, Gilmour was now likely out for the first round and Nolan iffy with a groin strain. But in goal, Toronto still had a Stanley Cup winner in Belfour going against a counterpart who had yet to win an NHL series.

"I feel maybe we are stronger mentally than the last two years," said

Cechmanek. "We have a good chance. We could lead or lose 4-0, but this year I will play very serious."

This was coming from the mouth of a guy who had requested leave during the four days between the end of the regular season and the playoffs.

"He said (while the Flyers were in Florida for the final two regular-season games), "I go home, take my family,"" recalls Hitchcock. "I thought he meant go home to South Jersey, but he was going to the Czech Republic.

"I said, 'No, you can't fly home and then come back and expect to play.' That shook me up. And he was really mad at me."

Hitchcock managed to remain publicly positive about his goaltender. "If it weren't for him, [our team] would have lost by seven goals every time (last spring)," said the coach. "His playoff performances were incredible."

Certainly Cechmanek had played better versus Ottawa in 2002 than the previous year against Buffalo, when the Flyers had given themselves a chance to win until the sixth and final game. But that Sabre series also had ended miserably in an 8-0 defeat, leaving nine Philadelphia holdovers from both flops with much to live down.

"This team has taken a lot of hits because of the way it went down last year," said Hitchcock. "We just want to prove that we can put up a fight."

Privately, the coach was extremely confident. "I felt like the Leafs had a lot of firepower, but our checking could frustrate and wear them down," he recalls. "They had people who could score, but we were a little bigger and deeper. I just felt like our structure could do the job."

And then a season of drilling deserted the Flyers in Game One at the First Union Center, when a river-hockey contest entirely to the Leafs' liking broke out.

Alexander Mogilny opened the scoring off a shorthanded two-on-one. Weinrich tied the game 1:12 later, in the final second of a Robert Svehla holding penalty, but Mogilny beat Handzus off the boards to put Toronto ahead before a falling Tie Domi launched a softie that Cechmanek managed to kick off Johnsson's skate to stake Toronto to a 3-1 lead.

Philadelphia bore down in a ferocious five-minute flurry. Brashear scored on a jam, then Desjardins tied the game on a rebound of his own shot that had left Nik Antropov writhing on the ice. But Brashear got called for boarding Aki Berg and Mikael Renberg fired a powerplay goal between Cechmanek's legs to restore Toronto's lead. Mogilny finished off his hat trick, and the 5-3 victory, into the empty net.

Just 15 Leaf shots had been enough to give them a 1-0 jump in the series. "They scored on every mistake we made," said Brashear and that wasn't entirely an indictment of Cechmanek, even if the goalie had been less-than scintillating.

"Not many shots, but I have to be better on the rushes," Cechmanek said. "I need help from my teammates, too. They didn't play very well."

Hitchcock wasn't sure what to think. "You look at the shot totals and probably say, 'Geez, Roman didn't play that well,' but I don't know how to evaluate it," said the coach. "They scored their goals on odd-man rushes, and when you give skilled people an opportunity, they can finish.

"But any time you only give up 15 shots, you are doing some things right."

Recalls Weinrich, "I vividly remember in the locker room that we were almost in disbelief that we lost. Everybody was like, 'We just got to continue to play that way and we're going to win.' We couldn't wait to get to the next game."

Toronto had capitalized better than Philadelphia. So Hitchcock shuffled the cards in his one-for-six powerplay, elevating Weinrich, the only Flyer scorer of a goal from the point, over Kapanen on the first unit and replacing Handzus with a still-rusty Gagne. While leaving only the Roenick-Amonte-Kapanen line intact, the coach challenged his team to bury the past.

"I thought we had played tentative, like bad things were going to happen again," Hitchcock recalls. "We had way too much stress.

"Stop worrying if [management was] going to blow this up and get rid of all of them. We just needed to play and needed to do it quickly."

In Game Two, Gagne got the message and, skating shorthanded because of a Williams penalty, forced a Brian McCabe giveaway, fired off of Belfour's chest and put in the rebound, all by himself. Five minutes later, he took the puck from Housley, enabling Roenick to chip over the goalie for a confidence-building 2-0 first-period lead.

Mogilny caught Cechmanek out of the net early in the second period on a wraparound goal, but almost before the fans could groan, Recchi's goalmouth pass went in off the struggling McCabe. Four minutes later, LeClair put a Weinrich powerplay rebound through Belfour's five hole and Philadelphia was up three goals.

"We dug in, really competed that game," recalls Hitchcock. Using both the Handzus and Primeau lines against the unit of Mats Sundin, Mogilny and Gary Roberts, the Flyers doubled the shots on the Leafs (36-17) for the second straight game, only this time they won, 4-1 to even the series.

"It was imperative that I have a better game," said Roenick, who wasn't the only one who did.

Pat Quinn called the mistakes by Housley and McCabe "egregious" and "almost unacceptable at the pro level." His team, which had lost Antropov in Game One, had been forced at every turn.

That continued early in Game Three at the Air Canada Centre. Domi, who had run at Gagne at the end of Game Two, tried again, only to get caught on a two-on-one. Roenick took advantage by feeding Amonte, who relayed to Weinrich coming late up the slot. Weinrich closed to the hashmarks and shot the puck in off the left pad of Belfour.

Williams, clipped by defenseman Aki Berg, continued into Belfour after a save and the goalie still was off balance as Williams chased the puck to the backboards. Desjardins moved in just below the circle and hammered Williams' passout to the short side for a 2-0 Philadelphia lead after only 8:02.

"They were unnerved, in my opinion," Hitchcock would say later. At least the Leafs should have been. But Amonte was light on the boards against McCabe and Robert Reichel was 10 feet behind Desjardins to tip a shot, and then put the rebound between Cechmanek's legs as he dropped down. Just 37 seconds after falling down by two, the Leafs were within a goal and storming.

Cechmanek had to make a sprawling save when Sundin beat Weinrich wide. Then, after LeClair went to the box, the Czech flashed the glove on Tomas Kaberle. Kapanen was penalized for tripping McCabe and, on the powerplay, Weinrich's stick broke in an attempt to lift Nolan's. As a result, Reichel had time to freeze Cechmanek with a fake shot and hit Kaberle, who was wide open at the post to tie the game, 2-2.

Late in the second period, Roberts overwhelmed Therien in the corner and Mogilny, his path cleared by Darcy Tucker's pick of Lapointe, went over Cechmanek's shoulder to put Toronto ahead, 3-2. It was already Mogilny's fifth goal of the series.

"Sick, sick talent," recalls Roenick. "He was strong, but that's not what beat you.

"Mogilny was one of the finest skaters that I ever played against and a smart player, too. He didn't get enough credit for how good he was."

Cechmanek slid out to keep Sundin from lifting in an insurance goal. After dropping his stick, the goalie made a glove save on Robert Svehla, then again kept the Flyers in the game when Tom Fitzgerald cut in after stripping Therien of the puck. Thus, when Yushkevich stopped a weak attempt by Kaberle up the boards and fired off Nolan's skate, Recchi pounced on the rebound 2:59 into the third period to tie the game, 3-3.

McCabe tipped away a Weinrich shot that had caromed into the low slot before Gagne could fire into an empty net. Belfour made a stop on Primeau on a give-and-go to the net and Desjardins broke up a scary Sundin-Mogilny two-on-one to get the game to overtime.

Johnsson had the best chance in it, hitting the post on a passout by LeClair. Roenick crushed Roberts in the back and Lapointe dumped Nolan with a stick in the face, neither foul being penalized. After 20 extra minutes, the teams had combined for 72 hits in the game.

A little more than four minutes into the second overtime, after Belfour made a big pad save on Williams off a Primeau feed, Mogilny tripped Roenick at the blueline. As their skates locked and Roenick struggled to stay upright, his stick flew up and caught the Leaf star in the face.

Mogilny lay bleeding on the ice with his eyes closed and was wobbly while being helped off, towel to his face. There was no penalty called for a foul ruled inadvertent and Hitchcock's players had gotten the guy killing them out of the game. But there was little opportunity to capitalize on his absence.

Sundin got wide on Yushkevich and carried around the goal for a stuffer, stopped by Cechmanek. While Renberg knocked Primeau down with a cross check, Lapointe was late to pick up Kaberle, who lifted Sundin's rebound over the goalie's butterflying left pad to win the game, 4-3, at 7:20 of the second overtime.

It was, of course, a quiet Philadelphia locker room. "Somber is a good thing," said Captain Primeau, determined to stay upbeat after a hugely draining loss. Despite every failed effort to score the winner during the third period and overtimes, much of the defeat still came back to not being able to manage that quick 2-0 lead.

"Some terrible things are going to happen to you in the playoffs and some of them are going to be emotionally crushing," Hitchcock told the media. "How you recover, that's what it's all about."

Recalls Roenick, "Hitch was really supportive after that game. He was probably as mad as we were that we let it get away, but he said we played really good for the most part and there was nothing we could do to change how it turned out. He didn't act like he felt down. That helped.

"Game Threes are always so big in a series. Instead of having the upper hand, we were in a [bleeping] hole. It's only one game's difference, right? But it's a totally different feeling, a total mental letdown, especially when you play for as long as we had. It wasn't that we didn't still think we could win, but it's just such a momentum destroyer to lose like that with control of the series at stake. It's tough to put it away mentally.

"You hate to use the word do-or-die but that's what Game Four pretty much was for us."

With Mogilny unlikely to play Game Four, Roenick knew he was doomed to lose the battle of public relations on the off-day, not that he deflected any of his villainy by telling reporters, "I did my job well, whether I meant to do it or not."

He recalls: "Total accident, falling down, stick coming up, just one of those things, but everything is a conspiracy theory when you are playing against Toronto, with their media.

"That's OK. I knew right away I was going to be a marked man—even more than usual for the playoffs—because it was a key player I put out. Darcy (Tucker) was such a competitor—a gamer in every sense of the word—that I knew he was going to try and return the favor at any cost."

Indeed, Mogilny, suffering from concussion symptoms, did not dress and, of course, Tucker left Roenick his calling card on the first shift, hitting him into the end glass with a forearm to the head.

"I remember my cheek hitting the glass, then it was almost like a blackout," recalls Roenick. "Literally, everything went black and then all the stars came in.

"I laid there for a moment, had to get my bearings. I remember that I could get back to the bench, but I didn't feel solid."

Linesmen had intervened as Amonte shoved Tucker, who also got an earful from Roenick after he had been helped to the bench. "I was [bleeped]," J.R. recalls, but today, he doesn't feel it was a dirty hit.

"What a lot of media guys who never played the game don't get is that there's a difference between hitting to hurt and hitting to injure," Roenick says. "[Tucker would] want to put pain in your body, but not maim you or knock you out for life.

"His stick? Yeah, sometimes, but I did that, too. For the most part, he hit clean, not from behind. He'd run you straight on and fight you, too, because if you are going to play that way, you have to take accountability for the way you play. I respected him for sure."

On the next shift, a determined Handzus pushed the puck down the boards through two Leafs and got it to Recchi, who caught Belfour, concerned about LeClair coming up the middle, deep in the net. Recchi went short side to give the Philadelphia a 1-0 lead after just 1:16.

Primeau nailed Tucker cleanly with the body. With five hits in the first two minutes, the Flyers were fully engaged. Renberg responded to a tug on the arm with a slash and went to the box. But Williams turned over the puck and Travis Green, Mogilny's replacement in the lineup, fed up to McCabe and went to the net to take a pass that came through Weinrich. Cechmanek dropped to his knees and Green went up high for a shorthanded goal to tie the score less than three minutes after Philadelphia had gone ahead.

Green then went to the box for elbowing Lapointe, but the powerplay lasted for only 11 seconds, when Primeau was called for marginally interfering with Belfour. Roenick, who had not missed a shift, rocked Wesley with a shoulder check and, in the first minute of the second period, was quickly on Belfour as he tried to clear up the boards from behind the net. J.R. stripped the puck, scored easily on a wraparound, and the Flyers, holding Toronto to just six shots in the first two periods, took a 2-1 lead into the break.

Only 1:30 into the third period, however, Tucker suckered Roenick into a retaliation penalty. "A sinking feeling, pit of your stomach," he recalls. "You sit there in the box thinking, 'Boys, please just kill this one off.'"

Just 21 seconds later, J.R. was doing the skate of shame. Desjardins tried to tie up Roberts coming out of the corner and had his feet swept from under him by the Toronto winger. Cechmanek, too, lost his balance in the takedown, and had risen only as far as one knee when Sundin shot over the goalie's shoulder to tie the game 2-2.

Philadelphia received a four-minute powerplay opportunity when Yushkevich bled, if only slightly, from a Fitzgerald high stick. As Roenick poked at a puck Belfour was freezing, he was rocked again, this time by Nolan, but having already been burned for one retaliation. J.R. did nothing and Primeau, off a Johnsson passout, put the team's best chance on the man-advantage into Belfour's chest.

When Johnsson's broken-down drive hit the fortunate Leaf goalie, the shots were 33-10 in favor of the Flyers. But the Leafs killed an eighth Philadelphia powerplay opportunity after Roberts slashed Johnsson. The Flyers had utterly dominated for 60 minutes, but any sense of their inevitability was mitigated by their lack of confidence in their goaltender.

"It was excruciating," recalls Roenick. "Just exhausting.

"Have you ever sat in a dentist's chair and you think you are relaxed until you realize you've been tensing up the whole time? That's how we felt every time Toronto went into our zone. Our hearts were racing.

"[The Leafs] could feel us coming at them and carrying the play, so, yeah, I'm sure they knew that if we got enough chances, they were in trouble, just by the law of averages. But I don't think they sweated it out every time the puck went in their end quite the way we did because they knew they had the better goaltender.

"With Cechmanek, we didn't know what we were going to get. Sometimes he could be really good. Or, he could implode on us. We just didn't know what to expect."

In the second minute of overtime, Handzus jammed at a puck Therien had forced to the goalmouth, but it slid under Belfour and rolled just wide of the far post of a mostly-empty net. On the same shift, Cechmanek held the post as Roberts, wearing Primeau like a blanket, tried a wraparound.

Gagne, cutting between the post and Belfour scrambling back into the net, knocked the goalie down and drew an interference penalty. On Toronto's powerplay, Cechmanek picked up Svehla's drive through traffic and then stopped Jonas Hoglund off the wing following a Yushkevich turnover.

The same goalies who allowed shaky goals over the 60 minutes were dominating the duel.

"Between periods our veterans just kept selling, 'Push, push, push, we can push these guys out,'" recalls Hitchcock.

When the tie was unbroken with 20 extra minutes, the Flyers and Leafs were playing only the seventh playoff series in Stanley Cup history with consecutive multiple-overtime games.

In the second overtime, Tucker was free in the slot off a faceoff and was stoned by Cechmanek's right pad. Ragnarsson first hit the post, then, on another drive, hit Primeau before Belfour got a piece of the redirection with the shaft of his goalie stick. The Leafs cleared the puck off the line and soon Belfour stopped Williams on a partial breakaway.

One mistake would put Hitchcock's team in the deepest trouble, down 3-1, but the players pushed aside their anxiety and weariness and continued to be in charge territorially. "It wasn't a nervous feeling but one of 'keep going,'" recalls Weinrich. "We were outplaying them and felt we deserved to win the game."

Williams, going to the ice after his shot was blocked by Kaberle, still got the rebound away, but Belfour stopped it. Cechmanek made a pad stop on Reichel after a slick Hoglund pass, and Yushkevich blocked a Sundin attempt after he beat Kapanen circling out from behind the goal.

Belfour's 64th save of the game, on LeClair off a three on-two feed from Handzus in the final minute of the second extra session, deflected up so that the goalie could glove it.

"I'd played five overtimes," said Primeau, one of six Flyers who participated in the 2000 marathon at Pittsburgh. "Three overtimes was nothing."

Only the second game in Philadelphia history to get that far began with Sundin's drive ticking off the edge of Cechmanek's pad and rolling wide. Coming way out in an attempt to foil Nolan, the goalie scrambled back to win the race to the far post after Nolan picked up the blocked shot and circled the net.

Primeau took an extra jab at Belfour when he froze a puck, and McCabe threw three punches, but referees Don Koharski and Stephen Walkom had thrown away their whistles. The chances were 56-29 for the Flyers when Belfour fought off a Primeau shot from a Johnsson drop pass on Philadelphia's 73rd shot on goal, a team playoff record.

Handzus got a piece of a clear by Berg, and Yushkevich corralled the puck at center, quickly countering to Recchi breaking down the right wing with LeClair coming up the middle. "I saw both Johnny and Michal coming and I just wanted to put it on net," Recchi would say later. He shot from next to the left dot and the puck, broken down by Belfour's pad, dribbled over the line just before the hungry LeClair, who had a step on Reichel, could have tapped it in.

There was only stone silence, no music being played at the Air Canada Centre. But Recchi, standing behind the goal line, did a little dance regardless as LeClair and Handzus led the mob to the goal scorer.

An NHL-record 75th shot by one team had won the game, 3-2, at 13:54 of the third overtime, evening the series 2-2. And that still wasn't the best thing happening to Recchi that week. His wife, Alexa, was due to give birth to their third child the next day.

"The greatest thrill in your life is your children," said Recchi, quite the endorsement of fatherhood considering he had just been the ultimate hero of one of the most relentless performances in Flyer history, under some enormous pressure.

"It was a season-long process and we believed once we got there, we'd be good," said Recchi. "We played a tremendous game tonight."

They did it walking on a tightrope.

"Just by history standards, if we go down 3-1 we're probably toast, but if you lose in double overtime, then in triple OT to go down 3-1, there is no [bleeping] way you are coming back from that, I don't care who you are," recalls Roenick.

"Instead, we had just stared down the barrel of that gun and had come out on top. We knew how demoralizing that had to be for them after having us dead in the water. All they needed was one goal, no matter how they got it, regardless of anything else you want to talk about like shots or scoring chances or whatever. That had to be devastating, especially since they knew the other team had felt that same way the previous game and yet came back and beat them.

"For them, it had to be like, 'These guys just took our best punches after we already knocked them down and they kept coming at us.'

"All these things are in your mind, even if you don't say them. And think about this: We had just played five overtimes in two games, so it was almost like we'd already played five-and-two-thirds games against each other. We felt like we knew each other inside and out, so the Leafs knew us well enough that going back to Philly tied at 2-2 made it very, very tough for them."

Hitchcock, too, thought his team had become destined to win this series, yet didn't see how they were going to win the next round. "I knew after Game Four whoever came out of this was going to have nothing left," he recalls. "It came to feel like a 12-game series.

"We weren't a quick team or a young team; it was demanding and draining. We had pulled back on our forecheck a little and took the boards away a lot as the series went on, so the puck ended up on the boards more. There were more scrums, more grunting and grinding, and some of their key guys were getting frustrated. We could see that if we just kept on, we were going to be okay."

Nevertheless, he predicted to the media another overtime before the series ran its course. "I can feel it," said Hitchcock.

Mark Recchi puts a triple overtime goal past Ed Belfour for a 3-1 win in Game Four of the first round of the playoffs.

Despite a cut upper lip and a puffy cheek, Roenick was one of the few Flyers to show up at the Skate Zone the next afternoon, where he announced no intention of getting tested for a concussion. "I am not going to let those doctors near me," he said. "They can only cause trouble for me right now."

Inquirer beat reporter Tim Panaccio, trying to do a little baseline testing of his own, asked Roenick to count backwards. "I'm not even going to attempt it," he said. "I feel pretty good today, and I'm not going to mess with it."

Unconcerned about his own head, he tried to get into Tucker's about a flop the Leaf center had taken in Game Four, attempting to draw a penalty from an Amonte hit. "I used to do that in pee wee, but I got ridiculed by my teammates and stopped," Roenick said. "I can't imagine what [the Leafs], as professionals, are saying about it."

Cechmanek showed up at the practice rink, too, despite his long night. "He had to be huge," said Hitchcock. "His confidence grew from that. Even talking to him today, he is a much more confidant guy, which is good for us."

The stork brought the Recchis a boy, Austin. But the Leafs also had a blessed event—Mogilny's return—for Game Five at the First Union Center, and Berg converted a three-on-two just 2:34 into the match.

But the Flyers killed off a Recchi roughing penalty. And when Tucker got called for closing his hand on the puck, Johnsson's shot through a screen caromed off Kapanen's stick, went through Roenick's legs, and over Belfour's glove to tie it 1-1.

Roenick stripped Kaberle and fed Yushkevich, who had jumped into the slot, putting Philadelphia, territorially dominating the first period, ahead 2-1. Just after Desjardins had made the final clear to take Handzus off the hook for a goaltender interference penalty, Williams jumped off the bench to steal the puck from Jyrki Lumme and fed ahead to Gagne. He shot off Kaberle then fought him off at the net, as well, to put the rebound between Belfour's legs for a 3-1 Flyer lead.

Toronto's back was broken. With an ineffective Mogilny off for four minutes after cutting Primeau with a high stick, Kapanen, who had scored only four times in his 28 regular-season games following his February acquisition, converted a Weinrich powerplay rebound. Philadelphia cruised, 4-1, over the tired-looking Leafs to create an opportunity to wrap up the series.

The team would have to do it without Desjardins, though. Early in the third period, his right foot was broken by a Svehla shot, putting the defenseman out for at least two weeks, when the bone would be x-rayed again. "I knew right away that it was pretty bad," said Desjardins.

It was worse for his team.

"A lot of times, parts are interchangeable; he was not a replaceable part," recalls Primeau. "He was just so calming, would never say anything in the room, just would listen to what you had to say and go out and do his job."

Hitchcock had no choice but to try to downplay the effect of losing his best defenseman. "Jimmy Vandermeer is ready to play," said the coach. "He has been captain on a Memorial Cup Champion (at Red Deer, Alberta) and knows what it is like in big games. He will be our most physical defenseman, a lot like Eric Weinrich."

Weinrich and Johnsson would take most of the duty against Mogilny, Sundin and Roberts. Hitchcock could only hope his new top pair would be as harassing as the fan in a Leaf jersey who walked up to the Flyer coaches sipping coffee at a Tim Hortons around the corner from the team's Royal York Hotel headquarters on the morning of Game Six and emptied a cup on the head man.

It hit Hitchcock mostly in the chest and he was unburned. "And then there was the one-and-a-half block walk to the arena," the coach recalls. "Nothing but abuse; it was not fun."

The desperate Leafs didn't figure to be any barrel of laughs that evening. Antropov, who was supposed to be out for the series, suited up. One more sign that, like their fans, the Leafs were not drinking decaf.

Hitchcock's team, having successfully killed an early Lapointe penalty, had been outchanced 6-2 when Brashear couldn't get the puck up the wall past Renberg. Cechmanek made a save on Reichel, but the winger reached partially over the net for the rebound and, in the process, knocked off the goalie's catcher.

Both puck and glove slid to the corner, where Ragnarsson retrieved the equipment and slid it back towards the crease. Cechmanek was in the process of picking it up as Reichel's shot flew over the goalie's shoulder and into the net for the first score of the game.

Late in the first period, after Gagne was in alone, but too close to lift a Primeau feed puck over Belfour's pad, Cechmanek got lucky when a Roberts wraparound went under the goalie's pad and just missed on the far side. After Philadelphia was penalized for having too many men on the ice, Ragnarsson saved a goal by deflecting a Mogilny try at the side of the net up into the screen. The Leafs, who had been outplayed badly in the previous two games, this time were getting the majority of chances.

Roenick, racing Svehla for a puck in the corner, tumbled as a result of a stick in the midsection, went into the boards head first, and then hit his face on the ice. He rose slowly but, after Kapanen had impressively ground down Mogilny along the boards at center, J.R. had plenty of energy to follow the Flyers' Flying Finn up ice, take his drop pass, and fire from just above the faceoff dot between Belfour's arm and body to tie the game, 1-1.

Cechmanek came out to stone McCabe, who had been sent in by Mogilny, before the goalie threw his stick at the puck trying to break up a Domi goalmouth pass to Reichel. Dan Marouelli called a penalty shot but, as the fans at the Air Canada Centre rose, Reichel made no move and just slapped the puck into Cechmanek 's chest to keep the score even.

In the third period, Kapanen's churning legs drew the first Toronto penalty of the game, by Sundin, but Philadelphia created no good chances on the powerplay. Belfour was alert on a deflection by Brashear from Murray, and then closed the five-hole on Gagne after a steal at center.

Vandermeer, disoriented on a hard hit by Fitzgerald, wobbled back to the bench, but not before Therien deposited Fitzgerald there, head over heels. The Flyers, standing up well on Mogilny rushes, held Toronto without a superior third-period chance until a minute to go in regulation, when Wesley had time to close to the top of the circle, but hit Cechmanek in the shoulder.

With Vandermeer unable to return, Philadelphia continued to play with five defensemen. In the overtime, Therien stayed with Mogilny one-on-one after Johnsson's miss had rimmed out of the zone and the Leaf star shot off the glass. When Toronto was penalized for too many men, Weinrich threw away the puck twice in 10 seconds, forcing Cechmanek to make stops on Sundin and Nolan. But when the Flyer goalie coughed it up as the penalty was expiring, Weinrich cleared the danger away.

Cechmanek, who was fortunate no Leaf was at the back post when a Wesley dump-in off the boards bounced out between the goalie's legs, then made the save of the game from his back by throwing a pad up on a Sundin backhand from point-blank range.

The netminder looked behind him when Svehla played a carom and shot from the circle, but made the stop and then another on a point-blank Roberts redirect of a Mogilny passout. At the other end, a Wesley sweepcheck denied Gagne just when it looked like he was in.

When the second extra period began, the two teams were playing the first series in NHL history to have three multi-overtime games. Cechmanek continued to come up huge, saving Ragnarsson when he fanned on an easy clearing attempt allowing Roberts to cut in, then stoning Reichel after he got outside.

At the other end, Roenick had a chance set up by Kapanen, but Belfour got it with his arm. Gagne also had the series on his stick off a Williams passout, but the winger's arm was hooked as he shot.

Thirty minutes of extra time had been played when Primeau, at the half-wall, couldn't bang the puck past Svehla. Cechmanek missed gloving a shot going wide and, at the other side of the goal, Tucker banked if off the sprawling goalie as he came across.

Yushkevich couldn't turn in time and Green swooped in to lift the water bottle with a backhander into the top of the net. At 10:51 of the second overtime, all of Cechmanek's efforts had been wasted. The Leafs had forced Game Seven with a 2-1 victory.

"The difference in the game was they had more players who were desperate," said Hitchcock. "But what are you going to say? It's a double overtime game on the road and one shot wins.

"We're going to put everything on the line (in Game Seven). Trust me on that."

The Leafs couldn't have had any players more spent than Roenick, still feeling the effects of his pitchforking by Svehla. "I had a lot of trouble skating in the second and third periods," J.R. told reporters. "I caught my leg really, really hard in the corner and hit everything on the glass.

"Nice to see Toronto fans like seeing people get hurt."

For four of the last five springs, Philadelphia fans had not liked seeing their team lose in the first round. Now they were one defeat away from hating it again. Television, plus a lacrosse conflict in Toronto, had dictated two two-day breaks in the course of the first six contests. For the first time in the NHL since 1950, a Game Seven would follow Game Six without a night off.

This was an absurdly short turnaround considering that just the regulation 60 minutes the following night at the First Union Center would make this the longest series in league history in terms of minutes played.

To make matters worse, both teams were on the tarmac at Toronto's Pearson International Airport for about 90 minutes before they could take off. It was at 2 a.m.—let the record show 15 minutes before the Leafs arrived at their hotel—that the Flyer bus pulled up at Philadelphia's Four Seasons Hotel in Logan Square, which they had booked for solitude and convenience.

In lieu of holding a morning skate, as per the team's usual routine, Hitchcock instead conducted a meeting.

"I'm not lost in a Game Seven," the coach, who was 2-0 in them at Dallas, later would tell Rich Hofmann of the *Daily News*. "I know you just can't get all emotional.

"There's a certain balance between emotion and execution, and execution becomes critical when your legs and mind are a little tired. So we went over a lot of stuff, every little detail.

"It was the longest meeting we'd had, but we wanted the players to feel confident what we were doing was right and then they could just go out and play."

Vandermeer, knocked out of Game Six, was ready to go. Hitchcock made just one other change in the lineup—Somik for Murray on the fourth line. His unshaken team was in no need for any further shakeup.

"Listen, you want to finish it off in Game Six and you hate to give a team like that another chance," recalls Roenick. "But this was nothing like after (losing in double overtime in) Game Three because, when we had gotten up 3-2 in the series, we knew we had two chances to win it.

"Game Seven at home is what you play for all year. We had played a hell of a lot of hockey against these guys. We knew we could beat them one more time."

Remembers Primeau, "If we were going to exorcise some demons, that was the matchup for us—a competitive team that other teams didn't want to play but that we had no problem playing.

"I gave them credit for pushing us to seven, but they had expended a lot of energy (in Game Six). I just knew we were going to win."

Perhaps that confidence seeped into the game presentation meeting, no attendees remembering why the decision was made to not have Lauren Hart sing "God Bless America," either solo or in duet with Kate Smith.

The First Union Center was wired regardless, but both teams looked tight in a whistle-prone first period. Handzus had the best chance, set up by a LeClair steal from Svehla, but shot wide. Kapanen's 17th hit of the series put down Mogilny. Williams was penalized for jumping on Belfour after he covered the puck, but Cechmanek made a powerplay save on Wesley off a Therien giveaway.

It was still scoreless into the final four minutes of the first period when Primeau dumped the puck to the corner, then cut off Belfour's attempt to clear up the opposite wall. The Flyer captain fed behind the goal line to Williams, who relayed through Kaberle to an all-alone Gagne, who had beaten Antropov to the slot. Gagne shot across Belfour's body, high to the stick side, for the game's first goal at 16:23.

In the final minute of the period, Lapointe pushed the puck past Nolan at center and raced ahead to feed it by Antropov to Williams, who got his stick down despite an attempted tie-up by Berg. The puck deflected past Belfour's stick side, about halfway up the net. Philadelphia had stunningly struck twice within 2:47 to take a two-goal lead into the locker room.

They still had to kill a carryover penalty on Weinrich for taking down Renberg and did, the Leafs managing no shots. The ice resumed tilting the Flyers' way as Primeau drew two Toronto penalties—a hook by Lumme and a gratuitous slash by Belfour—within 54 seconds.

The second penalty was expiring just as Yushkevich's keep-in turned up the puck for Kapanen, who tipped it to Williams. Primeau cut behind the net and tried to feed Gagne in front, but Kaberle deflected the puck off Mogilny and inside the post. Primeau's first playoff goal since the one in the fifth overtime three years earlier in Pittsburgh put Philadelphia up 3-0.

"I don't know if I was ever this nervous before games," the captain would say later. "My teammates bailed me out."

On the contrary, Primeau—scoring, drawing penalties, and running over any Leaf in his path—was dominating.

When he tied up Roberts at center ice, the Leaf retaliated and took a penalty, but Toronto got the next goal, a Roberts deflection of a Lumme point drive while Cechmanek was being interfered with by Sundin.

The irate goalie banged his stick on the ice at the non-call, but not to worry.

Less than three minutes later, Lumme, pressured by Lapointe,

Center Claude Lapointe corrals the puck and scores the final goal in a 6-1 Game Seven win to eliminate the Maple Leafs.

couldn't get the puck by Vandermeer, who shot. When Belfour failed to control, Lapointe put the rebound off a post, where it caromed to Recchi at the other one for a tap-in that restored the three-goal lead.

"When Mark scored that goal, the burden was lifted," Hitchcock would say. "We floated."

Wesley and a clearly frustrated Belfour, who elbowed LeClair in the corner, took penalties in the final minute of the period. Recchi's attempt was blocked by McCabe, but Belfour barely moved as the winger, still at a deep angle, nailed the net on the second try for his sixth goal of the series. In the third period, Lapointe, completing a three-point night, converted a two-on-one with LeClair.

"Never a Doubt" read the message from Signman Dave Leonardi, as the Flyers finished off the most grueling series in their history going away, 6-1, outshooting the Leafs 36-19 in Game Seven and bringing their favorable shot differential over the marathon 472 minutes of the series to 93. Philadelphia had outscored Toronto 14-3 in the final three games at the First Union Center.

Roenick, the compulsive hugger, gave Tucker a big one in the handshake line, no hard feelings. Hitchcock's team had embraced all the baggage that came from four first-round losses in five years to win the most redemptive victory for the franchise since Mike Keenan's first team in 1985, when the Flyers buried nine straight playoff game defeats with a sweep of three close games against the Rangers.

Quinn noted his opponent's burden and congratulated Philadelphia for shucking it off. "What happens in series that go long and hard is that mental toughness comes into play," said the Toronto coach. "In the last five years when they went out in the first round, the Flyers haven't displayed those things.

"Maybe they finally know how to play when the pressure is on. They did a heckuva job tonight. It could be the young kids, could have been the old guys, but they all looked pretty good as the game went on. Early on, we were fine, but they kept their game up and we didn't."

Hitchcock was like a teacher pinning stars on his pupils' heads.

"You don't get [a true) evaluation on your players until they're stretched right to the mental and physical limit," he said. "You have no idea what they have until they've stretched it to where you don't even know if they can get up anymore. And some players are never the same.

"You either get worse or better. I was curious to see what we would do, and we got better. So for those guys who have been around here, it means a lot. The baggage that you carry with you for not winning is a helluva burden and you notice the stress on the players. So I'm really happy that they not only won, but played their best game."

Primeau had carried the greatest load of the 11 holdovers from the Ottawa debacle of a year earlier. "We all know because of what happened last year there was a lot of pressure on me," he told reporters. "I had to meet that challenge head-on.

"For the health of our club, we needed to find a way past the first round. And, for me personally, I didn't want it to be my last game as a Philadelphia Flyer. Because of the stage we set and the way it came down, Ed Snider said if we don't have any success it would be the players who would be moved. Ultimately, being the most vocal, I was most probably the guy."

He wasn't the only player with permission to take the arrows out of his back. Recchi, who had gone scoreless like all the big guns in the Ottawa debacle and had endured long droughts during the regular season, had enjoyed his rebirth as a clutch scorer at age 35, thanks in part to a revamped workout regimen by strength and conditioning coach Jim McCrossin.

"There are always doubts that creep into your mind, but it was all pointed to one thing, playing well in the playoffs," Recchi said.

Weinrich recalls being happiest for someone who had been lost for the series in Game Four. "I really felt that we won that series for Eric Desjardins, too," Weinrich remembers. "That was a really good feeling for me to have him in the room when we came off the ice.

"For us to be moving on meant there was a chance he would be healthy enough to play again in the playoffs."

For only the second time in five years, the Flyers were advancing, and, despite it all, behind Cechmanek, too. "I am so happy," he said. "It's my first time going through the first round. I think that, in Toronto, a couple hockey experts don't trust me in this series."

The anxiety had been palpable. "There's always pressure," recalls Roenick. "But it builds every year you are not successful.

"I was always way more nervous in the first round than the second because I bowed out too many times early. I was in Phoenix for five years with mediocre teams, going in knowing you would be lucky to get out of the first round. Now I was on a team with expectations. And that made it harder.

"You lose in the first round, you might as well not even make the playoffs, in my opinion. You see a lot of first-round upsets almost every year. Get through that, and you can just play hockey again."

For all the talk about a lightened load, Hitchcock went into the next series, against Presidents' Trophy winner Ottawa, most worried about his players' heavy legs.

"The fatigue factor (that spring) was huge," he recalls. "We once had as many as 12 guys at a practice. The rest of the time there were only eight, nine, 10."

But if his team was tired, the coach swore he wasn't weary of Cechmanek's act, and had learned how to roll with his rolling goalie.

"My view with him is that there is always something bizarre going to happen so you just have to live with it," said Hitchcock. "I've never had a goalie who lost his glove and got scored on when he was looking for it, yet I've never had a goalie make that save he did on Sundin in overtime.

"You expect the unexpected so you don't get all revved up. That's what Roman is."

Perhaps the Flyers could live with Cechmanek's quirks this series better than the last. Ottawa goalie Patrick Lalime, virtually untested the previous spring, wasn't considered around the league to be money in the bank either.

No checks had bounced for the Senators—who had filed for bankruptcy protection in January—during their dominant regular season, or while bouncing the Islanders in five games. So Ottawa entered the quarterfinal rested, undistracted and as a clear favorite, not only because of the ease with which it had dispatched Philadelphia the previous spring. Already a fast and highly skilled team, the Senators had added grit at the trading deadline in Vaclav Varada and Bryan Smolinski.

"If you played hard against Toronto and competed in the right areas, you got scoring chances," warned Hitchcock. "You won't see those chances against Ottawa."

But at least the Flyers had the opportunity to work up some enmity for the Senators that had been absent 12 months earlier.

"I had more of a hatred for Ottawa the second time around than the first time," recalls Roenick. "I [bleeping] hated (Daniel) Alfredsson and all those guys. Losing built that emotion."

But not much confidence. "I remember I didn't like the matchup," recalls Primeau. "They had Stanley Cup caliber talent for a few years.

"As I look back, we couldn't figure out why Toronto always had such success against Ottawa (eliminating the Senators in 2002 and 2004), but I guess it was because [the Leafs] intimidated them.

"When we would try to intimidate the Senators, they'd just laugh at us. Then we would want to fight them and they wouldn't do anything, so how do you get under their skin? As much as Toronto was a good draw for us, Ottawa was a bad draw."

Nevertheless, on the first two Flyer shots of the series, the Senators looked like bowling pins begging to go down. Amonte, who had not scored in 24 shots on goal against the Leafs, got a step on Wade Redden to take a breakaway pass from Roenick and beat Lalime over his shoulder at 1:19.

Amonte then forced Karel Rachunek behind the net and Roenick's shot was deflected off the defenseman into the goalmouth, where Kapanen pounced. After 10:48, Philadelphia was leading 2-0 and had as many goals as it had scored in the entire series the year earlier.

The Senators, who had been off seven days, looked less than fully engaged. Early in the second period, Hitchcock's team pressured during a carryover penalty to Mike Fisher but couldn't get a third goal before Ottawa received a break to cut the lead in half. Martin Havlat's shot from straight up the slot deflected off Brashear's stick, then Johnsson, and Cechmanek was unable to close his legs.

Less than two minutes later, Marian Hossa circled around the goal almost out to the blueline with Weinrich unable to move the Ottawa star off the puck. Curtis Leschyshyn's shot from the circle caromed off Johnsson, then Smolinski, and Hossa converted to Cechmanek's short side to tie the game. When Vandermeer was penalized for tripping Varada, Radek Bonk beat Lapointe on the next faceoff and fed Alfredsson, whose 30-foot wrister went over Cechmanek's blocker. Three goals in 6:58 had put Ottawa ahead, 3-2.

Hitchcock called time out to pointedly remind the Flyers the series had started. They settled down, but other than a two-on-one stop against Handzus, fed by LeClair, Philadelphia had minimal chances the rest of the way. Hope for a comeback effectively ended when Hossa's passout, redirected by Zdeno Chara, hit Cechmanek's right skate as he turned, helping the puck over the line. Referee Bill McCeary waived off the goal but, after a review, it was credited, and the Flyers, 4-2 losers, had failed to take advantage of Ottawa's rust.

"[Cechmanek] is going to have to be better than he was today, I'm not going to hide from it," said Hitchcock.

Neither did the goalie. "I have to be better," he agreed and, in Game Two, he was. As was John LeClair of whom Clarke had said,"The defense is beating on him and he has to beat back."

Six minutes in, Cechmanek came way out to make one of his slid-

ing saves on Shaun Van Allen. Before a minute more had been played, Gagne, on a new line with Primeau and Brashear, walked out, used a Primeau screen on Wade Redden, and nailed the far side about half way up the net to put Philadelphia ahead, 1-0.

The Flyers let up on their forecheck, forcing Cechmanek to be at his diving, flopping best, acrobatically stopping Fisher, Bonk and Chris Neil. Through six powerplay opportunities, the Senators bombed away, but the goalie made a kick save on Redden, then stoned Hossa off a carom from the backboards.

Unable to cleanly glove a Bonk drive, Cechmanek stopped the Hossa rebound. Philadelphia entered the third period outshot for only the second time in nine playoff games, but its goalie continued to hold on, charging out to stymie Smolinski cutting off the wing, dropping down on a dangerous redirection by Alfredsson, and refusing to get flustered when run over by Magnus Arvedson.

The chances were 24-14 for Ottawa when Rachunek fanned on a puck and the embattled LeClair beat Redden's hip check and started a two-on-one with Recchi, Handzus trailing. Recchi faked, pulled the puck back and was almost to the goal line when he sent it under the dives of Fisher, Rachunek, and the flopping Lalime with 6:58 remaining.

The 2-0 series-tying victory was Cechmanek's triumph. He had seized the moment and, in the postgame, the Flyers took the opportunity to pump up his ego, Hitchcock even going as far as to praise him as a leader. "I know everybody looks for technical stuff in him, but his technique is athleticism," said the coach. "He just needed to let the play come to him, calm down; he's very good when he plays like that."

Johnsson had needed 25 stitches on the eyelid to close a wound from an uncalled Martin Havlat high stick. Sensing his tired team needed more than just home ice in Game Three to raise its emotional level, the coach used his postgame press conference to complain about errant Senator sticks, then with anger—real or feigned—walked away before the last question was asked.

Hitchcock was saving his best material to make Ottawa's alleged spearchucking the off-day story. Havlat said he had merely been trying to lift his stick over Johnsson's head and had gotten lucky that it wasn't called, but Hitchcock insisted it had been careless nevertheless.

"It came within an eyelash of ending his season and potentially ending [Johnsson's career]," said the coach. "Put your bloody stick down."

He claimed four cut Flyer faces thanks to Ottawa sticks, all of them uncalled. Primeau chimed in his annoyance at getting cut by Alfredsson on the first shift. "If you look at their past series, they've sent guys for stitches," said Primeau.

All this put the Senators, long accused of being wimps, in stitches. "I've never heard this about us before," Arvedson said. "If anything, people are saying we're too nice."

Hitchcock dressed Todd Fedoruk for Game Three at the First Union Center. On his first shift, he gave the puck away but, luckily, Alfredsson hit the post. Philadelphia was no more physical than it had been the first two games, but the team was more efficient, holding the Senators to just four first-period shots.

Amonte was tripped by Arvedson on a Roenick setup and Lalime made the save, but LeClair was lost by Senator coverage as he came off the bench to replace Kapanen and found the rebound before Leschyshyn did. At 4:35, the Flyers had the first goal for the third consecutive game.

When Roenick and Varada confronted each other at the end of the period, the teams played four-on-four to start the second until Lapointe was called for interfering with Todd White. On the powerplay, Alfredsson pounced on a shot Primeau had blocked and, before Cechmanek could reset himself, tied the game.

But Philadelphia bounced back to take another lead. Kapanen, set up by a good pass from Amonte, scored on a riser that ticked off Lalime's glove, his shoulder, and into the net.

Handzus missed on a two-on-one off a broken-down shot and was robbed by Lalime's left pad after a steal. But that was one of only three shots the Flyers had managed in the period when, in its final minute, LeClair wrapped up Chara as they went to the corner. LeClair, going in headfirst, got the worst of the contact with the boards and, in addition to a cut, a holding penalty that carried over into the third period.

It took only 22 seconds after the break for the Senators to take advantage. When Cechmanek dropped his stick making a paddle-down save at the post, Hossa circled the net and wrapped the puck to tie the score, 2-2. Lalime soon made a save on a LeClair blast from the top of the circle. But most of the few chances thereafter by both teams belonged to Ottawa.

In overtime, Cechmanek stood up to make saves on Hossa and Rachunek and got a piece on an Alfredsson drive from the top of the circle. The best Philadelphia chance disappeared when Amonte lost the puck on a backhand-to-forehand move.

Hitchcock's team had been outshot 6-2 when Varada played a Bonk dump-in and rimmed the puck to Redden, who, from a deep angle along the left boards, shot though three Flyers, the screening Varada, and Cechmanek's short side to win the game, 3-2, at 6:43.

"Under one guy's arm, between a stick and a body, then short side," said the Flyer coach after looking at the replay. "Unbelievable."

Also, distressing, since it was becoming more and more clear that his club would need superlative goaltending like Cechmanek had provided in Game Two in order to win the series.

Redden told reporters it appeared Philadelphia had worn down as the game went along. Yushkevich agreed, not something a player on the losing side often admits. "It seems like we're losing track of our games, losing focus," said the defenseman, who was playing with a separated shoulder. "Maybe we're getting mentally tired because of the series against Toronto."

The re-evaluation of Desjardins' foot had left no hope of getting him back before the Stanley Cup Final, if then. A plate was inserted and he was fitted with a cast. There was no cavalry coming. The Flyers would have to rescue themselves.

Hitchcock told his team, just 5-for-42 on the powerplay during the playoffs, that it had to shoot from some bad angles, just as Redden had done. The points were too well covered by coach Jacques Martin's use of the 6-9 Chara and 6-3 Chris Phillips. Philadelphia was afraid blocked shots would send the well-schooled Senators the other way. So, while the Flyers were not as totally befuddled negotiating the Senator trap as a year earlier, it still was exhausting work getting through center ice.

"It's very wearing," said Hitchcock. "When we get to the net, we're almost too tired."

To hang in, his players would have to keep their shifts short. A lead would help, too, and Handzus provided it in Game Four, winning a faceoff from Fisher and redirecting from well above the faceoff dot a shot that Therien had launched from along the boards. It flew over the shoulder of Lalime 17:06 into the first period.

"To be that far out, it was very lucky," Handzus recalls, but whatever the role of any unseen hand, Philadelphia, re-energized by a 1-0 lead, was prepared to use it.

Hitchcock went often to a fourth line of Lapointe, Williams and Somik and the Flyers chipped the puck out and made the Senators do all the work this time. "It's a lot easier to save your energy when you have the lead," Alfredsson would say. "You waste a lot chasing."

One minute into the third period, a Chara drive from 45 feet went off Cechmanek's skate, behind him, and just missed the opposite corner. The goalie got away with taking the net off as Smolinski circled for a wraparound, then made a diving arm save on Arvedson after being forced into a giveaway behind the net.

All the Ottawa chances were one and done, however. Philadelphia played almost perfectly through the last desperate minutes, forcing the Senators, having nowhere to go with the puck through center, into an icing with 1:23 remaining.

Primeau, who won 12 of 17 draws, mostly against Bonk, controlled two more in the defensive zone in the final two minutes. Ragnarsson made a good reverse to bank the puck out after Roenick missed the empty net. A superlative checking effort and Cechmanek's 1-0 shutout, his second of the series, tied it at two games apiece.

"They played hard, played physical and wore us down," Fisher said. "And they were more composed with the puck at the end."

The Flyers were getting tired of suggestions in the media that they were tired. "From the coach on down, the attitude was 'We're going to push through this,'" recalls Esche.

Having done it once, they still had to do it through two more wins, a daunting task. "They were a talented offensive team and played at a pretty high pace," recalls Weinrich. "After that first series, I was definitely dragging and I think a lot of guys were running out of gas."

Hitchcock started what had appeared to be the freshest guys—Lapointe, Williams and Somik—in Game Five at the Corel Center. It paid off when Brashear picked off a Neil pass up the middle, circled back into the neutral zone, and banked the puck off the boards to a breaking Lapointe behind Leschyshyn and Anton Volchenkov. Lapointe chased down the lead and scored off Lalime's shoulder just 21 seconds into the contest, the fifth time Philadelphia scored first in the series.

Twenty-one seconds later, Roenick stole the puck from Rachunek and shot from the dot, but Lalime dropped and made a pad save. When LeClair, going off the ice, half waved on a chance to backhand the puck deep, Redden stopped it, gave it to a countering Smolinski, who fired from 50 feet on the charging Cechmanek. The shot bounced off Ragnarsson's stick, the post, and went in over the goalie's shoulder at 7:15 to tie the game on just the second shot by Ottawa.

The Flyers weren't demoralized. Recchi hit the post after Primeau spun away behind the net, and Cechmanek robbed Havlat on a toe-drag move. But Yushkevich put his stick between Havlat's legs and Ottawa cashed in on the penalty. Primeau lost the draw to Bonk and Cechmanek didn't pick up Alfredsson's long drive through traffic. The puck whizzed past the goalie's left shoulder, putting Ottawa ahead 2-1.

In the second period, Primeau got bloodied in the face again, this time by the stick of Arvedson. It looked like Cechmanek, who made a good pokecheck when Varada beat Amonte with an inside move, would keep Philadelphia in the game until Arvedson dropped off the puck on a line rush, took Vandermeer to the net, and Havlat put in his own deep angle rebound that Cechmanek had been unable to control in his chest. The Senators went ahead 3-1 and the Flyers' play sagged. Roenick went to the box for high sticking Arvedson and, 27 seconds into the penalty, a Hossa passout trapped three Philadelphia players behind the net. Bonk beat Cechmanek's pokecheck at the side of the goal to make the score 4-1.

That was all for Cechmanek, but not for Ottawa. Peter Schaefer stole the puck from Johnsson along the boards, cut off the wing, and flipped a shorthanded backhander over Esche's glove to make the score 5-1. Somik's rebound goal got one back for the Flyers, but they had no energy to stage a comeback, only to provoke scrums at the end of a 5-2 defeat that left them one game from elimination.

"I don't know how you can fault [Cechmanek], the first two goals were deflections off a stick and off [Lapointe's] pants," argued Hitchcock. But the coach was grasping at straws and knew it.

"I thought we were coming on in the middle of the series, that we were getting a little more energy," he recalls. "But they had so many dominant players who were much quicker than we were.

"I said to [my assistants] once that it looked like we were rowing a boat. Exhausted. It would come out late in games, late in periods."

Nevertheless, Philadelphia had summoned the energy to play a stirring Game Four and had been at their best in a must-win Game Seven of the Toronto series. The Kate Smith-Lauren Hart duet, guaranteed to get hearts pumping, was cued up.

But fewer than three minutes into Game Six, Schaefer poked the puck away from Johnsson on a breakout. Williams lunged for Havlat and was beaten by a quick, blind, backhanded pass, leaving Schaefer all alone to sweep the puck by an overcommitted Cechmanek 2:41 into the game.

The Flyers had a chance to get it back when Van Allen was called for hooking. But Arvedson threw the puck off the sidewall for a breaking Fisher, who blasted the Senators' second goal, shorthanded, over the goalie's shoulder, 2-0.

The First Union Center fell silent. Brashear slew footed Neil and

Gagne's stick landed on Smolinski's shoulder, forcing Philadelphia to kill four minutes in penalties the rest of the period. There had been only one good chance, by Amonte off the rush, but Lalime kicked the puck out and Ottawa flipped it into the neutral zone.

Seven minutes into the second period, Arvedson took down Lapointe going to the net and the white-towel-waving crowd tried to coax the Flyers back into the game. But Lalime dropped down to stop Primeau's backhand, then made another save on Recchi during a scramble for a rebound.

When Brashear was called for mindlessly shoving Chara to the ice at the point while the Senators were cycling the puck out of the corner, the Philadelphia tough guy's second penalty of the game effectively ended it. Hossa sped outside Therien and Cechmanek kicked the shot up the slot, where Alfredsson fired right back to make the score 3-0.

Smolinski caught Cechmanek way out again, when White's pass went through Recchi for a tap-in to build the lead to 4-0. Handzus pounced on a deflected Williams pass and shot a backhander over Lalime's shoulder to get Philadelphia on the board but, midway in the third period, Havlat won a race with Therien for a flipped-out puck, waited for Cechmanek to slide, and had the empty net.

Whatever fans remained in their seats booed the goalie. "I know, I heard what people say," Cechmanek said after the 5-1 rout won the series for Ottawa in six games. "They hate me.

"I don't know why they hate me, hate our team."

Actually, they had loved the 2002-03 Flyers until the absence of Desjardins, disappointing specialty teams, a loaded Ottawa club, and the long, hard series against the Leafs wore Hitchcock's team down.

"Toronto was so physically tiring, I didn't think we had anything left," recalls Kapanen.

Ottawa, meanwhile, had Hossa and more Hossa in reserve.

"He was the most dominant player I ever coached against in a series," Hitchcock recalls. "We didn't have an answer for him."

Hossa was part of the reason Ottawa was at the top of an opportunity to dominate the Eastern Conference over the next few years, as Hitchcock emphasized at his postgame press conference.

"I just think we got beat by a better team," he said. "They close on you so fast and hard, you have no time to make any plays. Our focus moving forward is discussing how we are going to catch Ottawa.

"We needed a better start. When they got that lead, our guys who had quickness and puck strength earlier in the playoffs had nothing. Something I've learned is that you need a [relatively easy] series early on. But that takes nothing away from Ottawa. I thought they played great, the last two games especially. Over the series, their foot speed and size started to show.

"Our performance was heartfelt. We saw a lot of good things this year. You have to go through some tough times to build some resolve."

Primeau's worst fears had proven true. "They began to push it up and we didn't stay with their tempo," he told reporters. But today he believes that the Flyers also had been scarred from the debacle of the previous spring.

"Even if we were a resilient team in that series before the end of it, I still think we had a kind of a mental block against Ottawa," recalls Primeau. "Hitch saw it too."

The coach also witnessed a need for change that he outlined to reporters while his players gathered their belongings at the Skate Zone the day following their elimination.

"There are young players who have top-end talent that we need to work hard in developing," Hitchcock said. "We can't catch Ottawa if we continue to use the same guys in the same roles."

He praised Primeau for already accepting a checking role and suggested Recchi (age 35) and LeClair (soon to turn 34) had to follow.

"People have to accept less," said Hitchcock. "I don't think, quite frankly, we are going to get any better with our older players. They are who they are right now."

Of course Roenick kind of liked what he was.

"It was just another challenge by Hitch; something to think about over the summer," J.R. recalls. "He'd do this maniacal brainwashing thing where he'd get all this [bleep] turning over and over in your head about who you really were as a player and what you needed to be for the team.

"He wanted you a little apprehensive. But that's part of what made Hitch such a good coach. He wanted you to become the player—the complete player—you should be. He made you think. Making me think never is a good thing but no, seriously, Hitch is so good like that."

LeClair didn't shrug it off quite so easily. He realized that only his huge contract with three years to run was going to keep him in Philadelphia.

"I took it as, 'You're no longer useful to me,'" LeClair recalls. "Hitch is a good coach, but tough to like sometimes as a person.

"My shoulder still wasn't right; I couldn't handle the puck as well as I was used to doing and wasn't confident when I came back. So yeah, it's frustrating when your time gets cut."

The old goalie, Cechmanek, 32, was expected to learn new tricks, too. "I think he succumbed to the pressure," said Hitchcock, who added that "a look in the mirror" could enable the Flyers to go forward with the Czech.

"Eddie (Belfour) made changes in his game at age 32-33 to become a better goaltender," said Hitchcock. "I think Roman has tremendous competitive instincts, but aspects show up when you play the same team over and over again that you have to work on.

"I think he's a lot like our team. There's another gear that has to be obtained."

Clarke, however, had long reached the conclusion that an entirely new vehicle was needed in the nets, never mind Cechmanek's career goals-against average of 1.97—the lowest among NHL netminders with at least 150 regular-season games since 1943-44. Unfortunately, he had won only one playoff series in his four with Philadelphia.

"For me, it was over as soon as he asked out and tried to quit (the previous spring)," recalls the GM. "He was implying the team quit on him.

"We kept him another year because we had no good choice."

Clarke broke the news to the media when he spoke seven days following the Flyer elimination.

"It would be difficult to bring Roman back and I don't think he wants to come back," said Clarke after talking to the goalie's agent, Petr Svoboda. "You could tell by Roman's response at the end of the year—he felt fans didn't like him and that he was getting all the blame.

"He's runner-up for the Vezina one year, tied for the lowest goals-against in the league. And then his playoffs have been inconsistent. He shuts a team out one night and when you get down to the nitty-gritty, he lets in a soft goal. It takes so much out of your team."

Both Hitchcock and Cechmanek, who felt they had spoken productively on breakup day about the mental steps the goalie had to take, were surprised. Svoboda insisted that, unlike a year ago, he had not sought a trade for his client. "Bob called me, I didn't call him," said Svoboda. "Roman never said he didn't want to come back."

Regardless, this wasn't Cechmanek's decision to make. On May 28, he was traded to Los Angeles for a second-round draft choice. "This is great for me," Cechmanek said. "Maybe I play different hockey now."

Hitchcock, too, realized divorce was best for all parties.

"I liked Roman," the coach recalls. "He was a little bizarre at times, but he played good for me.

"But his personality was creating a division, guys wondering

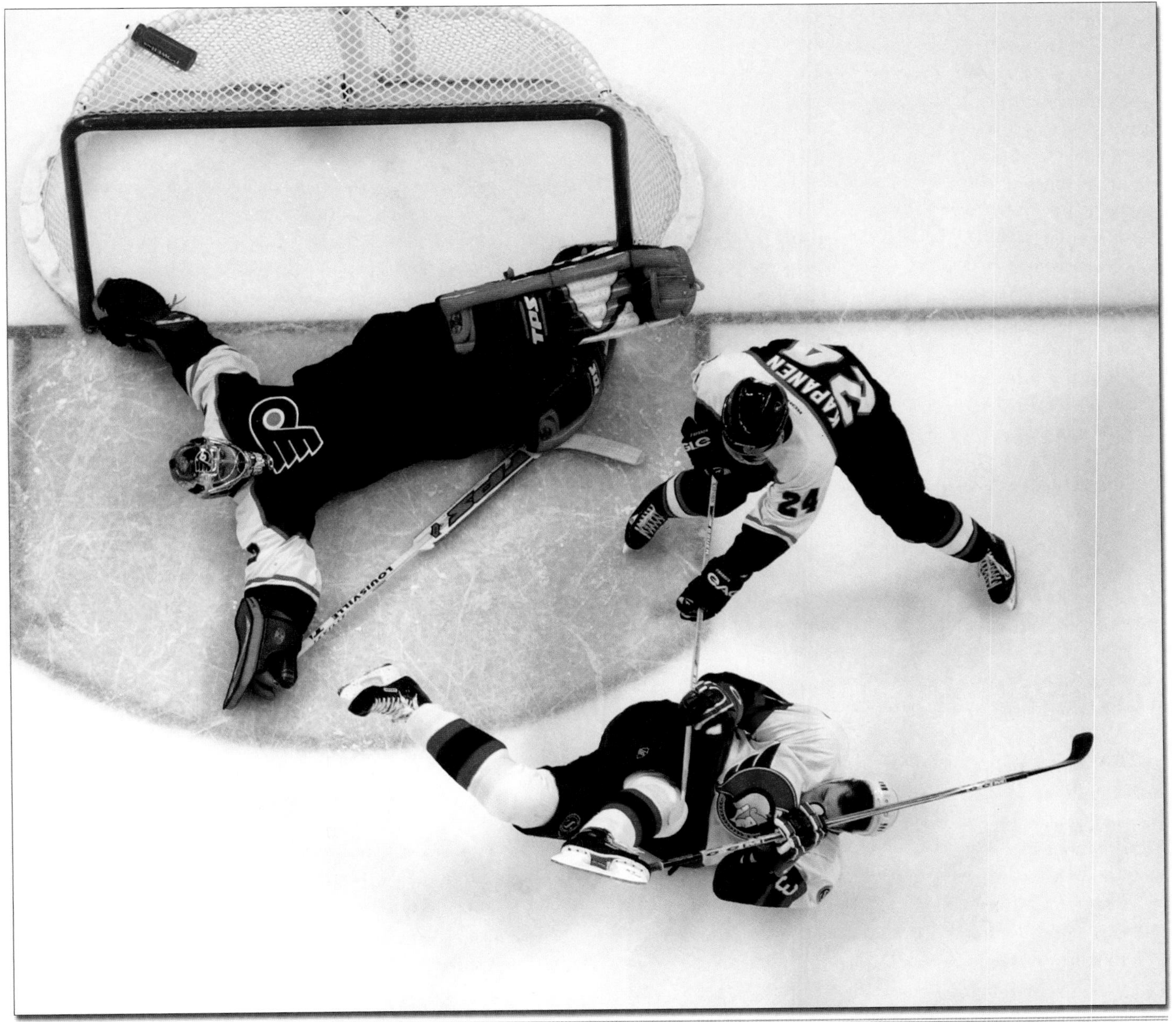

Zdeno Chara is checked by Sami Kapanen as Roman Cechmanek smothers the puck en route to a 2-0 shutout win in Game Two of the Eastern Conference semifinals vs. Ottawa.

whether he was dialed in or not. And Esche just kept working and becoming more popular in the locker room.

Remembers LeClair, "I didn't hate him. Some guys hated him."

Among those was Roenick.

"I didn't like his attitude," J.R. recalls. "I didn't like his personality, didn't like the way he played the game, or anything about him.

"As soon as the year ended and the World Championships got closer, his head wasn't in Philly, more back home. I just didn't think his heart was in it to play as well as he could at the most important time of the year."

Brian Boucher, who had backed up the Czech for two seasons, felt Cechmanek's nonchalance was misinterpreted.

"Everybody has a different way of approaching the game," Boucher says. "Some people are fired up and others act like they don't care, but deep down inside they are passive-aggressive.

"I truly believe that to be the case with Roman. He really did care, but his teammates believed otherwise, and it's really tough to change a guy's mind or, really, 20 guys' minds."

Recalls Gagne, "During the season he won a lot of games for us. We always had a chance to win, so there was no problem with him. But in the playoffs, he started to do risk-taking we thought was dumb so the relationship wasn't as good.

"Did he quit (in 2002 in Ottawa)? I don't know. But for some of the guys on the team, the trust went away."

Esche believes that among the cultural differences with which Cechmanek struggled was the mentality of the fans.

"Roman never grasped that the position of goaltender in Philadelphia is much bigger than it is in other cities," Esche said. "It's paramount to the success of any organization, but there is so much attention paid to it in Philly, so much scrutiny of every goal, every game, every win and loss, and I don't think he could relate to that.

"For someone who didn't speak good English to feel that way, it makes you think, 'How much are you reading into this? Why are you worried about it so much?' I don't think Roman grasped that it wasn't personal, but just the way things are in Philly because of how passionate it is. Tough love, right? Roman didn't embrace it.

"I got about five extra starts that year at the last second because on game day, he'd be in the medical room for treatment and would say, 'No, I just don't feel good tonight, I won't play.'

"But listen, I did like Roman. He kept to himself, but there are a lot worse out there. And no matter what people want to say about him, he had some success with us. I got my name on a Jennings Trophy and got to go to an awards presentation, standing up there with Marty Brodeur, because Roman played pretty well."

In a 2008 interview with Radek Vokal of the Czech publication *Novinky Sport*, Cechmanek's opinions on his Philadelphia days pretty much reflected the reviews he had received.

"I wish we played better in the playoffs because we had some good teams, especially my last year," he said. "That's the one regret. We had good teams that should have played better in the playoffs. I count myself in that, of course.

"You get a little homesick. You try to learn a new language. The food isn't like it is at home. It's tough, but it's part of the job. I think the players tried (to be supportive) but they hadn't had a lot of Czechs or Slovaks or Russians on the team over the years so they didn't really understand everything that was involved in making the transition. I think perhaps a team like Detroit, with all the Russians they had, maybe they understood a little better.

"Clarke did bring us (he and Jiri Dopita) there and sign us, and we all wanted to win. But I do think the Flyers were less patient with Czechs and Russians. For example, they played Jiri as a third or fourth center and he performed the role they asked, but they criticized him for not playing like a first center. They were faster to get rid of the European guys.

"Fans are fans. They are passionate in Philadelphia. I think sometimes goalies get too much credit and too much blame. You can give up four goals and play good that night or have a shutout and not really have played all that good but you got lucky. That's hockey.

"But I also think people get influenced by what they read in the newspapers and hear on the TV and radio. A lot of the media there is very negative most of the time and rude, not very knowledgeable about hockey.

"They had an agenda because they like to deal with Brian Boucher or Robert Esche, so they wanted those guys playing instead of me. Maybe I did have a bad night, but you win and lose as a team. Another thing is they were always looking to start a controversy, even when we were going well. I think it's because it was easier to write about that sort of thing than to write about the hockey.

"When I first got there, I worked hard to learn as much English as I could. As soon as possible, I started to do interviews in English. But the media would get impatient, roll their eyes, and walk away. They would talk bad about me when I was standing nearby because they probably thought I didn't understand. So that made it tough. I'm not talking about everyone, of course, but a lot of the media in Philadelphia were hostile to the European players and me.

"But I think [the experience] was good overall. Clarke told me they wanted to go in a different direction and I was fine with it."

The GM told reporters he was in the market for a veteran to compete for the No. 1 job against Esche, who had compiled a 2.20 goals-against average and a .925 save percentage in 30 games.

The Flyers would drop $6.5 million in salary with expiring contracts over the next two seasons and, with labor Armageddon a year away, Clarke talked about the need to lose more.

So an "aging and unfulfilled" team, in the words of *Daily News* columnist Rich Hofmann, heard the clock ticking. But a bounce-back 2002-03 season had reestablished Philadelphia's hockey club as a team of resolve and bought its core players more time.

"We had made progress but it wasn't acceptable," recalls Primeau.

The window remained open.

MARK RECCHI
FLYER HERO #32

MARK RECCHI

Even after Mark Recchi scored 154 points in the 62 games of his draft season, there were 66 players taken ahead of him, largely out of concern that a 5-10, 185-pound winger wouldn't survive. But he outlasted them all.

Mike Modano, Teemu Selanne and Jeremy Roenick, great stars picked that year and iron men, too, didn't play as many games (1,652) or score as many points as did Recchi (1,533) during his astounding 22-season career. Most of his era was not friendly to little men, but The Wreckin' Ball turned that stereotype into a pile of rubble.

"I was hoping I would get five or six years; I never in my wildest dream imagined 22," recalls Recchi. "You take satisfaction in that, of course.

"To the people that believed in you and gave you opportunities, you appreciate it, for sure."

The Penguins selected him in the fourth round and quickly got all the thanks they needed when he contributed 34 playoff points towards their Stanley Cup in his third season. The next year, the Flyers traded Rick Tocchet and Kjell Samuelsson for Recchi in a three-team exchange and were quickly repaid when Recchi set a single-season franchise record for points with 123 in 1992-93. After trading him to Montreal for a king's ransom—Eric Desjardins and John LeClair—that would set up three deep playoff runs, Philadelphia then brought Recchi back to become an integral component for two of them.

Not only did No. 8 in the lineup appropriately turn into the eighth-ranked Philadelphia scorer of all time, Recchi also proved the Flyers' second-best-ever trading chip, after Bernie Parent, who was the bait to get Rick MacLeish in 1971. In both cases, the heavy cost of dealing two stars, eventually was paid forward by triumphant returns. Parent backstopped the Flyers to two Stanley Cups, and Recchi scored 19 playoff goals—including one in triple overtime at Toronto with the team trailing the series 2-1—in the course of Philadelphia winning five playoff series between 1998 and 2004.

"Mark's whole career was about clutch goals," recalls Keith Primeau, Recchi's captain and often linemate. While the Flyers didn't get all the best years of the NHL's 12th leading scorer in history, they enjoyed seven full seasons and parts of three others. Whether they were playing or trading Recchi, he was an enormous commodity and quite the teammate, too.

"Mark Recchi was brilliant," says Craig Ramsay,

the Flyer coach during the 2000 semifinal run, and an assistant in Boston as Recchi finished up as a 48-point Bruin and Stanley Cup winner at age 42. "He is a high-end person who cared about everybody around him and tried to make them better."

There was a lot of room for improvement in the Flyers during Recchi's first time around with them.

"I went from a Stanley Cup champion to a franchise that was rebuilding and restocking, so it was definitely going to be different," he recalls. "But I knew what kind of an organization Philadelphia was and actually had seriously considered signing with the Flyers as a restricted free agent (the Flyers had been prepared to offer Tocchet as compensation) the previous summer.

"Things happen for a reason; I wound up there anyway in a trade. When I got to know Rick, I was glad that he got his Cup (the Penguins repeated). He deserved it.

"The Flyers were just an okay team but with a lot of decent pieces. Rod Brind'Amour was there, Ron Hextall still was there, Kevin Dineen was a great captain, and Bill Dineen was a coach I really liked."

Recchi, who arrived in February 1992, provided offense that Tocchet couldn't and instantly improved the franchise's outlook to break a three-season playoff drought by the following year. But the front office tore up the team again—trading five players, two first-round picks and $15 million to obtain Eric Lindros, leaving the Flyers a lot thinner than had been Recchi's patience level with the process. Philadelphia wouldn't make the playoffs again for two more seasons, but Recchi got to play with the most fearsome performer in the game.

"Obviously, Eric was a huge power forward and created space for himself, but he was a great shooter too," recalls Recchi. "I always looked to pass first, but I could also shoot and he made plays as well.

"Eric and I had great chemistry. I loved playing with him."

Recchi followed up that 123-point season with 107 in 1993-94. When the Flyers started badly coming out of the 1994-95 lockout, their most valuable commodity besides Lindros was the guy who could bring the most in a multi-player deal.

"They made a good trade with Montreal," Recchi says. "But it ended up hard for me to leave Philadelphia as it had been to be traded there from a Cup winner in Pittsburgh. You're settled in, think you've done a good job.

"But I went to a great place in Montreal and had five great years there; I loved every minute of it."

Basically, he wouldn't have been Mark Recchi if he wouldn't have loved every minute in every place he played. He wanted to re-sign with the Canadiens, who instead decided they wanted to cut payroll and start a youth movement. At the cost of former first-round pick Dainius Zubrus, the Flyers brought Recchi back in March 1999.

"It was very exciting for me," he recalls. "I had loved the organization and now got an opportunity to play with the Flyers when they had a great team.

"Mr. (Ed) Snider was an amazing owner. Bobby Clarke, everybody there, wanted to win and was doing whatever they could to help you get it done.

"Unfortunately we just didn't get over the hump. We lost twice (in the 2000 and 2004 conference final) to the eventual winner, which was tough."

After the 2004 Game Seven loss to Tampa Bay, the Flyers, the lockout and salary cap looming, decided they couldn't fit a 35-year-old who had been making $5 million a year into their new budget. They didn't make Recchi an offer.

"I would have taken the home-town discount, but we never even talked money," he recalls. "It wasn't about the money to me; it never really was. It was always about making sure that I was in the right place for me.

"I turned down a lot more from a couple other places to go back to Pittsburgh. I would have done the same for Philadelphia. But they signed two bigger guys (Mike Knuble and Turner Stevenson), the direction they felt they had to go."

The Penguins, who had hit rock bottom, celebrated Recchi's return for the credibility it restored. Good things continued to follow him everywhere. When the lockout ended, the Penguins won the lottery to draft first and take Sidney Crosby. But when the opportunity came to be dealt to a Carolina team with a real chance, Recchi gladly waived his no-trade clause and ended up with his second Stanley Cup.

There may be no greater character reference in sport than when multiple teams want you back. After the Hurricanes' triumph, Recchi returned to Pittsburgh, where he had maintained a home throughout, for a third time, before signing with Tampa Bay as 40-year old. Either he happened into more places at fortuitous times than Forrest Gump or they became good spots in large part because Recchi was there. The Bruins traded for him in 2009 and, two seasons later, Recchi won his third Cup and rode off to the happiest of sunsets.

"Like I said, everything happens for a reason," Recchi said. And the best explanation for his being able to repeatedly extend his career was, in his words, "Hockey sense and compete level. And, I could skate."

Indeed, for a guy who looked like he was running on his blades, Recchi arrived quickly to the puck, with a center of gravity so low he was never overpowered by players who had pounds and inches on him.

A right wing with a left-handed shot, Recchi played most of his career on the off wing, which gave him a more open view of the ice. Despite that choppy stride, he was often one step ahead of those trying to stop him.

"When you are a read-and-react player, you go to the place where the puck is going to be and Mark always put it there," recalls Jeremy Roenick. "And, if you made a mistake, he would cover for you.

"He skated to the right places, put the puck there, too, and worked hard. Mark wasn't the fastest and biggest guy, but it didn't matter. If you got open, he'd get you the puck. His hockey IQ was so big."

So were his upper legs and gluteus maximus, the smaller players' best friends in the land of the behemoths.

"Obviously, top defensemen are going to be physical on you," recalls Recchi. "For a lot of my career I was playing against the top guy."

"Sometimes it's hit or be hit. I could pick my spots to play physically. Mostly, if you have good hockey sense, you're not going to get yourself in positions to get killed. When I did, I was lucky (never missed more than 11 games in any season), and didn't have anything major besides a few concussions.

"But the game changed in the latter parts of my career. You couldn't cross check, hook or hold anymore, so it actually wasn't as taxing.

"Back then, if you weren't strong in the upper body to fight through (obstruction), it didn't make a difference how quick you were. You had to be able to get off people. You'd battle in the corner for 45-50 seconds, never get the puck to the net and come to the bench exhausted.

"Now, you need more ass and legs. It's mostly about your legs and your core."

It's also about dedication to quintessential beliefs like: the team comes first, often a hard thing for gifted scorers to learn.

"When the players would bitch about the coach—and they always bitch about the coach—Mark would listen, then say, 'shut up and play,' recalls Ken Hitchcock, the man behind the bench when Recchi played junior at Kamloops, B.C. and with the Flyers. "He was a really good ally later in his career for a lot of us. My last year (in Philadelphia), we missed him a lot in the room."

Hitchcock had arrived in Kamloops a year after Recchi, a local kid, had been signed from under the nose of the hometown team to play in New Westminster, B.C. Hitchcock traded seven players to bring Recchi and a tough 20-year-old winger named Craig Berube to Kamloops.

"Even at that age I could tell he was vocal and involved, one of those types of players," recalls Berube. "Mark obviously had brains and played both ends of the ice.

"Over time he became a better goal scorer. What stands out the most for me though, was that he had a hockey player's mentality. He loved to play and was a good teammate."

Two years before Pittsburgh drafted Recchi, they had taken their first fourth-round gamble on another smallish, opportunistic, Hitchcock player—Rob Brown—and gotten 24 goals out of him as a rookie. They came back to Kamloops looking for another sleeper. "Eddie Johnston (former Pittsburgh coach and GM) was there to watch me all the time, so I kind of knew Pittsburgh was on the radar," Recchi recalls. "As long as I thought I was going to get drafted, I could care less when."

Everything happens for a reason, believes Recchi, today the Penguins' director of player development, but of course, he made things occur.

"Part of being a small player is that you find survival instincts," says Hitchcock. "Mark learned how to play a big man's game, so I've got all the respect in the world for him.

"In order to be a scoring player, you have to be selfish. But at the end of the day he became a role player and was really good at it. So he learned to adjust."

After the Flyers were eliminated by two teams (Detroit in 1997 and Buffalo in 1998) that played four-line systems, coach Roger Neilson, who would soon be forced by illness to yield the bench to Ramsay, asked his star-laden team to keep shifts short, allowing more players to be involved. Recchi immediately agreed to sacrifice ice time. When Hitchcock— not an easy guy to please—was hired in 2002, the Flyer who already knew him became his locker-room defender and oft-times interpreter.

If Recchi agreed with a plan, he bought in. Even though he first became a Flyer during a dip in their fortunes, he recognized, and helped sustain, their culture.

"I knew the history when I got there and saw quickly the commitment," he recalls. "You don't do what they did to get Lindros without wanting to win very badly.

"I was lucky never to have played in a bad place. I won with three other teams. But I was especially fortunate to play in Philadelphia for as long as I did. Being a Flyer meant everything to me."

KEN HITCHCOCK

TWO HUNDRED POUNDS MELTED OFF a once-sporting goods store manager before he was given the opportunity to freeze NHL millionaires with his glare.

One can only imagine the weight of a coach's words if at 476 pounds, teenaged athletes still took him seriously. The Kamloops (B.C.) Blazers didn't think any less of Hitchcock, even before there was a lot less of him. The team claimed five Western Hockey League regular season championships in six years and two berths in Memorial Cups.

"He was pretty good about the jokes," recalls Mark Recchi, the star of two of those Kamloops powerhouses. "(Teammate) Glenn Mulvenna and I once put on his pants for a picture, one of us in each leg.

"Back in those days, a coach told you what to do and you did it. But Hitch had such knowledge that he had our respect. Everything he told us to do worked. Actually, he wasn't much different than he was with the Flyers. He became a little more polished, but it was the same barking from the bench, the same attention to detail, the same coach trying to get in your head and stay there."

Obsessions with the game and success have put Ken Hitchcock's name on a Stanley Cup, earned him the fourth-most regular-season victories of all time, and, in 2004, pushed the Flyers to one of their most inspiring playoff runs. But another compulsion—eating—threatened to kill him.

At age 18, before the appetite got totally out of control, Hitchcock set the course record at Edmonton's Riverside Golf Club with a 66. He played the sport for two years at the University of Michigan before finishing up at the University of Alberta, earning a degree in marine biology. Hard to find a hockey coach with one of those, and almost as difficult to name one who never played the game at any seriously competitive level. But moonlighting from his job as manager of United Cycle in Edmonton, Hitchcock was so successful at the midget (age 14-16) level that his application for the Kamloops coaching job was taken seriously, which was a surprise to him.

"A guy named Bruce Haralson who scouted for Kamloops (and later the Penguins and Red Wings) convinced me I should at least interview," recalls Hitchcock. "That was the only reason I went.

"They showed me the list of people they were talking to, all established coaches in junior hockey. I thought there was no chance, went home and forgot about it.

"I loved coaching midget, loved playing golf. Through my tight friendship with the family that owned the store, I felt like the place was mine. People (from sporting-equipment companies) were approaching me about becoming a sales rep and that's probably what I would have wound up doing. I was shocked when I got the callback."

Hitchcock got the job, in large part because he would work for $20,000 a year, about half the going 1984 rate for the jack-of-all-trades a junior coach was required to be.

"I thought I was getting hired as the coach," he recalls. "Then they said, 'Okay, you're basically the director of player personnel, too." "We've got a business manager but you're doing everything else.'

"I'd done a bit of scouting for other (WHL) teams so I knew a little about the league. But I knew nothing about player lists, had never made a trade in my life, didn't know how to do anything.

"I just wanted 25 guys to coach and to be left alone, ya know? I didn't know where to point the bus. After the first exhibition game in Kelowna [B.C.], I went into a 7-11, got myself a sandwich, and went back on the bus.

"The next day I read a quote from a player, 'He's tough! We lost an exhibition game and he wouldn't feed us.'

"I didn't know you had to feed players at the end of the game. In midget, parents brought their kids to the game, took them home. I just thought everybody would bring their own lunches.

"I mean, that's how naïve I was."

The clueless coach read everything there was to read about the game and leadership and proved dumb as a fox. He played the jolly fat guy to townspeople who quickly learned to love him, while being a martinet to the players, most of whom hated him. Hitchcock learned to order them food after games but never fed them a line about how good they were. Rob Brown, the team's best player and the general manager's son, was thrown out of practice at least 20 times before eventually being made the captain.

Teenagers who wanted to go somewhere in the game listened and the rest were doomed to fall by the wayside anyway. Arena organists mocked Hitchcock with fast-food jingles as he waddled to the bench and an opposing coach once had pizzas delivered there in the middle of the game. Hitchcock's thick skin had to weigh at least 100 of his 450-plus pounds, until finally, that omnipresent voice in his players' heads rang a bell in his own.

Hitchcock says his epiphany came during a ferry crossing to Victoria, B.C. for a coaching clinic, when he had the choice of struggling up three flights of stairs to reach the upper deck or staying wedged behind his steering wheel and nodding off in his car.

Because it was easier, Hitchcock decided to stay put, but also that day he chose to live.

"I thought to myself, 'You're out of control,'" he recalls. "I'm just going to get bigger and when I get to be around 45, I'm going to die.

"They're going to have a little tombstone and a few people will come to the funeral and that's it. I'll have accomplished nothing."

Hitchcock ate salads, went on long walks and, through pledges tied to his weight loss, raised $48,000 towards the construction of a new rink in Kamloops. He eventually curbed his appetite for food, but not for winning. Russ Farwell, whose work with two opposing Western Hockey League teams had gotten him the Flyer GM job after Bob Clarke was fired in 1990, was so impressed with Hitchcock's brain that he could have had 10 chins and been wearing a stained bib during the job interview and still been hired as an assistant for coach Paul Holmgren.

"We were opponents, not friends," recalls Farwell. "But I had watched him work every possible angle"

With the Flyers for three years that first time around, Hitchcock survived Holmgren's firing but not Clarke's 1994 return. Though most of the baby fat was gone, he was thrown out with the bathwater when Clarke immediately brought in Terry Murray as head coach.

Dallas GM-coach Bob Gainey hired Hitchcock to coach the Stars' farm team in Kalamazoo (MI). Midway through Hitchcock's third season in the organization, he was promoted to run the NHL bench when Gainey wanted to focus on being the general manager.

Hitchcock won five division titles in seven years, a Stanley Cup in 1999 and reached another Final in 2000 before the team's decline began. Gainey was gone when Hitchcock was fired on a charge of wearing his players out with negativity, even though that same approach had gotten a lot of them championship rings.

"We were a really good team in Dallas because the leaders ran the club," Hitchcock recalls. "They were given the reins and ran with them. As soon as those leaders—(Guy) Carbonneau, (Craig) Ludwig, (Mike) Keane, (Darryl) Sydor—retired or left, chaos took over.

"We were in fifth place in the conference when I got fired and they finished 10th. But the one lesson I learned was needing to work harder on the existing leadership."

The Flyers' performance under Bill Barber in a 2002 loss to Ottawa—two goals in five games—was the perfectly-framed opportunity to bring in a new, tough, sheriff. Hitchcock never wore his championship ring, but its sparkle nevertheless caught players' eyes, just as Clarke had expected.

"I understood what the problem had been with Billy and knew Hitch would get us straightened out," recalls Clarke. "Lots of guys didn't like him but at least they knew what they were supposed to do. He was pretty direct with his approach to the game and the way he wanted his team to play."

Practically the only pats on the back Hitchcock gave the Flyers were public ones. No mistake went uncorrected and no effort went unchallenged, no matter how hard the players already thought they were working.

The military history buff had read more than one account of Ulysses S. Grant's victory at Vicksburg. Hitchcock demanded his own version of unconditional surrender, this time by his own troops.

"When you read what a coach says or watch the way he behaves around veteran players, you can tell right away whether he is afraid of them," says Hitchcock. "I mean, we can all admire players but you can't be afraid of them.

"It's not easy sitting out veteran players or telling one, 'You're a fourth-line player' when he thinks he deserves more. Or, saying 'Your career is on the line if you don't change.' You've got to have those conversations or else you get swallowed up.

"You've gotta put the team ahead of everything."

The Flyers coveted the organization that captain Keith Primeau had stated publicly they had not received from Barber.

"We had the team together for a while but hadn't won and we were getting a guy who had," recalls defenseman Chris Therien. Still, these players were unprepared to have a mirror held an inch from their noses practically every day.

"Listen, we wanted to win so we had to go along with it," recalls Simon Gagne. "We got better as a team and I got better as a player, but at the same time, he broke some of the guys.

"There were some who just couldn't play for Hitch, couldn't play under all that constant pressure. They were afraid to make a play at the blueline because if you turned it over, you were going to sit on the bench.

"There were guys who said, 'He's a [bleep]. He's [bleeping] crazy.' For the first two years, I'm telling you, it was almost a nightmare for me. But I have a lot of respect for Hitch because I became a better player. And you can look at other guys and some of them played their best hockey for Hitch, like I did.

"Sitting here today, if you ask me who was the best coach I've had, it was Ken Hitchcock."

As Hitchcock says, it's all about leadership. The Flyers, perceived to be whining, unaccountable, and ultimately bumbling mutineers who had cost Barber, a Philadelphia legend, his job, proved to have almost as many strong voices in the room as they had good players.

Because Recchi knew what was coming, he could remind boiling teammates that, in the end, the team would be better for all the anxiety. Primeau, the guy with the most at stake, had to do more than just put up and shut up; he needed to become Hitchcock's messenger.

"He had his leadership group of a captain, assistants, elder statesmen," recalls Primeau. "It didn't change much, just every once in a while he would add somebody.

"We would win a game, or lose, and the leadership group would have accounted for all the goals, and Hitch would say, 'It's not good enough. You have to be better.'

"We are like, 'We're doing our part; it's not us, it's the rest of the group.' And Hitch is like, 'You're not understanding it. It comes from you guys. The only way we get better is if you guys get better.'

"At first I thought it was argumentative. It took months for me to understand that concept.

"When he first showed up, I was 10 seconds late for a powerplay meeting and he absolutely went off on me. I felt demeaned in front of my teammates, but he was 100 percent right. I was late. Ten minutes or ten seconds, it doesn't matter. So I understood the message.

"After that, if we would go through tough times, I'd be like, 'Hitch, go at me. If you hold me accountable, everybody else has to be.' I think that's where Hitch and I were able to have such a good relationship. I was a strong conduit to the locker room. I could turn down his volume and deliver exactly what he was saying.

"I've had so many conversations with guys who played for him after I did that my cell became like a Hitch Hotline. I would tell them the same thing every time: 'Get past the delivery. Listen to the message, and understand that all he is looking for is more. Yeah, he could have taken a different tack, but this is how he's done it and had success.'

"So I am a Hitch protege. I liked his system. One of the first things he said when he got here was, 'I'll get the media on our side.' He understood how important that was to share his message as well."

In his first Philadelphia playoff, the same team that became fractured over its inability to score the

KEN HITCHCOCK
FLYER HERO #41

previous spring played three multiple-overtime games against Toronto and lost two of them. Nevertheless, the Flyers had little doubt they would win in the end, and did in Game Seven, 6-1.

The following spring, 2004, Hitchcock's team eliminated the Stanley Cup champion Devils, beat the Leafs again, and reached the conference final against Tampa Bay.

Even when the team's third best defenseman, Marcus Ragnarsson, joined its second best defenseman (Eric Desjardins) on the sideline while the No. 1 (Kim Johnsson) played with a broken hand, the Flyers fought back three times to tie the series and went to Game Seven in Tampa believing, in all their exhaustion, that they were inevitable. But they fell behind early, had little left for another comeback, losing 2-1.

With the lockout approaching, the veteran team knew that was its last, best shot and will take the heartbreak to their graves.

"It should have been us," Hitchcock mournfully said, before and after the Lightning beat Calgary in a seven-game Final.

With the free-agent signings of Peter Forsberg, Mike Rathje and Derian Hatcher, Philadelphia thought it had reloaded quickly following the lockout. Despite the loss of Primeau to another concussion and a massive number of other injuries, Hitchcock's team led the NHL standings in early January but played only .500 the rest of the way and were beaten badly by Buffalo in the first round.

Clarke tried to prop things back up with mid-career players who had none of traditional characteristics of Flyers. A 1-6-1 start lowlighted by an uncompetitive 9-1 loss in Buffalo doomed Hitchcock on charges that the fat man had worn thin.

Hitchcock was fired the same day Clarke, who had been the ultimate iron-willed leader on the ice, resigned, blaming burnout, a condition Hitchcock never has cited and never will. Just as in Dallas after he was let go, the team got worse. Philadelphia sunk to 30th in the league.

One month later, Hitchcock became coach of the Columbus Blue Jackets, and led them to their first-ever playoff berth. Since joining St. Louis in 2011-12, the Blues have gone 224-103-36 and reached the 2016 conference final.

When no NHL or European team wants him, Hitchcock will coach pickup games at midnight while most of the same players who once wanted to kill him still will be thanking him. The Flyers got everything they had wanted except the Cup, which is Hitchcock's only regret after going 131-73-28-22 and winning three playoff rounds in three-plus seasons.

"Losing that Game Seven was the worst of my time there," he recalls. "The best was just sitting in Clarkie's office every day talking hockey.

"At one point we had Clarkie, (Ron) Hextall, Dean Lombardi and myself in one office talking hockey every day. We had a great coaching staff—Terry Murray, Wayne Fleming, Craig Berube, Craig Hartsburg. Great minds, close friends, great teachers, fun to be around, the type of staff you wish you could coach with forever.

"I think working for Clarkie was one of the ultimate benefits of being in the league. You couldn't work for a more loyal guy. You talk about the right way to treat a coach and the right way to treat players and the right way to do things—that's a man that knew how."

So did Hitchcock, his players ultimately agreed, in many cases the hard way.

"He taught me a lot more than I thought I had the ability to learn," recalls Robert Esche, the goalie during the 2004 run. "He was extremely hard on me, but for someone who never played goal, Hitch had a gift to understand the challenges of it.

"Philadelphia is a tough place, but if you understand that and embrace it, it turns out that it's not as tough as you thought. Hitch had a part in getting me through that.

"When you came in for practice, you had to walk in the corridor by his office. I used to come in early, but it was impossible to come in earlier than Hitch. I mean, Hitch was always there.

"I remember once he was pissed at me for something. For 15 days in a row, I would say, 'Hi' to him as I walked by. He'd look up from his newspapers—he read them all—see it was me, say nothing, and just go back to reading.

"He used to get me going so much. One time I went in there determined to give him a piece of my mind, let him listen for a change, and then walk out. But what happened instead is what happened each and every time: You'd be in there for 20-30 minutes and would walk out saying, 'this guy is right.'"

Jeremy Roenick

Chapter 7 • 2003-04

"It Should Have Been Us."

THE **2001** TRADE OF CENTER **DAYMOND LANGKOW** to Phoenix had given Philadelphia the option of using the Coyote No. 1 selection in either 2002 or 2003. When that pick came up 19th overall the first year, general manager Bob Clarke had decided to save it in anticipation of a loaded 2003 draft.

Many veteran scouts believed 2003 would prove to be as deep in talent as 1979, the year the NHL lowered the eligibility age from 20 to 19, essentially creating a talent pool of two classes that produced a first round of three eventual Hall of Famers, nine All-Star game selections, and dropped Brian Propp to the Flyers with the 14th pick.

"Our guys came up with 22 [projected first-rounders in 2003], who were better than [the top-rounders selected] last year," said assistant GM Paul Holmgren as the draft, to be held in Nashville, approached with Philadelphia holding the 11th (from Phoenix) and 24th (their own) choices. The Flyers' second-round pick (61st overall) had gone to Montreal in the Eric Chouinard trade but Philadelphia had five third-round selections.

Clarke had chips to offer for an even higher pick than 11th, but couldn't find a trading partner that would allow him to take the one player he valued above all others—Cape Breton's Marc-Andre Fleury, believed to be the best goaltending prospect in a decade. "Darn right we would consider moving up, but it's not going to happen," the GM said on draft week. "Teams want way too much."

Pittsburgh dealt winger Mikael Samuelsson and an extra later pick to Florida and moved up from third to first, choosing Fleury. Carolina GM Jim Rutherford wanted both Flyer first-rounders and a player for the second pick. So Clarke quickly closed discussions with the Hurricanes, who selected center Eric Staal.

The Flyers liked Nathan Horton, taken third by Florida, a great deal, but believed the draft was deep enough to get a future star even with Philadelphia's 11th pick.

"Unless there was a deal that made sense, we were totally fine with staying where we were," recalls Holmgren.

Right wing Nikolay Zherdev was selected fourth by Columbus; winger Tomas Vanek fifth by Buffalo; left wing Milan Michalek sixth by San Jose; defenseman Ryan Suter seventh by Nashville; defenseman Braydon Coburn eighth to Atlanta, defenseman Dion Phaneuf ninth to Calgary; and right wing Andrei Kostitsyn 10th to Montreal.

"As always, we were looking to draft the best player regardless of position," recalls Holmgren. "But the defensemen we liked—Suter the best, then Coburn and Phaneuf—went one right after another, so our direction was pretty clear."

Guelph right wing Dustin Brown, Calgary center Ryan Getzlaf and Sault Ste. Marie center Jeff Carter, ranked second, fifth and 27th among North American prospects by Central Scouting, were the available objects of the Flyers' desire when the 11th pick came up.

"Getzlaf had good vision but he hadn't played well when our guys saw him," recalls Holmgren. "We liked Dustin a lot as a systems player, but Carter was a more attractive package of skills."

Carter was 6-3 with a long skating stride, a hard wrist shot and, from what the scouts could see, a work ethic that had improved steadily through the season for a Sault Ste. Marie club that won just 26 games. Not every NHL team had spent as much time watching Carter as had Philadelphia, whose assistant coach, Craig Hartsburg, had been behind the Greyhound bench during the big center's first junior season.

"We had a lot of viewings on Jeff and also some inside information because of Hartsy," recalls director of scouting Chris Pryor. "As the season went along, we thought Jeff was as good as anyone in the draft."

It had taken a while, however. "The first few times I saw Carter, he didn't do much," recalls Quebec scout Simon Nolet about his crossover trips to Ontario. "I could tell he had a chance to score goals but he was passive.

"Later on, Clarkie told me to go to Sudbury and watch him in the playoffs. I saw three of four games and it was a different player, much more active in every part of the game."

Ontario scout Dennis Patterson, who had seen Carter the most, signed off on him eagerly. "Big, skilled, great skater, could really shoot the puck," Patterson recalls. "He was a home run swing for us." And Hartsburg, with first-hand knowledge, thought the negative views of Carter's work ethic through the first half season were exaggerated.

"Great character, very persistent," said Hartsburg. "It's hard to find big guys who can skate like him. He has a great upside offensively."

Carter became only the second center (after Simon Gagne in 1998) drafted by the Flyers since Peter Forsberg in 1991. Brown went 13th to Los Angeles and Getzlaf 19th to Anaheim.

With the 24th selection, Philadelphia was intrigued with London right wing Corey Perry, ranked 35th by Central Scouting but considered a sleeper by multiple teams that had become more impressed with him over the second half of the season.

"Great hands and pretty strong, but Perry's skating was rough," recalls Holmgren. "We were most looking at (University of North Dakota center) Zach Parise and (Kitchener center) Mike Richards almost side by side."

Scouts universally praised the character of both, but Richards was ranked only 30th by Central Scouting because he was considered to be an average skater. His 5-11 build also worried teams that had typecast him as a tenacious checker of some scoring ability.

"There was some concern about Mike's feet," recalls Pryor. "Maybe that was a bigger issue for other teams than it was for us because we saw that he made up for it in other ways.

"We didn't see him as undersized exactly, but Mike was far from the biggest guy. His skating was okay, nothing special. But once the puck was dropped, he stood out because he played the game the right way. He was a smart player, a captain everywhere he went."

The Flyers selected Mike Richards 24th overall at the 2003 NHL Entry Draft in Nashville.

As a result, Patterson recalls thinking Richards probably was a safer pick than Carter. "We all had seen Richards play a lot and all agreed there was nothing not to like about him," recalls Patterson. "We had taken our big swing with Carter and didn't want to [gamble] with both picks."

Holmgren remembers thinking the opposite, only because of Richards' size and Carter's greater upside. But the Flyers were secure in the belief Richards' fire and all-around skills gave him a higher ceiling than just as a reliable player. "He was a great competitor with leadership potential, who played in every game situation," recalls Holmgren.

Philadelphia also liked the character of Ohio State center Ryan Kesler. But their guy at pick No. 24 was going to be Richards, even had Vancouver not taken Kesler with pick No. 23. The Flyers selected Richards four choices before Perry went to Anaheim and five prior to right wing Patrick Eaves, the son of former Flyer assistant Mike Eaves, who went to Ottawa.

"He does everything," said Clarke of Richards. "Kills penalties, blocks shots, takes faceoffs. We never felt he would fall that far in the draft to us."

Nolet had hoped to get even luckier if center Patrice Bergeron of the Acadie-Bathurst Titans, who was not even in *The Hockey News* top 100, fell to the third round. "Simon loved Bergeron," recalls Patterson. "We all did when we all saw him later in the season."

But Bergeron was snapped up by Boston in the second round, a whopping 24 picks before Philadelphia used its next selection on center Colin Fraser. Right wing Stefan Ruzicka, defenseman Alexandre Picard, center Ryan Potulny and right wing Rick Kozak rounded out their third-round selections.

Having done the usual round of interviews with practically every team that felt Richards and Carter might fall to them, neither player recalls anything from their sessions with the Flyers that made them believe they would be Philadelphia's choice. As one would imagine, draft day went faster for Carter than for Richards by 13 long picks.

"My agent (Rick Curran) kind of kept it from me; he didn't want to say top 10 and then you're disappointed," recalls Carter. "So to go 11th was pretty exciting. And I was excited to go to Philly, obviously an organization with a lot of history."

Richards, who had stopped following hockey in the media the day his surprise selection as the fourth-overall pick in the 2001 midget draft (by Kitchener) had not been well-reviewed, had read no pre-draft speculation. He had been told by his agent, Pat Morris, that he would be taken ninth by Calgary if the three defensemen—Suter, Coburn and Phaneuf—were all gone by that pick. Phaneuf was still there for the Flames, so Richards waited. And waited.

'You're going down and down, you wonder if it's going to happen," he recalls. "When it did, I was pretty nervous going up on stage, I remember that."

On June 21, 2003, the day of the draft, former Flyer coach Roger Neilson died at age 69 at his home on a lake near Peterborough, Ontario. Diagnosed with deadly multiple myeloma during 1999-2000 season—and crushed when Clarke would not allow him to resume his position as head coach following treatment—Neilson passed from a second cancer, melanoma (skin), seven months after he was inducted into the Hockey Hall of Fame.

A coach in Philadelphia for one full season and parts of two others, Neilson was one of the most inspirational, and ultimately tragic, figures in Flyer history.

"He was a sun freak," recalls Nancy Nichols, Neilson's long-time companion. "He went to Hawaii every year and bought a condo on a beach when he coached the Panthers.

"Of course, when I would ask him to put on sunscreen, he joked, but not really, 'I'm way too tough for that.' That's what ended up killing him, but his system was weak from fighting the myeloma, I'm sure.

"The ending was pretty awful. We would talk three or four times a day (from her home in Dallas), but he wouldn't let me come up, because if I did, he would have to think about [his illness].

"Instead, he said, 'I'll call you when I'm ready.' I didn't have a relationship with that doctor, so I was kind of out of the loop. But everybody knew he was sick, and these charlatans with herbal remedies took advantage of him while he was grasping at straws.

"He never was alone, though. He had coached so many players, touched so many lives, that there was a constant flow of people in and out of the house. When he said, 'I think it's time to come up,' I bought a ticket with an open return.

"Just like when it took him so long to go to the doctor with his symptoms when he coached in Philadelphia, he thought he was way too tough for painkillers. He was ripping off his morphine patches.

"That all went back to his religion: if this was what was handed to you—the way God wanted it—there would be a better time on the other side. Once, while the nurse was rearranging him, one of the patches fell off and I just put it on his leg because I couldn't stand to see him in so much pain.

"I slept on the bed with him, holding his hand, asking 'Roger, can you hear me?' And he would nod. When I would tell the nurse some old story about him, he would say, 'Don't listen to her,' like the tough old coot he was. Roger the Codger.

"He died 48 hours after I got there and it [bleeped] me off.

"He was just an incredibly brilliant, idiotic, stubborn and tender man. We butted heads all the time. Our relationship was like a 28-year-long hockey match where sometimes we would throw the gloves off but, you know, we were on the same team and the same line. He would be in his eighties now and I can only image what a jerk he would be. I've never met anyone quite so complicated."

Nor, she says, as revered.

Flyer president Ron Ryan and director of team services Joe Kadlec, Roger's driver for his chemo treatments in Philadelphia, were among the 1,700 persons who attended the memorial service Nancy planned and staged for Roger at Peterborough's North View Pentecostal Church on June 28. Three hundred of the mourners had to watch on closed circuit in two spillover areas on the church grounds.

According to a statistician Nancy had engaged, Neilson had coached more than 500 NHL players through 10 NHL stops, seven as a head coach. Counting junior and youth hockey, the number of young people whom he had mentored was in the thousands.

After a painful divorce from the Flyers, Neilson had finished his coaching career as an assistant in Ottawa.

"I was with him there the afternoon they drilled four holes in his head so they could overlay the images of his brain and target the radiation exactly," recalls Rob Campbell, Neilson's agent. "I'm taking him home from the hospital and he says 'Geez Rob, I got a headache.'

"I said, 'No [bleeping] kidding Roger, you got four holes in your head.' I was taking him home, but he said he wanted to eat, so we went to Tim Hortons and then he changed his mind, wasn't hungry. So we picked up medication at the pharmacy and he said, 'Ya know, I feel okay, let's go to the Senator game.'

"I said, 'Are you kidding me?' But he said 'I'm alright.' He walked in and news of that spread around the building. After the game, a number of players from the opposition came by and said hi to him in his office.

"Point is, he was very tough-minded. He could really suck it up and make it appear he was feeling better than he probably was. He was one of the most remarkable people I've met in my life, just full of energy and not a mean bone in his body."

Although he had been denied his first Stanley Cup ring by Ottawa's upset at the hands of the Devils in the 2003 playoffs, the Senators and coach Jacques Martin had put Neilson in charge for the final two contests of the 2002 season, enabling him to reach 1,000 games in the NHL. Undoubtedly, he enjoyed some additional level of satisfaction in the Senator playoff triumphs over Philadelphia in 2002 and 2003. But Nancy doesn't remember his expressing any bitterness towards the Flyers.

"I don't think he was feeling that good when he got to Ottawa, so finally he was thinking, 'Well, maybe I don't need to be on the bench,'" recalls Nancy. "So when the Senators said, 'You go upstairs,' he didn't put up a fight.

"I don't think he ever said, 'Oh yeah, the Flyers were right,' but I know he came to feel that way. It was a very emotional and complicated time in Philadelphia and to see Roger so crushed, it was heartbreaking. But he didn't like to have enemies and didn't like holding grudges. I believe it's fair to say he let it go."

Clarke never suffered any regrets about a decision he said was dictated by Neilson's rundown physical condition following treatment, as well as the team's success in the 2000 playoffs under Craig Ramsay. When Ramsay, Neilson's protege as a player and coach, stayed behind the Flyer bench to begin the next season, Neilson would have been welcome to remain as an assistant, but chose to move on to Ottawa.

"Somewhere along the line Roger thought I promised him a long-term contract," recalls Clarke. "I wouldn't make that promise and not fulfill it.

"I liked him; I don't care if he liked me. Eventually, I think we were okay."

So was Clarke with stepping down as team president in June 2003, replaced by Ron Ryan, who had been the Flyers' chief operating officer. Clarke never thought he much functioned as a president anyway, just a hockey general manager.

"The concept was read to Clarkie and his reaction was, 'Well, thank God. Ron's been doing all that work. I have nothing to do with any of that stuff anyway,'" recalls Ryan. "Bob supported me."

With the Collective Bargaining Agreement between the league and players' association expiring at the end of the upcoming 2003-04 season and Commissioner Gary Bettman—the inventor of the NBA salary cap when he worked as deputy commissioner there—insisting hockey owners were not going to do a deal that didn't provide them "cost certainty," pressure was on everywhere to reduce salaries. Teams only guessing as to how much they would be permitted to spend under a new system feared big contracts would leave them filling out their teams with bargain-basement players.

So just two seasons after signing John LeClair to a five-year $45 million deal—the largest in Flyer history—Clarke was trying to trade him.

"I was all for it, if they wanted to move me," recalls LeClair, who had fallen off to 18 goals in an injury-interrupted, 35 game, 2001-02. "Why would you want to stay someplace you're not welcome?

"Nobody wants to go to the rink every day and be perceived as a problem. But it wasn't going to be an easy task (finding a buyer)."

Philadelphia was letting go of Dmitri Yushkevich—the 31-year-old defenseman signed with Yaroslavl of the Russian League—and was also shopping 31-year-old Chris Therien in anticipation of a youth movement to complement blueline holdovers Kim Johnsson, Marcus Ragnarsson and Eric Weinrich.

Joni Pitkanen, the fourth overall pick in the 2002 draft, signed a three-year, $3.5 million, contract with an incentive package that could bring the total deal to $11.35 million. The Flyers believed Dennis Seidenberg, a sixth-round pick in 2001 out of Germany who had been up for 21 games in 2002-03 could eventually be a second-pair defenseman. And free agent signee Jim Vandermeer already had taken a regular shift after Eric Desjardins had suffered a broken leg four games into the playoffs.

Still, despite the insertion of two screws in that leg during the off-season, Philadelphia was not ready to move on without Desjardins.

"He has been our best defenseman for nine years and a tremendous help to a lot of our players," said Clarke, who on July 1, the first day of free agency, re-signed the 34-year-old for the same $4 million per season he had been paid for the previous two years. Even in belt-tightening days, the Flyers took care of a loyal soldier who had no desire to shop himself to other clubs. Desjardins was also given the option to activate a third year, at $3 million.

"It's a good compromise," said agent Bob Sauve. "If things are going good in the third year, he can try free agency again, but he's happy; Eric wants to stay in Philly."

So did Claude Lapointe, a significant playoff contributor the previous spring following his trade deadline pickup from the Islanders. Lapointe took a cut from $1.2 million to $1 million for each of the next two seasons, essentially ending the utility role of Marty Murray, who had dressed for just four playoff games. He was traded to Calgary for a sixth-round pick.

The Flyers also came to terms for two years with Sami Kapanen, whose deal would start at the same $3 million he had made the season before. Justin Williams, a restricted free agent because his three-year rookie deal had expired, got a raise from $975,000 to $1.02 million; Radovan Somik received two years starting at $650,000 and Eric Chouinard was extended for one year at $650,000.

To replace Roman Cechmanek, Philadelphia signed 35-year-old Jeff Hackett to a two-year, $6 million deal. Despite playing 14 NHL seasons, Hackett had been on only four playoff teams, just once as a starter.

A broken hand, a dislocated shoulder and a broken finger had plagued his last three seasons with Montreal and Boston. But there had been no specific chronic health issue to cause the Flyers doubt that Hackett could give them two decent years. With some hope that Robert Esche (12-9-3, 2.20, .907 in his first Flyer season) could develop into a No. 1 goalie, Clarke thought that not only was Hackett's price right, but his attitude, too, post-Cechmanek.

"His competitiveness, personality and everything he brings to a team besides stopping the puck is much different than we've had recently," said the GM. "And we're really looking forward to it."

So was Hackett, who had played with good friends Weinrich and Recchi in Montreal. He was joining by far his most talent-laden NHL team. "Definitely, I would like to have more playoff experience," he told reporters on a conference call. "That's why we play.

"I know it's in me because I've won at every other level."

Another bank merger turned the First Union Center into the Wachovia Center, much to Ed Snider's helplessness and displeasure. The building had its third name in seven years. "The [29-year, $40 million naming rights] deal looked so appealing (in 1994) that I took it and didn't think it out as properly and carefully as I should have," said the Chairman. "We did not anticipate these banks would merge. We probably should have."

On the other hand, Snider had no reason for regret about the development rights for the Sports Complex property he had gained in exchange for privately financing the Flyers' home. *The Philadelphia Inquirer*'s Larry Eichel was told by Snider he had an idea for "a magnificent sports bar."

The bar for the 2003-04 hockey team seemed uncomplicated to coach Ken Hitchcock. The Flyers had been eliminated the past two playoffs by Ottawa. "At our first meeting at training camp, Hitch set an objective of getting over this belief we couldn't beat Ottawa," recalls Weinrich.

The Senators had been upset in the conference final by the Devils, who went on to beat Anaheim for the Stanley Cup. Thus, for all the respect the team had regained in Hitchcock's first season, multiple powerhouse obstacles still remained. And the coach worried whether his aging team had the legs to leap them.

"I was seeing wear and tear on guys, like their minds wanted to do things but their bodies couldn't," he recalls. "So I was a little bit nervous.

"I just thought LeClair, Roenick, even Amonte had played so many hard minutes in such hard areas that it was going to be a challenge keeping those guys enthusiastic, especially since they were not having a defined role like in the past.

"I wasn't as worried about Recchi because he hadn't played such a physical role. But I really saw it with Roenick and LeClair because they were such warriors; I remember they were still beat up when they came to training camp."

At the time, Hitchcock identified the issue with Roenick's listless camp as attitudinal.

"Sometimes during exhibition games he treated it like it was an exhibition game," complained Hitchcock to the media.

That's what they were, believed Roenick, who thought he had earned the right to get ready for a 16th NHL season at his own pace.

"I've worked hard and tried to do what [the coach] wanted me to do, so if he's not happy, I think we have a big problem," Roenick told reporters. "I feel like I've gone far, far beyond what anybody thought I would do to accept playing Ken Hitchcock's system."

The coach took the team to West Point—where generally compliance is not up for discussion—to participate in four days of bonding exercises that were not likely to bring Roenick and Hitchcock eye to eye.

"Look, I admit that my ego was pretty big at that time," Roenick recalls. "I didn't want to play preseason games and, as much as I respected Hitch and knew what an upgrade of a coach he was, I didn't want to do certain things he'd want a third or fourth-liner to do.

"Looking back, I was an idiot and an egomaniac. But for him to say I wasn't working hard, I mean, what the [bleep]? It's preseason. By 2003-2004, it wasn't like I was fighting for a spot on the team; I was focused on being ready to go when the season started. So for Hitch to say those things, I thought was idiotic.

"If you really have to question whether I'm going to answer the bell for the season, then we've got a big problem."

Part of Primeau's responsibility as captain was to provide interpretation services for Hitchcock. "He's trying to present uncomfortable situations that guys wouldn't normally be presented (with)," Primeau told reporters. "That's how he finds out an individual's personality and character."

Recalls Roenick, "That's exactly what Hitch thrives on doing. I'm sure he was just sending a message, but then tell me that. Bring me in the office, we'll talk about it, and it's fine. But don't blindside me and call me out in the paper. Then you're going to get backlash. That's what he got."

Backlash applied towards the opposition was what the coach really wanted, along with a healthy team. Unfortunately, the Flyers would begin the 2003-04 season without Primeau, who tore rib cartilage during the preseason, and Brashear, who suffered a sprained MCL in a crash against the boards during a drill.

Also wounded was LeClair, who suffered a hairline fracture from a shot off his left foot; Radovan Somik, who would miss the first four-six weeks with a partial tendon tear in his lower leg; and, Lapointe who was absent from camp with a right ankle sprain suffered after tripping over his cat and tumbling down a flight of stairs.

But at least Gagne, who had undergone surgery in May to repair tears in two oblique muscles, was hale and hearty following a season of injury and innuendo.

"They had kept taking pictures and doing tests and everything had come up negative," he recalls. "So they couldn't say that it was a sports hernia.

"I kept telling them, 'It's killing me.' Finally I went to a specialist in Montreal who did an ultrasound they usually use for (pregnant) women and that's how it finally got detected. After I had the surgery, the doctor told me the lining was halfway torn, which was why I kept pulling my groin.

"When Hitch found out he said, 'I know now you weren't faking it. You really had a big injury. I am really sorry for questioning your character. I should have listened and handled it better.'"

Recalls Hitchcock, "He was our best player at practices and then would say he couldn't go in the games. When he had the surgery, I called him and said, 'We didn't question your manhood, just wondered what was going on and now we know.'"

Hackett debuted with two shutouts in his first two games, beating Buffalo 2-0 in the home opener, and then in San Jose, backstopping the eighth scoreless tie in franchise history. Roenick and Recchi each had three-point games in a 5-4 victory at Phoenix that left Hitchcock steaming over Coyote tactics that included a hit from behind by Shane Doan that would take Gagne out with a shoulder bruise. "Do we play these guys again in our building?" the coach asked, perhaps rhetorically. "Ooo, that's going to be a good game."

First to settle a grudge, however, was Cechmanek, who sent the Flyers down to their first defeat of the season, 4-0, by the Kings at Staples Center. "I showed them I'm not a bad goalie and I can play with anybody," said the jilted former Philadelphia netminder. But the real lesson for the Flyers was five straight second-period penalties resulting in one powerplay goal and too much defensive zone time, helping to stake the Kings to a 2-0 lead.

The rookie Pitkanen, hardly an instant sensation, was a scratch in Los Angeles in favor of Therien. "We're going to do this periodically," explained Hitchcock. He is going to be an impact guy in our franchise and we don't want him to get overwhelmed."

Pitkanen was back the following night in Anaheim, where Tony Amonte scored with just one second left to tie the game before a 4-3 victory went to the Ducks on Rob Niedermayer's overtime goal. Philadelphia had to come from behind again, twice in fact, to tie Carolina 4-4, on October 25 at the Wachovia Center.

"We're chasing games," said Hitchcock, but at least the Flyers weren't struggling for goals, which meant a case of TastyKakes donated to a charity picked by the scorer. The organization had renewed the sponsorship enjoyed with the Tasty Baking Company in the early days of the franchise.

By happy coincidence, LeClair, the old Canadiens killer, was ready to return for a 5-0 shutout of Montreal, but it probably wasn't happenstance when he scored an incredible 29th goal in 32 games against his former team. The Canadiens still couldn't move LeClair. Clarke had the same problem with Big John's hefty contract.

"I know what I can do," said the 34-year-old winger. "I see players who are messed up, who can't play the game because of the pressure that's going through their hearts.

"I'm pretty sound in my heart with what I've done and where I fit in."

Hitchcock had closed the previous season by talking about sizing down the roles of veterans, but Recchi, who had cut back on postgame and off-day gym work to save his 35-year-old legs, was thriving with 17 minutes per game, down almost two from the season before. He had 11 points in the first seven contests.

Conversely, it appeared that phasing in more responsibility for 22-year-old Williams, who set up two goals in the Montreal victory, was producing a maturing sniper. Or, perhaps the egg came before the chicken: was Williams's production earning him more ice time?

"Justin has a personality in the NHL now," praised the coach. "He is a tenacious, hard-forechecking, two-way hockey player turning his tenacity into scoring opportunities."

Williams wondered who was saying that and what had he done with Ken Hitchcock? "You don't get many compliments from him," said the winger. "That's huge coming from the guy that matters, the guy who puts you out there."

He scored again, as did LeClair, in a 5-1 pounding of Florida. But after jumping up 2-0 on the Devils at the Meadowlands, the Flyers, held to one shot in the third period by the Stanley Cup champions, lost when Mike Rupp put a savable winner past Hackett. "They got the break and scored," said Hitchcock. "That's why they're champions; they got it up another level and we were the first team to crack."

Philadelphia bounced back with a 7-1 win in Toronto, as six players scored. With Gagne and Brashear returning, Somik was the only Flyer still unavailable, enabling the team's relatively fine health to pay off.

Amonte scored early in the third period at Madison Square Garden to tie the game before Ragnarsson won it, 2-1, in overtime. Amonte then assisted on Roenick's goal in a 2-1 victory over the Islanders that was especially hard earned by Todd Fedoruk. He pounded Eric Cairns to the ice, only to see the Isle defenseman rise and land a haymaker, sending the Philadelphia enforcer to Cooper Hospital to repair four fractures in facial bones.

That was practically the only loss, however, as Hitchcock's team caught its stride. The coach was matching a Kapanen-Primeau-Gagne line against the opposition's top units. "To me, Keith should get huge votes for the Selke (Trophy) this year," claimed Hitchcock. Through November 11, the Flyer penalty killing was statistically tops in the league, and their powerplay fourth.

After blowing three one-goal leads against Vancouver, the last with 7.2 seconds to go when Todd Bertuzzi's goal cancelled out Desjardins' apparent late-game winner, Kapanen broke up a two-on-one in overtime and Gagne banged home a Ragnarsson rebound to give Philadelphia a fifth-straight victory, 4-3. Two of those wins had been Hackett's, but Esche had triumphed in his last five starts.

"Robert is at the right age, has the right level of experience and has tremendous ability," Hitchcock said. "He is just getting better and better all the time."

Esche fully understood the opportunity in front of him.

"I really had worked hard in the off-season," the goalie recalls. "We had a team that could go a long ways so I just wanted to be a big part of that."

The trust by his teammates was growing. Hitchcock recalls the only thing holding Esche back was an internal fire that could sometimes burn out of control, not doused with all the beer he drank.

"He was really a great athlete who could make saves that were incredible," the coach remembers. "But focus was going to be a challenge for him because he was so competitive."

Fedoruk, another guy who had trouble reaching his "off" button, had a new, titanium, face and, despite it all, a hankering to expose it to harm. "It will be even stronger, but I won't know what it feels like until I get hit again," he said while healing. "That will drive me crazy.

"I'll probably spend a few days punching myself in the face to see how it feels."

Hitchcock was not afraid to give a slap across its collective cheek to a team that was 10-2-4 in its last 16 games. Forever worried about complacency, he kicked the Flyers from the practice ice during a sloppy passing drill. "We were wasting our time," he explained.

Shocked or otherwise, Philadelphia booted one away the following night, when it took a 2-0 lead into the third period in Raleigh before Williams coughed up the puck and Carolina's Peter Wallin beat Hackett with just 2:19 remaining, producing a 2-2 tie. "It was the best road game we played this year, not even close, and then we made a silly mistake on their second goal," said the coach.

One way to stop these late recurring opposition comebacks was to attempt to shorten the game. The Flyers were leading Minnesota 3-1 in the third period on two Recchi goals when the Wachovia Center horn went off and the clock failed. Lou Nolan, the PA announcer, gave the time at 30-second intervals until the end of the 3-1 victory.

Hackett gave up two goals by Boston's Brian Rolston within 35 seconds. But Recchi's powerplay score broke a 2-2 tie and Philadelphia took over first place in the conference from the Bruins by holding them to two third-period shots during a 3-2 victory on November 22. Esche surrendered a first-period powerplay goal and nothing else in a 1-1 tie in Pittsburgh, and then Pitkanen's powerplay goal provided the difference in a 4-2 win over Carolina.

The unbeaten streak went to 12 when five straight second-period goals smoked the Islanders, 5-1, in Uniondale. "There is a trust now among everyone, players and coaches, that somebody is going to step up," said Hitchcock.

But when the Flyers finally lost, 4-1 in Ottawa, it was apparent the coach didn't trust his team to shake it off. He elevated Brashear to the Roenick-Amonte line, moving Recchi to a unit with Primeau and Somik.

"We've been looking at this for a week to 10 days, waiting to go at it," said Hitchcock. "We weren't playing 60 minutes and were getting away with it until we got a significant opponent."

"Whatever," said Roenick. "He's been dying for a reason to split us up," he said. "I don't think Hitch wanted us to get too complacent.

"That's called being a control freak, but I'm enjoying what he's doing here. If I'm miffed at him, he'd know about it, believe me."

Recchi had no complaints either, about being dropped with the checkers. "Doesn't feel like the fourth line to me," he said. "John and I have played together quite a bit and this really balances the lines."

The units needed even more retooling when center Lapointe, who had not shown up for a 5-2 win over Pittsburgh on December 3 and then sat out the next two contests with what the Flyers termed depression, voluntarily entered the NHL's Substance Abuse and Behavioral Health Program. The 15-year veteran had developed a cocaine addiction.

"I had used just socially a couple times since I was 18," he recalls. "I had a family and career, so when I was offered, I would say, 'No.' After I got to Philly—and I don't know why because hockey was going really well for me there—I said, 'Yes.'

"It was best team I ever played on, for the best coach—Hitchcock—and the best assistant coach, too—Wayne Fleming, who also had helped me so much with the Islanders. But away from the rink, I fell in with the wrong crowd.

"I was using and was depressed. I couldn't believe I could be this way at this point of my life, and was really worried about overdosing."

After meeting with the two doctors who administered the program (Brian Shaw from the NHL Players' Association, and David Lewis from the NHL), Lapointe was sent to a Narcanon rehabilitation center in Clearwater, FL for 28 days.

The Flyers were not permitted by the joint agreement to disclose the nature of their player's health issue. "There is nothing we can say," said Clarke. "Claude is getting the help he needs. We obviously support anyone who goes for help. When he's done, he'll be back."

Fedoruk, wearing a wire mask, returned for a game with the Coyotes in anticipation of the bloodbath Hitchcock had threatened following the nasty game in Arizona the previous month. Instead, Esche beat his Phoenix mentor, Burke, 3-2, in a contest containing just three roughing penalties.

"When you have your best friend across the way, that's really emotional pressure," said Hitchcock. "He had a difficult time [opposing Burke] last year. I think this shows Robert's maturity."

Esche suffered a groin pull while warming up for the December 6 start in Boston, but Hackett stepped in. Although the Flyers were outshot 15-3 in the first period, Recchi's second-period goal and Hackett's 38 saves produced a 1-1 tie.

LeClair's redirect from Weinrich with 1:13 remaining, giving Philadelphia a 3-2 victory over Montreal, was Big John's sixth goal of the season, but his 30th in 33 games against the Canadiens since they had traded him to the Flyers. "It's one of those things that's not explainable," he said.

Primeau woke up with a sprained wrist on December 10 in Columbus, couldn't make a shot or a pass in the warm-up and had to be scratched. Kapanen played without his usual linemate and minus two of his teeth thanks to an inadvertent Brashear high stick, but the Finn nevertheless jammed the puck past Columbus goalie Fred Brathwaite with 1:08 remaining to pull out a 1-1 tie.

"We get the other team's A Game every night and we're still answering the bell," said a proud Hitchcock.

When Hackett fanned on Scott Niedermayer's dump-in with 31 seconds remaining in the first period, the alarm was sounded again, and this time answered by Primeau's late goal to pull out a 3-3 tie at the Meadowlands. "[Bleep] happens, and that definitely was [bleep]," said the goalie. "After the period I said, 'Boys, I really need you.'"

He received no scoring help the following night at the Wachovia Center as the Devils won the rematch, 2-0. "We deserved a better fate," said Primeau. "But down the road nobody will care that we worked hard."

Attendance suggested that caring was down for the team in general, despite its 17-4-8 record. After selling out only 14 regular-season contests the previous year, up to 1,000 seats remained available on game days. 76ers vice president Dave Coskey was named president of a new Comcast-Spectacor marketing division and former Flyer Bob Kelly was hired as a community ambassador.

The organization was working in a tough economy. With war drums sounding at the expiration of the Collective Bargaining Agreement at the end of the season, so was Clarke. But after Chouinard, who scored just three goals in 17 games, had been sent to the Phantoms, the GM came up with $1.75 million for a one-year contract with restricted free agent Mike Comrie. In 2001-02, his first full season in the NHL, the 5-10, 185-pound center had scored 33 goals for his native Edmonton.

"A pure passer like this is hard to find in today's NHL," said Clarke, who compensated the Oilers with defenseman Jeff Woywitka, the 27th player taken overall in 2001, plus a third-rounder in 2005.

"We thought we had other young defensemen in Pitkanen, Seidenberg, and Vandermeer," recalls Clarke. "Woywitka wasn't developing into what our guys had expected."

On December 19, the Flyers twice came from behind against Tampa Bay to go ahead on a third-period goal by Roenick, but Martin St. Louis tied the game and then won it in overtime for the Lightning. Hours later, Brashear was pulled over by Waterford Township, NJ police after swerving over the centerline following an exit from a parking garage. He was charged with unsafe driving and refusal to take a blood-alcohol test, eventually underwent alcohol counseling, and had his license suspended for 180 days.

After missing six games, Esche returned to snap a five-game Philadelphia winless streak (0-2-3) with a 3-1 victory over the Islanders. But when the Flyers opened an eight-game holiday trip with losses in Atlanta (4-1) and Uniondale (4-2), they had gone 14 games without scoring first.

Kapanen broke that streak in Denver before having to leave the game with a bruised kidney. Philadelphia, meanwhile, took a 2-1 lead on a rare goal by Somik midway through the third period, but ultimately lost in overtime when Milan Hejduk scored.

Thus Hitchcock returned for the first time to Dallas—the city where he won a Stanley Cup—with only one Flyer victory to show over their last 10 games (including three ties, and three overtime losses), not that anybody in Dallas had been tracking it. "I went out to get coffee and the (counter) guy said, 'So coach, what have you been doing with yourself since we fired you?'" Hitchcock reported.

It was practically the only laugh he experienced during his visit.

"It was really hard, not fun at all," recalls Hitchcock. "I had a huge part in designing the locker rooms and lounge in that [new American Airlines Arena] and then, half a year after we moved in, I'm gone.

"So I look up from the wrong bench and see the banners and it was really emotional for me. The whole game felt like a bloody blur."

Philadelphia jumped up 2-0 only to fade in the third period again, as the Stars rallied with two goals to gain a 2-2 tie. But Hitchcock's team, still eight points ahead of its previous year's pace, finally broke out with five powerplay goals during a 7-2 New Year's Eve win in St. Louis.

Comrie started 2004 by scoring his second and third goals in four games as a Flyer to provide Hackett's margin in a 2-1 victory at Florida. But Primeau was lost in the game to a broken thumb on a hit by Jay Bouwmeester.

"To me, this is a tremendous opportunity for guys like Handzus, Comrie and Roenick, especially Roenick," said the coach, but instead Philadelphia was mauled, 6-1, in Tampa before LeClair's goal and Esche's 21 saves secured a 1-1 tie in Buffalo to end their 2-4-2 trip.

"He's no fun right now," said Roenick, serving again as Hitchcock's barometer. Williams (no goals in 22 games), Gagne (one in 22), and Amonte (two in 23) also were not laughing. But the coach was happy to see some joy in Lapointe, when the center was welcomed back to practice after 28 days of treatment.

"His whole disposition is different now; it's terrific," said Hitchcock.

Lapointe claimed to like the new Claude better, too.

"When you get to know yourself, when you go deep, it's pretty scary stuff sometimes," he told reporters. "Depression is pretty common and I learned how to deal with it; don't stay negative and don't use any excuses.

"I kind of dealt with it all my life and this summer it blew up on me. I learned a lot in 28 days."

But 28 of them were not enough, and Lapointe knew it.

"You have to stay that long or you lose your salary," he recalls. "But if you believe you need more, you won't get paid, so the program provides for the minimum help and that's it.

"You say the things that they want to hear. Deep down, there is a little voice telling you you're not okay. But there's a stronger voice telling you to get back to hockey and that if you use once, it's okay because you had learned a lot about yourself in 28 days.

"I was 35 years old and had been dealing with feelings of inadequacy off the ice for most of my life. You don't solve deep issues in 28 days. It took me a week and I relapsed, just didn't tell anybody."

A 49-shot bombardment only got the Flyers a 4-3 overtime loss to Florida in their return home. Shut out by Edmonton, 3-0, and shutdown except for Comrie's late goal in a 2-1 defeat at Pittsburgh, they went to Buffalo 3-6-4 in their last 13 contests and were wound as tightly as their coach.

Philadelphia was trailing 3-2 when Comrie took a four-minute roughing minor, Handzus boarded J.P. Dumont, and Therien speared Miro Satan. The Sabres scored twice on the resultant powerplays. They led, 6-2, when Roenick, who had been cut twice in the first two periods by inadvertent sticks by teammates Ragnarsson and Kapanen, skated into the Sabre zone and apparently was high sticked by Rory Fitzpatrick. The infraction was difficult to detect even on the replay, but the cut J.R. had suffered earlier re-opened,

When no call was made, Roenick, skated past referee Blaine Angus and spit blood. "That's three times now!" the Flyer said. "Wake the [bleep] up!"

Upon returning to the bench and learning he had been given an unsportsmanlike conduct penalty, J.R. threw a water bottle that bounced against the leg of Angus, who immediately ejected the enraged player. Roenick made no attempt to suppress his anger when speaking to the media following the 6-2 defeat.

"What's he looking at?" he asked into television cameras, ranting that Angus wasn't the only NHL referee who "sticks it to the Flyers any time they have the opportunity."

When Roenick was suspended by the league for one game, costing him $91,463.41 in salary, he went off again.

"I have seen guys throw things on the ice—water bottles, sticks, a coach throw a bench on the ice—and I have never seen a suspension for it," Roenick said. "Again, the NHL uses me as a guinea pig.

"They love to do it to me. They screwed me last year when they suspended me two games for hitting Mike Modano from behind.

"It's a double standard; there seems to be no feeling for the player, only for the referee. Certain referees provoke this kind of response from players. I'm the one who gets punished because they refuse to do their job correctly. Certain referees—and they know who they are—are held unaccountable for their poor, poor decision-making.

Says Roenick today, "It's not up to me to decide if Blaine Angus is a bad ref. But he did have a terrible game and missed a lot of calls. I wasn't going to take it."

Hitchcock was critical of Roenick, not Angus. "You don't want to see a player lose money and you don't want to see a player suspended, but we really need to emotionally disconnect."

Actually, the Flyers needed to get a grip on two fronts. While Roenick did one game of hard time, Primeau, able to hold a stick after missing six games, returned to score a goal while another by call-up Patrick Sharp helped Esche to a 4-1 win over the Leafs, only Philadelphia's fourth victory in 19 games.

"[Primeau] makes sure that every guy is ready," said Gagne. "You could see it. On the first shift, he was physical, and on his second shift, he scored the first goal."

The next night in Toronto, Handzus tallied twice and the returning Roenick once as Esche beat the Leafs again, 4-0. But the satisfaction of consecutive wins was tempered. Desjardins had bumped with Roenick in the second period and suffered a broken forearm.

'He was chasing Mats Sundin around the net," recalls Roenick. "I came in because I wanted to knock Sundin down, but he saw me coming and I ended up catching Desjardins with the brunt of it.

"I was looking to knock out their best player and instead, I take out one of our best. I was devastated."

To make matters worse, Ragnarsson also was lost that night to a left rotator cuff sprain, joining on the injury list Seidenberg, who had suffered a leg broken in two places the previous week in practice. Ragnarsson was expected back in about two weeks. But Clarke already had been shopping for a defenseman.

On January 20, before a 4-1 Wachovia Center loss to Montreal—in which the Flyers also lost call-up defenseman Jim Vandermeer to a shoulder separation—Clarke traded Williams to Carolina for defenseman Danny Markov.

"We were reluctant to make the trade because we like [Williams] a lot," said Clarke. "But Markov is a defenseman that fits into our top four and they are very, very hard to find no matter who you offer.

"It's our opinion that a top-four defenseman is more valuable to us than a third-line winger."

Markov, 27, who as a member of the Maple Leafs had been an object of Clarke's desire in the failed Eric Lindros trade talks, was locked up through the 2005-06 season at salaries of $2.7/$2.9/$3.1 million, making him even more appealing for a team with the contracts of the 30-something Weinrich and Therien expiring at the end of the season.

"There were some players offered to us who were in the last year or two of their careers, but that didn't solve our problem," said Clarke. "We had to look into the future for replacements and Markov fits."

The GM mentioned the potential of Sharp, who had just been returned to the Phantoms, as one more factor making Williams—who

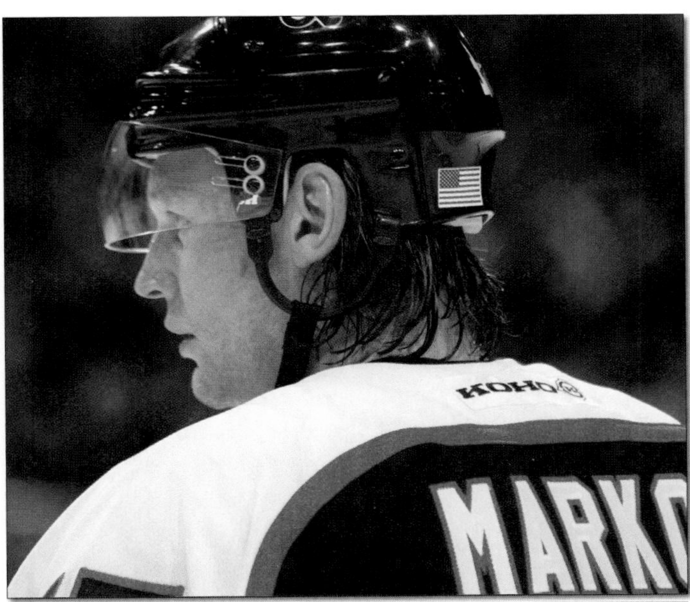

Danny Markov was acquired from Carolina in a trade for Justin Williams on January 20, 2004.

had 26 points in 47 games, but no goals in the previous 22 contests—expendable. "With the way Sharp and Fedoruk have played, we made the decision we could afford to give Williams up," said Clarke.

The GM broke the news to the 22-year-old before the morning skate. "He said, 'We traded you to Carolina. They want you to play tonight, here is (GM) Jim Rutherford's number,'" Williams recalls. "I said 'OK,' and out I went.

"I guess I was pretty shocked. When you are young, everything shocks you. I didn't think I was going to play in the NHL right away and didn't think I would get traded that quickly."

Like most high picks (28th overall in the 2000 draft) and instant successes, Williams, who scored 43 goals in 226 games with Philadelphia, thought he would be a fixture for a long time. But after missing 67 contests in three-plus seasons, the 180-pound right wing was dealt partly out of worry for how long he would last.

"The concern at the time was that Justin would be hurt often," recalls Clarke. "He was skinny and had the puck a lot. You always felt like you needed bigger wings."

Williams was averaging 15:41 in ice time, up slightly from the preceding season.

"I saw a really talented guy who still had a lot of junior in him," recalls Hitchcock. "He had tremendous skill and vision, was a fun-loving, loose, kind of guy, and you had to find a way to get some structure in there.

"I looked at it as, 'when he grows up, Willy's gonna be a good player.' But we had a ton of veteran right-wingers and he was getting pushed down to the third line. You are trading a young guy, but getting Markov for a few years.

"We felt like there was a little bit of an arms race going on between three or four teams and that we needed a huge defenseman that could carry a lot of minutes. Danny was a fierce competitor who was a No. 3 or a No. 4 (defenseman on the depth chart) at worst, because he could play on the powerplay too. He could really put us over the top and Justin was the price we paid."

Williams, who has won Stanley Cups in Carolina and Los Angeles and has scored more Game Seven goals (seven) during a 15-season NHL career than anyone in history, is not bitter about the too-few years he received as a Flyer.

"I loved it," he recalls.

"You always remember your first and this was a veteran group that taught me how to be a professional. I could look to my left at Rick Tocchet and to my right at Keith Jones, with John LeClair, Eric Desjardins and J.R. across the way.

"I've embraced the relationships created throughout my career and I have a lot of friends from here and still have a place in Ventnor, NJ.

"Hitch certainly was hard on me, but I feel I responded to that pretty well. You've got to expect to be yelled at every now and then and take it in stride. I don't regret any time I spent with any coach because they mold you into the player you eventually become. Hitch still is coaching and there's a reason for that.

"The game goes in cycles. It is less physical now. No one can foresee changes; it just kind of gradually happens. I had a tough little run with injuries in the middle of my career, but you learn throughout the years what you can and can't get away with. And I've always had the attitude that I'm going to prove somebody wrong."

Esche, who had played with Markov in Phoenix, didn't see any way Clarke could have gotten this deal wrong. "If I could hand-select a team, Danny would be on it," the goalie told reporters. "He skates like the wind, hits really hard and plays with a lot of talent and passion."

Markov recalls that his "conflict" with Carolina coach Peter Laviolette had reached the point where a trade was only a matter of time. "I walked on air that it was the Flyers," he remembers.

His wife Anna, with a one-year-old child and six months pregnant with a second, wasn't quite as thrilled. "She burst into tears but she quickly gathered herself," recalls Markov. "She knew this chance to play for a great team in the playoffs was better for me."

Clarke also picked up soon-to-be 30-year-old defenseman Mattias Timander from the Islanders for a seventh rounder. But even with two additions on defense, the absences of Desjardins and Ragnarsson made Therien, who had become the seventh guy, needed again.

Timander debuted, one game after Markov, on January 22 at Madison Square Garden, where Gagne broke a 1-1 second period tie and LeClair's 12th goal added insurance in Esche's 4-2 victory. He had started five consecutive games for a reason deeper than Hitchcock's increasing confidence. After Hackett's 9-2-6 beginning, he had one win in his last seven starts.

"He was a really good goalie and that changed like, overnight," the coach recalls. "After one warm-up, so many shots were going in that I remember somebody came up to me saying, 'Jeez, was Hackett out last night or something?'

"And then there were times during practice where he would just fall down."

Feeling fatigued and irritable, Hackett figured he was suffering from a mild flu or simply a mid-season slump. But five days after the 6-2 loss in Buffalo on the evening of Roenick's tantrum, the goalie got out of bed in the middle of the night to find the room spinning in circles to his right. Trying to enter the bathroom, he kept walking into the wall to the right of it, an exercise in futility that happened three more times in the morning.

"I was very scared," recalls Hackett, who actually remembers feeling relief when the diagnosis was positional vertigo. "I thought it might be something way, way worse."

Doctors could only guess that the condition was viral and had no idea how long it would take to clear up.

"Jeff and I were roommates in Montreal and, in Philly, I rode to games with him and Mark Recchi," recalls Weinrich. "Jeff became a little private when all that stuff was going on, guarded in what he was saying; I think he was having a hard time being around the team.

"He was a different guy in that time and it was hard to watch. I really felt for him.

Hitchcock recalls, "It was very unnerving to see a guy go through that, you know, where he couldn't move his head; even the shifting of his eyes was really troubling."

The Flyers called up Phantom veteran Neil Little to back up Esche, who, 6-1-1 in eight consecutive starts, was leading Tampa Bay, 1-0, before Gagne, trying to catch Cory Stillman on a breakaway, fell into the goalie, causing him to catch his foot against the post. Esche tried to soldier on before realizing he had to come out with what was diagnosed as a grade two MCL tear. Little surrendered two goals on eight shots in the 2-1 loss.

Antero Niittymaki, the Flyers' sixth-round pick in 1998 playing his second season with the Phantoms, was recalled to win his first NHL start, 5-1, over Washington.

"Very sound," praised Hitchcock. The following night, Niittymaki won again, 5-1, this time in Atlanta.

It had taken the Finn, who had been flabbergasted to learn of his draft as an 18-year-old in the sixth round in 1998, six years to reach the NHL. "Now, everybody knows when the draft is and you can watch it online, but back then you couldn't, so I wasn't really playing attention to it," Niittymaki recalls. "Next day, my dad called me and told me the news.

"You always dream. But I wasn't that big of a prospect. It was more like maybe get a chance one day to play Finnish professional hockey or for the national team. That was more realistic.

"Even after I got drafted, it wasn't really changing my goals, but things started to roll from there. Because of injuries, I got a chance to play for the big team (TPS Turku) and we won a championship that spring (2000). I had met some times with (Flyer European scout) Inge Hammarstrom, maybe Bob Clarke one time, and was close to signing with the Flyers then. But I had to do a year of military service, so we pushed it back a year. Because of that, I wasn't really having a good year. I thought maybe I had blown my chance. But then I had a really good year my third year, and almost made the Finnish National Team.

"So I signed. I knew it was going to be one or two years in the minors, but I expected to be a dominant (AHL) goalie right away. But the game was so different—more screens, more rebounds, angled shots; like I'd never seen before. I had played three years professionally and now I'm a rookie again, kind of tough to swallow for the first couple weeks but then I got used to it.

"I worked with (Flyer goaltending coach) Reggie Lemelin. He wasn't there (with the Phantoms) all the time, but we watched some video and he told me what I had to do differently if I ever wanted to make it. It got easier for me. I remember telling Paul Holmgren at our meeting after the first season, 'I'm a better goalie than this. I'll be ready next year.'"

In his second season with the Phantoms, Niittymaki was in the process of lowering his goals-against to 2.02 from 2.58 and raising his save percentage from .903 to .924 when he was called up for the emergency, which had Hackett's career in jeopardy at age 35.

Feeling the worst of his dizziness had disappeared, Hackett stopped 16 of 18 shots in a 5-2 Phantom win over Albany, but still knew he wasn't ready to return to an NHL goal.

"I felt distant; it was hard to focus," he recalls. "More than a full-blown episode, it was like drifting."

Clarke, shopping in the interim, had asked Hitchcock what he thought of Sean Burke, whom the forever belt-tightening Coyotes were trying to move. The coach endorsed Burke fully. When Clarke told Hackett the team couldn't wait on his recovery any longer, the goalie didn't plead for more time. The morning the players reconvened from the All-Star break, the Flyers announced Hackett's retirement after just 27 games with Philadelphia.

"They had to move forward, and I accepted what they decided," he recalls. "The Flyers were good people and I understood the position they were in.

"I don't think I felt completely right for probably a year anyway. Day to day, things were fine after a couple of months, but I never was at a high level of competition again after that, so anything I'm saying about whether I could have kept playing would be a total guess."

Hackett became the goaltending coach for the Avalanche from 2006-09. Today, he leads "a quiet life " and a healthy one in his native London, Ontario, where he has coached his two boys.

"I really was looking forward to that season, had a good feeling about the Flyers," he recalls. "I had been offered a contract (to remain) with Boston, but I talked with [Recchi and Weinrich] and really had wanted to play with some people that I enjoyed playing with in the past.

"I wish it worked out better for me, but I look at it more as a half-full thing. No, I didn't win a Stanley Cup, but I was in a Memorial Cup final, was on a World Junior Championship team (for Canada in 1988), and won an AHL championship (with Springfield in 1990).

"In the NHL, I played on an expansion team (San Jose); had some tough situations, but I have no regrets. Ultimately, you would love to leave on your own terms, but hockey has been very good to me."

Hours after announcing Hackett's retirement, Clarke dealt Comrie to Phoenix for 23-year-old winger Branko Radivojevic and Burke, reuniting the 16-year veteran with his greatest protege, Esche.

In 1990, a 12-year-old Esche, who grew up in Whitesboro, NY, had been gifted a stick from young Burke, the Devil goaltender, following a preseason scrimmage with the team's farmhands in Albany. Esche, who had played Tier II hockey near Ottawa and passed up scholarship offers at NCAA schools to join the Detroit Jr. Whalers, ended up being drafted by Phoenix, where he had backed up Burke for two seasons.

"For me, it's a huge thrill to come back to [the Flyers]," said Burke, who had started all five games during their 1998 first-round loss to Buffalo. "Me and Esche have a great relationship.

"I don't think any goaltending tandem gets along as well off the ice as we do."

In truth, being reunited with Esche was the only thing he liked about the trade.

"The reality was the (Phoenix) franchise was struggling and they basically said, 'We need to trade you, or we're not going to make payroll.'" Burke recalls. "At that point, you can't dig in and say, 'I'm not going anywhere.' So I agreed to be traded to Philadelphia, but Philadelphia was not what I wanted to do.

"I'd enjoyed to a point the experience I had the first time but [the Flyers disinterest in re-signing me] hadn't left a great taste in my mouth. Plus (in 2004), I didn't have any intention of being a backup. I was too good a player at that time."

Esche also was playing like a goalie too good to be a backup. But he nevertheless felt totally unthreatened by the arrival of his once-and-again mentor.

"When you first come up, you don't realize how far away you are from being a pro," Esche recalls. "I can look back and tell you that I don't know if I would have been an NHL player if not for Sean Burke; he kept me together at the start.

"Hitch told me they didn't want to put the entire burden, and all the accountability, on me. They needed a plan in case I couldn't carry the load, and I thought [the trade] was terrific. Sean was supportive of me and I thought the world of him. It was kind of a no-brainer."

The head scratcher was the Flyers bailing so quickly on Comrie, who had totaled nine points in just 21 contests with Philadelphia. But the ice time he was receiving, just 12:52 per game, down five minutes from what Comrie had enjoyed in Edmonton, was the tipoff that he was not a good fit.

"Our guys had liked him; we thought he would be able to score for us, set some plays up," recalls Clarke. "But as it turned out, I think he was better suited for playing in the West, where there was more skating room.

"You think you have plenty of character and size but need some goals, so you bring in a Mike Bullard or a Pat Falloon or a Comrie. But it usually doesn't work. It was a poor trade by me because that's not the kind of guy that Hitch likes. It's better to have a heavier guy that doesn't score than a guy like that who your coach doesn't want on the team."

Recalls Hitchcock, "Comrie was a center that wasn't big enough to play down low, so we ended up using him on the wing. You know, he was a really good player when he was with the Oilers. It was a size issue more than anything."

Roenick remembers it being more than that. "For a small guy, he was pretty effective offensively," Roenick recalls. "He was skilled and crafty, but wasn't the most intense guy.

"Mike kind of played hockey like it was a hobby. He didn't do it for the paycheck; he just liked to have fun making fancy moves, dangling up high, and was the same way in the locker room, happy-go-lucky.

"That was very un-Hitch-like hockey. He wanted more of a compete level and more commitment in tight checking games than Mike was going to give you."

Recalls Primeau, "They had me room with him, just like I had with young Justin (Williams). Eight in the morning, I opened the drapes and Mike is like, 'What are you doing?' He liked to sleep.

"I said, 'You gotta be professional, time to get up.' I was building a relationship with him; he seemed to be productive and then he was gone. It was one of the most bizarre things."

But no stranger than Burke finding himself returned to Philadelphia, brought back by the same GM who had no interest in keeping him the first time. "I liked Esche a lot, just never felt he was a No. 1," recalls Clarke. "Burke wasn't a bad goalie; he had had some success in the league."

Recalls Hitchcock, "Robert was the best athlete of any of our goalies, but he needed mental and physical refining. He was fiery, very similar to what Sean was early in his career, so he could help us with that.

"But I thought we were bringing Burke in to be our goalie in the playoffs."

The additions of Timander and Markov had convinced the Flyers that they could shed Weinrich and the remaining two months of their financial obligation to him. On February 9, the same busy day they dealt for Burke and Radivojevic, plus settled up with Hackett, Weinrich, 37, was traded to St. Louis for a fifth-round pick.

"When you get split up from your usual partner (Johnsson) and your minutes go down, you definitely sense that the coaches have lost some confidence in you," Weinrich recalls. "Even as a veteran, I definitely let it get to me and wasn't playing as well as I could.

"Anyway, I was kind of resigned to being the fifth or sixth guy (playing with the rookie Pitkanen). I took a shot off an ankle (against Tampa Bay on January 31) and it was pretty painful. I had trouble getting a skate on. So they had told me to stay home from a trip (to Atlanta for the final pre-All-Star break contest).

"When I look back on it now, part of the reason they wanted that x-ray was to see if I was tradable. We were at my wife's sister's place in South Carolina during the break when Clarkie called. He said, 'There are a few teams we could trade you to, what is your choice?'

"I thought St. Louis had a team with a good chance to go far in the playoffs. I always liked playing in that building, so that's what I chose.

"The day we came back from the break, I knew I was traded and still had to hang around the locker room until it went through. It was a really awkward time."

Primeau and Roenick, suspecting it might be their last All-Star

Game appearances, had made a point to enjoy the experience in St. Paul with their families and Roenick brought home his second shooting accuracy title.

As the schedule resumed, it appeared Niittymaki had been mistaken for a target by the Devils. With Burke arriving too late to get in a practice with his new team and Esche still out from his ligament tear, New Jersey shot 35 pucks into the Finn in a 4-1 Wachovia Center victory that put Philadelphia seven points ahead of the Devils for the Atlantic Division lead.

"He's technically sound with the puck, looks excellent," praised Hitchcock.

Two nights later, Burke made his Flyer re-debut in New York. The game was tied 1-1 4:09 into the third period when Petr Nedved beat Roenick on a faceoff. J.R. was looking through the Ranger center, trying to pick up defenseman Boris Mironov's point drive, when the puck crashed into Roenick's jaw. There had been barely time to flinch.

"I felt the shatter and, actually, I was lucky," Roenick recalls. "An inch lower and it gets me in the throat and crushes my larynx."

He lay motionless on the ice for several minutes then, spitting blood into a towel, was helped up by Philadelphia trainer John Worley and Ranger trainer Jim Ramsey. Primeau and Gagne helped Roenick onto a stretcher, where he sat as he was carried off, waving at Ranger fans giving a Flyer the only standing ovation in anyone's Madison Square Garden memory.

"He gets hit in the face and we're sitting on the bench thinking, 'Oh no, we're not going to have J.R. for the playoffs,'" recalls Primeau, who went out for the next shift. Thirty-two seconds of playing time after Roenick left, Primeau pivoted at center ice as Philadelphia was attempting to counter off a Ranger turnover and ran into Holik, who didn't see the Flyer center coming either.

Holik's elbow crashed the side of Primeau's head. The captain remained down for more than a minute until, as Primeau was resting on one knee, Ramsay and Flyer equipment manager Turk Evers tended to him while the Philadelphia bench castigated Holik, who insisted the contact was unintentional.

Four minutes after Primeau was helped to the locker room, Radivojevic forced a giveaway, and Kapanen pounced to put a shot in off the post, enabling the severely shorthanded Flyers to pull out a 2-1 victory.

"We had to play three lines and really dug in," said Lapointe, who took turns centering each one down the stretch.

Praised Hitchcock, "Our team and bench deserve an awful lot of credit. They sucked it up and played it out."

From New York's St. Vincent's Hospital, Roenick asked for PR director Zack Hill's telephone and proceeded to call *Inquirer* beat reporter Tim Panaccio. Thanking the Garden fans for a classy gesture, J.R. said that his head was clear, but his jaw unstable, and he then offered to take the writer "out for soup" soon.

Primeau rode the bus home suffering from a slight headache and a stiff neck, neither of which was sore the next morning. He skipped practice only because the trainers insisted on it as a precaution.

"My wife (Lisa) said, 'You don't look well,' and I'm like, 'I'm fine,'" recalls Primeau. "It wasn't that hard a hit.

"I get in my car to go to the [Wachovia Center] the next morning for [a matinee rematch with the Rangers], the first time I had driven since it happened, and all of a sudden I couldn't focus on the road. I broke out in a sweat and felt nauseous.

"I stopped at Starbucks and called John Worley from the car; I told him I felt motion sickness. He said, 'Turn around and go home.'

"I told him I would have Lisa drive me to the game. He said, 'Don't bother.' I had an unbelievable headache, couldn't function. I went back to bed, then went to see the neurologist and was diagnosed with post-concussion syndrome."

Roenick was released from the hospital Saturday morning following Friday surgery to repair a jaw broken in 21 places. "I remember seeing the x-ray and there was a perfect puck-shaped indention with all these spider-web breaks around it," he recalls.

J.R. had a cop friend come to New York to pick him up, and then received a State Police escort down the New Jersey Turnpike so he could arrive on time for the afternoon game. The television cameras found him in the owner's suite.

"I still was a little bit out of it," Roenick recalls. "And I couldn't look at the damage for a while.

"First time I [saw myself], I looked like Rocky Dennis from *Mask*. When they put me up on the arena video board, my face was so big and swollen that the whole place gasped. It was not a pretty sight.

"Everybody thought I was nuts, 24 hours after I had broken my jaw in 21 places, sitting up there watching the hockey game."

At least the contest was easy on the eyes. Sharp, recalled to take Roenick's place, scored twice as Burke completed the sweep of the Rangers, 6-2.

"I didn't want to be there," recalls Burke. "But after those two Ranger games, I remember thinking, 'Wow, this team, I just have to be good, not great, and it has a chance to win the Stanley Cup.'"

Of course, that was unlikely without Roenick and Primeau, but Clarke didn't merely hold his breath waiting on their return. He traded Vandermeer, a second-round pick, and 2003 third-round draftee Colin Fraser to Chicago for center Alexei Zhamnov and a fourth-round choice.

"The guy who knew (Zhamnov) better than anybody (from living in Winnipeg, where Zhamnov had once starred) was (assistant coach) Wayne Fleming," recalls Hitchcock. "And Wayne was pushing like crazy.

"He said, 'This guy's exceptional.'"

Zhamnov, 33, had scored 243 goals and 448 assists in 11-plus seasons for the Jets and Blackhawks, the later having obtained him, coincidentally, in exchange for Roenick, just as the Winnipeg franchise moved to Phoenix in 1996.

Having just lost Roenick—his best center and buddy—Amonte was getting a replacement who had helped him record three 40-goal seasons in Chicago. "I don't know if you could see me out there," the winger told reporters after practice at the Skate Zone. "I had a huge smile on my face."

So did Zhamnov, who had been in only three playoff series during his years in Winnipeg and Chicago but had not won a round. "It's been frustrating, especially when you see other guys leave Chicago and have an opportunity to compete for the Stanley Cup," he told the media. "I was there eight years and [the Blackhawks] are like my family, but it was time to leave."

When Burke let in five goals on 20 shots and lost for the first time in three starts, 5-2 to San Jose at the Wachovia Center, the fans wanted him to hit the road, never minding that he had just arrived. When the booing continued into, and after, a 4-3 loss to the Bruins, Fedoruk felt compelled to grab the microphone during a postgame shirt giveaway and tell the customers to knock it off.

"It made us all pretty angry," Hitchcock told the media. "Everyone in Philadelphia knows our situation.

"We have a lot of guys out and we're still fighting for first place. We need everybody's help."

Clarke believed the head coach could use more assistance, too. In the midst of the team's January struggles, the GM had asked Terry Murray, who had come back to Philadelphia as a pro scout after being fired as the Panther coach, to take a seat in the press box and report down to Hitchcock between periods. The Flyer coach welcomed the input and with Murray—at heart a coach, not a scout—wanting to be behind the bench during games and on the ice at practice, the job had evolved into a third assistant-coaching position.

No help would be coming from Primeau or Roenick for some time. Roenick went to his home outside Phoenix, where the full effects of the head trauma he had suffered—lightheadedness, nausea, dizziness and pain—set in.

"My brain stem had shifted from the impact," he recalls. A second MRI suggested there was a possible, ominous, cranial circulation problem. Advised not to travel, Roenick cancelled a visit to Philly to get rechecked by the Flyer medics and was talking about retiring. Meanwhile, every attempt Primeau made to build conditioning on the bike brought on a feeling of seasickness.

Ragnarsson, who had missed five games with a rotator cuff sprain, came back to score in a 5-4 February 21 win over Atlanta, a game decided when Gagne broke a tie with just 1:01 to play.

Zhamnov and Amonte tallied against their old Chicago mates in Burke's 3-1 win over the Blackhawks, then the goalie stopped 40 shots to make Gagne's eighth goal in 11 games hold up for a 1-1 tie in Ottawa. "Moral victories for us right now are good," said Hitchcock about the tie, but Philadelphia didn't feel ethically bound to take the high road over an incident during the deadlock.

Senator winger Martin Havlat had responded to a Recchi hook that sent both players into the board by slashing the Flyer in the head as they disengaged. "I wanted to hit him but not in the face; it was a bad decision," said Havlat after the game, apologizing for becoming frustrated with all the hooking that had gone on earlier. "I don't feel good about what I did."

Havlat, who had been suspended for two games earlier in the season for kicking Islander Eric Cairns, received a five-minute match penalty for attempt to injure and another two games from the league, penalties that did not satisfy Philadelphia.

"Someday, someone's going to make him eat his lunch," said Hitchcock. "This is something in my opinion that the players should take care of."

Recchi agreed. "He two-handed me across the face," said the winger. "He's known for it.

"It might not come from our team, but he better protect himself."

Recchi would miss no time, fortunately. Roenick got lucky, too, when an arteriogram revealed no blockages or aneurysms, although his return remained uncertain. But Esche was ready to play on February 28 against Boston, where Zhamnov scored in the third period to create a 2-2 tie that lasted only until Bruin Glen Murray won the game in overtime.

Gagne, put on a line with Zhamnov and Amonte, had a rare opportunity to score on his February 29 birthday and did it for the first time in his NHL career. But the Red Wings blew out his candles in a 4-2 victory at Joe Louis Arena.

The Flyers, Leafs, Lightning, Bruins and Senators all were within two points of each other for the Eastern Conference lead when Ottawa, Havlat's suspension just completed, came to the Wachovia Center eight days after the two teams had met in Canada.

Sean Burke's second stint with the Flyers began with back-to-back wins against the New York Rangers.

Markov's first-period score, a flip shot that netminder Patrick Lalime misplayed giving Philadelphia a 3-1 lead, was the 10,000th goal in Flyer history, making the team the fifth to reach the milestone. But that soon became a footnote.

Pitkanen, sent into the glass by Shaun Van Allen, was concussed and unable to return for the second period. Neither could Therien, who injured a shoulder in a collision with Marian Hossa, forcing Hitchcock—who remembered Kapanen had said during training camp that, as penalties demanded, he had played a few shifts on defense in Carolina—to move the winger to the blueline.

Recchi asked Havlat to fight on the first shift they were on the ice together. "I said, 'Let's just get it done,' and he wouldn't," recalls Recchi. "If he would have, nothing else would have happened."

The level of tension escalated with third-period roughing confrontations, first between Zhamnov and Daniel Alfredsson, then Sharp and Bryan Smolinski. But the only vengeance the Flyers had gained was a 5-2 lead on the scoreboard when, with 1:45 to go, Ottawa coach Jacques Martin put out enforcer Robert Ray and Hitchcock countered with Brashear.

Brashear shoved Ray in front of the net and the Senator tough guy answered with an elbow, causing Brashear to come back with several lefts, then a right that opened up a cut above the Ottawa player's right eye. "The Senators had just brought me back six games earlier," recalls Ray. "I was not in shape to be sent out there to start something and Jacques (Senator coach Martin) didn't believe in that stuff, anyway."

As Brashear, being escorted to the tunnel, verbally threatened the Senators, he was jumped from behind by Todd Simpson and Brian Pothier. When Sharp tried to come to Brashear's aid, Simpson knocked the rookie down and began punching, bringing Markov to the rescue. After Esche came the length of the ice to intervene, Lalime dropped his gear and the Flyer goalie gladly responded, while Radivojevic was rag-dolling Van Allen and Simpson decided to use his 50-pound advantage on Kapanen.

Three seconds after the penalties were sorted out and the puck was dropped, Chris Neil speared Somik, who tried to respond to little avail while Zdeno Chara tossed around Timander, setting off another round of fights.

On the next faceoff, Handzus engaged Mike Fisher, who flipped the big Philadelphia center onto his back. They received the sixth and seventh majors of the game and went to the locker rooms. But when play resumed and Recchi laid a hit on Wade Redden, the Senator defenseman grabbed LeClair, who engaged in the only fight of his Flyer career. While that wrestling match continued, Recchi threw down with Smolinski, the Senator center taking several shots before landing a right cross.

Only 24 seconds of playing time had elapsed since the first punch was thrown and still Ottawa was in a fighting mood. "We weren't known for that," recalls Ray. "I remember the other players were gleeful afterwards that they could fight like that." Jason Spezza went after Sharp, who fell on top and got in the last good punch.

Martin had kept Havlat safe by sending him to the penalty box to serve one of the penalties. "That coach is not stupid," Brashear said later.

There were three Flyers and two Senators left on the bench as the final seconds of Philadelphia's 5-3 victory finally ran out with the two teams having set NHL records for the most combined penalty minutes (413), most penalty minutes in a period (409), and most penalty minutes for one team in a game (Philadelphia's 213).

Clarke went towards the Ottawa dressing room to confront Martin—verbally, he was insisting—but was talked out of it.

"Obviously my teammates didn't forget what happened last week," said Recchi.

They had not, assured Brashear, confessing,

"I started it. Did you see the last game?

"I went out and fought a tough guy. Ray went after Sami Kapanen. They went after guys who don't fight. I could've fought one of their good players and hurt him, but I didn't."

That was Hitchcock's sentiment, too. "Their tough guy got beat up, then their next-in-lines fought two guys that don't fight."

Still, the coach claimed to be much more interested in the victory, his team's first in the regular season over the Senators in six meetings, with one more scheduled on April 2 in Philadelphia.

"We played a great hockey game," said Hitchcock. "We lost two defensemen and played on, established our game and created a number of opportunities for ourselves. I don't think the last five minutes should make you lose sight of that."

The injuries to Pitkanen and Therien were not long-term, but Ragnarsson had suffered a shoulder strain two days earlier, joining Desjardins and Seidenberg on the sideline. With Vandermeer gone in the Zhamnov deal, the Flyers had only two of their regular defensemen—Timander and Johnsson—remaining. Even after recalling John Slaney, Randy Jones and Freddy Meyer from the Phantoms for the game the next night in Washington, Philadelphia was a defenseman short. So Hitchcock used Kapanen there again.

"I said, 'We're in a tough spot, Sami, and need your help. Can you wiggle your hips and skate backwards?'" recalls Hitchcock.

"He said, 'Yup!'

Recalls Kapanen, "I'd been a quarterback on a powerplay since I was 16 years old, so I thought I could do it. I felt like I was a good enough skater to get there early and move the puck, spin around and make some plays.

"I don't think many guys could have gotten that done, but I felt like I could. It was a challenge to me. After the first 20 minutes, you kind of get comfortable. It was exciting, a different part of the game."

Brashear, apparently still in a foul mood from the previous night, committed a penalty that Cap Jeff Halpern cashed, then took a charging call and a game misconduct in the final minute. Handzus scored shorthanded with 26 seconds to play, but that was all the depleted Flyers got in a 2-1 defeat.

Clarke, his team 5-5-1 since losing Roenick and Primeau—and still having no idea when he would get either back—was determined to go down fighting, too. A day before the March 9 trading deadline, the GM came away from Glen Sather's Ranger estate sale—they were about to miss the playoffs for the seventh-straight season—with a considerable prize.

Vladimir Malakhov, a 12-year veteran defenseman, was acquired for a second-round selection and another of the five third-rounders the Flyers had drafted nine months earlier—winger Rick Kozak.

Clarke then dealt Therien, the longest tenured pro athlete in Philadelphia (almost 10 years) at that time, to Dallas for third- and eighth-round choices.

"When you are in these situations, money becomes a factor. To add a player, we felt we had to move a player," said the GM. "We didn't lose any size, but I think Malakhov is much better with the puck than Chris and a better skater.

"[Malakhov] played in Montreal in a very organized situation and was one of the top defensemen in the league. He was very good in New Jersey when they won the Stanley Cup (in 2000). It is the same type of atmosphere here. It will be good for him.

"Chris was a favorite of mine, played here a long time and played pretty well. But with Malakhov going into the lineup, Chris may not always be [dressing]. This is a really good opportunity for him. He and [Hitchcock] aren't the best of friends; it [would not have been] a good situation for him."

Therien looks back and concurs. "When Hitchcock sat me out (January 31) in Pittsburgh, I went to Clarkie and said, 'I cannot play for this [bleeping] guy anymore. He's the worst person I've ever been around.'

"Clarkie said, 'I'm not trading you; you're too important to the team.' I said, 'Too important? I'm a healthy scratch to this guy.'

"I don't want to say I gave up, but I put on five pounds. I'd just had enough of Hitch. But a week before I got traded, I was still playing against other teams' top lines every single night.

"When I [suffered a shoulder dislocation] in that Ottawa game and missed a couple of weeks, they asked me to take a (cortisone) shot to speed up [healing]. At that point, I was thinking I was not going to get traded. Weinrich was gone and I was not making that much ($2.6 million) for a team that had a lot of money.

"But Clarkie called me in and said, 'I've traded you to Dallas to give you a chance there.' And I said, 'Thanks, you've done me a favor.' I was proud to be a Flyer, but I couldn't take another day of Hitch.

"Dallas had [gone unbeaten in nine] when I got there, so it wasn't like Clarkie was sending me to the wolves or to some crap team that never had a shot. He did me the justice of going to the playoffs."

Hitchcock remembers Therien, 32, having a hard time keeping up. "Like any older player, he needed to be in twice as good of shape as when he first came to the league, and he just kept himself the same," the coach recalls. "So it became a factor from an endurance standpoint.

"Against skilled players, that gangly style would frustrate you with his long stick. He could defend. But towards the end he couldn't keep up.

"All of a sudden we've got Malakhov, Markov, Timander—who was another, strong determined, wide-bodied, guy—joining Johnsson, Ragnarsson, Desjardins, and Pitkanen. We were deep back there, had so many guys who could play a ton of minutes."

Malakhov had become the third Russian added in mid-season, much to the joy of Markov. "We all knew each other from the national team and we were all [in Philadelphia] without our families, which helped me mentally," he recalls.

The orange-and-black melting pot now consisted of 12 European players. Only the media was counting, however, obviously not the GM. "We've got Finns, Russians, Swedes and a couple of guys from Boston," Clarke smiled. "The rest are all English-speaking."

Historically, hockey players' language skills had conveniently deserted them whenever asked if they were suffering concussion symptoms.

Roenick, who returned to practice wearing a plastic shield to protect his jaw, reported he had been cleared to resume by a baseline test and was waiting only to have the wires removed.

"I'm smarter than I was before; this one knocked some sense into me," he joked, before adding, "It will be important to see how I respond (in practice)."

Primeau, too, passed a baseline test and returned to drills with the team on March 8.

"I've had some real good days, which are very encouraging, but there's times I don't feel myself," he said. "So I wouldn't say that I've been clear of symptoms for days or weeks on end.

"I'm going to be real honest. There have been times in the past that maybe I disguised a bit to get through it, but this one is different."

The following night, he got dizzy on the bus ride to the Meadowlands and was scratched, but the Flyers again responded without him. LeClair assisted on goals by Recchi and Johnsson and then scored his 21st of the season, into the empty net, to secure a 3-1 victory. At age 34, he had fulfilled Hitchcock's mandate of adjusting to a lesser role and enjoyed a solid and healthy season.

"John knew they were trying to get rid get rid of him, and the way he handled himself around the guys could have had a bad effect," praised Recchi. "He never once showed it.

"He was down and they were trying to kick him. He turned it into a positive. Not a lot of guys can do that."

Recalls Hitchcock, "He was banged up, sore every day. There was a period of time where my fourth line was Roenick, Johnny LeClair and Tony Amonte, the most expensive fourth line in the history of hockey.

"But they were also the line that I used on the second unit of the powerplay, so I was able to give those guys minutes that nurtured them along. They didn't have foot speed anymore, but they were smart and could still do things."

With Pitkanen, Ragnarsson and Markov back in the lineup, Kapanen returned to the wing. Therien, meanwhile, completed his rehab in time to play his first game for Dallas in the building that had been his home for nine-plus years. The Flyers killed off a six-on four that extended into the final minute, only to have the Stars' Brenden Morrow score with 35 seconds remaining to force a 2-2 Wachovia Center tie.

"The whole thing was just weird for me," recalls Therien. "At one point, I swear, I went to hit my partner, Sergei Zubov, in the corner."

Two nights later, two diving breakups by Handzus in the final minute led to an early third-period goal by Ragnarsson that held up for a gritty 2-1 victory over the Devils, the Flyers' second in four nights over their New Jersey nemeses, putting Philadelphia eight points up for the division lead with nine games to play.

"There was always this feeling that something bad was going to happen every game (against New Jersey)," gushed Hitchcock. "We don't believe that anymore."

Countered Devil general manager Lou Lamoriello with a smile, "For them to be talking about it, they must be thinking about it, right?"

Whether or not the cause of two goals allowed by Burke on the first six shots in Pittsburgh was a hangover from a couple of huge wins, the Flyers fought back. Zhamnov, who had scored unassisted to open the game, set up Gagne early in the third period for a 3-3 tie that clinched Philadelphia's 10th straight playoff spot.

"Zhamnov was one of the smartest, most skilled, most complete players I've ever coached," recalls Hitchcock. "And you never had to spend one second motivating or inspiring him."

But the coach did have to introduce him. A team with six in-season additions spent three days practicing and bonding at Amelia Island, FL.

"Crash course in chemistry," said Hitchcock. "It's not like we made all these changes in October; we made them in February and March through necessity. How quickly we can bring this group together is going to be the challenge."

When the Flyers went back to work four days later, the Leafs were no day at the beach. While Malakhov caught a deflection in the face and suffered a non-displaced jaw fracture requiring a plate and four screws—he nevertheless was expected back for the playoffs—Toronto jumped to a 3-0 lead on two goals by its newest acquisition, Brian Leetch, and hung on for a 3-2 Wachovia Center victory.

"We've had three facial injuries in the last six weeks," Primeau lamented as the count for man games lost to injury went to a whopping 222 for the season. "This stuff just doesn't happen (often)."

Esche shut out the Rangers, 3-0, and Burke won in Carolina 4-2. With the playoffs five games away, the wait for the return of Primeau and Roenick was going to the wire and J.R. figured it was time for the cutter.

"My wife Tracy was making me my dinners in a blender," he recalls. "She pureed steaks and chicken, seasoned it, and actually made it taste good, so I only lost about four pounds in the eight weeks.

"But it's not the same, so I'm counting down the days. They told me eight weeks, so eight weeks to the day, I went in to the locker room early (before the March 25 game against the Islanders) and told Jim McCrossin, 'I'm going to play tonight. I've been skating all this time. I'm ready.'"

He said, 'You've still got your jaw wired. You can't play like that.' So I said, 'Let's see about that.'

"They have the doctor come in. I say, 'You said eight weeks, Doc. Today is eight weeks. Cut these [bleeping] wires out. Please!'

"He said, 'Come to my office tomorrow morning and if you are fully healed, we'll give you novocaine and cut the wires.' I said, 'Hell no. You said eight weeks, not eight weeks and one day. Please, take the wires off right now.'

"I threatened to do it myself. The doctor—I don't want to say who—says, 'You win. I'll do it.'"

After a 19-game absence, J.R. was a sight for sore eyes, but the Flyers went down to the Islanders 4-2 on three eyesore goals allowed by Esche. One of them, by Adrian Aucoin, was from almost the red line.

"[Esche] is going to face this type of adversity," said Hitchcock. "We have to see how he reacts to it."

All hints from the coach suggested he wanted Esche to be the playoff goalie. "But we were holding our breath with him," Hitchcock recalls. "I went to Burke more than to Esche to ask how Robert was doing."

The man who knew best was Dr. Nathaniel Zinsser from the Center for Enhanced Performance at West Point, where the coach had taken his team for bonding exercises during training camp. Zinsser had worked with Army Rangers in addition to pro and Olympic athletes.

"Dr. Z is a sweet, awesome man," recalls Esche. "He helped me deal with my mental approach; actually that means he helped me deal with Hitch.

"I mean, I knew what Hitch was getting at. But I was such a fiery guy. I didn't know how to receive it. I didn't always take it well. Dr. Z always had the ability to keep me moving in the proper direction.

"Hitch was right from the beginning that Dr. Z could be a big help to us if we opened our minds to it. He didn't change my personality, just helped frame things in a way that really worked for me.

"Reggie (goaltending coach Lemelin) was terrific, a supporter of mine all the way through. Not for lack of effort but just the way I received the information sometimes, I know I wasn't the easiest guy to work with. But, as a result, I loved Reg and had so much respect for him.

"I always was a good puck stopper, but where I needed work was in reading the play. The stronger players know how to get themselves open and you have to pay attention to them."

Indeed, two nights following the Islander debacle, Esche was caught on his knees when Jaromir Jagr scored after faking a wraparound. Beaten later in the game through a screen by Holik from the blueline, Esche was yanked as the Flyers lost at home to the Rangers, 3-1.

"He has not played as well as we would like him to play," said Hitchcock, but, with the league's leading powerplay sputtering, he could say the same for more than just his goaltender. Philadelphia, 9-9-3 in its last 21 games, had lost all chance of catching Tampa Bay for the No. 1 seed.

Help was on the way, however. After multiple tries to crank up his workouts on the exercise bike, only to experience feelings akin to seasickness, Primeau finally reported no adverse symptoms. On March 31, he announced that his return from a 21-game absence would be the following night in Montreal.

"The ship has finally docked," said the captain. "I've strung together three days now where I haven't had the spinning.

"Last week, when I still was having problems, Joni (Pitkanen) elbowed me in the head and it didn't make it any worse. I'm not going to be able to tell until I get into those situations where I'm getting knocked around."

Desjardins' recovery from a broken arm had taken 10 weeks, two longer than expected, as he also announced his return for the Montreal contest. For both players, it seemed like now or never and, with three games remaining and the Flyers trying to hold off the Devils for home-ice advantage in the first round, the same seemed to hold true for the team. With goals by Gagne and Handzus and 41 saves by Burke, Philadelphia celebrated the return of its captain and anchor defenseman with a 2-0 victory at the Bell Centre.

Another win the following night at the Wachovia Center against

Ottawa would have allowed Hitchcock's team to catch the Senators for second place in the conference. But Esche lost sight of another long one—albeit deflected after leaving the stick of Antoine Vermette—and the Flyers, apparently all scores settled against Ottawa the last time, lost a peaceful encounter with just six minors, 3-1.

"[I'm] thinking about the playoffs and playing great and, for somebody who is probably not the brightest bulb in the chandelier, maybe I should just worry about what is going on right now," Esche told reporters.

With still a chance of falling all the way to the sixth seed, Philadelphia needed a point in Game 82 in Uniondale to hold off New Jersey for the division title and gain home ice in the first round. Before the overtime of a 3-3 tie forged by Johnsson's goal 4:20 into the third period, the Flyers got word that the Devils had lost in Boston, securing Game One in Philadelphia in a three vs. six first-round matchup against New Jersey.

Robert Esche fights for space with Jamie Langenbrunner of the Devils in Game Two of the Eastern Conference quarterfinals.

"We wanted in September to win the division; there is a sense of accomplishment with our players," said Hitchcock, whose 101-point team had finished 10-9-4 from the date Primeau and Roenick had been lost.

As the Islanders were three for four on the powerplay in the regular-season finale, the penalty killing had continued to struggle. So had Esche. Roman Hamrlik scored off the goalie's back, although he rebounded to make several good saves in the extra five minutes.

"Esche got really competitive toward the second half of the game and overtime, a good sign for us," insisted Hitchcock, the coach of a team needing traction.

The Flyers found a little. Primeau and Roenick had worked off some rust with a goal apiece in Uniondale and Philadelphia went into the New Jersey series having defeated the Devils in their last three meetings.

Some of that success probably was due to the absence of Scott Stevens, who, having been hit in the head by Tampa Bay's Pavel Kubina in the previous year's playoffs, had belatedly admitted to be suffering from post-concussion symptoms and left the lineup mid-season.

"Our 2003 team was a hard working one that never gave up, wasn't nearly as loaded as the one that won in 2000, which probably made Scotty's leadership more important than ever," recalls Patrik Elias. "So not having him was a huge loss.

"But we always thought we were a more disciplined team than the Flyers and that would only intensify during the playoffs. We still felt we could win just by going about our usual business."

Business as usual was going to be a greater challenge against a Philadelphia club that under Hitchcock had become more businesslike.

"Stevens was their leader and catalyst so [his absence] was huge for us," recalls Roenick. "But helping us more was that we had been playing the same system for two years.

"We had talent, leadership and coaching. There was no fear of the Devils. We embraced the idea of playing against them."

Recalls Primeau, "Zhamnov had filled a big hole; we were so deep now up the middle. We thought we had a legitimate chance of winning the Stanley Cup."

The Flyers had played 32 games during the season without Desjardins, experience that, sadly, would again come in handy.

His arm had felt weak during the three games since returning, and, after one-timing a shot during practice, he also had felt a stab of pain.

Two days before Game One, Desjardins was putting baseball gloves back on a shelf following a catch with his son when he noticed the angle of his arm was abnormal. When he shook it, the bone seemed to be moving. An image showed that the plate inserted on January 20 by Dr. John Taras at Thomas Jefferson University Hospital in Philadelphia had snapped and the radius bone was re-fractured at the site of the original break.

Dr. Taras said the bone surely weakened prior to Desjardins' catch with his son and that the 10 weeks it had taken to apparently heal should have set off a warning sign.

"I knew there was a risk to coming back, but that was a risk I was willing to take," Desjardins told reporters sadly. "This is the fun time."

A year earlier, it had been no barrel of laughs for the Flyers going down to the Senators in six after Desjardins' foot was fractured in Game Four of the Toronto series. But having gone 17-11-4 during his most recent absence, Hitchcock insisted his team would survive.

"He was a great luxury to have, but we beat (the Devils) three times when Eric was not in the lineup," said the coach. "He's out now (for six to eight more weeks) and we go back to the formula that worked before."

Burke (6-5-2, 2.55 and .910 since his acquisition) had been excellent in Game 81 in Montreal, so Philadelphia had one comfort in reserve as Esche (21-11-7, 2.04 and .915) was anointed the starter to begin the playoffs.

"Robert has improved dramatically if you look at the scope of the whole season," said Hitchcock. And despite Esche's late-year slump and his absence of any NHL playoff record, the goalie felt fully confident.

"Adam Patterson, our video guy, put together a highlight video for me set to a Foo Fighters song called 'It's Times Like These,'" Esche recalls. "I loved it.

"Visually, mentally, physically, I was really prepared. I took all the nervous and excited energy and was able to harness it into the relaxed energy I needed. It was probably the most in-the-zone I ever was in my career and that was a synergy of collective efforts by Burkie, Reggie. Dr. Z, Mark Recchi—my best friend on the team—and Hitch being hard on me.

"I will never forget going onto the ice (for Game One); there was just a feeling that things were going to go well. The crowd was electric. It just felt right for us, like the year before against Toronto."

Staked to a 1-0 lead when Gagne hustled off a Flyer defensive-zone faceoff win to beat Paul Martin to an icing and flick in a Kapanen rebound, Esche was sharp from the start. While Johnsson was in the penalty box for slashing Patrik Elias, the goalie threw his pad out on a Turner Stevenson redirection, stood up on Jamie Langenbrunner after a turnover by Timander, and then stopped John Madden after Malakhov lost the puck at the side of the net.

When Kapanen was called during the first minute of the second period for boarding Scott Niedermayer, Esche made seven saves, the best in throwing his right pad out on Stevenson. When Niedermayer went to the box for goaltender interference, the Philadelphia powerplay pounced.

Roenick kept the puck alive after Martin Brodeur lost his stick with an unsuccessful sweep check at the side of his net, then put a Zhamnov feed between the goalie's legs to make it 2-0.

Esche then killed another Kapanen penalty by stopping good chances by Viktor Kozlov and Langenbrunner. A unit of Kapanen-Primeau-Gagne did the defensive job against the top Devil line of Elias, Scott Gomez and Brian Gionta, then added a third goal three minutes into the third period. Primeau faked an inside move on Brian Rafalski, went wide, and had room to stay on his forehand when he cut in and beat Brodeur cleanly to the stick side.

The Flyers were in total command for all of 22 seconds. Esche made a strong pad save on Gionta from the top of the circle, but Markov lost Elias, who too easily put in the rebound to get New Jersey on the board. Just 35 seconds later, Roenick inadvertently deflected in Jan Hrdina's shot over Esche's shoulder during a scramble.

With 15 long minutes to go, it was suddenly 3-2. But Philadelphia was not rattled. Markov deflected a good Kozlov opportunity and Brodeur was forced to make big saves on Handzus and Malakhov. When Markov went to the box for holding Stevenson to prevent a two-on-one, Johnsson broke up the Devils' best chance—by Gomez—and Primeau had a block on Rafalski.

Thus, Esche's only save with Markov off was on Martin's long-distance drive, and the crowd, reenergized by an excellent kill, took the Flyers to the finish. Esche had to make only one more superior save, a glove on Sergei Brylin after a steal from Markov.

"[Esche] was the guy we've seen all year," said Hitchcock, about the 37-save effort—17 of them on four powerplays—that won Game One, 3-2.

"He had a rough, 10-day stretch, getting too far ahead of himself. Now, he's got a game under his belt."

It felt huge to the kid. "It was just one game," recalls Esche. "But it reinforced that feeling we had going in. This time, the Devils weren't going to beat us."

Not that the Philadelphia had any expectation of New Jersey doing a quick fade.

"What we will understand after two or three games in this series is that the defending champion doesn't go away easily," Hitchcock said. "This is really a series about resolve, not X's and O's."

Following his February return from a treatment center for depression and drug addiction, Lapointe had averaged 11 minutes per game of ice time and done his usual solid job in Game One. But it turned out to be the last contest he ever would play.

"I had relapsed during that week," Lapointe recalls. "I played the game and the next day called Dr. Shaw because I felt in danger and just wanted to be watched.

"When I met him at the (Newark) airport in New Jersey, he told me that under the terms of the agreement, for a second [episode], I was suspended for life.

"It wasn't like I got caught with drugs in my pockets after getting pulled over in my car, or at customs. That's what I thought was meant by a second [violation]. I asked for help because I knew I had a problem and got, 'You'll never play again in the NHL. See you later.' They didn't care what would happen to me.

"I remember Bob Clarke telling me how disappointed he was in me. Hitch called to express his concern and so did Sean Burke, and that was it from the Flyers. But I really didn't want to hear from anybody anyway. When you are depressed you want nothing to do with people who are happy because you are so ashamed.

"I had screwed up; I was in denial and angry. The Flyers had a chance to win the Stanley Cup and I wasn't allowed to be there; that just made me use more.

"We (wife and two boys) moved back to Montreal. I tried several rehab places but it did not work. Because money wasn't a problem, I could support my habit. It cost me my marriage and, for a while, my kids.

"For five years, once or twice a week, I wanted to take my own life. I had a lot of guilt. I had been a role model (as an Islander) for a lot of young people on Long Island, was involved in hockey schools and community work in Montreal. Being suspended, I lost my legacy, lost my credibility, and that really was hard on me.

"I went on like that for five years, until I met my present wife, Leora, and she started to open my eyes about how to live my life. She was my psychologist, my mentor. I had so many secrets with my ex-wife and today I have none. [Leora] put integrity back in my life and I have been clean for six years.

"When I look back at my career—14 years in the NHL for a 12th-round draft choice who was supposed to be too small (at 5-9)—I can be really happy about what I accomplished. And that seventh game against Toronto for the Flyers (a goal and two assists in 2003) was the highlight of it."

Hitchcock dressed Sharp in Lapointe's place on the fourth line for Game Two. Primeau and Timander took the first two penalties of the contest but the penalty killers held the Devils to just two shots for both opportunities combined. When Niedermayer got caught holding LeClair, Recchi one-timed the game's first goal through Pitkanen's screen.

Hrdina, lost by Timander, went to the net and beat Esche to tie the game early in the second period. But less than three minutes later, Amonte's deliberate miss from the left circle caromed off the back boards to the right post, where Roenick put the puck through the crease and between Brodeur's pads to Zhamnov. The Russian had an easy tap-in at the opposite post and Philadelphia led again, 2-1.

After Timander's slapshot from the right point midway through the third period made it 3-1, the Devils fought back one more time, Gionta converting a backhand pass from Elias with 5:25 to go, setting up another nervous finish. But Primeau, who had won just four of 18 faceoffs in Game One, dominated down the stretch, finishing the evening 14-for-22 on draws, as the Flyers claimed their second consecutive 3-2 victory and a 2-0 series lead.

"We're finding something out about ourselves right now," said Hitchcock. "The higher the intensity, the more composure we play with.

"The other thing we're finding out is that players who were missing (until late in the season), in particular Roenick and Primeau, are getting better every game."

Having the team's top two centers quickly back up to speed was a huge relief, of course, and still probably not as buoying as the play of Esche.

"You're looking across the way at Marty Brodeur, so as good as you feel about Esche going in, you're still wondering," recalls Hitchcock. "But the way Esche played in the first two games, I knew we were going to be in good shape.

"Stevens not being there, of course, made a difference. But they still had (future Hall of Famer) Niedermayer, and, even without Desjardins, we were deeper on the back end than they were.

"What I remember about Niedermayer is that if we were [behind], he played a conservative game, but if we were leading, that's when he scared us the most. A lot of times I had to put defending groups of five against him because he could do whatever he wanted. But we were playing so well and were so deep, I didn't think anybody was going to beat us.

"I changed the lines but really the players had taken control."

Brodeur felt it, too, as Philadelphia executed its game plan of shooting at his skates. "It's not that we thought his feet were slow, just that it is hard for any standup goalie to control those rebounds," recalls Primeau.

The Devil goaltender had always been quick to reach dump-ins and foil forecheckers, but the Flyer placements into the corners were mostly out of his reach. "I can't play the puck at all," Brodeur said.

Almost eight minutes into Game Three at the Meadowlands, Paul Martin grabbed Recchi to keep him from going to the net. On the powerplay, Roenick blooped a Johnsson rebound over Brodeur to give Philadelphia a 1-0 lead.

Esche got his glove down at the side of the goal to rob Elias, but the veteran Flyer killer won the next battle. He beat Roenick to the net to take a passout by Gomez, who had forced LeClair behind the net, tying the game.

Holding the home team's right to choose his poison, Devil coach Pat Burns had switched the Gionta-Gomez-Elias trio away from the Primeau line and matched New Jersey's best offensive unit against Roenick, Amonte and Zhamnov. Hitchcock didn't fight it.

With Hrdina off for hooking Sharp, Roenick forced Niedermayer into a second turnover on the same shift and Brodeur, anticipating a pass to Amonte, got fooled when Roenick instead skated out the other side of the net. The goalie awkwardly sprawled and was on his back when Amonte took J.R.'s pass and went high to restore the Philadelphia lead at 2-1 just 1:47 after the Devil goal.

But Handzus went off for interference on Stevenson along the boards and Markov, trying to clear a puck from his knees, only put it off the foot of Malakhov and right to Gionta. Esche was on both pads trying to cover as much of the net as he could when Martin lifted the puck high to tie the game again.

Later in the period, with Brashear in the penalty box for interfering with Brodeur, Elias's wide-angle drive changed direction dramatically off Johnsson's leg. With Gionta screening, Esche had no chance. New Jersey went ahead in a game for the first time in the series, 3-2.

After Zhamnov had been called for hooking, Esche made a superior drop-down save on Gomez. Primeau picked up the rebound and blew by Colin White, but a sprawling Brodeur made a poke check. Soon Elias, sandwiched along the boards by Kapanen and Markov, got the puck away to Gomez. His passout was redirected by a wide-open Gionta to put the Devils up 4-2.

Handzus had the best chance for the Flyers the rest of the way, but Brodeur stopped it with his pad. The Elias-Gomez-Gionta line had produced three of the four New Jersey goals, three on the powerplay, in a 4-2 triumph that cut Philadelphia's series lead to 2-1.

"In Philly, they got away with taking a lot of penalties and we didn't make them pay," said Brodeur. "They were flying high and hopefully we've put a little doubt in their minds."

Stevens reportedly was skating, not what the Flyers wanted to hear, although Burns, having zero expectation of getting his future Hall of Famer back, wanted to hear it even less. "Stop it, please," answered the coach to yet another Stevens inquiry. "End it, please."

Any hope by Philadelphia to put a quick zipper on the defending champion's season had been dashed by New Jersey's powerplay. But the Flyers hardly believed the worm had turned.

"[The Devils] were more vocal, seemed to have more confidence and a little bit more arrogance at home," Primeau told reporters. "But I think we battled hard and had chances."

Hitchcock didn't believe his team had played smartly, however, so he put his own brain to work.

After combining for 35 goals in the final 39 games of the season, the line of LeClair, Handzus and Recchi had been held goalless at even strength for the series by New Jersey's checking unit of Madden, Brylin and Jay Pandolfo. So the coach replaced Handzus with Primeau, the best Flyer so far in the series.

Two shifts into Game Four the switches paid off. Gagne forced Rafalski and Kapanen passed the puck out to Handzus, who was stopped by Brodeur. But Johnsson, hustling past Gomez, put in the rebound after just 1:18 to give Philadelphia a 1-0 lead.

Less than a minute later, Primeau was called for marginally interfering with Brodeur, but Esche made a point-blank save on Gionta as the winger went for the far corner, then gloved his deflection before the Flyers killed the second minute of the minor flawlessly.

Roenick lined up Gomez for a huge hit behind the goal. Esche stopped Madden in alone. During the first 10 minutes of the game, every shot the Devils had was a good chance, but the Philadelphia goalie stood tall, making his best save on a Brylin tip after he fought through LeClair. When Big John was flagged for a hook on the play, Esche made another huge save on an Elias redirection from Gomez.

Primeau, grabbed by Rafalski, threw the defenseman to the side, and forced Brodeur to make a save in the final minute of the period, the first good Flyer chance since their goal in the game's second minute.

Early in the second period, when Malakhov drove Jeff Friesen's head into the glass, drawing a penalty, Philadelphia did not allow New Jersey to set up. But at even strength, the Devils kept coming. Esche had to come across, beating Gionta to a rebound, then made a point-blank stop on Gomez.

In the first 13 minutes of the second period, the Devils outshot the Flyers 9-2 as Philadelphia clung to its 1-0 lead. Injury was soon added to insult when Gomez's shot rode up Johnsson's stick and bloodied his face. But Esche, making good saves on Friesen from 20 feet out, and then on a Stevenson wraparound, got his team to the second-period break still up a goal.

"We had possession time in their zone, felt we were fine," Primeau would say later, believing the shot totals of the second period—12-6 for New Jersey—were more lopsided than the play.

But whether or not it was from inactivity, Brodeur appeared slightly off balance on the sporadic Flyer chances over the middle 20 minutes. Leaning backwards as he stopped Kapanen coming off the side boards, the goalie got lucky as Gagne, trying to pull in the rebound, put the puck against the opposite post.

Thanks largely to the pressure of a LeClair-Primeau-Recchi line, Philadelphia had out-chanced the Devils 4-0 in the first four minutes of the third period when Roenick broke down right wing and fed Malakhov coming up the middle. The defenseman relayed to Zhamnov, who wasn't looking for a pass that hit his skate, but he kicked the puck to his forehand and, as Brodeur dropped down, put a shot between the goalie's legs. Ahead 2-0, the Flyers had insurance at last.

Luckily, Stevenson's shot went between Esche's legs, off his pad and just wide. Then, with seven minutes remaining, the Philadelphia goalie made a sprawling kick save on Hrdina. After Pitkanen went to the box for slashing, Elias fired a golden-looking rebound wide.

Big Primeau's arms seemed to spread from sideboard to sideboard. Soon after Esche came across on Gomez and then made a big glove save on a rising Elias shot, Primeau broke out, laid the puck off to Kapanen, and went to the net for a deflection. Kapanen's shot came up too high for Brodeur to control and, when the puck dropped to the ice, Primeau swept it into the goal with 3:58 left to play.

The Continental Airlines Arena began to empty long before Esche put an exclamation point on his 35-save, 3-0, shutout by snatching an Elias riser. In the goaltender's glove was a 3-1 series lead.

"[Esche] won the game for us in the second and we won it for him in the third," said Hitchcock. "[The goalie] was our best player, the only way you are going to win when teams are this even."

That was selling his 6-5 center a little short. One of the three stars for the third time in four games, Primeau's oft-concussed head was killing him all the while he was killing the Devils.

"It was bizarre," the captain recalls. "Maybe because my vision and head weren't great, I had to focus that much harder; I don't know."

Johnsson, with six points in the series, had been a dominant force, too. But the Flyers were startling—and impressing—their long-time nemeses with a show of restraint. "They weren't reacting (with penalties) the way we thought they would, like they always had against us," recalls Elias. "It throws you off."

Madden, a two-time Cup winner and a six-year veteran of wars against the Flyers, suggested the true star of the series was behind the Philadelphia bench.

"Since [Hitchcock] has taken over that hockey club, they are a much more disciplined team," he said. "I don't just mean about taking penalties but in having the third man doing the right thing, staying on the right side of the puck.

"He sends two guys in on the forecheck to the right side of the rink, our D swings it around the other side, and they've got a guy standing in the corner. They are confident because they have watched enough video to know where we swing the puck. It's like playing against yourself almost."

In the mirrors of the cramped visiting locker room at the Continental Airlines Arena, the Flyers liked what they saw, too.

"When their building goes silent and you can see in their eyes that they know they're not coming back, that's what playoff hockey is all about," recalls Roenick. "Winning on the road like that just can't be beat.

"That was a statement game for us. Now we're up 3-1 coming back to our building and no way were we gonna take our foot off their throat. Everyone goes into a game hoping to win, but it's a totally different mindset knowing you're going to win. You play looser."

To Hitchcock, the control freak, the greatest joy was that there had been nothing freakish about it. The Flyers had won, on structure, in the structure they had grown to hate off Exit 16W of the NJ Turnpike.

"That friggin' building, it was always so bloody cold," recalls the coach. "You had this little dingy dressing room and you'd go out there and the game would be over 10 minutes into the first period.

"It was really their team, though, not the building. They played so fast and with such precise execution that if you made a mistake, they made you pay for it seemingly every time. Their continuity overwhelmed you. So to play our best game in that building was really gratifying. I got beat [by the Devils] as a [Dallas] coach in the 2000 Final after they had beaten the Flyers, so to start winning games in that building was a good feeling."

Actually, in both 1995 and 2000, Philadelphia had won Games Three and Four at the Meadowlands and still lost the series, 2000 being the most haunting because Philadelphia had gone home with a 3-1 lead. Ten Devils who participated in that comeback were in this series four years later, although one of them—Malakhov—had switched teams. With Desjardins not available, the Flyers counted just four survivors. But, of course, the fans had long memories and this gave the media an obvious angle.

"I wasn't paying attention to it then because I was coaching in the West," recalls Hitchcock. "I just remember (Eric) Lindros coming back, getting [concussed by a Stevens check], and New Jersey winning the (seventh) game; so none of this hit home for me.

"But if our players weren't talking about it, there were people who were. So Clarkie told me, 'You need to put this to rest. Be defiant.'"

Jeremy Roenick celebrates what would prove to be Danny Markov's winning goal to eliminate the Devils.

Hitchcock feigned that the media had hit a nerve. "You do the worrying and we'll do the playing," he said. "This is a new team. We're not going to bring up some old, sad, story."

The Devils, remembering they had been written off four years earlier, didn't mind hearing the tale again. "Everybody thinks we're dead in the water," said Brodeur. "Sometimes that's the best way to play a game."

After a few failed early opportunities in the series-turning fifth game in 2000, the Flyer adrenaline had drained quickly as the Devils had gained confidence. But this time, Philadelphia kept hitting and pressuring, outshooting New Jersey 4-0 in the first seven minutes of Game Five.

The Devils didn't catch their breath until Ragnarsson was called for holding Gomez along the backboards. From his knees, Esche made a chest save on Gomez and use his stick to push aside a drive by Rafalski. Martin appeared to score through a screen, but because referee Don Van Massenhoven had just called a Friesen hook of Primeau, the goal was disallowed and the New Jersey powerplay was shortened by 32 seconds.

The Flyers didn't score on their 1:28 advantage. But seven minutes after the Devils killed it, Brodeur couldn't control a drive by Amonte from 45 feet. The goalie was bumped by White as Roenick picked up the puck and made a blind backhand pass to Amonte, who had closed to the bottom of the circle. Amonte faked a shot, forced Brodeur to commit, and passed to the opposite post to Zhamnov, who fumbled the puck but still got it over the line as Brodeur was diving back. Zhamnov had his seventh point of the series and Philadelphia the first goal for the fifth straight game.

Recchi just missed off LeClair's cross-crease setup before the period expired, but Zhamnov's line was enjoying a territorial edge against the Gomez line. The Flyers, placing their dump-ins more wisely than ever, were delivering wearing kinds of hits on the New Jersey defense, including some from a fourth line of Sharp, Radivojevic and Somik.

Amonte got away with taking down Gionta to keep him from reaching a Stevenson rebound, preventing a goal. Erik Rasmussen took a penalty for hooking Primeau at the top of the slot and the Philadelphia captain carried the puck in twice, only to have one attempt saved by Brodeur and the other blocked.

More than midway through the second period, Esche came across to stop Gionta, but Gomez pounced to make a quick backhand pass past Sharp to Niedermayer, who went around Brashear and shot low across the Flyer goalie's body to tie the game, 1-1.

It was the first point of the series by the dangerous Devil captain, and Kapanen, choosing to not risk any more, got called for holding the future Hall of Famer's stick. But New Jersey's powerplay, just 3-for-17 in the series, failed again as the teams went to the third period with one goal apiece.

Ragnarsson limped off after blocking a shot. Brodeur, falling backwards, had to trap a Zhamnov drive against his body. Appearing not to mind the goal Philadelphia's fourth line had given up, Hitchcock continued to play it and the response was two strong forechecking shifts. Eight minutes into a whistle-prone third period, the Devils had compiled practically no offensive zone time.

Brodeur covered up on both a LeClair walkout and a Handzus jam set up by Gagne, but the goalie appeared to rise slowly. Esche gloved New Jersey's first dangerous opportunity of the period, on White through traffic, with 5:45 to go in regulation.

Roenick won the subsequent draw, but Gomez broke up a pass to Amonte and Gionta dumped the puck back into the Flyer zone, where Malakhov quickly played up to Zhamnov. He turned and fed Markov, who had plenty of room through the middle but hit the blueline with White coming up on him fast.

"The defenseman was so close to me I could use him as a screen," Markov said later. But today, he insists he just shot, surprising both the defenseman and the goalie. Launched from well above the faceoff dot, the puck went through White's feet, hit low on the short-side post and caromed into the net.

Markov didn't see that the puck was in the goal until he was starting to circle it. "Never saw a guy jump so high in my life," Hitchcock would say.

Who at a hate-filled Spectrum on that January day in 1976 ever would have envisioned that three Russians would combine for a goal to make a Philadelphia crowd go insane with joy? The Flyers had the lead, 2-1, with 5:23 to go.

On the next shift, Niedermayer appeared to make Primeau woozy with a hard shoulder check at the blueline. With three minutes to go, Johnsson got hit in the right hand with a Jamie Langenbrunner shot.

Kapanen pushed the puck past White, but Brodeur stacked the pads to foil Gagne's bid for insurance. With the Devil netminder on the bench, the Flyers got one puck out of their zone off a Primeau faceoff win, but the next time in, Niedermayer pinched, shot, and Elias chopped down a dangerous deflection. Esche tracked the puck and kicked it away with a minute remaining.

On the next faceoff, Niedermayer picked up an Elias drive broken up by Timander, circled the net, and passed the puck out to Langenbrunner just 10 feet away, but Esche anticipated, butterflied, and got it.

Zhamnov tipped out a pass between the points. Primeau blocked a shot that put the Devils offsides with 15 seconds to play and then won a draw from Gomez back to Malakhov. Langenbrunner, desperately tried to backhand the puck into the Philadelphia zone but was forced by Gagne, and the puck went to Kapanen who scored into the empty net with one second remaining to a cathartic roar.

With a 3-1 win, and a five-game triumph, the Flyers had dethroned the champions on a late goal by a player who had scored for only the second time in his 46 NHL playoff games.

"Unbelievable," recalls Hitchcock. "Clarkie came in after the game, laughed and said, 'That's why we traded for that guy.'

"Danny Markov was one of our (cigarette) smokers—we had about four of them—but an old-school hockey player that looked like he could play all day. Oh man, he was so competitive and had galvanized our team so much that everyone was pretty excited to see him score that goal."

There were plenty of other reasons to be thrilled, such as the first Flyer win over their Devil nemeses in three playoff series. Two of the Philadelphia wins were by one goal, a third put away with an empty-netter, and the fourth had been 1-0 into the third period. Each time, the Flyers had held on with a steely resolve.

"That third period today was by far the best we have played all season," said Recchi. And the team had been fueled by the confidence of a first-time playoff starter in goal who had been better than a three-time Cup winner possessing the second-most playoff victories of all time.

"You can't blame Marty," Burns said. "[Markov's] was a pretty good low shot, and he didn't expect it.

"If it was a quarter of an inch on the outside of that post, it's not a goal."

Brodeur beat himself up regardless. "Bad goal, too far out," he recalls. Asked after the game by reporters to rate his performance, he said. "Average. Any series I don't win, I think I stink.

"I'm expected to win all the time. It's unacceptable not to produce. I'm a key player. I've got to do better than that."

He had given up 13 goals to nine against Esche, who made the bigger saves at the most opportune times.

"Goalies always say they are playing against the shooters, but I think you are playing against the other goaltender," Esche recalls. "You are trying to out-compete the other guy; you want all 40 guys on the ice and bench to think you are the best goalie.

"Listen, I am not an idiot. My career pales in comparison to what Marty Brodeur did. I grew up watching Marty (with the Devil farm team) in Albany and was in awe of how long he stayed at the top. He didn't even play that bad in the series, just not the way he always played. But for that one snapshot in time, it was different between him and me.

"I just think our team was really well prepared. Malakhov's breakout passes were right on the tape time after time. We had great puck support; they didn't get a lot of transition chances. There were no rebounds; guys were boxing out and clearing the puck. We didn't give up the blueline and when they did get in, everything was pushed toward the perimeter where I could see the shots.

"Kim Johnsson was fantastic; Zhamnov was terrific. Right down the line, we were spectacular, actually, as a team."

Indeed, all the in-season trade pickups—Markov, Malakhov and Zhamnov—had been everything Clarke had hoped. "Those guys came in and had a sense of urgency as if they knew they had the opportunity to finally get it done," recalls Kapanen.

So much for the myth that Europeans don't put the same value in winning the Stanley Cup as North American players.

"I know it hadn't always been the case with Malakhov to compete to his fullest, but he was just like a tower of strength," recalls Roenick. "And Danny, he was hard to play against because you had to fight him for every puck, every inch of space.

"He was mean in the corners, cleared the porch, pinned guys to the walls and cancelled them so our forwards could usually come get the puck."

The Flyers had scored the first goal in every game, and closed impressively. So Hitchcock glowed. "I observed the way New Jersey operates; you might as well learn from who played the best team game and then see if you can improve on it," the coach told reporters.

"Everybody knows when you're a champion, you don't win on talent but by doing everything necessary team-wise to win."

Early the next morning, Hitchcock got a call from Burns. Based on a brief conversation between the two following Game Five, the Flyer coach suspected this wasn't about further congratulations.

"During the series, I remember there were stories about Pat missing some practices and skates," Hitchcock recalls. "He and I had become really good friends in 1986 (when both had taken their junior teams to the Memorial Cup tournament), so I was asking what was going on and nobody was saying.

"We always had this thing where we would make eye contact and each of us would give the other a funny face, but during the series he was just staring straight ahead and looked white to me. When we shook hands at the end, he said, 'Hitch, I'm in trouble. I'll call you tomorrow.'

"He did at like 7 in the morning and told me he had (colon) cancer and was announcing it later in the day. He said, 'I've got a real battle in front of me.'

"That was really tough hearing that."

Elias recalls some of the Devils knowing about Burns' diagnosis during the series, but Brodeur doesn't remember being one of them. It was a hard spring in North Jersey, as it was in Ottawa, where the Senators couldn't get their terminally-ill assistant coach, Roger Neilson, his first Stanley Cup, losing to Toronto in six games.

The Flyers would have home-ice advantage in a second series against the Leafs in two years.

"Last year, [the seven-game Philadelphia victory] was tough to take, but it was a real high-quality series and I was told by many people that it was the best of the entire Stanley Cup playoffs," said Toronto coach Pat Quinn. "We beat each other badly enough that the Flyers couldn't advance in the next round."

Twelve months later, Philadelphia already had a significant casualty. Johnsson, who had been dominant in the New Jersey series, needed the insertion of pins to facilitate healing of the fourth metacarpal in his right hand. Unable to grip a stick, he did not dress for Game One.

Rather than dip into the Phantoms, Hitchcock decided to move Kapanen back to the blueline, where he had played two games during March when the team had four injured defensemen.

"It would hurt us a lot up front," recalls Hitchcock. "But, at the end of the day, if we couldn't get it out of our own end, we weren't going to beat anybody."

Game One began with the Flyers killing off penalties to Amonte and Primeau before Amonte pounced on a Roenick rebound and went up top from a deep angle to give Philadelphia a 1-0 lead at 7:14. The Leafs, playing the opener without star Mats Sundin, had managed only one shot in the first 14 minutes until Alexander Mogilny got wide on Ragnarsson and shot from almost on the goal line. The puck went in off Timander's skate to tie the game, 1-1.

Toronto clearly had set a strategy of pounding on Kapanen, who was playing mostly with rookie countryman Pitkanen on a third pair. "I expected them to come after me," said Kapanen, but the emergency D-man took the hits and, more often, spun away from forecheckers to make plays.

It was after Kapanen moved the puck ahead to Handzus, whose missed shot rimmed to Joe Nieuwendyk on the half wall, that Recchi created the next good Flyer chance. He bodied Nieuwendyk, allowing the puck to continue to the point to Ragnarsson, who fired off Nik Antropov's shin past goalie Ed Belfour's far side to give Philadelphia back the lead, 2-1, 15:13 into the second period.

When a Ron Francis shot off a Roenick giveaway changed direction off Malakhov, Esche was quick with his glove. The Flyers, who had looked a little rusty at the start, were beginning to impose their will and, at the end of an extended cycle, LeClair stickhandled to the slot past Nieuwendyk, where Gagne backhanded a rebound through Belfour's legs to extend the Philadelphia lead to two with just 4:25 remaining in the game.

Tom Fitzgerald came to Belfour's aid as he jostled with Somik and spent two valuable minutes in the box, helping the Flyers, who received a stellar 21 minutes from Kapanen, hold on for a 3-1 win.

Hitchcock braced for a fight he thought might even be harder than the one the previous spring. "Toronto has really changed its game," he said. "You are going to be gaining ice by the inch and not feet."

Game Two did not contradict the coach.

Brashear, on the ice late in a first-period powerplay because Fitzgerald's penalty for holding Handzus was about to expire, cross-checked Bryan McCabe and fought off the Leaf defenseman to put in a Recchi rebound with just two seconds left in the man advantage.

But with Sundin back in the lineup, Toronto dominated the second period, outshooting Philadelphia 11-1 and tying the game when Tie Domi's redirection of a feed from Clarke Wilm went over Esche's shoulder.

Huge pressure by a Flyer line of LeClair, Handzus and Recchi swung momentum back early in the third. When Wilm lost Recchi at center, he was taken down by Robert Reichel, creating a powerplay opportunity. Zhamnov, controlling the puck with his skate along the goal line, caught Belfour anticipating a pass to Roenick, who was battling Tomas Kaberle in front. The goalie was caught flush when Zhamnov's fourth goal of the playoffs went five hole with 11:35 remaining in the game to put Philadelphia ahead, 2-1.

At the end of another tremendous forechecking shift by Brashear, he was called for interfering with Brian Leetch. But the Leafs didn't get another sniff of the Flyer goal until after they had killed a Ken Klee penalty for pushing Recchi. Esche got his stick arm up to beat Wilm, who had a step on Ragnarsson. In the final minute, Mogliny was so sure he had scored, he lifted his stick, only to see the 15-footer hit Ragnarsson in the back. The Flyers held on, 2-1, to take a 2-0 series lead.

"Zhamnov is probably the most talented all-around player on our team," Roenick told the media. All around, the Russian was having the most fun, too, seizing an opportunity for which he had waited 12 dismal seasons in Winnipeg and Chicago. Never before had he played in the second round. "I really didn't have a chance to prove anything," he said.

Opportunity had come to Esche at age 26 and he was seizing it, outplaying a second future Hall of Famer in two series. Asked if his goaltender's inexperience made him nervous, Hitchcock said, "After last year?" referring to Roman Cechmanek.

What really gave the coach anxiety was a pattern of poor second periods, but he vowed his team would stay on the "right side of the fine line" for Game Three in Toronto.

It didn't, however. After a scoreless first period in which Philadelphia carried the majority of the play, a Zhamnov passout turned the puck over to a four-on-two. Sundin quickly relayed to Mogilny, who had two steps on Kapanen and beat Esche over the shoulder on the stick side.

Just 90 seconds after Mogilny's goal, Alexei Ponikarovsky got a step on Timander and scored on a redirection from McCabe to make it 2-0. Fedoruk turned the puck over at the blueline and Domi threw it on goal, off Malakhov, to Chad Kilger who had an easy backhand conversion at the side of the net to build the Leaf lead to three.

Amonte got one of those back on a gimme after a carom of a Pitkanen powerplay drive went off Zhamnov's face and dropped at the goal scorer's feet. But Markov, Brashear and Ragnarsson took frustration penalties, enabling Darcy Tucker to convert a Leetch setup on a five-on-three.

Donald Brashear opened the scoring on a powerplay in Game Two of the Eastern Conference semifinals.

Roenick went after Mogilny in the third period after the Toronto star had twice run Ragnarsson into the boards, one more reflection of how the Leafs had been the aggressors and the Flyers the retaliators during a 4-1 win that cut Philadelphia's series lead to 2-1.

"That was the most I've seen Bryan McCabe hit in a long time," said Roenick. "He didn't touch one person in the Philly games, not one."

The Leafs not only were taking the body, but also checking passports. "I think [the Flyers have] European defensemen and all we have to do is play together and keep being physical," said Antropov, who was born in Kazakhstan. "They can't handle it."

"That's ridiculous, that's all I have to say," replied Johnsson, who could hold a stick well enough to go back in the lineup for Game Three. Hitchcock moved Kapanen back to forward with Brashear and Primeau.

The coach wasn't just looking for scoring depth, but karma.

"I'm outside the (Royal York) Hotel, starting to walk back to the rink with Bob Cole from CBC," Hitchcock recalls. There's this roped off area and all of a sudden here comes the Dalai Lama, who had made a presentation at the University of Toronto, with (actor) Richard Gere following behind.

"What was I going to say to him? 'How's our forecheck?'

"Cole said 'Dalai, how are you doing?' and I just lost it; I couldn't stop laughing. He never acknowledged us, but a couple of the people following looked at us like, 'Who the hell are these guys?'"

The Dalai Lama and his entourage would have been rare people in hockey-mad Toronto to not recognize a member of the Flyers.

"The New Jersey series, you felt like it was two methodical teams trying to beat one another, but the second round, it was more like two circuses competing," recalls Esche.

"Between so much media taking over the room, fan tactics, and all the stuff between games getting magnified, it was crazy how many distractions there were.

"I dealt with idiots every day. This guy brings me like 15 or 20 cards to sign and when I do, he rips them up and throws them in my face. I almost doubled over laughing.

"You'd put a block on your hotel phone, but the managers must hate the Flyers because the phones still ring and ring. At all hours we've got people knocking on our doors. We had to get our own security on the floor."

But the Flyers didn't appear sleep-deprived at the start of Game Four. When McCabe whiffed on a clear, Gagne pounced and beat Belfour low to the glove side for a 1-0 Philadelphia edge at 7:44.

McCabe took a hooking penalty, giving the Flyers the chance to stretch the lead. But LeClair got called for marginally interfering with Belfour. On the four-on-four, the Leaf goalie made a pad stop on Primeau after his successful inside move on Kaberle and the game changed.

After Sundin's pass from the half boards to Mogilny hit Ragnarsson and went between Esche's legs to tie the score 1-1, Radivojevic, Malakhov and Primeau took three more penalties before the first period ended. All Philadelphia momentum died.

After the break, Sundin cut in on Malakhov and beat Esche through the five-hole again with a 20-foot backhander.

"Mats competed," recalls Roenick. "In addition to being strong and incredibly skilled, he would slash you right back; no [bleeping] way you were ever going to intimidate him.

"I had nothing but respect for the guy."

Sundin hit the crossbar on a breakaway in the final minute of the second period to keep Philadelphia within one. But Tucker's third-period redirection of McCabe's powerplay shot, the fifth deflected goal of the seven the Leafs had scored in the series, put the game away.

Although the shots in Toronto's 3-1 victory were even at 28, the quality of chances had not been. The two top Leafs—Sundin and Mogilny—had stepped up in both games at the Air Canada Center to tie the series, 2-2.

"Their best players were on the powerplay for the rest of the first period after we had built some momentum," said Hitchcock, not being clear whether he was upset with the calls or the shortage of discipline by his players. They were plenty mad at themselves, however, after Philadelphia had been outchanced and outplayed for the first time in the series.

"Guys like myself, Johnny (LeClair) and Rex (Recchi) have to step to the forefront and become the difference," said Roenick.

Otherwise, Belfour would, believed Hitchcock.

"On the flight back from Game Four," he recalls, "I said to the other coaches, 'We have to find a way to get to Belfour because right now he's got a hold on the series.'

"I could see our guys' heads shaking as they came back to the bench after scoring chances; he was getting into our heads and we needed a different mindset.

"I remember telling the guys, 'We have to get him at least a little bit worked up because right now anything he sees he's going to stop. Go to the net hard, put every puck from anywhere on the ice on goal.'"

Recchi, who had been under the weather with the flu, received a get-well present from McCabe, a gold-plated giveaway that the winger converted unassisted before four minutes had been played in Game Five at the Wachovia Center. On the next shift, Primeau knocked off Gary Roberts' helmet with a corner hit, and then, the next time out, delivered two more body blows to become the definition of the determination Hitchcock had told his team it needed.

Primeau whacked Kaberle in response to being held and both players went off for two minutes. On the four-on-four, Johnsson stepped up to pick off a Leetch pass to the slot and started the other way. Gagne took a drop pass and made a quick relay to Handzus, who shot through a screen as Johnsson crossed in front. The puck went right through Belfour.

Two goals in 1:52—and a 2-0 lead—had put the Wachovia Center in a frenzy that barely abated even when Recchi went to the penalty box less than a minute later. Primeau, playing mostly head to head against Sundin, leveled Mogilny behind the net and the Leaf powerplay, just one-for-17 coming into the game, never got set up.

After 10 minutes, Toronto had no shots on goal. Tucker tried to rally his troops by leaving his feet to nail Malakhov, drawing a penalty. A premature whistle by referee Rob Shick denied Pitkanen a powerplay goal, but the Flyers were too wired to be disappointed. When Gagne got called for a hold and McCabe tried to keep the puck in at the point, Primeau swept in, kicked the puck onto his stick, and was off.

Leetch made a half-hearted attempt to stop the runaway train, but Primeau went to his backhand and beat Belfour's pokecheck, making it 3-0.

The Leafs cashed in on the powerplay regardless when Nieuwendyk was gifted with a half-empty net, the result of a broken down Kaberle point drive. With just 35 seconds to go in the first period, Toronto had some life and soon received another break.

Esche, who had come into Game Five with a stiff neck stemming from a Game Four collision, became disoriented after being elbowed by Tucker in the first period. "I was dizzy as [bleep]," the goalie recalls. "The guys looked like they were skating a million miles a minute. It was like, 'Oh my gawd, what's going on?'"

The Flyer medical team refused to take any chances. Burke was in goal as the second period began.

Turned out, Hitchcock could have pulled a volunteer from the stands for all the chance the Leafs still had. In the first minute, Johnsson flew from behind the Philadelphia net past Roberts to feed Radivojevic, who headmanned to Gagne. He carried to the goal line and fed a backhand pass to Primeau, who had charged past Aki Berg into the slot. Belfour, who had been tracking Gagne, had no chance to scramble back. The Flyers led 4-1.

The ice-cold Burke stopped Antropov after a steal and the Flyer feeding frenzy continued. Skating four-on-four, Primeau circled the net and passed the puck out off the skate of Roberts into the slot, where Markov kicked it back to Radivojevic, who beat Belfour easily to the glove side, making it 5-1.

Kapanen was back on defense because Malakhov, hit in the head during the first period, was out for the game. It was being played almost entirely in the Toronto end regardless. Leetch tried to pin Somik behind the net, but Handzus walked out and had a ridiculously easy backhanded tuck past the clearly defeated Belfour to give Philadelphia a 6-1 advantage.

After Quinn pulled Belfour in favor of Trevor Kidd, Roberts got behind Amonte to redirect a Mogilny feed past Burke. But early in the third period, Primeau cut off a wraparound by Kidd, put the puck back down the boards to Gagne, and went to the slot to complete his hat trick off Gagne's passout.

Every time the ice girls and maintenance men would scoop up all the hats, a new barrage would come down to celebrate the 20th three-goal game in Flyer playoff history. It was estimated that more than 1,000 pieces filled the ice.

"Hitch wanted me go over to Lou (PA announcer Nolan) to ask the people to hold up and let's get this going again," Primeau said later. "I'm like, '*YOU* go tell them to get this thing going again.'"

The 7-2 rout, forged by one of the most dominant one-man performances in Flyer playoff history, left Primeau's team one game from advancing to the Eastern Conference final. "I've seen Mario (Lemieux) take control of games, being a presence everywhere," said former Penguin Recchi. "This one was right up there."

Said Primeau, "To be given this opportunity after everything, I just don't want to let it get by."

That was what the disgusted Leafs felt they had done in falling behind, 3-2, in the series.

"Probably my worst game as a professional," said McCabe. He and partner Leetch had been on the ice for 13 of Toronto's 19 playoff goals coming into the contest, but McCabe was minus-5 for the game and Leetch minus-4.

"We looked like Swiss cheese out there," said their coach. "We didn't have anybody that stuck to the basic principles of the game, just let it slide right outside the window.

"You talk about disappointing things, for a veteran team. . . "

It turned out that Esche, who was playing with a gradually worsening hip issue, did not have to deal with a concussion, too. He only had become dehydrated, like his quotes as the playoffs moved along.

Annoyed by end-of-regular-season criticism by the *Inquirer*'s Tim Panaccio—"I knew I was playing like [bleep], tell me something that I don't know," Esche recalls—the goalie had stopped answering the beat reporter's questions, before eventually receiving permission from Clarke to talk to all media members only after games.

With Esche's availability to play Game Six in question, Hitchcock was left to play pool reporter. Before the Flyers flew back to Toronto, the coach said his goalie's energy level was normal at practice, but that Malakhov was lightheaded and doubtful, making more minutes necessary for the rookie Pitkanen. As Pitkanen and Timander both were minus-five in the series, this wasn't good news. Hitchcock moved Kapanen back to defense and, for insurance, dressed Dennis Seidenberg, going with 11 forwards.

The coach stressed the importance of a good start. Not only did he get one, but also a game-opening goal from a very unlikely source. On an extended cycle that was largely the work of Brashear, Somik, dressing for just the fifth time in the 11 playoff games, bounced off Nieuwendyk along the wall, got the puck to Brashear and went to the net to receive Handzus's touch pass from behind the goal line. Wide open and just 15 feet away, Somik fired over Belfour's catcher to make it 1-0 after 9:55.

The ice time for the line of Primeau, Amonte and Roenick suffered from Hitchcock's mostly failed attempts to get them out against the Sundin line. But the blessing for Roenick, who had missed shifts in Game Five after being high sticked between the shoulder blades by Antropov, was considerable energy conservation.

Breaking two-on-two with Amonte, Roenick burst past Leetch, fought off the defender's desperate hook, and fired. Belfour made the stop but put the rebound right into J.R.'s path. He quickly banged his first goal of the series and 50th of his playoff career between the goalie's legs, giving Philadelphia a 2-0 lead at 15:30.

Belfour kept his team in the game with two quick saves on Roenick and the Flyers stopped forechecking through a four-shot second period, when they had to kill off minors to Timander and Pitkanen. Nevertheless, chances for the Leafs were minimal.

Leading 2-0, Philadelphia remained in control well into the third period. But with 11 minutes to go, Sundin beat Primeau on an offensive zone draw and Karel Pilar fired through traffic. The screened Esche reached at the last millisecond, but the puck beat his glove, bringing the Leafs to within a goal and the Air Canada Centre suddenly to life.

There were five minutes remaining when McCabe made a quick counter trapping Zhamnov at center and giving Mogilny room as he crossed the blueline. He carried deep and threw a backhand pass past Ragnarsson to Roberts busting up the middle.

Esche stopped Roberts' jam and Johnsson tied the winger up as they both went into the goalie. Handzus swung around to try to clear the rebound, but it caromed out too far for him as Sundin beat Recchi to the loose puck. Esche flung up his stick but the Toronto captain didn't miss. With 4:52 to play, a game that the Flyers had been leading almost from the start was tied, 2-2.

The Leafs, their fans in a frenzy, won the center draw and threw the puck in. When Philadelphia was outworked along the half wall, Esche had to stop a quick wrister by Sundin labeled for just inside the far post.

With Sundin waiting for Roberts' pass into the goalmouth, Zhamnov got away with a push from behind and the Flyers survived. There was a minute remaining when Malakhov fell down and Reichel came out from behind the net and found Domi, who had burst past Kapanen. With the Toronto fans on their feet for the kill, Esche made a left pad save from almost point-blank range.

In the final seconds, Antropov had Nieuwendyk breaking for the net on a two-on-one, but Johnsson broke it up. Philadelphia reached the regulation buzzer gasping.

"We could have been up by five or six after two periods, but Belfour had been standing on his head," recalls Hitchcock. "And all of a sudden it was again like we were skating uphill.

"The building was loud and it got really physical. The referees (Kevin Pollock and Stephen Walkom) had put their whistles away. Toronto was running the living hell out of us, firing everyone in on the forecheck. We had to take some risks to get them back on their heels.

"I remember saying, 'Look, we got out of the period. Whatever's been happening, we still only need one goal to reach the conference final. Let's go for it.'

"I don't know, it was just my respect for Belfour that was making me nervous. I thought if we didn't get him early, we weren't going to get him."

The previous spring, the Flyers had entered a Game Six overtime in the same building leading the series 3-2, feeling that no matter who scored the next goal, they ultimately still were going to be moving on to the next round. They do not remember being as confident a year later.

"When you are playing a team as competitive as that one, whom you beat the year before in a Game Seven, the Leafs are going to have memories," recalls Primeau. "This time I didn't like our chances in Game Seven."

Esche, on the other hand, liked them just fine, perhaps because he had been far and away the best Flyer in the final period.

"Our locker room was always kind of the same," he recalls. "There was never any panic in that room and sometimes that's the best voice.

"It was matter of fact, business as usual. They weren't worried for me and I certainly wasn't worried for them, not with all the All-Stars and (future) Hall of Famers we had."

In the first minute of the overtime, Belfour turned back a decent chance by Zhamnov. But then the Leafs quickly began to carry the play again.

Almost six minutes in, Esche gave the puck away from behind the goal to Ponikarovsky, but his shot hit a skate and caromed to the corner.

When Johnsson couldn't make a clear, Esche butterflied to make a right skate save on Pilar before Gagne, unable to get the puck past

Antropov, hustled back to the slot to tie up on Ponikarovsky. Toronto held the puck in for a full 90 seconds until Esche won a race to the post on Nieuwendyk.

When Philadelphia finally countered, Handzus's shot from the left boards deflected around the glass, where Kapanen, 20 feet inside the blueline, was attempting to control it, head down in his skates. Tucker, coming from 20 feet away, leaped and nailed the Finn with a shoulder to the head, lifting him into the air and dropping him to the ice as the Leafs cleared the puck.

"I saw he was coming but there was not a whole lot I could do," recalls Kapanen. "He left his feet and I'm not sure if it was his elbow or his shoulder, but he kind of hit me on the side of the head and part of my face."

Kapanen, on his back, rolled over to all fours, tried to grab his stick and rise, but collapsed.

"I had problems controlling my hands," he recalls. "I knew they weren't stopping play, so I was trying to get to the bench (25 feet away).

"I'm trying to skate, but my legs just gave out and I kind of fell down again. It seemed like every time I tried to go right, my body was going left. It was frustrating.

"Once I got going in the right direction, I kind of knew I was going to the bench and they (teammates) were trying to hook me in."

Kapanen rose for a fourth time, falling forward but able to maintain his balance at last. Primeau, standing at the end of the bench, hooked him towards the middle. "Fishing for my little buddy," recalls Primeau.

(Trainer) John Worley and Timander reeled Kapanen in while Reichel was closing to the top of the circle and firing. Esche made the save, and then was spinning when Handzus tied up another Domi chance to win the game.

Toronto's pressure was unabated until Berg, harassed from behind by Zhamnov, fanned on a shot. Recchi picked up the puck and, suddenly two-on-one with LeClair, closed to a place even with the hash marks and fired.

Belfour got a piece of the shot with his blocker, the rebound caromed out just past LeClair's reach and the Leafs carried back. Sundin tried to make a right-to-left move along the Flyer line, but Zhamnov poked the puck loose to Pitkanen, who quickly head-manned it off the right boards as both teams changed.

Roenick, who had just come on, had almost reached the Philadelphia blueline to help with the backcheck, but the neutral zone was so empty he had time to circle back and get the puck before it reached the Leaf blueline. For the second time in 10 seconds, the Flyers were two-on-one, Amonte coming up the middle, only McCabe back for Toronto.

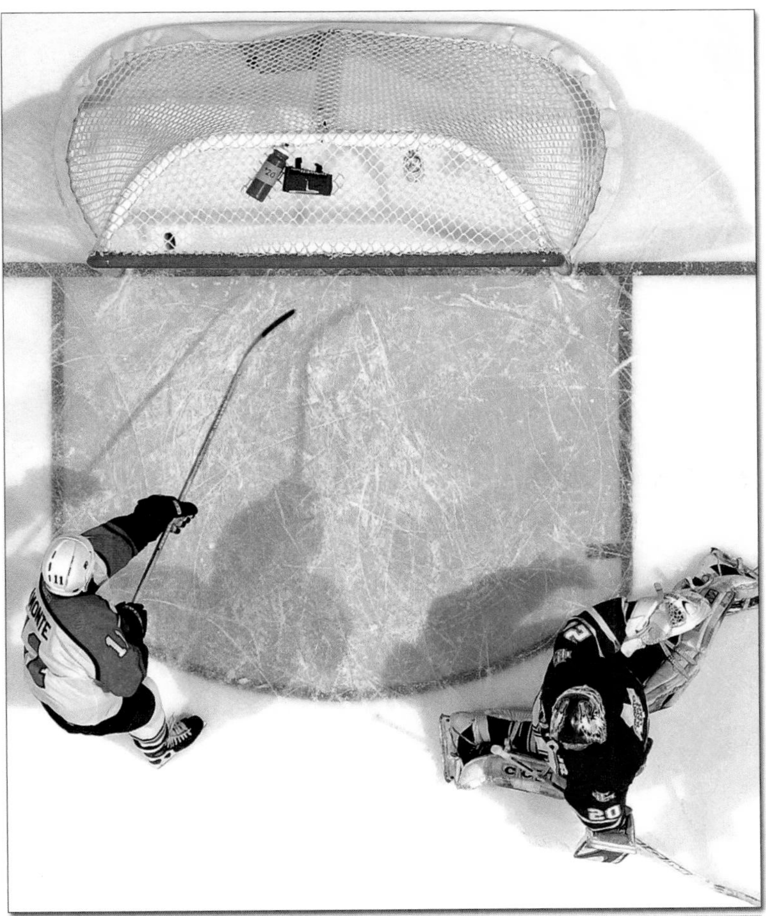

Leaf goaltender Ed Belfour and Flyer Tony Amonte follow J.R.'s Game Six series-clinching overtime winner into the net

Roenick closed all the way to the hashmarks before wristing the puck. The water bottle on top of the net jumped, the red light went on at 7:39, and J.R., cutting in front of the goal, was already into a toe dance before Amonte, just to be sure, put the puck back into the net.

The ongoing roar from the Tucker hit, plus the end-to-end chances of the remarkable, frantic sequence that followed, didn't drain for a second or two until reality totally silenced the Air Canada Centre. Ragnarsson reached Roenick, dancing at the opposite halfwall, with the first hug, followed by a mob of Flyers. They had won the game, 3-2, and the series, 4-2, putting the franchise in its 14th Eastern Conference final on what Roenick remembers as the shot of his lifetime.

"I was sitting at my locker at intermission going over in my head different scenarios for me to score and end the game," recalls Roenick. "I always did that.

"Knowing the (ex-teammate) goalie I was playing against helped me visualize, too. Eddie knew that shooting over his right pad was my go-to shot or else I'd pass. But this time, I visualized that I was going to shoot for the top corner instead.

"That's what happened. Exactly like that. The most perfect shot I ever made in my life. Eddie told me recently that he still has no idea how that puck got by him. He had the angle on it. He saw it. But it was just the perfect, perfect shot and the favorite goal of my career.

"After that hit on Sami, the building was rocking. It was

deafening in there. The Leafs were attacking in waves. Then, 45 seconds later, the building goes dead quiet, a thing of beauty. And if Sami just lies there like most guys would after getting hit like that, play would have stopped and I don't score the goal.

"Sami is one tough little mother. There is not one player today—not one—who would be able to make it back to the bench like Sami did after the way he got hit.

"He had the rubber legs and had to have a teammate pull him off—but he made it back through sheer will. Love that guy, yet another smart hockey player and a consummate teammate on a club with so many like that. But for as small as he was, Sami was a one-of-a-kind to be so fearless and smart."

Primeau, on the bench and looking into Kapanen's glassy eyes, was late to join the on-ice celebration. Kapanen was barred from participating. "I watched on the screen and jumped up and tried to go but John Worley just kind of pulled me down and said 'You're staying here,'" Kapanen recalls.

Esche had come up so big in the third period and overtime that he had free rein to go anywhere he wanted on the ice—and drink free beer at probably any bar in the Delaware Valley. He had played the game of his career to get his team within eight wins of Champagne.

"I remember thinking the biggest circus of my life is over, thank goodness," recalls Esche. And he wasn't the only Flyer to take additional joy in finishing the series at Toronto.

'They got hyped up to the moon and back up there," recalls Roenick. "I have to admit, I got satisfaction out of that, too.

"Not so much the Leaf players, because we respected the way they competed, but there was just a really obnoxious zoo of people up there, trying both years to make our lives miserable 24/7. All that did was motivate us even more. Scoring to knock them out was a big '[bleep] you' moment."

True to his personality, Kapanen refused to ever take personally what Tucker did.

"I never really accused him of a dirty hit, but you can see that he's leaving his feet and the hit is right on the head, so it was kind of dirty," he recalls. "By today's rules, it would be a major and a suspension, but at that time it wasn't even a penalty.

"I'm not complaining. We moved on (in the playoffs) and I had nothing more to say about that. When my son (Kasperi, Pittsburgh's first-round pick in 2014) was growing up, he said, 'I hope that Tucker is still playing because I'm gonna knock him out.'

"I told him not to focus on something like that. But I think it was kind of hard for him to see that happen to his dad."

Philadelphia had no such trouble viewing an act of such determination. The media replayed the sequence endlessly as a symbol of the resolve of a team that would next face Tampa Bay for the right to play for the Stanley Cup.

The Lightning, with only one regular defenseman—Jason Cullimore—injured, had enjoyed eight days off after sweeping Montreal while the Flyers had only one day off to lick wounds between series.

Despite balance problems and headaches, 48 hours between face-offs would have to be enough for Kapanen, who joined Primeau and Roenick on the list of Philadelphia players refusing to acknowledge their post-concussion symptoms.

"All that night (of the return from Toronto), I had this huge pounding in my head, but I never ended up going to a doctor's office or having a concussion test done," recalls Kapanen. "I didn't want to take myself out of the lineup."

The Flyers had lost all four regular-season meetings against the Eastern Conference champion Lightning, but Primeau had missed two of the contests, Roenick was absent for another, and neither Zhamnov nor Malakhov had been acquired before the season series was completed.

"We're a totally different team than what played them during the season," said Roenick, a fact that Vincent Lecavalier, then a rising 23-year-old Tampa Bay star, remembers acknowledging.

"Any win is a confidence builder, but I still kinda thought that we were the underdog in that series," he recalls. "A lot of people did.

"It was only our second year in the playoffs, going against Keith Primeau's big, strong team with experience."

Philadelphia was being portrayed as the grizzled bruisers, the Lightning as the young speedsters, which certainly played in Florida. "The people hated Philly because there was some history between the Buccaneers and Eagles," recalls Brad Richards, another young Tampa Bay star, but with his franchise on its first extended playoff run, there was little history to fuel on-ice venom. With Desjardins injured, the only roster survivor of the previous series between the two teams—a six-game Flyer triumph in 1996—was LeClair.

Hitchcock didn't like the brutes vs. prodigies spin regardless, and attempted to change it. "Some of the people who think we're the Broad Street Bullies have black and white televisions," argued the coach. "We're not that big; (more) a small, finesse hockey club."

But there was a big contrast at center ice, where Philadelphia had size, grit and wisdom, while the Lightning had burgeoning speedy stars Lecavalier, Richards and Martin St. Louis.

"They had a lot of firepower in the middle of the ice," recalls Hitchcock. "But I was more concerned with who was gonna play for us rather than who we were gonna play as an opponent.

"Because of what we'd gone through in the Toronto series, I was really nervous that we were going to be missing a lot of players. It was always, 'Who's gonna play? How much can he play? When can he play?' After Game One against Toronto, every day was like that.

"At times that (Leaf) series was so reckless, physical and nasty, it actually made you cringe. I remember talking to Pat Quinn at the World Cup (four months later, when they were together on Canada's coaching staff) and he said, 'If we had won the series, we couldn't have fielded 20 players. My team wanted to beat your team so badly that my players were not disclosing injuries, not coming into the training room.'"

During the regular season, the Flyers had lost 241 man-games to injuries to the Lightning's 34. Desjardins remained out at least through the conference final. But Tampa Bay's rust figured to be Philadelphia's advantage for Game One played at the St. Pete Times Forum.

Indeed, the Flyers carried the play in the first period, but all they had to show for it was a Kapanen goal disallowed because Primeau had slid into goalie Nikolai Khabibulin.

As a Ragnarsson penalty expired, Johnsson couldn't get the puck out and Fredrik Modin fed Dave Andreychuk, who came off the boards beating Roenick to the net, and then Esche's glove to the short side.

Philadelphia tied the game four minutes later when LeClair, sent in by Recchi, circled the goal, dug his failed stuffer attempt back out of the side of the net, and fed the point. Malakhov half fanned on the shot, but Handzus kicked it on net with his trailing skate and put in a backhander before Khabibulin could re-set himself.

Despite eight minutes of offensive zone time in the first 11 of the period, the Flyers soon found themselves trailing again. Recchi made the third of three consecutive Philadelphia giveaways, allowing Richards to come off the backboards and score.

The outplayed Lightning, leading 2-1, had been more opportunistic. A Flyer powerplay opportunity created when Andreychuk took down LeClair disintegrated into multiple blocked shots and a shorthanded chance for St. Louis.

Six minutes into the third period, Roenick flipped the puck over Pavel Kubina, and raced ahead, but only managed a jam shot into Khabibulin. Tampa Bay soon extended its lead when Chris Dingman, who had dumped a puck perfectly out of Esche's reach, beat Pitkanen to the net to put in Andre Roy's rebound before the goalie could come across, making the score 3-1.

Johnsson, crunched by Lecavalier against the boards, lost his sense of direction going back to the bench. Hitchcock's line juggling failed to turn up chances, as did a powerplay after Cory Stillman tripped Markov with 2:02 remaining in the game. The tiring Flyers managed just 11 shots over the last two periods. Once the Lightning cobwebs had cleared, they dominated in their 3-1 win.

By flipping the puck out, Tampa Bay had created some foot races and won them, but Hitchcock vehemently denied Philadelphia was facing a younger, faster, team. "They aren't young," he said. "They are 28.9 (average age) and we are 29.8, so don't give me that crap. They have guys like Andreychuk (38) who are older than dirt."

Actually, it was the youngest Flyer, Pitkanen, who had struggled the most.

"He's a 20-year-old kid that should be sunbathing in Helsinki right now," said Hitchcock, moving Kapanen, never mind the headaches he was hiding, back to Pitkanen's place on the blueline for Game Two.

"With all the excitement, I really didn't think much about (the health hazard)," Kapanen recalls. "The opportunity was taking over. Once I got on the ice, I felt OK to play."

Philadelphia, with another day to rest and build resolve to keep from falling behind 2-0 in the series, came out strongly in Game Two. LeClair, carrying into the Tampa Bay zone after Handzus won a battle along the boards, surprised Khabibulin with a wrister that beat him to the glove side on the game's first shot.

Lecavalier and Tim Taylor went off on penalties 1:23 apart. On the five-on four, Recchi tipped in a Ragnarsson point shot for a 2-0 Philadelphia lead.

Radivojevic was in the box for hooking and Ragnarsson was killing off the waning seconds of the penalty when his intended clearing pass nicked off Dan Boyle's skate to Timander. Timander led Kapanen, who poked the puck around Kubina, skated up the right wing and, when Darryl Sydor wiped out, elevated a wrist shot over Khabibulin.

It was the third Flyer goal on just five shots and Khabibulin's torment wasn't over. Malakhov's second-period wrist shot from the point, deflected in past the partially screened goalie.

Having stopped only eight of 12 shots by that point, Khabibulin was pulled by coach John Tortorella and replaced with John Grahame, who was beaten on a Handzus rebound and a Timander blast, off a turnover, through traffic. Philadelphia stunningly was up 6-0.

There wasn't any further talk about speed mismatches after Philadelphia's blowout 6-2 victory. There would have been more follow-up discussion about Khabibulin's failures, but Tortorella moved to take care of that by going to the podium on the off day and calling out Hitchcock for baiting Tampa Bay players from the bench.

"We knew going into the series that Bobby Clarke, their general manager, was going to be working as hard as he could behind the scenes, whining about this and that (to the officiating supervisors)," said the Tampa Bay coach. "We know Hitch is going to be talking

The Lightning and the Flyers mix it up in Game Two of the NHL Eastern Conference finals, a 6-2 Philadelphia win at the St. Pete Times Forum in Tampa.

about anything that is on his mind; we accept that.

"But when a coach starts bringing that dialogue onto the ice, behind the bench, more or less within earshot of the opposing team's players, it's wrong. Last time I looked, he's wearing a suit back there, same type of suit I'm wearing. He's not in the battle.

"It's gutless. He should shut his yap."

"I always yap," countered Hitchcock, a known baiter of the opposition, who had become annoyed with Tampa's Brad Lukowich for a temporarily-paralyzing stick jab to the back of Zhamnov's knee. "Tell [Tortorella] to mind his own business."

Clarke wondered why he also was being attacked, but seized the opportunity to return fire.

"I don't know what he's talking about," said the GM about his supposed lobbying efforts. "It sounds like a pathetic little man looking to get some publicity for himself."

Recalls Craig Ramsay, a Lightning assistant coach and former Flyer head coach, "John legitimately didn't like coaches [baiting the opposition], but he also made sure there was something else to be focused on besides our goaltender."

Whether or not that helped, Khabibulin bounced back and was sharp for the start of Game Three. And, apparently stung by Philadelphia's dominance in Game Two, a much more determined Tampa Bay team deflated the wired Wachovia Center early.

After Ragnarsson, hit on the hand by a Modin follow-through, went to the locker room, Esche had to glove a Modin riser from the top of the circle to keep the game scoreless. Recchi took a stick in the face from Kubina, who was penalized, but the Flyers only managed one weak attempt on the powerplay. When Stillman's drive from the top of the circle fluttered over Esche's glove at 12:56 of the opening period to give Tampa Bay the first goal, the Philadelphia netminder had surrendered his first softie in three rounds.

Meanwhile, Khabibulin stopped Primeau once after he pulled the puck inside Nolan Pratt and then again off a setup from the boards by Recchi. When Markov got called for holding, the Lightning pounced. Andreychuk's quick pass from the point beat Johnsson's stick to Ruslan Fedotenko, who had a step on Timander and fired off Esche's glove for a 2-0 lead.

Tampa Bay quickly tried to help the Flyers back into the game by getting caught with too many men on the ice, and then becoming shorthanded in the first minute of the second period as a result of a Kubina penalty for charging Amonte. But when a passout went off Taylor's skate and caromed to Zhamnov, Khabibulin came up with a big glove save, then another on a Malakhov hammer from the point.

Philadelphia took its own bench minor for too many men and also had to kill off a Primeau elbow of Roy's head. But Esche made his best save, paddle down, on a Lecavalier walkout and gradually the Flyers started to find energy. Pratt had to make a diving block as Recchi went to the net, Radivojevic shot over top on a golden Amonte rebound, Khabibulin stopped Primeau with the right pad and Somik hit a post.

When Kubina was sent off for tripping Brashear at the side of the net, the Philadelphia powerplay failed again, dropping to one-for-15 in the series. Still, the team had nine of the previous 12 scoring chances in the game when, in the first minute of the third period, Primeau pushed the puck down the boards past Cory Sarich and threw it out to Gagne. The pass hit Sydor and caromed conveniently back to Primeau, who swept in a gimme to cut the Lightning lead to 2-1.

The fired-up Flyers forced the puck into the Tampa Bay zone, where St. Louis fed past a pinching Markov to a flying Lecavalier, who had split Recchi and Malakhov. Lecavalier took the pass at the red line, blew in on Esche and, just 1:19 seconds after Primeau's goal, scored high to the glove side.

"Every time Marty (St. Louis) had it on the wall, I would take off full speed," recalls Lecavalier. "They were still cheering and announcing their goal when we made everything get quiet again, which was nice."

"I don't even know where he came from," Recchi would say after the game, and Philadelphia, down 3-1, lost its sense of direction.

After Taylor went to the box for interfering with Roenick, the Flyers managed only one drive, from 25 feet out, by Markov as the Lightning blocked shot after shot on the powerplay. Richards, set up by pretty relays from St. Louis and Roy, added a fourth goal with 11:20 to go and Tampa Bay handed Philadelphia its first home loss of the playoffs, 4-1.

Lecavalier's breakaway had been the backbreaker. "We had so many things going well," lamented Hitchcock. "That goal deflated us."

Really, though, the Flyers only had things going for about 10 minutes and were badly outplayed for the rest. "I felt we had them on their heels, unnerved (after Game Two), then didn't play as well in Game Three as we should have," recalls Hitchcock.

It had not helped that, for the first time in the playoffs, the opposition goaltender had been better than Esche, who was performing with a worsening hip. "Sometimes there was shooting pain down the left side into the leg, but I could deal with it," he recalls.

So could Khabibulin, easily, with a Philadelphia powerplay that managed just five shots in three opportunities.

"They are trying to stay in the shooting lanes all the time," said Malakhov. "We tried to make them move and it's not working."

Ragnarsson had surgery on his finger and was out for at least the series. Hitchcock had gotten through the rest of Game Three by spotting Timander on pairs of Kapanen-Malakhov and Johnsson-Markov, but Pitkanen would have to go back in for Game Four.

Flyer management premiered the giveaway of t-shirts at the door, forcing the Lightning to play under a sea of orange. The crowd was all-in, as seemingly had been Primeau since the start of the playoff, but it turned out nobody knew the limits of the captain's will.

He was double-shifted early in the game, when his recharged team dominated possession. Thanks to two Primeau hits, the powerplay asserted good pressure as Sarich was penalized for tripping Zhamnov.

With Gagne in the box on a double minor for drawing the blood of Sarich, St. Louis fed Lecavalier, who put the puck between his own legs and appeared to be one-on-one with Esche until Malakhov got back to knock the chance away with a sweep check.

As a result, when Modin put back a Kubina powerplay shot off the post to give Tampa Bay a 1-0 lead, Philadelphia had only fallen down by one. Esche kept it that way with saves on good chances by Fedotenko, Andreychuk and St. Louis.

The goalie risked bigger trouble with a penalized whack of Andreychuk, but on a short two-man advantage, Kubina missed on the long side and the puck rimmed out. With Tampa Bay firing wide two more times, the Flyers also survived the five-on-four.

Just back at even strength, Primeau, following as Kapanen was stood up at the blueline, cut to the middle and dropped the puck to the trailing LeClair. Kapanen had gone to the net to screen and LeClair's shot went in clean on the stick side, his second goal in three games after not having scored in the previous 16.

Tied 1-1, Philadelphia was all over the Lightning. Recchi, Roenick and Zhamnov produced a full minute of pressure before Timander's shot from up the slot was deflected once by Modin and then again by Recchi before trickling across the line under Khabibulin's glove.

Two goals in 2:15 had the Flyers ahead, 2-1. Primeau, still doubleshifting, was cruising for more, even as teammates took Tampa Bay's best body shots. After shouldering Fedotenko hard into the boards, Gagne went to the dressing room holding his left arm, although he soon returned to the bench. Pitkanen then got up looking disoriented after a sandwich hit by Dmitry Afanasenkov and Taylor, who left his feet.

Malakhov, giving as good as he got, snapped his stick in half with a cross-check of Modin and went to the penalty box. The outplayed Lightning had a chance to tie the game with its deadly powerplay, but pointman Andreychuk lost his footing, reached to try to keep the puck in, and only succeeded in knocking it up into the air.

Primeau, the minesweeper, gloved the puck down, broke out two-on-one with Gagne against Boyle, and wristed from the edge of the circle. The shot beat Khabibulin cleanly, high to the glove side, shorthanded manna from heaven, to extend Philadelphia's lead to 3-1.

A Markov block killed off the remainder of the penalty but Roenick, who hit a post, got caught holding Sydor. When the Flyers stopped Tampa Bay without a shot on the powerplay, Philadelphia remained in much better shape on the scoreboard than medically. Neither Pitkanen nor Roenick, the latter probably concussed on a first-period hit by Modin, returned for the third period.

Brashear took a penalty for interference, but Esche made a stick save on Lecavalier from the point and a pad stop on St. Louis from the slot before Gagne, playing without a stick, used his hand to clear the puck. When the Lightning came right back, Malakhov remarkably tied up Richards in the corner, then cleared the puck.

The Flyer powerplay failed on a 39-second five-on-three, and, on the five-on-four, St Louis, who had been well checked by Gagne, snuck behind Kapanen to shoot wide. After Roy put the puck between Markov's leg and skate, Esche flashed his glove.

As time began to run out on Tampa Bay, Timander was on the bench, too, with an apparent shoulder injury, leaving Philadelphia down to four defensemen when Markov got called for elbowing with 1:23 remaining.

With Khabibulin pulled, Primeau won a defensive zone draw cleanly from Andreychuk and got the puck out. But Lecavalier brought it right back and, from 45 feet out, lifted the water bottle with a rocket past Esche's stick side that cut the Flyer to 3-2.

Although the Lightning still had 33 seconds to get the equalizer, Primeau knocked down Boyle's attempt to start one last rush and then controlled the puck along the boards in the Tampa Bay zone as time ran out.

Philadelphia, the 3-2 winner, had evened the series on probably Primeau's best effort yet. Not only had he assisted on the tying goal and scored shorthanded to put the Flyers ahead, the captain repeatedly had crunched anybody in his path.

"Every time I came off the ice, I looked around to Hitch and wanted to go back out again," he said. "I felt I could have played 60 minutes."

The 22 minutes the stat guys recorded had seemed more like 60 to the Lightning.

"We felt him coming every shift," recalls Ramsay.

And the legend of Keith Primeau's 2004 playoffs grew.

"There are certain stages during a critical series when your captain has to step up. And he stepped up—again," said Hitchcock. This, despite the headache and blurred vision Primeau had been suffering since his return with three games remaining in the regular season.

Figuratively and literally, he was hungry.

"Whenever my head doesn't feel well, I eat," Primeau says. "After dinner, that spring, I would have a bag of Sun Chips and a pint of ice cream, which was ludicrous, but I was performing.

"Although my head wasn't great, physically I felt awesome. I was able to score a couple early in the Jersey series that alleviated me worrying about goals. I competed no harder than I had any other year, but I was scoring."

All but one of the Flyer goals in the series had been at even strength, while the Lightning powerplay was beginning to pick apart a Philadelphia defense that had completed Game Four without four regular defensemen. Nevertheless, the series was tied.

"We had Malakhov playing 30 minutes and that's a lot in a playoff game, when you're hitting and leaning on people," Hitchcock told the media. "That was almost superhuman, but it's the case with a lot of our experienced defensemen."

A video of the team's most inexperienced one—Kapanen, struggling three times to his feet from the Tucker hit, accompanied by the Rocky theme—drew a roar from the crowd every time it was shown on yhe center-hung scoreboard. And that was far from the only sight sending Ed Snider's heart soaring.

"I love this team," said the Chairman in the locker room. "We keep losing players and they don't quit, just suck it in and keep going.

"And I can't get over Primeau."

Roenick, who had suffered by his count the 19th concussion of his 17-season career, wasn't getting over his symptoms anytime soon. "I've got 30 hours so we'll see," he said about Game Five. "If we get six more wins, I won't have to worry about getting hit in the head except by a golf ball."

One had to be on the lookout, however, for flying verbal darts thrown by Hitchcock at Tortorella. "He's Italian, he's from Boston, he's probably a Red Sox fan, so he's got three strikes against him right there," giggled the Flyer coach.

But "The Great Tortellini,"—as called by Clarke—said he was going to shut his yap.

"Those comments (after Game Two) were made to protect my team and I would do it again," the Tampa Bay coach said. "But I've never been one to get involved in that stuff.

Mark Recchi is turned away by Nikolai Khabibulin in Game Five.

"It's about the players. I'm serious about that, so I'm out. Ken knows there are certain times you need to protect your hockey club. But this other stuff going on is a bit childish."

Roenick dressed for Game Five in Tampa. Pitkanen couldn't answer the bell, so he was replaced by 22-year-old call-up Seidenberg, who had played in only five regular-season games with Philadelphia because of a broken leg.

Tortorella, concentrating on his own team, never emphasized punishing the beat-up Flyer defense, just applying pressure as always. But of course, the Lightning players knew where Philadelphia was vulnerable.

"We were aware they were [shorthanded] back there, sure," recalls Lecavalier. "That's part of the playoffs, key injuries are sometimes why you win and lose.

"We were pretty healthy throughout the whole playoffs and had the luxury of winning the first two series [in nine games]."

Despite all that, in the first four games against Tampa Bay, the Flyers had a 66-52 edge in scoring chances. It only seemed like 65 of the 66 were created by Primeau.

"[Tortorella] always preached concentration on what we were doing, not what the other team was doing; he didn't get excessively caught up in the matchups," recalls Ramsay, whose job was to change the defensemen. "But Pratt and Sarich, who had done such a good job for us against Montreal, couldn't handle Primeau.

"So I went to Sydor, who was a huge addition (from Dallas, where he had won a Cup under Hitchcock) at the trading deadline and Kubina, who was a pretty big (6-4, 258-pound) boy."

Four minutes into Game Five, Sydor took a penalty for hooking Primeau well behind the play, but the Flyers were not even able to set up.

Again, the loser of the previous game had most of the energy to start the next one. St. Louis lifted the puck too high into Esche off a LeClair giveaway and the Philadelphia goalie had to make even stronger saves. One was with his blocker on Richards, another on Modin off an Andreychuk passout.

When Timander went off for hooking St. Louis, the Lightning broke through for a 1-0 lead, Fedotenko converting his own rebound of a tipped Boyle drive. It was Tampa Bay's fifth powerplay goal of the series in 20 attempts.

Roenick crushed Sarich with a charge behind the net, angering Tortorella when no penalty was called. St. Louis was put down along the boards by Primeau. When the Flyer captain received a retaliatory bump by Modin following a Philadelphia offsides, a scrum resulted in the Bolts getting an extra two minutes, enraging the Tampa Bay coach all the more.

Primeau, not happy with Modin, crosschecked him and then dropped his own stick, inviting a fight. Modin declined as Malakhov and Boyle went off for roughing, leaving the Flyers down four skaters to three as the second period began. Richards one-timed a return pass from Andreychuk high to Esche's glove side just 24 seconds after the intermission to build the Lightning lead to 2-0.

The Philadelphia goaltender kept it that way temporarily with an exceptional save on a Modin deflection. But in the fight for the rebound, Handzus took Modin down. Just three seconds after the penalty-box door closed, Richards, set up in the high slot by a clean Stillman faceoff defeat of Primeau, shot off the post and into the net.

The 3-0 Tampa Bay lead lasted only 1:44, when Handzus nailed Richards from behind, causing him to lose his stick. An Amonte pass probably intended for LeClair made its way through goalmouth traffic, allowing Amonte to score into a half-empty net, getting the Flyers within two.

Thirty-eight seconds later, they were down by just one. Primeau passed the puck to himself off the backboards and fed a passout to Sharp, who had position on Fedotenko to make the score 3-2 with half the game to play.

LeClair was stymied on a wraparound set up by the inexhaustible Primeau. Andreychuk, hooking the Flyer captain three times in the leg before he finally went down, took a second Tampa Bay penalty in the period trying to contain the Philadelphia star.

But despite some foolish penalties, the Lightning smartly fronted the big Flyer horses in front, deflecting away pucks before they became troublesome. The only Khabibulin stop during the Andreychuk penalty was on a deflection by Recchi off a Johnsson drive through a Handzus screen.

Philadelphia, finding a second wind, pounded away physically in the third period, but was having difficulty creating chances in a suddenly much tighter checking contest. Khabibulin stopped a Roenick one-timer off a Primeau steal from Lukowich with 14 minutes remaining, then barely got the handle of his stick on a Recchi crank from above the circle.

Primeau gained a half step on Modin, but Khabibulin got it with his left pad, then stopped an Amonte tip off a LeClair passout. Seidenberg had an opportunity thanks to a faceoff won by Handzus, but the Lightning goalie saw the shot even with LeClair flashing in front. Gagne, fed when Primeau chased down a dump-in, got a second chance by fighting off Sydor, but Khabibulin saved the rebound.

Handzus took out Modin and fired, but Richards tipped the puck away. After Roenick won two more faceoffs from Richards, Tortorella successfully switched to Taylor for the final two minutes. When Gagne couldn't beat Sarich to an icing, Hitchcock was unable to pull Esche, who had to make a final minute save on a Richards stuffer after a steal from Malakhov behind the goal.

With 27 seconds to go, Khabibulin gloved a turnaround shot by Zhamnov, giving the Flyers one last chance. But Andreychuk drew the faceoff back and Zhamnov couldn't keep in Tampa Bay's hard rim. Taylor hit the empty net on a two-on-one and the Lightning had survived a 15-shot Philadelphia third period to win 4-2, leaving the Flyers one game from elimination.

"[My players] don't have to do anything more than they have done already to prove to me they are special," said Hitchcock after a resolute, but failed, comeback. The absences on the back end had mostly shown up on specialty teams. The unavailability of Desjardins and the limitations imposed by Johnsson's hand had compromised a powerplay that was one-for-23 for the series. "You've got to make the other team feel like they can't take penalties," lamented Recchi.

You've got to make the other team feel like they can't take penalties," lamented RecchiAnd when the Flyers took them, they were increasingly defenseless. Tampa Bay had scored on three of four powerplay opportunities in Game Five and, after a slow start, was seven-for-23 in the series.

"I don't remember us talking about anything in particular we could exploit," recalls Richards. "We just had it going. And it was easier to get pucks through then than it is today."

He certainly wasn't making it look hard.

"Richards was playing the point, threading everything through," recalls Hitchcock. "I'll give them this, they were really good back there. We had to use our best penalty killer (Kapanen) on defense."

Nevertheless, the coach told the media, "We'll find a way around [the defenseman shortages] and will play very well in Game Six."

Primeau, certain of that, told a Tampa television station at the morning skate in Voorhees, NJ that he already was packed for Game Seven. It was now or never for more than just the next contest—actually, for a lot of Flyer careers.

With the owners and players at each other's throats, there probably wasn't going to be a next year for any club, let alone another chance for a core group in Philadelphia containing eleven players age 30 or over.

But as long as a lockout seemed inevitable, Primeau decided to use it to fire up the troops.

"I told the team we had a chance to be Stanley Cup champions for two years," he recalls. "Who gets to do that?"

Hitchcock tried to get Roenick going by subbing him for Radivojevic on the Primeau line with Gagne, who also was goalless in the series and having his feet put to the fire in the media by Clarke.

"He said, 'Simon has to decide: Does he want to be just another pretty good player or a great player,'" recalls Gagne. "'Does he want to be a difference maker like (Joe) Sakic or (Jarome) Iginla, or someone who waits for somebody else to make it happen?'

"At the morning skate, it's right there in the papers. But that kind of thing sometimes works for me. It fired me up, did what he wanted it to do."

To try to break the pattern of another lackluster start for Game Six, Tortorella started tough guy Roy; Hitchcock responded with Brashear. Pitkanen was returned to the lineup and Kapanen, replacing Somik, was back at forward.

On the second shift, Somik was waiting at the blueline for Seidenberg to dump the puck. But the young defenseman tried a pass to Kapanen instead, and St. Louis intercepted in front of the penalty box and fed Lecavalier, who looked off Taylor and beat Esche from 20 feet high to the side on the first shot of the game.

The Flyers had little time left to become discouraged. Khabibulin stood tall on Kapanen after he was set up by a falling Zhamnov's one-handed pass. But Philadelphia had plenty of remaining energy, which is another way of saying it had plenty of Primeau.

Roenick broke down the wing and fed inside to the Flyer captain, too big and irrepressible for Fedotenko or Kubina to handle. Primeau kicked to Gagne, who flipped the puck into the air onto his backhand and batted it out of the air into the top of the net. The gorgeous goal, Gagne's first in 18 games, was eye candy for the sorest of Philadelphia eyes, tying the contest 1-1, 5:55 after Tampa Bay had gone ahead.

The Lightning, unfazed, easily killed Andreychuk's penalty for slashing Johnsson, but even-strength play in the series still belonged to the charging Flyers.

Khabibulin was quick to a Roenick wraparound and Boyle tied up Primeau's stick on the rebound. But when J.R. slashed Sydor on the arm as he tried to go up the middle, the puck went right onto the stick of Malakhov, who, from the high slot, wasted no time hitting a breaking Primeau. He partially fanned on the sweep but still got enough on the puck to send it over the line for a 2-1 Philadelphia lead.

After losing a glove, Zhamnov was slashed by St. Louis on his bare hand, dirty business that had the Flyer center in the Tampa winger's face. Early in the second period, Esche put his stick in front of the face of Roy after making a save, and the Tampa Bay tough guy retaliated with a slash.

Esche next made a pad save on a 30-foot St. Louis blast off a diagonal Timander giveaway and Philadelphia got the puck to center, but Lecavalier picked it up. Timander, seeing St. Louis also coming, backed in and Lecavalier's shot grazed Timander's stick, then Esche's arm, before tying the game 2-2.

In a series of surges, the Lightning had the next one.

With Tortorella getting Kubina and Sydor out against Primeau's line on nine of 13 shifts, the Flyers went 12:18 with just one shot. The Wachovia Center was falling more and more silent when Zhamnov gained the line and fed left wing to Kapanen. From a deep angle and almost against the boards, Hitchcock's jack-of-all-trades put the puck between Khabibulin's legs to get Philadelphia back ahead 3-2.

That lead lasted less than three minutes. Recchi bumped St. Louis off the puck, but the Tampa Bay forward reached back to steal it and feed Andreychuk behind the goal. Fedotenko jumped into a big cavity between Pitkanen and Johnsson and scored off Esche's shoulder to tie the game 3-3.

Markov took a mindless high-sticking penalty against Fedotenko. On the first faceoff, St. Louis beat Handzus, and Fedotenko put a pass through Malakhov to Andreychuk on the goal line. Fedotenko went to the net on a give-and-go and scored his second goal in 2:18 from 15 feet out. Two goals on three shots had silenced the Wachovia Center and put Tampa Bay, leading 4-3, only 20 minutes from the Stanley Cup Final.

As the third period began, Hitchcock was double-shifting Primeau again on a line with Amonte and LeClair, making Tortorella choose his poison with the checking line of Andreychuk, Afanasenkov and Taylor.

Khabibulin made a kick save on a Zhamnov backhander. Sarich stopped Gagne's backhand passout to Primeau at the goal post. Esche batted away Modin's drive off a Pitkanen giveaway. The Lightning, so close to a series victory, mostly looked at the clock and tried to hang on.

Expecting Recchi to head for the far post, Khabibulin reversed quickly when the Flyer forward passed the puck out the other way and stopped Zhamnov with a chest save. The goalie also saw a Johnsson drive from the top of the circle at the last possible instant and made the save, then foiled Johnsson a second time after Zhamnov beat Andreychuk on a faceoff.

With 6:00 remaining, Khabibulin gave the puck away to Radivojevic, but Pratt dove to block it. When Gagne went offsides and a frustrated Roenick slapped the puck into the Tampa bench, J.R. got a hard stare from the linesmen but, fortunately, no penalty. The Lightning seemed to have the blueline secured. Philadelphia took three offsides in three minutes as the season drained away.

With 2:37 to go, after a lost draw at the Tampa Bay line, Timander broke up a St. Louis pass and rimmed the puck in hard. Gagne reached it on the opposite sideboard, only to be taken down by Taylor. But Roenick flattened Kubina and Timander, at the point, had barely enough time to send the puck back down the wall.

Primeau came in to help Roenick against St. Louis, who on all fours, tried to make a hand pass up the boards. Andreychuk couldn't reach it, so Timander had another chance, this time with room to close to the top of the circle.

Khabibulin had a clear view and made a pad save. But Primeau, at the post, kicked the puck with his right skate through the crease. "Oh, please don't go in, they're going to review it and it's going to be disallowed," the captain would remember thinking.

Instead, the puck was coming by the opposite post as he emerged from behind the net to make the tuck. Just 1:49 before the Flyer season would have run out, the game was tied, 4-4, and their bench jumping up and down for joy, like most of the people in the arena.

Markov gave Primeau a big kiss. There wasn't a hammer hard enough in Philadelphia to pound down the goosebumps. But after the third period ran out without a good chance for either team, the Flyers still needed one more goal.

In overtime, referees Kerry Fraser and Stephen Walkom put away their whistles and Philadelphia continued to apply most of the pressure. After Zhamnov was tripped, Johnsson took down St. Louis with no call. Zhamnov beat Andreychuk on a faceoff and Khabibulin made a save on Johnsson through traffic, then held the post on Kapanen off a passout.

Esche stumbled when Lukowich threw the puck up from the left boards, but the puck stayed out and hearts descended back out of throats. Nine minutes in, Primeau one-armed the puck around Boyle and Khabibulin stopped Roenick's rebound from a sharp angle.

Handzus's steal sprung a LeClair two-on-one with Roenick, who tried a toe drag, but Sydor checked it away. Fedotenko promptly gave the puck away at center, and Gagne, two-on-one with J.R., decided to carry in front on his backhand but was followed across by Khabibulin, who made a left pad save.

Eleven minutes in, the chances were 5-0 Flyers and the ice so tilted that Tortorella used his timeout with 7:17 to go. When the Lightning broke out three-on-two, Esche challenged; St. Louis's shot went wide before Gagne launched one through the feet of Lukowich and hit Khabibulin in the chest.

The Tampa Bay goalie had to make a save on Markov, too, after Primeau beat St. Louis cleanly on a faceoff. But finally, the Lightning busied Esche, who got his left pad out on a dangerous Lecavalier drive after Markov had run into the trap at center. St. Louis appeared to have Markov beaten until the defenseman dove and knocked the puck away. Pratt shot high and wide over the sliding Timander and Recchi.

Two minutes remained in the overtime when Gagne tipped the puck out of the Philadelphia zone and Johnsson dumped softly off Kubina's stick. Roenick fought off Kubina and, on his knees, pushed the puck to Gagne in the corner, who, pressured, tried to wind along the backboards. J.R. screened Sydor, letting the puck go to the more open Primeau, who, on the other side of the goal, drifted out a few feet above the goal line and fired.

The puck hit Kubina and went to Roenick near a post well covered by Khabibulin, so J.R. smartly spun and threw a pass across the goal-mouth to a wide-open Gagne. Kubina, who had gone out to meet Primeau, and Taylor, who had come too far across, had no chance to get back, as Gagne, with half the net open, instead put the puck back towards the desperate Khabibulin.

"I just shot as hard as I could," Gagne would say. It went through the goalie's legs at 18:16 of overtime and the Flyers, 5-4 winners, had forced a Game Seven in Tampa.

Gagne had both arms up. Roenick, cross-checked hard in the back by Kubina for spite as the light went on, was hunched over in pain but didn't go down until joining the Gagne-surrounding mob on the back-boards. Then J.R. collapsed, needing his teammates' support to reach the locker room.

Regulars at the Spectrum swore that the loudest that building ever had been was when J.J. Daigneault's goal had forced Game Seven against Edmonton in 1987. Gagne's goal, staving off another elimination 17 years later, set a new, deafening, standard for the eight-year-old Wachovia Center.

Primeau gave his arms one final pump into the delirious air before disappearing up the tunnel. Few fans left the arena for five minutes, celebrating only the ninth time in history that a team trailing in a Stanley Cup playoff game with less than two minutes remaining had won.

"In my opinion, this team's character was created because of the adversity we have survived," said Hitchcock. "You are going to have to stick a lot bigger stake in us than they did tonight if you expect us to quit."

Johnsson had played 37:22, Malakhov 35:47, Markov 33:49, and Primeau 25:21. Roenick, the ultimate survivor for all the head and body shots he had taken in playoffs over two springs, had been on the ice for 24:26.

"We couldn't afford to take one second off or we were heading to the bar," J.R. said.

Primeau's goal had been the ninth of the playoffs, which still represented only a fraction of his presence. The Flyers had not known such dominance of shifts since Lindros during the runs of 1995 and 1997. In Game Six, the unit of Primeau, Roenick and Gagne had been responsible for four of the five goals.

"The whole line was unbelievable, for the most part unstoppable," said Hitchcock. "I was so happy for Gagne because he's the guy we wanted and needed to step up and that's exactly what he did.

"He scored gritty points today, real gritty points."

Added Primeau, "The kid has more courage than most people. He's not as big as most guys, but he's driving right through so I know he'll get a chance to get the puck."

Considering the source, that probably was the greatest compliment Gagne received in his career.

"Over a whole playoff, I never saw anything like Keith," recalls Gagne. "He was great every game; like a monster on the ice.

"He dominated. It was amazing."

Primeau was so good that he even inspired the opposition.

"He was so big, physical and mean, so tough to play against that, honestly, he taught me a lot that series," recalls Lecavalier.

"I'm not as big or as strong as him, so I don't want to say I modeled my game after him. But I said, 'That [attitude] is something I have to try to become better.'"

The Lightning, who had been less than two minutes away from a berth in the Final, barely made themselves available to the media after the game. "We've got a Game Seven in our building to go to the Final," said captain Andreychuk. "Our guys are going to sit on that plane tonight, realize what happened, and we're going to get ready to play."

Roenick, meanwhile, was wondering how he could.

"Forget celebrating, I could (barely) get to my feet," he recalls. "I felt awful.

"In the locker room afterwards, I was thinking, 'We've got a Game Seven and I don't even know if I can do this. I had two concussions in the series.

"This was the biggest game of my life and I was in no state to play. But there was no way I would sit out and regret it forever.

"We were better than Calgary (which already had finished San Jose in the Western Conference final). You couldn't help but think the winner of our Game Seven probably was going to win the Stanley Cup."

Now, just to find the energy to do it.

"We'd all have rings and championships if this was easy, but it's not. So you just have to continue to persevere and battle," Primeau told the media. "Our guys will spend two days recovering, but they will [refill] the tank.

"We'll dig deeper than you could ever possibly imagine."

Tampa Bay, which had hung on after jumping to a 3-0 lead in Game Five, had not survived the Flyer desperation in Game Six. "Safe is Death," had been Tortorella's mantra with his team all season, and yet, so close to finishing off Philadelphia, the Lightning had died in Game Six by trying to play it safe.

"We were young and dumb and at times we played our age," recalls Richards. "But we also had the luxury of being up a game and being able to lose and learn from it.

"We saw what didn't work in Game Five or Game Six, so let's do something different."

Remembers Ramsay, "[Tortorella] was very calm about the whole thing. He said, 'We just had a great lesson in how to win, and that's not to sit back and be careful.'

"We just took it like it was another day."

Tampa Bay had another change to make besides its mindset—defenseman Jassen Cullimore, out since the first round with a wrist injury, was cleared to go.

Hitchcock felt he could trump that with the ace up his sleeve. "At two in the afternoon, we thought we had both Desjardins and Ragnarsson coming in (for Game Seven)," he recalls. "And then neither guy could get (medical) clearance.

"We thought they were close. But when we worked with them in the morning, they couldn't do the things to protect themselves, so we couldn't put them in.

"Whatever number of minutes we could have played either, or both, from a flexibility standpoint, that would have been immense. It would allow us to put Sami, our best forward that spring after Keith, back up front."

In Desjardins' case, it would have been asking a lot for someone who had played three games since January 17—and not one in six weeks—to step efficiently into Game Seven of a conference final. "Adrenaline carries you in that first game after you have been out a while; it's always a little bit later that you [hit the wall]," recalls Recchi.

"He was smart enough to keep it simple, move the puck, and help us defensively. He would have been fine."

Desjardins wasn't so certain. "I didn't feel exactly right to play," he recalls. "I didn't have much practice. It would have been hard after being out so long.

"It was a mutual decision between me and the doctors not to play. Especially after what happened after the first surgery—when they cleared me, I came back, and it broke again. The second time we wanted to make sure everything was perfect. Not playing would have given me another four or five days before the Final started. I think there was a 95 percent chance I was going to play in the Final."

Even without Desjardins for Game Seven, the Flyers still liked their chances for the reason Tortorella lamented at the morning skate. "We have had no answer for Keith Primeau," said the coach.

That wasn't entirely true. The Lightning had wrestler Hulk Hogan, a Tampa native who, following "The Star-Spangled Banner," asked into the public address microphone, "Are you ready?" and then tore off his shirt to juice the St. Pete Times Forum crowd for the first Game Seven in the franchise's 12-season history.

But Hogan couldn't play and neither did Desjardins, who skated in the warm-up as a carrot to teammates who likely would have him for the Final, if only the Flyers could get there. "I wanted to feel part of the team and maybe pump the guys up that I was close," he recalls.

Just one minute into the game, Sarich came across to hit Kapanen, but Zhamnov was able to cut through the vacated ice to create a chance. Recchi just missed on it, before LeClair, off a faceoff, was wide too, with a wraparound.

Radivojevic came off the sideboards to feed a Markov one-timer that Boyle tipped into Khabibulin's chest. The starts had not been good during the series for the winner of the previous contest, but, in the early going, the Flyers had the game where they wanted it—down low and at even strength.

With Philadelphia's powerplay 1-for-24 in the series, 0-for-the-last 18, and 1-for-37 going back to the previous round, maybe the law of averages would prove itself in the nick of time. While Lecavalier was in the box for knocking Gagne's helmet off with an elbow, Khabibulin had to make himself big when Johnsson perfectly led Recchi for a deflection.

But after Pitkanen had gotten tangled with Primeau, forcing Esche to make a chest save on Modin's shorthanded chance, a second Flyer powerplay opportunity—when Kubina was called for hanging on Kapanen as he was busting for a Recchi pass—produced no good chances.

The Lightning picked up the pace and Esche had to butterfly on Modin off a backhand feed by St. Louis, then stop a Richards rebound. As Primeau came together with Stillman, the captain's stick grazed the Tampa Bay player's face.

Typically for the series, it took the Lightning only 13 seconds to cash in.

Timander, not particularly hurried deep down the wall, had time to take the puck back, but went forward instead. Richards made a stop at the point, then fed Fedotenko who, from 20 feet out, artfully tipped the ninth Lightening powerplay goal of the series into the top of the net for a 1-0 lead after 16:46.

Philadelphia had come into the game with a 106-to-84-minute advantage in the offensive zone, but Tampa Bay was the better team now. Esche had to make a big right skate save on Roy after Andreychuk cut off another Timander force up the boards.

Hitchcock switched his two main defensive pairings, putting Malakhov with the struggling Timander and Markov with Johnsson. Primeau took advantage of a bad breakdown at center, feeding Gagne on a two-on-one. But Kubina prevented the pass and Khabibulin played the chance perfectly, taking Roenick's shot in the chest, then stopping Gagne's jam on the rebound.

Four-plus minutes into the second period, every member of the Lightning seemed covered as Stillman carried into the zone and dropped it to Richards. But his shot hit Malakhov and caromed off the backboards, causing the Flyers to break down.

The puck caromed off the skate of Johnsson and settled against the post as the defenseman couldn't stop, enabling Cullimore to feed the front of the net. From the closest of quarters, Modin, who had beaten Brashear and Handzus to the net, shoved the puck over the line to give the Lightning a 2-0 lead.

After Sydor pinched to force a Roenick giveaway, Esche kept his team in the game with a save on Lecavalier and Philadelphia responded. Handzus won an offensive-zone draw from Richards and kicked the puck to Johnsson, who took it at the right point, skated to the middle and fired. Sarich put his stick out and only succeeded in deflecting the puck between Khabibulin's legs. Midway through the contest, the Flyers were down only 2-1.

Esche, probably having his best game of the series, stopped Kubina through traffic from the top of the circle. Roenick picked up the rebound and led Primeau, who had a step on Kubina, and thought he had either drawn a penalty or tied the game. But his momentum took the net off and the goal quickly was disallowed.

Lecavalier did a spin-a-rama and went for the short side but was stopped by Esche, who also nailed a Sydor deflection, and then got lucky when Modin shot over top after another save on Lecavalier. But the chances were not frequent for either side.

"It was one of the worst Game Sevens I've seen, almost like both teams were flat," recalls Gagne. "I was tired and I think Tampa was too.

"There wasn't much emotion left on either side. I guess we had used up more than they had and they got energy from the crowd. But it was a pretty terrible game."

During the first minute of the third period, LeClair chased down

Pratt, stole the puck and centered, forcing Khabibulin to make a paddle-down save as Primeau tumbled over the goalie. Recchi was tripped by Lukowich as he drove the middle and Handzus pinched on a Sarich wraparound and fed a wide-open Amonte, who shanked the shot, then later fanned on a LeClair setup from behind the goal line.

Sydor hooked down Amonte, who was called for embellishment and did not argue. Sarich evened a score from Game Five with Roenick, leveling him on the four-on-four before Khabibulin fought off a Gagne laser from just inside the blueline.

Just as in Games Five and Six, Philadelphia was fast running out of time. But they also were now out of space as the Lightning, its lesson learned, squeezed the vise. "All I remember is we couldn't generate anything," recalls Hitchcock.

Johnsson and Modin went to a corner with arms locked, but Johnsson got the penalty at 7:17, so Hitchcock called time-out, trying to keep the frazzled Flyer penalty killers composed against a powerplay that had scored in five of its last six opportunities—and just 3, 13 and 20 seconds into the previous three. This one, Philadelphia killed off with an Esche gloving of a Stillman drive, maintaining hope.

Recchi, who seemed to have the freshest set of legs on his team, pounced with a quick follow-up shot after Handzus had lost his footing. But Khabibulin stopped, squared himself and made the save with 8:15 remaining in the game.

Down the desperate stretch, Esche, who came across to make a save on Richards fed by Stillman, was getting more work than his counterpart. Roenick lost the puck at the point and Fedotenko's backpass fed St. Louis. In a scramble for the rebound, Malakhov tried to freeze the puck under a surprised Esche and almost scored for Tampa Bay.

Kapanen flew into a corner trying to pin the much larger Andreychuk, who made the Finn miss. LeClair bulled behind the goal but

Lightning captain Dave Andreychuk looks for a loose puck in Esche's crease.

Stillman knocked the centering attempt away. Johnsson tried to pinch on a Primeau dump-in that went off Kubina, but Sydor got the puck up to Taylor, who made Esche play it with 1:20 to go, keeping the Flyer goalie in the net.

Gagne was offsides on a Kapanen dump-in. When Richards forced Roenick, and Johnsson suffered a gross giveaway, Esche had to do the splits on probably the best opportunity either team had in the third period.

Finally, Zhamnov got the puck into the Tampa Bay zone, but Kubina tipped Roenick's centering attempt away and Markov, forced by Afanasenkov, couldn't hold the point. With 10 seconds remaining, Zhamnov managed to get the puck past Richards to Recchi breaking through the middle. With the defense backed in, he got away a shot with velocity from 45 feet out, but Khabibulin routinely kicked it out and Kubina banged the puck, and Philadelphia's last hope, past Zhamnov with five seconds remaining.

As Richards missed the empty net, Johnsson, Recchi and Roenick, 2-1 losers in Game Seven, all were bent over at center ice from the biggest punch in the gut of their careers. The Flyers shook hands with the Lightning and went to their locker room to mourn.

"I told them I thought we performed at a championship level the whole playoffs," Hitchcock recalls. "I told them you can't do anything about the injury state we got ourselves in, and I told them how proud I was of them."

That was of little consolation to a team that strongly suspected it had taken its last, best shot.

"I don't know what happens now," said a teary Roenick, who had been to one Final in 16 seasons. "This is overwhelming.

"It's probably the most disappointed I've ever been for a lot of reasons. Our team was so close; we have such a good bunch of guys, and it just looked like it was going to be our year.

"Not knowing if there is going to be any hockey next year, not knowing how long that will last. . . At my age, after everything that I've been through, you kind of wonder if you can do it again. I don't know. I don't want to see ice or pucks for some time.

"I feel bad for guys like Primeau, who wished everything for us."

Primeau was feeling plenty bad for Primeau. "Close doesn't work," he told reporters. "It doesn't get you anything.

"It's not a good feeling and it gets harder every year. We've got a lot of older guys who really want to win. There is so much uncertainty around our group right now, it's hard to swallow. You start all over with 30 teams, a lot of good ones, and it just gets tougher and tougher.

"I don't know where we go from here, I really don't. We have well over a handful of guys that are 30 and older, so even if there is hockey next year, you just don't know. This was my best chance."

He recalls telling Sharp, who had sat on the bench for the entire Game Seven after scoring in Game Five, to "remember the feeling, to take advantage of the opportunities he would get in the game."

Goaltending being the bottom-line position, Esche, who had not matched his brilliance of the New Jersey and Toronto series, but still was Philadelphia's best player in Game Seven, blamed himself for the loss. "Obviously I'm just a little upset right now," he told reporters. "I don't know what to say; I'm really not smart enough to put it into words.

"It's just a tough thing right now, that's all."

It didn't get any easier in the subsequent days.

"The devastation just went through everybody and the plane ride was the worst of my life," recalls Roenick. "I felt like [bleep] physically, and emotionally I was even worse. I was beaten down, crushed.

"Listen, you can look back and rationalize. Tampa had a real good team, too. They were very, very lucky with injuries all year and we were severely depleted. So you can rationalize and make excuses, but in the end, it doesn't matter. We all knew this was the best chance we'd ever have, so close we could taste it.

"This was in addition to feeling like I'd been run over by a Mack truck multiple times. I had just enough in me to walk from the locker room to the bus. When I got back home, the only time in three days I got out of bed was to close up shop in Voorhees."

At break-up day, there was little talk about moving forward for a next season that had a good chance of not happening. There were only more laments about the most withering defeat of the 11 the franchise had suffered in five finals and six semifinals since last winning the Cup in 1975.

The 1999-2000 Flyers will take to their graves the failure to finish the Devils when they were reeling going into Game Five. But that was a powerhouse New Jersey team that—much like the Montreal, Islander and Edmonton dynasties—proved to have too much talent for Philadelphia.

In 2004, though, the Flyers and much of the hockey world felt Philadelphia had the best team. In addition to the absences of Desjardins and Ragnarsson, Johnsson, playing with a broken finger, had been a shell of the player who had dominated in the Devil series.

"Kim bit the bullet for us," said Hitchcock the day the Flyers packed up, and Johnsson hadn't been the only one. "We were all hurt," recalls Markov, who was playing with a bad shoulder.

That Tampa Bay powerplay had been deadly over many broken Philadelphia bodies.

"We didn't lose because we under-performed," Hitchcock told the media on breakup day. "We lost because we overextended people through necessity.

To not be able to come at them with anything close to a full roster on the back end was discouraging.

"We emptied the tank in Game Six. The board battles we won in Game Six and at the tail end of Game Five, we weren't able to win in Game Seven."

Hitchcock said he would be rooting for Calgary in the Final, and not out of spite. "If Tampa wins, we'll feel like that should have been us," he said.

Lecavalier remembers thinking that when the Lightning got by the Flyers, his club already had beaten the best team, beliefs that would be confirmed when Tampa Bay defeated Calgary in Game Seven, 2-1.

"I had felt all along whoever was going to win the East was going to win the Cup," recalls Primeau. "You still had to beat Calgary and

Jarome (Iginla) was playing well, but they weren't as good as us.

"If we had all our guys available, I feel like no one was going to beat us. Zhamnov, J.R., Johnny (LeClair), Recchi, Amonte, Gagne, top to bottom we were stacked. The chemistry, the leadership, the coaching was there.

"But a lot of teams can say they could have won if not for this or that. At the end of the day, Tampa had an unbelievable team, too, a lot healthier than ours, and they won."

It isn't just luck, however, that many members of the 2003-04 Flyers question, but decisions that had reduced the team's depth.

Clarke's pickups through the season—Zhamnov, Markov, Malakhov, Timander, and Radivojevic—had proven hugely successful. But the corresponding decisions to trade Eric Weinrich and Chris Therien for late-round draft choices consequently had forced the injured Johnsson, the marginal Timander and young Pitkanen and Seidenberg into longer, and sometimes overwhelming, minutes because of Desjardins' and Rangnarsson's absences.

Would one or two more veteran hands have made the difference against the nine powerplay goals the Lightning scored in 26 opportunities?

Clarke said publicly when he added Malakhov and traded Therien on the same day that financial considerations were a part of the latter decision. No one recalls, or will admit to Clarke being given directives to keep flat an NHL fourth-highest $68.1 million payroll for the remainder of that season. But it probably was the only time in franchise history that self-imposed financial inhibitions kept the Flyers from taking their best shot at a Stanley Cup.

"When I went to St. Louis, I ended up playing 25 minutes a night and had like 10 points in 24 games, so I definitely had a lot left," recalls Weinrich.

"I was watching the playoffs and you definitely have going through your head, 'What if I was still there?' Chris was texting me, saying the same thing.

"Those are all hypotheticals. All I can is that it was definitely tough to watch."

Recalls Therien, "I was so done with Hitchcock when I got traded that I was kind of happy. But I look back on it now and think, 'Geez, that didn't have to happen.' Eric and I were playing together, had a terrific plus-minus going, and two veteran defensemen that every team is trying to get end up being traded.

"I'm watching on TV and they had Sami Kapanen playing defense. That's what it's come to? I can't believe this is happening. One or two defensemen would have made all the difference in the world."

Gagne agrees. "You're a lot better having a guy like Eric Weinrich than three guys from the Phantoms," he recalls.

Hindsight, says Clarke, is 20-20. The team had every reason to believe Desjardins was coming back for the playoffs, that Weinrich would not have been happy with reduced or zero ice time, and that Therien was miserable playing for Hitchcock.

"We'll never know what would have happened if we had kept those guys, but when I made the deals, I thought we had really improved our defense and I was doing those two guys a favor," recalls Clarke.

Adds Hitchcock, "Eric wasn't happy because he wasn't playing, and nobody could predict what we were about to go through. When the trade was done, my thinking was, 'This is giving a veteran guy who I really like as a person a chance to continue his career.'

"I don't know if it's fair to say that would have meant winning the Cup. It is fair to say we needed a body or two back there.

"Or, we needed to buy one more day to get Desjardins and Ragnarsson back, just one more day."

Primeau doesn't recall second-guessing the salary-clearing moves when they were made.

"Those guys had been scratches," he says. "I guess Eric's trade surprised me because he was such a good guy, hard to find, but Bundy (Therien) had fallen out of favor with Hitch. At the time, no, I didn't think we were leaving ourselves short."

But it ended up that the Flyers did, leaving many members of that team wondering what might have been.

"Chris could still play at that point," recalls Roenick. "Maybe not as many minutes or as big a role as in all those years he was playing with Desjardins against guys like Jagr, but he still could play.

"Wino (Weinrich) was still real steady, such a smart defensive defenseman and good with the puck, too. In hindsight, if we still had Wino and Bundy with all those other guys we added who played real good for us, I think we would have won the Cup."

Recalls Esche, "Desjardins was a tremendous force. Rags was rock solid, and Kim was playing at an elite level before he got hurt. That is a lot to lose. We could have used two more veteran guys.

"We got a lot of scoring chances on Khabibulin and he made a lot of really tough saves. I wasn't quite as good as I had been back in the Jersey series. I felt maybe I could have done a little bit more.

"But, and I hate to keep going back to this, we ended up in mismatches at times, which is why we couldn't stop their powerplay. That's just the truth behind that series."

And that robs the members of the 2003-04 Flyers of practically any consolation for one of the bravest and most spirited playoff runs in franchise history.

"Khabibulin was good, but I don't think you can say he stole games in that series," recalls Primeau. "It was there for the taking and we were flat in Game Seven.

"I don't know, maybe it was fatigue."

The members of perhaps the best—and certainly the most regretful—of the multiple Philadelphia teams to come close since the 1975 Cup, will never know if they would have beaten Calgary, but will die believing it.

"I went to the Final (for the only time) with Chicago in '92, but that 2003-04 Flyer team was the best team I ever played for, bar none," recalls Roenick, "We had so many quality players who fit perfectly in their spots in the lineup.

"We had the goaltending. We had the coaching in Hitch.

"It's sad and really haunting to think about that year.

KEITH PRIMEAU

Bob Clarke's plan when he traded Rod Brind'Amour for Keith Primeau in 2000 was not fair.

The Flyers already had the biggest, baddest, and, arguably, best center in 6-4 Eric Lindros. Going forward he would be backed up by the 6-5 Primeau, a steamroller who followed a road grader and, flat out, the most flattening-up-the-middle combination that all the doomed Gumbys on ice ever would see. Even if it was the last thing they ever would see.

The hockey gods put their feet down, though. Primeau suffered a knee sprain soon after his acquisition and Lindros had two more concussions while playing his final year as a Flyer, allowing the two to team for only eight regular-season and two playoff games.

Of course, another reason Clarke had made the move was to have insurance against problems with Lindros's long-term durability and signability. So it turned out that the next best thing to a two-man wrecking crew was a one-man wrecking crew.

Sadly, Primeau also would have his career compromised by concussions, but not before wise hockey heads came together to declare Primeau's performance during the run to Game Seven of the 2004 Eastern Conference final astounding.

"It's something I have not seen either before or since in the postseason," said Primeau's teammate and good friend Sami Kapanen. "And it wasn't just the points (16 in 18 games) or goals (nine) he scored.

"Something was pushing him. It seemed like there was nothing that was going to stop him. He could take one or two players on his back and make a play, whatever it took to get it done. It was amazing to be part of that."

Phil Esposito, doing color commentary for the Stanley Cup championship Tampa Bay team that survived Primeau by one goal in Game Seven, told him he dominated more in one series than had even Bobby Orr, Wayne Gretzky and Gordie Howe.

Primeau's teammate, Jeremy Roenick, doesn't go back that far, nor was he quite willing to go that far, but isn't exactly damning Primeau with faint praise either in saying: "I played against Mark Messier in (the 1990 Western Conference final). He was almost psychotic, possessed, in the way he played.

"Prims in 2004 was the second-best I saw, and the best of any teammate I ever had. He was a man on a mission, dominant on draws, in every possible situation."

Primeau did all this despite having more of the headaches and blurred vision that had plagued him during the 2000 Conference final, problems that returned yet again after he was hit by Montreal's Alexander Perezhogin seven games into the 2005-06 season.

Although he waited 11 months for his symptoms to disappear before reluctantly announcing his retirement, Primeau's problems never have gone away, only lessened in frequency and intensity. Having been to hell and back multiple times, he co-founded "Stop Concussions" (stopconcussions.com) and has become an advocate for not doing what he did, even while admitting he probably would do it again.

"I wanted to show that I could play through anything, even if it was at the sacrifice of my health and well-being," he says today. "That's not the right approach for anybody.

"Nothing is more important than your health, right? It's really not. The game only lasts for a certain part of your life and then you gotta live the rest of it.

"My first sense when I was told that I was never going to get the opportunity to play again was relief. But my symptoms didn't all of a sudden go away. I still have them. So it's important that kids understand that real courage is having the ability to speak up and say, 'I don't feel well.' Also for parents to understand that they are putting their kids at risk by allowing them back on the ice.

"I say this sadly: I wouldn't change anything I did because that's who I am, that's what I wanted. I wanted to be on the ice with my teammates."

For that unflinching resolve, he is remembered as a top-tier all-time leader of the franchise that also brought you Bobby Clarke and Dave Poulin. To reach that supreme stature, Primeau travelled a long road from being a cocky third-overall pick in the 1990 draft by Detroit, to carrying an aging Flyer team on his back for a valiant last shot in 2004.

Miscast from the beginning as a dazzling scorer, frozen out in his early years by cliquish Red Wing veterans, Primeau blossomed in 1993-94 to a 31-goal season. "It was a roller coaster," he recalls of Detroit. "I loved the city, loved the (Mike Illitch) ownership and, at times, loved playing there. But at other times it was very stressful.

"I wanted to go back to junior my first year but they kept me. Then, the second year, they sent me to the minors and never discussed any of these things with me.

"When I would score two goals, they wondered why I didn't also get into a fight. If I fought, they questioned why didn't I score two goals. It was never enough."

Totaling only six goals in 64 playoff games with Detroit, he was considered one of the biggest perennial playoff flops during the early-to-mid-nineties.

"For my sanity and career, I needed to move on," he recalls, which he did to Hartford in a deal that brought Brendan Shanahan, the last piece of the Red Wings' Stanley Cup puzzle. With the Whalers (later the Carolina Hurricanes), Primeau made the playoffs in his third year with the franchise, then went goalless in a first-round defeat.

"I watched him in junior (for the Niagara Falls Thunder) and he was a grinding player who scored goals through hard work," recalls Clarke. "I always liked him a lot, just never saw him as a scoring machine."

Neither was Brind'Amour, but he was one of the hardest-working and most popular players in Flyers history. Regardless, Clarke felt Primeau had the size and wing span to become the more dominant two-way player. Primeau didn't hesitate to end his bitter money holdout in Carolina by agreeing to the deal, then Clarke instantly paid him star money to be a 25-30 goal scorer.

After the deal, Primeau missed 12 of his first 20 games in Philadelphia. For the 2000 playoffs, he didn't score through the first three games, nor again until the eighth period of the ninth contest until, rubbery legs all around him, he found a burst of energy, pulled up on defenseman Darius Kasparaitis, and nailed an astonishing goal under the crossbar behind Pittsburgh goaltender Ron Tugnutt to end the third-longest game in NHL history.

Five nights later, he was knocked unconscious by Penguin defenseman Bob Boughner's hit early in the Flyers' series-clinching 2-1 Game Six victory, but passed the rudimentary concussion protocol of the day and returned for the first game of the Conference final against New Jersey. There were as many people questioning his judgment as applauding his resolve, but though his headache was unrelenting, Primeau was undeterred.

"I should have taken the appropriate time to rest and get healthy and I didn't," he recalls. "I feel like that was the beginning of my demise."

Primeau followed up with his best goal-scoring season, 34, in 2000-01, but a knee sprain cost him time in March and his touch in the playoffs, when the Flyers lost in the first round to Buffalo. The next spring, when he questioned coach Bill Barber after the Flyers' collapse in a first-round series against Ottawa, Primeau was perceived as the leader of a bunch of grumbling mutineers who had scored two goals in a five-game series.

To be accurate, Primeau had jumped in to back up goaltender Brian Boucher, the teammate who first went public with criticism of the coach. But Primeau still unloaded on Barber hard for his failure to teach a system.

"Bill Barber the Hall of Famer and Bill Barber the coach were hard to separate and I wasn't thinking like that at the time," recalls Primeau. "I'm thinking of Bill Barber the coach and what was happening in our locker room.

KEITH PRIMEAU
FLYER HERO #34

"I made a conscious decision to support my goaltender. I should have just done that and it would have been the end of it. But I said we didn't have the structure we needed to win. That fell on Bill and I got crucified for it, rightly so.

"I didn't know for sure what was going to happen (Barber almost certainly was going to be reluctantly replaced by Clarke and Ed Snider). But, yeah, it came across like I was piling on."

When Ken Hitchcock took over, Primeau had a lot of living down to do. He did so fully, when the new coach delivered direction Primeau said the players had begged Barber to provide. Hitchcock counseled Primeau on leadership and gradually convinced him that less fixation on scoring would lead to more.

"I think Keith felt like he wanted to make a change," recalls Hitchcock. "He just didn't know where to go. He wanted some information.

"I'd give him reading on leadership and he really became a learned person. I was very impressed. He taught me a lot about how people can change. He found peace in being the guy that plays against the other team's best players. He had found a role where he didn't have to play on the powerplay and score.

"The pressure was off. His captaincy was empowered by really good support from the assistant captains so he wasn't looking over his shoulder and worrying about 'What do they think of me?' He knew everybody was following, so he started to play with the level of confidence that he was capable of. Then, he could take things to a whole other level.

"He could not get any points and still completely control the hockey game, physically and mentally. Once his value system changed, the frustration went away."

Snider had hired Hitchcock insisting that, next time, it would be players to go, not the coach. Primeau thought primarily that meant him. But fear alone did not cause him to live down his reputation as a coach killer, it was the relationship he forged with Hitchcock.

"I played for two of the greatest coaches in the game—Scotty Bowman and Ken Hitchcock—and loved both of them," he recalls. "So I had no problem with great coaching.

"I was just looking for information to share with the team and I never got that with Bill. Hitch was so black and white: 'this is what I need you to deliver; go do it.' And when I'd get resistance (from some players), my feeling was, 'Too bad, this is the message that was sent, and this is our job.'

"My relationship with Hitch worked so well. One time, when I was working hard but struggling, he called me in before a game in St. Louis and had me watch this two-to-three-minute video of my shifts. In them, I was swinging on a break to gain speed. He's like, 'You need to slow down. In your case, less is more.'

"I had heard him saying that before. But it was the first time where he actually showed me that I could be just as impactful by doing less. That really helped me sort out my game. I was running straighter lines.

"I had never considered myself one of those overtly offensive guys, a top-20 scorer, a guy skilled enough to carry the puck through the opposing team. I've always tried to do the right things away from the puck in the defensive zone but, at the same time, I didn't think of myself as a top defensive player. I came to love the challenge of playing against Mark Messier and Scott Stevens."

He similarly embraced the work demanded by T.R. Goodman (Pro Camp Sports, Venice, CA), the workout guru of multiple NHL stars.

"He's about realignment," says Primeau. "Hockey players use their forward muscles, hip flexors, and chest muscles but neglect their back muscles, shoulder and hip rotators."

"He tries to strengthen muscles that are little used and then build strength and endurance off that foundation.

"For me, it was transforming. I wish I would have found him when I was 18. I went to him trying to become a better player but he helped me with my long-term health. I always tell people from the neck down, I'm great today. I'm 44 and don't have any joint pain. I give him a lot of credit."

Primeau, concussed by an inadvertent collision with the Rangers' Bobby Holik on February 12, 2004 at Madison Square Garden, returned with symptoms only lessened, not gone, with three games remaining in the regular season. For six weeks, he chased his headaches with Sun Chips and ice cream and, through blurred vision, kept his eye unwaveringly on the prize.

It was perhaps the greatest individual triumph of will in Flyer history. Almost from the beginning of the five-game first-round triumph over New Jersey, Primeau was Philadelphia's best player. He turned the six-game victory over the Leafs with a hat trick in Game Five and, just when it didn't seem possible that he could play any better, he did, dominating shift after shift against Tampa Bay before scoring with 1:49 remaining to tie Game Six then helping to set up Simon Gagne's winner in overtime.

Game Seven in Tampa proved anticlimactic, and emotionally devastating. The Lightning, which jumped ahead 2-0, appeared one goal less exhausted than injury-decimated Philadelphia in winning, 2-1. Of six Final series losses and another six in the semifinals since the last Cup win in 1975, that one hurt the most because the Flyers believed they had the best team.

"Close doesn't work," a devastated Primeau told reporters after Game Seven. "It doesn't get you anything.

"It's not a good feeling and it gets harder every year. We've got a lot of older guys who really want to win. There is so much uncertainty around our group right now; it's hard to swallow.

"I don't know where we go from here, I really don't. We have well over a handful of guys that are 30 and older, so even if there is [no lockout] next year, you just don't know. This was my best chance."

It proved to be the last one, too. Had there been an NHL season in 2004-05, Primeau would have been unlikely to start it. When the NHL resumed in October 2005, he was ready to go and ecstatic after seeming to recover quickly from the Perezhogin hit. Primeau was able to finish the game and play two more before his symptoms re-emerged.

By the following summer, he felt well enough to plan a training session with Kapanen and a Finnish team but, almost at the last minute, was forced to concede that he wasn't ready. Primeau's reflexes were so compromised that Jim McCrossin, the Flyers head trainer and strength and conditioning coach, would not sign off on a return. On the eve of camp, Primeau retired.

"In a way, I was relieved," he recalls. "If somebody wouldn't have stopped me, I would have never stopped myself; I would have kept trying.

"At some point I probably would have said, 'I'm well

enough to play' and gone back out, even though it took me seven years to feel some semblance of normalcy after that last concussion. I never would have been able to play.

"By [the eighth and ninth year after retirement], I finally felt so good that [in the summer of 2014,] I started reaching out to NHL teams about [coaching or front office] jobs. My biggest fear has been making a commitment to do something and then not being able to fulfill it.

"Then, [in the fall of 2014] I hit my head again. I was in the locker room coaching my boys, had my skates on, and hit my head on the door jam, jamming all the muscles in my neck. I didn't hit it hard; it was just the way I did it that set me off again.

"I had a bad fall and winter. Headaches, pressure, blurred vision, fatigue, lethargy caused by strain on my eyes, and exercise-induced lightheadedness were the biggest symptoms when I retired. And, today, those are probably the same still. I don't get them as often, though."

His first year out, Primeau did studio commentating on Flyer telecasts, decided he didn't love it, and ceded the job to Chris Therien.

"I was still suffering and wasn't enjoying it, at least not at that point of my life," recalls Primeau. "The Flyers were losing. How many times can you say they need to play better, they need to play harder? I don't think it went over very well."

Primeau has found fulfillment shepherding his sons through minor hockey, coaching the Philadelphia Revolution out of Warwick, PA, and assisting at the boys' high school, Bishop Eustace in Pennsauken, N.J., He has a daughter at Villanova University, two sons playing with Lincoln, NE of the United States Hockey League on the way to scholarships at Canisius and Northeastern, and has received his degree in liberal studies from Neumann University.

"We tried to get our kids to understand the importance of education, which is hard to do if they look at (wife) Lisa and me without degrees," he said. "That's the biggest reason I did it. And I knew it would help me in the business world."

He has ambitions to being involved at a higher level of hockey.

"The competitive side of me wants the challenge of trying to coach or manage," he says. "One of the things I aspire to do is coach collegiate hockey. I love teaching the game, and know I could be successful. But again, if it doesn't ever happen, I'm okay with that as well."

He has something far better than the money in the bank: His faculties. May he never forget the spring of 2004.

"Considering the stakes and the incredible atmosphere, Game Six against Tampa might have been the best offensive game I ever played," recalls Primeau.

"What we did was a great accomplishment and memorable, but the only thing that puts a black cloud over it for me is that it didn't happen in a Cup-winning season. Who knows how many more special moments I might have had if I didn't have to retire due to injury.

"But do I feel fulfilled? Sure. I played the game for 15 years, and that's a long time. I was in the (1998) Olympics, the Stanley Cup Final and in All-Star games. So I never would say I have regrets."

Being unable to turn the clock back, he knows better than to beat himself up.

"I definitely know I've damaged my brain, but I don't live in fear of the future," Primeau says. "I guess I fear that when it does happen, how rapid the demise might be, but the cup is half full.

"I've got too much to live for to worry about it today."

JEREMY ROENICK

ALTHOUGH THERE NEVER WAS A CAMERA that Jeremy Roenick didn't seek or a microphone he declined, a player often perceived to be all about himself ended up making one of the most selfless gestures in Flyers' history.

When asked by general manager Bob Clarke to waive his no-trade rights so that his capped-out team could sign Peter Forsberg, Roenick made it easy.

"I'd take Forsberg over me," said Roenick, the compulsive truth teller. Out he went the next day in a deal to Los Angeles, nary a kick nor a scream, just a big wide smile in case Hollywood wanted to appreciate his magnetism, as had Philadelphia for three of the most productive years a big-ticket Flyer free agent ever delivered.

"Hey, if somebody gave you [$35] million, you would hug them, too," said Roenick after physically embracing Ed Snider at the introductory press conference. From that starting point, until his Flyer career ended in tears at their elimination in Game Seven of the Eastern Conference final in 2004 at Tampa, Roenick's feelings were unfiltered and his sincerity came to be unquestioned.

"He competed hard, would stick up for you, never took a night off," recalls Chris Therien. "He was one of the great players of the era and there wasn't a thing I didn't like about him."

Roenick was only pretty loud, no pretty boy. A magnet for attention, he also attracted multiple blows to the head, one slapshot to the jaw, and incessant nagging by a coach, Ken Hitchcock, who was entertained only by winning. Arriving for J.R.'s second year in Philadelphia, Hitchcock soon learned that along with the prestige and pressure of coaching this iconic franchise came a disco ball that Roenick had installed in the locker room for pregame entertainment.

"Aren't you ever serious?" the coach asked.

Only on the ice.

"He played with a lot of courage, a lot of pain, and was one of those players who was capable of doing a little of everything," recalls teammate, and sometime linemate, Sami Kapanen. "He had good tools, soft hands, was a really good playmaker and had the will to do whatever it took to win, including punishing you with a hit.

"He was always pushing harder and harder. He's so loud some people would say he's full of himself, but I found him fun to be around. He always was happy, always had stories about stuff that had happened to him, but it's not that he made himself so far above the other guys.

"He kept it loose, but once it was time to get it done, he was one of the best players."

Roenick's years in Philadelphia enhanced the Hockey Hall of Fame candidacy of a player who totaled 513 career goals and 1,216 points over 20 seasons. For the $21 million paid out before J.R.'s trade, Snider received a lot more than a big hug: 67 goals and 106 assists, reaffirmation in the wake of the nasty Eric Lindros divorce that the Flyers remained a preferred destination for free agents, and a pinpoint Game Six overtime shot in Toronto that punched the Flyers' ticket to a conference final.

Almost as important, in the view of Bob Clarke, the most seriously driven Flyer of all time, Roenick gave the team a sense of humor.

"Over a long time, our star players had always been pretty humble," recalls Clarke. "Guys like Tim Kerr and John LeClair were nice, quiet men.

"It was good to see a star player come through with zest and bite."

Who else but J.R. would dress for a warmup in a curly wig and an old set of long hockey pants, circa 1981, to lovingly mimic Clarke? Or suddenly counter the relentless jabbering of Hitchcock from the bench with, "Will you shut the [bleep] up, Hitch? I'm trying to play hockey here!"

While in a New York City emergency room awaiting the wiring of a jaw fractured in 19 places by a Boris Mironov slapshot at Madison Square Garden, J.R. asked public relations director Zack Hill for his phone and dialed beat writer Tim Panaccio to thank the Ranger fans for his standing ovation, then offered to take the reporter out soon "for soup."

"J.R. was an acquired taste for sure," smiles Keith Primeau. "I remember when we signed him, Rick Tocchet (Roenick's teammate in Phoenix) said, 'You'll love him at times and hate him at times.

"I came to understand what Rick meant. At times, J.R.'s colorful personality would be strenuous and other times he was exactly what the doctor ordered.

"I think the biggest advantage of having him was that everybody else didn't have to deal with the media. I didn't mind it, but there were guys who liked fading into the background."

J.R. was no backup singer in those pregame karaoke sessions. He didn't toe the union line during the season-long 2004-05 lockout, instead wondering aloud what was so terrible about a salary cap. Asked after scoring the opening goal in addition to the overtime winner in that Game Six for the odds of scoring his first two goals of the series in one contest, Roenick replied, "Pretty good, since I hadn't scored in the first five games."

Signed by Philadelphia at age 32, Roenick was not the 53- and 50-goal scorer that he had been as an eighth-overall pick by Chicago out of Thayer (Mass.) Academy. "He was a top-five player in the league then," said Eric Weinrich, a Roenick teammate both as a Blackhawk and a Flyer. "He could basically do anything out there, play power play, be physical, and fight when he had to.

"In Philly, there were moments you could see the old J.R. come out. And he was still the same person, signing every last autograph in the hotel lobby before going to his room."

Roenick adjusted to changes in the game and his body, but made no such accommodations in his personality.

"Everywhere I went, I took a lot of the tension that would normally be in a professional locker room and kind of eased it," he recalls. "I was the guy who tried to make people laugh or, if they were nervous, not so nervous.

"There were a couple quiet guys I'm sure I rubbed the wrong way, made them wonder if I had my head in the right place. But most [ex-teammates] would say, 'He's one of the best guys I played with and the most fun.'"

The media, too, had a blast chronicling the love-hate co-existence of two strong wills like Roenick's and Hitchcock's. The two eventually reached an understanding, sort of.

"Jeremy didn't have quick feet anymore but still had quick hands, great competitive instincts and hockey sense, so we had to find a way to use it," recalls Hitchcock. "On the powerplay, I wanted him to be at the net, but he wanted to be on the half-wall, so every time he would go stand there, I'd pull him off the ice. And he was really pissed off at me.

"This game went on for a month until finally he said, 'Screw it, I'll just play on the goal line,' and our powerplay became great.

"When he accepted being older, he became really effective as a goal-line player on the powerplay, a net-front presence at even strength, even a penalty killer.

"The year we lost to Tampa in the conference final, he pretty much had become a winger and was arguably one of our best forwards after Keith Primeau."

Roenick, having reached a Final in his third season and not gotten close to a Cup since, proved willing to bend to the coach's will.

"I wouldn't say I altered my game a lot because of Hitch, but I definitely tried to play within the confines of his system," recalls Roenick. "I would take a little bit more offensive chances and try to do things a little bit risky, but that's how I played all the time.

"I was pretty receptive to criticism. I had no problem calling myself out. It's always right for a leader to do that. But if I felt I was playing better (than a coach was maintaining), like it sometimes was with Hitch, then I would argue.

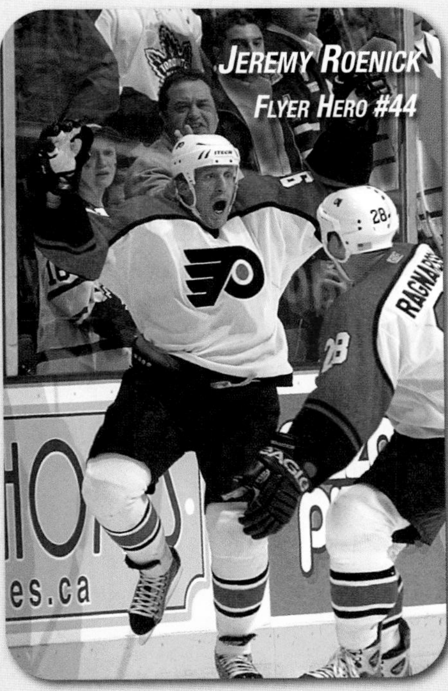
JEREMY ROENICK
FLYER HERO #44

"I wasn't always the greatest defender, but playoffs would be one of the times during the year when I would concentrate on it because the coaches always harped on it. I never felt like I was turned loose by Hitch. He always stressed defensive posture first and never offense. It was always, 'Let's be structured, let's be structured,' and I wasn't really a structured type of guy with anything in my life."

Certainly he was not exaggerating in that case, but Roenick often wasn't loath to embellish. The way J.R. tells it, he took it upon himself to cut the wires in his mouth so he could return to the lineup, as promised, on the 42nd day after suffering the fracture. Nobody in the locker room remembers it exactly that way. But even the guys who liked him better when he was unable to open his mouth knew that the drama king's desire to play was more than just sincere, actually reckless.

"I really didn't give a [bleep] about my well-being," J.R. recalls. "There was only so much I was going to listen to doctors."

"I never came back unless I knew I could be effective. I always thought that me at 75 or 80 percent was better than a lot of people at 100 percent and I wanted my teammates to follow my dedication."

Twice concussed, probably, during the Tampa Bay series, by Game Seven he was a wreck. "That summer was one of the worst of my life," Roenick recalls. "I didn't go outside much because the sun really bothered me.

"I slept a lot and still felt tired. I had headaches all the time, fights with my wife (Tracy), fights with my kids. I could barely play golf. It went on for six or seven months."

Had there been a 2004-05 season, Roenick undoubtedly would have been unable to start it. Finishing up with the Kings, Coyotes again, and Sharks, he had lost many of his skills, never his voice. Today, as a studio commentator for NHL telecasts on NBC, Roenick tells it like he always did, pulls few punches and has no regrets about what he put himself through, at least not yet.

"Right now I'm doing pretty good," he says. "Maybe ask me in 15 years."

Three seasons in Philadelphia was just a speck of two decades wearing five NHL uniforms. But, better late than never, Roenick was one of the best fits ever for a heart-on-its-sleeve kind of a town.

"I wasn't a good hider of my emotions," he recalls. "In Philly, I got to be really close to one of the best fan bases in all of sports. I loved their energy and enthusiasm and fed off it.

"There was always an electricity about being a Flyer. I loved the pressure and the style of play.

"Over the course of any day, in airports or wherever, I still run into more Flyer fans than fans of any other team. When someone tells me they are a Flyer fan, to this day, I will hug them. They are all wonderful to me.

"That's why that Game Seven in Tampa was worse than the broken jaw. I would have [suffered] 10 broken jaws if it could have changed the outcome. I wouldn't trade those years in Philly for anything, only wish we could have given those fans a Cup."

Derian Hatcher squeezes out impressive Pittsburgh rookie Sidney Crosby

Chapter 8 • 2004-06

Peter (Rabbit) Out of a Hat

WITH THE COLLECTIVE BARGAINING AGREEMENT due to expire on September 15, 2004, the NHL owners were determined, if necessary, to lock out the players to gain a salary cap. There was virtually no belief that the season would begin on time and skepticism as to whether there would be one at all. But whenever the Flyers were to play again, they wanted Keith Primeau leading them.

On June 14, 17 days before he would have become an unrestricted free agent, the organization signed their 32-year-old captain to a four-year, $17 million contract.

"I don't think you have any chance of being good without top leadership and Keith is a great leader," said general manager Bob Clarke. "Primeau is the player that we built this team around and will continue to do so.

"Now that we have signed Keith, it means that we can start filling in the other places."

Primeau, who took a cut from $5 million a year on his previous contract, told the media, "I knew that making a deal wouldn't be difficult."

Despite his expectation that the collective-bargaining process would almost certainly result in an across-the-board rollback of a certain percentage on any contract signed before the lockout, the captain had made negotiations especially easy for the Flyers. He knew there was a good chance of not seeing any of the $4.5 million for the 2004-05 season.

"I probably could have, or should have, waited until after the lockout to maximize," recalls Primeau. "I was having [post-concussion] symptoms, maybe that's why I rushed it, but I wanted to stay.

"The day I agreed to terms I was leaving a dentist's office (in Voorhees, NJ) to go back to [the Flyers Skate Zone] for the press conference and I got a call.

"The voice says, 'Keith, this is John Ferguson (Jr.), (GM) Toronto Maple Leafs. I'm calling to make sure this is your number for when I'm able to call you on July 1.'

"I had known they probably would be interested. Two years in a row we had beaten them out. I'm pretty sure they were prepared to offer me around $6 million a year. But I didn't want to go home (he was born and raised in Toronto). I wanted to stay here."

So did Simon Gagne, a restricted free agent subject to compensation. Waiting for the post-lockout market to declare itself, he took a one-year deal for $2 million. Sami Kapanen, who had finished the 2004 playoffs with post-concussion symptoms after staggering back to the bench following a second round Game Six hit by Toronto's Darcy Tucker, seriously considered retirement at age 30 to spend time with his family. But he had a change of heart and took a 50 percent salary reduction, signing for two seasons at a total of $3 million.

"I felt like my body had taken all this beating," recalls Kapanen. "I had small kids and wanted to spend more time at home. As the playoffs went on, win or lose, I'd decided I was done and, when it was over, told the players that at a team dinner."

Recalls Clarke, "I told Sami if he wanted to quit, then quit, but don't blame it on your family. It's not like you're going to spend 300 days of the year with your kids.

"In three or four years, do you want them to think 'Dad quit playing because of us?'"

The GM also used personal experience to talk Kapanen back. "He said he wished he had had a couple more years as a player, so I should make sure I was totally fine with retirement," recalls Kapanen. "I ended up signing an extension, kind of counting on there not being a season so I could take time off and recover."

The 27-year old Michal Handzus signed for three years at a total of $6.5 million, representing a raise of about $500,000 per year. The Flyers found the price right for free-agent right wingers Mike Knuble and Turner Stevenson, Knuble signing for three years at $6 million and Stevenson for three years at $3 million, those two deals ending the Philadelphia days of Mark Recchi.

"We thought he was going to be way too much," recalls Clarke about Recchi, who had been the Flyers' leading scorer the previous season with 75 points at age 36. But Recchi, who was coming off a $5 million-a-year deal, says the Flyers never inquired about his flexibility.

"I was always a hometown-discount guy my whole career," recalls Recchi. "Homer (assistant GM Paul Holmgren) tried to keep me patient for a while, but then they signed Stevenson and Knuble. I would have taken what Knuble got."

The 6-3 Knuble, turning 32, joining his fourth team in nine NHL seasons, was coming off years of 30 and 21 goals playing with Joe Thornton and Glen Murray on Boston's top line.

"For the first two years there, I was a plugger, third and fourth lines, in and out of the lineup," Knuble recalls. "Then I scored 30 goals out of the blue.

"My career had taken a different direction in a positive way and I wanted to keep going in Boston. I had close friends in a good town and was playing for [an historic] franchise. It was fun. But in discussions the Bruins had during the season with my agent (Kurt Overhardt), the offer they made was one they probably knew I wouldn't take, based on the success I was having.

"I think their approach to the lockout was keeping the core guys and then, coming out of it, to build around that, knowing how much money they'd have to spend.

"Under the old CBA, you had to be 31 to be a free agent. With a July 4 birthday, I had missed the July 1 deadline by four days (in 2003). Coming off that 30-goal season, I had to play another whole year before I could take advantage.

"So July 1 comes around and my wife Megan is due anytime with our third child. I'm on the golf course (in his native Grand Rapids, MI) and my wife calls me on the cell to say she's feeling a little funny, so I go home.

"I don't think her water had broken yet. In the meantime, I'm getting phone calls from Kurt, who says, 'We have an offer from the Flyers.' Philly was a team I would not have expected because I don't think I had played particularly well against them, not that it really matters because that's why you have scouts.

"Anyway, I was excited. There was always a little bit of drama around that franchise that caused you to ask guys who played there what it was like. I had been with Dan McGillis in Boston and he said it was a terrific place to play.

"I had been with Detroit when they had a lot of success and you think it's going to happen all the time. But when you are in the league more years, you realize how rare it is. Philly had just lost a conference final, was really close, another reason I was really happy. Keith Primeau was a monster.

"I remember being in the kitchen at around 7 and we're getting close with Philadelphia, and I'm saying to Megan, 'Hang on. Kurt's calling.' Her sister is there shaking her head at the whole scene.

"Megan finally says, 'We have to go now or I'm going to have this baby in the car.' It was probably a seven-to-ten minute drive to the hospital, hazards blinking, half-running (traffic) lights, cutting people off like I was a policeman.

"They got her in a wheelchair. Kurt was trying to tell Bob Clarke, 'We're not dragging this out; they're in the middle of having a baby.' And the cell service around all that electronic equipment in the hospital was terrible.

"We had Cole at 7:30 and probably committed to the deal around 9 or so. I became a father again and got the biggest contract I had ever signed. That is a great day.

"We have a picture of Cole coming home from the hospital in a Flyer hat that somebody had sent us. I don't really remember if Kurt was playing other offers or if Boston came back with one that morning. But three years at $2 million per was, I thought, fantastic money.

"I remember coming to Philly for a day in the middle of July and Mark (Recchi) was working out at the Flyers Skate Zone. He's the one who told me to live in Haddonfield, NJ, which turned out to be a life-changing experience for us."

In the 6-3 Stevenson, 32 years old, a 1990 first-round pick by Montreal and a 14-goal scorer for the Devils the previous season, Clarke had added a veteran grinder at what figured to be a cap-friendly price.

Since director of strength and conditioning Jim McCrossin also was certified as an athletic trainer, Clarke felt there was an overlap of responsibilities and dismissed John Worley, the head athletic trainer since 1995-96.

Philadelphia practically sat out the draft in the summer of 2004. Having traded away their first-round pick (which had turned into No. 25) as part of the Jeff Woywitka-for-Mike Comrie exchange with Edmonton, plus sacrificing their second selection to acquire Tony Amonte from Phoenix, the Flyers did not have a turn until No. 92, when they took winger Rob Bellamy, a Rhode Island high school player headed for the University of Maine.

Nevertheless, Clarke had added youth and speed to the organization with the June signing of center R.J. Umberger to a two-year entry-level contract. Umberger, a Pittsburgh native, had been the 13th overall choice in the 2001 draft by Vancouver, but had been unable to reach a contract agreement with the Canucks.

"After my junior season, I was ready to leave [Ohio State University]," recalls Umberger. "(Canuck GM) Brian Burke started at a really lowball offer of $700,000 when, at the time, guys taken even later into the first round were getting the rookie maximum ($1.13 million, plus bonuses).

"The Canucks weren't going to budge. Ryan Kesler (an Ohio State teammate) got drafted by the Canucks in 2003, the year I was ready to come out of school. He signed for $800,000 when I had been a higher pick and an All American.

"It dragged on. Burke made some personal comments and Kesler made some personal comments, for no reason. Around Christmas, at the deadline for rookie deals to switch over from three years to two, they made one last offer, but the way the contract was written, it turned out to be a worse deal, a real slap in the face.

"That year, I worked on my own off ice at the USA Hockey program. At the deadline, the Canucks lost Todd Bertuzzi (to a suspension for sucker punching Colorado's Steve Moore) and suddenly were hurting for the playoff push. So they traded Martin Rucinsky's and my rights to the Rangers."

If the Rangers didn't sign Umberger by June 1, they would get a compensation pick in the second round.

"I went to New York for a week, practiced and traveled with them, and actually came to Philly for a game. The Rangers wanted to sign me for a trial contract for the rest of the season, but I hadn't played all year and if I got hurt, my value would get worse. If I just waited until June 1, I could sign with any team that wanted me.

"Obviously, this is not the way you want to start your career. There are moments when you question whether you're doing the right thing. I had asked my agents (Mike Levy and Brian Long), 'Is there going to be a market for me afterwards?' They had a strong belief there would be. With the upcoming lockout, I would be starting the next season in the AHL and have a year of catch up, so I had that in the back of my mind.

"Everything happened for a reason. Bob Clarke called on June 1, Day One (of free agency for unsigned drafted players)."

The Flyers saw a rare opportunity. "It was like getting an extra No. 1 without having to trade anything," Holmgren recalls.

Toronto was among other teams thinking the same way. "There were a couple others, but Toronto and Philadelphia were the places I visited," recalls Umberger.

"I really was impressed with meeting Bobby Clarke and Ken Hitchcock. They told me how they were going to develop me and I'd heard nothing but great things about Philadelphia's organization.

"If I was going to start in the AHL, I would rather be in Philadelphia (with the Phantoms) than in St. John (New Brunswick, the Leaf affiliate). It was very nice knowing I could settle in Philly even if there wasn't an NHL season."

Also settled in Philly seemed to be the goaltending situation for a rare time. Robert Esche, who in June had undergone surgery in Pittsburgh from renowned hip specialist Dr. Marc Philippon to repair a torn labrum that had increasingly bothered him during the Flyer run to Game Seven of the conference final, looked like the No. 1 for years to come. With Antero Niittymaki deemed ready for the NHL after two seasons with the Phantoms, the Flyers chose to pass on bringing back 37-year-old Sean Burke.

It was the second time Clarke had acquired Burke in mid-season and then not offered him a contract for the following year. But unlike in 1998, when he was the starter during a five-game loss to Buffalo, Burke appeared in only one postseason game—in relief of a dehydrated Esche during Game Five of the Toronto series.

"I hated every minute (of the playoff run)," admits Burke. "I couldn't stand it, didn't want to be a part of it.

"I know that's going to come off sounding selfish. But I had no desire to sit on the bench every night and watch our team win games if I wasn't contributing. I came into Philadelphia and played well (6-5-2, 2.55, .910) but there just wasn't going to be the opportunity in the playoffs and that was disappointing because Ken Hitchcock had kind of made up his mind that he was going to run with Esche.

"My game was good enough at that point of my career—and I had enough experience—that I could have made the difference in winning the Stanley Cup. I had a lot of respect for Robert Esche; he's still a very good friend of mine and he played well. But I didn't feel that there was any reason for me to be sitting behind any goaltender other than maybe one of the top guys in the league.

"I don't believe that there's a goalie out there who had been a No. 1 guy who would rather sit and watch his team win. You'd rather lose and be in the battle. That's just the reality of being a goaltender.

"The only thing I really enjoyed about being there was that Robert was a friend of mine and I had other friends on the team like Recchi and Jeremy Roenick who were having the opportunity to go a long way in the playoffs. I believe to this day that team was Philadelphia's best chance to win a Stanley Cup in the last I-don't-know-however-many years. To have almost won with an inexperienced goaltender going into the playoffs, that's how good that team was.

"I thought we had taken the wind out of [the Lightning's] sails in Game Six, didn't think there was any way we were going to lose Game Seven. So give Tampa credit. But I was almost numb to winning or losing. I realized it was over and hadn't had a chance to contribute. I just wanted to move on."

So did Roenick from self-destructive behavior that made him the object of headlines. An FBI investigation into a touting operation for bettors, the Fort Myers, FL based National Sports Consultants, turned up evidence that Roenick had paid them between $50,000-$100,000.

Seven months earlier. Clarke had heard locker-room chatter of Roenick's sports gambling, and had confronted him. The GM had not informed the NHL because he thought it was not a league problem.

"J.R. said he wouldn't gamble anymore and I took his word on it," recalls Clarke. "It's easier to believe him. Are you going to make a big [bleep] storm out of something that may be nothing?"

Indeed, the disclosure drew no action by the NHL since there was zero evidence Roenick had ever bet on hockey or given any information on it to the touts. "I enjoyed [betting] but I don't think I had a problem," Roenick told *The Philadelphia Inquirer*. "I shut it off cold turkey."

The media field day blew itself out. But with no talks going on between the league and players' association, a big, black, labor cloud hovered over the second-ever World Cup of Hockey in late August and September.

Flyers Alexei Zhamnov and Danny Markov played for Russia; Handzus, Branko Radivojevic and Radovan Somik for Slovakia; Joni Pitkanen (Kapanen declined an invitation) participated for Finland; Kim Johnsson and Marcus Ragnarsson were in the lineup for Sweden.

Gagne was the lone Flyer representative for Canada, and when Roenick, still feeling the consequences of a hit during the Tampa Bay series by Fredrik Modin, declined his invitation, Esche, just two months removed from surgery, was the only Flyer playing for Team USA.

"They repaired my labrum, shaved my bone down so there was a little bit more involved than just a simple labrum tear," recalls Esche. "But the tournament was better than anything I had done in my career to that point, so I pushed and pushed against medical advice."

Esche lost a 2-1 duel to Canada's Martin Brodeur in a round-robin game, stopped 42 shots in Russia's 3-1 win over the Americans, then beat Russia's Ilya Bryzgalov 5-3 in the quarterfinals. "For the most part, I picked up where I left off in the playoffs," recalls Esche.

The American bid went to a semifinal against Finland at St. Paul (MN). "One of the most boring games ever played in professional hockey," recalls Esche. "After [Doug Weight] scored halfway through the game, [Finland] kept blocking everything.

"In the third period, (Teppo) Numminen shot one that bounced off the end boards, hit somebody's shin and bounced right to Olli Jokinen. Then Saku Koivu scored on a deflection."

The Finns had won, 2-1, with 12 shots. "It was heartbreaking because that was the end of an era for a lot of great American players (who had won the World Cup in 1996 and captured the silver medal at the 2002 Salt Lake City Olympics)," recalls Esche. Canada then defeated Finland in the final, Gagne finishing the tournament with two points in six games.

Primeau, still plagued by post-concussion symptoms that he had ignored while carrying the Flyers in the spring, didn't participate in the team's informal workouts to prepare for a training camp doomed for cancellation. Neither did Roenick. Because the expired CBA had stipulated that contracts of injured players would be honored during any lockout, the Flyers, hardly delighted at the prospect of paying Roenick $7.5 million for a year that wouldn't be played, argued he had passed the postseason physicals conducted by team physicians, Dr. Gary Dorshimer and Dr. Peter Deluca.

Roenick insisted he had reported his headaches and that they continued. "People have said to me all summer, you don't seem right," he said to the *Inquirer*'s Tim Panaccio. "That includes my wife, friends, and the media.

"If Clarke says there's no problem with me, he's crazy. I will not be able to play this year."

The matter was referred to noted concussion specialist Dr. Karen Johnston in Montreal. Over lunch with Flyer Chairman Ed Snider at the Capital Grille, Roenick apologized for comments he had made on an Arizona radio station about being traded back to the Coyotes and reiterated his desire to remain a Flyer.

"Sometimes I get caught up in who I am, who I am talking to, and situations," he told reporters. "I said things that were not very loyal to Clarkie or Mr. Snider and the team I play for.

"I don't want people to think I don't want to be a Flyer."

Said Snider, "I'm waiting for the medical reports. I'm a big fan of Jeremy Roenick's. We'll do what's right for him."

Snider added, "Jeremy doesn't have any kind of gambling addiction."

Eventually, the Flyers agreed to compensate Roenick $1.2 million of the $7.5 million obligation for the 2004-05 season. "There really wasn't a fight," he recalls. "There was a conversation and medical reports; it was really between the NHL and NHLPA.

"I didn't go outside much that summer because the sun really bothered me. I could barely play golf. I slept a lot but still felt tired and had headaches all the time.

"It was terrible. Fights with my wife. Fights with the kids. It went on for like six or seven months. The Flyers knew there was no way I'd have been able to begin that next season on time. They handled it with a lot of class in a totally first-rate way."

The rest of the Philadelphia players, warned for years by their union to save for this upcoming rainy day, knew they were not going to get paid one cent. "People talked two or three years ago about this situation, but now the time is here and it really hits you," said Chris Therien, who was an unrestricted free agent after finishing the preceding season with Dallas. "This is probably not getting done for a while.

"I had some potential offers, but once it got to August, teams weren't willing to do much. This is a terrible year to be a free agent."

It was going to be an even worse year to be signed for $9 million, as was John LeClair, and to not be able collect a dime. But a majority of owners were determined to shut down for as long as it took for the players to capitulate to team caps on spending and the players were equally determined to keep the marketplace for free agents unfettered. The likely devastating effects upon the sport were lamented by both sides, but as the day of reckoning approached, there were no negotiations.

"The popularity of hockey isn't that of the other major sports," LeClair told reporters after a skate at Voorhees. "It's a big concern for everybody.

"This is going to hurt the sport. It's not going to hurt it in Philadelphia until January. The first thing you hear on radio or TV here is the Eagles. But eventually, it is going to affect hockey everywhere."

With no counter-proposal from the players, and therefore, in Snider's mind, "nothing to discuss," the Chairman did not attend the September 15 Board of Governors meeting in New York to authorize the lockout. By proxy or in person, the vote by the owners was unanimous. Hours later, the clock struck midnight with the expiration of the old agreement.

Team members, not allowed into the Flyers Skate Zone, had packed their gear the day before and left with no plans to continue to practice on their own.

"I think what concerns everybody is to see how far apart we are and how strong both sides are in their opinion," said Eric Desjardins. Primeau added there would be no winner in any blame game to be played between the owners and players. "It's hard to explain to a blue-collar worker or layman that million-dollar players and million-dollar owners can't come to some sort of agreement," he said.

NHL Commissioner Gary Bettman authorized teams to begin releasing the arena dates for exhibition games. The Flyers, who had reduced their player salaries by $11 million to $57.39 million during the off-season, had the fourth-most favorable payroll-to-revenue ratio in the NHL in 2003-04 and stood to lose a lot more money than the small-market teams Bettman was championing. But Snider endorsed the cap although he believed the $31 million per team ceiling Bettman was seeking was unrealistic.

According to an NHL-commissioned report written by former U.S. Securities and Exchange Commission chairman Arthur Levitt, NHL clubs had spent 76 percent of their gross revenues during the 2002-03 season on player salaries, as opposed to a range between 50 and 60 percent for the other North American sports. Levitt wrote that the teams had lost $273 million collectively that year and only 11 of the 30 clubs were profitable.

The NHL Players' Association, citing discrepancies in the reporting of items like suite revenue in the "non-hockey" category, disputed the figures in the Levitt report about the league's overall health. But the Edmonton Oilers were threatening to fold if there wasn't a lockout, and were not the only team that stood to lose less money by not playing the upcoming season.

The owners had rejected two player offers that included revenue sharing, a "luxury" tax on teams that went over a team payroll threshold, a one-time five percent rollback in their pay, and cutbacks in entry-level contracts that had been capped since 1995. The players, standing on the principle of a free marketplace, were not ready to concede to limits on a team's total payroll. And owners, whose $300 million war chest available to its strapped teams dwarfed the players' assistance fund, were ready for battle.

The only real hope was that three months of bleeding by both sides would bring reasonable men to their senses by January so there would at least be a partial regular season and a full playoff, as had taken place with a 48-game season at the settlement of the 1994-95 lockout. In the meantime, the Flyers, who had not collected any season-ticket monies in anticipation of the stoppage, had no refunds to give.

The Phantoms were playing and were more interesting than ever because all NHL players still on entry-level deals (generally in their first three NHL seasons) were eligible to be sent down to the minors without clearing waivers. So Joni Pitkanen, Dennis Seidenberg and Patrick Sharp had the opportunity to continue their development in the AHL.

Veterans losing up to $50,000 a day (in the case of LeClair) were told they could rent ice at the Skate Zone at the discounted rate of $200 an hour. Instead, Primeau made arrangements for the Flyers—and ex-Flyers still living in the area such as Therien and Eric Weinrich—to skate twice a week at the Medford Ice Rink, where the ice was free, reciprocation for clinics that Therien and others had conducted there. The goalies were John Larnerd, a tryout with Atlantic City Boardwalk Bullies of the East Coast Hockey League, and Greg Cossaboon, a realtor who had played one year of club hockey at Rutgers and was 6-foot, 252 pounds. "This is the beer league," smiled Therien.

Todd Fedoruk, whose contract also was up, skated with a team of 15-year-olds in Washington Township, NJ. By October 13, the date Philadelphia was to have opened the season in Tampa, Michal Handzus, Radovan Somik and Branko Radivojevic had joined teams in their native Slovakia, Kim Jonsson had signed to play in Switzerland, and Knuble and Mattias Timander in Sweden.

All players had deals that would free them anytime the NHL began. But they could only wish, as Bettman began to cancel the season 15 days at a time.

Flyer assistant coach Craig Hartsburg resigned to coach his hometown Sault Ste. Marie Greyhounds. "Maybe they want to leave me," joked head coach Ken Hitchcock, who conducted clinics throughout North America and was a guest coach at Princeton University. Most Flyer staffers were re-assigned to duties with the 76ers, Phantoms, or the Wachovia Center. Coaches, trainers, and equipment personnel were paid, but the radio and television announcers were not. Jim Jackson did overnights on WIP Radio and Tim Saunders sold KIAs.

Clarke still had the Phantoms to watch, a scouting operation to run, and "rumors to spread on the phone." But he called it his "worst time in 30 years in the league" and otherwise kept his opinion of the mess to himself, as per the gag orders of Bettman.

Recalls Clarke, "I just thought the whole thing was stupid. Bettman would have worked with the players but NHLPA executive director Bob Goodenow just shut it down, thinking Bettman would cave."

No talks were being held. The NHLPA called its player representatives to a November 2 meeting in Toronto, after which Esche, the Flyer rep, unloaded on Bettman.

"We're talking to a madman, a guy with no rhyme or reason," the goalie said to a Toronto television station. "Personally, I don't even think he is a fan of the game.

"I think there are a lot of great owners out there, but there is a madman leading them down the wrong path."

Esche sounded more like Samuel Gompers than the reluctant rep he was. "I never really enjoyed it or wanted to do it," he recalls. "I had done it in Phoenix, so [Eric Weinrich] (Esche's predecessor) kind of had me helping out in Philly. Then, I officially became player rep when he was traded. But I was always hoping I could hand it off to somebody else.

"It wasn't like I didn't care, but it wasn't something I wanted to put a lot of focus and time on, that's for damn sure. The lockout kept going on and on and became more difficult and frustrating. That was when I started thinking, 'This is horrible. What the hell have I gotten myself into?'

"The players didn't even know that was going on. I remember getting calls from other player reps and they were saying, 'I don't know about you, but we're fine with a salary cap, it's only a matter of how it's going to work.'

"Then you talk to the PA and they were like, 'Who said they were fine with a salary cap?' And, 'Who gave you permission to talk to other team reps?' That kind of threw me for a loop. I can't talk to other team reps? What kind of system are we running here?

"Writers would call and I would tell them, 'I have no idea what's going on. If you know, please tell me.' But as far as what I had said about Bettman, that was frustration talking. I (later) got to be good friends with Gary and, especially, Bill Daly (then NHL vice president and chief legal counsel].

During the grim November, former Flyer Paul Coffey had been among the Hall of Fame inductees, as an NHL with no present and a questionable future only was able to celebrate its past.

In early December, the NHLPA made a proposal based on a luxury tax that increased the union's offer to roll back salaries from five to 24 percent and proposed a $45 million threshold for a luxury tax on big spending teams. Bettman called it a "big-time move." But the owners' counter offer still had a salary cap and the players, dismayed because they felt they had moved significantly, rejected it.

On January 4, Bud Poile, who as the first Flyer general manager directed perhaps the best expansion draft in the history of sports—Bernie Parent, Gary Dornhoefer, Joe Watson and Ed Van Impe were regulars on the Stanley Cup champions seven and eight years later—died of complications from Parkinson's disease at age 80 in Vancouver.

"I was rather impatient, I guess," the often impulsive, sometimes cantankerous Poile had told the *Inquirer*'s Frank Dolson in 1979. Indeed, Poile's dismissive demeanor towards an increasingly knowledgeable—and questioning—Ed Snider hastened the GM's firing midway through Year Three, when he was replaced by his good friend, assistant GM Keith Allen. Allen had been hired by Poile as the initial coach of the Flyers with the promise of a front-office job after two seasons.

Poile, who had played for four NHL teams, had been a successful GM in the Western Hockey League prior to being the first hire by Bill Putnam, the initial Flyer president. After his dismissal in Philadelphia, Poile became the first GM of the Vancouver Canucks and then, later, the commissioner of both the Central Hockey League and the International Hockey League. The father of David Poile, general manager of the Washington Capitals and Nashville Predators, had been elected to the Hockey Hall of Fame in 1990.

Many NHL players played in Europe during the lockout. Mike Knuble played with Linkoping in Sweden.

With Bettman and Goodenow getting nowhere by late January, Daly, Calgary owner Harley Hotchkiss, and an outside counsel, Bob Batterman, met with NHLPA president Trevor Linden, associate counsel Ian Pulver and senior director Ted Saskin to try to find some common ground that could save the season. Soon after the meeting, Daly gave Saskin a proposal that still linked a salary cap to revenues, and the players rejected it.

Knuble, playing for $10,000 a month with Linkoping of the Swedish League, had frustrations typical of even players who had found work.

"The $10,000 was clear of expenses but you are going to have pay taxes on that when you came back and then inevitably there was going to be a rollback in NHL salaries," Knuble recalls. "We work in such a small window of our lives, you were realizing how much money you were losing every day.

"I had been so happy to get to Philly, wanted to hit the ground running, and was so proud of my contract. But I was watching it get eaten away. My three-year deal was getting down to two, and we had offered a 24 percent rollback. It was really, really frustrating.

"You are literally straddling the ocean, one foot over there trying to be productive but always watching what was happening over here. You're living with the ups and downs of the negotiations, so it's a roller coaster for a lot of reasons.

"My family came over in October. We were living in a little apartment and it's dark at four in the afternoon, snowing like crazy. One of my goals had always been to play in Europe when my NHL days were over, but not while a big NHL salary was being eaten away.

"But I was able to get a sense for how out of their element European players must feel coming over here."

On Wednesday, February 9, Bettman said if the lockout were not resolved by the weekend, there would be no hope of saving the season. The next day, talks broke off again. At a union meeting in Toronto, Esche and Roenick joined players that included star St. Louis defenseman Chris Pronger in asking that the association consider a reasonable cap.

"I thought we still would be well paid and that the league needed a system that would allow more teams to be competitive," recalls Roenick. "In my last year in Phoenix, I saw what happened when a team had to dump players for financial reasons and it was not a pretty sight."

The leadership remained opposed. On February 14, the league dropped its demand that salaries could not exceed 55 percent of revenue, abandoning for the first time the notion of cost certainty. The union offered to accept a $52 million cap, again with the condition it not be linked to revenues.

When Bettman sent Goodenow a letter the next day with a final proposal of $42.45 million cap, the players made an offer of $49 million, which was rejected.

On February 16, Bettman announced the first cancellation ever of an entire season by a major professional sports league in North America. "Without question, this is the saddest day that I have ever had in my career in hockey," said Snider at a press conference at the Wachovia Center. "I am personally devastated by the outcome."

There was one last-ditch save attempt, a six-and-a-half hour meeting on February 19, attended by Wayne Gretzky and Mario Lemieux, bringing a flash of optimism that their presence could help bridge the apparent $6.5 million difference in cap figures.

"When I heard Mario and Wayne were going, there was no doubt in my mind there was going to be a deal done," Clarke said. But hope really had been a reach. Ultimately there were too many teams, determined to let stifling player contracts run out, that didn't want to play. And both sides felt they already had surrendered too much.

Snider blasted Goodenow. "The impression I got was that the union didn't want to make a deal," he said. "Maybe the rank and file does, but the leadership doesn't."

Said Esche, "I'm mostly embarrassed to be a hockey player right now. I am very scared for the sport I love."

The urgency to do a deal had passed. It would be almost summer until there would be any attempts to save the lockout from going into a second season.

In March, Bain Capital, a buyout firm, and Game Plan International, a sports financial consulting firm, both out of Boston, presented the NHL Board of Governors with an offer to buy out all 30 teams for $3.5 billion.

"I'm sure it probably had merit in many different ways for many different people," said Snider. "But it's not feasible for Comcast or me.

"You couldn't get 30 guys to sell their teams. You could go to the moon in a two-engine plane quicker than you could do that."

More feasible—and more meaningful to the grass roots growth of the game—was renting busses to take inner-city kids to the Flyers Skate Zone in Northeast Philadelphia to teach them to play hockey, an idea born out of Snider's philanthropy and his relationship with Philadelphia superintendent of schools Paul Vallas.

Because so many of the city programs had been cut, Vallas needed contributions from outside organizations to satisfy the state's physical education requirements. In 2005, the Ed Snider Youth Hockey Foundation was begun with about 600 kids being bussed twice a week for a total of 12 sessions.

Additional kids skating eventually would mean more of them watching. Phantom attendance, which had declined more than 4,000 per game from an average of 12,002 in 1998-99, rose only 400 per game during the NHL shutdown, despite the lockout putting more high-ceiling prospects in the AHL than ever before.

Umberger had scored 65 points in his first 80 professional games. "I had just come off a full year of not playing, so that was huge for me," he recalls. "Not only did (coach) John Stevens show a lot of faith in me, there were so many NHL guys in the league, it elevated my play and really put the questions of my sitting out to rest."

Center Patrick Sharp, who had played 31 regular-season and 12 playoff contests in the NHL the previous year, scored 52 points for the AHL team. Dennis Seidenberg, a veteran of 63 NHL games, won the Barry Ashbee Award as the top Phantom defenseman. Antero Niittymaki recorded a sparkling 2.07 goals-against average. Stevens' team won 17 straight games during October and November on the way to a second-place finish in the East Division.

With the circus regularly booked at the Spectrum for two weeks in April, early-round Calder Cup games had been annually moved to the bigger Wachovia Center. When the Phantoms, bolstered by five goals from Jeff Carter, the 2003 No. 11 overall pick whose Sault Ste. Marie junior team had been eliminated in the first round, advanced past Norfolk in six games, the AHL team moved across the parking lot for the duration of the spring.

The other Flyer No. 1 selection in 2003, Mike Richards, joined the Phantoms after having dominated 15 playoff games (28 points) for the Kitchener Rangers. "It was a unique situation," recalls Richards. "Essentially, I was taking the spot of somebody who had played all year, which is a little weird and not something I agree with, but it was a good experience to be introduced to pro hockey at its highest level during the lockout."

The Phantoms beat the Wilkes-Barre/Scranton Penguins in five, the Providence Bruins in six and then sweep the Chicago Wolves, drawing an AHL playoff-record 20,103 fans for the 5-2 Game Four victory that secured the franchise's second Calder Cup in its nine years of existence.

"It was my first real taste of a big arena and big crowd," recalls Carter, who scored 23 points in 21 contests. "Everybody wearing purple that last game, it was pretty neat."

Sharp put up 21 points—and two game-winning goals in the final—while Richards scored 15 in his 14 contests. Niittymaki, a once sixth-round pick out of Finland who outplayed countryman Kari Lehtonen, the 2002 second-overall pick, in the final, found that championship more gratifying than the two he had won as a starter in the Finnish Elite League.

"The Calder Cup was a way bigger thing for me," he recalls. "The season is much longer, you have to put in so much more work. It was one of the greatest moments in my career, winning that.

"If you didn't know better in those final games, you would have thought you were in the NHL playoffs. It was a great time for all of us."

Philadelphia fans had gotten a positive hockey fix, but of course the game and the business was anything but mended.

In late March, the NHLPA and the Players' Executive Committee had come up with the idea of a salary floor to accompany the ceiling sought by the owners, alleviating player concerns that small market teams would depress bidding. On April 4, the union privately presented the idea to the owners, who saw some merit to it. The NHLPA was further assuaged on April 20, when the owners decided to remove the threat of using replacement players in order to get the NHL started up again in the fall.

On May 5, the two sides began regular meetings on a new economic model and, under a virtual news blackout, they chipped away, a potential settlement not affected by Roenick, who said into TSN cameras at a Lemieux charity golf tournament near Pittsburgh that any fans wanting to blame the players for the cancellation of the previous season could "kiss my butt."

There was no kissing and telling behind closed doors, just a grinding away, point by point, towards a settlement. On June 9, *The Globe and Mail* reported that the owners and players had agreed upon a salary cap, and although Daly refused confirmation, he conceded that the talks had progressed to issues of player movement—free agency, arbitration and qualifying contract offers.

The Flyers weren't going to wait for the ink to dry before confronting what would become a league-imposed player budget. Clarke and his right-hand man with contracts, assistant GM Barry Hanrahan, who had used his lockout time to complete a law degree, asked for a meeting with Eagles vice president Joe Banner, the chief football executive and his assistant Howie Roseman, the administrator of the 10-year-old NFL salary cap.

The NHL was entering an even braver new world—the NFL does not have guaranteed contracts—but Banner shared his philosophy on managing a cap.

"What I remember getting out of it was allocating a budget by position; identifying your most important ones—in our case center, a top defenseman and goalie—and allocating a percentage towards them, then filling in the rest," remembers Clarke.

Recalls Hanrahan, "(Flyer president) Ron Ryan was in the loop of how the talks were going, so we had whispers of what the cap number was going to be. There was a lot to learn—like how your cap hit would be the average salary over the course of a contract, how much you could go over the cap during the summer, exemptions in case of long-term injuries, a lot of stuff.

"The other big point Joe Banner made was how reliant a cap makes you on player development. When you have to pay your stars, entry-level contracts help offset a lot."

The complicated negotiations between the players and owners were to continue for more than another month. The July 12 session, the culmination of 10 consecutive days of meetings, lasted until 6 a.m., then resumed at 11, ending with the announcement that after 10 months and six days, the lockout was over at last.

The players had conceded to a cap of $39 million, $8 million more than the owners were insisting upon when the lockout began. Nevertheless, salaries were rolled back 24 percent on existing contracts. Teams were required to spend a minimum of $22 million, which left a $17 million range. No player could account for more than 20 percent of a team's payroll, setting an individual player cap for the 2005-06 season at $7.8 million.

The cap would be adjusted annually, up or down according to league revenues. Players would deposit an adjustable percentage of their salaries into an escrow account and if the total player payroll of the 30 teams exceeded 54 percent of league revenues in a given year, the teams would share the money. At 54 percent or under, the players would divide it.

The Flyers, who had spent $68 million on players for their 2003-04 semifinal team, would have to shed $29 million to meet the first cap, but the new CBA provided significant help. Existing contracts were all subject to the 24 percent cut, but teams also had a one-time opportunity to release players by buying out their contracts for two-thirds of the remaining value.

The arbitration rights of those not yet eligible for free agency had been reversed. Clubs could now take players to the arbitrator for a binding decision.

The players made some gains, though. The minimum salary increased from $175,000 to $450,000, with further increases scheduled at two-year increments up to $500,000. The age of unrestricted free agency, 31 under the old CBA, would decrease over the length of the six-year agreement to age 27.

Testing for performance-enhancing drugs—a minimum of two random tests a year—was being implemented, with first-time offenders receiving a 20-game suspension, second offenses resulting in a 60-game ban, and a third violation banishing the player for life.

Roenick said the settlement was a "terrible deal" for the players, but 87 percent of them, having no stomach for the lockout going into a second year, ratified the agreement seven days after it was reached.

"Had we wanted to stay out into the next year, it would have put more pressure on the owners to play and we probably would have gotten a better deal," Roenick recalls. "But what were we, as players, going to stand for?

"It ended because of the players' passion to play. It was that simple. Players wanted and needed to play and that overruled the idea that we wouldn't accept a cap no matter what. Our careers were ticking away."

After claiming, for the sake of unanimity, that it was "a great deal for the game," Goodenow took the hit for the lost season and resigned on July 28, replaced by his head negotiator, Ted Saskin. Most of the 388 players who had gone to Europe during the lockout were homesick and all realized that 76 percent of their former salaries was a lot better than the zeros they had been paid for 2004-05.

There wasn't enough solidarity left to threaten the owners with a second lost season. But, of course, many players still questioned the negotiating strategy.

"When we offered that (24 percent) rollback in December, they just grabbed it and put it in their pocket," recalls Knuble. "Why our offer did not expire, I don't get that."

Nevertheless, he wanted to come home as much as anyone. Relief washed over the game. Clarke said he had some concern about bitterness affecting the players' attitudes, but predicted most of them would just be happy to be playing again.

That was the perception of captain Primeau and Hitchcock. As soon as the agreement was announced in principle, the coach called all his players one by one. He didn't sense much lingering animosity.

"I don't think it's going to be an issue," he said. "All they want to talk about is how excited they are to get back playing hockey."

As Kapanen summarized, "It's been a long year."

Most of the owners believed that, with spending limits in place, they had saved the league, but they feared a pyrrhic victory. "We were all scared," recalls Shawn Tilger, then the Flyer vice president of marketing and communications. The team, which would be cutting ticket prices by five percent, hoped that Snider's image as a dove would mitigate any anger towards management.

"I think everybody knew Ed Snider wanted to play and the Flyers wanted to play," recalls Peter Luukko, then the president and chief operating officer of Comcast-Spectacor. "We were known as a pro-player organization. It was Gary Bettman who took it on the chin for the league."

The NHL believed it needed to kiss and make up to the customers with a more wide-open product. Teams had averaged 2.46 goals per game in 2003-04, down practically a goal-and-half from the NHL's all-time high of 3.95 in 1981-82. So on July 22, the league announced significant rules changes, products of a Competition Committee that included Snider on behalf of the owners, Rob Blake, Jarome Iginla, Trevor Linden and Brendan Shanahan to speak for the players; Bob Gainey, Kevin Lowe, David Poile and Don Waddell representing the general managers; plus NHL director of hockey operations Colin Campbell.

Four feet were added to the offensive zones by moving the bluelines towards the red. The two-line pass was okayed; the red line now existed only for the purposes of calling icing. Players already in the offensive zone as the puck was cleared out, could avoid an offsides whistle by coming outside the blueline, essentially tagging up while their teammates maintained possession.

Teams icing the puck were no longer allowed to change personnel before the faceoff in the hope that tired players would give up more goals. Punishments were increased for fight instigation.

All players, not just goalies, would draw delay-of-game penalties for shooting the puck over the glass from the defending zone. Roaming, puck-handling netminders were confined to a trapezoid-shaped area behind the goal and had the size of their pads shrunk by 11 percent.

And the tie game became history with the institution of the shootout, should nobody score during a four-on-four overtime of five minutes. If tied after three shooters, the contest would continue with different shooters until one team scored in the round and the other didn't.

The order of selection of an Entry Draft held in the ballroom of the Westin Hotel in Ottawa, nine days after the settlement, was determined by the drawing of lottery balls, teams assigned either one, two or three based upon their number of playoff appearances over the last three seasons. Pittsburgh, one of four teams assigned three balls, won the drawing and center Sidney Crosby, the most highly anticipated prospect since Eric Lindros.

The Flyers, who drew the 20th selection, tried to move up for the second pick, hoping to take right wing Bobby Ryan of the Owen Sound (Ontario) Platers, a native of Cherry Hill, NJ. "But Burkie (Anaheim GM Brian Burke) wasn't trading," recalls Clarke, who also took a run at the third pick (Carolina's), hoping to draft defenseman Marc Staal, the brother of Hurricane center Eric. Marc Staal dropped to the Rangers at No. 12.

Clarke, his sights lowered, worked a deal with Florida to move down to No. 29, picking up an extra second-round selection in 2006, which he then traded for further middle-round picks.

"The three guys we liked were (center) T.J. Oshie, (of Warroad High School, MN), (defenseman) Matt Niskanen (of Virginia High School, MN) and (right wing) Steve Downie (of the Windsor Spitfires)," recalls Ontario scout Dennis Patterson. "We thought we would pick up an extra pick and still get one of them."

Oshie went to St. Louis at No. 24, Niskanen to Dallas on the pick right in front of the Flyers', leaving Philadelphia Downie, a 5-10, 192-pound right wing from the Windsor Spitfires who had scored 21 goals and 52 assists, and run up 179 penalty minutes with his junior club the previous season. "A young Rick Tocchet, that's what we're hoping for," said Clarke.

The first round was more than what Downie had wished for. "I couldn't believe it," he said after watching on television because only the top 20 prospects—and no members of the general public—were on hand for the hastily scheduled draft. "I thought I'd be going in the second round. I'm ecstatic and still in shock."

Downie had been deaf in his right ear since age 11. But the issues that had caused many teams to downgrade his promise were temper-related. He said the breaches of discipline stemmed from growing up without a father. Downie was seven years old and a front-seat passenger on the way to a hockey practice when his father, John, lost control of his car, crashed the vehicle, and died at the scene. Steve was uninjured, physically at least.

"We (he and brother Greg) had no father figure in our lives," said Downie. "My mom did an unbelievable job with us."

Said a crying Ann Downie, Steve's mother, "This is a dream come true. His dad is watching somewhere. He would be so proud."

With Carter, Richards, Umberger and Sharp on the way and Knuble expected to give the Flyers a veteran scoring presence off the wing at a friendly cap number, Clarke twice used his right to buy out contracts for two-thirds of their remaining value. Tony Amonte, who had a year left at $5 million plus, was let go at age 33 after 27 goals and 41 assists in 93 Flyer games. And with two years remaining at $9 million per, 34-year-old John LeClair, four seasons removed from the last of his five 40-goal-plus seasons, was neither surprised nor bitter to be let go after 333 Flyer goals and four end-of-season first All-Star berths.

"I was underpaid for a long time, then was overpaid," LeClair recalls. "It evened out."

Clarke felt the need to put his available cap money into his defense. Vladimir Malakhov, whose acquisition had been a godsend for the conference final run, made some sense for a short extension at a figure scaled down from the $3.5 million he had earned in 2003-04. But at age 37, he put off the Flyers about playing another year.

Meanwhile, Clarke was put off at the thought of being used to drive up the bidding on some of the best defensemen in the game. St. Louis, trying to trade Chris Pronger to get its cap under control, kept its rights to him with a $7.2 million, one-season, offer. And the Flyer GM thought Scott Niedermayer, an unrestricted free agent, would also get more than $7million.

"He wasn't going anywhere except to play with his brother (Rob in Anaheim)," Clarke recalls believing.

Six minutes after the noon start of free agency on August 1, Clarke called Pat Morris, the agent for 33-year-old defenseman Derian Hatcher, whose five-year, $30 million deal with Detroit had been terminated after just one season. Because of a torn ACL, he had played only 15 games for the Red Wings, but the lockout had been a rehabilitation blessing for him.

Hatcher, who had captained Hitchcock's Dallas Stars to the 1999 Stanley Cup and been a No. 1 pick of the Minnesota North Stars while Clarke ran that franchise, was familiar and attractive.

"I didn't have the guts to step up about Hatcher when we had the fourth pick in that (1990) draft (when the Flyers took Mike Ricci)," recalls Patterson. "Clarkie went to Minnesota, knew our list in Philly and took Hatcher (at No. 8)."

But destiny seemed to be guiding the defenseman to Philadelphia. "At that stage, I don't think Pronger was better than Hatcher," recalls Clarke.

Morris had already taken bids for Hatcher from the Islanders and Stars, the latter offering $14 million over four years. "For those same numbers, he'll come to you," Morris told Clarke. But Hatcher, who had been serious about a return to Dallas, asked for time to talk to his wife about her feelings on moving to Philadelphia.

While Clarke was waiting to hear back, Holmgren got a call from Art Breeze, the agent for 33-year-old defenseman Mike Rathje, a once third-overall pick by Flyer scout Dean Lombardi when he ran the Sharks. Breeze said his client, who had been an anchor of San Jose's defense for 11 seasons, was looking for a five-year deal to stabilize the lives of his five young children.

But Rathje was looking for more than just security—a chance to play for a championship in an iconic hockey atmosphere. "We also called Colorado and St. Louis," the player recalls. "But I wanted to go to a team where management tried to compete for the Cup every year.

"Last year I was in San Jose, we were in the conference final, but I knew my time there was up. You only get to be a free agent once or twice in your life and [the Sharks] weren't offering me fair-market value. So I was going to test the market. And the history of a team like the Flyers was really exciting to me.

"I'd been with San Jose as an expansion team. There, you don't really understand the magnitude of what it is like playing with the Flyers, Red Wings or Rangers, teams that had been around for a long time. I had played with (former Flyer) Dave Brown in San Jose and admired him. The whole atmosphere of winning around the Flyers appealed to me."

Hitchcock had spent seven years in the Western Conference, so he could pick out a winner from there. The coach enthusiastically recommended that Clarke sign Rathje.

"Both Hatcher and Rathje were bigger and stronger than Malakhov," recalls Clarke. "Better defensively, too."

Five years were a lot for a defenseman at the tail end of his prime years, but the new CBA allowed teams to spread out the cap hit. The five years, $17.7 million Clarke offered Rathje worked out to approximately the same $3.5 million a year the Flyers had offered Hatcher over four seasons.

With no word back from Hatcher, Clarke decided to commit to Rathje by late afternoon. Hatcher then called back to accept the Flyer offer at 11PM He was happy to land well.

"You never want to be bought out like I was with three years to go," Hatcher recalls. "I had bought a house in Detroit so it was a tough time, but I wasn't the only guy going through that during that summer.

"When it got to August, I thought the Dallas owner (Tom Hicks) was more interested in me than the general manager (Doug Armstrong). The Flyers, far and away, were my best option; nothing else was really considered.

"Players know what goes on inside every team in the league and Philadelphia always had a great reputation for treating its players well. And I've always had the utmost respect for Hitch. I had no issues coming back and playing for him.

"He's hard on people, but you forget. Sometimes you've got to step back, take a couple deep breaths, recharge your battery and everything is fine. And I knew exactly what to expect from him going into it."

For the approximate price of a Pronger, the Flyers believed they had received two big, veteran anchors. Hatcher had played 25 minutes per game in 2002-03, his final season with Dallas, and Rathje averaged 23 minutes in the pre-lockout year with the Sharks.

"The penalty killing will be pretty much perfect when I'm out there," Rathje told the media in a conference call. "I am very, very good defensively and can add a little bit on the powerplay, one part of the game I am trying to work on.

"I am a good guy in the locker room and good around young guys.

"That about sums it up."

Not quite for Clarke. He moved Danny Markov—who had expressed a desire to return home to Russia once his contract expired at the end of the 2005-06 season—to Nashville for a third-round pick in 2006, opening up $2.35 million in additional cap space.

"I got a call from Bobby Clarke informing me that, due to the salary cap, they have to trade me," recalls Markov. "It's too bad that my stay (34 games and 18 in the playoffs) was so short."

But it was memorable, as his late goal in Game Five of the 2004 first round finished off the defending champion Devils. "It was an honor to play for one of the great franchises and one of its most memorable teams," says Markov, who now does hockey commentary on Russian television and spends half the year in Florida.

Clarke proved correct about Niedermayer, who was offered the maximum $7.8 million and five years to stay with the Devils, but joined his brother in Anaheim for four years at an average of $6.75 million. Pronger, the other franchise defenseman whom the Flyer GM thought too expensive, was dealt from St. Louis to Edmonton for a package that included former Philadelphia first-rounder Jeff Woywitka. The Oilers signed Pronger to a five-year contract with a cap hit of $6.25 million.

The fallout from the Flyer moves had free agents Malakhov and Alexei Zhamnov leaving. Malakhov went back to New Jersey for a two-year deal at $3.6 million per and Zhamnov, with no room for him in a center ice of Primeau, Roenick, Handzus, Carter and Richards, went to Boston for three years and $15 million.

John LeClair chose Pittsburgh over offers from Boston and New Jersey, signing a two-year contract at $2.1 million per. Tony Amonte got a two-year deal, too, for $1.8 million from Calgary.

Todd Fedoruk was traded to Anaheim for a second-round draft choice. With Marcus Ragnarsson and Mattias Timander—the latter foregoing the second season of a two-year Flyer deal he had signed before the lockout—choosing to continue their careers in Sweden, Clarke, at the urging of Primeau and Roenick, brought back free agent Chris Therien, 34, at the cap friendly price of $500,000. "We felt that not only on the ice, but in the locker room, Chris was a big part of the team," Clarke explained.

Therien, who 18 months earlier hadn't been able to get away from Hitchcock fast enough, practically ran back to him.

"I had a few other teams that were talking about a little bit more money actually, but I had been out for year, didn't know how long I had left, and felt like I was going back to where I belonged," he recalls.

The miles of bad road between Hitchcock and Therien would be repaved, the coach believed, by the addition of Terry Murray as a full-time assistant coach. "He had his best years here under Terry," said Hitchcock.

Desjardins had a year left on his contract at $2.28 million and, at age 36, some gas remaining in his tank, even if it had taken months to refuel.

"I had driven home at the end of the (2003-04) season mentally drained from my (twice-broken) wrist (that had prevented playoff participation)," he recalls. "I remember calling my brother and telling him that was it for me.

"I didn't have the energy to train. I don't know what I would have done if that season had started on time. I didn't actually start working out until it was cancelled. I felt better by then and said, 'There is no way I'm going to end my career on an injury.'"

His presumed heir as a cornerstone defenseman—Joni Pitkanen—and Seidenberg provided the only youth on a blueline of Desjardins, Kim Johnsson, Rathje, and Hatcher. Clarke still had approximately $3 million in cap room for another forward or two, but not enough, presumably, for the best available—and probably the best in the business—center Peter Forsberg,

The Avalanche, which had made huge long-term commitments to Joe Sakic ($50.5 million) and Rob Blake ($40 million) before the lockout, had offered Forsberg, who had won Hart and Ross trophies and been on two Cup winners with Colorado, $13.5 million over four years. But it only could pay him $1.2 million for the 2005-06 season.

Clearly, Forsberg was moving on. The hockey world, Clarke included, wondered where, because almost 45 hours into the beginning of free agency, there had been no announcement of a signing.

"I was sitting in the office, about 9 or 10 o'clock (on the morning of August 4) when I said to (assistant GM) Paul (Holmgren), 'You think it would be worthwhile making a call on Forsberg?'" the GM remembers.

It was a rhetorical question. There was nothing to lose. Clarke dialed Forsberg's agent, the Winnipeg-based Don Baizley.

"What's happening with Peter?" the GM asked.

"We're close with one team," Baizley said.

"Would Peter be interested in coming here?"

"I don't know. But I will call him."

When Baizley reached Forsberg in Sweden, he thought it was because the agent had finalized a deal with Boston.

"The Flyers want to know if you're interested in coming to Philly," asked Baizley, who heard something like, "Oooo!" from across the ocean.

"He sounded pretty excited," recalled Baizley later.

Forsberg, a surprise sixth-overall pick by Philadelphia in 1991, remembers never having thought much over the years about what could have been had he not been included in the package that brought Lindros in 1992. But the opportunity to come full circle was one of his first thoughts. The Bruins had won the Northeast Division in the pre-lockout year, but didn't hold the same fascination for him as Philadelphia.

"It was a special feeling because I got drafted by the Flyers back in the day," he would tell reporters. But what appealed to him most was that Philadelphia was a team not only loaded but renowned for constantly reloading.

"I looked at their roster and it was pretty strong," he recalls. "And I know Mr. Snider has an organization that wants to win.

"They are a famous franchise with fans that are famous for being into the game. They like the physical part. I thought it would be a good

Peter Forsberg was the free-agent prize of 2005.

fit for me. I had told Don I didn't want to go to a Western Conference team. Going back to play in Denver so many times a season would have been hard on me."

An hour after he had hung up with Baizley, Clarke got a call back. Two years and $11.5 million, well under the individual maximum, would get his team the best center in the game, but also put the Flyers $2.75 million over the cap.

Clarke would need to clear not just money, but ice time. And he could do both in one move with the cooperation of Jeremy Roenick, who had a $4.94 million cap hit.

"I need a couple of hours to try and trade Roenick," the GM said to Baizley, who gave him three.

Clarke called Roenick at his home in Phoenix.

"Jeremy, we have another player coming in that puts us over the cap," said Clarke. "If you will waive your no-trade clause, I'll try to send you where you want to go."

"You signed that [bleeping] Peter Forsberg, didn't you?" Roenick asked.

Clarke said yes.

"Now I don't feel so bad," said Roenick. "I don't blame you, I'd take Forsberg over me any day."

Roenick asked to be traded to a Western Conference team. Before Clarke began to dial them, one by one, he and Flyer president Ron Ryan called Chairman Ed Snider for permission to go $2.7 million over the cap to sign Forsberg, within the rules as long as the payroll was down to $39 million by opening day.

"I told Mr. Snider we would be over by 10 percent, but I promised it wouldn't stay that way for long," recalls Clarke. "We had no fear we couldn't get under the cap. If I couldn't trade J.R., we had other options."

As the lockout had ended, Snider told Clarke, "Make sure we come back with a good team," instructions implied going into every season regardless. So the Chairman's pulse was racing, just like his GM's. Roenick was three years older than Forsberg and also coming off a concussion. Snider endorsed the move wholeheartedly.

Clarke called Colorado GM Pierre Lacroix, explained that he wanted to sign Forsberg, and offered Roenick to the Avalanche. Lacroix said he had no room for Roenick's salary, but Clarke didn't begin to look for another taker before calling Baizley to accept his terms for Forsberg. "I think he took $250,000 less from us than what [Boston] offered," recalls Clarke. Forsberg doesn't recall that, but, knowing where he wanted to go, money wasn't really an issue.

Clarke phoned Hitchcock, vacationing in Kamloops B.C. with the news, which Hitchcock refused to believe. The exasperated GM finally hung up.

"It was out of nowhere," recalls Hitchcock. "And I guess I didn't see how it was going to fit."

It was the GM's task to make it do so, better sooner than later. He made calls to Los Angeles and Vancouver, both of which were interested in Roenick. Kings GM Dave Taylor asked Clarke to take back a player—and a salary—but Clarke said that wouldn't work for him; he then called Phoenix, San Jose and Columbus (well, it was in the Western Conference).

The Philadelphia franchise didn't wait for the other shoe to drop before announcing it had bought a pair of Guccis. Fourteen years after drafting Forsberg, he was again a Flyer.

The Kings GM rose at 5:30 PDT to call Clarke on his car phone and tell him that his club would take Roenick without insisting Philadelphia take back a salary. When Clarke got to his office, he called Taylor back and gave Los Angeles an additional third-round draft choice.

For more reasons than just the sun, Roenick could live with a move west. Wife Tracy, daughter Brandi, and son Brett had decided during the lockout to move back to Phoenix year-round. Besides, J.R. was a Hollywood kind of guy who thought the Kings, third in the Pacific Division in the pre-lockout season, had some potential. But by no means had Roenick been looking forward to ending his time in Philadelphia.

"My heart hurts," he told reporters. "It's a tough place to leave, one of the best organizations in pro sports. The Flyers have done nothing but wonderful things for me.

"They will have such a great team this year and to not be part of that hurts a lot. But I never would stand in the way of getting the No. 1 player in the game. It was hard for Clarke to do what he had to do, but he tried to make sure I was well taken care of, something you don't get in professional sports. For that, I will be forever grateful.

"Obviously, Los Angeles is closer to my home. It's a place I wanted to play my whole career. It fits my personality."

Nevertheless, he looks back wondering why he was so magnanimous in waiving his no-trade.

"If I had to do over again, I would say, 'No way,'" he insists today. "It would have meant a lot to me to finish my career as a Flyer."

For the three years it lasted, one of the team's most expensive free-agent purchases ever had given the franchise its money's worth. "He was great, everything we thought he'd be," Clarke told the media. "J.R. never took a night off.

"He was exceptionally good with new guys. Sometimes we wish he would have thought a little bit more before he said things, but at no time did he ever not give to this organization. He was not a taker."

The vast majority of his Philadelphia teammates agreed.

"I played with J.R. both in Phoenix and Philly and loved him," recalls Esche. "I've never played with a player with a bigger heart and, in the locker room, there was nothing he wouldn't do for the other guys. He was always there for me.

"Look, J.R. is J.R. He's going to do his own thing. Maybe the rest of the league would look at the time he wore the (Bobby Clarke) wig and say he's just trying to get attention, not taking the game seriously. But very rarely did I ever see anyone who would out-compete J.R. He was fearless, always had your back. I think the world of that guy."

Snider called the opportunity to sign Forsberg "once in a lifetime" and sent Roenick away with heartfelt thanks. "I'm going to miss Jeremy," the Chairman said. "He played through a lot of injuries.

"Jeremy is a heck of a guy and also a class act the way he handled this thing."

Hugely popular with the fans, J.R. was the closest thing the Flyers had to a rock star since the full bloom years of Lindros. But, considering who was replacing Roenick, the only tears shed as he left town were his own.

"Peter Forsberg is one of the best players in the game," Clarke said before being unable to resist this semi-shot at Lindros: "Peter would have looked good in orange-and-black for the last 13 years."

Hitchcock, finally believing it was happening, still had a hard time fathoming his good fortune. "Some of the things we're doing are taking some people's breath away, I would imagine," said the coach, who, for seven years, had held his breath every time Forsberg came on the ice against the Stars.

"There is no way to box him out; you can't," said Hitchcock. "He is one of hardest-working one-on-one players in the league and has been for eight-to-ten years."

Clarke was living large, but looking small, in posing for pictures on August 10 with his two 6-foot-5 defenseman acquisitions at a Wachovia Center press conference. Hatcher was big enough to admit that he had suffered his share of bad days with the grating Hitchcock in Dallas. But his familiarity with the coach was a factor that had pulled him to Philadelphia.

The other reason Hatcher saw himself as a Flyer was because he fit the prototype. "It's just the way I always have played," he said. "I actually had someone tell me I should have been here my whole career."

Hatcher also was pumped about joining a team with Forsberg. "I think Peter is the best forward in the game, if not the best player," said the defenseman. "Not only can he do things with the puck that most players in the league can't, you've got to know where he is on the ice because he hits to make you pay a price."

The Flyers had reduced ticket prices by five percent to help bring back the fans. But they no longer needed to worry.

"Clarkie had called to tell me what he had done," recalls Peter

Luukko, then the president and COO of Comcast-Spectacor. "I called Shawn Tilger, (the Flyer vice president of marketing and communications) and said, 'Hey Shawn, you're a [bleeping] marketing genius.'

"He said, 'What are you talking about?'

"I said, 'We just got Peter Forsberg.'

"Clarkie had pulled a rabbit out of the hat."

Three days later, Tilger told the media that the Flyers had received 83,000 inquiries for full season tickets and partial plans since the lockout had ended and were on pace for their most renewals in five years. And this was even before grown men almost fainted at the incredible sight of Forsberg pulling on a Flyer jersey at his August 14 introductory press conference at the Wachovia Center.

"There's nothing not to like about his game," said Clarke. "We hope he's the finishing touch for our team."

It had always been the contention of Russ Farwell, the GM who made the Lindros trade along with then team president Jay Snider, that had Forsberg been willing to sign with Philadelphia in 1992, rather than stay in Sweden for another season, the organization would not have been looking to make the Lindros blockbuster deal.

"I made sure I got a no-trade clause so they wouldn't get rid of me again," Forsberg joked with reporters.

"When I grew up, I didn't think about playing in the NHL. I thought I'd play in Sweden. So when I got traded, I was just a young kid and it didn't bother me that much. But now that I've played 10 (NHL) years, I know this is an organization willing to do what it takes to win."

It also was one willing to take a calculated risk on a 32-year-old who, in 2001, didn't play in the last two series of Colorado's drive to a second Cup and then missed all of 2001-02 with a ruptured spleen and an ankle injury.

Half of Forsberg's 2003-04 had been lost to groin and hip issues. He had committed to give MoDo of the Swedish Elite League, adjacent to his hometown of Domsjo, the entire 2004-05 regardless of the length of the lockout, but was limited to 39 games because of a dislocated wrist and concussion. In his nine Colorado seasons, Forsberg had undergone 13 surgeries.

"There was a time when I had a lot of injuries; my feet hurt every time I went on the ice," Forsberg told the press conference. "And there was the spleen, so it was a little tough there for a while.

"But I sat out [2001-02] and I think that was good for me."

There wasn't a lot of money left for Esche, the incumbent Flyer goalie of two playoff series victories. But remembering the failure of a previous first-time starter—Brian Boucher—to follow up a semifinal run, Clarke wasn't about to lavish big money on another young netminder.

That seemed fine with Esche. He signed for $1 million a year for two seasons, a raise of $460,000, close to what he and Clarke had discussed before the CBA ratification.

"People were telling me I was worth $1.5 million or $2 million or whatever," Esche told the media. "But I just said, 'My heart is in Philadelphia.'

"Whether that's weird or whatever, I don't know."

Who wouldn't want to be a Flyer? The enthusiasm was barely muted when, on the day the players reported to the Skate Zone for physicals, Forsberg underwent a procedure to remove a painful bursa sac in his right ankle, an injury suffered during summer workouts.

Hatcher had sprained his good knee at a Colorado Springs training camp in August for players preliminarily selected to represent the USA at the 2006 Olympics in Torino, Italy. Thus, Forsberg and Hatcher were not among the 11 new faces—a two-thirds turnover in personnel from the highly successful pre-lockout club—on the ice for opening day of camp. "That's my job, to build chemistry quickly," said Hitchcock.

He meant inside the team, not between its fans and players following the labor shutdown. Even after the Forsberg signing, the organization made efforts to re-bond with the public by scheduling player appearances, including Esche throwing Flyer caps from a Zamboni circling Philadelphia's City Hall.

On Day One of camp, all seemed forgiven. An estimated 1,000 fans jammed the Skate Zone for an open practice and cheered when the team came onto the ice. "I said to Ron Ryan, 'There's our answer, huh?" recalls Luukko.

An intra-squad game at the Skate Zone hurriedly organized to benefit the victims of Hurricane Katrina was a sellout. The blessing from a year without NHL hockey was that no one, especially the players, took the game for granted.

"I'm really excited for lots of different reasons," said team captain Primeau. Pre-eminent among them was his health. He had been free of post-concussion symptoms for four months.

"If there wouldn't have been a lockout, I don't know if I would have been ready for September (2004)," Primeau recalls. "But while we were out, I healed up fine.

"I felt good, was able to train hard. The only thing I was nervous about was the next big hit."

Sami Kapanen believed he had only mildly hurt his shoulder during informal skates. But his camp physical showed the 32-year-old winger had been losing strength, necessitating surgery that would put him out until November. Brian Savage, a veteran of 11 seasons, nine of them with Montreal, was signed to a one-year deal for $500,000.

The Flyers took their boat, floated by big-name signings, to the Schuylkill River for a day of crew races, Hitchcock's latest team-building exercise. "We take players out of their comfort (area) and put them in a foreign element where they have to work together," explained the coach.

The game they had played almost as soon as they could walk seemed foreign enough to the defensemen through the exhibition season. Their ability to move forwards from in front of the goal had been virtually taken away by a crackdown on obstruction, announced via a formal letter and video from the league delivered during training camp.

"I remember Clarkie, Mr. Snider, Hitch, Forsberg and me previewing the video before we showed it to the team," recalls Holmgren.

"The longer it goes, Mr. Snider says, 'What the hell is this? We didn't sign up for this.' Clarkie is just shaking his head and Hitch is going, 'Whoa, we've got to make a lot of big adjustments here.'

"And Peter says, 'I love it. The game's going to be easier for me.'

On the spot, Holmgren called Colin Campbell, the league's director of operations and put him on speaker.

Recalls Campbell, "I said, 'Hitch, you were in one of the original meetings (during the lockout) with the coaches and told me you wanted all the hooking called.' I had said, 'Everything?' You said, 'Yes.' And I said, 'Whoa!'

"I said, 'Mr. Snider, I'll get you on a call with Rob Blake, Brendan Shanahan, Trevor Linden and Jarome Iginla (like Snider, members of the competition committee) and we'll review.

"We did that, and those guys authenticated [the committee's work]. Mr. Snider was fine then.

"The rule changes came in late July. We were working on the video the rest of the summer. There wasn't time to get it to the teams until training camp."

That wasn't of much consolation for Clarke. He had known about the rule changes, but not the obstruction crackdown, when signing Hatcher on August 2, in large part because of his strength in front of the goal.

"Not letting players battle in the corners and on the boards?" asked Hatcher, who was cleared medically to return for a September 29 exhibition game against the Devils. "Give me a break.

"Little pokes to the wrist, it's ridiculous. The NHL is trying to create this warrior image and yet they are taking a lot of that out of the game.

"But maybe I can now play another 15 years."

"There are no battles," complained winger Turner Stevenson. "The D-man now plays off you."

Amidst all these grumbles about the game losing its heart, Knuble's was palpitating. Suddenly short of breath, the 33-year-old went for an EKG, which was normal. The winger, who had suffered an episode of arrhythmia 11 years earlier, underwent a stress test, which did not identify a problem.

He guessed the cause was his usual 20 ounces of pregame Diet Coke. "But I ended up not changing anything and it was fine," he recalls.

Whatever Jon Sim, a former player in the Dallas system who had scored 35 goals for the Phantoms during the lockout, was drinking, it helped him score eight goals in the exhibition games and to secure a job with the parent team. To no one's surprise, neither Carter, coming off a summer bout with mono, nor Richards was deemed to need more time with the Phantoms, just as Forsberg required no introduction on opening night. Regardless, he received one, to a thunderous ovation.

"This is a hockey town," Forsberg would say after the game. "It feels good to be here; I felt comfortable right off the bat."

He looked it too. With the visiting Rangers leading 1-0, Forsberg swept in for a loose puck at center and perfectly led Gagne for a goal that tied the game, 1-1, and later set up Knuble's first Flyer goal on a five-on-three. Richards then tallied in his first NHL game, bringing the Philadelphia lead to 3-1.

Jaromir Jagr, however, put two third-period goals through Esche's armpits as the New York rallied to win the premier contest on the NHL's new cable affiliate—the Comcast-owned Outdoor Life Network—5-3. "Unfortunately we played bad," said Forsberg. "We got outworked in the third and there's nothing else to say." There was, however, a lot being said about the 14 powerplays awarded by referees Blaine Angus and Kerry Fraser. Little of it by the Orange-and-Black was complimentary, even though the Flyers received 10 man advantages. Esche said he didn't see either of the Jagr goals through the new parking lot in front of the net.

"I was shocked by how many fouls were being called away from the puck," Hitchcock remembers. "We had to make adjustments."

After receiving complaints about the new, no-touch, league during the preseason, the NHL had sent out a further directive saying contact by the defense in front of the net was legal as long as the stick or hands were not used. But it seemed like neither the defensemen nor referees had gotten the memo.

Rathje announced plans to test the limits of the new restrictions.

"I am going to go out and use two hands on the stick, control the play," he said. "From what they say, you can cross-check in the pants. We'll see what happens."

Hitchcock believed his defensemen were over-thinking the changes. Not one had taken any of the four Flyer minors in the opener. "It's really simple," the coach insisted. "Be physical.

"You can't hook or hold. Hands on the stick when you close in; you can't have it parallel to the ground."

Desjardins agreed. "You can push a guy shoulder-to-shoulder in front of the net and use your hands," he said. "They will still let us battle in front. They don't want us to grab guys around the waist and throw them out or cross check in the back. We have to be better at this."

Hatcher, serving a three-game suspension for a pre-lockout transgression while a Red Wing, would have to wait to begin the adjustment. Therien, playing in Hatcher's place, struggled in the season's second game, taking two penalties for horse-collaring that the Devils converted for a 2-0 first period lead. But Gagne, already hugely comfortable on Forsberg's left wing, scored his second and third goals of the season and Philadelphia went on to win, 5-2, behind Niittymaki.

"I felt like we had been afraid to play," said Hitchcock. "Once we got a little angry and (showed) the emotion, we started to go. I just think we stayed with it, played physical and within the rules."

Rathje and Hatcher, the two "dinosaurs," instantly were being scrutinized, but Rathje thought it was the officials who had to make the more daunting adjustment. "Of course, Hatch and I, being big men, were in the spotlight," he recalls. "They were trying to label us as old style clutch-and-grab, so we didn't do much of that.

"I don't think we had a problem, but the officials did. The experienced ones would call things within reason. The newer guys were calling everything left and right. One night there would be 15 penalties, the next night two or three."

But Knuble didn't believe it was just the officiating that had taken passion from the early contests.

"During the lockout, guys had been arm in arm with their opponents, everybody commiserating together," he recalls. "It was like you had gone to hell and back with your enemies.

Flyer fans were pleased to have the Orange-and-Black back after the cancellation of the 2004-05 season.

"There was a little bit of solidarity over that, so not a lot of fights. Games weren't very hostile. I think everybody was just happy to be playing.

"If some guys were mad, it wasn't at each other on the ice. I think some were (feeling) a little bit like, 'If we ended up with this cap, why didn't we do it earlier? We could have figured this out really fast and not missed a whole year.'

"Maybe that was a little bit of a distraction. And since almost any type of physical confrontation ended up in a penalty, the games were being defused.

"Coaches were harping on guys having to relearn their habits. If a guy got a step on Derian or Rath, they had always been big enough that they could get a stick on [opponents'] bellies and bring them right back. I felt they adjusted nicely, never thought for once that they were out of place.

"Meanwhile, for me and the guys who hung out around the net, it was great. Nobody could beat on you or obstruct you."

Esche, who whiffed on a goal by new Maple Leaf Eric Lindros in a 4-2 loss at the Air Canada Center, was struggling not only with screens, but getting used to the mandatory reduction in size of the catching gloves.

Three nights later, an equally hard adjustment for Flyer fans was the sight of John LeClair and Mark Recchi in Penguin uniforms. Their names were both cheered during the pregame lineup introduction—LeClair's especially large—and then again when Pittsburgh coach Ed Olczyk put them out on the first shift. It was business as usual for their ex-teammates—Gagne netted his fifth and sixth goals in four games and Hatcher scored his first for Philadelphia as the Flyers overcame a LeClair goal to take a 5-1 lead. But when the penalty killing broke down, Pittsburgh crept back to within a goal. Niittymaki, like almost everybody in the building, was watching a replay of a Forsberg move on the center-hung scoreboard when Max Talbot's dump-in from center ice went into the net to tie the game.

"It was a stupid mistake and it won't happen again," said the Flyer goalie, who was saved by Rathje's power-play score in overtime, giving Philadelphia, paced by Forsberg's four assists, a 6-5 victory.

"That's the new NHL baby," said Hitchcock. "I told them, 'Just keep going.'

"What are you going to do? It's a track meet and I'm too fat to run."

The Flyers did some team building with their most complete effort yet, a 5-1 win over the Islanders, before heading off to military history buff Hitchcock's favorite place—West Point—for some more off-ice fun and games.

Gagne and Knuble did not seem to need any bonding exercises with their new center. "The way Peter was thinking, the game was almost perfect," recalls Gagne.

"You can't just put the two best players on the team together and know it is automatically going to work. It's there or it's not; you can't teach that, and Peter always gave the puck to me just where I needed it to get a shot off fast. I played with some really good players before and after that, but nothing was even close to our chemistry."

Recalls Forsberg, "Simon had a quick release and saw the game really well. For the first couple of strides there was nobody that could catch him. I think he was the quickest winger I ever played with."

While Forsberg was marveling at Gagne's skills, it was his resolve that had won over Hitchcock. "When we need it, he steps up, whereas before he would just drift along," the coach told reporters.

All Gagne had ever wanted was to be respected by his coach. Finally, he had earned Hitchcock's full confidence.

"After the lockout, my relationship with Hitch got really good because he started to show trust in me," Gagne recalls. "If I made a mistake or had a bad game, I was right back out there.

"Hitch would even ask me questions about what [the team] should do. I was very happy."

Knuble, who had played in Boston for Pat Burns and Mike Keenan, understood that the key to dealing with Hitchcock was to concentrate on the message and shrug off its delivery. Laughter was one way of coping.

"One of Hitch's expressions was, 'Cut off the head of the snake,' as if this guy or that guy on the other team was the head of the snake," Knuble recalls. "So we had a lot of cutting-off-the-head-of-the-snake jokes in the back of the bus. One time, the snake had two heads.

"But for the first time, my opinion was being asked about things going on with a team, and I appreciated that. Then again, we were productive; there wasn't a whole lot to be negative about.

"I had played on an almost parallel line (in Boston) with Joe Thornton and Glen Murray, with a big, puck-controlling centerman and a goal scorer on one wing. I figured out I needed to go get pucks, be around the net, and try and create traffic. But Peter was great at mucking for pucks, loved the one-on-one battles, too. So I had to figure when to be near Peter and when to get away from Peter. There were times he wanted to take the guy one-on-one and find Simon.

"Peter could just do it any way he wanted to—run a guy over in the corner, hang onto the puck, feather passes, or shoot it. And he wasn't scared physically; wasn't gonna shy away from anything.

"He and Simon were like brothers from another mother. The game had opened up for Simon; he probably could get around the ice a little more unobstructed. He was as dialed in that year as ever in his career.

"It was an absolute honor to play with them. You didn't want to be that guy to slow those two down. If you come to the dance with the prettiest girl, don't do anything to piss her off."

Richards' second NHL goal was the first time a Flyer had scored three-on-five since Terry Carkner did it in 1991. It broke a 1-1 tie in a 5-2 win over the Maple Leafs. But there was no magic to save Philadelphia through five third-period minor penalties in Montreal, where a 2-1 lead disappeared on two goals by Mike Ribeiro in a 3-2 overtime defeat.

Primeau, however, felt one big triumph at the Bell Centre. With the Canadiens on a powerplay early in the third period, he was looking down between his legs too late to control a deep rebound of a shot by Saku Koivu when Alexander Perezhogin nailed the captain with a shoulder to the chin.

Primeau rose to all fours but no further as he was talked to by McCrossin for two minutes. The captain looked dazed, but not wobbly, in being escorted off the ice. After Perezhogin was hit by Hatcher and crosschecked by Knuble, the latter drawing a penalty, Primeau took the next shift and completed the game.

"I remember getting on the bus, calling my parents and wife, and being excited," he recalls. "I'm like, 'I took a hit and I'm good, what I needed. I'm over that hurdle.'"

Two nights later, Primeau played 14:35 and was plus-two as Forsberg scored with 49 seconds remaining in the third period to climax a two-goal rally, and Pitkanen jammed in a rebound in overtime to beat Florida, 5-4. The following evening, the captain was on the ice for 17:26 at Raleigh as the Hurricanes scored five third-period goals on Niittymaki in an 8-6 Philadelphia loss.

"We flew to Ottawa and I remember getting ready to go down for the morning skate—I was rooming with Mike Richards—when I called Jimmy (McCrossin) and said 'I don't feel good,'" recalls Primeau. "He pulled me out of the lineup."

The Flyers recalled Umberger who, in his first NHL game, was promptly crushed by Zdeno Chara behind the net. Goals by Carter and Gagne staked Philadelphia to a 2-0 lead even as Johnsson left in the first period with a groin pull, but the lead didn't hold. After Chara's 50-foot game tying goal went through Therien's feet and beat Esche, the goalie went to the bench during a timeout and immediately told his teammates, specifically Therien, to let him see shots taken from a distance.

"If he wants to see it, we'll get out of the way," said the defenseman, this snit by a Flyer goalie apparently much better tolerated by his teammates than the last one by Roman Cechmanek's during Philadelphia's 2001 playoff meltdown against Ottawa. Two goals by Knuble and 20 third-period saves by Esche gave the team a 5-3 victory over the Senators.

"He looked like the Robert Esche of 2004," said Hitchcock, a good sign since the Esche of 2005 had spent the lockout working out with the team at Colgate University and not playing any games. His rust had been showing.

"With my wife pregnant, I wasn't willing to go to Europe," recalls Esche. "I couldn't play for the Phantoms, not that I didn't desperately try. It was against the rules.

"The only team available was the Chicago Wolves (an AHL independent), but the Flyers told me they'd look at that negatively and I really couldn't blame them.

"So I got left out. When the lockout ended, it took me a lot longer than other guys to get going. "

Primeau's symptoms were similar to those he had suffered in the past. Dr. Gerri McGinnis, the neurologist at Thomas Jefferson University Hospital who had been on retainer by the Flyers since the controversy over Lindros's repeated head traumas, determined Primeau had suffered a concussion and whiplash from the Perezhogin hit.

The captain was placed on long-term injured reserve so that the team could otherwise spend his $3.4 million cap hit, but with the understanding a Primeau return would force them to shed salary to get back to the $39 million limit.

"The whiplash [is causing] an irritation and can slow down your circulation," said McCrossin. "Second, the muscles in the neck go up into the head. If they are tight, they pull down on the head and cause a headache.

"When Keith lies down, he feels like he's spinning. He also said his eyes feel busy. He may be focusing, but his eyes are going back and forth and they get fatigued.

"Each of the concussions Keith has had, the symptoms have been delayed.

"How many can he sustain? That goes to an individual and is beyond my scope. Keith's head is our first priority. There is life after hockey."

When Desjardins, who had been feeling good since his mid-lockout change of heart to continue playing, took an elbow in the head from Cap Chris Clark, the Flyers suffered their second concussion in four games. "A cheap shot," said Gagne, hot like his stick. He scored two more goals in the 8-1 victory over Washington and Carter netted two also, one off a steal from rookie sensation Alexander Ovechkin, the No. 1 pick in the pre-lockout entry draft.

The hit cost Clark a $2,000 fine but no suspension, much to Philadelphia's displeasure. "[Clark] had the puck, Rico (Desjardins) opened up to check him properly and got hit on the side of the head," Hitchcock complained. "These are the ones that can end careers.

"I don't think the guy in Montreal wanted to hit Keith in the head; it was a shoulder, not an elbow. The ones that concern me are when a player is in a vulnerable position."

It was going to be a while until Primeau walked back in the door. In the interim, Bill Logan of Langhorne, PA, was welcomed when he passed through a Wachovia Center turnstile on November 5 as the 25th millionth fan to attend a Flyer game in their 39-year history. The players gave him a 4-3 win over Atlanta while Snider presented Logan with a jersey signed by the team with "Million" and the No. 25 on his back. Logan also received prime-rate interest for a day on $25 million, plus a high-definition television.

The best thing on that TV continued to be Gagne, whose two goals in the victory over the Thrashers brought him to 15 in the first 12 games, while Forsberg's point total was 25, having been held off the stat sheet in just one contest.

"You would sit on the bench saying, 'Oh my god, what a player,' cheering like a fan because Peter was so unbelievable," recalls Handzus.

When six-game point scoring streaks of Forsberg, Gagne and Pitkanen came to an end, Sharp, heretofore getting only 7:42 of ice time, scored twice, Carter added another and Richards fought Islander tough guy Arron Asham as the Flyers rallied from a 2-0 deficit to a 3-2 Wachovia Center victory.

Gagne declined Hitchcock's offer of the captaincy during Primeau's absence. "It's short term and he will be back and be fine," said Gagne, feeling he had enough input with his new role on the "Gang of Seven" leadership council that consulted with Hitchcock.

"I told Simon we needed a representative (to the officials) during the game, but he was adamant," said Primeau. So the Flyers rotated nightly assistants, the As standing for a lot of the player grades, too, as the team continued to get clutch goals. Knuble beat the Panthers with 3.2 seconds remaining in regulation for a sixth straight Philadelphia win.

The streak ended with the Flyers seeming to get caught in a speed mismatch against the Lightning during a 5-2 loss in Tampa. Hitchcock disagreed with that analysis, drilled the breakout in practice, and two nights later, it appeared to have paid off.

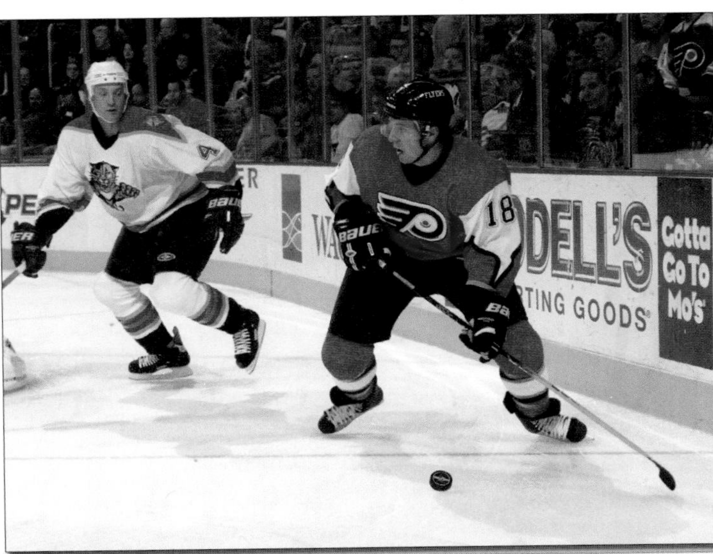

Center Mike Richards controls the puck against the Florida Panthers early in the 2005-06 season.

Philadelphia spent most of the first two periods in the Pittsburgh end while Crosby was trying to draw penalties. Already accused of diving on two other occasions by opponents, the rookie star doubled over after being engaged by Hatcher in the corner. There was no call on the defenseman, but Crosby drew one for embellishment in the second period, even though he was bleeding facially from an apparent grazing by Hatcher's stick.

"I hit him on the wall with my shoulder," recalls Hatcher. "I'm not sure, but I think he turned and cut his lip a little.

"The second time I went to lift his stick and missed, totally accidentally. I truly believe no one in the league would try to hurt someone with a high stick in the face. It was nothing like we were trying to intimidate him. When there's a chance to hit somebody, you hit him."

Pittsburgh coach Ed Olczyk didn't buy it. "It was welcome to the NHL, Philly style," he recalls. Crosby returned to score a second Pittsburgh powerplay goal within 56 seconds, staking the Penguins to a 2-0 lead until Forsberg made two of his specialty setups in traffic to feed Pitkanen goals that tied the game. Crosby had the last laugh though, sneaking behind Johnsson for an overtime breakaway winner.

Asked what he thought of the wunderkind, Hitchcock said, "I didn't notice him.

"You notice him on the powerplay. It's hard to notice the other team when you spend a lot of time in the other team's zone."

Olczyk was incensed. "I expect more from Hitch when it comes to that kind of stuff because to me that is a lack of respect," said the coach. "Worry about your team and let me worry about my team."

Recalls Hitchcock, "I said I didn't notice him and everybody went ballistic. The reason I didn't notice [Crosby] was that Pittsburgh was in D-zone coverage the whole game. And the other reason I didn't notice him was because the best player on the ice by a country mile was Forsberg. Nobody could get the puck off him. He was incredible."

Almost as astounding was the way the Flyers lost the next one. Up 5-3 with two minutes to go against Atlanta at the Wachovia Center, Radivojevic and Hatcher took penalties and a foul against Gagne headed for the empty net was ignored. Philadelphia gave up powerplay goals to Peter Bondra and Patrik Stefan and lost in overtime again, 6-5, on a score by Greg deVries.

Clearly the Flyers had missed Desjardins, who returned from a seven-game absence in Pittsburgh, where Crosby scored a powerplay goal but again went unnoticed as Carter, Handzus and Knuble scored in the third period, turning a 3-3 tie into a 6-3 Philadelphia victory.

Kapanen made his season debut on November 25 as the Flyers rallied from being two goals down for a 5-3 Niittymaki win in Boston. But Forsberg, who scored twice, left the game with a groin pull. This meant more ice time for the kids and Umberger stepped up with two goals against the Islanders. Nevertheless, his linemate Carter turned the puck over on a tie-breaking goal early in the third period and New York went on to a 4-2 Wachovia Center victory. Philadelphia won the rematch at Uniondale, though, 4-3, on tying and winning goals by Gagne, bringing his league-leading total to 23 in 23 games.

Esche was being outplayed by Niittymaki, who was receiving a more-than-expected share of the starts. "Obviously, Robert had a little edge because he had already had great playoffs the year before the lockout," recalls Niittymaki. "But I think Hitch liked me right away; he never really said bad things to me or about me."

Esche seemed to right himself with a 2-1 home win over the Devils but suffered a groin pull in the process. "That's the reality of taking a year off," he recalls. "There was a good chance it was related."

Niittymaki, beaten by Steve Sullivan and Paul Kariya, lost the first-ever Flyer shootout, 4-3, in Nashville on December 3, but Hitchcock praised the effort as his team tried to hold its own without Forsberg and Primeau. The captain showed up at a practice only because his wife Lisa said he needed something to do besides wait for his symptoms to subside. "They are not as severe, but, yes, they are prevalent," Primeau reported, but added, "People think I'm finished, but my whole intent is to play."

It was partly due to the team's belief he would return that, on December 5, Philadelphia traded Patrick Sharp and Phantom winger Eric Meloche to the Blackhawks for 22-year-old center-winger Matt Ellison. "We have lots of centers, even though we have some injuries right now," Clarke said. "We just felt Matt was a better fit for our team, although we realize we gave up a good young player."

Sharp, 23, who had been playing eight minutes a night, had three goals. "Patrick was a third- or fourth-line player at that time for us who was really struggling with the physicality of the NHL," recalls Hitchcock. "We were playing Umberger, a big body, ahead of Sharp.

"Our checking line with Radivojevic, Handzus and Ben Eager was good for us. We were about to send Patrick down. The next thing I knew he was traded."

Recalls Primeau, "I really liked playing with Patty during the 2004 playoffs. I thought, 'Put this kid with me and I can help him become a good pro.' And then I got hurt and Hitch never gave him the opportunities; they moved him while I was trying to come back."

Knuble recalls Sharp's frustration. "Patrick was my roommate, so I know he was in Hitch's office saying, 'You gotta let me play, I'm a good player,'" recalls Knuble. "And Hitch was like, 'You gotta show me something,' that never-ending circle.

"I remember Patrick asking me what it's like to be traded. You could tell he wasn't happy."

Sharp says that was not the case at all. "I didn't want to leave," he says. "A couple months earlier we won the Calder Cup in the same building with a lot of the same guys I was now playing with on the Flyers.

"I loved everything about living in Philadelphia and South Jersey. Even though I knew the trade probably was coming, I still was surprised and not happy."

Ellison had managed the same number of goals in Chicago as Sharp in Philadelphia—three. "The kid can play," said Hitchcock, who then played Ellison 6:35 in Niittymaki's 1-0 shootout win over Calgary, 5:06 in a 3-2 loss to Edmonton, and 5:43 when Forsberg returned to set up Radivojevic's goal in the final 53 seconds for a 3-2 victory over Minnesota.

Desjardins, back only nine games from his concussion, was lost for a projected eight weeks with a dislocated right shoulder suffered in the Edmonton defeat. "With all the stuff I've gone through, it's tough," he said. Just as difficult, considering the fine play of young Pitkanen, was the young defenseman's loss to a sports hernia surgery that would put him out for four-to-six weeks. Johnsson, who had emerged as the team's best defenseman before the lockout, was struggling to the point he had the A removed from his jersey by Hitchcock. Johnsson said he didn't mind.

With Gagne out for a projected 10 days with a slight groin tear, Hitchcock had no choice but to lean more on his kids, the farming of Ellison to the Phantoms after five games notwithstanding.

At 17-7-4, the Flyers were hanging near the top of the Eastern Conference standings in large part because of the tandem of Carter, who had eight goals and was being trusted for key faceoffs, and Umberger, who spent some time on the fourth line but was most productive playing with Carter.

"Jeff could carry the puck with such speed through the neutral zone, it simplified things," recalls Umberger. "You knew he was going to shoot.

"I went to the net a lot, and in the corners to dig out the puck. For some reason, we had a lot of two-on-ones where we found each other. It was fun."

Richards already was receiving key defensive assignments against top players.

"Carter and Richards were just kids learning, but they were close to Johnny (assistant coach Stevens), so they had real good value systems," recalls Hitchcock. "Richards had a lot of things to sort out about how we play down low in his own zone, but he still was such a fierce competitor.

"You could see both were going to be good players."

And both were mature enough to understand they needed direction.

"Maybe sometimes [Hitchcock] was tough to take," recalls Richards. But it was my first year in the league so I didn't know any different. He might have been hard on some players, but I don't think he was on me."

Umberger remembers he and Carter being in the coach's office practically every day. "Short leash, trying to make sure we weren't going to fall apart," Umberger recalls, but neither he nor Carter look back on the approach negatively.

"It was probably what I needed," says Carter.

"Hitch had a lot of older guys he trusted, so you know you have to work for everything that you get. I was 20 years old, looking up at Forsberg, Gagne and Hatcher. You have to kind of remind yourself every once in a while that you still have to do the work.

"They had me start on the wing, so I was learning a new position too. There were a lot of ups and downs, learning how to be a pro, and to have Mike going through the same thing helped. Being the lone young guy would have been tough at times for sure."

Carter and Richards seemed joined at the hip in sickness as well as health. On a night most of the Flyers were stranded because of a series of accidents on an icy Walt Whitman Bridge—necessitating a 33-minute late start against Vancouver—a shot by Seidenberg tore off a portion of Carter's left ear, requiring 52 stitches for re-attachment. Carter returned to play one 32-second shift late in the third period. Richards, meanwhile, had staggered coming away from a run into the boards by Canucks' Wade Brookbank in the second period and was done for the night.

They weren't the only casualties of the evening. Esche, who had returned to win the previous game, was seen by Hitchcock talking to McCrossin about his groin during a break and promptly yanked from what turned into a 5-4 Philadelphia loss.

Only 12 bodies were healthy enough to practice the next day. "This has to be some kind of record," said Forsberg.

Umberger scored twice centering a reunited Phantom line with Sim and call-up Eager to stake the Flyers to a 3-1 lead in St. Louis. When the energy of the depleted team ran low in the third period, Niittymaki's 16 saves preserved a 5-2 victory that ran Philadelphia's record to 19-8-4.

Richards returned after just one game. Gagne came back after five to score his 24th, helping the Flyers jump up 4-0 before holding on to beat Ottawa, 4-3. An 11-game trip, the team's longest since the Spectrum roof damage orphaned the club in Year One, started wildly in Pittsburgh, where Philadelphia blew a 3-0 lead into a 4-3 deficit before goals by Forsberg and Knuble rescued a 5-4 victory.

"Thirty-to-40 percent of our season has been timely goals," said Knuble, who had scored 13 that put the Flyers ahead in games. "To be where we are (first place in the Atlantic Division over the revived Rangers) is quite an accomplishment when you consider all we've been through."

For a team that was predicted to be caught in a time warp with the Hatcher and Rathje signings, Philadelphia was fooling them all. "We didn't fit the way the NHL was supposed to be played," recalls Hitchcock. "I felt like people were mocking us and then we shoved it up their butts.

"Both Rathje and Hatch could handle the mobility of the league because they were smart. We played them together and they were really an effective pair. Hatcher was so competitive, it was contagious to the rest of the team."

The kids continued to shine. On Boxing Day, Eager scored two goals in Niittymaki's 3-2 shootout win at Florida. The veterans stepped up too. Kapanen had overtime winners on back-to-back nights in Atlanta and Carolina. "They are relentless in their attack," admired Hurricane coach Peter Laviolette.

At 4-0 on the trip, the Flyers hardly were playing like accidental tourists. Upon the invitation of Brigadier General Jeff Hammond and Colonel Christopher Hughes, Hitchcock, the history buff, took the team sightseeing through the Pentagon before a game in Washington. "Having team experiences that are different and humbling, whether it's visiting a hospital or coming to establishments like this, serve as reality checks for our players," said the coach.

So did a 4-3 New Year's Eve shootout loss at the Verizon Center. "That's as dead as we have been in a month," said Hitchcock. But Carter's 10th goal and Niittymaki's 27 saves produced a bounce-back 1-0 victory in Boston.

Seidenberg was lost for two games to a knee sprain, so Philadelphia called up Randy Jones, another main man of the Phantoms 2004 championship who had been signed as a free agent in 2003 out of Clarkson University. Even with all the plug-ins, the Flyers continued to roll. Johnsson scored on a spectacular coast-to-coast rush and Gagne tallied off a set play seven seconds into overtime for a 4-3 victory in New York. The winger again had the winner in a 3-1 victory at Washington, this trip being so long it afforded the Flyers an opportunity to avenge a loss in the same city.

"Our veteran leadership was gone; we were just playing kids and winning games on enthusiasm," recalls Hitchcock.

The Flyers had gotten points in 14 straight road games before they finally lost one in regulation, 3-0, at the Meadowlands to Marty Brodeur. But when Knuble broke a 2-2 tie with a third-period goal and his teammates helped grind down struggling Chicago, 5-2, Philadelphia stood atop the NHL with 62 points. The Flyers' 17 points were the most ever collected on a road swing in NHL history, with one game remaining in Detroit.

"I can't remember when the trip started," said Hitchcock, although his team appeared able to play for two periods with total recall of what had gotten them to the NHL lead. Johnson, however, had to leave in the second after reporting concussion symptoms from an early first-period hit into the glass by Dan Cleary. Chris Chelios's shorthanded goal 15 seconds into the third broke a 1-1 tie and started a five-goal Red Wing third period that ended the 8-2-1 trip with a 6-3 loss.

Home—with a record regular-season crowd of 19,953—seemed sweet when Knuble and Forsberg scored in the final 2:36 to tie Colorado. But Rathje got called for hooking Joe Sakic, and Alex Tanguay stole the puck from Johnsson for a 4-3 Avalanche overtime victory. When Carolina's Rod Brind'Amour beat Niittymaki in a shootout, Philadelphia had suffered its third straight defeat, 4-3. Even worse, Forsberg was lost to a groin pull during the second period.

"It seems like every time we make a mistake, the other team scores," said Gagne, "which was the opposite case on the trip."

"I think a lot of times you find a way to battle through injuries and at a certain point, when you slowly come back to health and are finally relieved to have a full lineup, there isn't the same chemistry," recalls Knuble. "That's probably what happened to us."

Therien's 747th Flyer game made him the defenseman who played the most games in franchise history, passing Joe Watson. It only seemed like that many contests in a row for Niittymaki—actually 17 in the absence of Esche—as the Bruins sent Philadelphia down to a fourth-straight defeat, 5-2. "If I played well five days ago, I shouldn't play bad now," the goalie said, denying fatigue. "Physically and mentally, I feel fine."

Visits to more specialists only added to Primeau's frustrations and brought him no closer to a return. So on January 20, Clarke traded the 22-year-old Seidenberg to Phoenix for 34-year old center Petr Nedved.

"It was just a hope that Nedved would score some goals for a couple of years more than anything," recalls Clarke. "I always liked Seidenberg. That time (in 2003) he broke his leg at practice, I saw him reach down and snap it back into place before skating off. He was a tough bastard."

In other words, a Flyer to the core. "I loved it there," he recalls. "I would come back, if asked."

Seidenberg was dealt with the belief that the club had young defensemen just as good. "Because of the play of Freddy Meyer and Randy Jones, we could give up a young defenseman," Clarke told the media. "Not that we wanted to, but our theory was we needed more scoring ability and skill up front.

"[Nedved] was always a 20-goal guy with those Ranger clubs that weren't very good and never made the playoffs.

"I talked to Keith. None of us imagines that he is just going to wake up one morning and be ready to play. Too much of our scoring relies on just one line and we feel we also need a shot from the point on the powerplay. If we're going to do anything, we need to have two good powerplays."

Nedved had missed 19 games with injuries, scored only two goals and had asked to be traded to a team where he would be closer to his wife, Veronica Varekova, the Victoria's Secret model whose work was in New York. "I am pleased and happy to be coming to Philadelphia," said Nedved, who planned to live in New York and commute.

He assisted on Umberger's early goal in a 2-1 victory at Pittsburgh that marked the return of Esche and Pitkanen—as well as the absence of Johnsson, who, after playing three games following the Cleary hit, reported concussion symptoms and didn't dress. Also lost that night was Therien who, in coming back to pick up the puck, hit his head on Esche's shoulder and became disoriented.

Forsberg returned as the Flyers completed a home-and-home sweep of the Penguins, 4-2, on Knuble's late goal, but limped back out with another groin tear, this one on the other (left) side. The team's energy level fell "off a cliff," in Hitchcock's words, as Jan Bulis scored four times during Montreal's 5-3 Wachovia Center victory.

"The constant changing of the roster and lines is hard on everybody," said the coach. Philadelphia had Johnsson back for nine minutes of a 6-0 home loss to Tampa Bay, but he still didn't feel right and was shut down again.

Hatcher's head was pounding, too, from the shame at the Lightning rout. "This might be my all-time lowest defeat," he said of the seventh Flyer loss in 10 games and third in three games against the defending champions. "When I say every player should be embarrassed, I mean it."

Spoken like a captain, which he had been under Hitchcock in Dallas, and was about to become again on an interim basis. The team's backslide finally had caused Clarke to push his coach to formally replace Primeau for however long he would be out. "We are in a tough patch and need direction," agreed Primeau, who was kept in the loop in a meeting with Hitchcock and the GM. "Derian will demand a lot

Buffalo goatender Ryan Miller shuht down Mike Knuble and the Flyers 3-0 in Game Five of the Conference quarterfinals.

from the guys."

Whatever guys were left, that is. McCrossin took Forsberg to Duke University for a review with renowned groin expert Dr. William E. Garrett. Johnsson went to five doctors seeking answers about a dizziness that had begun even before the Cleary hit. Therien's light sensitivity was so severe he couldn't handle headlights to drive at night, further depleting the defense.

But there were extra bodies at forward. Jon Sim, an early-season revelation, had scored only once in his last 28 games and not dressed in five contests when he was traded to Florida on January 23 for a sixth-round pick.

Henrik Lundqvist, the rookie goaltender who had the Rangers on their way to a playoff spot for the first time in eight seasons, had an answer for every one of the Flyer shots on January 30 until, with New York up 2-0 midway through the third period, Pitkanen's goal ignited a comeback. Richards had an acrobatic redirect of a Meyer shot with 1:38 to play and Pitkanen's second goal, in overtime, gave Philadelphia a stunning—and seemingly buoying—3-2 victory at Madison Square Garden.

But the energy burst disappeared as quickly as it had come in a 4-2 loss at Buffalo. "Even when they are not shooting, [the Sabres] make you move so much," said Esche, who faced 37 shots. "These forwards are very underrated and some of the best in the game. I don't know if we can play that style of hockey."

Added Gagne after scoring his 35th goal, "We are having a hard time against fast teams. A pretty good example was Tampa Bay at home."

Poppycock, insisted Hitchcock. If you allow quick teams skating room in the neutral zone, they will make you look slow. "We came back (from the trip) so confident," said the coach. "I think there was a period of time we felt we could just throw our sticks on the ice and win. On the road, we dictated. Now, we're just chasing, giving up too many scoring chances early in games."

The 31-14-9 Flyers, who had won only six of 17 meetings against teams first or second in their division, had missed an NHL-high 354 man games to injuries in their first 54 contests. But the man they missed the most—Forsberg—still was hoping to play in the upcoming Torino Olympics, much to the unhappiness of Ed Snider, who said his best player shouldn't go unless he was 100 percent healthy.

"I'd like to play for my country, but if I'm not feeling healthy, I'm not going to go," Forsberg told reporters. "I don't care what other people are saying, whether it's pressure from Sweden or pressure from here."

The endless talk-show chatter over the issue served one constructive purpose, deflecting attention from Philadelphia having won only three of its last 12 games.

"You play good and it snowballs," recalls Clarke. "But when you're not that good, it ends and the snowball is rolling back on you.

"There is almost no way to stop it unless you get lucky in a trade."

The team's best effort in a month, according to Hitchcock, ended depressingly when the Rangers' Petr Sykora tipped in Martin Rucinsky's point drive with 42 seconds remaining to force overtime, which was won, 4-3, on a goal by Jagr while Pitkanen was in the penalty box.

"It's getting to the point where it's ridiculous," said Kapanen after the Flyers lost for the fifth time in six games, 5-0 in Montreal. "The other team is smiling and laughing skating off the ice.

"At least punish those guys when they have the lead. We just have to fight a little harder."

Hitchcock, sensing his team was mentally fragile, was trying to be supportive. "Hitch was one of those guys that lays off when things aren't going well," recalls Hatcher. "So really, he was fine, but there was so much pressure there to win.

"I mean we had been No. 1 overall. What the hell was going on? I think that team was in full-fledged panic during January and February. I don't think I've ever been on another team that held that many meetings. And it gets to a point you can only have so many."

The kids came through in a 5-2 win over the Islanders. Richards finished off the first regular-season hat trick by a Flyer rookie since Mikael Renberg in 1994 while Carter and Umberger had a goal apiece. When Desjardins returned after 29 games and Gagne scored a career high 36th goal, Savage put two in the net during a four-goal second period burst and helped a sharp Esche hold off Washington 5-4. But the goalie was yanked by Hitchcock after Philadelphia slipped behind Ottawa 3-0 in the final game before the Olympics. With the 3-2 defeat, the Flyers went into the 17-day break having fallen from first to fifth in the conference.

Handzus, who suffered a torn shoulder labrum at Ottawa, declined the invitation of Slovakia. Johnsson, his head hurting and his wife pregnant, was not playing for Sweden. Kapanen, chose to rest the shoulder that had kept him out until November, and Pitkanen (abdominal injury) turned down Finland. But Gagne reported for Canada, Niittymaki for Finland, and Esche, Hatcher and Knuble for the USA. Despite missing the final six Flyer games before the break—Forsberg flew to Italy hoping to play for Sweden, never mind an MRI showing the groin muscle tear had not completely healed.

"It's still not 100 percent but I'm going to fly over, rest a few more days, and see how it goes," he said. "If it feels 100 percent by the weekend, we will skate over there and get ready to play a couple of games. If it's not, I'm not going to play.

"It's not pressure from the Swedish team. I haven't read the Swedish papers all week and I'm trying not to read the Philly papers either. I don't care about that. It's me. I want to play for my country."

Snider, who had not discussed the situation with Forsberg personally, was conciliatory in the end. "Look, I don't think Peter will do anything to harm himself over there," said the Chairman. "This guy is really under pressure. He had a lot of pressure here not to go and he went anyway. That shows how strong a guy he is."

Added Clarke, "I think Peter knows what the results of the MRI were and the risks involved. He made the decision to go, so we wish him good luck over there, except against the Canadians."

Forsberg recalls his agent, Baizley, having the most influence on the decision. "We had lunch in Philly—I don't remember why Don was there—and he said, 'The Flyers signed you because they see you a winner, not the kind of guy who doesn't want to play in big games. They are not going to get mad, they're going to like it.'"

They didn't, but Clarke completely understood. "I don't think you can get pissed at a player for wanting to play," he recalls. "When I played, I would have played in a game anywhere, any time, any place.

"The Olympics can put a team in a bad spot. But I wouldn't want anybody telling me I couldn't play."

Forsberg went with Hitchcock's blessing, too. "Having been at the Olympics in 2002, I knew how much it meant," the coach recalls.

"Peter was a classy guy. If I had told him not to play, I don't think he would have. But I didn't think I had the right to do that."

Getting a huge opportunity when both Miikka Kiprusoff and Kari Lehtonen had to decline Finland's call because of injuries, Niittymaki shut out Canada 2-0 on the way to keying his homeland to a stunning 5-0 record in the preliminary round.

"Finland is a pretty hockey crazy country, so there's a lot of high expectations going in," Niittymaki recalls. "Now the two best goalies in [Finland] can't go because of injury so it's, 'Here we go, we have no chance.'

"But I was playing well in the NHL, so I knew that I could play there. I wasn't really that nervous. (Saku) Koivu, (Teemu) Selanne, (Kimmo) Timonen, and (Jere) Lehtonen had played together with the national team for so long, you almost feel like you're on a team that's been together for 10 years.

"You know, we weren't the best team on paper but, as a group, I don't think there was a better one.

The Canadians, for whom Hitchcock and Flyer assistant Wayne Fleming served under bench boss Pat Quinn, got shut out 2-0 by Switzerland in the preliminary round. With Gagne lost to a knee bruised in a collision with Darius Kasparaitis, Canada was eliminated in the quarterfinals by the Russians, 2-0, a shockingly disappointing performance.

The Americans blew a 2-0 lead into an opening game 3-3 tie with

Latvia and thereafter played every game, except for its lone win, 4-1 over Kazakhstan, from behind. They were eliminated, 4-3, by Niittymaki's Finland in the quarterfinals. As coach Peter Laviolette leaned on Rick DiPietro, Esche received only one start for the USA, a 5-4 loss to Russia during the preliminary round.

"When you're skating with all those [American stars] in the warm-up, it's certainly something more than I thought I would ever be a part of," recalls Knuble about his one Olympic experience.

"In (short) tournaments, if you are on, you're on, if you're not, you're not. We never built any momentum like [Team USA] did (to win a silver medal) in Salt Lake City. I think it was one of those years where the glory of the older group was gone, and the younger guys weren't ready yet.

"We didn't play well. Canada didn't either. I think that was our saving grace."

With Forsberg sitting out, Sweden suffered a shutout by Russia, but edged the USA, 2-1, and gained confidence. Forsberg returned against Latvia playing limited minutes, and the Swedes, though accused of tanking a 5-0 loss to Slovakia to draw a quarterfinal match with Switzerland rather than Canada, started to roll. Forsberg excelled on a line with Fredrik Modin and Mats Sundin in blowout victories over the Swiss and the Czechs to reach the gold-medal game against Niittymaki's Finns, who had shut out the Russians in the other semifinal.

Nicklas Lidstrom beat Niittymaki under the crossbar just 10 seconds into the third period to break a 2-2 tie and Lundqvist withstood a barrage in the final seven minutes as Sweden and Forsberg won the Gold, 3-2.

"We knew how good Team Sweden was, but you expect to win," recalls Niittymaki, who was named the MVP of the tournament. "Today you appreciate that silver medal and how well you did as a team, but it was tough to get over for a couple of weeks, I'm not going to lie to you."

Truth be told, with Gagne likely to miss some NHL games, the biggest interest the Flyers had in the result of the gold-medal game was to know that both Niittymaki and Forsberg would come home ready to resume the playoff push. "If I came back hurt it would be, 'Was it worth it?'" recalls Forsberg. "But I came back healthy, so it was."

Forsberg, earning his second Olympic gold medal, had been the shootout hero in the deciding game of 1994 against Canada. "This one was right up there with that one," he recalls. "And it had been five years since I had won anything (the 2001 Stanley Cup with Colorado), so it was good to get back on the winning track."

"The only bad thing is you win one day and go play another (NHL) game almost the next. There isn't a whole lot of celebration."

What little there was, Forsberg participated in with the Flyers' blessing. They excused him from practice the day before resuming their schedule at the Meadowlands so he could fly with the Swedish team to Stockholm for a rally in a downtown square. The party in Helsinki for the silver medalists was almost as enthusiastic.

In Philadelphia, there were parades—but only to doctors' offices. Gagne would not be available for three games; Primeau not for the rest of the season. "Although I have made progress in my recovery, I'm not symptom-free," he said on February 29. "I make this decision in the hope of prolonging my career and I'll continue to strive to return in the fall."

The Flyers had $2 million in cap room with which to approach the trading deadline, but were not going to come up with another Primeau, who also was missed in the locker room for his role in reducing tensions between Hitchcock and the players.

"Keith was a tremendous asset to both the team and the coaching staff," Hitchcock recalls. "A coach's job is to make players do what they don't want to do and have fun doing it. That's very hard.

"You have to find that person in the locker room able to understand the message. It was Keith."

Forsberg showed up at the Meadowlands jet-lagged and partied out. "Tired, I'm not going to lie," he smiled, nevertheless making one of his patented feeds in traffic on Brian Savage's game-tying goal in the second period. Esche was outstanding, but the team lost in the shootout, 2-1.

"To play as well as we did was a good start to this stretch," said Hitchcock, who proclaimed the division title as still the goal. But the Flyers smelled up the Wachovia Center in a 6-1 defeat at the hands of the first-place Rangers. Kasparaitis, who had ended Gagne's Olympics, tried to nail Forsberg, who ducked and then angrily confronted the long-time Philadelphia irritant. Hitchcock sent out Brashear, who unsuccessfully spent much of the rest of the rout trying to provoke Kasparaitis into a fight, the final refusal coming in the last two minutes, when he declined an invitation to drop the gloves.

"It was perfect the way they responded to me," gloated Kasparaitis. "I'm not fighting Brashear, that's not my game; I'll get beat up." Brashear received an automatic one-game suspension for instigating an altercation during the final five minutes of a game. Under a new rule, Hitchcock was held responsible and fined $10,000.

Brashear's $8,918.37 salary for one game went to the Players' Emergency Assistance Fund. Had there been a Flyers' Emergency Assistance Fund, DiPietro would have pitched some coins into the can by allowing two bad goals, but with both Nedved and Pitkanen in the box for high-stick fouls, the Islanders cashed a two-man advantage to break a 2-2 third-period tie and won 4-2 at Uniondale. "It was a stupid play and one of those things we have been doing lately," said Nedved.

The players told Hitchcock the next day they wanted a meeting, so he agreed, cancelling practice. "We have prided ourselves in making other teams crack," said the coach. "For the first time in a long time, the shoe is on the other foot and that is something that needed to be addressed today.

"I am not questioning the effort. But when the discipline leaves, sometimes the composure leaves. Penalties have hurt us."

Gagne's March 6 return reunited him with Forsberg and Knuble, the monster line during the first half. And Forsberg's goal, and Desjardins' first, staked the Flyers to a 4-2 lead. When Forsberg's penalty helped the Canadiens tie the game, he was saved by a Nedved shootout winner, but there was no reprieve from the pain in Forsberg's right ankle, which caused a visit to foot specialist Dr. Robert Anderson in Charlotte, NC. He recommended the star play with a custom-fitted brace to counter a chronic instability.

"Peter had to compensate for a high arch and it threw off his whole gait pattern, which is why he was having groin issues, too," recalls McCrossin.

Meyer, who had saved a loss to Carolina by redirecting a Rathje point shot with just two-tenths of a second left in regulation, took a penalty in overtime that Philadelphia killed before shootout goals by Forsberg and Gagne gave Niittymaki a 3-2 victory. "This should give us a lot of confidence," said the goalie. But the shootouts, in which the team was 5-5, mostly were giving the coach a pain in the butt.

"We spent way too much time working on that damn thing," recalls Hitchcock. "It was becoming a bigger deal than the game."

"We would have competitions (in practice) to see who could handle the pressure, had tryout after tryout, and always wound up with the same three or four guys.

"Here's what I learned about the shootout: It made overtime practically irrelevant. The overtimes had no scoring chances. Teams just wanted to get to the shootout."

As the trading deadline neared, Turner Stevenson, who had missed 33 games with a hip issue, was waived for cap-relief purposes. He cleared, remaining Flyer property. Clarke asked Pittsburgh about Recchi, who instead waived his no-trade to go to Carolina.

With Hatcher unavailable because of a bruised knee, Johnsson still out indefinitely with a concussion, and Rathje practicing sparingly with a torn hip labrum, Clarke obtained some defensive help—29-year-old Denis Gauthier from Phoenix for two second-round picks and Phantom winger Josh Gratton.

"[Gauthier] hits people," said Clarke, who also picked up winger Niko Dimitrakos, 26, from San Jose for a third-round choice. "He is highly skilled and probably an underachiever so far," said the GM.

Dimitrakos would fit right in then. The Flyers blew an early two-goal lead, then a 5-4 edge going into the third period, losing to the Sabres, 6-5, on Mike Grier's goal with four seconds to play. "We're not skating, hitting, doing anything," said Forsberg.

Gauthier debuted in Pittsburgh, where he refused to retaliate for Andre Roy's instigation, giving Philadelphia a seven-minute power-play. In it, they managed just one shot in a 2-0 loss to goalie Marc-Andre Fleury, the Penguins first shutout of the season. Forsberg said the team was playing "scared," and Hitchcock was asked if he was frightened the players had tuned him out.

"Oh, come on," he said. "You don't tune the coach out; this team has overachieved for most of the year.

"Be realistic. You're talking about changes in captaincy, injuries, all the things this team has gone through, and we're right in the mix. This is a whole new era and a bunch of new players, and we're trying to build the confidence to keep going."

In Florida, he gave the team a day off to forget its worries at the beach. Not only did no one suffer sunburn or coral scrapes, the Flyers played their best game in two months, running their record to 9-0-1 in their last 10 visits to the BankAtlantic Center with Esche's 4-0 shutout. Despite an almost-three-month-long skid, Philadelphia was back into a first-place tie with the also-sliding Rangers.

Advised not to play in back-to-back games and unable to take face-offs, Handzus returned at Tampa Bay, reducing the Flyer list of injured principals to Primeau and Johnsson. Gagne got Philadelphia off to a 1-0 lead against the Lightning, but Brashear, Gagne and Hatcher took consecutive penalties and Tampa Bay scored three times to control a 6-3 victory, its fourth straight decisive win over Philadelphia in the season.

A Carter-Umberger-Dimitrakos line enabled the Flyers to bounce back, each member contributing a goal in Niittymaki's 4-2 win at Atlanta. Gagne then became the 12th Flyer to reach 40 goals in a season in a 2-1 victory over the Devils. "Our tank is starting to fill up," said Hitchcock.

Some anger couldn't hurt. With Philadelphia trailing the Rangers 2-1 at Madison Square Garden, Ryan Hollweg sent Umberger flying face first into the boards with a hit from behind. During the resultant five-minute major, Knuble scored his 30th, and Handzus added another goal. With Umberger returning to the contest and Carter putting the game away with a fifth goal in six contests, the Flyers went on to a 6-3 victory that pulled them back into a first-place tie with New York. Hollweg was suspended for three games.

Gilles Lupien, the agent for free-agent-to-be Gauthier, told Clarke his client wanted to stay in Philadelphia, so the GM found a price that was right, locking the defenseman up for three years in a $6.35 million deal. "The kid is bright, he likes Philly, likes the organization," said Lupien. The defenseman, who delivered several punishing hits during his first six games in orange and black, was enjoying what he was seeing, and so was Hitchcock.

"Everybody was having a heart attack because our team wasn't playing that well, but Pitkanen, Forsberg, Gagne, Handzus, and Desjardins are just starting to get up to speed," said the coach after the Flyers scored four times in the first 8:33 to cool down the hot Senators, 6-3.

That was before Hitchcock's team started badly, then gave up two early third-period goals in a 3-2 loss to struggling Toronto, before being shut down by the Devils, 4-1, on April 1.

The Flyers looked engaged during a first-place showdown at Madison Square Garden, but the Rangers seemed to draw energy from a Hollweg-Richards bout as Philadelphia's 2-1 third-period lead slipped away on a Kapanen giveaway. Esche, who had given up nine goals to Jagr on the season, this time held him off the scoreboard on seven shots. "I think somebody other than Esche was in the net and they just put Esche's jersey on him," laughed Jagr after Sykora's shootout goal beat whoever that was, 3-2.

Nevertheless, it had been a good effort by the Flyers and they seemed to build on it. With Forsberg needing to sit out the April 7 contest in Buffalo because of a knee issue, Carter fed Umberger for an early goal and Philadelphia played its most complete game since December in winning for the first time in eight trips to Buffalo, 4-2.

With a first-round four vs. five matchup with the Sabres appearing possible, the Flyer victory seemed like a huge confidence booster. "We were very relaxed the whole game," said Esche, who, after speculating publicly earlier in the month that Niittymaki would be the playoff starter, had put himself back into consideration with a solid month.

The penalty killing, however, broke down again as the Leafs scored four goals with a man advantage in a 5-2 loss. "There wasn't a damn thing wrong with our five-on-five play; we go through a terrific (penalty killing) stretch (37-for-43) and then crash and burn, make the same mistakes all the time," seethed Hitchcock. "That really bothers me."

So did blowing a 3-0 lead against Pittsburgh, but after Crosby scored the second of his two goals, Carter's 22nd on a third-period powerplay pulled out a 4-3 victory. This didn't stop the Devils, who had been 19 points behind Philadelphia on January 6, from pulling into a fifth-place tie in the conference with a dominating 4-1 win over the Flyers at the Meadowlands.

"They're priming for the playoffs, and we might be waiting to throw the switch a little," said Hitchcock. "We're running out of time. It's not about wins and losses but about how we're playing."

Clarke didn't see it being good enough to survive a round.

"For me, those playoffs were hope without confidence," he recalls. "If you haven't been good, how can you be all of a sudden?"

So Clarke tried a shock treatment, blistering the team in a meeting. "It was as ruthless as I've ever heard," recalls Knuble. "He said, 'You guys aren't anywhere close to where you need to be right now.'

"We were a little bit like, 'What are you talking about?' We had just played Buffalo well, and, despite all the injuries, still had a chance at the division title and home ice with three games left. It always felt like we'd still be good enough. We were built big and strong, had two big anchors in Hatch and Rathje, and had young players who were playing well.

"What was hurting us was Peter. A lot of days, you didn't know if he was in the lineup or not, and that kind of messes with the psyche of the team. When you arrive at the arena wondering if a player of that caliber can go, it's a scramble for guys who don't know where they are going to be in the lineup, or even if they are going to be in there at all. That flicker of doubt messes with the psyche a little bit. We were always juggling."

After Gagne was presented his Bobby Clarke Trophy (team MVP) and Pitkanen the Barry Ashbee Trophy (best defenseman), goals by Carter and Dimitrakos gave their line with Umberger 20 in 18 games since Hitchcock put them together. Philadelphia pulled back to within a point of the Rangers and two ahead of the Devils with a 4-1 home win over New York in the regular-season home finale.

Again, what the Flyers showed you one night only made you wonder why they were a no-show the next. Esche, yanked after falling behind 3-0 at the Meadowlands, did a Roman Cechmanek-style meltdown at the bench, invoking an angry response from Brashear.

"He was very ticked off to get pulled and he was trying to fire up the bench," Brashear told reporters. "He was looking at me and I thought it was personal; then I sat next to him and he said it wasn't personal, just frustration.

"We were trying to follow up a good game against the Rangers with another one and had a bad performance from a lot of players."

Recalls Esche: "It wasn't directed at Brash. We got along very well. I said it to him because I thought he would back me up and it was a little bit of a misunderstanding in the heat of the moment. It ended real quick."

Despite their 5-1 defeat at New Jersey, the Flyers went into Game 82 at Uniondale with a chance to win the division. Carter's 23rd goal 11 minutes into the third period broke a 1-1 tie and Umberger impressively went left to right to beat DiPietro with a backhander for his 20th goal in a 4-1 Philadelphia victory.

With the Rangers having lost to Ottawa and the Devils trailing Montreal 3-1 with eight minutes remaining, the Flyers were congratulating themselves on their apparent title when, pizza in hand, they watched New Jersey come back to win its 11th straight, 4-3, forcing Philadelphia into a four vs. five matchup against the Sabres, starting in Buffalo.

"I don't believe in picking your opponent," said Hitchcock, stunned as anyone as the team boarded the bus to leave Long Island. "To me, everything was about getting home ice. So we have to start on the road and see where we go."

The Sabres wanted to go anywhere but Philadelphia, their star center Danny Briere recalls. "When we got on the plane in Montreal (after a 4-2 win, Buffalo's fifth straight), there were three options—the Flyers, Devils or the Rangers. When we landed in Buffalo, the pilot says, 'Good luck against the Flyers,' and the plane fell silent. It was, 'Oh, no, not the Flyers.'

"We were a young team in the playoffs for the first time (the Sabres, who had nine rookies, had qualified for the first time in four years.) And Gagne, Desjardins, Hatcher…they were just scary and physical. Forsberg probably was the best player in the league. That (April) game they beat us in Buffalo had been just like the playoffs, and we had barely touched the puck."

Philadelphia, 17-17-5 since January 11—when they had the best record in the NHL—finished 45-26-11, in ninth-place overall.

"I felt we could score, but couldn't defend," recalls Hitchcock, whose team had given up the 16th most goals in the league. The goalies had identical 2.97 goals-against averages and virtually the same disappointing save percentages (.897 for Esche, .895 for Niittymaki). Based on his performance in 2004, Esche was named the playoff starter.

"As soon as I show that I'm pissed just a little bit, everybody picks up on it," Esche told reporters. "But people misconstrue it.

"You have to be very calm, especially in the most clutch situations, because if opponents know that the goalie they're facing is calm in the heat of battle, that's a pretty intimidating thing."

The Flyers had scared no one in alternating victories and defeats over the last nine games. They, too, wondered what team would show up for Game One in Buffalo.

"I think it's scary," admitted Handzus. "I think everyone in the locker room knows something is not right.

"Momentum is the big thing in the playoffs. If you lose, it's hard to get it back. We need better focus."

Philadelphia also required more than just Forsberg's line to match up against four lines of Buffalo speed. The Sabres, who had six players with 20 or more goals, were among the top three teams in powerplay and penalty killing percentage, while the Flyers were 16th with a man advantage and a dismal 27th on the kill.

Johnsson, who had missed the final 31 games, wasn't coming back. Neither was Primeau. The experience edge Briere feared had also been mitigated by six Flyer rookies entering their first playoff series.

"If we're healthy we have an excellent chance to do some damage," said Hitchcock, whose NHL teams had won six of seven first rounds.

The coach knew the series would be lost without a strong Forsberg. So it wasn't a good sign when Ales Kotalik's stick found the Flyer star's midsection, causing Forsberg to turn the puck over in the slot, helping Tim Connolly to beat Esche up high with a backhander just 5:20 into Game One.

Desjardins, a step behind Briere, had to take the little Buffalo dynamo down to save a scoring chance, giving the Sabres a two-man advantage. A Hatcher break-up of a two-on-one and a good left pad save by Esche on Connolly allowed Philadelphia to kill the penalties, staying within a goal until Brian Campbell, fed up the boards by Briere, drifted to the middle, opening room for Jay McKee, who moved to within 20 feet and fired through Richards and Jochen Hecht. Esche, in his butterfly, never found the puck, which made the water bottle jump. Buffalo led 2-0, 4:43 into the second period.

Forsberg and Chris Drury, who had won a Stanley Cup together at Colorado, were going head-to-head. And Drury's linemates, Mike Grier and Derek Roy, were hitting Forsberg at every opportunity. When Knuble moved in to shove Grier after he shook Forsberg with a hit along the wall, the Flyer got the extra two minutes, giving the Sabres their fifth powerplay.

Three minutes after Philadelphia killed it, Forsberg backhanded the puck to Desjardins, who fed across to Gauthier. Goalie Ryan Miller butterflied to stop Gauthier's shot, but Knuble had a half-empty goalmouth on the rebound and cut the deficit to 2-1. Though outshot 27-12 through two periods, the Flyers still were in the game.

They remained there thanks to a good pad save on Connolly by the overworked Esche, who went to all fours to stop Drury, set up from across the crease by Grier. With nine minutes to go, Philadelphia was without a shot on goal in the third period but received a huge break when Sabre defenseman Toni Lydman, under no pressure, cleared the puck from just inside his blueline over the glass, drawing a delay of game penalty with just 2:38 remaining.

Hitchcock used his timeout. Forsberg took a long, lead pass and waited inside the Buffalo line before going to Knuble, who was almost on the goal line. He fed it though Henrik Tallinder's legs into the slot to the late-coming Gagne, who took the pass on his backhand, put the puck on his forehand, and tied the game off the post, 2-2, with 1:51 to play.

In the first minute of overtime, Lydman had to take down Gagne, set up by Forsberg, to prevent a goal. During the powerplay, the Flyers failed to manufacture a superior opportunity, but were starting to win some board battles.

Umberger hooked Paul Gaustad driving to the net, giving the Sabres a powerplay. But Gauthier, on all fours, got the puck to Desjardins for a clear, and Esche came across to stop Jochen Hecht on a two-on-one. Philadelphia was not only being out-skated, but out-hit when a Brian Campbell shoulder to the jaw flattened Umberger, who had been looking down to take a breakout pass from Dimitrakos.

McCrossin got the dazed rookie winger, bleeding from the nose, into a sitting position, but he had to be supported by assistant equipment manager Harry Bricker leaving the ice.

"I remember cutting across the ice and thinking I was going to get a clean breakout pass," recalls Umberger. "I wasn't expecting a defensemen to be right there.

"The next thing I remember was in the training room. Doctors snapped my nose back in place and woke me up. I was mad and wanted to go back on the ice, but obviously, they weren't going to let me."

The hit—clean in a time when contact to the head was allowed—and multiple replays of it shown on the scoreboard video screen at HSBC Arena juiced the crowd. But the Flyers had the next good chance. A Rathje shot deflected in front to Kapanen, who was stopped by Miller, paddedown, on the first shot. Facing a wide open net with the rebound, the Flyer winger hit the post.

The Sabres received their seventh powerplay opportunity of the game when Meyer hooked Jason Pominville at the net. Briere took a feed from J.P. Dumont, beat Richards coming out of the corner, and was stopped by Esche. Handzus tied up Briere on a Drury passout, but the Sabre picked up the puck and circled the net, only to have Esche do the splits and get his right leg against the post on the wraparound, a phenomenal save.

With the penalty up, Thomas Vanek hit the crossbar. Esche stopped Teppo Numminen from the point, gloved the rebound when it popped up, then beat a wide-open Hecht, shooting from the hash marks. The Flyer goalie had 54 saves when the first overtime ended.

In the second, Forsberg got away with taking down Tallinder and went to the slot to accept a Knuble pass. But Miller made a right pad save, and then fought off a Carter wrister on an end-to-end rush.

Forsberg beat two Sabres and Knuble fed out to Gagne, but Miller, busy for the first time in the game, made the stop. A Gaustad pinch on Hatcher turned up a Vanek chance, but Esche went paddle down.

One minute later, Numminen saved at the point and wound the puck down the boards. Richards tried to tip it on his backhand to Knuble, but Briere made a steal and got a shot off as he was being restrained by Desjardins. The referee's arm was up as Esche kicked the puck out to Hecht. Nedved took a bad angle in coverage and Esche was in his butterfly as Briere was wide open to redirect Hecht's cross-crease pass. Buffalo's 58th shot, a tap-in, won the opener, 3-2, at 7:31 of the second overtime.

"[Esche] was spectacular," said Nedved. "He gave us every opportunity to win the game."

Nevertheless, Philadelphia had lost and, even worse, had given little indication that it was Buffalo's equal. "It's a real gut-check time for us," said Knuble. "The good thing is they are probably as tired as we are."

Actually, the Sabres, 10 of them in their first playoff game, were ebullient. "We had stood up to the big, bad Flyers and found a way to win," recalls Briere.

Umberger had a concussion, a broken nose, and would fail the baseline test to play in Game Two. As for the rest of his team? Two years earlier, Philadelphia had bounced back from a double-overtime loss in Game Three in Toronto and evened the series in Game Four in triple overtime. But there were just six members of that team still on this one to draw from the experience.

Hatcher was not one of them, but as the captain and the survivor of multiple Cup grinds in Dallas, he spoke as soon as the team got to the locker room, reminding players to immediately prepare for the next game. "I've been in a lot of overtime games with Hitch and won some, lost some," said the defenseman. "I personally don't think this is devastating."

The Flyer on-and-off-again penalty killing had stopped all nine Sabre advantages, but all those minutes in the box had limited attack time. "We have to do a better job five-on-five, said Hitchcock. "This is where we have a chance in this series.

"We weren't ready for the pace at the start of the game. We will be this time."

Or so he thought. On the first shift of Game Two, Hatcher led Gagne by too much on a breakout and Roy got the puck in front to Grier. He missed the net with Esche down and out. But, on the second shift, Dumont beat Desjardins at the blueline and Gauthier, anticipating a pass, took himself out with a slide, enabling Dumont to keep carrying and roof the puck into the net on Esche's stick side.

Gagne then hooked Roy and went to the box. Tim Connolly played a Briere miss that rimmed to the point, carried to the slot and, when Kapanen slid, gave Drury half the empty net to sweep in the puck. The Sabres led 2-0 after only three minutes.

Hitchcock immediately called time out and spoke pointedly to his team. Nevertheless Meyer dangerously crosschecked Kotalik into the boards from behind, putting the Flyers down a man. They killed the penalty with no Buffalo chances and had an opportunity to stop the bleeding when Hecht and Vanek took consecutive Buffalo penalties, but Miller stopped Richards off the rush.

Vanek had just stepped back on when, after a faceoff in the Sabre end, Dimitrakos didn't pick up Lydman on a breakout, creating a three-on-two with too much speed for Philadelphia to handle at its line. Kotalik's one-timer of a Connolly pass beat Esche between the legs to make the score 3-0.

Two minutes later, Richards was bumped off the puck at the blueline by McKee, and Gaustad's quick relay trapped Pitkanen and Kapanen in the middle, letting Pominville to get wide and slap the puck from the hashmarks over Esche's glove. The hemorrhaging Flyers were down four goals before 15 minutes had been played. The fans, reminding Esche he had been chosen over Miller for the U.S. Olympic team, mocked him with chants of "USA! USA!"

When Forsberg, frustrated by the score and an uncalled Roy hold, bumped the Sabre after he had cleared the puck while lying on the ice, Roy got up to retaliate and was charged by Esche. "It was nothing he did, I was just trying to spark the team," the goalie later said.

As the linesman held Roy, Esche was unable to land any punches. But Hatcher saw an opportunity to avenge Campbell's Game One hit on Umberger, catching the defenseman in the face with an elbow. Thus, after Rathje grabbed Dumont as they went together into the boards, Philadelphia faced a five-on-three.

Hatcher had just stepped back onto the ice when Gauthier was caught too high and Briere fed the puck through the crease to Drury for an easy tap that boosted the Sabre lead to 5-0.

Hitchcock yanked Esche—who had given up the five goals on just 10 shots—for Niittymaki to start the second period. Gagne used a Knuble screen to score in the first minute, but Gauthier took a hooking penalty then a major for a hit from behind on Vanek. When Meyer, worrying Briere would try a wraparound, left Dumont, he was alone to take a passout and scored easily to re-establish Buffalo's five goal lead, 6-1.

Nedved scored on a Desjardins rebound in the third period, but Pominville answered once, then again, to complete a hat trick. Eager, dressed in place of Brashear, hit Campbell from behind in the waning moments of the mortifying 8-2 loss that sent the series to Philadelphia with the Sabres holding a 2-0 advantage.

"It is my responsibility to get the team ready, so this is on me," said a red-faced Hitchcock. "We were embarrassed for our fans and for the City of Philadelphia at the way we played."

He apologized to everybody but Buffalo coach Lindy Ruff, who said the frustrated Flyers had "acted like idiots."

This was not exactly what Hitchcock wanted to hear. "Tell Lindy to [bleep] off," he said as he left the podium. "To mind his own [bleeping] business."

But it was good business, recalls Briere. "It was clever by Lindy; he put pressure on himself, gave us the chance to relax and just play without the spotlight being on us."

It didn't appear the Sabres needed any diversionary tactics. "If they get to use their speed, they are good. And yeah, they did," Forsberg said. "You get down 3-0 and start taking chances, you play into their hands.

"At least we're going home. If we win the next game, we're right back in the series."

Bad decisions by Flyer forwards up ice had helped expose the team's defense as slow. But at practice the next day in Voorhees, the players were dumbfounded that they could have been so terrible.

"They are spreading us out, then pull up and slip the puck behind us," said Knuble. "You see them standing between the blue and red lines, with three guys across ready for the break.

'You have to keep guys coming over the top. Don't give up the odd-man rush. Don't lose guys on the forecheck. If you do, their fourth guy drops in for the attack.

"They catch you in over-pursuit. They give you one wide pass and everyone closes in on that side and then they say goodbye to the other side. We've got to know where we are on the ice and not have a big gap between the defense and forwards."

Jeff Carter and Buffalo's Toni Lydman fight for the puck in front of the net in Game Three.

"In Buffalo, Chris (Drury) was playing against Forsberg," recalls Briere. "In Philly, it was clear from the first shift that, with last change, Hitchcock wanted Forsberg against me.

"I had played just five (playoff) games four years earlier. This was my first playoff round really. On the second shift, Forsberg bee-lined me and crushed me in the corner, the best player in the league trying to take out the best player on the other team. Well, maybe I wasn't, but that's the way I saw it and that probably was [Forsberg's] intent.

"It was the wakeup call to me; how we need to play in the playoffs. After that it was, 'I'm going right back at him.'"

The Sabres had held the puck in the Philadelphia zone for the entire first 1:25 of the two-minute powerplay until Hatcher's outlet from the back wall sprung Savage, who blew by Connolly through center on a two-on-two, shot from the top of the circle, and beat Miller to the short side. The Flyers had scored 19 shorthanded goals, second in the league, through the regular season, none bigger than this one, which tied the game, 1-1, and excited the crowd.

Esche got his team through the remaining 26 seconds of the powerplay with a stop on Briere from the top of the circle, and then made a big blocker save on Campbell after Pitkanen was called for closing his hand on the puck.

Forsberg took a hit from Gaustad along the halfwall and received a big cheer for not going down. Only 15 seconds later, Knuble ran at Lydman well after he had gotten rid of the puck, but Philadelphia killed the penalty, thanks to a Hatcher break up of a two-on-one pass and some Buffalo fumbles at the point.

Early in the second period, another mindless penalty, by Savage for a hook in the neutral zone, put the Flyers in the soup again. But Gagne stole the puck at the Philadelphia line and sent Richards away on a two-on-one shorthanded chance that ended when he hit the post.

The Flyers were reenergized nevertheless. After Esche beat Vanek to the post, Forsberg, getting outside of Grier, tried to hit Knuble in the middle. The puck went off McKee's leg and bounced up, faster than Miller's glove, high into the net to give Philadelphia its first lead since the series began, 2-1.

Now, the Sabres were becoming frustrated. Tallinder got caught holding Handzus at the corner of the goal and Dumont took a penalty for pushing Rathje into Esche. Buffalo had killed both advantages though, when Forsberg, behind the goal line, retrieved a blocked Knuble shot and scored his second banker of the game, this one off Kalinin, to stake the Flyers to a 3-1 lead.

"Sometimes you are lucky and sometimes you are very lucky," said Forsberg. But his quick hands had beaten too many unsuspecting defenders during his career to put it all on good fortune.

Later in the second period, Handzus got away with a spear of Du-

Whether or not Philadelphia had been exposed as terminally slow, its players were fast to grasp the reality of the situation. "I felt like I'd had a pretty good rookie year—23 goals," recalls Carter. "I was pleased with that.

"Then you get to the playoffs. Everybody warns you that it's quicker, faster and harder, but until you are actually in the middle of it, you don't realize how big a step it is."

The Flyers, having spent 43:38 in the penalty box to Buffalo's 14:47 in the first two games, obviously had to get better control over their emotions.

"Me included," said Hitchcock, who met with Clarke and Snider. No minutes from that session were forthcoming, but the embarrassment was deep and went all the way to the top of the organization.

Campbell—Public Enemy No. 1 in Philadelphia despite repeatedly stating his regrets over Umberger's injuries—didn't pile on about the Flyer transgressions.

"That was a frustrated team," he said about the repeated avenging runs at him. "I think if it's a one-goal game, it doesn't happen."

Of course, a one-goal lead in Philadelphia's favor would be a huge help in keeping the Wachovia Center crowd, pumped by a Kate Smith-Lauren Hart "God Bless America" duet, into the game. For further inspiration, Umberger was back, too. But Buffalo struck first for the third straight contest.

Maxim Afinogenov bounced off a Carter check in the corner, fed Kotalik at the side of the circle, and his savable turnaround shot beat Esche on the short side after just 2:37.

The Flyers continued to invite disaster. Hatcher had the slippery Briere apparently pinned in the corner when Forsberg left his feet to hit the Buffalo star.

mont, who had to be helped up the tunnel, and Hatcher left Afinogenov slumped in the corner. "We have passion out there, we want something," Forsberg, his team outhitting Buffalo 17-6 for the game, said on the CSN Philadelphia telecast between periods.

While Dumont came back for the third, Numminen did not, for undisclosed reasons. The Sabres cut the lead to one off the rush, when Savage let up on Kotalik and Connolly swept in Kalinin's feed before Esche could come across.

For all the talk about the Flyers being unable to handle Buffalo's speed, Philadelphia had four odd-man breaks to the Sabres one. But before Nedved took a penalty for tripping Roy in the corner, Esche had to make stops on Afinogenov from 15 feet off a diagonal pass, then on Campbell from the top of the circle.

When Roy was called for embellishing a Forsberg knockdown, the Flyers, who had taken just one shot on goal during the third period, ran a careful powerplay. Esche held the post on Vanek and then, in the final minute, butterflied to stop Afinogenov after he had gotten a step on Hatcher.

Two #23s: Chris Drury of the Sabres ,ixes it up with Denis Gauthier in Buffalo's series-clinching 7-1 win in Game Six.

Forsberg kept up pressure in the Sabre zone to keep Miller from being pulled, then came all the way from behind the Buffalo goal to tip a Knuble center-ice breakup to Gagne, who, with the goalie finally on the bench, shot into the empty net from 80 feet.

Forsberg had scored only twice in the game. But the fans, either believing the final goal was his or paying homage to one of the most dominant two-way individual performances ever in a Flyer playoff contest, rained down hats to celebrate the 4-2 win that cut the series deficit to 2-1.

"Forsberg can win a game by himself," said Ruff, not exaggerating by much. But it had been a determined, team-wide effort by Philadelphia to hit the smaller Sabres and, despite many mindless penalties, to successfully kill all seven Buffalo powerplays.

"We played the way we had to," said Hitchcock. Now his team had to do it again to tie the series.

Numminen, diagnosed with a heart arrhythmia during Game Three, was scratched for Game Four. Nevertheless, the Sabres came out determined to take control that had eluded them two nights earlier.

On the second shift, Kapanen had to hook Kotalik to save a likely Buffalo goal. The Sabres missed the net on the first three attempted shots of the powerplay, but the fourth attempt, by Rory Fitzpatrick, who had replaced Numminen, was redirected from the hash marks by Vanek for a 1-0 Buffalo lead at 2:34.

Although Briere took a penalty for hooking Handzus, the Sabres had the best opportunity during the two minutes when Grier snuck behind Kapanen. Esche made a right pad save. But when Handzus gave away the puck behind the Buffalo net and Desjardins only got a piece of Tallinder's attempted lob up the middle, Briere, leaving the box, had another breakaway for Buffalo. Esche did the splits and made a right pad save, but the chasing Desjardins lost his edge, crashed into the goaltender, and pushed the puck across the line giving the Sabres a 2-0 lead.

It took Forsberg less than two minutes to recoup one of the goals. He bobbled the puck in gaining the Buffalo zone but immediately stole it from Lydman, circled the net, and led all five Sabres on a merry chase two-thirds of the way to the blueline before cutting back towards the goal again. Thus, Desjardins was left wide open at the point for Forsberg's diagonal feed. The Buffalo players who weren't chased Forsberg were screening Miller as Desjardins' slapshot cut the lead to 2-1.

The Flyers killed a Dimitrakos hooking penalty, allowing just one shot. Forsberg, breaking up a two-on-one, made the defensive play of the game, exploding back on Hecht after he had pushed past Hatcher.

In the second period, Forsberg picked up the puck in his own zone, made a shoulder feint that left Connolly flatfooted at center, and fed ahead to Pitkanen, who turned up just inside the line. He tried to hit Gagne coming hard on the other wing but the puck bounced fortuitously off Roy's skate to Forsberg in the high slot. He quickly slapped the puck past Miller's glove side to tie the game, 2-2.

Miller kept it even with a huge pad save on Handzus off a gold-plated Fitzpatrick giveaway. Esche answered on Pominville when Desjardins' stick got caught in the boards behind the net.

Radivojevic, one of the best Flyers on the ice, drew a hooking call on Kalinin but, when Forsberg got bumped off the puck, Roy was away on a shorthanded breakaway. Hooked by Pitkanen, Roy was awarded a penalty shot but was forced by Esche to the backhand and missed high and wide.

Kapanen had to break up a Drury shorthanded rush caused by a Pitkanen giveaway, but the young Philadelphia defenseman was playing assertively as his team carried the play.

Early in the third period, after Pominville went to the box for hooking Savage in the high slot, Nedved pounced on a Meyer setup that had gone off McKee to put Hitchcock's team ahead 3-2.

A penalty on Carter for interfering with Afinogenov shortened a Flyer powerplay. So when Rathje, who gave the puck away and was forced to hook Kotalik, joined Carter in the box, the Sabres had the opportunity to exploit a five-on-three.

Briere jumped on a deflected Drury shot with three seconds remaining in the first penalty, tying the game, 3-3, and giving Buffalo two whole minutes to exploit another man advantage. But Desjardins, taking most of the shifts with Gauthier against the Briere line, made a big block on the Sabre captain and a Kapanen interception killed the rest of the penalty.

Carter, undeterred by a Fitzpatrick breakup of his two-on-one with Umberger, stymied Roy at the Philadelphia line and sent his partner away again, this time two-on-two with Desjardins. Umberger shot from the top of the circle and the puck sneaked between Miller's stick arm and his body to put the Flyers ahead again, 4-3, with 10:09 remaining.

The finish was frantic. With Esche overcommitted on one side of the net, Nedved saved a goal. So did Rathje in lifting the puck from Dumont as he broke in. The clock was down to 2:05 as Esche boxed down a deflected Fitzpatrick flutterball and fell on the puck, before making a point-blank pad save on Kotalik off a passout.

In the game's 58th minute, Buffalo couldn't break the Flyer trap at center, forcing Miller to stay in his net. When he finally went for the bench, Knuble's backcheck on Afinogenov freed the puck for Forsberg, who capped his brilliant three-point night—and a career 10th multiple-goal playoff game—into the empty net.

The 5-3 Philadelphia lead, and a Fitzpatrick penalty, appeared to seal the deal until Meyer and Pitkanen allowed Grier to sneak away for a shorthanded goal with 19 seconds remaining. Back to within one, the Sabres forced a faceoff in the Flyer end, but Briere was penalized for tripping Richards, moving the final draw to center ice. Philadelphia had outlasted Buffalo, 5-4, and tied the series 2-2.

"We did some things that really make you shake your head," said Hitchcock. "So did they. I'm not sure I liked that shorthanded breakaway goal with 19 seconds left."

Esche hadn't loved four breakaways and a penalty shot, but he had stopped three of the five one-on-one chances. "I'd like to think our team is capable of handling whatever is thrown at us," said the goalie.

That included hard shoulders to the chin. Umberger, whose line with Carter and Dimitrakos was productive for the first time in the series, said he was happy to get his first playoff goal and even happier television could show him doing something rather than getting drilled by Campbell in Game One.

The potent Sabre powerplay was only 5-for-32 in the series, a necessity for the Flyers as they continued sentencing themselves to the box. They went back to Buffalo for Game Five with long memories of the Game Two shellacking. "We got killed there the last time, so we have to come out and show right off the bat that we want to win this game badly," said Forsberg.

Thanks to Ruff, the Sabres had become equally committed to demonstrating that consecutive Philadelphia victories had not turned the series.

"Everybody had been kind of depressed and Lindy said, 'You lost two games, they didn't beat you,'" recalls Briere. "And then he showed a video of all our turnovers from not wanting the puck and shying away from the physical stuff.

"He showed us like 80 clips from the last two games, just about every one of us in at least one of them. Then he said, 'You guys have a decision to make. You are better than them. Now it's deciding if you want to play. If you stop turning the puck over, you are going to beat them.'"

Drury told ABC's Cammi Granato that he saw determination in Forsberg's blue eyes during the two games in Philadelphia that had not been there for the first two in Buffalo. There was no such glimmer from Hitchcock when he went into the training room and saw McCrossin working on Forsberg. "Jimmy shook his head at me," recalls Hitchcock. "I knew Peter would be on one leg."

The Flyers barely had the puck for the first four minutes of Game Five. Desjardins had to take down Kotalik going to the net to save a goal. On the powerplay, Pitkanen and Kapanen backed off Connolly, who was able to close to within 15 feet and beat Esche's glove to give the Sabres another 1-0 lead.

Carter took a hooking penalty that Philadelphia killed with little problem, but it took the Flyers 12:45 of the first period to generate a shot. When they finally applied some pressure, Tallinder pushed Forsberg off the puck behind the goal. Philadelphia was penalized for too many men on the ice and Esche, attempting to clear up the boards, hit Rathje in the back and the puck caromed into the slot. But the goalie atoned with a terrific left pad save on Kotalik that kept the Flyers within a goal.

When Roy received a penalty for shooting the puck over the glass, the Philadelphia powerplay—a weary 3-for-22 in the series because of all the Buffalo shot-blocking—only passed the puck around the perimeter.

Richards finally put Miller to work with a shot from the dot. But a powerplay created by a Briere tripping call ended when Connolly took a dive that sent an innocent Forsberg to the box. Two minutes later, he exited to get nailed by Dumont.

The first Flyer chance from the slot in the game—a Savage rebound of a Nedved shot—took 35 minutes to generate. Somehow still down by only a goal, Philadelphia had a chance to catch its breath during a late second-period delay for a glass repair. In the final minute, however, Savage got pushed into Miller and was called for goaltender interference. On the powerplay, Connolly got the puck past Desjardins, walked off the boards and fed Briere, who, with Nedved sprawled, threw across on his backhand to Dumont for a virtual tap-in.

Forty-eight seconds before intermission, the Sabres had a 2-0 lead that felt like five, so few chances were the Flyers generating. In the third period, Dumont fed a breaking Briere. He controlled the puck with his skate, then fed it through Meyer to Afinogenov, who had a step on Dimitrakos and scored easily.

It would be inaccurate to suggest that the goal, which boosted the lead to 3-0, put away the game because the Flyers had never been in it from the first shift. The shockingly dismal 3-0 defeat had left Hitchcock's team one game from elimination.

"[The Sabres'] tenacity and hunger, not their speed, controlled the game," said the Philadelphia coach. "This was the best they've played in the series.

"They forced us to make soft plays with the puck at inopportune times. We lost too many board battles because of it."

Added Gagne, "Everything was a second too late for us. If you're late ßon the first pass, you're going to be late through center and so there's going to be five guys in front of you."

The Flyers had surrendered the first goal in all five games, and Hitchcock joked with television voice Jim Jackson about having the Wachovia Center put a Buffalo goal on the scoreboard before the match began so his team would know it was time to start playing. The coach then pulled Dimitrakos from the lineup in favor of Eager, hoping the kid—or if not him, Kate Smith and Lauren Hart—would jump start the home team.

Philadelphia took two icings in the first minute before a good forechecking shift by Handzus and Richards forced McKee to take a holding penalty. But after Miller made a save on Gagne off a Forsberg passout, the Flyers had no more powerplay chances before confusion on a line change caused them to take a too-many-men penalty.

Richards tipped the puck to himself and fed Hatcher on a two-on-one shorthanded break, but Miller closed the pads. After Philadelphia killed the penalty with no Buffalo shots, Miller had to stop Savage off a Kapanen passout.

The Sabres didn't have a good chance for the first six minutes, until Esche made a good stick save on Pominville off the wing. So the Flyers had the decent start they craved until Knuble picked up a rebound and tried to bank it off the backboards, only to commit the first of three consecutive Philadelphia turnovers. The other two were by Gagne, then Desjardins, who was stripped by Roy.

"The Sabres were real quick; all series long we didn't have time to make plays on the back end," recalls Desjardins. With both he and Gauthier caught behind the net, Roy relayed to Drury, who fed across to a wide-open Grier for a slam dunk 11 minutes into the contest.

The only Flyer response came from Esche, who stopped Kotalik off a passout to keep the score 1-0. Philadelphia generated nothing before Pominville skated off the boards away from Carter and fed Kotalik, who fired from the faceoff dot between Esche's legs to build the Buffalo lead to 2-0.

In the final minute of the period, Forsberg, at the halfwall, tried to lead Meyer coming up the middle on the breakout and missed. Drury picked up the puck and threw it in front. Esche made a save on a Grier tip, but Roy pounced on the rebound and got it by the goalie's short side, one more pin in the Flyer balloon as they went to the first intermission down by three.

"We did everything we wanted to do at the start of the game," Hitchcock would say. "Then it was over so quick, just bang, bang, bang, that everyone was in shock."

When Kapanen drew a Lydman tripping penalty in the first minute of the second period, Philadelphia didn't generate a shot. Worse, as soon as the advantage expired, the team got caught on a change. Tallinder banked the puck past Hatcher to Lydman, who carried it through a wide-open neutral zone with only Desjardins back. Pominville fired from the faceoff dot right through Esche for a 4-0 lead.

The Flyers, being heavily booed, did nothing during a Taylor Pyatt hooking penalty. Dumont won a battle with Richards on the halfwall and threw the puck ahead to Briere, two-on-one with Afinogenov against a backpedalling Pitkanen. Briere had an easy pass across to Afinogenov, who made it 5-0 with Buffalo's fourth goal on its last six shots.

Esche, yanked by Hitchcock, broke his stick on the wall in the corridor, in full sight of the television camera.

Radivojevic, his path cleared by Richards taking McKee to the net, beat Miller with a backhander late in the second period to get Philadelphia on the scoreboard. But less than a minute later, Forsberg couldn't control Gagne's pass up the boards and the parade of two-on-ones continued. Niittymaki stopped Roy, but Gauthier couldn't clear the puck and Drury, with no other Flyer having bothered to come back, had three tries to make one good for a sixth Sabre goal.

As the third period began, about a third of the seats were empty. During a four-minute Buffalo powerplay, Meyer was stripped by Grier, who fed Drury to complete the 7-1 season-ending disaster. "That was probably the single most embarrassing moment that I've had in my whole career," said Hatcher, to which he adds today, "probably still stands true."

It was the second rout that Philadelphia had suffered in a Game Six elimination to the Sabres over five years, but the 8-0 loss in 2001 had been an anomaly in an otherwise close series. This time the Flyers had been dominated in all four of the Buffalo victories, including the double overtime.

"Losing in the first round, there's nothing you can take out of that," Knuble told reporters. "Part of being an athlete in Philadelphia is there are extremely high expectations and demands from the fans and organization.

"When you don't deliver, you question yourself as a player."

This certainly had not been Forsberg's expectation when he had signed on. "Everyone feels brutal right now," he said.

"It's tough when you get down all six games. The (Sabres) got to use their speed really well."

Indeed, it had taken the Flyers apart. But with no Primeau and a hobbled Forsberg, Philadelphia had little chance to play to its size and strength.

Forsberg today doesn't recall his groin or ankle being particularly troublesome during the playoffs. It was the cumulative effect of the double overtime Game One and the uphill climbs in Games Three and Four, he says, that wore him down by the final two games.

But he wasn't the only one out of gas.

"I passed the (concussion) test, but it isn't [as extensive as] it is now," recalls Umberger. "I shouldn't have played.

"If I would tilt my head, I felt like it would pull me to the ground. I felt lightheaded and just not myself. I went over to the World Championships when I still wasn't feeling right, so I came home.

"I couldn't work out or anything. It wasn't until probably the end of July or early August that I was symptom-free."

Umberger and Carter had played just one good game each and the other key rookie, Richards, had struggled almost throughout, leaving just the Forsberg line against four for Buffalo.

Recalls Hatcher, "When young guys have to play a lot, they tend to wear down because they are not used to that pace and the bigger bodies. If you have a full team, you can play them less."

At breakup day, Hitchcock admitted fearing the Flyers would be overmatched.

"Look, I know how hard we had to play to win this series," he said. "Not a lot of people thought we could win.

"But we could have played better from the red line back as a group. From the coach's desk, you're measured by the way you check. Your offense comes and goes. We didn't check well enough to control the series."

Hitchcock, who had one season remaining on his contract, would be back, assured Snider. "He has a pedigree of being a fine coach, including with us, and he didn't suddenly go brain-dead," said the Chairman.

Clarke, addressing the media the day after Hitchcock, said he would talk to his coach about an extension.

"It wasn't his fault, he didn't have enough horses," the GM recalls. "It was kind of a broken team, one with lots of cracks in it.

"After so many years, instinct tells you when coaching is an issue. Problems between players and coaches don't heal. But I guess I wasn't convinced totally. He still was a good coach and I wanted to give him a chance."

Esche felt the fallout from the lockout and salary cap had turned over too many new players.

"We were excited about all the guys we signed," the goalie recalls. "But it was a different team.

"It was pretty unrealistic to think we were automatically going to have success just because we brought in big-name players. You still have to learn to be a team. It didn't have that same feeling as '04. In the big picture, it's easy to see why we would start out great and then finish like that. We weren't ready to win yet as a team.

"That's the reality, not Peter Forsberg's or anyone's fault. It was amazing Peter played as well as he did considering everything he was going through."

Recalls Gagne, "After the lockout, our team was a little too much about offense. We got caught up in the new system and the new rules. Then we didn't have Johnsson and Desjardins for a lot of the season, and Primeau for almost all of it. That was a lot of big-game experience to lose from our team.

"Everything was focused on one line and Peter started to have injuries. So it wasn't just one thing, it wasn't Robert Esche's fault."

Esche had been spectacular in the marathon Game One and mediocre thereafter. Up and down through the season, he had not clearly established himself as the No. 1 goalie over Niittymaki. But Clarke had more serious shopping needs in other areas.

"The defensive defenseman is becoming almost an obsolete player now," he told reporters. "He can't touch the forward who throws the puck in. You have to rely on quickness and positioning more."

Still, with three and four seasons remaining on the big deals of Hatcher and Rathje, respectively, Clarke refused to say signing them had been a mistake. "Rathje played from January until the end of the year with his back shot full of needles every game," said the GM. "He'll be fine."

Today, Clarke says, "Rathje had played [80 games] the year before, so if we had required physicals (before a trade in those years), he probably would have passed. We hadn't been the only ones trying to sign Hatcher and Rathje. The league completely changed the game on us with no warning."

Actually, both the veterans had adjusted fairly quickly before their play deteriorated. "The second half of the year was not very good for Hatch," said Clarke. "We will sit and talk to Derian; he can still play in the league."

Rathje and Hatcher were among 15 players who would need at least a clean-up postseason medical procedure. The list included Gagne, Kapanen, Handzus, Stevenson and both goaltenders.

Johnsson had struggled before a concussion took away his second half. "It was the first time we've seen Kim as an inconsistent player," Clarke told reporters, before pondering aloud his dilemma with the upcoming unrestricted free agent.

"It's been two-and-a-half months (with lingering symptoms)," said Clarke. "I don't know what to do with him.

"If he gets cleared in a month or so, how much do you pay him? What if he takes a hit the first day of practice and is done again?"

Although Primeau was signed for another two years, he posed a similar question. Should the Flyers wait for him or move on?

Clarke was clear the team would not be keeping Brashear and Savage, and wasn't certain Radivojevic would be back.

Six days after the season ended, Philadelphia's chance at a quick resurrection suffered another huge setback. Forsberg told Clarke he would miss half of the next season because surgery was needed on both ankles, one after the other, to correct the congenital condition causing his feet to lean inward, making them an increasingly bad fit in his skate boot.

"It's a bad situation that I have to get fixed," Forsberg said. "When I come back I will be a better player."

It was imperative that he return to a better team, making it obvious that the GM had work to do. But Clarke increasingly wondered whether he was the man to do it.

Peter Forsberg wore the captain's "C" for 2006-07

CHAPTER 9 • 2006-07

The Season from Hell

IN MANY WAYS, THE **2005-06 FLYERS,** who had undergone 15 post-season surgeries and seen six of their first- and second-year players become overwhelmed in a first-round loss to Buffalo, had proven to be both too old and too young at the same time. The club needed some strong mid-career additions. But, after winning only three playoff series in the last five springs with veteran-loaded teams, Ed Snider vowed he wasn't interested in any quick fixes.

"We got carried away wanting to win Stanley Cups," the Chairman said on June 7 at the Flyers Skate Zone in Northeast Philadelphia, where he and 200 children from city schools celebrated a successful first year of Ed Snider Youth Hockey. "We are going back to our roots.

"We're not going to trade picks anymore or trade our kids ever again for veterans. If it takes us longer, then so be it, but we are not going to give away our future. We're going to start building our team the same way we won our two Cups."

This was news to general manager Bob Clarke. "We never had that conversation," he recalls. "I read about it.

"As long as I was GM, Mr. Snider never told me I couldn't do this or that. We had good young players, we just had to develop them. And even if we used picks to try to win in some years, we always had extra ones."

Clarke had traded some draft choices and young players for temporary gain. A first-round selection, plus 1999 22nd overall pick Max Ouellet, went for rental Adam Oates in an unsuccessful attempt to save the 2001 season. Right wing Justin Williams, a sharp find with the 28th pick of the 2000 draft, had been dealt for veteran defenseman Danny Markov, a key contributor to the 2004 conference finalists, who quickly became a cap casualty.

But Williams had been only one of the excellent, mid-to-late, Flyer first-rounders on a list that included Simon Gagne at No. 22 in 1998, plus Jeff Carter and Mike Richards at Nos. 11 and 24 in 2003. All the more reason, Snider felt, for Clarke to trust his scouts to pick a Cup team. In the upcoming draft, Philadelphia was again picking 22nd, the same spot where it had obtained Gagne. Could the club become that fortunate once more?

Assistant GM Paul Holmgren, who ran the drafts, held a briefing with beat reporters before the June 24 proceedings at Vancouver's General Motors Place. The Flyer system needed defensemen, but after Erik Johnson—expected to go No. 1 to St. Louis—the 2006 pool of blueliners appeared thin.

"The top five [selections] would be sort of no-brainers," recalls Holmgren. "Everyone pretty much had Johnson, (center Jordan) Staal, (center Jonathan) Toews, (center Nicklas) Backstrom and (right wing Phil) Kessel, maybe not right in that order but in their top five."

Toews, the No. 1 player on the Philadelphia list, was selected third after Johnson went to the Blues and Staal to the Penguins. Backstrom became the third straight center chosen when the Capitals took him fourth before Boston opted for Kessel. The Flyers also liked right wing Kyle Okposo, who went seventh to the Islanders.

Then Holmgren and his scouts waited, confident that the 165-pound, 38th ranked, player in North America by NHL Central Scouting, would still be there for them at No. 22.

"I had never seen Claude Giroux play," recalls Clarke. "But when one of your scouts like Simon Nolet stands up that strongly for a player and your other scouts love him, too, you are going to take him."

Nolet, the Quebec scout, had gone out on a limb for Gagne eight years earlier and felt almost as good about Giroux, a center for the Gatineau Olympiques of the Quebec Major Junior Hockey League. "Gagne had slipped to us because he wasn't that big," recalls Nolet. "But he was bigger than Giroux, who we didn't have (rated) nearly as high."

"I liked Giroux; he was competitive, and had great hockey sense."

Philadelphia's other two principal Canada-based scouts—Dennis Patterson from Ontario and John Chapman from Western Canada—easily were won over on their trips to Quebec.

"When a guy like Gagne or Giroux comes along, that talent jumps out at you and you have to go with your gut or else you might get burned," recalls Patterson. "Jerry (Melnyk, the late Flyer head scout from 1984 to 1996) would say, 'When all is said and done, there's no substitute for talent.' I always tried to keep that in mind."

The game was changing, and with it, the team's way of thinking, in part because of Gagne. At Patterson's urging, Holmgren went to Quebec to watch Giroux during the playoffs; he was both intrigued and frightened.

"Five-foot-10 isn't terribly short," recalls Holmgren. "The main concern was his weight; I'll bet Claude really was 155 pounds.

"I would think teams ahead of us liked Claude, too. But I'll bet there were six or seven that had one or two guys a little bit higher because Claude's size was such a concern. I don't know that for certain, and it's a moot point, but that's the way the draft works.

"Because we also liked (center) Patrik Berglund (who would go 25th to St. Louis), we actually discussed whether we could get Claude in the second round. But we thought better of it.

"We hoped he would grow a little more and fill out. His size scared the [bleep] out of us, frankly. But he was ultra-competitive and had a sixth sense about him for coming up with pucks and making plays. He either had the puck or was working his ass off to get it. He didn't score goals yet, but Simon said he would.

"At the end of the day, we liked so many things about him; we believed we could work around the size if we had to. I remember Claude's confidence when we interviewed him at the combine. We ended up being very comfortable with him."

When selection No. 21, which belonged to the Rangers, came up, GM Glen Sather walked to the Philadelphia table and offered to flip picks so that Clarke could take Bobby Sanguinetti of Lumberton, NJ, a defenseman for the Owen Sound (Ontario) Attack.

Holmgren remembers suspecting New York might have been trying to get an extra pick before taking Giroux. Regardless, the Flyers had no interest in selecting Sanguinetti in that spot. "I told Glen, 'You take Sanguinetti if you want him,'" recalls Clarke. "So he did."

Recalls Holmgren, "It was made a big deal out of that that day and has been ever since that we wanted Sanguinetti and it's just not true. We liked him, but not at 22 in the first round."

The Flyer brain trust then gave their pick to the messenger and walked to the stage.

"I remember I said to Clarkie, probably four times, 'From Gatineau of the Quebec Major Junior Hockey League, Claude Giroux,'" recalls Holmgren. "And once you are up there, it's on the screen in front of you. If you forget, just look down."

Clarke not only forgot Giroux's name, he failed to remember to look down.

"Philadelphia selects from Gatineau of the Quebec League…" the GM said, before freezing. "I forget," he said as he turned to Holmgren and asked, "Who did we take?"

"Claude Giroux," Clarke finally said with a self-deprecating chuckle.

"Right up there on the board in front of me and I didn't look," Clarke laughs today. "I just went blank."

In the stands, Giroux had mentally checked out too.

From his interviews at the combine and with pre-draft speculation, Giroux believed his best chance to be selected in the first round—the only round of the initial day—was by either Montreal (which took defenseman David Fischer at 19) or the Rangers. "I remember looking at my dad and saying, 'I don't think I'm going to be drafted today.

"The Flyers were next and I'm thinking they are never going to draft me because I'm way too small. Then Clarkie said my team and stopped.

"I thought he was going to change his mind."

The happy prospect didn't stand on ceremony as he came up to put on the winged P and shake hands. "I think it was a plus, actually," Giroux reflects on Clarke's brain lock. "A lot of people were talking about it so I was more in the news than I should have been, taken that late.

"I still give it to Clarkie about that once in a while."

Before addressing the media, the GM had been told that what's-his-name could play.

"A smallish junior, but he has tremendous hockey sense, skill and intelligence," Clarke told reporters. "He's very competitive."

That was the skinny on one of the skinniest kids the big, tough, Philadelphia Flyers ever had selected. A classic late bloomer, unselected in the midget draft, Giroux had made Gatineau on a tryout at the beginning of his first NHL Draft-eligibile season and, after a modest start, put up 39 goals and 64 assists.

"I was never on the (draft) radar until the end of that year," he recalls. "Then I saw that maybe I was going to get drafted in the first round, or at start of the second, and I was like, 'Whoa!'

"I looked up who was playing in the NHL after they got drafted in the second round and there were plenty of guys. So I was like, 'I have a chance!' I got a boost from that and became more motivated.

"At the (Scouting) Combine, I think I had 22 teams talk to me. My English wasn't that good then and I was really nervous. You just want to look like you're a competitor.

"After the Flyers took me, (director of scouting) Chris Pryor asked, 'Do you remember our interview?' I said, 'I must have thought you didn't like me because I don't.'"

In his best English, Giroux, called a "new age player" by Holmgren to the media, told reporters, "I work hard, have a lot of heart, like to have the puck on my stick and make great passes to my teammates."

The next day, Philadelphia selected Austrian right wing Andreas Nodl 39th and American defenseman Michael Ratchuk 42nd,the latter chosen with a pick obtained from Los Angeles for allowing Dean Lombardi—who had scouted for the Flyers for two years following his dismissal as Sharks general manager—out of his contract to become GM of the Kings.

Lombardi had taken Ron Hextall—Philadelphia's director of player personnel for four seasons—with him to become assistant GM in Los Angeles, a step towards Hextall's ambition to run a team one day.

"It still was the hardest decision I ever made in my life," recalls Hextall. "You have to think about (uprooting) your kids, and then there's this organization and my loyalties.

"Working for the Flyers was hard to give up. In the end, I felt like I had to get going if I wanted to be a general manager. I was the third guy here behind Clarkie and Homer and I felt like it was going to be that way for quite some time."

Hextall was replaced by Dave Brown. Initially furious with Clarke at being transferred from assistant coach to scout in 1997, Brown had developed into a trusted evaluator.

There were changes near the top of the organization as well. President Ron Ryan, 67, announced his retirement after 18 years as the business head of the operation. "It's something that was time for me to do," said Ryan, who was moving to Palm City, FL to spend more time with a 16-year-old daughter who was having personal issues.

Peter Luukko, 46, the president and chief operating officer of Comcast-Spectacor, was absorbing Ryan's duties with the hockey team.

Luukko, who got his start in arena management as the marketing director for the New Haven Coliseum and became assistant director of the Providence Civic Center, had been running the Los Angeles Coliseum and Sports Arena when they came under contract with Spectacor Management Group, at the time partially owned by Snider.

Luukko was appointed president of the Spectrum in 1993. It was at his suggestion that Snider, who by then had sold his share in SMG, got back into the arena-management business. With the Flyers scheduled to leave the Spectrum in 1996, Luukko also had presented to the Chairman the idea of buying an American Hockey League franchise to play in the building.

From there, Ryan had shepherded the birth of the Phantoms. "It's one of the proudest things for me on my watch," he recalls. "It worked out great in (player) development, in terms of growing hockey interest in the community, and for the Spectrum. At the beginning, we were putting 15,000 people in that place regularly."

Behind the bench, assistant coach Wayne Fleming accepted a similar position with Calgary to be closer to his family. To replace Fleming, Clarke promoted John Stevens, who had been head coach of the Phantoms for six seasons. "I think there always was a feeling John was going to be head coach of the Flyers one day," recalls Clarke, who retained Terry Murray as the other assistant under head coach Ken Hitchcock. Craig Berube, who had been a Phantom assistant under Stevens for three seasons, was promoted to head coach of the AHL team.

Jim (Turk) Evers, an equipment manager for 23 years, retired and was replaced by Derek Settlemyre, who was promoted from the Phantoms.

Chris Therien's second stint with Philadelphia, which brought his total years of service on the defense to 11 seasons, ended.

"My sister Sarah, my only sibling, died a sudden cardiac death that June," Therien recalls. "I was in a deep and private personal place.

"Lou Lamoriello, who had coached me at Providence, really wanted to sign me (for the Devils), but he was trying to shift some money around and that fell through the cracks. Pat (agent Morris) had gotten me two tryout opportunities; one, I remember, was with Columbus.

"The way I was feeling mentally, I wondered about my chances and decided not to go, but as it turned out, I probably would have made their team, so I kick myself for that one a little bit. I should have sucked it up and been a little bit more of a man about it, but I was dealing with a personal thing."

As it was, 11 years in the NHL was an impressive career for a sixth-round draft choice. Therien, best remembered for his successful matchups against Jaromir Jagr, was an effective, puck-moving, first-pair partner for Eric Desjardins on a Stanley Cup finalist, plus two more semifinalists. Bundy—nicknamed after Al, the father on the television comedy "Married With Children"—played more games on the Flyer defense than anyone in the team's history and, before his trade to Dallas in 2004, had the longest tenure of any active professional Philadelphia athlete.

"I take a lot of pride in my career; I think the biggest thing is having played that long in a city where the fans can be so proud and at the same time so loud," Therien recalls. "It's hard enough to play in a lot of cities, but when you hang around Philadelphia for a long time, it leaves a mark of endurance.

"I was surrounded by a lot of great players. I appreciate more than anything in my career the commitment from an organization that tried every single year to give us, and the city, a chance to win a Cup. You can't ask for anything more than that."

Therien was not the first—or last—big man to frustrate fans with his gentle nature. But his 10-year tenure on Flyer broadcasts—studio commentator, radio color and, currently, rinkside reporter—is an extension of the popularity he enjoyed in the locker room.

"Chris was one of my favorite teammates ever," recalls Jeremy Roenick. "Lots of fun to be around, made everyone laugh.

"He didn't mind being the whipping boy, took whatever got dished out, and gave it right back. And he could play."

So could Donald Brashear, probably the most feared Flyer fighter ever. But his ice time had dwindled in 2005-06 to 8:36 per game in the final year of his contract, so he was not offered another. After three full seasons and 50 games of a fourth, the team was saying goodbye to a strong cornerman, in addition to a pugilistic presence.

"There had been an offer (from Philadelphia) early in my last year, a low one, and then not another as my ice time went down," recalls Brashear, who lives in Quebec City, where his company, Brash87, markets itself as providing affordable, quality, hockey sticks. "I thought I would be moving on, but still, it was disappointing.

"The day I got traded to Philadelphia was the happiest one of my life. It came out of nowhere and they had been one of the teams that, growing up, I wanted to play for.

"I wanted to be a tough guy, a protector, and play physically. Every once in a while they are going to send you out to drop the mitts. But fighting had become entertainment and, too often, you had to do it for no good reason.

"I was one of the best scorers on my team as a young kid. It was important for me to show that I could play with good players and put the puck in the net. I was given that chance with the Flyers. My best year in hockey was 2002-03 when I had 25 points playing on a regular line with Keith Primeau."

With Brashear's $1.748 million salary off the books, and the cap increasing from $39 million to $44 million, the Flyers had the potential to spend as much as $6 million during the summer of 2006 on unrestricted free agents.

"I have no intention of spending $6 million on one player," Clarke said of an unrestricted group headlined by defenseman Zdeno Chara (signed by Boston) and winger Mike Grier (by San Jose). "There are lots of affordable guys out there.

"Part of our handicap is we don't know what it will cost to re-sign (restricted free agents) Gagne and (Joni) Pitkanen (plus Antero Niittymaki and R.J. Umberger), so we have to guess."

Clarke didn't have to worry about fitting in Kim Johnsson. After missing the final 31 games of his fourth Philadelphia season with post-concussion symptoms, the defenseman signed on July 1 with Minnesota for $19 million over four years.

"(Agent Rick) Curran asked for $3 million from us," recalls Clarke. "If his concussion was legitimate, you can't pay him $3 million. But Minnesota did and more.

"Something fishy was going on. He wasn't going for treatment, doing anything, just stayed home and didn't play. In my opinion, he basically quit. I think he had a $4-5 million offer from Minnesota during the Olympics and didn't want to come back and get hurt."

Curran vehemently insists Minnesota made its offer after contracts expired at the end of June. "It was the biggest surprise when I got a call from Minnesota on July 1, telling me what they were prepared to pay Kim," recalls the agent. "I had no (prior) relationship with them, had never asked what they would offer, so Bob is wrong.

"I have been doing this 40 years and would never do that to anyone, and especially not to Bob. When I was negotiating with him, it was at a figure I thought would be the market for Kim. When [GM Doug Risebrough] called, I immediately told Kim he was not going to get a better offer."

Clarke could not have done much better in his 2001 trade of an oft-concussed Eric Lindros than acquiring Johnsson as the centerpiece of the Ranger package. Acquired along with Jan Hlavac (who was moved after 31 games for Brashear) and Pavel Brendl, Johnsson added puck-moving skill, defensive efficiency and, by 2004, had supplanted Desjardins as the best Flyer defenseman.

As the Flyers dethroned the Devils in the first round that spring, Johnsson starred, only to suffer a broken hand in the clinching Game Five. He returned during the Toronto series at reduced efficiency, but remained in the lineup until Philadelphia was eliminated in Game Seven of the conference final.

Keith Primeau announced his retirement just before the start of training camp.

In Johnsson's place, Clarke signed 30-year-old free-agent defenseman Nolan Baumgartner, a Washington 1994 first-rounder who had been a career minor league call-up until emerging as Vancouver's top scoring defenseman the previous season. Baumgartner received a two-year, $4.8 million deal.

"I didn't think he would be better than a fifth or sixth, but I thought he would be a decent player," recalls Clarke, who picked up another defenseman, Lars Jonsson, Boston's unsigned seventh-overall pick in the 2000 draft. At age 25, the Swede had decided to give the NHL a shot.

With Peter Forsberg, who had undergone surgery on his right heel on May 15, expecting to need until December to have the other foot similarly fixed, plus lingering uncertainty over the return of the concussed Primeau, Clarke needed to add depth at center.

He signed Randy Robitaille, an 11-year veteran of seven teams who had scored 40 points in 67 games with Minnesota the previous season, to a one-year deal. "A real good skater who plays both ends of the rink; we believe he will give us more offense," said the GM, who also reached an agreement with Mark Cullen, who had been played 29 games with the Blackhawks after being signed as a free agent out of Colorado College. "Mark is a smart, skilled, and on the cusp of becoming a real solid player under the new rules," said Holmgren.

The off-season priority—speed—also was reinforced with the signing of 34-year-old winger Geoff Sanderson. Coming off 25 goals in 2005-06 with Phoenix, he took a two-year, $3 million contract.

But the most exciting summer "acquisition" became Forsberg's sudden availability. According to Dr. Robert Anderson, who had performed the operation on the star's right foot, the anticipated surgery on the left one would not be necessary.

"The ligaments in the left ankle are not nearly as bad as the ones on the right," said Flyer head athletic trainer Jim McCrossin. "Dr. Anderson believes we are going to be able to strengthen his left ankle to the point where he can play."

Said Forsberg, "If we could avoid it, that's what I wanted and what the team wanted. If I have any problems with it, maybe we can do [the second procedure] at the end of the season."

One major Flyer anxiety appeared eased, leaving unresolved the status of the concussed Primeau, who had lasted nine games of the 2005-06 season.

He recalls, "I had started skating in the spring and (*Philadelphia Inquirer* beat reporter) Tim Panaccio is writing, 'Primeau's coming back.' I was just trying to get myself back eventually but thought, with the team struggling, maybe I could help get some guys going.

"I was giving it to Joni (Pitkanen) to the point that one day he skated by Sami Kapanen and said, 'I hate that [bleeping] guy,' because I was so relentless on him. But all the speculation (about a return) was becoming a distraction, so I pulled myself off, just kept riding the bike."

Nasal surgery in May had left Primeau preliminarily encouraged, but lingering symptoms caused him to scrap his plans to spend a pre-training camp month in Finland practicing with Kapanen.

"The (departure) date was closing in far too quickly," Primeau said after conferring with Flyer physician Dr. Gary Dorshimer. "I continue to believe I'm on the last stretch of my concussion symptoms, but just don't know when the remainder are going to disappear."

The captain kept working out through the summer, even organizing the pre-camp skating sessions at the Skate Zone for Flyers and ex-Flyers who still lived in the area.

"I was maybe 85 percent and fooling myself when one day in (late) August, I went into Jimmy McCrossin's office," recalls Primeau. "(Defenseman) Freddy Meyer was walking out.

"I told Jimmy, 'I feel good. I'll be ready for camp in September.'"

McCrossin told Primeau that he would have to wear a white jersey with a red cross on it to warn players not to hit him.

"Then he looked at me and said, 'Keith, we applaud your effort and courage, but as a medical professional, I could never give you my clearance to play again,'" recalls Primeau.

"Later, Jimmy told me that Freddy had just told him my reaction times were so bad that 'he's going to hurt himself out there.'

"It was the first time I had been in touch with reality in the last few months."

Recalls McCrossin: "Freddy had reiterated what we already knew from talking to doctors and Bob Clarke—Keith wasn't getting better."

Primeau, nevertheless, thought he had nothing to lose by giving himself at least until camp, and received no pressure from Clarke to decide earlier. "Whatever time he needs, he gets," said the GM. "Having given what he did to this team, we feel we owe it to him."

"Having waited this long, we certainly can for another month, but we're not very optimistic right now."

Clarke could clear $3.16 million in cap room at any time by putting Primeau on injured reserve. But finding a replacement for a player of such importance would have been a reach at any point. The GM felt Forsberg and second-year centers Carter and Richards, both first-round picks, still made the Flyers strong up the middle. So on August 3, Clarke traded restricted free agent Michal Handzus to Chicago for 27-year old left wing Kyle Calder, who had played six seasons for the Blackhawks and scored 26 goals the previous year.

"We ended up using Michal a lot on left wing when he is really a center and plays his best there," said Clarke in a statement. "Calder is a player we have coveted for a long time. He can score, kill penalties, and play on any of our top three lines."

Calder came with the recommendation of Holmgren and former director of player personnel Ron Hextall, who had watched the winger perform well on a line with Carter and Richards for Canada at the 2006 World Championships in Latvia.

Calder, who would be making $2.95 million, called the Flyers "one of the teams I wanted to come to. The dream is finally here."

Handzus could hardly say the same about the Blackhawks, who had made the playoffs once in the previous eight seasons. But he wasn't surprised to be moving on.

"I knew I might be gone," he recalls. "But it was tough to leave.

"I loved Philly, loved the players, loved the fans, and liked Hitch, even if a lot of guys didn't. I grew up where coaches yelled all the time so I never thought he was bad, and I would listen anyway because he knew what he was talking about.

"I think the Flyers were one of the better organizations I ever experienced and I played my best hockey there. To be on a team that wanted to win every year was like a dream for a player."

Recalls Clarke: "We offered Michal a tryout, but he wanted a contract. I didn't think we had a fit, so I thought I was doing him a favor."

Handzus, who scored 146 points in 237 gritty games in Philadelphia and added 18 in 31 playoff games, had been the kind of Flyer for which the organization never minded doing a good turn. "Low maintenance," recalls Hitchcock. "I loved coaching him."

Remembers Jeremy Roenick, "I played with Michal in Phoenix and Philly and loved him. He was strong on his skates, made good plays, and was responsible defensively, plus he had a great little sense of humor.

"I always was amazed at how he was so quiet but had an edge to him on the ice. He would do anything to win games."

Handzus, however, wasn't the toughest goodbye in the summer of 2006. Desjardins, at age 37, retired.

"The new rules had really sped up the game," he recalls. "I felt a step behind the whole year.

"It felt great to play in the playoffs again (he been injured midway through the first round of 2003 and had missed all of the 2004 postseason), but it was upsetting to get beat (by Buffalo) like that. The last four or five years I had gone under the knife practically every year; I was having a lot of chronic back pain, too.

"I didn't know what to do (about continuing), but the Flyers kind of made the decision for me when they didn't offer anything at first."

Clarke recalls Desjardins asking for time to think. As he did, Detroit, Edmonton and Montreal—the city where Desjardins grew up and won a Stanley Cup—all inquired about his interest in continuing. He didn't seriously consider any of them.

"I was a Flyer for 11 seasons and am still a Flyer today," says Desjardins. "I didn't want to play for another team.

"Maybe if the Flyers would have offered me something at the end of the year, I would have thought about changing my mind and playing another season. When [Clarke] called, it came too late. I wasn't going back. I'm happy with the way it played out, though, don't regret anything. It was the right decision."

Perhaps the best one Clarke ever made as general manager came after he had been told in 1995 by Montreal GM Serge Savard that Mathieu Schneider was not available for trade, but that Desjardins was. Acquired with John LeClair in the deal that sent Mark Recchi to the Canadiens, Desjardins won seven Barry Ashbee Trophies in anchoring the Philadelphia defense for 11 seasons and played on both the Stanley Cup finalist and semifinalist teams. The Flyers will forever wonder what might have been in 2004, had Desjardins not been lost for the entire Philadelphia run to Game Seven of the semifinal because of a broken arm.

"Smart player, so dedicated; I think we could have gotten another year out of him," recalls Clarke. After a summer of stalled negotiations with Gagne, Clarke flew to Montreal three days before training camp. In a three-hour session with the star winger and his agent Bob Sauve, a five-year, $26.25 million contract was negotiated.

"The same agent had gotten (Calgary's Alex) Tanguay something like $5.12 million per year, more than he was worth, and Simon was the better player," recalls Clarke. "I said we shouldn't be held to [more than] what Calgary gave Tanguay.

"We ended up giving Simon the same, and that was a fair contract for us."

Gagne agreed. "I always wanted to get this done," he said. "I love the place and the fans."

Holmgren thought Ryan Kesler, the Canuck first-round pick in 2003, might like it too. The assistant GM urged his boss to extend a one-year, $1.9 million offer sheet to the center, who was a restricted free agent.

"Hexy (before leaving for L.A.) and I were pounding on Clarkie trying to get him to do that," recalls Holmgren. "He liked the idea but was hesitant. We talked him into it.

"We should have done a three or four-year deal. It was too easy for Vancouver to match (which it did, rather than take a second-round pick)."

Recalls Clarke, "Paul, who (as Team USA assistant coach) had Kesler at the World Championships, was right; Kesler was young and strong and would have been a really good signing."

For a second consecutive summer, Flyer fans' heads were spinning from all the player changes, both real and attempted, but Primeau's dizziness after exercise was unaltered. On September 14, the day before the opening of camp, he announced his retirement at age 34, ending a 15-year NHL career.

"I didn't want to become a distraction again," Primeau told the media. "I'm sorry I couldn't overcome this injury and dragged this out; I did it all with the best of intentions.

"This decision will allow me to live a normal life and hopefully, with time, few reminders of my injuries."

The permanent absence of Hitchcock's locker-room conscience, the hero of the 2004 semifinal run, created a leadership void. Opportunity knocked for players to step up, but despite the immediate naming of Forsberg as the new captain, camp opened with little sense of closure and rebirth.

Hitchcock, who was headed into the final season of his contract, received a two-year extension at the same $1.12 million he had been paid in 2005-06. He took it as a vote of confidence. "It took 30 seconds," reported the coach. "Clarkie and I are good friends; I am tied to him.

"When you make the decision to play younger players (seven rookies received at least 25 games in 2005-06), you want to be around when they mature."

But the coach was less excited about the veterans Clarke had obtained that summer.

"I knew a week into camp we were in trouble," Hitchcock recalls. "I remember telling Clarkie, 'these guys we brought in aren't Flyers.'

"They were not up to the standard of play we'd grown accustomed to here. We had needed to upgrade and had downgraded. This wasn't a very competitive team."

Clarke didn't become defensive, one more sign to him that he had become uncompetitive, like too many of his acquisitions.

"That summer, I did things because I knew how to do them," he recalls. "There wasn't a passion to do them. There's a difference.

"That was a summer of almost indifference by me, even though I showed up.

"There was no enthusiasm at that training camp; guys were just going through the motions. That was the way I felt about myself, too. I should have been raising the roof."

Actually, Clarke did, suggesting that some defensemen should feel "lucky" that Jonsson, the only impressive newcomer during a 1-6-1 preseason, wouldn't be available by opening night because of a right ankle sprain.

"He said 'somebody was lucky,' not that Jones was lucky," huffed defenseman Randy Jones, who had played 28 games with Philadelphia the previous season. "He could have meant me or somebody else.

"Every time on the ice, I have given all I have."

Another of the suspects, Baumgartner, took the criticism better. "I totally agree with [Clarke]," he said. "As a hockey player you don't mind being called out every once in a while."

Clarke not only called out, he called up Jay Grossman, the agent for Brian Leetch, to see if the Ranger great who had played the previous season with Boston, had any interest in continuing. Leetch, who had already declined a return to the Rangers, said he was done at age 37. Mike Rathje, just 32, and headed into the second season of four-year deal with the Flyers, was not nearly as prepared to walk away, but the failure of a cortisone injection to relieve the pain down into his legs put his career in jeopardy.

Minus Cullen, whom Clarke stunningly waived before opening night, Hitchcock took the team to the Naval Academy for bonding, even though he suspected this boat wasn't going to float. Having previously indicated that Philadelphia was not going to carry an enforcer, the team had lost enough board battles during the preseason to warrant Hitchcock's request to keep Riley Cote, who had 259 penalty minutes and just three goals the previous season for the Phantoms.

Forward Matt Ellison, farmed to the Phantoms just five games after his acquisition for Patrick Sharp the previous December, had not come close to earning a job with the Flyers and was headed back to the AHL, all but closing the book on an NHL career. As Sharp would blossom into a three-time 30-goal-plus winger on three Chicago Stanley Cup teams, his trade would prove to be probably the worst waste of a good prospect in Flyer history.

"Obviously, I blew the deal," Clarke recalls. "But Hitch wouldn't play Sharp."

More ice time in Sharp's two partial seasons with Philadelphia might have convinced the GM to hang onto a third-round draft choice of some promise. But Sharp wasn't as advanced as Richards and Carter, and Hitchcock, hired to win, wasn't as prepared to give the kid time to grow.

"Patrick was afraid to make a play," recalls Gagne. "He'd turn the puck over at the blueline and end up sitting on the bench, just like it had been with Justin Williams."

No hard feelings, insists Sharp today. "The team was competing for first place in the conference," he recalls. "It was a numbers game; the Flyers were stacked up the middle.

"I didn't want to leave. Even though I saw it coming, it still was a shock. But it turned out to be the best thing that could have happened. I went to a team where I was able to fail for a couple years and make a lot of mistakes.

"It's untrue that I had a bad relationship with Hitch. I played for him in the World Championships, won a gold medal with him in the Olympics, and have had good conversations with him. I credit Hitch and John Stevens with helping me become an American Hockey League all-star and an everyday NHL player."

Petr Nedved had been one for 16 seasons, scoring 99 points in one of them. Hitchcock was trying to squeeze one more year from the 35-year-old by making him a defensive center to replace Primeau. "I've never really played this kind of role before," said Nedved. "It's a challenge."

Challenged Clarke: "Is he going to make the commitment with his teammates? That's always been one of the questions Petr has faced. Are you going to be part of the team?"

After having commuted from Manhattan following his trade from Phoenix the previous January, Nedved had moved to South Jersey following the end of his marriage to supermodel Veronica Verekova.

Coming out of camp, the players were so lacking in unity that Hitchcock tried to buy them time, telling the media the team would require at least 10 games to get its act together. Nothing that happened in the season opener at Pittsburgh convinced anybody otherwise. The Flyers lost 4-0 for more reasons than failing to capitalize on 40 shots and nine powerplays against goalie Marc-Andre Fleury. The Penguins jumped up 3-0 by scoring too easily off transitions and goalie Robert Esche was not sharp.

Philadelphia was much better in its home opener against the Rangers. Nevertheless, a 4-3 third-period lead disappeared when Adam Hall shot the tying goal in off Robitaille's skate. Forsberg, citing a lack of confidence in himself and his sticks, begged out of the shootout until five other Flyers had taken their turns. Marcel Hossa won the game, 5-4, for New York, by beating Niittymaki through the five hole on the 26th shot.

"I thought there were better shooters out there and I've been struggling scoring," said Forsberg, who added, "I got new sticks today and I was not really comfortable with them."

Hitchcock shrugged. "It's not that big a deal," the coach insisted. "Look, when he doesn't want to be the shooter, he doesn't want to be the shooter."

Three nights later, at least one of those sticks seemed to work fine as Forsberg beat Henrik Lundqvist three minutes into the game, then added two assists in a 4-2 victory at Madison Square Garden. The Flyers had played a complete game. But the relief didn't last even 24 hours.

The following night at the Wachovia Center, Montreal's Michael Ryder scored 37 seconds into the game, the Philadelphia powerplay went 0-for-8, and the team was listless through most of a 3-1 loss.

Two days later, on Friday, October 13, Clarke phoned Luukko.

"He said, 'I need to come over and see you,'" recalls the COO. "I didn't think much of it, there was all kinds of stuff we used to talk about.

"He walked in and, out of the blue, said, 'With the changes in the game and everything, I think it's time for me to resign.'

"It really caught me off-guard. I said, 'Are you sure this is really what you want to do? Why don't you think about it and maybe we'll talk tomorrow?'

"He said, 'No, I mean it. I've thought it through.'

"We sat in my office for three hours, talking about hockey and our kids, making small talk for a while, and then I'd ask him again. I kept saying, 'Listen Bob, I'm with you no matter [what you decide.]' If he had changed his mind overnight, that would have been great as far as I was concerned. I like Bob a lot and certainly enjoyed working with him.

"He was very clear—that's what he wanted to do. Feeling the way he did about the game, he wasn't up for the job anymore.

"I didn't think for a second he was resigning because he was afraid of getting fired. That's just not him.

"When he left, I called Ed and said, 'Bob wants to resign. I think we should meet.' Then Ed had the same thing with Bob, asking him, like I did, whether he was certain."

Clarke remembers his reasons being more varied than just his frustration with the sport and the way it was being administered. "It was an accumulation of things, I guess, but that was part of it," he recalls.

"I think the league has done an incredible job with the financial end of the game. Everybody—managers, coaches, scouts, and players—makes tons of money and has good pensions.

"But the actual on-ice product, I didn't like the way it was going. Decisions were being made not by people managing in hockey, but by the front office of the NHL. When Brian Burke worked for (NHL Commissioner Gary) Bettman, Burkie [established that] you can't protect yourself anymore; you have to take the hit. Well, that's high school hockey, not NHL hockey.

"You can hit me, but I have a right to protect myself, too. He took that away and that's when the hitting started getting out of hand. More hits, harder hits, after there hadn't been any concussions to speak of in our day.

"When Bettman put in the two referees, it was because the league didn't want the players protecting themselves, looking out for each other. That became strictly the league's job.

"And then, of course, Bettman fell in love with taking the red line out and all these new rules, which led to more, and harder, hitting than ever. Now that concussions and injuries are rampant, they're trying to solve the problem by sending players to the rubber room for 15 minutes if they get hit in the head. But [the league] caused it all."

Clarke also believes that the lack of challenge he was feeling about his GM duties had something to do with the absence of any place left for him to rise in the organization.

"I talked to Mr. Snider about this," Clarke recalls. "When he brought me back from Florida (in 1994), he said, 'You can be president.'

"I said, 'No, I'll just be the GM.' He said 'No, you can be president so when you're tired of being GM, there will be a job for you.'

"In 2003, Mr. Snider called me in and said, 'We're going to name Ron Ryan the president. Do you have any problem with that?' I said, 'No, I think it's a great idea. He should be the president and make more money. He's doing all the work and, besides, Ron and I had talked and he was going to retire in two or three years anyway.'

"So when Ron retired and they made Peter president, I kind of felt like I was moving backwards in the organization. That wasn't an exact reason for me. But when I had enough of being the manager, there was no place else to go in the organization; I was pretty much done.

"I liked Peter. He was easy to get along with. When he became the president, I never felt like there suddenly was another layer between Mr. Snider and me. It was nothing like that at all. It was just that after [33] years here, I wasn't going anywhere, was just going to manage until it was done, and then I would be gone. And that's what happened. I wasn't power hungry or anything like that. I just made the decision quicker than I thought I would have because I didn't have the enthusiasm I needed to keep going.

"The game was being run out of the offices in New York. Any say we had (in the game) pretty much had been taken away. There was hardly reason for the managers to get together anymore and I missed that. At one time, general managers were pretty [tight], but by the end, there were so many new ones, I had lost that sense of closeness. There was a time when you would talk to every GM within two to three weeks, but with 30 teams you might not talk to some of them all year. And I only had a few friends there anymore anyway.

"When I started (as GM in 1984), July was always taken off. When it ended for me, you didn't get one day away. Time in the car used to be time away but, with cell phones, everybody went everywhere with his phone. I didn't want that anymore every day.

"I'm quite sure Mr. Snider knew enough about me that when I went to see him (after meeting with Luukko], he knew I was done. He accepted that I had lost interest. You don't make a decision like that out of thin air. But he told me to take a week anyway.

"My recollection is he then told me that once I was totally sure, to get away for a month and then, if I wanted to do anything, I could still be part of the team. But I didn't want to have any responsibility at that point.

Paul Holmgren was promoted to general manager after Bob Clarke resigned. Coach Ken Hitchcock would be replaced by John Stevens soon after.

"It's always easier after you make the decision. But it wasn't easy. I don't think relief is the right word; it was almost like being a little numb inside. Whatever emotions you have, you are restricting them. It always takes a while to sink in."

Holmgren flew home from a scouting trip after getting the stunning news in a call from Luukko. Clarke reiterated his reasons to his assistant GM and close friend of 31 years.

"With what I know now, I can look back and see there were signs Bob was. . .I don't know the right word to use. . .getting burned out," recalls Holmgren. "But I didn't think his work habits were slipping.

"He would leave his office early in the afternoon a lot, but he was always reachable, always answered his phone, got his messages."

"I had known his enthusiasm for the game was waning. Clarkie was more of a purist about hockey in the way we grew up with it. He's all about toughing it out, finding a way, playing gritty, and getting to the dirty areas to score. In the regular season, you don't see that any more.

"The league has the referees call all these useless penalties. The poor defensemen aren't allowed to play defense. You can't touch anyone in front of the net, and you can't hold up their forechecker so you can break out of the zone. There are a lot of smart coaches in this league. They've figured how to stop you from scoring."

Essentially, the time Clarke had been asked to take was time for Luukko and Snider to decide whether to take the outgoing GM's recommendation and give the position to Holmgren.

That job looked bigger by the game.

Mike Knuble's two goals had the Flyers up 2-1 deep into the second period at New Jersey, but Jamie Langenbrunner and Brian Gionta deflected in Brian Rafalski drives. Philadelphia was unable to get off a shot in the first 15 minutes of the third period, suffering a 3-2 loss that dropped the team's record to 1-4-1.

"I remember talking with Hitch after that game," recalls Gagne. "He said, 'Gags, tell the guys, 'Don't quit, we're right there. We just need to clean up a few things that we can fix. We'll be fine.'"

Esche, starting for the first time since opening night, held his team in the game during a scoreless first period at Buffalo. But 37 seconds into the second session, Thomas Vanek put in his own rebound, Pitkanen and Richards took back-to-back penalties, and the Sabres cashed in both the five-on-three and five-on-four. After Jaroslav Spacek shot a one-timer past Esche to make the score 4-0, the Flyers stopped competing.

"I figured Hitch has got to pull me at some point," recalls Esche. "But he kept me in and at the end of the night, it's 9-1. That was really embarrassing."

The goalie tossed equipment in a rage that followed perhaps the most mortifying loss suffered by the franchise since its earliest years.

"It was the accumulation of everything I had seen since Day One of training camp," recalls Hitchcock. "We looked like we didn't believe in ourselves; you could see that with the people we brought in."

Actually, the players the team brought back didn't have much more confidence than the ones they had brought in. "Typical Philadelphia Flyers hockey game right there," said Richards. "We got behind the eight-ball, had a little bit of pressure on us, and folded."

Forsberg, rarely a locker-room orator, spoke following the game. "I have never lost by that much in my entire career," he relayed to reporters. "I told them I don't want that to happen again.

"This wears on you. It's not fun. Esche has not played for four games and gets thrown in and hung out to dry. We didn't stand up; we let them keep on doing it to us.

"You can't do too much because that is bad sportsmanship. But we should have taken some runs."

Snider said some unsportsmanlike things during an animated phone call to Hitchcock. "It wasn't that unusual for us to talk," recalls the coach. "He was embarrassed, but so was I."

The coach was also fearful of losing his job. To Ed Moran, *The Philadelphia Daily News* beat reporter, Hitchcock privately expressed concern that he wasn't going to last 10 games. And that was without knowing Clarke had resigned, making the coach's tenure that much more precarious.

The day after the Buffalo debacle, Clarke pointedly shook up the roster while dropping no hints of his imminent departure.

He waived Nedved, who was minus-7 in six games, Niko Dimitrakos, and Baumgartner, who had been Philadelphia's biggest off-season acquisition. Called up were Stefan Ruzicka, the Phantom leading scorer in the early going, defenseman Alexandre Picard, and left wing Ben Eager.

"The way these (waived) players were playing, they forced us to choose between sitting and waiting for them to come around or attacking the problem," Clarke told reporters. "A couple of these [call-ups] had very good training camps.

"The reality is that the top players are all still here. We have six or seven guys who scored 20-plus goals and we expect them to play better. But it's time to put the young kids in and bring the energy level up.

"Buffalo is the best team in the league right now. How come instead of it bringing out our best, it brought out our worst? You're supposed to want to play the best team, and we looked like we didn't."

Two nights later in Tampa, Rathje played for the first time since the season opener but the Flyers fell behind 2-0, and continued to look spiritless in a 4-1 loss, the club's ninth straight to the Lightning.

At least Forsberg's wrist, which became jammed as he braced himself against the wall on a first-period check by Tampa Bay's Paul Ranger, was not broken. But Forsberg couldn't play the following night against the Panthers, when a 2-1 lead created by Gagne's second-period powerplay goal was answered within 34 seconds, again deflating the confidence of Hitchcock's team in a 3-2 defeat.

Philadelphia had been bad around the opposition goal and worse around its own, coverage breakdowns killing the team even though the energy had improved since the Sabre rout.

"Other than the Buffalo game, we've been getting pretty much everything from everybody," insisted Hitchcock after the loss in Florida. "Play as hard as we did and [lose], that hurts a lot, especially back-to-back."

Clarke had called the coaches together on the Florida trip to announce his resignation. Hitchcock knew the ice had gotten too thin to support him, but was unsure when he would crash through.

The firing was "in the works," Holmgren recalls, before he was officially appointed interim GM. But he agreed Hitchcock should be replaced.

"Ken was committed to some of our young guys more than others," recalls Holmgren. "I remember talking to some of the players about Hitch to get their feeling for him, and they were getting burned out.

"His style is very grating. I think there was tension from the losing, too; it wasn't just because of Hitch. But all that barking wears on you.

"I like Hitch for the most part. When Clarkie wanted him (in 2002), he sent me (and Ron Hextall) over to Sweden; I was the one who convinced Ken to come here. I think he's a great coach, but he's got a pretty short shelf life because he's maybe a little too relentless with the psychological stuff. If you have a team that's right there, and you just need that extra push, Hitch is a good choice."

Clarke, who had not confided his potential resignation to Hextall before he left for Los Angeles—"What if he stayed hoping to move up and I changed my mind?" Clarke asks—also didn't consider Hitchcock's fate when making the decision to step down.

"It was selfish on my part to decide I had enough," recalls Clarke. "I didn't think I'd be costing Hitchcock his job, so I guess I only thought about myself.

"If I had stayed, I wouldn't have fired him, but I wasn't going to stay for that reason. I don't think Mr. Snider would have put pressure on me (to make a change). But after two or three weeks, something would have happened. You couldn't continue the way we were.

"It was a fractured team, no spirit, no personality. The players had to really work to get some emotion into their game and you can't win that way."

There were no serious discussions about replacing Hitchcock with anyone besides John Stevens, who, after six years coaching the Phantoms, had been promoted to Flyer assistant at the beginning of the season.

"Johnny was smart, hard-working, well-organized and competitive," recalls Holmgren. "He had a good system and presence about himself with his players.

"He'd won a Calder Cup with the Phantoms with [11] members of our [2006-07] team, so there was a built-in trust factor. To me, it was a no-brainer to hire John."

With a five-day break between the game in Sunrise and the next one at home against Atlanta, it also seemed logical to Holmgren, Snider and Luukko to make the change immediately so that Stevens would have four full practice days before his debut.

When Holmgren called Stevens on Saturday and asked to meet late that night at a Blackwood, NJ, diner, the assistant suspected it had something to do with a coaching shakeup.

Holmgren told Stevens the head position was his and that the task was to get several floundering young Flyers to play for him as they had with the Phantoms.

"He thought with a voice they respected and had won with before, it would kind of free them up so they could just go play, as opposed to maybe squeezing the sticks too hard," recalls Stevens.

"For me, it was a very difficult meeting with Homer. I was excited for the opportunity, but I idolized Clarkie and felt just as responsible as Hitch for the way the team was playing.

"Usually you go through camp building momentum. You see your team taking shape. But this one just had no identity. We weren't a great defensive team, we weren't a smash-mouth team, weren't a speed and skill team. That Buffalo loss was the real eye-opener of what we weren't.

"Primeau had been the locker-room lieutenant. Keith not being there, I believe, sent the whole thing into a tailspin."

Holmgren called Hitchcock to his office in Voorhees, NJ, on Sunday morning. "He told me he was making a change and that was it," recalls Hitchcock.

"I knew he was going to want his own guy. I was connected with Clarkie."

Except for four seasons in the early nineties, Philadelphia's link with Bob Clarke was a 33-year iron bond. Sooner or later, Hitchcock's dismissal had been expected, but not the franchise icon stepping away on his own volition. When both were announced at a late-morning press conference on Black Sunday, October 21, 2006. The sight of one of the most passionate figures in NHL history, explaining he didn't care to continue, was jarring.

"From the end of last season on, the decisions that had to be made, I was letting other people make them," Clarke told the gathered reporters. "I wasn't doing the right job for the organization.

"Mr. Snider is a friend and the best owner in professional sports and didn't deserve this. The fans didn't deserve it and the organization didn't deserve it.

"Even the day-to-day stuff, when we had to change a trainer or change people, I let Paul do it. I should have recognized this earlier. The draft usually is a time when the Flyers are very active in moving picks and players. When I left the draft, I realized I had been a bystander. Not on the phone, not running to tables, almost like I was bored. When I got home, I thought, 'something's not right.'

"We played a few games and nothing changed. I wasn't tired or stressed, just had lost interest. It wasn't because we lost some games; it was not wanting to do what a general manager has to do if you are going to be successful.

"Teams that stuck with people in my position too long ended up in real bad shape for a lot of years. I wasn't going to keep the job just to say I was the GM."

Despite having produced three Stanley Cup finalists and four more semifinalists through two terms totaling 18 seasons as GM, Clarke said he had "deep regrets" for failing to win a championship. "My responsibility was to try and win the Stanley Cup and I didn't deliver."

At the press conference, Snider called it "a difficult day" for the organization.

"When a man can sit up here and say he hasn't done the job, it shows what kind of man he is," the Chairman said. "He came to that realization himself and was man enough to do it, that's why I respect Bob Clarke so much.

"I have always known I would not have to fire Bob Clarke and that he would fire himself."

Asked whether he felt the players had begun to tune out Hitchcock, Snider replied, "Yes. We have a lot better talent on the team than we have shown so far."

When reached by reporters, Hitchcock—who recorded a .614 winning percentage in three-plus seasons, squared the Flyer image with their fans in the aftermath of the soulless Ottawa 2002 playoff debacle, and led the team to within one game of the 2004 Stanley Cup Final—thanked Snider for the opportunity. Hitchcock also said the implication/suggestion that he had lost the players was unfair.

"You can find people to say that anyplace, anywhere, anytime," the coach said. "You have to look deeper, a lot deeper, if you are willing to do it.

"I know what went on."

Today, Hitchcock says, "You always hear afterwards that the coach has lost the team, or they tuned him out. There were guys on that team that quit on each other, not on me."

Not all of the players were relieved at the demise of Hitch, the Big Bad Witch. When Hitchcock rose at 5:30 the next morning to go for a walk, outside his Medford Lakes, NJ, home was a tearful Pitkanen, waiting in his car to say goodbye to the only NHL coach he ever had.

"We talked and I wished him luck," recalls Hitchcock. "I loved Joni.

"He's a different guy, low key, some think aloof. But he would light up when you talked to him about personal things like fishing or the house he was building on the river [in Northern Finland].

"He also is one of the most unique individuals I've ever met in my life because the next day, he could give you exactly what happened on every shift he played without looking at the video."

Only a savant would have remembered Holmgren's previous experience as an NHL general manager—the 1993-94 season with the Hartford Whalers. So with an understanding that his hand had been on multiple Clarke moves at the end of his reign, plus an initial inclination to bring in fresh thinking, Luukko and Snider made the interim GM no promises. At the press conference, Luukko said Holmgren would be "evaluated from today as we move forward."

Said the Chairman: "Paul and I haven't had a chance to really sit down and talk about his ambition and the entire situation. We're going to have some discussions in the future and announce what the situation is."

This was the second time in Philadelphia that Holmgren was dangling, the first being in his coaching days after Clarke was fired by Jay Snider following the 1989-90 season. Left to the decision of new GM Russ Farwell, Holmgren had survived a year plus 24 games.

Stevens, a first-time NHL head coach, effectively was week-to-week too. Even so, the message GM and coach delivered to the team before the initial practice was to chill out and have fun.

"It was a very somber mood with the players because nobody likes to see people lose their jobs or step down," Holmgren told the media.

"In terms of impact, generally there's a little more spark when something like this happens because we all have to accept some of the blame, even the players.

"That's one of the things we talked about. Now, what are we going to do about it?

"You get to the point where there's so much tension—and not just in the young guys. I think we need to relax and play. It's a results-oriented business but, at the end of the day, it's still a game. These players have enjoyed playing all their lives and I think we need to get back to that somehow."

Stevens, 40, a once third-round pick by the Flyers who played 53 NHL games, was forced to retire from a respected AHL career by an eye injury and had become head coach of the Phantoms when Bill Barber was promoted to the Flyers in 2000. The 16th bench boss in the history of the Philadelphia franchise had paid his dues by teaching many of these Flyers how to pay theirs.

"When you deal with young players at the pro level, you have to make them feel comfortable," Stevens told the media. "The thing we demand is work ethic. Mistakes are going to happen.

"My belief is: you show the players the value in the way you want to play, reasons why you want things done. Then they start to figure out the rest for themselves.

"If you are 45 seconds into your shift and are one-versus-three at the offensive line and trying to beat everybody, I am probably not going to be tolerant of that. But if you are in an offensive situation and try to make a play and turn the puck over and skate like crazy to get back, this is what we want from our players."

As fits the age-old pattern of coaching changes, Stevens had been chosen because he was perceived to be an opposite in personality from the man he was replacing.

"It's not that Hitch didn't have up-tempo practices," Stevens recalls. "I know he was demanding on the details. But he came to Philadelphia when the Flyers were an older team and we had become a younger one. So we ramped up the execution and fundamentals.

"I have a deep intensity about the game and have a different way of presenting it. But there was no conscious decision that I'm going to try to be different.

"We thought our execution and energy level was poor. We wanted to pass the puck better, do everything quick tempo and upbeat from Day One."

Richards today says he doesn't believe Hitchcock was too hard on him, but his weariness was evident. "[Stevens is] not the kind of guy who is just going to bark at you," Richards told reporters after practice. "When something needs to be said, he will tell you, show you the video.

"If you are constantly saying things in the dressing room, we might not take every word to heart. But when someone who doesn't say much says something, you are going to listen."

Gagne had become one of Hitchcock's trusted advisors, but he remembered becoming unnerved by the coach early in his career. "When I had Hitch for the first time, it was my fourth year in the league and it felt like my first," Gagne told the media. "It was very tough.

"I can't imagine how those young guys here got through it the last couple of years. John Stevens will be calmer. He will allow young players to make mistakes."

Despite all the off-season changes, Philadelphia still was the same one-line team that had gone down to Buffalo the previous April. Ten of the 15 Flyer goals during their 1-6-1 start—the worst since the 1989-90 season—had been scored by Forsberg, Gagne and Knuble, so, at his first practice, Stevens broke up the line to try to spread experience and confidence throughout other units.

Holmgren admitted that the off-season had not been productive.

"Sanderson has given us some speed," evaluated the interim GM. "Robitaille, when he's had the opportunity to perform, has been okay. Baumgartner had a real good year last season in Vancouver, but it hasn't happened here.

"For the most part, I don't think we did a great job."

The plan had been short-term supplements to what Clarke and Holmgren felt was a good base of veterans and young players. "We thought we had a lot of good young kids coming in, and we had Gagne, Knuble and Forsberg," recalls Holmgren. "So we believed we could set things up for both the short and long term."

The future had been compromised by the Williams and Sharp deals. But recent first-round picks Carter, Richards, Pitkanen and Umberger remained, and most of the veteran signings had been for one year. Even if Forsberg re-upped at an anticipated $6 million a year, the Flyers figured to have $15 million-plus in cap space to use in the summer of 2007.

But the first objective was to save the 2006-07 season.

"We all believe we are not as bad as we've played," Holmgren told the media. Berube, promoted during the shakeup from Phantom head coach to a Flyer assistant position, was put in charge of improving a 4-for-55 powerplay, even though he had played on few in his career. "He's relentless in looking at video and he has great people skills," endorsed Stevens.

Longtime Phantom assistant coach Kjell Samuelsson was promoted to bench boss of the AHL team.

Unfortunately there were no sure-fire strategies in any coaching manual for replacing your best player. Recalls Stevens: "My very first game I was told that Peter was ready to go, but when the media talked to him he said, 'Hopefully I can go tonight.' So, of course, the reporters all came back to me and said, 'We thought Peter was playing.'

"I learned right away that Peter himself never knew, even right up through warm-up, because he was having so many issues with his foot. If a great player doesn't know if he's in or out, it plays with the confidence of your team.

"The young guys may have been a little intimidated by him but they loved him, just like the older guys respected him. Not having Primeau there made everybody lean on Forsberg."

Forsberg did play in Stevens' coaching premier game against Atlanta and scored a third-period goal. After Thrashers coach Bob Hartley unconventionally lifted Johan Hedberg for a cold Kari Lehtonen to play the shootout, Niittymaki won it, 3-2, a bizarre victory to start the Stevens era.

Two nights later, the Flyers were humiliated 8-2 by Pittsburgh and called a players-only meeting. "This just can't happen again," said Forsberg. "It's not for lack of trying; it's just that we were giving up way too many two-on ones, three-on-twos."

Said Stevens, "Sometimes when you don't score, it saps the life out of you. This gives me a real opportunity to sit down with these guys and figure out where we go from here."

They would do that without Knuble, who needed surgery performed by Baltimore hand specialist Dr. Thomas Graham to repair a fracture on his left middle finger.

Stevens called together the remaining leaders to ask what kind of identity they felt the team needed. The conclusion was predictable: There still was playoff-level talent on the team if it could do a better job in the defensive zone.

"Yeah, it's a (2-7-1) hole," said Forsberg. "But we can't give up on the season. I'm not. And it's my job to make sure [my teammates] don't think that way either."

Snider had quickly concluded he wanted a new direction. While Pittsburgh was clobbering Philadelphia, the Chairman was in New York meeting with Colin Campbell, the former Ranger coach who, as NHL executive vice president and director of hockey operations, had worked with Snider on the league's Competition Committee.

In subsequent talks with Snider the following week, while Esche was shutting out the struggling Blackhawks, 3-0, and the Flyers were losing for the tenth-straight time to Tampa, 5-2, Campbell was offered the general manager job. On Saturday, November 2, he had left his Ontario farmhouse and was enroute to Toronto's Pearson Airport to fly to Philadelphia to accept the job when he had a change of heart.

"The main numbers were done between Ed and myself," Campbell recalls. "I was going to Philly to finish the details with their lawyers.

"I just decided it wasn't a good fit for me. I hadn't felt comfortable with the whole situation with Bob Clarke stepping down, didn't feel he was ready. I thought he was going through a tough time and just wanted a breather. I didn't want to go there thinking Clarkie had made a mistake.

"I liked their talent, guys like Richards and Carter. I thought they needed goaltending but had a real good base, and I wasn't scared off (by the terrible start) at all.

"They had made a lot of decisions over the years regarding people that had a Flyer background so I didn't know if they were ready for a non-Flyer, particularly an ex-Ranger. I had a good job with the league and always had been supported by Gary Bettman, so it wasn't like I had been looking for work when Ed called. I had a desire to get back into the competition at some point, but just didn't feel this was the right spot.

"I was wrong. Clarkie had had enough and was ready to step back. So to this day, I have second thoughts.

"I did complete the trip. I went to Philly and told Mr. Snider that I wasn't ready to load my wife to Philadelphia and move off my farm. He said, 'We have [bleeping] farms here.' I never told him the real reason why."

Snider asked Campbell, as he had Clarke, to take a week and think about it. He agreed, but his mind was made up as the news leaked out. Holmgren was blindsided by a call from a *Canadian Press* reporter asking for a comment about Campbell becoming the new GM of the Flyers.

"I didn't tell anybody, was very sorry it got out and Homer had to go through that," recalls Campbell. "I hadn't gotten as far as staffing with Ed, but certainly Homer would have been a huge help to me."

Crestfallen, Holmgren nevertheless called Campbell to offer support during the change-over and to learn of his status.

"I told [Campbell], 'If you're coming to the Flyers, I'll do whatever I can to help with the transition," recalls Holmgren. "If you want to talk to me about staying on as your assistant and going back to the role I had under Clarkie, we can talk about that. If you want to go in a different direction, I'll understand but I'll do whatever I can.'

"He told me, 'Homer, the only way I'm coming to Philly is to watch a game.'"

Snider issued a statement the following day. "I considered Colin and we had a discussion about the general manager's position," the Chairman said. "Paul Holmgren will continue as the interim general manager."

Holmgren told the media, "It's part of the process that Mr. Snider and the organization are going through." Then he lied. "I don't think it's awkward."

Actually, it was painful, like watching every step forward the Flyers appeared to take morph into a face-first pratfall the following game. "We allowed Tampa Bay to dictate," Stevens said after the loss to the Lightning. "Why we came out the way we did is a mystery."

Henceforth, the exact nature of player injuries would remain undisclosed to the public by decree of Holmgren. When Carter had to leave the ice during the Tampa Bay defeat, the affected area was not detailed, only announced as a lower-body problem. The interim GM wanted to protect players from cheap shots.

Meanwhile, a seething Forsberg wanted to protect himself from himself, bolting from the Wachovia Center without comment after drawing a game misconduct in protesting a high-sticking call.

"Sure we're a little frustrated," said the captain after Philadelphia played better, but could not prevent Washington's first win at the Wachovia Center in 26 visits (0-15-10), 5-3. "But to be honest, I don't think we're playing good enough to win a hockey game."

Certainly Esche (1-3, 5.32 GAA and .726 Sv%) was not. Neither was a 7-for-87 powerplay, its continued failure ruining an improved performance in a 4-1 Air Canada Center loss to the Leafs. "The effort is there, but the finish is not," said Stevens after the game. "Nothing against Ben Eager, but when he is your only goal scorer, it's a concern."

Recalls Stevens: "We thought we could get them going. But, when you look at that team now, we had one guy (Pitkanen) we could put [at the point] for the powerplay. He was just a kid and, quite honestly, Joni had not been our first powerplay guy with the Phantoms (during the

2004-05 lockout). John Slaney, a career minor-league guy, was."

When the coach attached a plastic "Shooter Tutor" in front of the net at practice and asked players to hit five shots in succession into the openings in the upper corners, only Eager was able to succeed.

Carter's leg proved broken, leaving him out for an expected six weeks. So Nedved, who had been made an example following the debacle in Buffalo but had accumulated eight points in seven games for the Phantoms, was returned to the big team.

"It's easy, you walk 20 yards (from the Phantom rink at the Skate Zone) and you're right back up," Nedved laughed.

"Obviously, I was disappointed the way things went. This was not the way you want to end your career in the National Hockey League."

Said Stevens, "He's here because he didn't mope. He is a veteran presence and right now that's important."

The coach wanted to put Nedved into the same checking role that Hitchcock had tried out of camp, and attempted to appeal to the 34-year-old center that it could buy him extra years in the NHL. "His numbers had fallen off, but he was big, could skate, and knew the game and the league," recalls Stevens. "But he didn't think he could do it and wanted no part of it."

Not that the 3-10-1 Flyers, their best young players struggling, couldn't still use a goal or two from a veteran. Three of Pitkanen's eight points in the first 14 games had come during the win in New York. Carter had six points, but Richards and Umberger only three each.

"After the concussion (suffered during the 2006 Buffalo series), I wasn't able to train until August," recalls Umberger. "When I came to camp, my VO2 test was just awful, and when I played my first exhibition game in London, it was like, 'I don't want to get hit.' I was gun-shy for a while and it lingered all that year. I never got any momentum.

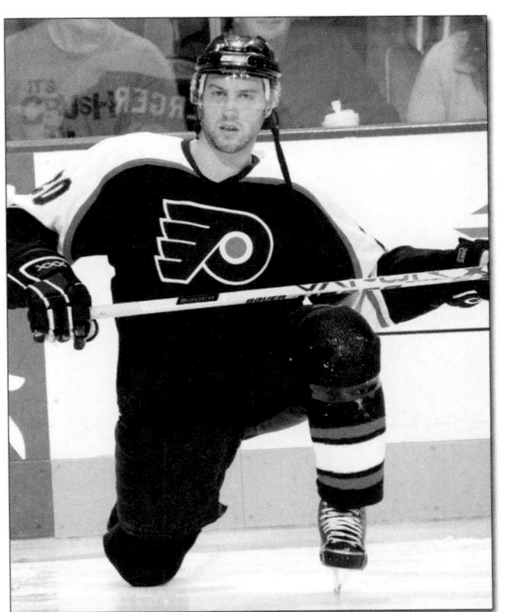

Injured in the 2006 playoffs, R.J. Umberger was one of several Flyers who struggled in 2006-07.

"I also didn't start playing with Carter (who was moved to a line with Gagne) and had some frustration with that. I was put on the third line and thought the chemistry we had shown the year before wasn't being used.

"But really, none of us young guys was ready to take over."

Despite his offseason ankle surgery, Forsberg's foot still would not rest comfortably in his skate boot, so when he went for a scheduled follow-up with Dr. Anderson in Charlotte (NC), the captain took assistant equipment manager Harry Bricker along.

Forsberg kept playing, but not to the standards he set for himself. "I don't know if it is confidence, but we are not playing physical at the beginning (of games)," he said after another catatonic start resulted in a 3-1 home loss to the Islanders. "If you are going to win games, your best players have to be your best players, and I am definitely not doing that right now.

"We are getting killed. I can't blame it on anyone else but me."

Actually, there was plenty of blame to go around, as finger-pointing began. "No one is helping each other right now," said Hatcher. "Everyone is covering their own hide."

At least one booty was shaking, that of portly season ticket holder Shawny Hill, whom the roving camera in the Wachovia Center stands captured dancing high up in Section 219 during the Islander loss, never mind a 3-0 third-period deficit.

"There was a bus group in the two rows in front of me that had left after two periods to beat the traffic," recalls Hill, a Rowan University student whose season tickets had been in the family for 15 years. "This was the first time I had the whole row in front of me to dance."

"Right after I did, Gagne scored, so they showed me again. Soon an intern ran up to me with Shawn Tilger's business card."

Tilger liked the energy and decided to make Hill's act a third-period staple. The next game, it seemed contagious—the Flyers rallied from a 3-1 deficit to take a 4-3 lead against Buffalo on Robitaille's third-period goal. But old nemesis Danny Briere both tied the game and won it, 5-4, in overtime.

Despite the return of Knuble, Philadelphia folded again in Pittsburgh, 3-2, on rookie Evgeni Malkin's late goal, the Flyers record falling to 3-12-2.

"I got a call from Mr. Snider," recalls Holmgren. "And I'm getting an earful about how bad the team is."

"I said, 'Well what do you expect? You've got an interim GM, which meant John is an interim coach. It's a rudderless ship.' So he took the interim tag off me as GM."

This was not announced to the public, however. Holmgren, on double-secret probation as were the Deltas in *Animal House*, remained working on an assistant GM salary. "I felt like I could help get us back on track if we gave it some time," he recalls. "But I also knew it was out of my hands, so I just focused on one day at a time."

They were depressing days. Defenseman Denis Gauthier made an effort to play with a bad shoulder but ended up needing surgery to repair a torn labrum. Stevens tried shock treatments on Kyle Calder, who had three assists in 16 games after scoring 26 goals the previous year in Chicago, benching the winger for three games. "The thing that made him a good player was his second and third efforts," said Holmgren. "We haven't seen that here."

The Flyers also had not witnessed one of Forsberg's patented spin-a-rama moves since the season's infancy. But fitted with a new orthotic wedge, he wheeled for a goal in Anaheim as Philadelphia stunningly broke out of a six-game winless streak to a 7-4 victory. The following night in Los Angeles, the Flyers followed up with their first back-to-back wins of the season, coming from behind on two late third-period goals by Umberger for a 4-3 victory.

Just as quickly as they had started to feel better about themselves, the players were overwhelmed 6-1 in San Jose. "It was pretty obvious we got away from what had given us success in the last two games, which was taking care of the puck," said Knuble. "We can be proud of what we did this trip but the bottom line is we're still in last place."

And they likely would stay there unless Forsberg, whose foot rolled in his boot, resulting in a slip into the boards and a hard hit from Pittsburgh's Brooks Orpik, could be himself again. "When I get off the ice now I feel like the worst player in the league," he said glumly the day after a 5-3 loss to the Penguins at the Wachovia Center. "I feel like I know what I should do and I'm not able to do it."

Some nights he could. Forsberg had a goal and an assist before Richards' first score in 46 games broke a 2-2 tie in a 3-2 home victory over Columbus, spoiling the debut of Blue Jackets' coach Ken Hitchcock. He had been out of work just 29 days. "With him coming back, [the win] was a little bigger," said Forsberg. "I think it would have been real tough for us if we had lost this game."

When Niittymaki followed up with a 4-2 win in Montreal on November 25, Philadelphia was 4-2-1 in its last seven and apparently gaining some traction. Three rookie call-ups, Jonsson, Alexandre Picard (third round, 2002) and Jussi Timonen (fifth round, 2001), had provided some resolve to the defense, Timonen in particular seeming to have energized his Finnish countryman, Pitkanen.

When Nashville made a rare Wachovia Center appearance—these were the days of fewer inter-conference games—Timonen was pumped to play for the first time against Kimmo, his older brother by eight years. Nevertheless, the Flyers lost 3-2 when Rathje, who had been playing on painkillers, made a blatant turnover to Paul Kariya, who fed Martin Erat's overtime winner.

"I was having all kinds of problems trying to skate," recalls Rathje. "I had pain in my hip and then my foot went numb, so I was trying to skate against the fastest guys on the planet on one leg.

"My tailbone always was inflamed. I had to put on a lidocaine patch each game. I remember doing stuff I probably shouldn't have been doing so I could stay in the lineup. But I was committed, partly because we had started off so [badly].

"Finally I told (trainer) Jimmy McCrossin, 'I gotta stop and find out what the hell's going on here.' Jimmy was really good to me and Homer was as positive as anybody could be. He had to retire (at age 29 from chronic shoulder issues), so I was talking to a guy who had gone through it."

After Rathje's problem puzzled specialists on both coasts, he finally was diagnosed with piriformis syndrome, a condition in which the sciatic nerve is compressed or otherwise irritated by the piriformis muscle, causing pain, tingling and numbness in the buttocks and into the leg.

"The doctor told me that most people get it from a big blow to your hip area in a car wreck," Rathje recalls. "I don't know if there's ever been any other NHL player that has been diagnosed with it.

"They talked about surgery but I was 32, later in my career, and the doctor didn't want to risk cutting my sciatic nerve and leaving me crippled."

The Flyers placed Rathje on injured reserve but held off putting him on the long-term-injury list so that they could remove his salary against the cap.

"There are still some avenues we are going to explore medically," Holmgren said before adding, "I don't think there is a doctor so far that has told Mike if he had surgery, it would guarantee fixing the problem.

"We all feel for him…the pain he's gone through. You have to start to look at life as a person and not a hockey player."

Given a complete chance to run with the goaltending job after Esche underwent sports hernia surgery on November 29, Niittymaki beat the Islanders, 3-2. When Todd Fedoruk, who had been brought back to Philadelphia from Anaheim two weeks earlier in a minor-league trade, scored the game-opening goal and an assist in his re-debut against New Jersey, the Flyers were two minutes away from a sixth win in eight games when Knuble gave the puck away on Brad Lukowich's tying goal. The Devils won, 4-3, in the shootout.

"Those are the reasons we are where we are right now," said Stevens, meaning 30th in a 30-team league. "That's twice in the last week where we had a self-inflicted wound and lost a hockey game."

Holmgren, short of help in the front office due to his ascension and Hextall's preseason departure for Los Angeles, added Don Luce, a long-time front-office fixture in Buffalo who had become a victim of budget cuts, as director of player development. Chris Pryor was promoted from pro scout to director of hockey operations. Dave Brown, who had moved up to director of player personnel when Hextall left, remained in that position.

"Basically, Chris had been doing things for me that I had done for Clarkie," recalls Holmgren. "I had known Donnie a little bit over the years and always respected his work from a player assessment and development standpoint."

Two months had passed since Clarke's resignation, but he was suffering no remorse. "It was the right decision," he reiterated to reporters. Still wanting to be around the game, Clarke was appointed senior vice president, essentially to serve as a special advisor to Holmgren.

"Why would we just let Bob Clarke go and not keep him involved for his knowledge and experience?" Holmgren says today.

"He remained connected with a lot of managers in the league. He's still a great judge of the game who picks up on the idiosyncrasies of what's really going on with your team. So of course I wanted him around.

"He's been through a lot in this game. And to me he'll always be Mr. Flyer."

Clarke still enjoyed watching, even if the team he put together wasn't easy on the eyes.

While Niittymaki was good, he was not good enough to prevent a second loss to the Devils in two days, 2-0 at the Meadowlands. Richards and Sanderson both suffered groin tears that would require sports hernia surgeries that were projected to keep them out for three weeks. So just when there had been a glimmer of light at the end of the dark tunnel, injuries began to hit a team not nearly deep enough to withstand them. Another long losing streak began.

Forsberg, who had been to doctors and orthotic specialists in Nashville, Cleveland and Arizona without finding a solution, decided he couldn't play without finding a skate boot, or device to put in it, that would stabilize his right foot and ankle.

"We sent three team doctors and Jimmy [to Montreal] to try to get him a skate that would work," recalls Stevens. "I'm willing to bet they went through three or four hundred pairs of skates that year.

"Peter was an unbelievable competitor, but he was never there to practice, and that was a huge problem.

"I know it really bothered him that the team was in that state and that he wasn't healthy to make a difference every day. I've never in my life seen a guy compete harder when he could play or one who was more frustrated than Peter that year.

"I think the fact that Primeau wasn't there affected Peter in more ways than people realize. He always was a world-class player but had another guy with him. In Colorado, he and (Joe) Sakic were unbelievable. Here, Primeau had carried a lot of responsibility against top lines and top players.

"Gagne had a hip flexor and refused to say anything about it because we had so many guys going in and out of the lineup. He was our best player and tried to lead the team."

A perfect storm of bad breaks and miscalculations had sent this Titanic to Davy Jones' Locker, but mortified veterans still refused the lifeboats.

"I remember Joni came in one day and couldn't practice because he wasn't feeling well," recalls Stevens. "Hatcher was all [angry] about it, saying, 'the way I was brought up, you practice.'

"Mike Knuble loved the game and showed up every day ready to work. He was one [veteran] extremely well respected by the younger guys. He was a great (generational) bridge, and was a better player than I had realized. If you would have put him on the third or fourth line, he probably couldn't play in the league. But in your top six, he played like a star.

"I never have seen a player complement skilled players like Mike; he helped connect the dots. He took great pride in winning a puck battle in the corner and making a play off the walls. He stood in front of the net and got 15 powerplay goals just from being there."

"You always have upfront leaders and a secondary core. And Mike was one of those important secondary guys.

"Another guy the losing really bothered was Sami Kapanen. It killed him to see the team at that level. Whenever I said the team was not working hard enough, he took it personally, even though he was doing everything he could."

But the Flyers didn't have enough Kapanens and Knubles, and especially suffered for having that summer traded Handzus, another gritty player whose absence was compounded by the loss of Primeau. "Two huge guys down the middle no longer there," recalls Stevens.

"Handzus was the ultimate pro. He played hurt and nobody worked harder day after day. Losing him had a big effect.

"Sanderson, Robitaille, Calder had no impact. None of them had anything to do with building an identity for that team, a huge problem.

"Paul was realistic and very supportive. He understood our personnel had to get better but he also knew our young guys would become good players. Because of that, at first we thought we could get the team going, but we didn't play good enough defense. Here and there we could do it, but over a period of time or on a longer road trip, we weren't even close.

"Pitkanen and Forsberg had some chemistry. I realize they had a good year coming out of the lockout. But Joni was an extremely difficult player to integrate with the team. He had a superior skill level in terms of ability to skate and join the rush, but a good player is always predictable to his teammates and unpredictable to the other team. Pitkanen may have been the opposite.

"He didn't like to let his guard down and engage with teammates. That's something we worked extremely hard on when we had him in the minors and we continued to do that with the Flyers. But he played the game a little too much on his own agenda.

"It wasn't a close team. From talking to guys, I realized players didn't know much about each other; like [the fact] that Mike Rathje had twins. Meyer was paired up with Derian, but Freddy didn't know Hatch's wife's name or any of his kids. I thought that was odd."

Fourteen of the 20 players who dressed for a 5-3 home loss to Washington on December 9 had been Phantoms within the last 18 months. With Pitkanen and Rathje out, Meyer played 25 minutes on defense. "I'm one of the veteran guys now," he laughed. "I can even sit in the back of the bus."

Nedved was thrown under it for the second and final time. Holmgren had seen enough, waiving the veteran despite having Carter, Forsberg and Richards all out of the lineup.

"(Ottawa GM) Bryan Murray had called and told me, "If you put [Nedved] on re-entry waivers, we'll claim him," recalls Holmgren. But Edmonton, lower in the standings, had first dibs, and snatched him.

The Flyers wanted to take a look at Ryan Potulny, a Hobey Baker Award finalist at the University of Minnesota and a third-round pick in 2003. He was not ready for the first or second lines however, so Stevens moved Gagne to the middle for the first time since 2001, his second season in the NHL.

Philadelphia took what it had to New York and battled the Rangers hard, but there was no consolation in a 3-1 defeat. "Another loss," said Umberger, who had the goal. "I don't know if there is anything to feel good about."

At 8-18-4, all pretense that the team could crawl back into the race was gone. Sidney Crosby scored a goal and five assists in Pittsburgh's 8-4 win at Mellon Arena, pushing him to 29 points in 13 career games against Flyers. "He's got to be excited to see us coming on the schedule," said a glum Knuble.

"What can you do? If you show up and work hard, but are not as good as the other team, you can live with that."

Niittymaki had played the game as if in a fog. When one enveloped Philadelphia International Airport, the charter had to land in Newark, NJ where the team waited for a bus and finally arrived home at 4:30 a.m. But even if the Flyers were 16 points out of a playoff spot, Holmgren had to sleep at night. On December 16, he traded Meyer and a third-round pick to the Islanders for defenseman Alexei Zhitnik, never mind the 34-year-old had two years remaining on his contract at $3.5 million per.

"We did it to try to make the team better, not to acquire a trading asset," recalls Holmgren. "Alexei was a solid pro."

Stevens was happy to get the help. "He can make the people around him better," the coach told the media. "He protects the puck and makes simple plays. When young players see that it, it kind of makes things look easy."

Zhitnik was not joining the Philadelphia club that he had battled in five playoff series while with the Sabres, but said he didn't mind. "I've been on bad teams at Buffalo and I was on a good team when they went to the Final," he said. "Take one shift at a time, one game at a time."

One move at a time for Holmgren, who had the full GM title but no contract extension at GM-level pay as his makeover of the team began. But he was forming an important bond with his bosses.

"That year I got to know Peter Luukko very well," Holmgren recalls. "Whatever significant thing I wanted to do, I would make two phone calls—one to Peter, one to Mr. Snider. In terms of the day-to-day, I talked to Peter more regularly, but Mr. Snider always knew what was going on.

"He'd call me from time to time or I'd call him and tell him what we were doing. Peter didn't insulate him from me. In fact, Peter helped open those lines of communication.

"Peter loved to suit up himself and play; hockey was big in his own family. So he was another guy with a lot of passion for the game and that wasn't a bad thing at all."

Forsberg's quest to quiet his barking dogs next took him to Montreal, where Bauer manufactured a special order skate that it hoped would stabilize his heel. The captain tried it out in Washington and was able to pivot like the Forsberg of yore until he was smacked by Alexander Ovechkin in the first period and had to leave the 4-1 loss with a suspected concussion.

"It would benefit us the most if we went into these games mentally without Peter in the lineup and then, if he shows up, it's a bonus," said Knuble. "We can still have a lot of good days without him as long as everybody isn't looking over their shoulder thinking, 'Where is he? Is he coming back?' We were kind of in the same situation with Keith last year."

A 2-1 defeat by the Stanley Cup champion Hurricanes was the Flyers' seventh straight, a new club record in the franchise's 40th season. "We killed way too many penalties and flat out didn't compete," said Stevens.

For a second-straight year, the team was on pace for 300-plus man games lost to injury. But at 8-21-4, the losing rate was unprecedented. In 1969-70, the franchise had recorded its fewest wins ever—17—but, thanks to 24 ties, had competed for a playoff spot until the final day of the regular season. Even during the five-year stretch from 1990-94 that the team missed the playoffs, the farthest out the Flyers had finished was 12 points. Never had the club been this buried, or humiliated, in its history.

"It was hard," recalls Stevens. "But that was a good learning experience for me too, to get your head up every day, go to the rink, take on the criticism, and try to make your team better. That was the coaches' attitude the whole year."

Holmgren still was trying to help ease the pain. Even with Carter having returned on December 19 against Carolina, Philadelphia had a desperate need at center. So the GM made a second deal that week with Islander GM Garth Snow, moving Robitaille and a fifth-round pick for the 28-year-old Mike York, who had scored 61 points in 2001-02 on a Ranger line with Eric Lindros and Theo Fleury.

"We feel his competitiveness and versatility bring us a little more than Randy—a good player for us, but not a guy who fits into a third or fourth-line energy role," said Holmgren.

York became the 10th Flyer with a contract expiring at the end of the season, which really had become Holmgren's scoreboard as he prepared for the July 1 start of free agency.

A 6-3 loss to Ottawa was the sixth straight at home, another club record. "We haven't been good at home or on the road," shrugged Stevens, as his team headed out of town for the next eight. Even with the fans' anger dissipating as a sense of reality settled in, most glimpses of competency were coming in away games.

"We didn't believe we could win every night, so there was probably added anxiety in front of our home fans," recalls Stevens.

"I don't remember the fans of Philadelphia being brutal. I just remember them being honest. If they booed, they had every right to boo, and I think the players felt that way, too."

Forsberg was back as the team's road trip began at Florida, but Niittymaki had to leave after two periods of the 3-1 loss with a recurrence of the hip problem for which he had gotten an injection during training camp.

"I knew I had a chance to be the No. 1 guy so I took the shot instead of the surgery," he recalls. "We decided to move the surgery until after the season.

"I'm not saying that I played bad because of the hip. But I think mentally it was there all the time. I had to do extra work just to make sure I was able to practice and then we started the season really bad.

"I played a lot of games we weren't even close to winning. It wasn't fun. Maybe I should have done the surgery right away."

Esche, rehabbed from his sports hernia procedure, made his first start in 40 days and held off a late Lightning rally for a 4-3 victory that snapped the losing streak at 10 games. "I was sore, but I was seeing the puck well and didn't think much about it," said the goalie, staked to a 4-1 lead with the help of three points by the amazing Forsberg.

Niittymaki went to Nashville and specialist Dr. Robert Byrd for an injection of cortisone while Esche gave the team an unexpected shot in the arm, stopping 40 as the Flyers welcomed winger Dmitry Afanasenkov, a waiver wire pickup from Tampa Bay. Then, on New Year's Eve, the goaltender survived five second-period powerplays to stun the defending champion Hurricanes, 5-2, in Raleigh.

"Esche was sometimes outstanding," recalls Stevens. "And then sometimes it seemed like he lost his game, which was unfortunate."

The goalie still had it in Uniondale, where he backstopped Philadelphia to a 3-2 win, but the candle of hope flickered out again when Forsberg left that contest with a groin pull undoubtedly caused again by his unstable foot.

"We thought we had it licked, but there still is some motion in there," said McCrossin. He went with Forsberg to Temple University to try further orthotic inserts and then—following a 3-2 Flyer defeat in Forsberg's absence at Madison Square Garden—with the team to Boston for a meeting with Dr. Thomas Gill, a foot and ankle specialist at Massachusetts General Hospital.

Philadelphia lost at the Fleet Center, 4-3, then Forsberg didn't dress in Ottawa, where a lot of Flyers who had felt hopeful during good periods, were startled back to reality in a 6-1 pounding.

"I let in six goals, so I don't think I competed hard," said Niittymaki. "But I don't think there were too many guys who competed hard."

Hatcher was especially distraught. "We have a surprisingly good knack of getting disorganized on the ice," the defenseman said. "And it's just positional play.

"I've never been through anything like this and I don't think most of the other guys in here have either. That's something we talk about literally every day. We have 40 games left; we can't go through 40 games like we are right now."

He was even too embarrassed to make his customary Starbucks stop on the way to practice. "It's one thing to lose, but I think it's a lot in how you lose," Hatcher recalls. "At least you have to play hard and try to do the right things.

"When you have four, five or six guys that aren't pulling their weight, it's tough. When you are going good, you can't tell anything about a player. When things are going bad, that's when you can.

"There were definitely players who weren't good for the team. Everyone wants to [win], but some weren't willing to go the extra mile. Between stuff they were doing on the ice and saying things like, 'I'm happy I got a point tonight,' there was a lot of that going on.

"Younger guys coming up don't think about the mental part of the game. It's a process of learning. That's why you want them in the right culture. There were times our kids probably were overwhelmed between the pressures and everything else. That can make them not want to be at the rink.

"I'd say, 'try to get better. If you lose, go out with some passion and emotion. The season is not done, so quitting is not acceptable. We've got to play, might as well play as hard as we can, do the things Johnny wants us to do.

"The energy Johnny brought to the rink every day was unbelievable. He loved the game and personally, I liked him, as I think most players did. I thought he handled it great. I really do."

Although Philadelphia played with much more determination to close the trip in Washington, Esche performed so poorly that, following the 6-2 defeat, he felt the need to apologize to his teammates. So it went: On the nights the Flyers played hard enough to stay in the game, they would be foiled by terrible penalties, a horrendous powerplay or weak goaltending.

Umberger remembers Knuble doing his best to boost spirits. "He was always upbeat, always positive, always putting things in perspective," recalls Umberger. "He'd say, 'Enjoy yourself. If you're struggling, simplify. Think only about getting five shots on net tonight.' I sat next to him, so I'd pick his brain.

"But we just weren't good enough. And when it got that bad, it probably brought out the worst in a lot of people."

Alongside the absence of talent and heart, there was virtually no esprit de corps.

"We needed some of those younger guys to have more of a bite in the locker room and take more responsibility," recalls Stevens. "But they were looked at not as teammates, but as threats.

"It's not that they didn't get along or that they despised each other, [it's just that] the bonding and affection wasn't there."

Neither a pregame ceremony thanking Desjardins nor the return of Forsberg could inspire the Flyers, who opened a homestand with a 4-1 loss to Montreal. Philadelphia put up more fight against Pittsburgh, but Jordan Staal broke a 3-3 third-period tie and the Flyers went down once more. "It was one of our better home games but I guess that doesn't say a whole lot," said Forsberg.

By January 18, Philadelphia had won only three times in its own building. "It's abominable," said Holmgren.

So was York, who had two points and was minus-7 in 12 games as a Flyer. "He was in no physical condition to help us," recalls Stevens. "He couldn't skate anymore; we had to scratch him half the time."

This made welcome the simultaneous returns of Richards and Sanderson for a January 20 game at the Meadowlands. Philadelphia took a 3-2 lead during the third period on a goal by Gagne and was 20 seconds away from victory when Brian Gionta scored on Niittymaki, then did it again to win the shootout. The Finn had not won in his last 14 starts and the Flyers had lost their last eight.

"I'm miserable," Snider told the *Inquirer*'s Michael Klein. And misery loved company.

"It was horrible," recalls Holmgren. "Thank God for Shawny, the dancing guy. That year he was our Most Valuable Player."

Forsberg practically was beside himself. When the club returned from the All-Star break with a 2-1 loss to the Rangers, he was so worried about exploding on the officials, the captain asked Knuble to "drag me out of there and keep me quiet."

Sure enough, the next night in Atlanta, Forsberg boiled over from several non-calls of stick fouls against him and responded with three crosschecks before finally getting whistled for a hook. His protestations got him slapped with an unsportsmanlike conduct penalty, causing Stevens to bench his star for the remaining three minutes of the second period. Nevertheless, two Carter goals and Niittymaki's first win in 59 days allowed Philadelphia to snap its second nine-game losing streak of the season with a 2-1 victory.

"We can't afford to be shorthanded and have our best player in the box for four minutes," said Stevens. "Peter needed some time to regroup."

But for the long term, would the franchise be better off regrouping without him? As the February 27 trading deadline approached, Forsberg would not commit to a contract extension.

"We have to figure out the foot situation and there's no need to talk about anything else," Forsberg told reporters after meeting with Holmgren on January 29.

The GM said he empathized. "He wants to get back to being a good player (first)," Holmgren told the media. "Every time you talk to Peter at length, you find out how proud a man he is and how frustrated he is by this whole ordeal. Basically, he tells you he is the reason the Flyers are where they are."

The organization still was prepared to make a substantial offer for a 33-year-old player with a chronic physical issue. "Even Peter at 60 percent or 75 percent would have been pretty good," recalls Holmgren. "But Peter had to play to the standard he set for himself, which also meant the team was winning."

Podiatrist Dr. Frank Tursi made more adjustments to the center's boot during the skate the next morning, and that night against Tampa Bay he was Forsberg again, with jump unseen in months, plus a goal that put Philadelphia up 3-2 in the third period. The Lightning won the shootout, 4-3, but the captain was encouraged. "I think I had more chances than in the last 10 games," he said. "It was fun to feed my linemates, have balance, and not be scared out there."

Two days later at New Jersey, he again put the Flyers up in the third period, in this go-around, 5-4. But for the second occasion in two games against the Devils, Philadelphia was tied in the final minute and lost in OT, in this instance on a winner by Brad Lukowich. "We seem to find a way to lose at the end every time," said Forsberg.

Finally, they didn't. When Niittymaki relieved Esche, who left with neck spasms after facing just six shots, the Flyers rallied for their first win of the year after trailing going into the third period, winning 5-2 in Atlanta. Philadelphia then came back from being two goals down in the third period to force overtime against Pittsburgh, but lost to the Penguins for the seventh time of the season, 5-4, on Crosby's shootout goal.

Tired of seeing improved efforts get away for lack of a well-timed save, Stevens tried goaltender Michael Leighton, a 1999 sixth-round draft choice by Chicago whom Holmgren had claimed off waivers from Nashville in January. Gagne, who admitted his surgically-corrected hip still was bothering him, scored with 4:55 remaining to tie the Blues, then beat them 27 seconds into overtime for the first Flyer victory at home in 14 tries.

Two nights later, after a pregame ceremony to thank Primeau for his dedicated service, Philadelphia won again behind Leighton by an astonishing 6-1 over powerful Detroit, with Gauthier, who went after Andreas Lilja for a dangerous hit on Gagne, sticking up for a teammate like the players had not been doing all year.

The 15-33-8 Flyers were 4-2-4 since the All-Star break. Why wouldn't Forsberg want to remain a member of this juggernaut?

"I am pushing him," said Gagne. "I would do everything to get him to sign here."

Despite the organization's three-year offer starting at $6 million and escalating to $6.5 million per season, Forsberg remained non-committal.

"I need to play a little more to know if it's going to be 100 percent," he told reporters. "I don't want to go through this again next year.

"I want to get my foot fixed. I've stood by that all year. It's not like I've said I want to leave. I like it here."

Logically, top free agents would be more willing to join a team with Forsberg on it, so trading him for prospects wasn't an obvious move for the GM. Never before had the franchise been a seller at the trading deadline, and it was taking their Chairman time to grow accustomed to the idea.

"I was open to going in either direction," recalls Holmgren. "Mr. Snider did not want to trade him and wanted to meet with Peter alone.

"Mr. Snider could be very convincing, so I set it up. I don't think he told Peter anything different than the rest of us were saying, but it was coming directly from our owner: He wanted Peter to stay."

Recalls Forsberg, "I still remember when I was called into Mr. Snider's office. He said, 'We don't trade good players, ones we like. It's not what we want to do.'

"I had to tell him that if they traded me, it wouldn't necessarily be the end. I could come back that summer as a free agent.

Snider still didn't want Forsberg to enter the market. But the player wasn't prepared to sign.

After the meeting, the team issued a terse statement that discussions would continue. So did Holmgren with trade talks, even though his options were limited by Forsberg's full no-movement clause.

"Peter and I had a good relationship through the whole thing," recalls the GM. "It was up to him.

"When teams would call, he'd let me know how he felt about potentially going there. He didn't want to go to Detroit or Toronto. Colorado called kicking the tires.

"In the end, he'd only go to Anaheim, San Jose, or Nashville. Nashville had Kariya—a guy Peter was interested in playing with—and they had a good team he could help in the playoffs."

With Anaheim GM Brian Burke, Holmgren asked about recent first-round picks Ryan Getzlaf and Corey Perry, winger Chris Kunitz, and goaltender Ilya Bryzgalov.

"But Burkie wasn't as interested as was (Nashville GM) David Poile," recalls Holmgren. "David and I must have talked every day for 40 days.

"He asked what the (health) situation was. I told him that Peter really wants to play, but these issues are ongoing and he's not sure about what he's going to do for next year. But David had a real good team that year and was going for it."

Poile doubted he would be able to sign Forsberg, but pressed on despite the player's health issues and Holmgren's steep asking price. "It took so long because Paul asked for so much," Poile recalls. "I thought he would be talking to other teams, but I felt for sure we were the leader in what we were prepared to pay.

Poile was willing to move either of two defenseman the Predators had taken in the 2005 draft—Ryan Parent (first round, 18th overall) or Cody Franson (third round, 79th).

"There wasn't that huge of a disparity between them, but Parent (pronounced PAIR-ehnt) was the guy we wanted a little more," recalls Holmgren. "He was a very good skater with good size (6-3) and he defended very well. We thought he'd get a lot better with the puck."

Poile was willing to move left wing Scottie Upshall—the sixth overall pick in the 2002 draft, who, in his second professional season, had not found a place on the top two Nashville lines behind Kariya, a three-time first team NHL All-Star—and Erat.

"We liked Scottie's energy and speed," recalls Holmgren. "He had a little bit of nastiness to him and could score a few goals. He was a good fit for us."

San Jose was offering draft selections, not players. Holmgren wanted picks from the Predators, too, and because their upcoming No. 1 figured to be almost in the second round, Poile was willing to move it, even though Forsberg was refusing to be anything more than a rental for the rest of the season.

"Hockey 101 for managers is never trade your younger players until you know how they will turn out," recalls Poile. "Upshall would have been fine for us for many years.

"Franson had more offensive ability than Parent, but we thought Ryan would be a fine defensive defenseman. With a No.1, too, there was no doubt we were overpaying. I still thought [Forsberg] was worth it.

"We were getting a rock star. I thought it was going to create a buzz that would have a big carryover effect for the franchise in our market whether we could keep Peter or not."

Having negotiated for a No. 1 pick, plus the sixth and 18th players taken in previous drafts, Holmgren had done well. But Snider still wanted Forsberg to be the centerpiece of the rebuild.

Twelve days before the trading deadline—and 60-90 minutes before Philadelphia's February 15 game with Toronto at the Wachovia Center—Holmgren met with Snider as the Chairman dined in the VIP lounge. "He asked me, 'Before we do this, can we get (agent) Don Baizley on the phone one more time to try to get them to commit?'" recalls Holmgren.

"I did that. Don told me they'd be glad to sit down after the season and talk to us, but they couldn't commit at this point.

"So Mr. Snider reluctantly said, 'OK, Homer. If you really think you've got a deal that's good for us, go ahead.'"

Forsberg, collared by reporters on his way into the building, had said, "I'm sure it will all be settled by the weekend. I don't know if it's a deadline, but everybody wants it settled as soon as we can."

Holmgren, with no good reason to wait and risk Forsberg getting hurt, acted within an hour, calling back Poile and dealing the center to Nashville for Parent, Upshall, and first- and third-round picks in the 2007 draft.

Forsberg already had completed the warm-up when he was pulled from the lineup by Holmgren.

"I've never seen a guy yanked out of the locker room as you are lacing up your skates for the game," Knuble told reporters after the Flyers fell behind 3-0 in the first period on the way to a 4-2 loss to the Leafs. "It was tough to take, a shock for us.

"Paul didn't even say where Peter was going. We had to dig around a little to find that out. It was surreal. He couldn't have been traded on an off-day, right? It had to be five minutes before a game. Obviously, we were a little rattled during that first period. The team was starting to build something and now your captain is gone."

"It was difficult," Stevens would say. "There wasn't much time to come up with a plan, not much time to adjust the lineup.

"He's a world-class player and I'm really sad to see him go, but I understand the situation. It is what it is, we have to deal with it."

It wasn't fun for Forsberg, who said he was "shocked" a trade came so soon, even though he had approved his destination. "Today is not a good day," he said.

Holmgren dealt with the fallout.

"We've gone round and round with Peter over the last fair amount of time about making a commitment to us in future years," the GM told the media. "We all tried. We ganged up on him.

"We didn't want to do this deal, but we couldn't afford not to do it in the end for the betterment of the franchise's future. The timing of it might not have been great, but a good deal was on the table that we couldn't pass up.

"We appreciate everything Peter Forsberg has done for us and the franchise over the last year. He's been a tremendous player, a tremendous person, and we wish him nothing but the best."

Snider echoed Holmgren that the Flyers had no option but to do the deal. "If Peter finished out the season with us and decided to retire, we had nothing," said the Chairman. "We are going to miss him in the short run, but in the long run we'll be fine."

As far as the players were concerned, they had seven long weeks to go in a miserable season with only Scottie Upshall coming in to replace one of the league's best players.

"Parent is a shutdown defenseman," said Holmgren. "I don't believe he is far away from the NHL." But the prospect was remaining with his junior team in Guelph (Ontario).

Perhaps it wasn't over in Philly for Forsberg who, after saying he would miss Gagne and Knuble—"we jelled perfectly"—raised the idea with the media, just as he had with Snider, about coming back as a free agent. Certainly this was what a woebegone team that went 15-20-5 with Forsberg and 0-13-3 without him wanted to hear.

"Simon and I hope his No.1 choice will be Philadelphia," said Knuble. "The door is always open.

"We have his email. Come July 1, we'll call him. Maybe Simon and I will fly over to Sweden and surprise him."

Then Knuble added bravely, "We want to keep getting better. We want to be a team worth coming to."

The Central Division-leading Predators finally had become one of those in their eighth season. "Has there ever been a better player traded at the trade deadline than Peter Forsberg?" said Poile, whose team never had won a playoff series. "My answer to that is, 'Probably not,' and the price we paid was very high.

"I think this is a clear message that we are aiming to be the best, and certainly hope this translates to more fan support from our community."

Coming out of the lockout, the Flyers had been nervous about their fans' loyalty, but the surprise Forsberg signing had blown away any bitterness. For half the 2005-06 season, as the team surged to the top of the NHL overall standings, the future Hall of Famer and, perhaps the best Swedish player ever, had landed in nirvana.

"In the beginning it was fantastic to be here," he recalls. "Then it kind of went downhill and got worse and worse.

"I had the big surgery—they actually cut the whole heel off and moved it over—but it didn't help. So I felt I was struggling.

"I look at my points—115 in 100 games—and it wasn't that bad. But I thought I could have done so much better. I didn't want to sign anything and not be worth the money. I got so frustrated with my health. My time in Philadelphia ended disappointingly, but I'm still really glad I got to experience that franchise. Mr. Snider and the fans cared so much; it was my kind of place."

Parent, who had excelled along with partner Marc Staal in a defensive role in the 2006 World Junior Championships but was sidelined with a bulging back disk at the time of the deal, said, "It was an honor to be part of a trade with someone of [Forsberg's] caliber."

Upshall welcomed the fresh chance. "Obviously, you're going to have a hard time replacing a guy like Peter Forsberg," he told reporters. "I just want to come in, get the train turned around, and help the Flyers be what they have always been."

Forsberg's foot had become Philadelphia's crutch. Holmgren tried to kick it from under the arms of his beleaguered players in a locker-room meeting the day following the deal.

"Homer said, 'You guys are the team,'" recalls assistant coach Terry Murray. "There was a change of attitude. Now the players wanted to grab ownership and you could sense that intangible. To me, that was a critical turning point, no matter how many games we lost the rest of the season."

The next day in New York, the Flyers looked reenergized. Fedoruk pounded away on Jagr, Umberger scored shorthanded in the first period, and Gagne's 31st goal of the season gave Philadelphia a 3-1 lead. Upshall, debuting on a line with Carter and Richards, scored during a third-period powerplay on a wraparound and Niittymaki was withstanding a 23-shot third period when Knuble and Ranger Brendan Shanahan turned near the blueline without seeing each other and collided headfirst.

Two 230-pound men were flat on the ice—Knuble face down, Shanahan on his back unmoving. Within two minutes, McCrossin got the bloodied and groggy Knuble to his knees and helped him off the ice. But Shanahan stayed down virtually motionless until his head and neck were stabilized and he was wheeled off.

Knuble suffered fractures of the right cheekbone and right orbital bone that were going to require surgery. Shanahan had a severe concussion.

"To see two veteran, respected, guys down and seriously hurt, it was an ill feeling on both benches," recalls Stevens.

Those ill feelings were dwarfed by those in Knuble's head. "It certainly was a long train ride home," he remembers. "I had avoided anything really big, injury-wise, to that point, but I guess you play long enough, your number comes up."

Shanahan says it was the only time he lost consciousness in his career. He laughs at the irony of it being caused by an ex-teammate. "I played with Mike at Detroit and we used to tease him that he took one of us out every practice," recalls Shanahan.

Certainly that kind of collision wasn't what Hatcher had in mind when he said after the Flyer 5-3 victory, "We want to see guys hitting." But nobody contradicted him when the defenseman called it "the best game we've played."

Two nights later at the Wachovia Center, the team started slowly, took too many penalties, and lost 6-3 to Boston as if the win in New York never had taken place.

In Buffalo, Umberger called out Brian Campbell, whose hit had concussed the winger the previous April, and won a narrow decision. Nevertheless, Stevens had to yank Esche in a 6-3 defeat. Niittymaki's glove, an ongoing issue, betrayed him on Rod Brind'Amour's early goal in Raleigh, but Picard's score with four minutes remaining tied the game, 2-2. Philadelphia went down regardless, 3-2, on Blake Wesley's goal 16 seconds into overtime.

Night after night the Flyers got off to slow starts. But Holmgren was full speed ahead on the youth movement.

Atlanta, leading the Southeast Division and under pressure to solidify the viability of the franchise with a deep playoff run, wanted veteran help on defense that Zhitnik could provide.

GM Don Waddell offered 22-year-old Braydon Coburn, the eighth-overall pick in the loaded 2003 draft. Had Coburn still been available when Philadelphia picked 11th that year, they would have taken him over Carter. Now they could get Coburn, who had divided his season between Atlanta and its AHL team in Chicago, in a one-for-one swap for Zhitnik, a 34-year-old journeyman. Holmgren jumped on it.

"Coburn was a big defenseman who could really skate and was a terrific kid," recalls Stevens. "That was a big building block."

Within nine days, the GM had acquired defensemen who had gone eighth (Coburn) and 18th (Parent) in recent drafts. "Coburn has tremendous size (6-5), skates and moves the puck well," the GM told the media. "We've been interested in him for a long while. I love him."

Zhitnik had been flipped after 31 games for a significant piece in the rebuild, but Holmgren wasn't looking at the 34-year-old Hatcher as a similar commodity. When there were expressions of interest in the veteran, he was called to Holmgren's hotel room.

"I remember Paul saying he really didn't want to trade me but he had a deal with Anaheim," Hatcher recalls. "They would end up winning the Stanley Cup that year, not bad, right?

"He said, 'think about it for a few hours.' The trade must have been pretty close. I called him back an hour or two later.

"For whatever reason, I didn't want to go. I felt like, 'I'm in this mess; instead of just bailing out, let's fight through it and try to get better.'"

Kapanen was all in, too, re-signing for $2.77 million over two years. "It was an easy decision," he said. "I believe we will be back contending next year and my family loves it here."

Knuble also took a two-year extension at $2.8 million per season. "Paul's message to me was, 'We're going to get this together and we want you to be a part of it,'" Knuble recalls. "I was like, 'I get it.'

"We'd had injuries and some bad personnel moves, but the core group was good. I felt the season was an anomaly that would be fixed. Some teams you feel like never are going to get fixed.

"Paul was saying in effect, 'We're tying some wagons to you.' That should mean something. It becomes your team. Derian and I wanted to see this through."

Gagne, who had signed a five-year deal before the season, wasn't going anywhere, nor was that his desire.

"I had a really good relationship with Paul at that time and had really good discussions with him almost every week," recalls Gagne. "I knew it wasn't going to be a three-season [rebuild]. The trades he already had made were a good sign.

"I knew we would go after this guy and that guy and get back to the playoffs right away. So I told [teammates], 'If you want to be here next year and be part of a good team, you have to show something now. You're playing for your jobs.'

"We would lose and they would be out afterwards, laughing and having a beer and just kind of not being affected by it. There were guys who just wanted to be traded, who didn't really get what was going on. The Flyers are a team that hates to lose and we had guys who didn't seem that bothered by it.

"I tried to be a leader, spoke up more in the dressing room. I was like, 'take some pride. We're [bleeping] dead last.'"

Some players didn't get a say in whether they wanted to stay. Baumgartner, farmed to the Phantoms in mid-October after being the biggest blueline acquisition of the summer, was picked up by Dallas on waivers.

"He was pretty smart with the puck, but just lacked too much foot speed for today's game," recalls Holmgren. "If you could still pick (forecheckers) and give him time back there, he would have been able to play.

"We had a year (under the obstruction crack-down) to see that before we signed him. We just misjudged what he could do."

Holmgren traded the disappointing Calder (21 points and minus-31 rating in 59 games) back to Chicago—which then moved him onto Detroit—obtaining 25-year-old defenseman Lasse Kukkonen and a third-round draft choice.

"Calder should have been better here," recalls Holmgren. "He had some personal issues that he was not dealing with very well."

Kukkonen, a fifth-round pick by the Blackhawks in 2003, had some skating limitations, but he had been an effective partner of Pitkanen's in Finland. The Flyers were desperate to get more out of a fourth-overall pick who they had expected to become their defensive anchor.

The construction had to be from the back end out, starting in goal. "The decision had been made that Esche was not going to be the guy moving forward," recalls Stevens. "I think we all felt we needed a goalie.

Simon Gagne sccored 41 goals in the midst of a very difficult season for the Flyers. He would be at the core of a rebuilt team goiing forward.

"Nitty had played at a really high level for me in the minors. I had envisioned him getting back to when he won that championship, but even when he played well, he'd still lose. So sometimes we'd put Esche back in. Neither goalie ever took the net and stole it that year. We needed our goalie to be our best player."

On the morning of the deadline, Philadelphia obtained 29-year-old Martin Biron, an upcoming free agent, from Buffalo for a second-round pick in 2007. Biron, who had become Ryan Miller's backup, was believed in many circles to be the best goaltender in the NHL who was not a starter.

"We needed some stability back there," recalls Holmgren. "Nitty was still a young guy but he had the hip issues, and Eschie had kind of peaked.

"Marty wasn't the starter in Buffalo because they had (Dominik) Hasek and were developing Miller. But Donny Luce knew Marty from way back.

"For someone who was going to be an unrestricted free agent at the end of the season, we tried to do it a little cheaper than a second-round pick. But at the end of the day we thought it was worth it. We felt like we had a pretty good chance to sign him."

In announcing the trade, Holmgren acknowledged the risk of the pick. "Hopefully, he will like the direction we're going in," said the GM.

Biron (134-115-25, 2.53, .896 for his career and 12-4-1, 3.04, .899 for that season) had been called in before the Sabres' morning skate in Toronto and told by coach Lindy Ruff not to go on the ice because the team was close to dealing him.

"He asked me how I felt about being traded," Biron recalls. "I thought that was funny because it wasn't my decision.

"If I wasn't traded then, I still would have been looking over the summer for a place to be a No. 1 goalie.

"A half hour later, Darcy (Buffalo GM Regier) told me where I was going. I was pretty excited it was Philadelphia because Don Luce was there. He had been the guy on stage when the Sabres drafted me (16th overall in 1995). I respected him a ton.

"The Flyers' record didn't scare me. I knew Simon Gagne really well from junior and they had just gotten Coburn and Upshall, so I knew they had a lot to look forward to and I was excited about the opportunity."

Having failed to move Esche at the deadline, Holmgren reduced the team's glut of goalies by exposing Leighton to waiver claim. He was taken by Montreal while the mentally-exhausted Niittymaki, though still with Philadelphia, was at least taken from his misery.

"To be honest , when they [traded for Biron], it was kind of a relief," Niittymaki recalls. "The hip still hurt and we were losing every game.

"Basically, you're going out there hoping that nothing bad happens and you're not going to get pulled. It wasn't fun.

"Johnny Stevens said, 'Just work hard. Marty is going to play and we'll see what happens next year.' I was like, 'thank God somebody else starts playing right now.'"

Holmgren didn't write off the shell-shocked Finn. "We still have high hopes for Niittymaki," said the GM. "This has been a tough year for him as well as everybody else."

Biron, who didn't bother to go home to Buffalo and pack, got to Boston ahead of the Flyers, who arrived late after losing to the Islanders, 6-5, in overtime. Following practice in the morning, he told reporters he was open to foregoing free agency. The two breakaways Biron faced in the first eight minutes the next day, both resulting in goals by Mark Mowers, didn't change the goalie's mind. Philadelphia bounced back to beat the Bruins, 4-3, on Upshall's breakaway goal with nine seconds remaining in overtime.

"One-handed move, just like Peter Forsberg, around Tim Thomas," recalls Biron. "Afterwards, the room was buzzing."

Mostly about the new goalie. "Marty gave us such a lift," raved Stevens. "He showed his composure and experience when we got down."

Biron lost a shootout at Pittsburgh as the Penguins completed an 8-0 sweep of the season series, 4-3, but then beat the Devils, 5-4, in overtime, on Gagne's 36th goal of the season. The goalie's puck-handling issues notwithstanding—the Flyers lost to Florida 2-1, when his early third-period clear went off defenseman Randy Jones' leg and into the net—Biron played like an upgrade, and so did the other first manifestations of the Holmgren remake.

Upshall had five goals and three assists in his first 11 games. "Scottie has a bubbly personality, lots of energy, and a terrific skill set," recalls Stevens. "Even though he was coming to the worst team in the league, he was so excited to get an opportunity to play."

Indeed, Upshall, quickly a fan favorite, felt he had joined a bear not in hibernation, but only taking a quick snooze. "It was an honor to put on a jersey that carried so much tradition," he recalls. "It felt like there was chemistry to be built around the group of guys that they were going to keep."

Kukkonen's enthusiasm was contagious, too. "He was awesome," recalls Stevens. "He's not a big defenseman and a great skater but whatever he lacked in skill level, he was one of the most competitive guys we had and just an absolutely terrific teammate.

"He would block shots, give you everything he had every shift. Guys loved him. He was a good add for us."

Snider and Luukko had been won over by Holmgren. On March 15, the GM signed a contract extension. It only lasted through the 2008-09 season, still the barest vote of confidence, but most importantly, he was getting more time to turn things around.

"Paul was in a tough position, but right away he thought about the long term," explained Luukko, who cited the advantage of rebuilding with a GM who had been running drafts and knew the prospects and young players around the NHL.

Added Snider, "In this year of transition, I think Paul has moved quickly and decisively to better our team on the ice and position ourselves for the future. He is very deserving of the opportunity to be our general manager."

Holmgren and his bosses were solidifying a healthy working relationship.

"I grew up loving and playing the game," recalls Luukko, "so I had enough knowledge where I could be either dangerous or helpful. My whole style—and, frankly, I learned much of this from Ed—was to ask, 'What do you feel we have to do to get to the next level and how can I help you?'

"Homer and I were great for brainstorming. He said things like, 'You've started businesses; I want to run my structure by you.' So I was always a sounding board, never overstepped the bounds. That's what you have your GM for. An Ed expression was, 'You hire good people and let them do their jobs.'

"I wasn't Paul Holmgren's or Bob Clarke's boss. I was their partner.

I remember sitting together for hours with Paul talking about the plan. At the end of the day, he had a great one.

"Many times Paul would call me and say, 'I'm thinking of doing such-and-such, maybe we've got to get Ed on the phone.' I'd say, 'Call him, drop him a note.'"

By extension through Holmgren, Luukko and Snider also were confirming their belief in Stevens. To keep his team focusing through an interminable season, the coach had been assigning point targets in five-game segments. Now Stevens knew he would at least last the five games.

"That whole year, we all felt like we always were a day away from the whole thing being blown up," the coach recalls. "So when [the contract extension] happened with Homer, it was obviously done with confidence that we were going in the right direction."

Stevens long before had wiped clean the NHL standings board in the locker room, trying to get his team just to play the next game hard. From the beginning, Murray was a huge ally and advisor.

"Murph was very generous in sharing his experience as a head coach," recalls Holmgren. "Terry did legwork in preparing the team, and together they came up with their game plans."

They had a good one for Atlanta, at least. As Knuble returned on March 15, the Flyers completed a difficult-to-explain season sweep of the Southeast Division leaders, 3-2, with Hatcher scoring a goal.

It was the only victory in a seven-game stretch by Philadelphia, which lost Upshall to a shoulder separation, then Fedoruk to a stunning knockout by New York's Colton Orr just 21 seconds into a March 21 game at Madison Square Garden.

Orr was in coach Tom Renney's starting lineup because Fedoruk had repeatedly body-checked Jagr during the previous Flyer visit and 5-3 victory. The Ranger tapped Fedoruk on the leg in an invitation quickly accepted. After tying each other up briefly, Orr got his right hand free to throw two glancing blows, then connected to the jaw with a haymaker. Fedoruk went to the ice unconscious, lying face up, his left hand raised at a right angle and twitching.

Silence fell over the Garden as a stretcher was brought out. "It was my first game back (from the Knuble collision)," recalls Shanahan. "You're always a little nervous about that and then you see a guy get knocked out on the first shift. It was unsettling."

Fedoruk regained consciousness while still on the ice and protested being wheeled off on a backboard, but was overruled, of course. He was aware of what had happened to him during the short ambulance ride to St. Vincent's Hospital, where no facial fractures were found, probably because of previous work performed on him. While playing for Anaheim five months earlier, Fedoruk had needed reconstruction after a fight with Minnesota's Derek Boogaard.

"The (three) surgeries he's had, Todd basically has a titanium face," said Holmgren after the 5-0 Flyer defeat. "When Fridge came here, I thought he might need the entire season to get over it. He will. I know the mentality he has."

As a precaution, Fedoruk was held overnight at St. Vincent's. "I do think anybody would be tentative," he said after being released the next day. "When you change your style a little bit you leave yourself vulnerable, and that's what happened to me last night. I will get back on track; I have had worse things done to me than this."

Indeed, it probably wasn't as bad as the figurative shot in the solar plexus that Esche, third man out of the goal, was taking daily.

"At the end, I wasn't allowed to skate in practice," he recalls. "I don't know whose decision that was, but it made sense. They had their two guys for next year and I was not going to be one of them.

"I just skated with the extra players and stayed out of the way. But I still looked at myself as a true Flyer and it hurt a lot, even if I wasn't crying about it. It wasn't easy to move on.

"Hatch, a great teammate, helped me get through a lot of things. Whether I was burned out from the last couple of years or wasn't at my best physically, or both, that year I couldn't play.

"My first few seasons with the Flyers, we had such strong leadership on the team. That helps you a lot. The last year it was like every man for himself."

Holmgren thought Esche had begun to think in those terms. "I like Robert, he's a very competitive guy," recalls the GM. "But I don't think he handled his tandem that well near the end and it affected Niittymaki and the team."

Niittymaki says he got along fine with Esche. "We had beers together on the road and never had any arguments," the Finn remembers. "I think it was a good relationship."

Recalls Holmgren: "Nitty is being kind. I remember calling Esche up—I was on the West Coast scouting juniors—and kind of reading him the riot act. I said, 'You might not play (anymore that season) and you had better not make any waves or I'll make sure you never play in the league again.'

"I got my point across. Robert is a good guy deep down, but he wasn't kind to Nitty."

While some veterans were territorial about jobs that weren't likely to keep going forward, Carter and Richards—twin draftees of the same year and already the team's two top centers at age 22—were fast friends being forced to grow up quickly.

"I don't think the league overwhelmed them at all," recalls Knuble. "Jeff had 37 points that year with a bad team and Richards 32 playing in every situation possible. You knew they were going to be players."

Richards doesn't recall struggling to put it all in perspective because he was too inexperienced to have one. "When you're young like that, you don't think of the big picture," he remembers.

Carter had not scored in 15 games until enjoying consecutive three-point nights in a 4-3 loss to the Islanders and a 5-1 win over Carolina. "You love the game, but when things are that bad and you know you're out of the playoffs by Christmas, it wears on you mentally," he recalls. "It's tough to get up and go to the rink."

But the young Flyer suffering the worst growing pains was Pitkanen, who was leading the club in turnovers and not lugging the puck, which should have been his strength. "Last year, before he got hurt (sports hernia surgery), he was great," Holmgren told reporters. "This year, he's sometimes up, sometimes down, but I'd like to think that last year was the Joni we're going to see.

"We tell him all the time to take the puck and go. He's still a good defender, he really is. We think he could be more creative and should shoot the puck more.

"He's a really nice kid but a loner in a lot of ways. Because of his age, because of where he's from (Oulu, almost in the Arctic Circle), because of his shyness, we're going to continue to work with him."

Holmgren's gamble of a second-round draft choice for Biron paid off on March 27, when the team announced his two-year, $7 million deal. The goalie had not been tempted to test the market after July 1.

"I didn't know what free agency was going to be like and I felt like I needed to be loyal," recalls Biron. "The Flyers had traded a good pick for me.

"They had good young guys and cap room, and planned to be aggressive. I knew Philly was going to be a real good spot for the next few years."

He had won three of his first five starts. But the March 28 win over Carolina at the Wachovia Center was the team's only victory in a stretch of 10 games.

Shawny Hill kept dancing though. And for the most part, the season-ticket holders continued to show up. "There were only about 1,000-1,500 no-shows more than normal toward the end, which was amazing," recalls Luukko.

Still, the loyalty wasn't being rewarded. Too many players just wanted the season over. "It's up to the older guys to help people realize there are things to play for at season's end," said Knuble, who, like Hatcher, was trying to take leadership in the absence of an official captain.

"There is a reason why there are captains. Any team will benefit from a consistent presence."

Stevens had reasons for not naming one to get through the year. "It was so late when Peter got traded and there was so much transition going on," he recalls. "More changes were coming in the off-season; we were better off waiting."

Change is good, decided the Philadelphia veterans as they played their last-ever game at the Meadowlands on March 30, and lost it 3-1. Having gone 22-44-6-2 there over regular seasons dating back to when the Colorado franchise moved to New Jersey in 1982, the Flyers looked forward to trying their luck at the new Prudential Center in Newark starting in the fall.

That said, it is the losses that make the wins special. While some of Philadelphia's greatest triumphs had taken place at the Meadowlands—five in eight playoff games and the birth of the Legion of Doom—there were no memorable wins during the season from Hell.

Losing to the Islanders, 4-2, at the Wachovia Center on April 7, the 2006-07 Flyers were assured of having the fewest points in franchise history. It was not the way Hatcher wanted to commemorate his 1,000th NHL game, nor Gagne his 40th goal of the season, but the team's two most consistent players had earned a little consolation for a season of pain.

"People are going to remember the Stanley Cups," said Gagne, who, despite a groin issue, had not bailed out of the lineup down the endless stretch. "And the other thing they will remember is this year. It's not fun when your name is part of that."

Stevens never made avoidance of the ignominy a motivation. "I don't think it mattered whether you're the worst or the second-worst," he recalls. "We were trying to win every game."

In Game 82, Biron had fun beating the Sabres, the disinterested Presidents' Trophy winner, 4-3, but to the nine Flyers who had endured the entire season, the only significance to the game was that it set the team's final point total at 56, two fewer than the 1969-70 Flyers—who went 17-35-24 for 58 points and were eliminated on the final day when Bernie Parent allowed a goal from center ice by Minnesota's Barry Gibbs.

The longest six months of Derian Hatcher's life were over. "I never saw anything like this coming," he said. "It's tough to put in words.

"You always had hope, even when we were 1-6-1, that we were going to turn it around. I did, anyway. We played somewhat better towards the end, but still weren't a very good team."

Philadelphia had finished with 56 points—11 fewer than the 29th-place Coyotes—and missed the playoffs by 36. Following the coaching change, Stevens' team had gone 21-42-11. "He came into a hornet's nest," Hatcher told the media. "I think he was a little overwhelmed at first, but he did take control, I definitely saw that transition. By the end of the year, he had a grip on things."

Holmgren agreed Stevens had been put in a virtually impossible spot. "I think John is a tremendous young coach," the GM said. "I like his style and I know he'll be better next year. Getting a training camp under his belt and having things in place the way he wants will make a big difference."

Sanderson was the sole survivor of the preseason moves made by Clarke. There had been 301 man-games lost to injuries and a franchise-high 49 players used. The Flyers could only hope a group of them would become better for their hard-earned experience. "We were too young in a lot of areas this year," Holmgren said.

Moving ahead, the core consisted of forwards Gagne, Knuble, Richards, Carter, Umberger, Kapanen and Upshall, plus Hatcher, Coburn, and Pitkanen on defense, and Biron and Niittymaki in goal. Holmgren considered it a good start towards respectability.

"Clarkie felt like he left things in a bad way," Holmgren recalls. "But we had a number of kids and Gagne, Knuble and Hatcher still were good players. And we had cap room."

The organization never had suffered any problem getting some of the league's better players to take its money. But Snider feared the worst record in the league would scare them away.

"I remember Ed telling me, 'It's really risky what we're doing here,'" recalls Luukko. "He asked, 'Who in their right mind would come play for us?'

"I told him, 'they'll come here because of you and your reputation.'

"He said, 'Yeah, that's nice.' And I said, 'No, I mean it.'

"We're going to get free agents because of our history. One year is not going to destroy the reputation of you and this team."

PAUL HOLMGREN

THE FLYER PRESIDENT WORKED HIS WAY to the top tarting from the bottom of a pile of brawling players.

In March 1976, a skate blade creased Paul Holmgren's right eye during an altercation in an American Hockey League game in Springfield, MA. When the right wing was called up to the NHL a few days later, he hid the fact that his vision was compromised.

As it turned out, that was not even the worst of it. After making a memorable Flyer debut by bulldozing Ranger star Phil Esposito onto his backside, Holmgren showed up for a team meeting at a Boston hotel the following night with his eye suddenly so swollen that he had to be rushed to the Massachusetts Eye and Ear Infirmary. During emergency surgery, the rookie suffered a reaction to the anesthetic that twice forced operating room personnel to re-start his heart.

Before his career could even begin, Holmgren had to beat death, but it has returned to repeatedly confront him. At age 15, he came home from school to see the priest's car in front of the house. His brother, Dave, 23, had passed away from diabetic complications that had left him blind the final four years of his life. Paul lost another brother, Mark, to the effects of diabetes at age 49, and a sister, Janice, to cancer at age 42. He is the only one of four siblings to make it to age 50.

"When I was 49, I was scared to death," he said. "Really, every headache I feared might be a tumor."

The fact that he is going strong at 60 still sometimes surprises him. If Holmgren covers his left eye, he cannot make out your face, but all he has been through helps him see the big picture at 20-20. Ultimately, he has been fortunate. So have been the Flyers that his eye for talent remains uncompromised. As director of scouting and assistant general manager, he endorsed the drafting of Claude Giroux, Mike Richards and Jeff Carter; as general manager, he executed the signings of Danny Briere, Scott Hartnell and Kimmo Timonen, plus the trades for Wayne Simmonds, Jake Voracek, Sean Couturier and Brayden Schenn.

Inheriting the worst team in Flyer history after Bob Clarke quit in October 2006, Holmgren signed and traded the club back to the semifinals the very next season and to the Final in 2010. It was a remarkable turnaround and Holmgren laid the groundwork for it with no reassurance that he was anything more than a temporary GM.

During his career, Holmgren has often been underestimated, much to Philadelphia's benefit. Other than Chairman Ed Snider and Clarke, who brought Holmgren back to the organization twice—in 1985 as an assistant on the bench, and in 1995 as director of pro scouting—the franchise has not had a more constant presence. No player or employee has better exemplified toughness and loyalty—the primary qualities of being a Flyer.

"Mr. Snider and Clarkie gave me opportunities," said Holmgren. But it was he who made the most of his chances. The biggest thrill of his career remains playing in his first NHL game. Everything that has followed has been a bonus. "It truly has been beyond my wildest dreams."

In 1975, the Flyers took a month to call Holmgren after drafting him in the sixth round. When the World Hockey Association's Minnesota Fighting Saints, who had not paid their players for a month, folded in mid-season, Holmgren assumed Philadelphia—venturing a sixth-round pick on a rare American without knowledge he had signed with the rival league—had no interest. He was planning a return to the University of Minnesota to play baseball when Flyer GM Keith Allen offered a contract.

One of Holmgren's best skills, as would be endorsed by anyone who ever has worked with him, is listening. But was he hearing this right? Was he being offered a chance to play for the Stanley Cup champions?

PAUL HOLMGREN
FLYER HERO #8

"I had no confidence," he recalls. "Whenever I passed the puck, I thought I should have shot it; when I shot it, I thought I should have passed it."

From Day One, Holmgren was big, powerful and so earnest and respectful that he became more to Clarke than a teammate. "Clarke went out of his way for every new guy," recalls Holmgren, but the bond between the two was almost instant and deep. In Holmgren's case, it grew because of Clarke's diabetes.

"We talked about the disease, and Clarkie was a big help to my brother Mark," said Holmgren. The best player the Flyers ever had played 15 years against considerable odds. Holmgren also had a handicap to overcome, deepening the relationship.

When struck in the same eye by a racquetball during the summer of 1976, surgery, prayer, and exercise were again needed. Holmgren would cover his good eye and watch television with the other one and doctors who first measured his vision at 20/300 were amazed when it apparently improved to 20/30. "Actually, they never changed the chart, so I memorized it," Holmgren said. He could not tell if a puck was on the ice or six inches off it, but he certainly didn't need a dog to lead him to the net. Or, for that matter, to the doctor's office.

In 1978, Holmgren suffered a chipped vertebra and was declared out for the season. Regardless, he was in the lineup for the next game. His strength of character was matched only by the power in his upper body. "He ran into me one time at practice and every part of me hurt," said coach Fred Shero. "Even my hair. I didn't know hair could hurt."

Fearless and reckless, conditioned well above the standards of the day, Holmgren threw his 200 pounds around rinks for nine Flyer seasons. His final statistics—144 goals, and 179 assists in only 527 career games—suggest he was an average, oft-injured and penalty-prone performer whose minutes (1,684) more than tripled his final point totals. But that impression would be wrong. During his two peak seasons, 1979-80 and 1980-81, Holmgren scored 30 and 22 goals, respectively, and was among the better right wings in the game.

He protected his smallish, persistently annoying linemates—Ken Linseman and Brian Propp—from physical harm, and cleared room for them and himself with a temper that drew two lengthy suspensions. One was for six games in 1978 for cracking Ranger Carol Vadnais over the helmet with a stick; the other, in 1982, for five games after shoving referee Andy van Hellemond at the end of a fight with Pittsburgh's Paul Baxter.

"I'm not proud of all the stupid stuff I did," Holmgren said. Even back then, the soft-spoken and reflective guy bore little relation to the one who would snap. Still, the short fuse often served him well because of the fear it generated in opponents. Holmgren missed being on the second Cup team by a year, and being a part of another championship in 1980 by just two wins, but he had every quality of the most willful of the Broad Street Bullies, especially playing through shoulder issues that ended his career prematurely.

"He was all beat-up and gave the Flyers what he had," remembers Clarke. When coach-GM Bob McCammon thought there was little left, he traded Holmgren home to Minnesota just before a February 1984 Spectrum game against the North Stars. Not wanting to distract the team, McCammon decided to announce the deal after the game but, upset he wasn't dressing, Paul had left the Spectrum and received the news on the car's radio.

Holmgren lasted only 27 games with the North Stars before his shoulder drove him into retirement at age 29. On Clarke's recommendation, Holmgren was hired by Keenan as an assistant coach in 1985, and then, in 1988-89, became his replacement. As a rookie boss, Holmgren directed the aging nucleus of Keenan's two-time finalists to a last hurrah—a first-round upset of Washington, and a Game Seven win over Mario Lemieux in Pittsburgh—before losing to Montreal in the semifinals.

Barren drafts, the franchise's first playoff miss in 18 years, and bad communication between Clarke and team president Jay Snider led to Clarke's firing in April 1990. New GM Russ Farwell kept Holmgren on but, following the team's late-season collapse in 1990-91, he was dismissed after an 8-14-2 start in December 1991.

Hired by the Hartford Whalers, Holmgren did two stints behind their bench, and one as GM around a stretch at the Betty Ford Clinic following a drunk-driving crash. His wife, Doreen, and the Whalers supported him through what he calls "a dark period of my life," but he was able to find strength and put his self-destructive behavior behind him. Twenty-two years sober, he still attends Alcoholics Anonymous meetings a few times a week.

Clarke, who returned as Flyer GM in 1994, brought Holmgren back in 1995-96 as player personnel director and then promoted him to assistant GM. When Clarke resigned suddenly in October 2006, he recommended that Holmgren take over the reins, but Snider and CEO Peter Luukko did not immediately accept the suggestion. Both had wanted to go beyond the organization for a fresh outlook.

Holmgren learned from a reporter that Colin Campbell, the NHL's vice president and former Ranger coach, had turned down Snider's offer to become Flyer GM. With no vote of confidence, Holmgren sifted through the wreckage from the perfect storm that sent the team to the bottom of the league and started the rebuild. One day and deal at a time, he won Snider and Luukko over with trades for Braydon Coburn and Marty Biron—using the prospects and picks obtained by dealing Peter Forsberg—and then sold his rebuilding plan to free agents Timonen, Briere and Hartnell.

When it became clear to Holmgren that the contender he had built was minus one big piece, he showed the courage, over Snider's skepticism, to trade three first-round picks to obtain Chris Pronger, who anchored Philadelphia to the 2010 Final.

A season later, after becoming troubled by the team's direction, Holmgren traded Richards and Carter for four players who are part of today's nucleus. When Pronger's career ended prematurely, the GM took a run at replacing him with restricted free-agent Shea Weber, signing him to a front-loaded offer sheet that was looked upon as predatory by many in the NHL. Nashville was forced to match.

Over time, Holmgren came to feel that the hostility his move generated around the league compromised his ability to function. He also feared losing assistant GM Ron Hextall, whom he had brought back from Los Angeles a year earlier as a successor-in-waiting, to another franchise. So Holmgren, with Snider's endorsement, hurried along the process and stepped upstairs at the conclusion of the 2013-14 season.

"Homer would do everything he could, turn over every rock," says Hextall. "He was creative, always trying to find ways to make the team better."

A cost of that became cap-choking contracts Hextall inherited for Scott Hartnell, Vincent Lecavalier and Andrew MacDonald that have precluded big moves over the last two seasons to make the Flyers elite again. Regardless, a big expenditure on a free agent has never been part of Hextall's plan. He does not believe he took the job wearing handcuffs.

"I said this when I took over: Look at the young pieces we had in place—Giroux, Voracek, Simmonds, Couturier, and Shayne Gostisbehere coming," says Hextall.

"Before I came back to Philadelphia, I interviewed for another GM job—I won't say where—but it was not a good situation at all. When I took over here, I felt like I came in at a good time.

"I think Homer did a helluva job. That turnaround (in 2007-08) was incredible. Two more wins in 2010—if you remember, a few of those games really could have gone either way—and Homer would have become the GM who brought the Flyers another Cup."

It was Snider, not Holmgren, who wanted to sign a big-ticket goalie in 2011. The consequence was Ilya Bryzgalov and an expensive buyout, but Holmgren does not regret anything he did to almost win a championship.

"A lot of the reason we [had to juggle to stay under] the cap was because we had really good players that were on long-term injury reserve—Pronger, Mike Rathje, Derian Hatcher," Holmgren recalls.

"We did the best we could. Could we have done better? Probably. There were some situations in dealing with people I could have handled better. I give myself a B. We didn't win the Stanley Cup.

"I'm not going to beat myself up over contracts. If you are afraid to keep a player off a career year (in the case of Hartnell), how do you maintain a contender?

"Contrary to what some people might say, I never liked giving up picks for short-term guys. I am a believer in building through the draft and player development as much as possible. Sometimes stuff happens—injuries, a need for depth—and it makes sense to try to help out your team. But I never had a strategy to trade picks. We always did it reluctantly.

"Our scouts have done a good job at identifying young guys who come into the system other ways—college guys like Matt Read, or European players like Pierre-Edouard Bellemare or Michael Raffl, who develop a little later. So that offsets trading some of those picks. But at a certain point, yeah, it takes its toll to trade off second- and third-round picks with too much frequency."

The job of team president being largely Holmgren's to shape, he has endeavored to make the staffs on the hockey and business sides more interactive. From the first time Holmgren made an opponent pay for messing with Clarke, through his legendary lifting of Mike Bullard by the throat for breaking curfew during the 1989 semifinal run, to giving up the GM position because he thought Hextall would do a better job, the team always has come first.

USA Hockey officials have repeatedly chosen Holmgren—the 2014 Lester Patrick Award winner for service to hockey in the United States—to serve in managing and coaching capacities for the Olympics and World Cups. They have learned what the Flyers have known: Holmgren is the easiest of people to work with but never a pushover.

"Claude Giroux, who had just made the team coming out of training camp (in 2009) said, 'Mr. Holmgren, I'm thinking of living in Olde City,'" recalls Luukko. "Paul said, 'Claude, you've got two choices—Voorhees or Adirondack.'

"Claude said, 'I think I'll like Voorhees, Mr. Holmgren.'

"Paul would be a great leader in war because he doesn't get too high or low. I never really saw him yell and scream."

The look in his eye that opponents dreaded has made raising his voice unnecessary.

"I don't think I'm aggressive by nature," said Holmgren. "Most people who know me say I am a calm, quiet guy, but if you are competitive, stuff sometimes happens. I have been known to do stupid things playing pickup basketball."

Don't mess with Mr. Holmgren or his Flyers. Serving the organization for four decades has been a privilege, so having the big title gives him no sense of entitlement. He has earned every responsibility given to him in shaping this proud franchise.

Dismayed Wasjington fans watch Joffrey Lupul celebrate his Game Seven overtime goal during the 2008 Eastern Conference quarterfinals. Flyers won 3-2.

Chapter 10 • 2007-08

With A Vengeance

As the general manager of a team that had finished dead last in the 2006-07 season, Paul Holmgren had needs at practically every position and approximately $15 million in salary-cap room with which to fill them. He also had a marketable commodity in defenseman Joni Pitkanen, who had asked to be traded.

"To this day, I have no idea why," recalls Holmgren. "I know he especially liked (Ken) Hitchcock (the coach the Flyers had fired in October), but if he didn't like (successor) John Stevens, that didn't make any sense."

Or, maybe it did. "I'd had Joni in the minors and liked him, but he never embraced the team game we [insisted] was necessary," recalls Stevens. "Maybe he didn't appreciate being told that; I don't know, he never said."

The Flyers, who had traded winger Ruslan Fedotenko in an exchange of first-round picks that enabled them to select Pitkanen fourth overall in the 2002 draft, were frustrated, but still not anxious to give up on him.

"Joni was one of those guys who always seemed to leave you wanting more than what you got from him," recalls Holmgren.

"He could skate with anyone, had high-end puck skills, a heavy shot, a little bit of nastiness from time to time, and could eat up all the ice time you gave him. But after one really good year for us with Peter Forsberg, Joni went sideways or even backwards a little.

"You could see he had another level, so we still wanted to keep him. But he wasn't buying it."

Even had Pitkanen wanted to stay, he was not maturing quickly enough to fill the team's immediate need for a cornerstone defenseman.

Soon after Nashville's five-game first-round upset by San Jose, Predators' GM David Poile received a call from Holmgren asking whether Nashville was going to be able to keep Kimmo Timonen—a 32-year-old defenseman considered the best of the offensive defensemen who could reach free agency on July 1—and 25-year-old left wing Scott Hartnell—a six-year pro who had been the sixth-overall pick in the 2000 draft.

"If you let us try to sign them before July 1, maybe there is something the Flyers can do in terms of compensation," Holmgren told Poile.

The Predators, for sale by owner Craig Leipold, had no money budgeted to sign Timonen or Hartnell. "It was a painful time," recalls Poile. "We were just getting by (financially) and I was being given no guidance or direction (about the franchise's future).

"It clearly was the best thing I could do to get assets for the two players. Paul stepped to the plate."

Back in February, Holmgren had traded a second-round pick for another upcoming free agent, Buffalo goaltender Martin Biron, hoping that if the goaltender finished the season with Philadelphia he would want to stay. It worked. Biron had re-upped without testing the market.

"Other teams had made those kinds of trades (for free agents-to-be)," recalls Holmgren. But not many, actually. For an exclusive, pre-July 1 window to negotiate with Timonen and Hartnell—whom Poile informed Holmgren were best friends and road roommates—the Flyer GM was willing to return the first-round pick he obtained from Nashville as part of the February trade that sent Peter Forsberg to the Predators. It had turned into the 23rd selection.

"David would get that pick if I could sign both of them," recalls Holmgren. "It was lesser [selections], a third-rounder as I recall, if I could only get one.

"There also was a price if I didn't sign either."

There was no alternative defenseman of Timonen's ability available by trade or free agency, the reason why Holmgren was willing to give up the valuable rebuilding asset of a first-round selection. But there was a strong chance of three attractive centers coming on the unrestricted free agent market on July 1—Buffalo's Danny Briere and Chris Drury, plus New Jersey's Scott Gomez. So the Flyers had a Plan B.

"If we couldn't sign Timonen and Hartnell, we would have cap room for two of those centers instead of one," recalls Holmgren. "And based on the conversation we were having about Pitkanen, we knew there was a good chance we were going to get a winger back in that deal."

Granted, there was no guarantee Briere, Drury or Gomez would be coming to Philadelphia. There was only an intelligent guess by the Flyer brain trust that the signing of Timonen, who had just finished fifth in the 2006-07 Norris Trophy balloting, might help reel in one of those centers. So on Friday June 15, Poile and Holmgren agreed on the terms of the conditional draft choices. Holmgren was given 48 hours to make the deals, or else Poile would move onto the next suitor, which the Flyers later found out was Edmonton.

Poile called the players' two agents—Allan Walsh for Hartnell, Bill Zito for Timonen—and told them their clients' rights had been transferred to Philadelphia. "We were preparing for July 1 and were very surprised," said Zito. "But we had nothing to lose."

Walsh wanted $4 million a year for Hartnell, a 22-goal scorer in 2006-07. Timonen was going to cost in the range of $6 million per season.

Holmgren called Timonen, who happened to be visiting Forsberg in Sweden.

"Why would I want to sign with you guys?" asked Timonen. "You were the worst team in the league last year."

"He really hit me with a hammer," Holmgren recalls. "But it was a good question."

"I said, 'We don't plan on being the worst team in the league next year. Feel free to talk to anybody you want about our kids. We have good ones here. We're trying to sign Hartnell, too. And we are going to be active for one of those centers.'

"We talked for about half an hour. I ended up throwing a lot of [bleep] out there that I didn't know I could make come true. But I was going to try.

"I never brought up Jussi (Kimmo's younger brother by eight years, a Philadelphia draftee who had played 14 games and 46 with the Phantoms the previous season). Kimmo probably knew Jussi wasn't a full-time NHL guy."

Holmgren found Hartnell instantly sold on the Flyer brand. "He seemed to know about our history, never asked those questions that Kimmo did," recalls the GM.

"From the beginning, I felt more confident that we were going to get Scotty than I did about Kimmo. With Scotty, it was just a matter of the money."

Hartnell, who had not been out of the first round in any of his six seasons with Nashville, checked the Philadelphia roster on-line and saw enough talent to convince him it was an up-and-coming team. "The Flyers always were in the hunt," he recalls. "Plus, I was flattered that they had made the trade for me.

"I looked at some other cities that might be interested after July 1 and, hands down, Philadelphia was the best. With the history and everything, it was a no-brainer."

He called Timonen. "I said, 'You'll never guess what's going on. They've traded my rights to a team that's made a really good offer to sign me before July 1.'

"Kimmo said, 'Oh really? The same thing is happening to me.'

"I asked, 'What team are you talking to?' He goes, 'Philadelphia.' I'm like, 'No way! I'm talking to Philly, too.'

"That definitely was comforting to me, even though there was no certainty he was going to sign."

Flyer winger Sami Kapanen shared ownership with Timonen of the KalPa Kuopio Finnish club, after playing together there and on the national team. Kapanen put in a good word about Philadelphia.

"Sami said it was a great place to play and a great place to live," recalls Timonen. "And he said to believe Homer—the Flyers were going to do anything to try to get better.

"That was probably the biggest thing. I didn't want to come to a team where the illusion just keeps going and we just slowly get better. I went through that in Nashville and it was no fun."

Except to talk about his big plans, Holmgren had little leverage in contract negotiations. "We had kind of set the market for [Hartnell] at about $3.75 million, but Walsh never budged off the number he wanted for him," recalls the GM. "We ended up stretching [the deal's length] to help from a cap standpoint."

Willing to front-load the deal to $5.2 million in its first season, Philadelphia took its total offer up to $25.2 million over six seasons to ease the cap figure to $4.2 million. Hartnell accepted the terms on Sunday, within the 48-hour window set by Nashville.

Recalls Hartnell: "I called Kimmo and said, 'I have to take this deal. I don't think I'm going to get a better one. It's going to be great; you have to come, too.'

"He was laughing." But not yet committing.

"Bill Zito wasn't giving me a whole lot of help in talking Kimmo into coming here," recalls Holmgren. "Bill was like, 'You are going to have to talk to him again. I can only tell him so many things. Let's try to negotiate [the money.]'

"He knew other teams were going to be lined up."

Zito wasn't budging on an average $6 million a year, so the Flyers added two more seasons to lessen the cap hit.

Holmgren tried to reach Timonen several times on Sunday, but he was pondering, not answering. "I was home, just didn't have my phone on," Timonen recalls. "When I checked messages, there was a bunch from the Flyers."

Poile gave Holmgren a one-day extension. Philadelphia had not counted on Jussi's presence in the organization to influence Kimmo's decision. But, fortunately, it had become a factor.

"When I told my dad (Jukko) that I had a chance to go play with Jussi, he was so happy, he couldn't talk," Kimmo would say.

After three days, Timonen was hearing what he had hoped.

"I had wanted to test the market, but when I heard all this talk about the team getting better, it got me excited," he recalls. "Scott had committed. I thought, 'Let's do this together.'"

On Monday, Zito called Holmgren to accept his six-year $37.8 million offer. Timonen would be paid $8 million for the first two seasons, $7 million for the next two, and the cap hit would be $6.3 million.

The Flyers were taking a risk that a 5-foot-10, 32-year-old defenseman would prove effective until age 38. "I didn't worry about that at all," Holmgren remembers. "Our scouts all liked him.

"This was a smart, two-way, guy who could move pucks and be good on our powerplay."

The simultaneous announcement of the deals brought Holmgren admiration throughout the hockey world for getting ahead of the market to land its best defenseman and a winger entering his prime years. It was acknowledged that Philadelphia had overpaid by at least a little and possibly by a lot. But the GM had to give Gomez, Briere or Drury, evidence that it was not going to take three or four years for the Flyers to contend.

"[Hartnell's] numbers have improved every year and he is still on the upward swing," Holmgren told the media. "From a character, grit, and skill standpoint, he's going to be a tremendous addition for us.

"Timonen gets the puck out of his own end and helps out offensively. He is one of the better two-way defensemen in the game. He is not a very big man, but he is smart."

Timonen called it "an awesome day for me and my family" and a "once-in-a-lifetime chance." Hartnell said he had been swayed by Holmgren's level of commitment.

Factoring in the Philadelphia-Nashville trade in February, the Flyers had received Timonen, Hartnell, Scottie Upshall, Ryan Parent and a third-round pick from the Predators for Forsberg, who was a free agent after having played just 17 regular-season and five playoff games for the Predators.

The Flyers announced Hartnell and Timonen on Monday June 18, hours before the lottery was held in New York to determine Philadelphia's spot in the 2016 draft.

The bottom five teams of the 2006-07 season had a chance at winning the weighted drawing for the first pick. The only thing that finishing 30th out of 30 guaranteed the Flyers was that they could not drop below second. The extra numbers assigned them for being last still only provided a 26 percent chance at going first.

The hockey gods, apparently believing that Philadelphia's precipitous drop in 2006-07 had been a fluke, decided that the Blackhawks, who had missed the playoffs eight times in nine seasons, had suffered enough. Chicago, the fifth-worst team, hit on its eight percent chance, and got the first pick.

Holmgren, who had declined to attend, was content to take the news—good or bad—in a phone call.

"Peter (Luukko, Comcast-Spectacor president) asked me if I wanted to go," recalls the GM. "The accounting firm watches over everything; no need to be there.

"When you are the worst team in the league you don't want to parade around."

Second would be the highest pick the Flyers had since 1975, when they had traded up to first and selected Mel Bridgman. But to Holmgren and his scouts, it was a clear loss. They believed that right wing Patrick Kane of the London Knights unquestionably was the best prospect in the draft, never mind he weighed 162 pounds and was ranked second by NHL Central Scouting among North American prospects to center Kyle Turris of the Tier II Burnaby Express.

"When a player is that good, you don't worry about the size," recalls Holmgren. "Kane had escapability, excellent awareness of everything going on around him and really tremendous hands. We all knew he was going to be special."

There was little chance the Blackhawks would pass on the one player in the draft the Flyers believed was capable of becoming a superstar. "Having the No. 2 pick is good, but it's not like there's a (Evgeni) Malkin or Jordan Staal at No. 2 this year," Holmgren advised reporters at a pre-draft briefing.

Philadelphia scouts loved the size (6-1, 187), play-making ability, and speed of Jakub Voracek, a Czech Republic-born right wing of the Halifax Mooseheads, but questioned his finishing skills. To Holmgren the choice came down to Turris or prototypical power winger, 6-3, 200-pound left wing James van Riemsdyk of Middletown, NJ, who had scored 31 goals playing 49 games on the Under-18 team of the U.S. Hockey Development Program.

"I didn't see John LeClair as a young player, but our scouts say [van Riemsdyk] is ahead of John at that age," Holmgren told reporters. "I would say that he's probably got better hands in maybe making a play (than LeClair), but maybe not his ability to finish.

"Van Riemsdyk is a hard-working kid at both ends and he's going to put up numbers."

The Flyers had gone away from the big-and-strong organizational stereotype in successfully gambling on slightly undersized players like Simon Gagne, Justin Williams and Claude Giroux (the 2006 first-round pick who had scored 112 points in 63 games for his junior team in Gatineau, Quebec in his post-draft season). But Holmgren and director of scouting Chris Pryor went to Columbus for the draft having decided on van Riemsdyk as the best player available to them, should they keep the second selection.

"(Edmonton GM) Kevin Lowe had three first-round picks (Nos. 6, 15 and 21) and wanted to move up to the second spot, probably to take Turris," recalls Holmgren. "He called and offered the six and the 21.

"I said, 'Give me all three of your picks and we'll do it.' Maybe I was being a little greedy, I don't know. If we had gotten the sixth pick, we probably would have taken Voracek. But we really liked (defenseman) Ryan McDonagh, too.

"We liked Turris, just liked JVR a little more. Kyle was skinny, almost Giroux-like, if taller. JVR had a bigger frame and was more dynamic."

Once Chicago took Kane, van Riemsdyk—a lifelong Ranger fan headed for the University of New Hampshire—was not surprised when Philadelphia called out his name. "I had a pretty strong feeling it was the Flyers just by how they talked to me (at the Scouting Combine)," he told reporters.

Turris went to Phoenix with the third selection, Voracek to Columbus with the seventh, and McDonagh to Montreal with the 12th.

For the sake of his draftee's feelings, Holmgren told reporters the Flyers would have not have taken Kane over van Riemsdyk. "He's big, can skate, has good hands," the GM said. "He continued to get better as the year went on. I don't think he is done growing."

At the draft, Holmgren, who had never acknowledged publicly Pitkanen's request to be traded, negotiated a deal that would send him to Dallas for 28-year-old winger Niklas Hagman and 34-year-old defenseman Philippe Boucher. The trade was about to be consummated when trainer Jim McCrossin got tipped that Boucher's shoulder was significantly damaged.

"Somebody whose conscience bothered them," is all McCrossin will reveal about his source. The Flyers pulled out, much to the anger of the Stars' front office.

"[GM Doug] Armstrong was [bleeping] angry," recalls Holmgren. "I said, 'Doug, you had better talk to your doctors.'

"Kevin Maxwell, a good friend who had scouted for us and was working for Dallas was really hot and started to tell me off.

"I said 'Maxy, you had better get your facts straight.' He ended up apologizing."

As it turned out, Boucher would need season-ending surgery by December and would last only 79 games over two seasons until retiring.

Holmgren turned to Edmonton, the other serious bidder for Pitkanen.

"The Oilers couldn't or didn't want to sign Jason Smith (their 33-year-old defenseman and captain)," recalls the Flyer GM, "We thought for a couple years he would be a good, steady, defenseman."

To satisfy Philadelphia's requirement for a young player with growth potential, Oiler GM Kevin Lowe was willing to include 25-year old winger Joffrey Lupul, who had been the seventh selection, three behind Pitkanen and one behind Flyer winger Upshall, in the 2002 draft.

After being acquired the previous season from Anaheim in a package for defenseman Chris Pronger, Lupul had dipped from 28 goals to 16 with the Oilers, his hometown team.

"He could skate and shoot. When he played for Cincinnati against the Phantoms, we liked what he brought," recalls Holmgren.

"If I also gave Kevin a third-round pick, he would take Geoff Sanderson and give us a $1.5 million cap break. We had liked the Dallas deal just a little better. But we liked this one, too. These were good fits for us."

On the night of June 30, Lowe and Holmgren agreed to a deal of Pitkanen, Sanderson and a third-round pick for Smith and Lupul. Because the summer grace period allowing teams to be up to 10 percent over the cap would begin on July 1, Holmgren asked to announce the deal after noon the next day, when free agency began.

It figured to be an anxiety-filled, and potentially franchise-turning, afternoon. Recalls Luukko: "There haven't been three marquee guys like Gomez, Briere and Drury available at one time since that year, and probably never will be again. Teams have been locking up their good young players with long-term contracts."

Among Holmgren confidants, there were slight differences as to the order of preference. Gomez was the youngest—by three years over Drury and by two over the soon-to-turn-30-year-old Briere, no small consideration.

Perhaps because Briere had scored 18 points in 16 career games against Philadelphia—adding nine in Buffalo's six-game playoff triumph in 2006—he was Chairman Ed Snider's preferred choice. But amongst the brain trust, it was unanimous that all three were worth big money.

Holmgren believed his best chance was Briere for two reasons: Biron—who had been Briere's roommate in Buffalo—and Don Luce—who had been the Sabre head of player development before joining the Flyers in the same capacity the previous season. But unwilling to assume anything, the GM was going to make offers to all three players, even though the team could comfortably fit only one under its cap.

There was also speculation that Briere and Drury, the one-two center combination in Buffalo for three seasons, might want to move somewhere together. Philadelphia didn't want to risk losing its first choice and then come in too late for the second and third.

"We could have maneuvered enough cap room after the fact to take two," recalls Holmgren, who then laughs. "Had all three accepted, the Phantoms would have had a pretty good team that year."

It was Luukko's idea to have high-level Flyer representatives present the offers personally to all three free agents, along with a bonus. He had the finance department cut checks for $5 million and was booked to go to Los Angeles—where Briere would field offers from the office of agent Pat Brisson—when Holmgren, worried about communication gaps amidst the need to make fast decisions while also clueing in Snider, decided to put out the bids from his Voorhees office.

Briere had gotten a Philadelphia pitch from Biron but could only guess which teams would make offers. Having gone to arbitration for Briere's 2006-07 $5 million salary, the Sabres had not been allowed to negotiate an extension until after January 1, by which time they had approached Drury, who asked them to keep the team strong by signing Briere, too.

"When nothing happened (for either center), Chris said he would like to go someplace with me," recalls Briere. "New York seemed like the place where that was most likely. I knew he had grown up as a Ranger fan (in Connecticut).

"The Sabres ended up making an offer to me with about five days to go (before July 1). I don't know why they waited so long. While it had always been my intention to keep them in the loop, by that point, I was going to see what was out there."

Because the Flyers believed they were near the top of Briere's list, they put out their first two offers just after 12 p.m. to Gomez and Drury, trying for a quick gauge on their interest in coming to Philadelphia.

The Canadiens had a representative show at up at 9 a.m. (PDT) in Brisson's office with jerseys, books and videos. "Very impressive," recalls Briere. Although his first three preferences were the Flyers, Canadiens and Rangers, he never noticed that Philadelphia was not among his initial bidders.

"Everything was just happening so fast," Briere recalls. "Teams were calling one after the other. Most offers were for above what I thought I would get, and I had been told I would get a lot."

Within the hour, Holmgren had called Brisson with a five-year offer that averaged $7 million per season.

"I didn't know the Flyers would be one of the teams calling on that day, but I had hoped so," recalls Briere. "I really believed in what Paul Holmgren was doing with his team; the good, young players they had, the trades they had made at the deadline to get Coburn and Upshall, then Timonen and Hartnell. My good friend Marty was here, and I had played in the World Junior Championships with Simon Gagne (in 1997).

"My heart wanted to go to Montreal because I grew up watching them. And they had a decent team. But the one part that scared me was raising kids in that environment. In Quebec, there's Bill 101, where if both parents are French-Canadiens, like us, the kids have to go to a French school.

"My boys (aged nine, eight and seven) had started school in the States. They understood French and could speak it a little bit, but going to school and taking all their subjects in French is a different story.

"We had a lot of people that were willing to help us out and make that work, so it wasn't going to stop us. But it was a concern.

"People thought that I didn't want to go to Montreal because of all the pressure of being a Francophone and taking a huge contract there. Actually it was the other way around. I think it would have been pretty cool.

"So once the Flyers made their offer, it was coming down to the team I wanted to go to versus the team I grew up cheering for. There were a lot of emotions [making] the decision so tough.

"But when it is going to be [a seven-year] deal, it's not just the first year that matters. You've got to look three or four years down the road and, to me, the Flyers were the team going in the best direction. The more I looked at it, it was the right place."

An hour after the Flyers made the offer to Briere, they were called by Drury's agent, Mark Witkin, and told they had not made his client's short list. By that time there was only one team on it—the Rangers. When Drury told Briere he was leaning to signing with New York, Briere told Brisson: "Take me out of the Rangers, I'm going to let Chris go there.

"At that point, I didn't think they would have room for two of us," recalls Briere.

He was wrong. The Rangers were well along on also signing Gomez, who, after playing seven seasons for the Devils in the shadow of New York City, desired to be in the real thing. "I had a lot of respect for the Flyers; wasn't worried about that season they were coming off at all," Gomez recalls. "I just really wanted to play in New York."

Briere had been the Rangers' third option. "We believed all along he was going to go to Philly," recalls New York assistant GM Jim Schoenfeld. Indeed, Briere wasn't looking for the brightest lights, or for the most money.

"I had 14-16 offers, all of them for so much. I couldn't believe people would pay me that much to play a game I loved," he recalls. "In fact, the Flyer offer was for a little too much to make me comfortable.

"I remember telling Pat, 'Okay, I've decided. Make a deal with the Flyers. But the average is too high. I want that lowered.'

"I thought if the Flyers could use an extra $500,000 to get an extra player or a better player somewhere, we would have a chance to have a better team. I knew they weren't going to pocket that money and save it for rainy days.

"Pat looked at me, shaking his head, and said, 'Okay.'

"The Flyers came back with (an average) $6.3 million, with an extra year added. Pat said, 'No, that's too low.' But I said, 'I'm happy with it.'"

By front-loading the deal with a $10 million first-year salary and tapering it down to $4 million in the final two seasons, Philadelphia was able to give itself some protection from getting stuck with an unmovable salary in Briere's declining years. "I remember (Ranger GM) Glen (Sather) called and asked, 'How did you get Briere's cap number so low?'" recalls Holmgren.

By 3:30 p.m., for a total of $52 million over eight seasons, the Flyer deal with Briere was done. Pretty much so was the rich guy for the day.

"I went back to the hotel and just laid down on the bed," Briere recalls. "I felt like I had been working out for 10 hours straight. It was one of the best days of my life and probably the most stressful one."

An elated Holmgren had plenty of strength remaining to call Gomez's agent, Ian Pulver, and withdraw Philadelphia's offer. The Phantoms weren't going to be 82-0 in 2007-08 after all.

By the time Holmgren met with the media late in the afternoon to simultaneously announce the acquisitions of Briere, Smith, Lupul, and the official registrations of the Hartnell and Timonen contracts, the Flyers had improved themselves dramatically with a center coming off a 95-point season, a blueline catalyst, a veteran glue defenseman, and two scoring wingers entering their prime years.

Briere followed Jeremy Roenick (2001) and Forsberg (2005) as Philadelphia's third exhilarating free-agent center catch in six seasons. "The opening up of the game is better for smaller, quicker players and Danny is one of the quickest in the game," said Holmgren in making the announcement. "He has creativity, can score, and has a real knack for toughness in the offensive zone.

"We felt it was very important to try and snag one of those centers. With [Jeff] Carter, Mike Richards, and R.J. Umberger, we have good, young players. In order to elevate them, we needed someone with a strong sense of purpose—Danny Briere will help in that development."

Holmgren called Smith, who joined Timonen and Briere as the third former captain the team had added in two weeks, a "throwback player."

"He's a warrior, a character defenseman," said the GM. "Not great offensively, but he can make a good first pass and complement an offensive guy."

Briere reiterated to the media that he entered the day with the Flyers at the top of his list because of what Biron had told him about the organization and its future. "I was a little afraid the last few days [that] they would not call or be interested in me," he said.

Lupul told reporters he would not continue to be the flop he was in Edmonton. "I was coming off the playoffs in Anaheim where I thought I played the best hockey I ever played, but things didn't seem right from the get-go," he said. "I got frustrated, then confidence became a factor.

Deal done. Danny Briere's signing gave the Flyers strength down center.

"It's a lot different going from Southern California, where no one knows hockey much, to Edmonton, where every person in town knows who you are."

The 23-year-old left wing had been at his cabin in Silver Lake, Alberta with Upshall when informed of the deal by Edmonton GM Lowe. Best friends since age 16, when they had been in Canada's camp for the Under-18 World Championships, they had now become Flyer teammates.

"I wasn't surprised to get traded after the year I'd had," Lupul recalls. "And Scottie didn't give me any time to be disappointed."

Not only was it good to be coming to Philadelphia, Lupul said to the media in a conference call, but it was good to be going anyplace with Smith. "He was probably the best captain I've ever had," Lupul told reporters. "He sticks up for his teammates and will do anything to win."

The Flyer transformation begun in mid-2006-07 had brought in eight new faces, nine if you counted Holmgren's, with the corners of his mouth turned up again. Asked to provide input at a marketing meeting for a slogan about the upcoming season, the GM suggested, "We're coming back with a vengeance."

Brian Boucher didn't know about the vengeance part. But having bounced from Philadelphia to Phoenix to Calgary to Chicago to Columbus, the goaltender was happy to be coming back, even to play for the Phantoms. "It's not how I envisioned my career going," said the 30-year-old Boucher, a rookie hero of the Flyers' 2000 conference final run. "But I'm grateful for the chance to come back to a place I enjoyed so much and hopefully resurrect my career."

Boucher was signed to an AHL contract to provide experienced emergency backup because Antero Niittymaki, anticipated to be Biron's backup, had undergone a second hip surgery in two years. Despite his shaky health and a .894 save percentage in 2006-07, the Flyers still believed the 27-year-old Finn was a keeper.

"I know it surprised some people [to learn] they would give me a new contract after the disaster year," recalls Niittymaki. "But I knew I was good enough and that I could slowly get my confidence level up.

"Marty was the guy, so I would be able to focus on practice more than if [I was] playing most of the games. I planned to work my butt off and see what happened."

Robert Esche, unable to attract any NHL interest after his struggles of the preceding season, went home to Utica, NY, and opened a restaurant before taking a deal with Kazan of the Russian Super League.

In August, Rick Tocchet was sentenced to two years probation for bankrolling former New Jersey state trooper James Harney in a bookmaking operation between 2002 and 2006—years the former Flyer served as an assistant coach with Colorado and Phoenix.

As a first-time offender, Tocchet escaped jail time or even punishment by the NHL because there was no evidence he bet on hockey or did anything to influence its outcomes. "I'm sorry I was involved in this," said Tocchet to Judge Thomas S. Smith in a Mount Holly, NJ, courtroom.

Shawn Tilger, the Flyer vice president of marketing and communications, was promoted to vice president of business operations while several positions also changed on the coaching level.

Craig Berube and Joe Mullen switched places, with assistant coach Berube going back to the Phantoms to add more head-coaching experience to his resume while Mullen was promoted from the AHL team to improve the Flyer powerplay. Of the 502 career goals that had earned Mullen's 2000 induction into the Hockey Hall of Fame, 150 had come on the man advantage. "We thought Joey would give us some insight," recalls Stevens.

Mullen, who had served the Penguins as a coach both in Pittsburgh and at Wilkes-Barre/Scranton, was let go during a regime change in 2006. At that time, he had written every NHL organization for a job with the exception of Montreal and Philadelphia. "Those teams were known for hiring from within and I didn't have any connection with either," he recalls.

It turned out he did. When the Flyers fired Ken Hitchcock and Berube moved up from the Phantoms to assist John Stevens, Kjell Samuelsson, the new coach of the AHL team, was given a list of possible candidates by Holmgren from which to pick his assistant.

Samuelsson didn't know anybody on it, so he asked Holmgren if Mullen, a teammate on the 1992 Stanley Cup champion Penguins and a respected rival during his time at Wilkes-Barre/Scranton, could have the job.

Decimated by call-ups, the 2006-07 Phantom powerplay had not done much better than that of its parent team, but Mullen was wanted for the big club by Stevens and Holmgren.

"I was on vacation when I got a call from Paul saying he wanted to move me up," recalls Mullen. "I said, 'sounds terrific, but I'd like to talk to Kjell; he kind of got me into the organization and now I am being moved up ahead of him.

Kjell told me, 'these chances don't come every day; you gotta take them when you can."

Mullen became Stevens' eye in the sky, while former Flyer Jack McIlhargey, a coach with the Canucks and in their system for 18 years, joined holdover Terry Murray on the bench. "I didn't know Jack; he was Paul's suggestion," recalls Stevens. "We had a good talk on the phone.

"He was a former Flyer with passion, and a little older guy with insight."

Restricted free agent Upshall re-upped for two years and $2.45 million. Dmitry Afanasenkov left for Moscow Dynamo and Ottawa signed Niko Dimitrakos. Tough guy Todd Fedoruk's second Philadelphia run ended when he signed with Dallas.

"Everything changed for me with (Derek) Boogaard [a knockout that resulted in facial fractures while Fedoruk was playing with Anaheim in 2006]," recalls The Fridge, one of the most willing combatants in Flyer history. "I couldn't take shots the way the way I used to.

"I used to try to take punches because 90 percent of them are glancing blows anyway; if you see them coming, you move just a little and take them on your forehead and come back. But because of the injury, I wasn't as offensive as I had been.

Back with Philadelphia, Fedoruk then suffered a one-punch knockout at the right hand of Ranger tough guy Colton Orr at Madison Square Garden in 2007. "Orr happened because of Boogie," Fedoruk says.

At the invitation of Holmgren, Mike Knuble and Hartnell joined the GM and Forsberg at Pine Valley, NJ, for a round of golf, fellowship and gentle arm-twisting to convince the star to return to Philadelphia.

Forsberg, who had scored 15 points in 17 regular-season games and then added four more during Nashville's first-round loss to San Jose, remained uncommitted for the 2007-08 season because of his still-troublesome foot.

But that hardly put a dent in Flyerland's optimism. From his office overlooking the practice rink at the Flyers Skate Zone, Holmgren delighted in the boisterous enthusiasm coming from the informal workouts by pre-camp arrivals.

"They were hooting and hollering and having a blast," he recalls. "I called Mr. Snider, held the phone up and said, 'Listen to this!'

"I couldn't help myself; I felt so excited about what we had done."

Hartnell had shown up early because the only person he knew on the team was Timonen. Umberger, who had started the previous season behind in conditioning because of post-concussion symptoms, was raring to go after a full summer of workouts with a personal trainer.

"When we had started adding pieces towards the end of the season, things were starting to make sense," Umberger recalls. "And playing against Danny, I obviously knew we were getting a game changer.

"There was going to be competition at camp. There was a lot of buzz."

But not enough of it to keep bachelor newcomers Hartnell, Upshall and Lupul in the New Jersey suburbs, where most Flyers had opted to live since the early days of the franchise. The young players followed in the footsteps of Forsberg, and took places in Olde City Philadelphia, where the not-so-old could have more fun.

Camp opened with Claude Giroux, the team's 2006 first-round pick, sprinting to the front of the fitness-testing mile run that the Flyers conducted on the track at Eastern High School in Voorhees, NJ. After not even being able to finish the run at development camp two months earlier, the kid lapped many in the field. "I can't believe the gains he has made from summer to now," Stevens said.

It wasn't the top prospect's only impressive accomplishment—he won the "Hart Trophy" named after the late broadcaster Gene Hart, as MVP of the intrasquad tournament. "He wants the puck all the time, plays without fear," said Stevens. But with no room for a 19-year-old on the top two Flyer lines, Giroux was sent back to Gatineau for further development.

"I will go back to junior and get better," he vowed.

Lupul and Upshall came up with wrist injuries as the result of hits during an exhibition game in Ottawa, where R.J. Umberger also fractured his pinkie when it got caught in his uniform as he threw a check. Pictures showed only a severe sprain in the case of Lupul, but Upshall had a broken navicular bone that sent him with Umberger to Baltimore, MD, where surgery was performed on both players' hands by specialist Dr. Thomas Graham.

Upshall was expected to miss the first month; Umberger perhaps only the first week, but the game in Ottawa took a further toll. Steve Downie, apparently seeking retribution against a Senator—any Senator—after being driven face-first into the glass by Cristoph Schubert, delivered a flying shoulder check to the head of Dean McAmmond.

Although contact above the shoulders was not automatically illegal, this hit fit the criteria for discipline the NHL had laid out in a video shown to the players at the beginning of camp. Downie had left his feet, specifically targeted the head, and hit an unsuspecting player.

"Steve just happened to be the first guy," recalls Holmgren. "At the hearing, I said to Colin (Campbell, the NHL disciplinarian), 'You're not thinking about something stupid like 20 games, are you?'

Colin said, 'No, but a lot of people are.' So I said, 'You're listening to a lot of people? Apparently, this isn't your decision.'

"He got [bleeping] mad at me. Sure enough, Downie gets 20 games."

Said Campbell in handing down the fourth-longest suspension in league history, "People don't think we have been tough enough on head shots."

Holmgren gritted his teeth and told the media, "My reaction is it seems like a lot of games, but Colin Campbell is in a very difficult position and we respect his judgment. I was with Steve during the hearing and after the verdict. He is very upset and understands the ramifications."

Downie phoned McAmmond (who would miss the first 10 games of the season with a concussion) and apologized. It was accepted, but not before Senator enforcer Brian McGrattan said, '[Downie will] get what is coming to him next time we play him, that's for sure.' Campbell called McGrattan with a warning that further threats could result in disciplinary action.

Downie was a first-time offender in the NHL, but had a significant record of suspensions in junior. "I think for the good of Steve Downie, he needs to be suspended for a long time," said Ottawa coach John Paddock. "Probably hockey is the most important thing to him. Take it away so hopefully he remembers.

"I think this kid is the kind of player every team in the league wants. But we all know his history in the OHL. You have to have control."

Said Stevens, "He's going to need some direction and discipline on and off the ice. But to me, he's the kind of kid you work with all day long because he wants to play."

At age 32, Mike Rathje, was no youngster, and certainly needed no direction, only a body that still would stand up to the rigors of NHL play. Having missed the final 57 games of the previous year with piriformis syndrome, a hip condition, the defenseman had undergone surgery for a double hernia and worked through the summer to make one final try.

"At one point I had a Botox injection and felt great," recalls Rathje. "I skated and was back to my normal self.

"I was like, 'this is it, I'm good to go.' Then, a week later, bam, it started again and I was like, 'Aw [bleep.]'

"I knew it was grim, but I had to try. So I trained the best I could. We played Washington (in the preseason) and I tore my groin. I was like, 'there's no way I can do this.' I went up to see Homer and told him I couldn't.

"My chances hadn't been good, so my wife had taken the kids back to be in school in San Jose. One of the toughest days of my life was cleaning up the house in New Jersey and getting all the stuff out to drive it across the country with my brother-in-law. I shed a tear. We had such a good thing going. My wife really liked it.

"I was blessed to play for the Flyers. The greatest thing probably in my career was being able to play for a team with such tradition."

After a fight with the carrier that insured their largest contracts, the Flyers were able to recoup much of the $10.5 million they owed Rathje for the remaining three seasons of his five-year deal. But they had lost a good player before his time.

"Mike was okay enough with the puck, but his main value was as a big defender who could skate," recalls Holmgren. "He probably really would have helped us.

"He had been a big, happy-go-lucky guy and was just miserable because of the pain. It was sad to watch."

Today, Rathje lives in San Jose where, after running a trucking company in Western Canada for several years, he is a partner in six restaurants. He still feels some pain in his hip, but would settle for that if doctors could fix issues with his neck.

"I'm in pretty rough shape actually," he says. "I've had three neck surgeries in the past five years.

"The first fusion helped for only a couple months. I went back and they fused another disk and it was good for seven months. But this past year, all of a sudden it came back. So now I have a big pain in front of my neck with rods and six screws.

Jason Smith became Philadelphia's prototypical Canadian captain.

"My last surgery was September (2015), so I'm still recovering. I'm down to one Vicodin a day from four, so maybe that's a good sign.

"I've asked myself a few times, 'Was it worth it?' Right now, I'm not sure. You're supposed to enjoy your retirement, but it's tough having four kids and being half-crippled. I coach my daughter's hockey team, which is great. If I didn't have that, I don't know what I'd do. I'd probably be pulling my hair out."

Even with Rathje retiring, Philadelphia still had extra defensemen. Denis Gauthier was outplayed by Randy Jones in the preseason and his $2.3 million salary was creating a cap issue. He was sent to the Phantoms, giving Jones the sixth spot on defense behind Timonen, Smith, Derian Hatcher, Braydon Coburn and Lasse Kukkonen.

The injuries to Upshall, Umberger and Lupul helped center Jim Dowd, a Brick, NJ, native and 15-year veteran of nine previous NHL teams, earn a place on the roster. Center Denis Tolpeko, a free-agent signee who had spent 2006-07 with the Phantoms, also made the team, as did Jesse Boulerice, a once-Flyer draftee who had reached the NHL for a full season and parts of two others with Carolina.

Stevens, wanting to see what the summer brought, had not named a captain following Forsberg's trade in February. Regardless, many of the strongest candidates for the position were incumbents. Richards had asked for the position with Forsberg's departure; Gagne led the team in seniority and was its most established star; Hatcher had held the position on the Cup-winning 1999 Dallas Stars.

"We thought down the road Richards was going to be the guy," recalls Holmgren, "but we didn't think it was fair to give it to him just yet.

"Derian had experience and would have been good, but because of [knee issues], we didn't know how much he had in the tank. We talked a little bit about Simon (who two years earlier had turned down the position on an interim basis after Keith Primeau had been lost to a concussion), but we didn't think it would affect him by not being captain. He would still remain part of the leadership group.

"Danny had been captain in Buffalo, as had Kimmo in Nashville, and Jason Smith in Edmonton. In camp, Jason had been the first guy on the ice at every practice. The young guys followed him around. He had captain written all over him."

When Stevens asked Gagne, he thought Smith would be a good choice. Knuble felt Smith was out of central casting.

"He looked the part, you know," said Knuble. "Gritty, blocked shots, looked mean, had a missing tooth; he was your prototypical Canadian captain."

Stevens had made up his mind practically from the first exhibition game. "Jason was blocking shots and battling like it was the regular season," the coach recalls. "It became unanimous, not just from the [brain trust] watching but from the people inside the locker room. We all knew who the captain already was."

On October 1, Smith became the 16th Flyer to wear the C, and the first player earning that honor in his first season wearing orange-and-black since Lou Angotti in Year One. The August informal workouts attended by more than 20 of his new teammates had given him a good feeling about the group and a head start in learning how to lead them.

"I had competed a lot against Kimmo, Hatch, Hartnell, Upshall (in the Western Conference) and played with Joffrey," Smith recalls. "I was surprised to be picked, but was really confident I knew enough about the guys to do the job."

Stevens knew too well the bad work habits that had helped sink the 2006-07 Flyers and noted publicly during the preseason that he still was seeing inconsistent efforts. But a makeover with 12 new players who had not started the preceding year with the club had so clearly upgraded the team that it flew to Calgary for the opener with expectations substantially raised.

"It's all on paper; we have not yet turned it around," said Snider. "But I'd be extremely disappointed if we haven't."

Added Luukko, "Our rebuilding process wasn't years, it was one year. We're ready to compete."

Certainly Timonen, Briere and Biron hadn't signed up for any long-term project. "People in this room feel this organization has laid it out for everybody to be successful," said Biron.

The only prediction Holmgren risked publicly was that his team would be playing "meaningful games in March."

There was expectation throughout the hockey world that the Flyers would make a significant jump. But the near-40 points of improvement that a playoff spot would require was too daunting for most prognosticators to believe likely.

Hatcher noted that the yearly assumptions of Philadelphia being a contender had become a thing of the past. The players had to make good on what Holmgren had done.

"We should want to be a team that, a year from now, has people saying, 'You guys are tough to play against,'" said Hatcher on the eve on the opener. "By no means are we even near that.

"It is essential that we get off to a good start."

That could be accomplished only if the team's new big tickets instantly could handle the pressure. Briere was a $10 million player in Forsberg's old spot between Gagne and Knuble, the team's two best finishers. But not to worry about someone who had averaged a point per playoff game in leading Buffalo to conference finals the previous two seasons.

During the first game's third shift, Briere won a faceoff from Wayne Primeau, took a feed by Knuble and beat Adrian Aucoin out from the back of the net. Calgary goalie Miikka Kiprusoff won the race to the post, but Briere kicked the rebound onto his stick and banged it in for a 1-0 lead. Knuble, set up in the slot by Gagne, one-timed a five-on-three goal after eight minutes to make it 2-0.

Mike Keenan's Flames fought back for a 2-2 tie on two powerplay goals by Daymond Langkow. Overtime loomed when Anders Eriksson backhanded the puck into a group of players in front of the Philadelphia bench trying to change. The puck caromed to Gagne who had Briere breaking in the middle of the ice with three Flames in hopeless pursuit.

Briere took Gagne's pass at the hash marks and fired under the crossbar on Kiprusoff's glove side with 1:48 remaining. The new-look Flyers had looked spiffy in a 3-2 victory. And with two goals, Briere had the fast start he wanted.

"You could not have scripted it any better," he told reporters. "You don't want to go five, six, seven (goalless) games and start chasing, with pressure building up."

Not since 1986, when Ron Hextall debuted with a breakaway stop on Wayne Gretzky in a 2-1 win over Edmonton, had a 1-0 Flyer record felt so good.

"It felt like a weight was lifted off our shoulders," said Biron. "We weren't going down the same path we had the season before."

There was only one sense of dejà vu experienced during the trip. While in Edmonton, the Oilers showed a pregame video tribute to Smith, their former captain, one of the city's most beloved players since its Stanley Cup days. It made his eyes water while standing on the blueline awaiting the anthems.

"I'm not one to cry very often but I almost had some tears," he recalls. "It was great to be recognized, but I'm thinking, 'Boy, this is going to be a tough one.'"

Holmgren remembers that it was. "His first shifts were horrendous," the GM recalls, but Smith had plenty of company. The Flyers allowed 16 scoring chances while managing only four shots on goal in the first period.

They rallied from a 2-1 deficit to a 3-2 lead on goals by Briere and Gagne, but with Smith on the ice for a second goal-against of the game, Sanderson tied the score with five seconds remaining in the second period.

The winner, by Pitkanen, went in off Knuble's stick before Sanderson scored again into the empty net. Revenge was served cold by two ex-Flyers in the 5-3 Oiler victory.

"I'm embarrassed with the way things happened there last year," said Sanderson. "I'm not going to lie to you, it's sweet."

Because the 2006-07 Flyers had operated as strangers, Stevens took advantage of three off-days before a game in Vancouver by taking his players to Whistler, British Columbia for bonding exercises. They included building Lego models that projected what each person wanted the team to be.

"I would think we want to be a pyramid, a team with a strong base," said Hartnell.

The Lego set also had parts to build airplanes, tanks and cars. Asked what kind of car the Flyers would want to be, Gagne said, "That would be a tough one. I would think it would be European. We've got lots of Finns here."

Stevens reiterated the value of these games to a team that too often the previous season had taken its toys and gone home. "It really has come out here how close this group is already," said the coach. "I think this experience fast-tracked how much they think of each other."

Recalls Richards: "That whole group bonded immediately."

Umberger, Vancouver's 2001 first-round pick, hadn't exactly developed the same kinship with the Canucks. GM Brian Burke, since departed, had made Umberger a lowball contract offer, then traded away his rights. "I've got a history here," said the winger, who, making his season debut with the splint removed from his broken finger, scored the second of four Philadelphia goals in the first period of an 8-2 rout at Rogers Arena.

With Briere scoring his fourth goal, Carter his second and Richards adding two, things couldn't have been going any better for the team until Boulerice, who had been exchanging unpleasantries with Ryan Kesler through much of the third period, cross-checked the Canuck in the face.

"I reacted in a bad way," said Boulerice, who was cut no slack by Stevens.

"Unacceptable," said the coach. "We had the game in hand."

Holmgren, who as Team USA GM had helped select Kesler for the 2006 World Championships, waited outside the Canuck locker room to get the word he was not seriously injured. In fact, he would not miss a game. But at the hearing, Holmgren threw Boulerice, who in junior had been charged with assault for a stick attack, on the mercy of the court.

"I had signed him because he had always been a good teammate, plus having an unpredictable player is sometimes not a bad thing," recalls the GM. "But I said (to Campbell), 'I have no defense.'

"I might have given Jesse 30 for that one."

He got 25. Like Downie, who had 17 remaining on his suspension, Boulerice had to be carried on the roster, making Holmgren juggle to stay under the cap.

Three nights later, Smith's first goal as a Flyer, into the empty net, secured a 3-1 home-opening victory over the Islanders before a sellout crowd. Although there were 1,400 empty seats for the next home game against Atlanta, it didn't bother Biron, who recorded his first Philadelphia shutout. Carter was on fire, netting his fourth goal in the season's first five games, a promising contrast to having scored only 14 times the previous year.

"Jeff has all the talent in the world, but confidence was the thing last year," said Knuble. "He had a six percent shooting percentage."

The Devils, just like the Thrashers, shot zero percent against Biron as he picked up his second consecutive whitewash. "When there are tough shots and he makes it look so easy, your confidence keeps growing," said Briere.

Biron's self-assurance, in turn, was getting a boost from goaltender coach Reggie Lemelin. "My hometown (Lac St. Charles, Quebec) is like 10 minutes from his hometown," recalls Biron. "The rink I skated in as a kid is now called the Reggie Lemelin Arena.

"I grew up watching him on the Bruins but never had met him before I got to Philly. The new-age goalie coach is very different from Reggie; much more technical and structured. He would sit down and calm me down. He was more of a friend, a support guy, that put me in the right place mentally."

There was little trespassing on Biron's space as he stopped 42 shots by the visiting Hurricanes. Gagne's goal 48 seconds into overtime won the game, 3-2, to push both the goalie's record, and the team's, to 6-1.

In 2006-07, it had taken the Flyers 23 games to win six times. But as the team hit the road for the next eight contests, Snider knew better than to get carried away. "We have a good team," said the Chairman. "How good, I don't know."

It couldn't possibly be as good without Gagne. In Sunrise, he took a hard check from Jay Bouwmeester on the first shift and, after playing a few more, decided the pressure in his head would make it wise to call it a night. "The game was going too fast for me at that point," Gagne said after his teammates erased one two-goal deficit, but not a second, in a 4-3 loss.

Gagne woke up the next morning in Tampa feeling fine, but his lightheadedness returned as the day progressed. He compared it to the feeling one might get after having a few adult beverages and said the good thing was not having to pay for them. "Personally, I think I will be all right this weekend," he said after two Lightning powerplay goals helped send Niittymaki to a 5-2 loss in his first start of the season.

When Gagne was not all right by Saturday afternoon, he was scratched in Boston. Biron stopped Phil Kessel on a penalty shot to make Richards' sixth goal of the season and Lupul's fourth hold up for a 2-1 victory. But Bruin Patrice Bergeron was hit from behind into the boards by Jones and taken off on a stretcher with a concussion and broken nose.

Jones, shaken by word that Bergeron would be out until at least January—as it turned out, he was finished for the season—argued he had no intention to injure. Campbell agreed but added, "He did deliver a hard check to a player who was in a vulnerable position." Jones, banned for two games, became the third suspended Flyer of a season that had not reached November.

Said Holmgren, "In fairness to [Campbell], I think he had a hard time making this decision. Randy was just a little too aggressive on the player, who, in [Campbell's] viewpoint, was in a vulnerable position."

Hatcher, who had played all 82 games the previous year, was not going to be able to do so this time. Recurring fluid buildup on a right knee that had been reconstructed in 2003 was forcing the defenseman to undergo arthroscopic surgery to repair cartilage. He would be out two-to-four weeks. "I'm not worried because it felt so good before this," said Hatcher.

Gagne had plenty to worry about though. He flunked the baseline neurological test and remained out, even though the club was refusing to call it a concussion.

Upshall, out since the preseason with a wrist sprain, was ready to return to the lineup. So was Briere to his home province, despite the likelihood he was going to get booed for turning his back on Quebec and signing with the Flyers.

Indeed, *les citoyens* were not kind during the 5-2 Philadelphia loss. "Actually it was a lot of fun early on," said Briere, who assisted on Richards' first-period goal. "I can't get easy motivation like that in every building.

"Obviously I'm disappointed with the way I played and with the results. We wanted to show them the real Flyers."

The real Flyers were starting slowly almost every night, just like the real bad Flyers had done the previous season. They also were taking too many penalties. Briere and Stevens drew unsportsmanlike conduct calls as Gagne's return from a four-game absence fizzled in a 2-0 loss at Madison Square Garden to Henrik Lundqvist. But at least Gagne got all the way through the game without suffering any post-concussion symptoms.

"If I'm fine when I wake up, that will be a great sign," said Gagne. "Every day now is a test."

That applied to the team, too, which, after the fast start, had won only two of its previous six games. There were reasons for this beyond 11 of the first 15 contests being on road. Briere, the No. 1 center, was proving not to be a great fit with the team's top two wingers and was being booed by impatient Philadelphia fans.

"Danny and Simon Gagne both were give-and-go, jump-through-a-hole kind of players, so they didn't end up being as great together as we thought they might be," recalls Stevens. "We put Mike Richards, more of a puck-possession guy, with Gagne."

Placed between Umberger and Lupul, Briere understood. "Listen, I played on a team last year where our supposed third line could have been the No. 1 on most teams," he said. "What matters is finding chemistry."

The Flyers had it in Pittsburgh, where Briere forced a turnover by Sidney Crosby on the first shift to set up a Lupul goal, Carter and Richards both scored, and Philadelphia, despite taking nine penalties, won 3-1. The Penguins had swept the eight-game season series in 2006-07. "A lot of guys weren't here for what happened last year," said Briere. "It wasn't even discussed."

Gagne had felt another headache on the flight to Pittsburgh, but dressed and played until being hit in the neck by Gary Roberts during the third period. "Right away all the symptoms came back," recalls Gagne, who was not well on the late night flight to Newark and felt dizziness the next day.

Without Gagne and Kapanen, who had suffered a strained right knee in Pittsburgh, the first Flyer game at the new Prudential Center went like too many had gone against the Devils at the Meadowlands. Biron was pulled after giving up three first-period goals and Philadelphia closed the trip at 3-5 with a 4-1 defeat.

While former Flyer MVP Eric Lindros announced his retirement from hockey at age 34—injuries had limited him to 49 games the previous season at Dallas—Holmgren met with another former captain, Forsberg, to take his temperature about returning. Forsberg, who was in town with a youth team that contained his godson, was planning to give his foot a test in an upcoming tournament in Finland before deciding whether to attempt an NHL comeback.

The City of Philadelphia's ice rinks appeared to be past the point of any return when Mayor Michael Nutter announced all would have to be closed because of budgetary constraints. The Ed Snider Youth Hockey Foundation, which had been running programs out of Scanlon Rink in the Kensington section of the city for a year, was planning to build a facility in South Philadelphia for the burgeoning youth program. Instead, Snider Hockey stepped forward with a last-minute offer to renovate and operate four existing open-air facilities.

"We decided we could do more good in the neighborhoods," said Snider.

The Flyer defensive zone was improving as well around Timonen, for more reasons than his skill level.

"He brought a level of calmness to the team," recalls Umberger. "Kimmo had everything under control—he slowed the game down and it proceeded the way he wanted it to.

Timonen sped up his scoring pace, however, with a four-point night that included his first Flyer goal in a 5-2 victory over the Penguins. Upshall made up for the time he had lost with his second and third goals in a 3-2 win over the Islanders, a game won on a third-period shorthanded goal by Richards, his 10th score in a 17-game-old season.

Counseled by Keith Primeau, the oft-concussed former Flyer, to not return until feeling 100 percent, Gagne was playing a computer game designed to improve his focus and decrease his dizziness. "One thing that is helpful is that I don't feel any pressure from the team to come back," he said.

Tolpeko's mid-third period goal rallied Philadelphia to a point against the Rangers, but New York won in the shootout, 4-3, against Biron. The Flyers began to suffer for lack of a big save.

"When a guy's a backup for a long time you kind of get a backup mindset," Stevens recalls. "Marty had to go through a process.

"We constantly grinded him on staying focused every day. And there were a lot of puck mishandles by both goalies getting us into trouble."

Niittymaki failed to stop the only two shots he faced against the Devils, who then scored four goals off Biron, in a 6-2 Wachovia Center loss that dropped Philadelphia's record to 11-7-1. The fresh talent no longer was masking the reality of the team's relative inexperience.

"There were a lot of guys feeling their way," recalls Holmgren.

Among them was Hartnell, whose two lone goals in the first 19 games were into empty nets. Playing with Carter and Lupul, the left wing had managed just four assists.

"Obviously it was big money for me and I felt a lot of pressure right away," Hartnell recalls. "It was different here than in Nashville.

"I was coming off the ice between the first and second period of my first exhibition game in Philly and I hear someone say, 'Come on Hartnell, hit somebody!'

"I turned around and looked at Mike Knuble. He said, 'Get used to it.' My next few shifts, I made a couple of big hits to try to make that fan happy.

"It was just a different level here. Fortunately, I wasn't the only new guy. Kimmo, Danny B. and Jason, being the new captain, were getting more media attention than me."

That didn't last. The Flyers were in the third period of a 6-3 loss in Boston on November 26 when Hartnell plowed into defenseman Andrew Alberts, who was on his knees against the backboards. Alberts hit his head on the boards and Campbell nailed Hartnell with the fourth Flyer suspension of the season, a two-gamer.

"The puck was bouncing and he was in a vulnerable position; my hip was near his head," Hartnell recalls. "I shouldn't have [hit him]. Obviously, I didn't try to hurt him, but it looked bad on film."

At the hearing, Campbell conceded Holmgren's argument—Hartnell had tried to stop—but the winger nevertheless had made contact with the head of Alberts, who fortunately, did not miss a game.

"Like the Randy Jones hit on Bergeron, it wasn't dirty but it had bad results," Holmgren recalls.

Among those consequences was the hockey world beginning to wonder if Philadelphia was trying to goon its way back into contention.

"They are all different; there is no pattern and I think it's ridiculous to think like that," Holmgren said to the media. Hartnell, hardly contrite at the time, vowed to reporters he would change nothing in his game. "You can't worry about the repercussions when you finish a check like that," he said. "I'll still play hard every night."

The silver lining to his punishment was an arena seat next to his dad Bill on the annual father's trip, this year to Raleigh.

After a 13-game absence, Hatcher made it back into the lineup just in time to open the scoring in front of his Pop. But perhaps because Derian had not scored in his previous 123 contests, Eric Hatcher had not wagered $10 in the first-goal pool.

On the ice, the sons were playing a game of chance, too, allowing the Southeast Division leaders to pump 41 shots at Biron. The goaltender stopped 40 in a 3-1 win that left the Flyers, for all their ups and downs, third in the NHL with 30 points.

"I think it's wonderful we are where we are," said Stevens. "Sometimes we forget that we have a new team here and a lot of young players."

Or as Upshall put it, with apparent sarcasm unintended: "There's no question we're a good team. We prove that every second game."

It only seemed like a Philadelphia player was getting suspended every other contest. Riley Cote was next—three games for elbowing the Stars' Matt Niskanen in the head during a 4-1 loss in Dallas.

"I would not think either the coach or general manager are instigating [these repeated incidents]," said Campbell. "But the Flyers certainly are not behaving the right way."

Niskanen did not miss a game, but that hardly was the point when one team had earned five suspensions in its first 25 games. NHL Commissioner Gary Bettman called Holmgren.

"He thinks, like I do, that these are coincidences, different situations that have to be viewed differently," the GM said. "But the question was raised about ramifications if it happens again so, obviously, we are under watch.

"This has been addressed (with the team) and will continue to be addressed. We want to play a physical style, but we've got to play within the rules. This is just going to have to stop."

Paul Kelly, executive director of the NHL Players' Association, alleged a pattern. "It does concern me that a number of these incidents have involved the same franchise," Kelly said. He called for the league to take a tougher stance on repeat offenders, never mind Boulerice was the only one of the "Flyer Five" to ever have been suspended before by the NHL.

With Downie's 20-gamer served, he was called up from the Phantoms. "It's kind of funny that he's back after everything that's happened," said Hatcher. "He was kind of the poster boy for this."

Downie was not among the Flyers who combined for nine minors in St. Paul. But they killed two five-on-threes and, with the help of a third-period goal from outside the blueline by Coburn on Niklas Backstrom, Philadelphia beat the Wild 3-1 behind Niittymaki.

Two nights later in Denver, Biron lost for the sixth time in eight starts, 2-1, but Lemelin did not want to hear or read any discussion about which of his students was No. 1. "We have a nice, calm, situation in net and you guys want to stir things up," he complained to media questioners.

A little controversy sometimes can rouse the soul. When the Penguins came to town on December 11, it didn't matter much what goalie was in the net for Philadelphia. After Umberger scored consecutive goals to break a 2-2 second period tie, Lupul added his third of the night as the Flyers opened up a 6-2 lead.

Lupul had completed a hat trick—and Philadelphia's first six-point night since one by Eric Lindros in 1997—when Biron was tripped by Crosby and steam-rolled by Georges Laraque, who also broke his stick over Kukkonen. Soon Carter was pounding Ryan Whitney in one corner while Hartnell pummeled Colby Armstrong in another. Umberger, a Pittsburgh native, completed the second Flyer hat trick of the night on a final-minute powerplay in an 8-2 rout.

"I don't want to hear any more talk about our team and how undisciplined we are," said a steamed Stevens afterwards. "[The Penguins] get one penalty on a play where they could have had two or three, and there were three broken sticks on the ice.

"It's ridiculous, in my opinion."

Replied Penguin coach Michel Therrien, "Are we talking about the same team that had five players suspended this year? It's a lack of respect to do what [Stevens] did. You don't send your best powerplay on the ice at 7-2."

Actually, you might, if it meant getting a player a hat trick. Another reason might be disliking a particular opponent. "These heated rivalries are the ones you get up most for," said Richards, who, playing between Umberger and Lupul, added three points to bring him to 34 points in 28 games.

As a restricted free-agent-to-be, Richards had the leverage, in addition to the production, to obtain a 12-year, $69 million, contact extension that would begin with the 2008-09 season at a salary of $5.4 million, a raise from the $940,000 for which he was playing in 2007-08.

"I love the city, love the organization and, given the opportunity, I am excited to be here for the next 12 years," said Richards, set for life at age 22 thanks to negotiations completed between agent Pat Morris and Holmgren.

Coburn, also scheduled to become a restricted free agent at the end of the season, didn't hit nearly Richards' jackpot, but received a two-year, $2.6 million, deal that seemed to protect both player and team depending on what the 22-year-old defenseman might, or might not, become.

"It's difficult to put a number on what he could be worth in a few years," said Holmgren. "Right now he plays a lot of minutes, is on the powerplay, and kills penalties, but is he going to be the kind of defenseman that puts up big numbers? We don't know."

Stevens thought he had a good idea. "We are just scratching the surface," said the coach. "He's at full speed in three strides and can do it with the puck."

The red-hot Lupul's second hat trick in three games, achieved midway though the third period against Carolina, pulled the Flyers into a 5-5 tie before Rod Brind'Amour won the shootout with a goal that ticked off Biron's glove, onto his back, and into the goal. Brind'Amour, believing he had been stopped, skated away without realizing he had won the game.

A 4-2 loss to the Devils was Philadelphia's fourth in five games. But Briere thought he saw progress, sort of. "Before, we were taking nights off completely," he said. "Now, every game we're taking a period where we're kind of in a daze."

Two nights later, against Phoenix, it happened again when a Jones giveaway at the blueline led to a Fredrik Sjostrom shorthanded goal, sparking the Coyotes to a 3-2 comeback win, the fourth successive Flyer loss. Nevertheless, Stevens, working on the final year of his contract, received a substantial Christmas bonus—he was extended through the 2008-09 season, with a raise from $600,000 to $650,000.

That saved the coach from having to answer questions about his job status. The guy getting grilled, however, was Holmgren, in this case by the NHL, because the Sabres had filed tampering charges over his signing of Briere. Based largely on some enthusiastic comments made by Biron before the July 1 signing date about his ex-roommate's prospects for joining him in Philadelphia, Buffalo was alleging premature contact.

"I had to sit for something like six hours with [league-hired interrogators]," recalls Holmgren. "I wasn't worried, we hadn't tampered. How could I be responsible for something Marty Biron said?"

Biron was questioned, too, before the NHL found no wrongdoing.

With Stevens having already benched Kukkonen for one game, and Hatcher's knee health an ongoing concern, Holmgren had to do some investigating of his own to obtain defensive depth. On December 19, he brought back Jim Vandermeer by trading winger Ben Eager to Chicago.

Danny Briere's first game against his former team was a 3-2 loss to the Sabres on December 21, 2007.

Vandermeer, 27, had played only 47 regular-season and eight playoff games in a Flyer uniform before being dealt to the Blackhawks for Alexi Zhamnov in 2004. Thus, his homecoming was not nearly as emotional as would be the return of Briere and Biron to Buffalo for the first time wearing Philadelphia uniforms.

"It's going to be a little weird obviously," Briere said. "There are still a lot of good friends on the other side."

He had a few in the stands, too. The "Briere Bunch" seated in an upper corner of HSBC Arena cheered him. Otherwise, he was booed every time he touched the puck while recording one shot on goal and a minus-2 rating. Biron, who unlike his friend had not left as a free agent, was treated more kindly, except by a bounce of the puck. He surrendered a pinball goal by Jochen Hecht with 2:51 remaining as the Sabres won, 3-2.

"[The fan reaction] was about what I expected," said Briere. "It was a fun game, apart from how we found a way to lose another one."

The following night, in a rematch with Buffalo at the Wachovia Center, shorthanded goals by Carter and Richards 55 seconds apart brought the Flyers back from a two-goal deficit. Philadelphia took a 5-4 lead on Timonen's powerplay tip-in early in the third period and subsequently had a four-minute man advantage. But the Flyers did nothing with it and an arguable icing call resulted in Thomas Vanek's redirection to tie the game with only eight seconds remaining.

Ryan Miller stoned all three Philadelphia shooters, including Briere, in the shootout, before Ales Kotalik won the game 6-5, sending Stevens' team to its sixth-straight defeat. The Flyers were 0-for-3 on shootouts for the season and 5-15 since the tie-breaker's introduction in 2005-06.

"I'll take the blame for it," Briere said. "I've had three chances [this season] and haven't scored. Before I got here, I was about 50 percent on shootouts."

It wasn't a merry Christmas for a team that was 10-13-4 since its 6-1 start. From a scheduling standpoint, it wasn't a typical holiday either. Instead of heading out for usual away games during the last week of December and the start of January, the team played a December 27 contest at home. As Lupul scored twice, Philadelphia exchanged all the gifts it had been granting the opposition for a solid effort in a skid-ending 4-1 win over Toronto.

The weather in Tampa was not needed to heat up the already-sizzling Lupul. He scored his third point of the night, on a penalty shot, in a 4-2 Biron victory. The Flyers followed up with Niittymaki's 38-save, 1-0 shutout of Florida, the goal scored by Hatcher off a nice pass from the boards by recall Stefan Ruzicka.

An Atlantic Division separated by five points top-to-bottom remained a dogfight and the Devils wanted Hatcher remanded to a pound, accusing the defenseman of biting center Travis Zajac's finger during a second-period tussle. Hatcher said Zajac's finger barged, uninvited, into his mouth during a rake across the face. "If he's cut, then good," said the Flyer. "I didn't bite him. He almost took my tooth out." Down the hatch went Philadelphia, 3-0, to Marty Brodeur.

The loss still was gnawing at Hatcher the following night in Toronto. He leveled Alex Steen, and then bounced into Lupul, who hit the ice headfirst and had to leave the game. When Kapanen suffered a headache and lip lacerations that required 25 stitches from a deflected Richards pass, the Flyers were subjected to friendly fire yet again. Already without Gagne and Upshall (ankle sprain at Florida), Stevens' team was down four regular forwards. But Downie popped in a rebound for his first NHL goal, Richards scored on the powerplay with 2:51 remaining, and Niittymaki, facing a franchise-record 56 shots, beat the Leafs, 3-2.

"Nitty was unbelievable," the coach marveled. "He looked really confident."

Downie, on the other hand, mostly looked relieved after he was let off with a stern Campbell warning for a sucker punch on Toronto's Jason Blake.

"Steve is walking a fine line there, which is basically what he was told," said Holmgren. "My conversation with him was a little harsher than Colin Campbell's."

The injuries required both the recall of Ryan Potulny and additional duties for Hartnell, who had scored only five goals in his first 35 games. Used to kill penalties for the first time all season, he scored shorthanded for his 100th career goal, plus added two assists, in 4-1 victory at Atlanta.

The left wing was just getting warmed up, though. Two nights later, as Gagne returned from a 26-game absence, Hartnell's natural hat trick brought Philadelphia back from a 2-0 deficit to a rousing 6-2 win over the Rangers at Madison Square Garden.

"Hockey is a weird thing and confidence is a weird thing," Hartnell said. Actually, he wasn't much less streaky than his team, which had won the last three to get to the season's halfway point at 22-15-4. The Flyers were 22 points ahead of their previous year's pace and solidly in playoff position.

The modest three-game winning streak ended when Niittymaki gave away the puck on an overtime winner by Boston's Aaron Ward at the Wachovia Center. But the goalies continued to pick each other up. After sitting for four games, Biron won in Washington, 6-4.

Hartnell's second hat trick in nine days beat the Islanders at Uniondale, 5-3, and a 6-1 demolition of conference-leading Ottawa made Philadelphia 9-1-1 in their last 11. "Hockey is so much more fun when you're playing like this," said Kapanen.

The eternal spoilsports from New Jersey chased Niittymaki with a five-goal first period during a 7-3 Wachovia Center victory, the Devils' 17th against the Flyers in 20 meetings over three seasons. "They have our number," said Briere. "We have to find a way to get it out of our heads, I guess."

The Penguins, who had swept all eight games against Philadelphia in 2006-07, looked a little spooked themselves one year later. Thirty-four seconds after Ryan Whitney's goal forced a 3-3 tie, Knuble scored to give the Flyers their third victory in three tries against Pittsburgh, 4-3.

The sizzling Hartnell scored with 29 seconds remaining to beat Los Angeles, 3-2. And though Stevens' team went for a sleepwalk through a 4-0 home loss to the Rangers, Knuble scored all three goals during a 3-0 win over Anaheim and then Niittymaki beat Atlanta for the seventh straight time, 3-2, on Downie's winner with 4:29 remaining.

Largely on the strength of the Timonen-quarterbacked NHL's best powerplay, Philadelphia was 30-17-5, had the fourth-best record in the NHL, and led a tight Atlantic Division by two points. It was a good time to celebrate the franchise's revival and honor its past by making Ron Hextall the first inductee into the Flyer Hall of Fame in four years. But following the ceremony, a flu-ravaged team fell into a 4-1 hole it couldn't escape in a 4-3 home loss to Washington.

Lupul returned after missing 14 games, but Coburn limped off with a ruptured blood vessel in his buttocks as the Ranger shot blockers frustrated the Flyers, 2-0, at the Wachovia Center. Gagne suffered the "worst headaches I ever felt" following the game, which puzzled him since he hadn't been hit. The following night in Pittsburgh, he was sent to the locker room after an early collision with Staal. It was clear Gagne's concussion symptoms had returned. On the fourth try, the Penguins claimed their first victory of the season over Philadelphia, 4-3.

"We're not getting the bounces we got a couple weeks ago," lamented Hartnell. "We've got to get prepared differently for these games and bear down around the net."

In Uniondale, the Flyers didn't bear down around their own goal either, as turnovers and lost battles brought a 4-3 defeat, even if Briere scored for the first time in eight games.

"This reminds me of that (six-game) drought we had at Christmastime, always a little bit short," said Briere. "We know what we're doing wrong. It has to run its course."

Not yet it didn't. Terrible giveaways by Vandermeer in the first period, then Kukkonen in the third, plus a lackluster initial 40 minutes, sent Philadelphia to its fifth-straight loss, 5-3, to Tampa Bay. "Two goals were absolute gimmes," Stevens said. "We tried to outscore the other team and not check the other team. We're taking penalties because we're reaching, not working."

In Montreal, Hartnell appeared to score with 1:07 remaining to pull out a point, but referee Dave Jackson, alleging goalie Carey Price was pushed into the net, waved off the goal and refused to ask the Toronto control room for help, even though the video showed the puck already was in the goal when Price was shoved.

"The puck went in the left side," said Hartnell after the 1-0 loss, the Flyers' sixth straight. "The ref was on the right side and could not see it. They don't even give us the courtesy of going upstairs. It's really frustrating. We had a lot of chances."

Lupul, who had suffered a high ankle sprain, Downie (concussion), and Hatcher (knee soreness) were all missing for the rematch with the Canadiens the following night in Philadelphia. With the score 1-1 in the final seconds of the first period, several Flyers absent-mindedly rushed to join a scrum that never fully developed in the corner of the Montreal end. As a result, Francis Bouillon converted a three-on-one with 1.2 seconds remaining before the intermission.

"Just a killer. At the end of the period, you can't stop playing," said Stevens after his team, 5-3 losers, dropped to seventh in the conference.

The Flyers had plenty of offense and a mentality that they could score themselves out of trouble. It was an ongoing struggle to get them to play smarter.

"It was still a young team that didn't always recognize when to attack and when the puck had to go in deep," recalls Stevens. "Our penalty killing was fine but we were shorthanded 100 times more than some teams. If you have given up 15 more powerplay goals, what does your percentage matter?

"We weren't disciplined. The other thing that came up a lot was just getting ready to play. But it still was a lot different than the year before when we thought we couldn't win. This year, we thought we were capable. These (February) losses were close ones."

The coach continued to come to work with the same intensity that had gotten him through nine- and 10-game losing streaks in 2006-07.

"He had a passionate belief that with discipline, trust and confidence we would turn it around," recalls Smith. "He kept talking about the details, the process, and working through it.

"He didn't beat you down, bury you, banish you to the press box. He wasn't vocal and fiery, but when the fuse did go off, the energy that players want to see in coaches came across. I think he truly believed in our group."

A belief in the coach, forged by many of these players during their Phantom years with Stevens, was mutual.

"Guys respected him and knew what we were going to get from

him," recalls Carter. "John was the right coach for us at that time."

In Ottawa, Timonen's goal late in the second period and Upshall's early third-period deflection rallied Philadelphia to a 2-2 tie. With Tolpeko out with a concussion, the team called-up top prospect Claude Giroux—whose junior team in Gatineau was located only 15 miles from the Canadian capital.

Giroux had a chance to put the Flyers ahead, but the puck rolled off his stick. Nevertheless, Stevens tried to boost his failing shootout unit by using the kid in his first NHL game. "We knew how talented and deceptive he was and [Ottawa goalie Ray Emery] didn't know him," recalls the coach. "So I took a calculated guess."

Giroux tried a backhander and missed. "Happens, I guess," he said. Timonen was the only goal scorer of the three for the Flyers, who went down, 3-2, suffering the team's eighth straight loss. "We've got to build on the point," Stevens insisted. "We were down 2-0 and regrouped."

Giroux, who was allowed one more game under the terms of his emergency recall, flew back to Philadelphia with the team. Two nights later against the Sharks, he made a diving backcheck to prevent a goal by Joe Pavelski.

Knuble scored in the final six seconds of the second period to tie the game 1-1, but Milan Michalek scored a softie on Biron before defenseman Doug Murray's centering pass went in off Briere's shoulder. Giroux went back to Gatineau having played nine minutes in each game while the losing streak went to nine games with the 3-1 loss to San Jose.

"Obviously we're not playing with a lot of confidence right now, and it's affecting our work ethic and our execution level," said Smith.

"It's pretty much rock bottom. You can only talk so much; it's time to take action."

Added Stevens, "You can't walk away from a fight. This is a challenge and right now it seems like we have too many guys waiting for someone else to step up and make a difference. When the passion and emotion aren't there, you're not going to win a hockey game."

Briere's third goal in 16 games—and the team's first on the powerplay in 19 opportunities—gave Philadelphia its first working lead in six contests, 1-0 over Florida. Richards, the team's leading scorer, suffered a partial hamstring tear early in the third period on a hit by Bouwmeester, but the Flyers needed only one more clear to win the game.

They didn't get it. Hartnell's lob from the corner was knocked down by Steve Montador and Bouwmeester scored on Niittymaki off Parent's skate to tie the game, 1-1. When Olli Jokinen's overtime goal gave the Panthers a 2-1 win, Philadelphia's best effort since the 10-game losing streak began was ruined.

"I should have ate it in my skates or just held it in the corner," Hartnell said. "I didn't know how much time was left. I'm super frustrated. I wasn't hard on the puck and it cost us a game and a point."

While Richards was expected to be out three-to-four weeks, Gagne had been advised by concussion specialist Dr. James Kelly to shut it down for the rest of the season. "He said if you want to play another five or 10 years, you need to give it as much time as possible," recalls Gagne. So the Flyers, who had slipped a point out of a playoff spot with 20 games remaining, were without both their star winger and leading scorer.

"There's no sense waving the white flag," said Holmgren. "Everyone else is just going to have to pick it up."

The GM looked for some pick-me-ups. With Hatcher's availability game-to-game and Tomas Kaberle, an object of Philadelphia's desire going back eight years, refusing to waive a no-trade clause, Holmgren spent a third-round pick on 36-year old King defenseman Jaroslav Modry, getting back a third-rounder from Calgary for the struggling Vandermeer.

Forsberg ended months of speculation about the location of his comeback by choosing to return to Colorado, rather than the Flyers. Despite 115 points in 100 Philadelphia games, he had been so distraught about missing so much playing time with his foot issue that he couldn't stand the thought of coming back to disappoint again.

"It felt safer to go to Colorado, where I had been so many years," recalls Forsberg. He would participate in only 11 games in two separate tries with the Avalanche before retiring in 2010.

"I still have problems," says Forsberg, elected to the Hockey Hall of Fame in 2014. "Walking is fine, but it's no fun to skate anymore so I don't do it often. It's frustrating, but some people have it worse."

As the trading deadline neared, Holmgren picked up 24-year-old Norwegian right wing Patrick Thoresen off waivers from Edmonton and recalled Boulerice from the Phantoms. Neither was another Forsberg, but then again, Biron hardly had been Bernie Parent during a skid seemingly without end.

As a result, that season's annual Flyers Wives Fight for Lives Carnival seemed interminable.

"We've lost 10 straight, have fallen out of the playoffs, and we've got to smile through this?" Biron recalls thinking. "Guys were just miserable.

"Nitty and I had to take shots from fans for like four straight hours. That's worse than two or three overtimes because you're sliding down to let goals in. Then there's that 40-year-old who thinks he should be in the NHL taking a full slapshot at your head.

"I was exhausted. After it was over, I remember flying to Buffalo thinking, 'How are we going to play tomorrow?'"

Not well, it appeared at the start. Derek Roy put a goal between Biron's pads 6:31 into the game. When Clarke MacArthur made it 2-0 just 11 seconds later, Stevens used his timeout to convince his team it had been more unlucky than bad.

"We came out with the energy we wanted and got caught with a couple pucks in our net," the coach recalls. "I looked around the circle (of players gathered around the bench) and there was belief we could get back in the game. Guys were rallying each other."

Remembers Smith, "The message was, 'stick to the structure and trust what we're doing. Don't give up the next goal.'"

The Flyers did regardless. Jason Pominville shrugged off Smith to build the lead to three. But on the next shift, Carter rattled the boards with a hit on Nolan Pratt, and then took a breakaway pass from Knuble to beat Miller and put Philadelphia on the board.

"Carter had a look in his eyes of real determination that said, 'We're coming back,'" recalls Stevens.

Just 1:48 later, Thoresen forced a turnover and Hartnell scored from just inside the left hash mark. The Flyers were down only a goal.

"This is it," said Smith between periods. "It is time to win."

Philadelphia carried the play in the second period. "I just remember how badly we wanted to win that game," recalls Umberger. After Jason Pominville cleared the puck over the glass 12 minutes into the third period, it took Umberger only 16 seconds on the powerplay to tie it, 3-3.

By making a point-blank save on Carter in overtime, Miller got the game to a shootout. In the first round, Biron stopped Tim Connolly and the Buffalo goalie beat Timonen. After Ales Kotalik scored the first goal, it was Carter's turn.

"Jeff had asked Danny how to beat Miller," recalls Biron. "Danny said 'Make it look like you're going top shelf to the glove side. He will put his glove up and, if you go underneath, you'll beat it.'

"That's what Jeff did. He scored and was laughing going back to the bench."

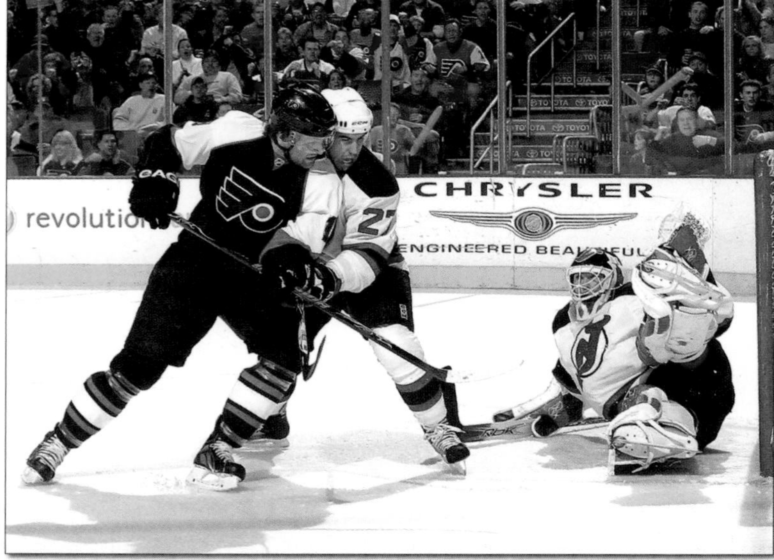

Scott Hartnell opened the scoring in the first of two shutout wins to conclude the 2007-08 season. The Flyers would go on to defeat New Jersey 3-0 and Pittsburgh 2-0.

Roy missed the net. Briere now could win the game.

"Ryan would have my number more times than I care to admit," recalls Briere. "But at that precise moment, there was no other place I wanted to be.

"I wanted to be the guy making a difference."

Deafening boos were raining down as Briere moved in. "Because Ryan knew me so well, he probably thought I wouldn't try the move I did so often in practice," recalls Briere.

But he did, faking going to the backhand and pulling the puck onto his forehand. Briere had a puck-sized opening between Ryan's left pad and the post and tucked in the winner, the 4-3 victory ending the losing streak at 10.

"The crowd was dead silent," Danny recalls. "That was a good feeling."

It got even better after the game, when Holmgren announced he was sending defensive prospect Alexandre Picard and a second-round pick to Tampa Bay to bring back center Vinny Prospal.

"With the loss of forwards due to recent injuries, we felt that we needed to add some help to that position," the GM said in a statement. "We believe Vinny will bring experience with the ability to produce offense."

Although Prospal, 32, was having a career goal-scoring year with 29, the non-contending Lightning wanted assets for him before his contract expired at the end of the season.

Drafted by the Flyers (third round, 1993) and traded to Ottawa in the 1998 deal for Alexandre Daigle, Prospal said he was happy to return. "I am glad that I am going to an organization that I already have been involved with," he said.

In truth, Prospal, content to play out his career in the Florida sunshine with linemates Vinny Lecavalier and Martin St. Louis, wasn't at all happy to be back in Philadelphia. "I called him and said 'Welcome back,'" recalls Holmgren. "He said, 'I don't want to be there.'

"He was really upset that Jay (Feaster, Tampa GM) had traded him."

At least Prospal had come to a team in playoff position, which the Flyers regained when Timonen set up goals by Dowd and Knuble in a 3-1 Wachovia Center victory over Ottawa.

"With all the guys out, Kimmo has really taken ownership in our team," praised Stevens. "It doesn't always show up on the scoresheet, but his presence, confidence and demeanor have been very important to us."

The team received seven points from the Upshall-Carter-Knuble line in a 4-1 win on March 1 at Uniondale. But the following day at Madison Square Garden, Niittymaki allowed four goals on the first 15 shots and the club was playing from behind again. Carter scored his third goal in three games to pull Philadelphia into a 4-4 tie before Marcel Hossa won the shootout for the Rangers.

It was Biron's turn to get yanked in a 5-2 home loss to Buffalo. But Carter's 25th goal with 1:54 remaining rescued a 3-2 win over Tampa. Then Briere, cooking with Prospal, had one of four powerplay goals in a 4-1 victory over the Islanders.

For a guy who wanted out, Prospal was teaming with Briere and Hartnell like a guy who was all in. "Instant chemistry," recalls Briere. "I loved his enthusiasm. When he scored a goal, he looked like a five-year-old."

With five wins in seven games, the pep seemed back in the Flyers' step, but they couldn't handle the prosperity. On March 11 in Toronto, Briere's tip-in of a two-on-one pass from Prospal had just put Philadelphia up 3-0 early in the third period when Upshall took an unnecessary penalty for holding Blake's stick well behind the play.

Mats Sundin scored a powerplay goal through a screen by Alexei Ponikarovsky, and the Leafs, who had badly outplayed the Flyers, were within two goals. After Sundin beat Thoresen on a faceoff, Pavel Kubina scored from the point, and then Jones, under pressure, banked the puck off the boards right to Jeremy Williams, who beat Biron from the face-off dot to the stick side. The game was tied.

Biron, down and seemingly out, saved his team a regulation loss by remarkably throwing up his waffleboard to rob Ponikarovsky, but the overtime remained a Toronto shooting gallery until Kubina, standing behind the Philadelphia goal, banked the puck off the toe of Jones and by Biron. Despite their three-goal cushion, the Flyers, 4-3 losers, had been fortunate to get a point out of a contest in which they had been outshot 55-25.

The following night at the Wachovia Center, Philadelphia managed only 20 shots as the Leafs completed the home-and-home sweep, 3-2. "The emotion this time of year should be ramping up and it's not for our team," said Holmgren.

In Boston, Richards returned after missing 10 games to score a goal, and Briere redirected a Prospal feed for the seventh goal by the line (with Hartnell) in the nine games since it had been put together. Philadelphia took a 2-1 lead in the third period.

But after goalie Tim Thomas had stoned Carter, Umberger and Richards on insurance bids down the stretch, Andrew Ference tied the game with 27 seconds remaining on a goal that bounced off Smith, then Carter, the latter standing in the crease for no apparent good reason. Aaron Ward scored his second overtime game winner of the season against the Flyers as they lost, 3-2.

"We have to find a way to close games," said Briere. "This can happen once in the while, but for us, it's way too often. We're throwing away valuable points."

While insisting he liked the way his team competed in Boston, Stevens benched the penalty-prone Upshall in Pittsburgh. Losing Hatcher with a hairline leg fracture, and Umberger, who suffered a partial MCL tear in his left knee, Philadelphia was routed 7-1.

"I thought we did the things we needed to do (in the first period)," said the coach, putting the blame on Biron for allowing two goals on just four first Penguin shots. Regardless, it was yet another bad start and there was little energy once the team had fallen behind. The Flyers were 5-11-5 since February 5.

"This time of year, if you don't have full intensity, you're not going to win games," said Holmgren. "It has to come from the coaches, but it comes down to the players, too."

With nine games to play, Philadelphia was hanging onto eighth place by one point over Buffalo and Florida, and two points over Washington.

It was too late to change any more players, so Stevens decided to switch around their locker-room seats. "We had a quiet group, so we wanted to get them talking a little more and just change things up," he recalls. "I was driving home (after landing from Pittsburgh) when I called (equipment manager) Derek Settlemyre and said, "I want everybody coming in tomorrow to be sitting some place different.

"They came in and wondered, 'What's going on here?' But I didn't say a word, just ran the practice, and thought there was a buzz."

Two nights later, Biron's seat was on the home bench when Stevens glanced into the stands before the opening faceoff against Atlanta and saw a sign: "Changing the chairs in the locker room is like changing the chairs on the Titanic. Ship's going down."

The coach had to laugh, however temporarily. After only 58 seconds, Niittymaki gave up a goal by Chris Thorburn on a deflection off Timonen. Six minutes later, Richards' 25th goal, on a Lupul rebound, tied the score, 1-1. Then, with three seconds remaining in the second period, Carter scored to put his team ahead.

Prospal built the lead to 3-1 off a give-and-go with Briere. The Flyers were in complete control into the final minute, until the Thrashers pulled their goalie, forced a giveaway from deep on the sidewall, and Ilya Kovalchuk closed to within 10 feet to score his 50th goal of the season.

Suddenly flummoxed, Philadelphia couldn't freeze a dump-in along the boards. Slava Kozlov centered the puck to Kovalchuk, putting the potential tying goal on the stick of the league's best scorer. But Niittymaki, continuing to be Atlanta's greatest nemesis since William Tecumseh Sherman, made a left pad save on Kovalchuk with two seconds remaining, beating counterpart and countryman Kari Lehtonen for an uncanny ninth time in nine head-to-head matchups.

"The thing I'm most happy with is they got a lucky bounce early in the game on their second shift and the emotion on the bench was terrific," said Stevens.

Knuble was most happy about the Flyers winning. "I would have dug a hole in the ice and climbed in it if Kovalchuk had scored again," the winger said.

With opponents having scored four goals on the season when his team's goalie was pulled, Stevens felt the need to practice five-on-six.

Late games continued to be a scramble. Briere's goal 10:50 into the third period put Philadelphia up 2-0 on the Rangers at the Wachovia Center. But Biron gave up a floating wrister from near the point by Marek Malik before Nigel Dawes, left wide open in the high slot, scored off Thoresen to tie the game.

Briere put back a Hartnell rebound with 3:37 remaining to seemingly rescue the night until Jaromir Jagr's backhanded rebound ricocheted off Smith to bring New York into another deadlock with 1:51 remaining. Fortunately, in overtime, Richards pulled a puck onto his backhand and scored on Stephen Valiquette to win the game, 4-3.

"I had that move in my head," said Richards after it had saved the Flyer head cases. He was fast becoming Philadelphia's Mr. Clutch, but the team needed another one of those in goal. Biron bounced back with his most solid outing in a month as powerplay goals by Briere and Prospal keyed a 4-1 victory over the Islanders.

"Marty seems like he is getting more confident as we move along," said Stevens. Indeed, although beaten again by Jagr just 1:41 into a return match on March 25th at Madison Square Garden, Biron was perfect thereafter. At 7:32 of the third period, Briere scored his 30th off a give-and-go from Prospal—their 10th goal together since the trade. In overtime, Smith picked off a Sean Avery pass and fed Richards, who leaned off Malik and fired a backhanded shot over Henrik Lundqvist's glove hand to win the contest, 2-1.

"Huge," said Briere. Finally, it had been the Flyers' turn to come from behind.

They did it again three nights later at Newark, tying the Devils on Knuble's conversion of Richards' drop pass with 56 seconds remaining. In the shootout, Briere and Carter scored on Brodeur, but Richards did not, while Biron was beaten by all three Devil shooters in a 5-4 loss. Philadelphia was a point ahead of eighth-place Boston and three in front of ninth-place Washington with four games remaining.

The final-minute heartbreakers had suddenly become the comeback kings. At Uniondale, Niittymaki gave up the first two goals and the Flyers trailed 3-2 when Thoresen stripped Radek Martinek, setting up Richards' game-tying goal with 4:22 to go. This time, Philadelphia won the shootout on a goal by Briere. The "gutsiest effort of the year," according to Stevens, left the Flyers with a chance to finish as high as fourth and as low as 10th.

Upshall was benched in Pittsburgh. "Tough to do because we loved his energy," recalls Stevens. "Scottie was upset. One night he was a fourth-line checker who finished every check and then the next night he was first-line guy trying to dangle through everybody. We didn't know what we were getting from night to night.

"He said, 'I'll be what you want me to be.' I said, 'that's the problem, you should already know. We want you to be an energy guy who will turn over pucks and provide secondary scoring.'"

In Upshall's place was Umberger, returning after a six-game absence. But an opportunity to clinch a postseason berth slipped away on four Penguin powerplay goals in a 4-2 defeat that dropped Philadelphia to ninth place, a point behind Washington.

But the Flyers still were in control of their own destiny heading into the final two contests. And destined was exactly the way the players felt in their home locker room before playing New Jersey in Game 81.

Briere, suffering a charley horse from a Jarkko Ruutu hit in Pittsburgh, and Kapanen (flu-like symptoms), were scratched. But their teammates could feel an intensity that hadn't been present for most of the season.

"We knew it was a playoff game for us and we were desperate," recalls Timonen.

"It's hard to describe that feeling. But as a player, I knew we were ready to go, if only we directed the energy the right way."

Management passed out thundersticks at the doors, and Kate and Lauren fired up the crowd. The Flyers, who would be in the playoffs by the end of the evening if they beat the Devils and Carolina lost to Florida, owned most of the motivation over a New Jersey team playing only for home-ice advantage in the first round.

On the second shift, Brodeur read a two-on-one pass from Carter and robbed Upshall, but Philadelphia kept coming. Umberger chased down a blocked Prospal shot and quickly threw the puck to the front of the net and off the stick of defenseman Mike Mottau as he jostled for position with Hartnell. The puck caromed past Brodeur for the first goal of the game.

"Only one I ever scored in my entire career against Brodeur," recalls Umberger.

He had picked an excellent time for it.

After stealing the puck from Carter, John Madden cut to the slot and Timonen slid helplessly by, but Biron made a pad save on the 15-footer. The Flyers, who outshot the Devils 14-6 in the first 20 minutes, led 1-0, and were happy to learn in the locker room that the Hurricanes trailed the Panthers, 2-1.

New Jersey managed to get the puck on goal only three times in a 25-minute stretch during the first and second periods. But when Coburn dragged down Jamie Langenbrunner at the second period buzzer, the Flyers started the third with a 31-12 shot advantage and still only a one-goal lead.

Philadelphia blocked three shots in the first minute of the powerplay, then another as it expired, but for the first time the Devils were winning board battles. Biron had to make a big save on a Patrik Elias wraparound.

Almost midway through the third period, Kukkonen was penalized for tripping Johnny Oduya behind the net, but Biron butterflied on Dainius Zubrus's redirection; as Richards picked up the rebound, he had his stick broken in half by a Travis Zajac slash. On the four-on-four, Carter beat Elias on a faceoff and passed the puck out to Upshall, whose quick release beat Brodeur's glove high to put Philadelphia ahead, 2-0.

The two teams still were both short a man when Richards carried down the left wing and hit Lupul coming up the middle past an inattentive Paul Martin. When Lupul fired past Brodeur's pad, two goals within 37 seconds had given the Flyers a 3-0 lead and turned the Wachovia Center into a madhouse. With a minute remaining, the crowd rose and roared until Biron's 3-0 shutout was complete.

While Upshall, who had been a healthy scratch in the previous game, told CSN Philadelphia interviewer Steve Coates on the ice that, "A lot of things built up inside of me that I wanted to get out tonight," his teammates were in the locker room watching Florida hold on for a 4-3 victory over Carolina that put the Flyers back in the playoffs after an absence of one year.

It had only seemed like five years to the 11 survivors of 2006-07.

"Everybody was high-fiving, celebrating, going crazy," recalls Umberger. "We had snuck into the playoffs, but it was a big deal after what we went through the year before."

Smith, one of the players brought in to, as he says today, "put the Flyers back where they were supposed to be" recalls having the most fun looking at the faces of those who had suffered the most. "It was great to see the excitement of the guys who had gone through tough times," he recalls.

Nobody in that locker room would better appreciate perseverance than Smith. From separate Devil hits during the first and second periods, the defenseman had suffered dislocations in both joints that connect the collarbone to the sternum.

Easing the pain, even if temporarily, was not just the playoff berth, but how his team had gained it. Philadelphia had its best performance of the season when under the most pressure.

"We dominated from start to finish," recalls Stevens. "There was such energy and emotion that everything just clicked."

Richards called it "close to a perfect." Snider, who had watched 40 seasons, agreed. "I don't think I've ever seen a team play a better game that was so crucial," the Chairman said. "They weren't afraid or nervous."

Perhaps that was because the Flyers essentially had been playing playoff contests for more than a month, just to qualify. "It really does harden your team to the pressure," recalls the coach.

With no possible home-ice advantage at stake in Game 82 against the Penguins, Philadelphia had a one-game break from that stress for Smith and Briere to heal. In a pregame presentation, Richards, finishing with a team-leading 28 goals and 47 assists while playing in both offensive and defensive situations, was awarded the Bobby Clarke Trophy (Team MVP), and Timonen the Barry Ashbee Trophy (Best Defenseman). Biron went on to shut out Pittsburgh, 2-0, earning his team the sixth seed and a match-up with Washington, the Southeast Division Champion.

The Capitals, who had won 11 of their last 12 to squeeze past Carolina, had been 27th in the league in 2006-07. So the Flyers fortunately were matched against an opponent with even less playoff experience than themselves.

This was the first series for 15 Caps, including Alexander Ovechkin, the first overall pick in the 2004 draft who had become the NHL's leading scorer with 65 goals and 47 assists in his third season. Goaltender Cristobal Huet, who had keyed the late surge after being acquired at the trading deadline from Montreal, had made the postseason for only the second time.

Counting Hatcher, who was hoping to return by the second round, there were nine Flyers with postseason experience, but only five had participated in Philadelphia's last postseason appearance in 2006. If Stevens' team had a meaningful edge, it might be its second-rated powerplay going against Washington's 25th-best penalty killing unit.

But the most intriguing plot in this first meeting between the two franchises since 1989—when the Flyers won in six to avenge their Game Seven overtime loss the previous spring—was the depth of a Philadelphia club with six 20-goal scorers versus the star power of Ovechkin.

It was Stevens' pre-series practice to have each player prepare a verbal presentation in front of the team about a member of the opposition, usually his proposed matchup. Timonen could have filibustered about the speedy, shifty and physical Ovechkin. "He's the best in the league; it will take more than one player to stop him," said the defenseman. "It's going to take five."

Actually, it was going to be five against Ovechkin and Mike Green, a 56-point defenseman adept at joining the rush.

Briere was ready-as-vowed for Game One at the Verizon Center. Smith claimed to be too, despite pain to the contrary.

"I can't afford to dress a defenseman that I might lose after a couple of shifts," Stevens told his captain.

"If I start the game, I will finish it," said Smith.

He recalls: "I was always a believer that if you aren't going to harm yourself and you can play, you do. The game is supposed to be fun, but we are earning a great living doing it, so you find the willpower to push through."

He convinced the coach. "Our doctors said it was about the most painful injury you can have," recalls Stevens. "I just couldn't believe his pain threshold."

Knuble was out of the box for slashing Nicklas Backstrom, but not yet back in the play, when Donald Brashear put in a rebound of a blocked Tom Poti shot to give Washington a 1-0 lead after only 3:16. Five minutes later, Briere beat Brooks Laich on a draw and Prospal tied the game 1-1 from above the circle.

The Flyers dominated the opening minutes of the second period. But the Caps took back the lead, 2-1, on their first good chance of the session, their fourth line striking for a second time when Biron gave too much room on the short side to David Steckel.

Smith had just broken up the last rush of a Washington powerplay when Briere bolted from the penalty box, straddled the blueline as he took a pass from Knuble, and, from the faceoff dot, beat Huet to the stick side to tie the contest, 2-2.

When the Cap defense left too much open in the middle, Briere found Prospal, who fired through Huet's five hole to give Philadelphia its first lead, 3-2. After Matt Cooke went to the box for interfering with Coburn, Richards threw a cross-crease pass to Briere, who, thanks to Hartnell's screen, had a half-empty net to score his second goal and build the edge to 4-2 after two periods.

But control was short-lived. When Modry couldn't handle a back pass from Smith along the back wall, Sergei Fedorov stole the puck and chipped a pass through Prospal to Green, who was practically alone on the weak side. The NHL's leading goal scorer among defensemen didn't miss, cutting the Flyer advantage to 4-3 before the third period was two minutes old.

Less than five minutes later, Green fired again, this time hitting Thoresen in the protective cup, leaving him in agony on the ice as referees Brad Watson and Wes McCauley refused to interrupt Washington's possession with a whistle. "They didn't think it was serious," Richards would report later. As Thoresen writhed, Green was able to fire over Biron's glove to tie the game 4-4.

The clock was under five minutes when Kukkonen received a terrible return pass from Modry and was caught flat-footed by Ovechkin. The superstar stripped Kukkonen clean, Biron flopped and Ovechkin went high, putting Washington up, 5-4, with 4:32 remaining.

Kukkonen broke his stick in self-disgust. "I thought [Ovechkin] was coming from the other side, and he sneaked behind me," the defenseman would say. "I have to make a stronger play there."

With only a minute remaining in the game, Carter had the puck lifted as he started a rush, leaving Biron unable get to the bench. When he finally did, Ovechkin ran over Richards and lobbed the puck out, enabling Washington to hang on for the win and 1-0 series lead.

"The frustrating part is we gave them a couple of goals they didn't have to work for," Briere said. "Overall, we played a hard game."

Actually, they did for only two periods, after which the Flyers had stopped getting pucks deep, begging for an ultimate opportunist such as Ovechkin to beat them.

Thoresen's injury opened up a spot for Umberger, Stevens' utility winger, on a line with Richards and Lupul.

"I had 50 points in the regular season and because I got hurt and came back with three games to go, I started the series on the fourth line," recalls Umberger. "It's the playoffs, so wherever you play, you have to figure out a way to make a difference."

He did early in Game Two. Sprung on a stretch pass from deep in the defensive zone by Coburn, Umberger split defensemen Jeff Schultz and John Erskine to beat Huet over the shoulder with a wrist shot. Hartnell took two penalties, but Biron stopped Ovechkin through traffic, then Backstrom on the rebound. When Knuble forced Green into a giveaway and fired, Carter put in the rebound and Philadelphia went up, 2-0, 15:17 into the first period.

The Flyers clogged the neutral zone, took only three penalties the rest of the way, held the Caps without a shot in a seven-minute stretch of the second period, and looked like they had been checking away playoff games for years. Biron's first playoff victory—a 24-save, 2-0 shutout—evened the series, 1-1.

As the father of two, he was an older pro in the delivery room, where his wife, Anne Marie, was scheduled for a Caesarian section between Games Three and Four.

"But they had to move it up," Biron recalls. "We could do it on the off-day after Game One or after Game Two, but the way I played in Game One, no way was I going to go to the coach and tell him I was going to miss practice the next day.

"So, great, I had a shutout in Game Two. We were standing by the bus after the game, when I told Johnny Stevens, 'I won't be at practice tomorrow; we're having a baby.' He laughed, guess it was okay."

Anne Marie delivered Emily Marie the next day. As a bonus, The Stork also brought Stevens twin bundles of joy—Hatcher and Thoresen.

Thoresen's testicular injury was much less serious than first feared. And with Philadelphia relying on so many playoff babes, Hatcher figured to be a godsend.

Biron spent the afternoon of Game Three with his wife and infant daughter at the Voorhees campus of Thomas Jefferson University Hospital, and then got stuck in I-295 gridlock. He was in serious jeopardy of being late for the warm-up.

"I moved to the shoulder, put my hazards on and just went," he recalls. "A few cars saw me coming and tried to squeeze me out, but I put the pedal to the metal.

"I closed my eyes thinking, 'I might be going into the ditch. But I have to get to this hockey game.'"

He made it in time to get conked on the side of the mask with an early shot by Alexander Semin. "Saw stars," Biron said afterwards, but it was the Caps who played the first period like they didn't know what was hitting them.

As much as the Flyers controlled play, it took them more than 16 minutes to jump ahead. Briere accidently kicked the puck away from Coburn during a breakout swing behind their own goal but the defenseman quickly retrieved to find Prospal at center. Suddenly Philadelphia had a three-on-two and Briere buried Coburn's pass over Huet's shoulder.

The Caps tied the game only 1:11 later when Eric Fehr's quick wrister caught Biron sliding the wrong way. Still, the Flyers kept coming. Briere carried the puck into the Washington zone on a three-on-two and Prospal threw a circle-to-circle pass to Hartnell, who one-timed a shot over Huet's left shoulder. One shift later, Dowd stole the puck from Jiri Jurcina and fed Kapanen, who beat the goalie to the short side for a 3-1 lead at the first-period break.

Philadelphia squandered a second-period powerplay when Hartnell, who had taken an Erskine elbow for the team, interfered with Huet just 14 seconds later. After Hatcher shoved Green from behind, the Caps couldn't cash in on a brief two-man advantage. But with Hartnell back on the ice, Green scored on the five-on-four through a Backstrom screen to put Washington within a goal.

Both teams continued to ask for trouble with penalties. Poti was in the box for a stick tug in the neutral zone when Briere, set up by Richards in the slot, restored the lead to two in the final 10 seconds of the second period.

Having been pushed by Laich against the camera mounted in the back of the Flyer net, Timonen could not return for the start of the third period. Green missed a golden chance at the backdoor with Umberger off for hooking Ovechkin, but the Caps' dynamic defenseman was undeterred. Working a give-and-go with Laich, Green fed diagonally to a wide-open Shaone Morrisonn, whose shot was tipped out of the air by Laich, past Biron. Washington, though outchanced 26-14, was within one, with 4:34 remaining.

Richards stepped up, stealing the puck from Morrisonn in the neutral zone and, when tripped from behind by Green, earned a penalty shot. Only Eric Lindros had ever been successful at a postseason penalty shot in five Flyer attempts.

"You don't know what the goalie is going to do," Richards would say later. "You're worried about the ice, and the crowd is going crazy. It's nerve wracking. But once I touched the puck, I kind of had a feeling what I was going to do."

He faked a forehand, dropped his shoulder, and put his first NHL postseason goal between Huet's legs on the backhand. And on the way to the bench, Richards scooped up a small handful of ice shavings and tossed them into the air.

"I'm an idiot," Richards would say. "I mean, act like you've scored a goal before."

But having extended the lead to 5-3 with 2:59 to go, he had never scored a bigger one. Knuble, half-fanning on an attempt from the blueline, trickled the puck into the empty net to put away a 6-3 victory and a 2-1 series lead.

"The Flyers are outworking and outhitting us," said Cap defenseman Steve Eminger.

Stevens had matched two lines, centered by Richards and Carter, against Ovechkin to supplement the work on defense by Timonen, Coburn and Hatcher. "They're not giving me space to shoot the puck," the Russian said. "They just skate with me."

Predicting that Philadelphia was on borrowed time, Washington coach Bruce Boudreau said, "My history with Ovie is that you can't keep a good man down."

Brave words, considering the treatment his Caps were receiving from the Wachovia werewolves.

"[The Capitals] entered the playing surface like Russell Crowe entered the Colosseum in *Gladiator*," wrote Mike Wise, the *Washington Post* sports columnist. "Flyer fans didn't want to beat Washington as much as bludgeon, emasculate. Many of the women and children looked is if they could work security for Megadeth."

Tilger read the column with, uh, interest. "I think our fans should know about this," he said. Many of them already did. In addition to an email bombardment from insulted fans, Wise received a few phone threats at his hotel. After he had checked out and gone to the Wachovia Center for Game Four, the journalist was told by co-workers that three scowling gentlemen of size had been in the lobby asking for him.

The Flyers decided to distribute copies of the column to the fans, but *The Post*, fearing for Wise's safety, threatened the team with copyright infringement. Placing excerpts of the piece on the center-hung scoreboard was fair game, however. Wearing a Megadeth jacket and a mullet, Ike Richman, the Comcast-Spectacor public relations vice president, stalked Wise in the press box.

"Of all the towns in North America that wouldn't get satire when it comes to sports, Philly would be one," recalls Wise. "They take their teams so seriously, which is great, too.

"At that point of the series, the Caps were getting outworked by a much more intense team. That was my column: the difference between the two teams was reflected in the atmosphere of the two buildings. Look at the slogans of the two franchises that year: One was 'Rock the Red;' the other 'Vengeance!'

"I got my baptism into what Philly fandom really is. It was a little frightening actually."

Tongue in cheek, Luukko threatened legal action against the newspaper. But it was Ovechkin who should have been suing his teammates for non-support. The Flyers had eight players with as many goals in the series as Ovechkin, who had scored only once.

Carter got his second just 42 seconds after the Game Four puck drop, converting a Green turnover forced by Knuble, by shooting across Huet's body from the edge of the circle. Briere was off for holding Semin's stick when Ovechkin, who had been moved from the point of the struggling powerplay to the wing, fed Backstrom at the back door to tie the contest, 1-1.

Despite the return of quarterback Timonen, Philadelphia did nothing with three consecutive Washington penalties that including 44 seconds in five-on-three advantages. The Capitals got their turn when Briere high sticked Steckel well behind the play and Hatcher broke his stick on Backstrom. Given 1:48 to work the two-man advantage, the Caps needed only 13 seconds. With Smith preoccupied by Laich in front, Ovechkin fed the opposite post to Semin, who did not even need to one-time the pass to put Washington up 2-1.

Making no mistale: Mike Richard scored on his Game Three penalty shot vs. Washinton to put the Flyers up 5-3.

Hatcher got away with drawing blood from Jurcina before Modry—playing despite the death of his father from colon cancer in the Czech Republic—drew out Poti and threw a beautiful pass to a wide-open Carter at the goalmouth. He had an easy redirect to tie the game 2-2.

Biron gave the lead back to the Capitals by failing to track an Eminger toss-up from the half wall. The momentum changed, with Washington carrying the play for the first time since late in Game One. Hatcher took a big hit from Ovechkin and, in the final minute of the second period, Biron came out to stop Semin, wide open at the edge of the circle.

Early in the third, Biron left a big rebound on a Green shot and got lucky when Ovechkin, the puck bouncing in too tight for him to get full arm extension, shot wide.

Almost halfway through the period, Huet flung up his glove to stop Upshall off a Carter passout and the Caps cleared the puck, only to get caught with two many men on the ice.

The Flyers, however, had too many men not thinking. Biron had to stop Semin on a two-on-one shorthanded opportunity and needed Briere to clear the rebound from in front of an open net. The subsequent rush was broken up, but Umberger prevented a Poti clear and Richards won the race to the puck in the corner. Briere sneaked from along the backwall to the far post and, off a beautiful seam pass from Richards, banged in the tying goal from a tough angle with 9:59 remaining.

One minute later, Jones hit the post. When Upshall forced Fedorov and fed a wide-open Knuble, Huet made a phenomenal diving save, then got his pad on a Knuble deflection of a Modry drive. Biron answered with a slick glove save on Steckel off a Matt Bradley passout, but Philadelphia, presented a gifted powerplay when Timonen's accidental trip of Biron was attributed to Viktor Kozlov, didn't do much with the opportunity.

In overtime, Carter didn't man the point on a Timonen pinch, sending Ovechkin out two-on-one with Fedorov, but Coburn smothered the Washington star's shot. Biron, at his best since allowing the Eminger goal, dragged his right pad on Semin from the top of the crease and then stopped Poti in alone. When a Semin shot off a faceoff trickled through the goalie, Carter saved the game by tying up Kozlov.

The Flyers went to a second overtime for the 11th time in their history having held Ovechkin to just one shot in the game. But five minutes into the period, Stevens' team had applied little pressure until Huet made a stick save on Jones off a diagonal feed by Hartnell, then a stop on Hartnell after Modry turned up a chance with a pinch.

On the next shift, Richards hit Lupul with a backhand pass at the blueline. Huet came to the top of circle, cut down the angle and made the save, but Philadelphia had forced a faceoff in the Washington end.

Fedorov pulled the puck back, but Jones jammed an attempted clear down the boards to a battling Knuble. Upshall joined the forecheck and quickly fed Knuble at the right post. Although Huet butterflied to make the save, Carter was on the puck quickly.

He fed through the legs of Jurcina to Knuble, still at the same pipe behind Ovechkin.

Huet got his toe out on the backhander. "I couldn't believe he had stopped that one," Knuble recalls. But on the rebound, the winger took the time to put the puck on his forehand and, as Huet pitched forward, shot high into the net.

Carter, who had been the best player on the ice, leaped. Knuble tilted his head back and thrust his arms skyward. Signman raised "Thrilla in Phila." The first multiple-overtime game in the history of the Philadelphia's 12-year-old arena had been won, 4-3, at 6:40 of the second session, giving the Flyers a 3-1 series lead.

Asked if his first sudden-death playoff score was the greatest thrill of his life, Knuble replied, "There is not much bigger; the birth of your kid maybe. It's just a huge feeling to hear the building going crazy."

Stevens warned that the Capitals weren't dead, but at least one of them believed they were. "This was the first time I had ever been up in an NHL playoff series," recalls Umberger. "I remember thinking, 'We got this.'

"I don't know if the whole team felt that way. Maybe."

That appeared to be the case at the start of Game Five in Washington.

The Caps signaled their determination early. During the first minute Semin responded to an Upshall trip with a shove, and Erskine got the extra two minutes for coming to his teammate's aid. Although the Flyers had an early powerplay, Huet stopped both Knuble on the doorstep and Briere on a partial breakaway.

Six minutes in, Carter took a penalty for interfering with Green. Only 30 seconds after that, Timonen was caught flat-footed and had to hook Ovechkin on his hands. On the five-on-three, Backstrom, alone at the post behind Modry, put in a Semin pass and Washington had the 1-0 lead they craved.

Philadelphia then went an 11-minute stretch of the first period without a shot on goal. "Never been forechecked that hard in my life," recalls Stevens, whose team was still being badly outplayed early in the second. Kozlov won a battle with Timonen behind the net and put the puck between Carter's legs to Fedorov breaking off the sidewall. Ovechkin ran a pick on Coburn in front of the goal and Fedorov beat Biron to the stick side, giving the Caps a 2-0 lead.

The Flyers, who had managed one shot in the last 25 minutes, were doing little with a Morrisonn penalty when they got a break. Fedorov was whistled for a phantom hold of Coburn and, on the two-man advantage, Prospal converted a Briere pass through the crease to cut the edge to 2-1.

Biron made a big pad save on Ovechkin, who had gone around Lupul following a Carter giveaway, so Philadelphia was still down only a goal going into the third period. The Flyers woke up and played most of the first six minutes in Washington's end but Briere, alone in front, tried to go backhand-to-forehand and lost the puck.

Three minor penalties set back Philadelphia's catch-up efforts—Upshall took his third of the game, this one for interfering with Huet; Jones tripped Bradley; and, when Hartnell had to take a hooking penalty to prevent a Steckel chance, the Caps cashed in on the third opportunity. Semin took a drop pass from Green and used screens by Laich and Ovechkin to restore Washington's lead by two.

They needed that insurance. Only 44 seconds following Semin's goal, Hatcher made a stop at the point, took a chance by going to the net, and Prospal found the big defenseman in the slot. Huet was beaten low to the glove side, cutting the lead to 3-2 with 4:33 remaining.

The Flyers had one good chance thereafter, by Coburn after Carter won an offensive zone draw, but Huet made the stop. In the final 10 seconds, Briere's one-timer off a Timonen feed was deflected by Poti, enabling the Caps to hang on for a 3-2 victory that cut their series deficit to 3-2.

"Their season was on the line, so they really came at us hard," Stevens said. "To me, that's a lesson we learned that won't happen again. We've got to initiate."

Terminating the Capitals was a job necessitating even more output than the big guns of Lauren Hart and Kate Smith. While Miss Smith was never known to have been an aficionado of Megadeth, the band's music blared during the Game Six warm-up.

Stevens couldn't replace the net presence of Knuble, who, popping up from a slide after Green had faked a shot in Game Five, had suffered a partial hamstring tear during the first period. He was out indefinitely. But the coach did try to pick up the energy level by dressing Cote.

Sure enough, he drew an interference penalty from Bradley only 2:59 into the contest, generating the start Philadelphia needed. Timonen missed the net from the top of the slot but Richards picked up the puck off the backboards, circled the net, and put the Flyers up 1-0.

In Knuble's absence, Umberger moved to the line with Richards and Thoresen then blew by Eminger, but was stopped by Huet's right pad. In turn, Biron anticipated and came across to beat Ovechkin off a centering pass by Fedorov.

Upshall took yet another penalty, this time putting his stick between the legs of Fedorov, and the Caps powerplay, four-for-10 since Ovechkin had been moved from the point to the wing, had an opportunity. But Philadelphia killed it and another penalty on Jones for interfering with Bradley at center ice.

When Semin, battling with Kukkonen, came back at the defenseman with a hard crosscheck, the second period opened with the Flyers having 1:22 left on the powerplay to build their lead. They did. When Steckel drifted to take away a pass to the point, Briere was left wide open at the edge of the circle to beat Huet's glove to put Philadelphia up 2-0.

The Caps were caught with too many men on the ice, so the Flyers quickly had another powerplay opportunity. But Lupul, goalless in the series, was stoned on a diving save by Huet.

Philadelphia then killed a Coburn penalty as Biron made two saves on Semin from the faceoff dot. Nine minutes into the second period, an Eminger breakout pass trapped Prospal, and the Caps broke out three on two. Laich then dropped the puck to Semin, who fed Backstrom, and the center completed the gorgeous tic-tac-toe play before Biron could come across. "It wasn't just that they scored the goal," recalls Stevens, "it was the way they scored it—almost like they were toying with us.

"I know our confidence was a little shaken."

Trailing only 2-1, Ovechkin dropped the puck to Green at the line and deflected the return pass on goal. Biron gloved that one, but Washington kept up the pressure. Laich pinched to force a giveaway by Briere, and Erskine, wide open at the point, fired through a crowd. Biron flashed up his glove again but only knocked the puck down, and Semin quickly pounced to tie the game 2-2 in a suddenly silent building.

When Steckel hit the post following a Jones giveaway with less than two minutes to go, the Flyers were fortunate to get out of the second period even.

Coburn, set up by a Carter pull-up off the rush, had a chance to change the momentum during the opening seconds of the third period; he beat Huet's glove, but not the post. After Timonen's shot was blocked by Ovechkin, the puck caromed into the high slot to Kozlov, who quickly relayed to the superstar flying on a breakaway behind Coburn. The Russian whirlwind dropped his shoulder, shot on the forehand, and beat Biron high to the glove side to put Washington ahead, 3-2.

Held to only one goal in the first five games, Ovechkin was dominating, forcing Prospal to take a hooking penalty. Morrisonn stupidly chopped Upshall's stick in half, allowing Philadelphia a countering powerplay opportunity. Green went to the locker room with a leg injury, giving the Flyers another break. But three times on the four-on-three, Briere failed to handle a pass. When Coburn played the puck prematurely on a change, he was called as the sixth man on the ice, and the Caps had an opportunity to salt away the game.

Fedorov stripped Carter at the blueline, and Laich walked off the sideboards to feed Ovechkin. He unleashed a howitzer past Biron's short side to build the Washington lead to two with 9:19 remaining.

Philadelphia generated little down the stretch as the stunned crowd streamed out. Ovechkin, with two goals in the series-tying 4-2 win, had become a runaway train while the Flyers had to board one for Washington. Game Seven would begin in 21 hours.

"It's an opportunity we have let slip away here," Stevens said. "But there's nothing more we can do right now besides get our rest. I have yet to see us not get off the mat."

Many members of the team had not packed. "I was one of them," recalls Stevens. "Maybe my wife had given me a shaving kit and another tie. To me, if you had packed, you were figuring we weren't going to win Game Six."

It had never occurred to Biron that Philadelphia wouldn't.

"When we lost, it was the most defeated I have ever felt after a hockey game," the goalie recalls. "I'm listening to my music on the train, thinking, 'How did we let that slip away? How are we going to win a Game Seven in that crazy building in Washington?'"

Before boarding the train, Richards had expressed to the media the feeling that the back-to-backs might work in the Flyers' favor. "No time to dwell on it," he said bravely.

Upshall recalls being confident. "I didn't think for one second we were going to let the opportunity slide," he remembers but, having taken five minor penalties in the six games, this was a player apparently not equipped with an alarm.

Because of the travel and next-day game schedule, there would be no morning skate, just a meeting at the team's Mayflower Hotel headquarters. On the train, Stevens was asked by the team leaders to keep his remarks short. "They said they knew [the Caps] really well by now, so I just hit a couple key points," recalls the coach. "That's the way we did it, just a few adjustments.

"I felt good about our team. They didn't look nervous or worried. They looked excited."

In the morning, Stevens told his players that it was them against everybody who was writing them off. Then, unable to nap, the coach walked the 40 minutes from the hotel to the Verizon Center.

He recalls Richards as instrumental in getting Flyer chins off the floor. "I don't remember anything specific, but with a few words during a timeout or a tap on the shin pads, Mike always was one of the best I've ever been around.

The wisecracking Hartnell was a valve releasing some pressure, too. No matter how they had gotten to Game Seven, everyone seemed to fully understand that with one more win, they were in the next round.

"You can over-analyze looking too much into 'the mood' in the room," Smith recalls. "But I think there was trust that we were a better team than Washington and would play a good game."

If the Philadelphia players were aware that Huet was 1-6 during that season on back-to-back nights, it couldn't have been much consolation. Biron was 1-5. Regardless, by game time the Flyer goalie's head was on straight. "If I can just play a little better, we have a good chance," he recalls thinking.

Stevens replaced Cote with Downie, who was making his postseason debut, on the fourth line with Dowd and Kapanen. The 13th Game Seven in team history—Philadelphia was 6-6—began with a good early chance off the wing by Lupul, but the team quickly got into penalty trouble.

Hartnell was called for interfering with Eminger, and Hatcher for a face wash of Laich along the halfwall. On the five-on-three, Biron made a glove stop on Semin and Ovechkin fired wide from the slot, but Backstrom retrieved the puck off the backboards and beat Jones and Biron to the opposite post for a 1-0 Washington lead after 5:42.

The Flyers didn't give up a good scoring chance on the five-on-four. Still, the Caps applied pressure until Semin hooked Richards as he picked up the puck in front of the net. The powerplay gave the Flyers a chance to catch their breaths. But they did better than that. When Erskine lost his stick 10 feet above the circle, Upshall fired through Umberger's screen and Huet's pads to tie the game 1-1, 15:38 into the first period.

Fedorov drew a double minor for inadvertently cutting Upshall and, 18 seconds later, Richards was tripped by Steckel while gaining the zone. Philadelphia now had a five-on-three opportunity, but Prospal hit the post, Poti blocked a Carter drive and the struggling Lupul missed a half-empty net on a rebound as the first penalty expired. The five-on-four also passed without a superior chance.

Early in the second period, Biron came across to thwart a Laich backhander. Downie took a penalty for hooking Eminger, but Richards drew one right back from Fedorov after fleecing him of the puck.

Huet stopped a Briere screamer from the top of the circle to keep the game tied. Coburn stuck like glue to Ovechkin, following him all over the defensive zone in one memorable possession before forcing the puck out to center. Hatcher then made a sliding block to break up a two-on-one Ovechkin feed for Backstrom.

Nine minutes into the second period, Biron fed ahead to Thoresen, who gained the blueline and relayed to Kapanen. Green broke up a centering pass as Thoresen crashed into Morrisonn and, together, they plowed into Huet. From the lower edge of the circle, Kapanen shot the puck into a wide-open net. Ovechkin argued for goaltender interference, but there was no review. On a score from the fourth line, assisted by the goaltender, the Flyers led 2-1 midway through the game.

Less than four minutes later, Downie lost Boyd Gordon, and then had to take him down in the goalmouth. The Caps held the puck for the entire powerplay without getting a good look. Philadelphia cleared it as the penalty expired but Kozlov brought it right back in. He was chased by Downie, leaving Ovechkin time and space in the middle to beat Biron high to the glove side and tie the game 2-2 with 4:31 remaining in the second period.

Early in the third, Briere put a drive off the handle of Huet's stick. A minute later, Biron made a pad save on Poti. Hartnell was hammered along the boards from behind by Jurcina and appeared injured but, when the puck came back to the Flyer winger, he rose, shot again and was stopped by Huet.

Whenever possible, Boudreau tried to get Ovechkin away from Timonen and Coburn and just from the volume of the star's shifts, the coach sometimes succeeded. Midway through the third period, Ovechkin had nine chances.

A Biron giveaway led to a Green try at the point, but the puck deflected high over the net and, on the resultant faceoff, Laich played the puck off the boards to a wide-open Erskine. He fired from just outside the top of the circle and Biron made a pad stop, pulling in the rebound before Semin could reach it.

With three minutes remaining, Timonen gave the puck away up the slot to Ovechkin, who tried to hit Fedorov breaking for the half-open goal but missed the connection.

Double overtime joy, Game Seven vs. Washington.

The 30th Game Seven overtime in NHL history—and second for the Flyers, who had lost on Dale Hunter's goal against the Caps at Landover in 1988—began with Upshall beating Jurcina down the wing, then being unable to get full wood on his own juicy rebound, the puck popping up for Huet to easily glove.

Ovechkin, from 35 feet out, was stopped by a cool Biron positioned perfectly at the top of his crease. Erskine batted down a Hatcher clear and shot, but Biron fought off the puck through traffic before Erskine got away with a trip on Kapanen to prevent a two-on-one.

Four minutes into sudden death, Fedorov beat Carter with a move, forcing Biron to make a right pad save on Ovechkin. Umberger deflected away a potential rebound and started out of the zone, only to have his right skate tripped by Poti. Paul Devorski, the trailing referee, made the penalty call.

To a Philadelphia team that had been outshot 29-14 over the second and third periods, not only was this a chance, but perhaps the last chance.

"I remember thinking, ''this is what we have been waiting for, we're going to score,'" recalls Biron. "I just had that feeling."

Prospal won the draw at the Washington line and Briere carried the puck in. Lupul and Richards shot wide, then Lupul worked a give-and-go with Briere on the goal line, but the puck was deflected away.

Huet butterflied to stop a Richards one-timer from above the dot, and the Caps got a clear off the faceoff. But Umberger brought the puck back in and dropped it to Coburn, whose drive through traffic hit Huet in the mask and deflected up into the netting, so the Flyers had another faceoff in the Caps' end with 35 seconds remaining on the penalty.

Richards won it cleanly from Gordon, but Huet found Timonen's shot through a Briere screen and covered. Stevens, annoyed that Prospal had not carried the puck from the sideboards towards the goal as the coaches had preached, substituted Lupul.

Fedorov pulled the next draw back from Richards. But Lupul beat

Morrisonn to the puck along the back wall, and fed Richards on the goal line, who then found Briere coming up the slot. Jurcina blocked the shot but the puck bounded to Timonen who was 45 feet out.

"They had done a good job blocking my shooting lanes all series," Timonen would recall. "I was open that time."

He cranked a one-timer, and Lupul, crossing in front, ever so slightly tipped it. A butterflying Huet made the stop with his left pad and looked to the left for a rebound that lay instead at his skates.

"Pucks hadn't been bouncing my way," Lupul would say. "That one bounced right on my backhand." He pounced on the puck before Jurcina and slid it around Huet's outstretched right pad and into the net. At 6:06 of overtime, Lupul's first goal of the series had won it for the Flyers.

While Huet broke his stick over the goal, Lupul threw his in the air and, with both arms up, danced to the sideboards as Timonen won the race to the hero and jumped into his arms.

In the visiting management booth high above the Verizon Center, Holmgren leaped and hit his head on the low ceiling. Then he lifted Luukko off the ground.

The Philadelphia players poured off the bench, Stevens bouncing up and down in joy behind it, while assistants Murray and McIlhargey pumped their fists before joining McCrossin and Settlemyre in a group hug.

"I couldn't get down to [the celebration] fast enough," Biron recalls. "It took me a while because a couple players came to see me on the way.

"I remember thinking, 'I've got to get to that scrum.'"

In a silent elevator filled with Washington personnel, Holmgren felt just as much in a hurry to reach the visiting locker room.

Before the handshake line, Ovechkin, having scored nine points over seven games in his first playoff series—more than Gordie Howe, Bobby Orr, Bobby Clarke, Guy Lafleur, Wayne Gretzky, Mario Lemieux or Sidney Crosby—put his hands together leading the Washington fans in applause for how far their team had come. But the Flyers, only one year earlier the worst team in the NHL, were going farther—to a second-round matchup with No. 1 seed Montreal.

After the handshake line, Jones stood behind the bench, slapping each teammate with a hard high five as they came by to go up the tunnel to one of the happiest locker rooms of their lives.

"Coach had me out almost the whole powerplay," Lupul told reporters. "He showed a lot of confidence in a guy who hadn't scored all series. But it's not how you start, it's how you finish.

"This is the type of goal you think about growing up. It's probably the highlight of my career so far."

Certainly Briere, who had 11 points in the series, believes today he never has recorded a greater second assist.

"How much better does it get than winning a Game Seven on the road in overtime when everybody thought you were dead?" he recalls. "In my home is the picture, one of the best I have, of me jumping on Joffrey in the corner with the fans behind us.

"The faces are priceless. You know, I can sit there for 20 minutes and just look at all the faces one by one; they're just devastated."

In eight seasons at Nashville, Timonen never had been to the second round. "I see that puck go in, it's unbelievable," he said. "[I was] so tired, mentally and physically."

He could have fooled Stevens. "Timonen was unbelievable. He looked like he could play all night out there," said the coach, who had used the Finn for 28:24 in Game Seven on top of 27:05 in Game Six. "He contributes in all situations, wanted to be the guy. He really stepped up for us and brought Coburn along with him.

"And I guess Marty (39 saves) answered those questions about back-to-back. He was terrific. You learned that this team has got the heart we always said it had. It's a resilient group. We're a relatively new team and you need things like this to create a bond."

Win or lose, Holmgren had long-before formed one with Hatcher, the 35-year-old warrior who a year earlier had turned down the opportunity to be traded to a contender because he wanted to be part of the turnaround. Hatcher was getting his knee drained in the training room when the GM looked inside the door.

"That smile I shared with Paul is what I will always remember about that locker room," says Hatcher. "I don't think we had to say a word to each other.

"Everyone was so happy, so relieved. But finally it was like, 'All right, get our stuff and let's go to Montreal.'"

On the train ride home, Flyers who had won the 2005 Calder Cup under Stevens remembered that, after each successful playoff round, the coach had brought in a cake with the team's picture on it.

To emphasize collaboration, Stevens had assigned each Phantom an ingredient from a cake recipe to bring to the locker room. But on this occasion, players arriving home from Washington in the wee hours had to be on the charter for Montreal by 2 p.m. for a game the following night. So the Flyers, into the second round for the first time in four years, enjoyed their just desserts on the plane.

Hartnell, who had risen early enough in the day to accompany Lupul to an Olde City barbershop, decided on a whim to get his Afro straightened. Hartnell addressed the media that met the team at Pierre-Elliott Trudeau International Airport with his hair flat and at shoulder length.

"Once I wash it, I'm sure she'll go back to the ol' Afro," said Hartnell, a male referring to his hair in feminine terms.

"He looked like Joe Dirt from that movie, had the guys just dying," recalls Stevens. "Who takes time to go do this for the sake of getting a few laughs from his teammates? That was Scotty."

Four losses in four regular-season games against Montreal weren't scary enough to curl the hair of the bold Flyers. The Habs had traded Huet to Washington at the deadline to go with 20-year-old Carey Price, who had backstopped his team to a 3-1 series lead against Boston in the first round before giving up four third-period goals in both Games Five and Six. Price then finished off the Bruins with a 5-0 shutout.

The Canadiens—meeting Philadelphia for the fifth time (3-1 Montreal) and the first occasion since the 1989 Eastern Conference final (won bythe Habs in six games)—were smaller than the Capitals and reliant on the NHL's best powerplay. But for the second consecutive series, the Flyers were facing a club not much more playoff-tested than themselves. The Boston series win had been Montreal's first in three springs.

Game One at the Bell Centre was Philadelphia's third contest in four nights, but adrenaline appeared to get the players off to a good start. Thirteen minutes into the contest, Umberger tried to hit Thoresen on a rush and the puck went off defenseman Patrice Brisebois, on the near post, and in. Three minutes later, after 30 seconds of pressure from the Philadelphia fourth line, Dowd took a passout from Downie and one-timed the puck to Price's stick side to build the lead to 2-0.

Briere was still booed every time he touched the puck for having signed with the Flyers rather than the Canadiens. "I'm taking it as a compliment," he insisted.

In the second period, Kukkonen had to take down Andrei Kostitsyn, who was awarded a penalty shot, but Biron didn't buy any of the winger's fakes and got the right pad down to make the save. Kostitsyn did not go quietly into the night, however. He created a turnover at center, and then followed on a broken line rush to score during a delayed penalty on Coburn.

With the lead down to 2-1, Coburn stopped Tomas Plekanec with a pokecheck on a semi-breakaway enabled by a Jones cough-up. Philadelphia continued to attack. Carter knocked the stick out of Price's hands as he saved a hard wrister. And when Mike Komisarek was penalized for an after-the-whistle hit on Upshall, the Flyers had a chance to extend the lead.

Instead, Montreal tied the game, 2-2, on a shorthanded, controversial, goal. Biron played a Tomas Plekanec drive with a shoulder and Kovalev appeared to bat the rebound down and into the net with a stick that was above the crossbar. But after a long review, the score stood.

Nineteen seconds into the third period—and with seconds remaining on a Komisarek penalty—Price dropped a Coburn riser into the shin pad of Lupul. No kicking motion was needed to get the puck to trickle over the line and Philadelphia was back in front, 3-2.

Price fumbled another one, this time by Carter, four minutes later, but nobody could reach the rebound. As the Canadien goalie got his pad out on a dangerous Timonen deflection, the Flyers hardly were sitting on their lead.

With 1:30 remaining Biron made a pad save on a Saku Koivu backhander and Hartnell soon blocked a point shot. But on the next Montreal rush, Richards stuck out his leg near the Philadelphia blueline to try to stop the shifty Alexei Kovalev and was called for a trip, even though the replay showed it was Richard's shoulder, not his extended leg, which had taken the Canadien down. With Price pulled, Montreal would have a two-man advantage for the final 1:09.

Hatcher got one puck out, then covered another in the corner with 31 seconds remaining. Stevens took his time out. But Carter's stick broke on the faceoff against Koivu, and Kovalev jumped up to roof the puck to Biron's glove side to tie the game, 3-3.

In overtime, Canadiens coach Guy Carbonneau started his fourth line. Richards was forced along the halfwall, and though Hatcher broke up a centering attempt, a hurried Kapanen couldn't get the puck past Andrei Markov at the point. There were four Flyers caught above the top of the circle when Markov fed Tom Kostopoulos alone in front of Biron. The goalie got his shoulder in front of the shot, but on the second whack Kostopoulos scored.

Forty-eight seconds into overtime, Philadelphia stunningly had lost a Game One, 4-3, that they had led with 29 seconds remaining.

The arguable call on Richards had not only put the Flyers down a skater but also denied them their best faceoff man on the critical draw. But Richards didn't complain.

Stevens recalls: "I remember very well that Mike told the media, 'I put the referee in the position where he had to make a call.' He basically stood up and said, 'My fault.'

"I thought that was important in helping us rally around each other. We'd won a game in Washington where the cards were against us. I think the group was starting to grow up."

The coach noted the arguable calls, but didn't dwell on them. "We certainly didn't get any breaks tonight," said Stevens. "But I think we can play better and will."

Biron remembers thinking: "We had played well enough to win and I made a couple of mistakes. Dejà vu. Like in Game One against Washington.

"The [Kostopoulos] goal in overtime was a bad rebound, and I didn't love the Kovalev goal to tie it. I should have been better and knew I would be, like against Washington."

What, the Flyers worry? When Umberger circled out of the corner and beat Price over the shoulder at 5:53, the team had its second fast start in two games.

The Montreal goalie appeared rattled. When Mathieu Dandenault was called for tripping Richards, Price went to his bench on the delayed call, even though the penalty was on his team. On the powerplay, Carter fired from below the dot, and the puck deflected off the stick of defenseman Roman Hamrlik and Price for a 2-0 Philadelphia lead.

Briere saved a goal by turning away Kovalev's wraparound after Biron overcommitted. But the Flyers got caught with a too-many-men penalty, and then Coburn shoved Kovalev as he fished for a rebound, putting Philadelphia down two men for 1:08.

With Biron flopped, Smith cleared away a puck as the first penalty expired, but the Canadiens scored on the five-on-four. Koivu, on his knees behind the goal, banked the puck away from Kukkonen and Biron guessed wrong on which post to cover. Koivu beat Smith to the far pipe and stuffed in a goal to cut the lead to 2-1.

Biron recovered to make a big pad stop on Bryan Smolinski coming up the middle and got the paddle down on Kovalev, who had performed some of his trademark fancy stick handling on the way to the slot. The goalie had also just made a pad save on a back-footed attempt by Koivu when the Flyers extended their lead to two.

Hartnell, on a line with Prospal and Briere for the first time since Game Six of the Washington series, forced a giveaway at center by Komisarek and Briere, sent in by Prospal, shot the puck in off the right pad of Price to make it 3-1.

Biron kept it that way by stoning Plekanec on a breakaway. When Maxim Lapierre gave the goalie a glove rub in the face after a save,

Hartnell leveled the Canadien forward, taking a roughing penalty. But Markov missed off a backdoor pass before Biron made his best save yet, getting his pad out on Plekanec, and then snatching the pop-up out of the air.

Montreal got to the goalie early in third period, though. Christopher Higgins, poke-checked by Coburn on a carry into the Philadelphia zone, followed up and, with Lupul failing to close, got the puck to Markov for a tip-in that cut the Flyer lead to 3-2.

Umberger was sent off for interfering along the halfwall with 11:37 to go, but the Canadiens missed the net on two opportunities during the powerplay and Philadelphia kept itself at even strength down the stretch.

The clock was under three minutes when Umberger stopped Kostopoulos at center and carried back into the Montreal zone. Price made the save but Umberger got a piece of Markov as he tried to clear it, and Upshall put the puck back on goal. Price tried to catch the puck a little too casually and Umberger's stick was quicker. He knocked down the puck, which slid against the post and then off the Hab goalie's pad and into the net, giving the Flyers some breathing room with a two-goal advantage.

At the buzzer, Kostopoulos sucker punched Timonen. "He deserved it," claimed the Canadien coach. That was highly arguable, but there was no disputing Biron earning most of the plaudits for Philadelphia's 4-2 victory that tied the series at one game apiece.

"I knew Montreal would play better and that to get a split out of here, Marty would have to be our best player," said Stevens.

It would either have to be the goalie or Dave Mustaine, the lead singer and guitarist for Megadeth, who had been located by Richman playing a gig in Columbia, MD and happily agreed to record a message for the center-hung scoreboard.

"Hey Flyer fans, you can work security for me anytime," said Mustaine, wearing a Jason Smith jersey. "Get up, get loud, and make some freaking noise!"

Fans were offered a link on philadelphiaflyers.com to download "Megadeth Security" iron-ons, but despite management's best fire-up efforts, Game Three began without a full pedal to the heavy metal. Markov and Steve Begin hit posts while Philadelphia killed a full two-minute five-on-three. Biron then stopped Koivu on a breakaway coming out of the penalty box, allowing the Flyers to scramble through 20 scoreless minutes.

Philadelphia's first shot in more than 13 minutes, by Upshall off a rush with Lupul, beat Price through a screen for a 1-0 lead 7:04 into the second period. With Kukkonen off for a stick hold, Price's glove betrayed him once more as Richards scored shorthanded. Then Umberger, shooting as Carter's wraparound caromed out to the left circle, scored to give the Flyers a third goal off their last seven shots; the score was now 3-0.

Hartnell crushed Philadelphia's public enemy No. 1—Kostopoulos—with a body check, whether Carbonneau thought it was deserved or not. But as the third period began, the Canadien coach believed Price had earned a yanking in favor of another rookie, Jaroslav Halak.

It seemed to change Montreal's karma, albeit the hard way. Francis Bouillon had his face driven into the glass by Hatcher, who was given a boarding major and game misconduct.

On the powerplay, Plekanec shoved the puck over the line following a Biron save of a deflected point shot, and then Koivu put in a rebound of a Markov shot. The pair of goals, 72 seconds apart, had suddenly cut the Flyer lead to 3-2 with 11:19 to go.

Jones blocked shots by Kostitsyn and Koivu before Kovalev shot wide on Montreal's best chance down the stretch. The Flyers only had to kill one more powerplay, on Kukkonen for interfering with Begin, before being cut a huge break by a Canadien too-many-men penalty with 3:36 remaining.

Stevens conservatively used Thoresen, Kapanen and Kukkonen on the second shift of the powerplay and, with Halak pulled, Timonen blocked shots by Markov and Mark Streit. Philadelphia survived a 17-2 shot disadvantage in the third period to hold on for a 3-2 victory and a 2-1 series edge.

"A win of desperation," Stevens called it.

The most desperate guy in the house had been Hatcher, staring at the television in the locker room. "I told some of the players that watching that last 15 minutes was a lot more tiring and mentally exhausting than playing it," he said.

Regardless, it takes more energy to come from behind. Through three games, Montreal had the majority of opportunities, but never the lead during regulation time.

"I was like a fan reading about and playing in the series at the same time," recalls Biron, who had grown up as a Nordiques fan/Canadien hater in Quebec City. "All the stories: 'Is Price hurt? Why can't he catch the puck? Oh, he's getting a new glove. Will Carbonneau bring out his lucky tie? Did they make the right decision to let Huet go?'

"It seemed like all that stuff had gotten into their [players'] heads."

Certainly there was little good going on inside of Price's. "I am 20 years old, better that these things happen to me at 20 than 30," he told reporters.

Better they didn't happen to him at all. Or that Umberger never had been born. He had four goals in the first three games of the series. Stevens' jack-of-all-trades was coming up aces no matter where he was used.

"Left wing, right wing, center, it didn't matter; all got me more playing time," Umberger recalls. "I just wanted to be on the ice."

When Knuble's hamstring was pronounced good to go for Game Four, Umberger went to the Richards line with Lupul.

Richards was in the penalty box for a boarding penalty against Higgins when Carter blocked a shot by Streit, soloed shorthanded, and went to the backhand. Halak made the save to keep the game scoreless.

Biron responded with a pad save on a redirection by Plekanec. The infernally irritating Kostopoulos, jabbing at Biron as he froze the puck, suckered Kukkonen into a penalty, but Philadelphia killed it.

Seven minutes into the second period, Lapierre stole the puck from Lupul behind the net and found Kovalev in the slot. Biron made a pad save and the Flyers came up ice, Briere leading a three-on-two from the right wing. Lupul took defenders to the net, leaving a lane for Briere to hit Umberger with a cross-ice pass. He rifled his fifth goal of the series under Halak's arm and Philadelphia had drawn first blood for the fourth-straight game.

Biron flashed his glove on a Kovalev rebound, and then made an arm save on Streit after Timonen had tipped another Kovalev try into the slot. Outshot 28-17, the Flyers nevertheless took a 1-0 lead into the third period.

Umberger slashed Kovalev after he had beaten Richards to get to the slot but the Canadiens were kept to the outside on the powerplay, not threatening until Biron made another save on Kovalev, this one from the point. Philadelphia cleared the puck out to center, where Hartnell forced a giveaway by Smolinski and Prospal led a three-on-two. When his wrist shot from the top of the circle hit the post, Hartnell jammed in the rebound for a 2-0 Flyer lead.

With seven minutes remaining in the game, Philadelphia had limited Montreal to four shots in the period and seemed to have complete control until a Smith clear landed in the Flyer bench, bringing the face-off back into the Philadelphia zone. Plekanec beat Briere on the draw, Josh Gorges fired, and Plekanec's shot went off Hatcher's shins and between Biron's legs, pulling the Canadiens to within one.

Thirty-seven seconds later, a Streit point shot went off Jones and fell at the feet of Koivu, who slid the puck along the ice and into the goal to tie the game, 2-2, with 6:24 remaining.

The Prospal-Briere-Hartnell line had been burned for a second time on the same shift. And it was the third time in the series Montreal had scored twice in proximity to erase a two-goal Flyer deficit. "It had happened to us the entire season, giving up [leads] in the last minute and such," Knuble would say. "We would keep going."

Again, the Canadiens helped Philadelphia restart its engines. Begin almost sent Kapanen, who had just dumped the puck and was about to come off, through the open bench door. Luckily, the Flyer hit against the boards, and Begin, called for interference, landed in the penalty box.

On the powerplay, Prospal forced Markov into fanning on a clear. Richards pinched on Kostopoulos and Prospal's shot from the top of the circle was blocked by Komisarek, but the puck bounced under Halak's stick to Briere. Scoring his eighth goal of the playoffs, from almost along the goal line, Briere put Philadelphia back ahead with only 3:38 to go.

Richards was a demon, making Montreal play along the back wall in its own zone as the clock ticked down, and then, with Halak pulled, forcing the puck out of the Flyer end following a Carter faceoff win from Koivu.

When Timonen blocked another Canadien attempt out of the zone, Streit took his time chasing the puck and drew an icing call. But off the faceoff, Umberger tipped the puck out to center and raced ahead. His shot was blocked by Streit, but Umberger retrieved the puck, circled the net and scored the putaway goal.

Umberger became the first Flyer to score in five straight playoff games since Brian Propp in 1989. And his team, a 4-2 winner, was one victory from the conference final.

"It's a very good feeling, especially after being on the ice for those two goals that let the Canadiens back in the game," Briere said. "All I kept thinking was, 'We have to get that lead back.'"

Although Montreal had again outshot Philadelphia substantially, rallying once more from a two-goal deficit, the Habs kept getting thrown from the seesaw.

"Timely goals, that's what that whole series was about," recalls Streit, but that was another way of saying it was about timely saves, too. And the Flyer goalie was riding a wave of confidence.

"When you win people want to give you flowers; when you lose, the vase is coming at you," Biron said. "That's the way it is. You take some praise and leave some. You read a little, surf a little and go back to work."

Maybe he took a few phone calls as well.

"In the hotel in Montreal, Reggie (Lemelin, goaltending coach) came over to me and said, 'Got someone on the phone for you,'" recalls Biron. "I take it from him, and a voice says 'Marty? Ray Bourque here. Remember what Reggie is telling you about the series we won (with Boston) against Montreal (in 1988). You guys do the same thing here.'

"I'm like 'Absolutely, Sir!'

"Who gets a call from Ray Bourque before a game?"

Not Price apparently, although the kid goalie had a chat with Carbonneau and was told he was the Canadiens' goaltender for better or worse.

Given a chance to close out the Washington series in five games, the Flyers had been at their worst, but Stevens thought his players would be better for the experience. "A team thinks about winning and loses sight of the process," he recalls. "Once you have been through it, you learn how to deal with it."

Would Price, also? After Timonen had forced a Kovalev giveaway early in Game Five at the Bell Centre, the goalie stopped Richards on a shorthanded chance with Thoresen in the box. Montreal failed to get set up until there were 30 seconds left on the penalty, but nevertheless took their first regulation lead of the series when Plekanec redirected a Brisebois shot past Biron.

After Prospal hooked Guillaume Latendresse along the half wall, the Canadiens had a chance to go up two. But Biron got his pad out as Plekanec tried to hit Hamrlik for a backdoor redirect, and Kostitsyn shot the puck under the goalie and against the opposite post.

Umberger wasn't hitting any posts. Celebrating his 26th birthday, he was intent on blowing out the flickering candle of Montreal's season. The winger banked the puck past Brisebois to create a two-on-one with Lupul, beat Hamrlik, and shot on the backhand. Price made a left pad save, but Umberger received a second chance as he was falling over Hamrlik. From one knee, the winger shoved in the rebound to even the game, 1-1 after 10:20 of the first period.

The tie lasted only 1:08. Coburn stood up Plekanec on a one-on one-rush, but Lapierre won a battle with Timonen behind the goal and jammed the puck in off Kovalev's right skate to put the Canadiens back ahead, 2-1.

Price missed an attempted catch of a Carter drive and was fortunate the puck hit the side of the net. Biron couldn't control an Kostitsyn rebound and had to make a falling backwards save on Komisarek though traffic. But the goalie didn't close his legs on a Higgins shot off the rush, allowing Montreal to extend its lead to 3-1, 8:15 into the second period.

The Canadiens couldn't stand prosperity. Komisarek responded to a stick in the Adam's apple by Briere with an elbow to the Flyer's face and, as usual, only the retaliator was caught. Price then hooked Knuble's arm, pulling off his glove, creating a 55-second five-on-three for Philadelphia. Nevertheless, the Montreal goalie stopped Prospal on a carom off the backboards, and then foiled Briere from point-blank range on the five-on-four.

The penalties had just been killed when Price made an arm save on an Umberger rebound. But Lupul chased down the puck and Umberger pinched down the boards and fired high. Richards put his glove up and ever-so-slightly changed the shot's direction to fly under the crossbar on the stick side. After a long review, it was determined that the puck had been merely deflected by Richards, not batted, and the Flyers were back within a goal.

A little more than a minute later, Price stopped Hatcher, who had been sent in by a Richards feed from the sidewall. The puck went off the backboards and out the other side, where Hatcher was on Hamrlik before he could clear. Umberger swooped in and wrapped the puck under Price, who, on one knee, didn't get the paddle completely down. R.J.'s ninth goal of the playoffs had tied the game 3-3 with 4:16 remaining in the second period.

R.J. Umberger #20 and Mike Richards celebrate a goal during the Flyers' 6-4 win that eliminated the Canadiens in Game Five of the Eastern Conference semifinals.

"We just had their number," recalls Umberger. "Their goaltender couldn't stop anything, Marty was on fire, and I just kept on scoring.

"I remember thinking how much fun this was. I thought, 'We can win the Stanley Cup this year, it's really possible.'"

Kovalev had a chance in the slot to break the tie, but lost control as Coburn closed in, enabling Timonen to counter quickly to Hartnell flying up the left wing. Price challenged, but left too much room on the far side and, from the faceoff dot, Hartnell blew a slapshot under the goalie's glove. Three Philadelphia goals in 2:58 had put the team up 4-3.

The stunned crowd gasped but the Canadiens were not done. On the third shift of the third period, Kostitsyn took a drop pass from Plekanec off the rush, used Timonen as a screen, and fired over Biron's glove to tie the contest 4-4.

The bigger and more physical Flyers were allowing Montreal to come through center with too much speed. But by now, Philadelphia was willing to trade chances. In the next eight minutes of play, there was one whistle.

Prospal picked off a pass by Sergei Kostitsyn and, with Richards running blatant interference most of the way up ice, got the puck to Briere, who deked and went to his forehand. Price did the splits and kicked the puck away.

With seven minutes remaining in regulation, Smith's stick came up too high on Kostopoulos after he had created a chance by beating Knuble, putting Montreal on the powerplay. Streit got the puck down the boards and centered to Higgins, but Richards got his stick out to stop the first shot and Biron butterflied to stop the second, giving the Flyers an escape. They did again when Latendresse sent Jones spiraling with a pull-up move and hit the post behind Biron from 20 feet out.

The clock was under four minutes when Knuble dumped the puck. Upshall, going in hard against Bouillon, lost his balance but popped to his feet after hitting the boards. As a result, Bouillon could only clear as far as the opposite corner, where Carter picked up the puck and fed Kukkonen at the point.

Upshall, standing at the edge of the crease, had his stick up anticipating a chance for a redirection, but Kukkonen's shot didn't make it through traffic. Carter chased the puck down 40 feet up the slot, turned, and, in one motion, fired through Knuble and Gorges. With three Canadiens caught up high, this time the puck got through to Upshall and, on his backhand, he tipped the puck past Price's stick side.

Leading 5-4, Philadelphia was 3:04 away from the conference final.

Umberger got one puck out, Hatcher another, Knuble one more. Off a faceoff at the Flyer line with 2:11 to go, Richards won the draw and forced the puck over the blueline. When Markov dumped it in, Richards got a standoff in the corner against Higgins and Lupul cleared the zone.

Markov flipped over Timonen's head into the offensive zone, but Upshall went high, too, on a clear and the puck died before the goal line, saving an icing. The only save Biron had to make in the final minutes was a right pad on Kovalev, and Carter got to the rebound first, banking the puck out and letting Knuble drive for the empty net.

Higgins dove and blocked the shot, and his stick caused Knuble to stumble. But he stayed on his feet, made a recovery off the backboards, and tucked in the insurance goal with 50 seconds remaining.

"The seconds are ticking off and I'm thinking my hometown is going to be nuts because we all grew up watching the Nordiques and hating the Canadiens," recalls Biron. "This is pretty major for a Quebec City kid to be helping to make this happen."

Biron thrust his glove into the air as Coburn played the puck to the corner at the buzzer, the goalie's teammates racing off the bench to surround him. One year after being 30th in the NHL, the Flyers, 6-4 winners of Game Five, were in the final four for the 15th time in their 40 seasons.

"I remember doing an interview on the ice with Elliotte Friedman of *Hockey Night in Canada*, and the crowd being so silent," Upshall recalls. "Eliminating the Canadiens in Montreal is not something everybody gets to do."

Having done it with these teammates makes the memory that much better to Lupul. "We had such a good group of guys," he recalls. "We were all kind of the same age and had so much fun coming to the rink that it was pretty cool to win the playoff series with those guys."

The Flyers had been so opportunistic that the Canadiens couldn't help but feel star-crossed.

"We have pressure, pressure, pressure and then they get a deflection for a winner," said Koivu, the Montreal captain. "That was pretty much the whole series in one minute.

"They did a lot of good things, but it felt like luck wasn't on our side."

Throughout the series, Stevens had believed his team was doing more of those good things than the Canadiens were acknowledging. "From the comments they were making, I don't think they respected us," the coach recalls. "But what I remember most about that locker room was that we hadn't surprised ourselves at all."

Timonen spoke the bottom line. "Marty was better than Price and that's the biggest reason we're still playing," said the defenseman.

Another was Umberger, whose eight goals in five games were the second most—to Tim Kerr's 10 in a seven-game series against Pittsburgh in 1989—that a Flyer had scored in a series.

"R.J. was a possessed man," said Stevens. "We moved him around and he didn't even bat an eye."

Philadelphia, seemingly unable to do anything wrong, was not intimidated by the challenge of a Penguin team that had sailed through their series against Ottawa and the Rangers in only one game over the minimum. Stevens' team had won five of eight regular-season meetings with its cross-state rival.

Obviously, the focus was going to be on stopping Crosby, that responsibility largely to fall on Coburn, Timonen and Richards.

"The first year, there was criticism of how [Crosby] handled himself on the ice," said Richards. "As the second year went on, he got better. Now he respects everyone, gets along with the referees."

The task of containing the Pittsburgh whiz was complicated by the presence of a second star, Evgeni Malkin, who had been dominant during the first two rounds. After the Penguins' 4-3 win on February 10 at Mellon Arena, Malkin had told reporters he liked neither the Flyers nor getting pelted with trash in their arena. Asked to add a little more fuel for the fire before Game One, Malkin said through an interpreter, "I don't like anybody. Whether I like them or not, we have to play them."

Because of Pittsburgh's struggles prior to the arrival of Mario Lemieux, the two franchises born in 1967 had not even met in the playoffs until 1989. The Penguins had not won any of the previous three series (1989, 1997 and 2000). But the finicky on-ice personality of Crosby and same-state rivalry made the matchup about more than just two rising young teams trying to reach a Stanley Cup Final.

As much as it would hurt to get this far and lose to Pittsburgh, even more painful was Timonen's ankle. After taking a Markov shot in Game Four against Montreal, it was getting progressively worse.

An MRI was negative, but on the day before the opener, Timonen went to see Dr. Ronald Fairman, chief of vascular surgery at the Hospital of the University of Pennsylvania. He diagnosed a blood clot.

Timonen was warned that if there was another blow, the clot might break up and cause a circulation problem so severe that it could result in amputation. The defenseman was put on blood thinners and would be re-evaluated in 10 days.

This was the second clotting incident of his NHL career, and by far, the worst-timed.

"We were on the plane waiting to leave for Pittsburgh when we found out," recalls Holmgren. "I remember Mr. Snider went right to the hospital to sit with Kimmo."

Timonen needed cheering up. "It's the most disappointing thing in my hockey life for sure," he told reporters. "I didn't expect this; it's an awful feeling."

The Flyers flew to Pittsburgh on a charter of pain.

"It was like a morgue," recalls Stevens, who dressed Modry in Timonen's absence. "Kimmo was like a father figure, our Mr. Calm. We're going against Crosby and Malkin and he's not there."

The Penguins struck first in Game One. After Thoresen overskated trying to take Kapanen's pass out of the air, Ryan Malone picked up the puck and, when Kapanen chased to the other side of the rink, Pittsburgh had a three-on-two. Petr Sykora was alone at the net to pull out Biron and roof a backhander at 6:19.

Philadelphia fought back quickly. Richards, set up by Umberger's pass between Rob Scuderi's legs, circled the net, and put the puck in off goalie Marc-Andre Fleury's right pad. Referee Mike Hasenfratz initially waived off the goal, but his ruling was reversed in Toronto and the game was tied, 1-1.

A little more than four minutes later, Scuderi batted down Umberger's goalmouth pass, but he got the puck back and put it on net. With Fleury down, Lupul had two jabs on the backhand before Richards swooped in on his forehand and put the Flyers up 2-1.

"I'm thinking, here we go, right where we left off against Montreal," recalls Umberger, a Pittsburgh native. "I'm riding the high of my life, thinking we're going to [go to the Final] in front of all my family and friends."

Biron gave the lead back 1:21 later, however. Playing a Crosby dump-in, the goalie failed to leave the puck for Smith and inexplicably tried to backhand it up the opposite boards. Marian Hossa retrieved and hit Crosby, who beat Coburn to the front of the net for an easy redirect that tied the game 2-2.

It appeared Philadelphia was at least going to get out of the first period with a tie until Upshall gave the puck away to Ray Whitney at the Penguin blueline. The winger made a stretch pass to a streaking Malkin, who shot from the dot and beat Biron to the stick side to put Pittsburgh ahead, 3-2, seven seconds before the break.

With Orpik off for holding early in the second period, Malkin's shorthanded chance ended when he was crushed by Richards into the end boards. Malkin rose slowly as the Flyers took the puck back up ice, where Briere fanned trying to hit Knuble. Sergei Gonchar threw the puck past a diving Jones to Malkin who was still gathering his senses at the Philadelphia line. On a breakaway, he slapped the puck past Biron's stick side to stretch the lead to two goals.

The Flyer powerplay did nothing with a third-period Whitney tripping penalty. Umberger stole the puck from Sykora to create Philadelphia's best chance of the final 20 minutes, but it was foiled by a Fleury pokecheck. For the third straight series, the Flyers had lost Game One, this time 4-2.

"We were sloppy," said Hatcher. "Both teams were, to be honest. We didn't do anything clean or crisp."

"They're an opportunistic team. You give Malkin chances like that, this guy scores."

Feeling like his team had played nervously and looking for a spark, Stevens scratched Thoresen in favor of Downie. But disaster struck early in Game Two when Coburn was hit in the face with a deflected Hal Gill point shot and, after staying down for many minutes, left the ice bleeding into a towel. Already minus Timonen, Philadelphia was now without both of its first-pair defensemen.

Soon, the team was in penalty trouble that was unaffordable. Knuble was caught crosschecking Jordan Staal four seconds before a Carter tripping penalty expired and then, during the five-on-four, Kukkonen tipped Crosby's drive from almost against the boards. Biron couldn't track it, allowing Pittsburgh to jump up 1-0.

Early in the second period, the Flyers caught a break when the puck, backhanded by Gonchar, was covered over the line by Biron's glove but had not been visible on the replay. The goal was disallowed. So when Scuderi failed to clear past Modry at the point and Lupul beat Gill in the corner to feed Carter's goal from the edge of crease, the game was tied, 1-1.

Hatcher used his chest to push Malkin off the puck, but the defenseman's stick was between the Penguin's legs so it was called a hook, much to Philadelphia's displeasure. On the powerplay, Crosby beat Carter off the boards and Hossa reached around Kukkonen for Malone's rebound to put Pittsburgh back up 2-1.

Biron, throwing a suicidal clear up the middle of the ice directly to Crosby, made a diving, highlight-reel save on the Penguin star to keep the Flyers close. Hatcher took another penalty by cross-checking Staal in the final two minutes. But Richards picked off a Malkin pass along the blueline, flipped to the forehand to beat a flat-footed Gonchar, and then pulled away for an electrifying game-tying shorthanded goal with only 24 seconds remaining in the second period.

Going into the third, Philadelphia had committed only five turnovers through two periods. But Downie didn't get all of an attempted clear from the boards along the sidewall and Roberts saved Hatcher's follow-up attempt. Laraque fought off the check of the much smaller Kapanen and got the puck behind the goal line to Roberts. His quick pass beat Downie, and Max Talbot was alone in the slot for a one-timer to put Pittsburgh back ahead, 3-2, with 11:09 to play.

Downie slammed his stick against the glass in disgust and his team did not get another good chance. Carter won a draw from Crosby in the Penguin end with 43 seconds remaining, but Briere was forced behind the goal and the Pittsburgh captain flipped the puck out. When Richards couldn't control the bounce, Staal had a clear path to the empty net and put away the Penguins' second consecutive 4-2 victory.

Although there were no fractures in Coburn's face, 50 stitches had been required and his eye was swollen shut. Twenty-year-old Ryan Parent was put into the lineup, despite the fact that he had not played since the first game of the Washington series.

Returning home to the Wachovia Center for Game Three, Stevens praised the efforts of the five defensemen who had had carried the load after Coburn's early Game Two exit. "I thought they played big minutes," said the coach, but 28:30 was too much for Hatcher, whose knee was being drained after almost every game.

"I watched them do it once," recalls Knuble. "Just nasty. It looked like dark urine that had been outside in a bottle for about a month."

"That's why it felt so good when it came out," laughs Hatcher. "I was like two different people."

Smith needed an anti-inflammatory shot for his collarbone injury before every game and couldn't practice. "I could hang onto my stick and had full power in my hands," he recalls. "But I had to be aware of not getting myself into a vulnerable spot to get hit."

Actually, the mid-chest location of the dislocations made every spot in his body vulnerable. "Jason lived a few houses up from me so we would have a few beers together after games sometimes," recalls Briere. "It even hurt him to lift his glass up to his mouth. But he didn't miss a game.

"Jason was the toughest teammate I ever had. Kimmo would be 1A."

Somebody, somewhere was sticking pins in a Flyer doll. The team's two best remaining defensemen were taking needles to stay in the lineup.

"Obviously, it's tough," Stevens lamented. "Coburn is an all-situation player for us. But we are capable of getting more from a forward group that has been our strength all year."

The coach couldn't expect much more from Richards, who already had scored three goals in the series and had a 63 percent success rate on faceoffs in Game Two. Carter had been effective, too, despite some missed chances.

But Briere, who had been elbowed in the back of the head by Malkin—"For a few minutes there I was in la-la land," Danny confessed—did not escape scrutiny. His line with Prospal and Hartnell was minus-seven with no points through two games.

The Flyers had exceeded expectations in getting this far. Could the home crowd, Kate and Lauren will them farther? It wasn't likely to happen without a good start.

With Hatcher in the box for a marginal hook of Malkin, Whitney's pass attempt for a wide-open Crosby hit Smith and trickled into the goal at 5:03. Less than two minutes later, Hossa went the length of the ice, made a move on Carter, shot out of Kukkonen's legs, and beat Biron to the glove side. The Penguins had silenced the house by scoring on two of their first four shots.

Stevens' team didn't let down. Briere gained the zone and Umberger, quicker than Malkin to the post, successfully followed up on a Prospal stuffer to cut the lead to 2-1. Hope was engendered going to the second period, but the Penguins settled into coach Dan Bylsma's 1-2-2 deployment and stifled Philadelphia at center ice. Carter, set up by Upshall gaining a step wide, had the one good Flyer chance of a three-shot second period.

Hurt by the absence of a puck mover on defense, Philadelphia nevertheless made a push in the first seven minutes of the third period, but the best chance, by Hartnell, hit a post. The team remained down a goal when Downie, who had just stolen the puck from Sykora, pulled up inside the Pittsburgh line and tried to hit Carter.

Malkin picked off the pass and led a rush that Kapanen broke up. But his outlet attempt hit Carter in the skate and Sykora trapped Hatcher with a pass to Malone. He spun on his backhand and scored, making it 3-1.

Whatever air still was left in the Wachovia Center had rushed out before Gill threw the puck out of the Penguin zone to Hossa, who scored into the empty net to wrap up a 4-1 Pittsburgh victory and a 3-0 lead in the series.

"We put [Downie] back out there because he's a big-game player, but he's got to learn from his mistakes and obviously he hasn't," said Stevens. "A flat pass in the offensive zone with Malkin on the ice hasn't worked all series; I don't know why [Downie thought] it was going to work now."

For the second straight game, the rookie had made a late, killing giveaway. "We were down a goal and I tried to make a play," said a downcast Downie, who admitted his confidence was shaken. But the Penguins had used their early lead to severely limit Flyer options.

"They're creating offense from the checking side of the puck and pouncing on turnovers," said Stevens. "We hear about their offensive game, but they are committed defensively right now."

In this series, unlike the last, the timely goals and saves belonged to the opposition. "It seemed like we had to work 100 percent harder to get half the results," recalls Biron. "Pittsburgh was really good."

Hartnell tried to rally the troops. "It's frustrating to me that they've already picked the final—Detroit and Pittsburgh," he said. "It gets our blood boiling a little bit. We have to play like we've got something to prove."

Stevens benched Downie in favor of Cote, moved Briere on a line with Richards, while putting Prospal with Lupul and Umberger. The coach also turned the inspiration for Game Four over to Timonen in his street clothes.

"He stepped into the room and read the starting lineup," Umberger would report later. "The way he did it, with the emotion he showed, it gave me goose bumps."

Timonen told his teammates to go have fun. And they did.

Fleury turned back a good early chance by Hartnell. Although Briere was caught tripping Staal, Richards stole the puck from Malkin for another shorthanded breakaway and, when Richards' shot hit the post and Hossa raced back through wide-open spaces, Biron made a blocker save to keep the game scoreless.

Evgeni Malkin was one of six Penguins to score in Game Five of the Conference Finals.

"That got me into the game," Biron would say later. "The whole penalty kill was big for the team."

Thirty seconds after Briere stepped back on the ice, a Lupul shot, defected by Gill at the point of contact, flew up over Fleury's shoulder to give Philadelphia a 1-0 lead. And the Flyers kept coming. Richards, who drew a hold by Gonchar, put in a rebound with three seconds remaining on the powerplay to make the score 2-0.

The period was almost in its final minute when Carter stripped a flat-footed Hossa at center and led a rush. Fleury butterflied and made a right pad save, but Carter had half the net to put in the rebound and build the lead to three.

The rattled Penguins took the next three penalties. Fleury had to make a spectacular sliding save on Briere on a three-on-two. Richards lined up Kris Letang for a rattling body check and Upshall won a race to cancel an icing as Philadelphia took its 3-0 edge into the third period.

In the first two minutes, Biron made a glove save on Gonchar despite traffic, but Pittsburgh broke through regardless. Staal, cycling with Talbot on the sideboards, reversed on Kukkonen and found Tyler Kennedy in the right circle. Biron made a right pad save as he was leaning off the post, but Staal got a second whack while going by the net, and put the puck off the top of Biron's pad and into the goal at 3:16.

Though the Penguins, down only two, started to surge, the Flyers had the best chance of the next 10 minutes when Fleury stopped Upshall from in close. Two minutes later, Kukkonen kept Kennedy from cutting off the goal line, but Talbot was first to the puck. When neither Hartnell nor Briere took Staal, he put his second goal in 11 minutes past Biron from 15 feet out to cut the lead to 3-2 with 5:49 remaining.

Scuderi had a chance to tie the game off a Smith giveaway, but Biron made the stop. Philadelphia stayed relatively composed into the final two minutes, when Crosby beat a Jones stick check, got inside Richards, and shot while he was falling. Biron made a left pad save and, with Fleury pulled, Hartnell sneaked up on Malkin, stole the puck and Lupul hit the empty net.

In the final seconds, Richards and Crosby traded slashes off a faceoff and, when Malone left his feet to hit Hatcher after he had stopped a Staal rush, the defenseman exacted his revenge with some punches. But the Flyers, 4-2 winners to cut Pittsburgh's series lead to 3-1, had already demonstrated an intention to go down fighting.

"We got pucks deep, got on top of their defense, and had a third guy high," Hartnell said. "We didn't really give up any odd-man rushes until we got a little nervous at the end."

Coburn was still suffering post-concussion symptoms that ruled out his availability for Game Five at Mellon Arena. But Timonen was taken off blood thinners and deemed good to go.

To have any chance of getting the series back to Philadelphia, the Flyers needed the same energy with which they started Game Four. But when Knuble hooked Talbot just 2:18 into the game, it took the Penguins just 12 seconds of the powerplay to jump ahead, 1-0. Crosby's point drive was legally redirected past Biron by Malone's planted left skate.

Richards had a chance on the next shift, but Fleury made a pad stop and Pittsburgh, determined not to let Philadelphia off the hook again, was doing most of the hitting.

Malone stood up Biron off a dump-in, and the goalie lost his stick. He scrambled back into the net but, having no idea which post would be challenged from behind the goal, was used as a pinball pylon on Malkin's bank shot that made the score 2-0.

Three minutes into the second period, Fleury had to be good on a one-timer by Briere off a Richards pass, then again on a Hartnell rebound. But Crosby soon lifted Richards' stick to foil a rush and countered quickly into the Flyer zone. The play was broken up, but Crosby chased it down and fed a Hossa one-timer past Biron's short side that built the lead to 3-0.

Biron knew it was over. "I had run out of steam, everybody had run out of steam," recalls the goalie, who had no chance when Malone broke down Gonchar's wrister from the point, changing the puck's direction on a fourth Penguin goal.

Talbot pounced on Parent, and then Timonen, before either could settle the puck, giving Staal the chance to turn the game into a 5-0 rout with a backhander to the stick side. Although outshot only 25-21, Philadelphia rarely threatened before or after Pascual Dupuis' third-period goal set a 6-0 final, an abrupt ending to a season of rebirth.

"It's disappointing when it's over, a little tough right now to look at the big picture," Briere said in the locker room. "I'm sure when we look back, it was a good step in the right direction for this organization."

Stevens called Pittsburgh, headed for a Final against the Red Wings, the best team in the conference. The coach said the Flyer "spirit was a little bit broken" as Game Five moved along but that he realized his team was overmatched.

"I don't remember our team being tired," Stevens recalls. "We just couldn't handle those injuries on the back side.

"Carter was criticized because he had some key opportunities to score in some of those games and didn't, but I still thought he played well. The biggest thing in that Series was that Marty wasn't as good as he had been against Montreal. We needed him to be great again."

Holmgren told reporters his team required more depth and speed. He vowed not to lose Carter, about to become a restricted free agent. "We'll sign or match," said the GM.

Holmgren's eyes welled up when talking about Hatcher and Smith to Rich Hofmann of *The Philadelphia Daily News*. "In my mind, they brought toughness to a new level."

On breakup day Smith, an unrestricted free agent, expressed a desire to return. "I'm happy here; my family is adjusted here," he said. "This team kind of cracked the seal on the possibilities of what it can do.

Another talented young forward was on the way in Giroux, and Gagne said his concussion symptoms were subsiding while his excitement was growing.

"I'm very happy with the way things are going right now," the 28-year-old left wing said. "We have players who are going to be here for a long time."

Hatcher, headed into the final season of his contract, said he wanted to fulfill it, but wasn't certain that he could.

"Some nights you feel good and some you don't," he said. "The toughest part was going out there every night not knowing. There are times you get sick of the needles. I want to play, but I know my knee might not let me.

"I have played hockey since I was two years old. It's part of me. I think that's why I don't want to think about it, but I know I will have to do that soon."

For now, he just wanted a little time to feel good about how far the Flyers had come.

"Whether you lose the last game 1-0 or 6-0, it doesn't matter," recalls Hatcher. "You're out and it sucks.

"But especially because I was near the end of my career, I look back on that year with a lot of satisfaction. I was part of the bad, stuck it out, and we had a really good run.

"I had won a Stanley Cup (in Dallas). But this almost was more gratifying."

Aaron Asham and Jared Ross

Chapter 11 • 2008-09

In the Pitts of Their Stomachs

The lightning-quick rebuild that Flyer GM Paul Holmgren had engineered in the 2007-08 season put him in a salary-cap quandary. Entering the summer, he not only needed to re-sign rising star Jeff Carter, a restricted free agent, but shore up a defense that no longer could be anchored by the hobbled 35-year-old Derian Hatcher and the 34-year-old Jason Smith.

Smith, an upcoming unrestricted free agent, had not jumped to sign a three-year, $9 million, extension the GM recalls offering during the season. As it progressed, the general manager changed his mind about a commitment of that length.

Washington's Steve Eminger, a 25-year-old former 12th-overall pick, was a less expensive alternative behind holdovers Kimmo Timonen, Braydon Coburn, Randy Jones and Lasse Kukkonen. On June 20, the day of the Entry Draft in Ottawa, Eminger was acquired from the Capitals, along with a third-round choice, for Philadelphia's first-round selection, 27th overall.

"Eminger had played pretty well against us in the playoff," recalls Holmgren. "We thought he would be a good fit as a fourth or fifth guy. We asked Mike Richards (a junior teammate with Kitchener) and he endorsed it."

Holmgren gave up the late first-round choice knowing he could get a higher one back. The cost for that, however, would be R.J. Umberger, whose 10 playoff goals during the semifinal run essentially had priced him out of a future with the team. "I knew, and Homer knew, I was in line for a big raise," recalls Umberger, who had made $1.5 million in 2007-08 and was seeking a deal of at least $3 million per season. "According to my agent (Mike Levy), the Flyers wanted to keep me and were going to try to move other pieces."

When Holmgren couldn't make that happen, his best deal was with Columbus, which, wanting to reunite Umberger with the coach of his rookie Flyer season—Ken Hitchcock—was willing to trade the second of its two first-round picks, 19th overall. Holmgren, also parting with a fourth-rounder, closed the deal with Blue Jackets GM Scott Howson on the draft floor.

Together, the Ottawa and Washington trades relinquished Umberger, added Eminger, and enabled Philadelphia to move up eight places in the first round. The team decided to take Luca Sbisa, a 6-2, 190-pound, Italian-born defenseman from the Lethbridge Hurricanes, over rearguard Michael Del Zotto of the Oshawa Generals, who went to the Rangers on the next selection.

"We liked Del Zotto, but (scout) Mark Greig, who lived in Lethbridge (Alberta), really loved Luca," recalls Holmgren.

Umberger, an Ohio State graduate, thought he had said goodbye to Columbus. "My initial reaction was, 'Yuck, Columbus, one of the worst teams in the league,'" he recalls. "Then I had a phone conversation with Hitch and he got me extremely excited. I felt like he was going to utilize me a lot."

Carter was locked up with a three-year, $15 million contract on June 27th. The Flyers beat by four days the start of free agency, when they might have had to match an offer from another club or accept a number of draft choices (the higher the yearly salary, the better the picks) for the 23-year-old center. "I'm pretty sure Vancouver was ready to do an offer sheet," Holmgren recalls. "We would have been forced to give him a lot more money."

"We would have preferred a five-year deal, but ended up settling on the three. It wasn't that difficult."

Carter made it simple. "I said from Day One that I didn't want to go anywhere," he told the media.

Vinny Prospal felt otherwise. During his first conversation with Holmgren after being acquired from Tampa Bay at the 2008 trading deadline, the center had made clear his wish to be a member only of the Lightning. Thirteen points in 17 playoff games positioned on a line with Danny Briere didn't change Prospal's mind.

He was so anxious to return to Tampa, in fact, that Prospal jumped the July 1 start of free agency in conversations with the Lightning. It was only out of the goodness of Holmgren's heart that he accepted a seventh-round draft choice, rather than file a tampering charge. "It wasn't Jay (Feaster, Lightning GM)," recalls Holmgren. "He was embarrassed. I could have held them up for more but I didn't because of him."

On July 8, Smith signed a two-year, $5.2 million deal with Ottawa. He recalls: "We ended up exchanging a brief offer (with the Flyers after July 1), but it was something that was, I guess, middle of the road. "I'm sure they looked at it as trying to get [a deal] done, but it wasn't a real serious negotiation.

"Obviously there was a lot of youth in the organization. It would have been great to stay, but the year I had there was outstanding."

The feeling was mutual. "Jason played his heart and soul out for the Flyers," recalls Holmgren. "He was awesome."

Smith, captain of the Philadelphia team that made a 39-point jump in one year, had played the entire 17-game postseason run of 2007-08 despite separations of the sternoclavicular joints.

"Jason would do anything for his teammates and play through anything, which inspired everyone around him," recalls Richards.

Richards, the team's leading scorer with a 75-point season in 2007-08, was a captain-in-waiting, another reason Holmgren could afford to let Smith walk. Primary in practically every decision the Flyers made that summer, however, was the $50.3 million cap for 2008-09. It had gone up $6.3 million over the preceding year, but Holmgren had to spend much of the increase to fill out his team.

Needing almost a complete makeover was the fourth line. Unhappy in that role, Sami Kapanen, 34, decided to walk away from the final year of his contract to play for KalPa Kuopio, the Finnish club in which he had an ownership stake with Timonen. "Sami and John (Stevens, Flyer coach) butted heads a lot," Holmgren recalls. "It wasn't fun dealing with both those guys. Sami thought he was better than a fourth-line guy and John didn't."

Kapanen remembers there being another concern beyond playing time—his children, who were entering their teen years and losing language skills they would need for the family's eventual return to Finland. "I thought if we were going to go home, we should go now," recalls Kapanen, who is still an owner, and now an assistant coach, for KalPa Kuopio. But while the mighty-mite winger says he had fun being part of Philadelphia's return to contention in 2007-08, he admits being frustrated with his usage.

"I still felt like I could do so much more," he says. "I was having a hard time staying focused.

"[Stevens] was making his decisions based on what he thought was best for the team—trying to win hockey games—something I understand better now since I have become a coach. At the time, I didn't feel I was being treated fairly, but I never wanted it to be an issue with the team."

After scoring 110 points in 311 Flyer games, adding nine playoff goals in three substantial Philadelphia postseason runs, and providing an iconic moment for the franchise in his determination to get back to the bench after being knocked woozy by a high, hard check from Toronto's Darcy Tucker during the 2004 Toronto series, Kapanen could not go away angry.

"It means the world to me," he says of his five years being a Flyer. "Throughout my career, the one thing I always tried to bring to my team was passion. Feeling that from the Philadelphia fans probably was the best part of being there.

"When Joffrey Lupul scored against Washington in the Game Seven overtime, that was really, really big. Maybe the greatest moment was that (semifinal) run in 2004; at the same time, it probably was the worst moment when we just couldn't squeeze any more from our tank in Game Seven (at Tampa)."

The fourth line also lost Patrick Thoresen, who requested a doubling of the $500,000 Philadelphia had paid him after his waiver-wire selection from Edmonton, but was turned down. He signed with Lugano of the Swiss league.

The foot-soldier replacements were winger Arron Asham, who was coaxed away from the Devils for two-years at a total of $1.34 million, and 34-year-old journeyman center Glen Metropolit, signed for two years at $1 million each. The Flyers also added depth on defense with 28-year-old Ossi Vaananen, a seven-year veteran of Phoenix and Colorado who was brought in on a one-year, $1 million deal.

Holmgren had to give the Kings a second-round pick to get them to take the year remaining on the contract of veteran defenseman Denis Gauthier, who had played with the Phantoms in 2007-08. That cleared another $2.2 million in cap room that helped keep Jones for $5.4 million over two years and re-up Riley Cote for three-years at $1.65 million.

Coach John Stevens was extended through the 2010-11 season. But changes were needed on his staff when Terry Murray left to become coach of the Los Angeles Kings. Craig Berube, who had spent 2007-08 as head coach of the Phantoms, moved up to the big club to fill Murray's assistant position. John Paddock, a player and AHL coach with the Flyers during the eighties and recently fired as head coach by the Ottawa Senators, was hired to coach the Phantoms.

Holmgren, as had Stevens, received his just reward for the 2007-08 turnaround—a three-year contract extension. "He brought us back to respectability," praised Chairman Ed Snider.

The next goal was consistent contention, and that meant locking up core players for the upcoming years. Although tight against the 2008-09 cap, Holmgren anticipated $4 million-a-year in room for winger Joffrey Lupul in future seasons, signing him to a four-year, $17 million contract extension beginning in 2009-10. "It is not something that I was really expecting this summer," said Lupul, who would play for $2.3 million in the coming season. "I'm really thrilled. Five more years with Philadelphia is great."

Wondering where there would be room for him on the Flyers, Stefan Ruzicka, a third-round pick in 2003 who managed just 17 points in 55 NHL games with Philadelphia over three seasons, decided he had a brighter future with Spartak Moscow of the Kontinental Hockey League.

Through all the comings and goings during the summer of 2008, the departure announcement that struck the saddest chord was that the 42-year-old Wachovia Spectrum would be closing its doors forever at the conclusion of the 2008-09 Phantom season.

"It's my baby, probably the best thing I ever did," said Chairman Ed Snider. "But we're at a point where a lot of money would have to be put into it to bring it up to snuff with all of the modern technology."

As the Flyers searched for new housing for their AHL team, one of the final heroes of their beloved first home, Eric Desjardins, decided to come back to the organization as a player development coach. "It was good to go away and take that break," said Desjardins, who had retired in 2006. "But after two years, it's time to do something."

Brian Propp, for seven years the color commentator on radio, left the booth. "We both thought it was time to go in a different direction," said COO Shawn Tilger. After two seasons of postgame and between-periods studio work on Comcast SportsNet, Chris Therien, another long-time Flyer, took the seat next to play-by-play broadcaster Tim Saunders.

"It meant travelling to every game, but my family still thought it was a good idea for me," recalls Therien, a Philadelphia defenseman for 11 seasons. "Jonesey (Keith Jones, the team's television analyst) pushed me to take it as well."

Richards officially was named the 17th Flyer captain three days before the opening of camp. "At this time, we think that he is the right guy to lead us," said Holmgren. "He is a hard-nosed kid and has the skill and drive that it takes to excel."

Timonen and Briere, who had been captains in Nashville and Buffalo. respectively, were willing to serve if asked, but said they agreed with the choice. Richards, headed into his fourth-season, welcomed the veteran help. "There are so many leaders here," said the 23-year-old Richards. "You worry more about yourself and then help out where things are needed. I am just going to do the same things I have done throughout my life."

Holmgren hoped that did not mean a continuation of Richards' indifference to off-ice training. He was getting the job, the GM said, because "when the game starts, he's the guy you want leading."

So had been Hatcher, the once-captain of a Stanley Cup winner in Dallas and an inspiration during the preceding playoffs when he averaged well over 21 minutes per game on a knee that was drained after each of the 17 contests. As feared, the summer had not brought improvement. The Flyers announced Hatcher would not be ready for camp, and wondered if he ever would be again.

"Due to the class and character of Derian, we believe that it is important to continue to let him try to make his way back and give him as much time as he feels necessary to make a (retirement) decision," Holmgren said. "As of now, he still wants to play. Presently, our doctors don't believe he can."

There was considerably brighter news. Simon Gagne, whose 2007-08 season had been shut down from February 10 on because of post-concussion symptoms, was not only good to go for the beginning of camp, but proclaimed himself stronger than ever. Under the care of Dr. Scott Greenberg, the eight-year veteran had undergone prolotherapy, a non-surgical form of treatment that utilizes injections to reconstruct and regenerate ligaments and tendons. "Body-fat wise, I'm better than I was a year ago," Gagne said.

So was Steve Downie, who, 18 pounds lighter than in his rookie season, entered his second by scoring a pair of goals in a 4-1 exhibition victory over the Devils at the Wachovia Center.

Not as impressive was Claude Giroux, even after coming off an amazing 17 goals, 51 points, and a +33 rating in just 19 postseason games for his Gatineau junior team. The removal of four wisdom teeth prior to training camp had set back the superb 20-year-old prospect. "I just ate ice cream, watched TV and got a lot of rest," he reported.

The rookie who stole the show during camp was Sbisa, who had been expected to be at least two seasons away from competing for a job. "The first thing you notice is his fitness level for a young player," praised Stevens.

A preseason game against Carolina at the Spectrum—complete with a $19.67 priced ticket and pregame ceremony including 21 members of the Stanley Cup teams and eight other former captains—had sold out so quickly that the Flyers scheduled a second contest at their doomed birthplace, against the Phantoms, at the end of camp. Fans who hadn't been in the old arena for years were making it clear they were going to miss the place.

"Any material things in life will eventually have to go," said Bernie Parent. "But the one thing you can't take away are the beautiful memories that we have of the people, the crowds, the building, and winning the Stanley Cup."

When the Flyers lost the second game at the Spectrum to their farm team, concluding a so-so camp, goalie Marty Biron was in no mood for nostalgia.

"It seemed like our play was spiraling out of control and we couldn't stop it," Biron recalls. "We took a picture after that game—the Phantoms team is smiling and the Flyers look like we are about to jump off the Walt Whitman Bridge. That's how bad of a feeling it was."

Holmgren, who had challenged his players during May exit interviews not to rest on their laurels, felt they had come to camp ready to compete. "Judging by their fitness results, intensity, effort and dedication (during the preseason), I think they took it upon themselves to make sure that we are ready," he said.

No sense of entitlement would be fostered in Flyers—or future Flyers—who came not so well prepared. Giroux was sent to the Phantoms. "His eyes watered up; he was really devastated," recalls the GM. Instead, the big team kept Jared Ross, an Alabama-born-and-hockey-educated (University of Alabama-Huntsville) center.

Giroux still had his whole career ahead of him, unlike 39-year-old Jim Dowd, a Brick, NJ, native who had given Philadelphia 73 games during the 2007-08 season and scored a playoff goal. He was let go after attending camp on a tryout basis.

Twenty-year-old Ryan Parent's bid to claim a spot on the defense was set back by a torn right shoulder labrum that would put him out for 12-14 weeks. Incumbent Jones had a torn labrum, too, this one in his right hip, and was likely to be out of the lineup for nine weeks. So Sbisa made the final cut, however temporarily. The rules allowed a 10-game look for players with remaining junior eligibility, without clubs enduring roster and salary implications. "It's something we'll have to monitor on a daily basis and see how Luca's doing," said Holmgren.

With Smith gone, Hatcher unlikely to be able to play, and Jones hurt, the blueline was so thinned that Stevens decided to split up his first pair of Coburn and Timonen. Vaananen was put with Timonen, Coburn with Eminger, and Sbisa with Kukkonen.

It was a defense only a hockey mom could love. The most famous one in the nation—Republican Vice Presidential candidate Sarah Palin—was invited by Ed Snider to drop the puck on opening night against the Rangers, a move the team Chairman insisted was apolitical. "We were so excited when she talked about hockey moms in her acceptance speech," the Chairman explained. "She did a great service to our sport. This is all about having fun with what she said."

Democrats and independents, not happy to see the Flyers politicized, didn't agree, their booing of Palin drowning out the cheers.

"Now that I know who she is, to have someone like that drop a puck at a hockey game is obviously big for us," said Richards. "I'm Canadian, so I don't pay attention to too much political stuff."

The captain's opposition on the ceremonial draw, Scott Gomez, was an Alaskan like Palin. He gave the Veep wannabe a peck on the cheek, apparently unaware that during a pregame tour of the Flyer locker room, she had written on the whiteboard, "Let's Go Boys!"

The boys, including six new ones from the 2007-08 conference finalists, didn't seem too inspired by this. The Rangers, who had already played three games because they had opened the season with a pair of contests against the Lightning in Prague, chased Biron with four goals on their first 14 shots. NY backup goalie Stephen Valiquette, who had won 10 games total in the NHL, improved his record to 5-1-1 against Philadelphia by holding on for a 4-3 victory. Asked to explain his success in the City of Brotherly Love, Henrik Lundqvist's understudy on the hated Rangers said, "Maybe it's watching *Rocky* before the game."

Or maybe the Flyers just weren't ready to play, which continued to be the case in their second game. A 2-1 lead against Montreal disappeared with two goals 44 seconds apart during a 5-3 Wachovia Center loss that put Philadelphia, after just two games, 10 points behind 5-0 New York.

Holmgren tried to shore up his defense by picking up 6-5 Andrew Alberts from the Bruins for minor leaguer Ned Lukacevic and a conditional draft choice. Said the GM: "He's a big kid, skates well, and is competitive."

Forgiving, too, apparently. The preceding season, Alberts had been kneed in the head by Scott Hartnell, resulting in a two-game suspension for the Flyer winger, but the newcomer insisted bygones would be bygones. "I saw [Hartnell] in the hallway and we laughed about it," said Alberts.

Also not holding a grudge was Bill Barber, who, after being fired as Philadelphia's coach in 2002, had declined a Snider offer to move into another capacity and instead became director of player personnel in Tampa Bay for six seasons. Unhappy with the direction of a new Lightning ownership headed by former Flyer Len Barrie and Oren Koules, Barber had resigned and was rejoining the only team for which he ever played, as a scouting consultant. "It's great to come back home where I belong," he said.

The Flyers were struggling during the early going. Late second-period goals within 21 seconds by Carter and Gagne rallied them from a 2-0 deficit in Pittsburgh, but Pascal Dupuis beat Antero Niittymaki from a bad angle with 11 seconds remaining in overtime to give the Penguins a 3-2 win. Whatever progress the team could claim from that season's first point in three contests was fleeting. Philadelphia was outshot 17-3 in the first period and fell behind 2-0 during a 5-2 loss at Colorado.

"We're playing like it's preseason," said Gagne. "We don't battle. [If] we keep playing like that, it's going to be tough to win a game this year."

At the team's hotel, Stevens met with captain Richards and assistants Briere and Timonen.

"We talked, and I think everyone's on board with what we need to do," the captain said. Richards, Gagne and Carter had accounted for nine of the team's 10 goals, but scoring really wasn't the first problem. "We're turning the puck over in critical areas and not winning loose pucks," said Holmgren.

Downie, not getting much ice time, was sent to the Phantoms, replaced by Andreas Nodl, a second-round pick in 2006. Niittymaki stopped 40 shots to get the team a point in a 5-4 overtime loss at San Jose, earning a second consecutive start when the Flyers returned home to complete a two-game set against the Sharks. But he gave up four goals in the first period and was relieved by Biron, who was beaten by 39-year-old Jeremy Roenick for the winning shootout goal in a 7-6 loss that dropped Philadelphia to 0-3-3.

"This most likely will be my last game in this building, and it's a nice way to finish," said Roenick, who received a huge ovation when shown on the center-hung scoreboard during a first-period stoppage. "This city really means a lot to me."

When Briere was lost for a month following surgery for an abdominal muscle torn in the home San Jose game, the Flyers called up winger Darroll Powe, signed a year earlier as a free agent out of Princeton University. But in the absence of a star scorer, it was Richards who stepped up, having four assists in a 6-3 win at Newark that not only broke a 12-game winless steak on the road against the Devils but also gave Philadelphia its first victory of the season.

The next day at the Wachovia Center, the Flyers and Devils were 2-2 in overtime when a smoke bomb was thrown on the ice during a stoppage. It took five minutes to clear the air but less than a minute after the resumption of play for Carter to redirect a Vaananen drive for a 3-2 win and a sweep of the home-and-home. With the help of fans, police eventually identified and arrested Earl Greene of South Philadelphia, who was charged with causing and risking a catastrophe, possession of an instrument of crime, recklessly endangering another person, disrupting a public event, and disorderly conduct.

The play of Sbisa, which was making Kukkonen an extra man, caused Holmgren not to wait the full 10-game trial before announcing that the 18-year-old was going to get a further look. Sbisa's partner on the second Flyer pair, Vaananen, gave the kid an A and not just because he had one in his name to spare. "He's only 18, but you don't notice that," the Finn said. He plays with such confidence. The really good thing is he likes to talk a lot."

Niittymaki might have been in conversation with Georges Vezina, Jacques Plante and Glenn Hall as far as Atlanta was concerned. Behind two-goal games by Gagne, Knuble and Lupul, the goaltender stretched his record to 10-0 against the Thrashers with a 7-0 win at Philips Arena.

Stevens decided to move game-day skates from the Flyers Skate Zone in Voorhees, NJ, to the Wachovia Center, a move endorsed by a growing contingent of players living in Olde City Philadelphia, but not by Gagne. "It takes me five minutes and I'm here (to Voorhees) in the morning," he said. "I'm the type of guy who likes to sleep a lot."

The coach tried to wake up the slow-starting Lupul by dumping him to the fourth line. But fortunately, the Flyers dozy start had stayed largely under the Delaware Valley's radar, thanks to a deep Phillies postseason run. After it culminated in the baseball club's first World Series title in 28 years, a minute-long video played on Wachovia's center-hung scoreboard drew a standing ovation from Flyer fans. There was another at the end of the game when Carter's second overtime goal in two home contests, and his eighth score of the young season, beat the Islanders, 3-2.

"He's in such good position and so sound defensively. I think the big key with Jeff is that he worries about defense first," Stevens gushed.

But that put Carter in the minority on a team with a 3.64 goals-against average.

"I'm not happy with the play of our forwards," said Holmgren. "They are not helping our defense." Philadelphia spotted Edmonton a 3-1 lead in a 5-4 home loss and then gave Ottawa its first two goals in a 4-1 loss. The Flyers had fallen back below .500.

Philadelphia's 46 percent rate of faceoff success, 27th in the league, brought Bob Clarke on the ice at the invitation of Stevens to show the players how No. 16 used to do it. The senior vice president, happy enough to offer his two cents when it was sought by Holmgren, had turned down an invitation to interview for the Maple Leaf GM job.

At age 56, Clarke was a little too old to suit up. But Holmgren thought the club could use a veteran presence on the ice and in the locker room. After 36-year-old free agent Mats Sundin did not include Philadelphia on the list of teams on which he might play one more year, the GM had exploratory talks with 40-year-old Brendan Shanahan, who had not been re-signed by the Rangers. "He's been on three Stanley Cup championship teams and his presence would be invaluable," said Holmgren. But the Flyer cap issues made a fit problematic, and Shanahan, who also had some interest from the Devils, was not ready to commit.

What Philadelphia needed most was a puck-moving defenseman who could handle top-four minutes. On November 7, Holmgren obtained one—sending Downie, Eminger and a fourth-round pick to Tampa for 24-year-old Matt Carle and a third-rounder. "He'll help us get out of our end a little quicker and he can join the rush," said Holmgren about Carle, who wondered what the rush had been for the Lightning to move him. Following a summer trade from San Jose, the former second-round pick of the Sharks had been a member of the Lightning for just 12 games.

Tampa Bay owners Barrie and Koules had been angered that Feaster, the team's recently resigned GM, had taken on Carle's four-year, $13.75 million, deal in the trade with San Jose. New general manager Brian Lawton had been told to unload the contract.

"It was little bit weird," recalls Carle. So was arriving in Philadelphia on November 7 with the Lightning for a game the next night, and then getting a call he was going to be playing for the other team. "I got picked up by (Flyer director of team services) Bryan Hardenbergh and taken to the (Hampton Inn) in Voorhees," Carle recalls. "The next morning, John Stevens picked me up at the hotel and brought me to the game skate."

The key to the deal for the Lightning was Downie, whose discipline issues had made him a chancy first-round pick by Philadelphia. In the opinion of Stevens, bad third-period giveaways in consecutive games of the Eastern Conference finals the previous spring had made the kid a risky lineup choice. In 38 games over a season-plus, Downie had 84 penalty minutes, but had produced only 12 points despite good hands and hockey sense.

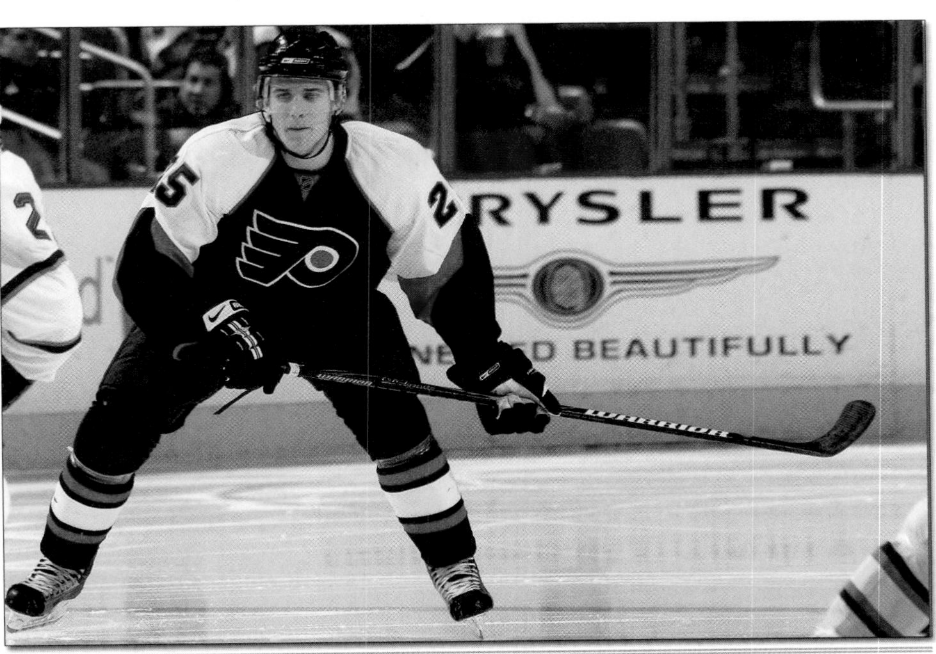

Former Hobey Baker Award winner Matt Carle was acquired from Tampa Bay in November.

"He was young, immature and undisciplined to a fault," recalls Holmgren. "At times, he couldn't help himself. But I was a fan of Steve's passion for the game. We were trading him for a defenseman who could do a lot of things for us.

"I had been talking to Tampa about Matt since that season started. It took time to work out how we were going to fit him [under the cap]."

The Flyers did by moving Eminger's $1.2 million, Downie's $585,000, and sending down minimum salary ($475,000) rookies Boyd Kane and Nate Raduns, both of whom had played just one game.

Paired with Coburn, Carle played 25 minutes in his Philadelphia debut. "I was worried that their guys calling for the puck would be the voices I was used to and that I would give it to them," he recalls. The newbie didn't fall for any dirty tricks during the 2-1 loss in which Prospal scored the winning goal. Carle was named the third star and Briere, returning after missing just six games, scored the only Flyer goal.

He got another one at Uniondale three nights later, but his groin

problem was ongoing, forcing him to leave the game. Richards got the eventual winner in a 3-1 Philadelphia win, accomplished without third-period help from the benched Hartnell. "It didn't look like he wanted to play tonight, so we went in another direction," the coach explained.

Said Hartnell, "I have no problems sitting if he doesn't think I'm doing a good job. You just deal with it and work hard in practice. I'm a positive person; even watching on the bench, it's a good feeling to win."

In Pittsburgh, Gagne joined Barber, Propp and Rod Brind'Amour as the fourth Flyer ever to score two shorthanded goals in one period. But Richards gave away Sidney Crosby's game-tying goal with just 2:33 remaining and Alex Goligoski, the sixth Penguin to get a chance, broke a scoreless shootout to give Pittsburgh a 5-4 victory.

Enforcer Cote, out with a torn oblique muscle, was placed on the long-term injured-reserve list. His role was filled by call-up Josh Gratton, who fought Montreal's feared Georges Laraque before Carter's 11th goal of the season proved to be the winner in a 2-1 Bell Centre victory. Philadelphia's first triumph against a team with a winning record was keyed by the play of Carle.

"I thought Matty was tremendous tonight," said Stevens. "I know he's known as an offensive guy, but he had a lot of poise under pressure going back for pucks. He's really solidified things back there and he's a guy that is going to play in all situations. He definitely makes us better."

The following night at the Wachovia Center, the Flyers went to 27-3-3-1 lifetime against the Thrashers as Niittymaki beat them for the 11th time in 11 starts, 4-3, on Lupul's third-period goal. "The game was on the line, we were a little bit tired, and Joffrey looked like he wanted to make a difference," said the coach as his team moved back over .500 with the win.

Lupul was back in Stevens' good graces while Hartnell credited himself with having been the whipping boy responsible for whipping his teammates into shape. "I think [my benching in Long Island] had an effect on the team," he said. "Now we've had two games in a row with 60-minute efforts and guys not taking shifts off. That's what we're going to need to take this team to the next level."

With the Coburn-Carle pairing showing promising results, Sbisa had a new partner in Timonen, plus new digs. The kid moved into the Cherry Hill, NJ, home of Allison Staffin, who had previously billeted teenaged Flyers Maxime Ouellet, Justin Williams and Todd Fedoruk.

Biron's 40-shot shutout and Carter's two goals—bringing him to 13 in the 18-game season—stymied the Sabres 3-0 in Buffalo. "Jeff is playing big minutes against top lines every night, kills penalties, and he is still putting up offensive numbers," said Stevens. "I think he's rounding himself into one of the better two-way players in the league."

In that regard, Carter was joining his good buddy Richards, who scored to beat Phoenix, 4-3, in overtime and, with Gagne's help, was reinvigorating Knuble. "Mike looks like he's reborn since we put [him] back together with Gagne and Richards," Stevens said after the veteran winger scored two goals, including the game winner, in a 4-3 home victory over Dallas. It was a good arrangement for Gagne, too. The winger extended a point streak to nine games in scoring twice and setting up Carle's first Philadelphia goal in a 3-1 win on November 26 in Raleigh.

Scoring like the explosive 1975-76 team—and looking like them too in debuting retro orange jerseys to be worn in selected games—the Flyers were temporarily waylaid by Sergei Samsonov's overtime goal in a 2-1 home loss to Carolina, completing a home-and-home.

The winning streak was over at six and Carle was out with a back issue. But the karma hadn't run out, and on December 2 against Tampa Bay, Hartnell threw in some chutzpah, too. With the score tied 3-3 in the final 20 seconds of regulation, Ryan Malone blocked a Sbisa shot and broke away. Biron made the save but, because Hartnell had tossed his glove at the shooter, Malone received another chance on a penalty shot. "I'm not sure what Hartnell was thinking," said Stevens. "Actually, he wasn't thinking."

Biron got enough of Malone's second attempt to send it wide, and Richards' second goal of the game, on a powerplay in overtime, gave the Flyers a 4-3 victory. "Looking back, it was kind of stupid," said Hartnell.

Briere had tried out his sore groin for the second time in 17 days, which also proved to be foolish. He came out in the second period. An MRI taken the following day showed a bad strain that would leave him out a projected four to five weeks.

Two nights later, Biron made the next big Philadelphia error, mindlessly clearing an icing touchup away from Coburn, allowing old Flyer killer Patrik Elias the chance to tie the game for the Devils, 2-2, with 1:30 remaining on the clock. Alberts' turnover in overtime helped Elias score again, sending Stevens' team down to a ridiculous 3-2 home defeat. "That (icing) should be as automatic as reaching for the brake when you see a red light," said the annoyed coach.

"We're wondering how we lost that game, especially when it's against the Devils," said Hartnell, who had a second-period goal wiped out on an early whistle.

Generally, Philadelphia was overcoming its lapses with confident special teams. Richards' fourth shorthanded score of the season, tying him with Gagne for the league lead, got the Flyers to a second overtime with the Hurricanes in eight days. This one went to Philadelphia, 2-1, when Carter beat Brind'Amour on a faceoff and scored his third sudden-death goal of the season. "Special teams are going to really enhance your chances of winning, but I don't think you can rely on them, just like I don't think you can just rely on your five-on-five play," warned Stevens.

Cote, back within a month from an oblique muscle tear, drilled Jon Sim along the wall, stole the puck, and fed Asham for a goal as the Flyers stretched their record to 14-7-6 with a 4-3 Wachovia Center victory over the Islanders. Powe added his first NHL score. "I think our fourth line all year has been tremendous," praised the coach.

Two nights later, the fourth game in 16 days against Carolina, none of the lines was impressing the coach as Philadelphia and Niittymaki entered the third period down 5-1 at home. "Stevens came in and basically said we were playing like a bunch of pansies," Hartnell would say.

As the lone Flyer goal scorer through two periods, he was perhaps the guy with the confidence to light a spark. Hartnell tipped in an Alberts drive, and then put in a carom off the glass to complete his hat trick, bringing Philadelphia to within two, 5-3. The crowd stirred and Upshall put in a rebound of a Kukkonen shot to make it 5-4 with five minutes remaining.

There was 3:37 left when Gagne was tripped by Brett Carson. He had just completed serving his penalty, but was not yet back in the play when Gagne scored off a passout from Knuble to tie the game. With the fans in a frenzy, the Flyers survived a too-many-men penalty in overtime before shootout goals by Richards and Gagne against goaltender Michael Leighton and two Niittymaki stops produced their 6-5 victory.

It was only the second occasion in franchise history—the other was an 11-6 victory at Detroit in 1988—that the Flyers had come back from four goals down to win a game, and the first time they had done it in a third period. "I just asked them to go out and play 20 minutes the right way," said Stevens. "I never had any idea that we could come back from that kind of a hole against a team that had been playing so well."

The comeback had been a snapshot of a surge that had lifted the team to 15-7-6 from an 0-3-3 beginning. Knuble's two goals and two assists by Carle in his return from a five-game absence keyed a 6-3 victory over the Penguins. Richards and Gagne each scored once and set up another goal in a 5-2 win on December 16 over Colorado. "We didn't get the start we wanted this year," said Timonen. "But we never stopped believing and we're playing as a team very well."

The win streak ended at five with a 5-2 loss at Montreal. But after Niittymaki, taking on the full workload while Biron struggled with a long and severe case of the flu, held the Caps scoreless in a 25-shot first period, Philadelphia pulled away for a rousing 7-1 Wachovia Center victory. "I've seen him good, but he was great today," marveled Stevens about his goaltender.

After missing the season's first 24 games, Randy Jones returned in a 3-2 shootout loss to the Devils, replacing Sbisa, who had appeared to be tiring. Upshall was lost to a knee sprain that would leave him out about 10 days, but his teammates were playing with too much confidence to be disturbed. After Ottawa scored twice in the third period to force a 4-4 tie, Gagne's goal with 5:30 remaining sent the Flyers on to a 6-4 triumph.

"Last year, maybe this is a game we lost," said the coach. "A lot of our young guys have matured and we've got a really strong veteran presence that can bring a sense of calm in those situations."

Giroux had taken his 31-game diversion to the Phantoms like a big boy, scoring 33 points. On Christmas morning, he was home in Ottawa when Holmgren called to tell him to be in Chicago the next day as the Flyers began a six-game trip.

"We were just starting to make breakfast; I waited until the whole family was together at the restaurant for lunch when I told everybody I was going up," Giroux recalls. "They all got really excited. It wasn't just my moment. With all the sacrifices my family had made for me, this was for all of us."

Less than two minutes into the game the next night, Philadelphia was already behind 1-0 when Giroux gave the puck away at center to Patrick Kane, who fed Patrick Sharp for a goal. "It's pretty funny now," recalls Giroux. "At the time, I didn't think so.

"Chief (Craig Berube) just gave me a pat and said, 'shake it off kid.'"

He didn't really, but neither did anyone else on what had become a long day. Not permitted by the CBA to travel or practice on Christmas Eve or Christmas, the Flyer had risen early on the 26th to fly and get in a morning skate, but when a stalled plane on a Midway (International Airport) runway caused the team's charter to be diverted to O'Hare, the club's bus and equipment truck were left waiting at the wrong airport. The workout was scrubbed and the players had no legs—and just one second-period shot—during a 5-1 thrashing by the improved Blackhawks. "It looked like we were too ready to use [travel] as an excuse," said Stevens.

Philadelphia suffered worse than just the rout and Giroux's gaffe. In blocking shots, Timonen came out of the contest with a chip fracture of his right ankle and Hartnell with a broken toe, while Carle limped out again with an ankle issue.

After a postgame flight to Columbus, the Flyers were an easy mark the following night for a 20-save shutout by rookie goaltender Steve Mason in the first-ever Blue Jacket win in eight tries against Philadelphia. "We're in a tough stretch; sometimes fatigue sets in and guys get hurt. All the more reason we have to play tighter hockey," said the coach.

A two-day break, the team's first in two weeks, allowed the club to get in a full practice in Vancouver. "I can't remember our last one," said Carter. "Felt good to get back to basics."

It was even more soothing to get back Carle, Hartnell and Timonen the following night. Assisted by Giroux's first NHL point, Carter scored his 27th goal of the season to start the Flyers to a first period lead that Biron made hold up for a 3-2 victory. There was a cost to it, though. After a hit by Kevin Bieksa on the first shift, Gagne left with a shoulder injury.

Giroux took his spot on the line with Richards and Knuble but, two nights later in Anaheim, suffered a concussion when elbowed in the head by the Ducks' Corey Perry. Biron, nevertheless, earned a 5-4 win, thanks to three assists and a shootout goal by Richards.

Perry was suspended for four games, which was of no help to the Giroux-less Philadelphia team the following day in Los Angeles. Kings' rookie winger Wayne Simmonds broke a tie and Jonathan Quick stopped Carter and Richards in a shootout as Stevens' team fell, 2-1. "Big point for us," said the coach, thrilled with the response despite the loss. "We asked huge minutes of some of these guys."

Another Flyer went down. Winger Jon Kalinski, a sixth-round pick on his second call-up of the season, took a hit to his left thigh in LA, and, upon the team's return home, was experiencing pain far worse than a charley horse. Kalinski underwent three surgeries during a nine-day stretch at Virtua Hospital Marlton (NJ) for "compartment syndrome," a condition that causes severe pressure on fibrous tissue that can cause irreversible damage if not treated immediately. Dr. William DeLong saved Kalinski's career, but he would be out for months.

Gagne, however, was back as the trip closed in Washington with Coburn's third-period goal saving a point in a 2-1 shootout loss. Home wins against Minnesota and Toronto briefly moved Philadelphia into first place in the Atlantic Division. Things also seemed to be looking up for Briere after a couple of tune-up games with the Phantoms. But then his groin issues flared again, forcing an additional surgery expected to

leave him out another four weeks. This was all the more reason Holmgren believed Brendan Shanahan might be a good fit to finish the season, but he decided to sign with New Jersey.

"There had been one point where Paul made an offer to me and I was hesitant," said Shanahan. "Another time, when I called him and said, 'I'm in, I'm a Flyer,' he then had something else going on. We both had good respect for each other from our time in Hartford, but it seems we were never on the same page on the same week.

"Since I was living in New York with my family, the Devils' situation was a little better for me."

Giroux returned after five games in a 4-1 loss at Tampa, when Timonen took a puck in the face for 25 stitches. But the resolute little defenseman was back the following night in Sunrise, when Gagne scored during both regulation and the shootout to trip the Panthers, 3-2.

In the final game before the All-Star break, Philadelphia had its foot out the door one period too soon. The Thrashers scored three third-period goals in six minutes to tie the game 3-3, but Knuble saved a happy vacation—and kept the team two points behind the division-leading Devils and one back of the Rangers—with two late goals that provided a 5-3 win. Niittymaki was 12-0 lifetime with a 1.76 GAA versus Atlanta, and 48-56-21 (3.13) against everybody else.

Carter was the Flyer representative at the All-Star Game in Montreal, where players took their annual vacations from checking during a 12-11 win for the Eastern Conference. The rest of the Philadelphia team had a five-day holiday between two Florida trips, which left little excuse for the mid-winter blues.

At Sunrise, Giroux beat Panther netminder Tomas Vokoun on a breakaway for his first career goal. "I think it's every kid's [dream] to score in the NHL," said the rookie after a 3-2 loss. "Now that I've got that out of the way, I can keep playing better."

Carter and Richards continued to set an excellent example. Both scored twice in support of Niittymaki as the Flyers bounced back to win in Tampa, 6-1. The following night in St. Louis, Coburn and Jones were too weak from the flu to play, and the second-ranked powerplay in the NHL looked sick, failing to score on 11 advantages in a 4-0 loss.

Sbisa, who had seen some time on the wing but then had sat out for 10 consecutive games, played against the Blues. Two days later, as Ryan Parent returned after missing 49 games following shoulder surgery, Sbisa was sent back to his Lethbridge junior team. Holmgren worrying aloud about the just-turned-19-year-old's ability to handle the demotion after being given an NHL job from his first camp. "I have my concerns about what this does for his development," said the GM.

Jones returned after just one game, but Coburn was still on his back, joined by Richards and Upshall as Philadelphia opened a home-and-home with the Bruins, losing 3-1 at the Wachovia Center. In Boston, Biron was yanked after allowing three goals in the first period, but Niittymaki was flawless the rest of the way as the Flyers fought back from a 3-1 deficit on goals by Metropolit and Hartnell. Jones, booed throughout the contest because his hit from behind had put Patrice Bergeron out for the previous season, bounced in a 4-3 overtime winner off Bruin defenseman Andrew Ference.

Like clockwork, Niittymaki won at Atlanta, 3-2, but stumbled in a 5-2 home loss to Ottawa. Stevens went back to Biron, who had lost four straight following his prolonged bout with the flu, and he beat the Islanders 5-1.

Richards, eight pounds lighter from the bug, returned the following night at Madison Square Garden to take a breakaway pass from Coburn, beat Lundqvist on a breakaway, and become the first player ever to score three three-on-five goals during his career. Biron's 35 saves and a three-point night by Giroux, gave Philadelphia the 5-2 victory.

Rookie Claude Giroux playued 42 games for the Flyers in 2008-09.

"We moved [Giroux] to center (on a line with Powe and Upshall) and like what he's done," said Stevens. "He's good in his own zone and is a lot stronger on the puck than he looks."

Biron then stopped 39 Sabre shots as Richards' five points, including an NHL-leading sixth shorthanded tally, produced a 6-3 home victory. "Our game plan was to get our forecheck going, get pucks and traffic to the net, and keep it simple," said the captain, for whom things were not as uncomplicated as they appeared. He was playing the season with torn labrums in each shoulder, yet keyed a 75-second cycle in the second period that forced five Buffalo failures to clear before Coburn scored.

"Best shift I have ever been part of," said Gagne. "Chance after chance for more than a minute, maybe a little bit tired by the end, but finding a way to get that goal."

Against Pittsburgh, Biron found an odd way to cough one up in front of the largest home regular-season crowd in Flyer history—19,992. Richards' third shorthanded goal in three games had sparked a rally from a 3-1 deficit to a 4-4 tie when the goalie came out 30 feet to beat Dupuis to a puck and save a breakaway. But fearing a delay-of-game penalty, the goaltender decided to keep the puck moving with a behind-the-back pass to Richards, but flubbed it, allowing Dupuis to feed Crosby at an empty net and win the game 5-4.

"Get it to the corner, get it to the boards, even let it stay alive and let the guys recover," Biron lectured himself. "But I kind of got anxious and got rid of it. It ends up losing the game."

Three nights later at Washington, with Timonen now stricken by the flu, the Flyers again rallied with three in the third, this time within 3:19 on goals by Hartnell, Carter and Asham. Niittymaki made 35 saves and the Flyers won, 4-2, before Biron bounced back, delivering a 2-0 home shutout of the Kings.

To make salary-cap room for the return of Briere, Philadelphia waived Vaananen, who had dressed in only two of the last seven games, and Metropolit. Vaananen was claimed by Vancouver, Metropolit by Montreal with the Canadiens in town to play on February 27.

"It is a crazy game," said Metropolit, who played 11 minutes for the Habs and wound up on the winning side, 4-3, after the Canadiens converted an interference penalty on Upshall into an overtime powerplay winner by Mathieu Schneider. "But I don't know if it can get any crazier than this."

Holmgren still didn't have enough cap room to fit Briere. So the GM temporarily sent Giroux to the Phantoms along with Kukkonen, who had become a seventh man. Nate Guenin, a lower-salaried defenseman, was called up for a game at Newark to fill in for Timonen. Holmgren's hocus pocus was keeping his team compliant, but at long last, under one of the shells was Briere, ready to go after a 36-game absence. He looked rusty in his return, but the Flyer wheels were squeaky all around during Marty Brodeur's 3-0 shutout.

Timonen came back March 3 in Boston from a four-game absence, allowing Holmgren to return Guenin—along with Jared Ross for the eighth time that year—and bring up Giroux. Knuble, who had become familiar with life on the fringes during his first six NHL seasons before suddenly developing a scoring touch, celebrated his 800th NHL game with a three-point night in Philadelphia's 4-2 win at TD Garden. "That's probably 799 more than I ever thought I'd play," said Knuble.

Despite cap issues, the Flyer GM kicked tires at the trading deadline and wasn't just looking for retreads. He asked Florida general manager Jacques Martin about the availability of 25-year-old Jay Bouwmeester, once a third-overall pick. "We had one conversation," recalls Holmgren. "Jacques called back close to the deadline and said, 'So, you ready to do that deal for Giroux and a first?'"

"I said, 'What?'"

Holmgren also had one talk with Anaheim GM Bob Murray about 34-year-old Chris Pronger, who had anchored the Ducks to the 2006 Cup but, making $6.2 million, was projected to be a $7 million-a-year keep when his contract ran out after the 2009-10 season. Murray had won a championship and felt a package of younger players would help him towards another one. Holmgren felt he would have to subtract too much of his team too late in the season to add Pronger. "I remember telling Bob, 'I can't see how we could ever do this now. If he's still [available] in the summer, we'd be more than happy to talk about it.'"

The Philadelphia GM did make a move, however, just before the 3 p.m. March 4 deadline. He created a significant $400,000 in cap room by trading Upshall and a second-round pick to Phoenix for left wing Daniel Carcillo, whose 174 penalty minutes had put him well on his way to leading the league for a second-consecutive season.

"He also scored 13 goals last year," Holmgren said. "Carcillo is a good player who happens to be tough and aggressive, that's the bottom line.

"We think he can play with our top nine forwards. The fans are going to love him. Trust me."

They also had enjoyed the irrepressible Upshall, as he had enjoyed playing for them. The winger was getting his hair cut when Holmgren telephoned. "It was well after 3, so I was pretty rattled," Upshall recalls. "I was crushed, really upset.

"Paul said he had to do it for cap reasons. That's hockey. I had a blast in Philadelphia. I had a great time living in Olde City, and it was an honor to wear the jersey. The highlight of my career was scoring goals in those [2008] playoffs."

Upshall had one in Game Seven versus Washington and the series winner in Game Five against Montreal, so he wasn't going to be quickly forgotten. Remembers Holmgren: "A couple days after the trade, somebody passed me driving into [the Wachovia Center] and they must have recognized me. All of a sudden, a girl is holding this Upshall jersey in the back window. He was a popular guy.

"Scottie is a ninth or 10th forward, skilled enough to move up in your lineup. He was really good for us. Lots of life, I'd take him back."

San Jose had to take back Holmgren's other deadline acquisition, defenseman Kyle McLaren, when the 31-year-old defenseman failed his physical because of a hand injury suffered during a December AHL game.

When Briere's groin began bothering him again during a 5-1 home loss to Calgary, he feared his season might be over. The following day, his concern lessened, but he had to be shut down again temporarily. As had been the case most of the season, there were plenty of players to pick up the scoring slack. Lupul, assisted by Carcillo's first point as a

Flyer, joined Carter, Richards, Gagne, Hartnell and Knuble as 20-goal scorers during Biron's 4-1 win over Nashville.

Two goals apiece from Carter and Hartnell spearheaded a 5-2 victory over Buffalo as Philadelphia, which had fallen seven points behind surging New Jersey in the Atlantic Division, maintained a tentative hold on fourth place in the Eastern Conference, which would mean home-ice advantage in the first round.

Advancing in the playoffs would be problematic though, without a healthy Briere, who returned in a 2-1 loss on March 12 to Washington. "I had more power, more jump, didn't feel like I was lagging behind when I had the chance to jump in the hole," he said.

That was encouraging, and so was the play of Biron, as he continued his resurgence from an up-and-down first 40 games. His GAA dropped to 1.73 and his save percentage soared to .948 for the last five contests during a 39-stop, 4-2, home victory over the Rangers. "Probably his best performance of the year," said Stevens.

It has been 11 games since the Flyers had given either of their goalies a lead after one period when goals by Hartnell and Lupul carried them to a 2-0 edge deep into the second at Detroit. But when Henrik Zetterberg scored 11 minutes into the third, the Stanley Cup champions rallied and stretched a streak of winless Philadelphia visits to Joe Louis Arena to 16 (14-0-2] with a 3-2 defeat.

Stevens said his players "had some work to do" to be as good as the Red Wings. The Flyers, 4-5 in their last nine contests, quickly rolled up their sleeves again. Briere scored twice within 2:05 to erase a 3-2 deficit in a 6-4 victory at Buffalo, and Gagne and Hartnell each had powerplay goals during a 3-1 win at Pittsburgh that pushed Philadelphia two points ahead of the Penguins and back into fourth place.

The following day, Carter scored his 40th and Gagne his 30th just 2:06 apart in the third period as Biron out-dueled Brodeur in a 4-2 home victory over the Devils. "We really feel like we're starting to get into that groove," Carter said. "We're playing solid D; guys are leaving it out all there, and Marty's standing on his head."

Speaking of heads, Hartnell had one of the most prominent ones in town, so the Flyers decided to have some fun with his bushy, carrot-top, curls by giving out imitation wigs to the first 5,000 fans, plus all kids, at the March 26 contest against Florida. He was not tipped off about the promotion before he took the ice for warm-up.

"You come out and there's all these kids around the glass with big, curly, hair. It's pretty cool," said Hartnell. "I'd never seen better hair on fans in my whole career."

Cutting it a lot closer than his 'do, Hartnell scored with only four seconds remaining in the second period to pull Philadelphia into a 2-2 tie with the Panthers. But Florida goalie Craig Anderson was superb in a 4-2 win that snapped the Flyer win string at three.

Hair like Hartnell's was not meant to be kept under a hat. But when one was sent to Carter to autograph, the team decided that the first star of the game would wear it during postgame interviews. Meanwhile, radio color commentator Chris Therien opined that Giroux, who had eight points in his last 10 games, was a player upon which the franchise could eventually hang its hat. "He could be a top-five player in the league," projected Therien, while Stevens added that it was not too soon to compare the kid's hockey sense to that of Peter Forsberg.

"You have to be ready all the time because chances are Claude will get you the puck," said the coach. Giroux had put on 20 pounds since his 2006 draft, adding strength to his tenacity and hockey sense, characteristics the team had loved when drafting him. "Even in practices, I'm still learning little details," said the rookie.

For most of two seasons, the Flyers hadn't much bothered with trifles like jumping ahead and staying there, as most games are won. But they consistently had shown comeback capabilities. Two goals by Lupul, around one by Hartnell within 3:55 of the third period, turned a 2-0 deficit at Uniondale into a 3-2 lead. Even after Islander Mark Streit tied the game, 3-3, Briere and Richards had shootout goals to give Philadelphia a 4-3 victory.

A 3-1 deficit was finally insurmountable in a 4-3 home loss to Boston. But when the Flyers were bad from practically start to finish in a 3-2 loss at Toronto on April 1, it was time to stop fooling around.

"For a team that's battling for home-ice advantage and even still battling for the division, what with the way Jersey is slumping (with seven consecutive losses), this is unacceptable," said Lupul. "Our execution was poor and our passing was the worst I've seen it all year. We didn't even really work that hard."

Holmgren voiced his displeasure to Stevens. "He called me upstairs and we had a long conversation," recalls the coach. "It was one of those we've-got-to-get-going meetings with a sense that changes will be made if we don't."

Carter's first NHL hat trick, Briere's four points, Hartnell's 30th goal, and a three-point night by Giroux keyed an 8-5 home win in the second game of the home-and-home with the Leafs. But having led 6-0, an 8-5 win still left a sour taste.

"We were always six or eight points behind Jersey and four or six points ahead (of fifth) with games in hand," recalls Briere. "You get casual, [as if] it's not a big deal when you win or lose. And sometimes you lose that intensity."

Behind Niittymaki in Ottawa, Philadelphia had to rally from another bad start and took a 3-2 lead on Gagne's early third-period goal. But they quickly gave it back on a Carter giveaway, went 0-for-5 in the shootout, and lost 4-3.

With the playoffs only four games away, the Flyers had dropped four of their last six. But it wasn't the coach who was being tested for ulcers. After Giroux had experienced three weeks of G.I. tract discomfort, nothing ominous was found and he was put on medication.

In a pregame ceremony before a home contest with the Panthers, Richards and Timonen were presented their second consecutive Bobby Clarke and Barry Ashbee trophies, respectively. Carter went on to score his 45th goal seven minutes into the third period, and Philadelphia beat Florida, 2-1, clinching a playoff berth with three contests to spare. "Marty looked like himself tonight," said Stevens after Biron made 29 saves. "This was a very important game for him."

With Parent needing to rest a troublesome groin, the Flyers were so tight against the cap that they couldn't call up a Phantom. Instead, they recruited a local amateur—David Sloane, who had played at Colgate and been an invitee to a Philadelphia training camp—to play gratis in a 2-1 loss at Madison Square Garden. The kid did get to keep his jersey though after his 6:44 of fame.

Biron shone in the defeat at New York and then needed to be good again when his team started terribly at Uniondale. But after the Flyers made second-period goals by Lupul, Knuble and Gagne hold up for a 3-2 victory against the 30th place Islanders, Stevens was accentuating the positive.

"I thought we did better as the game wore on," the coach said. "I have seen the focus get a lot better this week, a sign that the playoffs are getting close."

The victory assured a four vs. five first-round matchup against Pittsburgh. Philadelphia would be playing Game 82 at the Wachovia Center against the Rangers—whose playoff position was locked up—needing one point to obtain home-ice advantage through the first two rounds.

Parent, who had played 13 minutes against the Islanders, was sore again. Since amateurs were allowed only one game, Sloane could not be used again. So the GM had to sign another guy off the street—Jamie Fritsch, who had just completed his career at the University of New Hampshire.

"It wasn't a great situation I put us in," recalls Holmgren.

Briere set up Giroux at 5:26 of the first period to give Philadelphia the initial goal but, with Timonen in the box for clearing the puck over the glass, Brandon Dubinsky tied the game 1-1 with a deflection of a Derek Morris point shot. After Carter beat Lundqvist through a screen to restore the lead, Dubinsky scored the only shorthanded goal the Flyers allowed all season to tie it 2-2.

Briere redirected an Alberts shot to give Philadelphia its third lead but the Rangers, with little to play for, didn't go away. Early in the third period, Sean Avery shot a savable puck past Biron from the top of the left circle to tie the contest yet again.

With 11 minutes remaining, Fritsch (the amateur recruit), taking one of his nine shifts in the game, was beaten wide by Aaron Voros, then used as a pylon by Blair Betts, whose bank shot went off the amateur and past Biron. New York now led 4-3, and when Knuble was wide with the best Flyer chance thereafter, Philadelphia had kicked away the home-ice advantage almost the length of the Pennsylvania Turnpike.

"Chance to get home ice, for me to get my 30th win, to go the whole year without allowing a shorthanded goal, and I give up a bad one," recalls Biron after the 4-3 defeat. "We failed at everything."

Briere remembers wondering why so few of his teammates were not beside themselves, like he was. "Why wouldn't you want to start the playoffs at home?" he recalls. "We were very casual about it and I couldn't understand why."

With a fresh start just three days away, this was no time to mourn. "I was [bleeped]," said Holmgren, but Stevens had to spin the squandered opportunity positively.

"It's probably my fault, because nothing for me ever comes easy," said the coach. "I think it's almost our destiny, to be honest with you.

"This group has always found hard ways to [succeed]."

Stevens was counting on some good, old loathing of the Penguins, who had won last year's five-game conference final against the Flyers, to get his club psyched for the rematch. "The rivalry is well known," the coach said. "The teams don't like each other very much. Any time you play two years in a row in the playoffs, the emotions roll over."

Both franchises had ended the season with 99 points, but Pittsburgh had finished a blistering 18-3-4 after replacing coach Michel Therrien with Dan Bylsma. Philadelphia had gone a mediocre 13-10-2 down the stretch. The season-series had been 2-2-2, whatever that meant. "You start at zero again," said Gagne.

The Flyers had actually spent the season beginning at minus, trailing after the first period in 30 games. They had rallied for nine wins and five overtime losses, but this was not a formula for success against playoff-caliber teams.

With Parent back in the lineup, they had their full complement of players for Game One, but again started poorly. Asham, tired at the end of a long shift, was called for holding Ruslan Fedotenko in the neutral zone. "Undisciplined penalty," Stevens would say. "That's the worst-case scenario, starting like that."

It took the Penguins all of 15 seconds to convert. Sergei Gonchar fed through Hartnell to a streaking Crosby, who executed a quick give-and-go with Evgeni Malkin at the side of the net. Crosby kicked the puck forward, tucked it around Biron against the post, and got a carom off the back of the goalie's right skate into the goal, giving Pittsburgh a 1-0 lead.

Late in the first period, Hartnell, who had hurried Rob Scuderi into a giveaway, was in too tight after receiving a pass from Richards and lifted the puck into the mesh above the glass. Marc-Andre Fleury was run over by Hartnell's momentum and the Flyer forward went to the box for goaltender interference, effectively killing the first signs of a Philadelphia surge.

Early in the middle frame, Jordan Staal poked away an attempted Coburn pass down the boards and the Penguins broke away on a three-on-one. Tyler Kennedy decided not to pass and largely fanned on the shot, but got just enough on it to fool Biron between the legs with a change of speed to make the score 2-0.

Giroux was tackled by Gonchar, and then, after sliding into Fleury, crosschecked by the goalie, but Pittsburgh did not get a penalty. The Flyers did receive a powerplay, however, when Brooks Orpik elbowed Lupul in the closing seconds of the middle session.

With the man advantage to start the third, Philadelphia put four shots on Fleury and Richards fired off the crossbar. But any momentum the Flyers were gaining ended when Hartnell stuck his leg out on Kris Letang, putting the Penguins back on another man advantage. Philadelphia killed it, but soon Knuble's attempt at a bank pass caromed to Malkin in front. He skated around Biron's poke-check attempt and flipped in a backhander at 6:28 of the third period to build the lead to 3-0.

Mark Eaton, firing from the point, off a Crosby faceoff win over Giroux, scored off the Flyer's stick to make it 4-0. With Fleury penalized for tripping Giroux, Gagne broke the shutout with 4:35 to play, way too little and too late for Stevens' players to do anything more but send some messages that they were going down hard, even though they really hadn't. In the final 19 seconds, Philadelphia, shorthanded eight times in the contest, took 21 more minutes in penalties. And that did not include a punch to Max Talbot's head by Carcillo, which went undetected by the referees.

"We know that's their style," scoffed Fleury, who had ample reason for condescension after Pittsburgh's dominant 4-1 victory in Game One. "That's how they play."

It certainly wasn't Stevens' idea. "I like Scotty Hartnell's emotion, but [after 16 minutes of penalties] he's got to find that line of discipline, and I really didn't think he did tonight," said the coach.

Carcillo was suspended for Game Two and Stevens was fined $10,000.

"We held a conference call Monday with the general managers and coaches of playoff teams and told them explicitly we would not tolerate attempts by clubs to 'send a message' late in a game when the outcome had been determined," said Colin Campbell, the NHL's top hockey operations executive. "Organizations—players and coaches—will be held accountable for such actions."

Timonen got the day off from practice because of a sore thigh caused by a Chris Kunitz hit and Jones went home to be with his family mourning the death of his grandmother. Both Flyers were coming back for Game Two. To replace Carcillo, Stevens dressed Sbisa, recalled from his junior team, to play the wing.

Playing a defenseman up front was not going to make a bit of difference for Philadelphia if it didn't smarten up. Asked to relay to the media the coach's off-day message, Richards said in a word, "Discipline."

Hartnell, the team poster boy for putting the Flyers in bad positions, quickly atoned in Game Two. He deflected in Carle's point drive seven seconds into a first period penalty on Mark Eaton.

Leading 1-0, Philadelphia had Pittsburgh largely bottled up until Byslma put Crosby and Malkin on a line with Bill Guerin. The 17-year veteran winger took a pass from Malkin on a line rush and beat Biron with a quick release with 3:32 remaining in the second period to tie the game 1-1.

The Flyers dodged a bullet in the opening seconds of the third period when Staal, left alone in front, had much of the net empty, but hit Biron's right pad. Philadelphia then took the lead back when Giroux fed Powe, whose right-circle drive flew past Fleury's far side at 2:09.

Eleven minutes into the period, Fleury stopped Carter's bid for an insurance goal by going post to post to make a sterling pad save. With 4:04 to go Staal was half-holding Carter's stick as he in turn was marginally hooking the Penguin center, but the Flyer was the one called for the penalty. Twenty-seven seconds into the powerplay, Letang's point shot went off Coburn, then Malkin, and past a helpless Biron to send the game into overtime at 2-2.

Philadelphia had the first big opportunity of sudden death when Hal Gill was called for crosschecking Briere. But the Flyers failed to register a shot before Knuble's slash of Orpik during a front-of-the net battle, took 31 seconds off the powerplay. Just one second before Pittsburgh was about to go up a man, Giroux slashed Kunitz, giving the Penguins a five-on-three.

Biron stopped Malkin, who then had a shot blocked by Coburn. Timonen got in front of a Gonchar drive and Philadelphia got the puck out once. But Crosby won a draw from Carter and Gonchar sent a point pass to Guerin near the bottom of the left circle. He stepped towards the slot, faked a cross-crease pass to get Biron leaning, and whipped a shot past the goalie's short side. The second five-on-three overtime goal in NHL playoff history since 1933 had beaten the Flyers 3-2 and put them down 2-0 in the series.

An incensed Timonen chased referees Bill McCreary and Brad Meier, telling them they had taken the game away from Philadelphia and earning himself a misconduct penalty. The Carter call had been marginal and Knuble's had been a result of give-and-take in front of the goal. But there wasn't much arguing the Giroux penalty that had put his team down by two men, not even by the perpetrator.

"I was just trying to jam [Kunitz's] stick and mine broke," said the crestfallen rookie. "My guess is I went a little too hard. The refs saw that my stick broke and they had to call it.

"Dumb play. I've let the guys down here and I have got to put that behind me."

This figured to be difficult. The Flyers had been the better team for the majority of the game.

"We did all the right things," said Richards, who, on anti-inflammatory medication for two torn shoulder labrums, played 26-plus minutes and had a team-high seven hits. "It's a tough pill to swallow after how hard we worked and how it finished."

Just keep doing what you are doing, preached Stevens. "We've certainly proved we can mount an attack," he said.

A year earlier, Philadelphia returned home for Game Three against the Penguins in the same 2-0 hole. The players received the usual encouragement from "God Bless America" and a wired house, yet had given up the first two goals of the game within seven minutes. So this time the team, which Richards would later say appeared remarkably confident in the pregame, needed an early reward.

Carter provided it, taking a drop pass from Lupul, faking Gonchar to his knees, and then flipping a backhander past Fleury's blocker after just 2:59. Two minutes later, Staal was sent off for holding Alberts, and a Richards pass for a cutting Gagne bounced in off Gill. Two goals on two shots had given the Flyers a 2-0 lead.

Kunitz tried to rally the Penguins with his second hard hit on Timonen in three games, this one an elbow to the head that brought in Hartnell to engage the Pittsburgh winger in a fight. "I couldn't believe it was actually possible Timonen got up and finished the game," Hartnell would say later. A Letang hit on Giroux during a delayed penalty caused Powe to go after the Penguin defensive catalyst and had Giroux ending up on top of Kennedy as they traded punches.

In the final minute of the period, Talbot eliminated Coburn with a solid forecheck and Fedotenko found the loose puck in the left wing corner. He whirled and sent a cross-ice pass that somehow found its way through Gagne, Richards and Carle to the right circle and a wide-open Malkin, whose one-timer beat Biron between the legs at 19:48. Cutting the lead to 2-1 was a huge boost for Pittsburgh as it went to the break and, only 13 seconds into the second period, Scuderi's shot from

Martin Biron and Jeff Carter celebrate after defeating Pittsburgh 6-3 in Game Three of the 2009 Conference quarterfinals.

the point through Guerin's screen went past Biron on the short side to tie the game.

"We had done a lot of good things so we weren't worried," Carter would say later. "We knew we just had to stick to the game plan."

Four minutes into the second period, Briere picked up the rebound of a Powe shot and sent a pass past Orpik and Staal to Giroux, who had an empty net for his first postseason goal, restoring the Philadelphia lead at 3-2. Richards was in the box for holding Malkin when Giroux stole the puck from Gonchar, spun past Letang, reversed his direction and fed out from behind the Penguin net to Gagne at the far side for a slam-dunk shorthanded goal. "I'm not sure there are many players who are capable of making plays like that," Stevens would say of the rookie, whose goal and assist had restored a 4-2 lead.

Early in the third, Alberts's one-timer deflected off Talbot to Jared Ross, whose first NHL goal, on his seventh call-up of the season, squibbed between the left arm and pad of Fleury to make the score 5-2. Malkin had a powerplay goal before Gagne's second score of the game, into the empty net, cemented a rousing 6-3 Philadelphia victory that cut Pittsburgh's series lead to 2-1.

"We knew they would come out charging in the first period," said Crosby, "and that's what they did."

Actually, the Penguins had handled it, fighting back for a 2-2 tie, but the Flyers had not become rattled. "You saw the desperation that carried on through the game," said Biron after stopping 26 of 29 shots. "The emotion was definitely there and that's the way we've been successful all year."

Timonen was plenty emotional about Kunitz, whom he accused of two attempts to injure within three games. "You can tell that for sure," said the defenseman. "I didn't even have the puck; it was in the corner."

Stevens, who had seen his team fall victim to too many letdowns, warned against another. "We got one game and now we have to leave it behind," said the coach. Too often, Philadelphia's self-assurance had turned to arrogance as players had waited for the game to come to them in first periods and fallen behind. But coming off consecutive strong performances, the Flyers started well again in Game Four, registering multiple body checks and the game's first three shots.

Letang and Malkin took penalties to sandwich one by Alberts, and, on the four-on-three, Fleury stopped Giroux on Philadelphia's best chance. The Flyers killed a holding call on Parent for grabbing Malkin, the Penguins one on Matt Cooke for hooking Powe, and the second period began scoreless.

It didn't remain so for long. Kunitz, holding the puck in the faceoff circle, got Timonen to slide and flipped a pass to a hard-charging Crosby, who lost his edge and went in feet-first on Biron, the puck going off the Pittsburgh star's skates and winding up in the back of the net.

"It's a dangerous play when you're kicking the puck around the crease and it's not the first time he's done that," Biron would say, but replay officials in Toronto ruled there had been no intent to boot the puck. The goal stood and, 3:19 into the second period, the Penguins had a 1-0 lead.

Just over four minutes later, Ross got in teammate Jones's way, and with too many Flyers on the wrong side of the ice, Kennedy was wide open to lift the puck over Timonen's block attempt. Biron was not completely set and Pittsburgh went up 2-0.

Philadelphia poured 15 second-period shots at Fleury to the Pen-

guins' six at Biron but couldn't cash in on two powerplays. In the third period, with Pittsburgh killing an Eaton penalty for tripping Giroux, Carter hit the post.

Finally, Carcillo knocked in a Richards rebound and the lead was cut to 2-1 with 8:16 remaining. The Flyers continued to pressure, but Carcillo's was the only shot of 19 in the third period that they could make count before Talbot hit the empty net. Fleury had 45 saves in the 3-1 victory that put the Penguins up 3-1 in the series.

"We had great second opportunities and they got the bounces tonight," said Richards, who, like most of his teammates, seemed more encouraged by their strong play over three consecutive games than disheartened by facing elimination.

"I think we were the better team," said Timonen. "If we can keep that up, I'm sure we'll bring the series back here."

A year earlier, battered Philadelphia had stayed alive in Game Four with the help of a Penguin let-up, and then had little left during the 6-0 demolishment it suffered in Game Five. But this time, the Flyers had a complete lineup and more reason to believe.

"It's a deep hole, yes," acknowledged Richards. "We also started the season 0-6. Pretty big hole there, too."

Actually, they had started 0-3-3, but one should never contradict a captain in the middle of an inspirational message. Going back to Pittsburgh, Biron could have used a lift. He had a record of 4-8-2 in 14 regular-season career games at the Igloo and still was looking for his first playoff victory there after four tries.

"I lost the first NHL game I ever played there," he recalls. "Never liked that place."

The Penguins appeared determined to extend Biron's misery, but he stopped 15 first-period shots. Early in the middle session, Byslma put out Malkin, Crosby and Guerin against Philadelphia's fourth line of Carcillo, Ross and Asham, but this time, there was no mismatch. Carcillo stole a drop pass by Guerin, carried the puck along left wing and dropped it to Asham, who used Eaton as a screen to beat Fleury and give the Flyers the precious first goal.

"You could feel our energy jump," Knuble would say. Biron, looking quick to the puck, was even faster into the face of referee Eric Furlatt. The goalie protested Malkin's game-tying goal saying that it had been kicked in. After a lengthy review, the replay officials in Toronto agreed, and Philadelphia still led 1-0.

While Scuderi was off early in the third period for holding Carter, Fleury stretched his right pad on a Hartnell rebound of a Carter drive, and then beat Lupul on the second carom. But when the penalty expired, Carle picked off a backhand pass up the wall by Philippe Boucher, stickhandled around Dupuis, and fed Powe, who put the puck into Giroux's wheelhouse at the left circle. He overpowered Fleury and the Flyers had breathing room at 2-0.

With 10 minutes remaining, a Pittsburgh dump-in that Biron was chasing took a bad bounce into the crease, but the goalie got lucky when the puck hit the post. Miro Satan pounced on the rebound, but Biron got his right pad against the pipe to preserve the two-goal lead. Seven minutes remained when Hartnell gave Boucher no room after a keep at the point. Carle picked up the puck and hit a breaking Richards, who teed up a slapshot from the left circle. Knuble slapped home the rebound to build the lead to 3-0.

Penguin fans began to leave the building. Biron stopped 28 Pittsburgh shots in the 3-0 shutout that sent Philadelphia home for Game Six, just as Timonen had promised. "Finally, Mellon Arena is smiling at me," recalls Biron. Not only were the Flyers alive, they also had largely outplayed the defending Eastern Conference playoff champions in four consecutive games.

"We were more excited to win than nervous to lose," Giroux said. "That's important. We're just having fun right now and can't wait to get back home and play in front of the fans."

Many of them were surprised to see their team again before October. At the start of Game Six, Talbot seemed especially shocked that Richards still was playing. Nonetheless, seventeen minutes into the first period, the Flyer captain stole the puck from the feisty Penguin and went five-hole on Fleury. The goalie closed his pads, but Knuble beat a diving Talbot to the puck and lifted a backhander high into the net to give Philadelphia a 1-0 lead.

Lou Nolan still was announcing the goal to the Wachovia Center crowd when Briere trapped Pittsburgh players during a shift change, and hit Giroux with an outlet pass. He jammed on the brakes at the top of the left circle and sent a gorgeous cross-ice feed to a streaking Lupul, who quickly rifled a pinpoint shot from the right faceoff dot over Fleury's glove and under the cross bar with 1:21 left in the first period. Philadelphia took a 2-0 lead into the locker room.

Four minutes into the second, with Crosby off for slashing Carter, Timonen lugged the puck from behind his own net and hit Briere in full flight through center ice. He dished to Gagne on the left wing, sprinted past a flat-footed Orpik, and finished off the give-and-go goal—the first Flyer powerplay score in 18 advantages—by beating Fleury's left pad.

The crowd was roaring and the Penguins, down 3-0, should have been reeling. Just eight seconds after the goal, Talbot, lining up against Carcillo for a blueline faceoff following an offsides, either saw an opportunity to spark his team or wanted to avenge the head shot that had gotten the Flyer winger suspended for Game Two. After several seconds of goading by Talbot, Carcillo responded and threw the Penguin around like a rag doll.

Carcillo, waving skyward as he was being escorted to the penalty box, asked for more noise. Talbot responded with a hushing gesture. On the next draw, Malkin bulled his way through Richards, carried the puck into the Philadelphia zone and, from behind the net, reversed on Carle to skate out front. Biron made a save, but Malkin dove and poked at the rebound before the goalie could cover it. The puck trickled under Biron's body and came to rest under his outstretched right pad, where Fedotenko pushed it into the cage to cut the lead to 3-1 just 29 seconds after Briere had scored.

A frustrated Coburn, who felt the puck had been covered, threw Fedotenko backwards onto his rear. Players on both teams paired off, but Coburn and Malkin were dealt the only minors. On the four-on-four,

Scuderi broke up an attempted Gagne pass from the half-wall that trapped Jones and sent Fedotenko and Kennedy away on a two-on-one with Timonen back. He sprawled to take away the passing lane, so Kennedy fired. Biron blockered the puck, but Eaton batted it out of the air to pull Pittsburgh within a goal at 3-2.

Timonen blocked an attempt by Kunitz to tie, but Carle took down Staal, drawing a penalty. With the Flyers shorthanded, Biron made three saves, but just 17 seconds after the successful kill, Alberts tripped Miro Satan. Again, Philadelphia killed the penalty, Biron stopping Malkin twice and Staal once. But when Fedotenko went to the box for crosschecking Gagne, the Flyers couldn't seize the opportunity to regain momentum. Their only shot on the powerplay was from the point by Carle.

Fedotenko's penalty had just expired when Letang poked the puck past Hartnell and up the boards to Guerin, who threw up a backhander from the outside of the left circle that ricocheted off Timonen and into the air. Biron reached up, but the puck hit his wrist and Crosby batted it out of the air to tie the game 3-3 with 3:01 remaining in the middle period. "To hear a little silence was gratifying," Crosby would say.

There were no parachutes attached to stomachs free-falling all over the Delaware Valley. A little more than two minutes into the third period, Orpik won a race to a loose puck and banked a pass to Malkin as he picked up speed through center ice. When Parent and Timonen backed in, Malkin left a drop pass for Gonchar, who, from the top of the right circle, blew a slapshot past Biron to the blocker side, giving the Penguins a 4-3 lead.

Philadelphia still had 17:41 to fight back but managed only four shots, none threatening. With Biron pulled, Crosby deflected a Carter center-zone pass into the Flyer end. The Pittsburgh star retrieved his own rebound behind the goal, circled out, and put away the 5-3 victory into the empty net.

As the Penguins celebrated a six-game triumph and their comeback from a 3-0 deficit to clinch it, the Flyers could do nothing but blame themselves for the most sickening playoff-game collapse in their history.

"We gave them life," Briere said in a crushed locker room. "We lost our focus after scoring the third goal and let one turn into two and eventually three. Up 3-0, all we had to do from that point on was just play solid hockey."

Instead, a team that had looked unshakable following defeats in Games Two and Four suddenly unraveled during Game Six in the apparent emotional wake of the Carcillo-Talbot bout.

"I guess he felt he needed to do something, and I was pretty confident I wouldn't lose the fight," Carcillo said. "I can see where fighting might get them going. If you show up, it doesn't matter if you win or lose.

"In hindsight, maybe I shouldn't have fought. I don't know."

The Pittsburgh players thought the bout, such as it was, had turned around everything.

"I think it was the right time," said Talbot in the locker room. "The crowd was into it. Sometimes you lose momentum. This time it gave us a little bit."

Most of the involved Flyers refuse, in retrospect, to blame Carcillo. "I don't really think that had anything to do with [the comeback], to be honest," recalls Richards. "Carcillo beat him up pretty good."

Says Holmgren: "I think it's unfortunate that people remember it that way. Our poor play and their lucky goals on bounces around the net came together at the same time. I can still see that one Crosby knocked out of the air."

Biron disagrees, feeling the bout changed everything.

"I remember [thinking], 'Why? Why are you fighting him there?'" recalls the goalie. "Maybe I wasn't focused enough to not let it bother me. But I remember thinking that wasn't the right timing.

"Didn't matter who won the fight or not. Talbot was there to get his team fired up and in the next five minutes after that, Pittsburgh seemed to be coming on really strong.

"It was up to me and everybody to respond, and we didn't."

The Penguin stars had taken it from there.

"To me, that fight could have really turned the series in our favor, or could have turned it in their favor, depending on either team's response," recalls Stevens. "It's what Malkin did next, going ahead with the puck on the faceoff against Richards, so determined in getting to the net, that I'll never forget.

"There were goals from loose pucks around the net and goals batted out of the air. But Malkin turned the whole game around."

The Flyers, nevertheless, had remained ahead 3-1 with 35 minutes to recover in an elimination game and never showed any response. "Everyone says it was the Carcillo fight, but to me, it was the way we reacted that disappointed me," remembers Stevens. "We weren't ready for it.

"It was a big-time missed opportunity."

To understand what had been lost, Philadelphia didn't need to watch Pittsburgh go on to win the Stanley Cup six weeks later. In a league where teams often have to fail in order to learn how to succeed, the Flyers had become another example.

On break-up day, Stevens called it a year of growth. But after only a four-point regular season gain over 2007-08, the failure to advance a round, and an almost incomprehensible implosion just when the team had appeared to have turned everything its way, progress in 2008-09 was a hard sell.

"You can't hold anyone accountable unless you look in the mirror first," said Richards. "I probably wasn't the most focused guy, either. It's something that I need to learn from and just not let it happen again.

"I think it hurt us down the stretch when we had to call people up. As much as it's a learning process for me, maybe it's the same thing for Paul, not giving us a little extra cap space."

Talented enough to outplay the eventual champions of 2009, the team had demonstrated its capabilities and immaturity at the same time. "We did ourselves in, not only at points of games, but points of the schedule," recalls Holmgren. "We had seen signs of this for two years."

Giroux was a huge addition to a deep group of skilled forwards, but a defense meek around the net needed a stabilizing presence and so did the locker room. Holmgren was in the market for the player who could solve both problems.

Ville Leino

Chapter 12 • 2009-10

From 3-0 Down

Even before Pittsburgh used its first-round victory over the Flyers as a springboard to the 2009 Stanley Cup, general manager Paul Holmgren had counted two Penguin superstars to none for Philadelphia.

"They had (Sidney) Crosby and (Evgeni) Malkin, the two best forwards in the game, and we had to play them all the time," recalls Holmgren. "In order to win the Stanley Cup, we probably would have to beat Pittsburgh in whatever round."

The Flyers, who had lost in a perfunctory five games to the Penguins in the 2008 Eastern Conference final, had outplayed them in large portions of a six-game defeat in 2009. But the blown 3-0 lead in Pittsburgh's 5-3 clincher was a painful extension of the maturity issues that had been plaguing Philadelphia in the two seasons since its reemergence as a contender.

While the Penguins got some lucky bounces during the Flyer collapse, it was disorder in front of Philadelphia's goal that allowed Pittsburgh to take advantage.

Fortunately, the most commanding defensive-zone presence in the game had become available to fix that problem.

In 15 NHL seasons, Chris Pronger had won both Hart (MVP) and Norris (Best Defenseman) trophies. Six other times, he had finished in the top five of the Norris balloting. After anchoring Edmonton to within one game of the 2006 Stanley Cup, Pronger had taken Anaheim to the championship the next season.

His career 142 goals and 464 assists represented only a tip of the scariest iceberg in the North American hockey sea. The reach of the 6-6, 220-pound defenseman and a mean streak documented by eight career suspensions essentially had created a moat around Pronger that made him practically inexhaustible for 27-30 minutes a game. Time and space define the functionality of any player. Because he had been given so much room, Pronger, about to turn 35, had plenty of years remaining, Holmgren believed.

"He was very into nutrition and fitness," recalls the GM. "I didn't think he had changed much from 18 to 35.

"When things were going crazy and you were having trouble in your own end, Pronger would go out there and all of a sudden the game would slow down."

"He was a special player. We were going to take our swing for the fences."

Holmgren, who coached Pronger at Hartford in his first two NHL seasons (1993-95), had made an initial call to Anaheim GM Bob Murray before the March 2009 trading deadline. Pronger's contract was expiring following the 2009-10 season. Were the Ducks going to extend him? Or, with a Cup already won, would they recycle him into younger assets?

The conversation was reasonably short. Both GMs were reluctant to tear up contending clubs so soon before the playoffs. The Flyers also needed to subtract $6.2 million in salary to fit Pronger's current salary under the cap. When Murray asked if the Flyers would be interested in talking again over the summer, Holmgren agreed that would be the opportune time to make a deal.

When Scott Niedermayer, the Ducks' other future Hall of Fame defenseman, subsequently committed to play another season, Murray could maintain a good team, save the $7 million per year Pronger would command on a new deal, and get considerable retooling pieces at the same time.

The trade talks came as no surprise to Pronger. "I knew at the deadline they were shopping me," he recalls. "I was told Philadelphia was one of the teams. There were some in the Western Conference too, just didn't know if those were actual destinations or they were being used to see what Anaheim could get for me from the Flyers."

No team was going to give up significant assets for the defenseman without a commitment beyond the upcoming season, so Murray had given suitors permission to talk to Pronger's agent, Pat Morris, about a contract extension. Pronger knew the Flyers always had been willing to pay their stars.

"But I really didn't know their team," he recalls. "Playing in the West, you lose touch with the East; for a while we only played one division in the other conference in a given year.

"I knew the Flyers were a contender again and thought highly of Philadelphia as a hockey city. When you get a chance to play in that kind of market, it's exciting."

Holmgren and Murray talked sporadically during May, and then became serious in the weeks leading up to the June 26 Entry Draft in Montreal. Holmgren had to lose some salary to fit Pronger, so he pushed Joffrey Lupul, who had an extended cap hit of $4.2 million and had scored nine goals for the Ducks during their conference final run in 2006. "[Murray] wasn't excited about it, but Joffrey had matured, so

Bob warmed up to him," recalls Holmgren.

Lupul's was the only contract of size Murray was willing to take on. He pushed for young assets or future ones. Holmgren, who was getting a monster defenseman back, was willing to include Luca Sbisa, the club's first pick in 2008 who had already played 39 NHL games but was not projected to make the 2009-10 club.

Murray demanded Philadelphia's first-round pick—21st overall—in the 2009 draft, and also negotiated with Holmgren for a conditional, pick in 2010—a third rounder that would become a No. 1 should Pronger deliver what the Flyers hoped, a Stanley Cup.

Ed Snider had declared during the summer of 2006 that Philadelphia would no longer be trading draft choices, but Holmgren and Comcast-Spectacor CEO Peter Luukko brought the Chairman on board, convincing him that Pronger was worth the sacrifice.

Recalls Holmgren: "I talked to Mr. Snider, Luukko, the coaches and (director of scouting) Chris Pryor. We agreed that if you get a chance to get that type of defenseman who can make big plays and play that many minutes, you have to do it. We had Kimmo Timonen, but needed one more top guy."

Lupul, 25, and Sbisa, 19, had been first-rounders, so essentially Holmgren was giving up three of them. But the 2009 pick was 21st overall and the 2010 choice would be 30th should the Flyers hit the jackpot and win the Cup, so these were not blue-chip picks. Philadelphia had other trading assets and perhaps could get a first-rounder back at some point.

Through the grapevine, Holmgren had heard San Jose and Washington were bidders, and Luukko believed St. Louis—where Pronger had played nine seasons—was interested in getting him back. But the Flyer GM went to the draft confident. "Pretty hard to top what we were willing to give up," he recalls. On Wednesday (the draft was Friday), I thought we were pretty close."

Fifteen minutes before the start of the draft, on the Bell Centre floor, Murray demanded the condition be dropped on the 2010 pick, making it a certain first-rounder.

Holmgren had no Plan B. There was only one Chris Pronger. The GM was out of leverage, out of time, and would be out of his mind, he believed, to let the quintessential cornerstone defenseman go to another team, especially if it was a conference rival like Washington.

"I couldn't say to Bob, 'Hold on, I've got to call my owner and see if he's OK with the extra pick,'" recalls Holmgren. "I didn't feel like there was time to process all of that."

He agreed on the spot, and then called Snider to tell him the good news. The Chairman didn't think it was so good, though. He was furious that his GM had agreed to guarantee the 2010 first-round pick without permission.

"I'll talk to you later," Snider said tersely to Holmgren.

In announcing the blockbuster deal—probably the second-biggest in franchise history to the one in 1992 for Eric Lindros—Holmgren described Pronger as a player who "can make life miserable for the other teams."

Just as Snider had the capability to make life miserable for his general manager. Back in Philadelphia, the Chariman unloaded on Holmgren and Luukko. "You guys think you [bleeping] own this team?" he said.

When Pronger was introduced to the media at a Wachovia Center press conference on July 7, Snider said all the right things. But when asked to talk about the acquisition as a great moment in Flyer history, he couldn't help himself.

"This better be," the Chairman said. "We gave up a lot."

Holmgren had no doubt that four first-round picks (counting Lupul and Sbisa) and the additional third-round 2010 pick included in the deal (which also brought minor-league throw-in Ryan Dingle) were worth it for a player who would make everybody around him better. Pronger's arrival would take some opposition attention away from Timonen and help to slot Braydon Coburn and Matt Carle to their capabilities in a top four that could be as good as any team's in the league.

Pronger put on an orange and white jersey with the No. 20 his father wore as a senior amateur. "I took his number, not his game," the defenseman laughed.

There were smiles everywhere. Not since the days of Mark Howe had the Flyers possessed a player so capable of controlling the defensive zone. Pronger's 1,457 penalty minutes suggested it would be accomplished with different means, however. Asked what statement he would want to make to foes like Alex Ovechkin and Crosby, Pronger teased: "I think you know the answer to that."

Reminded that Peter Forsberg, Paul Coffey, Dale Hawerchuk and Adam Oates were other future Hall of Famers who had been acquired late in their careers in failed attempts to end a 34-season Stanley Cup drought, Pronger said, "My job is to break the trend."

Adding that he hoped to finish his career in Philadelphia, Pronger said he was not going to play as long as Chris Chelios (age 47), but that 40 was a reasonable expectation. The defenseman claimed that his dedication to his body had paid off with him feeling "24." That afternoon, Holmgren and Morris left the press conference and negotiated a deal that backed up the Flyer belief Pronger could anchor them into his fifth decade.

"My early conversation with Pat, right after the trade, was that we had a young team we want to keep together, so we wanted to get the cap number at just under $5 million if we could," recalls Holmgren. "Pat had other clients on the team, like Mike Richards. He understood."

They celebrated at dinner with Snider and then the next day announced a seven-year, $34.9 million extension to begin in 2010-11. The deal was front-loaded to pay Pronger $7.6 million the first two years, with declining salaries until he would finish up at age 42, making $525,000.

"I think both parties wanted to get it handled in a timely fashion," said Pronger. "Knowing they have me in place, the Flyers can make moves either this year or next year."

Circumstances were demanding goaltending changes immediately.

Marty Biron had backstopped Philadelphia's resurgence to contention and won two playoff series in 2008. But initial talks for an extension of his expiring two-year deal had left a wide disparity between the goalie's expectations and what the club felt was workable.

"I would have signed Marty, but we certainly couldn't afford the number he was looking for," recalls Holmgren. "We tried a couple times during the year. One deal was two years for $3.5 million, and then, all of sudden, [agent Gilles Lupien] asked for five years at a significantly higher number. We didn't have a good feeling about being able to continue with Marty."

Holmgren had not waited until Biron's contract ran out at the end of the 2008-09 season to begin to look elsewhere. The most talented goalie on the market, at the likely best price, was Ray Emery. But he had baggage.

Emery had gone 33-16-6, 2.47, .918 during 2006-07 with Ottawa, whom he then carried to the Stanley Cup Final with a 13-7 record, a 2.27 GAA and three shutouts. But the next year, he began behaving erratically, repeatedly showing up late for practice and getting into fights with teammates. He later estimated the number of times he and his Lamborghini were pulled over by policemen at 30. After a road-rage incident, a senior citizen accused Emery of threatening to kill him.

After the Senators bought out the remainder of his contract, Emery signed with Atlant Mytischi of the Kontinental Hockey League, where, after being pulled from a game, he took a swing at a trainer who tried to put a hat on the goalie's head, and then chased him up the tunnel.

Holmgren's interest in the goaltender went back a year, when he sought information from Phantom coach John Paddock, who had coached Emery both at Ottawa and for their farm team at Binghamton. Turned out, he had just committed to the KHL, but Paddock, who had been fired in the midst of some of Emery's chaotic behavior, did not tell the Flyer GM to steer clear.

At the worst of Emery's behavior in Ottawa, Paddock had told the *Canadian Press* that the goalie "wasn't preparing to play, not taking the game seriously." But those problems were not seen prior to, or during, his successful 2006-07 season, so Paddock encouraged Holmgren to check the goaltender out.

"When his life was in proper working order, he was a quick, big (6-2), gritty goalie," recalls Paddock. "His disciplinary stuff on the ice (several fights with other goalies) really came from his pure competitiveness.

"When Paul asked me if I would want him on my team, the answer was yes, but with some qualifications. I said, 'You need to see if he wants to pay the price, on and off the ice, to be one of the top goalies in the NHL. If you believe that, you should go for it.'"

Holmgren flew to Ottawa in March, after the early end of the KHL season.

"We were at Ray's condo for four or five hours talking about where he was in life," recalls the GM. "He opened up to me."

Emery told Holmgren he had come to camp following the playoff run out of shape, had allowed his frustrations with a poor season to result in bad behavior, and that he felt responsible for the firing of Paddock, a coach who had been good for his career. The goaltender said he realized that one more opportunity in the NHL might be the last he would receive.

Holmgren sought the opinions of former teammates, coaches, and trainers and came to a conclusion that Emery was a good person who had made some bad choices. When Snider and Luukko expressed skepticism, the GM had Emery come to Philadelphia to meet with them and they were impressed.

"He had been a number one goalie in the league, been to the Stanley Cup Final, had a decent year in Russia," recalls Holmgren. He was only 26.

"I think people deserve second chances."

Emery was signed to a one-year, $1.5 million deal. "The novelty of going out or doing certain things wears off," the new goalie told the media.

"I'm always changing it around. I've learned tons of lessons. I realize I had a great thing going and lost a lot of people that I enjoyed hanging out with. I want to get back to having those good relationships. I think that's the reason I'm going to change."

Biron had become aware of the Flyers' interest in Emery even while the 2008-09 season was continuing. "It was not easy to learn that," Biron recalls.

"Paul had said to me after the Washington series [in 2008] something like, 'Marty, you just earned yourself a long time with us. It's not a matter of if we sign you to an extension, but when.'

"It never happened. And I think my play fell. [Maybe] it was because of expectations (raised by the semifinal run) or the change of the team's makeup. I'm not trying to use excuses, but I was disappointed we weren't talking about my future.

"Maybe that put added pressure on myself, and it kind of started the beginning of the end for me in Philadelphia. I remember telling my agent, 'Why don't we do it over five to six years, start at $5 million and go down to $600k.' But I never got any numbers.

"Business is business. I ended up switching agents (to Peter Fish of Boston-based Global Hockey Consultants). Even on the morning of July 1 (when free agency began), I thought we still were talking to the Flyers."

Another goaltending spot was open. The dysplastic hip that had been endured for several years by Antero Niittymaki forced a decision on the backup's future.

An examination during the season by Dr. Bryan Kelly, a renowned hip specialist at New York's Hospital for Special Surgery, had yielded a poor prognosis. During a speakerphone call in Holmgren's office between Dr. Kelly, the GM, (head athletic trainer) Jim McCrossin, and Niittymaki, the 28-year-old goalie was informed the ball of his femur was severely deteriorated and that he would need hip replacement surgery in the foreseeable future.

"Niittyß broke down crying," recalls Holmgren. "I felt so bad; he was one of my favorite guys.

"I said, 'If you need to retire from playing, we will find a job for you.' But he wanted to continue to play."

That was because Niittymaki, somehow, was having his best NHL season.

"Everyday it took an hour to get ready for practice," he recalls. "I hoped the shots came to the right because my left leg wasn't working as well. I wouldn't even call what I was doing a butterfly. I was only going down because there was no range of motion anymore.

"I took a lot of pills. On the day I went to see [Dr. Kelly], I told the cab driver to drop me about three blocks away and I would walk, but then I had to stop and take a break.

"The doctor looked at my x-rays and MRI and said, 'I'm surprised you are walking.' But I was having a good year (finishing 29-15-8 (2.76, .912). I didn't have to change the way I played, just had to be a little bit more patient, read the plays better, and I think that made me a better goalie. The biggest thing was when things weren't going well, I had learned how to get back on track."

Walking was much harder on the hip than skating, enabling Niittymaki to keep playing. He went with McCrossin to see Dr. Michael Millis at Boston's Children's Hospital, who had enjoyed some success with an operation that moved the pelvis to make it a better fit. "But the doctor told me if I did that, I would be done playing," recalls Niittymaki.

He remained under Dr. Millis's care for the rest of the season, driving to Boston with McCrossin for periodic checkups and drainings. "Normally, the hip joint should have about 5 cc of fluid," recalls McCrossin. "Every few months, Dr. Millis would take out 30 to 50, and Nitty would feel better."

As nobody ever had continued to play the sport following a hip replacement, Niittymaki decided to keep going as long as he could and have the replacement after his career ended. "We couldn't take a chance any longer with him," recalls Holmgren.

The GM had moved onto exploring two former Flyers who had once keyed the team to semifinal berths—Robert Esche and Brian Boucher. Esche, a hero of 2004 who had angered Holmgren with his treatment of Niittymaki as they competed for the No. 1 job in 2006-07, had found his game again by playing two years in Russia.

"I talked to him for a couple hours last week and he's a different guy," Holmgren told the media. "He struggled with a lot of things towards the end of his time here, but family is bigger in his life now."

Instead, the GM decided to bring back Boucher for a third tour with the organization. After starring during the 2000 run, struggling as a sophomore, and losing his job to Roman Cechmanek, Boucher had been traded to Phoenix, then done short stints with Calgary, Chicago and Columbus before signing an AHL contract with Philadelphia in 2007-08. A strong half-season's work with the Phantoms earned Boucher another NHL shot with San Jose, where he had played 27 games over two seasons.

"My confidence was back," recalls Boucher. "But Jonas Gustavsson was the big free agent that summer, off a great World Championship, and the Sharks were going to try and sign him. So I wasn't their first priority.

"I was a backup at that stage. If somebody had interest in me, I couldn't sit around too long or the music was going to stop without there being any chairs left."

When Holmgren made a two-year, $1.9 million offer on the first day of free agency, Boucher grabbed it. "I'd loved it when I came back two years earlier to the Phantoms, but I had wished it was the Flyers," he recalls. "Now I could play for them again. The most success I had had in my career was with Philadelphia; I was fired up."

Three weeks later, Biron also took what he could get—a one-year, $1.4 million deal with the Islanders. "Every day I was calling my agent and there was nothing," he recalls. "You see on the ticker that this guy has signed and that guy has signed, so what am I going to do?

"Finally, I could either go back to Buffalo to be a backup or do one year on Long Island, where it was going to be me and Dwayne Roloson, playing 1A and 1B. I decided to take a shot there."

Biron finished his Flyer career with a 65-47-16 record, a 2.71 goals-against average and .915 save percentage in two-plus seasons. He ranked third in franchise history in save percentage and 10th in shutouts (seven) and was a star in playoff series wins over the Capitals and Canadiens.

Most important, in the recollection of coach John Stevens, was the credibility Biron brought to the Flyers' rebuild. After being acquired at the trade deadline of the miserable 2006-07 season, he decided to re-up without testing free agency.

"That was really important for us that he liked what was going on," remembers Stevens.

Biron went on to play three more full NHL seasons with the Islanders and Rangers. Today he works in Buffalo as an instructor for the Academy of Hockey, while doing television and radio commentary. During his playing career, nothing ever came close to his 2007-08 season in Philadelphia, and when the Flyers lost in the conference final to Pittsburgh that year, he remembers wondering if anything ever would again.

"I was thinking, 'Who knows, I may never even make it back to the playoffs, let alone this close to the Cup," he recalls. "And that's what happened, I was never a No. 1 again.

"You know what my best Philadelphia memory was? [The overtime win in] Game Seven in Washington was up there, but it was the first time being on the Flyers when they played "God Bless America." I was in my crease right where Lauren Hart sings, so not only could I hear her through the speaker, but her actual voice. The hair on my neck was standing up and I had goosebumps.

"All those years I was with Buffalo and we played Philly so often in the playoffs, we hated the big, bad Flyers and their big, bad fans. I'm glad I got to experience it from the other side. There are a lot of good people in the organization, people I still talk to."

Niittymaki found work, too. On July 10, he signed a one-year contract with Tampa Bay. "I understood the Flyers couldn't take a chance on me, but I was really disappointed," he recalls. "I had been expecting to stay and maybe even challenge to be No. 1."

He played two more seasons in the NHL, had the left hip replaced, and still played another year in the minors, as well as one more in Finland until the right hip forced a second replacement surgery. When Niittymaki retired, he took Holmgren up on his offer of a job in the Philadelphia organization and scouted for two seasons before becoming the general manager of TPS Turku, the most successful team in the Finnish league's history.

"The Flyers mean a lot to me," he says. "They gave me a chance to play (as a sixth-round pick) and then to work for them.

"If you treat them well, they treat you well."

That was what Ian Laperriere always had heard while playing 15 seasons with the Blues, Rangers, Kings and Avalanche. During that time, Holmgren had often been told there was no harder worker or better teammate in the league. "I coveted him for a long time," said Holmgren in signing the 35-year-old right wing to a three-year, $3.5 million contract, despite the paltry seven goals Laperriere had scored in 2008-09 with Colorado. The GM felt the signing strengthened the fourth line and penalty killing considerably.

Laperriere had turned down a bigger offer from Phoenix. "Winning is everything," he said on July 15, when introduced to the Philadelphia media. "I've played many years and a lot of games, but I don't have any bling-bling to show. I told my agent (Pat Brisson), 'that's why I want to go there.'"

Pronger had been added for his voice as well as his long, mean stick. But Holmgren wanted as much professionalism in the locker room as possible. Social media reports of nightlife by the growing contingent of young Flyers living in Olde City Philadelphia, were troubling the GM and his coach.

"The issue has been raised by John [Stevens] and myself with all the players," Holmgren told Wayne Fish of the *Bucks County Courier Times.*

"I think this all falls under the umbrella of discipline. On-ice discipline is not overstaying your shift. It's off-ice discipline to take better care of yourself the night before a game. That's a natural maturation process that a lot of our younger players are still going through.

"We've addressed that. We'll see how it goes this year. All our players have been talked to about it. Is it an issue? The fact that we've talked about it, I guess it is an issue."

Certainly it never had been with Mike Knuble. But with Holmgren's expectation that James van Riemsdyk, the ready-to-turn-pro 2007 first-round pick, would make up for some of Knuble's usual 20 goals, and the team being tight against the salary cap, there was not enough money to keep the 36-year-old right wing for a fifth Flyer season.

"I was willing to take a little bit less just [to avoid] the hassle of moving and starting over," Knuble recalls. "My kids liked where they were going to school, and that was worth a hometown [discount], but I wasn't going to bend over backwards."

He had contract conversations with Holmgren into the morning of July 1. Knuble wanted the same money ($2.8 million per year) he had earned on his expiring deal, while Holmgren was skeptical the 36-year old winger could get that much on the open market. Regardless, Holmgren didn't have it to spend.

Knuble was proven right. He signed a two-year $5.6 million deal with Washington that virtually duplicated his expired Flyer contract.

"We put a lot of time and effort into bringing Mike back and, to his credit, he put a lot of consideration into hanging around," recalls Holmgren. "In the end, Washington's offer was probably too good for him to refuse. We couldn't afford it cap-wise, so I don't think we could have played it any differently."

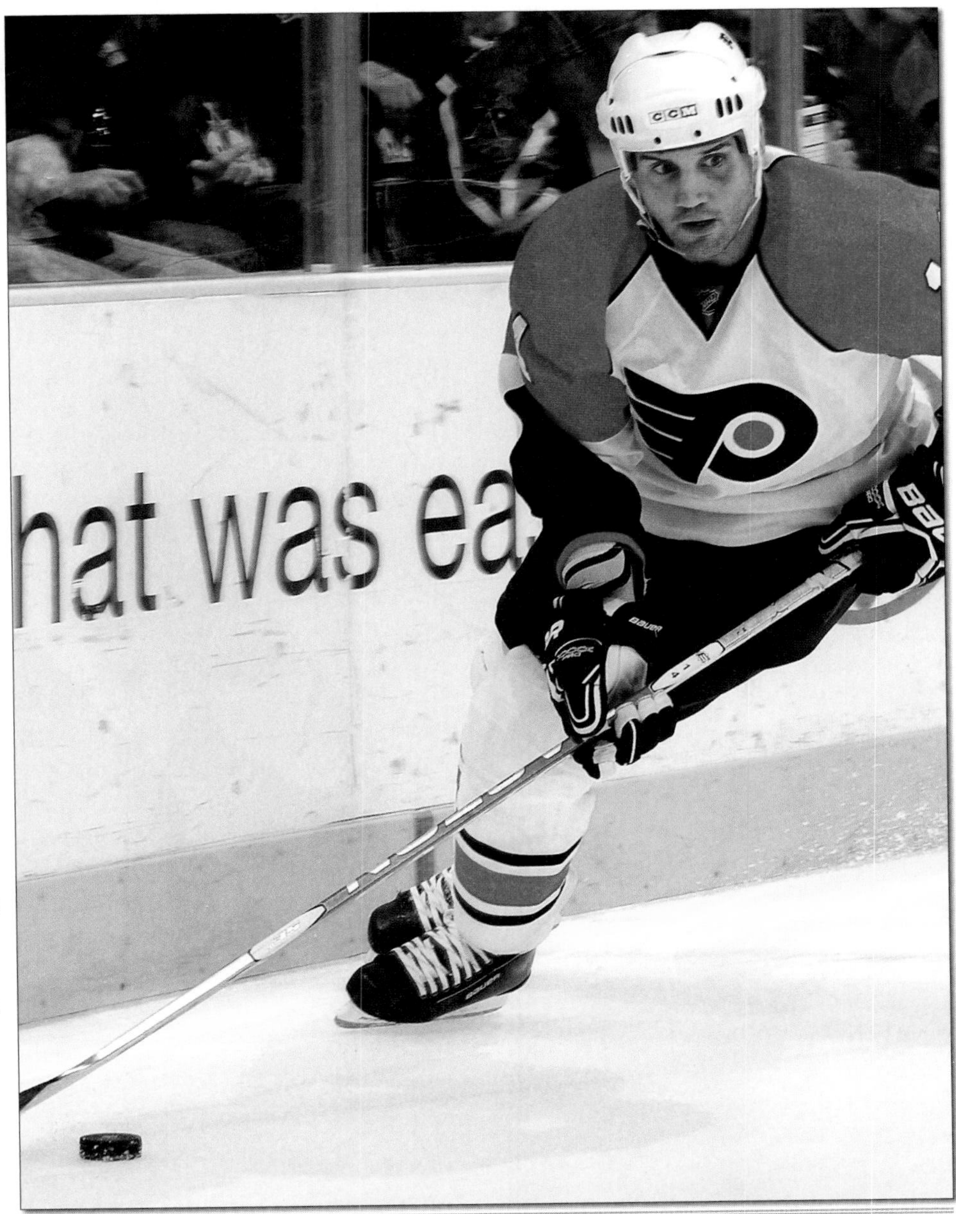

Ian Laperriere joined the Flyers after 1,001 games with other NHL teams.

Knuble scored 118 goals and 111 assists in 338 games with Philadelphia, and added six goals in the playoffs, including one in double overtime against the Capitals. He was a shoulder to lean on for teammates, a voice of reason in the media, and a player who fully grasped the privilege of being a Flyer.

"It was tough to go," recalls Knuble, today a coach with Detroit's AHL affiliate in his hometown of Grand Rapids, MI. "I liked my role and how I was treated by the organization. Those were my most productive years.

"The Flyers are not an original six team but they had that feel. We made a lot of good friends away from the game. My family had a good time."

By re-signing with Philadelphia in the midst of the 2006-07 collapse, Knuble had taken some ownership in restoring the franchise to contention.

So had Derian Hatcher, who, in turning down the opportunity to be traded during that season, was rewarded with Philadelphia's 2007-08 rebound. The Flyers ultimately benefitted for having signed Hatcher coming out of the lockout. Initially presumed to be stuck in a time warp as the NHL cracked down on physical aggression by defensemen, Hatcher had adapted well.

But after spending the 2008-09 season in a failed rehab, Hatcher, 37, underwent knee-replacement surgery that ended his playing career. He was taking over as player development coach from Eric Desjardins, who, after a year of counseling Philadelphia draftees, had decided he didn't want to travel.

"I was proud to retire as a Flyer," recalls Hatcher, the team's 14th captain. "I played my 1,000th game right at the end of that really bad year, and when the team did a presentation for me on the ice, the fans were unbelievable to me.

Peter Zezel had enjoyed impressive longevity, too, going on to play 15 seasons after being traded by the Flyers. But his most successful teams were the first five in Philadelphia. The city's hockey fans were stunned and saddened by his death in the summer of 2009 from hemolytic anemia at age 44.

"I spoke to him last week when I first learned he was having troubles," said Snider. "He was hopeful, as was I and all of those who loved him. Peter was a good friend of mine. This is a real tragedy."

After being traded to the Blues for Mike Bullard in 1988, Zezel spent time with the Capitals, Leafs, Stars, Devils and Canucks. In 1999, he requested a trade from Vancouver to either Toronto or Buffalo so that he could be closer to a niece dying from cancer. When a trade sent him instead to the Anaheim Ducks, he retired to run the Peter Zezel Hockey and Sports Camp near Toronto.

In 2001, Zezel had been near death from the rare blood disease that would claim his life, but made a complete recovery. Eight years later, he began suffering severe headaches and required chemotherapy and the removal of his spleen. Brain hemorrhaging caused Zezel to lapse into a coma, and his parents had taken him off life support so that his organs could be donated.

Zezel never married. The thought of him not being the marrying kind brought smiles to the faces of everyone who knew him and the multitude of females who wished they did.

"He was a living matinee idol," Rick Tocchet told Tim Panaccio of CSN Philadelphia. "When we would go to bars, guys would want to talk to me about my fights, and the girls were all over him. I would get his overflow."

Zezel had a role in the 1986 hockey movie *Youngblood*, starring Rob Lowe and Patrick Swayze. Not only did he have good looks, but the ability to make a look-off pass. Strong faceoff work also earned him a spot on two Stanley Cup finalists in his first three Flyer seasons. The second-round pick in 1983 played 310 of his 873 career NHL games for Philadelphia, scoring 91 goals and 170 assists.

"Pete had a huge heart," recalled Dave Poulin, the captain of Zezel's Flyer teams. "He was a fun-loving guy but he really cared for his teammates, on and off the ice. He was also great with kids and kind of a big kid himself. He took things to heart and I think Mike Keenan knew that in the way he coached Peter."

With the Spectrum awaiting the wrecking ball, the Flyers had explored moving the Phantoms to Boardwalk Hall in Atlantic City while continuing to practice in Voorhees, NJ. But Rob and Jim Brooks, the sons of Bob Brooks, the once-chief financial officer for Westinghouse Air Brake in Pittsburgh and an investor in both the Penguins and Pirates, had a better idea.

Impressed by the popularity of the Penguin farm team at Wilkes Barre/Scranton, and intrigued by a survey that projected the Lehigh Valley as an even better market for a team, the Brooks brothers had purchased the Phantoms in April for $3.1 million and moved them to Glen Falls, NY while developing an arena in downtown Allentown. Comcast-Spectacor gained a 10-year contract for food service and ticketing at the proposed new facility.

The Adirondack Phantoms anticipated a three-year stay at the aged Glens Falls Civic Center. Paddock, the AHL team's coach for the final year at the Spectrum, would not be going with them. He had accepted Holmgren's offer to become the Flyer assistant GM.

Holmgren had tried to replace Paddock with Peter Laviolette, who was fired by Carolina in December 2008, 18 months after leading the Hurricanes to the Stanley Cup.

"I had gotten to know Peter a little at the Olympics in Torino (where Laviolette was the USA coach and Holmgren assistant GM)," recalls Holmgren. "He wanted to keep his options open in case an NHL job became available; he had some television stuff to tide him over, so he wasn't going to take the Phantoms job.

"But we sat for three or four hours in Montreal at the draft, and I got some nuts and bolts about how he thought. It was food for thought for me down the road."

Holmgren hired former Flames coach Greg Gilbert to replace Paddock behind the Phantom bench, and also changed the Flyer goaltending coach. Rejean Lemelin, who was in the position for 15 years, was replaced with Jeff Reese, who played 174 NHL games, mostly with the Maple Leafs, and had worked with the Lightning goalies for 10 seasons. He had been fired by the new Tampa Bay ownership soon after

GM Jay Feaster had resigned.

"We needed someone in a full-time, everyday role, studying video and debriefing goalies after the games," recalls Holmgren. "I knew Jeff from when he played for the Whalers. He had been praised for his work with (Nikolai) Khabibulin in Tampa that helped the Lightning win a Stanley Cup.

"Bill Barber (Lightning director of player personnel from 2002 to 2008) was all positive about Jeff, and so was (former Lightning coach) John Tortorella."

In August, Pronger, Richards, Jeff Carter and Simon Gagne were invitees to an orientation camp in Calgary for Canadian Olympic Team prospects. The 2010 Winter Games were to be held during February in Vancouver. Gagne, who had undergone right hip surgery in May, tried out the repairs, felt tightness in his groin, and came home to get checked by Flyer doctors. He took an injection of his own blood—a process called platelet rich plasma—to speed recovery.

Who wouldn't have been eager to be part of a 2009-10 Flyer team containing Chris Pronger? An estimated 2,000 fans showed up for the first day of camp to watch drills at the Flyers Skate Zone practice facility in Voorhees, NJ. "You see that and get the extra adrenaline going," Laperriere said.

Snider felt it, too. When *The Hockey News* picked Philadelphia to win the Stanley Cup, the Chairman apologized for the dressing down he gave Holmgren in the belief too much had been given up in the Pronger trade.

"Obviously [the magazine's] not partial. It's a good feeling that people think we've done the right things and are on the right track," Snider said, adding that he had not been so excited for the start of a season "in a long, long time."

One step at a time, Pronger cautioned. "You certainly don't want to be picked last," he said. "Usually that means you are in for a long haul.

"But June's a long ways off. To play under that scrutiny and that pressure each and every day is exhausting. You've got to be able to make your mistakes and learn from them. There a lot of new faces here, guys playing in different roles. At the end of the day, we expect to see a big difference from September to hopefully May and June. That's how good teams are built, through a gradual process."

As an example, Carle, Pronger's partner from Day One of camp, had never played a first-pair volume of minutes. At three-four, Timonen and Coburn had proven contrastingly effective with ample time together the previous two seasons. So Stevens and Holmgren spent training camp mulling options for the last two spots.

Included were four-year veteran Randy Jones; Ryan Parent, a prime acquisition in the Peter Forsberg trade; Ole-Kristian Tollefsen, a Norwegian defenseman signed as a free agent after four years with the Columbus Blue Jackets; Oskars Bartulis, a third round pick in 2005 out of Latvia; and Danny Syvret, a once third-round pick by Edmonton who had spent the 2008-09 season with the Phantoms after being acquired for center Ryan Potulny.

Jones was sent to the Phantoms, saving $2.75 million against the cap, and Bartulis was returned to the farm.

Van Riemsdyk scored three goals in the preseason and made the team, as did two free agents—center Blair Betts, who came to camp on a tryout basis after four years with the Rangers, and center Mika Pyörälä, a 28-year-old Finnish free agent with no North American experience.

On opening night, eight players had changed from the 2008-09 line-up. But one thing had not. The Flyers, constantly shorthanded for the last two seasons, had to kill nine penalties. Nevertheless, Emery debuted with a 2-0 shutout in Raleigh. When he beat the Devils, 5-2 in Newark, Philadelphia had won back-to-back road games to start a season for the first time in their history.

Richards' hat trick and four second-period assists by Carle—tying an NHL record—enabled the Flyers to reach overtime of the home opener against Washington and, from there, Danny Briere's goal won it, 6-5. But Betts, who had been anchoring a strong fourth line with Dan Carcillo and Laperriere in the infant season, fell awkwardly on his stick in taking a defensive-zone faceoff and suffered a shoulder dislocation expected to keep him out for a month.

The first loss of the season, 5-4 in Pittsburgh when Coburn gave the puck away to Tyler Kennedy for the winning goal, wasn't easy to swallow. Afterwards, the Penguins' Kris Letang held up a bandaged finger and hinted that he had been bitten by Scott Hartnell. "I think he knows what he did," Letang said before Hartnell's denial gave reporters something to chew on. "He had his hands in my face doing the face wash and we're rolling around," said the Philadelphia winger. "I can't say what happened.

The following day, his denial was a little stronger. "His bare hand scratched my face, and that's about it," said Hartnell, and NHL vice president Colin Campbell bought it, not finding enough evidence to warrant supplemental discipline.

When Anaheim came to town, Lupul, the former Flyer and Olde City resident, was asked if he had become a Duck because too many good times had rolled. "The reason I was traded was to get Chris Pronger," Lupul said. "Richie (Mike Richards) and Carter told me people have been talking about [the nightlife], but they are all professionals. Never once would they put themselves ahead of the team."

After Anaheim's Teemu Selanne made a 2-0 third-period Philadelphia lead disappear with consecutive goals six minutes apart, then scored again to win the shootout, 3-2, Lupul relayed his exchange with the media to Richards. The Flyer captain called the press box and requested that reporters focus on other subject matter, but his appeal was ignored.

Rows with the media notwithstanding, Stevens thought some rowing of boats would build camaraderie. With a five-day break before a game at Florida, the team arrived early and went out onto Biscayne Bay for a 4.5-mile race. The coaching staff's boat beat the fastest player boat, Pronger's, by three minutes.

After Philadelphia lost, 4-2, to the Panthers, Stevens shook up the lines, leaving only the Hartnell, Carter and Briere unit intact and merging Gagne and Richards with heretofore fourth-liner Arron

Asham. "He's got more skill than people think," said Gagne.

Dave Schultz, never a top six forward, once scored 20 goals in a season. But that was not the preeminent reason he had been elected to the Flyers' Hall of Fame. With his induction coming on November 16, The Hammer held his press conference from the Spectrum's penalty box.

"It wasn't as crowded as being on the bench," Schultz said nostalgically. "I would have a towel and a Coke. It was relaxing."

The scheduling of only one game in 11 days threatened to give the players too much downtime, but they appeared to use it well. With Tollefsen replacing Parent, who had suffered a groin pull at Florida, Philadelphia beat Boston, 4-3, on Giroux's lone goal for either team in the shootout, making Dollar Dog Night (21,235 sold) at the Wachovia Center a delicious success.

Jeff Carter and Arron Asham after a 3-2 win over the New York Islanders on March 9, 2010.

When Asham scored for a third straight game, Briere tallied twice, and van Riemsdyk scored his first NHL goal on a breakaway against Florida goalie Tomas Vokoun, the Flyers avenged their loss in Sunrise with a 5-1 victory that ran their record to 5-2-1. "Something you dream about your whole life," said van Riemsdyk, whose line with Carter and Briere had recorded 20 of the 38 Philadelphia shots on goal.

The hardest shot of the evening, however, was a body blow by Richards. Catching David Booth coming across the middle of the ice with his head down, the Flyer leveled the Florida winger with a shoulder to the head. He lay motionless on the ice, was taken off on a stretcher and spent the night at Pennsylvania Hospital. Severely concussed, Booth would not return until January, but because shoulder contact is legal and there was no rule against hits to the head, Richards wasn't fined or suspended.

Boucher got the first start of his return to Philadelphia against San Jose, for which he had played the previous season-and-a-half. He allowed four goals on 28 shots in a 4-1 Wachovia Center loss. "All four were awful," he said after the game. "I'll be better."

The team could only hope the same for Gagne, whose quickness seemed to have been left on the operating table during summer hip surgery. Off to the worst start of his 10-year career—one goal and four assists in the first nine games—he lasted just one shift in the third period against the Sharks. Gagne, who had undergone a repair for a double sports hernia three years earlier, was again diagnosed with a rupture. After consults with doctors in Philadelphia and Montreal, the left wing underwent surgery in the Canadian city and was expected to be out for six to eight weeks.

When a 2-0 lead at Washington blew up into a 4-2 loss, the winning goal scored by Alexander Semin going in off Timonen's knee, the Flyers had won only two of their last seven games. "Every time bad breaks happen, I'm on the ice," said Timonen, who after 10 games was a combined minus-15 with partner Coburn. The 43 shots Philadelphia had launched at Washington goalie Jose Theodore were no consolation to Pronger.

"You can have all the effort you want, but if you don't win, you don't win," said the defenseman. "It's no secret where a lot of the goals are scored in this league. We have to get dirtier."

Stevens cancelled a scheduled off-day and ran a practice with extra skating. "You have to maybe do a little more to make sure the near-misses turn into goals," said the coach, turning up the volume to the point where the players thought it best to turn off the stereo in the locker room.

"It's kind of good," smiled Laperriere. "The music we listen to is awful."

With Gagne on long-term injured reserve, the Flyers had $5.25 million in extra cap room until he returned. Holmgren asked for re-entry waivers on Jones, who had been stashed with the Phantoms because of his $2.75 million cap hit. But the defenseman was claimed by Los Angeles, so Philadelphia not only lost the player, but also had to carry half of his cap obligation.

"I thought the teams with an interest wouldn't have the room to claim him," said Holmgren. "That's the risk you take. He certainly would have helped us."

A groin pull suffered by Briere in Washington required an injection and rest, but Parent and Betts were ready to go on October 31 against Carolina. Coburn broke out of his doldrums with two goals 90 seconds apart and the Flyers ended their three-game losing streak with a 6-1 victory.

Across the parking lot, Pearl Jam was wrapping up four shows—and the Spectrum 42 years as America's Showplace—with a three-hour-and-35-minute concert. Snider had invited several thousands of his closest friends for a January 17 bash with his favorite band, Earth,

Wind and Fire, for a final, final farewell. But while the doors were closing forever, customers still could take with them more than just memories. Arena seats were available at RememberTheSpectrum.com for $295 each, or $395 for a pair.

When the Flyers put up six goals for the second straight game—this time in a 6-2 victory against the Rick Tocchet-coached Tampa Bay Lighting—it appeared the offense finally was cooking. Thanks in part to the powerplay time van Riemsdyk was getting in the absence of Gagne and Briere, the rookie had 13 points in the first 12 games.

"He has a unique ability to protect the puck and has a sense of where people are," said Holmgren. "His play away from the puck has been good, too. We're pleasantly surprised at how James has done."

The Carcillo-Betts-Laperriere unit, which enjoyed a five-point night in a 5-2 victory at Buffalo, was also a revelation. Certainly Philadelphia was getting better performance from its fourth line than from the rotating cast of the third defensive pair. When Tollefsen suffered a concussion in a 2-1 shootout win against the Blues, Bartulis was recalled from the Phantoms.

Briere scored twice in his return as Emery, receiving treatment for groin discomfort, beat the team that let him go—Ottawa—5-1, at the Wachovia Center. Boucher then stopped 39 shots to defeat the Kings, 3-2, at the Staples Center. But when Emery lost 6-3 at San Jose and 3-1 at Phoenix, the goalie was yanked after allowing four goals on 17 shots in a 5-4 defeat at Colorado. The Flyers had not only lost three straight games, but Betts (again) and Darroll Powe to shoulder injuries. Briere was also given a two-game suspension for leaving his feet to hit the Avalanche's Scott Hannan just after he scored a goal.

The grateful, shorthanded Flyers got by the Islanders, 2-1, on Thanksgiving Eve, but on Black Friday, there were no bargains to be found as Philadelphia lost 4-2 to the Sabres. That contest is best remembered as the day Laperriere went shopping for pain. Late in the first period, he went to his knees to block a shot from Buffalo's Jason Pominville and took a puck square in the mouth, breaking bones at both the top and bottom of his jaw, and knocking out seven teeth—five real and two false. Laperriere required 80 stitches.

"I went down, saw my teeth on the ice," recalls Laperriere. "I'm bleeding, and [bleeped], cause I put myself in that position."

Briere, serving the final game of his suspension, came into the training room as Laperriere lay on the table. "You'll be all right," Briere said.

Laperriere wasn't buying it. "Look at me!" he demanded, spitting more blood.

"No, I can't," Briere said.

Laperriere insisted he wanted to go back into the game.

"(Trainer) Sal Raffa looked at the doctors like, 'Is he for real?'" recalls Laperriere. "But I'd had plenty of concussions, so I knew what they felt like. I didn't have one."

He returned for four shifts in the third period and then didn't miss a game while waiting for his dentures. The dentist called one day to tell him that the package containing them had arrived ripped, opened, and empty. They had apparently been stolen in the mail.

"Who the [bleep] would do that?" Laperriere asked.

"They're made with gold," said the dentist.

A story like that makes one never want to smile again. Two weeks later, the replacement bridge arrived.

In the meantime, the Philadelphia offense had completely lost its bite. "I'm not disappointed with the effort, but we have to find a way to sharpen up offensively," said Stevens, after the Flyers outshot the Thrashers, 34-18, but were shut out 1-0 in Atlanta, a fifth loss in six games. "Sometimes there's a fine line between scoring and not scoring, and we have to start crossing that line."

Holmgren had been aggravated for two years by Philadelphia's inconsistency, but says he had not gone into the season thinking coaching was part of the problem. "I thought we had to improve the team," he recalls, and the GM had significantly done so with Pronger's arrival. But a club that had repeatedly scored its way out of trouble had stopped attacking.

Stevens' conservative, one-forechecker system hardly had held the Flyers back in the previous two seasons, when the team twice finished fifth in the league in goals. "I know we put a lot of time into working on our rushes during those years with Johnny," recalls assistant coach Joe Mullen. But as confidence eroded, the system suddenly appeared too conservative.

"It seemed like we were in neutral, not good either offensively or defensively," recalls Holmgren. "I had liked the defensive structure John had given us. We had offensive players who were cognizant of playing defensively, but they had become stuck in the mud.

"Players sometimes get bored playing a certain way. They need a new challenge."

A few hours after the Black Friday loss to the Sabres, Holmgren had called Laviolette, who was working as a studio analyst for TSN in Canada. Known for his aggressive offensive philosophy, Laviolette was asked by the Flyer GM to watch his team and report back with an opinion.

Snider offered the obligatory statement backing the embattled Stevens, whose soft-spoken manner was an issue in the fan chat rooms.

"To fly off the handle and do something out of character because of frustration isn't going to help anybody, although I do think we're being demanding and we need to be demanding," Stevens said. "Playing well and losing isn't good enough."

When the season had started, Stevens didn't have to be told by his superiors that any allowances for the youth of his club had been used up. "I had a real sense we had to get off to a good start and be a serious contender that year," he recalls. "We couldn't go through the inconsistencies we had before.

"Clearly, we'd improved our team adding a guy like Pronger. This year had to be a big step in terms of performance or, without question, changes would be made."

He didn't know how much time he had. The 38-shot effort the Flyers put into their 3-0 Wachovia Center defeat by Vancouver on December 3 was not going to be looked upon as encouraging, not when it was the fifth loss in six games and the second consecutive one by shutout.

The players called a postgame meeting. "Basically, it was about what me and Chris (Pronger) have been saying," Briere reported. "We have to play with more passion. You have to stop blaming everybody and get a good look at yourself in the mirror.

"If you're willing to do a little more, it's going to go a long way."

Holmgren had gone back decades with Stevens, who, except for six years in the Hartford system, had been in the Flyer organization since 1984. Together, they had endured the 2006-07 collapse and brought the team out of it to a semifinal berth the next season. Emotionally, this was a brutal call for the GM. If he were to change coaches, it wouldn't just be because he felt the team needed a more offensive or emotional leader, but one who would hold players' feet to the fire.

"Mike Richards was the captain, and John wasn't pushing him to be the best player at practice," recalls Holmgren. "How are the other players going to view that? Over time, the accountability drops off; I think that's what started to happen."

During TSN's telecast of the Toronto-Columbus game, commentator Bob McKenzie mentioned that Laviolette, sitting there on the panel, would be a top candidate to coach Philadelphia should Stevens be let go. Off the air, Laviolette asked McKenzie, "Do you really think so?"

"Lavvy," McKenzie responded, "This stuff doesn't just fall from the sky."

Recalls Laviolette: "I wasn't going to say anything about the one conversation that I had with Paul because some things don't materialize and it's just best to stay quiet. I wasn't lying to them at the time. I had no offer."

Following what Stevens recalls as a good practice the day after the Vancouver loss, the coach and Holmgren discussed whether they would return callups Jon Kalinski and Andreas Nodl to Adirondack. Then the GM went back upstairs to his office. "I remember thinking about [a coaching change] again, top to bottom," he recalls.

"I told Clarkie how I was agonizing over it, laid out to him all my thoughts, both ways. He said, 'I think you know what you have to do.'"

Holmgren telephoned Laviolette, reaching him at Toronto's Pearson Airport as he prepared to board a flight to his home in Tampa. He quickly agreed to the base dollar figures of the GM's three-year contract offer. Unable to get another flight because he had cleared immigration, Laviolette called his wife Kristen with the news, asking her to pack a bigger bag and bring it to him at the Tampa airport so that he could fly right back out to Philadelphia.

In his two previous NHL jobs, Laviolette had ended an Islander seven-season playoff drought and coached the Hurricanes to the Cup. But he didn't look at all NHL jobs as created equal. "I was really excited for the opportunity because it was a big-market team," Laviolette recalls.

Holmgren had no such enthusiasm for his walk downstairs to do "the hardest thing I've ever done in my life."

Stevens was on the phone in his office. He gestured, asking whether Holmgren needed him to hang up, but the GM indicated no, to finish the call. When Stevens hung up, Holmgren said, 'John, I've got to make a change.'"

Recalls Stevens, "My first thought was, 'We're making that change with a guy going to the minors.' That lasted about half-a-second."

After 263 games over four seasons as coach of the Flyers, Stevens had been fired. Both men fought back tears.

"It was actually a little bit emotional for both of us," recalls Stevens. "But my mind immediately went to 'Who knows about this? When are you announcing it? I don't want my family hearing this from anybody but me.'"

Stevens went home to tell his wife Stacy. She went to their son Nolan's hockey game in Pennsauken, NJ, while John drove to John Jr.'s contest in Vineland, NJ. They successfully got both boys home before anyone could break the news to them.

"I got fired in my hometown, in the public eye," recalls Stevens. "I can handle it, but it's tough on your family. Anybody in the business will tell you that."

Late the following night, when they were confident nobody would be around, Stevens and Stacy went to the Skate Zone to drop off his laptop, clean out his office, load up the truck, and leave 19 years in the organization behind them.

"People reach out to you in those situations," he recalls. "Bob Clarke was amazing, absolutely amazing. Ken Hitchcock…I could go down the line. People in the hockey community are wonderful."

"It's interesting. You learn a lot about your relationships with your players by the calls you get and the calls you don't get. Sometimes the guys you're hardest on are the ones that call first.

Stevens compiled a 120-109-34 record and directed a resurrection from a 56-point crash that led all the way to a conference final. He says something he would have liked to do over was work harder on a relationship with Timonen in order to bring out more leadership.

"Kimmo is an extremely intelligent and well-respected player," recalls Stevens. "I think I would have forced him to be a little more involved in getting more out of our team."

"The other thing was the integration of a young captain and Pronger. I don't think there were problems, but there were perceived to be problems. You had a guy come in who was a very strong personality and I think I could have done more to foster and fast-track that [relationship], as opposed to just letting it go through a natural progression. It was a challenge to get young players to take on ownership. I think I could have done more.

"But if I went back and coached that team again, would I use a different forecheck? No. We were an aggressive team. One year (2008-09), we scored 15 shorthanded goals."

There were players who felt encumbered by Stevens' system, but none who didn't respect him. "I think the guys liked him," Briere recalls. "Sometimes it's just a spark that you need.

"You need to scare the guys with a coaching change, because players know they won't blame the coach again. The next time it's going to be their asses."

Understandably, the Flyers who had played for Stevens as Phantoms were the saddest to see him go.

"Johnny was great for me," Carter recalls. "He taught me how to play the game the right way.

"In junior hockey, you get away with so much, cheating for offense when you should be taking care of your own end. He worked with me on being in the right position."

Richards probably was the closest player to the departed coach. "It was tough for me because we had a pretty good relationship," he recalls. "But I don't think I was shocked at all. I'm not saying anything bad about anybody, but Philadelphia might be a little impatient with a lot of things. The reality is when you lose a bunch in a row, it's time to make some changes."

Laviolette wanted to turn a team loaded with good forwards into an attack machine. Breaking forechecking habits would take time. But when the 17th Flyer coach was introduced at an 8 p.m. Wachovia Center press conference—still looking refreshed by the challenge even at the end of a Toronto-to-Tampa-to-Philadelphia day—he made clear his expectations for an immediate upgrade in work ethic.

"I think that you have to be tough on players," Laviolette said. "I also believe in the human side of things. I think if you can get to the human side, then you can be tough."

"I understand in Philadelphia there's an expectation for success."

Holmgren addressed that. "I certainly recognize that my neck is on the line here," said the GM. "I asked myself, 'Did we overrate our team? Do we have the right mix?'

"I believe we need a new voice at this time."

To Laviolette, Holmgren had praised assistant coach Craig Berube and asked that he be kept on. The new coach readily agreed. When Carolina GM Jim Rutherford called to ask Holmgren if he had any interest in re-joining Hurricanes' assistant Kevin McCarthy with Laviolette, Holmgren did.

"I knew Kevin (as a Flyer defenseman, then their director of pro scouting) of course," said the GM. "I didn't have any problem with the work of (assistant coach) Jack McIlhargey, but it's not fair to stick a coach entirely with assistants he doesn't know."

McCarthy was hired to replace McIlhargey as coach of the defensemen. When McIlhargey's contract ran out at the end of the season, he was re-hired by Holmgren as a scout.

As Laviolette took over a 13-11-1 team that was tied for 10th place in the conference, time was not a luxury. The new coach had only a morning skate to prepare for his first game, and he tried to make the most of it.

"He had 11 drills on the board," Briere recalls. "And we were figuring, 'OK, normally you go about 10 minutes a drill, so we're going to be on the ice for almost two hours.'

"Even if you cut it in half you're still on the ice for an hour, which is way too much for a game-day practice. He ran those 11 drills in about 17-18 minutes. It was go, go, go, non-stop. No time to catch our breath."

Only 57 seconds into Laviolette's debut, the Flyers had the wind knocked out of them again. The initial Washington shot of the game, by Tomas Fleischmann, beat Emery. Pyörälä tied the game at 12:06 of the first period, ending a 172:10 drought. But two minutes later, Carcillo, responding to a body check by Matt Bradley, threw punches at the Caps' center, who didn't drop his gloves. Given a nine-minute powerplay—two for instigation, two for cross-checking, and five for fighting—Washington scored three times to go up 4-1. Emery was yanked after giving up five goals in an 8-2 rout.

Richards made a point of talking to Carcillo. "All I can do is hold people accountable; I don't think it will happen again," said the captain.

Even less pleased was the new sheriff. "The whole thing never should have happened," Laviolette said. "We got hit; we should have skated away and kept playing. I've never seen a nine-minute powerplay."

In losing for the seventh time in eight games, the Flyers had saved the worst performance yet for their new coach's first game. "A horrible, horrible feeling," Laviolette recalls. "I mean, that was just Day One, but it certainly wasn't the way the script was supposed to go."

The next morning, he set about changing it. In an 80-minute practice, the longest one so far of the season, the coach did the drills with the players. Asked what had been accomplished, Laviolette laughed: "I really proved that I'm out of shape, first and foremost." But it was clear he was trying to raise the tempo so Philadelphia could more relentlessly go on the attack.

"Teams that play pretty good hockey have a certain identity, whatever that identity might be," he said. "It might not be systems, it might be an attitude. Today is the first step to try to get there, but you're not going to climb the mountain in one day."

Two nights later in Montreal, the Canadians were held to 13 shots. It would have been a big step forward except that the Flyers managed only 15 as Boucher was beaten 3-1.

"We didn't give them a whole lot," Pronger said. "But we didn't win the game."

Philadelphia did win the next one, however, 6-2, over the Islanders at the Wachovia Center as Richards, Giroux, and Carter all broke out with two-goal games to give Laviolette his first victory.

"[Richards] is a leader and he played like it," said Pronger. "He got us off to a great start and continued to play both ends of the ice very hard.

"He's been highly regarded for his passion for the game. Tonight is something to build on for him."

The same went for Boucher, who stopped 22 in the first game of what appeared to be the start of a long run for him in goal. Emery underwent surgery on his groin at Hahnemann University Hospital in Philadelphia and was expected to be out for six weeks. "We tried to approach it through rehab and cortisone injections, but it progressed," said Holmgren.

Laviolette celebrated his first Flyer victory by putting the players through five-minutes of starts and stops the next day. Discipline was the ongoing focus. He was not happy with the three penalties his team took in the second period of a 2-0 home loss to Ottawa, or with Briere for a hold and then a crosscheck he committed against Jamie Langenbrunner during a 4-1 defeat at Newark. Briere paid the following day with a multi-lap skate at practice, while the rest of the team watched before they were ordered to do the same.

"When somebody takes a stupid penalty, the players can't just accept it and move on," recalls Laviolette. "There has to be peer pressure.

"When you're in [22nd] place, you gotta figure out how you're going to turn this around."

Briere understood. "It makes you think twice," he said.

Meanwhile, the team's ongoing offensive problems were stemming from over-thinking. Only once in the last nine games had Philadelphia scored more than two goals.

Maybe a little sightseeing would help. In Boston, the Flyers took a tour of Fenway Park, which was being set up for their Winter Classic contest against the Bruins two weeks hence. Apparently pumped, Laviolette's team rallied with three goals in the third period—one by van Riemsdyk and two by Timonen—to win the next night, 3-1, at the TD Garden. But 24 hours later in Pittsburgh, they were taken apart by the Penguins, 6-1.

"It's really disturbing," said the coach. "You take a small step forward, [then] you take a big step backward. We didn't compete."

Holmgren moved to get an experienced backup for Boucher during Emery's absence, bringing back Michael Leighton by claiming him again on waivers, this time from Carolina. The 28-year-old goalie had played four games for the Flyers during the 2006-07 season, before he had been claimed by Montreal.

Once a sixth-round pick by Chicago, Leighton had recorded a 3.10 goals-against average and .896 save percentage in just seven games for the Hurricanes, who split his $600,000 cap hit with Philadelphia.

"I had been tossed around a lot for three or four years," he recalls. "Carolina said they were going to put me on waivers, so my agent called around and Paul Holmgren said he would pick me up.

"I thought I would be there a few weeks until [Emery's injury] healed, and then go to the minors."

With Betts back in the lineup, the Flyers put up a much better fight against Pittsburgh in the second game of the home and home, but Boucher was beaten for two shootout goals in the 3-2 loss. Gagne returned after missing 25 games following sports hernia surgery and shook off the rust to assist on a Pronger goal. But that was the only one the team got as they were defeated 2-1 by the Rangers.

The losses seemed endless, but Laviolette, teaching a left-wing lock that simplified defensive responsibilities while turning the center and right wing free to chase the puck, stuck to the means that had earned him a Stanley Cup ring at Carolina.

"He demanded a lot and was harping all the time on hard work," recalls Briere. "But he also understood we had a long ways to go and was very understanding of that."

When the Panthers came to town, for their first meeting with Philadelphia since the Richards hit to the head of David Booth, the Flyer captain only had to wait 3:42 for Bryan McCabe's invitation to fight. Not a punch landed cleanly before McCabe was wrestled to the ground. Laperriere tried to inspire his slumping team with three separate fights, earning an automatic game misconduct. But Philadelphia, which lost Boucher to a lacerated right ring finger, went belly-up for the 14th time in 17 games, 4-1. "We got down a goal and it went south pretty quick," said Laviolette.

The booing was so bad, the Flyers probably would have been better off down south, at least until a sewage pipe burst in the visiting locker room at the St. Pete Times Forum, forcing cancellation of their practice. The following night, however, the team didn't stink out another joint. After the Lightning wiped out a 2-0 lead with two-second period goals, Betts broke the tie midway thought the third, and then Richards put away Leighton's 5-2 victory. "Minor step," said Laviolette, who got Powe back after missing 16 games. "We need major ones."

Three nights later, Philadelphia blew a 3-0 lead in Raleigh against the worst team in the NHL. But in the shootout, Leighton stoned the latest in a long line of clubs that had rejected him, while Briere and Richards, both 0-for-6 so far on the season, scored to give the Flyers a 4-3 win.

When they followed by defeating the Islanders in a 2-1 win at Uniondale, perhaps the worst was over. "We played freely," said Laviolette. "Of the three (straight) wins, tonight's was the best."

The fourth one was even better—Gagne's third career hat trick sparking a 6-0 Leighton shutout at Madison Square Garden that pushed the 19-18-1 Flyers into eighth place in the conference. "I definitely feel more comfortable with the more games I play," said the goalie. "I haven't gotten an opportunity like this in the NHL in a long time."

It would have meant a great deal to Boucher, the pride of Woonsocket, RI, to get the start in the Winter Classic at Fenway Park on New Year's Day. His finger had healed, but Laviolette wasn't toying with the team's run. "You're playing whoever is the hot hand at the time," recalls the coach. "We had a lot of climbing to do."

Philadelphia was making its debut appearance in an outdoor game. (No, they never got to play in the Spectrum after part of the roof blew off in 1968.) And none of them ever had performed before an audience of 38,112. As they walked out from the visiting dugout and onto the rink, each Flyer got a tap on the pads from Clarke, as each Bruin did from Bobby Orr.

Carcillo had told NBC a day earlier that it was his intention to participate in the first fight ever in the three-year-old history of the Classic. He caught the eye of Bruin tough guy Shawn Thornton during the warm-up to make an appointment. They went toe to toe during the first period.

Boston goalie Tim Thomas, unnerved by a Hartnell strafing, was slashing the Philadelphia winger in the back when Syvret spun and scored through the legs of Carter to put the Flyers ahead 1-0 in the second period. "I was excited to get my first (NHL) goal—and it just happened to be outdoors and at Fenway," Syvret said.

After Thomas stopped Giroux and Asham on breakaways to keep the Bruins within a goal, a Timonen penalty gave Mark Recchi the opportunity to redirect a feed by Derek Morris to tie the game with only 2:18 remaining. After Philadelphia had to kill a penalty in overtime on Briere, he missed two golden opportunities before Marco Sturm tipped in a David Krejci shot to give Boston a 2-1 victory.

The linesmen had missed the Bruins having a sixth man on the ice at the start of the rush, all the more reason for the Flyers to hate the loss even as they had enjoyed the spectacle.

"The experience is once-in-a-lifetime," said the Massachusetts-born Laviolette. "Fenway Park. Bruins. Flyers. Forty thousand people on a perfect day. You couldn't ask for anything better for the game of hockey.

"For our organization, players, fans, it was just unbelievable to be a part of it."

It feels that way to Pronger today. "I grew up playing on an outdoor rink," he recalls. "Being out in the cold, wind blowing on your face, gets the youthful enthusiasm back in your game.

"It is hard when the fans are screaming and the coach and media are all over you. At times the game is not fun, and it has to be fun. This felt like a pond hockey game outside."

Back inside, Leighton was yanked after surrendering two early goals at Ottawa. Boucher then provided little relief in the 7-4 loss that ended the unbeaten streak at five. But Philadelphia bounced back to defeat Toronto, 6-2, then beat the Penguins in Pittsburgh 7-4, despite the best efforts of Fox Sports Net producer Lowell MacDonald Jr., who withheld a replay showing a contested third-period Gagne score until after the officials reviewing in Toronto ruled no goal. Only then was it shown that the puck had crossed the line. The network suspended MacDonald.

The Flyers averaged six goals per game during a win streak that stretched to four contests with victories over Tampa Bay and Dallas. "You need a lot of energy to play [Laviolette's] system," said Gagne, who had 13 points in his first 12 games back from surgery. "Early on, we were a little tired."

Emery returned sooner than expected from his groin repair. So when Leighton lost for the first time in 11 starts, 4-0 at Toronto, the coach went back to his No. 1 guy only to have only to have Emery stop just 17 of 22 shots during the 5-3 defeat in Washington.

Goaltending wasn't the only postgame topic in the visiting locker room of the Verizon Center. *The Philadelphia Inquirer*'s Sam Carchidi, annoyed to read an accusation by Richards in *The Hockey News* that the Philadelphia media "seem to just make things up to take a negative spin on things," asked the captain what he was talking about.

Although gossip about fun times in Olde City—and one video of Richards and Carter at a college party—had made its way onto social media, little, if any, had been reported on mainstream sports pages and broadcast outlets.

An annoyed Richards didn't answer Carchidi's question, instead asking another reporter to intercede on his behalf before walking away and then sending word through the Flyer PR staff that he would never talk to Carchidi again.

Richards told Holmgren about the incident on the train ride home. "He's the captain of our team," the GM said to the media the following day. "He's going to be put in the position where he's got to answer difficult questions.

"I think over the course of time, Mike will get better in dealing with those questions as they come up. He's an honest, young man and I'm sure he was stating his feelings. I don't think it's any big deal."

Privately, Laviolette had asked all his players to make pledges of abstinence from alcohol.

Meanwhile, there weren't any secrets about who was the No. 1 goalie, despite Leighton's fine run. Laviolette went right back to Emery following his Washington loss. R.J. Umberger's two goals erased a two-goal Columbus lead, but Carter quickly untied the game by shooting

In front of Fenway Park's famed Green Monster outfield wall, the Flyers celebrate a goal against the Boston Bruins in the 2010 Bridgestone Winter Classic.

and scoring directly off a faceoff, startling center Sammy Pahlsson and goalie Mathieu Garon.

"I might have seen it done once, maybe," said Blue Jackets GM Scott Howson after the 5-3 Philadelphia win. Certainly he never had witnessed it by Carter. "I've come close a couple of times, but I never scored on it before," said the center.

After tallying just once in a 23-game stretch, van Riemsdyk was cooking again. His fifth goal in eight contests and Emery's 24 saves produced a 2-0 home win over the Rangers. Next, Emery robbed Carolina's Rod Brind'Amour in the final 23 seconds to preserve a 4-2 victory over the Hurricanes and, after giving up three in the third in Atlanta's 4-3 Wachovia Center win, bounced back to beat the Islanders 2-1.

Since their Christmastime turnaround, the Flyers were 12-5-1. "They believe they're going to win before they go out on the ice," Laviolette said.

Due in part to Syvret being out with a shoulder separation—but largely because no third defensive pair was engendering much faith—Holmgren signed 25-year-old defenseman Lucas Krajicek. The former first-round pick by Florida had been released by the Lightning after he had quit the farm team at Norfolk.

Emery shut out the Flames in Calgary, 3-0, for a fifth win in his last seven starts, lowering his goals-against average to 2.64 and raising his save parentage to .905. But following the contest, the goalie came to McCrossin reporting pain shooting from his right hip to his knee.

"The whole pelvic area had been going funny on me that year," recalls Emery, but McCrossin suspected this was something a lot more troublesome than a further aggravation stemming from Emery's groin surgery. "It was a sign something major was going on," recalls McCrossin. "I thought it might be a fracture."

For the first time in nine games, Laviolette went back to Leighton, who suffered an excruciating loss, 1-0, in Edmonton on ex-Flyer Ryan Potulny's goal with 17 seconds remaining. Suddenly getting no offensive support, Leighton closed the trip with a 2-1 loss in Minnesota.

Back in Philadelphia, Emery went for an MRI that revealed a devastating diagnosis—avascular necrosis, a genetic condition in which the femoral head (ball) in his right hip was deteriorating—the same affliction that had drastically shortened the football-baseball career of Bo Jackson, one of the most gifted athletes of all-time.

Dr. Thomas Byrd in Nashville, a frequent consultant of McCrossin, recommended Dr. David Ruch at Duke University, who did a bone graft one month later in hopes of avoiding a full hip replacement. The odds against Emery ever playing again were considerable. The crease of a team expected to win the Stanley Cup was in the hands of Leighton—a goaltender who had been waived four times and traded twice in seven seasons.

Krajicek's addition had left no spot for Tollefsen. He was moved to Detroit for 26-year-old left wing Ville Leino, who had just seven points in 42 games for the Red Wings and hadn't dressed in their last seven contests.

Richards' third-period powerplay goal capped a rally from a 2-0 deficit to a 3-2 victory over the Devils at the Wachovia Center, and two nights later in Newark, before 5,580 who braved a snowstorm, Philadelphia came from 2-0 down against New Jersey again, this time winning in sudden death on Gagne's first goal in 13 games. "You don't do this against the New Jersey Devils too often," said Pronger. "It was a good test to show what we're made of."

The Flyers survived a late rally by Montreal in a 3-2 home win and then, with the help of Briere's hat trick, blew out the Canadiens, 6-2, the following night at the Bell Centre. Philadelphia hit the February Olympic break at 32-25-3 and held fifth place in the East, although having only a five-point lead on ninth-place Atlanta.

While there was not a Flyer on Team USA for the 2010 Winter Games, Timonen was playing for Finland for a fourth time and Bartulis was suiting up for Latvia. Philadelphia stars Pronger and Richards were on the Canadian team, for which Carter agreed to go as an alternate should Ryan Getzlaf be unable to play through an ankle sprain.

Playing on home ice naturally added urgency to Canada's bid for men's hockey gold. So did the country's 2006 quarterfinal elimination by Russia at the 2006 games in Torino, Italy. But in any international tournament, the Canadian players were made to feel like their birthrights were at stake.

"Whether it's Vancouver or not, if you don't come back with the gold, it's going to be, 'What's wrong with Canadian hockey?'" said Pronger.

He was hearing that already in the preliminary round. Brian Rafalski scored two goals and set up a Langenbrunner third period tip-in to key a 5-3 win by the USA over Canada. The host club was forced into an elimination game against Germany. The Canadians won it easily, 8-2, and then, in the quarterfinals, avenged their Russian defeat of four years earlier, 7-3.

Timonen's team was eliminated by USA, 6-1, in one semifinal, and Canada squeaked by Slovakia, 3-2, in the other, to set up a rematch between the USA and Canada for the gold medal.

In the first period, Richards forced Erik Johnson into a giveaway, fired, and Jonathan Toews put in the rebound to put Canada ahead, 1-0. Corey Perry's goal in the second made the score 2-0. But five minutes later Ryan Kesler cut the lead in half and Zach Parise's rebound goal with 24.4 seconds remaining stunningly tied the game, 2-2.

At 7:40 of overtime, Canada's Sidney Crosby took a give-and-go feed from Jarome Iginla and beat tournament MVP Ryan Miller between his legs to give Canada the gold medal. "It was the quickest game I've ever been in," said Richards of the most watched hockey contest in the U.S. since the Miracle on Ice game against Finland in the 1980 Olympics at Lake Placid. "It was perfect to play in.

"You could kind of feel the waves on the bench. It was unbelievable to be a part of it."

After the medal was placed around his neck, Richards reached over to shake hands with Pronger, who was adding a second gold to his 2002 medal in Salt Lake City. "I don't think it gets any better than that," he recalls. "Pretty compelling end, winning in overtime against the U.S. team that had beaten us in the round robin."

Timonen, who won the third Olympic bronze medal of his career in Finland's 5-3 victory over Slovakia, was on an inglorious 4:30 a.m. flight the next morning with Richards and Carter to connect to Tampa for the resumption of the NHL schedule.

The Flyers beat the Lightning, 7-2, with Richards having a hand in the first four goals. But the following night in Sunrise, he was no national hero to David Booth, just the guy whose shoulder-to-the-head had put the Panther winger out for 45 games. As soon as Booth had a chance in the opening period, he dropped his gloves for the first time in his career and challenged Richards.

"I just asked him if he wanted to, and he was good enough to give me my shot," said Booth. "I don't really know what I'm doing when I fight. I just wanted to get it off my chest.

Richards, who had emailed Booth following the incident with an expression of concern, landed one punch before the Panther wrestled his way on top. Neither player showed any desire to prolong the bout, but Booth won the evening, scoring a goal and three assists in Florida's 7-4 victory.

"It's over and you move on," said Richards.

So had Holmgren without any further changes to his team as the trading deadline passed that day. The GM had taken his best shot 25 days earlier in picking up Leino, but Laviolette apparently was unimpressed, refusing to take a look at the winger. Finally, hearing "we can't get the puck off this guy" reports from his assistants who were working with extra players after practice, Laviolette inserted Leino for the first time in Florida and he scored.

Emery had been put on long-term injured reserve, creating $2.8 million in cap room, but Holmgren did not try to use that money on goaltending help. "Leighton (13-3-1 with a 2.18 goals-against average and a .926 save percentage) has been playing very confidently and I see no reason for that to change," said the GM.

The netminder was unable to hold a late lead created by an unassisted third-period Richards goal, and lost 3-2 in overtime at Buffalo. But he bounced back to beat the Leafs, 3-1, and then the Islanders, 3-2, when Richards' attempted pass went in off defenseman Mark Streit's stick. It was Philadelphia's 15th straight win against New York, the longest streak ever by the franchise against any opponent.

The Flyers were 20-8-2 since their Christmastime turnaround. But they suddenly were terrible in a 5-1 home loss to Boston. "We hung Michael out to dry," said Laviolette.

Two days later, with Philadelphia trailing the Blackhawks 2-1 at the Wachovia Center in the final three minutes, Hartnell took a 130-foot pass from Timonen and, leaning off Chicago defenseman Brent Sopel, tied the game. When Pronger won it, 3-2, in the final two seconds with a slapshot off a rush with Giroux, the team had earned its most exhilarating Wachovia Center victory in at least two seasons. But the next day, the Flyers played with little emotion in a 3-1 loss at Madison Square Garden.

"We were hard to read," Briere recalls. "I believe we had big-game players and sometimes it's tough to keep that high going. What made us so good on some nights made us also look really bad on the off ones."

Carter's 33rd goal gave Philadelphia a 1-0 lead on March 16 at Nashville, but Steve Sullivan and Martin Erat banged in two goals within 2:31 to put the Predators ahead. Two minutes later, Leighton came out of the net to play a bouncing dump-in, was bumped by a forechecker, and fell backwards on his left leg. Unable to continue, he was replaced by Boucher, who had been in just three games, all in relief, since December 21.

Just 20 seconds later, Jerred Smithson put in a rebound, but Boucher turned back the next 22 shots as the Flyers rallied on third-period goals by Gagne and Pronger to tie the game 4-4. The only goal of the shootout, by Erat, sent Philadelphia down to a 4-3 defeat.

Leighton was sent home to be examined. "I didn't think it was that bad," he recalls. "Then Paul Holmgren called. The doctor told him I tore my ankle in three different places.

"It was devastating. Things had been going so well for me, finally." Leighton, diagnosed with a high ankle sprain (tears of the ligament that connects the tibia with fibula), was expected to be out a minimum of six weeks.

Having received his big chance when Boucher was injured in late December, it was now Boucher's turn to get a break. But after months as the third wheel, he was rusty.

"In that stretch Ray (Emery) was back, it had been hard for me to even get reps in practice," Boucher recalls. "But with them both out, who were they going to give it to after me? I knew I was going to get a good run at the job.

"I didn't have to look over my shoulder, wondering if I was going to be in there the next game. That helped."

When he won in Dallas, 3-2, on Hartnell's third period goal, Boucher's record on the season improved to 5-12-2. But the Thrashers completed a sweep of the season series with Philadelphia by winning on back-to-back nights and, worse, in the second game, Carter suffered a broken bone in the arch of his left foot. His consecutive game streak over at 286, the team's leading scorer would be out for three to four weeks.

The Flyers were shut out, 2-0, at Ottawa. They next were leading a Minnesota team out of the playoff race when they let up in their own building, eventually losing in overtime, 4-3, when Kyle Brodziak's 37-footer bounced up off Boucher, rolled down his back, and went off his skate and in. The goalie was 1-4-1 since taking over and repeatedly giving up long goals.

Nevertheless, he wasn't the subject of the team meeting called after the defeat.

"At home, up 3-1 against a non-playoff team, it's got to be money in the bank, that's what Chris (Pronger) said," Hartnell told reporters. "It's almost embarrassing, losing like that."

Said Laviolette, "A meeting is talk. Let's see if it translates to the ice."

The coach sat Boucher and gave backup Johan Backlund, a free-agent signing who had played 41 games with the Phantoms, the start in Pittsburgh. But he got hurt, too—a groin pull in the second period—and Boucher had to finish up the 4-1 loss, the last Philadelphia ever would suffer at Mellon Arena in 43 seasons of visits (44-58-2; 7-8 in the playoffs). In the fall, the Penguins would be abandoning The

Igloo in favor of the new CONSOL Energy Center.

The Flyers had lost five straight, and their margin over ninth place had shrunk to four points. In another meeting, Richards told his teammates to forget the playoff picture and concentrate only on the Devils, their next opponent.

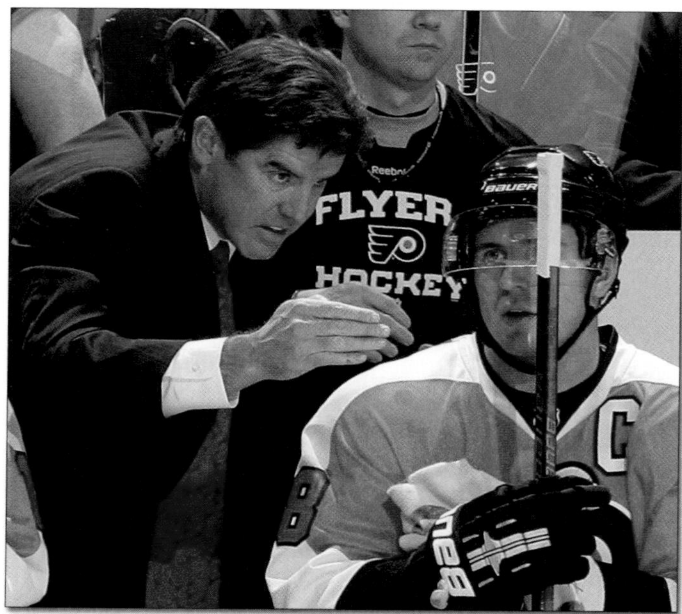

New head coach Peter Laviolette and captain Mike Richards discusses strategy.

"Everyone was focusing on the big picture," the captain said. "I just wanted to settle everything down. Just take it game by game."

His teammates appeared to follow his advice. Carle's drive in the first minute went in off the glove of Marty Brodeur, and Leino added a goal less than eight minutes later and Philadephia, blocking 26 shots, was in control almost throughout. Boucher was sharp in the 5-1 win that seemed to get the Flyers back on track.

But their train derailed at Uniondale when Blake Comeau's shot from the right boards two minutes into the game deflected in off Briere and, five minutes later, Comeau swung one out from behind the net and used Krajicek as a pinball pylon. Totally discombobulated by the two unlucky goals, Philadephia fell behind 5-1 in a 6-4 loss, the Flyers' first in their last 16 games against the Islanders. "Nauseating," recalls Laviolette about that defeat.

At home against Montreal, Richards whiffed on a clear, enabling Tomas Plekanec to put the Canadiens ahead nine minutes into the game. Philadelphia poured 35 shots at Jaroslav Halak, who stopped all of them, defeating the Flyers 1-0. The loss to Montreal left Laviolette's team in eighth place, just two points in front of the charging Rangers.

"I don't think we gave up more than six quality scoring chances the whole night," the coach said. "You play a game like that, you expect to win. It's frustrating for everybody."

With four games to go, Philadelphia had won just one of its last eight contests.

Against the Red Wings, the magic of Kate Smith and Lauren Hart helped Carcillo score after just 17 seconds. Giroux then broke a 2-2 tie—and a 14-game goalless streak—in the second period. Asham added what proved to be the winner in a critical 4-3 victory. "That's the way we need to play every night," said Laperriere.

To do that, the Flyers needed goaltending, and Boucher was rising to the occasion. He stopped 23 as Philadelphia nursed Giroux's first-period goal until Richards hit the empty net in a white knuckle 2-0 win at Toronto. "We can't take our foot off the gas now," said Boucher. "We've been doing that and have been paying for it."

With the Flyers and Rangers set to play a Friday/Sunday home-and-home to close the season, Philadelphia needed one win to get into the playoffs. Carter, cleared to return for the first game at Madison Square Garden, would be available to help.

Forty-seconds in, Richards intercepted a Marc Staal clear out of mid-air and fired his 30th goal of the season over Henrik Lundqvist's blocker. On the following faceoff, Aaron Voros went to the box for high-sticking Carcillo, giving the Flyers a chance to add on. But New York killed the penalty and, when Carcillo's stick drew blood from Brandon Prust, Chris Drury converted a pinpoint pass from Erik Christensen through three sets of Philadephia skates to tie the game, 1-1.

The Rangers took over the game, grabbing the lead less than three minutes later when enforcer Jody Shelley scored off an Artem Anisimov faceoff win over Richards. Outshot 12-4 in the first period, Laviolette's team didn't start the second one any better. Marian Gaborik raced past Carle and left the puck at the post for Brandon Dubinsky, who shoved it in before Boucher could reset himself.

Down 3-1, the Flyers fought back. Briere scored with a one-timer from the top of the circle, and Richards on a breakaway to tie the score 3-3 with less than six minutes remaining in the second period. But just 2:13 later, Gaborik picked up a puck that had hopped over Pronger's stick, and fired. The shot grazed Carle's stick enough to rise over Boucher's glove, putting New York back in front, 4-3.

Down the stretch van Riemsdyk, a half-empty net in front of him, was robbed by Lundqvist's left pad. Philadelphia, outshooting the Rangers 23-13 over the last two periods, were defeated 4-3, paying dearly for its inexplicably timid first 20 minutes.

"We came out for the first period a little like deer in the headlights, waiting to see what was going to happen," Laviolette said.

By losing eight of their last contests 11 contests, a once 10-point lead was gone. The Flyers would have to beat the Rangers at the Wachovia Center in Game 82 to get in. Laviolette told his players to "embrace the opportunity" to play one game for a playoff spot and, in those words, that's what many of them told the media they would do. But the train ride home was mostly silent.

"I remember Kimmo standing up and going, 'Guys, really? Come on,'" Pronger recalls. "We win and we're in."

He left out the part about what might happen if the Philadelphia lost. The team built to win, picked to win, was one defeat from not even making the playoffs.

Holmgren, who had the most pressure on him of anyone, also was in an embracing mood. "If you can't give your best in this situation, there's something wrong," the GM said, trying to rally the troops. Something had seemed wrong much of the season, but with one chance left, Laviolette believed there had been a purpose to all of his team's travails.

"Everything you do is preparation for something else," he says today. "Whether it was for the playoffs or, if we didn't get in, for being better for the experience the next season.

"There is always stress, and that game was probably the most stressful I've ever been in. We were either in or out, like a Game Seven without the buildup of Games Five and Six. So it was heavy. But I liked our team and thought we would play well."

At practice, the coach and his assistant, Mullen, pulled Briere, Richards, Carter, Giroux and van Riemsdyk aside to watch video of Lundqvist, an acknowledged master at shootouts.

"[Laviolette] basically told us to pick one move and practice it," Briere recalls. "He kept the five of us out for extra work. I probably took eight-to-ten breakaways just doing the same move."

When Boston beat Montreal on Saturday night to jump three points ahead of the tied Rangers and Flyers, for the first time in its history, the NHL had a head-to-head matchup on the final day of a regular season for one playoff spot.

As Boucher drove into the Wachovia Center, he found some fans not exactly embracing the opportunity. "People had paper bags over their heads because they thought we were going to blow it," he recalls.

The heat was on, but Hartnell and Asham still went to the hot tub to treat whatever was ailing them at the end of a long regular season.

"You nervous?" Hartnell asked Asham.

"No," Asham replied. "Mark my words: Whoever wins this game is going to win the Stanley Cup."

"Well, it's going to be us," said Hartnell.

New York, on a 7-1-1 roll, did not agree.

"I think we were pretty confident," Ranger Jody Shelley recalls. "We had won the game before. The pressure was on the Flyers, I thought, because they had huge expectations. We were supposed to have been out of it when we lost to Boston (on March 21) to fall 10 games out. Here we were, one win away."

Before the biggest regular-season game in Philadelphia history, Pronger joined Mark Howe as the second defenseman in team history to receive both the Bobby Clarke and Barry Ashbee Trophies in the same season.

Kerry Fraser, refereeing the final game of his 30-year NHL career, dropped the puck a little after 3 p.m. Within minutes, New York had the start it wanted, Shelley was in behind Parent to redirect Michal Rozsival's slapshot from the point after 3:27.

But down to their last chance, the Flyers chose now over never. The team they had expected to be all season showed up, leaving it up to Lundqvist to keep the Rangers in the game. Fighting off rebounds, finding pucks through screens, Lundqvist fought off everything but the mid-period shot of Carle's that hit the post and trickled wide. Philadelphia outshot New York 18-4 in the first period, and didn't allow one Ranger attempt in the final 13 minutes.

Voros, trying to get a spark out his team, challenged Laperriere to a second-period fight and the Flyer obliged. As he was escorted to the penalty box, Laperriere clapped his hands and yelled, "Let's go!" to the crowd. He was preaching to the choir. Philadelphia had no intention of letting up.

P.A. Parenteau took down Carcillo, putting the Flyers on the powerplay, but Lundqvist stopped Pronger and Briere to keep New York ahead. Boucher, with no margin for error the way his counterpart was performing, made four saves while Krajicek was off for tripping Anisimov. With Christensen penalized for slashing Carle, Carter and Briere missed the net around a Lundqvist save on Gagne from 12 feet, and the Rangers got out of the second period still up a goal.

"They couldn't touch the puck, they were chasing us all over the place," recalls Briere. "I felt like we were toying with them."

But Philadelphia was still trailing 1-0. "Trust the process," Laviolette reminded them, "the results will come your way." If the Flyers continued to go the net, eventually, they would get the rebound, the screen, the deflection, or just wear Lundqvist down.

At 5:39 of the third period, Parenteau tripped Giroux in the neutral zone and went to the box. Lundqvist made a stop on Pronger before Anisimov stole the puck from Carter in the neutral zone and looked for a shorthanded chance. But Carter sneaked up from behind the New York center and stole the puck right back.

He went down the right wing and passed to Hartnell, at the halfwall, who took a look and fed through traffic to Briere for a one-timer. Lundqvist anticipated and came across to make the save, but the rebound popped into the slot for the charging Carle, who had time to put the puck on his backhand and hit a half-empty net at 6:54 to tie the game at last.

"Gotta be the biggest goal I ever scored," recalls Carle, but not if the Flyers failed to finish the job. Beaten on a tip by Gagne, Lundqvist was rescued by the crossbar. But he still had enough left to make his best save yet, on a van Riemsdyk turnaround through a screen, before stopping Giroux on the rebound to get the Rangers into overtime.

For New York, the entire purpose of the extra five minutes was to get through them without being scored upon. "Coach [John Tortorella] even said, 'Don't totally sit back, but don't let it end here because we have a big advantage in the shootout,'" Christensen would admit later.

The overtime, in which neither team had a good chance, ended with Philadelphia having totaled 47 shots on goal, almost double New York's 25. But the Rangers still had the Flyers where they wanted them. Lundqvist's 142 of 188 shootout attempts represented the best shootout percentage of any active goaltender. Boucher had surrendered eight of 17 in his career. In five seasons of shootouts, no NHL team had a worse record than Philadelphia's 15-27.

"How can it come down to this?" Snider wondered aloud to people in his box. Boucher kept his thoughts to himself because some of them weren't good.

"I knew Lundqvist was the best shootout goalie in the National

Hockey League," recalls Boucher. "For me to say I felt confident, I'd be lying to you.

"I didn't claim to be a great shootout goaltender. I wasn't a starter at that point of my career, so I wasn't in a lot of those situations. You don't know how you're going to handle the pressure right?

"But as an athlete, you can't ask for a better situation. This is a chance to put your stamp on a game, on a season. I was excited. Nervous as hell, but you don't want to run away from that opportunity."

Laviolette chose Briere, Richards and Giroux; Tortorella bypassed his top three scorers—Marian Gaborik, Vinnie Prospal and Brandon Dubinsky—in favor of Christensen, Parenteau and Olli Jokinen, who had superior shootout records.

"Please score and take the pressure off me," Giroux told Briere, the first shooter, who was 40 percent for his career, but only one-for-five in 2009-10.

Briere did exactly what he had practiced, faking a shot, and taking a step to his right. When Lundqvist had to put out his pad to cover the bottom part of the net. Briere then went high and beat the goalie's glove.

The sense of dread in the building was gone. The Flyers led 1-0.

Erik Christensen, 53-percent in his career, one-for-three on the season, drifted to the right and tried to go left on Boucher to the stick side, but the goalie blockered the puck away to preserve the 1-0 lead.

Richards tried to get Lundqvist moving with a stutter step and went stick side, but the goalie got a piece of the puck with his right pad and sent it wide.

On the bench, the season totally out of his control, Carle felt sick to his stomach. Asham and Hartnell dealt with the anxiety by remembering their pregame talk in the hot tub and alternating saying, "We gotta win the Stanley Cup!"

Parenteau went wide left, cut through the goalmouth to get Boucher to open up and succeeded, the puck catching the cuff of the goalie's glove but with enough on it to carom high into the goal. The shootout was tied 1-1 headed into the final round.

Giroux, two-for-four on the season, two-for-seven in his career, approached Lundqvist slowly. He looked low blocker and saw no opening, then searched high glove and found nothing there either.

"He looked pretty big in the net," recalls Giroux. "I tried to slow down and give myself a little more time and went five hole."

It beat Lundqvist clean and put Philadelphia just one Boucher stop away from the playoffs.

"Oh man, they skipped over Gaborik!" the goalie thought when he saw Jokinen skating in circles in his own zone waiting for the linesman's signal to pick up the puck.

"I'd never seen that," Boucher recalls. "And I'm thinking, 'He's confident.' But all right, here we go.

"I told myself, 'Just stay patient, don't make the first move. There's just as much pressure on the shooter as there is on the goaltender."

Jokinen had scored only four goals in 25 games since his February 1 acquisition from Calgary. But he was five-for-nine in shootouts on the season.

He started at his own goalline, blazed down the right wing and tried to get Boucher moving so he could slip the puck through the goalie's five-hole. But it wasn't a confident move and Boucher's pad was there. "It wasn't a very tough save," he recalls.

As he rose out of his butterfly, pumping his arms, the goalie stumbled as the building rocked with relief and joy. Briere won the race off the bench to embrace Boucher, the third stringer who had just out-dueled a shootout master. Snider high-fived everybody around him in his suite as the sustained roar suggested that the Flyers had done a lot more than simply qualify for the playoffs.

"It must be great to win a Cup and to be in that clinching game," recalls Boucher. "Probably tenfold to winning the game that day. But for that moment, right there, that was for me like winning a Stanley Cup.

"It had been a hard year, a difficult year with ups and downs, injuries, and a lot of doubt. And I was able to come through in the clutch, what every athlete wants to do."

Asked to reflect on the narrowest of escapes and the absurdity of having a season come down to a skills competition, Boucher said, "I guess you don't ask how. We're in."

But Holmgren recalls glancing across a crowded press box elevator at Ranger GM Glen Sather and only imagining the pain.

As Snider told reporters, "Truthfully, I don't like New York. But I really feel sorry for them, because it's a tough way to lose the season."

But if it had seemed ridiculous to have the regular season decided by three players per side, the Rangers had been trying to get in on the strength of one—Lundqvist. After getting outplayed that badly, they could not complain about losing in a shootout, when it had been their best chance.

"I was pretty tired," Lundqvist admitted. And that was because for 65 minutes—and in the nick of time—the Flyers had become the team they had been expected to be all season.

"At the end, we played pretty good hockey to get in by our fingernails," Holmgren said. "Our key players stepped up."

Added Laviolette, "I thought we were fantastic for 65 minutes and a shootout. I think we got rewarded."

For once, an opportunity against long-time nemesis New Jersey seemed like a payoff. The final-day win over the Rangers had jumped the Flyers over eighth-place Montreal and set up a two-versus-seven matchup with the Devils, a team Philadelphia had defeated in 2009-10 in five of the six regular-season meetings.

Old Flyer killers Marty Brodeur and Patrik Elias still were in place from New Jersey's 2000 team that came from 3-1 down to beat Philadelphia in the conference final, and the Devils' 2004 club that the Flyers eliminated in the first round. New Jersey had won only two series since their last Stanley Cup in 2003.

"The game changed on them, you've got to remember that," Pronger told Sam Donnellon of *The Philadelphia Daily News*. "They had older guys on the back end when there was a lot of holding and hooking. Marty [was allowed by the rules] to go to the corner and get every puck."

GM Lou Lamoriello also had made a major change in the Devils personality with his addition of winger Ilya Kovalchuk in a February trade with Atlanta. Selflessness and discipline had made the Devils greater than the sum of their parts. Now they were trying to integrate a superstar who needed big minutes.

Despite Kovalchuk's point-a-game production since the deal, the 103-point division champions had gone only 13-9-5. And now he was going to have to deal with Pronger.

"I don't know what to do to tire him out," said New Jersey coach Jacques Lemaire about the huge Flyer defenseman. But Pronger certainly had ideas about handling the Devils.

"Play hard on their top players," he said. "Wear on them. You may not get them in Game One or Game Two, but hopefully, by Game Five or Six, the price they've had to pay [will have] taken its toll. Our physical style should be conducive to that."

Boucher, who was a rookie star of the 2000 run that ended so disappointingly, would now get another chance at New Jersey, an unimaginable scenario during the years when he had kicked from organization to organization, and even as recently as mid-March, when he was Philadelphia's third-string goalie.

"It's hard when you jump right to the top," he said. "You would rather have a nice steady progression to your career.

"But you learn, and time flies by. It's been 10 years between these experiences. If I have to wait another 10 years for the next one, I don't think I'll be in the NHL."

Gagne, also a first-year player in 2000, was the only remaining Flyer from the 2004 club. There wasn't much postseason history between the two teams' players.

In fact, after dominating the Rangers in Game 82, Philadelphia didn't even recognize itself as the team that had underachieved practically all year. Laviolette's club bussed up the New Jersey Turnpike for Game One at the Prudential Center, feeling already tested by its travails.

"It's like your playoffs already started," said Gagne. That said, the Flyers managed only four shots in a scoreless opening period, earning a tongue lashing from their fiery coach.

When Dainius Zubrus took the second Devil penalty midway through the second period, Pronger, being used on the powerplay in front of the net, backhanded in a rebound of Richards' shot and Philadelphia led, 1-0. Almost seven minutes later, Richards took a spin-around backhand pass from Laperriere and ripped a slapshot in off Brodeur's leg.

Down 2-0, New Jersey's coach largely abandoned his tactic of trying to sneak out Kovalchuk at the end of Pronger's shifts so his star would still be out there against the next pair. Pronger never seemed to leave the ice anyway, playing 30 minutes as the Devils failed to seriously threaten before a carom goal by Travis Zajac off Laperriere with 2:43 remaining in the game.

Boucher was required to make just one save after that as his 2-1 victory gave Philadelphia a 1-0 jump in the series. Although the Flyers, managed only 14 shots, they had not been outworked.

This shootout goal by Claude Giroux on April 11 clinched a playoff berth for the Flyers in the final game of the regular season.

"I think we played good hockey but, as always, it comes down to the goalie making saves," Laviolette said. "It's nice to have one with confidence."

Boucher was tested more in Game Two. With Kovalchuk in the box early for elbowing, Carle was unable to control a point pass from Pronger, and Zach Parise broke away to roof a shorthanded goal.

Giroux set up an Asham goal, then redirected a shot by Carle to give Philadelphia a 2-1 lead after a period. But Colin White beat Boucher between the pads to tie the contest and Andy Greene deflected home an Elias drive to put New Jersey ahead, 3-2.

Pronger tied it again on the powerplay before the second period was over. But late in the third, a minute-long cycle by the Devil line of Elias, Dainius Zubrus and Parise wore out the third Flyer defensive pair of Parent and Bartulis, enabling Zubrus to whack in a rebound. Kovalchuk completed a three-point night into the empty net and the Devils had evened the series 1-1.

"We were in position, but got out-muscled," said Laviolette about the game winner. "We need to tie up sticks a little better."

The coach substituted Krajicek for Bartulis in Game Three at the Wachovia Center.

Brian Rolston's powerplay goal with Timonen off for hooking Parise gave New Jersey a 1-0 lead 7:13 into the first period. But a minute later, Devil Matt Corrente high-sticked Timonen, and Giroux redirected a Timonen powerplay point drive to even the score 1-1.

Early in the second period, Giroux forced a Mark Fraser turnover, and Richards, fed by Carcillo, broke the tie over Brodeur's blocker. Coburn was off for interference when Rolston beat Boucher from the point with a cannon shot to make it 2-2, but only the scoreboard was even, not the play, as the game progressed. Managing just three third-period shots, New Jersey relied mostly on Brodeur's brilliance to survive penalties on David Clarkson and Rob Niedermayer and get the game to overtime.

Less than two minutes into sudden death, Clarkson took another penalty, this one for interfering with Asham in the neutral zone. The Devil winger had just come back onto the ice when Gagne pinched down the boards to force the puck to Richards, who was stronger than White at the New Jersey post. Brodeur stopped the first Richards jamming attempt, but the Flyer captain got the second one into the slot, leaving the Devil goalie on one knee while Carcillo, his eyes as wide as the open net, banged in the 3-2 winner at 3:35 of overtime.

"I'm kind of shaking right now," said Carcillo. "It's everybody's dream to score a goal like that."

Somebody was destined to be the hero, Laperriere had told Carcillo on the bench. "He said, 'I got it,'" recalled Laperriere. "Sometimes it might not be the goal scorer who gets the goal."

Always at playoff time, it is the player with second effort who makes the difference. With two goals and four assists over three games, Richards had points on six of Philadelphia's eight goals in addition to doing all of his defensive work.

"[Richards] has the worst body on the team, but he puts himself in front of anything," Laperriere said. "He might not be as flashy as (Sidney) Crosby on the other side of the state, but he's as effective. Or even more."

New Jersey, outplayed in Game Three and down 2-1 in the series, pushed back harder in the first period of Game Four. When Coburn and Pronger took penalties 1:08 apart, Kovalchuk had room to cut to the middle and beat Boucher with a wrist shot to the blocker side through a screen.

A prone Brodeur reached up to make a spectacular catch of a Gagne drive to keep the Devils ahead 1-0 midway through the second period. "Best save I ever saw," exclaimed Gagne. But during a Niedermayer penalty for interference, Carter circled out of the corner and, from above the dot, fired over Brodeur's glove with a screaming wrist shot to even the game at 1-1.

Briere untied it off the rush on a four-on-four, going under the crossbar from the edge of the circle to beat the Devil goalie in the final three minutes of the second period.

It had taken two pinpoint shots by accomplished snipers to beat Brodeur and put the Flyers up 2-1, but perhaps he was wearing down. Four minutes into the third period, when Carcillo walked out from behind the net and fired from along the goalline, Brodeur did not close his legs. The puck banged off his pad and trickled into the goal to put Philadelphia up 3-1.

To add to his indignity, Brodeur's mask was knocked off during the play by teammate Salvador's inadvertent high stick. The goaltender never had appeared so vulnerable and Kovalchuk, repeatedly stopped by a cool Boucher on mostly solo rushes, had never looked so frustrated. The Devils were done even before Briere, picking up a Pronger blast that had hit Carter on the foot, added the fourth goal midway through the third period. After the Flyers cruised, 4-1, to take a 3-1 series lead, the Devils GM threw a jar of jelly against the visiting locker room wall.

"The Flyers got a bad goal by me early in the third period and it changed the whole intensity of the period," said Brodeur. "When it got hard, we didn't play.

"They're keeping everything simple, playing pretty safe, and we're the opposite, trying to force it."

He mostly meant Kovalchuk, but Elias recalls there being a trickle-down effect to his line, too.

"You know all the minutes [Kovalchuk's] going to get and all the situations he's going to be on the ice," Elias recalls. "That was hard for some of us.

"From a team perspective, we'd always counted on every one of the guys. Then, all of a sudden, you're depending so much on one. Maybe some players thought he was going to do it on his own. It wasn't fair to him and it wasn't fair to the team."

Pronger recalls: "[The Devils] felt defeated. You could tell. They had moments where they got a chance or two, but we controlled the play. They were doing a lot more receiving than giving. That is how our team was built, to wear teams down."

Philadelphia, however, was running out of bodies. The Pronger shot that resulted in Briere's second goal had fractured Carter's foot.

"It was broken in three or four different spots, so I had to get a plate and a bunch of screws," Carter recalls. "They pretty much told me

I was done for the season."

Gagne played one shift and took a Rolston second-period shot on the foot. His was broken too. After consulting with a specialist, the Flyer underwent surgery the following morning.

"Every day counted," Gagne recalls. "They could put in two pins and then, if it healed quickly, maybe I could be back in two or three weeks. Either that, or I could rest, let it settle down, and maybe come back even sooner.

"But if I did [the latter] and it started hurting again, I would be out for the playoffs. I had a better chance with the surgery."

In Carter's absence, Giroux was being moved from right wing to center. He didn't care which wingers he was between as long as there was melted cheese in the middle of two pieces of toast for him to eat before every game. The grilled cheese sandwiches were not as good as the ones his mother made back in Hearst, Ontario, but that was Giroux's routine and he was sticking with it.

Daniel Carcillo celebrates his Game Three overtime game winner vs. New Jersey in the Eastern Conference quarterfinals.

So was Lemaire to his belief that the Carter and Gagne injuries were fantasies. "[Bullbleep]," he said, when asked about their absences.

Kovalchuk, trying to rally his teammates, guaranteed a victory to keep New Jersey alive. Carcillo almost helped make the Devils' star a prophet by tripping Paul Martin 0:43 into the game, but Philadelphia killed the penalty. Less than a minute after Carcillo returned, Giroux made a spanning pass to Briere, whose backhand redirection landed just inside the post before Brodeur could get there.

The Flyers nursed their early 1-0 lead into the second period. Boucher made a poke check on Parise on a semi-breakaway. Briere cleared a puck that had been jammed to the net by New Jersey's Martin off the line. Parise hit a post, then Elias fanned on an empty net on the rebound as the Devils' frustrations continued.

Eleven minutes into the second period, Richards fired a shot off the rush, got his own rebound off a Salvador block, and shot again. The puck deflected into the high slot to Giroux, who put a screamer into the top corner on Brodeur's blocker side to give Philadelphia a 2-0 lead on only its second shot of the period.

Less than a minute later, Dean McAmmond cut Asham, giving the Flyers a four-minute powerplay. Briere's shot from the right circle was blocked, but Hartnell dug the puck out of traffic in front and Briere quickly snapped in Philadelphia's eighth powerplay goal of the series to make it 3-0.

Midway through the third period, the Flyers were killing a van Riemsdyk penalty when Laperriere went down to block a point shot by Martin and got hit just above the right eye.

The winger jumped to his feet and started skating to the bench. Blood began pouring from his face as he crossed the blueline. Before McCrossin could reach him, Laperriere collapsed.

"Can you see my eye?" he asked the trainer. "Yeah, it's there," said McCrossin.

"I couldn't see anything out of my right eye," recalls Laperriere. "That wasn't a good feeling. You see blood everywhere, you think the worst."

Doctors were waiting for him in the medical room. He was concussed and cut for 60-70 stitches, but the eye was not damaged. His vision started to gradually return as doctor worked on him.

Pronger blocked another shot just seconds after Laperriere left with his face a bloody mess. "Guys see that and only want to push harder," Pronger said.

New Jersey, however, had no push left.

"I remember feeling that they were going to turn it up at some point and that we've got to be ready for whenever that burst comes," recalls Briere. "And it never did."

Ten years later, Boucher finally had finished off the Devils, 3-0, to win the series in five games.

"You never know when you are going to get a chance to be in a situation like this," he said. "I'm so grateful.

"I've had people ask me if this would take away what happened 10 years ago. Not really, that still stings. We were on our way to the Final and we lost. But this feels nice to move onto the second round."

The Flyers had done it in a way that suggested they had been the second seed and the Devils the seventh, not the other way around. They had killed 28 of New Jersey's 32 powerplays. Giroux, with two goals and an assist in Game Five, had stepped up magnificently in the absence of Gagne and Carter.

"Two months ago, [Giroux] told me he wanted more responsibility and we revisited that this morning," said Laviolette. "In a big situation, he was a very, very good player for us."

The Devils had a hard time grasping they had been beaten so routinely. "I just don't believe it," Brodeur said. "We had a hell of a team here.

"For whatever reason, we never got to the level we needed to play at in the playoffs. This is three years in a row we accomplished nothing."

Elias remembers being handled by a relaxed and confident underdog. "Sometimes when you go through all the pressure of just getting [to the playoffs], you feel like you have nothing to lose and play free," he recalls. "The Flyers had no extra baggage. That's when a team can be most dangerous."

Remarkably, Laperriere made himself available to the media, saying he had played his last game without a face shield. "It was bad luck tonight, but it was my last warning," he said. "Call me dumb, call me stupid, but it took this to realize my eyes are important. I want to watch my kids grow up with both eyes."

He said his wife had been asking him to wear a shield for years. "It was just a stupid macho thing in my head," the 35-year-old veteran said. "If I'm still going to be willing to fight anybody, I'll just have to take the helmet off."

But Laperriere added he would continue to block shots without fear. "That's what I do," he said. "I don't think twice. The day I stop doing that, I'll retire."

Naturally Laperriere—who had finished a game in November after suffering two jawbone fractures and seven lost teeth—fully expected to play in the next round. But two days later, the winger confessed to Holmgren he "just wasn't feeling right." A Pittsburgh specialist confirmed through a CT scan that the winger's brain was bruised. He would be out at least until undergoing another scan in four weeks.

The good news was that the Flyers' chances to still be playing in four weeks had improved. Their presumed second-round opponent—121-point Washington—was upset by eighth-seeded Montreal in seven games, matching seventh-seeded Philadelphia against sixth-seeded Boston, a team only three points superior to Laviolette's club during in the regular season.

After splitting four series in five years during the seventies, the Flyers and Bruins had not met in the playoffs in 32 years, a long gap for enmity-building purposes. In recent seasons, Bruin fans had gotten into booing Randy Jones, but the defenseman, whose hit had put the fine Boston center Patrice Bergeron out for the rest of 2007-08, had been waived earlier in the year.

It was hard for Flyer fans to hate a team with Mark Recchi, a one-time Philadelphia star who had scored 18 goals for the Bruins at age 41. Pronger and Zdeno Chara, two huge defensive anchors with mean streaks, could eventually stir some loathing but, in the meantime, Laviolette was having difficulty finding the Bruin who most earned Richards' defensive attention. With Marc Savard having missed half the season with a concussion, Boston's leading scorers—Bergeron and David Krejci—had just 52 points.

As timely as Philadelphia's scoring had been to eliminate the Devils, the Flyers weren't exactly coming into Round Two with a full battery of blazing guns. Not only were Gagne and Carter out of the lineup, but Hartnell hadn't scored in his last 17 games, and van Riemsdyk had hit the rookie wall, tallying just once in 25 contests.

Leino, about to dress for his first playoff game in Laperrier's place, was put on a line with Hartnell and Briere, who had become a center because of Carter's absence.

The longer the layoff between series—Philadelphia, first to advance to the second round, had to wait eight days for Washington and Montreal to finish—the greater the odds for Gagne to return sometime during the playoffs. But rust obviously had gathered on the Flyers as Game One began at TD Garden against a Boston team that had eliminated Buffalo in six.

Trying to hit Carle on the first shift, Bruin forward Marco Sturm injured a leg. But his replacement on the Bergeron line, Steve Begin, converted a rebound at 2:39. Bergeron then beat Briere on a faceoff and banged in a rebound to put Boston up 2-0 after a period.

Philadelphia got on the board through some strong cornerwork by Richards, setting up a Parent point shot that got through traffic and goalie Tuukka Rask midway through the second period. After both Carcillo and Richards drew roughing penalties for a confrontation with Savard, Miroslav Satan scored on the powerplay to put the Bruins up 3-1, but Pronger overpowered Rask with a one-timer on the powerplay to again cut the deficit to one.

Krejci picked up a broken down Satan shot, faked Boucher to the ice and went around him to put Philadelphia down by two for the third time in the game. But Richards converted a Briere passout on a powerplay with 7:23 remaining, to make it 4-3. After Briere took a feed from Pronger, splitting Boston defensemen Dennis Wideman and Matt Hunwick, the Flyer knocked in his own rebound to tie the score 4-4 with 3:22 remaining, forcing overtime.

The Bruins bombarded Boucher early in the extra session, leaving Pronger on the ice for what he remembers as almost a three-minute shift. "About a minute in, I was in front of the net when there was a scrum," he recalls. "I was on my knees, got bent backward, and heard a big crunch.

"It didn't feel very good for the next five to seven minutes. Eventually, the feeling returned and I was able to get a little bit of strength back."

Boston had already fired 14 shots at Boucher in the first 13 minutes of sudden death when the goalie attempted to make a clear to Briere waiting near the boards. Wideman pinched to turn up the puck and Savard, playing his first game in 55 days, one-timed a bouncer from the far edge of the circle. He got all of it, beating Boucher over his shoulder on the short side, to win the game, 5-4, at 13:52 of overtime.

"I think we should be pretty pleased with the way we played our second and third periods," Boucher said. "Once we got our legs about us, we battled back."

When Johnny Boychuk's goal sneaked through from the point 5:12 into the first period of Game Two, Philadelphia had to rally from an early deficit for the second time in two contests.

Richards picked up the puck behind the goal, circled out, and snapped a 35-footer past Rask to tie the game, 1-1. Satan got one through Boucher's legs midway though the second period and the Bruins led again, but Briere came out of the penalty box, formed a two-on-one with Leino, and beat Rask from the faceoff dot to make it 2-2.

A too-many-men-on-the-ice penalty, and the second hooking call of the game on Briere, made it difficult for the Flyers to generate offense in the third period. Their comeback again got them nowhere when Milan Lucic's turnaround 30-foot slapshot with 2:57 remaining gave Boston a 3-2 victory and a 2-0 lead in the series.

It was a second consecutive biting loss, and after the game, Carcillo said he had the teeth marks on his hand to prove it. He blamed Savard.

"The last time I was bitten was in grade school," the Philadelphia winger said. "Pretty cowardly."

Savard contended that Carcillo tried to rip his teeth out.

"Yeah, that's what I do," Carcillo said sarcastically. "I try to rip people's teeth out."

Better than getting your heart ripped out. The privilege of last change at home was expected to help solve the Krejci-Satan-Lucic line, which had figured in five Bruin goals in the first two games, so the Flyers were not dismayed by their 2-0 deficit. "We deserved better," Briere recalls. "We still felt pretty good."

So, surprisingly, did Gagne's foot when he met with Dr. Steven Raikin of the Rothman Institute for a follow-up.

"There's no way you can play yet," Gagne was told. "I will see you in another week."

That would be just in time for golf season if Philadelphia, playing catch-up to no avail in Games One and Two, didn't start working with some leads. "Your bench runs a little different when you are ahead," said Laviolette. "We won't feel like we have to get certain guys back out there—and maybe that will keep them fresher for the third period."

His team got the start it wanted in Game Three at the Wachovia Center. Giroux forced a giveaway by Adam McQuaid, took a quick headman pass from Betts, and broke out two-on-one with Asham, who converted off the glove of the diving Rask just 2:32 into the contest. But just 1:39 later, Krajicek was forced into a giveaway and then beaten to the net by Blake Wheeler for a deflection that tied the score.

Five minutes had been played when Krejci, looking to make a play from one step over the Boston blueline, was leveled with a body check by Richards. The puck, however, already was away to Lucic, with Richards and the pinching Carle both trapped. Lucic threw a breakaway pass by Pronger to Satan, who deked Boucher and slid the puck in on his backhand to put Boston up 2-1.

Krejci went to the bench, not to celebrate with Lucic and Satan. "I thought it was a head injury," Lucic recalls. "I think I said to him, 'suck it up, suck it up.' I had no idea it was his wrist."

The Bruin center did not return. With Boston getting a breakaway off his devastating hit, Richards had lost the battle, but the Flyers were trying to make this a seven-game war. They outshot the Bruins 11-1 in one stretch of the period, forcing Rask to stop Carcillo on a semi-breakaway before Asham twice hit the post.

When Begin went off for tripping Asham six minutes into the second period, the center-hung scoreboard showed a video tribute to Laperriere, then cut live to the winger, his eyes bloodshot, standing in the Zamboni tunnel. As the ovation swelled, the "toughest man on hockey" as termed by *The Hockey News*, didn't look so tough anymore as he fought back tears. His face, although a mess, had become the face of this playoff drive.

"I said to myself, "There's no [bleeping] way I'm not coming back," Laperriere recalls. "There's something special here."

He was not referring to Rask. But the Boston goalie was playing extraordinarily, turning back four Philadelphia shots on the powerplay to preserve a 2-1 lead into the second-period break. Early in the third, a Chara drive hit Pronger high in the chest and bounced at the feet of Recchi, who converted before Boucher could reset himself to put the Bruins ahead, 3-1.

Flyer pressure twice forced Boston to shoot the puck over the glass during the third period. During the second penalty, Laviolette pulled Boucher and put in Backlund for 90 seconds to give his first powerplay unit a rest. It didn't work and, eventually, Bergeron hit the empty net to put away a 4-1 Boston win.

By the end of the night, Krejci was in Baltimore, MD, having surgery on a dislocated wrist by a specialist at Union Memorial Hospital. The Flyers, meanwhile, were ready to commit themselves to a psychiatric ward. After largely carrying the play since the first period of Game One, they trailed in the series 3-0.

"I don't like the scoreboard," Laviolette said. "I liked the way we played."

Richards said what captains of teams down 3-0 have said since the advent of the best-of-seven series. "It might look like a mountain if you look at the whole thing," he said. "If you break it down, it's just one game after another.

"Hopefully, we can create some of the bounces that they've been getting so far."

Hartnell, who had slumped to 14 goals from 30 the previous regular season, had not scored in 20 contests. He had been given only 13 minutes of ice time in Game Three.

"Lavvy told me I didn't do [bleep]," Hartnell recalls. "I'll remember that until the day I die.

"It was a tough year for me. I was going through a divorce, so where the focus should have been on hockey, it was on other things. It was pretty hard to deal with that and to be on every game like you are supposed to be during the playoffs.

"When we were down 3-0, he questioned if I wanted to win, and it got pretty heated. I don't think there were any swear words going back and forth, but I was insulted that he would question my character."

The latest x-ray of Gagne's foot had shown more healing. So the day before Game Four, the winger tried on his skate in the company of McCrossin, Holmgren and Dr. Raikin.

"I wasn't feeling any pressure to play," Gagne recalls. "When I first broke it, I couldn't put any weight on it; they had told me it was going to be a few weeks.

"I remember watching (part of) Game Two on television with my one-year-old son, then taking him swimming. I wasn't even thinking about playing. I had been riding the bike a little but no hard training or practicing. I just figured I would do what [Holmgren] wanted and show him and Jimmy (McCrossin) that I still couldn't skate."

But he could, even though it hurt. Gagne was asked to try again the next morning at the game-day skate. It hurt more than the first time, but the doctor said the bone had hardened enough that playing wouldn't set back his recovery as long as he could tolerate the pain. Assured his foot would be numbed for the warmup, the winger said he would give it a try.

He did and was surprised.

"It was way better than it had been in the morning skate," Gagne recalls. "So I tell Jimmy and we talk to the doctor, and we decide I am going to play.

Only the 1942 Maple Leafs and 1975 Islanders had ever come from being behind 0-3 to win an NHL playoff series. Of the 111 teams that had fallen behind three games in the 35 years since New York, only 37 had even survived Game Four.

"Right after 'God Bless America', some fan leaned over and was like, 'Don't get embarrassed; don't get swept at home,'" recalls Carle. "I'm like, 'Alright, let's just win this game and get it back to Boston.'"

The Flyers were all over the Bruins early. Rask made a glove snatch of Leino on a two-on one, Giroux missed a breakaway, and a van Riemsdyk shot at an empty net was saved by Chara's skate. When Asham didn't pick up Bergeron coming through the middle, Boucher stopped the breakaway, but Recchi picked the top left corner with the rebound to give Boston a 1-0 lead.

In the last minute of the first period, Rask's legs couldn't close in time to foil a quick Briere release on a slapshot from the edge of the circle. The game was tied. When Pronger, off a faceoff win by Gagne, scored a deflected goal 4:28 into the second period, his team had its first lead of the series, 2-1. Giroux, off a smart Hartnell kick across the goalmouth, made it 3-1.

The Bruins found some luck and life. Michael Ryder's stick broke as he shot, but the puck bounced off the backboards and as Boucher tried to cover the jumping bean, the goalie knocked it into his own net to cut Philadelphia's lead to 3-2. Early in the third period, with Leino in the penalty box for hooking, Lucic's tip of a Wideman powerplay drive broke down past Boucher to tie it 3-3.

If the Flyers were going to survive, they had to make their own luck. Gagne's pain forced him to the bench, but with 5:40 to play, Leino deftly redirected a Pronger drive high into the net to give Philadelphia a 4-3 lead.

It was nursed into the final minute. With Rask off for an extra attacker, Savard beat Richards on a faceoff, and Timonen left the front of the net in an unsuccessful attempt to keep the puck in the corner, while Powe got caught too high expecting a pass to the point. Recchi was so alone near the right post he did not even have to one-time a diagonal feed by Bergeron to tie the game, 4-4, with 32 seconds remaining.

The Flyers had worked too hard and were too close to a reward to take such a kick in the solar plexus. But no matter what they did, Boston seemed to always have an answer.

Laviolette knew he had to chase any fatalistic thoughts from his players' minds.

"The most important thing going back into the overtime was to completely wash out everything that happened in the game, the good and the bad, just leave it," he would say later.

Certainly Briere was buying. "It was unbelievable, all the breaks they had been getting up until that point and then they tie it up late like that," he recalls. "But we wanted to keep playing, so that's all we thought about."

On a high wire with no net below, Philadelphia didn't dare look

Simon Gagne's goal past Tuukka Rask at 14:40 of overtime gave the Flyers a 5-4 win over Boston in Game Four of the Eastern Conference semifinals.

down. Powe was called for boarding Savard, who took the only two shots of the Bruin powerplay as the Flyers efficiently killed it.

On the bench, Gagne flexed his foot and found the pain not nearly as intense as when he had come out of the game. He told McCrossin, and Laviolette sent Gagne back out. On the next faceoff, a Richards win, Gagne fired what appeared for a split second to be the game winner until Rask remarkably kicked out his right pad to make the save.

Chara carried out looking to make a play, but Richards knocked the puck off the defenseman's stick and quickly got it back on a touch pass from Carle. Richards pulled up at the halfwall and perfectly fed a speeding Carle, who relayed to Gagne, at the right post, behind both defensemen. He redirected the puck under the diving Rask's glove to give Philadelphia a 5-4 victory and another game, two nights later in Boston.

"Let's face it, it's (just) one goal," said Gagne. "But maybe now I'll have a chance to score a bigger goal that that."

Carle's feed on the gorgeous winner gave him the first four-point playoff game by a Flyer since Recchi's in 2004. "Matty was outstanding," said Laviolette. "Our guys put in a gutsy effort."

Since 1975, only seven teams of 109 that trailed in a series 0-3 had survived through Game Five. But Laviolette's club figured it wasn't playing the odds, only the Bruins. "There was nothing great about them," Gagne recalls. "We were down 3-1 and thought we should be ahead."

Six minutes into Game Five, Leino redirected a Pronger drive to give Philadelphia a 1-0 lead for the first time in the series. Boucher was looking his sharpest yet, when at 4:35 of the second period, he butterflied to save a Savard 20-footer and was bent over backwards by the weight of the tumbling Parent and Satan.

Boucher threw off his gloves, screaming in agony.

"I was in so much pain, I thought I blew both my knees out," he recalls.

As Pronger went to the bench to fetch McCrossin, the defenseman said, "Better bring a gun to put him out of his misery."

"It's over Jimmy, it's over." Boucher said when the trainer reached him.

"OK, let's just get you off the ice," said McCrossin.

On the training table, he was writhing in pain. "Oh my God," Boucher said to two attending doctors. "Please just tell me it's not my ACLs."

Fortunately it was his MCLs, which wouldn't require surgery, but Boucher, likely out for the playoffs, wasn't feeling particularly lucky. Neither was Leighton, who, having been out since March 16 with a high ankle sprain, was dressed as the backup for the first time in the series. Although still wearing a cast off the ice for protection purposes, he had been a full participant in practices for a week.

"My fitness was through the roof because I was doing cardio the whole time I was in rehab," Leighton calls. "But all that time, I couldn't do anything with my legs."

Now he had to come in without the benefit of a warmup. "It wasn't easy," he recalls. "If I let in a couple of soft goals we were done.

"My mindset was to [minimize] the pressure. How many teams come back from 0-3? We're in Boston, odds are we're going to lose on the road, so just go and play your best and hopefully it turns out well.

"Obviously I wanted to win, but that took some pressure off."

Thirty-two seconds after coming in, Leighton made a routine save on Bergeron. The next Bruin shot, by Trent Whitfield, was five minutes later. On the following shift, Leino circled out from the goal line to the blueline, picked up a puck that had hit Shawn Thornton, and fired from 40 feet. Briere picked the shot out of the air and threw it across to a wide-open Hartnell, who scored his first goal in 22 games to give the Flyers and Leighton some breathing room at 2-0.

With Begin in the penalty box for boarding Giroux, Gagne, a hot stick with a hot foot, snapped in a Richards passout to build the lead to three going into the third period. Boston, totally contained, was getting no energy from an emptying TD Garden. When Wideman's stick snapped at the point, Gagne pounced, broke out solo, leaned off Hunwick, and stuck a dart past Rask's short side.

Leighton stopped 14 of the 23 Bruin shots in the first shared playoff shutout in the NHL since one by Jacques Plante and Charlie Hodge in 1955. With a dominating 4-0 victory, Philadelphia had narrowed Boston's series lead to 3-2.

"We've been playing these types of (pressure) games since Christmas," said Laviolette. "Maybe we're conditioned to it.

"I've got to give credit to the players. Ultimately, when you're thrown lemons, it's the players that have to make lemonade. They won't stop playing."

Leino, who had a goal, an assist, and made multiple plays in traffic, was earning the coach's trust. And Leino's faith was growing. "It's a lot easier to believe now than when we were down 3-0," he said.

After appearing so determined to finish the Flyers off in Game Four, it had been a curiously flat effort by the Bruins. "We definitely would have liked to have tested [Leighton] a lot more," said Boston coach Claude Julien. "When you're outworked, you don't get shots, get frustrated, and take (10) penalties like you saw us do tonight.

"They are getting on our D quick. We are going to have to figure out a way to get some [pucks] through."

Boston had lost Krejci and Sturm while Philadelphia had gained Gagne and a reawakening Hartnell. The Flyers had reason to believe they had both destiny and superior firepower on their side.

"Why not us? Why not our team?" Briere told reporters. "We've never quit all year."

In 1975, after coming back from 0-3 to beat Pittsburgh, the Islanders rallied from that same deficit against Philadelphia, only to lose Game Seven. Since then, no other team of the 111 that dropped the first three in a series had lasted past Game Six.

Granted, 19,929 believers hardly were interested in the laws of probability while roaring at the completion of "God Bless America." But that decibel count still couldn't match the one created as Timonen made a passout between his legs, Gagne and Carcillo kept the puck alive during a goalmouth scramble, and Richards snapped in the game's first goal at 6:58 of the first period.

Five minutes later, Lucic poked the puck from Powe and Whitfield had a shorthanded breakaway. Leighton cut down the angle just as he had been working on it with goaltending coach Reese, and took the puck in his chest. Leighton made seven stops in the second half of the first period to get the game to intermission with the Flyers leading 1-0.

When the center-hung scoreboard camera cut to Boucher standing in the Zamboni entrance during the second period, the ovation swelled and his eyes filled with tears. Leighton, now holding the baton in the season-long goaltending relay, made big stops on Wideman and Satan to keep Philadelphia up a goal.

Late in the second, with the Flyers skating four-on-three, Richards fed Briere on a give-and-go. Boychuk deflected the return pass, but Briere quickly pounced and beat Rask's glove from the circle to make the score 2-0.

Vladimir Sobotka hooked Leino on a breakaway, giving the Philadelphia winger an opportunity to both beat his childhood Finnish friend, Rask, and put the game away. But Leino did neither as the Boston goalie made a windmill catch and then stopped Briere on a breakaway.

With Rask pulled, Lucic flicked home a broken down shot by Wideman to cut the lead to 2-1 with 1:00 to go. But after Richards won the center-ice faceoff, the only puck the Bruins got on goal before the clock ran out was a 155-foot prayer by Chara in the final eight seconds. By blocking 30 shots, Philadelphia had won, 2-1, to even the series, 3-3, and earn the opportunity of a lifetime.

Nobody grasped the significance of what the Flyers had a chance to accomplish better than Briere, who was watching games every night, listening to every historical nugget as it was reported. "I was very well aware," recalls Briere, still the same newspaper junkie he had been growing up. "Whatever the year, whether we still were playing or not, I always was watching playoff hockey.

"I love it. Some guys don't like to watch other teams play. But that time is magical to me."

Without the help of any known sorcerer, Philadelphia was one win away from following the 1975 Islanders, 1942 Leafs and 2003 Boston Red Sox, as teams that had advanced despite an 0-3 start. That was in 281 combined series in the NHL, NBA and MLB.

"I'm sure there's a lot of pressure on [Boston]," Briere made certain to say on the off day.

But it didn't look that way as Game Seven began at TD Garden. Hartnell helped lower the anxiety level in their building by getting called at 5:19 for high sticking Hunwick. Only eight seconds later, Ryder ripped in a powerplay goal off a deep Chara rebound to put the Bruins ahead.

Briere, angry that the Flyers had come too far to get off to a start like this, took his stick to Wideman and went to the box at 7:41. Philadelphia killed the penalty without a shot until Wideman pushed past Carle down the boards and centered to Lucic at the back door behind Giroux. Lucic had an easy redirect and, at 9:02, Boston already had a 2-0 lead. Laviolette considered calling timeout, but feared the Bruin fans were too loud for his players to hear him.

The Flyers dodged one bullet when Savard picked a puck out of the air and put it off the goalpost. Boston had four of the next five shots as Philadelphia's three games of resolute comebacking were unraveling quickly.

Timonen pinched even though Powe had possession along the halfwall so, when Lucic stole the puck, both Flyers were trapped on a Boston two-on-one. Lucic, using Savard only as a decoy, was shooting all the way. He fired a wrist shot from the right circle between Leighton's legs, building Boston's lead to 3-0.

The goalie had little chance on the first two goals, but this one was a routine shot. "A stake through-your-heart kind of goal," recalls Leighton. "I was thinking I was going to get pulled."

Backlund, the backup, had played 41 minutes for Philadelphia that season, and only one minute in the playoffs. Laviolette had no intention of making a change.

As Lucic taunted the Flyers with, "How do you like that? You [bleeping] guys are done!" Laviolette used his time out.

"When it got to 3-0, I had to do it, no matter how loud it was," the coach recalls. He was animated and encouraging, holding up his index finger. "Get one goal before the end of the period," he told his team, promising that if they could, they would win the game.

Timeouts are for different things," Laviolette recalls. "Sometimes you want to give your team [bleep], sometimes you want to pump them up, sometimes you want to tell them what they did wrong, or how to fix something.

"That one was just about being really positive. If we could go into the locker room at 3-1, we could win the game. That was in the message—just forget what happened."

Erasure had become a Philadelphia specialty over the course of the trying and inspirational season. Laviolette specifically told Leighton that he had to move on.

"You never want your coach to give up on you," the goalie recalls. "If he would have just stood there with his arms crossed or not even called a timeout, that would have been him saying, 'We're done.'"

The Flyers decided they were finished only with Lucic's insult. They had 5:50 left in the first period to work up a good grudge and get back in the game.

"We got [bleeped] off about what he said," recalls Gagne. "We [drew] energy."

Ryder, from 25 feet, had a good chance to make it 4-0, but was turned back by Leighton. At the other end, a determined Richards plowed into Wideman, then bounced off flying. But the defenseman only got his clear halfway up the boards, where Giroux was waiting to quickly throw a subtle backhand pass to van Riemsdyk coming off the same wall.

The rookie winger did a curl-and-drag on the sliding Mark Stuart and shot, the puck catching just enough of the defenseman's stick to change the trajectory past Rask's pad. On van Riemsdyk's first goal of the playoffs, Laviolette's team had followed his directive, cutting the lead to 3-1.

Briere doesn't remember it improving the mood much at intermission. But van Riemsdyk certainly seemed pumped. He stole the puck and forced a Rask save after just 50 seconds of the second period. One minute after that, Parent missed connections with Hartnell down the boards, but Briere won the race to the puck behind the net. He fed Leino, who walked out, spun to his backhand, and shot while falling. Rask made the stop, but the rebound came to Hartnell 15 feet out. He roofed the puck on his backhand and Philadelphia trailed only 3-2.

Twelve thousand fans who had gathered to watch on the center-hung scoreboard at the Wachovia Center erupted. Their Flyers were coming back.

Less than six minute later, Briere burst into the Boston zone, took a feed from Hartnell, and left Andrew Ference sprawling. Briere circled behind the net untouched, came out the other side, and banked the puck off Hunwick's pads past Rask at 8:39 to tie the match, 3-3.

The only sounds in the building came from the Philadelphia bench and the smattering of Flyer fans. "At 3-3, I think it was clear to everybody that it was over," recalls Briere.

"I think the Bruins were all frozen (at the prospect) of history."

Philadelphia, having outshot Boston 11-6 in the second period, came out for the third feeling invincible. The Flyers outhit the Bruins 9-4 in the first nine minutes of the period, and outshot them 4-3, not counting a post hit by Pronger. When Chara put one off the iron, too, more than ever, this comeback for the ages was not for the faint of heart.

Rask stopped Richards from 25 feet out, and Asham on a wrap-around. Leighton's only save of any difficulty in the period was on a 17-foot backhander by Wheeler.

With 11 minutes to go, Savard went to the Boston bench with his stick up signaling he wanted to come off, and then changed his mind. Sobotka, who had followed Savard's directions and jumped on, was all the way across the blueline before realizing he was the sixth man. The Philadelphia bench was yelling, and the linesmen acknowledged the obvious. The Bruins would be shorthanded for two minutes.

Giroux beat Begin on the faceoff. Stuart blocked a Carle drive. Gagne passed to Leino, who, unchallenged behind the net, found Richards alone along the half wall. The captain wristed one towards the net.

Gagne reached out trying to create a deflection, but the puck got by him to Stuart who, preoccupied with Leino, could only stop it. Gagne, standing at the edge of the circle, had time to put the puck on his forehand and go over Rask's blocker into the far side of the net, giving Philadelphia a 4-3 lead with 7:08 remaining.

Leighton figured it would be the longest 7:08 of his life. "Everytime I looked up, the clock had moved only 10 seconds," he recalls.

With 3:40 to go, he kicked away a redirection by Savard, crossing in the high slot.

The Flyers got the puck deep into the Boston zone with two minutes remaining. Giroux personally kept it along the backwall for 17 seconds, forcing Rask to remain in his net.

After the goalie was finally able to head for the Bruin bench, a puck caught in the netting beside Leighton to give Boston a faceoff in the Philadelphia end with 53 seconds remaining. Savard tied up Giroux and the Bruins, having the extra man, controlled. But they didn't get a good look until the final 10 seconds, when the puck wound around to Chara wide open at the right point.

He missed to the far side. At the opposite point, Wideman fired, but Giroux knocked down the Bruins last, desperate chance and calmly flipped the puck out.

Before it had even cleared the zone, Gagne's stick was up in celebration, Leighton was leaping into the arms of Richards, and the Philadelphia bench was a backslapping, shoulder pads-pounding, fraternity of joy.

Rallying from three goals down in games, and from three down on the scoreboard, the Flyers had pulled off the ultimate comeback in NHL history with a 4-3 Game Seven victory and 4-3 series triumph.

"This is a fantastic achievement in every single way that you can imagine," said a tearful Snider in the locker room. "I never, ever, in my wildest imagination thought that we could spot the other team three goals in their building and come back and beat them.

"I've never seen a team like this. I mean, it's like a storybook."

Gagne, playing with a broken foot, had scored the overtime goal that had kept the Philadelphia alive in Game Four, and then, the Game Seven winner.

"To think about what we did is crazy, just crazy," Gagne recalls. "I had been unable to do anything for a week and a half. But then, not only am I playing, I'm able to [score four goals]. That was almost too good to be true."

After flunking a goaltending trial in Chicago, Leighton had gone two years without appearing in an NHL game while being passed around by four organizations. After the best chance of his life was heartbreakingly ended with an injury suffered three weeks before the playoffs, he had come in from the cold to bring the Flyers back.

Hartnell, his desire questioned by Laviolette, had become a force in the comeback, contributing a goal in Game Seven. "I've obviously envisioned in my head what a Stanley Cup celebration would be like," he recalls. "That night was probably pretty close to being like that.

"Everybody was hugging each other. It was a great, great moment."

It didn't require Champagne—taboo by NHL custom until the Cup is won—to be celebrated as the ultimate triumph. But from an historical standpoint, it was. Nineteen years had passed since a team came from three goals down to win a Game Seven.

The players felt like it was a two-cork night when they learned eighth-seeded Montreal, which had eliminated top-seeded Washington in Round One, had just knocked off No. 2 Pittsburgh in Game Seven, earning a berth in the conference final against Philadelphia.

"We were like, 'We don't have to go through Sid (Crosby),'" Hartnell recalls. "We had played well against Montreal. It was like, 'Oh my God, we're going to go to the Final.'"

In 1979, Boston's chance to topple a Montreal dynasty had similarly been lost on a late third-period Game Seven too-many-men penalty. But the shared infamy was of no consolation to the crushed 2010 team. "Disappointed doesn't begin to explain it," Boychuk told reporters.

Lucic was gracious. "They came at us and came at us," he said of the

Flyers. "They were relentless."

So would be the Bruins' guilt for being unable to finish off Philadelphia when the team was most vulnerable. "I think that we were really comfortable, thought there's no way they're going to come back on us just because it was 3-0," recalls Lucic. "And losing Krejci in Game Three changed everything. He had been dominating."

While playing for the Flyers in 2003, Recchi had experienced ultimate joy with a series-turning triple-overtime goal in Toronto, and then scored twice as Philadelphia won Game Seven. In 2010, he suffered the definitive devastation of his career.

"It was as bad as it gets in terms of how you can feel," he recalls. "I mean, you can't even imagine being up like that and then, four straight, you're out. It was terrible.

"We weren't very good at Game Five and that was the big difference. It was like we were a little bit deflated after losing Game Four. For whatever reason, we just didn't play well."

For the first time since the league began seeding teams one through eight in 1994, the seventh team had home-ice advantage in a conference final. But any depiction of the Flyers as a Cinderella team was a misrepresentation. The preseason pick to win the Stanley Cup by *The Hockey News*, they entered the 16th semifinal in their 42 seasons more appropriately cast as a sleeping giant awakened.

Montreal, which had ridden rookie goalie Jaroslav Halak after Carey Price had faltered, was better depicted as the club defying the odds. In the absence of top defenseman Andrei Markov, who was injured in Game One of the Pittsburgh series, 6-7 journeyman Hal Gill had frustrated Pittsburgh's Crosby, but the Habs also received help from struggling Penguin goaltender Marc-Andre Fleury to win the final two games.

Two diminutive wingers—Brian Gionta, 5-7, and Michael Cammalleri, 5-9—were the biggest Montreal guns. The Canadiens were without a true offensive star, leaving Philadelphia little reason to believe it wouldn't prevail against a smaller, and less offensively gifted, opponent.

"I don't know if [the confidence] was all because of physicality," Briere recalls. "I grew up watching the Canadiens and, as successful as they were against Boston, they always struggled against the Flyers. I remember wondering, 'Why can't they beat the Flyers?'

"There was no doubt in my mind we were going to win. I was already starting to think what it would be like to play in the Stanley Cup Final for the first time."

With Price on the bench and Markov injured, the Game One Montreal lineup contained only six players from the team that had been beaten in five games by Philadelphia in the 2008 second round. There were seven holdovers on the Flyers.

Each squad was coming off a Game Seven triumph, but while the Canadiens had four days to refocus, Philadelphia had only two. Whether that was a good or bad thing remained to be seen, as period one at the Wachovia Center was a mixed bag. The Flyers were outshot 13-6, but, thanks to Scott Gomez's penalty for an after-the-whistle shove to Richards, Philadelphia led, 1-0, on Coburn's powerplay rebound.

Thirty seconds into the second period, van Riemsdyk worked a give-and-go with Giroux and scored between Halak's legs. Maxim Lapierre, engaging in more of Montreal's mindless after-the-whistle macho activity, this time against Parent, had just stepped out of the box when Briere made the score 3-0. Gagne converted a boarding penalty on Andrei Kostitsyn to build the lead to four.

Coach Jacques Martin yanked Halak, but Price allowed two more during Leighton's 6-0 shutout—the first solo blanking of his career after having shared the one in Boston's Game Five with Boucher. The line of Hartnell-Briere-Leino had each contributed a goal, with Hartnell up to three goals and five points in the last four games after having had his desire questioned by Laviolette midway through the Bruin series.

"In a meeting, [Laviolette] said, 'I knew you had it in you. That's how I felt was the best way to get it out,'" Hartnell recalls. "I told him, 'I didn't like it at the time, but I respect you for being honest with me and getting me going.' It was all good between us after that."

The next day, Laperriere—out four weeks after blocking a shot with his face during Game Five of the New Jersey series—returned to the ice wearing an oversized helmet. "I look like the (Flintstone's) Great Gazoo, but who cares?" Laperriere said. "I would have never dreamed about skating this soon or even this year."

A six-day bout with vertigo had been fixed by a procedure that balanced the crystals in his ear. He considered himself fortunate to have suffered no long-term impairment in what he called his "tiny, little brain."

"[Doctors] told me if you want to get hit in the head, you want to get hit in the front," Laperriere said. "If you go any further back, you're in trouble. I could have been blind, could have lost movement in the left side of my body."

Carter, who had been out with a foot fracture since Game Four against the Devils, also skated for 15 minutes with director of player personnel Dave Brown. "Brownie looked faster than Jeff," joked Holmgren. Carter's return was not considered imminent.

The Canadiens, shorthanded six times during Game One, had the first powerplay opportunity of Game Two, a Krajicek slash of Gill. But their opportunity disappeared when Gomez went off for hooking Giroux. On the powerplay, he made a pretty pass to Briere, who scored his ninth goal of the playoffs off the underside of the crossbar.

Montreal, nevertheless, was the better team in the first period. After Leino got caught holding Plekanec, Leighton had to stop six shots on the powerplay and make 16 saves for the Flyers to go to the break leading 1-0.

Philadelphia continued to nurse that slimmest of margins for more than 14 minutes of the second period, until Richards drew a Gionta hold and Gagne, scoring his sixth goal in six games, put away a Leino rebound.

The Flyers, increasingly in control as the game moved along, were able to put the contest away with 9:36 to go in the third period when Halak's glove betrayed him on a harmless-looking Leino shot from the bottom of the faceoff circle.

With a 30-save, 3-0 victory, Leighton joined Bernie Parent as the only Philadelphia goalie ever to record back-to-back shutouts in the postseason.

"Tonight, Michael looked as good as I've seen him," said Laviolette. "He was very calm and relaxed; in complete control of that net and everything that went on around it."

Added Timonen, "Today we had one good player out there, obviously Leighton, and the rest of us were average."

The Canadiens had controlled enough of the play for their coach to state that special teams were the only difference in the series. This was just another way for Martin to say that his team had to stay out of the box. But the Habs also had to get some saves.

In Game Three at the raucous-as-usual Bell Center, Halak denied Giroux on an early tip-in attempt. When P.K. Subban's shot went off the shin of Pronger to Cammalleri for a tap in on the weak side, Montreal had its first big break of the series and initial lead, 1-0.

Tom Pyatt took advantage of a Pronger giveaway to make it 2-0 after a first period in which the Canadien shots practically doubled the Flyer tally, 17-9. In the second, Dominic Moore beat Leighton between the legs and Gionta and Marc-Andre Bergeron added third period goals around one by Gagne. Philadelphia got clobbered, 5-1, and had its series lead cut to 2-1.

"They handed it to us right from the get-go," said Richards. "Maybe we were a little too full of ourselves. I don't know if we thought it was going to be easy."

It was getting more difficult for Pronger, who was on the ice for three of the Montreal goals. Transcutaneous electrical nerve therapy was helping the knee that had been injured during the overtime in Game One of the Boston series, but it still required periodic draining. "After we took out the fluid, I could get my range back," he recalls.

The Flyers needed their mojo back, too. Outplayed for much of Game Two, and all of Game Three, they were fortunate to still be up 2-1. "They really kicked the [bleep] out of us," Laviolette recalls about Game Three. "In every facet of the game, they were the better team."

He called a meeting that stressed getting back to basics.

Nobody in the history of the game had ever been more basic in his approach to hockey than the relentless, fearless Laperriere.

Four separate neurologists compared his tests to a baseline established during training camp and cleared him to return. Laperriere did not tell them that he also had passed in the immediate aftermath of the accident, making the recent tests worthless.

"They didn't have anything to compare, because my tests were normal even two days after I took that puck, when I was concussed for sure," Laperriere recalls.

"I felt bad because I lied to them. They need to find a real test, but that's a different story. I had been playing 16 years in The Show without ever having a sniff (at the Cup), and now I was six wins away. [Chasing that dream at practically all cost] is in our DNA, the way we are. That's why I came back.

"Was I taking a big risk? Probably. But I don't regret it at all."

Reinserted into the lineup in place of Carcillo—"Hardest decision I ever had to make," said Laviolette—Laperriere got his competitive juices going again by shoving with Roman Hamrlik along the boards in the neutral zone. Both players drew roughing penalties. By then, the Flyers already had blocked five shots, making a statement that the Canadiens were facing a different beast than in Game Three.

Carter, cleared to play much earlier than expected and put on a line with Gagne and Richards, undressed Travis Moen with a move at the blueline and fired point blank. But Halak made a pad save and Briere fired the rebound over the net.

Philadelphia kept up the pressure. Richards' passout found Leino alone at the circle, but Halak got a piece of the drive with his glove, the puck trickling behind him. Off the scramble, Carter had a second chance, but Gill stretched out along the goalline to save a goal. At the other end, Krajicek gave up the puck under pressure following a

Michael Leighton denies Montreal's Brian Gionta in Game Three of the Eastern Conference finals.

dump-in, and Kostitsyn was alone at the left circle for a backhander. He was stopped by Leighton, who then beat Moen on the rebound to keep the first period scoreless.

In the second, the Flyers stayed patient and flawless. Sergei Kostitsyn, forced by Asham along the boards at center, gave up the puck easily to Timonen, who quickly fed ahead to Giroux breaking at the blueline. Josh Gorges, compromised by a loose strap on his skate, couldn't turn with the speedy center putting Halak at Giroux's mercy. He stuck a dart over the goalie's blocker and Philadelphia led, 1-0, 5:41 into the period.

Forcing Montreal at every turn, the Flyers were running a clinic while equipment managers Derek Settlemyre and Harry Bricker were racing back to the hallway to sharpen skates. A mysterious powdery substance in the corridor leading to the bench caused Hartnell, Powe and Giroux to miss shifts. Richards would say later that his blades needed sharpening five times during the game.

But it was the Canadiens who were skating in sand. Pronger, rebounding from his worst game of the playoffs with his best performance yet, caught Montreal in a change with a pass to a breaking Leino. He sped outside Gorges and, in alone, deked as if to come across the goalmouth. As Halak butterflied to try to protect both posts, he couldn't cover the short one, enabling Leino to slide the puck between the pipe and pad to build the Philadelphia lead to 2-0.

The Bell Centre was filled with the sweetest sound a visiting hockey team can hear—silence. The Canadiens had nowhere to go and their fans had nothing to cheer during a second period in which the Habs were outshot 13-1.

In the third, Halak tried to keep his team's hopes alive with a pad stop on Briere after a spinning backhand pass by Hartnell. But with the clock ticking down under three minutes, Leighton stifled Montreal's best chance since the first period, a jam by Lapierre.

With Halak pulled, Coburn one-armed the puck up the boards to Giroux, who brushed past Hamrlik at the Philadelphia blueline and held off Moen to slide the puck from the halfwall into the empty net.

Leighton recorded a remarkable third shutout of the series, 3-0, but the mere 17 shots he had to save and the 27 the Flyers blocked were reflections of an utter shutdown. Philadelphia took a 3-1 series lead with a defensive masterpiece.

"We were trying to make too many plays at the blueline and against this team, they are going to step up," said Gionta. "They've got guys that can make plays when you turn pucks over."

Just when the Canadiens appeared back in the series, they had been utterly smothered.

"Arguably our best game of the playoffs," recalls Pronger, who played 31:07. "We dominated them."

Laperriere had played 9:13 and Carter 13:51 during their re-entries into the lineup. "Jumping right back into a series like that is as hard as it gets," Carter recalls. "But I thought I could be out there contributing."

Every player had done his job in an ultimate team effort that sent the Flyers home for Game Five with an opportunity to wrap up the series. Laviolette's club considered itself warned: Montreal also had looked finished when down 3-1 to Washington and 3-2 to Pittsburgh.

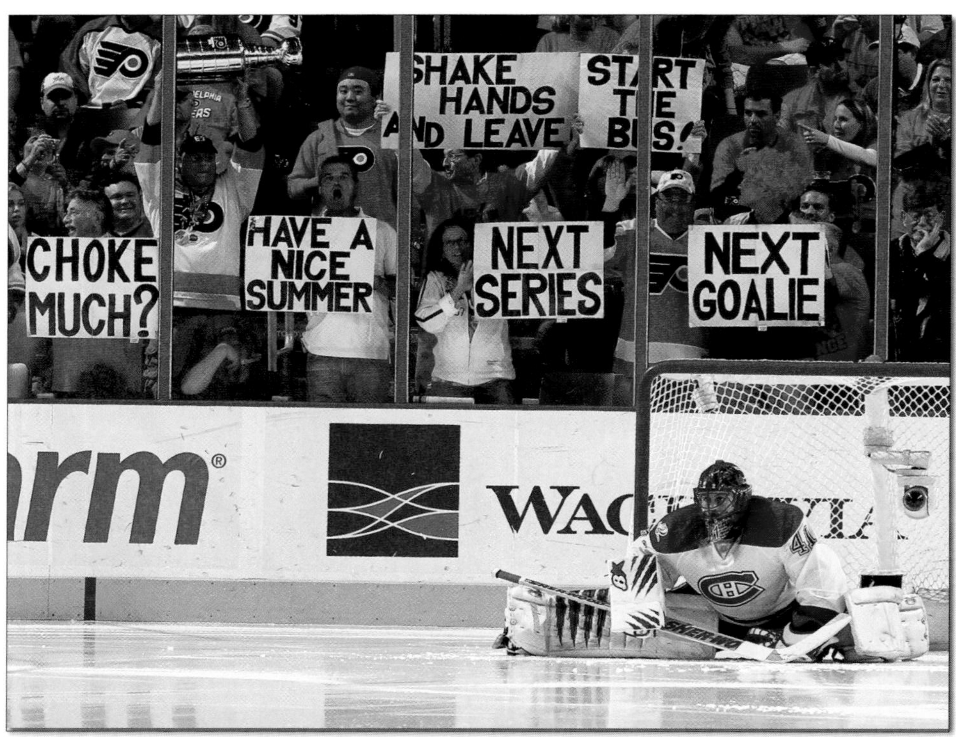

Flyer traditionalists give Mntreal goaltender Jaroslave Halak the full sign treatment at the start of Game Five.

"Their backs have been against the wall a few times in these playoffs and they've always come out and played extremely well," Pronger said. "We need to understand that."

Indeed, the din from "God Bless America" had not subsided when the Habs showed they would not go quietly. Pronger tried to hit Powe with a two-line pass at the Canadien line, but Hamrlik intercepted and fed a two-on-one with Gionta and Gomez. When Betts left the middle open to chase Gomez, Gionta took a return pass and ended Leighton's shutout streak with a shot between the legs just 59 seconds into the game.

The 1-0 hole threatened to get deeper when Timonen got called for roughing Gomez, but Richards knocked Bergeron off the puck at the point and led a shorthanded break, requiring Halak to make a pad save on Coburn.

Montreal came back up ice and Bergeron was stymied by Richards' backcheck. Having done plenty for one shift, the captain was about to go to the bench when Giroux, standing in the corner, lobbed the puck out.

It didn't have enough steam to travel the length of the ice. Richards changed his mind and took off. In a foot race with not just Hamrlik but Halak, Richards dove as the three arrived at the puck near the top of the circle almost simultaneously. All lost their balance, but the puck slid through, leaving Richards as the only one headed in the right direction, an empty net in front of him.

Rising quickly to his feet, all Richards had to worry about was avoiding the lost goaltender stick. The captain picked up the puck, skated to the goalmouth, and guided in a backhander to tie the game 1-1.

"It was just lucky," Richards recalls. "Somehow it ended up on my stick."

With a full-extension dive, he had made his luck. And his effort had earned the goal a place among the most memorable in franchise history. Not since Rod Brind'Amour scored twice on the same penalty-killing shift to put away Pittsburgh in 1997, or perhaps even 12 years earlier when Dave Poulin scored three-on-five to send Quebec home in 1985, had the Flyers and their fans had been so electrified by shorthanded magic.

With the help of a penalty to Carter for tripping Cammalleri, and a second for too many men, the Canadiens survived its rocking from the Richards goal. When Gorges was penalized for holding Gagne in the neutral zone, Montreal blocked three more shorthanded Flyer chances to go to the locker room still tied, 1-1.

Three minutes into the second period, Laperriere juiced the crowd by blocking a Subban shot and Philadelphia dumped the puck into the Canadien end. After taking a hard bump by van Riemsdyk, Kostitsyn couldn't get the puck past Carle at the point. He quickly relayed to Asham waiting behind the defense in front of Halak.

"I only have one move," Asham would say, but it looked well practiced and Halak bought it. The winger went forehand-to-backhand-to-forehand again and fired over the flopped goalie into the top of the net to put the Flyers in front, 2-1.

On the next shift, Carter dropped a backhand pass for Timonen cutting down the left wing boards. The defenseman fed Richards behind the net and went to the goalmouth, taking Gill with him and screening Halak's vision as Richards fed in front to Carter. He went to one knee to one-time the puck by Halak's glove. A masterful three-way passing play had put Philadelphia up 3-1.

Halak beat Asham on a breakaway to keep the Flyers from pulling away. Leighton had to be alert to stop Gomez after Coburn overskated a dump-in off the backboards, and later, the goaltender tracked Subban's drive all the way through traffic.

Montreal wasn't surrendering. Subban, stronger than van Riemsdyk behind the goal, grabbed the puck and fed through the legs of Coburn to Gomez, who had been left uncovered by a drifting Giroux. Gomez's quick 10-footer beat Leighton to the stick side, cutting Philadelphia lead to 3-2 with a long 13:07 to play.

Cammalleri had a chance just 30 seconds later, but was turned back by Leighton. When Pronger tempted disaster by drawing a four-minute penalty for accidentally cutting Subban, Betts and Laperriere blocked shots until Laperriere took the pressure off by drawing a trip from Glen Metropolit, leaving Montreal one-for-22 on the powerplay for the series.

As the anticipation built and the noise crescendoed, the Canadiens didn't get another shot until the clock was down to three minutes.

Timonen blocked a Cammalleri drive while Halak was on the way to the bench, Richards won two faceoffs from Plekanec and, following the second, Gagne forced Gorges at the point enabling the Flyers to break out.

Richards knocked over Plekanec and, from his stomach, fed Carter coming up the middle to the empty net. When he scored to put away the 4-2 win, the 19,986 fans, who had been holding their breaths for 13 years since the franchise's last berth in a Stanley Cup Final, exhaled a virtual twister throughout the Delaware Valley.

The Canadiens, defeated in five games, shook hands and went to the locker room to praise their opponent. "That is a very disciplined team," said Cammalleri, while the Prince of Wales Trophy for the Eastern Conference champions sat on a stand, waiting for the Philadelphia captain to pick it up. Or not.

After consulting with his teammates, Richards ignored superstition and accepted it from NHL vice president Bill Daly. Despite a long-held belief that the conference championship trophies were toxic, Crosby had held it in 2009 and the Penguins had won the Cup regardless. Besides, after all the Flyers had survived, they were of a mind to defy broken mirrors, litters of black cats, and even the Chicago Blackhawks, their opponent in the Final.

"My first instinct was to grab it," Richards said after not passing the trophy to any teammate, instead taking it directly up the tunnel to the locker room. "Obviously, it's not the trophy we want, but we haven't done anything conventionally all year, especially in the playoffs. We might as well go against the grain one more time."

Whatever their captain wanted to do, his teammates were following. "If I had to put my money on one player tonight to lead us to the win, I'd easily have put my money on Richie," said Gagne.

A shorthanded goal to add to the franchise's video collection of great moments, followed by two assists—the final one from his stomach to put away the game—put Richards' performance in the conversation with Keith Primeau's in 2004 as an inspiration for a deep Philadelphia playoff drive.

Ed Snider didn't stop there. "[Richards] reminds me of a young Bobby Clarke," said the beaming Chairman after shaking every Flyer hand in the locker room and Richards' the hardest. "He's our captain for a reason and showed it tonight."

It had also become apparent why Laviolette had placed such value in getting Laperriere—whose inspirational value was much beyond a fourth-line winger and penalty killer—back into the lineup at mid-series. Having played more games than all but two active NHL players (Hamrlik and Owen Nolan) without reaching a Final, Laperriere had made one at last.

"That's the toughest hockey player I've ever seen," said Snider. "And

Mike Richards celebrates after scoring a goal in the first period as Marc-Andre Bergeron of the Canadiens looks on in Game Five of the Eastern Conference finals. The Flyers' 4-2 win would put the team into the Stanley Cup Final for the first time since 1997.

that's saying something because I've seen a lot of them."

Pronger, who had keyed the effort to hold Cammalleri to just one goal in the series, had reached his third Final in five seasons. The only way he had not exerted his dominance was during the short debate on the ice about giving the Wales trophy a hoist. "I would rather not, just based off past precedent," the defenseman recalls. "But there have been years where the guy has touched it and won."

Laviolette said he wasn't superstitious, just proud of how his team continued to knock down its challenges.

Giroux offered a perspective to match his play—beyond his years. "You could probably make a movie out of this," he said. "It's a great story."

The Flyers were the first team since the 1959 Maple Leafs to reach the Final after making the playoffs in their last regular-season game. Leighton was the fourth goalie—joining Patrick Roy, Miikka Kiprusoff and Dwayne Roloson—to take a team this far after starting his season with a different organization. Laviolette became the eighth coach to take over a club mid-year and produce a finalist.

"It's probably our most exciting season ever since the first Stanley Cup," Snider said. "What these guys have done, and what they've been through, it's incredible."

Since the 1997 Final loss to Detroit, the Flyers three times had been turned back in the semifinals, but their frustrations had been dwarfed by decades of pain suffered by the Blackhawks. Like Philadelphia, Chicago had lost in five Finals since its last Stanley Cup win—in 1961—but only one of those defeats, in 1992, had occurred since 1971.

The Blackhawk franchise, which had missed the playoffs nine out of 10 seasons between 1998 and 2008, had been revived largely by its draft of winger Patrick Kane with the No. 1 pick in 2007, the year the Flyers had the worst record and came in second in the lottery. Philadelphia's choice—van Riemsdyk—came into the Final as a streaky rookie, but Kane had quickly become a superstar.

Jonathan Toews—Kane's center and the third pick in the 2006 draft—had developed into perhaps the best two-way forward in the game; and Duncan Keith, a second-round draft choice in 2002, had become an anchor defenseman. The previous summer's signing of 30-plus goal scorer Marian Hossa had created a dynamic second line with Troy Brouwer and Patrick Sharp, the best young player the Flyers ever traded away.

Chicago, 112 points strong through the regular season, had beaten Nashville and Vancouver in six games, and then swept San Jose to come into the Final as a 2-1 favorite in Las Vegas for the Stanley Cup. But those odds seemed inflated by Philadelphia's seventh-seeded status as the postseason began. That inconsistent team had disappeared six weeks earlier. Most of the prognosticators gave the Blackhawks only a slight edge. And as usual, Briere was reading every word.

"All the media was saying that Chicago was a little better," he recalls. "I was okay with that. New Jersey and Boston were supposed to be better and we found ways to win those two series.

"The one thing that worried me a little was that we had played three similar teams, system wise—all trap teams. Chicago was a totally different type, a lot more creative up front and still with a lot of depth."

It was one thing to trap the trappers, as the Flyers had done in Game Four to take command of the Montreal series. But the Blackhawks were going to be coming quicker.

"They were a team that liked to swing things back and come at you through the neutral zone with speed," recalls Laviolette. "Defensively, we knew we had to be good."

That had become problematic as the coach had lost trust in his third defensive pair. Pronger, on a knee that required periodic draining, probably needed to be playing less, but Parent and Krajicek had been on the ice fewer than six minutes each in the clinching game of the Montreal series.

Despite seven Flyers over age 30, Pronger was the only one who had won a Cup. But John Madden, Tomas Kopecky and Andrew Ladd were the only players with rings on the Blackhawks, so there was virtually no edge in experience or in goal, where Chicago's Antti Niemi, an undrafted free agent, had taken over for Cristobal Huet in March.

Leighton was a waiver-wire wonder, but his .948 save percentage demonstrated he hardly had been a passenger in this Philadelphia ride. It probably had been since Ron Hextall's heyday that the Flyers were close to a championship without facing a more accomplished goaltender on the other side.

Blackhawk coach Joel Quenneville didn't see an appreciable advantage for his club. "My God, the Flyers had a good team," he recalls. "They had three lines that could all go, a useful checking unit and Pronger. All the assets were there."

The NHL, gifted with a Final between two traditional franchises from top-seven television markets, had most of the elements to make it one of the most watched in history. Missing only was a recent rivalry. The one playoff series between the two teams was a 1971 sweep by the fabled Blackhawks of Bobby Hull and Stan Mikita in Philadelphia's fourth season of existence. Rocky Wirtz, Chicago's principal owner, did what he could to stoke a little loathing by throwing away all his orange ties and directing the clients of his liquor distribution business to promote the (tomato juice) Bloody Mary over the (orange juice) Screwdriver.

On the secondary-ticket market, seats for the games in Philadelphia were going for an average of $587; in Chicago it was $766. As the anticipation built, Gagne looked over the sea of reporters at a press conference in the Windy City the day before the first contest and had an epiphany.

"I think it's just starting to sink in," he said. "To see all this media and attention, I realize that after 10 years, I'm finally here."

Perhaps that was why both teams looked awestruck as Game One began. Leino's drive from the circle went in off Niklas Hjalmarsson to give the Flyers a lead after six minutes. But just 1:08 later, Brouwer drifted away from Asham in the high slot and beat Leighton on the stick side to tie the match 1-1.

With Kane in the box for slashing van Riemsdyk, his good friend from the USA Hockey development system, Coburn fumbled the puck at the point and Dave Bolland broke away to beat Leighton between his legs.

The Blackhawks led 2-1, but on the efforts of Hartnell, Philadelphia came right back. On a powerplay, he converted a rebound of a Pronger one-timer to tie the score, and then stole the puck from Kane so that Briere could bang in his own rebound with 27 seconds remaining in the first period. The Flyers took a 3-2 lead into the first intermission.

A minute into the second period, Pronger missed a poke check along the boards and Betts got caught in no-man's-land as Chicago broke out two-on-one with Sharp and Hossa. Leighton appeared to be expecting a pass when Sharp beat the goalie's glove on the short side to create a 3-3 tie.

Betts atoned, unassisted, off a Brouwer cough-up along the boards, beating Niemi to the far side. Philadelphia led again, 4-3, but Krajicek failed to react on a Kopecky passout and Kris Versteeg easily swept in the puck to create the game's fourth tie, 4-4.

Half the game had not yet been played. "Oh my God, that was nuts," Quenneville recalls. "The goalies couldn't stop the puck and everything went in."

Brouwer was left all alone by multiple Flyer spectators for an easy conversion of a Hossa passout to put the Blackhawks back up, 5-4. Philadelphia's defensive-zone coverage was horrendous, but Leighton also wasn't riding to the rescue, so Laviolette went to Boucher, who hadn't played since tearing both MCLs 19 days earlier. The Flyers responded again, Asham beating Niemi off a cross-ice feed from Briere to tie the game 5-5.

On adrenaline, but minimal practice time, Boucher butterflied to stop a Bolland redirection. The play tightened up; the next mistake probably would mean the game.

Midway through the third period, Hjalmarsson struggled with a bouncing puck at the point, but Bolland saved it. Thinking the puck was out, Gagne got caught in the neutral zone, and then didn't come back hard as Versteeg's pass through Coburn found Kopecky one-on-one with Boucher. The goalie challenged, so Kopecky, in the lineup only because of an injury to Ladd, went around Boucher to put Chicago ahead, 6-5, with 11:35 remaining.

"I thought he might have run out of room, but he made a pretty good play," recalls Boucher. "You don't expect him to be open on a cross-ice [pass], but he had the poise to not shoot it, just made a pump and deke."

Niemi tracked a Richards drive through traffic with Gagne at the post ready to pounce, and then gloved a screamer from the high slot by Briere with two minutes to play. The last 13 shots of the game were taken by the Flyers and the Blackhawk goalie stopped them all.

After Pronger's shot in the final seconds was blocked, appropriately by Bolland—whose line with Kopecky and Versteeg had been the difference in the game—the Philadelphia defenseman denied Chicago the winner's usual pleasure of retrieving the puck. Pronger picked it up instead.

The Flyers had been good with it, horrendous without it, losing Game One, 6-5, and squandering an opportunity to get a jump in the series.

"We were a little bit too loose in front of our net," Laviolette understated. "We left too many point-blank opportunities, sometimes with [defenders] there."

Philadelphia had not taken one penalty. Nor had one player on a top line scored any of the 11 goals in what ended up being the highest-scoring game in the Final in 19 years.

"To have two big-market teams playing a wild game to start it off was amazing," Briere recalls. "We didn't come up on top but realized we were right there with them."

The Flyers also understood they couldn't win like this. "We need to play with a little more gusto in our own end," said Pronger.

Carcillo, swallowing what he called "the most bitter pill" when he was scratched in Game One, replaced van Riemsdyk on the Richards line for Game Two. Bartulis replaced Parent, who had played 41 seconds and been on for the first Blackhawk goal, on the third defensive pair.

But the biggest change in the second contest was the return of two fundamentally sound teams that apparently had been kidnapped before Game One.

Game Two looked much more like a playoff match. Both goalies were also sharper. Leighton tracked a dangerous Kane drive through traffic 17 minutes into the first period. Niemi stopped Hartnell twice, one on a Carcillo-fed breakaway, the other on a setup by Asham. But Philadelphia managed only three shots in the first period and, for most of the second, was not generating much either.

Leighton stoned Keith from the slot following a good pass from Sharp. Niemi used his right pad to stop Richards, and then stretched his glove on a one-timer by Asham to keep the game scoreless.

The period was in its final three minutes and the Flyers were coming on when Sharp, standing at the top of the circle, one-timed a pass from pointman Brent Seabrook. Leighton butterflied to make the save and Brouwer took a whack at the rebound, but it landed at the feet of Hossa, unchallenged by a passive Krajicek. Hossa's shot hit Leighton's pad and bounced high into the net to give Chicago a 1-0 lead.

On the next shift, Dustin Byfuglien picked off Asham's lead pass at center for Gagne. He carried the puck in and dropped it to Ben Eager, who used Carle as a screen. "I didn't see him release it," said Leighton, who was beaten over his glove. Two goals in 28 seconds had put the Blackhawks up 2-0.

A minute later, Leighton kept the hole from deepening by making a left pad save on Brouwer off a steal from Richards. The third period began with Philadelphia trailing only by two.

With Sharp in the penalty box for tripping Briere, Gagne beat Niemi with a one-timer from the left circle to cut the lead to 2-1 at 5:20. The Flyers, outshooting Chicago 15-4 in the third period, came hard, but Keith tied up Gagne at the side of the net to prevent a rebound on a Timonen try. With two minutes to go, Leino pulled the puck inside Brent Sopel and was in, but Niemi trapped the shot against his body, the last good Philadelphia chance of many down the stretch of a 2-1 defeat.

"That was us, that was our game," said Timonen. "We didn't play it enough in the first two periods."

At the buzzer, Pronger picked up the puck again, this time not unobserved. Eager left the happy Blackhawk celebrants to confront the Flyer defenseman, who shot the puck at Eager, and then threw one of the white waving towels given away at the doors that had been tossed onto the ice. Both players were given misconducts.

In the locker room, Pronger threw the puck in the garbage can. "Where it belongs," he said, and then sarcastically answered questions from members of the media intrigued by his hijinks.

"That was great for us," Briere recalls. "We don't have to talk about why we lost the first two games. The focus is all on him, on why he's stealing the pucks, and where are the pucks. He's taking all the heat, so smart on his part."

The Philadelphia horse—Pronger followed a 31-minute Game One with an almost 28-minute Game Two—had turned Trojan horse for a team going home down 2-0. In 33 Finals where a team had held serve in the first two games at home, only twice had it not won the series.

Briere thought the Flyers had gone overboard in their efforts to tighten up in Game Two.

"I thought we were way too conservative in the first two periods," he said. "We didn't give them much. I understand that, but it's not really our type of hockey. We didn't forecheck."

Having been swept by Detroit in 1997, Philadelphia's streak of losses in Finals was at seven, going back to Game Seven in Edmonton in 1987. They needed more than Pronger's impish sense of humor to change the karma.

"I thought we played well enough to get two (wins in Chicago)," recalls Laviolette. "I don't think our guys thought [the Blackhawks] were better than us."

The Flyers had been playing Michael Jackson's "Don't Stop Until You Get Enough" in the locker room and wearing similarly-inscribed t-shirts since the beginning of their run. They intended to follow their own advice.

The two teams flew at each other from the start of Game Three. Kane came closest to scoring, hitting a post on a rebound from Byfuglien, but Philadelphia was carrying more of the play. Almost 15 minutes into the period, Briere burst past Keith into the offensive zone and fired, the rebound bouncing out to Giroux, who fed Coburn's one-timer. Niemi made another stop, but Hartnell's remarkable behind-the-back blind pass to Briere enabled his easy tap-in for a 1-0 Philadelphia lead.

In the first minute of the second period, Niemi made a point-blank save on Gagne. Richards, set up by Leino, had an empty net and missed, not a good idea, because there was only so long the Flyers were going to keep Kane pointless in the series. The Chicago star picked up the puck behind the net, skated out into the left circle and fed cross-ice to Keith, whose shot went off Carter's stick, blooped over everybody's head, and dropped behind Leighton into the goal to tie the game 1-1.

The 6-5 Byfuglien, Quenneville's antidote-of-choice for Pronger, crawled under his skin far enough to draw a slash from the big defenseman and a two-minute penalty. After the Blackhawks fired six shots at Leighton during the penalty, it was Pronger's turn to exploit Byfuglien. He was called for slashing Pronger, who, on the powerplay, wristed a puck from straight up the slot that Hartnell deflected on goal.

The puck so barely trickled over the line that Hjalmarsson was able to whisk it out before referee Bill McCreary could get a good look.

Play continued for another 90 seconds and the penalty was killed before there was a break for McCreary to get on the phone with

More overtime heroics: Claude Giroux scores on Antti Niemi of the Chicago Blackhawks to win Game Three of the Stanley Cup Final 4-3.

Toronto. The replay showed the puck on its end, with visible space between it and the goalline—the Flyers led, 2-1.

Sopel scored with a point blast off Madden's clean faceoff win over Richards, and the two teams went to the third period tied 2-2. Two minutes in, Leino, usually the Fort Knox of puck protection, wriggled his way to the slot, but this time was pilfered by Eager. He tipped the puck ahead to Toews, who quickly fed to Kane before Coburn could turn. Timonen, who had pinched without support, had no chance to catch up as Kane roared in and beat Leighton between his blocker and pad to put Chicago ahead, 3-2.

The Wachovia Center fell silent. For 20 seconds. Leino, on a mission of redemption, came through center, dished to Giroux and went to the net. Giroux threw the puck ahead and it ricocheted off Sopel and the pad of Niemi right back to Leino, the puck magnet, who had an empty net in front of him to quickly re-tie the game, 3-3. "Everything he touches seems to be working for him," said Giroux.

Philadelphia became the aggressor again. With eight minutes to go, Niemi butterflied on Giroux from the slot and gloved a Coburn rebound. There were four minutes remaining when Brian Campbell's stick broke and Leino again fed Giroux, but the defenseman recovered to kick the puck away. Twenty five seconds before the end of regulation, Keith was stopped from the high slot by the right pad of Leighton, only the fourth Blackhawk shot of the period to the Flyers' 15. "We felt that we created so much that it was just a matter of time," Briere would say later.

Four minutes into the overtime, Carter forced a giveaway by Keith and Gagne fired. The puck slid against the post and along the goalline as sticks went up in celebration. But the replay showed the puck never had entered the net.

The letdown fans barely had settled back in their seats when the Blackhawks made a poor line change, leaving them mostly in chase as Carle entered the zone and pulled up. Bolland let Giroux go to to the net to cover Carle, who delivered a pass perfectly for Giroux to redirect between Niemi's legs. At 5:59 of overtime, Philadelphia had won, 4-3, to cut the Blackhawks' series lead to 2-1.

"The guys didn't want to come back again from 3-0," said Giroux. "In Chicago, I don't think we played close to what we should have been playing. Any time we face adversity, we find a way to get it done."

It was the third-straight one-goal result in a series of big momentum swings. Every time the Blackhawks had appeared dominant, the Flyers had re-taken charge, a reflection of their playoff path. "Down 2-0 for us is comfortable," said Laviolette. "We're okay with that. We know how to battle through it."

Quenneville, wanting a little more size for that fight, dressed winger Ladd and defenseman Nick Boynton, mostly to contend better with Pronger. Philadelphia, however, started fast in Game Four. Three minutes in, Carter had an empty net on a rebound, but Seabrook made a block with his skate. On the next shift, Leighton stuffed Toews' point-blank attempt, then dove to beat him to the post as he circled the net with the rebound.

After Briere drew a high-sticking penalty by Kopecky, Richards sneaked up on Hjalmarsson behind the net, stripped him, and startled Niemi on the short side for a 1-0 Flyer lead. Leighton, looking his sharpest of the series, did the splits on Keith while Timonen was in the box for hooking Hossa.

Off a van Riemsdyk passout, Briere spun and fired. When the puck went off Hjalmarsson's stick at the post, Carle quickly put it into the net to make the score 2-0 on two unassisted goals.

But four minutes later, Chicago struck back. Keith pinched on Hartnell along the wall and relayed cross-ice to Sharp. With Coburn crossing in front to cover Hossa, Leighton picked up the puck late and Sharp's wrister sailed through to get the Blackhawks on the board, 2-1.

Hartnell helped get that goal back less than a minute later, pulling up on Sopel, feeding back to the rushing Timonen, who found Giroux hiding in plain sight at the left post. He swept in Timonen's feed with 37 seconds remaining before intermission to boost the lead to 3-1. Fourteen hits and four takeaways had fueled a dominant Philadelphia first period.

The amazing Leino made it 4-1 by pulling up on Boynton, firing as Carle went to the net, and getting lucky when a drive going wide caromed off Versteeg's back and past Niemi. It was the seventh goal and 16th point of the playoffs for a player whom Laviolette had not dressed for the first four games of the initial round.

With nine minutes remaining in the game, Briere had a chance to seal the deal but hit the post. And soon, 4-1 didn't look like such a comfortable lead anymore.

Hartnell ignored warnings given to both teams by referee Stephen Walkom to not bang sticks against the boards and was called for unsportsmanlike conduct, giving Chicago an unnecessary powerplay. When Coburn was penalized for holding Kane 1:03 later, the Blackhawks would have a two-man advantage for 45 seconds. It took just 12 for Bolland, waiting at the back door, to redirect a Keith feed and make the score 4-2.

Leighton turned back Byfuglien from the slot and the Flyers got through the Coburn penalty unscathed. But Campbell gained the zone and threw the puck ahead for Toews, who took Timonen to the net and got the break that was intended. The shot bounced off the stick of the defenseman and past Leighton to pull the Blackhawks within 4-3 and turn knuckles white all over the Delaware Valley.

Carle almost immediately rushed the puck back up ice to try to restore some breathing room, but was stopped by Niemi, who did a snow angel to keep it out. With 1:50 remaining, Seabrook's attempt to find Toews at the far post hit Coburn's skate and bounced fortunately wide.

Richards won a defensive zone draw with 25 seconds left in the game. When Keith couldn't settle down the bouncing puck, Carter soloed to the empty net to put away a 5-3 victory and tie the series 2-2.

Pronger, who was plus-four and blocked three shots, conceded the game puck to Hartnell. Chicago had more important things to worry about. "I thought we were very generous in the first period," said Quenneville, whose team lost its 10th straight game in Philadelphia.

The Blackhawk coach decided to shake up his lineup. With Kane minus-six in the series, Toews minus-three, and their linemate

Ville Leino and Danny Briere celebrate Leino's third-period goal that gave the Flyers a 4-1 lead in Game Four of the 2010 NHL Stanley Cup Final. The Blackhawks would make it close as the Flyers would need an empty net goal to win the game 5-3

Chicago's Patrick Kane celebrates after scoring the Stanley-Cup winning goal in overtime in Game Six of the 2010 NHL Stanley Cup Final.

Byfuglien's physicality being neutralized by Pronger, Quenneville moved Sharp up to the big line and put Byfuglien with Versteeg and Bolland.

It wasn't really going to change the matchups, which Quenneville controlled at home regardless. But the changes seemed to re-energize Chicago, forcing Leighton to be good early in Game Five. Seven minutes into the contest, the Flyer goalie came across to foil Sharp's bid off a backdoor pass to Kane. Philadelphia then had to kill a Krajicek penalty for crosschecking Kopecky.

"We survived the first six or seven minutes and they didn't score," Laviolette said later. "I thought that would be the worst of it."

When Bolland went to the box for crosschecking Leino, the Flyers had a chance to do better than just survive. But they didn't get a shot, let alone a lead.

Bolland had just stepped back on the ice when Hartnell's stick came up on Sharp, putting the Blackhawks on the powerplay. On their first shot, Versteeg's passout ticked off Pronger to Seabrook 30 feet from the goal. His shot then went off the Flyer defenseman again on the way to beating Leighton 12:17 into the period.

Three minutes later, Pronger got a piece of a Sopel try from the point and Leighton swept the puck behind the net, from where Bolland quickly banked in Chicago's second score off the goalie's skate. It stayed 2-0 for only three minutes, until Versteeg went left to right, taking Pronger with him, and shooting back across everybody, including Leighton, who seemed to not pick up the puck before it was by him.

Down 3-0 on three goals within 5:58, Laviolette went to Boucher as the second period began. He had not yet made a stop when Briere jammed the puck through Niemi hugging the post, allowing Hartnell an easy tap-in at the back door to get Philadelphia on the board.

Boucher came out to foil Hossa on a semi-breakaway. Philadelphia almost had the lead down to one when Powe lobbed to Betts, who had a step on Toews at the far post. But Niemi came across and made the save.

On the next shift, Carle got caught at center by a Sharp pass and Ladd broke in one-on-one against Pronger. He blocked the shot but the puck came right back to Ladd, who threw it across to Kane, untended by Briere. Boucher dove in vain across the goalmouth as Kane boosted the Blackhawks lead to 4-1 at 3:13 of the second period.

The Leino-Hartnell-Briere line immediately went back to work, busying Hjalmarsson and Campbell in a goalmouth scramble, enabling Timonen to jump into the slot and beat Niemi on the stick side.

The score was 4-2 and apparently about to turn 4-3 when Gagne, with Seabrook in the box for closing his hand on the puck, hit a wide-open Richards at the goalmouth. The pass was just a little too tight into the captain's body, however, keeping him from facing the net. His redirect went back into the fortunate Niemi.

Byfuglien crunched Pronger hard, knocking him over backwards. But Boucher kept the Flyer hopes alive by butterflying on a circling Kane from the high slot and then beating Toews on a two-on-one. Pronger took a penalty for hooking Kane, however, and Byfuglien was alone in front for an easy redirect from Toews that boosted Chicago's edge to 5-2.

Six minutes into the third period, Philadelphia cut it to two again when Niemi left a rebound of a Krajicek shot and van Riemsdyk, back in the lineup after a two-game benching, scored from 18 feet out. The Flyers had a powerplay, too, after Versteeg slashed Pronger, but managed only one shot on it. With just under four minutes remaining, Kane burst past Asham, led a two-on-one and dropped to Sharp, who shot from the hashmarks and beat Boucher to the blocker side. Chicago led 6-3.

Briere needed stitches because of an uncalled high stick by Keith, further annoying the steaming Flyer coach. "They said it was on a followthrough, not sure I understand the call," Laviolette would say.

Gagne, open on a crisscross with Leino after Keith suffered a broken stick and Seabrook lost his balance, again brought Philadelphia back to within two before Byfuglien hit the empty net and Eager picked up the puck. The Blackhawks, 7-4 winners, had taken a 3-2 lead in the Final. "This was the pace we were looking for the entire series," said Quenneville.

Pronger, plus-seven in the first four games, had been on the ice for six of the seven Game Five goals and in the penalty box for the other. The defenseman had been played like a pinball pylon on three of the scores, which largely were bad luck, but his knee injury (in Game One of the Boston series) was catching up to him and he wasn't moving as well.

"The fifth game was probably the worst I felt," he recalls. "It had been hit 1,000 times, or whatever. The (transcutaneous electrical nerve) therapy is supposed to work for 28 days and we were past that."

Pronger had been too good to wind up as a victim. The same went for the Flyers who still were only two games away from the Stanley Cup and deserving all the support they were getting from their coach.

Asked on the off day which goalie would be play Game Six, Laviolette feigned indignation. "Our goaltender has the best numbers in the playoffs," he said. "I didn't think I had to announce it."

Richards had one goal in the series and Carter none. Together they were minus-11. "Mike has proven in everyone's eyes a big-time player," said Laviolette. "I would expect a big game from him tomorrow.

"Jeff doesn't have a lot of time under his belt (after returning midway through the Montreal series). I think he was making strides up until [Game Five].

"In general, we weren't good enough as a team. It didn't seem like anybody brought their best game. But I've learned that one playoff game doesn't have much to do with the next one. I lived it in (the) 2006 (Final). We (Carolina) went to Edmonton in Game Six and really got outplayed. In Game Seven, we probably had our best game of the year.

"There are seven separate chapters in this book. I'm certain Chris Pronger will have a big game and lead the way. But we need to make sure we have all hands on deck."

With common sense suggesting Pronger was playing injured, the defenseman was asked about his status for Game Six. "Day-to-day with hurt feelings," he smiled.

Quenneville didn't have to soothe or protect any egos after Chicago's best performance of the series. "I thought we had better speed, better attack, more consistency, more pressure," he recalls. "We didn't have to defend as much as we had been.

"And then we got a great start to Game Six."

Leighton was fortunate early. Keith and Kane hit posts and Toews fanned on a bouncing rebound with the goalie sprawled. But Philadelphia had some chances too. Niemi made a stop on a point-blank tip by Carter from Gagne. Leino, set up by Briere, was tied up in the goalmouth by Keith.

The Flyers dodged a Pronger penalty with only one Blackhawk shot and managed none themselves while Sopel was off for interfering with Giroux. But when Pronger went to the box for a second time, for high sticking Versteeg, Chicago took advantage quickly. Toews won the faceoff from Betts and found Byfuglien in front for a backhander that gave the Blackhawks a 1-0 lead at 16:49.

Chicago was dominating, outshooting Philadelphia 17-2. But Leino drew an interference penalty by Sopel and, this time, it was the Flyers striking quickly on the powerplay. Briere, set up by Pronger, hammered a shot from the top of circle and Hartnell put in the rebound to tie the game, 1-1, 27 seconds before the first period expired.

On the opening shift of the second, Gagne picked off a Kopecky pass at center, went in alone and fired for the stick side, but Niemi made a blocker save. On a four-on-four created in part by a mindless Hartnell penalty for high sticking Hjalmarsson, Leighton followed Ladd across the goalmouth to keep the score 1-1.

Keith's skates locked with Hartnell's, sending both players flying and enabling Krajicek's stretch pass to get to Leino at the Chicago line. He went in on a virtual two-man breakaway with Briere, who took the pass from the lower edge of the circle and roofed his 12th goal and 29th point of the postseason to put Philadelphia up 2-1.

Only nine seconds later, Coburn was called for crosschecking Ladd. When Hossa took a penalty for running over Leighton, it appeared the Flyers were off the hook but, with the two teams skating four-on-four, Keith took advantage of the extra room. The defenseman carried into the Philadelphia zone and fed in the middle to Bolland. He quickly relayed to Sharp, who beat Leighton to the short side, tying the game, 2-2 at the midway point.

It wasn't a good goal. But Leighton had no chance on the next one, a Ladd redirection of a Hjalmarsson drive that left the Blackhawks, up 3-2, 20 minutes from the Stanley Cup.

Although outshot 27-13, after two periods, the Flyers had come too far to surrender. They came hard.

Briere, working a give and go with Gagne, had room on the far side but just missed on his backhand. Leighton kept his team alive by stopping Toews who fired from 30 feet up the slot on a Hossa pull-up at the halfwall.

With the clock just under five minutes, Coburn pinched down the boards to force a turnover by Ladd, and Richards had a good whack at the loose puck from 20 feet. Niemi closed his pads.

Just nine seconds later, Pronger passed from the sideboards, the puck got tangled in Keith's skate, and Richards poked it to Giroux. But he couldn't get enough elevation to beat Niemi's butterfly.

Toews beat Briere on the ensuing faceoff and Chicago cleared the zone. But Leino brought the puck past All-Star defenseman Keith, then by the Selke candidate Toews and passed out to Hartnell, who had position on Hossa in front of the goal.

"I knew it was going to come to me," Hartnell recalls. The puck bounced off the winger's shin pad, caromed off Keith and then Hartnell's stick, to sneak inside the far post and tie the game with 3:59 to go.

The Flyers had made one more comeback and the Wachovia Center was a nuthouse. Hartnell, who had taken a hit from Toews a split second too late to prevent the goal, got up faster than the Blackhawk captain, who wound up under Giroux. Toews, his knee injured, struggled back to the bench.

With 90 seconds remaining, Richards strong-armed Hjalmarsson and fed Giroux. He quickly relayed to Carter, who had time to circle out from behind the net to 17 feet up the slot, leaving Niemi at the mercy of one of the league's best snipers.

"I would put my money on Jeff Carter any day of the week," Laviolette recalls. "That kid could shoot pucks."

Niemi butterflied and pitched forward. "He didn't even save it," Carter recalls. "I hit him in the head."

Chicago made it to overtime with Toews taking just one more shift.

Twenty seconds into sudden death, Richards stepped in front of a Keith pass for Seabrook, tipped the puck to the corner, and then stole it from Niemi. The Philadelphia captain centered off Keith's stick to Giroux at point-blank range, but Niemi made the save with his right pad.

At 2:35 of the extra session, Toews took his second shift since the collision, lost a faceoff to Richards, and went off immediately.

Almost four minutes had been played when Kane fired from 52 feet and missed the net, but the Blackhawks applied pressure. Ladd tied up Coburn along the backboards and Powe blindly threw the puck up the left boards, where Campbell was waiting at the point.

He faded towards the middle to open room for Kane, waiting along the wall. The Chicago star took the pass and did a head fake on Timonen to gain a half step down the boards, but the defenseman allowed no room to cut in, so Kane shot from the lower edge of the circle.

"Kane was coming down the wall and I knew that he had pressure on him," recalls Leighton. "I knew that there were guys coming towards the front of the net.

"I leaned on my right leg a little bit to push towards the traffic in front and he threw a quick shot at my feet."

The goalie wasn't square to the shooter and his stick not against the ice. The puck went under him, skimmed just inside the goalline, landed inside the far post, and became stuck underneath padding.

Kane's arms were up instantly. He continued around the back of the net and, throwing his gloves and stick, raced the length of the ice towards Niemi, the Chicago players pouring off their bench in a merry chase.

"I don't think any of us knew it actually went in," Brouwer would say later. "We just followed the flow."

While mobbing each other at the opposite end of the ice, the Blackhawks were stealing glances at the officials.

Gagne, the closest Flyer, asked Leighton where the puck was.

"It's in the net." Leighton said. "Under the padding."

When one of the linesmen asked the same question, the goalie lied. "I don't know," he said. As the official looked first in the mesh, not under the padding, Leighton tampered with the evidence, lifting the goal off the magnets and kicking the puck into the corner.

"Obviously they were going to check the video," he recalls. His only hope was that the replay would not be clear.

But it was. The Blackhawks had won the Stanley Cup.

"The worst feeling of my life," Leighton remembers. "To come so close and have it end on a goal like that was just terrible."

On the bench, Pronger was dumbfounded. "It's in? How did that go in?" he wondered, and then, realizing that how didn't matter, put his head down on the boards.

For two months, Briere felt as if he had been starring in a blockbuster "2010 Flyer Story," and was just following the director's orders. In disbelief, he stared at the Chicago celebration. "This was not in the script," Briere recalls thinking. "It's not written this way.

"I think I was more in shock at that point than devastated."

The fans mustered a supportive "Let's go Flyers!" chant even before the player handshakes. Most of the audience stayed to watch Toews, the Blackhawk captain and playoff MVP, accept the Stanley Cup from Commissioner Gary Bettman.

From Chicago's point of view, the 16th overtime Cup winner in history had happened in the nick of time. "I don't think Jonathan could have played Game Seven," recalls Quenneville.

The Blackhawks, in no hurry to interrupt a night that would last forever, partied on the ice and in their quarters for hours; the Flyers went to a crowded home locker room filled with media, but empty in feeling.

"I not only realized the game was over, but the series and my career, too," recalls Laperriere, who had played through concussion symptoms. "Down deep, I knew it was over for me."

Recalls Pronger, "I have an ice bag for my knee in the training room and Lappy is in there crying."

"You hear stories about guys who get to the Final their first years in the league and never get there again. These chances don't grow on trees. I don't think young guys realize how difficult it is to get there."

Carter, 25, already understood fully. "That was as tough as it gets," he recalls. "It is so much harder if you get that close and have it slip away.

"It probably makes you stronger in the long run, but so many guys never get another chance."

Timonen had played 11 seasons to get that opportunity, and looks back at it as squandered. "We didn't play like we did against Boston," he recalls. "It disappointed me."

As Gagne looks back, the Flyers had hit the wall. "Now I can see we were emotionally and physically exhausted," he recalls. "That comeback against Boston drained a lot of energy from us, and having to come back from 0-2 against Chicago took away the rest.

"The tank was empty for a lot of guys, including me. The Blackhawks had more left than we did. But if we got the goal in overtime in Game Six anything could have happened in Game Seven. So to get far and have the balloon just pop, it's tough to swallow.

"You are so drained, almost too tired to think about it. For me, it took a week or two to totally sink in. And then it felt horrible. It was one of the worst summers ever."

Recalls Pronger: "Your body is running on adrenaline for two months. You play, get a day off, do maintenance. Then it's over. There's a little grace period where your body is asking, 'Are we not still doing this?' and then realizes it can relax. That's when things start to swell up and get sore. The adrenaline shifts off and the pain comes."

Leighton has wrestled with the emotional ache ever since.

"The first couple days, I was hanging out at my house," he recalls. "When one of my good friends invited me to a Phillies game, I told him I didn't want to be in public.

"He said, 'No, you need to get out,' and he convinced me. During the game, they showed me on the [video scoreboard] and I got a standing ovation. After the goal and the loss, to see how much they appreciated what we did and what I did was unbelievable. It was big, changed the way I thought a lot of people were looking at me.

"It's going to be hard for the rest of my life. People always are going to remember me for that goal. I know that. But what happened at the Phillies game made me feel a lot better about the whole year.

"I helped the Flyers come back from 3-0. I had three shutouts in a series. I played in the Stanley Cup Final. Not many goalies in the NHL can say they did all that, including ones that make $5-$8 million a year.

"Regardless of how that year finished, I looked at it as successful for me. I didn't win a Stanley Cup and that was disappointing. But I was there. I lived it."

Michael Leighton and Patrick Kane exchange congratulations and consolation in the handshake line after Chicago's Cup-clinching 4-3 win in Game Six of the Final.

SIMON GAGNE

On one of the most fortunate days in Flyer history, Simon Gagne slipped to 22nd in the 1998 draft because a number of teams were worried about the 160-pound player's ability to withstand body contact. Eye contact, however, never was a problem.

"When I sat with him, he would look right at me," recalls Rick Tocchet, whose career was winding down while Gagne became a rookie sensation in 2000. "He was taking it all in. I loved that; he was a sponge.

"He could have come in all cocky, maybe gotten away with a little bit, but he was respectful. And when he hit the ice in practice, he would do some magic stuff."

Over 11 seasons, Gagne did pretty well in the games, too. His 264 Philadelphia goals included years of 47 and 41, plus two more of 34 and 33. The left wing's 32 playoff scores included one in Game Four overtime that kept the Flyers alive against Boston in 2010, and another in Game Seven of that series to climax the comeback from an 0-3 deficit. He also scored the 2004 sudden-death goal to force Game Seven of a conference final against Tampa Bay.

For a lightweight, that is a ton of accomplishment. And Gagne's injuries held him back from doing even more. One of six career concussions stopped his participation in Philadelphia's 2008 semifinal run and a sports hernia took away almost half of his 2003 season. Even physical problems suffered by linemates kept the winger from greater glory.

He and Peter Forsberg, in the words of their linemate Mike Knuble, were like "brothers from another mother" until Forsberg missed 20 games the season of Gagne's 47 goals and was barely available the following year before being traded in February. For as long as it lasted, the Gagne-Forsberg-Knuble line was as good as the two most celebrated in Flyer history—Bobby Clarke-Bill Barber-Reggie Leach and Eric Lindros-John LeClair-Mikael Renberg.

Gagne's principal Philadelphia centers—Forsberg, Keith Primeau and Mike Richards—found him to be more than just a finisher. He could create, too, with speed and hockey sense.

"Good with the puck and without the puck," recalls former GM Paul Holmgren, now the team president. "Above-average skill and a very good skater.

"In my opinion, Simon was almost underrated as an all-around player. He really came into his own in the (2002) Olympics on a line with Joe Sakic. That's where everyone took pause and said, 'Hey, this guy's really good.'"

Bob Clarke, the GM who drafted Gagne, insists Gagne would have been even better if left in the middle, the position he played starring with the junior Quebec Remparts. "Instead of sending him back (in 1999-2000) to junior (because of a center-ice position loaded with Eric Lindros, Rod Brind'Amour and Daymond Langkow), Roger Neilson put Simon on the wing," recalls Clarke. "It hindered his development, but he never wanted to go back.

"Teams are always looking for a centerman, and he would have been one of the best in the world. I think we screwed up."

Maybe. But the Flyers lived 11 seasons with an error in judgment that resulted in 535 points in 691 games. Not only did Gagne's numbers grow, but so did his entire game. He was made better at both ends of the ice after Ken Hitchcock took over as coach in 2002.

"He had come in as a scorer and had the attitude of one," recalls Hitchcock. "But all the goals he was going to score weren't going to make a difference if I couldn't make him a player.

"From the red line in, he was always on the move; any 50/50 puck, he was gone. But when you're up against top talent, you can't win like that. I needed to see someone who was committed to all three zones.

"He really was a sensitive guy. But I kept pushing and demanding because I thought he was capable of a higher level of compete. Playing with Keith, who made the same adjustment, had something to do with Simon buying in. Once he did, I'll bet I had no more than five conversations with him the rest of the time we were together. I just backed off and let him play. He was dialed in, committed."

It was a frustrating process for both coach and player.

"At one point, I didn't think I could play for Hitch and almost asked to be traded," recalls Gagne. "I must tell you, he was mostly a nightmare.

"For awhile, I was in his office almost every day. It was always about negative things. But I wasn't the only one in there, and I think we all knew in the back of our minds, he was doing it for a reason. We had asked for a change to a coach who had a good system and structure. Hitch had won a Cup, so he came in almost with a free card to do whatever he wanted. I remember Clarkie told us, 'You guys asked for this.' And he was right.

"If you tell me now to name my best coach, it was Hitchcock. Before the (2004-05) lockout, I was a good young prospect and maybe an all-star, but I wasn't totally grown up as a player. I was always a two-way guy, but Hitch helped me take it to the next level."

As it turned out, Gagne had the skill and grit to play for any coach in any situation, and he came to take pride in his versatility above all. The No. 9 ranked goal scorer in Flyer history came to feel exactly as did No. 1, Bill Barber.

"You want to feel trust from the coach and teammates," Gagne recalls. "When you get it, you want to show you deserve it. To help stop a goal feels as good as to score a goal."

Lessons about professionalism began long before the arrival of Hitchcock. Gagne's father, Pierre, was the property of the AHL Quebec Aces when the newborn Flyers bought the Aces as their development team in 1966. Dad never played a game for the NHL club, so a sense of entitlement was not among the things the Quebec City police sergeant passed along to his son on a small backyard rink.

"Looking at his scrapbook, I knew he had played the game, so he could teach it to me," recalls Gagne. "The coaches in minor hockey helped me a little bit, but my father had the biggest influence.

"When I was a young kid, the game was easy. But when I was 14 or 15, I had my ups and downs. Some people were saying I was too small, but my dad helped me get through the times when I had doubts. He pushed me to another level, but it wasn't crazy father stuff. He made sure I had fun."

Simon Nolet, Pierre Gagne's teammate on the Aces, made it to the Flyers, played on their first Cup team, and eventually became their Quebec scout. He pushed GM Bob Clarke to use a first-round pick on a scrawny kid for better reasons than just an old friendship.

As Dennis Patterson, Philadelphia's Ontario scout recalls: "When I went to see Gagne the first time, I told Simon Nolet, 'this guy didn't get off the bus tonight.' Nolet said, 'I'm telling you Dennis, he can play. He's one of the best guys we could get this year.'

"That was good enough for me. If I hadn't seen Gagne again, I would have been behind taking him anyway because that's how much I trusted Nolet."

The Philadelphia organization did not interview Gagne before taking him. And the young player was never aware of the friendship between his father and Nolet until after his selection. "My dad told me, 'You were meant to be a Flyer,'" Gagne recalls.

It became so important to him that, at the end, he stubbornly refused to leave. Soon after the 2010

Stanley Cup Final, during which he had returned with an incompletely healed foot, Holmgren was on the phone pushing Gagne to waive his no-movement clause so he could be traded to relieve the team's cap problems.

For obvious reasons, he felt betrayed. By the end of the summer, Gagne realized that he didn't want to play where he no longer was wanted and accepted a deal to Tampa Bay. A year later, as a fourth liner with the Kings, he won the Cup that had eluded his Philadelphia teams. Everything happens for a reason.

Holmgren brought Gagne back during the lockout season of 2012-13. He wished to play another year and finish his career, in perfect symmetry, as a Flyer. But after a long delay over the summer, the GM went in another direction and more bad feelings followed. Still, too many good things happened in Philadelphia for Gagne to hold a grudge.

Upon his retirement following the 2014-15 season with Boston, Gagne was invited onto the Wells Fargo Center ice one more time to receive the love of his fans. He attended the memorial service for Ed Snider. He sat for five hours at a Quebec City coffeehouse being interviewed for this book. When his dad said Simon was destined to be a Flyer, that meant for life.

Having been born on February 29, 1980, technically he was playing for them at age five. "Always hoped I would get a few extra years to my career out of it," he laughs. The time in Philadelphia went by fast because, with the exception of the collapse in 2006-07—when Gagne distinguished himself with 41 goals and a stiff upper lip—he always was playing for a contender.

"Before the salary cap, every summer the Flyers tried to get the best players," he recalls. "It was almost like an all-star team.

"Every year, we were in the top three, top five, to win the Cup, but something always would happen. In 2004, when Hitchcock said it was the best team he had as a coach, the top three defensemen got hurt. It was almost like luck was against us every year."

Regardless, the most fortunate day of his life, he believes, was the day he fell to the 22nd pick and became a Flyer.

"I remember my first playoff game," Gagne says. "There was a big party outside the arena. Lots of people, music, two-and-a-half hours before the puck dropped. And this was only the first round. I realized 'Wow, what a city to play in!'

"All the time I was there, I saw Barber, Clarkie and (Bernie) Parent, Joe Watson, and (Bob) Kelly. They all stick around. And the fans—people say they're crazy, but they love the Flyers.

"So I got to play for those guys in the jersey that always will be No.1 for me. We had four long playoff drives, even if they all broke my heart in the end. Got a gold medal for my country. Got my Stanley Cup eventually.

"While I always thought I would play in the NHL, it could have been as a third- or fourth-line guy for teams that didn't win. So I could not ask for more than I got out of my career."

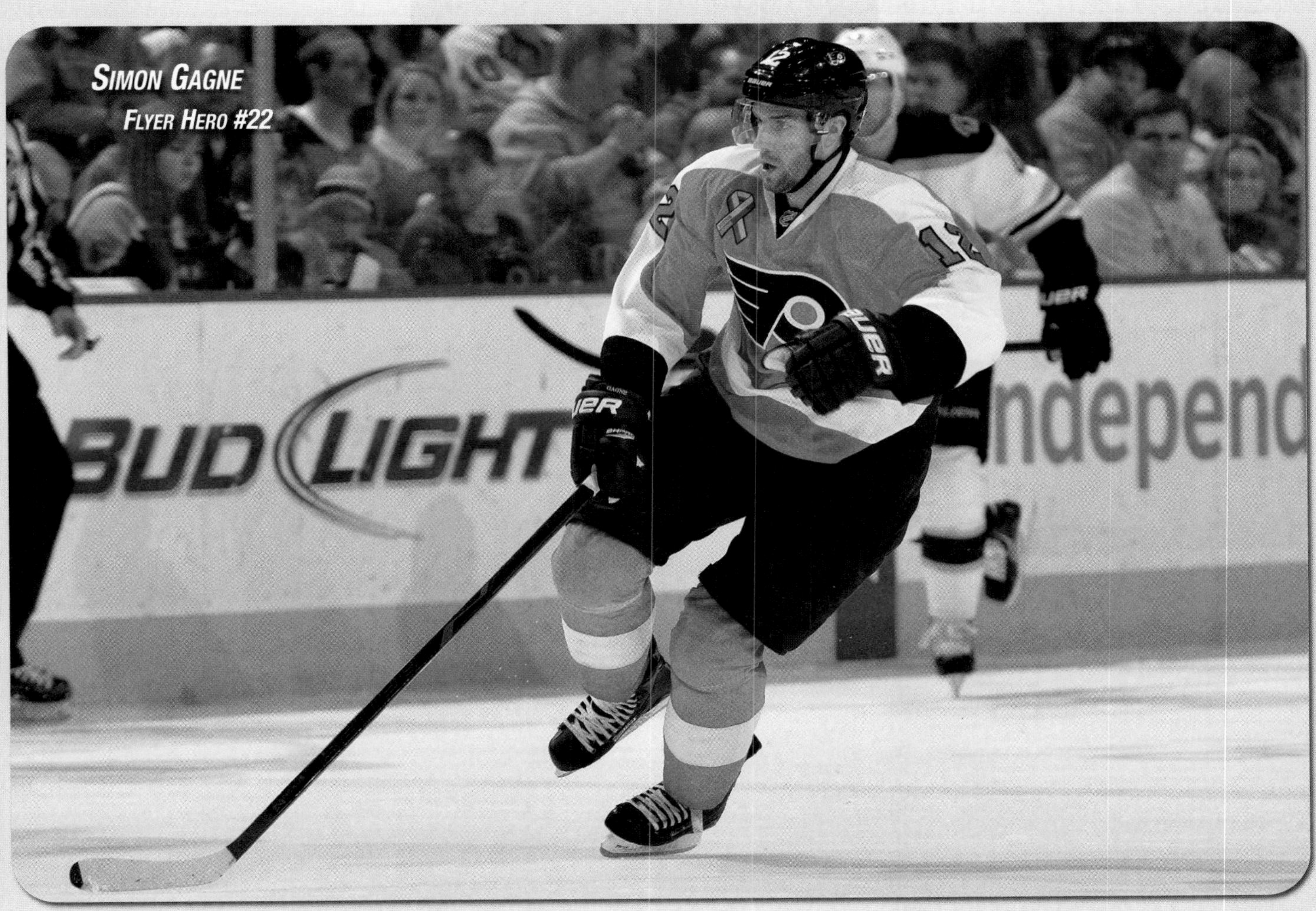

SIMON GAGNE
FLYER HERO #22

DANNY BRIERE

Just as he uncannily sensed where the puck was going, Danny Briere had an extraordinary instinct that the Flyers would prove the best fit for him.

"All I knew about them [in 2007] was what I saw from the outside," he recalls. "And it was the best decision I ever made. I believed in Paul Holmgren and where the organization was going."

Undeterred by the fact Philadelphia was coming off the worst season in its history, Briere picked the Flyers from a dizzying number of free-agent offers, an expression of faith that was an extension of his unblinking self-confidence. At 174 pounds, the center and sometime right wing wasn't even as big as the chip on his shoulder. Yet, for 17 NHL seasons, he was unfazed by the size of the brutes surrounding him. Thanks to the fast hands of the best veteran free-agent forward Philadelphia ever signed, the Orange-and-Black enjoyed one of the great clutch scorers for six years.

During the playoffs, when space is more difficult to find, Briere scored 37 goals and 35 assists in 68 games as a Flyer, averaging 1.05 points per contest, much higher than his 0.78 mark during regular seasons. In the franchise's history, only Eric Lindros, Peter Forsberg, Ken Linseman and Briere ever have averaged better than a point per playoff game.

He did it with speed, hockey sense, a low panic threshold around the goal, accuracy and attitude. Plenty of attitude. At 5-9, Briere carried his stick all the way up to 6-3 and didn't hesitate to use it for protection. He was known to go high with more than just his patented shots under the crossbar.

"There are a lot of guys out there who take liberties on players my size," he recalls. "They don't have the [courage] to do it with bigger ones because they will have to fight, or back up what they are doing.

"There were times I took bad penalties to get somebody for something they did to me earlier in the game. I would wait for the right time to let them know I didn't forget; to tell them that the next time we got in the corner together, they would have to play me as though I was 6-4, 225.

"The emotion that drove me also got me in trouble. Sometimes I went overboard. I went to give [Buffalo's] Chris Butler a shot back and ended up giving him a stick in the throat. I didn't mean to do that, but he never touched me again.

"Early in my career, [Calgary's] Bob Boughner would run after me. One day, on a power play, I shot at his head, skated by and said, 'You come after me again, next time I am not going to miss. After that, he seemed to leave me alone.

"That's how I survived playing with big boys. I was suspended three times [total of seven games], but honestly, I don't regret any of them. It gave me a chance to skate a little bit more freely."

Briere never totaled fewer than 69 penalty minutes in any of his full seasons with Buffalo or Philadelphia. And even that unabashed recklessness was dwarfed by his fearlessness of failure.

"I wanted to be the guy that was either going to make the play or be in position to finish that play," he says. "And if I didn't do it on one night, it just meant that I was one opportunity closer to scoring the next time. The way I figured it, my chances had just gone up.

"I grew up watching playoff hockey. I dreamed of making the play to win the playoff game, to score

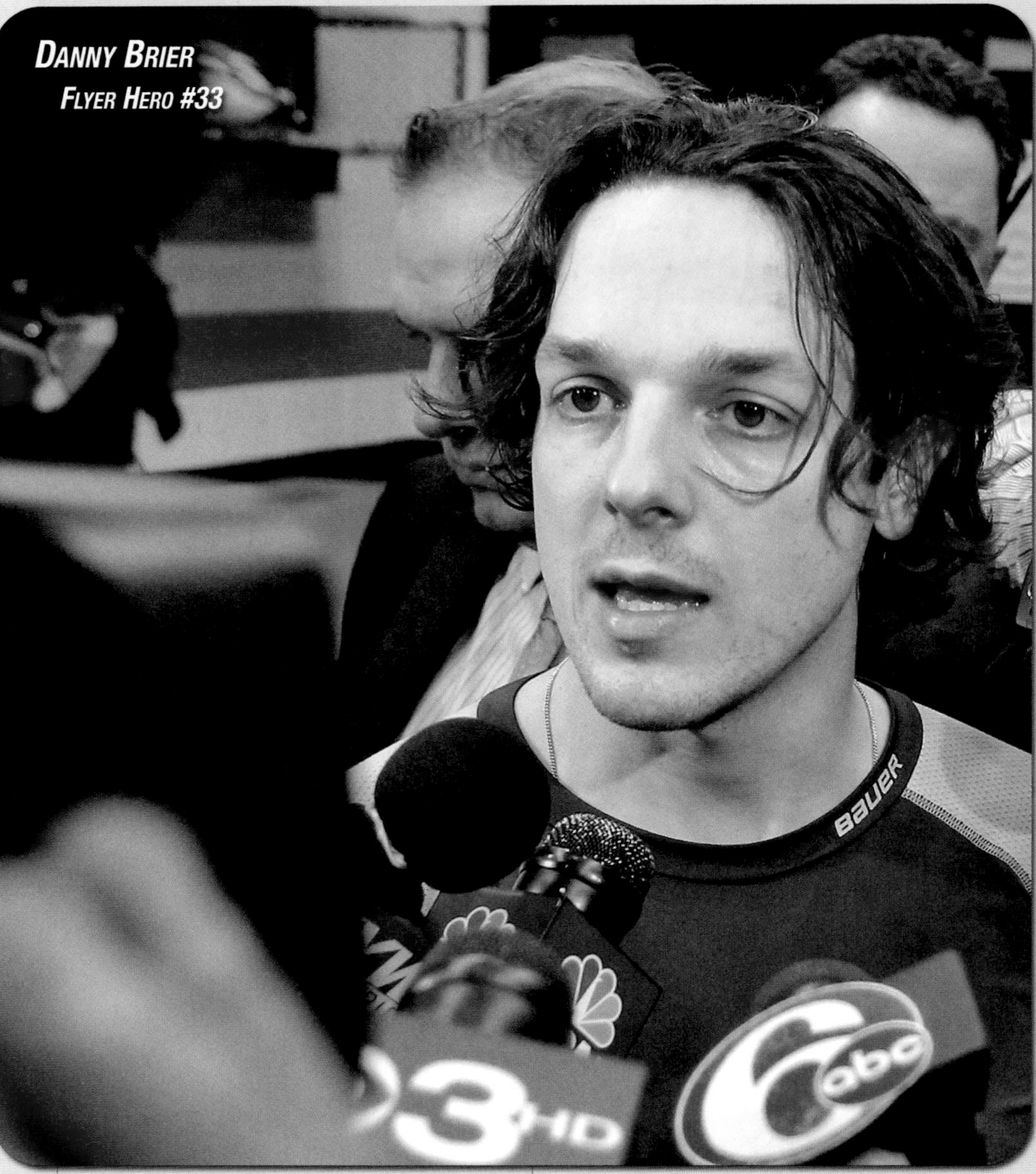

Danny Brier
Flyer Hero #33

a goal in overtime. I lived for those moments. They drove me.

"I'm a big fan of the game. That helped me. On our off days, I loved to watch other teams to study goaltenders and defensemen, see where I could take advantage of certain things.

"During the regular season, when it's a different team every other night, you are readjusting. For some, that makes it easier to score. But for me, it was harder. When you play the same team over and over again, you are able to find the crack in the armor. Maybe that's one of the reasons I got better as a series went along."

In his first game after signing an eight-year, $52 million deal, Briere scored two goals, including the winner in the final two minutes. He totaled 72 points in 79 games during 2007-08 and added another 16 in 17 playoff contests as Philadelphia went to the Eastern Conference final.

Injuries (he played in only 29 games in 2008-09), switches to the wing, experimentation with various linemates, and a painful marriage breakup kept Briere from exploding until the 2009-10 playoff run. He scored in a shootout on New York's Henrik Lundqvist, enabling the Flyers to qualify on the final day of the regular season, and put in the tying goal as they rallied from a 3-0 deficit to a 4-3 win in Game Seven at Boston. A magical line with Ville Leino and Scott Hartnell, thrown together in the second round because of injuries, helped Briere earn 30 points in 23 playoff games, and his 13 points against Chicago came within one of Wayne Gretzky's record in a Final.

There was a just one series of the seven Briere won and five he lost in a Philadelphia uniform in which he flopped—Boston's sweep in 2011–and he had plenty of company that time. The Flyers got bang for their big bucks while Briere was serving as one of the greatest off-ice ambassadors for an organization that never has had a shortage of them. If it weren't for the Philadelphia hockey writers' desire to move around their yearly Yanick Dupre Class Guy Award, Briere would have owned that plaque for six years.

"One of the nicest men you will ever meet," said Holmgren. "He showed up and worked hard every day, never said a bad thing about any of his teammates, cared about the organization, and went wherever we asked him to go.

"He was a good dad (to three boys), great with the fans. On the ice, he met every expectation, actually exceeded them."

Briere made a career of being underestimated. Born in Gatineau, Quebec, across the river from Ottawa, he is the son of homemaker, Constance, and an insurance agent and former junior player, Robert. There is a picture to prove young Daniel was skating on the frozen backyard pool at 26 months.

"Dad put me on the ice early," recalls Danny. "He wasn't pushy, didn't need to be; I always wanted to play."

"I had friends who didn't want to get up at five or six in the morning to go to practice. Those guys aren't involved in hockey anymore.

"I wasn't always the best kid at my age, but I showed some skill, so a lot of coaches put me in favorable positions to succeed. My first year of midget (15-16 year olds), we had a couple of kids over 200 pounds on our team. I would say the average was 170-175 pounds. I weighed 129, but was able to stay free of major injuries and kept moving forward.

"Because of my size, everyone was telling me I'd never play pro. I was a good student, so a big issue for me was to make sure my education was going to be taken care of. I went to visit Maine and Clarkson. We were in very advanced talks with Harvard and other schools, but college hockey was not as big to us back then.

"I knew a few words of English to make sentences, but going to school using a different language scared me. Now I realize, what did I leave on the table? But Drummondville (of the Quebec Major Junior Hockey League), which had taken me sixth in the midget draft, guaranteed they would pay for my [college]."

Briere finished high school in Drummondville and took a few university-level courses, but hockey was going too well to leave much time for higher education. "I got to Drummondville at the perfect time," he recalls. "Ian Laperriere was going pro and they had a big hole in the middle on their first line. I didn't think I'd be near the top of the leaders and scoring in the whole league, but I was. Second year of junior, my draft year, was even better.

The Winnipeg Jets selected Briere 24th overall, one month before relocating to Phoenix, where he bounced up and down from the minors for three seasons. "Part of it was still filling out," he explains. "I was 158 pounds when drafted and probably wasn't ready to play against men until I was 22 or 23.

"But I also needed an attitude readjustment. Until Phoenix, everything in my life had been without obstacle. The last time the Coyotes sent me down, they had to get waivers and I cleared. It's a big wakeup call when you realize that no one wants you. I didn't have the excuse anymore that Phoenix wasn't letting me play.

"I'm not the only [prospect] who ever went through something like that. I was just fortunate enough to be able to [apply myself] before it was too late."

Having finally established himself with 32 Coyote goals in 2001-02, he had signed a new contract and bought a house, when the team, wanting to get bigger up the middle, traded him to Buffalo for Chris Gratton. Sabre coach Lindy Ruff threw responsibility at Briere and he blossomed into the leading scorer on a team that beat the Flyers decisively in the first round and reached a conference final in 2006.

When his contract was up, Buffalo couldn't or wouldn't keep him. Philadelphia won the auction due to close ex-Sabre friends working here—Marty Biron in goal and Don Luce in the front office—and because two good young centers, Mike Richards and Jeff Carter, already were in place, giving the Flyers the kind of depth up the middle which helped Briere thrive in Buffalo.

"Right from the beginning, I felt at home," he recalls.

In 2013, after an injury-and-lockout shortened season, Briere's time in Philadelphia ended with a buyout of the remaining two years on his contract. When informed of the decision by Holmgren, neither player nor GM was able to hold back tears. Briere got in a year with Montreal—his second choice when he opted to come to the Flyers—and then one last season in Colorado before hanging up his skates.

He kept his Haddonfield, NJ, home and considers his years with Philadelphia closest to his heart. At Holmgren's invitation, Briere is sampling and studying several aspects of the Flyer business operation as a possible post-playing career.

Just having him around makes the organization more fan-friendly. Despite the boos he heard through his injury-plagued second season, Briere turned the die-hards around by playing hurt and hard, becoming one of the most beloved players in franchise history.

"The fans of Philadelphia have a bad reputation and, honestly, I don't see it," he says. "Even in tough times, they always had our backs. Whenever they were unhappy, they would let us know, but every season they were there and my interaction with them was just amazing.

"Philadelphia means everything to me."

CHRIS PRONGER

EVEN IF HE HAD KNOWN THEN WHAT HE DOES NOW, Paul Holmgren says he would have gone for it. For one full season and a magical 2010 playoff run, Chris Pronger was worth the four first-rounders (two future, two recent), the initial wrath of Ed Snider for surrendering so much, and the $26 million payout to a player who was finished.

There was only one Chris Pronger. And for however long he lasted, the Flyers had him, smoking the Devils, coming back from 0-3 to beat Boston, getting to a Final for the first time in 13 years and coming within two wins of the Stanley Cup.

"We took our swing for the fences to get a special player," recalls Holmgren, then the GM. "For a 6-foot-6 guy with that arm length, nastiness, and ability to control the pace of the game, I would do it again. He was given so much room and respect that he could have played at a high level into his forties.

"You can't control injuries."

As it turned out, the July 2009 trade that sent late first-round picks in 2010, 2011, winger Joffrey Lupul and defenseman Luca Sbisa to Anaheim did not leave Philadelphia with a haunting void of young players. Holmgren traded Jeff Carter for Jake Voracek and the eighth-overall pick in 2011 that became Sean Couturier. Lupul has become an oft-injured, second-tier scorer, and Sbisa is a marginal defenseman.

But what the Flyers gave up is a separate issue from what they have missed since Pronger's career ended in November 2011 with a severe concussion. During the summer of 2012, Holmgren took one more home-run cut for an anchor defenseman, signing restricted free-agent Shea Weber to an offer sheet, but Nashville matched.

The search for another top guy remains ongoing. Selecting blueliners at No. 7 (Ivan Provorov), No. 11 (Sam Morin), and No. 17 (Travis Sanheim) in the 2013-15 drafts, Philadelphia has been trying to shorten its odds of getting another Pronger, but that's a reach, pun fully intended. Pronger's arms seemed to stretch from sideboard to sideboard, and he influenced games both by what he did and what opponents feared he might do.

"Another good thing about getting him was how great it was not to have to play against him anymore," recalls former Flyer winger Scott Hartnell. "It was always going to be a tough night in front of the net with crosschecks and sticks in the back of the leg.

"If you dumped it in his corner and went at him, he probably was going to knock you down. Every one of his passes was on the tape. You couldn't really put any pressure on him."

Teammates couldn't escape Pronger's intimidation in the locker room either, another big reason Holmgren made the blockbuster deal after two seasons of inconsistent, immature play by a talented team.

"Pronger was quick to point out when somebody screwed up," recalls Holmgren. "A lot of players, especially young players today, don't take that sort of thing very well, so Chris rubbed some people the wrong way. But it was always for the right reasons. He only cared about winning.

"He wasn't the type of leader who would try to get everybody together (for team meals). He had his own routine, was very into fitness."

Pronger was almost as deep into sarcasm, with both teammates and reporters, being especially playful with the latter. "What are you going to ask me today? Let's give them a sound bite," Pronger sometimes would tell CSN Philly's Tim Panaccio, but not all insults were set up in advance or directed at people who could take them.

"He didn't have any filter," Flyer coach Ian Laperriere, a teammate of Pronger's, recalls. "I played with him when he was 18 years old (on Canada's World Junior Championship team) and with the Blues, and Prongs has always been Prongs. It took a while for the guys to respect that, but they always respected his game. How can you not?"

Pronger had not been been treated gently by Brad McCrimmon, his initial NHL defense partner in Hartford, or by coach-GM Mike Keenan after being traded to St. Louis. "The best teams are the ones where players apply peer pressure, hold each other accountable to a high standard," Pronger says. "If it ruffles guys' feathers after they've been shown a successful way to play, then tough. I am my own worst critic and I hold other people to that level.

"I played with a broken hand (in 2010-11) for probably two or three weeks. It was my top hand, so I couldn't shoot and I kept dropping my stick. Against Edmonton (on March 8), we were winning 4-1, and it's late in a shift when G (Claude Giroux) tries to stickhandle through three guys at the red line instead of dumping it in and allowing me to change. He loses the puck, they come in on a three-on-two, and now I've got to hit the guy with my hand that's killing me.

"I was [bleeped] off. We had talked about this stuff a year earlier and now we're reverting back? You need to know what is going on around you. You might be fresh, but everyone else might be tired. I just told him he needed to get the puck in deep and let me change. We were up 4-1, didn't need another goal.

"That is what good teams do. That was the extent of the message. G didn't like that I yelled at him on the ice. I didn't like that he turned the puck over. Don't turn the puck over and I won't yell.

"On good teams, stuff like that happens all the time. It lasted about a minute and a half. But the media heard it (as reporters were being let into the locker room) and it was 'omigawd,' there had been this big brawl.

"As the season went along, what do you think G did in that situation? He dumped the puck."

The closest of families have arguments. Giroux, who became the captain, says he learned much about leadership from a provoked Pronger as well as the veteran who remained cool under pressure.

"We lost a game in the playoffs and I was ready to break all my sticks," Giroux recalls. "I look over at Prongs and he's all calm, had already put the game behind him, getting ready for the next one."

When Pronger arrived, Philadelphia had Mike Richards as captain. "Homer told me to support Richie and help him grow as a leader," Pronger remembers. And despite innuendo to the contrary, that's what happened. Richards' sudden trade in June 2011 had nothing to do with the locker room being too small for the two of them.

"I think [having Pronger] was good for us," Richards recalls. "He was a more vocal leader and I was a more quiet one, leading on the ice. I'm not sure how people in the media thought we had a bad relationship."

Pronger says, "I never had an issue with Richards. We had the same agent (Pat Morris), and I never heard from him or Richie that there was a problem.

"We weren't going out to dinner every night. I had a family and kids. He lived downtown, was at a different stage in his life. Because we weren't seen around the rink holding hands, people thought there was a rift."

Teammates felt the two complemented each other well. "Mike didn't like dealing with the media, so Chris took a lot of that pressure away," recalls Danny Briere. "It took the heat off all of us."

Pronger was a heat-removal specialist. By picking up pucks at the buzzer that Chicago had rightfully claimed as souvenirs with wins in Games One and Two of the 2010 Final, he annoyed the Blackhawks and distracted the media's focus away from the two Flyer losses. Suspended eight times during his career, he had been called a lot worse than just

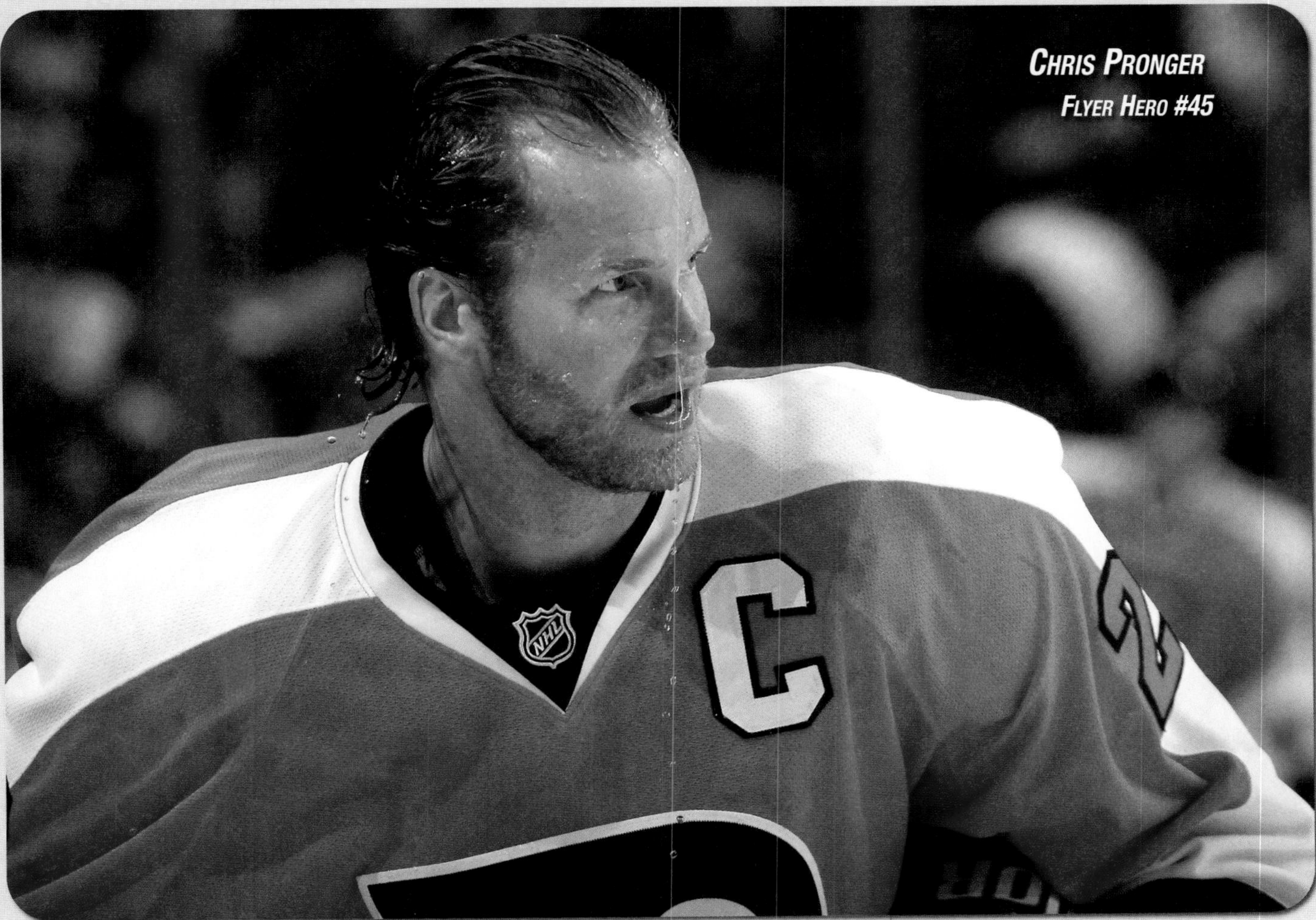

CHRIS PRONGER
FLYER HERO #45

obnoxious.

As intractable and indispensible as Pronger had remained while playing on a knee that had to be repeatedly drained over that season's last three rounds, the ultimate demonstration of the defenseman's value came the following spring when a twice-fractured hand had healed enough to take a regular shift in Game Seven against Buffalo. The Sabres never went near him during his 17 minutes, and Philadelphia controlled the game, winning 5-2.

He hurt his back, however, and didn't play again after the first game of the next round, when the Bruins, who had crumbled at the hands of a Flyer team anchored by Pronger the previous spring, this time won in a sweep.

By the start of the 2011-12 season, the defenseman had successfully undergone the removal of a disk fragment that was pressing against a nerve, and the Philadelphia club was revamped around a series of trades. "My back and knee felt great, I was moving really good," Pronger remembers. "I was 37, but didn't feel old by any stretch of the imagination. We made those deals—Jags (Jaromir Jagr) came in—and got off to a great start. Everything was falling into place."

And then it happened. On October 24, Pronger was struck in the eye by the stick of Toronto's Mikhail Grabovski as he followed through on a shot, and the Flyer left the ice screaming from the pain and terror.

At first he seemed fortunate. The blood drained from his eye during his eight days in bed exactly as hoped, and he was back in the lineup in just over two weeks.

"I only had two practices," he recalls. "I felt like awful with a headache but assumed it was my eye. I thought I was going to puke out there but figured it was because I was out of shape. I tried to come up with excuses, like maybe it was due to the visor. Headache? Take an Advil and let's go. I had that mindset."

He played five games with big minutes as the symptoms worsened.

"Finally, in Winnipeg (on November19), the crowd seemed really loud to me," he recalls. "I was dizzy, falling down, not seeing the puck, making plays that weren't me, had a lack of perception of where everybody was. I was going to get creamed.

"After the game, I said I couldn't play like this. Had the protocol (concussion) testing and it was really bad."

And it stayed that way for the better part of two years. "Eye was still blurry, had a headache," Pronger recalls. "I would get sick driving my car, got angry when the (three) kids were screaming; I became agitated really quickly.

"Because you can't play, you don't want to be around the rink. What the hell am I going to do down there? I'm spending time at home in dark rooms because my eye was sensitive to light, but what's making you feel a little better is actually making you depressed. Bright lights gave me a headache, so I almost never went outside.

"I got bored; I wanted to read, but the headache would start. I didn't want to stop because I was into what I was reading, but before an hour went by, I would have to quit. I learned to keep it to 20 minutes.

"By the next season, I hadn't been to a Flyer game live since it happened, so I came to Philly (the family had moved back to St. Louis). I'm watching and my eyes got sore from the lights. I went to Toronto with the team and my eyes were so tired, and this time burning, that I couldn't keep them open on the bus ride to the hotel. It was painful to keep them open, just so I could walk.

"I was depressed, living like a hermit. I drank a little, not much because I was spending a lot of time with the kids. For a while, I ate badly. But I cleaned that up, got back on a pro diet and it helped a little bit. But I still had the odd blow up. Golfing one day, my head was pounding out of my skull; I almost drove to a nearby hospital. I got home, grabbed the hand of my wife (Lauren), and put it on the back of my head. She could feel my headache.

"The process is exhausting. You can either not try anything and get stagnant, or continue to push the threshold. Push too hard, you blow up.

"It took a year and a half before I could do much. Homer called and asked me to watch some junior kids."

In 2015, in his first year of eligibility, Pronger went into the Hockey Hall of Fame with symptoms eased, but not gone.

"My eye doesn't move properly," he says. "I'm still very sensitive to light. I get headaches; I'm sometimes still a little fumbled in the head. You get used to it after awhile. You don't have a choice."

It's ironic that a player suspended eight times during his career would become a judge and jury in the NHL Department of Player Safety. The Flyers traded his rights to Phoenix in 2015 entirely for cap purposes. It was clear almost from the time he last left the ice that his career was over.

That reality proved much easier for him to live with than post-concussion symptoms.

"I was still playing to try to win again, end it on my terms, complete the saga," he recalls. "But I'd played 19 years; it's not like my career got cut short.

"If it had happened when I was 25, I'd be [bleeped] off. But there is nothing I didn't do in the game. I was fortunate enough to win a Stanley Cup (Anaheim 2007), felt that euphoria of being the last team standing. I won (two) Olympic gold medals (in 2002 and 2010), a Norris and a Hart Trophy (both in 2000). I don't feel like the game owes me anything. I had a prosperous career."

Only for Philadelphia Flyer purposes did it not last long enough.

PETER LAVIOLETTE

There is always a time to attack. Even the most conservative of coaches preaches seizing opportunities that spring from sound positioning in the neutral zone, advocate defensemen getting up in the play when forwards are in proper positions of support, and want the second forechecker to move in when the first one comes up with the puck.

After that, however, players usually are left to rely on their instincts. Danny Briere had been in the NHL for 10 full seasons before he had a coach like Peter Laviolette, who worked on scoring goals at even strength. Possession of the puck is nine-tenths of hockey law, Laviolette believed. A good offense can be the best defense. But he also believed the game should be fun.

"[Coaches] think about how they can keep the puck out of the net, and he did, too," recalls Mike Richards. "But he concentrated a lot more on how to enjoy the game and score goals because everyone loves doing that. He always looked at different and creative ways for players to use their offensive skills."

Two seasons after John Stevens had taken the Flyers to the Eastern Conference final, GM Paul Holmgren believed they had become, in his words, "stuck in the mud." That hadn't been the case the previous season, when Philadelphia countered effectively off Stevens' neutral-zone defensive lockdowns to the fourth most-goals recorded in the league and its sixth best powerplay. But in December of 2009, when the team was struggling with one win in seven games and had been shut out in the last two, Holmgren took a Flyer envelope stuffed with skilled forwards and decided to push it.

"I had been here three years and it was up and down hockey every time," recalls Kimmo Timonen. "We needed a higher demand level."

Stevens had been a father figure to the young players, many of whom he had coached with the Phantoms. But when Laviolette replaced him, with Philadelphia standing 13-11-1 on December 4, 2009, these guys were about to enter a different world.

There had been no sitting back for Laviolette's 2005-06 Carolina Hurricanes. The slowest they moved all year was in their convertibles at the Stanley Cup parade.

"When Lavvy took over, there was no trying to make everybody feel good," recalls Briere. "It was get on board and go as hard as you can or you're going to be left behind."

Laviolette's system wasn't a tough sell. Who doesn't like to score? But muscle memory had to be changed on a team accustomed to stopping, not going. The Flyers struggled early in the process—2-7-1 in their first 10 games—which was to be expected. But no one anticipated they would become frozen again down the stretch. Although back in playoff position by February, the team still almost missed out, needing to win three of its last four contests to qualify.

There were many nights Laviolette insisted he still liked his club when there had been little about it to enjoy. He had unequivocal trust in his left wing lock, which made the left wing defensively responsible and allowed the right wing and center to chase the puck. More than a belief in the system, the players needed to have faith in themselves and each other.

"He was so passionate about being here," recalls Scott Hartnell. "Yelling, chomping on his gum, there was just so much enthusiasm.

"To me, it was totally different and exciting. He wanted us to take our chances. He used to (derogatorily) call working the puck around the boards from player to player a "high-school cycle." All you would do is tire yourself out until you lost the puck. He was all about creating confusion, allowing our forwards to become lost in their zone."

With good games followed by bad games, the Flyers had a hard time finding themselves. With one remaining chance to get in, they did on a shootout, after playing their best 60 minutes of the season. The anvils lifted from their shoulders, the team was on its way to the Stanley Cup Final and one of the best coaching eras in franchise history.

Laviolette, 145-101-29 in Philadelphia's regular-season play, took his first team to within two games of the Cup and, over four seasons, won five playoff rounds, more than any other Flyer coach besides Fred Shero (13), Mike Keenan (6), and Terry Murray (6).

The fans liked Laviolette not only for the number of wins he produced, but for the passion with which he succeeded. Down 3-0 to Boston during the 2010 run, the coach never let his players feel inferior to the Bruins, nor, after they fell behind 3-0 in Game Seven, let them congratulate themselves for a good, failed, try. Laviolette called the most celebrated time-out in team history to ask for just one goal before the end of the first period and got it, from James van Riemsdyk, sparking the comeback to a 4-3 victory, the NHL's first rally from an 0-3 series deficit in 35 seasons.

Laviolette was not shy. Just days after taking over the reigns, he singled out a star, Briere, to skate laps in front of the team as punishment for careless penalties. When Claude Giroux knocked down Sidney Crosby and then scored seconds into the 2012 clinching Game Six, Laviolette said his captain was "the best player in the world," as if Giroux had, that day, taken the throne from Crosby.

Annoyed with the trap employed by Tampa Bay, Laviolette once ordered Chris Pronger to pull back the puck into the defensive zone and just stand there with it for minutes on end, trying to either embarrass coach Guy Boucher for his excitement-killing tactics or draw him into attacking. When Pittsburgh coach Dan Bylsma sent out his tough guys against Philadelphia's good guys in the final minutes of an already-decided regular-season game, Lavvy got hotter than lava, banging a stick on the boards and screaming at his counterpart.

Laviolette's teams lived on those emotions, but then died without them in 2011, when the Bruins had their revenge in a four-game sweep. In 2012, the thrilling win over Pittsburgh left the Flyers flat against a methodical Devils team in the next round, when Laviolette was outcoached by Pete DeBoer in a five-game New Jersey victory.

The shortened lockout season that followed left little time for a bad start. But Philadelphia had overcome one to climb back into playoff position before injuries foiled the charge. When Pronger, who was unable to participate in the 2011 Boston series, was lost for good with a concussion the following November, Holmgren sensed that a diminished Flyer defense needed more than what Laviolette's style of play was providing.

The GM suggested changes to a more swarming kind of defensive zone coverage, but Laviolette only half-heartedly endorsed the recommendation. Training camp had been sluggish, and the team's play in the second and third games of the season was practically catatonic when Holmgren decided Laviolette's time was up. Craig Berube, the elevated assistant coach, demanded more accountability in all three zones and, just as in Laviolette's first season, Philadelphia rallied to make the playoffs.

It wasn't the first time Laviolette had been fired, but it probably was the most painful. "I really liked it in Philadelphia," he recalls. "I liked the passion of the sports city that it is. I loved the fans because they care. But if it's not working anymore, I get it; Paul had to make a change."

Laviolette was only out of work until May before being hired by Nashville, which had been out of the playoffs in consecutive seasons. The Predators haven't missed in the two years since. The man knows how to rally troops.

In a speech before Game Six of the 2012 Pittsburgh series, Laviolette asked everyone to play their best for just one afternoon. It was the most inspirational pregame oratory Briere had ever heard.

Not always kind to his players in private, Laviolette still was liked by them. He had their backs in the media and was always advocating success. The best Flyer performance of the 2010 run—a 3-0 win in Montreal that gave them a 3-1 lead—followed their worst performance—a 5-1 defeat in Game Three.

That said, Laviolette's best work probably was done in 2012. With captain Richards and leading sniper Carter both suddenly traded, four talented, new, young players—Sean Couturier, Wayne Simmonds, Brayden Schenn, and Jake Voracek—had to be integrated into important roles while Giroux grew quickly into the captaincy. Philadelphia finished with 103 points and Giroux 93 personally, his best-ever statistical season.

"Lavvy really pushed me to be the best I could be," Giroux recalls. "I learned a lot from him. He motivates guys."

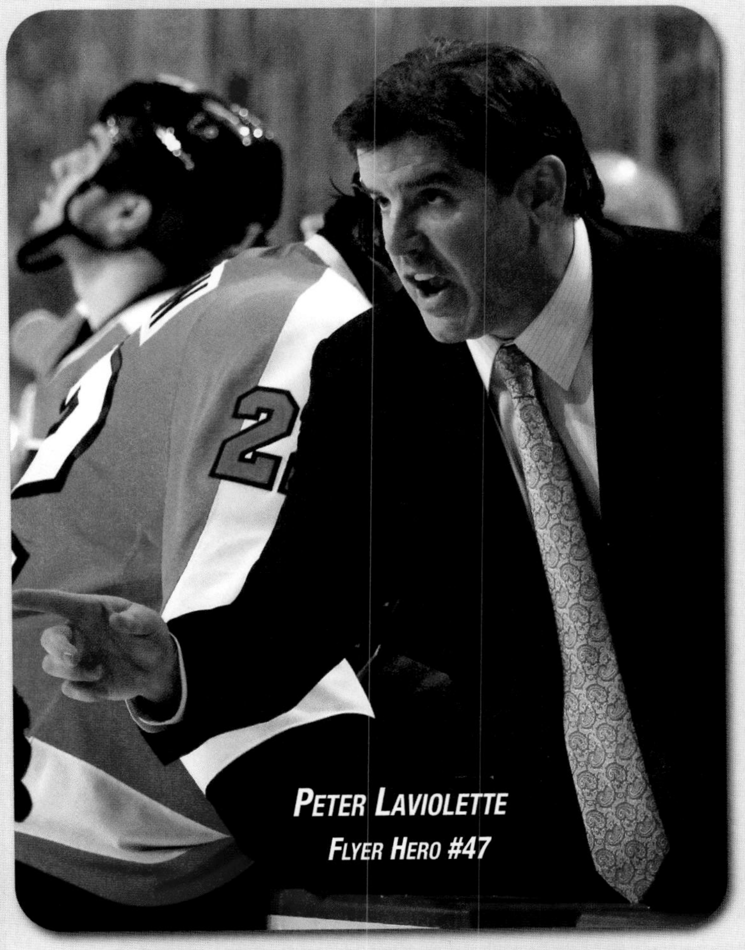

Relentless in doing so, Laviolette won more regular-season contests behind a Flyer bench than anyone besides Shero and Keenan. "Even in my role, I would leave his office fired up that we were going to have a great night and win," Holmgren recalls. "He did that every game."

Laviolette has said that coaching is having your team believing that on a given night, it can overcome anything. His Islanders overcame a seven-year playoff drought to qualify in back-to-back years. Only one of his four Carolina clubs made the playoffs, but it went all the way, a triumph of faith as much as talent.

It's not supposed to get any bigger than winning a Cup, yet it wasn't until he got to Philadelphia that Laviolette, who played at Westfield (MA) State College, on three USA Olympic teams (captain in 1994) and lasted 12 NHL games as a defenseman with the Rangers, felt he had finally made the big time.

"I'm a New England kid, grew up in a big sports market watching rivalries like Philadelphia and Boston," he says. "You start [behind the bench] in the East Coast League (Wheeling, WV), kind of work your way up, and when you get an opportunity in a market like Philadelphia with a lot of tradition, it felt like the next step for me.

"For an opportunity to coach a team like the Flyers, I'll always be grateful. I liked working for Ed Snider, liked the fans, like the area.

"We had some success, but didn't get all the way. In the end, that hurts the most."

PETER LAVIOLETTE
FLYER HERO #47

Sergei Bobrovsky

Chapter 13 • 2010-11

Glove Triangle

Headed into the summer of 2010, the Flyers' obvious need was for a No. 1 goaltender. Re-signing Ray Emery, attempting a longshot comeback from avascular necrosis in his right hip, was not a viable option. Michael Leighton, who had been so solid in the conference final and so shaky in the Stanley Cup Final, was an impending unrestricted free agent. The organization was content with Brian Boucher as a backup or as a split-time starter with the right partner, but not as its undisputed starter.

Before the June 25-26 Entry Draft in Los Angeles, general manager Paul Holmgren made two conditional trades of seventh-round picks to have a pre-July 1 window to sign two impending unrestricted free agent netminders—San Jose's Evgeni Nabokov and Dallas's Marty Turco.

Neither option panned out because "Nabokov was going to Russia, and Turco wanted too much money for too many years," recalls Holmgren.

The GM took a similar run at upgrading his team's defense. He traded a conditional 2011 draft pick to Nashville along with former Predator prospect Ryan Parent (originally acquired by Philadelphia in the Peter Forsberg trade) in exchange for impending unrestricted free-agent shutdown defenseman Dan Hamhuis.

"(Nashville GM) David Poile couldn't sign Hamhuis, so he was offering a signing window," recalls Holmgren. "Rather than taking a draft pick, I asked, 'Would you rather have Ryan Parent back?' He said, 'Yes.'

"Ryan had good tools and he worked hard, but puck skills held [him] back."

The Flyers forechecked hard to sign Hamhuis, who took calls from Mike Richards and Chris Pronger, but was unmoved. "Our pitch was: We would have won the Stanley Cup if you played for us last year; we tried it with four defensemen, basically, and got to Game Six," Holmgren recalls.

Through agent Wade Arnott, Hamhuis expressed concern that his role in Philadelphia would not be big enough since the organization already had Pronger and Kimmo Timonen. The defenseman wasn't sold on the GM's vision of him as a shutdown blueliner who would play about 20 minutes per game.

At the draft, Pittsburgh GM Ray Shero gave Holmgren a third-round pick to try to negotiate with Hamhuis, but the Penguins couldn't tempt him either. On July 1, he signed with Vancouver.

For the second straight year, due largely to exchanges made in the 2009 Pronger trade, the Flyer braintrust watched as the first and second rounds of the 2010 Draft took place without them. The top Philadelphia pick, 89th overall, was Quebec Major Junior Hockey League center Michael Chaput. Prep school defenseman Nick Luukko, son of Comcast-Spectacor president Peter Luukko, was also selected, 179th overall, by the organization even though Luukko had asked Holmgren not to take his son. Dad feared there would be too much pressure on Nick as a member of the Flyer organization and wanted to avoid the predictable peanut-gallery squawking about the pick being made solely out of nepotism.

"It had nothing to do with Peter being Nick's father," the GM said. "We liked him and thought he had a chance to play pro hockey down the road."

That summer, Holmgren faced a difficult salary-cap situation that had only a bleak solution—Simon Gagne would be asked to waive his no-movement clause.

There was no doubt that Gagne, the longest-tenured Flyer, had shown decisively during the club's playoff run that he still was a valuable player. The winger was in a precarious spot, however, as an injury-prone, 30-year-old entering the final year of a contract that carried a $5.25 million salary cap hit.

It was going to be tough to retain him once he became an unrestricted free agent after the 2010-11 campaign, and Philadelphia had important young players soon requiring extensions. Jeff Carter, making $5 million in the upcoming final season of his contract, would become a restricted free agent in the summer of 2011, as would Claude Giroux, who would be due for a substantial raise from the $821,667 he would make in 2010-11.

Two top-four defensemen—Braydon Coburn ($3.2 million) and Matt Carle ($3.43 million)—plus playoff hero Ville Leino ($800,000) were going to become unrestricted free agents the next summer, too.

Gagne's no-movement clause—meaning he had to approve any deal—greatly reduced the potential trade market. So did a medical history of 84 missed games over the previous three seasons. League-wide knowledge of the Flyer salary-cap issues also compromised the team's bargaining position.

Gagne had hoped to spend his entire career in Philadelphia. "I got drafted there. I grew up as a player there. I was happy in Philly. I felt like I gave the Flyers everything I could," the winger recalls.

Having played through severe injuries in the playoffs multiple times to score some of the franchise's biggest goals, Gagne felt betrayed when Holmgren asked him to agree to be traded.

"You know, it was Homer that asked me to play when I had the broken foot," he recalls. And I did it—for him, for me, for the team, for the fans.

"After we were so close, and I felt like I was a factor for our team to get to Game Six of the Final, I was hurt, thinking, 'Why me? I've been here for 10 years. Didn't I just play my best hockey for you when I had a pretty serious injury? What did I do wrong?'

"Paul said I did nothing wrong, that it was just a business decision they had to make. But I didn't understand it. At first, I almost felt like it was a joke. Then I got really mad at him and said, 'I refuse [to waive the no-trade clause].'"

The once rock-solid relationship between Holmgren and Gagne deteriorated quickly.

Gagne recalls: "Homer kept calling. It wasn't very friendly or nice. We had some '[Bleep]-you!' battles back and forth on the phone, and it got to where, at the end, there was no going back. It all went downhill between me and Paul."

Holmgren also remembers the unraveling of his relationship with Gagne as one of the most unpleasant times of his GM tenure.

"It was contentious, with Simon and (Gagne's agent, former NHL goaltender Bob) Sauve," he recalls. "I don't necessarily regret the decision (to pursue a no-movement waiver and a trade), but I probably regret the way I handled it.

"If I went to Simon earlier and was a little more upfront, maybe it would have been better. He did a lot for the Flyers. I wish I could have a do-over on that."

The Bruins had interest in Gagne. They also had a player to offer who could fit Philadelphia's immediate need—veteran goaltender Tim Thomas, the NHL's 2008-09 Vezina Trophy winner. Thomas, 36, had been temporarily displaced as a starter by the much younger Tuukka Rask as the previous season progressed and was agreeable to waiving his own no-movement clause to come to the Flyers.

The salary cap, however, remained a problem. Thomas carried a $5 million hit of his own, and his contract through the 2012-13 season made it a virtual wash with Gagne's salary, which would only have worsened the team's longer-term cap woes.

"We couldn't do it," Holmgren recalls. "It was a money-for-money trade offer." And Philadelphia still had not received Gagne's formal agreement on a no-movement waiver. The process dragged on for several weeks.

"At the end," recalls Gagne, "I called my agent and told him, 'If they want me to be gone, then I'll get the [bleep] out. But if I'm going to get rid of my no-trade clause, then I want to pick where I'm gonna go.' I told him to call different teams and find the best fit—almost like I was a free agent—and then tell Homer that's where I'm going.

"I never thought that was the way things would end. It sucked. But even though I didn't like what Homer said, he was straight with me.

"I had some really productive talks with (Lightning GM Steve) Yzerman. But it took a good month-and-a-half because there were things they had to work out salary-wise and Tampa Bay wanted to throw some money back to the Flyers."

Holmgren recalls that it took additional cajoling to persuade Gagne to accept the trade. "(Tampa stars) Vincent Lecavalier and Martin St. Louis both called him."

While waiting, Philadelphia upgraded its blueline, trading a 2011 second-round pick to the Lightning for 24-year-old defenseman Andrej Meszaros, and signing 38-year-old unrestricted free agent defenseman Sean O'Donnell to a one-year, $1 million contract.

The 6-2, 223-pound Meszaros, a former Ottawa first-round pick in 2004, brought a booming shot and an imposing physical game. As a young player with the Senators, Meszaros thrived in a pairing with countryman Zdeno Chara. Thereafter, he struggled with inconsistency. After going to Tampa Bay in 2008-09, he dealt with both injuries and erratic performances and was considered largely a bust. The defenseman carried a $4 million cap hit through the 2013-14 season and the Flyers decided to take a chance on his high-caliber skills reemerging around a better surrounding cast.

A pairing with the steady O'Donnell—one of the sport's most respected veteran defensive defensemen and locker-room leaders—had the potential to be a large-scale upgrade that would provide depth behind Philadelphia's established pairings of Pronger-Carle and Timonen-Coburn.

"(Assistant GM) John Paddock coached Meszaros in Ottawa, and they loved him," Holmgren recalls. "When the opportunity came up to move just a draft pick, it was a no-brainer. O'Donnell had played in Anaheim on that [Cup-winning] team with Pronger. Prongs was a big proponent of getting him."

The GM also locked up restricted free agent Coburn through the 2011-12 season at a $3.2 million cap hit.

The Flyers added winger Jody Shelley as an unrestricted free agent, beating the Ranger offer of $825,000 by signing him to a three-year deal at a $1.1 million cap hit per season. Shelley, an enforcer who had scored his only two goals of 2009-10 during the final weekend of the regular season in a game against Philadelphia, was another well-respected, veteran leader. Holmgren believed the 34-year-old was also a better overall hockey player and, arguably, a more effective fighter than Riley Cote, who soon announced his retirement as a player at age 28 to become an assistant coach with the Phantoms.

Shelley recalls: "The Flyers were my team growing up [in Manitoba]. I was a huge fan of Lindros, John LeClair, the Legion of Doom. When I was a kid, I loved the logo. For them to make me a three-year offer, it was exciting."

For the GM, too. "Even though [Shelley] was a fourth-line guy, toughness was still important then, and Jody was probably the toughest in the league," recalls Holmgren. "He could also play eight or 10 minutes."

Shelley's arrival spelled the departure of Arron Asham, who signed with the Penguins. "I think we all liked Asham, but you were always holding your breath on whether he was in good shape or not," Holmgren explained.

Philadelphia retained the most unpredictable and skilled of their tough-guys, inking restricted free agent Dan Carcillo to a one-year, $1.075 million contract. The team also re-signed checking line forward Darroll Powe to a one-year, $725,000 deal.

Having no other goaltending options, the Flyers decided to stick with the status quo by committing to the 29-year-old Leighton with a two-year contract at a cap hit of $1.33 million.

"We had just improved our defensive depth in front of our goalies," the GM remembers. "And Michael and Boosh had gotten us to Game Six of the Final."

Recalls Leighton: "They gave me decent money, and Holmgren said, 'If you perform in the first year, then we'll give you a lot more money to extend you. We need to make sure you're a starting goalie in this league and we will give you a year or two to make certain that you are.' That gave me confidence that I could be a starter."

The Gagne deal still was hanging when Philadelphia made a surprise signing to try to replace his offense. Obtained was the massively talented but aloof Nikolai Zherdev, a once fourth-overall pick by Columbus, to a one-year, $2 million contract. After the Rangers, for whom he had scored 23 goals in 2008-09, walked away from an arbitration award in the player's favor, the 25-year-old right wing returned home to Russia in 2009-10, producing 39 points in 52 games for KHL club Atlant Mytishchi.

"It was a pretty good low-risk gamble on a highly skilled, talented guy," Holmgren recalls.

With Gagne only willing to go to Tampa, and the Flyers unable to take on a major long-term salary, Philadelphia took what they could get for him—defenseman Matt Walker and a fourth-round pick in 2011. Walker had been signed by Tampa Bay in the summer of 2009 to a four-year contract carrying a $1.7 million cap hit and an annually escalating real-dollar salary that peaked at $2 million in 2012-13. Holmgren figured Walker could at least be a useful defenseman to provide third-pairing caliber veteran depth, some added physical toughness and size (6-4, 215 pounds), plus a right-handed shot on an otherwise all left-shooting blueline corps.

Holmgren unconvincingly tried to publicly spin the Gagne deal as a hockey trade that added to the Flyer depth on the blueline. But with his hands tied, the GM had few options and was unable to obtain anything close to the assets that may have come back had there been a more open field of potential trade partners and/or a less confining salary cap situation.

When Pronger's knee remained swollen while on vacation with his family, the defenseman underwent an MRI that disclosed loose bodies. Arthroscopic surgery was performed in late July.

"It didn't get much better or, really, any better at all," he recalls. "I don't know if I could have sped up the process (for an earlier surgery)."

With his team coming off a playoff run that achingly had fallen two wins short of the Stanley Cup, coach Peter Laviolette used the opening of training camp to try to publicly quash any notion of a carryover effect, whether positive or negative.

"That's over and done," Laviolette said. "Every season, we start again with the same goal. You can't dwell on last season."

While most of the veteran players skated in Voorhees before camp, Richards did not show up until the required reporting date. Never a workout enthusiast, he arrived in less-than-peak physical condition.

Leighton's back, sore during the playoffs, had started to trouble him again.

"I finished 2009-10 and the doctor said, 'You have a muscle strain in your back, go get some rest,'" recalls Leighton. "So I rested.

"Through the summer, I worked out, felt fine, signed my contract. X-rays before training camp showed I had a bulging disc, but no big deal. I was told to just keep doing core strengthening. So I went through camp and felt great.

"I want to clear this up: There was a lot of media controversy that I was hiding an injury when I signed the deal, and then came forward and said my back hurt. That was total BS. The Flyers knew that my back was sore during the playoffs. It wasn't a surprise."

Leighton played without incident in his first preseason outing, but during his second, against the Maple Leafs, he was in considerable distress.

"I did the exhibition game and all of a sudden, boom!" recalls Leighton. "It was like something just exploded in my back. I'm not sure how it happened. The extent of the injury [at the start of camp] wasn't anywhere close to what it ended up being in that exhibition. It went from an 8% injury to 100% when I herniated it."

Discectomy surgery was performed by Dr. Alex Vacarro at Methodist Hospital in Philadelphia. Holmgren said he did not believe Leighton had been duplicitous and the goalie's return was expected in late November-early December.

Third-string Johan (Back-up) Backlund was behind schedule in his recovery from off-season hip surgery, leaving Philadelphia with a gaping hole in goaltending depth apart from Boucher.

The Flyers, however, had a solution already in-house—22-year-old Russian goaltender Sergei Bobrovsky, who stole the show with an outstanding preseason.

"He was (Semyon) Varlamov's backup for the World Junior team, so he had played at the highest level for the Russians," Holmgren recalls. "Our guy Kenny (Hoodikoff, the Russia-based Flyer scout) saw him a lot and so had (European scout) Ilkka Sinisalo.

"'Bob' played on the worst team in the KHL, but his save percentage was always great. (Flyer goaltending coach) Jeff Reese liked what he saw on tape.

"We had competition to sign Bob—L.A. and another team. I like to believe that we offered him the best opportunity to play; that's what we pitched. But did any of us come to camp thinking he could come play right away for us? No. I don't even remember talking about it. He was going to play for the Phantoms."

Despite a language barrier, a strong working relationship developed quickly between Reese, Boucher and Bobrovsky.

"There was a lot to like right away," recalls Reese. "Naturally athletic, competitive, and eager to learn. He absorbed things fast and had an outstanding work ethic."

Boucher publicly predicted future NHL stardom for Bobrovsky, calling him "really fantastic."

"I meant it," Boucher recalls. "His English was not very good, but we communicated through hand gestures. I like Bob a lot. Good kid, hard worker."

Professionalism had marked the careers of two veteran forwards who unfortunately came to the end of their playing careers during camp. Bill Guerin—a 429 goal-scorer in the NHL who had not been offered a contract by any team at age 39—was released after attending on a try-out basis.

Ian Laperriere, with two years remaining on his contract, suffered recurring post-concussion symptoms from the puck he took in the face during the 2010 playoffs. "He played a game in Toronto," recalls Holmgren. "The next night in Minnesota, he came to me before the game in the press box and was crying. I knew it wasn't going to be good. It was kind of sad."

Laperriere's lone remorse from 15 seasons of board work, penalty killing, shot blocking, and fierce body checking was that only one year was spent in Philadelphia.

"It was my shortest time here compared to the other clubs I played for," said Laperriere, one of the best teammates the Flyers ever had, in announcing his retirement. But I'm just glad I had a chance to wear the orange-and-black. "Nothing compares with the way the Flyers care about their players.

"At the end of the day I'm lucky because I played close to 1,100 games. As a little boy, I was hoping to play one."

Walker reported to camp with the same hip and shoulder issues that he apparently had while at Tampa Bay. "I had asked Yzerman, 'Are there any injury issues?'" recalls Holmgren. "He said, 'No, he's fine.' Then we trade for him and find out that's not the case."

Philadelphia changed its trade policy, requiring physicals before finalizing transactions.

In a preseason game against Minnesota, Walker fell awkwardly during a fight with the Wild's Matt Kassian and was out indefinitely.

With both Walker and Pronger (still recovering from knee surgery) unavailable during training camp, Oskars Bartulis got a reprieve, making the team as the seventh defenseman.

Laviolette stunned everyone, especially Boucher, by starting Bobrovsky as the Flyers opened the 2010-11 regular season and Pittsburgh's new CONSOL Energy Center.

"I knew he had a great camp," Boucher recalls. "But I was a little bit surprised because he's a young kid."

The rookie almost single-handedly kept Philadelphia in the game early, making 15 saves to get to the first intermission scoreless. "He didn't look nervous," Danny Briere would say later.

Early in the second, Briere deftly redirected Richard's wrist shot on the powerplay for a 1-0 advantage. With 2:45 remaining in the period, Blair Betts put home a Powe rebound to make it 2-0.

Tyler Kennedy took a cross-ice feed from defenseman Paul Martin and beat Bobrovsky 44 seconds into the third period but Giroux stole the puck from Kris Letang and, short-handed, restored the Flyer two-goal lead.

Alex Goligoski converted on a Meszaros penalty to cut the gap, but thereafter Bobrovsky slammed the door, debuting with a 3-2 win.

"Definitely an impressive first game for Bob," said Scott Hartnell, who was credited with a game-high five hits. "Really, we couldn't have asked for more."

Two nights later, Briere's third-period goal forced overtime in St. Louis before Blues defenseman Carlo Colaiacovo hammered the ricochet of a blocked Alex Steen shot over Boucher to win the game, 2-1.

Pronger received a 36th birthday gift when he was cleared to play in the next night's home opener against the Avalanche. The Eastern Conference championship banner, raised at the Wells Fargo Center—Wachovia had been bought out, giving the 14-year-old arena its fourth name—received a big ovation, just not as large as the one given to Laperriere to mark his retirement.

"It brought tears to my eyes. I don't have words to describe how much all the support means," he said, as both Philadelphia and Colorado—his previous club—honored him for his contributions.

Giroux tallied his second shorthanded goal of the young season, Carter scored a pair, and Powe hit the empty net as Bobrovsky's 25 saves gave the Flyers a 4-2 win.

When the Penguins came to town, Crosby turned Giroux and Richards penalties into back-to-back powerplay goals in the 5-1 Philadelphia defeat.

Through five games, the Flyers had been penalized a league-high 42 times. "Whether they are questionable [penalty calls] or deserved, we're going to the box, and it's ended up costing us," said Laviolette. "It taxes the penalty killers; it taxes the defensemen. We're not scoring five-on-five, and that doesn't help, but now we're on defense again.

"We have to do a better job in the battles for the puck. I'm not happy with where we are offensively as a group. We have to generate more."

Every defensive mistake was proving costly. Anaheim's Ryan Getzlaf stripped Giroux of the puck to score, and a rusty-looking Pronger was beaten along the wall on another goal by Teemu Selanne.

"I don't think I ever said I was 100 percent," Pronger said. "[The knee] is getting a little bit stronger, but some days feel better than others."

A three-game losing streak ended with a 5-2 win over Toronto. Not Walker's issue, however. In Nashville, Dr. Thomas Byrd repaired a torn labrum and bony impingement in the defenseman's right hip. He would need 10-12 weeks to recover.

Laviolette was not pleased with his team's effort during a 2-1 loss in Columbus. "We played mindless hockey without any energy, without any passion," he said, and Timonen agreed.

"We are not very hard to play against right now," said the defenseman.

O'Donnell changed that. With Philadelphia down 1-0 at home against the Sabres, the veteran defenseman dropped the gloves with Cody McCormick in a bout that brought a heretofore silent Wells Fargo Center crowd to its feet and his teammates to life.

On the powerplay, Briere jammed his own rebound past Ryan

Miller to tie the game, and middle-period goals by Zherdev, Powe and Giroux put the Flyers in the driver's seat in Bobrovsky's 6-3 win.

"Sean picked a great time to get a fight going," Giroux said. "We started playing after that."

When Laviolette's team returned to Pittsburgh for the second time in a month, the Penguins knew who Bobrovsky was. Matt Cooke, who had been accused by Richards during their previous meeting in Philadelphia of avoiding a fight, this time took the Flyer captain on six seconds into the game. Seventeen seconds later, Pittsburgh enforcer Deryk Engelland defeated Shelley, requiring him to go to the locker room for stitches above the left eye.

There were 12 minor penalties during the rest of the game and Giroux took advantage of two of them with shorthanded and powerplay goals. Six-for-six penalty killing, and a 26-save performance by Bobrovsky added up to a 3-2 Flyer win. "A lot of fun," said Carcillo, who, after being scratched for three of the previous games, scored a goal and played the villain for booing Penguin fans.

On October 30th, Briere received a three-game suspension for cross-checking Islander Frans Nielsen in the face. But Philadelphia was starting to find the net even without him.

The Flyers scored 24 times over a six-game winning streak, all with Bobrovsky in goal, to push their record to 9-4-1. Not coincidentally, Pronger had started to play close to his customary form, and the addition of Meszaros and O'Donnell had given the team an ability to roll out three reliable defense pairings. The changes started to make a huge difference.

Carter, after posting just two goals and three points through the first eight games, was on a tear as Giroux's right wing, rattling off six goals and 12 points during a 9-0-1 run. On November 11, he recorded a natural hat trick in an 8-1 road pasting of Carolina. Giroux already had 10 goals and 11 assists, while Richards had posted at least one point in nine of 10 games.

Even Andreas Nodl, playing on Richards' left wing by the captain's request, seemed to be fulfilling the promise that made him a second-round pick in 2006. He had returned from shoulder issues to compile six goals and eight points during his first 14 contests.

Briere and Hartnell, who had played the 2009-10 season through marital break-ups, had largely picked up with Leino where the unit had left off during the playoffs.

"Those guys are very easy to play with because they are so skilled," Hartnell said. "They are also real hard workers. I just try to bang some bodies around and get to the net. There's just been really good chemistry. Who knows why?"

Laviolette remembers recognizing Leino's skill level as soon as the Flyers had acquired him in February 2010. "I liked our lineup at the time, and he had to wait for his opportunity," the coach said. "But I didn't realize he had such a tremendous compete level on the ice. He fights for space and is very hungry for the puck. If it's not on his stick, he'll go get it."

After beating the Panthers and Ottawa, Philadelphia was shut out

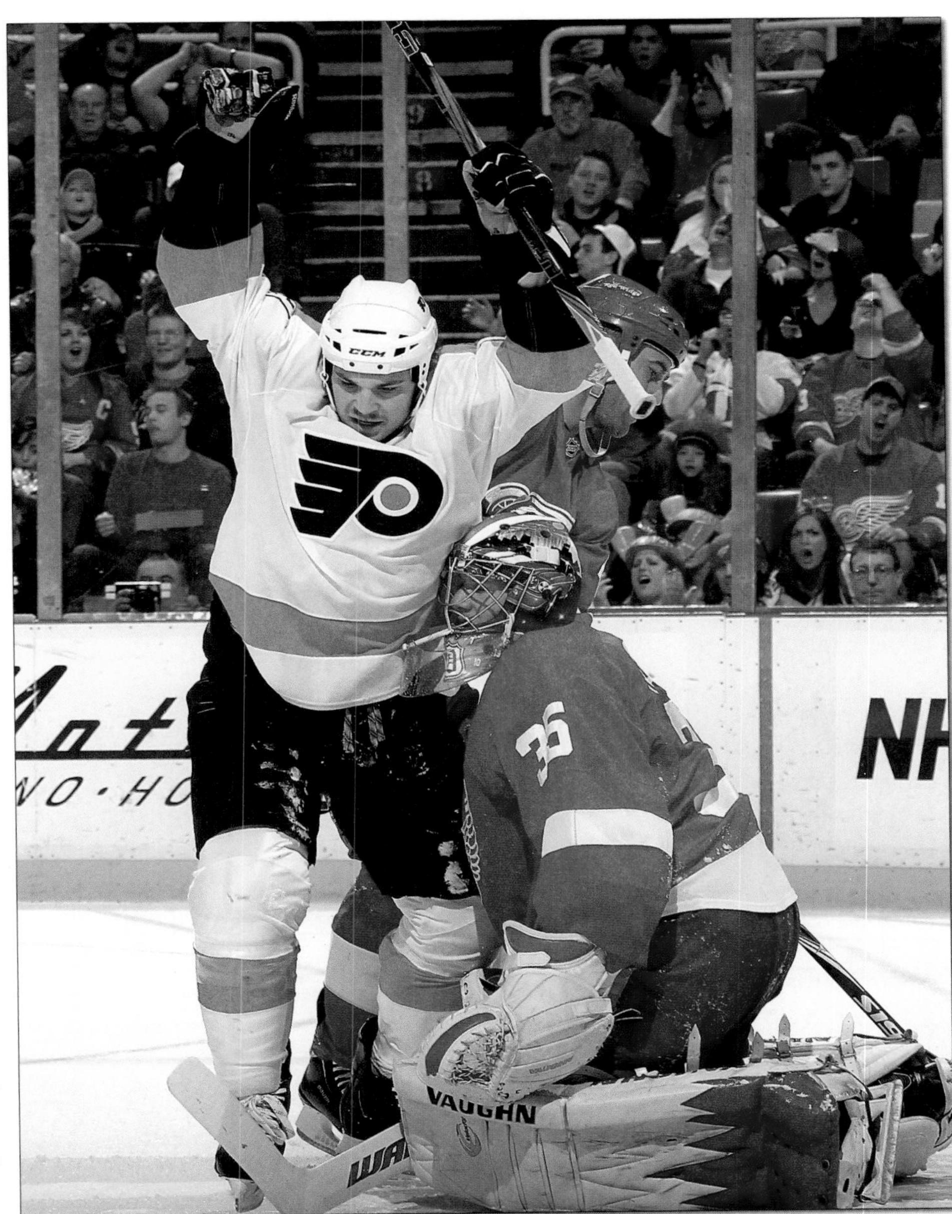

Despite playing only 57 games, Daniel Carcillo was one of three Flyers with more than 125 minutes in penalties in 2010-11.

Before the Spectrum was demolished, Snider Youth Hockey players lowered the club's championship and retired number banners.

in Montreal, 3-0, despite putting 41 shots on goaltender Carey Price.

Visiting Tampa Bay, the Flyers had outscored the Lightning 5-4 in the first period when Laviolette yanked Bobrovsky. But Boucher, playing for the first time in over a month, wasn't much better. In the second period, Richards received a double-minor for carelessly clipping Pavel Kubina, and Steven Stamkos completed a hat trick with 1:01 left before intermission to tie the game, 7-7. Nate Thompson's third-period strike won the wild game for the Bolts, 8-7.

At Washington, 3-1 and 4-3 third-period Philadelphia leads slipped away when the Caps scored three powerplay goals, one of them off Giroux's protective cup. But in the shoot-out, Boucher stopped three of the deadliest offensive players in the world in succession—Nicklas Backstrom, Alex Ovechkin and Alexander Semin—to make Briere's second-round goal stand as the game-winner.

"It wasn't our best hockey," said Boucher, "but we found a way. These are games you have to win against the good clubs."

The Flyers planned to be one of those teams for a long time. Giroux, 23, was signed to his first big contract—three years, $11.25 million—and the franchise committed to Carter for a massive 11-year, $58 million extension.

"I wanted to stay there for the long haul," Carter recalls. Both he and Richards, who had signed a 12-year contract in 2007, had no-trade clauses that would kick in before the 2012-13 season.

As Holmgren looked ahead, Flyer Chairman Ed Snider took the beginning of the demolition of the Spectrum as a chance to look back. But he had a hard time actually watching the wrecking ball hit the building on November 23, 2010.

"To me it's not a celebration," Snider told NHL.com, "but in another way it is. I'm very emotional about it."

Following a ceremony that included beloved athletes Bernie Parent and 76ers Hall-of-Famer Julius Erving, it took more than a half dozen swings of the orange wrecking ball before any noticeable dent was made in the tough-to-the-end, 43-year-old home of the Broad Street Bullies. Demolition was expected to take four to five months. Planned for the site was a retail restaurant and entertainment development called XFINITY Live.

After rallying from a 2-0 deficit to a 3-2 win over Montreal, then blasting the Wild in St. Paul, 6-1, Black Friday turned unprofitable. In a 2-2 overtime, an apparent powerplay goal by Richards was disallowed because the officials ruled Pronger was face-guarding Calgary goaltender Miikka Kiprusoff even though the Flyer appeared simply to be using his stick to direct traffic. Calgary won a shoot-out and Pronger was seething.

"There was no explanation on the ice because they know they screwed up," Pronger hissed. "I wasn't turned around waving at him. It's infuriating."

The next day at Newark, Briere's third-period powerplay goal forced overtime, but Philadelphia lost another shootout 2-1. A 3-0 shutout loss to Boston's Tim Thomas brought the Flyer winless streak to three.

"I think anytime you've lost a few games, you look to your captain to step it up," said Laviolette, and Richards did, breaking a third-period tie in a 5-3 home win over New Jersey.

The next day at Uniondale, Briere stepped up similarly, snapping a 2-2 tie with 5:44 remaining in a 3-2 victory, Philadelphia's 21st in its last 23 meetings with the Islanders.

Richards' apparent overtime winner on San Jose's Antero Niittymaki proved on replay to be a split-second late, and the ex-Flyer goalie won the shootout 5-4. But when Briere scored his 15th and 16th goals of the season at Toronto, Philadelphia had its bounce-back 4-1 victory.

Denied once by the clock, another time by a questionable penalty, Richards finally got his overtime winner to beat the Bruins 2-1 in Boston. "I guess the third time's a charm," he said.

Not as fortunate was Shelley when he faced NHL justice for boarding Adam McQuaid in the second period. The Flyer enforcer received a two-game suspension.

Bobrovsky's two wins in two tries against Pittsburgh notwithstanding, Laviolette stayed with the hot Boucher and, again, the Flyers broke a third-period tie, this time on a Hartnell powerplay goal as Philadelphia made it 3-0 against the Penguins on the season. With their 3-2 home win on December 14, it was the earliest date that the Flyers had reached 20 wins since 1986.

They were, however, about to learn whether their pace could be sustainable without Pronger, who suffered a broken right foot blocking a second-period shot in a 5-3 Philadelphia victory at Montreal. Following surgery, the Flyer defenseman was expected to be out of the lineup for a month.

Walker, who had yet to play since his summer acquisition for Gagne, was unavailable to serve as Pronger's replacement—the defenseman's hip required a second surgery.

Leighton's September back procedure was deemed successful, however, and he was prepared to play following a conditioning assignment with the Phantoms. But the goalie now had to wait his turn behind Bobrovsky and Boucher.

Zherdev scored twice against the Rangers—the team that rejected him after a hefty arbitration reward two years earlier—giving the winger four goals in three games. "It's really great that I score," he said. "It doesn't matter what team it's against."

Philadelphia, 7-0-1 over the preceding eight games, and 22-7-5 for the season, was cut no slack by its booing fans in a 5-0 pre-Christmas shellacking by the Panthers. "We weren't able to get up for this game," said O'Donnell. "It shouldn't happen, but we're human beings."

Boucher gave up four goals in the first 5:21 of the second period as the Flyers opened a five-game road trip in Vancouver. Laviolette went to Bobrovsky, who gave up two more in a 6-2 loss, the first time Philadelphia had failed to gain a point in its last 15 visits to British Columbia.

Laviolette turned to Leighton in Los Angeles. The netminder struggled, but a four-point night by Richards allowed the Flyers to win 7-4.

The next night—New Year's Eve—Bobrovsky was bombed 5-2 in Anaheim, but goaltending was not the only problem. "I don't like the way we played," said Laviolette. "The second period was nonchalant and flat for us."

On a fourth game in six nights, the Flyers had enough left in their legs to overtake 22 years of frustration in Detroit. James van Riemsdyk's ninth goal in 18 games and scores by Carcillo and Carter jumped Philadelphia to a 3-0 lead that Boucher held for a 3-2 victory, his team's first at Joe Louis Arena since November 1988 (0-16-2).

Boucher followed up with back-to-back wins over the Devils, making Leighton, more than ever, the odd man out. He cleared waivers and was sent to Adirondack.

Vice President Joe Biden, the former Delaware senator, visited the Philadelphia locker room after the home win over New Jersey, telling Briere he was the favorite player of his wife, diehard Flyer fan Jill Biden, who kept a Briere bobblehead figurine on the nightstand.

"You're the guy!" Biden said to a smiling Briere.

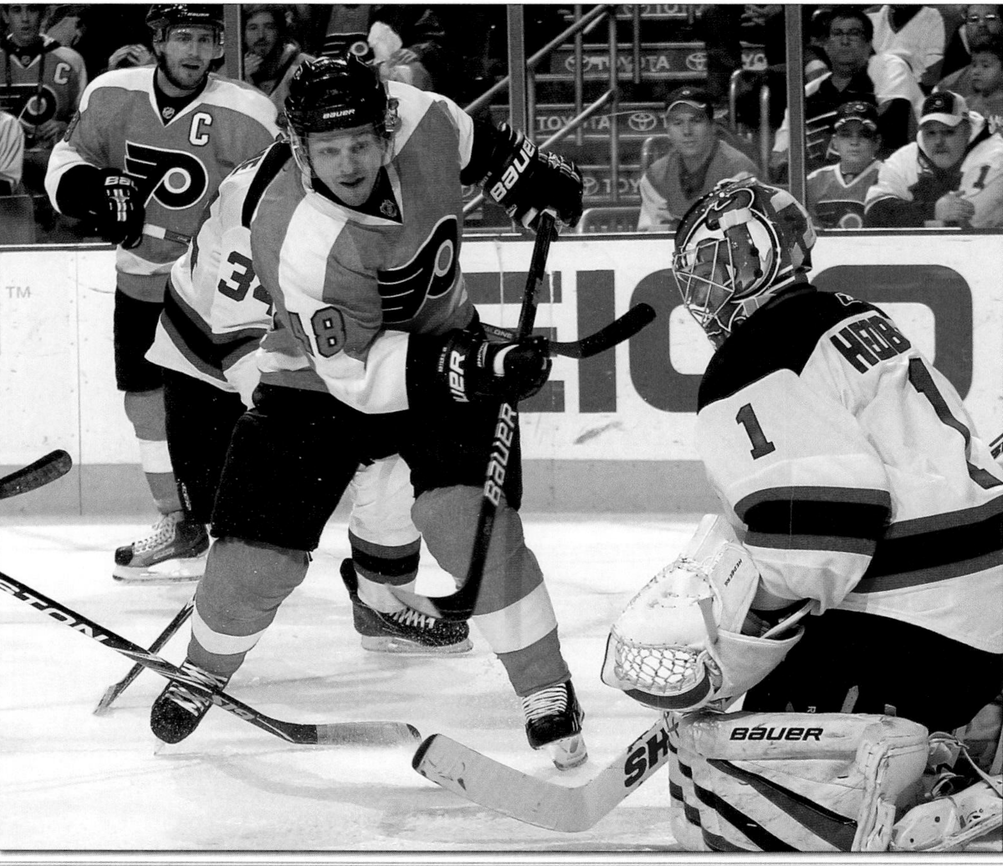

Danny Briere tries to put the puck past New Jersey's Johan Hedberg. Briere, Claude Giroux, Jeff Carter amd captain Mike Richards (shown in this photo) combined for 118 goals in 2010-11.

Philadelphia had lots of guys going well. Leino scored the winner in a comeback 5-2 win in Buffalo and Briere had a goal for a fifth consecutive game in a 5-2 triumph at Atlanta. Boucher's 34-save, 3-2 win at Madison Square Garden finished up a stretch of 9 out of 10 games on the road. Since the Flyers had won seven of them, Laviolette booked the team in a hotel the afternoon of a home game with Washington, and Meszaros' goal in overtime won the contest, 3-2.

Holmgren, his team first-place overall after having put together a semifinalist and finalist within the last three seasons, earned a three-year contract extension.

Pronger, who rejoined the lineup after 13 games for a 6-2 win in Ottawa, was back in time for a return to Chicago, the scene of his worst nightmare—the 7-4 loss in the previous season's Game Five Stanley Cup Final in which he was minus-five. This time, he was plus-two as Philadelphia, getting four assists by Giroux and 30 saves by Bobrovsky, beat the Stanley Cup champions 4-1.

"We know how last year ended," said Carter. "[The win] obviously was nice."

Said Laviolette: "It's about looking forward, not looking back. I'm really happy we won the game because we maintained our position in first place this year."

There was no letdown two days later. Five players scored and Pronger had four assists as the Flyers earned their 1,000th home win and capped a hugely successful January (10-2) with a 5-2 victory over Montreal.

Briere's 26 goals earned him a replacement spot in the All-Star Game in Raleigh, joining Giroux and Laviolette, also first-time honorees. Philadelphia enjoyed the break with a 33-12-5 record. "We were winning, and the right way, too, most nights," recalls Laviolette.

Walker, who had played sparingly in four January games, was sent to the Phantoms after he cleared waivers, the Flyers having received almost zero value besides the cap savings in the Gagne deal. "If Matt Walker had been healthy, I think the trade would have been better," said Holmgren. "Well, maybe a little."

Bobrovsky, who had shared the goal equally with Boucher during January, was lifted after giving up three goals in the first period of a 4-0 loss in Tampa. But he bounced back two nights later at home to beat Nashville, 3-1. "Clearly the Flyers are the deepest team in the Eastern Conference," said Predator coach Barry Trotz. "They are just tremendous."

Bob Clarke, presented before the game with his retired No. 16 banner that had hung at the Spectrum, agreed, saying this version of the team had "pretty much every ingredient you could want. Everybody from my era is hoping that they win the Cup."

Behind Boucher, Philadelphia rolled 3-1 over Dallas and 2-1 over

Carolina. Powe scored shorthanded on a penalty shot in a 4-3 shootout win over Tampa Bay, Timonen getting the winner in the seventh round.

On February 14, Holmgren traded first- and third-round picks to the Leafs for 24-year-old right wing Kris Versteeg, a two-time 20-goal scorer, who had been a cap casualty in Chicago. "Versteeg had been good against us in the Final, was a guy you could use different ways," Holmgren recalls.

Carolina chose Philadelphia's February 18 visit as an appropriate night to retire the jersey of Rod Brind'Amour. Eight years a Flyer and the captain of Laviolette's 2006 Hurricane Stanley Cup team, Brind'Amour had retired at the end of the 2009-10 season. Erik Cole's late goal gave Carolina, for which Brind'Amour was working in player development, a 3-2 victory.

At Madison Square Garden, O'Donnell suffered a knee injury on his first shift of the game and was expected to miss two weeks. Philadelphia cleaned up a 3-1 trip with Boucher's pristine 4-2 triumph. It was only the third time in Flyer history that the team played a game without a penalty.

O'Donnell's absence gave playing time to Bartulis, but two games later, he was driven into the boards by Coyote Scottie Upshall during a 3-2 loss to Phoenix and needed surgery that was expected to leave him out 10-12 weeks.

Down two defensemen, Holmgren picked up 32-year-old Nick Boynton off waivers from Chicago. The GM also acquired 6-5 left winger Tom Sestito, 23, from Columbus, in exchange for the rights to Michael Chaput (Philadelphia's third-round pick in 2010) plus minor-league right wing Greg Moore. Sestito was sent to the Phantoms.

Zherdev, who had neither dressed in six games nor engaged with teammates much all season, was waived at his request, after Holmgren had unsuccessfully tried to find a trading partner. "His work ethic has probably dropped off," said Holmgren. "Right now, he's not fitting in."

When no other team picked up Zherdev, he remained with the Flyers.

Philadelphia blew leads in home losses to Toronto, 3-2, and Buffalo, 5-3. "Little mistakes are costing us," Pronger said. "We're playing teams that are battling for their lives."

An abysmal 7-0 loss in New York City brought the losing streak to four games.

"We're at the stage now where it's a test of our character," Pronger said. "We've got to understand it's going to take some hard work to get everybody on the same page."

They did for a period against Edmonton, outshooting the Oilers 17-1, but the energy dissipated again, resulting in lots of work for Bobrovsky. The win and the 4-1 score flattered a sloppy effort. As the locker-room doors opened to the media, Pronger was heard shouting, "Some people just don't learn!" at Giroux, who had made three egregious turnovers.

The next day, Holmgren said Pronger was being a leader and Giroux merely a young player needing to be led. "I think it's great," the GM told reporters after practice. "Nobody likes the way we've been playing, and it just came to a head in that particular instance, I'm sure.

"Claude Giroux wants to win, but sometimes he needs to hear from the older guys on the team how it's done. Claude maybe didn't like being spoken to like that, but I think he understands what's being said to him, and he'll benefit from that."

The slap to the young star's face was only figurative, not the reason why Pronger's hand was killing him. The pain had been persisting for six games while an X-ray and MRI both failed to disclose any serious problem. Finally the defenseman sat out a 3-2 win at Toronto—Giroux, apparently not pouting, had a goal and an assist—but one game's rest did little to alleviate Pronger's discomfort. The Flyers still were without him as they wasted a Leino hat trick in a 5-4 home overtime loss to Atlanta.

When a CT scan revealed a hairline fracture, surgery intended to hasten the recovery was performed in Cleveland by specialist Dr. Tom Graham; Pronger was expected back for the playoffs less than four weeks away. To fill in, Holmgren recalled from the Phantoms defenseman Erik Gustafsson, a free agent signed out of Northern Michigan University who had a fireplug build (5-10, 180 pounds) and an ability to move the puck.

"Without Chris, we needed our other main guys—Timonen, Coburn, Carle, Meszaros and O'Donnell—to carry the load," recalls Holmgren.

Carter's two goals helped the team to a 3-2 win at Florida, and Leino's shootout goal in the sixth round got Philadelphia past the Stars, 3-2, in Dallas. But that was the only win of four consecutive games that went to shootouts. After the fourth—a 2-1 defeat at Pittsburgh—Laviolette complained, "We got beat in most areas. If it wasn't for our goaltender (Bobrovsky), we wouldn't have gotten any points tonight."

Having received three solid years from an undrafted college player—Princeton's Darroll Powe—the Flyers were staying active in the collegiate market. Gustafsson was up with the big team, and Philadelphia signed two more when their final NCAA seasons ended. Brown forward Harry Zolnierczyk was projected to fill a Powe-type roll on the fourth line, but Bemidji (MN) State's Matt Reed, 24, was on the radar screens of multiple teams as a potential top-nine center or winger.

"Matt was at the Ranger camp the previous year and I know they tried to sign him," recalls Holmgren. "He went back (to college) for one more year, basically because that would move him beyond the entry-level contract requirement. He wouldn't need to sign a two-way deal (which universally calls for players to take a substantial pay cut if playing in the minor leagues). He played his cards right; had a good senior year.

"We'd all seen Matt play. We had him in for a game (during the Montreal series in 2010) and I remember introducing him to Mr. Snider. Ross Fitzpatrick was doing a lot of college scouting for us then, and put time in on Matt. He called me and said, 'We gotta [make an] offer on him. The Rangers already offered a million dollars to sign.'

"We made our offer ($2.7 million over three years) and ended up getting him."

Read can remember calling his parents the day after his Philadelphia visit and telling them that he wanted to play for the Flyers. "[Ten months later] they were knocking on the door," he recalls. "It was an easy decision.

"Chris Pronger and Mike Richards called me. Obviously they were being told to do that, but no other team had their players make those calls like the Flyers did. It told me how the organization was run.

"Chris told me he had played with multiple teams and that the Flyers were like a big family; he said that Ed Snider would do anything to win.

"The offers were very similar, all just under a million dollars (a year). Three of them were for one-way contracts, the fourth for more money, but a two-way deal. (Agent) Neil (Sheehy) told me to sleep on it. I had a great sleep and woke up with the right feeling. I knew exactly what I was doing."

Read signed with Philadelphia and was sent to the Phantoms to complete the season while the parent team kept muddling along.

A hat trick by van Riemsdyk, his first in the NHL, during a 4-1 win over the Islanders at Uniondale, lifted the Flyers to their 18th 100-point season and kept them in first place in the Eastern Conference. But after losing 2-1 at home against the Bruins, Philadelphia had won only seven of its last 18 games.

Leino's two goals and an assist sparked a third win in three tries in Pittsburgh's new digs, 5-2. But 43 shots against Atlanta goalie Chris Mason only got the Flyers a 1-0 defeat. "Now's the time of the year where you're going to have to score on second and third opportunities," Richards said. "We have to be hungrier."

Desperate for offense, Laviolette dressed Zherdev for the first time since March 6 for a game at the Prudential Center. He fed Carter for a tap-in to knot the game, but Philadelphia lost 4-2 on a Patrik Elias hat trick. The conference lead over Washington had shrunk to one point.

"We keep talking about being the top team in the league, but we haven't played that way," said Timonen.

Against the Rangers, Zherdev redirected a Giroux setup past Henrik Lundqvist at 4:32 of the third period to force OT, but Bobrovsky lost a shootout and the Flyers were defeated 3-2. Next, four unanswered tallies sent them down to a miserable 5-2 loss at Ottawa.

"It was a big game for us, and pretty much the whole team came out flat," said Giroux. "We've got two games left. I don't think you can turn on a switch when playoffs come, so the next two games are going to be huge."

Philadelphia placed Leighton on re-entry waivers to get the goalie onto the playoff roster. He cleared and rejoined the team. The Flyers also announced that Pronger had a "minor setback" in his injury rehab. The defenseman thought he would be able to play in the first round of the playoffs, but wouldn't guarantee Game One. "I guess you'll have to wait and find out, won't you?" smiled Pronger, who often delighted in teasing the media.

The losing streak went to five games when a 3-2 third period lead evaporated into a 4-3 overtime loss in Buffalo that killed Philadelphia's last chance to win the conference title.

"It's so frustrating," said Briere, who scored his 33rd goal of the season after missing the previous two games with a minor groin pull. "We're not looking at positioning now as much as trying to come up rolling to start the playoffs."

On April 7, the Flyers and the hockey world were stunned to learn about the death of Edward John (E.J.) McGuire, who had served terms as a Philadelphia assistant under Mike Keenan and Bill Barber. McGuire had kept private his struggle with leiomyosarcoma, a rare cancer, almost until his passing at age 58.

McGuire had also been an assistant with the Blackhawks and Senators, plus an AHL head coach for the Bruins, Rangers and OHL Guelph Storm. For his final seven years, he was director of the NHL's Central Scouting Service. The brightest of coaches, he did the Xs and Os and much of the video study for Keenan and Barber, but as the sweetest of men, he kept the players feeling appreciated and informed.

"The Flyers were the favorite team E.J. worked," recalls Terry McGuire, his wife. "And it wasn't just because he met me here.

"The first time he came to Philadelphia, it was his entree into the pros, and he was like a kid, working for Bob Clarke and meeting Joe Watson and Bernie Parent."

"The second time, he had been around and had come to realize just how well the Flyers treat people."

Before the home finale, Giroux won the Bobby Clarke Trophy as the Flyer MVP. Meszaros celebrated his initial Barry Ashbee Trophy as the top defenseman with two goals that helped the team come back from a 4-3 deficit to a 7-4 win over the Islanders.

"Problems? I don't really remember the problems," Hartnell laughed, before adding, "It's a big relief."

A smiling Snider made the locker room rounds shaking hands and doling out thanks. "I think they're more ready than last year's team," the chariman said, never minding that the victory was the first in six attempts and only fifth in the last 15 contests.

Philadelphia, 47-23-12, and Pittsburgh, 49-25-8, finished with the same amount of points (106), but the Flyers won the Atlantic Division title by virtue of having five more regulation and overtime wins. Both teams had 106 points, one fewer than Eastern Conference champion Washington.

The Sabres, Philadelphia's first-round opponent, had gone 15-5-4 in the final 24 games of the regular season to claim the seventh seed. Since the two teams' last playoff series in 2006—a six-game Buffalo victory that brought the all-time series to 5-3 for Philadelphia—only six Sabres and two Flyers (Carter and Richards) remained. A rivalry that developed from the two franchises meeting five times between 1997 and 2006 understandably had ebbed as the personalities had changed.

Nevertheless, Ryan Miller, the 2010 Vezina Trophy winner and Olympic tournament MVP, was in goal for Buffalo, just as in 2006. And in a recurring theme over decades, Philadelphia went into a series at a seeming disadvantage in the nets.

Bobrovsky's play had tailed off like the rest of the team's down the stretch—21-6-3, 2.42 GAA, .920 save percentage before the All-Star break and 7-7-5, 2.84 GAA, .907 afterwards. Boucher's numbers—11-

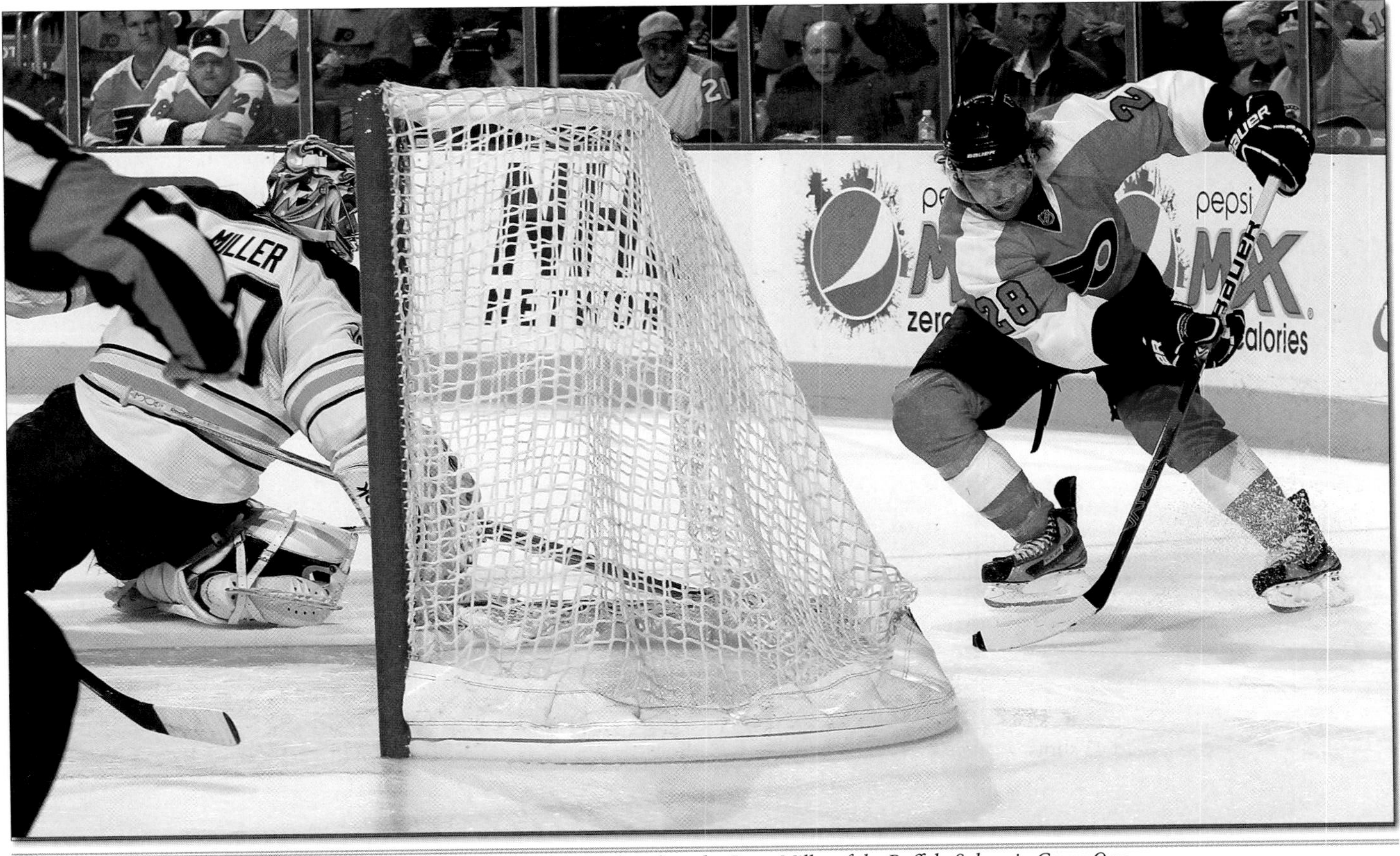

Claude Giroux handles the puck behind goaltrender Ryan Miller of the Buffalo Sabres in Game One of the Eastern Conference quarterfinals. Miller would record a 1-0 shutout in this game.

6-2, 2.41 GAA, .914 before the break to 7-4-2, 2.44 GAA, .914—had barely changed. But Laviolette was starting with Bobrovsky, the acknowledged No. 1 during the season.

With six 20-goal scorers to four for the Sabres, the Flyers, statistically the third-best offensive team in the league, had an edge in firepower. But any defensive advantage would depend on Pronger's availability. Out since his March 6 hand surgery, he had hoped to have a regular-season game or two for a tune-up. That had not occurred because the bone had re-broken, a fact Philadelphia was hiding from the media. As the opener approached, he was able to hold a stick and planned to play.

Asked on the day before the series opener by CSN Philadelphia's Tim Panaccio to rate his level of pain on a scale of one to ten, Pronger teased, "Ten right now because I'm talking to you."

It hurt to look at the Flyer record since February 24, just 7-8-5. But Laviolette thought his club had enough to beat Buffalo with or without Pronger. "You build the whole team so that when it takes the ice, it feels invincible," the coach recalls. "It was tough without him, but I still believe we thought we could win."

Laviolette's faith in his depth on defense hardly was as unshakable. For a sixth man, the coach chose April call-up Danny Syvret over the rookie Gustafsson or the veteran Nick Boynton.

In a Game One played without Pronger at the Wells Fargo Center, Bobrovsky matched Miller's saves, 10-for-10, making rapid-fire stops on Patrick Kaleta, Nathan Gerbe and Paul Gaustad to keep the game scoreless.

Miller denied van Riemsdyk on a wrap-around attempt following a steal by Giroux, and then fought off a difficult 15-foot deflection by Carter.

The nets remained empty through nearly 46 minutes until Gaustad won a board battle with Carle, and Kaleta converted a rebound of Marc-Andre Gragnani's drive from the top of the circle to give the Sabres a 1-0 lead.

Tyler Myers tripped Leino and went to the penalty box with nine minutes to play, but Carter's miss of the net on the powerplay was the 11th errant shot for Philadelphia on five man-advantages. The Flyers didn't get another superior chance before Miller finished off a 35-save, 1-0 shutout that gave Buffalo a 1-0 series edge.

"I think four or five times tonight I missed tips," said Richards. "We just have to find those pucks (around the goal)."

There was no faulting the effort.

"Ryan played great for the Sabres; sometimes a goalie will steal a game like that," recalls Briere. "But we felt like we were the better team. There were some adjustments we could make—getting more traffic, shooting a little faster, those sorts of thing. We weren't feeling down."

Bobrovsky had been good, just not quite good enough, which he acknowledged in a reluctant interview given through Russian-speaking reporter/translator Natalia Bragilevskaya. "I can't be happy when we lost," said the goalie.

Four minutes into Game Two, Giroux snapped a 20-foot wrister from the right slot past Miller for the first Philadelphia goal of the series. He pounded the glass to celebrate the breakthrough. But with Timonen off for hooking Tyler Ennis, Bobrovsky over-committed on an anticipated right circle shot from Gragnani and was fooled by a pass to Thomas Vanek. His path to the goal cleared by a collision between Betts and Meszaros, Vanek beat a lunge by Coburn to tie the game 1-1.

When Gaustad crosschecked Briere during the ensuing faceoff, Hartnell went to his teammate's defense, but had his jersey pulled atop his head. He lost the bout badly. Carcillo, following up on two tries by Versteeg, put in a rebound to restore a 2-1 Flyer lead. But with Powe off on a needless crosscheck of Cody McCormick, Bobrovsky left open the short side for Vanek to stuff in his second powerplay goal of the game, evening the score 2-2 before 10 minutes had been played.

When O'Donnell coughed up the puck at the offensive blueline, the Sabres broke out on three-on-one. Bobrovsky dropped to his butterfly early and Andrej Sekera roofed a short-side shot for a third Buffalo goal on only seven attempts.

Laviolette went to Boucher. If the purpose was to get his team's attention, it seemed to work. Within a minute of the change, Meszaros collected a Buffalo turnover forced by Giroux, and van Riemsdyk made a sharp inside cut on Chris Butler to wrist a puck in off the post and forge a 3-3 tie.

Coming off a mild-mannered 1-0 game, the two teams had combined for 30 penalty minutes, 28 credited hits, three goals apiece and 23 shots in a wild first 20 minutes. And this was with Philadelphia failing to score on a 1:43 two-man advantage with Gerbe and Myers in the box.

"I think it was a little bit too much Flyer hockey in the first," O'Donnell would say. "We needed to kind of settle down."

Philadelphia failed on their second two-man advantage of the game—and third for the series. But with Steve Montador in the penalty box for tripping van Riemsdyk, Leino snapped a shot of a toe-drag move from the hash marks that deflected off Mike Weber and back across Miller's body to put the Flyers ahead, 4-3.

Less than two minutes later, Carle took advantage of a Sabre overload on one side of the ice to find an easy offensive zone entry for Hartnell. Briere redirected a Hartnell shot for a 5-3 Philadelphia edge.

With Timonen penalized during the third period, Boucher made back-to-back, tough, shorthanded saves on Drew Stafford from the slot. But nine seconds after Timonen came back on, McCormick crashed the net and tipped home a Rob Niedermayer centering pass to cut the Flyer lead to one goal.

Timonen, being slammed by Mike Grier, accidentally flipped the puck over the glass from the defensive zone, but Philadelphia held the Sabres to just two shots in a flawless penalty kill. Boucher made tough stops on Niedermayer and Stafford down the stretch and the Flyers evened the series 1-1 with a 5-4 victory.

They largely had Boucher to thank.

"It takes a special kind of person to come in while we're down 3-2, in front of 20,000 fans, during a big game," said O'Donnell. "He was one of the reasons why we played with a little more composure in the last 45 minutes."

Laviolette expressed confidence in both goalies, of course. "If you are trying to find the number one, we have been struggling with that question the entire year," the coach said. "Bob always comes back and answers the bell in the next game." Nevertheless, the coach was staying with Boucher for Game Three at Buffalo and dressing Leighton, not Bobrovsky as the backup. Laviolette made one other lineup change—Zherdev for Andreas Nodl.

The series' two primary irritants—Carcillo and Kaleta—jostled and jabbered early in Game Three. There was no fight, but Carcillo won the battle—only Kaleta was penalized. Carter capitalized, beating Miller under his blocker with a wrist shot that went off Weber to give Philadelphia a 1-0 lead.

Boucher had to scramble to keep the Flyers ahead, denying Gaustad after he had stripped Carle. When Coburn was called for interfering with Kaleta, Stafford took a pass from Jason Pominville and beat Boucher's blocker with a turn-around shot from the slot to tie the game, 1-1.

Hartnell interfered with Stafford and then, during the delayed penalty, pushed the net off its magnets to draw a double penalty. A busy Boucher fought off a Vanek deflection from 10 feet and then denied Gaustad and Brad Boyes from the slot to get Philadelphia to the first intermission tied, 1-1, despite a 16-6 shot disadvantage.

In the second period, the Flyers pushed back. Hartnell stole the puck from Butler and feathered a pass to a wide-open Briere, who snapped in the lead goal from the slot. Versteeg pressured McCormick into overskating the puck and Zherdev redirected a Richards pass past a helpless Miller to create a 3-1 lead. But Boucher left a fat rebound of a Tim Connolly flip from a bad angle and Gerbe quickly pounced to pull Buffalo within a goal at the second intermission.

Early in the third period, Philadelphia survived a Timonen holding penalty on Connolly. But Gragnani drew a slash from Zherdev, and then a charge from Powe, setting up a 1:15 five-on-three opportunity.

Boucher killed it by taking an Ennis shot on the mask and then, the strap broken, quickly pulling it off to draw the intended whistle and ire of the Sabre fans. "It was loose and I felt it was kind of unsafe," the goalie would say.

Boucher made 11 of his 35 stops in the third period to nurse the one-goal lead before Timonen hit the empty net from the red line to put away a white knuckle 4-2 victory that gave Philadelphia a 2-1 series lead.

"Boucher won this one for us," Hartnell said. "They came at us pretty good."

As Game Four began, the Flyers were the aggressors, but Miller robbed Richards from close range and van Riemsdyk on a shot ticketed for the top corner. Boucher handled deflections by Boyes and Kaleta but had no chance when Ennis made a blind backhand pass off the backboards to Niedermayer, whose quick relay across the goalmouth set up a Pominville tap-in for a 1-0 Buffalo lead.

Carter limped off with an apparent right knee injury after a late first-period collision with Myers and did not return for the second.

Miller, so good in the opener and so pedestrian in Games Two and Three, was playing like a Vezina Trophy winner again, making three straight denials of van Riemsdyk. Boucher was sharp, too, but the Sabres had the lead and a confident goalie to hold it.

A five-minute penalty Richards took for elbowing Kaleta that bridged the second and third periods took valuable time off Philadelphia's comeback attempt. But with nine minutes to go, Syvret intercepted a clear and fed Briere alone in front. He went forehand-backhand-forehand, but Miller stood his ground and gloved the shot. Richards and Hartnell also had prime chances down the stretch, but Miller completed his second 1-0 shutout of the series, tying it 2-2.

"We had the game down there and couldn't get it by him," lamented Laviolette.

Richards, still seething about his penalty, was asked if he felt the teams' growing mutual animosity.

"Yeah, when you're allowed to get away with murder out there," said the Flyer captain.

Regardless, Laviolette felt his team could use some more emotion. With Carter unable to play in Game Five, he gave the spot to forward Zac Rinaldo, a sixth round pick in 2008 who had already built a reputation in junior and the AHL for his recklessness.

"Zac is a good skater and we thought he could bring us some energy," the coach said.

But the enthusiasm drained from the Wells Fargo Center early in Game Five. Boucher came off the post to allow a goal by Ennis from a severe left side angle after just 2:24 and, 1:27 later, Vanek banked in a shot from behind the net off the goaltender's leg. Philadelphia was already in a 2-0 hole. During a four-on-four, Briere was sent off for goaltender interference and Gragnani, scoring from 33-feet out, put Buffalo up 3-0 at 15:36.

Boucher was pulled, Leighton came into his first NHL game since December 30, and the Flyers started to claw their way back. At 8:12, van Riemsdyk stepped out of the corner to put in a Meszaros rebound. Less than two minutes later, Meszaros hammered a center point shot through traffic to cut the Buffalo lead to 3-2.

Early in the third period, Versteeg forced a Butler turnover behind the net and Richards found Briere open at the right post. He beat Miller's desperate dive and tied the game, 3-3.

Leighton made a spectacular save on Ennis from the goalmouth and denied a tricky backhander by Niedermayer. Miller made three separate stops on a buzzing Zherdev, who drew a holding penalty from

Michael Leighton saw his first game action since 2010 when he replaced Brian Boucher in in Game Five of the Eastern Conference quarterfinals.

Jordan Leopold with 2:22 remaining in regulation. On the powerplay, the Sabre goalie stoned van Riemsdyk from point-blank range.

In overtime, Philadelphia generated four of the first five attempts on goal before Leighton left a rebound of a point shot by Weber and Ennis got away from Carle to tuck in Buffalo's 4-3 winner at 5:31.

The fans filed out silently. This was the sixth occasion in Flyer history the team faced elimination in a Game Six on the road. Philadelphia had won just two of those contests—1968 at St. Louis, and 1981 at Calgary—and had not captured either series.

Boucher praised his teammates for their comeback effort and Leighton for cleaning up the mess. "It was my responsibility tonight," Boucher said, "and I'd very much like to redeem myself."

Laviolette decided instead to stick with Leighton. The coach, who had hoped to get through the series without rushing Pronger back into service, had medical clearance to use him in Game Six, but the defenseman's hand was weak and his game rusty after 47 days on the shelf. At least, he could be a presence on the powerplay but, to be safe, the coach dressed seven defensemen, including Syvret, who had skated a mere 2:59 in Game Five.

Pominville was unable to play for the Sabres as they went for the kill. In the second minute, Hartnell and Gaustad dropped the gloves and tussled behind the Flyer net, both going off for roughing. On the four-on-four, Niedermayer roofed a shot from near the right faceoff dot over Leighton's glove for a 1-0 Buffalo lead.

Miller made a tough pad save on a pinching Coburn before Carcillo was called for a crosscheck on McCormick. On the powerplay,

Vanek's weak tip of a Myers setup from the right circle trickled past Leighton's skate at 8:41. Philadelphia was down 2-0 before Pronger took his first shift.

Leino controlled the puck off the sideboards and Briere flipped Hartnell's rebound over Miller's glove to cut the gap to 2-1 at 14:53. When Connolly was called for crosschecking and Butler shot the puck over the glass, the Flyers had a two-man advantage for 35 seconds, but couldn't score, also failing on the five on four.

Soon a Pronger slash of Myers and a Meszaros high stick of Gragnani put Philadelphia down two men. Myers fed Vanek, who jammed the puck between Leighton's pads to put the Sabres up 3-1.

Leighton, the third goalie started in the series by Laviolette, became the third one to get yanked in mid-game. "I hadn't played, had barely practiced, but I think adrenaline took over when I came into Game Five," recalls Leighton. "I just never felt good in Game Six."

Boucher was getting his shot at redemption, albeit from a two-goal deficit. The Flyers, who had outshot Buffalo, 17-8, in the first period, desperately needed some stops.

The Sabres also required some to put Philadelphia away, but instead, Miller let Laviolette's team back into the game. Forty-nine seconds into the second period, Giroux won an offensive left circle faceoff from Connolly and van Riemsdyk wired a savable wrist shot from above the hash marks cleanly past the Buffalo goaltender to cut Buffalo's lead to 3-2.

Van Riemsdyk drew a holding penalty on Leopold and, fifty-five seconds later, Briere took a cross-ice pass from Meszaros, faked, held, then fired his second goal of the game and fourth of the series through traffic to tie the game 3-3 midway into the second period.

Boucher made a good stop on Ennis from inside the left hash marks and then, spun around and dove to smother the rebound off Carle.

The Flyers continued to make their lives as difficult as possible. Versteeg was penalized for a chop on Kaleta. Fifty seconds later, Richards recklessly boarded Connolly from behind, putting him out of the game with a concussion.

Philadelphia's captain was lucky to escape without a major and game misconduct while the team was fortunate that Boucher and the penalty killers rose to the occasion. Giroux and Betts blocked shots, and Boucher made saves on Stafford, Gragnani and Myers before Laviolette used his timeout to give his penalty killers a breather. When play resumed, Boucher made stops on an Ennis deflection and a dangerous 20-foot shot by Vanek.

The Flyers had killed both penalties when Gerbe, given way too much room by the backing-in O'Donnell and Meszaros, fired off the rush and O'Donnell's stick, from 40 feet up the slot. The puck flew over Boucher's glove with 3:51 remaining in the second period.

Philadelphia had put in too much work to be behind again, 4-3. The situation almost got worse when Boucher turned the puck over in the waning seconds before intermission, but the team survived the period down only a goal.

Twenty minutes from an early summer, the Flyers regrouped and attacked as the third period began. With the back door left open, Boucher had to make a sliding save on a knuckling Stafford shot off a two-on-one and then was fortunate when the puck hit iron.

Butler, struggling to contain a dogged van Riemsdyk, took a holding penalty. The Sabre defenseman was coming back onto the ice, but his team was unable to get a change, as Richards willed the puck past two Buffalo players and got it to Zherdev who had a step outside Gaustad. Miller stopped the shot, but Leino reached the rebound and got it out to Richards, who, with four Sabres overloaded on his side of the ice, found Hartnell coming up the slot. He got just enough on it for the puck to trickle past the downed Miller, tying the game 4-4 with 9:17 remaining.

Boucher, trying to feed a breakout to Betts, almost gave it right back. But Boyes, who had stolen the puck from the goalie, fired wide of the net. Giroux forced a giveaway, but Miller stopped van Riemsdyk.

Down the stretch, van Riemsdyk awaited chances on two outnumbered breaks but passes from Giroux and Briere missed the mark, enabling Buffalo, outshot 14-6 in the period, to get the game to overtime.

Two minutes after it began, Boucher cleanly corralled a good Sabre chance—a Gaustad tip-in attempt of a Kaleta shot. Soon Leino, overhandling the puck, lost it, but Vanek missed the net and Timonen carried back up-ice and dropped to Versteeg. Gaustad blocked the shot, but the rebound came right back to Versteeg who fired again. Richards kept the puck alive amidst the scramble in front and fed Leino near the right post.

The winger was denied by Miller and Butler tried desperately to whack away the rebound. But the Buffalo defenseman's stick hit Leino's skate instead, enabling a second try past Miller's dive. At 4:43 of overtime, the Flyers and their fans could breathe again. A relentless, 49-shot effort while backed to the abyss had kept Philadelphia, the 5-4 winner, alive for a Game Seven.

"My heart definitely skipped a few beats today," said Briere after executing another vintage playoff performance. His linemates, Leino and Hartnell, had made some gaffes but saved the day with clutch plays, as they did during the 2010 drive to the Final.

Pronger, used for only 4:33 and entirely on powerplays, joked about having a new physical problem—a sore back from sitting on the bench. But his teammates had bought time to help get their anchor defenseman back up to speed. 'We've been through a lot of ups and down but always seem to come through in the clutch," said Pronger.

The Flyers had made enough mistakes, including their usual quota of unnecessary penalties, for the Sabres to feel like they had allowed their favored opponent to slide off the hook. But Buffalo coach Lindy Ruff found no fault with his team's effort. "We emptied the tank," he said.

Miller had enough energy left to bitterly complain about the Richards hit on Connolly, who would join Pominville on the shelf for Game Seven. "If Mike Richards thinks we get away with murder, what did Richards do?" asked the goaltender. "Mass murder? The league has to take a look at that."

The NHL took no further action.

Laviolette, breaking usual policy, announced Boucher as his starter for Game Seven. The identity of the backup seemed almost as impor-

Ville Leino's goal at 4:43 of overtime sparked this celebration and gave the Flyers a 5-4 win, forcing a Game Seven showdown in Philadelphia.

tant, considering the way the series had progressed, but the coach wouldn't give that one away.

The series had turned into a twisted tale of Philadelphia goalie pulls. But Miller, despite two 1-0 shutouts, had been neatly as erratic as his revolving door of counterparts.

Bobrovsky, not Leighton, was on the bench as the Wells Fargo Center rocked in the aftermath of Kate Smith, Lauren Hart, and "God Bless America." Richards felt the vibe, too, landing a big hit on Sekera in the opening half-minute, and Pronger, out during even-strength play, snapped a shot on goal during his first shift. During a four-on-four, Miller fought off a van Riemsdyk deflection and Carle attempt from the doorstep. The goalie then committed grand larceny on a point-blank Richards chance from a Butler turnover.

The Flyers had racked up a 15-2 shot advantage before scoring on their 16th try. Briere cleanly won a right circle faceoff back to Coburn, whose seeing-eye shot tipped off Mike Grier's glove and wobbled past Miller with 18.5 seconds remaining in the first period.

Briere impishly taunted Miller, his former teammate and good friend by patting the back of the dejected goalie's head. Philadelphia went to intermission with a 1-0 lead.

When Giroux was called for holding up Leopold in the neutral zone one minute into the second period, Boucher denied Ennis from near the right post. Myers interfered with Zherdev to prevent a cross-crease pass from Briere, who, on the powerplay, won another draw, then stashed home his sixth goal of the series on a rebound from Richards to make the score 2-0.

After Butler got the gate for hooking Briere, Miller made a diving blocker save on him. But the Sabre goalie had little chance on van Riemsdyk's successful deflection of a Giroux wrister from the left circle at 10:19 of the period. Philadelphia was up 3-0, thanks to the point work and, particularly, the defensive-zone presence of Pronger.

Carle and Coburn took penalties just 14 seconds apart to give Buffalo a chance at a final-minute goal and some life headed into the third period. But Boucher made good stops on Stafford and Jochen Hecht from in tight.

In the second minute after the break, Leino took a quick countering pass up the wall from Carle and, from outside the left faceoff dot, blew a slapshot past Miller high to the long side to build the Flyer lead to 4-0.

Ruff pulled Miller for Jhonas Enroth and Myers scored from the right circle at 6:33 to get the Sabres on the board. With play getting ragged at both ends, Laviolette felt the need to call a timeout before Buffalo crept any closer. Carcillo did not let that happen, putting away his own rebound to build the lead to 5-1 and then skating by the Sabre bench to taunt the defeated opponent.

The Buffalo players barked back but managed only a goal by Boyes with 4:39 to go before the clock ran out on a dominating 5-2 Philadelphia victory. The game probably had been decided as soon as Pronger went out for his first shifts. The Sabres barely went near him during his 17:27 of ice time.

"In the big games, we show up," said Briere. And that included Boucher, who had survived his gross hiccup at the beginning of Game Five to ride to a stirring rescue.

"I've had to deal with adversity a lot," said the goaltender. "And somehow I keep sticking around. Even when things are down, I always try to say [they] find a way to work themselves out. And in this series, they did."

When the Boston beat Montreal the following night in Game Seven overtime, the Bruins moved into a second-round matchup against the Flyers with much to live down from their 3-0 collapse against Philadelphia the previous spring.

"We were hoping the Flyers were going to win because we wanted them in the next round," recalls winger Milan Lucic. "We wanted to take that confidence and swagger they were able to gain on us and wash it completely away."

Briere expressed no fear of skating into a hornets nest. "Playing against the Bruins always seems to bring out the best of this team," he said. "With the rivalry and how physical they are, you cannot take a period off because they will make you pay.

"Hopefully, we don't spot them a three-game lead again this year."

The Bruins, who had suffered a critical loss in Game Three of the 2010 series when Richards' open ice hit broke center David Krejci's wrist, had him back in the lineup for this go-round. They also had deepened themselves up the middle with the additions of Nathan Horton and Rich Peverley. Boston's defense was strengthened when Tomas Kaberle arrived in a February trade with Toronto, and veteran goalie Tim Thomas, a finalist for his second Vezina Trophy, had taken over for young Tuukka Rask.

"Thomas is a completely different goalie than what we faced in the first round," said Briere.

"Ryan Miller is big, tall, and plays the percentages. You need a perfect shot to beat him. Tim Thomas is smaller and all over the place. You never know what he is going to do.

"One thing in common is that they are competitive. Sometimes with a guy like Thomas you will be facing an empty net and the next thing you know he will come out of nowhere. You have to be ready to bury your chances."

Carter, one of Philadelphia's best gravediggers, was not ready to participate in Game One. Neither, really, was Pronger, who had felt his back give out during the second period of Game Seven of the Buffalo series, but was determined to play in the opener regardless.

The results were disastrous. On the game's second shift, Pronger was beaten down the wall by Krejci, who scored on a juicy Horton rebound left by Boucher.

Briere converted a rebound of a Coburn shot during a four-on-four to tie the game 1-1 at 11:02, but the Bruins were controlling the play. Horton, on a feed by Krejci, bulled his way to the slot and beat Boucher's glove with 36 seconds left in the first period to put Boston ahead, 2-1.

Thomas twice denied van Riemsdyk early in the second, but Mark Recchi, typifying the Bruin effort, scored on a third rebound to open a 3-1 lead.

Thomas made saves on rapid-fire chances from close range by Briere, van Riemsdyk and Richards during a Johnny Boychuk penalty before Krejci tipped home an Adam McQuaid point shot to make the score 4-1. After Brad Marchand put in a rebound off a Patrice Bergeron redirect to build the Boston lead to 5-1, Laviolette switched goaltenders for the fourth time in eight playoff games.

"Certainly, you don't want to do that," the Flyer coach would say after the game. "Based on the way we played, the team deserves most of the responsibility (for the change).

"Too many easy goals, too many easy plays. We weren't strong enough right in front of our goaltender."

Van Riemsdyk put a rocket past Thomas, and Richards scored on a five-on-three to pull Philadelphia back within 5-3, but Marchand converted a wide-angle centering attempt that had gone off Pronger and the Bruins were never really challenged. Gregory Campbell's goal put away a 7-3 rout.

Pronger doesn't know to this day why his back went out, but speculates that perhaps it was from sitting hunched forward on the bench between scant shifts in Game Six against Buffalo. Regardless, he had a serious problem, and, as a result, so did the Flyers.

"I couldn't use my leg," Pronger recalls. "I was done."

Having gotten the Sabre series to Game Seven without their cornerstone defenseman, Philadelphia came out for Game Two determined to overcome his absence once more.

Zherdev sprang Giroux to a two on one with van Riemsdyk, who took a perfect feed and beat Thomas's sprawl at the left post after just 29 seconds for a 1-0 Flyer lead.

Shelley, dressed in place of Rinaldo, boarded McQuaid, but on the powerplay, Boucher stopped point shots from Boychuk and Dennis Seidenberg. When Campbell was penalized for holding Carcillo at 8:49, van Riemsdyk poked in a rebound of a Timonen center point blast on the powerplay.

Two goals by JVR, his sixth and seventh of the playoffs, had given Philadelphia a near-perfect start. But less than four minutes later, Chris Kelly crashed the net and knocked in a rebound. Then, with 5:45 remaining in the period, Boucher was beaten glove side from the deep slot by a 37-foot Marchand wrist shot to tie the game, 2-2, and quiet the Wells Fargo Center.

Eleven minutes into the second period, a Boychuk slapshot bent back Boucher's catcher and hyperextended his wrist, forcing him to the locker room in favor of Bobrovsky. Bob's head was bobbing when Krejci soon hit the post, but the cold goalie looked good when stopping him again and then denying a deflection by Lucic.

Van Riemsdyk, bulling down the wing like Eric Lindros and fending off defenders like Peter Forsberg, was playing the game of his 21-year-old life as the crowd chanted "JVR! JVR!" and the Flyers carried the play during the second period. "To hear that and be a part of it was very special," van Riemsdyk would say later.

After Boucher re-entered the game to start the third period, van Riemsdyk led another charge, weaving at will through the defense, getting off a backhand attempt, and forcing Thomas to make another outstanding save.

With a surge of energy, Philadelphia peppered Thomas, who turned back Richards on four shots and Giroux and Briere three times apiece, a number of them prime chances. After Zdeno Chara gratuitously roughed Briere with 2:39 to go, Thomas made three more saves, tracking two of them, by Meszaros and Timonen, through heavy traffic.

In the final seconds of regulation, Briere was the first to a loose puck but it went on edge and was blocked by Seidenberg. Despite a Flyer shot advantage of 22-7 in the third period and 44-36 for the game, the score remained 2-2.

Laviolette double-shifted van Riemsdyk in the overtime, trying to end it. Richards, contributing his best all-around performance of the playoffs, was beaten by Thomas on backhanders that represented the captain's ninth and 10th shots of the game as Philadelphia ran up a 10-3 shot advantage through the first 13:30.

En route to a Stanly Cup win, the Bruins proved to be too much for the Flyers, sweeping them four-straight in the Eastern Conference semifinals. Here left wing Daniel Paille skates with the puck against Matt Carle in Boston's 5-1 win in Game Four.

A year after his legendary timeout in the same building in Game Four, Laviolette didn't wait to fall behind 3-0. He called his reeling team to the bench. As the period progressed, his players gained a measure of equilibrium, but their breakouts were labored and any forechecking pressure was not sustained.

"It had nothing to do with our guys not wanting it," recalls Hartnell. "It was just that Boston was really good. When we had the puck, we were getting hit. It was tough to play that way."

A powerplay opportunity from a goaltending interference call on Lucic produced no Philadelphia shots on goal. The Krejci and Bergeron lines were getting the better of the Richards and Giroux units.

After Thomas denied Briere from close range during a Bergeron penalty that bridged the first and second periods, O'Donnell dropped the gloves with Horton trying to give the Flyers a spark. But Syvret, attempting to force a cross-ice feed to Carter, was intercepted by Boychuk. The Bruins broke out three-on-two and Daniel Paille snapped a 25-footer past Boucher to build a 3-0 lead.

None of the goals that the Philadelphia goalie gave up were his fault until, on the fourth one, he went down early and opened up the five hole for Horton. Down 4-0, Laviolette changed goaltenders for the third-straight game and fifth time in the playoffs, going to Bobrovsky.

Meszaros beat Thomas from near the left hashmark to get Philadelphia on the board, but Boston conceded a dozen, mostly perimeter, shots in the third period. Chara completed the 5-1 rout on the powerplay, putting the Flyers down 3-0 in the series.

"It's not the start we envisioned," Boucher understated. "After that, we settled down a bit, and then it got away from us late in the second."

Ed Snider visited the locker room to try to rally the troops.

"I never think this team doesn't fight," the Chairman said. "Last year, we showed fight throughout the playoffs. It's very much the same squad. They're not ever going to quit."

In 2010, close and largely luckless losses in the first three games had convinced Philadelphia it was not an inferior team to Boston, but this time, the Flyers had been blown out twice and were stoned by an accomplished goalie in the other loss.

"It was just very deflating," Hartnell recalls. "After every game, we felt like a speed bag. As much as you want to say, 'OK, we're down 3-0, so let's do it,' you can't. Totally different year."

Boucher came out to set up a dump-in for Coburn who, trying to wrap the puck around the wall to Timonen, badly missed connections. kkHorton stepped up along the right half boards to intercept and fed Krejci, who ripped a 27-footer over Boucher's shoulder and hit the inside crossbar.

The puck caromed right out of the net and play initially continued. But the goal, at 14:00, was quickly confirmed on replay. All the Flyers' 54 shots had gotten them was a 3-2 defeat and a 2-0 series deficit.

"We deserved better," said Briere as his team, down in another series, put on a brave face about all the confidence it had gained from adversity.

"We have to go in to Boston, and play the same way we did tonight," said Timonen.

Privately, many wondered if it was possible. "That loss was a gut punch," Hartnell recalls.

Behind a white-hot goaltender, the Bruins had just shaken off Philadelphia's best performance of the playoffs. Pronger was gone for the duration. And the odds of coming back from 2-0 against a wiser, deeper, version of the Bruins were even less than they had been at 3-0 a year earlier.

At least the Flyers had Carter back for Game Three at TD Garden. But just 30 seconds in, Chara closed to the top of the circle to take a pass from Marchand and hammered a drive into the top corner for a 1-0 lead. On the next shift, Krejci slipped away from Giroux and Meszaros on the halfwall, went to the net to gain position on Coburn, and jammed in a goalmouth feed from Lucic for a 2-0 lead. Only 1:03 had been played.

Whether over-confidence on the Bruins' part really had anything to do with turning the series a year earlier, there was no chance of it happening this time.

"I remember we were all talking about it," recalls Lucic. "Let's not drag this out any longer than we need to and give them any hope."

Lucic did his part, converting the third Bruin powerplay opportunity of the game 12 minutes into the first period for a 1-0 lead on Bobrovsky.

Philadelphia had been generating little until Versteeg finished off a two-on-one with Richards at 13:32 of the second period. Largely because of Bobrovsky, the Flyers managed to go into the third period tied 1-1.

But the rookie goalie cracked early when Boychuk knocked down a bouncing puck off a Michael Ryder faceoff win against Carter and fired an unscreened 59-foot slapshot that went over Bobrovsky's glove to the short side. Down only 2-1, Philadelphia had no good chances thereafter.

Carle turned the puck over just outside the defensive blueline and Horton fed Lucic's breakaway goal with 4:57 to play. Boston tacked on empty-net goals by Marchand and Paille to complete a 5-1 final and a humiliating 4-0 sweep.

"We had a tough injury to a key player, but we should have been better than that," recalls Laviolette. "It was awful and embarrassing."

The Bruins talked about lessons learned, keeping any thoughts about revenge to themselves. More than an object of hate, the Flyers had become Boston's rite of passage. "This is something that has been hanging over our heads for more than a year," said coach Claude Julien.

Recalls Lucic: "To be in the same situation we were in the year before and be able to finish it off was sweet for us. But there was no bad blood or chirping because there was none of that coming our way in the handshake line the year before.

"They were classy about it and for the most part we were as well. There was definitely respect from both teams through both series."

The Bruins, who had won eight of their last nine games since losing the first two of the Montreal series, had greater ambitions than burying Philadelphia. As it turned out, for the third-straight year, the Flyers had been eliminated by the eventual Cup winner. Boston went on to their first championship since 1972 with a seven-game triumph over Vancouver in the Final.

"Coming out of that (2010 collapse), they didn't change a whole lot in the summer, didn't fire their coach, or trade their best player," recalls Laviolette. "Struggle sometimes leads to strength—the first thing that went through my mind when they won the Cup. We got beat by a better team."

The Bruins had been the superior club since March, actually, making Philadelphia's slide easily datable to its prolonged loss of Pronger. As Laviolette had noted before Game Four, "You notice the impact a guy like Chara has on the other side. He and Chris have the same style, play the same way."

Pronger's absence caused Timonen and O'Donnell to wear down and put too much responsibility on Meszaros. But beyond missing the defenseman's size, strength, reach and skill, the Flyers had also felt the loss of his edge. They had become a finesse team.

Five days after their elimination, Pronger had a disk fragment removed from his back by Dr. Frank Cammisa in New York. Recovery was expected to be complete. Richards and Meszaros (wrists) and Versteeg (sports hernia) also underwent procedures.

Holmgren's plan to make Bobrovsky the No. 1 goaltender in 2011-12 was abruptly changed by a frustrated Snider. "We are never going to go through the goalie issues we've gone though in the last couple of years again," the Chairman vowed to *The Philadelphia Inquirer*'s Sam Carchidi.

Snider called Bobrovsky the "goalie of the future," and promised the Flyers would sign or trade for an accomplished No. 1 netminder. "We can make anything work, even with the cap," the Chairman said.

"The extremes from their goalie to ours had an effect on our team. I don't look at it as, 'Why did this guy have only one goal?' or, 'that guy played that way.' The bottom line is when you have [an opposition] goalie playing out of his mind, that confidence spreads to the whole team. And when your goalie is not playing well..."

Laviolette acknowledges, "We were all probably a bit impatient" with Bobrovsky, whom he thinks became a victim of a long, first NHL season. "He was a young kid in a man's game."

Regardless, Holmgren had wanted Laviolette to stay the course with the rookie netminder. The GM strongly disapproved of the coach going to a cold Leighton after Boucher's hiccup early in Game Five. But goaltending and Pronger's absence were not the only factors in the early Flyer demise. Many key forwards had come up empty.

Leino was inconsistent in the second half. Versteeg had not proven worthy of a first-round pick. Van Riemsdyk, who seemed to exhaust himself during his spectacular effort in Game Two, had remained a streaky enigma two years into his NHL career.

For the second straight postseason, Carter had suffered a significant injury and struggled upon his return. Richards also had not been the difference-maker he was in three previous playoffs. Fairly or otherwise, the captain's leadership had come under more scrutiny with the retirement of Laperriere and the absence of Pronger.

CSN Philadelphia's Tim Panaccio reported the coach and Richards weren't talking by season's end, although Laviolette vehemently denied the relationship was nearly that troubled. "If you ask me if we were talking at the end of the season, the answer is yes," the coach said.

"I have a relationship with Mike and I think it is something we can work on over time. All relationships are built. You don't come in and put your hand on someone's hip and say, 'You and I are best friends.' I can't speak to how he handles you [media] guys, but I can tell you the players respect Mike.

"There were games down the stretch where we weren't happy. I wasn't happy; Mike wasn't happy. We were inconsistent. Mike is a good, quiet leader. When he is going and our team is going, he is usually the guy leading the charge. Since I've been here, he's done a good job."

Today, Richards disputes the notion that he and Laviolette were not on the same page. He had made the adjustment from the more cautious system of coach John Stevens and had come to relish Laviolette's emphasis on attack.

"He always said that he wanted to play good defense, just less of it," recalls Richards. "Lavvy is an extremely smart coach. He just looks at the game in a different light."

The captain also disputes the notion that he and Chris Pronger did not get along, saying he was entirely comfortable with Laviolette using Pronger to keep his finger on the pulse of the locker room, including being the bad cop when necessary.

"I think he leaned more on Chris for all that stuff than he did me," Richards recalls. "I don't know if that was because I was a younger captain or if he had more confidence in Chris. That wasn't a bad thing. Chris was a very knowledgeable guy."

Pronger insists he had complete respect for Richards. "I had no problem with Mike," Pronger recalls. "I said it then, and I'll say it now. I don't know where [the media] gets a lot of this stuff. It just wasn't true."

In interviews for this book, Hartnell, Laperriere and Boucher backed that up. Pronger was more assertive than Richards, but there is no record of them clashing or resenting each other.

"I think you always are going to have a slight disconnect with older guys versus younger guys," Boucher says. "The guy who's married is not out at night with the young, single guys.

"It's not an easy thing for somebody to say, 'Look, you've got to commit yourself a little more,' (as Pronger would do). Those are hard conversations.

"But in terms of being divisive, that was blown out of proportion. I think they respected one another's efforts."

In Holmgren's view, too, the locker room was fine. But the GM had come to believe that the Flyers, just one season removed from a berth in the Stanley Cup Final, needed significant changes on the ice.

Scott Hartnell, left, and Brian Boucher (#33) console Sergei Bobrovsky after the Flyers were eliminated by Boston 5-1 in Game Four of the Eastern Conference semifinals.

Jaromir Jagr

CHAPTER 14 • 2011-13

"Watch This First Shift."

FOR THE MOST PART, ED SNIDER LET HIS GENERAL MANAGERS have the final say on all hockey matters. But after Philadelphia used three goaltenders during the 2011 playoffs and lost in the second round, the Flyer Chairman demanded the team find a long-term solution in goal.

While the franchise had gone on deep playoff runs before with Brian Boucher, Robert Esche and Martin Biron, none had ever been considered an elite goalie. Not since Ron Hextall in the late 1980s had Philadelphia boasted a clear-cut starter. For the past two decades, the team had tried various combinations of two- and three-headed monsters, and it worked with Boucher, Ray Emery and Michael Leighton in 2009-10. But when Boucher, Leighton and rookie Sergei Bobrovsky combined for a 3.14 goals-against average and a save percentage of .894 in the 2011 postseason, Snider had reached his boiling point.

Both Holmgren and goalie coach Jeff Reese liked Bobrovsky, who was coming off a promising NHL rookie season at age 22. But the Chairman did not want to give the still-unproven youngster the responsibility of backstopping a Stanley Cup drive.

"He pounded on the desk and started yelling," Holmgren recalls. "He wasn't yelling at me; I just happened to be in the room. He was yelling about the situation."

With the gauntlet thrown down, the Flyers set about acquiring a veteran Number One goaltender with a track record.

Snider sat in on every meeting as Holmgren and his braintrust considered all their options. They quickly realized that a bona fide starter would not be available via trade.

The top free-agent goalie available was 31-year-old Ilya Bryzgalov, who had been a Vezina Trophy finalist in 2010. Bryzgalov had been a workhorse for the Coyotes, playing more than 200 games the previous three seasons. Bright, eclectic, sensitive and quirky, Bryzgalov fit the stereotype of the eccentric goaltender.

"Everywhere I played, I tried to feel like a lone wolf," recalls Bryzgalov. "I did my job, never got close with anybody, but I always got along with everybody. I don't know, it's just me. I never get attached to anyone."

The Coyotes, between ownership groups, were being run by the NHL. With constant relocation rumors surrounding the team, Bryzgalov was looking for stability. Rather than lose him in free agency for nothing, Phoenix traded his negotiating rights to Philadelphia on June 7 for two third-round draft picks. The deal gave the Flyers a head-start on getting Bryzgalov signed before he hit the market on July 1. Philadelphia had made similar moves, trading for the rights to Kimmo Timonen and Scott Hartnell in June 2007 and then successfully signing them both prior to free agency.

Bryzgalvov, his wife Zjenia, and his agent, Rich Winter, flew in to tour the Flyer facilities and meet their front-office and training personnel. The courtship continued at dinner with Snider, Holmgren and assistant GM Barry Hanrahan.

"I don't know how the seating got arranged, but Ed was sitting by Rich Winter," Holmgren recalls. "I had the feeling the deal was already negotiated before I got in there."

The two sides eventually worked out a front-loaded nine-year, $51 million deal in order to set the cap hit to $5.6 million.

"Mr. Snider was never like, 'save the money,'" Bryzgalov recalls. "He was always giving the best to the organization. He spent his time. He spent his everything. The team was his life and soul."

Bryzgalov's contract left no room for Ville Leino, who signed a whopping six-year, $27 million deal with Buffalo, or Kris Versteeg, who was traded to Florida for second- and third-round picks in 2012. The GM also gained a bit of cap space by not offering contracts to Sean O'Donnell, and Dan Carcillo (both of whom found work with the Blackhawks) or Nikolai Zherdev, who signed with Mystischi of the KHL. Nick Boynton retired.

Brian Boucher, the odd man out behind Bryzgalov and Bobrovsky, took an offer from Carolina, ending his third tour of duty with Philadelphia. This one had been interesting.

In 2010, Boucher won a shootout over the acknowledged master, Ranger Henrik Lundqvist, on the final day of the regular season to get the Flyers into the playoffs, then backstopped the team to a first-round win over the Devils. The following spring, he twice rode to the rescue when Bobrovsky and Leighton faltered in a first-round series against Buffalo.

"Every time I got traded from here, I missed it so badly," recalls Boucher, currently an analyst for Comcast SportsNet and NBC Sports. "I'm honored to have played for [Philadelphia] multiple times. It's my home."

Holmgren had created enough space to fit Bryzgalov's contract under the team's cap, but the deal was going to limit the GM's ability to make other significant changes. "Drastic ones," he remembers. "I felt we needed to get bigger on the wing."

Claude Giroux appeared ready to become a No. 1 center, so Holmgren decided to put Jeff Carter and Mike Richards in trade discussions.

Carter was about to enter the second year of an 11-year contract, and Richards had nine years remaining on a 12-year deal. For two headliners, each had relatively friendly cap hits of under $6 million. Most important to the Flyers—both players had no-trade clauses set to kick in for the 2012-13 season. So this was the most opportune time for Holmgren to fully explore the market.

For the second-straight spring, Carter had come off an injury to put up disappointing postseason numbers. But Richards had played poorly enough to make management wonder if the peak years of a player never committed to off-ice conditioning were already behind him. There was some belief within the organization that Richards—a late first-round pick projected to be an above-average, third-line center—had overachieved, and might have a short remaining shelf life as a top performer.

"Richards was brutal [in the Boston series]," Holmgren recalls. "He was brutal in the Buffalo series, too. I remember somebody saying to me at the GM meetings during the Final that year, 'What the [bleep] was wrong with Richards?'"

The two biggest suitors to emerge were Los Angeles and Columbus. Both clubs were building and wanted to accelerate the process with an impact player.

"I thought Richards was the perfect fit for us as a number two center behind (Anze) Kopitar," recalls Kings GM Dean Lombardi. "Richards brought skills we needed on both sides of the puck. And he was 26, not 32.

"I wasn't crazy about trading younger players, but Mike had built an MO as the ultimate competitor and winner. I figured it was time (nine years since the Kings last playoff series win). We needed to take a step."

Holmgren wanted to get young players of potential who did not yet carry big cap hits. He asked Lombardi for 20-year-old center Brayden Schenn, who had been the fifth pick in the 2009 draft, and 23-year-old right wing Wayne Simmonds, who had scored 14 goals the previous season, his third in the NHL. And then the Flyer GM didn't budge.

"I never really changed my price," Holmgren recalls. "I laid it out for Dean right from the get-go who I wanted. When it finally hit the end, I said, 'this is what the deal is.'"

In talks with Columbus about both Carter and Richards, Philadelphia had asked GM Scott Howson for 19-year-old Ryan Johansen, the fourth-overall pick in 2010, and the Blue Jackets' first-round selection in the upcoming draft. Having surrendered first-round picks in 2009 and 2010 for Chris Pronger, and another in the 2011 draft for Versteeg, Holmgren prioritized getting one back.

The imminent Bryzgalov deal and its cap implications had made Carter a subject of speculation as the NHL gathered in St. Paul, MN for the June 24-25 draft. Richards, at his cottage in Kenora, Ontario, had heard that scuttlebutt about his good friend before receiving a call from his own agent, Don Meehan. "He was talking about me being traded," recalls Richards. "That caught me off-guard.

"The next morning, Donnie called back to say that I was traded.

"I called Jeff and said, 'I don't think you're being traded.' He said, 'What? Why?' I said, 'Because I just got traded.' Then he called me back like a half hour later saying he got traded, too."

After Holmgren had agreed with Lombardi on the Richards deal for Schenn, Simmonds and a second-round pick, the Flyer GM called Howson.

"Scott said, 'so you've traded Richards?'" Holmgren recalls. "I said, 'Yeah.' And he said, 'Are you still okay with trading Carter?' So he was nervous. I said, 'Yeah, I'm probably still looking to trade him.'"

Howson insisted he wasn't going to part with Johansen, but agreed to Holmgren's close second choice—right-wing Jakub Voracek, a three-year pro who had been the seventh-overall pick in the 2007 draft. Forty-five minutes after the Richards transaction, Holmgren completed a deal with Columbus, trading Carter for Voracek, plus the eighth and 68th picks in the next day's draft.

"I was in shock," Richards recalls. "I never expected to be traded—one, because I never heard it anywhere, and [two], Paul promised me when I signed that he wouldn't ever trade me."

Remembers Carter: "I'd just signed that deal to potentially stay there for the rest of my career. I didn't even have a chance to play a game. It was tough to swallow."

As Holmgren met the media in St. Paul, the GM had a lot of explaining to do.

"When you make a commitment to go out and acquire an upper echelon goalie, you're going to have to pay him," said Holmgren.

"I had said that we needed to get a little bigger up front, especially on the wings. With the additions of Voracek and Simmonds, we got two [6-2] guys who can play in our top nine forward mix.

"Brayden Schenn is a little bit of a diamond in the rough. He is probably the best young player outside the NHL who is not playing regularly. Do we take a step back with him? I don't know. He's a tremendous young player.

"Claude (Giroux) has emerged over the last couple of years. He was tremendous last [season]. And James (van Riemsdyk), I can't say enough about how James played in the playoffs. We hope that ascension continues.

"I like our team right now. Different, but I like the make-up. A lot of things could happen between now and the start of training camp, and we'll see where that leads."

Holmgren choked up three times talking about Carter and Richards. "Both Jeff and Mike have been good players in our organization for the last six years and they're both good kids.

"They were extremely upset. It was a call that was tough for me to make and tough for them to receive. You're around this business long enough to know it's a business."

Two days later, *Philadelphia Inquirer* gossip columnist Dan Gross said the club was largely motivated by concerns over the reputed hard-partying ways of the two players. The *Inquirer* story harkened back to coach Peter Laviolette's so-called "Dry Island pledge" where the team's

23 players were asked—on five separate occasions—to voluntarily write their uniform numbers on a locker room dry-erase board, thereby committing to abstain from alcohol for a month. Numbers 17 (Carter) and 18 (Richards) were among those that did not appear on the board.

"Obviously, we're going to go out and have some beers and what-not," recalls Carter. "But the way that the media made it seem and everybody [reacted], I think it was totally blown out of proportion. I don't think it was warranted."

Holmgren vehemently denied that Dry Island had anything to do with the deals. "Preposterous" is the word he used to describe the Gross report, which had cited two unidentified Flyers who had played with the team in 2010-11.

"That's our locker room, our inner sanctum, our board," the GM said. "Someone's crossing a line here."

Today, Holmgren will not discuss if off-ice considerations factored into the deal. Whether or not the team would take a step back in favor of the long run, he had made a hockey trade and restocked the Philadelphia cupboard with highly regarded youth.

Voracek might have become a Flyer four years earlier had the GM been able to complete a deal with Edmonton to move up in the draft.

"We liked that he was a big winger with puck friendliness," Holmgren recalls. "Not necessarily a shooter, but he could make a lot of plays at high speed. I think we were all tantalized with his ability and him being on the verge of coming through."

Voracek, who had averaged 44 points in his first three NHL seasons with the Blue Jackets, was working out in Montreal when he learned of the trade from Howson.

"[Howson] did what he thought was right for the team, but it was hard," Voracek recalls. "On the other hand, I was pretty excited to be going to a contender."

Philadelphia, suddenly holding the eighth choice in the following day's draft, was looking at prospects that had once seemed beyond its reach. But always prepared to trade up should the opportunity arise, the team assuredly knew who Sean Couturier was.

At the start of the year, the Drummondville Voltigeurs center had been the consensus candidate to go first overall. Big-framed with off-the-charts two-way instincts and back-to-back 96-point seasons to his credit, he was touted as a player with equal ability to score and prevent goals.

However, a bout with mononucleosis, a slow start before regaining his strength, and some lingering concerns about his skating meant Couturier was no longer the undisputable top pick. Even so, he was expected to be off the board before it was the Flyers' turn to select.

Philadelphia had not interviewed Couturier at the NHL Scouting Combine. "We were on (Swedish defenseman Jonas) Brodin, big time," recalls scout Dennis Patterson. "He was probably going to be our pick."

The team also liked Niagara IceDogs (OHL) defenseman Dougie Hamilton. But Holmgren wondered how far Couturier might fall. "We just traded two [bleeping] centermen," the GM told his scouts who were focused on the two defensemen. "Maybe we better start looking at this Couturier."

The Flyers quickly arranged time with him on the eve of the draft, which broke remarkably well for them. Five centers—Ryan Nugent Hopkins (first to Edmonton), Jonathan Huberdeau (third to Florida), Ryan Strome (fifth to the Islanders), Mika Zibanejad (sixth to Ottawa), and Mark Scheifele (seventh to Winnipeg)—were taken in the first seven selections. "Couturier kept falling and falling and, suddenly, he's there for us," Patterson recalls.

Couturier—whose father, Sylvain, played 33 games with the Kings after being taken 65th overall in 1986—had seasons of plus-55 and plus-62 at Drummondville.

"I'm pretty reliable defensively, and offensively I'm pretty good at protecting and controlling the puck," he told reporters. Couturier said he thought he might be Philadelphia's pick when the team wanted to meet with him after making the trade.

Hamilton went ninth to Boston, and Brodin 10th to Minnesota.

The Flyers did not a have a second-round pick. With the third-round selection acquired in the Carter deal, the organization chose Sault Ste. Marie Greyhounds center Nick Cousins, an agitating forward with a knack for scoring despite below-average size and skating.

"Dennis Patterson said, 'this guy will figure out a way to play,'" recalls Holmgren. "When I saw Nick (in junior), the only thing I remember is everybody on the other team wanted to kill him."

There were similar sentiments in Pittsburgh for Jaromir Jagr. On July 1, the five-time, first-team All-Star turned down an offer to return to the Penguins and signed with their hated Philadelphia rival. Holmgren had pulled off another stunner.

Jagr, 39, who was returning to the NHL after playing the previous three seasons in the Kontinental Hockey League, had listened to offers from Detroit, Montreal and the Penguins before agreeing to a one-year, $3.3 million deal. It was not the highest bid he received, but Jagr, the five-time NHL scoring champion, saw his best opportunity with the Flyers.

"If I went to Pittsburgh, there were so many (star) players there, I didn't know if I was going to get ice time early in the season," he recalls. "I hadn't been in the NHL for three years, and nobody knew how well I could still play.

"Philly had just made trades for new guys, so I felt that I was going to have the same opportunity as them. I just wanted to play.

"(Agent) Petr (Svoboda, former Flyer defenseman) had recommended [Philadelphia] to me. I looked forward to playing with [Giroux]. But it wasn't just G; it was guys like (Danny) Briere and Hartnell. Guys like Voracek coming in."

After scoring 646 goals and 1,599 points in 1,273 regular-season games in the NHL, and another 181 points in 169 playoff games, Jagr almost surely had lost a step, but none of his mystique.

"You're talking about having a chance to play with a legend," Briere recalls. "This was pretty special. I started looking forward to it right away."

Not half as much as Voracek. He had grown up in Jagr's hometown, Kladno, come through the same development program and, as big wingers who relied on their size and finesse to advance and protect the puck, had similar styles.

"For every single Czech guy, Jagr was the hero," Voracek recalls. "He was the best player in the world for eight or nine years."

Pittsburgh lost another fan favorite to Philadelphia when center Max Talbot, who had scored both Penguin goals in their Game Seven win over Detroit for the 2009 Stanley Cup, took a five-year contract across the state at a $1.8 million cap hit.

"To me, rivalry also means respect," Talbot said. "You kind of learn from those tough games that there's a lot of good players."

Philadelphia gave van Riemsdyk a six-year contract extension, with a raise from the $1.65 million he would earn in the upcoming season to an average of $4.25 million over the course of the deal. Voracek and Simmonds, both restricted free agents, signed quickly—Voracek for one year at $2.25 million, Simmonds a two-year package for $3.5 million.

Unwilling to stretch the budget to accommodate the raise from $725,000 sought by Darroll Powe, Holmgren traded him for a third-round pick to Minnesota, which gave the fourth-line forward a three-year deal at an average of $1 million.

The Flyers re-signed Andreas Nodl to a two-year deal worth $845,000 per season, added veteran blueliner Andreas Lilja for two seasons at a $750,000 cap hit, and brought back Tom Sestito on a one-year, $550,000 contract.

During Labor Day weekend, Holmgren was injured while biking in Avalon, NJ, sustaining a broken shoulder, busted ribs and various cuts requiring stitches. "I have no idea how it happened," he says today. "The first thing I remember is waking up in the ambulance and they were cutting my clothes off." No other vehicles or pedestrians were involved. Fortunately, the GM was wearing a helmet and did not have any serious head injuries apart from a gash.

Wounds suffered by the hockey world on September 7, however, were everlasting. A plane carrying the Lokomotiv Yaroslavl team to its KHL regular-season opening game in Minsk crashed shortly after takeoff killing 44 persons, including coach Brad McCrimmon.

Mark Howe's superb partner on Stanley Cup finalists in 1985 and 1987 had gone to Russia to further his ambition of running an NHL bench. He left behind a wife, two children and devastated Flyers of his era who remembered him as the perfect offensive and defensive complement to Howe and one of the best teammates they ever had known.

"Brad was one of my three closest friends," Howe said a few hours after the crash. "A man of his word, the best partner I ever had on the ice, but a better husband, friend and father off the ice."

"It's really tough," said former Philadelphia right wing Rick Tocchet. "He took me under his wing and taught me how to be a pro.

"I'm scratching my head as to why he never got an opportunity in the NHL. If you sat down with Brad McCrimmon, he knew hockey as well as anyone I know. That's what I'm sad about. He should have been a coach in the NHL."

Holmgren was released from the hospital after three days and planned to make his usual rounds during training camp. Pronger was recuperating nicely, too, from back surgery in the spring. On September 9, he skated for the first time, and eight days later, became Richards' replacement as captain with Timonen and Briere named alternates.

During camp, it soon became apparent that Couturier's play, especially without the puck, was as strong as had been advertised heading into the draft. From the outset, Laviolette placed him in a variety of game situations, including the penalty kill.

A second standout rookie was 24-year-old forward Matt Read. Signed in March, Read had thrived in his late-season stint with the Phantoms and obviously had the speed and puck skills to play immediately in the NHL

The coach also liked what he saw from 21-year-old forward Zac Rinaldo, who had played two games with the Flyers during the playoffs. The task was to get him to play with greater discipline.

"Zac knows that and we're working with him," Laviolette said. "He brings a lot of energy. He has to channel it [positively]. He wants to learn and is an enthusiastic young man."

Although Hartnell had to leave an exhibition win over Detroit with an elevated heart rate, an examination by a cardiologist found no abnormalities. "It gets in your head a bit—are you working too fast?" he said upon his return. "But the test was OK and I feel good."

In a visit to Philadelphia before the regular season began, Brendan Shanahan, the league's chief disciplinarian, had shown the team a video demonstrating a new standard of legal bodychecking.

"I remember walking out of the room next to coach Laviolette," recalls Jody Shelley. "I said, 'they're going to make an example out of some idiot.' He said, 'Damn right they are.' Guess who the idiot was?"

Shelley received a 10-game suspension from the NHL—including the first five games of the regular season—for hitting Toronto's Darryl Boyce from behind during a preseason game. Sestito, challenging Shelley for a job, also received two-games for boarding Ranger forward Andre Deveaux.

Neither incident generated as much attention as one during a Flyer preseason game in London, Ontario. As Simmonds stepped onto the ice to take his turn during the shootout, a spectator threw a banana at him—a gesture aimed at black players that is more common to European soccer leagues.

Simmonds, undaunted, skated in and scored. "I don't know if it had anything to do with the fact I'm black," he said. "I certainly hope not.

"When you're black, you kind of expect things. You learn to deal with it."

The perpetrator, Christopher Moorhouse, 26, was cited with a "Provincial Offense" and "engaging in a prohibited activity under the Trespass-to-Property Act." He was fined $200. Attorney Faisal Joseph claimed his client's act was not one of racism, but rather as an overzealous Red Wing fan determined to see the club win a preseason shootout.

Team loyalties were more genuine when the Flyers, Rangers and NHL Commissioner Gary Bettman met with the media on September 26 at Citizen's Bank Park to officially announce the Winter Classic scheduled in Philadelphia for January 2. In addition to the main event and the return of weekly episodic "Countdown to the Winter Classic" shows on HBO's 24/7 program, there would be an alumni game between the two franchises on December 31 and an AHL match between the Phantoms and Hershey Bears on January 6.

Snider and Ranger GM Glen Sather kidded, sort-of, about the longstanding rivalry between their two teams as well as exchanging barbs harkening back to Flyer battles with Sather's championship Edmonton teams of the 1980s.

After Sather predicted a New York win at the Winter Classic and a New York Yankees World Series victory, he added that his teams had "kicked the hell out of [Philadelphia] in two Stanley Cups."

Snider said Sather was confusing his Oiler dynasty with the Rangers. "When he said, 'We kicked the hell out of you in two Stanley Cups,' he wasn't talking about the Rangers," said the Chairman. "I remember kicking the hell out of the Rangers on the way to our Cup!"

As opening night of the regular season approached, the Flyers farmed Harry Zolnierczyk and Erik Gustafsson. Schenn was also sent to the Phantoms. The bonus structure of the deal he signed with the Kings had provisions based on spending the entire year on the NHL roster. By being assigned for even one day to an AHL roster, his cap hit would drop significantly from $3.11 million to $1.7 million.

Holmgren then had what he deemed a "difficult conversation" with fourth-line center Blair Betts, as he placed the 31-year-old on waivers. The GM had grown fond of Betts during his two Flyer seasons as he fought through shoulder and knee issues. "With Lavvy's system, it's real high-energy, so you have to be able to roll four lines," Holmgren said. "Betts could play against anybody."

But with his spot already jeapordized by the Talbot signing, Betts had also been outplayed during camp by Couturier and Read. Montreal claimed Betts, but he failed his physical. Returned to Philadelphia, he was placed on long-term injured reserve for the year.

The Flyers took nine new faces to Boston for the opener, an early opportunity for the holdovers to gain a small measure of vengeance for the second-round sweep in the 2011 playoffs by the Bruins, who went on to win the Stanley Cup.

"I'm actually really glad we get to play Boston first," Briere said. "We know what happened, and that was tough to take. It's a new [year] and we're glad to put that behind us right away."

Not so fast, actually. The pregame ceremony celebrating the first Bruin championship since 1972 seemed even longer than Philadelphia's summer. The start was delayed by half an hour.

The Ilya Bryzgalov era began with Boston's Brad Marchand converting during a Rinaldo penalty 9:42 into the game. But Jagr, taking a pass from Pronger, perfectly led Giroux for a powerplay goal to tie the score, 1-1.

"Not even Mario Lemieux could make those plays," Jagr, who had just recorded the 1,600th point of his regular-season NHL career, teased Giroux on the bench.

Three seconds before intermission, Voracek's turn-around shot beat Tim Thomas through the legs, and the Flyers nursed a 2-1 lead through two scoreless periods to a victory.

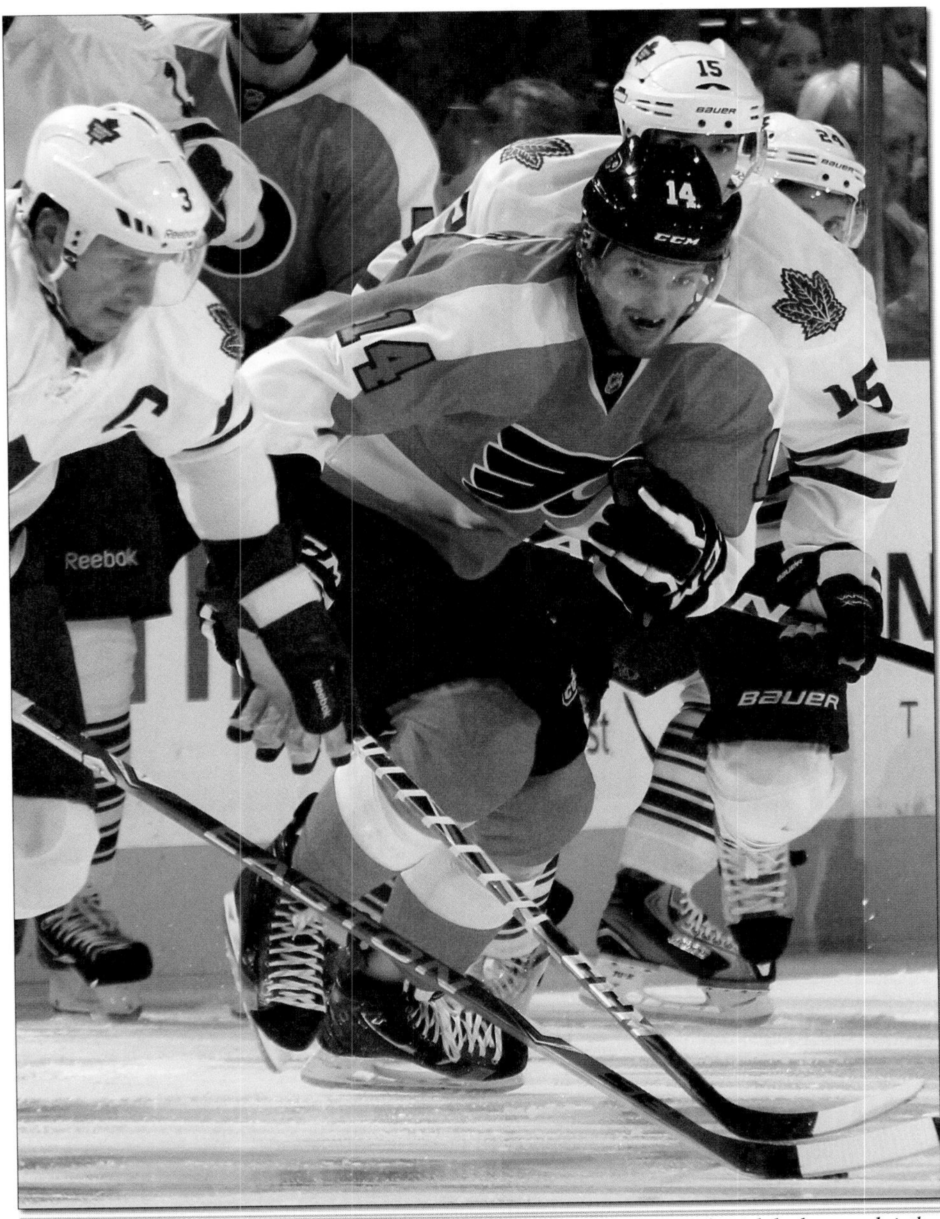

The Quebec Major Junior League's top player in 2010-11, Sean Couturier was the eighth player and sixth center taken in the 2011 NHL Entry Draft. His father, Sylvain Couturier, also played in the NHL.

"It was a big night for Boston, but we came here with business to do," Bryzgalov said. "We did not come here to celebrate with them."

Two nights later, Philadelphia jumped on the Devils in Newark, dominating the opening period with 13 shots and taking a 1-0 lead on Giroux's second goal of the season. In the third period, both Read and Simmonds scored their first Flyer goals, and Simmonds landed two heavy blows in a KO of David Clarkson. Bryzgalov stopped all 20 shots he faced for his second win and first Philadelphia shutout, 3-0.

"My first thought was, 'Wow! He is the real deal,'" Briere recalls. "I had talked to some ex-teammates of his. They all had good things to say. I was thinking, 'My God! This is going to be a fun season. He's dominating in that net.'"

The Flyer home opener against Vancouver on October 12 was more of a track meet than a goaltending duel. The Canucks battled back from deficits of 2-0, 3-1 and 4-2 to tie the game early in the third period, but Andrej Meszaros quickly answered with a shot off the rush past Roberto Luongo for a 5-4 winner. Giroux, enjoying instant chemistry with Jagr, scored in his third straight game and added two assists.

Philadelphia was off to a 3-0 start when Mike Richards came home with the Kings. As the former Flyer captain stepped onto the ice, he received a loud ovation from most of the crowd, which also cheered a still photo and message posted on the center-hung scoreboard during the first stoppage of play. "Thank you, Mike Richards, for all your contributions and service to the Flyer organization and our fans," it read.

After that, the Philly faithful booed lustily every time he touched the puck. "He spent six years here and was the face of the franchise," Pronger said. "I think the fans showed their appreciation, and then they got over it quickly."

The Flyers were down 2-1 with seven minutes remaining in regulation when Richards was sent off for hooking. On the seventh Philadelphia powerplay, Matt Carle took a tape-to-tape pass from van Riemsdyk and tied the game. But in overtime, Richards made amends, wristing a shot that Jack Johnson tipped home, sending the Orange-and-Black to its first defeat of the season, 3-2.

Newcomers sparkled in a 7-2 road rout of the Senators. Couturier and Zolnierczyk, who was recalled from the Phantoms, both scored their first NHL goals, while Read got his second during a four-point game. Talbot notched his first as a Flyer, Giroux scored his fourth goal in five games, and Bobrovsky turned back 21 of 23 shots in his first start.

Schenn's four goals in three games at Adironcack earned him a quick promotion. He debuted in Philadelphia's 5-2 home loss to Washington.

Against St. Louis, a mix-up between Bryzgalov and Coburn cost the Flyers a tap-in goal by Matt D'Agosinti during a 4-2 home defeat. "Somebody yelled, 'I'll get it,' and didn't," Bryzgalov explained.

Asked if he was referring to Coburn, Bryzgalov said, "Yeah, I guess him.

"We need to have simple words: 'Play it,' 'Leave it' so everybody understands everybody. Not everybody's own words."

Coburn said he didn't feel thrown under the bus by a teammate. "I thought he'd make a different play, but that's on me," he said. "I have to be on my toes there. It was a miscommunication, I guess. We'll get better at it."

Laviolette remained displeased that his team had been outplayed by a Blues club that had arrived in Philadelphia at 3 a.m. The coach turned a planned optional skate into a full practice ahead of the next match at home against Toronto.

With 8:03 remaining in the first period, Bobrovsky steered aside a shot by Nikolai Kulemin into the left circle. The Leafs' Mikhail Grabovski swung at the bouncing puck, which deflected away, but his follow through caught Pronger's right eye.

"I still remember the screams," Pronger's defense partner Carle told *Sports Illustrated* in 2015. "Prongs never let you know he was hurting, even when he blocked shots, fought, got slashed. That was the scariest thing I've seen."

Pronger immediately threw his gloves to the ice and slid into the corner as play was halted, the crowd falling silent. Covering his eye with his right hand, he almost immediately rose and, hunched over, hurried up the tunnel.

"As I saw the stick coming, I moved and the heel hit me directly in the eye," recalls Pronger. "[I] couldn't see, so I wasn't sure what was going on. Blood was rushing into my eye. I was checking my orbital. I was in a little bit of shock, scared."

The postgame prognosis was reassuring—Pronger would spend a few days on bed rest and miss three to four weeks of action.

"There's a lot of swelling," said Holmgren after Jagr's first two goals as a Flyer gave them a 4-2 victory. "The hope is that there's not a lot of blood buildup there where it will create issues.

"I think he was very scared and rightly so," added Holmgren, who, as a rookie in 1976, suffered a skate cut in the eye that required emergency surgery and left him with compromised vision for life. "When something like that happens to your eye, you're worried about what's going on. I think he settled down over a period of time and was fine when he left."

Pronger saw an eye doctor each of the next four days. The swelling and pressure had to lessen and the blood drain before a complete diagnosis could be made.

"I was in that mindset of, 'How am I going to get back? When can I play?'" he recalls.

Without its captain, Philadelphia got thumped in Montreal, 5-1. To make matters worse, Schenn suffered a broken bone in his left foot against the Canadiens and was projected to be out four to six weeks.

After being virtually impregnable earlier in the month, Bryzgalov had yielded 10 goals in a three-game span. The coach gave Bobrovsky the starting nod as his team returned home to play the transplanted Atlanta Thrashers—now the Winnipeg Jets.

Winnipeg jumped out to a 5-1 lead on Bobrovsky, but Laviolette's team recovered with goals by five different players, two by Briere, to take a 7-6 advantage in the third period. Bryzgalov yielded the next two goals, but van Riemsdyk tied the game before Andrew Ladd's score with 1:06 remaining sent the Flyers down to a maddening 9-8 defeat.

"I have zero confidence in myself right now," Bryzgalov said. "We score eight goals and we are still losing. It's obviously a terrible goalie and that's me. I am the reason we lost the game tonight. I am lost in the woods right now."

Boucher returned to Philadelphia with the Hurricanes and allowed only a Hartnell score through two periods. With the game tied 1-1 in the third, a pair of goals by Jagr bookended scores from Talbot and Giroux, giving the Flyers a 5-1 win.

Bryzgalov, back into the win column with 24 saves, was asked if he was out of the woods. "I found the way pretty quick, huh?" smiled the goalie, who had been beaten only after Hartnell had slid into him prior to a Jussi Jokinen shot. "I found a compass."

Jagr, meanwhile, discovered a new butt for jokes—the balance-challenged Hartnell. "Hartsy scored two tonight," Jagr laughed. "One for them and one for us."

After the game, Pronger gave an update to reporters for the first time since his eye injury. "It's not bad," he said. "It's still a little blurry because of the eye drops and things that I have to take to relieve some of the swelling and pressure."

Bryzgalov staved off a Sabre rally for a 3-2 win in Buffalo. But the following night at home against the Devils, Philadelphia couldn't hold 2-0 and 3-2 leads and, despite Bobrovsky's 36 saves, lost 4-3 on Patrik Elias's shootout goal.

With Bryzgalov back in the net, the Flyers strafed Columbus goalie Steve Mason for seven goals on 28 shots in a 9-2 Wells Fargo Center win.

Holmgren lengthened the services of the already longest-tenured Flyer, Braydon Coburn, for four additional seasons with a contract that averaged a $4.5 million annual cap hit. "The Flyers are like a family," the defenseman said. "Here is where I feel like I can also play my best hockey."

After missing just six games, Pronger returned wearing a visor at Tampa Bay on November 9. The captain looked like his old self, logging 25:22 of ice time and hacking his way to a couple of stick infractions in a 2-1 overtime loss.

He played another 24:13 at Sunrise, where Read's penalty-shot goal gave Philadelphia a 3-2 victory, and then had three assists during a 5-3 victory in Raleigh. But he still was suffering headaches and nausea while riding a bike and had difficulty driving, symptoms he couldn't blame on the annoying visor.

"I didn't know what was going on," he recalls. "I felt like crap."

Read's sixth goal, with 19 seconds to play, gave Bryzgalov a 2-1 home win over his old Coyote mates. Jagr, who had 13 points in his past 10 games, suffered a groin pull and couldn't make the trip to Winnipeg.

Pronger did, but wondered why. Despite gritting his way through 27 minutes of ice time, he vomited between periods. "Ultimately, I said I couldn't play like this," he remembers. "I was going to get hurt. Somebody was going to cream me.

"The [concussion specialist] took one look at me and was like, 'What's wrong with you? How can you be playing?'"

There was no timetable for a return. As his symptoms worsened, Pronger had much greater anxieties than his next game.

"My eye wasn't working right, it was still blurry," he recalls. "I got sick when I was driving, pissed off when my kids were screaming, was agitated quickly.

"I didn't want to be around the rink because I couldn't play. I'm thinking, 'What the hell am I going to do down there?' So you drive yourself deeper, get depressed.

"Suddenly, I'm sitting there like, 'Is this the end?'"

Holmgren recalled defenseman Marc-Andre Bourdon, a third-round pick in 2008. Without Pronger and Jagr, as well as Coburn, who suffered a bruised kidney against the Jets, Philadelphia and Bryzgalov dropped a 4-2 home decision to Carolina.

Jagr returned two nights later in Uniondale, only to leave in the second period with a groin injury, and the Flyers also lost van Riemsdyk to a concussion. But Bobrovsky rode to the rescue of Bryzgalov, who had allowed three goals on just nine shots, and Coburn, in his return, assisted on the tying and winning goals by Briere in a 4-3-overtime victory.

Giroux's 12th and 13th goals of the season and 23 saves by Bobrovsky backboned a 3-1 Black Friday victory over Montreal, but a depleted Philadelphia team was shut out by Lundqvist, 2-0, the next day at Madison Square Garden.

"When we did get shots, Lundqvist had no problem seeing them," said Laviolette. "We needed to do a better job getting guys to the net."

Jagr returned on December 2 in Anaheim to score two powerplay goals and start the Flyers back from a 3-0 deficit. Hartnell tied the game with just over three minutes remaining and Giroux scorched the 4-3 game winner past Jonas Hiller in overtime.

"It was a great comeback," said Bryzgalov, whose NHL career had started with the Ducks. "We don't give up, just keep playing."

In his return to Phoenix, the city where he had played for the past three-and-a-half years, Philadelphia buried the Coyotes quickly with a four-goal outburst in the opening period. The Bryz turned back 36 of 38 shots in the 4-2 win.

"I was surprised. They booed me a little bit," he said. "I did a lot of good things for Phoenix and I appreciate what Phoenix did for me."

With van Riemsdyk back in the lineup, the Flyers made another 3-0 deficit disappear in Buffalo, Giroux getting the overtime winner and three assists in a 5-4 victory.

When Philadelphia returned home to take on the Penguins, there were many new eyes in the locker room. An HBO crew would be omnipresent for the next three weeks to film segments of the "Road to the Winter Classic" show. The cameras also captured the fourth straight Flyer win, 3-2, their sixth in the past seven games, as the team's record rose to 17-7-3.

"Jags was excited to play the Penguins because he played there so long," Talbot said. "He had so many great moments there."

Jagr had six goals and seven assists in his past 10 games. Fanatical to the point of midnight skating sessions and workouts, and in better physical condition than he'd ever been in the prime of this career, Jagr, 39, retained almost freakish lower-body strength that made him difficult to separate from the puck.

Against Tampa Bay, he scored his 656th career goal, tying Brendan

Shanahan for 11th place on the NHL's all-time list, and Briere remained hot with a goal and an assist. All was going extremely well until, in the last minute of the second period, Simmonds tried to hurdle Giroux to avoid a center-ice collision, and inadvertently kneed the league's leading scorer in the back of the head, putting him out of the 5-2 victory with a concussion.

In Washington, Hartnell extended a goal streak to five games in a 5-1 win, while in Montreal, Meszaros scored with 12 minutes to play, producing a 4-3 victory that raised the team's record to 20-7-3.

After the game, Holmgren acknowledged Pronger was lost for the season. "Where there was hope, now there is not," said Laviolette sadly.

Added Hartnell: "He's a presence in the room and on the ice. When he is in the lineup, he really brings of lot of intangibles a lot of guys can't bring. This is devastating, to say the least."

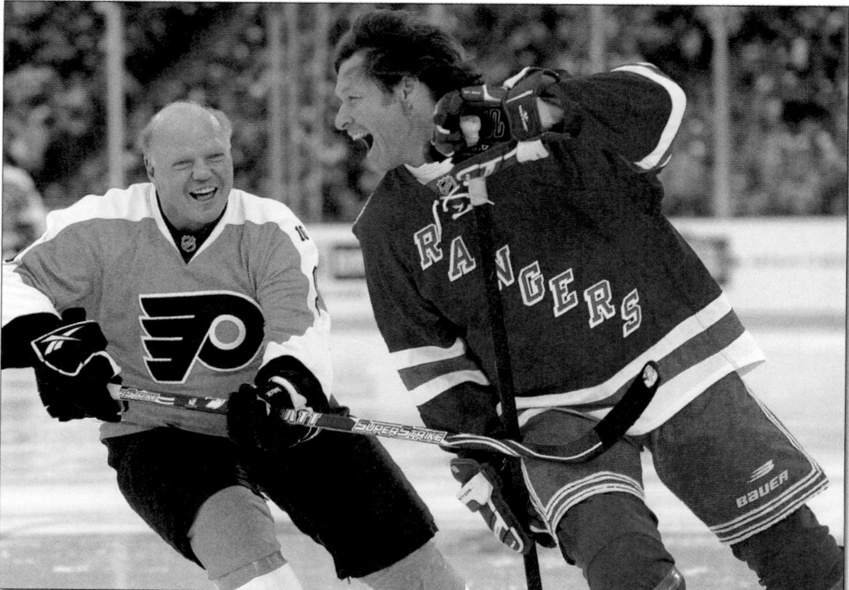

Bob Kelly and Ron Duguay enjoy a laugh during the Legends Game that took place prior to the 2012 Bridgestone NHL Winter Classic at Citizens Bank Park.

Perhaps a little comedy might help. Bryzgalov became the breakout star of the HBO series with a philosophical monologue.

"I'm very into the universe, like how it was created," the goalie said. "Our solar system and galaxy are so small, you can't even see it. So we have some problems here on Earth to worry about? [We're] like nothing. Don't worry, be happy right now."

Owning up to his reputation for being enigmatic, Bryzgalov said there were many facets to his personality.

"I have many faces, masks," he said. "In home, I have one face. Public, I have other face. On ice, I have different face. Day off, I have fourth face. With you [TV reporters], I have fifth face."

The Flyers fell face-first in a 6-0 wipeout at home to the Bruins. "Tough day for us," said Laviolette. "Not typical of the way we were playing or executing."

Daniel Briere's last minute goal saved a point in a 3-2 shootout loss at Colorado. But all seemed well again when, after missing four games, Giroux returned with a four-point night—a goal and three assists—in a 4-1 win at Dallas.

Jagr challenged Giroux to do it again as Philadelphia next played in New York. "It's tough to score four points here," Jagr said with the HBO cameras rolling, pausing before adding, "I did it (playing for Pittsburgh against the Rangers)."

Neither did this time. Bryzgalov stopped just 20 of 24 shots as New York won, 4-2. At Tampa, the goalie then gave up five on just 16 Lightning attempts in a 5-1 defeat.

As long as the Flyers kept piling up wins, Bryzgalov could be as colorful and offbeat as he desired. But his comments were starting to distract his teammates. Bobrovsky's win in Dallas was Philadelphia's only victory in five games.

Believing that the attention paid to his segments on 24/7 was much ado about nothing, Bryzgalov today says: "I want to ask you what I said wrong? OK, we're hockey players, but why do we have to concentrate only on hockey? I might have some interests. I read the books. I like the universe because that's how everything [was] created, even the planet Earth, you know?"

Planet Pittsburgh once rotated on Jagr, so of course, he was booed heavily at the city's first sighting of him in a Flyer uniform. He saluted, then scored; so did the other turncoat—Talbot—as Philadelphia got back on track with a 4-2 victory in the final game before the Winter Classic.

On the afternoon of December 31, a crowd of 45,808 packed Citizen's Bank Park to see the Flyer and Ranger alumni face off. With Mike Keenan behind the Blueshirts bench, Pat Quinn coached the Orange-and-Black.

The most thunderous ovations were given to Bernie Parent, captain Bobby Clarke, and Eric Lindros, who made his first appearance in a Flyer jersey since Game Seven of the 2000 Eastern Conference Final.

Parent, wearing his old-school style pads and familiar white mask, initially resisted playing in the game because he was afraid of embarrassing himself. He was 66 and had not appeared in so much as an alumni game since his career-ending eye injury of 1979.

Facing his fears head on, Parent decided to participate. Hearing non-stop chants of "Ber-nie! Ber-nie! Ber-nie!" like it was the mid-1970s all over again, No. 1 played the first five minutes of the game. He sprawled to make one save. Ranger alumnus Ron Duguay got a breakaway against the Hall of Fame goaltender, but gently guided a flip shot directly into the center of standup goalie Parent's pads, bringing another roar from the crowd.

"The five minutes that I was given on the ice during the Winter Classic Alumni game, surrounded by the best fans in America, were exhilarating and liberating," Parent later wrote for *The Philadelphia In-*

quirer. "The feelings were equal to what I had felt after winning those back-to-back Stanley Cup championships."

Lindros, who accepted a personal invitation from Holmgren to participate, had played eight seasons with Philadelphia. After disagreements with the organization over the treatment of his multiple concussions, he left on bad terms in 2000 and was traded to New York. But asked by a TV reporter if he had given any thought as to which team he'd represent, Lindros just chuckled.

"No, this was a no-brainer," he said. "My best years and memories were here."

Mark Howe's goal on a penalty shot paced the Flyer alumni to a 3-1 win. The hero had trouble walking for the next several days, but figured it a small price to pay. As the Ranger alums gathered for postgame food and drink, there was some grumbling about the uneven distribution of ice time. Keenan had been trying to win.

The next day was almost all about fun, as Briere, and other players with children had the ice for a post-practice family gathering.

"That was the highlight of both Winter Classics I was in," Briere recalls. "My kids loved it. We were out on the ice for at least an hour after practice."

The 6-foot-5 Coburn used the opportunity to take his infant daughter, Rory, out for her first skate. "She liked it, liked the wind in her face a little bit," Coburn said. "She was looking around at everything. That was really cool.

"People said to my wife (Nadine), 'Weren't you scared with Braydon out there on skates holding the baby,' She said, 'I'd be more nervous with him in shoes.'"

That same day, goaltending coach Reese informed Bryzgalov that Bobrovsky would be the starter for the next day's Winter Classic. Minutes later, the "backup" took the liberty of informing the media.

"I have great news and even better news," Bryzgalov said. "OK, great news: I'm not playing tomorrow. Good news: we have a chance to win the game.

"[I will need to] make sure I don't forget early in the morning my thermos. I'll put some nice tea and enjoy the bench. It'll be Earl Gray probably. Lemon, lots of sugar. Sweet. I hope I have enough for the whole game.

"It's supposed to be colder tomorrow, so we'll see. I'll probably make sure I have enough towels. I always wear long underwear and I usually wear lingerie, too."

Turning serious, Bryzgalov added, "I'm a human. I'm not made from steel, but it is what it is, and I had a good practice again. We [will] just keep moving forward and there are lots of games in front of us. Lots of hockey. I heard it was still the main goal in Philadelphia to win the Stanley Cup."

Laviolette, seething that Bryzgalov had revealed the plan, had little tolerance for his sideshow. The coach claimed no decision had been made on the starting goaltender while the players were happy it was going to be Bobrovsky.

"I think it might be good for Bryzgalov to get a wakeup call," Hartnell said. "Work on some things and get back to being the goalie that he can be and that we all know.

Added Timonen, "As a coach, I would do the same thing. You reward players who play well and work hard. It doesn't matter if it's the Winter Classic or whatever."

Bryzgalov admits today that being bypassed for the Winter Classic stung more than he let on publicly. "I was really disappointed," he recalls. "Of course I wanted to play that game. Lots of friends came from Russia to watch me."

Unaware at the time if teammates misinterpreted his frustrations, Bryzgalov insists it never bothered him if they did.

"I don't know what they thought," he recalls. "When I brought the thermos to drink, [in front of the] cameras and everything, G asked me in the locker room, 'Bryz, you're not going to take that thermos on the bench, are you?' I said, 'Obviously I'm not.' He said, 'OK, thank you.'"

Only two points separated the second-place Flyers (22-10-4) and the division-leading Rangers (23-9-4) as the crowd of 46,967 watched the Winter Classic on January 2. It was officially 41 degrees at the 3 p.m. faceoff, but the temperature dropped considerably as the sun went down, and wind made it colder still.

Briere remembers: "It was a hard game to play. The fans were so far away; you felt like you were playing in a big bubble in the middle of a huge stadium. The sightlines were a little bit different. And we had to deal with shadows for part of the game."

After being stopped by Lundqvist on a first-period breakaway, Jagr suffered a strained left calf and was lost for the contest. The game still was scoreless past its halfway point when Schenn stashed a rebound of a Carle drive past the Ranger netminder for the rookie's first NHL goal. "Pretty special to get it in that game," Schenn recalls.

Less than two minutes later, Giroux took a short feed from Talbot on a rush and quickly went to his backhand to beat Lundqvist to make it 2-0.

But on the next shift, Michael Rupp's savable shot from the hashmarks beat Bobrovsky low to the glove side. Rupp celebrated with a mock Jagr-style salute, then struck again early in the third period from a terrible angle when Bobrovsky didn't seal the post.

Three minutes after the Rangers tied it, Ryan Callahan's passout set up Dubinsky at point-blank range. Bobrovsky made the save but had no chance on Brad Richards' rebound. New York led 3-2 with 14 minutes to go.

The Rangers killed a Ryan McDonagh penalty for clearing the puck over the glass. When Callahan and Timonen were sent off on coincidental minors with 1:06 remaining, the Flyers pulled Bobrovsky and attacked five on four.

Lundqvist made a pad save on Voracek. The puck narrowly eluded Hartnell's follow-up attempt, bounced over Briere's stick, and lay partially uncovered near the sprawled goalie's pads.

The play was blown dead with 19.6 seconds remaining. Referee Dennis LaRue ruled that McDonagh put his hand on top of the puck in the crease, which called for an automatic penalty shot.

"I'm not sure if NBC got together with the refs and wanted to turn this into an overtime game," New York coach John Tortorella would gripe afterwards. "I'm not sure if they had meetings about that or what."

Laviolette selected Briere to take the penalty shot.

"At the bench, Claude (Giroux) wasn't confident about taking a penalty shot against Lundqvist," Briere recalls. "So Peter looked at me and said, 'Danny, you're taking it.' I was feeling good. I had beaten him in 2010 when we got into the playoffs in the shootout (as had Giroux). That's all I was thinking about.

"My plan was to try to surprise him with a quick shot. The hole was there [between the pads], but I missed it by a little bit and he made the save."

Philadelphia pressured for the final 19 seconds but had one shot blocked and missed the net with the other. The final horn of the 3-2 defeat sounded, and fireworks went off over Citizens Bank Park, but Laviolette's team had nothing to celebrate. It had blown a 2-0 lead and missed the chance to move into a first place tie with the Rangers.

"It sucked," the coach recalls. "It's bigger than a regular game. We all wanted to win it."

Bryzgalov was back three nights later surrendering one bad goal but, thanks to a last-minute powerplay score by van Riemsdyk, beating the Blackhawks, 5-4, in their first Wells Fargo Center visit since Game Six in 2010.

In Ottawa, Briere had all three goals, including the overtime winner with just six seconds left as the Flyers won 3-2. But the following night at home, Bryzgalov was booed heavily as Philadelphia blew a 4-2 lead over the Senators into a 6-4 loss.

"If you play a helluva game and the team wins, all the team is good; nobody mentions me," Bryzgalov recalls. "If we lose, everybody starts blaming [me]. It's just not fair. We play as a team, win as a team, lose as a team."

The Flyers bounced back as a team. Couturier had the winning goal in both a 2-1 road win in Carolina and 3-2 victory on Long Island, thanks to 35- and 33-save performances, respectively, by Bobrovsky. Unfortunately, van Riemsdyk, hit twice in two games, was shut down with concussion symptoms.

Two days later in Nashville, Bryzgalov was back in the net and Couturier's goal streak grew to four, but Philadelphia lost 4-2. Bryzgalov's record was now 16-10-3 and Bobrovsky's 10-3-1.

Couturier, who had made the team largely because of defensive savvy well beyond his 18 years, scored in a fifth consecutive contest, bringing his season total to 10, as the Flyers beat the Wild, 5-1, at Wells Fargo Center.

"He's never on the wrong side of the puck," Laviolette said. "His goals have been impressive."

After the Islanders ended a four-year, 13-game losing streak in Philadelphia, 4-1, things started even worse at Newark when Briere was concussed on a hit by the Devils' Anton Volchenkov and Jagr was lost again with a groin injury. But Hartnell juiced the powerplay with two goals in a 4-1 victory.

The carrot-topped winger stayed hot with a natural hat trick—the Flyers' first since Mikael Renberg's 17 years earlier—in a 6-5 shootout loss at home to Boston. With 25 goals after 46 games, Hartnell was on a pace to smash his previous season high of 30 in 2008-09.

Partly because of injuries, there were eight rookies in the lineup when Giroux scored the only goal for Philadelphia in Bryzgalov's first shootout victory of the season, 3-2, at Florida.

Hartnell was a first-time All-Star at the game in Ottawa, where the proud—and mic'd up—winger had a pair of assists and the memorable quip of the game—"Suck it, Phaneuf!"—to longtime nemesis Dion Phaneuf. Giroux, making his second All-Star appearance, had a couple of goals while the rest of the Flyers took a break at 29-14-5, good for second in the Atlantic Division, three points behind the first-place Rangers.

The trading deadline was still five weeks away, but Holmgren had a mind-blowing idea that would have gotten more attention than anything another contending team could do to improve its chances.

Having watched Lindros at the Winter Classic alumni game, the GM could not help but wonder if the soon-to-be 39-year-old had some gas left in the tank, despite having been out of the NHL for nearly five years. In the ultimate test of whether by-gones could be by-gones, Holmgren wanted to bring the estranged former Flyer captain back to Philadelphia.

Flyer vice president Bob Clarke, outspoken and bitter at Lindros for almost two years leading up to his July 2001 trade to the Rangers—but an advocate for Lindros's Hall of Fame candidacy—thought a return was a good idea. Holmgren, whom Lindros had trusted above any member of the Flyer brass as the relationship deteriorated, made the call.

"I told Eric, 'Look, we don't need you to be the focal point of our team anymore,'" Holmgren remembers. "I said, 'Maybe you can get in shape, play eight, nine, 10 minutes a night, but get out there on the powerplay with Jags. Take one last kick at the can and maybe we can win a Stanley Cup together.'"

Clarke, who was just as acrimonious toward Lindros as Snider, volunteered to make the sell to the Chairman.

"Mr. Snider once said he'd trade his own mother for the Stanley Cup," Holmgren says. "I think he'd have been OK with it, and both Clarkie and I thought Eric could have helped make our team a little deeper."

First, however, Lindros had to be sold on the idea.

Holmgren recalls: "Eric said, 'I don't know, Homer. I've got this elbow issue going on. I need to think about it.' He said he'd also need to get back in hockey shape, drop weight and do hard skating. But I remember the elbow was the main thing he mentioned."

Lindros gave it some thought, but declined the offer.

As the schedule resumed with three home games following the All-Star break, Jagr was back in lineup, but became one of three Flyers beaten by Jets goalie Ondrej Pavelec in a shootout. Winnipeg's Brian Little scored on Bryzgalov to win the game, 2-1.

In a 4-1 victory over Nashville, Simmonds recorded his 14th and 15th of the season, Read his 16th, and Giroux ended a month-long goal drought. "When we play like this, we can beat any team," Timonen said. "Now we have tough back-to-back games (against the Devils and Rangers). That will be a good test, too."

They flunked. Bobrovsky was bombed for six goals on 23 shots as Philadelphia fell behind 6-0 in a 6-4 loss to New Jersey. At Madison Square Garden, another comeback failed. After Simmonds' early third-period powerplay goal tied the game, 2-2, New York pulled away to win 5-2.

Briere was back against the Islanders after missing six contests, firing two of 45 Flyer shots at Evgeni Nabokov. But he stopped them all, and three shootout tries too, in a 1-0 defeat.

Against Toronto, Hartnell scored a goal and dropped the gloves with Phaneuf, while Bobrovsky made second-period tallies by Giroux, Schenn and Talbot hold up for a 4-3 home victory. Philadelphia still couldn't beat the Rangers, however. Three powerplay goals at the Wells Fargo Center gave New York a seventh straight win over the Flyers, 5-2, dropping them to 2-3-2 since the All-Star break.

"I was a little disappointed with the effort, actually," Timonen said. "(Playing) the top team in the conference, I was expecting more."

After 2-1 and 3-2 leads slipped away into a 4-3 loss in Detroit, Holmgren said, "There are areas we would like to address." And he did.

Four days later, on February 16, the GM acquired defenseman Nicklas Grossman from Dallas in exchange for the 2012 second-round pick acquired from L.A. in the Richards trade and the 2013 third-rounder received from Minnesota in the Powe deal.

Possessing imposing size (6-4, 230), muscle, and a willingness to block shots and do the grunt work, the 27-year-old Swede had been an effective player with the Stars, but he was about to become an unrestricted free agent.

Bryzgalov, back that night for a home game against Buffalo, spotted the Sabres a 2-0 lead by the first intermission. But two goals apiece by Simmonds (who hit the 20-goal mark for the first time in the NHL) and Talbot paced an explosion, as did a five-assist night for Giroux in a 7-2 blowout.

In Pittsburgh, Grossman debuted with eight hits, three blocks and zero giveaways, JVR returned after missing 15 games, Jagr tallied twice in 18 seconds, and injury call-up Eric Wellwood scored his first NHL goal. But Bryzgalov gave up shorties to Jordan Staal and Matt Cooke, and Bobrovsky surrendered the final three goals in a 6-4 defeat.

"It's easy to find a scapegoat, to put it at one guy," Bryzgalov said. "I was frustrated with my game. I will continue to work."

After the loss, the Flyers announced the acquisition of 34-year-old defenseman Pavel Kubina from Tampa Bay, in exchange for Phantom winger Jon Kalinski, a second-round pick acquired in the Versteeg deal, and a fourth-round pick. To make room for the 6-4, 258-pound Kubina, who had been a major factor during the Lightning's defeat of Philadelphia in the 2004 conference final, the Flyers assigned Bourdon to the Phantoms.

Kubina, reluctant to waive a no-trade clause, had been a tough sell on Philadelphia. "We basically agreed on a trade, then he didn't want to come here," recalls Holmgren. "He was crying on the phone, all upset with (GM Steve) Yzerman. So I finally said, 'Fine.' And we didn't do the deal.

"Then it came up again. He finally thought about it. Petr Svoboda, his agent, talked him into coming here."

Grossman, meanwhile, had quickly stepped into a key penalty-killing role and assumed defensive shutdown duties. Before long, he had a four-year, $14 million contract extension in addition to an extra letter in his name.

While playing in Sweden and through his time in Dallas, the defenseman's surname had been spelled with only one 'n' even though his parents had used two. Young and not wanting to complain, he never bothered to ask for a change.

Flyer director of team services Bryan Hardenberg noticed the discrepancy on the player's passport and the team quickly made the correction. "I was just happy to have a jersey with my name on it," the properly-named Grossmann said.

Simmonds' goal with just 10 seconds remaining in regulation, and then Jagr's in overtime, spelled temporary relief from all the losing as their team outlasted the Jets, 5-4, in Winnipeg. Philadelphia also rallied on two third-period goals by Hartnell for a 5-4 shootout win in Calgary. But these feasts turned to famines in a 2-0 loss in Edmonton and a 1-0 defeat at San Jose.

The leaders of the Flyer locker room had a discussion with Bryzgalov.

"Our team wasn't doing great," recalls Briere. "There was a lot of frustration. It was a lot about stuff that came down from Bryz being made a special feature on the Winter Classic."

Bryzgalov, by his own account, found himself more at odds with his coach than his teammates.

"I wouldn't say I had an easy relationship with Lavvy," Bryzgalov remembers. "Lots of times we disagreed."

Laviolette wanted his defensemen to block shots. Bryzgalov wanted them out of the way so he could have a better view of the puck. Goaltending coach Reese believed it was the netminder's responsibility to find what worked within the system the head coach put in place.

Asked about his relationship with Reese, Bryzgalov today says: "I have nothing to say about him. Nothing good, nothing bad."

Philadelphia received a pair of goals from the versatile and consistent Reed, and Timonen earned his 500th NHL point in a 6-3 home win over the Islanders. But the Flyers lost both Meszaros to a herniated disk in his back and the luckless van Riemsdyk to a broken foot.

Three nights later in Washington, Bryzgalov recorded a 34-save shutout that included a dozen in the final period to preserve a 1-0 win.

"We've seen all kinds of Bryz this year," Briere told CSN Philadelphia. "He's never the same. But the last couple of weeks, he's actually been a great teammate and hopefully, he stays that way. It's been fun having him around."

On March 6, the Flyers honored Mark Howe's Hockey Hall of Fame induction by retiring his No. 2 jersey. With the Red Wings, for whom Howe had worked since leaving Philadelphia in 1992, in the house, the greatest defenseman in team history joined Bernie Parent (No. 1), Bobby Clarke (No. 16), Bill Barber (No. 7) and Barry Ashbee (No. 4) in receiving the franchise's highest honor.

"When I first came to Philadelphia back in 1982, it was as if I was born to be a Flyer," Howe said. "The orange-and-black began to flow through my veins and instantly consumed my heart."

Detroit outshot Philadelphia 39-23, 21-6 in the third period alone, but could only get a pair by Bryzgalov, who was mobbed by teammates after the 3-2 win. Voracek had to leave the game in the second period after being blasted by Niklas Kronwall and was out indefinitely with a concussion. Jagr also didn't finish the Detroit win due to a hip problem.

He returned for the next game, when Bryzgalov heard chants of "Bryz! Bryz!" while shutting out Florida, 5-0, at the Wells Fargo Center.

"It's very nice and very kind from them," Bryzgalov said. "From hate to love is one step." Then he added, "Same in the other direction."

To forgive is divine. Lindros gladly accepted Holmgren's invitation to don a Flyer uniform and join their morning skate in Toronto.

"It doesn't surprise me," Jagr said. "It's a family organization and everybody is friendly. He is a big part of Philadelphia Flyers history. It's great to see it."

Wearing a big grin throughout and after the session, Lindros joked with Jagr and took good-natured ribbing from Hartnell about his conditioning. A giddy Rinaldo, who grew up idolizing Lindros, had the ex-Flyer autograph a stick.

Afterward, Big E stressed that he was happy to be retired. "When you get older, you realize that there's more to life than going out and playing the game," Lindros said. "The game is fantastic, but there's many more things to do. I'm a fortunate guy."

That evening, Bryzgalov turned aside all 29 Leaf shots and Giroux (4-for-6 on shootouts for the season) pulled off a nearly impossible lateral deke on Jonas Gustavsson to put Philadelphia ahead, 1-0, in the shootout. "It's not fair," said Bryzgalov after stopping Phil Kessel to preserve the 1-0 Flyer victory. "[Giroux] did it a couple times [in practice]; it's unreal."

Bobrovsky's first start in 10 games, a 4-1 loss at New Jersey, ended a five-game Philadelphia winning streak. In the second half of the home-and-home with the Devils, Bryzgalov recorded his third consecutive shutout, 3-0, tying the franchise record of John Vanbiesbrouck, who did it twice.

Bryzgalov's consecutive goalless minutes stood at 196:13. He would need to go 31:29 in the next game, at Uniondale, to top Vanbiesbrouck's franchise record set in October 1999.

Bryzgalov came within 6:30 of a fourth-straight shutout when Michael Grabner scored at 249:43. The goalie settled for the longest streak of consecutive shutout minutes in Flyer history and a 3-2 victory, Philadelphia's eighth in 10 games.

"It's a team accomplishment," said Bryzgalov.

Added Laviolette: "He comes to work every day, always very focused. He's really the one who kept us in games early in the season. Now you're seeing what Bryz can do when we play well in front of him."

Voracek and Timonen, who had missed five games with a back injury, returned to the lineup on March 17 in Boston. Read's second-period score made him the first Flyer rookie to have 20 goals and 40 points since Carter in 2005-06, but Philadelphia lost the shootout, 3-2.

The following day, the Penguins, with Sidney Crosby playing in his third contest since returning from a month of concussion symptoms, came to the Wells Fargo Center with an 11-game winning streak and a three-point lead on the Flyers for home ice in the first round.

Early on, Rinaldo was cut in the mouth by an inadvertent, but careless, Hartnell stick and soon his teammates were equally as negligent in the defensive slot. Craig Adams was left alone on a first-period tip-in that gave the Penguins a 1-0 lead, and Evgeni Malkin was able to bull his way to the front of the net to score in the final minute of the second period. Philadelphia was looking up at an 0-2 deficit, but a needless Zbynek Michalek slash on Voracek opened the elevator door. On the penalty, which bridged the intermission, Timonen scored on a point drive to cut the lead to 2-1.

Three minutes later, Hartnell took a pass from Giroux on the goalline and, 15 feet from the net, pinpointed a shot over Marc-Andre Fleury's shoulder to tie the game. In overtime, Hartnell scored from the high slot with just one second remaining to give Philadelphia the 3-2 win.

In a year of multiple comebacks, this was the most exhilarating one yet. Hartnell celebrated with high fives to fans before heading down the tunnel to the locker room. "It was a playoff game," he said. "Odds are that we are going to end up with these guys in the first round."

With 10 regular-season contests remaining, the Flyers (42-22-8, 92 points) were two points behind Pittsburgh and three behind the Rangers.

On March 20, Kubina was back against Florida when the Panthers, outshot 36-13, scored on the only two good chances they had to beat Bryzgalov, 2-1, at the Wells Fargo Center.

Two nights later, he made 30 saves—including on a second-period penalty shot by Marcus Johansson—and three stops in four shootout attempts in a 2-1 home victory over Washington.

But Bryzgalov, struck on the foot during the warm-up for the March 26 home game against Tampa Bay, gave up five goals on 15 shots in a 5-3 loss. An MRI disclosed a chip fracture. With 12 days left in the regular season, doctors predicted it would take seven to ten for the goalie—10-2-1, with a 1.43 goals-against average, a .947 save percentage, and four shutouts in his last 13 starts—to feel comfortable enough to play.

Bobrovsky had not started in 18 days, but his teammates made his re-entry easy, steamrolling the Leafs, 7-1 in Toronto, as Bourdon returned from concussion issues to play 20 minutes.

Against Ottawa at the Wells Fargo Center, Simmonds took one in the face—a Schenn riser that caused a seven-stitch cut above the eye before deflecting into the goal—to start the team back from a 3-0 deficit. When Couturier and Coburn added goals, Philadelphia saved more than just face—a point in the standings, despite a 4-3 home shootout loss.

Two of the four remaining games were in Pittsburgh, where the Flyers had won all four contests since the CONSOL Energy Center opened. Philadelphia, three points behind the Penguins, would need to sweep against their likely first-round opponent to get home-ice advantage.

The Flyers, down 2-0 before five minutes had been played, rattled off goals by Giroux, Talbot, Simmonds, Voracek and Bourdon on Fleury to take a stunning 5-2 lead.

After Steve Sullivan scored to pull Pittsburgh to within 5-3, Crosby was crosschecked in the back by Schenn. When Voracek scored an empty-net goal with 1:15 left to put Philadelphia up 6-3, Penguin coach Dan Bylsma sent out his fourth line against the second Flyer unit. Moments after Briere took a pass at his own blueline, he was leveled by an open-ice hit from Joe Vitale.

"The game was pretty much over and I kind of let my guard down," Briere recalls. "I should have known better because messages were going to be sent with us [probably] playing them in the playoffs."

The players paired off. Laviolette screamed at Bylsma and smashed a stick on the glass between the players' benches. Standing on top of the boards, Laviolette and Penguin assistant coach Tony Granato exchanged heated words before the Flyer coach was pulled away by assistant coach Craig Berube.

"Those (fourth-line) guys hadn't been out there in 12 minutes," seethed Laviolette after the game. "It's a gutless move by their coach."

After the melee, Hartnell taunted Pittsburgh fans behind the Philadelphia bench with Hulk Hogan's famed cupped-hand-to-the-ear gesture. Chris Kunitz scored a meaningless goal in the final minute as the Flyers won, 6-4, even though they had been outshot, 47-26.

Bylsma, insisting that the Vitale hit on Briere was clean, felt that Schenn's crosscheck was the true catalyst for the hostilities. "It's clearly a cheap shot, a guy targeting a player well after the whistle," said the Pittsburgh coach,

Echoed Crosby, "It's pretty cheap. He skates 10 feet in between the whistle. I don't know. If that's a sign of what's to come, it's going to be a pretty tough playoff series."

Crosby was unhurt, while Briere would miss the final three games of the regular season with an injured shoulder. He felt like he'd taken one for the team.

"They gave us easy ammunition to go into the first round with the mindframe we needed to have," recalls Briere.

Bryzgalov returned ahead of schedule on April 3 against the Rangers at the Wells Fargo Center and gave up four first-period goals, marking the seventh time in the last 10 games Philadelphia had fallen into at least a 2-0 hole.

"I don't know what we've got to do," said Giroux. "Drink one more cup of coffee? We've got to find a way to get a better start."

New York clinched the top seed in the Eastern Conference and completed a sweep of the six-game season series against the Flyers with a 5-3 win. "This means to beat us in the playoffs, they are going to have to beat us 10 games in one season" said Voracek bravely. "I don't think they can do that."

After Giroux was presented with his second consecutive Bobby Clarke Trophy, and Timonen received his third Barry Ashbee Trophy in a ceremony that preceded the final home match of the regular season, Bryzgalov tuned up for the playoffs with a 25-save, 2-1 victory over Buffalo.

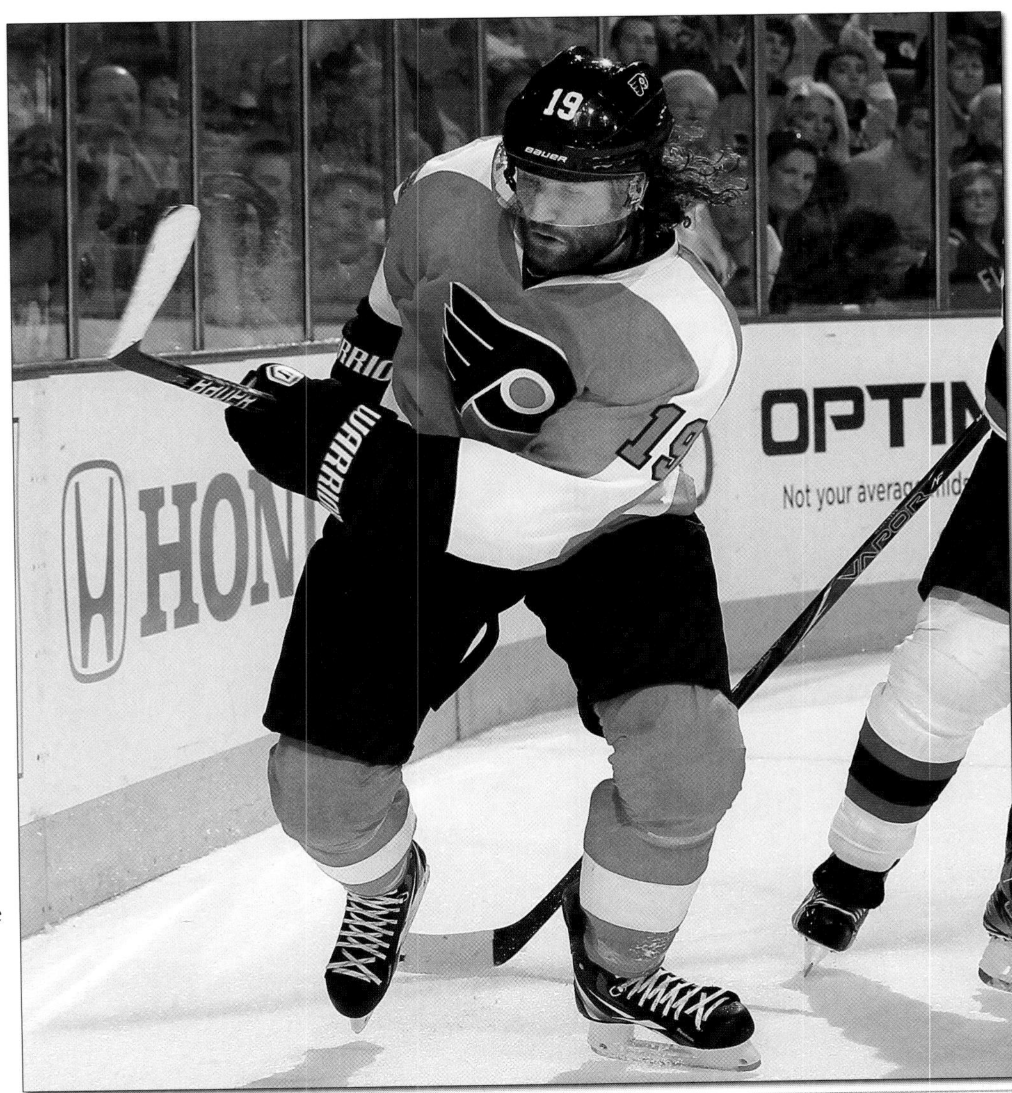

Scott Hartnell scored a career-high 37 goals in 2011-12 and added three more in the playoffs.

When Philadelphia returned to Pittsburgh for its last game before the playoffs, it was already locked into a four-versus-five matchup with the Penguins that would be sending them back to CONSOL Energy Center for Game One.

Laviolette rested Giroux, played Bobrovsky, and dressed Zolnierczyk, who sought out Vitale and dropped the gloves at 2:22 of the opening period. By 11:15, Rinaldo had been tagged with a checking-from-behind major and game misconduct for a hit on Michalek.

The 50th goal of the season by Art Ross Trophy winner Malkin (109 points) helped Pittsburgh to the 4-2 win. Giroux finished third with 93 points.

The Penguins ended the season with 108 points, five more than the Flyers (47-26-9). Philadelphia, however, had won eight of the last 12 regular-season head-to-head meetings, restoration to some degree of bragging rights after being beaten by its cross-state foe in both the 2008 and 2009 playoffs. Because of those two series, Pittsburgh had surpassed the Rangers as the Orange-and-Black's No. 1 rival.

Crosby, the best player in the sport and one of its most demonstrative, also had much to do with stoking the fire of Flyer fans. Together with Malkin, the Penguins had two of the five biggest stars in the game.

Asked if he feared Pittsburgh's tops-in-the-NHL attack (3.43 goals per game to the Philadelphia's second-ranked 3.22), Bryzgalov said he was only frightened of "bears in the forest."

Both teams needed more growl in front of their nets. The Penguins were 15th in goals allowed, the Flyers 20th. The return of Grossmann, now sporting two bulky knee braces, would help. So might the presence of the rookie Bourdon, who had been so solid down the stretch that Laviolette bumped Kubina for Game One.

Briere, with a shoulder injury described by his team as an "upper-back contusion," was ready to go. Sort of.

"If it were the regular season, I probably would have given it another week or two," he recalls. "I had a hard time. I couldn't even practice. But when you get out there and the energy starts flowing, you find a way. I was fired up emotionally."

The Flyers were spending enough time in Pittsburgh to buy, rather than rent. With a 5-1 record at CONSOL Energy Center since it had opened, they felt at home, so perhaps Laviolette's players had their feet up on the furniture as Game One began.

The Penguins came hard and with speed. Crosby beat Coburn out of the corner, picked up a Kris Letang point shot that had hit Grossmann and, just before getting drilled by the defenseman, lifted in a quick backhander to create a 1-0 lead after 3:43.

A little over four minutes later, Letang made a quick counter from deep in the Pittsburgh end that enabled Jordan Staal and Tyler Kennedy to break out two-on-one. Jagr let up on his backcheck and Kennedy, from 15 feet out, had an easy finish of Staal's feed.

Laviolette, who had become well-practiced on timeouts when down 0-2 in the first period, called another and his players reassembled. Nevertheless, in the final minute of the period, Pascual Dupuis' pass-out went off Bryzgalov's stick, up his back, and into the net for a 3-0 lead.

"Sitting in here (at the period break), we were saying we've [come back] all year, let's start with a goal," Briere would say.

He scored it, too, albeit with help from the linesmen. Vitale couldn't control an Arron Asham pass through center and Schenn quickly relayed to Briere, who was blatantly offsides as he took the pass. Without apology, he roared in on Fleury and beat him to the glove side at 6:22 of the second period to get Philadelphia on the board at 3-1.

Bryzgalov became fortunate when Staal rang a shot off the post early in the third period, but the goaltender kept his team in the game with a sparkling glove save on Sullivan from the slot.

Fleury made a point-blank save on Voracek off a Wellwood passout, and then a terrific catch on Carle. The Flyers kept coming regardless.

Briere stole from Letang behind the Penguin goal, cycled with Schenn, and fired from three feet off the boards. The puck went between Crosby's legs and by Fleury's glove with 11:43 to go and Philadelphia was within a goal.

"When we scored to make it 3-2, we could sense the panic on their side," remembers Briere. "They were just trying to hold on."

Pittsburgh's hands were full with just Briere. He forced Fleury to make a save on a 13-foot backhander, and then drew an interference penalty from Brooks Orpik. On the powerplay, Jagr gained the zone, and Hartnell perfectly led Schenn moving laterally through the slot. Fleury had no chance as Schenn's redirect slid by the goalie's pad to tie the game, 3-3, with 7:37 remaining in regulation.

Early in the overtime, Staal could not eliminate Voracek along the boards. He fired from a deep angle and Fleury redirected the puck to the other wall, where Carle quickly threw it back towards the net. Letang tried for a block and instead tipped the puck off Fleury's pad. Voracek burst past a flat-footed Staal to sweep in the winner at 2:23.

Voracek's first NHL playoff goal had given the Flyers a 4-3 victory, a 1-0 lead in the series, and, like the hero said, "the kind of moment that doesn't disappear out of your head."

Heads were exploding all over The Burgh as a result of Briere's offsides goal that started the comeback. The NHL had no defense. "There's no other way to explain it but a missed call," said director of hockey operations Colin Campbell the following day. "We're as upset as Pittsburgh almost."

Bourdon had an even bigger headache after becoming concussed for the second time in two months. Kubina rejoined the lineup for Game Two.

Crosby took a tip pass from Dupuis, went by Carle, and converted a give-and-go pass from Sullivan at 15 seconds to put the Penguins ahead, 1-0. Timonen had his clear up the boards stopped by Letang, then surrendered inside position to Kunitz, who redirected a James Neal feed to make it 2-0 at 9:27.

Bryzgalov did not come unhinged. He stopped Kunitz, who was given a boulevard up the middle by Giroux, and then made a highlight reel glove save on Letang off a brilliant Crosby diagonal setup. Still down 0-2, Philadelphia had no doubts about its ability to come back.

Grossmann was in the box for holding Neal when Talbot forced Crosby into a giveaway just inside the Flyer blueline and sent Giroux on a breakaway. Fleury made a sliding right pad save, but left a wide open net for the trailing Talbot, who cut Pittsburgh's lead to 2-1.

In the final minute of the first period, Dupuis chipped the puck past Lilja, creating space for Crosby, who went right to left and dropped to Paul Martin. He used Schenn as a screen to score on Bryzgalov's stick side. Thus Philadelphia went into the break down by two at 3-1. But what was another goal between these clubs?

Five minutes into the second period, with Crosby in the box for running a pick on Grossmann, Voracek made Orpik buy a head feint, pulled the puck around the sliding defenseman, and fed Giroux in the slot. He beat Fleury high to the stick side to cut the Penguin lead to 3-2.

A little more than a minute later, Couturier threw the puck out on his backhand to hit Talbot on a breakaway. Fleury stopped that one and Bryzgalov countered by using his catcher to bat away a Sullivan try from almost point-blank range.

In this kind of game, even down a man, there was plenty of room to operate. After Crosby drew an interference call on Schenn, Giroux took a give-and-go pass from Talbot and one-timed a shot inside the post on Fleury's stick side. The second shorthanded Flyer goal of the game had tied the score, 3-3.

There was still 1:49 remaining on the Schenn penalty, so Laviolette left the same four penalty-killers on the ice. Malkin won the draw from Giroux and pushed past him, creating a three-on-two. Malkin threw a backhand pass to Neal who shot and Bryzgalov made the save, but the rebound dropped perfectly into the path of Kunitz, who scored just six seconds after Philadelphia had tied the game.

Bryzgalov, behind again 4-3, smashed his stick on the crossbar and flung it into the corner. The Flyers were about to end the second period down a goal when a Talbot tip pass sprung Couturier, who dropped to the point. Coburn cranked and the shot caromed to Couturier, who had half of an empty net to even the game, 4-4, just three seconds before the break.

Bryzgalov gave it back 1:04 into the third, when Kennedy scored from almost against the boards. But Pittsburgh's 5-4 lead lasted a mere 17 seconds, until Couturier picked off a D-to-D pass by Ben Lovejoy, broke in alone, froze Fleury with a deke, and fired by his right pad to make the score 5-5.

"Fighting back like that is not easy," Laviolette would say afterwards, but Philadelphia was making it look like child's play.

Bryzgalov, alternating clunker goals with brilliant saves, made a stop on Adams from just 15 feet out. "You have a choice to give up or to win the game," the goalie would say.

The Flyers were playing like losing never crossed their minds. Jagr gained the zone, fought off Lovejoy, wrapped the puck around to Giroux, and went to the front of the net. When Kubina's point shot was stopped by Fleury, Jagr spun and scored on the rebound giving the Philadelphia its sixth goal, but first lead, 6-5.

Bryzgalov preserved it with two minutes to go by making a good stop on Kunitz after Carle gave the puck away to Letang at the point. Voracek skated down the rebound, wheeled to Giroux and the gambling Penguins were caught.

Two-on-one with Couturier against Letang, Giroux waited and led the rookie perfectly for his tap-in behind Fleury and a hat trick that extended the Flyer lead to 7-5. The kid then reciprocated by feeding Giroux's third goal into the empty net. Philadelphia had stunned Pittsburgh 8-5 to take a 2-0 lead in the series.

Asked if he had ever seen a wilder game, Jagr, the oldest Flyer ever to score a playoff goal, rubbed his grey postseason stubble and laughed, "I have been playing a long time," he said. "I don't remember."

The Penguins, who had blown three leads—and four in two games—were going to have a hard time forgetting what had transpired. "I wouldn't say they are in our heads," Crosby said. "I would say we've had two good starts and then we just got off our game."

Giroux's six points in a playoff game set a new franchise record, beating the previous mark of five shared by Reggie Leach, Bob Dailey and Mark Recchi. The Giroux and Couturier hat tricks were also the first time in Philadelphia history that two Flyers had scored three goals in the same postseason game.

For the fourth time in a month, Philadelphia had spotted Pittsburgh two goals and come back to win. Yet the Penguins still had no compunction about scoring first. Despite the roar of 20,092 Flyer fans wearing orange Hulk Hogan-inspired T-shirts—a reference to Hartnell taunting Pittsburgh fans after the April Fool's Day brawl—Staal's wrist-shot through a screen on a four-on-four hit Bryzgalov in the shoulder and trickled in to put the Penguins up 1-0 after 3:52 of Game Three.

When Voracek went to the box for high-sticking Michalek, Giroux pushed ahead with Talbot on a two-on-two shorthanded opportunity. Fleury couldn't cleanly glove Giroux's shot from the dot, and Talbot, being flattened by Matt Niskanen, took a whack. As the goalie tried to cover, the puck went off the heel of his catcher and inched across the line to tie the game, 1-1, at 6:44.

Niskanen immediately crosschecked Giroux, who responded with a shove, but Niskanen received an extra minor. Forty seconds later, Letang crosschecked Couturier to set up a five-on-three. Philadelphia converted when Hartnell picked up the rebound of a Jagr drive and made a heads-up pass across the crease to Briere, who had most of the net open to put the Flyers ahead, 2-1.

Three minutes later, all three Pittsburgh forwards were caught low as Schenn picked up the puck near the blueline. Leading a three-on-two, he fed across ice to Simmonds, who relayed perfectly to Briere for an easy finish at the goal.

Philadelphia led 3-1. And the Penguins were getting annoyed. At the next whistle, Crosby twice jabbed at Bryzgalov's glove along the ice. When Giroux responded by pushing the Pittsburgh captain from behind, Crosby retaliated by shoving Giroux's head against the glass as various players pushed and shoved.

No penalties were given immediately, but Giroux and Crosby continued to jaw at another. When things settled down, Voracek leaned to pick up his discarded glove near the faceoff circle, but Crosby petulantly knocked it away. Timonen skated over to bark at Crosby, who decided to fight Giroux. What ensued wasn't exactly Ali-Frazier, but as Laviolette would say afterwards, it's the thought that counts in the postseason.

"A couple of the best players in the world dropping the gloves and going at it," the coach said. "Would I rather have G keep his gloves on? Sure. But when he's fighting Sidney Crosby, that's playoff hockey. That's this series."

Voracek tangled again with Sullivan, while Letang rag-dolled Timonen to the ice—a secondary fracas that automatically warranted game misconducts for both teams' best defensemen.

Two minutes later, Schenn left his feet to steamroll Martin and was called for charging. Asham retaliated by crosschecking Schenn and then connecting with a right hand to the back of his head, earning the Penguin forward a match penalty for intent to injure.

The loss of a catalyst like Letang figured to cripple Pittsburgh's catch-up capabilities. But so far in this series, nothing figured. The Flyers missed Timonen too. Lilja and Carle collided as they were being split by Neal, who beat Bryzgalov between the legs. The Penguins were down 3-2 with 4:43 to play in the first period.

That score held up all of 23 seconds, until Briere knocked the puck away from Derek Engelland behind the goal and Reed walked out to shoot right through Fleury's butterfly, restoring a two-goal Philadelphia advantage, 4-2.

Somehow, almost 15 minutes went by without another goal until, with Grossmann in the box for kneeing Neal, Pittsburgh crept closer again. Neal found the middle of a spacious Flyer penalty-killing box, took a feed from Malkin, and shot from 15 feet through Bryzgalov's legs to bring the visitors back to 4-3 with 9:29 left in the second period.

Kunitz was penalized for tripping Wellwood, and Read one-timed a dot-to-dot Jagr powerplay feed to extend Philadelphia's lead to 5-3. But only 1:22 later, Neal fired from the top of the circle off Bryzgalov and then Voracek. The puck landed against the post where Staal had an easy tap, closing the gap to 5-4.

No one had been hit in the head for almost a period, but the defenses remained dizzy. In the 39th minute of play, Simmonds opened up breathing room again, taking a breakaway pass from Coburn and beating Fleury with a backhander to build the lead back to 6-4. "Every time they scored, we answered right back," Read said. "That was big."

Brent Johnson, replacing Fleury to start the third period, was greeted with a deadly Giroux one-timer after Jagr held off Dupuis with one arm. Ahead 7-4, Bryzgalov gave the Penguins no more cheap goals as the delighted Flyer fans chanted, "You can't beat us!" down the stretch.

With 5:22 remaining in the third period, Neal dropped Couturier with a blindside hit. No penalty was called, but Couturier lay prone on the ice and had to be helped back to the dressing room.

Thirty seconds after play resumed, Neal headhunted Giroux, who managed to avoid the brunt of the hit but had his helmet knocked askew before stumbling. Again, Neal escaped without a penalty, so he took license to try again, taking a run at Voracek near the Pittsburgh bench, this time receiving a charging minor and a challenge from Simmonds.

Hartnell needed no further excuse to go after Crosby and Craig Adams jumped in, throwing punches as Giroux yanked Crosby away, leaving Hartnell and Adams to go at it.

When all the penalties were sorted out, Neal, Engelland and Adams received misconducts, as did Simmonds. Philadelphia was also given a powerplay, which Talbot used to score on a turnaround, extending the lead to 8-4.

Rinaldo wanted to make the Penguins' surrender unconditional. He crosschecked, and then engaged Kennedy, earning 14 penalty minutes by the time the Flyer winger was escorted to the tunnel.

Philadelphia fans, who had gotten their money's worth, stayed to the end of the wild 8-4 win, even if many of the players had left. The final totals: the Flyers scored eight goals on 34 shots and amassed 89 penalty minutes, while Pittsburgh had four goals on 35 shots with 69 penalty minutes.

Crosby bristled when asked if his team, down 3-0 in the series, was losing its poise. "You can make a story all you want about us getting frustrated," he said. "They're doing the same things we are. It's intense."

Asked about pushing away Hartnell's glove, Crosby said, "I don't have to sit here and explain why I pushed a glove away. They are doing a lot of things out there, too.

"You know what? We don't like each other. Was I going to sit there and pick up his glove? What was I supposed to do?"

Well, skating away was an option, as Hartnell pointed out.

"I think we made it a point to walk away every time, and I think Crosby started almost every scrum," added Hartnell. "If they're trying to get under our skin, they're not. They're just getting more frustrated with themselves, which is great."

The NHL suspended Asham for four games, plus Neal and Adams for one each. Up 3-0, it was Philadelphia's intention to make sure the three Penguins had played their last match of the season.

"All three games were kind of weird," Giroux said. "I guess I like weird games because we always finish by winning."

So far, anyway. The Flyers got off to a good start in Game Four. Just 17 seconds in, Sullivan high-sticked Giroux, who, after some good work along the backwall from Simmonds and Jagr, put one between Fleury's legs on the powerplay to give the Philadelphia a 1-0 lead.

After Bryzgalov muffed a Dupuis shot in the midsection, Malkin's rebound goal, his first goal of the series, tied it 1-1. With Coburn in the box for holding Sullivan, Niskanen one-timed a powerplay goal before Bryzgalov could come across, and Pittsburgh was on top, 2-1.

Again the Penguins couldn't stand prosperity, Within 50 seconds, Kunitz was penalized for holding up Coburn in the neutral zone, Orpik cross-checked Briere, and Cooke high-sticked Hartnell. On the five-on-three, Timonen blew one between Fleury's pads from the top of circle, and then, on the five-on-four, Simmonds turned at the pipe and hit Voracek coming on the weak side. He had an almost entirely empty net to put the Flyers up 3-2, with 4:08 remaining in the first period.

The lead lasted 27 seconds, until Crosby tipped a Niskanen shot under the bar to tie the game again 3-3. On the following shift, Staal manhandled Kubina behind the net, and converted a little shovel pass by Eric Tangradi to restore a 4-3 Pittsburgh lead.

With Giroux in the box for high-sticking Orpik, Letang scored on a one-timer off a dot-to-dot pass by Crosby to make it 5-3.

"You got Malkin and Crosby on the ice," Bryzgalov recalls. "You give them that chance and what do you expect? We were just not thinking."

If any Philadelphia players were of the opinion that a timely save or two might help, they kept those thoughts to themselves. Even so, beaten for five goals on 18 shots, Bryzgalov was pulled for Bobrovsky, who received no better support. With Grossmann off, Staal was alone at the hashmarks following a Carle giveaway to make the score 6-3.

When Sullivan blew a powerplay goal over Bobrovsky's glove the rout was on. The Penguins, though still down 3-1 in the series, had stayed alive with a 10-3 victory.

"We all need to be better at what we do," Laviolette would summarize. Fleury had settled down in the second and third periods, so if the Flyers were going to continue to trade chances and take penalties, they were inviting the high-powered Pittsburgh team back into the series.

Because Grossmann had been concussed by a Malkin elbow, Gustafsson went into the lineup for Game Five, when Neal and Adams returned for the Penguins.

Engelland burst the sudden sanity of a scoreless first 10 minutes by roughing Briere. Carle converted from the top of the circle through a screen, giving Philadelphia a 1-0 lead.

When Malkin went off for roughing Schenn, the Flyers had two more good chances, but Fleury stopped Coburn and then Read on the rebound.

With Coburn in the box for a neutral-zone foul, Sullivan one-timed from the edge of the circle a Letang feed to tie the game 1-1. But Pittsburgh took another penalty—Adams for slashing Jagr. It took only 10 seconds of powerplay time for Briere to put a saucer pass over Orpik's stick to Hartnell, who put Philadelphia back up, 2-1, before the end of the first period.

As the second period progressed, an actual playoff game, complete with saves and checking broke out. It took a stretch pass across two zones from Kennedy to spring a chance by Staal, who roofed his sixth goal of the series to tie the game 2-2.

Three minutes later, Kennedy, standing in the right circle, was given way too much room by the Briere-Jagr-Schenn line. Off a passout by Cooke, Kennedy beat Bryzgalov to the stick side through traffic to put the Penguins ahead, 3-2.

Bryzgalov kept the score right there, with a third-period glove snatch on Neal, and Laviolette's team pushed confidently for a tying goal. When Kennedy took a penalty for slashing Hartnell, and the Flyers put seven shots worth of pressure on the powerplay, but Fleury made a glove stop on Read from the slot and then stretched remarkably when Briere appeared to have an open net on the rebound.

All the slipping and sliding Fleury had done for four games was slip-sliding away. Down the stretch, he made a point-blank save on Hartnell off a Talbot passout and then flashed his glove on Voracek after he had circled out. With Bryzgalov pulled, Philadelphia didn't really get a good look. At the buzzer of Pittsburgh's 3-2 victory, Giroux broke his stick over the net in frustration.

With 14 third-period saves, Fleury had been the biggest difference. "He won the game for them, pure and simple," said Hartnell.

Laviolette had no complaints about his team's effort. "The pace was still fast and furious," he said. "It was physical; we just couldn't get it in the back of the net as often."

The Penguins, however, had gotten it done—in this case without a point by Crosby or Malkin. Pittsburgh had willed itself back to only a 3-2 disadvantage in the series. "Our defense made hard and good plays," said Bylsma.

Asked if the pressure was now on the Flyers, Giroux said, "I like pressure. If it is on us, that's good."

But the question was how much of it the Flyers could withstand in their own end.

Grossmann's injury had put them down to rookie Gustafsson and part-timers Lilja and Kubina behind Timonen, Carle and Coburn.

The last thing the Flyers needed was a Game Seven. "The Penguins were back in the series," recalls Giroux. "We didn't want to return to Pittsburgh. We had to stop them.

"In the rest of the series, we had not been sharp in the first five minutes. I remember talking to Jags and Hartsy that we needed a good start.

"It just happened I was getting a coffee in the locker room when Lavvy was having one. I asked 'Who's starting?' He said, 'I'm not sure yet.' I said, 'I would like to start, just to get the ball rolling.' I wanted to make sure the team was ready to go."

Similarly, Laviolette didn't want to save his best oratory for being down 0-2. After the warm-up, he stood in front of his club and posed questions.

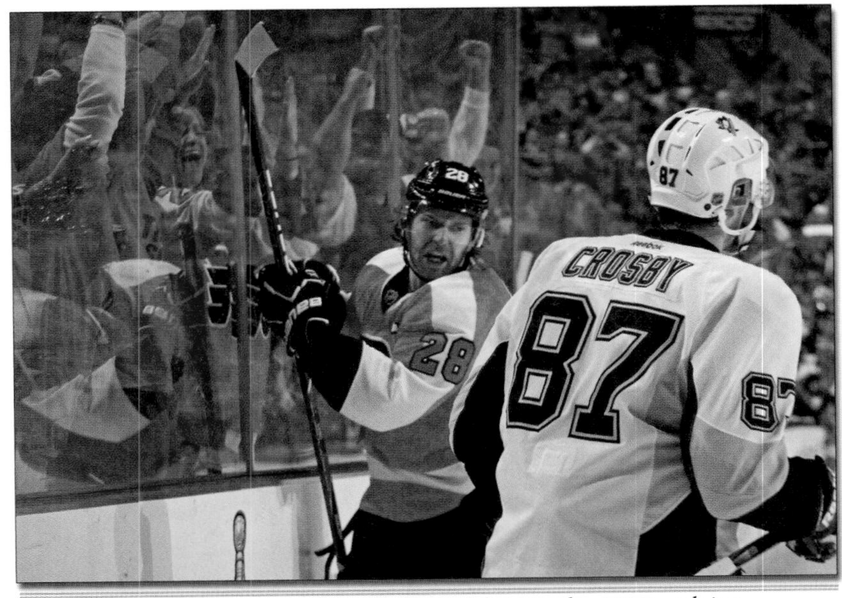

Claude Giroux decked Sidney Crosby and then scored just 32 seconds into the first period of Game Six of the Eastern Conference quarterfinals.

"Can you, Danny Briere, play the best game of your career?" he asked. "Is it possible that Claude Giroux can do that, too? Can everyone here play the best you ever have played for this one game? Because if you do that, it doesn't matter if we're short on the bench. If you do that, we will win.

"You don't need to do it for a whole season or for every game of a whole series. Just one game. Here. Today. Can you do that?"

Briere was awed, "That was just the most amazing speech I'd ever heard before a game," Briere recalls. "It gave me goosebumps."

Giroux had them, too.

As Lauren Hart was walking off on the red carpet to a huge roar, Giroux said to Briere, "Watch this first shift."

"Just don't take a penalty G," Briere said. "We can't start with a man down."

Recalls Giroux, "The whole crowd was going nuts. I was excited, pretty pumped up. Everything happened quickly, to be honest."

Giroux pulled the opening faceoff away from Crosby to Gustafsson. When the young defenseman cleared the puck to the other line, Giroux lined up Crosby and right in front of the Pittsburgh bench, put him to the ice with a hard shoulder check.

Giroux went down too, but popped up first. The Penguins carried up ice and Bryzgalov gloved a soft shot by Dupuis. Crosby won the draw but had the puck poked up the wall past him by Jagr, who forced Letang, and then Sullivan into a giveaway inside the Pittsburgh line.

Giroux picked up the puck, closed to the top of the circle, pulled up, let Sullivan drift idly by, and wristed the puck past Fleury's short side after 32 seconds to put the Flyers up 1-0.

Giroux pumped his arms and pounded the glass while shouting, "Let's go!" at his teammates on the bench. There was no chance they could hear him through the bedlam of the Wells Fargo Center but after what he had just done, they were ready to go wherever Giroux wanted to lead them.

"You could not be numb to that," Briere recalls. "Every single one of us was fired up."

As it turned out, Briere took the early penalty that he had warned Giroux to avoid, but Bryzgalov came across to foil a Malkin one-timer off a Kunitz feed, then made himself big on a Crosby redirect from Sullivan.

Twelve minutes into the game, Cooke took a penalty for interfering with Schenn. On the powerplay, Fleury got his blocker on a Giroux one-timer from Voracek, but the puck dropped in the crease behind the goaltender. Vitale, trying to clear it off the line, kept the play alive for Hartnell, who jammed in Philadelphia's 12th powerplay goal of the series at 13:01 to put his team up 2-0.

The Penguins, who had not responded to Giroux's leveling of Crosby with even an angry word, seemed curiously passive, the Flyers getting the majority of the good chances. With Simon Despres in the box, Simmonds couldn't tee up a bounding Voracek rebound at the side of the crease, so the score remained 2-0 into the second period.

The hot and cold running Fleury stopped Briere bursting in alone, then surrendered an unscreened 45-foot goal by Gustafsson that boosted Philadelphia's lead to 3-0. But with Timonen in the box for holding Malkin, the goalie came right back to save Crosby when he gave away a Couturier shorthanded breakaway.

Malkin picked up the rebound and, with Lilja in full retreat, skated all the way to the faceoff dot before shooting right through Bryzgalov at 8:34 of the middle period, cutting the lead to 3-1.

Pittsburgh's little glimmer of hope lasted only 36 seconds. Voracek, coming off the wing to the post, dropped to Briere, whose quick shot went off Michalek and trickled over the line to build the lead back to three goals.

"[Malkin] skated by me and I saw his face," Bryzgalov remembers. "I thought, 'they're done.' He was, like, on empty."

The Flyer goalie did not have to make a difficult save the rest of the way. Schenn sealed the 5-1 win, and a six-game triumph in the series, with an empty netter. "I don't think it could have worked out any better," Giroux recalls. "It was pretty much fun."

Philadelphia had 40 blocked shots, recorded 32 hits, 10 takeaways and won 55 percent of the faceoffs. Coburn had logged 29 minutes, Couturier had performed beyond his years against Malkin, and Giroux, with three points to lift him to 14 in the series, had authored a new chapter in the franchise's thick volume of playoff lore.

"His game tonight was monstrous, it really was," said Laviolette. "When the best player in the world comes and tells you, 'I don't know who you are planning on starting tonight, but I want that first shift,' that says everything you need to know about Claude Giroux right there.

"Line matchups didn't matter at that point. He wanted to make a statement."

Hartnell called Giroux, "Probably the biggest competitor that I have ever played with."

That was no secret to Orpik. "[Giroux] was the best player on the ice in the series," said the Penguin defenseman, while Laviolette was revealing a covert operative—Talbot, with four goals in the series, had provided his coaches with the book on his ex-teammates that helped bring them down.

"You get a player that is well-versed on the opponent, you spend a lot of time with him," said Laviolette.

Bylsma congratulated the Flyers, but added he "couldn't wish them luck." Looking back, he believes they had more than their share of it in the series.

"They didn't have a lot going on (in Game One) until Danny Briere was clearly offside by four feet and went in to score on a breakaway, and it's 3-1," Bylsma recalls. "They won in overtime, and it turned into a hectic, crazy series. I always think back to what would have happened if that was called offside and no goal."

Philadelphia waited four days for the three other Eastern Conference series to go seven games before drawing a matchup with the sixth-seeded Devils. They had won their final two first-round contests in double overtime to survive the Florida Panthers and produce New Jersey's first playoff-series victory in five years.

The Flyers and Devils had been separated by just one point during the regular season, and there was not that much difference in style.

New Jersey was attacking more under new coach Pete DeBoer, but had not given up their trademark defensive structure.

In the 2010 first round, Ilya Kovalchuk, a brilliant individualist acquired at the trading deadline, had proven to be a misfit in that system and the team a shell of its old self in a five-game Philadelphia victory. But as the fifth series in history between the rivals (2-2) began, old Flyer killers such as Marty Brodeur and Patrick Elias were to be dismissed only at Philadelphia's own risk.

Laviolette's team certainly suffered no lack of knowledge about a divisional foe they played six times every season (3-3 in 2011-12). But the Devils hoped the Flyers were at least emotionally unprepared.

"We thought they might have a letdown after that series with Pitt," recalls DeBoer. "With Giroux and Crosby fighting, coaches going at it (in games late in the regular season), that was a war. We thought maybe we could take advantage of that.

"The other thing was that Philadelphia had all left-handed defensemen. We thought if we could get pucks in behind them and run good forechecking routes, they would have a hard time getting out of their end."

Helped by the seven-day gap, Grossmann and van Riemsdyk were ready for Game One. The extra time didn't do much for Talbot, who sustained a chipped tooth from a Carle shot in practice and had to undergo a root canal, but the center was fine for the opener, too. "Fortunately it was [Carle], so it was a muffin," Talbot joked.

Regardless, the first period at the Wells Fargo Center was like pulling teeth for the Flyers. New Jersey had the initial 10 shots of the game and, three minutes in, scored the first goal, by captain Zach Parise off a Read giveaway behind the net.

Laviolette's team increasingly found their legs, however. Voracek caught the Devils pinching and sprung Briere for a breakaway goal to tie the game eight minutes into the second period. Just 37 seconds later, Voracek hurried Brodeur into a giveaway to Carle and van Riemsdyk scored for the first time in nearly four months to put Philadelphia up 2-1.

The Flyers killed a Wellwood penalty for tripping Parise, but when Carle hooked Adam Henrique, Travis Zajac was alone at the post for a tap in off a pass by Parise to tie the game, 2-2.

After Andy Greene was called for hooking Talbot early in the third period, Giroux won a faceoff from Henrique and one-timed a Timonen setup to put Philadelphia ahead again, 3-2. That lasted only until Voracek gave away the puck at the point and was trapped by David Clarkson's quick pass to Petr Sykora, who shot from just inside the circle to tie the game once more, 3-3.

To get the game to overtime, Brodeur had to foil two van Riemsdyk

Giroux, Voracek, Simmonds and Hartnell celebrate Hartnell's first period powerplay goal that made the score 2-0 against the Penguins in Game Six. The Flyers would eliminate Pittsburgh in this game, winning 5-1.

breakaways. As the Flyers' rust came off, New Jersey was looking like a team worn down from being pushed to the limit in the first round. A little more than two minutes into sudden death, Briere redirected with his foot a Carle setup under Brodeur's stick to apparently win the game, but a kicking motion was clear on the replay.

Briere shook his head in disapproval when the control room in Toronto ruled no goal, but after the game would admit the call was obvious. "I needed to stop pouting and get back to my focus," he would say. When a Marek Zidlicky wraparound was stopped by Carle at the point, opportunity knocked again.

With van Riemsdyk in Brodeur's lap, Briere's slapshot sailed in from 50 feet to win Game One, 4-3, at 4:36 of overtime.

"Everyone expects [heroics] from him by now," said Laviolette of Briere, who scored his seventh goal of the playoffs. Brodeur had no hope that two goals within two minutes would be disallowed, despite evidence that this one shouldn't have counted either.

"Van Riemsdyk pushed my stick over when he came across," the goalie said. "He didn't do it on purpose, [but] it prevented me from making the save. Especially after disallowing one goal, they wouldn't do that twice in Philly. That's for sure."

Kovalchuk, trying to play through a groin pull, was not dressed for Game Two, replaced in the lineup by rookie defenseman Adam Larsson, who had been a scratch throughout the Florida series. Defenseman Peter Harrold moved to the wing.

The Flyers started better this time. Read, set up by a backhand pass from Schenn, hit the outside of the net, but then put a rebound from an even tougher angle inside the near post to give Philadelphia a 1-0 lead.

Protecting it soon became almost the entire responsibility of Bryzgalov.

The goalie made a good stick save on Alexei Ponikarovsky after a steal from Lilja and then had an even better one off Ponikarovsky on an Henrique rebound. Henrique spun off Coburn for a turnaround shot in the slot and Bryzgalov butterflied to get that one, too, as the Flyers went the first 18 minutes of the second period without a shot, yet still went to the intermission up 1-0.

"I didn't sense frustration," DeBoer would say. "We were comfortable with how we played. It was just a matter of keeping going."

Three minutes into the third period, a Harrold shot from a deep angle was stopped by Bryzgalov, but Zubrus got to the rebound first in the high slot and made a behind-the-back feed to Larsson, who rang one up over Bryzgalov's glove to tie the game, 1-1.

Any response by Philadelphia was negligible. Parise sealed off the wall as Grossmann unsuccessfully tried to get the puck out and the Couturier-Talbot-Wellwood line covered nobody. Bryzgalov, suddenly one-on-one with Parise at point-blank range, went for a poke check and missed, allowing a hard-charging Clarkson to put New Jersey ahead, 2-1, before impaling himself on the goal.

The Devils, owning the front of the net, added an insurance when Zajac retrieved a Stephen Gionta jam, circled behind the net, and wrapped it around the opposite post.

A distraught Bryzgalov stayed on one knee until after the center-ice faceoff. Three straight even-strength goals had put New Jersey in control, 3-1.

When Dainius Zubrus took a penalty for holding Giroux with 4:25 to go, Bryce Salvador picked up a broken-down pass by Giroux and hit the net from 166 feet. The stunned Flyers had little possession of the puck for the final two periods of a dominating 4-1 Devil win.

Giroux had a quick talk with Bryzgalov before his consoling teammates gathered around him after the buzzer. The goalie had been Philadelphia's best player by far.

"Bryz was phenomenal tonight," said Laviolette. "We were not skating the way we needed to be."

No tangible explanation for the Flyers getting outshot 35-20 at home was forthcoming.

"It's all about the will and desperation," Briere told reporters. "We have to get that back."

It appeared Philadelphia was working towards that as Game Three at the Prudential Center began. Simmonds drew a trip by Henrique in the neutral zone and, on the powerplay, Jagr kept the puck alive along the backboards so that Briere could feed Schenn's goal from the slot. The Flyers led 1-0.

Brodeur kept his team within a goal by coming across to rob Simmonds on a two-on-one. Coburn tripped Zubrus, and, on the powerplay, Elias, firing without a screen from the top of the circle, tied the game, 1-1, off Bryzgalov's arm.

On the following shift, Zajac freed the puck along the wall to spring New Jersey on a three-on-two. Philadelphia chased the puck en masse, allowing Kovalchuk to walk right up the middle. From only 18 feet away, he beat Bryzgalov's glove for a 2-1 lead at 12:53 of the first period.

Four minutes into the second, Voracek circled the net and found Carle, who beat Brodeur cleanly from the top of the circle to tie the game. 2-2. It looked like the Flyers went ahead when van Riemsdyk put in a rebound, but appearances were deceiving. The goal was waved off because Schenn had run into Brodeur.

Trying to beat the Devil goaltender, who then came across to deny Voracek, was getting old fast.

The third period began in a 2-2 tie and New Jersey soon broke it. Lilja couldn't handle a hurried pass from Carle, and Elias fed Parise, who scored on a wraparound between Bryzgalov's legs as he tried to seal the post.

With 12:31 to go, the Devils were up 3-2. Three minutes later, Kovalchuk hit the crossbar and Philadelphia skated back up ice. When Brodeur juggled a van Riemsdyk drive from the sideboards, Briere's quicksilver hands banged the puck between the goalie's leg and the pipe to even the game again, 3-3.

New Jersey was in trouble for most of the overtime. Brodeur had to make an early gamesaver on a Voracek turnaround, and it took seven minutes for the Devils to generate a shot. Zubrus boarded Carle and went off for two minutes, and so did Salvador for clearing the puck over the glass, but New Jersey survived both penalties without the Flyers getting the puck on goal.

Parise, one-on-one with Timonen, went for the roof and the win, but Bryzgalov made a shoulder save.

Seventeen minutes had been played when Kovalchuk took advantage of Philadelphia change with a feed to a breaking Ponikarovsky, one-on-one with Lilja.

The winger was kept to the outside and Bryzgalov made the stop, but Ponikarovsky quickly stashed the rebound between the goalie's pad and the post at 17:21. The Devils had won, 4-3, to take a 2-1 lead in the series.

Kovalchuk, with a goal and two assists, was the best player on the ice, but Briere recalls, "Right to the end of that game, I thought we were the better team."

That may have been, but all the club had gotten out of its effort was a sense that New Jersey had absorbed Philadelphia's best punch and won regardless.

"The Flyers were a team that always played with some swagger," recalls DeBoer. "I think we planted some doubt in their minds.

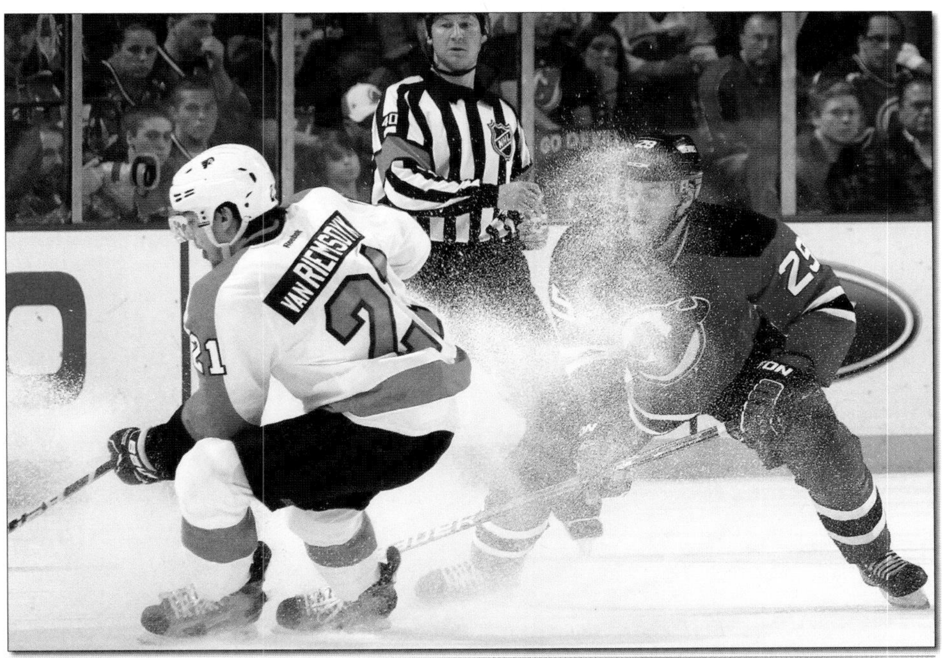

Showered in snow, Mark Fayne of the Devils tries to check James van Riemsdyk in Game Four of the Eastern Conference semifinals.

"Our big guys were playing exceptionally and our possession players like Zubrus and Ponikarovsky were becoming huge. The more we had the puck, the more we could make guys like Giroux and Jagr play in their end, which was the best defense we could have.

"Philadelphia definitely played a wide open brand. That's Peter Laviolette hockey and, when it is going, it is unstoppable. But we got in between them and slowed them down. We controlled the neutral zone."

After four minutes of Game Four, the Flyers had been outshot and outhit 3-0. Laviolette felt compelled to use his timeout while the contest still was scoreless.

Perhaps the breather helped. Or, maybe the Devils bailed Laviolette's team out in the early going by taking a penalty. Zajac went to the box for holding up Briere and, on the powerplay, Hartnell's tip of Giroux's shot from the circle put Philadelphia ahead 1-0.

Two shifts later, Lilja tripped Henrique, giving New Jersey a man advantage. On a faceoff in the Flyer end, Giroux tied up Zajac, took a return pass from Talbot, split Zidlicky and Kovalchuk. and went in alone. Brodeur made a save, but Giroux stayed with the rebound to flip it over the goalie's pads.

It was a brilliant goal but, leading 2-0, Philadelphia built nothing off of it. The Devils still had 1:47 to exploit the Lilja penalty and did easily. Sykora got behind Carle for a redirect of Zidlicky's drive to pull New Jersey to within 2-1.

Less than three minutes later, Zidlicky beat van Riemsdyk to the net to redirect a Salvador drive and the Flyer lead was gone before the end of the first period.

Thereafter, Philadelphia chances were few and far between. Sykora foiled the best opportunity by tying up Hartnell in a goalmouth scramble early in the second period. On the day Brodeur was turning 40, it was the Flyers looking old and tired.

Nevertheless, Bryzgalov kept his teammates tied until late in the second period, when Sykora got the puck past Coburn in the neutral zone, creating a three-on-one. Timonen broke up a pass to the goalmouth, but Sykora retrieved and fed Henrique behind the net. Schenn and Hartnell were already going into their breakout swings, leaving Zubrus all alone to take Henrique's passout and put the Devils ahead, 3-2.

The second period was in its final seconds when Giroux, not particularly liking the way things were going and annoyed by an apparently clean Mark Fayne hit to the shoulder, turned away from his protests to the referees and targeted Zubrus, hitting him with a right shoulder to the head.

The New Jersey winger went down on all fours for a full minute until he was helped up. Giroux received only a two-minute penalty.

Zubrus, the long-ago Flyer first-round pick (1996), returned for the third period, and remained key to shutting them down. Timonen was called for holding Henrique with 3:36 left, costing Philadelphia two valuable minutes of catch-up time. But the club had been mounting no charge regardless.

With Bryzgalov pulled, Briere was stripped by Zubrus and had to trip him on the way to the empty net. The puck slid in, however, and the Devils had taken a 3-1 lead in the series with a 4-2 victory.

"What can I say?" Briere asked the media rhetorically. "We didn't expect to be [in this position]. We are just not making plays."

Not only did the Flyers, outshot 43-22, look completely stunned and befuddled, Giroux seemed clueless that he had committed a suspendable offense. "It was a quick play and hockey is a quick game," he said. "I think I should be fine."

He was not. NHL vice president of player safety Brendan Shanahan called Giroux's hit "reckless," and suspended him for Game Five.

In a video released by the league, Shanahan noted Giroux's anger after Fayne's check, building the case that Zubrus had been head-hunted. Giroux had told both the media and Shanahan, "That's not the kind of player I am. I was just trying to finish my hit."

The first suspension of Giroux's career had come at the worst possible time. Unlike the previous round, he would not be available to knock down the other team's best player, score a first shift goal or turn around a series.

Rinaldo did what he could, leveling Anton Volchenkov six minutes into Game Five. Philadelphia took some inspiration, and Talbot the puck from Kovalchuk. Briere passed in front and Talbot put in Schenn's rebound through a scramble to give the Flyers their fourth-straight game-opening goal and a 1-0 lead.

It lasted just 1:09. Henrique pulled up along the wall and hit the late arriving Salvador, who skipped a shot that bounced over Bryzgalov's shoulder, off the post, and into the net to tie the contest 1-1.

Three minutes later, Timonen dropped the puck back to Bryzgalov, who tried to send it up the boards to van Riemsdyk. The pass hit Clarkson's right skate and caromed through the netminder's pads and into the goal to give New Jersey a 2-1 lead.

"I hit him on his stick and it went into the net," Bryzgalov said. "It could have gone anywhere—in the corner, higher or lower—but it goes straight between the legs."

Whatever air Talbot's goal had pumped back into the Philadelphia balloon totally rushed out. Flyer opportunities thereafter were minimal.

At 4:56 of the third period, van Riemsdyk mindlessly held Elias in the Devils end, and New Jersey, the smarter team in addition to being the better one, took advantage quickly. Zubrus beat Talbot on the draw and Kovalchuk rifled in an apparently unscreened point shot to build the lead to 3-1.

The Devils continued to make Philadelphia defensemen play dump-ins on their backhands and to limit the outlets. The only good look the Flyers had with Bryzgalov pulled was when van Riemsdyk was allowed to go to the net in the final five seconds. Brodeur turned it away easily and a postseason that had started with the loudest bang had ended in a whimper. Just as New Jersey, smothering 3-1 winners in the clinching Game Five, had plotted.

"We knew they were limited in their options," recalls Brodeur. "Pete was really on the ball making adjustments and we didn't get into the little games Philadelphia wanted to play. We had really good penalty killing and gained momentum from special teams."

DeBoer believes the Flyers may have been suckered by their success. "Looking back, the best thing that could have happened to us was losing Game One," recalls the coach. "It maybe gave them a little false sense of security that this was going to be an easier series than Pittsburgh.

"We played better and better after that. We made a conscious effort to stay out of the scrums and the emotional stuff that they had fed off of in the Penguin series. We had enough guys who remembered 2010 to get some extra motivation from that, too. The Flyers had beaten the Devils badly the last two times they had played them in the playoffs (also 2004).

"It was really like a perfect storm that hit them."

Philadelphia tried to summon some thunder and lightning, but instead wound up wading in hip-deep rainwater. "A big part of it was emotion," Briere recalls. "New Jersey was almost acting like it was preseason, skating away, but between the whistles, their team outworked us.

"We played right into their hands. Just the opposite of what happened in the Pittsburgh series, Then, the panic set in."

Recalls Bryzgalov, "Maybe it was in the back of our heads, like, 'We got this, what's the problem?'

"We didn't find the right adjustments. Maybe we were empty on emotion."

In many ways, the script had been flipped from the 2010 series, when the Devils had become stunningly demoralized as the games moved along. This time, it was Giroux's turn to say in a near-whisper, "It should have been a tighter series."

Bryzgalov's giveaway goal to Clarkson, who might have been New Jersey's best player, had been particularly unfortunate. "Except for a play here and there, Bryzgalov was pretty good in that series," recalls Holmgren. "Goaltending did not cost us."

Immaturity had. "That was the most fun I ever had in a season," recalls Simmonds about the most offensive-minded team he ever played on. When the Devils made the going tough, Philadelphia's group of young forwards was unable to adjust.

As the walls closed in, the oldest Flyer, Jagr, appeared no wiser than his younger teammates. But he thanked them, regardless, in what sounded like a possible goodbye following Game Five.

"I've won some Cups and some trophies, but I loved this season," he said. "From the organization to the last player on the team and the fans, they were so nice to me."

The Devils beat the Rangers in six games and went to the Final, where they lost to the Kings, who had reunited Richards and Carter. That made Philadelphia's summer even longer as it threatened to become a winter without hockey.

The Collective Bargaining Agreement was up and the owners were seeking a reduction in the players' 57-percent share of hockey-related revenues, plus other concessions. The possibility of the following season starting late, or not at all, loomed.

Just because Holmgren didn't blame Bryzgalov for the Flyers' second-round fizzle didn't mean he was pleased with the goalie's first season with the team. "His performance was all over the map," Holmgren recalls. "Just here, there and everywhere in between."

Having made a massive financial commitment to Bryzgalov, the GM traded Bobrovsky to Columbus on June 22, the day of the first round of the NHL Draft in Pittsburgh. Philadelphia received 2012 second- and fourth-round picks, as well as a fourth-rounder in 2013.

"His agent (Paul Theofanus) was saying Sergei was willing to be a backup for one year, but not two or three," recalls Holmgren. "He was threatening not to re-sign with us when his contract was over (at the end of the upcoming season) and go back to Russia and play. So he was demanding a trade."

The Blue Jackets wanted Bobrovsky because they had lost faith in Mason, the NHL's top rookie in 2008-09, who had struggled to a sub .900 save percentage cumulatively over the past three seasons. To back up Bryzgalov, Holmgren brought back Michael Leighton on a one year, $900,000 deal.

The Flyers, holding the 20th choice in the first round, had three targets—Finnish forward Teuvo Teravainen (second on Central Scouting's European skater rankings), Russian goaltender Andrei Vasilevskiy (first among European goalies) and Oshawa Generals center Scott Laughton (28th on the North American list).

"We loved Scott by the end of the year," Holmgren recalls. "We saw a little bit of Mike Richards in him, but a better skater than Mike."

As Teravainen began to drop from his projected selection range, the Philadelphia GM talked to Calgary, who held the 14th pick, about the possibility of moving up six spots. But the Flames elected to trade the selection to the Sabres, who selected Latvian center Zemgus Girgensons.

Teravainen dropped all the way to 18th, where Chicago took him just before Tampa Bay grabbed Vasilevskiy.

Laughton had interviewed with the Flyers three times before the draft. "So you can guess they were interested," he recalls, "but you never know what is going to happen. I think I took 15 or 16 washroom breaks before they called my name."

The Penguin fans packing CONSOL Energy Center booed when Holmgren and director of scouting Chris Pryor stepped on stage, then cranked it up louder as Holmgren announced Laughton and he put on the jersey.

"I just kind of laughed at it," Laughton said. "It added fuel to the fire. The rivalry is alive and well."

The next morning, before rounds two through seven, Holmgren dealt van Riemsdyk to Toronto for defenseman Luke Schenn. Over three seasons in Toronto, the brother of the Philadelphia's Brayden Schenn had not yet lived up to the lofty expectations that came with being the fifth pick in the 2008 draft, just as van Riemsdyk, the second pick in 2007, also had struggled through a disappointing 2011-12.

Van Riemsdyk's scoring had dropped by 10 goals from 21 in 2010-11 because injuries had limited him to just 40 games. His efforts had been inconsistent, but Holmgren was not let down, just prioritizing defensive help. "There was no disappointment at all with James' development. We knew Pronger was more than likely done and we were afraid about losing Carle in free agency. We thought adding a strong defensive defenseman was the way to go."

Holmgren and Toronto GM Brian Burke had been talking about the exchange for multiple months. The Schenn brothers, of Saskatoon, Saskatchewan, became the fourth Flyer sibling act, following Wayne and Larry Hillman, Joe and Jimmy Watson, and Ron and Rich Sutter.

"We were excited," recalls Luke. "And our parents were really excited."

With the second-round pick obtained for Bobrovsky, Philadelphia took another goalie, Anthony Stolarz of Jackson, NJ, who at 6-6 was ranked fourth among North American goaltenders by Central Scouting.

In the third round, with the 78th-overall pick, the Flyers selected Shayne Gostisbehere, a 5-10 defenseman out of Union College. He was ranked 148th among North American skaters by Central Scouting, but considerably higher than that by Philadelphia scout John Riley.

"You would leave a game saying the little guy is pretty good despite all these reasons he shouldn't be," Riley recalls. "There had never been a kid from Florida in the NHL. He had already gone untaken through one draft, and he's from Union College, which isn't what Union is in hockey today.

"I just kept coming back to his hockey IQ, his agility, his skating ability and the fact that he could shoot a puck. I mean at that size, how did he get that much torque on it? But he did.

"I was a regional scout. It was my job to promote the guys that are in my area. You become a little attached. It really was Pryor who sold Homer on Shayne."

Riley had met with Gostisbehere at a Schenectady, NY bagel shop. The young defenseman thought it was one of his best pre-draft interviews and felt the Flyers were one of the teams most interested. But although the draft intelligentsia had him as a third or fourth rounder, he chose not to attend the proceedings in Pittsburgh because his mother feared a long, devastating day.

From his home in South Florida, Gostisbehere was watching the draft on television when his name was called. "I jumped off the couch," he recalls. "I mean, literally, I jumped off the couch. The Flyers are a team with so much history, so much going for them."

As free agency began on July 1, Holmgren had multiple balls in the air. He put out 12-year offers exceeding $80 million to two unrestricted free agents—blueliner Ryan Suter and center Zach Parise. Suter, 27, was one of the premier offensive defensemen in the NHL. Parise, also 27, had just helped New Jersey eliminate Philadelphia in the 2012 playoffs.

The GM took his shot without having reason to believe the Flyers were at the top of either player's list. Both chose to return to their upper Midwest roots, signing with Minnesota.

The same day, Philadelphia lost Carle to a six-year, $33 million contract with Tampa Bay. According to Holmgren, that was significantly more than what Carle and his agent had agreed to take from the Flyers a few months earlier. This was a tough loss for more reasons than forfeiting a 27-year-old puck mover in his prime. At the trading deadline, Holmgren had turned down offers for Carle, always intending to re-sign him.

"(Late in the season) I gave him a number and said we could do it over six years," the GM recalls. "I asked if that sounded acceptable and he said, 'Yes.'

"I talked to his agent, Kurt Overhardt, and he said, 'Fine, put it in writing and we'll get something done.' I thought we had a deal. In my mind, we did.

"When Matt signed with Tampa, the agent's retort to me was, 'Well, you never followed up.' Shame on me, but in my mind, a deal's a deal.

"As we got into the draft and the time where teams could talk to free agents, Matt and his agent had expressions of interest from other clubs. They decided to back out of the deal they verbally agreed to."

Although Jagr's numbers had trailed off over the second half of the season, Holmgren wanted the winger back and asked for more time to fit him under the cap, relative to other moves. But on July 3, the veteran star agreed to a one year, $4.55 million deal with Dallas, which represented a $1.25 million raise over his 2011-12 salary with Philadelphia.

"That was more than we could afford to do at that point," Holmgren recalls. "Jaromir brought a lot of value beyond his stats, but we were in a precarious spot with the cap and couldn't stretch it at that point."

For an anchor defenseman, however, the Flyers were willing to spare no expense. With Pronger's career likely over, Carle gone, and Suter deciding instead on the Wild, Holmgren contemplated making an offer to Nashville's Shea Weber, a two-time Norris Trophy finalist who was a restricted free agent.

Weber had a big frame (6-4, 236 pounds), a scorching 100-plus mile-per-hour slapshot, plus a willingness to deliver hits and block shots. He also had the ability to absorb heavy-duty ice time. Via free agency or trade, there would not be another defenseman of this caliber available in the foreseeable future.

"I'm not saying Shea was a Pronger, but he's pretty close," Holmgren says.

Weber, 26, a year away from unrestricted free agency, had been unable to come to an agreement with the Predators. But obviously the loss of Suter made retaining Weber more critical than ever.

Holmgren exchanged trade proposals with Nashville GM David Poile. They were unable to come to terms, leaving Philadelphia to ponder harder than ever the ramifications of making an offer to Weber, which the Predators would then have a right to match, or take four first-round draft choices as compensation.

Considered a hostile and inflationary move, there had been only six offer sheets signed by players since the current CBA had gone into effect in 2005.

Six years earlier, the Flyers had taken a shot at RFA Ryan Kesler, but the Canucks had matched. "We made it too easy for them," recalls Holmgren, who wasn't going to make that mistake again.

Snider was prepared to deal with the fallout. "He said, 'It's your decision, do whatever you want,'" recalls Holmgren.

Weber flew to Philadelphia and met with the Chairman, GM and the coaches. He liked what he heard and saw. It was a no-lose situation for him—he would get the money whether it was paid by the Flyers or the Predators.

Holmgren took a trip to the Jersey shore to spend time with his grandchildren. No sun and sand for him, however. "[Nashville] knew the offer sheet was coming and there was a period of about 10 to 12 hours where we were negotiating about a trade. I never left my bedroom that day.

"It didn't come to fruition, so we filed the offer sheet."

It was the most poisonous pill in hockey history. During the wee hours of July 19, Weber signed a 14-year, $110 million offer sheet via fax. To make it as hard as possible for Nashville to match, $80 million was due over the first six years of the deal. The signing bonus alone, to be paid over several summers, exceeded Weber's salary for those years. The cap hit was $7.85 million per season.

Poile, a longtime friend and frequent trading partner with Holmgren, was incensed. The CBA gave him seven days to match or take the picks.

Neither GM was available for comment as the long week progressed. Five days into it, Holmgren went golfing with assistant equipment manager Harry Bricker, goalie coach Jeff Reese and director of team services Bryan Hardenbergh.

The GM's cell phone rang as he stepped up to the tee. It was (assistant GM) Hanrahan, back in the office. "This tee shot is either going to go 300 yards, or it's going to go 30 yards under the ground," Holmgren said to Bricker as he excused himself to take the call.

"We just got the fax," said Hanrahan. "They matched."

Outside of Philadelphia, there was no sympathy for the losing Flyers. Poile will not talk about the offer sheet to this day.

"I'm not going to apologize," Holmgren says. "We didn't break any rules. One thing I learned from Clarkie is play to win."

Philadelphia spent some money on extensions for some of its top players. Voracek, 23, and Simmonds, 24, signed deals that locked them up through a good portion of their prime years—$17 million over four years for Voracek; six seasons at $24 million for Simmonds.

Hartnell, 30, coming off his best year—37 goals and 67 points—was given six years and $28.5 million.

"If you avoid signing a player because you're afraid he just had his career year, you're going to lose a lot of good ones," says Holmgren, who felt the cap hit, $4.75 million, was reasonable. "No regrets. I'm a big Scott Hartnell fan."

Laviolette also was rewarded, in his case for having the only team in the NHL to reach the second round in each of the previous three springs. The coach received a three-year extension.

Meanwhile, Terry Murray, fired by the Kings six months before they won the 2012 Stanley Cup, came back to the Flyer organization—willing to ride busses at age 62 to develop prospects as head coach of the Phantoms.

"I took some time to think about it," Murray said. "I decided that I'm a hockey coach; I love to coach. The Flyers mean a lot to me. I probably wouldn't have done it for any other team."

Ian Laperriere, who had been on long-term injured reserve for two years with post-concussion symptoms, made his retirement at age 38 official and then, 17 days later, became director of player development, hitting the road to counsel Philadelphia's draftees.

"Lappy's sharp and has a knack with younger players," Holmgren recalls. "He was tailor-made for the job."

The final year of defenseman Oskars Bartulis's contract was bought out so he could sign with Donbass of the KHL. Holmgren, who had added his righty-shooting defender in Schenn, added another in Bruno Gervais, a six-season Islander, in a two-year deal for $1.65 million.

The GM also brought back winger Ruslan Fedotenko, who 10 years earlier had been traded to Tampa to acquire the fourth-overall pick the Flyers used on Joni Pitkanen. Pitkanen never had come close to meeting expectations and, upon his request, was traded in 2007 for Joffrey Lupul and Jason Smith. Twice Fedotenko became a playoff nemesis to Philadelphia—for Tampa Bay in the 2004 Eastern Conference final, and Pittsburgh in the 2009 first round.

"I was excited to come back," Fedotenko recalls. "The fans were great to me.

"When I would play here (with other clubs), there would be signs like 'Welcome back Rusty' and 'We miss you Rusty.'"

Meszaros was recovering well from back surgery when he suffered a torn Achilles on August 7 while training in his native Slovakia. He underwent surgery and was expected to miss at least the first half of the season. Lilja, who had a year left on his contract, underwent hip surgery and was projected to be sidelined for October and November.

On September 14, with no progress made in the labor negotiations, the Flyers assigned all their NHL roster players on entry-level contracts—Couturier, Brayden Schenn, Gustafsson, Rinaldo and Wellwood—to Adirondack so that they could play there during the stoppage. The lockout went into effect the next day.

NHL Commissioner Gary Bettman arrives for a negotiation session with the NHL Players' Association in New York City on December 4, 2012.

Giroux and Briere signed to play in Germany. Three went home to the KHL—Voracek with Lev Prague, Fedotenko with Donbass Donetsk, and Bryzgalov with CSKA Moscow. Read went to Sweden, and Simmonds to the Czech Republic, where in a road game, he was the subject of racial taunts. "Ignorance," he said. "I don't let it bother me."

Coburn, Philadelphia's player representative, stayed home to keep abreast of the negotiations and to train. "I tried to focus on what I could control," he recalls. "I enjoyed being able to spend some extra time with my family."

When Hurricane Sandy ravaged the eastern seaboard on October 29, causing $71.4 billion in damage, Hartnell helped organize a benefit game at Atlantic City's Boardwalk Hall that drew over 10,000 fans and raised more than $500,000.

As negotiations dragged on, Commissioner Gary Bettman continued to lop off chunks of the schedule, including the Winter Classic and All-Star Game. The lockout in 2004-05 had been about free-market principles—the institution of a cap the players believed would greatly depress salaries. This one was strictly over the two sides' shares of the take, so a compromise to save part of the season had seemed likely all along. But with no agreement in sight going into December, the hockey world was getting nervous. Games through January 14th had been cancelled.

Labor strife in the professional arena wasn't going to set back the sport at the grassroots level. The four rinks owned by the City of Philadelphia—Simon, Scanlon, Laura Sims and Tarken—that were to be closed in 2008 before the Ed Snider Youth Hockey Foundation agreed to renovate, enclose and manage them, had been completed by 2012. The program, which was using participation in the game as an educational incentive for inner-city youth, had become a phenomenal success.

Giroux, who had signed to play in Germany to keep in shape and see the world, saw stars after getting hit in the neck and head, and returned home for evaluation. Fortunately, he was not concussed. Briere, playing for the same team, sustained a fractured wrist.

Bettman set a January 11 deadline to avoid the cancellation of the entire season. In the wee hours of January 6, a tentative agreement was reached. The salary cap had been cut from $64.5 million to $60 million (with a new floor of $44 million). Over the next two seasons, each team was permitted to buy out two contracts at two-thirds of their value and not have that money count against the cap. To prevent grossly front-loaded deals like Weber's, a contract could have no more than a 50 percent variance in salary over its length. And none could go longer than eight seasons.

A 48-game schedule, featuring only intra-conference games, was slated to begin on January 19.

As camp opened, Briere was not ready to participate. With Meszaros's availability for the first game uncertain, Holmgren picked up defenseman Kurtis Foster, 31, who had played a total of 51 games with three NHL franchises. To add depth behind Bryzgalov and Leighton, Brian Boucher was brought back to the organization for a

fourth time and assigned to the Phantoms.

Replacing Pronger as captain was the 25-year-old Giroux. "We have some veterans who have been captains and could be again, but I think they realize, with us, that this is Claude's time," said Snider. "He is our leader, without a doubt our best player, and one of the premier players in the NHL right now."

G became the 19th player to wear the "C" in franchise history. "There have been a lot of great captains here in the past," Giroux said. "Along with this comes a lot of responsibility, which I am prepared for."

Players had returned from Europe, or backyard hammocks, in a wide range of conditions. "Jakey [Voracek] and I are candidates for the fat club," Hartnell said.

Laughton, able to play through the lockout for his junior team in Oshawa, had an impressive first Flyer camp and was in the lineup between Read and Simmonds on opening night.

Fans proved to have memories as short as the training camp. After three lockouts in 17 years, the Wells Fargo Center was filled for the opener against Pittsburgh.

Philadelphia fell behind 2-0 after just seven minutes. Giroux cut that lead in half at the 23-second mark of the second period, but the Flyers lost 3-1. The next afternoon in Buffalo, three powerplay goals sank them 5-2.

Hartnell, hit in the foot by a Timonen shot during the third period of a dismal 3-0 loss in Newark to the Devils, was going to be out four to eight weeks, so Holmgren signed 40-year-old Mike Knuble to a one-year, $750,000, contract.

Bryzgalov stopped 18 shots as Philadelphia, swept by the Rangers the previous season, beat them, 2-1, to get into the win column. Unfortunately Meszaros suffered a separated shoulder on a hit by Ryan Callahan and would be lost for two months. Briere was back the following game, however, and the team celebrated with Read's first NHL hat trick, Tye McGinn's first goal, and Luke Schenn's initial one as a Flyer during a 7-1 win at Florida.

Leighton's first appearance in the Philadelphia net since the 2011 playoffs was a 5-1 loss at Tampa Bay. Briere pumped 10 shots at Henrik Lundqvist at Madison Square Garden, but Timonen's powerplay goal was the only one in a 2-1 loss. When the Caps scored twice in the third period to beat the Flyers, 3-2, in Washington, Laviolette's team was 2-6 with one-sixth of the season already gone.

Bryzgalov had barely played in Moscow during the lockout, but was a bright spot in the early going. "I feel totally comfortable now here," the goalie said. "I understand the Philly media. I understand the Philly fans right now. I know what to expect from everybody."

This was a good thing, as Leighton got scratched with what was announced as an upper-body injury. The team recalled Boucher.

Knuble got his first goal of his second Philadelphia go-round as the team bounced Carolina 5-3. Two scores by tough guy Sestito defeated Tampa 2-1 and Briere's overtime winner beat Carolina, 4-3, as the Flyers climbed within one game of .500.

But momentum was fleeting. Boucher was in relief of a yanked Bryzgalov when van Riemsdyk beat Luke Schenn cleanly off a rush for a goal in a 5-2 Leaf win at the Air Canada Center. While Philadelphia bounced back to win 3-2 in Winnipeg on McGinn's early third-period goal, a 3-1 lead at Newark turned into a 5-3 loss, and was followed by a 4-1 stomping in Montreal.

"It's not acceptable the way we played tonight," Giroux said. "It's not just two or three guys. It's the whole team. We're not winning enough battles, not competing. We're just going through the motions."

With a third of the season already gone, the Flyers were 6-9-1.

Bryzgalov needed only 19 saves to shut out the Islanders 7-0, at Uniondale. Voracek, having shed the extra poundage picked up from his mother's home cooking during the lockout, had a hat trick in a 6-5 win in Pittsburgh. But every step forward seemed accompanied by one backwards. Read, Philadelphia's leading goal scorer with seven, tore a muscle in his ribcage and was expected to miss the next six weeks.

Grossmann did what he could to rouse his team from an 0-4 hole at home against Florida, dropping the gloves with veteran enforcer George Parros. But the Flyers lost 5-2. Voracek stayed hot, setting up Giroux, Brayden Schenn and Simmonds for powerplay goals in a 5-3 victory over Winnipeg, and Hartnell returned a week ahead of schedule. But McGinn, who had been making a strong push for a full-time roster spot, sustained a fractured orbital bone in a late first-period fight with Toronto's Mike Brown during a 4-2 home loss and was expected to be out more than a month.

Holmgren needed bodies. As with Knuble, the GM leaned towards a familiar one, reacquiring Simon Gagne from L.A. in exchange for a 2013 fourth-round pick.

Gagne, who won a Stanley Cup with the Kings in 2012, had missed considerable time in recent seasons with ongoing concussion issues and surgery to remove a two-inch mass from his neck. In his happy homecoming, a 4-1 win over Washington, he scored a second-period powerplay goal that drew a sustained ovation.

"I scored bigger goals in my career, but that one was special," Gagne recalls. "The way the fans were so happy for me, I will never forget it."

Sestito and Leighton had to be waived in order to send them to Phantoms. Vancouver claimed Sestito, but Leighton cleared.

Bryzgalov made 33 saves and Simmonds scored his third game winner in as many contests as Philadelphia beat Ottawa, 2-1, to get back to 11-11-1. At Madison Square Garden, a good start evaporated into a 4-2 loss thanks to two bad line changes that resulted in Ranger goals. Then, back at home against Pittsburgh, Bryzgalov stopped just 12 of 16 shots as the Flyers failed to hold a 4-1 lead, losing 5-4.

"I don't know why we stopped playing," Hartnell said. "It's embarrassing to the fans and to one another.

Philadelphia got Meszaros back after a 21-game absence, as well as Read, a month ahead of schedule. But the team was lifeless in a 3-0 loss at Boston. "After 1-0, we stopped competing," Laviolette said through gritted teeth.

The Flyers were four points out of a playoff spot, but had four teams to go over and 22 games remaining. "I'm not good at math but if you look at it, we have to win games right now," said Gagne, whose powerplay goal and a shorthanded one by Talbot helped Philadelphia to a 3-2 win over Buffalo.

Bryzgalov's 2-1 shootout salvaged a split of a home-and-home against the Devils, and the Flyers played one of their most solid games of the season against Tampa. But they lost it, 4-2, and then failed to close out Pittsburgh. A late slashing call against Simmonds enabled Crosby to tie the game before Kennedy won it for the Penguins, 2-1 in overtime.

Laviolette's team had no battle in a 5-2 home loss to the Rangers. After coughing up a third-period lead against the Islanders, Hartnell's goal with 30 seconds to play saved a point. But the second one got away in a 4-3 shootout loss that left Philadelphia second-to-last in the Eastern Conference with just 15 games remaining.

Coburn separated his left shoulder during the Islander loss, joining Grossmann (concussion), and Meszaros (shoulder separation again) as out for the remainder of the season.

With the Flyers afforded two buyouts by the lockout settlement, Briere, 34, endured questions about his future. He had not scored in 13 games before being lost indefinitely to a concussion suffered during practice.

Bryzgalov's save percentage was .899 and there were seven seasons left on his deal. There was even less question he was going to be bought out than there was about Briere.

"You try to play your best and everybody is talking about the buy-out," Bryzgalov recalls. "Every day they ask me, 'What do you think?'

"I say, 'I don't care. If you buy me out, I will go somewhere. Just [bleeping] leave me alone and let me do my job.'

"Do you want your goalie being like a thousand needles, stressed out? What is the point of all this? No matter how thick is your skin, your kids are asking, 'Dad, what's going on?'"

Knuble, a repeated healthy scratch, scored a first-period powerplay goal and Philadelphia won for the first time in two weeks, 3-1 at home over Boston. It triggered one last stand.

Voracek pounded on Washington's Steve Olesky in retaliation for an open-ice hit on Giroux, whose powerplay goal and an assist on Timonen's goal with 10 seconds remaining enabled Fedotenko to beat the Caps 5-4 in overtime. The most exhilarating win of the year was tempered by the loss of Talbot to a broken tibia suffered in a knee-on-knee collision with Mike Green.

Holmgren claimed forward Adam Hall off waivers from the Lightning and traded Zolnierczyk to the Ducks for enforcer Jay Rosehill. The GM then made a more interesting move. On April 3, deadline day, he acquired 24-year-old goaltender Steve Mason from the Blue Jackets in exchange for Leighton and a third-round 2015 draft pick.

Mason, the NHL rookie of the year in 2009, had lost his No. 1 job in Columbus to Bobrovsky. But he was 24 years old, and came with a high recommendation from St. Louis coach Ken Hitchcock, who had been the Columbus coach during the goalie's initial burst of success. After considerable film study, Flyer goaltender coach Reese endorsed the idea, too. Philadelphia was hoping a change of scenery would revive the career of a netminder desperately waiting to be rescued.

"I had been in contact with my agent (Anton Thun) a little up until trade deadline day and had been told there was some interest from a couple of teams, the Flyers being one of them," Mason recalls. "On deadline day, my bags were packed for a game to St. Louis, but I was secretly hoping that I would be playing for another team the next day.

"I went home while waiting for the plane to leave. Finally the agent calls and says, 'We've got a deal in place with the Flyers if you'd agree to go there.' I said, 'Yeah, absolutely. Let's do it.'

"Paul Holmgren called right after that, saying the Flyers were happy to have me. I didn't have a no-trade, didn't need to give my approval. He just wanted to know how comfortable I was with coming there. Bryzgalov was signed for a long time, but Homer wanted me to know there was potential for me being re-signed if things went well.

"I just wanted a fresh start. It was over for me in Columbus. Even during pregame introductions, when they announced the starting goalie was Steve Mason, the crowd would boo. Being young and booed on your home ice was tough for me. It takes a lot to play a solid game if you don't have support from your home fans.

"My time in Columbus started when I was 20 years old, and I got traded at 24. Looking back, I wish I had the opportunity to play in the American Hockey League to grow. I needed to go through struggles outside of the spotlight of the NHL."

"There were times (while going 60-73-19 over his final three Columbus seasons) I felt better, but I just couldn't find consistency. You get really depressed. It got to a point where I had a sick feeling every morning just going to the rink. Hockey wasn't fun anymore. Had the trade not happened, I was done with the game. I was looking at what I was going to do with the rest of my life."

Leighton moved on knowing his Philadelphia legacy, unfortunately, was defined by the bad-angle goal that gave Chicago the 2010 Stanley Cup. But he also was in the nets when the Flyers became the third team ever to come back from an 0-3 deficit to win a series and three shutouts during the Eastern Conference final against Montreal. There has never been a more successful waiver-wire pickup in franchise history.

"As disappointing as was the way it ended, that year defines my career pretty much," Leighton recalls. "I'm grateful the Flyers gave me a chance.

"They stuck with me and the team really played well when I was in the net. From the Winter Classic to the playoffs, that whole story is going to be the greatest hockey memory of my life. And that's what I'm known for. When I tell people who I am they say, 'Oh you're the Flyers' goalie,' and not, 'You played in Carolina,' or 'You started in Chicago.'

"Obviously, the goal is what I'm known for, too. I met a Flyer fan not long ago who thanked me for the season and everything I did. There are others that say, 'You're the guy who lost it for us.' But everyone who thanks me makes me feel good.

"I enjoyed my time in Philly. Everyone loves to play there. If you're losing or not playing well, it's a tough city. But I'm always going to be proud to say I put on that sweater."

Humbled, but not quite ready to surrender, the 2012-13 Flyers took one last shot at saving their shortened, disjointed, season. Third period goals by Simmonds, Gustafsson and Voracek rallied them to a 5-3 vic-

tory over Montreal. The following night, Rosehill was among the scorers in a 5-3 win at Toronto. Four straight victories had pulled Philadelphia to within two points of eighth place in the conference with 11 games remaining.

In Winnipeg, Fedotenko's third goal in five games got the team off to a 1-0 lead, but Bryzgalov gave up four goals on 12 shots so Laviolette went to Mason in the third period. The game was gone, but the newcomer stopped all nine of the shots he faced. Three nights later, Bryzgalov's string of 22 consecutive starts ended when Mason got his first as a Flyer.

"We lost (4-1 at the Islanders), but I played well," recalls Mason. "From that point on, I felt comfortable again.

"A lot of it had to do with Jeff Reese. From the beginning, he was instilling belief in me. He didn't try to change much. Instead, he said, 'Whatever you feel comfortable with, we will try to make it better.' I really enjoyed working with him.

"The first time I put on the Flyer sweater, it was already a different feeling. I'll never forget this: One time driving to Columbus (from home in suburban Toronto) the border guard asked where I was going. When I said 'Columbus' he asked why and I said, 'I play hockey there.' He said, 'Oh, they have a farm team?' I said, 'they've had an NHL team for eight years.'"

"Everybody knows the Philadelphia Flyers. Everybody who comes in the door is proud to be part of that tradition."

Mason's start on Long Island was reported by WPEN-FM (The Fanatic) as a disciplinary measure against Bryzgalov after he allegedly fell asleep during a team meeting. Laviolette vehemently denied the report. Knuble said the meeting was too short for anyone to have dozed off.

"Not unless they're narcoleptic," Knuble said. "You hardly even sat down for it. That's asinine."

Bryzgalov was back in the nets the following game, stopping 31 in a 3-1 home loss to Ottawa. Two nights later, Mason yielded a single goal, just enough for him to be bested in Buffalo, 1-0, by Jhonas Enroth.

Briere returned after 10 games, but at 17-21-3, Philadelphia had fallen nine points back of a playoff spot with seven games remaining. Mason stopped 38 shots in an impressive first Flyer victory, 4-2, at Wells Fargo Center over the Rangers. But a New York win over Buffalo eliminated Philadelphia with three games remaining.

Mason won his last four starts. "Last game, at Ottawa, I was going for my 100th win, so it was big for me personally," he recalls. "We got outshot (44-25), but we won (2-1). It was a nice way to finish.

"Not knowing where I stood going into next season, it gave me confidence."

The win over Ottawa pushed the Flyers record to 23-22-3, the only time during the season they were above .500.

Voracek received his first Bobby Clarke Trophy as the team MVP. Timonen, who had missed only one game despite a nasty bout with planter fasciitis in his heel, was honored with his fourth Barry Ashbee Trophy as the club's best defenseman.

The special teams—Philadelphia was third on the powerplay (21.6 percent) and fifth on the penalty kill (85.9 percent)—were good for most of the shortened season. But the Flyers had finished a mediocre 19th in even-strength goals.

There were significant needs to address on the blueline, but four nucleus veterans—Giroux, Voracek, Simmonds, and Schenn—were under 26. "I don't look at it like, 'Holy mackerel, we've got to blow this up and start all over again,'" Holmgren told reporters.

Laviolette, who had always believed the best defense was a good offense, told the media he had made a slight adjustment in coverages to "add an extra layer of protection" in the defensive zone. But he added his belief that the problem wasn't the system, but too many turnovers leading to counterattacks.

Pronger, who had been a system unto himself in the Philadelphia end, never was going to play again. The Flyer defense, not particularly nimble, arguably needed more help from the forwards and coaches to compete in a league where defensive structure increasingly ruled.

"Lavvy was starting to get under a lot of pressure to play a more defensive system," Briere recalls. "It's hard to change a system when you've only got about a week of preparation before a season. We tried to adjust, but it didn't work."

Holmgren thought part of problem might have been Laviolette's ambivalence about changing.

"We talked to him and told him we would need to make adjustments and pick up the team defense aspect," Holmgren recalls. "He said he would do it, but I don't think he was ever really sold on it."

By the time the season ended, the GM had made his decisions on utilizing the two amnesty buyouts. One was a lot harder than the other.

Briere was called to Holmgren's office and given the news that after 124 goals and another 37 in the playoffs, the most productive free agent the franchise ever signed was no longer a Flyer.

"Danny Briere is one of the nicest men you will ever meet," says Holmgren. "He worked hard every day and never said a bad thing about any of his teammates.

"He did whatever we asked, was great with the fans; the media guys all liked him. Good dad. Active in the community. You want to keep people like Danny.

"We both shed a tear or two."

By buying out the final two years of Briere's eight-year, $52 million contract, the team would save $6.5 million against the salary cap in the 2013-14 and 2014-15 seasons.

"It wasn't an easy thing for them, either, meeting with me and having to break the news," Briere told reporters. "But they did it with a lot of class.

"I'll always be grateful for that and also my time here as a Flyer."

Holmgren had seen enough from Mason (4-2-0 with a 1.90 GAA and a .944 Sv%) to be confident about going forward with him as a starting goalie. Buying out Bryzgalov would mean paying out $23 million over 14 years ($1.64 million per year), but the cap savings would be nearly $6 million a year for the next seven seasons.

Snider had become resigned to the buyout.

"He wanted to know our reasoning," Holmgren recalls. "After we went through it, he was on board."

Bryzgalov remembers that late in the year Holmgren told him that a buyout was not going to happen.

"At the end of the season me, Lavvy, Paul, Jeff Reese, the coaching staff, we're supposed to have a meeting," the goalie recalls. "And I say, 'It's too emotional right now, let's take some time. In a few weeks when everything is cooled down, I will tell you what bothers me, you will tell me what bothers you, and we try to find a solution.'

"When I come to that meeting, it's only Paul Holmgren. I say, "Where is everybody?' He said, 'We decided to buy you out.'

"I say, 'Okay.'"

Holmgren told the media, "Obviously it's a costly mistake that we made, but we have to move forward. I still believe he played pretty well, but in a salary-cap world, you need to make decisions from time to time that put you in a better position.

"I think Ilya is a colorful guy. Does he say things out of the blue sometimes? Absolutely. But I don't think he's any different than a lot of other players I have been associated with. I didn't have an issue with that. This is strictly a business decision."

Bryzgalov was 52-33-10 with a 2.60 goals-against average and a .905 save percentage as a Flyer. Ultimately, the cap amnesty was an opportunity the team couldn't pass up after he had been a less than the dominant goaltender for two seasons. Bryzgalov had been at his best in a more structured system in Phoenix. So he was being let go because of a shortage of saves, not friends.

"Hockey players are bred to think and talk and act for the team first," Briere recalls. "Bryz didn't always go by that. But I never thought that he was a bad guy."

Bryzgalov has maintained his Haddonfield, NJ, residence and has no hard feelings for the organization. But he does feel his career was shortened and his reputation tarnished by his time with Philadelphia.

"If I stay in Phoenix, I would be continuing to play right now," Bryzgalov, 36, says. "The media created a bad myth about me; GMs and people who don't know me say, 'We don't want to deal with that.'

"They say I was asleep in the meeting. We got a two-minute meeting, you know. How you even come up with that? It's just ridiculous. Nobody says, 'No, it's not true,' so you start to look like a freak.

"But I never regretted that I came here. I am really proud I played for the Flyers. I didn't picture our relationship was going be over like that; I pictured we'd win the Stanley Cup. But I still wear the jersey sometimes when I'm out. Always will with honor."

Winner of the Calder Trophy in 2009, Steve Mason joined the Flyers in a trade at the deadline that sent Michael Leighton to Columbus. Mason would allow just 12 goals in 378 minutes played in 2012-13 and would become the club's No. 1 goaltender in 2013-14.

MIKE RICHARDS

SLOW FEET, NEVER COLD ONES, were the cause of Mike Richards slipping to the Flyers with the 24th pick of the 2003 draft. Mike Stothers, the former Philadelphia assistant coach who was the bench boss at Owen Sound during Richards' junior days in the Ontario Hockey League at Kitchener, called him, "the closest thing I'd ever seen to Bobby Clarke."

Philadelphia would be the hardest place to live up to a declaration that bold. But in his peak years, Richards' good hands, accurate shot, superior hockey sense and, most of all, relentless drive, made him no cheap knockoff of the greatest Flyer of all time. In fact, Richards proved to be one of No. 16's most worthy successors.

"The bigger the game or the situation, the better Mike responds," said Peter Laviolette, the coach of the 2010 team Richards captained to the Stanley Cup Final.

Richards wore the C for three seasons, leading Philadelphia in points twice, in hits by a forward three times, and in contest-turning plays on more occasions than ever have been counted. He scored his first NHL playoff goal on a penalty shot to put away a Game Three win over Washington during the first round in 2008, and went on to key a semifinal run with 14 points in 17 playoff games that spring.

During the 2009-10 drive to the Final, Richards scored one of the most exhilarating goals in team history—shorthanded, after tumbling over goaltender Jaroslav Halak—to erase a 1-0 deficit in the semifinal-clinching Game Five over Montreal. Richards totaled 23 points in 23 postseason games that left Philadelphia just two wins short of the Cup.

He played hurt. Both shoulders needed surgery after Richards scored five points during a six-game elimination by the Penguins in the 2009 playoffs. And he inflicted pain upon the opposition. Richards' leveling of David Krejci with a clean, hard, open-ice body check fractured the first-line Bruin center's wrist and turned around the 2010 series in which the Flyers became the third team in history to rally and win from an 0-3 deficit.

The greatest shorthanded threat Philadelphia has had since the combination of Dave Poulin and Brian Propp, Richards is the only NHL player to have scored three career goals with his team down two skaters. In 2009-10, one of the years he led Philadelphia in scoring, Richards lost the Frank Selke Trophy (best defensive forward) to Detroit's Pavel Datsyuk by just three voting points, recognition of his all-around value.

"We used him more like a defenseman on the (powerplay) point," recalls Flyer assistant coach Joe Mullen. "But he was almost like a weak-side point guy because of his great vision and ability to get his shot through. If your center got thrown out (of a faceoff), you could always put Mike in to take it. He did everything."

Teammates loved him for all the ways he helped produce wins, as well as for the encouragement he lavished upon them. "Because he's such a good player, his influence went a long way," Laviolette said. "He constantly stuck up for [them].

"If somebody had a bad game or a bad shift, he made sure he smoothed things out with a pat or some positive feedback. I saw that a lot with him."

Recalls Danny Briere: "Mike was a natural leader. Because he was so young (23) when he assumed the captaincy, he might have missed a couple of steps on the learning curve, like how to handle the media. But he had the respect of every one of us and was really well-liked."

In his passion for the game, Richards was a Canadian prototype. Born in Kenora, Ontario, a town of 15,000 close to the Manitoba border, as the middle of three sons, he was on skates at age three. Norman Richards, Mike's father, was employed at the paper mill, the town's biggest employer until it closed in 1985; his mother, Irene, worked at a grocery store. The Richards clan pitched in with two other families to help maintain an outdoor community rink.

"We played inside for the games, otherwise we were outside, even when it was minus-30, or minus-40," Mike recalls. "You layered up—long johns, wool socks.

"[Few] had ever been to the NHL out of Kenora. I didn't think about making it until my cousin Jeff (Richards) got drafted by Sault Saint Marie of the OHL. Our teams never got to Toronto (a 24 hour drive) to play; Kenora was in the Manitoba (Tier II) league. We had no OHL orientation."

A local tipped off the Kitchener GM, who made the trip to watch the kid and then made him the fourth-overall pick in the OHL midget draft (at age 16). Richards was stunned. He played hockey because he loved it, but had yet to be consumed by it as a potential career. "My parents always taught me to have fun," he recalls.

Leading Kitchener to a Memorial Cup was both a good time and additional exposure to scouts who saw him as smallish (5-11) grinder with an oversized heart who wouldn't be able to get around the rink fast enough to put up big point totals. Thirteen picks earlier, the Flyers had taken a big potential scorer in Jeff Carter; they figured if a third-liner was all Richards ever was going to be, he still would be a very good one.

Richards didn't get caught up in proving anybody wrong, just kept playing the way he always had, one game at a time. Much less interesting to him were the practices, workouts and the culture of conditioning that was taking over the game.

He embraced the camaraderie of the beer-and-chewing-tobacco culture of hockey days gone by. After 60 hard minutes, he wanted to go to the bar, not the gym. When the season ended, that was time to recharge at his cottage outside Kenora, not work five hours a day with a trainer.

"Fishing on the lake for eight hours a day took precedence over being in the gym," said John Stevens, who coached Richards with the Flyers and Phantoms. "I would never call Mike a poorly conditioned athlete, but he was probably average.

"My vision for him was that he take that part of his game more seriously, especially in the off-season, to get to an elite fitness level."

Young Flyers who had traditionally bought places near the practice rink in Voorhees followed Peter Forsberg's lead to Olde City Philadelphia, where it was good to be young, single and a millionaire.

In the days of the Broad Street Bullies, there were no tweets of the goings-on at Rexy's, the favorite Flyer South Jersey hangout. Times had changed. A cell phone photograph surfaced showing Richards, Carter, Joffrey Lupul and Scottie Upshall enjoying themselves with co-eds at a college party, one of a series of social media "reports" that caused Richards to bristle at the invasion of privacy and what he called an exaggeration of his after-hours lifestyle. In a *Hockey News* article, he accused the Philadelphia media of writing fiction about him. When confronted about that allegation by one beat writer, Richards froze out the reporter for months.

Given the captaincy at age 23, he was proving mature enough to handle it only on game nights. "He was so good on the ice at that point that we thought he would grow into the rest," recalls Flyer president Paul Holmgren, then the GM.

"Ideally, you want your captain to be your hardest-working guy at practice and in all situations, like Clarkie always was. Mike never really got to that level as a captain, but it didn't affect his leadership because everyone liked and respected him.

"He was never in great shape at the start of training camp. It was OK, but he didn't take it to the level that other really good players do now. Mike was like,

'I'm OK.' What he put into it probably would have been really good back in the seventies, but it's a new game.

"At the end of the day, he's a gamer. He shows up and does what you want him to do when it's all on the line.

"But I think back to the Final in 2010. The Blackhawks played above the speed limit. Mike was OK in some of the games, but in others, he couldn't keep up. He was brutal in 2011 against Boston (a Bruin sweep). I can remember people from other teams asking me what was wrong with him."

No-trade clauses in long-term Richards and Carter contracts were going to kick in with the 2012-13 season. Claude Giroux was ready to become the No. 1 Flyer center. With Chairman Ed Snider insisting Philadelphia get a veteran upgrade in goal, Holmgren needed cap room to sign Ilya Bryzgalov. From an immediate standpoint, the GM thought his team required more size on the wings. For the long term, he wanted to replenish the youth traded two summers earlier to obtain Chris Pronger.

So in June 2011, Holmgren stunningly traded Richards to Los Angeles for Brayden Schenn and Wayne Simmonds. On the same day, the GM dealt Carter to Columbus for Jake Voracek, an eighth-overall pick that the Flyers used the next day to take Sean Couturier, and a third-round pick that turned into Nick Cousins.

"I'm saying today the same thing I did at the time," recalls Holmgren. "We needed to get bigger and to address our goaltending issues.

"There was other stuff going on, but I don't want to talk about it. That stays with me. I liked both those kids."

Within nine months of the trades, the Kings obtained Carter and won the 2012 Stanley Cup, repeating in 2014. Richards played a much more critical role in the first championship than the second, by which time he was on the fourth line. In June 2015, he was arrested by the Royal Canadian Mounted Police for attempting to cross the border with oxycodone, a controlled substance, without a prescription.

The Kings terminated the remaining seasons of a 12-year contract he had signed with Philadelphia in 2008, a deal that had $22 million remaining on it. After the NHL Players' Association filed a grievance, an undisclosed financial settlement was reached.

Los Angeles GM Dean Lombardi received the championship(s) that he wanted from the Philadelphia deal, and Carter continues to play at a star level for a contending Kings team. Nevertheless, right after the settlement, Lombardi told Lisa Dillman of *The Los Angeles Times* he was devastated by the Richards "tragedy."

"In terms of the total package, Richards never was the player for us in LA that he was in Philly," recalls the GM.

"Knowing what Mike had been and seeing it progressively go downhill because he wouldn't or

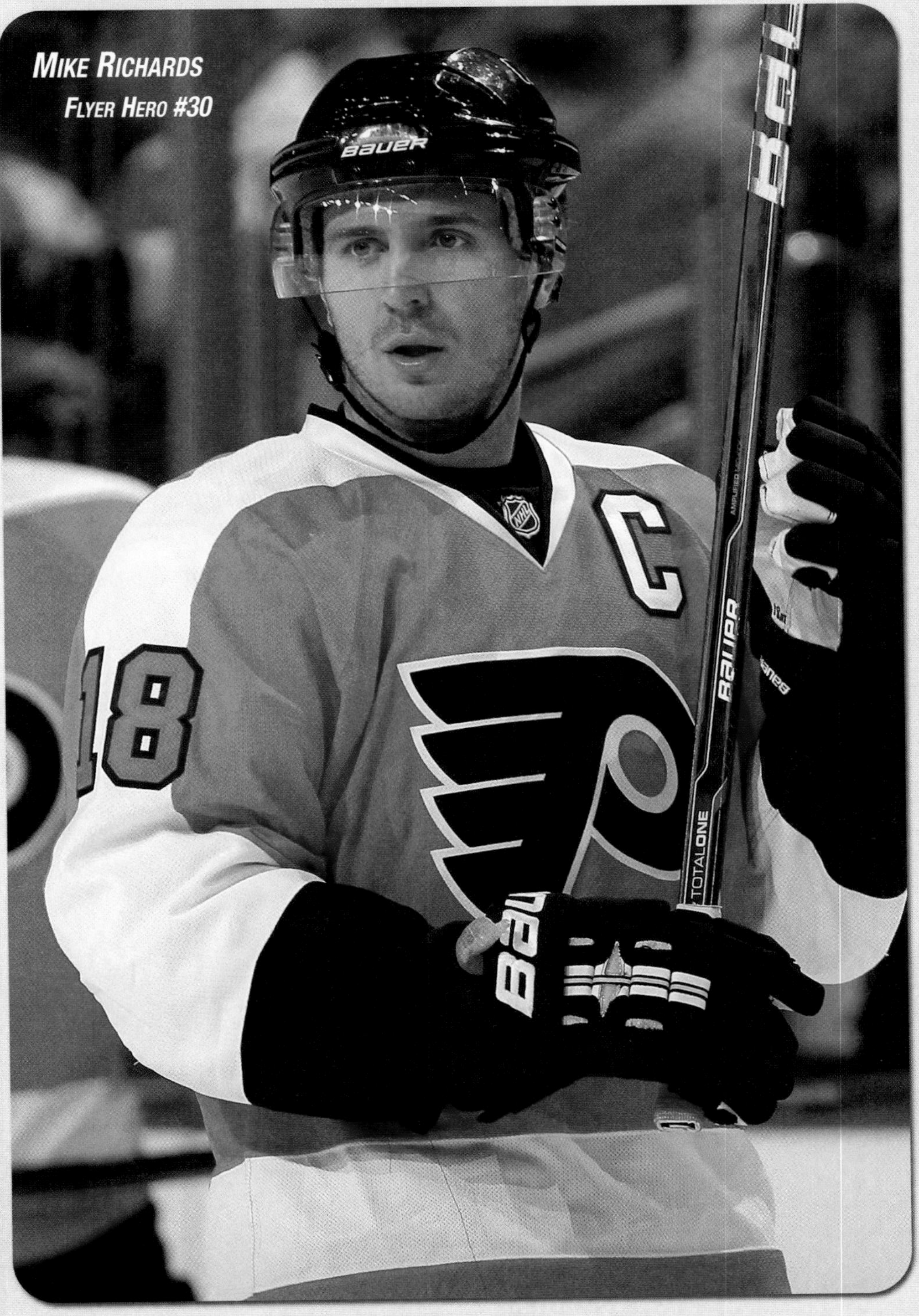

couldn't help himself—or embrace being helped—that's my regret; not the trade. He brought the competitive impact that we needed.

"I loved this kid. He was my type of player."

When cleared by the NHL to participate, Richards signed a contract with Washington for the remainder of the 2015-16 season. As a 30-year-old fourth-liner, he played against the Flyers in the first round, attracting a minimum amount of attention from their fans only five seasons after being Philadelphia's best all-around performer.

In Simmonds and Schenn, the Flyers received two nucleus players on a playoff team while Richards was delivered to the right place at the right time. "It's hard to argue [the trade] didn't work out the best for me," he says. "But I still miss Philly, have lot of friends there.

"You'd have to ask Paul for the reasons he made the deal. I don't know. I do know what being a Flyer meant to me. It's pretty cool to have my name on the wall of their dressing room as a former captain of a team with that much tradition."

WAYNE SIMMONDS

Going into his second year of eligibility for the NHL Draft, Wayne Simmonds was not in Central Scouting's top 210 North American prospects. Even after the Kings took him in the second round, he remained the ultimate sleeper. At his first rookie camp, GM Dean Lombardi found Simmonds one morning snoozing in a car.

"No, I wasn't quite homeless, had about $1,000 to my name," he recalls. "My (Toronto) friend (the Blues') Chris Stewart and I were staying in Anaheim, had a long drive in Stewie's brother's girlfriend's car [to the Kings practice facility in El Segundo] in brutal traffic and wanted to be there early."

It dawned on Lombardi that this kid was different. "Wayne wanted to be there first thing every day," recalls the GM. "He was very raw but embracing a long process a lot of guys would find daunting.

"Nowadays, there are these elite programs for kids ages 14 and up, and they come out of them feeling like they already know the game. They aren't used to being criticized. Wayne and other late-bloomers who go through a draft or two and don't get picked have a different mindset about being coached. You don't get the backtalk or the entitlement.

"No one ever coddled Wayne as a player. No one put a mindset in him that he was above coaching or the team. He believed it was on him to prove himself.

"There's a lot of cost in playing hockey, especially these days. Wayne did not have access to those resources growing up as a player. But what he did have—and still does have—is an endless well of desire and commitment. He's really a throwback to another era."

In practically every Flyer generation—from Gary Dornhoefer to Paul Holmgren to Rick Tocchet to Mike Knuble—the team has had self-sacrificing, workaholic right wings who finished plays that they often started out of the corner. Not one of these players was a high draft choice; all overcame a physical issue, a size liability, or a skating deficiency to become quintessential power forwards. Simmonds, just as self-made as any of the above figures, also has overcome bigotry and financial hardship to become Philadelphia's first minority star.

Turned out, no adversity could withstand his two greatest assets: family and community.

"The majority of whatever came into our household probably went into my hockey," Simmonds recalls. "I couldn't give you a dollar amount, but I know it was ridiculous.

"I'm really, really grateful to my brothers and sister. They could've been really mad at me for taking up the family's money, but they were always gracious about it. My family's not the jealous type.

"My parents told me, 'You've always gotta work twice as hard as the person beside you, because he's the one trying to take your dream.' There's not enough room for everybody to play in the NHL, so I did everything to be better than that next guy. If I didn't have his skill level, I'd work harder than him. That was one thing I could control every day."

Cyril Simmonds was a construction foreman who brought two kids from a previous relationship into a blended family of five children growing up on the east side of Toronto.

"We're all pretty tight, I don't consider them half-siblings at all," says Wayne. Cyril married Wanda, an office worker for the City of Toronto, when Wayne was 11 years old, not that making it legal changed anything.

"Seemed like it was just E.L.E.—everyone loved everyone," recalls Simmonds. "I lived in culturally-mixed neighborhoods—white, black, some Asian. Toronto is a melting pot with every ethnicity you can think of. People got along pretty well and helped each other.

"Anne and Big Mike Heron, parents of my still best friend Mike, lived around the corner, so they would pick me up, take me to games, flip-flopping the transportation with my parents.

"I had the same coach in every league I played in between ages six and 16—Mike Hutton. His oldest son played on my teams. Every day I'd be at his house after school and Mike would be on me about my homework, like he was my dad. He was awesome, cared about everybody. He passed away from lung cancer. I owe a ton to him.

"There were others. When I was 15 and picked to play AAA—where the best kids at that age played—I knew we weren't going to be able to afford it. A couple of my cousins helped me out, and the construction company my dad worked for sponsored me."

As part of the arrangement, Simmonds would be on construction job sites during the summer months.

"I got up with my father every morning, like 4:30 or 5 and would work until 5 or 6 cleaning up all the scraps from the electricians and guys building the houses. That's when I really realized how tough Dad's job was, and what he did to provide for the family. I didn't want to go back and do that for a second summer. It made me want to be a hockey player even more.

"That has been my life goal since I watched my older brother Troy play junior. My fallback was to be a firefighter, because I like helping people. But that year, when I started playing AAA, was when I really began to think I could make something out of playing hockey. I started to get scouted by a lot of junior teams.

"Mike Futa, the GM at Owen Sound (OHL), came to my house and said he was going to draft me. I said, 'Don't even bother.' I didn't play AAA until I was 16, so I was a year behind, thought I needed college hockey to catch me up. Mom liked the idea of me going to school anyway. I had a scholarship at Bowling Green State University, but Futa drafted me anyway and convinced me to come to Owen Sound.

"We had an unbelievable team and I had a pretty good rookie year (23 goals) as an 18-year-old. A week after it ends, Futa got named head of amateur scouting for L.A. I'm like, 'He's leaving? He's the only reason I came here.'

"Mike told me he'd take care of me, whatever that meant. Maybe I'd get like a free-agent tryout or something like that? I wasn't invited to the (NHL Scouting) Combine. Had two interviews with Atlanta, did a test for New Jersey. So I thought I was going to get drafted by the Thrashers or Devils in a late round."

With the financial assistance of Stewart's family, friends since youth hockey, and their agent Eustace King, Simmonds was in Los Angeles working with T.R. Goodman, a fitness guru to hockey stars, on the day of the 2007 draft.

"A little after 7 in the morning, I was driving on the 405 with Chris, on the way to working out, when the phone rang," recalls Simmonds. "It was my agent telling me, 'You just got drafted.' I'm like, 'What do you mean? It's only the second round right now.' He said, 'Yeah.'

"Me! Wayne Simmonds, 61st pick to the Los Angeles Kings. I kept driving three exits past where we were supposed to get off, Stewie laughing at me all the way. My mom called me two minutes later crying."

Simmonds did okay at his first training camp, at least for a guy who weighed 150 pounds. But, as expected, he went back for one more season of junior.

"Next year, I was a lot more ready," he recalls. "First exhibition game, I got in a fight with Shane Hnidy and after that never let my foot off the pedal.

"I scored a couple goals, played sound, good, defensive hockey, and got into two or three fights during camp. Everyone was saying, 'You're going to have to play in the AHL.' I'm like, 'Why, cause you did?'

"I wasn't trying to be cocky or anything like that. I just knew what I had to do, provide a little bit of toughness and energy. And I was lucky that L.A.'s team wasn't too good at that time."

He scored nine goals as a rookie under coach Terry Murray. "Every other day I was in his office, looking at a video at what I had done wrong," recalls Simmonds. "He definitely made me accountable, but he was playing me against top lines, so I knew he had faith in me."

Despite feeling the effects of meniscus cleanup surgery, Simmonds scored 30 goals over the next two years and was a brick in the foundation of the contender the Kings were building. Then, he became the cost of Lombardi's desire to accelerate the process. In June 2011, when the GM sought Mike Richards as the finishing piece of his Stanley Cup team, Flyer GM Paul Holmgren set a stiff asking price of Simmonds and Brayden Schenn, the fifth player taken in the 2009 draft.

"We tried to keep Wayne out of the deal, but Homer wouldn't move," recalls Ron Hextall, then the Kings' assistant GM.

Simmonds was at his uncle's cottage, suffering sporadic cell phone service, when Holmgren got through with the news of the deal before Lombardi did.

Players say the first trade always hurts the most; after that, they understand it's a business. Nevertheless, Simmonds was glad it was Philadelphia.

"I was a kid during the Legion of Doom days. The Flyers were one of the teams you always followed," he recalls. "I loved the way they played, thought it would be a good fit."

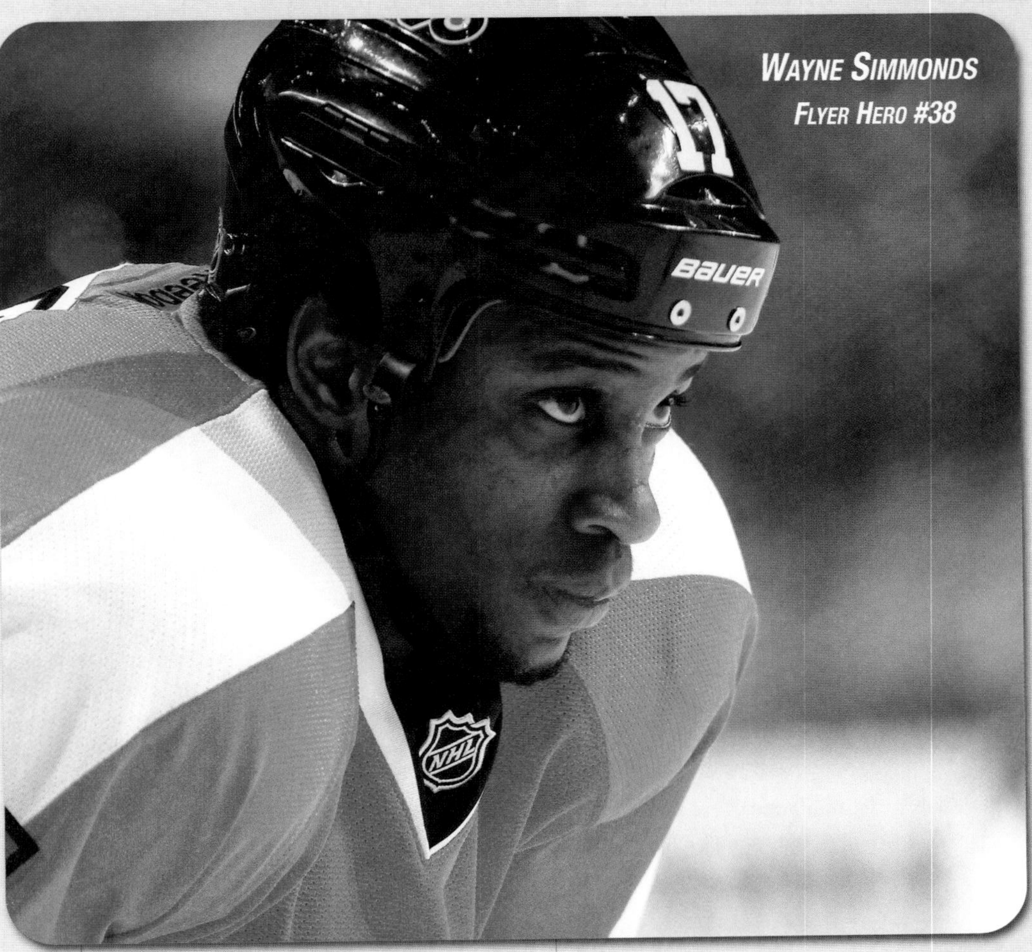

WAYNE SIMMONDS
FLYER HERO #38

Indeed, anchoring a second line and being a key to the first-unit powerplay, Simmonds has been everything Philadelphia believed it was getting. Fifty-nine of the 132 Flyer goals he had scored going into the 2016-17 season came with a man advantage, a too-high ratio reflective of the club's struggle to find Simmonds a playmaking center. But then again, the back pressure is so relentless in today's NHL, there are not many lateral plays to be made at even strength. Whichever team jams the front of the net best usually will win. And despite the skinniest legs in the game, maybe in the human race, Simmonds will not be moved.

"Got em' from my dad, his whole side of the family," laughed Simmonds. "As hard as I've worked on them, I don't think they will ever change."

Three-year-olds draw thicker legs with crayons—two long poles, interrupted slightly by knees—yet somehow, these rods seem planted eight feet into the ice. Just try to move him.

"The rules have changed a bit to help players like him, but its not easy to just stand there and watch pucks whizzing by your head," says assistant coach Joe Mullen, who runs the Flyer powerplay. "But he's willing to get hit with one, and he can make passes and tip pucks.

"If the puck hits the goalie, he finds it; if it goes behind the net, he can recover it."

Simmonds grinds away in the great Philadelphia tradition of forwards who will not go away.

"He's an important guy for us, not only because of what he does on the ice in terms of goals and assists, but also in maintaining our identity as a team hard to play against," says Hextall, the Flyer GM. "You take Simmer out of our equation, our club has a different look and feel to it.

"He's one of the hardest-working players on the team, cares about his teammates, wears his heart on his sleeve.

"The diversity part, that's great. But I've never viewed him in any terms except as a huge player for us."

Nevertheless, it is a step forward for the franchise to have a magnet for new fans and an inspiration for future Flyers.

"I've joined the board of the Ed Snider Youth Hockey Foundation," Simmonds says. "It's an honor.

"I remember being young and wide-eyed when I saw an NHL player. Seeing the way those kids look at me is very satisfying. It's very important to give back to the community.

"Jarome Iginla (Colorado's future Hall-of-Famer) is a huge reason why I play the game the way I do. Willie O'Ree, too. My parents thought it was important to teach me the name of the first black person in the NHL both so that I knew my roots and also to see that it was possible for me to make it.

"Willie lives in San Diego. I met him my first year in Los Angeles and worked with him on the *Hockey is for Everyone* campaign. He is an awesome human being.

"Being a black hockey player, when all you saw around me was white kids, I'd sometimes be called names and stuff like that. It happened all the way up. I don't think it's ever stopped.

"I had that unfortunate incident (at an exhibition game) in London (Ontario) during my first year here, where I got a banana thrown at me. When I was in the Czech Republic during the lockout, I had fans chanting racial slurs towards me.

"When I was younger, stuff like that used to drive me crazy. I'd always try to [respond] physically. But my parents did a good job of teaching me that you really hurt them best when you put a couple of pucks in the back of the net and they lose the game. So, after a while I became like, 'Whatever.' I didn't even bother with it anymore, even though I still get subtle (verbal) jabs.

"I'm not an idiot. I can tell when somebody's trying to demean me. But I have a huge support system of family and friends, a lot of good people in my corner of different races and types. That's how the world works best."

SCOTT HARTNELL

Charisma counted as we numbered the team's 50 top heroes. So we cannot begin to give Scott Hartnell his due without mention of the 'do. It was flaming orange to match the team colors, bigger even than his attachment to Philadelphia, and not really meant to be hidden under a helmet.

But according to the coach under whom Hartnell had his most success as a Flyer, he was a main man for more reasons than his mane.

"He's a good hockey player," says Peter Laviolette. "He can bring physicality, can score goals, and goes to the hard areas. But what stands out is that he's probably one of the best teammates that I've coached or seen. He's a caring person."

More than being good around the net, Hartnell was good just to be around.

"Fun-loving guy," says R.J. Umberger, witness to a personality change on the team after Hartnell brought more than 24 goals in his initial Philadelphia season, 2007-08.

In the few hours available between the joyful train ride home after the Game Seven overtime triumph in Washington and the flight to Montreal to begin the next series, Hartnell decided to have his Afro straightened. His hair flopped to his shoulders like it was trying to draw a penalty, robbing the impromptu press conference the Flyers held upon their arrival at Pierre-Elliott Trudeau International Airport of all sense of decorum.

"Had the guys just dying," recalls John Stevens, Philadelphia's coach that season. "Who takes time to go do this for the sake of getting a few laughs from his teammates? That was Scotty."

No big deal, the winger insisted. "Once I wash it, I'm sure she'll go back to the ol' Afro," said Hartnell, referring to his hair in feminine terms. Indeed, the natural perm returned, saving a Philadelphia landmark.

The following season, the team secretly ordered orange wigs and used them as giveaway items before a home game. The Flyers skated out for the warm-up to see 5,000 Hartnells—any goalie's worst nightmare—but the funniest sight ever at the Wells Fargo Center. "Good-looking crowd," acknowledged the real Hartnell.

Vanity became him. As frustrated as the fans could get with Hartnell over bad penalties and horrendous slumps—and the coaches and management about his wavering attention to conditioning—it was difficult to stay angry even before he would rattle off a fast seven goals in eight games. The left wing tried hard, too hard, sometimes. The confidence would come and go like his latest style.

That cliche about it being time to look in the mirror? He did, literally.

"One year, I kind of had a tough start and we were losing," he recalls. "After a big loss, you didn't really want to go out for dinner in Philly. So I stayed home.

"I looked in the mirror and hair's everywhere. I said, 'I should just cut it right now.' I [decided] that if I still felt like that way in the morning, I would go get it done.

"I woke up and said, 'Yeah, it's time,' so I went to a barber. It looked like there was five pounds of it on the ground. I donated it to Locks of Love—they make wigs for kids who lose their hair during chemotherapy.

"It felt kind of light. The next day, everyone was like, 'Who's the young kid?'"

Eventually, the head of Olde City—figuratively we mean—grew a ponytail. "Long or in a ponytail, the hair was kind of my trademark," he says.

In 2011-12, several years before spending his final Flyer season in a crew cut, Hartnell became known for something other than being hirsute. On Twitter, a fan started counting how many times the winger would fall to the ice during a game and in a season. Occupational hazard—you go to the front of the net, you inevitably are going to wind up on your butt—so never had he considered himself prone to being prone. But he decided not to get all insulted about it and joined the fun. "Hartnell Down!" became a phenomenon.

"The fans had fun with it," he said. "I heard there were Hartnell Down drinking games where every time I fell, they had to take a shot or chug a beer or something like that.

"When I started my foundation, I donated every time I fell. We raised a lot of money."

He could drop anytime, anyplace on a rink. But it could have also been called "Hartnell: Hard to Keep a Good Man Down!" He rose repeatedly to become one of the franchise's greater playoff heroes, scoring third-period goals to force overtime in a 2011 Game Six at Buffalo (a Flyer win) and a 2010 Game Six against Chicago (a loss).

That wasn't all. Hartnell also chipped one in during the 2010 Game Seven comeback from down 3-0 in Boston, rang up a beauty off a rush to give Philadelphia a lead in the clinching Game Five at Montreal in 2008, and jammed in a precious rebound off a scramble as the Flyers put away the Penguins in Game Six of 2012.

He endured hard times to eventually enjoy those moments. In his first Philadelphia season, it took Hartnell until November 24 to score into anything other than an empty net. In going through a divorce in 2009-10, he had only 14 goals the entire year, and then was so bad during the first round against New Jersey, that his will to succeed was challenged by Laviolette. After both Jeff Carter and Simon Gagne were lost to injuries in the same game, the coach put Hartnell with Briere and mid-season depth pickup Ville Leino. No. 19 went on to score eight goals during the balance of the drive to the Final.

When he was on, as Hartnell was practically the entire 2011-12 season in scoring a career-high 37, he was one of the deadliest snipers the Flyers ever had. The turnaround one-timer from the edge of the circle was deadly and, at his confident best, Hartnell's instincts in front of the net—whether to put back a rebound or to find a wide-open Briere, Leino or Claude Giroux at the opposite post for tap-ins—could be uncanny.

Such intuition is not really learned, al, though both of Hartnell's parents were educators. His mother, Joy, was a special-needs teacher, and his father, Bill, an elementary-school principal in Lloydminster, Saskatchewan, where the family moved when their youngest of four children, Scott, was eight years old.

"As a kid I got pounded a lot by my brothers," Hartnell recalls. "Charley horse punches, noogies, everything. But I always kept coming back for more.

"I was five and seven years younger than my brothers (Chad and Devin). I would watch them play bantam, peewee, and junior, and lean over giving them high fives as they were going on and off the ice. I always was looking at how they skated, how they made plays; I was just in awe of them. Those were some of the best days of my life."

The brothers were good enough to earn scholarships at Colorado College and Michigan Tech, but the best hockey genes were saved for the baby of the family. Scott grew up bigger than his brothers, both of whom recognized early on that the kid had superior skill and hockey sense and helped guide him on his path to a pro career through Junior A.

"My parents and my brothers are probably the biggest people in my life getting me to where I am today," said Hartnell.

"When I went to play junior at Prince Albert (Saskatchewan), my mom and dad were there every step of the way. It's about a three-and-a-half-hour drive for them from Lloydminster, and they didn't miss too many games. They would leave at 11 p.m. after games, get home at 2:30 a.m. and then be up for school."

SCOTT HARTNELL
FLYER HERO #49

An 82-point season in his draft year got Hartnell picked sixth-overall by Nashville. He was in the NHL the next season, progressing over six years with the Predators into a consistent 20-goal scorer. As his second NHL contract ran out, the team was for sale and its future in Nashville uncertain. Faced with losing both Hartnell and his road roommate, Kimmo Timonen for nothing in free agency, GM David Poile took a first-round pick from Philadelphia GM Paul Holmgren in exchange for negotiating rights prior to the July 1 start of free agency.

Timonen, skeptical of signing with a team that had stunningly sunk to the bottom of the NHL that season, needed some convincing by Holmgren that there was a plan to turn it around quickly. Hartnell, who had grown up knowing the Flyers as the team of Eric Lindros and John LeClair, couldn't wait to sign.

It turned out to be a superior move, both for the franchise with a heart, and a player who wore one on his sleeve. Probably the best game Hartnell ever played was the Game Six against Chicago, when he scored a goal and an assist to keep Philadelphia alive through an early Blackhawk onslaught. With 3:59 remaining, Hartnell was—where else?—on his back after tying the game, forcing the unfortunately-fated overtime goal by Patrick Kane that cost the Flyers the Cup.

Every generation of players since the Broad Street Bullies has had at least one deep playoff run that turned into both their best and worst Philadelphia memories. Departing without a ring was hard on every Flyer, but after Hartnell's seven years, 156 regular-season and 19 playoff goals, just leaving was hard. He was traded to Columbus in the summer of 2014 to bring back Umberger.

"I had signed a (six-year) contract hoping to finish my career in Philly," he recalls. "I loved playing there, loved the team, the guys. Loved the chance we had every year to win.

"Hearing, 'We appreciate everything you've done, but it's time to move on' was really hard to listen to. It was tough cutting the cord. I'm not sure I ever completely did.

"First time I put on that jersey, I wanted to make Philly proud. I felt that every time."

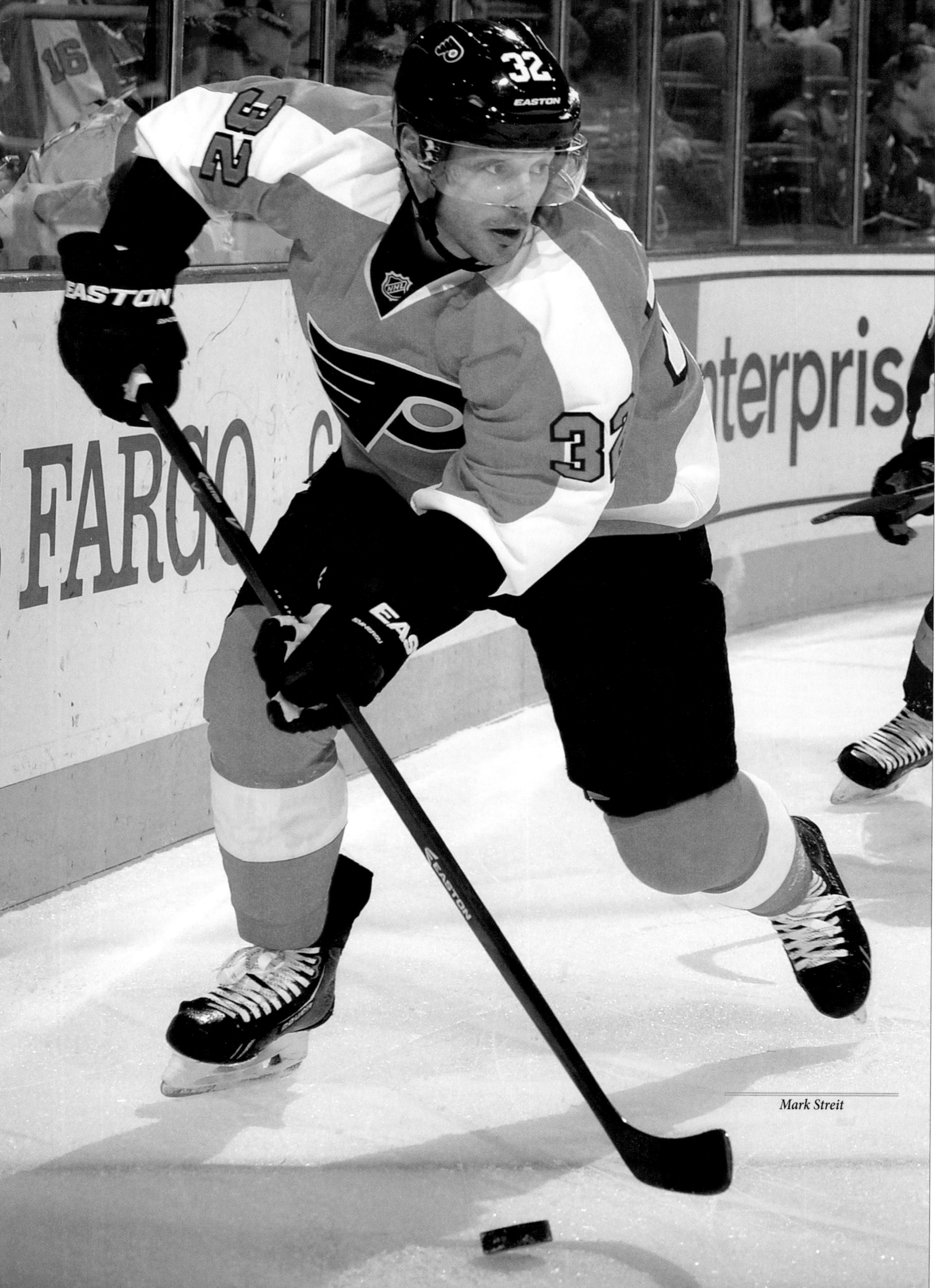

Mark Streit

CHAPTER 15 • 2013-14

The Guarantee

WITH SIGNIFICANT CAP ROOM OPENED UP by the buyouts of Ilya Bryzgalov and Danny Briere, GM Paul Holmgren was anxious to rectify Philadelphia's absence from the postseason during the shortened 2012-13 season.

The club's most obvious need was on a defense still reeling from the loss of Chris Pronger's career to concussion symptoms. In the summer of 2012, the organization had tried to plug the huge hole with free agent offers to Ryan Sutter, who went to Minnesota, and Shea Weber, who signed and then was lost when Nashville matched. However, a year later Holmgren found a good defenseman who was unrestricted in free agency and unbridled in his enthusiasm to become a Flyer.

Even at age 34, Mark Streit of the Islanders projected to be the top defenseman on the market come July 1. Drafted at age 25 in the ninth round by Montreal, the Swiss-born Streit had not come to the Canadiens until he was 26, leaving low mileage on his odometer from playing five seasons in the less demanding short seasons of the league in his native country.

"Once I realized I was moving on from New York, the Flyers probably were at the top of my list," recalls Streit. "We didn't beat [Philadelphia] much but I always liked coming to the Wells Fargo Center.

"It was always a storied franchise. The commitment to winning was humongous. When (Islander GM) Garth Snow called and said, 'the Flyers want to trade for you before July 1,' that was exciting."

On June 12, Holmgren dealt minor leaguer Shane Harper and a fourth-round pick to the Islanders for 19 days of exclusive negotiating time with Streit. Through agent Pat Brisson, Streit signed a four-year, $21 million contract on June 28.

"A powerplay guy," said Holmgren. "He gave us another option with Kimmo (Timonen)."

After competing for seven years against hard-nosed Devil right wing David Clarkson, Philadelphia was interested in the upcoming free agent. But priorities changed with the June 27 announcement that Tampa Bay had used one of the buyouts allowed by the lockout settlement to rid themselves of the final seven years of Vincent Lecavalier's contract.

Lecavalier, 32, had scored 32 points in 39 games of the lockout-shortened season, his 14th with the Lightning.

A delegation of Holmgren, Comcast-Spectacor CEO Peter Luukko, and coach Peter Laviolette went to New York City to meet with Lecavalier and his agent, Kent Hughes, who were meeting with several teams, the most prominently mentioned being the Maple Leafs, Canadiens, Stars and Red Wings. Holmgren and Luukko turned the pitch over to Laviolette.

"I watched Vinny's eyes go from normal size to huge listening to Lavvy," Holmgren recalls.

Lecavalier wanted to go to a traditional hockey market and play in a system where a 383 career goal scorer could thrive. The Flyers met both criteria. When a five-year, $22.5 million deal was announced on July 3, Hughes said he had discussions with more than a dozen teams and that Philadelphia had been at the top of the list from the beginning.

The remainder of the available cap room largely went to lock up Claude Giroux for eight seasons—the maximum allowed under the new CBA—at $66.2 million, making the captain's average salary of $8.25 beginning with the 2014-15 season the highest in 46 years of Flyer hockey. Giroux was being paid $5 million for the 2013-14 season. He had missed only five games in the previous four years while averaging more than a point per game in the playoffs.

"A high quality young man who has blossomed into our best player," said Holmgren, who then scraped together his remaining pennies to sign free-agent goaltender Ray Emery for one year at $1.65 million.

Emery's first Philadelphia tour, in 2009-10, ended with a devastating diagnosis of avascular necrosis in the hip. A bone graft performed by Dr. David Ruch at Duke University Medical Center saved his career.

"The doctor told me the procedure wasn't meant for playing sports; it was more to save the hip," said Emery. "If I played, it was going to be a bonus."

The goalie was in a hospital bed in his parent's living room for three weeks and then watched the Flyers go to the Final without him. "I was happy for the guys, but at the same time, you want to be part of it," he recalls.

His good fortune with the operation, and dedication to the rehab paid off in February 2011, with a contract offer from Anaheim, where he won seven of nine starts. Emery then signed for the lockout season with Chicago, where he went a sparkling 17-1 with a 1.94 goals-against-average playing for the Stanley Cup champion Blackhawks.

"If he wouldn't have gotten hurt (in 2010), I think we would have won the Stanley Cup," said Holmgren. As far as Emery was concerned, that door was not closed.

"It felt unfinished," he says about his decision to come back. "I liked the culture, the gritty attitude of the team. The management, coaches, trainers were all still here from my first time around, so I knew what to expect, and I was excited about that."

The $3.15 million that Philadelphia budgeted for Emery and holdover Steve Mason made them one of the lowest paid tandems in the league. Holmgren said both would compete for the starting job.

The Flyers had the 11th pick at the Entry Draft at the Prudential Center in Newark and a plan to stock defensemen. The organization had only two prospects of any note on the blueline—Shayne Gostisbehere of Union College and Marc-Andre Bourdon, who had played 45 games with the 2011-12 parent team, but had been set back by repeated concussions.

Seth Jones, the top-rated defenseman, was taken fourth by Nashville. Philadelphia liked three others—Darnell Nurse of Sault Ste. Marie (OHL), Rasmus Ristolainen of TPS Finland, and Samuel Morin of Rimouski (QMJHL).

Nurse went No. 7 to Edmonton and Buffalo took Ristolainen at No. 8. Dallas GM Jim Nill offered the Flyers the 10th-overall pick for winger Brayden Schenn, which would have given Philadelphia consecutive first-round choices.

Montreal GM Marc Bergevin dangled Max Pacioretty and the Canadiens 25th-overall pick for Wayne Simmonds and the Flyers' 11th selection. Holmgren, who felt Simmonds was better than Pacioretty, discussed the offer with his staff, but upon learning the Canadiens were also interested in Morin, Holmgren turned down the deal. The 6-foot-6 Morin, who had a meteoric rise in the rankings during the second half of the season, became the tallest first-round pick in Philadelphia history.

"Don't get me wrong, he's not Chris Pronger yet, but Sam just keeps getting better all around," said Quebec scout Simon Nolet. "He's a good kid; works hard and really wants it bad. He's learning what he can do with his size. Strong, too."

Morin had racked up 117 penalty minutes in just 46 games, and scored the highest of any prospect at the NHL Combine in anaerobic testing.

In the second round, with the 41st pick, Holmgren took another defenseman—Robert Hagg, who averaged nearly a point-a-game with MoDo in Sweden's junior league, but had slipped in the ratings after earlier being considered a first-round pick.

Mike Knuble, 41, had retired at the end of the 2012-13 season. But Simon Gagne, 33, wanted to come back and was told by Holmgren he would try to create space, perhaps even as late as opening day, when it was permissible to put Chris Pronger on long term injured reserve. Gagne, who had contributed a point in seven of the Flyers last 13 games, decided to wait, wanting to finish up with the team for which he had once starred.

Time marches on, but the celebration of one of the most important figures in the organization's history began anew with the July 9 election of Fred Shero to the Hockey Hall of Fame.

Chairman Ed Snider had relentlessly advocated for the induction of Shero—the coach of Philadelphia's two Stanley Cup teams—since his death in 1990.

"There's no sense looking back as to why it didn't happen sooner," Snider said. "Today's a happy day to celebrate the fact that a guy who deserves it immensely has finally been elected to the Hall of Fame."

Shero had been passed over so many times that Ray Shero, Fred's son and general manager of the Penguins, was completely surprised by the call. "A coach had not been inducted for a long time (Herb Brooks, 2006)," Shero recalls. "It never seemed to be happening, so I wasn't expecting it at all."

He got the call while on a beach with his children and was thrilled to tell them first. "My oldest was born in 1995, so they only knew their grandfather from the stories," recalls Ray. "It was really great for me and them to have his career [memorialized] again.

"He never was one to promote himself, never kissed anybody's butt; it was always about the players. But he would have been very proud. He had been proud to go into the Flyer Hall of Fame."

On July 15, the organization announced the return of Ron Hextall as assistant GM and director of hockey operations after seven seasons in the same positions with the Los Angeles Kings. Conversations between Holmgren and Hextall, who had worked together in the Philadelphia front office from 1999-2006, had taken place over the preceding year.

"I met Mr. Snider for lunch," Holmgren recalls. "We talked about a bunch of different things and I convinced him that bringing Hexy back was a good thing. Mr. Snider said, 'I gotta go to the bathroom. When I come back, I want you to tell me what you think it's going to cost.'

"So he comes out, and I said, 'It's probably going to cost about $400,000 a year.'

"Mr. Snider said, 'Really? Is he worth it?'

"Mr. Snider wanted you to fight for what you believed in. I said, 'Yeah, he's the best guy for the job.'

After we had the press conference, he said, 'this guy is a smart guy.' I said, 'Yeah, he is, and he's going to do us good.'"

With John Paddock having been reassigned as an assistant coach during the lockout season, Holmgren had an opening for another assistant general manager (alongside cap specialist Barry Hanrahan). With his children out of the house, a move back to the place Hextall had left seven years earlier only for the sake of career advancement was feasible.

"It was my gut feeling to come back," recalls Hextall. "To this day, I can't give you a better answer than it felt right.

"I guess we'd accomplished the goal in L.A. we set out to accomplish—we won the Cup in 2012. I don't want to say the job was finished because there are always new challenges, but the timing was right to come back. This is the only place I'd have even considered a lateral move.

"The offer was what it was—to be assistant general manager. Absolutely, 100 percent, nothing was promised to me."

Hanrahan would continue to focus on the salary cap and Paddock would fill multiple roles. "I would find things for John to do—special assignments or whatever," recalls Holmgren. "He is a valuable and knowledgeable guy."

The good news of Hextall's homecoming was followed by bad news from the golf course. Giroux damaged the extensor tendons in his right index finger when his pitching wedge snapped and shattered as he shanked a shot at a course near Ottawa. Although no bones were broken, the doctors thought he would miss training camp.

Gagne waited the summer in vain. Just before camp, winger Daniel Cleary, a 15-year veteran, accepted a three-year contract worth $2.75 million per season. Since this was going to put the Flyers approximately $1 million over the cap, the plan was for Cleary to report without a contact, then sign on opening day, as soon as it was permissible to clear room by putting Chris Pronger on Long Term Injured Reserve.

But Cleary did not show up on the initial day of camp, opting instead to take a one-year deal to remain with the Red Wings. Ultimately, the Flyers decided not to spend the money, saving the camp room to promote from within.

"I kind of put all my eggs in one basket because there was no other place I wanted to go," recalls Gagne.

"Paul said 'don't worry' he was going to move some money.' and I was willing to take that chance. We had been talking every week that summer.

"The cap went down and all the free agents were signed. I wound up with a lot of (camp) invitations but no guarantee and decided not to play.

"I was [bleeped off], Homer has said he never promised a contract but he was very positive about it and changed his mind in the end.

"I decided not to talk about it with reporters. It would be stupid to close the door on so many good years with the Flyers for maybe an extra one or two. It's behind me now."

With the Flyers Skate Zone locker rooms undergoing remodeling, the preseason was slated to be split between the Wells Fargo Center and the Herb Brooks Arena in Lake Placid, NY.

Laviolette felt uneasy about the disruption and maintained that the workouts were much quicker in a less cavernous setting.

"I don't think training camp was great," he recalls. "There were a lot of things that I wanted to do and we didn't. It could have been better."

To complicate matters, several players contracted the flu during the trip to upstate New York. The team's 1-5-1-preseason record was only a surface reflection of the overall organizational sense that time was not being utilized well. But with Bryzgalov sitting at home in Haddonfield collecting $1.64 million a year for the next 14, at least Snider had a sense of closure to a disappointing chapter and was optimistic about the future in goal.

"I don't care who you're playing with, for Emery to win 17 games and only lose once (the previous year in Chicago) is pretty amazing," the Chairman told the media. "And I think Mason really has changed—what we saw at the end of last year wasn't a fluke. So I am very optimistic about the goaltending."

Thirty-eight-year-old Hal Gill, a well-travelled 6-7 veteran of 1,102 NHL games invited to camp on a try-out basis, was signed to a one-year, $700,000 contract to provide defensive depth. Right wing Adam Hall, 32, who had played the final 11 games of the lockout season after being claimed on waivers from Tampa Bay, gained a fourth line spot.

Mason was in the net, and Giroux good to go, when the Flyers opened the 2013-14 season at home against the Maple Leafs. Lecavalier debuted by setting up Brayden Schenn's first Flyer goal of the season but Dion Phaneuf intercepted a Max Talbot clear, enabling Phil Kessel to score on a rebound. After Simmonds was beaten by Jonathan Bernier on a penalty shot with three seconds to go in the second period, Philadelphia faded. Dave Bolland beat Mason from point-blank range 2:30 into the third period, then added an empty-net goal in Toronto's 3-1 victory.

The major Flyer failing had been their 1-for-7 powerplay, so Laviolette moved Jakub Voracek to the third line with Sean Couturier in an attempt to rouse some offense. "Even in practice, we're firing Scud missiles and they're smashing off the glass," the coach said, "Put it between the red bars somewhere."

Laviolette announced Emery would be the starter in Montreal, where new Canadien Briere would play his first game against his former club since it reluctantly bought out his contract.

Habs fans had relentlessly booed Briere during his Philadelphia years for having rejected a Canadien offer. Now it was Lecavalier's turn after making the same decision. Emery, surrendering only a goal by Brian Gionta after he had overpowered Streit to a rebound, kept the Flyers down only 1-0 into the third period, but nine Canadien powerplays, and a Philadelphia failure to convert more than one (by Lecavalier) of five powerplay opportunities turned into a dismal 3-1 loss.

"We'll look at the video," said Giroux. "It has to change."

It didn't the following evening in Raleigh. The Flyers were not nearly as much in the game as a 2-1 loss suggested. Trailing by a goal the entire third period, their comeback efforts totaled three shots.

"The final push is missing," Timonen said. "When you have to make a statement, for some reason, we haven't been able to do that.

"There's going to be ups and downs in a season, and this is the first test for us as a team. It's about sticking together, sticking to the game plan, and putting the work boots on. If we start blaming people and not playing as a team, we're going to be 0-6 soon."

Laviolette was asked if his forwards were pressing. "Could be," the coach said.

On the plane ride home, Holmgren sat in silence. Laviolette's teams had always been known for their high energy, but there was little of that since the beginning of camp. Holmgren and others had asked the coach to pull back some on the all-out attack system that had worked well when Pronger manned the defensive zone. Laviolette had agreed, but without enthusiasm.

"I'd had a fleeting thought about making a change over the summer," recalls the GM, "but I liked Peter and thought he deserved another opportunity.

"We made some changes [in the off-season] that got us all excited. To start training camp and the year with Peter was the right thing to do at the time. But I just didn't like what I was seeing."

Early the next morning, October 7, Holmgren called assistant coach Craig Berube into his office and told him he was the new head coach on a two-year contract. The GM then called Laviolette, asked him to come to a meeting, and said he was being relieved of his duties.

The conversation between Holmgren and Laviolette lasted only a minute. The GM thanked the coach for all he'd done and wished him well. Laviolette simply said, "OK," and left.

He pulled two of his kids out of school, packed, and took them and his wife Kristen to visit an older son attending Proctor Academy in Andover, New Hampshire.

"No cable, no *NHL Network*," Laviolette recalls. "I wasn't watching anything.

"When you get let go, it's never painted as a good picture. It's always about the things you did wrong. Whatever, I get that. I don't really care."

He denies having been distracted by a $3 million lawsuit he and Kristen filed that month against the Bank of America, alleging the Laviolettes had followed the institution's advice to leverage the $8 million equity they held in three homes into failed, high-risk, investments.

Laviolette believes it was simple: he lost his job because the Flyers missed the playoffs and had a bad start to the following season.

"I liked the way we played in the opener," he remembers. "A (Toronto assistant coach) called me and said, 'You should have beaten us 5-0.'

"Montreal had a real good team that outplayed us for sure. Carolina was waiting for us, for a 5 p.m. start after we got in at 3 a.m. We just didn't play well, had no jump.

"But when the GM says it's time for a change, that's his call. If it's not working anymore, he has to move on.

"I believe in attacking. When a coach is standing in front of you preaching something, you know whether he believes it or doesn't believe it. If I'm not sure, that comes off quickly in a locker room.

"I am 100 percent sure in the style I want a team to play. All my teams have had success that way, so that's what I want to do. If it's not working anymore, I get it.

"I think the world of Homer. I loved the fact when I was talking to him, it was not only to my GM and boss, but someone who had been a coach. He always treated me fairly and also with respect. I have absolutely nothing but good things to say about him.

Laviolette, fired three games into his fifth season, had gone 145-101-29 and taken Philadelphia to within two games of the Cup. He won five playoff rounds. He was not doomed by an 0-3 start, but because those three games seemed like a continuation of the team's performance during the preceding season. It had become a fair question whether the system Laviolette was teaching worked for the current Flyer personnel.

"In today's NHL, in the last five years, it's all defense," Matt Read recalls. "Videos and everything are all defense, back checking, back pressure, defensive zone. Laviolette did teach that, but he also preached how to score goals, how we can gain separation in the offensive zone.

"He wanted us to score. Your defense will take care of itself if you're playing smart and the right way. I think guys were cheating (defensively) too much. He tried different things to fix it, and maybe it slowed down our game.

"[Laviolette] was a very well-spoken, knowledgeable coach. If you didn't have a good game, he wasn't afraid to pull you aside and talk to you for thirty seconds. He would say the right things and get you re-motivated, get you to put your thinking cap back on. I respected him a lot.

"Being my first (NHL) coach, I thought he showed up to the rink every day with the right attitude and was teaching us the right way to play hockey. Things just didn't go the way that everyone wanted it to. Maybe it was time for a change but for me, it was sad. He gave me my first opportunity to play in the NHL."

Read texted Laviolette and thanked him, acknowledging that he probably wouldn't be where he was without the coach's help. But even his biggest supporters understood the firing.

"I think the combination of our D-zone with his offensive style of attack just never really came together," recalls Brayden Schenn. "That's kind of how it all went down. He was offensive-minded and guys had a lot of success under him.

"We didn't have a very good preseason. It was a different feeling. You could tell the pressure was rising. Then we had the 0-3 start and you could sense something was going to happen."

Berube, the new coach, did not anticipate a change, however. "It was surprising," he recalls. "Usually you give it a little more time than that.

"You always think that maybe you'll get the opportunity (to become a head coach), but it was a tough deal. Lavvy was good to me. You don't want to see a coach get fired. I don't, anyhow. That's not the way I work. It was a tough situation, but management was obviously displeased the year before not making the playoffs. And Mr. Snider was unhappy with training camp. [That] had a lot to do with it.

"I think our big problem was going over to the (Wells Fargo) Center to have camp. It's dead in there, and it's hot. You only have one ice surface rather than two. I don't think camp was great and we just didn't get off to a good start."

At the press conference, Holmgren called the move a "gut decision."

"We're not playing well enough to win in the National Hockey League," the GM said, "and that's got to change. Whether it's fresh ideas or a new voice, that's up to Craig. That's his job. But I didn't like the direction the team was heading. We needed a change.

"Craig is one of the smartest hockey guys I've ever been around. He's a no-frills, no-BS guy."

Snider told reporters that the coaching change was Holmgren's call all the way. "If the general manager feels he has to make a change, I approve it," said the Chairman. "It's as simple as that."

Bristling at a suggestion that the Flyers were promoting too much from within and needed a culture change, Snider said, "We haven't won a championship, [but] we've been in the Stanley Cup Final a lot of times and we've been in the playoffs a lot of times. The culture is to win. That's our culture."

Laviolette's long-time assistant Kevin McCarthy was also let go. Paddock, as suggested by Holmgren, agreed to become coach of the defensemen. Ian Laperriere was moved from director of player development to be another assistant on the bench, while Joe Mullen was retained to run the power play and be the "eye-in-the-sky," Jeff Reese stayed on as goaltending coach.

Kjell Samuelsson was promoted to director of player development, assuming Laperriere's previous responsibilities, and Derian Hatcher was retained as Samuelsson's right-hand man.

Berube's immediate challenge was to restore player confidences that had begun to wane during the previous year. With three days to prepare for his first game, the Chief—as he had become known over 1,054 games of locker room leadership as a player with five NHL teams and seven seasons working in various coaching capacities for Philadelphia—adjusted the team's forechecking and pinching strategies. Laviolette's bread and butter left-wing lock was cancelled and the centers given more defensive responsibility.

"I really stressed the third man high and holding that position while the other two forwards worked to cycle down low," Berube recalls. "I'd had enough of the odd man rushes."

A difference was immediately noticeable in Berube's debut against Florida. When Brayden Schenn scored from the slot in the opening five minutes, the Flyers had their first even-strength goal of the season. Coburn scored into the empty net after Tim Thomas suffered a groin pull to make it 2-0 before the ten-minute mark. Although the 0-for-5 powerplay still needed work, Mason stopped 34 of 35 shots in Philadelphia's 2-1 win.

"It's not so much a defense-minded approach," the coach said. "We want to be aggressive on both sides of the puck. I want them to play the team game all the time, to understand that they don't want to let their teammates down or leave [their] goalie out to dry."

The Flyers largely outplayed Phoenix in a 2-1 home loss. But as Berube was demanding more defensive responsibility, the offense was going to suffer until the hesitation came out of the players' games.

Michael Raffl, a 24-year-old Austrian winger signed as a free agent over the summer, had started camp promisingly before tailing off in the final week. But as Scott Hartnell suffered an upper body injury in the Phoenix game, Raffl was recalled from the Phantoms and made his debut in Detroit.

Berube was prioritizing an improvement in discipline. That might take a while. Three Red Wing powerplay goals in seven opportunities doomed Philadelphia to a 5-2 loss at Joe Louis Arena.

Back home, the Flyers took only three penalties against Vancouver, but lost energy in the third period, as a 2-1 lead turned into a 3-2 loss. Full period letdowns were a recurring problem. Bombarded by 17 Pittsburgh shots and three goals in the second period of a 4-1 home loss, Mason called out his teammates for playing "terrible hockey."

At 1-7, Philadelphia was suffering the worst start in team history. Giroux, coming off his summer golf accident, had no goals and just two assists in the first eight contests, but as Berube drilled his players during a welcome six days between games, the captain decided to step up.

"When you have the record we have right now, you're a little frustrated and you try to figure out what's going on," Giroux said following practice on October 22. "There's a lot of hockey left to play here. How many points are we off? Six? Even with the start we had, we're that close.

"We'll take it game by game and we will make the playoffs."

Either a solid week of intense workouts was beginning to get a re-

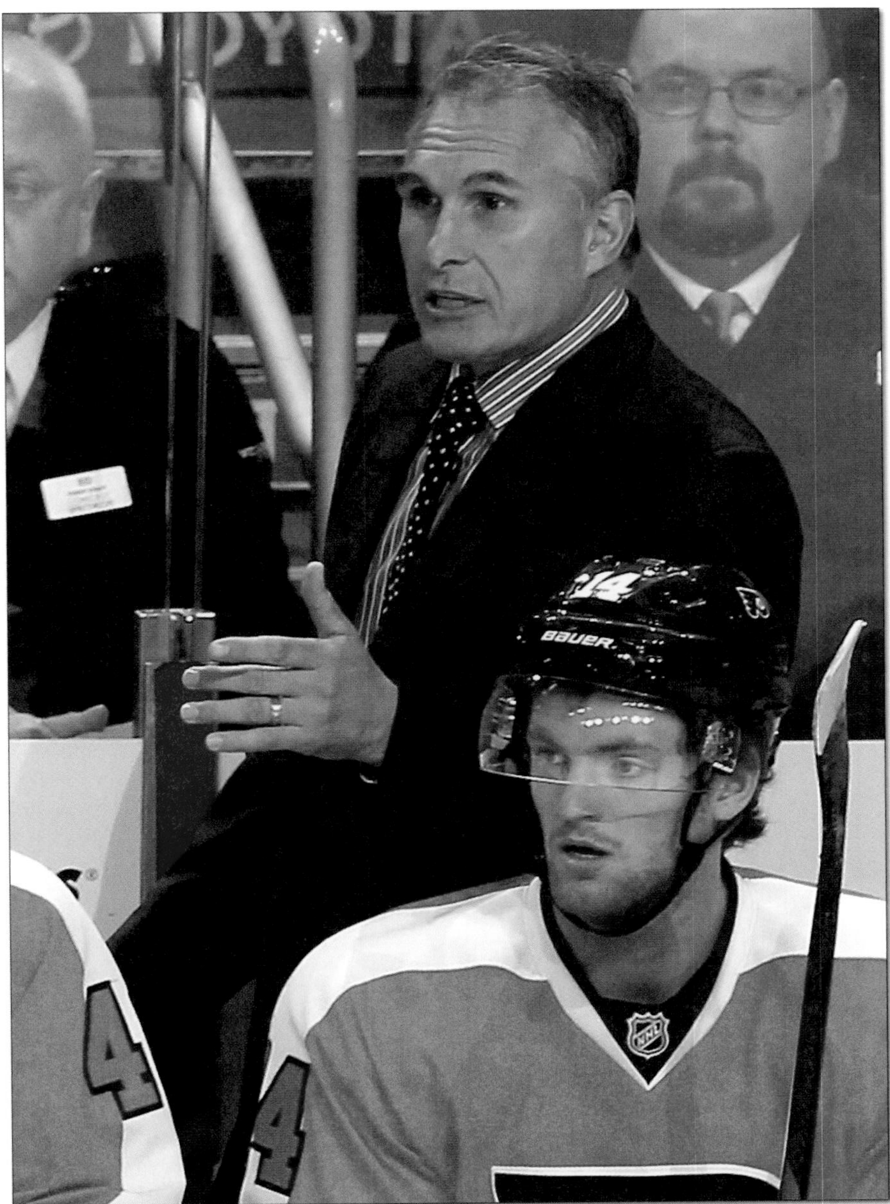

Newly appointed head coach Craig Berube wanted the Flyers to pressure the puck carrier and prevent odd-man rushes, making them better able to protect a lead.

sponse or the Rangers, who dragged a 2-6 record into town, showed up in the knick of time. The Flyers used a shorthanded breakaway goal by Reed, a seeing-eye long distance goal by Coburn, and Mason's 31 saves to break a four-game losing streak with a 2-1 victory.

When Lecavalier's hat trick sunk the Islanders, 5-2, at Uniondale, Philadelphia avoided becoming the first NHL team since 1940 to not score three goals in any of its first 10 games. But after jumping up 2-0 on Anaheim, the Flyers faded again into a 3-2 loss.

With the hope of adding some skill while not sacrificing grit, Holmgren traded Max Talbot to Colorado to re-acquire Steve Downie, Philadelphia's first-round pick in 2005. Frequently an on-ice disciplinary problem during his initial run with the Flyers, Downie had seemed to settle down, establishing his worth with a 22-goal season for Tampa Bay in 2009-10, but subsequently hit a valley after tearing his ACL.

Berube had coached Downie, who is deaf in his right ear, for a short time with the Phantoms and liked both his potential as a playmaker and fearlessness.

The following night, the Flyers had badly outplayed Washington for the first period at the Wells Fargo Center until giving up a late first period goal. They rapidly started turning over pucks and completely fell apart. The Caps were leading 5-0 at the Wells Fargo Center and the fans chanting, 'Fire Holmgren!' when Downie dropped his gloves with Aaron Volpatti and was penalized for instigation. Troy Brouwer converted the powerplay to make it 6-0.

After Joel Ward completed a hat trick for a seventh Capital goal, Simmonds went hunting. He ran over Steven Oleksy while chasing down a loose puck in the Washington zone, and then slammed into Tom Wilson along the boards. Wilson and Simmonds began swinging wildly at each other while Emery, who had replaced Mason after the third goal, raced toward Washington goalie Brayden Holtby to challenge him to a fight. The surprised Holtby was not interested, but Emery pummeled him anyway.

The clock wound down on Philadelphia's 7-0 defeat, its biggest shutout loss since 1994.

"When you're getting slapped around like that, it's a response from an embarrassed hockey team," Holmgren said.

Asked if he heard the fan vitriol directed at him, the GM added, "If I were sitting in the stands, I'm not sure I'd be chanting, but I might be thinking the same thing. It's part of the business."

NHL Commissioner Gary Bettman said there was no rule that allowed the league to suspend Emery. Media criticism for the goalie's behavior would have made a Broad Street Bully blush. But the Flyers were unrepentant.

"Even though the crowd booed us the whole game, it felt like a win after that little scrum," Hartnell said. "We love it. Fans love it here in Philly. It's part of our heritage. We feed off it."

At 3-9, the only shame the team felt was over its record.

"It can't get a whole lot lower, can it?" Berube asked.

The following night, the coach started Emery at Newark, where the Flyers received a first period tip-in goal by Brayden Schenn. By not turning over the puck once the entire game, Philadelphia nursed the lead into a 1-0 win over the 3-6-4 Devils. Emery had to stop only 14 shots.

"Ray's been a winner and a battler his whole life; I knew he'd have a good game," Berube said. "The guys were very frustrated and upset at the game against Washington. I knew the focus was there."

The Flyers would need more than one win against an equally struggling opponent to be convincing that a turnaround had begun. At Raleigh, they played almost as tightly as they did in Newark and took a 1-0 lead on Hartnell's powerplay tip-in of a Timonen shot with four minutes remaining. But Jordan Staal beat Mason from the top of the circle with just 53 seconds left on the clock, and Streit's giveaway on Manny Malhotra's goal in overtime sent Philadelphia down to a disheartening 2-1 defeat.

Two nights later at the Wells Fargo Center, Adam Henrique's redirect on only the second shot of the game gave New Jersey a 1-0 lead. This time, the Devils took charge, limiting the Flyers to just 22 shots, none of them threatening, in a 3-0 loss that was the team's most lifeless yet.

"It's my job to get them to play better," said Berube, and it also was the players' responsibility to take accountability. They called a postgame meeting. When the doors opened late to the media, the still-goalless Giroux declined to speak. But the next day at practice, the Chairman did.

"When Paul let Peter Laviolette go, I said we can't fire all the players," Snider told reporters. "I'm hoping that they'll snap out of it and show us the kind of talent they've shown in the past and that we believe they still have.

"We all know what they can do. It's not like they're all new guys. Everyone knows what kind of talent Claude Giroux is. Jake (Voracek) scored 22 goals last year."

Through 15 games, the Flyers had scored only 22 goals, only one by Voracek and still none by Giroux. "I think we've got good young players in place and I'm patient in that regard," said Holmgren.

The following afternoon against Edmonton, Philadelphia jumped up 2-0 on goals by Jay Rosehill and Hartnell, but were hanging on 2-1 in the third period when Giroux carried the puck from his own zone, cut to the middle and beat goalie Devan Dubnyk to the stick side. Not only was it the captain's first goal, but his team's initial clutch third-period score of the season.

"To see all the boys on the bench being happy, that was really fun," said Giroux after Lecavalier's sixth goal assured a 4-2 victory.

"I think the team was waiting for G to get going, and obviously when he scored the goal against Edmonton, it elevated his game," Berube recalls. "He started leading by example. You need your best player to be your best player."

Leadership can extend beyond a lifetime. A charter jetload of Broad Street Bullies and Flyer staffers were Snider's guests for Fred Shero's Hall of Fame induction in Toronto on November 11.

"When he wrote on the board 'Win and we will walk together forever,' it wasn't so significant at the time," said Clarke in a video message that preceded Ray Shero's acceptance speech. "But now that we're older, it is, because he was right.

"He deserves to be in the Hall of Fame because he was the greatest innovator of his time. And a winner."

An organization of such heritage never has taken its downturns lightly, always adding to the stress level whenever confidence is low. But the victory over Edmonton seemed to finally relieve some tension. Lecavalier scored for the sixth time in seven games, and Mason stopped all 24 shots in a 5-0 win at Ottawa. When Brayden Schenn scored twice in a 2-1 road win over the Metropolitan Division-leading Penguins, Berube's team had its first triumph over a quality opponent.

Giroux's early goal ignited a 5-2 win over the Senators, and two goals by Read helped Philadelphia to a 4-1 home win over the Sabres. When the Islanders chopped a 3-0 deficit at the Wells Fargo Center down to 3-2, the Flyers demonstrated their new resiliency in a 5-2 victory.

"They believe they can win," Berube said. "We killed off two big penalties there in the third; huge kills. We were on our heels, but did what we had to do to win the game."

The unbeaten streak ended at seven with a lackluster 3-1 loss at lowly Florida. "Who are we to overlook anybody?" asked Berube. Another poor start two nights later at Tampa, leading to a 4-2 loss, made only a Lecavalier goal in his homecoming worth the trip to the Sunshine State.

The team bounced back though. Couturier's unassisted shorthanded breakaway goal proved the winner in a 2-1 Black Friday home win over Winnipeg. A six-game trip began the following night in Nashville with Lecavalier's shootout goal providing a 3-2 victory, but after struggling with some back pain over the last few games, he was found to have a non-displaced fracture that was expected to keep him out of the lineup for at least three weeks.

Wayne Simmonds was one of seven Flyers to finish the season with 20-or-more goals.

Fortunately Couturier stayed hot, contributing four assists as Philadelphia won for only the second time in its last 19 visits to Joe Louis Arena, 6-3.

The Flyers had stabilized themselves back to .500, 13-13-2, when their hierarchy underwent a significant disruption. Comcast-Spectator president Peter Luukko announced his resignation on December 2, citing family reasons and other business opportunities.

On the recommendation of Comcast chairman and CEO Brian Roberts, Snider asked the recently-retired Dave Scott, the former top official in the company's cable division, to take Luukko's place.

"I had been in the cable business for a log time, thought it was time to do something different," recalls Scott. "I was 60, wasn't going to just lie on the beach. When Brian, and then Ed, who I knew just a little, called, it just sounded so interesting."

Gary Rostick, who had been the chief financial officer of Comcast's business service division, was appointed the new chief financial officer at Comcast-Spectacor.

On the ice, Raffl's first NHL goal helped the Flyers to their only other point on the road trip, a 5-4 shootout loss in Ottawa. The team was overwhelmed in Dallas, 5-1, and in Chicago, 7-2, to close the journey.

The first home game after a long trip is usually a motivational minefield. Nevertheless, after returning to Philadelphia in the wee hours, Berube had his team prepared the very next night. Raffl, moving up to the top line, scored in the first period, and his new center Giroux tallied in the second. With assists on both goals by Voracek, the Flyers ruined Danny Briere's homecoming with a 2-1 win over the Canadiens. "That's a character game there," said Mason.

A 4-1 third period lead in Washington distressingly disappeared into a 5-4 shootout loss. But in the second half of the home-and-home, Philadelphia used a five-minute penalty (on Tom Wilson for hitting Brayden Schenn from behind) to score two powerplay goals and pull away to beat the Caps 5-2.

Down 3-0 at home to Columbus, and trailing 4-1 with less than five minutes remaining, the Flyers rallied. Giroux set up Voracek's goal to start the comeback, tied the game with 3:46 to go, and then picked up a rebound of a Streit shot, and, while falling, roofed a backhander over Columbus goalie Curtis McElhinney's glove and under the crossbar with 1:38 remaining. The 100th goal of the captain's career was the most visually astonishing yet.

"He put all 20 of us on his back," said Hartnell.

Two nights later in Columbus, as Lecavalier returned, late second-period goals 20 seconds apart by Simmonds and Couturier rallied Philadelphia back to a 2-2 tie, but the team crashed in a 6-3 loss.

The Flyers weren't always efficient, but they were resilient. Two goals by Simmonds helped them to a 4-1 home win over Minnesota that pushed Berube's club over .500 at 17-16-4.

A six-game trip started in Edmonton with two Simmonds goals for a third straight contest, Hartnell's late tying score and shootout markers by Giroux and Raffl on old friend Ilya Bryzgalov in Mason's 5-4 victory.

At Vancouver, Luke Schenn accidentally knocked the puck into his

own net to put the team down 3-2 with 2:22 to go, but brother Brayden scored in the final minute and Lecavalier's shootout goal made Mason the winner again, 4-3. "For the guys to show that kind of resiliency after a pretty deflating goal is nice," said Mason. "Realistically, I don't think we could have done that two months ago. We were pretty fragile then."

Emery rang in a happy New Year with a 4-1 win at Calgary. By going 17-7-4 since the 3-9 start, Philadelphia had moved into third place in the division and—under the revised postseason format that rewarded the three division winners and two wild cards—was in playoff position.

In Colorado, the Flyers fell one goal short of a comeback in a 2-1 loss, but down 3-2 in the third period at Phoenix, Simmonds scored on the powerplay, then Voracek off a steal from Keith Yandle. Giroux's empty-net goal finished off a rousing 5-3 win.

Ray Emery had earned a share of the Jennings Trophy with Corey Crawford in Chicago in 2012-13 before joining the Flyers where he would appear in 28 games, posting a 2.96 goals-against average and two shutouts in 2013-14.

The captain's resurgence did not get him a place on the Team Canada roster, announced on January 7, for the 2014 Olympic Games in Sochi, Russia. Unlike the centers selected—Sidney Crosby, Ryan Getzlaf and Jonathan Toews—Giroux couldn't bring a good Flyer linemate with him; instant chemistry being the priority of GM Steve Yzerman in the absence of preparation time. Voracek would be playing for the Czech Republic.

Giroux took his disappointment out on the Devils, scoring the tying goal early in the third period as Philadelphia won at Newark, 3-2, on Brayden Schenn's overtime goal. "Anytime somebody takes something away from you, you want to prove them wrong," said Giroux. "But I put that behind me.

"It's a fun game, I'm not going to stress myself."

For the second time in the season, the Canadiens were rested and waiting as the Flyers played at home the night following the completion of a six-game trip. Once more they professionally ground down Montreal, in this instance with Andrej Meszaros—who had been restored to the lineup by an injury to Erik Gustafsson—contributing three assists in a 3-1 victory.

A top-four defense of Timonen, Coburn, Streit and Nicklas Grossmann lacked a true anchor and, except for Coburn, foot speed. Holmgren was shopping for a partner for the struggling Luke Schenn to upgrade the third pair. But the team defense was improved under Berube's system, and the powerplay and penalty killing both hovered in or near the top five of the league.

Philadelphia's goaltending, which had been outstanding since the start of the season, finally faltered a bit. Mason gave up five goals in 17 Lightning shots and got the hook in the 6-3 loss that ended a home winning streak at 10. Emery then allowed three in the first 10 minutes of a 4-1 defeat in New York that had the Rangers leap over the Flyers into second place in the division.

At Buffalo, Mason let in three goals on just 19 shots, but his teammates came from behind twice before Lecavalier, scoring for the first time in 12 games since his return, won the game 4-3, with 15 seconds remaining. Mason returned the favor against Nashville with a 34-save effort that earned the club a point in a 3-2 home shootout loss.

Holmgren was impressed enough by Mason, an upcoming restricted free agent, to give him a three-year extension worth $12.3 million. The announcement on January 18 called for a celebration, but instead, Mason was pulled after the Islanders went ahead 4-3, but Voracek and Raffl goals, and another by Giroux into the empty net, brought Philadelphia back to a 6-4 victory. During the rematch at Uniondale, leaks continued to spring up in the Flyer defense and forward lines as two third-period goals against Emery wiped out a 3-1 lead, resulting in a 4-3 shootout loss.

Emery was a victim of non-support in a 5-2 defeat by Sergei Bobrovsky and the Blue Jackets at Columbus. "Sloppy hockey," said Brayden Schenn before it got worse. Mason was yanked again in 6-1 home shellacking by Boston that lengthened Philadelphia's 0-3-1 losing streak. "We're going away from how we were winning games," said Giroux.

Detroit came to town without Pavel Datsyuk, Henrik Zetterberg and Johan Franzen, but Mason still needed 33 saves to right himself with a 5-0 shutout, good for everybody's soul before the Flyers headed to California for contests with three Stanley Cup contenders.

In Anaheim, Philadelphia gave the overall-standings leader a good effort in a 5-3 loss, dropping Berube's club to 3-6-2 in its last 11 games. "That's a very good team over there," said the coach. "We played with them, but that's not good enough."

Thirteen shots proved plenty in Los Angeles, where Simmonds scored on the powerplay in the second period against his ex-mates, and Giroux put away into the empty net a 34-save Mason masterpiece, 2-0, over the Stanley Cup champions. "I know we didn't create a lot offensively, but we capitalized on the powerplay goal, which is huge," said Berube. "I like the competitiveness of the team right now."

It carried over at San Jose for yet another big third period—four goals—in a 5-2 victory, the tenth in which the Flyers had trailed sometime in the third period and the first for them against the Sharks in 13 contests going back 14 years. "This was one of those games where I was just telling myself to keep it at two goals," said Mason. "The way the guys were playing it was only a matter of time before they found the back of the net."

The following day, February 3, former Philadelphia GM Keith Allen died at an assisted living facility in Delaware County. The architect of the two-time Cup winning Broad Street Bullies, and one of the most brilliant general managers in the game's history, died of chronic obstructive pulmonary disease at the age of 90.

As Snider noted in his eulogy at the Bryn Mawr Presbyterian Church, a bold and brilliant series of Allen trades and draft choices not only had made the Flyers the first of the 1967 expansion teams to go all the way, but the only one of the six that even had a winning record the year of Philadelphia's first championship.

"I can't remember one player he traded away in his 14 years as GM that we would come to regret," said Snider. "In our sport, I have not seen a track record like this since.

"I was thrilled when he was inducted into the Hockey Hall of Fame (1992), almost as grateful as I am today in looking back at our phenomenal working relationship."

Snider and Allen had shared a vision not only of how to build a winner but also of a working relationship with the players that was practically new to the game. The same was true of their special GM and owner bond. The Chairman told mourners that a year after the Flyers traded Dave Schultz, Snider urged Allen to bring back the popular enforcer. Weary of the pressure, Allen snapped, "You want him so goddamn badly, I'll get him for you."

"To me," explained Snider, "that said, 'You're the owner, but this is against my better judgment.' Far be it from me to question that, so I backed down."

Cool and calculating as a GM, warm and beloved as a father figure even by players he traded away, Allen was memorialized as both a boss and a parent by the youngest of his three children, Blake.

"Right now, Dad probably has St. Peter's No. 1 draft choice," he said. "If he is looking down on us all today, at his family and dear friends gathered in this beautiful place in his honor, he's probably shaking his head in that humble way he had, knitting an eyebrow and thinking, 'Not bad...'"

Mason's 38 saves in a 3-1 victory over Colorado to start a homestand weren't too shabby either.

When Steven Stamkos had to pull out of the Olympics because of injury, there was a ray of anticipation that Giroux might be the replacement. But Yzerman, the Lightning general manager, chose another of his players—Martin St. Louis.

"I didn't give myself hope," Giroux said. "I didn't want to be disappointed again."

His friend, however, saw the letdown. "We went out to lunch at our normal pregame spot," said Hartnell. "He was a little quiet. We all know how much he wanted to go."

Once again, Giroux expressed his frustration with a strong performance. His third period shot off Hartnell produced the winner in a 2-1 victory over Calgary.

The Flyers split for their 19-day Olympic break in the best of moods, including the Chairman.

"I love where we are right now," Snider said. "I think our goaltending, the way we're playing, and the system Craig Berube has instituted are outstanding. I've got my fingers crossed."

Philadelphia was not represented on either the Canadian or U.S. teams at Sochi. But Meszaros played for Slovakia, Raffl for Austria, and Streit for Switzerland. Timonen's Finland team and Voracek's Czech Republic club had realistic medal hopes.

Streit's team upset the Czech Republic 1-0, and hung in with the Swedes in a 1-0 loss, before being eliminated by Latvia. Voracek had a goal and an assist in five games as the Czechs got past Slovakia in the medal round before being eliminated by the U.S. in the quarterfinals, 5-2.

Canada struggled past Latvia, 2-1, in the quarters, then got a goal from Jamie Benn and threw a 1-0 blanket on Team USA in one semifinal. Sweden outlasted Finland, 2-1, in the other but then couldn't solve another spectacular defensive effort by the Canadiens, who won the gold medal, 3-0.

In the bronze medal game, the disappointed Americans were easy prey for a veteran and proud Finnish team, 5-0. Timonen, adding a third medal to the bronze he won in Nagano in 1998 and his silver in 2006 at Torino, brought his prize to the Skate Zone as the Flyers reassembled after the break.

"I kept reading that some of you thought we didn't have a chance," he teased reporters. "It was like a dream come true. It was emotional for me and everyone there. I knew it was going to be my last time putting that jersey on."

Berube gave the 38-year-old Timonen the first game off as NHL play resumed. He was missed as the Sharks scored five second-period goals in a 7-3 rout at the Wells Fargo Center. "We had a week to practice, our effort was pretty crappy if you ask me," said Mason.

The Flyers faced 17 games in the next 30 days and had a remaining schedule that included five matches against Western powerhouses in addition to Eastern teams competing with Philadelphia for the same playoff positions. A postseason spot looked daunting, but one game at a time, the Flyers were proving the skeptics wrong. With Simmonds breaking a second-period tie, Mason bounced back for a 4-2 home win over the Rangers. The following afternoon, third period goals by Voracek and Giroux and a shootout winner by Lecavalier produced a 5-4 thriller in Washington.

"Coming through in one of the biggest moments of the year is great to see," said Mason. "For us to be able to force overtime and then get a second point against a divisional opponent right behind us, that's huge."

So was the need to add to add another solid veteran defenseman. At the trading deadline, Holmgren dealt a third round pick in the 2014 draft and a 2015 second rounder, plus minor leaguer Matt Mangene, to the Islanders for 27-year-old Andrew MacDonald.

Working ahead as usual on an expiring contract, Holmgren hoped to be able to sign the upcoming unrestricted free agent, a strong second-pair blueliner who had not been as effective when given bigger minutes on Long Island but still led the league in blocked shots. "A solid two-way defenseman who brings us depth and experience," he was called by the GM.

"I was really excited," recalls MacDonald. "Between the crowds and the Flyers' style of play, games Philly were always easy to get up for."

To make room, Holmgren traded Meszaros, a healthy scratch in 20 games, to Boston in exchange for a third-round pick.

MacDonald debuted against the Capitals, who needed to get back the two points the Flyers had taken from them in a late rally two days earlier. But as Giroux scored twice, and Voracek and Raffl once each to build a 4-0 lead, Washington managed just eight shots through two periods.

As Philadelphia began to sit on the 4-0 lead, the Caps made it back to within 4-3 before Voracek scored with 8:09 to play. That breathing room lasted barely two minutes before Brooks Laich's goal turned knuckles white again at the Wells Fargo Center. Downie, who had been struggling with a concussion and hearing loss in both ears, put his first goal since December 11 into the empty net, and, with a sweep, the Flyers had dealt a severe blow to Washington's postseason chances.

An uphill climb from an early 2-0 deficit at Toronto was climaxed by Coburn's goal with 2:32 remaining, enabling Philadelphia to pull out a point even though losing in overtime, 4-3, on Joffrey Lupul's goal. When Jaromir Jagr brushed past Streit for a third-period score in a 2-1 New Jersey win at the Wells Fargo Center, the Devils had pulled within two points of Berube's third-place team in the multi-club race for the third automatic playoff spot in the division.

To dedicate an eight-foot statue of Fred Shero—created by South Jersey sculptor Chad Fisher—outside of XFINITY Live complex, the Flyers chose the morning of a Penguin visit so that their iconic coach's son Ray, the Pittsburgh GM, could participate in the ceremonies. He spoke of the dominance of his father's teams, reiterating that not only did they win two Stanley Cups, but also "kicked the crap out of the Soviet Red Army."

"And Pittsburgh!" Snider shouted from the front row. There were laughs all around, but none from the conference leading Penguins that night. As in days of yore, the Pens were kicked, 4-0.

The following afternoon at the CONSOL Energy Center, two Simmonds powerplay goals helped stake Philadelphia to a stunning 3-0 lead. Reed's second shorthanded tally in two days held up for a 4-3 victory and the second sweep of a home-and-home against a division rival in two weeks.

It didn't seem like it could get any better than that, but it did. The Flyers erased an early 2-0 deficit to the Blackhawks with two Hartnell goals before the first period break and won, 3-2, with just five seconds remaining in overtime on an end-to-end rush by Giroux. It was the captain's 51st point since December 11, the most of any player in the league.

His team, 18-2-1 in games during which he scored a goal, continued to roll at home. Dallas fell, 4-2, on a pair by Simmonds. So did St. Louis, 3-1, as Voracek and Hartnell took turns setting up each other. Philadelphia, winner of five straight, was 38-25-7 and holding a three-point lead over Columbus, the closest divisional and wild card pursuer.

Berube's club was 13-3-1 in its last 17 games before the Kings visited, bringing Jeff Carter for his first Wells Fargo Center appearance since his trade 21 months earlier. His goal, and another in the third period off a mix-up between Hartnell and Timonen, cooled down Philadelphia, 2-1. "I know Jeff wanted this game bad," said Justin Williams, another ex-Flyer with a Kings' Stanley Cup ring.

Two nights later at Madison Square Garden, Philadelphia lost again, 3-1, falling three points behind the Rangers in what was shaping up to become a battle between the two teams for home ice in a first-round series. "They checked well and we kind of just let it happen," said Berube. "Not enough fight tonight.

"This time of year things tighten up and you don't get easy goals. You've got to get to the net, get rebounds."

The coach dropped Lecavalier, goalless in six games and, according to Berube, struggling in every zone, onto the fourth line, but moved him back to center, his natural position, after a season spent mostly on the wing. The veteran responded with the game-opening goal in a 4-2 home win over the Leafs.

"He came out with an attitude," said Hartnell. "He was all over the puck, and playing great defensively. You can take [the demotion] two ways. You can sulk and be a baby about it, or do what he did."

Two days later, against Boston, Lecavalier continued to respond, opening the game with the 400th goal of his career and then climaxing his team's third-period push (17-6 in shots) by tying the game 3-3 with 15 seconds remaining. The Flyers dominated the overtime, too, but Giroux was their only scorer in a 4-3 shootout defeat.

In St. Louis, a goalless 65 minutes sent Philadelphia to another shootout, which Emery lost, 1-0, on goals by T.J. Oshie and Kevin Shattenkirk while Ryan Miller was stopping both Giroux and Lecavalier. The offensive frustration was building, but again one point was better than none, as the Flyers, still four points ahead of fourth-place Columbus with six games to go, inched closer to a playoff spot.

When the Blue Jackets visited on April 3, they scored a powerplay goal, Philadelphia did not, and 37 saves by Sergei Bobrovsky in his Wells Fargo Center return sent the Flyers down to a second-straight shutout loss, 2-0. Philadelphia finally got back on a scoreboard with second period goals by Simmonds and Rosehill that created a 2-2 tie at Boston, but Johnny Boychuk and Milan Lucic scored 31 seconds apart in the third to send Berube's team to its sixth loss in seven games.

"I thought that we competed hard through two periods and were in good shape," said the Flyer coach. "We had to go out and initiate the third period and didn't."

His team still held third by two points and had a cushion of three for the final wild card spot. But the club's game the next night at home against 21-47-9 Buffalo was not one to be squandered. Reed's first period goal kept the panic down and as Braydon Schenn became the sixth Flyer to reach the 20-goal mark, Philadelphia breezed, 5-2.

"I think it really helps," Berube said. "You lose shootouts, it feels like a loss. We didn't score at all in the one at St. Louis, and then didn't win the next two. This was important to get the guys' spirits back up."

Morale got another boost when a Devils loss to the Rangers put the Flyers in position to clinch a playoff spot with a win at 28-43-8 Florida. Just two minutes in, Lecavalier became the team's seventh 20-goal scorer, and then Giroux tallied twice on a wrister and then a one-timer in the second period to help build a 4-0 lead.

It was too early to celebrate, however, as Philadelphia was outshot 16-3 in the third period. But after the Panthers crept back to within two goals, call-up Tye McGinn put away a 5-2 victory and the Flyers' 37th playoff spot in 46 years of competition.

In many ways, this was the most difficult ever earned. Since the NHL began rewarding a point for overtime losses in 1999-2000—making it harder to close ground in a race—no other team had ever recorded nine points or fewer in its first 15 games (3-9-3) and made the postseason. From that start, Philadelphia had gone 38-20-6, earning 16 points from 100-point teams since the beginning of February, and running a gauntlet of playoff-bound clubs in the final 29 games.

The Flyers had done it with reliable goaltending, deep scoring, and a defense most personnel evaluators around the league had thought was not good enough to support a postseason qualifier. With 12 holdovers from the team that had missed the playoffs in the shortened season of a year earlier, and a new system installed without the benefit of a training camp, Berube, had done a superior job.

So had the players. The coach told them to be proud. "They went through a lot," Berube told reporters. "They're a good group of guys, good character, and they deserve a lot of credit."

No one earned more than Giroux, who had expressed confidence at a point when both he and the team were playing with practically none. He had delivered like a superstar.

"People looked at me with crazy eyes when I said [we would make the playoffs]," the captain said in the happy locker room. "I just believed we had a good team. We had four lines rolling, eight defensemen that can play a lot of minutes, and two good goaltenders."

Recalls Simmonds, "It was a great statement that G backed up. And then we, in turn, had to back him up. We really took that to heart.

"Chief came in and said, 'You got to play defense, defense, defense.' We couldn't keep playing the way we did when we had Pronger and (a younger) Kimmo back there, and could sort of freelance. But I also think that no matter what the message, hearing a different voice helped."

A 4-2 Philadelphia loss at Tampa Bay and the Rangers 2-1 win over Buffalo eliminated the last chance to have home ice in the first round. But as the Flyers went to Pittsburgh, they still needed one victory in their final two games to stay out of the wild card and avoid matchups with either 117-point Boston or 109-point Penguins. So, after using Emery against the Lightning, Berube went back to Mason.

With 3:33 remaining in the second period and Philadelphia leading 2-1 on two goals by Voracek, Jayson Megna knocked MacDonald into Mason, snapping back his head. The goalie finished the period but began to suffer a headache and nausea during the intermission.

Emery came on, giving up two goals, including one in the final minute to Kris Letang that tied the score, 3-3. But Streit continued the remarkable Flyer run at CONSOL Energy Center (11-3, counting playoffs since its opening) with a 4-3 winner in overtime. It secured Philadelphia's two vs. three matchup with the Rangers beginning in New York.

Before the season finale at Wells Fargo Center the following afternoon, Giroux, who had finished third in the NHL in scoring behind Crosby and Getzlaf, was presented his third Bobby Clarke Trophy as team MVP. Timonen won his fifth Barry Ashbee Trophy—one behind Eric Desjardins all time—as best defenseman.

Among the regulars Berube rested in a 6-5 shootout loss to Carolina was Emery, who had become the likely goalie to start the playoffs.

Mason's symptoms, exacerbated by reading, watching television, or driving, were not constant, allowing for hope that he could still play in the series. "I would feel fine for portions of the day and then, out of nowhere, fall off," he recalls. "Concussions are a waiting game. There's nothing you can do but sit and hope."

There would be no delay until July 1 for MacDonald to find out his market worth. It was not going to be better than the six years and $30 million he was offered in negotiations by assistant GM Hextall, so the defenseman signed two days after the season ended. He played well in the 28 games since his acquisition and, in a sense, doubled his value by steadying partner Luke Schenn. Holmgren felt MacDonald's age, 27, was right for the big commitment in years and dollars.

After leading Union College to the NCAA championship in a Frozen Four played at the Wells Fargo Center, Shayne Gostisbehere, Philadelphia's best defensive prospect, passed up his senior season, signing an entry-level contract. "I talked it over with my parents and I'm just ready for the next step," he said. Gostisbehere was going to play with the Phantoms for their three remaining games.

Somehow, the Rangers and Flyers, who played seven times in the playoffs in a nine-year period between 1979 and 1987, had met only once in the postseason since then, a five-game Philadelphia triumph in the 1997 conference final.

Under first-year coach Alain Vigneault, New York's strength remained goaltender Henrik Lundqvist and a defense anchored by Ryan McDonagh, Marc Staal, Dan Girardi and Anton Stralman. Discipline was going to be a factor for Philadelphia, the most penalty-prone team in the NHL, going against the ninth-least penalized.

The gentlemanly Rangers were unlikely to engage in anything self-defeating, or, for that matter, rivalry-inducing, part of the reason why Pittsburgh had surpassed New York on the Flyer hate list. Going in, this matchup was almost strictly business. Philadelphia had the most players in the NHL with 20 goals, but couldn't count on its fifth-

ranked powerplay to make the difference. The Rangers had the third-best penalty killing in the NHL.

"Their 'D' and goalie obviously were their best players," Berube recalls. "I talked about puck possession and told our team, 'You've got to chip pucks a lot against these guys and make them turn and go back and take the body.'"

Seven minutes into Game One, Hartnell did as directed. He shouldered McDonagh off the puck as he played a dump-in and fed MacDonald, who rifled his first goal as a Flyer off Martin St. Louis on Philadelphia's initial shot of the series to produce a 1-0 lead.

Four minutes later, Benoit Pouliot won a battle with Coburn in front of the net and backhanded the puck to Mats Zuccarello, whose shot caromed off Derick Brassard and Timonen, dropping in the crease to give Zuccarello a second chance. He scored easily to tie the game 1-1.

The Flyers were largely outplayed for the first two periods. But it still was deadlocked into the third when right wing Jason Akeson, a 24-goal scorer for the Phantoms whom Berube had decided to dress over McGinn, attempted a stick lift, lost his balance and, while going down, clipped Carl Hagelin's face, drawing a double minor.

On the first powerplay, Brad Richards put in a St. Louis rebound. On the second, Richards fed a beautiful cross-ice feed to Derek Stepan in front of a practically empty net to put the Rangers up 3-1.

Philadelphia, hamstrung by not only the Akeson penalty but slashing calls on Giroux and Rinaldo, had just one shot in the third period and only 15 overall. Hagelin added an even strength goal with 4:08 to go in a 4-1 New York win that Berube found particularly annoying.

"There's no reason for it," the coach said of the penalties. "You've got to control your emotions." He then called out the Giroux-Hartnell-Voracek line, which had produced only two shots, both by Hartnell. "They didn't produce, didn't get pucks on net," Berube said.

Akeson, who had played two prior NHL games, was the fall guy in the media for the loss, but the Flyers didn't generate enough attack to believe they should have won.

Four minutes into Game Two, the struggling Coburn led Hall by too much with a pass through center. The Rangers countered quickly, trapping Rinaldo, and Stepan found St. Louis wide open from 20 feet to put New York ahead 1-0 after just 4:08.

With Couturier in the box for roughing Girardi, Benoit Pouliot converted another pass to a virtually empty net, this one by Brassard. Just like in Game One, Ranger goals in close proximity had put Philadelphia in a two-goal hole.

"I didn't think we were playing that bad," Berube would say later. "They had just capitalized on two mistakes."

Emery, getting across his crease to foil Stepan, didn't make a third one and the Flyers broke back up ice. Hartnell led Voracek, who had a step on McDonagh and room to cut in. Lundqvist put his paddle down, but Voracek went around it, scoring a brilliant goal to cut the lead to 2-1.

Early in the second period, Hartnell drew an interference penalty from Stralman. On the powerplay, Lecavalier won a draw from Stepan and shot from 40 feet. The rebound caromed perfectly off Kevin Klein to where Akeson could sweep it in and tie the game, 2-2.

After Emery made back-to-back saves on good St. Louis chances, Pouliot drilled Lecavalier against the halfwall. The referee's arm was up on a delayed penalty as Raffl led a rush so, with nothing to lose, Luke Schenn jumped up into the play. Hall's rebound bounced fortuitously onto the defenseman's backhand and he banged it home to put Philadelphia ahead, 3-2.

Thanks to Emery, the Flyers had scored the only two goals of a second period in which they had been outshot 17-9. His teammates took over from there, playing a superb third period, limiting New York to just seven shots.

The Rangers helped when their extra man left too early as Lundqvist was being pulled—a too-many-men penalty left them shorthanded for the final minute push. Simmonds was stronger than St. Louis to hang onto the puck at center and hit the empty net to complete a stirring comeback 4-2 win that tied the series 1-1.

Philadelphia's first victory at Madison Square Garden in 10 visits belonged to Emery really. With 31 saves, he had been the difference. "He battled all night," said Luke Schenn. "With the amount of penalties we took (nine), he was huge for us."

As a result, Mason, who had passed the concussion protocol and was ready go for Game Three, was not going to be rushed back.

Emery couldn't stay hot, though. Less that four minutes into Game Three at the Wells Fargo Center, Rick Nash threw a puck on goal from deep along the boards that the goalie failed to cleanly glove. At the other side of the net, Stepan quickly pounced to give New York a 1-0 lead. When St. Louis redirected a Girardi drive at 10:24, the Rangers had an early 2-0 advantage for the second straight game.

Just like in New York, the Flyers quickly responded. After Giroux knocked down McDonagh as he carried the puck out of the defensive zone, Voracek tipped the puck out of the reach of Richards and then took a quick feed from Giroux to break down the right wing. Giroux drew coverage to the net, leaving Streit steaming up the middle to redirect Voracek's feed and pull Philadelphia within 2-1 going to the intermission.

Five minutes into the second period, Girardi's 45-footer seemed to be picked up late by Emery, and the Rangers led 3-1. Giroux soon drew two penalties—one a roughing call on Dan Carcillo, the other a charge by Derek Dorsett—but New York had four blocks without allowing a shot on the first powerplay, and smothered another four amidst two Lundqvist saves on the second.

The Flyers were dominating possession, but the Rangers were not breaking. Midway through the third period, Brian Boyle stole the puck from Brayden Schenn and perfectly led Carcillo, who had beaten MacDonald to the net, for a redirect that boosted the New York lead to 4-1.

Berube pulled Emery for Mason, more to give him some work than to inspire a turnaround. Philadelphia had 32 shots on goal, missed the net on 20 more, suffered two hit posts and 28 blocks by the Rangers in a 4-1 defeat. The Flyers were down 2-1 in the series.

"Everything has to happen quicker," said Timonen. "If it means moving the puck sideways or whatever, we have to get some shots through."

Philadelphia's powerplay had gone 0-for-5. "It's so predictable what we're doing with Giroux and Timonen," said Berube. "We've got to get it in [Voracek's) hands more.

"We've had a lot more offensive zone time. But it you don't get to the net, you're not going to score."

Mason had only been forced to stop four shots in relief, but was happy for any game action and pleased by the absence of any recurrent symptoms. He was ready to start Game Four, when Dominic Moore quickly hooked Rinaldo to give the Flyers the first powerplay opportunity. Voracek, Hartnell and Lecavalier all missed the net, though, and Moore came out of the penalty box to surprise MacDonald and take off down the left wing. He shot from a bad angle and Mason covered the post, but not the rebound, as Moore recovered the puck, continued around the net, and beat the goalie with a wraparound giving New York a 1-0 lead.

Later in the period, Pouliot had a step on Coburn, but Mason came across with a denial and Philadelphia countered. Akeson's shot missed the net, but Read was quicker than John Moore to play the carom off the backboards before Lundqvist could come across. The game was tied 1-1.

With Dominic Moore in the box for crosschecking Giroux in the second period, a Voracek rush was ended by a bump from Stralman. Nevertheless, Akeson kicked the puck to Streit at the point. Voracek got up and sneaked behind the defense to redirect a drive by Brayden Schenn, putting the Flyers ahead, 2-1.

Mason, who had been out for 10 days and was unable to practice for most of them, looked sharp regardless. When McDonagh stole from Read, beat Coburn to the net, and went to his backhand, Mason reached out his stick and spectacularly batted the puck out of midair.

Grossmann, going to the boards with Brassard, crashed, had to be helped up and couldn't continue in the game, forcing Philadelphia to play with five defensemen for the duration. But with the help of another huge point-blank save by Mason on Zuccarello, setup by Brassard's passout, the Flyers protected impressively.

In the reverse of the previous game, the Rangers had carried the play but Philadelphia stayed in control. Recording his first career playoff win (1-4), Mason stopped 37 shots and his teammates blocked another 14—five by MacDonald—for a 2-1 victory.

The series was even, 2-2, even without Giroux having scored a goal. "I think he can be more patient," Berube told reporters. "[Big scorers] can get impatient, because it's all about you guys writing he is not scoring and not doing enough."

Grossmann's torn tendons left the coach with a Game Five option of young Gustafsson or Gill, the aged, 6-7 veteran of six teams and 110 playoff games. The coach went for size and experience in what figured to be a limited role.

"Skydivers jump out of planes because they get a rush," Gill said after practice. "I play hockey in the playoffs. That's the high we look for."

Putting the big guy into a Game Five after having dressed only six times all season was a leap of faith without a parachute.

Regardless of lineup, the Flyers, who had given up the first goal in three straight games, had to hit the ground running. But after doing nothing with two early Hagelin penalties, they fell behind again. Staal's shot off a drop pass from St. Louis rode up Coburn's stick and changed direction on Mason, giving New York the 1-0 lead.

Philadelphia received a huge break in the second period when referee Justin St. Pierre blew his whistle before St. Louis put away what should have been a live puck behind Mason. But that did nothing to change the momentum. J.T. Miller retrieved a Hagelin miss and passed through the goalmouth, where Voracek swung and missed and Gill was slow to react. Richards, coming out from behind the net, scored before Mason could get to the post, and the Rangers led 2-0.

Eight minutes later, Coburn put a routine D-to-D pass into the skates of Gill, who had little chance to save himself from a Dominic Moore steal and Mason from a breakaway goal that made it 3-0.

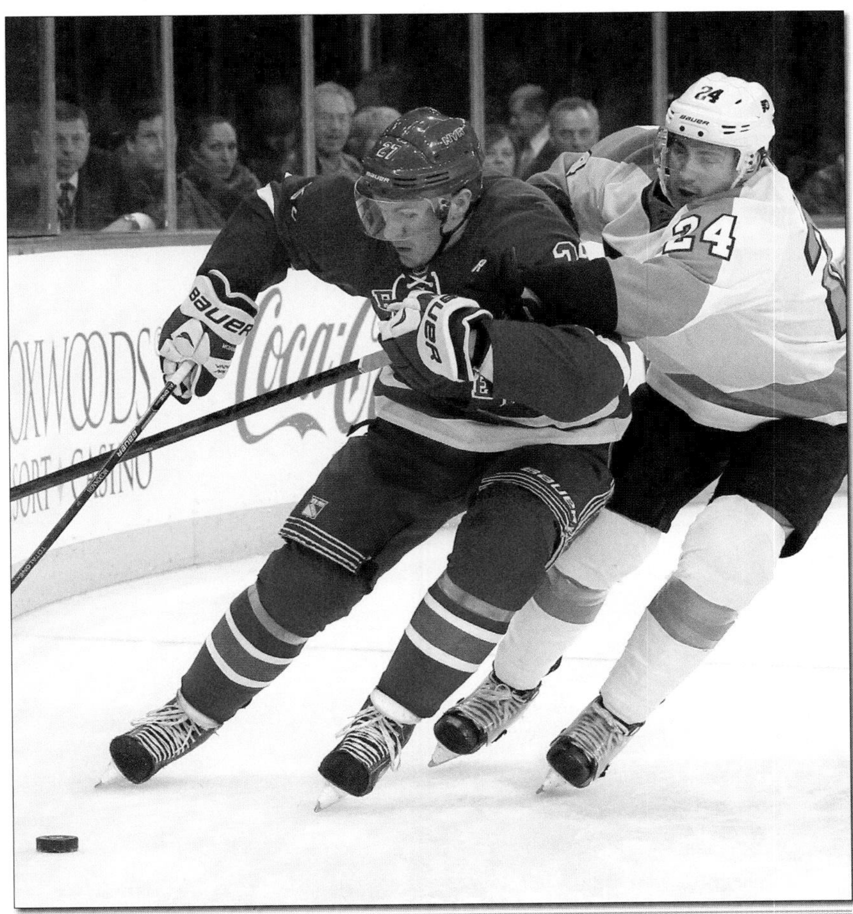

Matt Read checks Ryan McDonagh of the Rangers in Game Two of the Conference quarterfinals won by the Flyers 4-2.

Before the period ended, Stralman was penalized for running into Mason and, on the powerplay, Lecavalier's drive from the top of the circle deflected past Lundqvist to get the Flyers on the board at 3-1.

It took them more than 18 minutes of the third period to creep closer, however. With Mason pulled, Giroux put his first goal of the series, a one-timer from the edge of the circle, through Simmonds' screen and past Lundqvist. But Philadelphia didn't get another good chance. Timonen was bumped off by Dominic Moore, who fed Boyle for an empty-netter that put away New York's 4-2 win and 3-2 series edge.

"It's frustrating always playing catch-up," said Hartnell.

In a series of big swings in the play, the Flyers had not been able to quickly gather themselves through adversity, plus the Ranger quickness was resulting in easier chances than Philadelphia was getting.

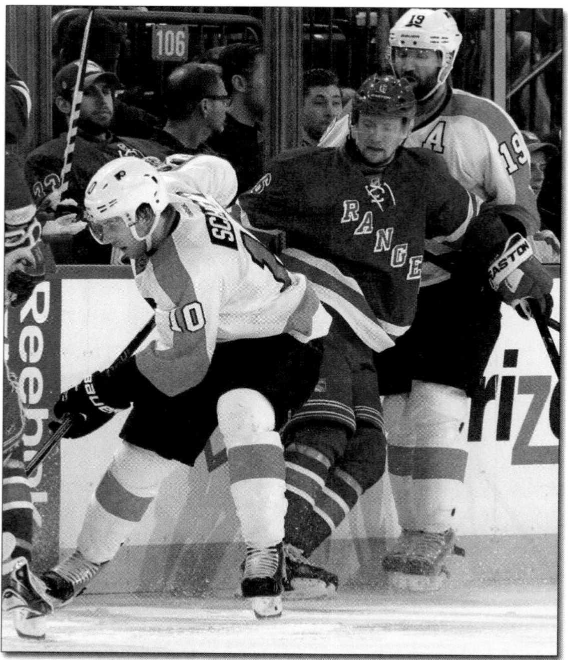
Brayden Schenn and Scott Hartnell battle with Anton Stralman in Game Seven in New York. The Rangers won 2-1.

Gill was out and Gustafsson in for Game Six, when the Flyers flirted with another early deficit. Zuccarello hit the post off a MacDonald giveaway behind the net.

New York may have been a little faster and more efficient in its own end but was not proving to be smarter. Pouliot took an offensive zone penalty for holding Giroux. On the powerplay, Lundqvist came across to rob Simmonds, but the Rangers couldn't get a clear and the Philadelphia winger received another chance. Set up by Hartnell, Simmonds kicked a puck onto his stick, outworked Stralman, and wrapped the puck around Lundqvist to give the Flyers a precious first goal.

Mason flashed his glove on Stralman, who was in the clear at the hash mark, to preserve the 1-0 lead. Early in the second period, Brayden Schenn stole the puck from Girardi to create a two-on-one, and Simmonds put in the rebound to make the score 2-0.

With Gustafsson off for high sticking Dorsett, Richards sent in Pouliot with a long stretch pass. But Mason, looking more confident with each game, brought the crowd to its feet with a sensational glove save. Gustafsson had just come out of the penalty box when Hartnell whacked the puck away from Zuccarello and Coburn threw ahead to Gustafsson 10 feet behind John Moore. The young defenseman roared in and shot the puck through Lundqvist to make the score 3-0.

The New York players could not hide their frustration. Dorsett drove Streit into the end boards, and, on the powerplay, Simmonds completed his hat trick by stuffing in a beautiful pass from Voracek for a 4-0 Philadelphia lead. Caps rained down and Vigneault threw in the towel, deciding to save Lundqvist for Game Seven the following night and going to rookie Cam Talbot for the third period.

The Rangers kept coming, though, and Mason continued to deny them, stopping Hagelin on a breakaway after a steal from Brayden Schenn. Stepan's line, which had accounted for 14 points in the prior four games, was checked efficiently by the Couturier-Read-Akeson unit.

Finally, Hagelin got a rebound past Mason with 6:34 to go, so Vigneault, trailing by three, pulled his goalie, enabling Giroux, who knocked down a Staal clear at the point, to hit the empty net with 4:11 remaining. Before Zuccarello scored on a passout in the final minute, Boyle began preparing for Game Seven with several overhand rights in a fight with Hall.

The most convincing win for either team in the series went to the Flyers, 5-2, for more reasons than Mason's brilliance.

"The passion, skating and tenacity were really good tonight," Berube said. "We stuck our nose in there around the net."

Berube's players got on the train for the game the following night with reasons up and down the roster for feeling good. The team's powerplay had clicked two out of three times, and Mason had outplayed Lundqvist. After a season's worth of clutch wins, this club had come to expect them.

"We were confident," Voracek recalls. "We knew it was going to be hard, but it might have been harder for them than for us, to be honest, because they were at home, were favored, and had to win."

Having already won Game Sevens in the first round the previous two seasons, the Rangers had already proven excellent under pressure. But Berube also thought being he underdog team on the road, could work for his club.

"They had everything to lose; we had nothing," recalls the coach. "I thought they were nervous and we didn't take advantage of it.

"We should have really went after them a lot harder in the first period."

The only penalty for either side, which went to Rinaldo for holding up Richards in the neutral zone, was killed without a New York shot on goal. But as the period moved along, Philadelphia was showing more cracks than the Rangers.

With four minutes remaining, a breakout pass by Coburn was behind Brayden Schenn. When Stepan picked it off and sent in Nash, Mason had to make a superior glove save. In the final minute before the intermission, a Hartnell cross-ice giveaway at center sprang a Hagelin chance that went off Gustafsson, forcing Mason to stretch high to keep the puck from blooping in.

Just 39 seconds into the second period, New York made a bad change, getting caught with too many men on the ice. The Flyers had an opportunity to get ahead and failed miserably. Hartnell had Philadelphia's only shot of the two minutes, during which time Nash, shorthanded, had the best chance, only to be denied by Mason.

The penalty had been over for 19 seconds when MacDonald turned over the puck, forcing Mason to make a save on Brassard. Zuccarello chased down the rebound on the sideboards and threw a quick pass through Couturier to Carcillo behind Coburn. The scrappy ex-Flyer, a scratch in Games Five and Six, had an easy redirect to give the Rangers the precious first goal.

Philadelphia sagged, managing only one shot in the next five minutes. After Hartnell unsuccessfully tried to kick the puck ahead at center, Mason had to do the splits to stop a superior chance by St. Louis.

With 8:37 remaining in the period, Pouliot was called for interfering with the Flyer goaltender, giving Philadelphia another opportunity to change the momentum of a period rapidly going from bad to worse. But Stralman and Stall blocked shots by MacDonald, who was then stripped by McDonagh, forcing Mason to stop the defenseman on a two-on-one.

New York had been back to even strength for a minute when Stralman made a point save of a wraparound by Read. The defenseman got the puck down the boards to Brassard, who threw it cross-ice past Rinaldo's desperate dive to Pouliot for yet another Ranger backdoor goal, building their lead to 2-0 at 11:46.

Flyer chances were minimal. Giroux, on a passout from Voracek with four minutes remaining in the period, had Lundqvist flopping, but shot wide. Mason, meanwhile, stopped a wraparound by Nash, then his rebound, before standing up to stop Boyle on a setup from Dorsett. During a second period in which Philadelphia had been outshot 18-5, only Mason had kept the game from turning into a rout.

"We were on our heels the whole time," Berube would say.

Still, New York fully expected the Flyers to summon energy for the third period. And they did. Hartnell sent Pouliot to the ice with a booming check. Seconds later, Akeson took a breakout feed from Coburn, skated down the right wing, and fired from the top of the circle. The shot was blocked by Staal, but Akeson one-timed the carom over Lundqvist's blocker at 4:32 to give Philadelphia a lifeline, trailing only 2-1.

A shot by Simmonds from the point hit high off Lundqvist and dropped to the crease, but the goalie covered up just as Brayden Schenn arrived. When the whistle blew, bodies were stacked in the net behind the Ranger goalie.

With 7:20 to go, Giroux pushed past John Moore, but the puck rolled as the captain went to shoot and it fluttered high into Lundqvist's chest.

The desperate Flyers kept pushing, winning faceoffs, creating traffic, but New York wasn't panicking and good looks at the net were non-existent. Vigneault used his timeout as 2:19 remained on the clock. With just under two minutes left in the game, Mason skated to the bench for an extra attacker. "We were positive we were going to tie it up," Giroux said.

Berube called a timeout with 1:13 to go to give his big guns a breather, but there was nothing doing in front of Lundqvist. When the Rangers iced the puck with 12.4 seconds left, Dominic Moore beat Giroux on the draw and New York cleared, appearing to ice it with 2.7 seconds to go, but that call was reversed and the final faceoff took place at center ice.

It was over. The Rangers had won the game, 2-1, and the series in seven.

Snider came to the stricken locker room to thank the players for their efforts in saving what had looked like an utterly lost season. But having been just one shot away from extending it, there was little immediate consolation for the Philadelphia team.

"You come so close," Voracek told reporters. "It's the worst feeling ever. We didn't play good enough in the second period to win that game."

Berube also lamented that "big sag," as he called it, but said he was proud regardless.

"We went through a lot this year," said the coach. "We stuck together and went to a Game Seven. There's a lot of character in our locker room."

The pain didn't lessen when New York beat the Penguins and Canadiens to reach the Final before losing to the Kings. "You see the Rangers rolling and rolling," Mason recalls. "It very easily could have been us."

New York had controlled more of the play during the series, but had been made to break down in Game Six, so it hardly had been a case of the Flyers being fortunate to extend the series to the limit. "After Game Six, I thought we were going to beat them," recalls Berube. "We didn't score on those powerplays and let down. It was disappointing."

It also was not completely surprising. Philadelphia had saved one of the most satisfying regular seasons in its history by coming from behind a soul-stirring 11 times in the third period to win games, but against playoff teams, that rarely was going to work.

So there was obvious work to be done in building an elite club. But Mason had stabilized the goaltending, and the core players—particularly the young forwards—had learned a lot about themselves thanks to two heroes of the recovery—Berube and Giroux.

"Chief was intimidating," Read recalls. "He said all the time simply, 'If you're not going to play the right way, I'm not going to play you.' I think he got the best out of some players and put us in the right direction."

Recalls Voracek, "He was hard on me, and I really liked it. Sometimes when someone's hard on you, it can be really annoying as a player. But he got the best out of a lot of us."

The rest of the confidence came from the captain when he insisted a 1-7 team was going to make the playoffs.

"We didn't make Giroux eat his words," Hartnell said. "When you say something like that, you've got to back it up. And we did."

RON HEXTALL

THE TEARS WERE BARELY DRY when Ron Hextall miraculously appeared, like an even-up call from above.

"You don't replace a Pelle Lindbergh," Bob Clarke said after the Flyers lost the reigning Vezina Trophy winner in a November 1985 automobile accident. Yet somehow, one season later, there was Ron Hextall, out of the sixth round and like a dream.

He debuted in the opening game of the 1986-87 season against the Oilers at the Spectrum by stoning Wayne Gretzky on a breakaway, and winning, 2-1.

"Who the hell are you?" asked Gretzky.

"Who the hell are you?" shot back Hextall.

He was big (6-3, 192), quick, antagonistic, colorful, innovative, tireless and, at age 22, ready to strap one of the NHL's strongest teams to his back. Hockey never had seen a package like this. Hextall chopped at opponents' legs like a lumberjack, played his stick in cadence against the goalposts between faceoffs as if it was a xylophone, and whipped outlet passes for fast breaks like he was Kareem Abdul-Jabbar.

Eight months later in the Final against Edmonton, Hextall held Philadelphia close in three games that it rallied to win from two-goal deficits and got the Flyers to a Game Seven against hockey's greatest-ever offensive machine.

"As good as Lindbergh was [during the 1985 drive to a Final against the Oilers], he wasn't at the level Hextall was in 1987," recalls Gretzky. "When a goalie is playing like that, it changes the atmosphere in two locker rooms.

"We rarely spent much time on video of opposing goaltenders. But he was one that we did, not so much to talk about where to shoot, but how he handled the puck so well. We wanted to keep it away from him as much as possible or put him on his backhand."

In the 57th minute, Glenn Anderson scored to put away a 3-1 win and Edmonton's third Stanley Cup in four years.

Philadelphia never has gotten that close again. Nor has Hextall ever been able to get himself to view the video of that game, even though he won the Conn Smythe Trophy as playoff MVP of the most compelling Final in history. "If I watched it, I'd cry my eyes out again just like I did that night," he says. "I do that just when I've seen clips of it.

"That's something I'll take to my grave. It's not that I regret anything we did as a team, just the final result. If I'd won a Cup as a player, that probably would lessen the [pain]. But when you play [13 years] and you don't win…

"I'm getting upset as I think about it right now. And how many years later are we?"

Maybe it won't hurt so much after he assembles the next Flyer Stanley Cup team. But knowing the general manager, probably not. Hextall does have a ring—earned in 2012 while assistant GM of the Kings—but is the first to say you can't compare the gratification of helping to put together a successful club to being a member of one.

"I don't mean to downplay what we did in L.A.," he recalls. "We rebuilt the Kings over six years, so there was a certain amount of satisfaction from the work we put in. When I look back at my career in hockey, it will be one of the highlights for sure.

"But it's different when you're not playing."

Then again, so is the Philadelphia GM. "He was nuts," says Kjell Samuelsson, once Hextall's teammate, today one of three directors of player development. "Now, he's calm and easy-going. I can't believe this is the same guy."

Dean Lombardi argues the transformation is not that acute. When he left an advisory position with Philadelphia in 2006 to become general manager of Los Angeles and took along Hextall, the Flyer director of player personnel, to be the Kings assistant GM, Lombardi wanted a right-hand man with passion as much as brainpower.

"He is not a stoic thinker at all times," the Kings' GM said. "In the moment, Ron still has the intensity; I saw that in meetings. But now, he can take a step back, weigh things and let his homework and reasoning be determining factors. It's a good combination for a hockey executive."

Paul Holmgren became a big fan working alongside Hextall for seven years in the Flyer front office, understood the role he played in L.A.'s championship, and brought him back in 2014 as Philadelphia's assistant general manager. A year later, when Holmgren proposed yielding his GM chair to Hextall and stepping upstairs into the vacant club presidency, Ed Snider's arm didn't need any twisting. Nor, during the final year of the Chairman's life, did he have to be sold on Hextall's recipe to slow cook the organization's third Stanley Cup.

"You can't build quickly, it just doesn't happen," says Hextall. "All the dynamics have changed.

"The Blackhawks and Kings (three and two Stanley Cups, respectively, in this decade) built slowly, methodically, the only way to do it in the cap world."

The goalie who loathed giving up goals even during practice now has the patience as a general manger to execute a long-term plan. After Hextall had engaged in a much-resented holdout for a renegotiated contract in 1990, there is an additional irony. Even as he stuck to his principles, Hextall insisted he wanted to be a Flyer for a life. With a few interruptions, that is the way it has worked out.

Having been included among the five players in the 1992 deal with Quebec that brought Eric Lindros to Philadelphia, and after being reacquired by Clarke in a 1995 trade with the Islanders, Hextall got his wish of retiring as a Flyer in 1999, when he then began his front-office training as a scout.

Hextall left for the Kings in 2006 reluctantly, only for the purposes of career advancement, and demonstrated an uncommon loyalty when he returned to Philadelphia seven years later for essentially the same-level job he held in Los Angeles. Not promised an eventual promotion to become the Flyer GM, he came back for no better reason than wanting to be here.

"There's something in your blood and heart about the team you came up with," Hextall says. "I still have that for this franchise and it's never going to go away."

Maybe that blood doesn't boil like it once did, but back in the day when Hextall was whacking away, his temper was a curious phenomenon. His grandfather, Bryan Hextall, Sr., a Hockey Hall-of-Famer, was a perennial Lady Byng candidate. He would admonish both his son, Bryan Jr. (738 penalty minutes in seven NHL seasons), and grandson Ronald for using their sticks on anything other than a puck, and would then throw in the odd reprimand for uncle Dennis (1,398 minutes in 12 seasons), too. The real firebrand in the family, according to Ron, was Grandma Gert.

Grandpa and Dad were both centers. But whenever Ron would accompany his father to practice, Bryan would notice his son's little face pointed only toward the goaltenders. "In school, everybody else would be working and I'd be drawing pictures of Tony Esposito and Jimmy Rutherford," Hextall recalls.

His mother, Fay, whose wrist shot tested five-year-old Ron in their driveway, said she saw a single-mindedness that someday would make him exactly what he intended to be. "He had a love for the game that, frankly, I didn't see in too many of the players that his father played with," she recalls.

Dad overcame his initial objections to having a goalie in the family on the condition his son play other positions first to develop his skating. "I always thought Ronald would make a great defenseman," Bryan said. When boredom overtook the kid between saves, a third defenseman is what he became, coming out of the net to play the puck, sometimes skating it as far as the red line, the goaltender's legal boundary.

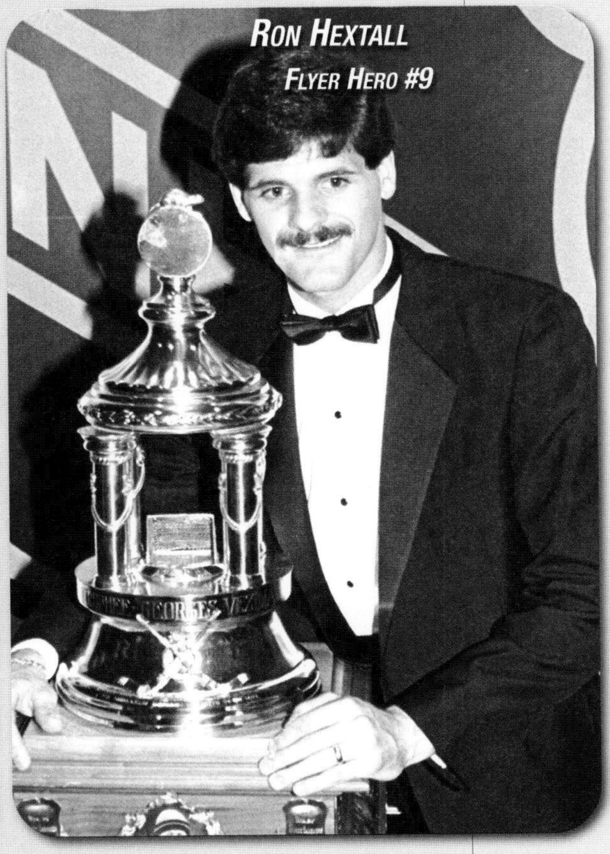

"Wouldn't you like to keep going?" Fay would ask, but he couldn't be talked into a position change, or into surrender while backstopping a bad Brandon (Manitoba) Wheat Kings team to an ugly 5.71 goals-against average (and an even-uglier .859 save percentage) in his draft year. That didn't help Hextall's prospect status or his mood as he raged against crashers of the crease.

"What I liked about him was what everybody else didn't," said Jerry Melnyk, the late Flyer scout. "A lot of people thought he was loony."

In working up from the minors, Hextall refined his style but hardly his temperament, and certainly not his drive. "I felt sorry for him because I knew no goalie could ever have a year like that again," recalls teammate and Hall-of-Famer Mark Howe, but Hextall wasn't afraid to try to top it. Upon accepting the Vezina Trophy after his rookie season, he announced intentions to try to become the best goalie ever.

Hextall did fulfill one grand ambition by becoming the first NHL goaltender ever to shoot and score a goal—on December 8, 1987, in a game at the Spectrum against Boston. Two years later at the Capital Center against Washington, he became the first netminder do it in a playoff game.

In the next round, Ken Wregget stepped in for the injured Hextall and stoned the Penguins in Game Seven at Pittsburgh, but Hextall was back by Game Four of the Montreal series, and unable to turn either the tide or the other cheek when he had a chance to avenge a Game One elbow by Chris Chelios that had sent teammate Brian Propp to the hospital. In the final seconds of the Canadiens' clinching victory, Hextall took the law into his own hands and his blocker to Chelios's head.

The goalie, who had been suspended (eight games to start the next season) during the 1987 Final for a gratuitous whack at the leg of Edmonton's Kent Nilsson, this time earned a 12-game penalty and more public scorn for what he did to Chelios. Public opinion did not discourage him from asking the Flyers to renegotiate the eight-year contract (but paid over twenty) that he had signed after his rookie season. But when Clarke refused to re-do the deal, Hextall hired the contentious Rich Winter for representation and did not report to training camp, enraging the organization further.

Coaxed back by captain Dave Poulin in November, Hextall eventually signed a contract more in line with his market value. But he suffered repeated groin and hamstring pulls—probably a result of his attempts to stay in shape running the steps of the Brandon arena—and subconsciously compromised what had been a near-flawless style. Out of the lineup for all but eight games, Philadelphia's 1989-90 season was effectively ruined, and two more non-playoff seasons followed from Hextall's up-and-down struggles to restore his lost promise.

His inconsistency, an expensive contract, and the organization's desire to make a new start, punched the goaltender's ticket out of town. Although Hextall appeared to have found himself again during a strong regular season in Quebec, he suffered a poor playoff, and then struggled in the postseason after a trade the following year to the Islanders. His career was at a crossroads when Clarke, back with the Flyers as president/GM after a 1990 firing he had bitterly blamed on Hextall's holdout, found the Islanders desperate to move the goalie and willing to take an inconsistent Tommy Soderstrom in return.

"I was so happy, I would have run back to Philadelphia," recalls Hextall. Coach Terry Murray kept a lid on expectations by declaring the goalie an upgrade, no savior. The Flyers wanted him back mostly because of his competitiveness. "He added a lot of the ingredients I thought were missing on the ice and in the dressing room," Murray recalls.

Hextall's balance—his primary strength in 1987—was a memory, and his right hip no longer worked very well, so the goaltender reduced his crouch and better distributed his weight. Murray urged the 30-year-old to conserve energy by eliminating many of his superstitious rituals. Philadelphia's increased scoring capacity extended Hextall's margin for error and lowered his temptation to overtry. He stood up much more and, as scoring ebbed in the league, began putting up the best numbers of his career in getting the Flyers to the 1995 semifinals and then sharing responsibilities with Garth Snow on the 1997 Final team.

"I had to cheat, stay to one side a little, because I knew I could only move a certain way," he recalls. "It was hard, but you deal with what you've got and try to be the best you can be."

Hextall's villainy ebbed as he matured, but then he always was a different person off the ice. Even when thought to be out of his mind, the only thing he minded was the media suggesting he was a 24-7 jerk, not just a miscreant for two-and-a-half hours in the arena.

A devoted husband to Diane, a former competitive figure skater, and a doting father to four children, Hextall had his off-the-ice priorities in order. On the ice, he would save his defensemen steps by coming back for the puck, and spared them any blame. The netminder never allowed a goal that he did not consider to be primarily his fault.

Hextall finished up his playing career in 1998-99 as backup to John Vanbiesbrouck and eagerly accepted Clarke's offer of a scouting position. The hardest part of leaving the ice was not the pay cut, but never winning a championship. "If you've given everything you've got, you shouldn't come out of something with regrets," he says today. "But not winning the Cup is a disappointment, it just is. That's why you play every year."

He had a seamless transition to being a working

stiff, perhaps because he always was one, even as a star. "I'm the type of guy that when something is over, you move onto the next stage," he says. "I'm not big on living in the past, and I'm not real hung up on what people think. I believe my teammates will say I was a pro, which, to me, is the highest compliment you can get."

He brought the same worker mentality into the office. As it turned out, Hextall dragged himself away from the Flyers for the purpose of career advancement unnecessarily. Three months after he went to the Kings, Clarke suddenly resigned, and Holmgren ascended to the GM's chair, which would have opened up the assistant GM position for Hextall here in Philadelphia.

Regardless, working seven years in Los Angeles, he received the training he wanted, while the Kings were deriving the benefit of his experience in a winning culture.

"I wanted him because he had credibility, a work ethic, and an understanding of a franchise's need for a defined culture," says Lombardi.

"People called us Flyers West, which was fine. We needed that Philadelphia-type of identity that Clarkie had started and which transcended generations. Hexy was a big part of that. Bringing him along certainly enhanced what we wanted to do.

"What impressed me the most was that he was willing to get in the trenches. A lot of top ex-players don't want to drive their truck four hours to scout games, file reports, make lists, and learn the other parts of this business from top to bottom. He did."

Hextall could have done those same things here, but perhaps the experience of taking over a rundown franchise and building it from the ground floor up, instilled in him an additional layer of patience.

Certainly, the Hextall of his twenties wasn't thinking of long-term implications committing acts that brought him 26 games in suspensions during his career. But he claims to have been basically a mellow dude even back then.

"When I was on the ice, I was in that environment for a reason—to compete," he said. "It's not like I had a split personality, it was just a function of time and place. I don't think I ever was that guy people saw on the ice.

"Of course, I'm more mature. You look at certain things a little differently and maybe you reorder some priorities. That's just life experience, though. I don't think I'm that different."

KIMMO TIMONEN

ASKED LATE IN HIS 16-SEASON CAREER for his most gratifying accomplishment, Kimmo Timonen answered as decisively as he moved the puck.

"That I'm still here," he responded. "Nobody wanted to give a 5-foot-10 guy a chance except for (Nashville GM) David Poile, and I have played close to 1,100 games.

He wound up with 1,108, almost half of those for Philadelphia. It's hard to remember a single one of them being subpar, except perhaps by the Finn's own high standards.

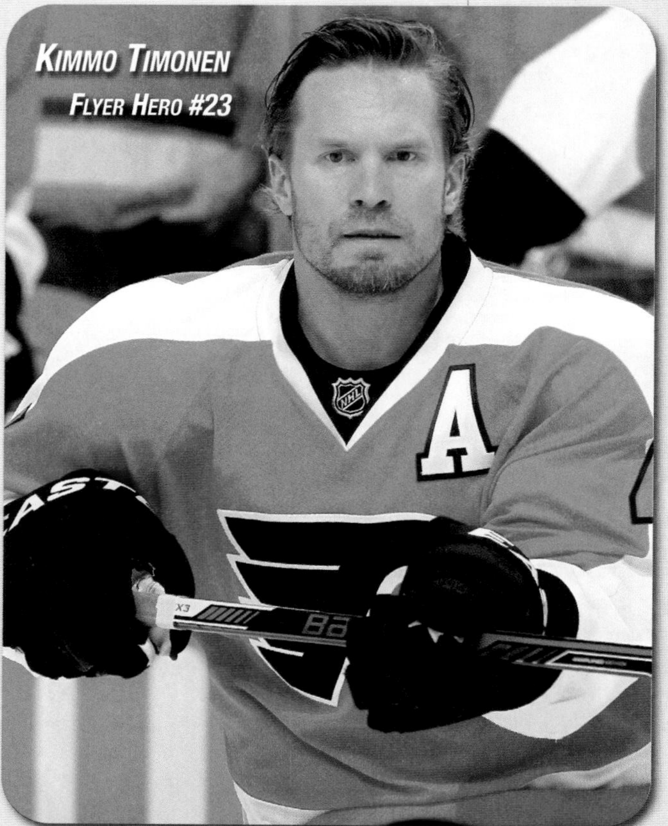

Little guy, huge impact. The highest he ever finished in the Norris Trophy balloting was fifth, during his final season in Nashville, but you couldn't measure his value in voting or scoring points. Timonen was the most important addition at any position towards turning a 54-point Philadelphia disaster in 2006-07 into a Stanley Cup semifinalist in just one year because he made the other players around him better.

"You wondered, 'How can a guy this small be so good defensively?'" said Danny Briere, a teammate for six seasons. "First, there was the sacrifice part of it, his willingness to block shots (averaging over two a game for three years).

"I saw Kimmo play through pain. Everybody knows about his blood-clot issues (costing Timonen his entire final Flyer season), but they should have seen some of the other stuff he endured.

"He wasn't just courageous, though. He was efficient—good at reading rushes, cutting off passes on two-on-ones and three-on-twos. And he'd rarely turn the puck over, so we weren't stuck in our zone for 60 seconds."

The Flyers studied advanced metrics in Timonen's final seasons. Thiugh his skills had began to decline, he demonstrated an uncanny ability to anticipate where a rebound was going. The five-time Barry Ashbee Trophy Winner as the Flyers' best defenseman had a low center of gravity that kept him upright after collisions with taller players, Popeye arms that kept attackers away from the net, and a level of conditioning that enabled him to outlast opponents who outweighed him by 20 pounds. Timonen played 24:41 per game through three postseason series in 2007-08, and 26:38 through four rounds in 2009-10.

"He and (longtime partner) Braydon Coburn gave us big minutes against top guys," said John Stevens, the coach of the 2007-08 team. "Kimmo played the game with such intelligence, didn't race around trying to do a million things. He exuded a calm that relaxed everybody."

Did this guy even sweat in the sauna? Timonen was the coolest man in the house.

"When our players were all wanting to rush up the ice, he'd pull the puck back as if to say, 'Let's come up together, the right way,'" recalls assistant coach Joe Mullen. "Once we got into the (offensive) zone, he never forced things. He could both shoot and pass, saw the ice very well, took control."

Timonen quarterbacked a Philadelphia powerplay that was one of the top three in the NHL three times, top seven two more seasons, and only once finished in the bottom half in percentage.

"He would skate through the middle of the ice with his head up and then take a slapshot or make a pass without ever looking at the puck," recalls Briere, who scored 307 career goals. "I'd say, 'I gotta try that,' but I'd have to look at some point. I wasn't able to do it.

"Kimmo could walk the blueline, feel the puck and when it was time to let go…zoom. From the stands, it looks second nature to do it without looking down, but it's tough to have confidence that the puck is not going to move on you.

"His shots were not blocked. If he didn't have a line to the net, his passes would always be the right things to do."

For consistency, durability, diligence, leadership and skill, only Mark Howe (plus-349 for his Flyer days with .80 points per game) clearly surpassed Timonen as the best defenseman Philadelphia ever had. Figuring out who belongs next between the excellence of Eric Desjardins, Jimmy Watson and Timonen is a subject more worthy of celebration than debate.

Watson played on the best teams the franchise ever had, so his plus-295 as a Flyer dwarfed Desjardins' plus-143 and Timonen's plus-44, but Desjardins (.53 points per game) and Timonen (.52) were much higher point producers.

In whatever order you might want to rank these rocks, they compose a top four that ate serious minutes, won playoff games, and had to be extremely efficient to leave Joe Watson and Van Impe as your third pair on the all-time Philadelphia blueline. That's six deep, players with whom you would want to dig a foxhole. The common thread is there was no guesswork if you were their partner.

"You knew what you were getting from Kimmo every game," said Howe, now director of pro scouting for the Red Wings. "If you are a coach, that is golden."

It also was worth a silver and three bronze medals in the Olympics for tiny Finland, where Timonen, the son of an architect father and banker mother, came up in the system of his hometown team, KalPa Kuopio.

"In Kuopio, they like hockey and it's cold. What else can I say?" Timonen laughs. Today, he owns the club with his former Flyer teammate Sami Kapanen. Back in Kimmo's development days, even as a prodigy playing professionally at age 16, he was trying to make the national team, not thinking much about the NHL.

When the Kings made him a 10th-round selection in 1993, he suddenly knew what else he wanted. But after looking at Timonen in camp just once, Los Angeles had zero intention of signing him.

"It's a slap in the face, but what can you do?" recalls Timonen, who made the his national team and played in the 1998 Nagano Olympics. Poile, the GM of the new Nashville Predators, watched the defenseman in a tournament in Switzerland and told him that he would make a deal for his rights. Better late than never. Timonen anchored the defense of a slow-cooked expansion team for eight years.

By 2007, the Predators were regularly making the playoffs. They also were for sale and seemed likely to be relocated.

It broke Poile's heart to be unable to keep his upcoming free agents, but the GM did what he could to recoup, giving Holmgren pre-July 1 negotiation rights to the defenseman and winger Scott Hartnell in exchange for getting back the No. 1 pick the Flyers had received from Nashville four months earlier for Peter Forsberg.

The negotiations with Timonen weren't really about money, more a case of the Philadelphia GM selling Timonen and Hartnell on the Flyer plan to quickly change over the worst team in the league. Hartnell believed in the Philadelphia brand from the beginning. Timonen took some coaxing.

The biggest gamble was making a six-year, $37 million commitment for a smallish 32-year-old player. Holmgren looked at the defenseman's track record—since joining the Predators full time, Timonen had played 82 games twice and had never been absent more than 10 times in a season—and took a measured chance that paid off. Because of the clots, Timonen was absent during the first four games of Pittsburgh's five-game victory in the 2008 semifinals, and for his entire final Flyer year at age 39. Otherwise, he never missed more than six games in any Philadelphia season.

"Early in the Nashville years, I played through things because I thought I was going to lose my spot," he said. "So I learned how to cope with tiny injuries.

"You have to be lucky, but you have to be smart, too, on how you go into corners and get the puck, read the play, know where the other guys are. Everyone is smart out there, but I had to be especially."

Kapanen, Timonen's business partner, watched this triumph of intelligence and willpower waving the Sinirstillppu—the blue cross flag of Finland—all the way.

"Kimmo proved all the people wrong," said Kapanen. "He's right there with Teppo Numminen as the best defensemen our country ever has produced and may be a little ahead because Kimmo had a little more offense in his game.

"As far as being beloved in our country, he'd be right at the top of the list with Teemu (Selanne), Saku (Koivu), and Jari Kurri. Kimmo is so easy to like. Anybody who takes the time to talk to him can be amazed at how polite and easy-going a person he is. He's fun to be around; you find yourself in a better mood. Not everybody has that ability.

"There are times when the [bleep] hits the fan in the locker room and nobody knows what to say. Or, maybe they do and don't speak up. Sometimes you just need that one veteran guy who has his head screwed on straight, and that was Kimmo.

"He demanded a lot from his teammates while always being positive. He really didn't say a lot, but when he did, everybody paid attention. It wasn't what he said so much as the way he said it—the tone and body language. It could be as simple as saying, 'We're OK. Everybody just needs to relax,' and everybody would go, 'Whew.'

"Kimmo settled Hartnell down all the time. I know he helped Mike Richards when he was named a young captain."

At age 39, Timonen signed for one more season (2014-15), only to be diagnosed over the summer with recurring clots. It was assumed that the blood thinners required to treat the problem would make it too dangerous for him to return to the ice. But of a mind to go out on his own terms, or be traded for one more shot at a Cup, Timonen persisted with the doctors and GM Ron Hextall.

In February, he was given the okay to play and was traded to Chicago for two draft picks. Timonen got to live the happily-ever-after of a hockey player's dreams—going out with a Stanley Cup—his victory cheered in Philadelphia as the second best thing to the Flyers winning it.

Even in the highest places, Kimmo was loved. When the Blackhawks visited the White House, President Barack Obama singled out Timonen for being an inspiration.

"He already had a great career before last season," said the President. "He'd been to a Stanley Cup Final, an Olympic final and a final at the World Championships and lost them all.

"But in his final NHL game, at age 40, Kimmo finally hoisted the Stanley Cup. He has been able to stick with it, consistently contribute, and make a huge difference."

Obama clued the nation into what Philadelphia already knew.

JAKE VORACEK

THERE WAS PLENTY for Hanna and Miroslav Voracek to be unhappy about during the time they lived under the communist regime in Czechoslovakia. So when their son, Jakub, was able to experience childhood in a free Czech Republic, one rule was pre-eminent in the family's apartment.

"My mom and dad never complained, and they never wanted to hear it from me," recalls Jake. "If I came home unhappy about something, they'd always tell me not to [grumble], just to work hard. That's why I'm where I am now."

The people who really have something to complain about are defensemen trying to knock Jake Voracek off the puck. He is another big, strong, Flyer right wing from a long line of them, including Paul Holmgren, the general manager who traded for Voracek in 2011. Gary Dornhoefer and Rick Tocchet were other tireless workers with strong finishing skills, as is Wayne Simmonds. Reggie Leach was a pinpoint shooter, and Tim Kerr a scoring machine parked in the slot. But none has had the speed and elusiveness of Voracek.

"He uses his (6-foot-2, 208 pound) body really well to come up with the puck and protect it," said Holmgren. "He can use that big butt of his to knock a guy off the puck, and has the speed and change of direction to keep it.

"He is a dynamic player."

In 2014-15 Voracek led the NHL in points through much of the season before finishing in a tie for fourth. He was chosen as a first-team NHL All-Star, won his second Bobby Clarke Trophy as team MVP in three seasons, and appeared established at age 25 among the elite performers in the league. But his 2015-16 season was a struggle almost throughout.

In the course of scoring just one goal in his initial 30 games, Voracek first lost the privilege of playing on the top line, and then, his sense of direction when reunited with Claude Giroux, this time on the left wing. Voracek adjusted to the change, however, and was looking much more like his old self until missing nine games in late February and March with a foot injury.

He struggled thereafter but kept shooting, the same as through the entire ordeal. Voracek recorded only eight fewer shots on goal than the 221 he compiled during his All-Star year, while scoring half the number of goals (11).

"I wouldn't use it as an excuse, but with me, everything always came automatically," the winger said after totaling only 55 points, 26 fewer than in 2014-15. "Sometimes, before I passed the puck, I was thinking, 'What if I hit something?' or 'What if the puck doesn't make it there?'

"I wasn't very confident on that foot during the playoffs. My game is built around the first three steps, cutting and crossing. When you have two or three quick steps, you're used to getting great acceleration from the other players and then you have more time to make the play. If you don't create that separation, you start missing passes and you're not in the place you're used to being.

"But that's not an excuse for me to have one point in the whole (Washington) series. Injuries are going to come and go. You have to find a way to compete better. You learn the hard way sometimes."

So did coach Dave Hakstol.

"I bounced him around the lineup and, as I look back on it, I don't know if that helped him," he said. "We were looking for balance, in addition to getting Jake going. So part of the thinking process became [using] Jake as the kind of player who could make [others] around him better, just like Claude does.

"Going forward, I think Jake is a right wing."

Voracek never showed a bad side, no matter what side he was playing. Bad beard maybe, because it became as scraggly as his numbers. But in the worst of times, he remained the best of people with the media and his teammates.

"When we had a good start and things weren't going great for him, he was happy that the team was doing well," said Hakstol. "When we hit a tough stretch, it wasn't about his individual stats not being what he wanted; [it was] about not helping the Flyers.

"At the end of the season, his numbers weren't terrible, just not what he would expect of himself or what our team needed. But it was an opportunity for him to continue maturing. And he is the type of person who will react the right way from that type of year."

In the summer of 2015, Voracek signed an eight-year, $66 million contract. If the pressure to earn that money wasn't the cause of his struggles, then it probably became an effect. The additional stress he felt, however, was not compounded by impatience from the fans. The net may have been shrinking on him, but not his credibility with the customers who could see how hard he was working. "You just have to stick with it," Voracek said at the peak of his struggles.

Sticking with it has been a Voracek strength since the first time he put on skates, a Christmas present from his parents, at age three-and-a-half. "I would fall backwards and hit my head on the ice," he recalls, "but the next day, I wanted to go again."

His father, Miroslav, worked in the state-run steel plant of Kladno, a mill town 30 minutes from Prague. When capitalism returned, he bought a restaurant at a bargain price and today, owns two.

"It was hard work, but with the amount of money I'm making since I've been in the NHL, it's become more like a hobby to them," says Jake. "They have a nice house in Kladno with a yard; they have come a long way from the apartment."

So has their second child, born 13 years after daughter Petra, especially considering the NHL became a belated goal. Jake was playing with older kids in organized hockey from first grade on, and was good at tennis and soccer, too. But Jaromir Jagr, who also grew up in Kladno, was Voracek's first inspiration for hockey to become his "everything." Another incentive came in 1998, when a five-year-old democracy of 10 million persons won the gold medal at the Olympic Winter Games in Nagano, Japan. Most of those people took to the streets waving flags and honking horns, prompting an eight-year old to fantasize.

"That became my dream—to win an Olympic gold medal one day," Voracek remembers. "I never thought about the NHL."

National Hockey League games featuring prominent Czech players were on television live, albeit at 2 am. But it wasn't until 16-year-old Voracek's Kladno junior team won the national championship and the Halifax Mooseheads selected him in the first round of the Quebec Major Junior Hockey League's Import Draft that an opportunity to play beyond the Czech Republic seemed viable.

"My agent, (former Flyer) Petr Svoboda, said there were a few teams in the NHL that would like to draft me, and that I should go to Halifax," said Voracek. "Hockey-wise, it was the right decision and I knew it. I had never been in any trouble as a kid. My parents knew they could trust me.

He went to Halifax, sight unseen, at age 17, without a word of English in his vocabulary. "That's when you've got to find out how strong you are as a human being," Voracek said.

"The hockey was tough, much more physical. I got smoked with my head down a few times during the first five games, got absolutely killed. But right away, I had an 11-game point streak so that helped. In Europe, you don't get respect until you're old enough. Over here, you get respect by how you play.

"I was a Mama's boy and thought it would be tough being away. But we skyped and the team let me miss a couple games to get home for Christmas. I wasn't homesick at all. I was on a mission."

He was fortunate to have a coach, Cam Russell, who had played 10 years in the NHL, and blessed with a resolve to throw himself into a new culture. Voracek did interviews and engaged teammates in English almost from the start.

"If you want to learn, you can't be shy that somebody's going to laugh at you," he said. "If they see you're trying to talk to them, they're going to help you out.

"You're around it every day, so you pick it up pretty quickly. Movies with sub-titles helped because you could see the words in addition to hearing them. There was one other Czech guy on the team, Jiri Suchy. He helped me out whenever I was around him."

Within two months of his first season in Halifax, Voracek was being talked about as a high first-round selection. The Flyers, who had the second pick in 2007, liked everything about him except a shot he tended to push, not snap, at the net. They took James van Riemsdyk instead. Columbus selected Voracek seventh, especially nice because the team was hosting the draft that year.

"Everybody was cheering, it was pretty great," recalls Voracek. A year later, he was in the NHL at 19, and getting a crash course in professionalism from coach Ken Hitchcock.

Voracek scored 39 goals over three seasons with the Blue Jackets. Columbus wanted to win sooner, rather than later, however, and in June 2011 coveted Jeff Carter badly enough to give up Voracek and the seventh overall pick in the draft the next day. Philadelphia used that pick on Sean Couturier, a two-for-one that made the team younger, deeper, and poised to get all the best years of Voracek's career.

He scored in his Flyer debut, on Tim Thomas in Boston, and had the overtime game winner in the series-turning Game One as Philadelphia upset Pittsburgh in 2012. Voracek shed 10 pounds before his breakout 2014-15 season and it seemed to give him an extra half step. Strength makes him a hybrid, but the legs turn on his game. "When he is going at his top level, he is so [talented] and unpredictable," says Hakstol.

The only element to Voracek's game that has not earned an A is finishing ability. Last season was subpar, but he also has yet to break 25 goals in a good year. The voice of reason suggests he is not a sniper, but the voice of Hakstol—the one that is in the players' heads—will not put a limit on what Jake, still only 27, can do.

"Aim and release are things anybody can continue to work at," said Hakstol. "No question, more than a scorer, Jake is a skater and playmaker who dictates a pace, whether it is from his strength down low or off the rush.

"But he and Giroux can make things happen at a pace that is difficult to defend. Jake is a great player. And I don't think bigger scoring numbers are out of the picture for him."

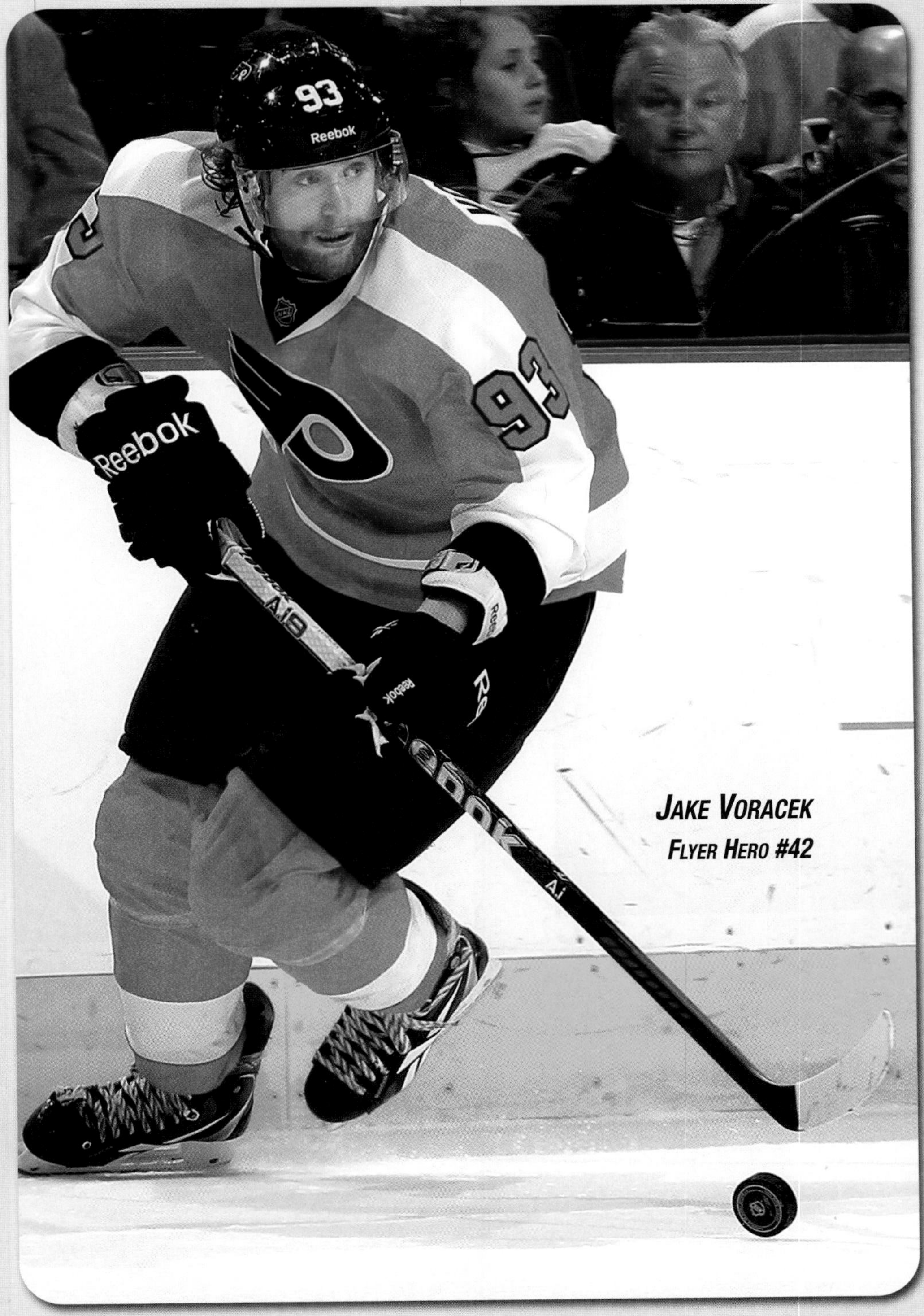

JAKE VORACEK
FLYER HERO #42

Jake Voracek

Chapter 16 • 2014-15

The Long-Term Plan

Ron Hextall had resigned in 2013 as Kings' assistant general manager to take the same position in Philadelphia with no finite promise that he would eventually become the general manager. But GM Paul Holmgren had brought Hextall back with the belief his ascendancy was inevitable. And during the 2013-14 season, Holmgren became increasingly convinced it should happen sooner rather than later.

After nine years on the job, Holmgren was not feeling burned out. But he was questioning his functionality in the aftermath of the 14-year, $110 million offer sheet the Flyers made in 2012 to sign restricted free agent Shea Weber away from Nashville. Bitterly, the Predators had matched the heavily front-loaded offer and retained one of the league's best defensemen. They had many sympathizers around the NHL.

"Even though [RFA offers] are within the rules, they are really frowned upon," recalls Holmgren. "My relationship with a lot of [other general managers] changed.

"It's hard to do this job if you have a bad relationship, or at least a perceived bad relationship, with any number of GMs."

He told Chairman Ed Snider that perhaps Hextall should become the Flyer general manager at the end of the 2013-14 season, and inquired about other roles for himself within the organization. The Flyer presidency had been open since Peter Luukko's departure in 2013.

Snider was not a hard sell on the idea. "Pretty smart guy," the Chairman had said to Holmgren about Hextall, but the move was left up to Holmgren, and Hextall was clued in throughout.

Recalls Holmgren: "In all of my conversations with Hexy during that year, he kept asking me, 'Are you sure you want to do this? Are you sure you are ready?' And I was pretty sure I was. It was during the last 10 games of the season that I started to push the envelope.

"Then (Canuck president) Trevor Linden called during the playoffs asking for permission to interview Hextall for their GM job. I knew there would be other calls. That probably put me over the top, but I knew it was going to go that route anyway."

Hextall was confirmed as the seventh Flyer general manager and Holmgren as the new team president at a May 7 press conference at the Wells Fargo Center. "I think Ron's going to be a star," Holmgren told the media. "He's more than ready, has been for a few years."

Said Hextall, "When Mr. Snider and Mr. Holmgren brought me in the other day and talked about offering me the job, not only did I reach my goal of being a general manager, but I got my dream job. I've got a special feeling about this organization and I am absolutely honored and thrilled today to be sitting here."

Hextall, 50, said he "would have to be an idiot" not to consult Holmgren, who was stepping upstairs after producing a Stanley Cup finalist and another semi-finalist in his 10 seasons as GM. But the president made clear that this was no new, layered structure. "All hockey decisions fall in Ron's lap," Holmgren said. "He has full authority and autonomy."

Snider denied rampant speculation that he had instigated the moves, and Holmgren reiterated that he had been their sole catalyst.

"I started talking to [Hextall] about this in December, and I went to Mr. Snider about it in January," said Holmgren. "Just to dispel any doubt about what's going on, this is a good thing."

Not a good thing, however, were the cap issues the new GM was inheriting. The $69 million ceiling for the 2014-15 season was $2 million lower than expected because of the plunge in the Canadian dollar. "We've got to find a way to get below it," said Hextall.

The new GM's vision was to build the team through the draft, with select fits of free agents.

"I knew we couldn't do anything significant about [the cap situation] in the short term," he recalls. "So I decided, 'OK, we'll just try it with what we have and flesh this thing out.'

"There is no quick fix in pro sports when you have a cap. You can't do it. But we had a competitive team and good young pieces. Our course of action was to be methodical and just keep building."

Four days before the 2014 NHL Entry Draft and a week before free agency was to begin, Hextall traded 32-year-old Scott Hartnell to Columbus to bring back former Flyer R.J. Umberger and a fourth-round draft pick in the 2015 draft. The cap hits of Hartnell ($4.75 million) and Umberger ($4.6 million) were similar, but Umberger's contract was expiring in three years and Hartnell's in five.

Umberger, suffering shoulder, back and finger issues, had often been a scratch towards the end of the 2013-14, but Hextall hoped he would add some versatility. Only once in six full seasons with Philadelphia had Hartnell failed to reach 20 goals. But with seven Flyers having attained that mark the previous year, the GM believed the team could withstand the loss of production in favor of a better-conditioned, less penalty-prone player.

Anything Hextall wanted to do that put his team in better position down the road was fine by Snider, who was 82 years old and in remission following bladder cancer treatments.

"What do you need from me?" the Chairman asked Hextall.

"I need you to be patient," the GM replied.

"What, I'm not patient?" Snider laughed.

In truth, he was ready to endorse a more forward-thinking approach.

"People think that Mr. Snider and Homer are going to lean on me to speed things up," Hextall told reporters. "They've been phenomenally supportive of who we are, where we're going as an organization, and what we're going to be."

A big splash at the 2014 NHL Entry Draft, held for the first time in Philadelphia on June 27-28, would have instantly labeled Hextall as a mover and shaker. He did make several attempts to select higher, including one to get the first player taken in the draft—defenseman Aaron Ekblad, who went to Florida. But when a deal was rejected by Florida, the draft instead turned into a declaration of the new GM's long-term plan.

With good defensive prospects Shayne Gostisbehere, Samuel Morin and Robert Hagg already in the system, Hextall added one more with the 17th pick by selecting 6-3, 190 pound Travis Sanheim of the WHL's Calgary Hitmen.

"This kid just rose and rose," said the Flyer GM about a player who had gone from being ranked 167th by Central Scouting to 53rd in the second half of the preceding season. Most teams had him ranked still higher. "He's a really good skater, a kid with range who moves the puck well. We made our pick and got a call right away [from a team wanting] our guy for two picks."

The departure of 26-year-old defenseman Erik Gustafsson to Avangard Omsk of the KHL opened up a spot and cap room, enabling Hextall to sign Nick Schultz, once a stalwart of the Minnesota defense, to a one-year, $1.25 million contract. Schultz, 31, was coming off a sub-par year with a poor Edmonton team and fared no better after a late-season trade to Columbus, but Hextall was hoping a chance to play on a winner, and in an improved structure, would revive the career of a former captain.

"The Oilers had a bunch of skilled, young players who didn't play the way our coaches coached," recalls Hextall. "Schultzie is a very structured player, so I thought he'd be fine here.

"He's a great defender, good stick, blocks a lot of shots, and he's still pretty mobile, even now. Above all, we wanted to add character, and Schultzie is a character player. It was a one-year deal, there really wasn't much risk."

To better all these defensemen, both future and present, Philadelphia hired Gord Murphy, 47, as an assistant coach.

Murphy, who played three-and-a-half seasons with the Flyers between 1988-92, had been an assistant for 11 seasons in the NHL. He replaced John Paddock, who was not reassigned after having served the organization in multiple capacities during different stretches going back to his playing days (1976-80).

"It was pretty surprising and tough in the moment," recalls Paddock. "When you're fortunate enough to come back (after being fired as head coach in Ottawa) to what you call your hockey home, it was a hard time for me for sure. We were coming off a successful season.

"But things worked out. It was only a month later that I got the call from Saskatchewan (to become coach and GM of the WHL's Regina Pats), which has turned out more than good.

"The Flyers were always great to me. Once I got past the initial stage (of the firing), I didn't have any problems with it at all. Things were always done right there. They didn't strive for second place and they cared for people."

Ross Lonsberry was a valuable member of Philadelphia's two Cup winners, but this was just the first of many reasons to mourn his death, at age 67 in Acton, CA, after a nine-year battle with cancer.

"Salt of the earth," said Orest Kindrachuk, Lonsberry's teammate on the 1974 and 1975 Stanley Cup champions. "A true friend if you needed help. Nothing phony about Ross."

Lonsberry, who scored 32 goals in 1973-74, averaged 24 during his six seasons with Philadelphia. He was one of the most selfless players on a team filled with them. A big scorer coming up in the Boston system, he happily took a defensive role on a line with Rick MacLeish and Gary Dornhoefer.

"We complemented each other so well," recalled Dornhoefer. "We stayed together what, six years? How often does that happen?

"Ross could score, but he wasn't interested in stats. He wanted to win. He could kill penalties, do whatever Freddie Shero wanted him to do. And Ross was so consistent, he never took a night off. As a teammate? If you had gripes against Rosscoe, you needed to get into another line of work."

Lonsberry, traded to Philadelphia from the Kings with Bill Flett in 1972, and then to Pittsburgh alongside Kindrachuk in 1978, returned to Southern California after hockey to run a successful insurance agency.

It was in the hope of adding another worker in the mold of a Lonsberry that Hextall signed 29-year-old Pierre-Edouard Bellemare from the Swedish Hockey League. Despite the fact that only three players born in France ever had appeared in more than 200 NHL games, the Flyers considered the 6-foot, 196-pound Bellemare ready to skate for them immediately.

"The level he was playing at (during prime development years) wasn't great, so his progression was intriguing to us," recalls Hextall. "Our guys always had liked him, and it got to the point where they felt he could help us out.

"He was in a pretty good situation in Sweden, making a decent chunk of money playing 45 games a season, living a good life-style. Yet he still was really hungry to play in the NHL. That was an attractive thing for us."

After considering a short list of goaltending options, Hextall re-signed Ray Emery, 31, to a one-year, $1 million deal for a second season as the backup. "It's a role I'm used to," said Emery. "If Steve (Mason) has the season he had a year ago and I'm able to stop some pucks when I get in there, I'll be happy."

The organization was not at all amused when Claude Giroux was retained by police after he jokingly grabbed the rear end of a male Ottawa police officer during Canada Day celebrations in the ByWard Market area of Ottawa. No charges were filed.

"I sincerely apologize to my fans, teammates, and the Philadelphia Flyers organization," said the captain in a statement. "I have the utmost respect for law enforcement and apologize to the Ottawa Police Department, and specifically the individual officer."

Kimmo Timonen's off-season was going even worse than Giroux's. Re-signed for another, probably final, year for $2 million, the 39-year-old defenseman reported from Finland in early August that he had developed blood clots in his right leg and both lungs.

There was considerable question whether he would be able to play again, so Hextall reached out to Donnie Meehan, the agent for defenseman Michael Del Zotto, a 2008 former first-round pick of the Rangers. His development stalled, his contract about to expire, and his lifestyle an apparent issue, Del Zotto had been traded to Nashville midway through the season. The Predators decided not to keep him.

"We did our homework and it came up fine for the most part," said Hextall. "There were things you find with a lot of young men, nothing too crazy.

"We had called [Meehan] when Del Zotto became a free agent. Meehan asked, 'Where is he going to play?' They didn't like the numbers game. When Kimmo went down, the situation changed. We signed him that day."

The defenseman had enough interest from other teams to draw a one-year, $1.3 million deal from Hextall, which was half of what Del Zotto had made on his previous contract.

'He gets up and down the ice pretty fast," said coach Craig Berube.

Bellemare was not the only potential fourth-line addition. Ryan White—a 151-game NHL veteran, late of the Canadiens—was signed to a one-year, $513,000 contract; Chris VandeVelde, a former University of North Dakota player and once-Edmonton draftee who had been an 18-game call-up from the Phantoms in 2013-14, was retained on a one-year, $575,000 deal; and, Zac Rinaldo was re-upped for two-years and $1.6 million. Tye McGinn was traded to San Jose for a third-round pick in 2015.

With the new PPL Center in downtown Allentown, PA, finally completed five years after its conception, the Flyers were able to move their AHL affiliate—the Adirondack Phantoms—from Glen Falls, NY, to just 68 miles from the Wells Fargo Center.

"The whole symmetry between the (renamed Lehigh Valley) Phantoms and the Flyers is going to be a lot better," Hextall said.

The arena, which officially opened on September 10, 2014, had major-league facilities with a big, minor-league capacity—9,046 fans, including standing room. After five non-playoff seasons as a lame duck in an aged and distant facility, the organization was thrilled to be in Allentown. An agreement was also reached for the Reading (PA) Royals to become Philadelphia's East Coast Hockey League affiliate.

As the rookies reported to the Flyers Skate Zone in Voorhees, NJ, Snider predicted a breakout season for Jakub Voracek. "He has a chance to be a superstar," said the Chairman, who spoke to reporters at length about the club's new direction.

"I think Ron has established a philosophy that is probably long overdue," Snider said. "I have probably been a little too anxious to win another Cup.

"I was very patient when I was young, when we built the winners. We let the other five teams trade away their draft picks and some of their top kids, and we didn't do that. We were not successful for the first four or five years, and then all of a sudden, we were the best.

"So Ron Hextall has done a good job, in my opinion, in establishing what we want to do for the future."

Despite Philadelphia's significant 39-21-7 run to a playoff position after a 3-9-3 start in 2013-14, the GM was wondering if that progress was sustainable.

"I think we came back (in the third period) 11 times," Hextall recalls. "If you're playing from behind a lot and you need comebacks, there aren't going to be very many years where you're going to end up winning a lot of those games.

"You give your team credit for battling, but you also have to look at it like you were fortunate to run into a lot of teams that weren't doing their job very well in closing us out. There's a certain amount of luck involved. If you bank on that every year, you're not going to be successful.

"So we made the playoffs, but are we really as good as we think we are?"

At the time, Hextall tried to be more optimistic. "I don't think we're an elite team right now," he told the media. "But I think we can come right under that—and those teams all have a chance of winning. You can never go into a season thinking you're not going to win.

"The game is so tight right now and there are so many little factors that play into winning and getting momentum going. Once you get it going, teams are hard to stop. So never say never. I think we have a real good team."

During the first training camp session, Giroux had to leave with a groin injury but was back on the ice six days later and able to play in the team's final two preseason games.

The farming out of Jay Rosehill at the end of the postseason meant Philadelphia was going to open without an enforcer for the first time since the team's infancy. "Jay does maybe the hardest job in pro sports and he does it very well," Hextall said. "He fights for the team, and when he sits out, he has a good attitude.

"But given our cap—there are ramifications with keeping 23 players—we felt this was the right way to go for now."

Bellemare had demonstrated speed and defensive ability as projected, culminating his unlikely journey from France, through Sweden, to the NHL.

"I'm 29 years old," he said. "They're taking me because they need me to do [an immediate] job. I signed with the Flyers (over Montreal) because they were very clear what my role was going to be."

Before the season opener in Boston, Berube took his team to Cape Cod, MA, for some bonding—a trip pronounced a success even if the deep-sea fishing portion of it had to be cancelled due to choppy waters.

Just as long as Philadelphia didn't have a third consecutive rough start.

"We have new guys on the team, and it's important they get to know each other," said the coach.

Five fresh faces—Del Zotto, Bellemare, Schultz, Umberger and Blair Jones, a 28-year-old center/left wing—were premiering in Flyer uniforms, while Wayne Simmonds and Mark Streit donned the As, replacing Hartnell and Timonen as assistant captains.

Philadelphia was defeated in Boston, 2-1, on Chris Kelly's goal with 1:51 remaining. The team also lost Braydon Coburn with a foot fracture.

Schultz went into the lineup for the home opener, when the Flyers, with the help of two goals by Simmonds, rallied from a 3-0 deficit, then again from 4-3 to tie the Devils on a score by Vincent Lecavalier. But quickly Streit was caught on a pinch and Mason was beaten from just above the right faceoff dot. He then allowed a goal on a savable shot from the top of the circle by Dainius Zubrus in what ended up a 6-4 defeat.

Against Montreal, Simmonds had two more goals, but big defensive breakdowns did not enable Emery to hold a 3-0 lead in a 4-3-shootout loss as Lecavalier, who had three points in three games, suffered an injured left foot.

After another bad first period, Voracek's third-period goal saved a point against Anaheim, but Philadelphia, with the worst shootout record of any NHL team since its institution in 2005, lost another one, 4-3, to stay winless in its first four games.

"For me to stress my team over [shootouts] doesn't do anything," said Berube. "You just keep working on it."

VandeVelde was recalled to replace Lecavalier in Dallas, where Mason was yanked after three second-period goals. But the Flyers fought back to force an overtime which Giroux won 6-5 with one of his patented left circle drives.

"Ugly," the captain called the victory, but Philadelphia's place in the standings looked a lot better without that zero in the win column. In Chicago, Mason got the start and was bombed for three goals on 19 Blackhawk shots in a 4-0 loss that dropped the Flyers to 1-3-2.

The following night in Pittsburgh, Bellemare's first NHL goal staked Philadelphia to 2-1 lead. Giroux fed Umberger to break a 2-2 tie, and the Flyers went on to a 5-3 win, improving to 10-1-1 in regular-season games at the CONSOL Energy Center. But Andrew MacDonald's foot was injured blocking a shot, expected to leave him out for four weeks. With Coburn's absence expected to be extended, the Flyers were seriously short on defense.

"I can tell you I'm hoping to get a defenseman for a hell of a lot less than $2 million," Hextall said. When he couldn't, the GM called up Gostisbehere just three games into his AHL career. "Unfortunate," said the general manager, determined not to rush any prospect. Gostisbehere played an uneventful 12:27 as Emery made 37 saves to send Detroit to its ninth-straight loss on Flyer ice since its last win there during the 1997 Stanley Cup Final.

Emery had all three Flyer wins in the club's 3-3-2 start. Mason's save percentage was .878 as he struggled with the Wells Fargo Center's new LED lighting system, designed to substantially reduce glare.

"It's just a weird glow out there," said Mason. "With how bright it is, you'd think it would be clearer."

Berube saw no need to be illuminating about any long-term goaltending plan. He would choose his goalie according to which one currently was giving his club the best chance.

"Nobody's bigger than the team," said the coach. "Nobody. We've got two good goalies. I used them both last year and I'll use them both this year."

Mason vowed to be patient. "You can't argue when the team is doing well," he said. "You just have to bide your time and wait."

Philadelphia recalled defenseman Brandon Manning, an undrafted free agent with three years of Phantom experience, and sent down Gostisbehere. "[Shayne] might be the first kid I ever dealt with who knows exactly where he is at as a player and where he needs to be to get better," said Hextall after breaking the news to the rookie. "I am almost taken aback by his understanding."

Manning had an assist as Emery was beaten by two power-play goals in a 4-3 loss at Tampa. Afterwards, Hextall announced he had found his less-than-$2 million defenseman, signing 11-year veteran Carlo Colaiacovo, who had played 25

Free agent Michael Del Zotto bolstered a Flyer defense corps that had sustained injuries early in the season.

games with St. Louis in 2013-14, to a $625,000, one-year deal.

Mason returned to the net against the Panthers, and the Flyers got Lecavalier back, but the powerplay went 0-for-6 in a 2-1 loss.

Voracek scored twice in a 4-1 home victory over Edmonton, running a scoring streak to 11 points in the last six games, and pulling even with Sidney Crosby for the league lead in points at 18. Del Zotto got his first Philadelphia goal in a 4-1 Wells Fargo Center win over Florida. Voracek then added three more assists, two of them on Giroux goals, as the Flyers piled up a 4-0 lead and held on for a 4-3 home victory over Colorado.

Berube's team had won six of its last eight to climb to 7-5-2. But the news wasn't all good. Two of the goals against the Avalanche had been scored while Nathan MacKinnon was in the box for five minutes after a hit on Luke Schenn, who was projected to be out two weeks with a shoulder problem. He was joined on the sideline by Michael Raffl, who had blocked a shot against Edmonton with his foot, and would miss four weeks. And then, news came in from Lehigh Valley that Gostisbehere had suffered an ACL tear and was going to miss the rest of the season.

At least Coburn had been able to return against Colorado. And Philadelphia's six-day break would allow fewer games to be lost by the wounded, which included Umberger, who had just one goal and two assists in 14 contests. Mason's old roommate in Columbus had reported to camp without disclosing a bad back.

"I started working out in the summer and it just got worse and worse," Umberger recalls. "When I got on the ice here a couple of weeks before camp, I started thinking, 'I don't know how I'm going to do this, let alone finish the season.'

"I wish I would have been more honest with Philly, but I passed the physicals and was looking for a fresh start. You don't want to tell them how bad your back is hurting and that you can't work out as hard as you want.

"My life at home was awful. I couldn't bend over; I'd have to lay on the floor and play with the kids."

When Columbus came to town to end the schedule break, Umberger was still in the lineup but in no condition to show up his old team. Hartnell, who received a video tribute in his first game back to the city where he spent seven years, received a big ovation, but there were no hands for the Flyer penalty killers, who gave up three goals. Philadelphia lost 4-3 to the Blue Jackets, who were missing eight of their regulars. The following night in Montreal, Berube's team again gave up three powerplay goals during Emery's 6-3 defeat.

The Flyers sent the little-used Jones to the Phantoms, but then, concerned after Giroux was limping in practice, recalled Scott Laughton, their 2012 first-round pick, from Lehigh Valley. Giroux turned out to be good to go the following night at Madison Square Garden, but most of his teammates only went through the motions in a 2-0 loss to a Ranger team without Henrik Lundqvist and Ryan McDonagh.

"Our first line (Giroux, Voracek, Brayden Schenn) competed, in my opinion," said Berube. "I didn't see much after that except our goalie. [Mason] played a helluva game.

"What really upsets me more than anything is being soft in our own end. We're not being physical, not closing in on people fast."

From the empty outer visiting locker room, where the media waited for the players to come out and speak, Hextall could be heard screaming at his team.

"Are you [bleeping] kidding me?" he shouted, tossing a trashcan. "That's [bleeping] embarrassing! Jesus [bleeping] Christ!"

Reporters got the G-rated version. "I just said I was very disappointed," Hextall told them. "We didn't come out hungry enough. We've got to be a lot better than that."

As Mason recalls, "Sometimes you've got to realize the importance of games, and not [need] your GM to come in and say things that we should have already known. That should have been an easy one to get up for."

Perhaps a blast from Philadelphia's past would shake up the suddenly reeling club. John LeClair and Eric Lindros were inducted into the Flyer Hall of Fame before a November 22 game against Minnesota. Originally scheduled to be honored on separate nights, it was their idea to go in together, which was appropriate.

Lindros, who had left the Flyers on terrible terms, received unconditional love from the fans. He returned the sentiment.

"Night in and night out, you guys brought passion and energy every game," he said in his acceptance speech. "We felt you, we played for you, and whether it was a chat on a street, or down an aisle in a grocery store, you couldn't get away from the energy.

"It was fantastic; it was everywhere. I just want to say thank you so much for the memories, your support, and again, for this night."

LeClair thanked the fans, too, but showed the most gratitude for his former linemate and co-honoree. "Big E raised my game to another level," said LeClair. "And the fact of the matter is, he raised the level of everybody he ever played with.

"The seven years we were able to play together was an unbelievable ride. I've been fortunate enough to play with one of the best NHL players to ever lace them up. We loved winning together and hated losing even more."

Getting MacDonald and Luke Schenn back, Philadelphia played with considerably more heart and dominated much of the game against the Wild. In the end, however, the team still couldn't get out of its own way. Jason Zucker got behind Luke Schenn with less than a minute remaining and scored to beat the Flyers 3-2.

The losing streak ended at three. Voracek's two assists brought his NHL-leading points total to 29 in a 4-2 victory at home over Columbus.

The following day, Sunday, November 24, former Flyer coach Pat Quinn passed away at Vancouver General Hospital from multiple complications from an intestinal illness. Clarke said that Quinn, who led Philadelphia to an NHL-record 35-game unbeaten streak in the 1979-80, and to the Stanley Cup Final that same season, was an offensive innovator comparable to 1980 Olympic mastermind Herb Brooks. Holmgren remembered crying on that 1982 day when Quinn was fired in the midst of a late-season slump.

"He was a great man with vision and intelligence," said Bill Barber.

"He and Fred Shero were two best coaches I ever had."

Mason seemed all the way back to form, stealing a point with 46 saves in a 1-0 shootout loss to the Islanders at Uniondale. Too many other Flyers were lagging behind as plummeting confidence led to low energy. "We don't have enough guys that compete hard enough, that show enough urgency throughout the game," Berube said.

Raffl returned earlier than expected for a dismal 5-2 loss in Detroit. "I think we need to look at ourselves in the mirror here," said Giroux, "[We need to] show a little attitude."

He did not mean a defeatist attitude. Philadelphia gave up a power-play goal for an almost unbelievable sixth-straight game and scarcely tested goalie Cam Talbot in a 3-0 Black Friday loss to the Rangers. The team's effort the next day was barely better in a 5-2 loss at Madison Square Garden, the third Flyer loss to New York in eight days and the team's ninth defeat in 10 games overall. Snider and Hextall were forced to give Berube a vote of confidence, never a good sign.

Jason Akeson, pointless in 12 games of limited ice time and, as a defensive liability, not really a good fit on the fourth line, was sent to Lehigh Valley.

At San Jose, the coach benched Del Zotto and Lecavalier, the latter for the first time in his stellar career. "It's very hard to take," Lecavalier said, perhaps even more so because he hardly was the only player not producing.

In three-plus seasons, Sean Couturier had teased with spurts of offense, but his primary role was checking the opposition's top line. So there was a glaring need for a second-line center to team with Simmonds, who was only scoring on the powerplay.

In nine games, Philadelphia had received just two goals from forwards not on their first line until Couturier scored to give them a 1-0 lead over the Sharks. It was the only time the Flyers had tallied first in a road game all season, and it jump-started nothing. The players hung on to the bitter end, when they gave up a Patrick Marleau breakaway and allowed Matt Nieto to put in the rebound with 11 seconds remaining for an excruciating 2-1 loss.

At Anaheim, Philadelphia blew a 3-1 lead into a 4-3 deficit, saved a point on Simmonds' goal with two seconds remaining, and then lost the shootout, 5-4. "We're up 3-1, we've got to shut the door there," said Berube. "We let them back in the game with defensive mistakes."

But at least the Flyers appeared to be skating again. Giroux and Simmonds scored, and Mason was superb, stopping 37 shots in a 2-1 victory over the Stanley Cup champion Kings at the Staples Center, ending Philadelphia's six-game winless streak.

"It's always frustrating when you're losing, but by the same token, it happens to teams," Snider said in the locker room. "If we hadn't given up that goal with 12 seconds to go [in San Jose], we would have not lost in regulation in any of the games on the trip, so I'm very proud of this team."

Two days later, December 8, Snider called all his children individually to tell them that despite chemotherapy and radiation treatments, his bladder cancer had metastasized. Doctors were estimating he had a year to live.

"He had an even tone of voice, but a monotone," recalls Jay Snider, Ed's son and former Flyer president. "I could tell he was shaken.

"I knew from the experience with my mother (Myrna, Snider's first wife, who had died from lung cancer seven months earlier) that this was the end. It just is."

At Columbus, Brayden Schenn scored with 56 seconds remaining in regulation for another last-minute point saved, but a 2-1 loss in overtime was one more point that got away. The Flyers had won only four of their last 15 games and had fallen to 9-13-5 and 13th place in the conference.

Lecavalier had been scratched for four games. "I don't want to be a distraction," he said. "That's not my style. It's not a time to say things I might regret and that's definitely not going to help the team.

"I'm not going to lie and say I didn't come here for Lavvy. But that's last year. It's a different system and it is what it is. It's my job to try to work with it and do my best."

Couturier's first-period shorthanded goal sparked a 4-1 Wells Fargo Center win over the similarly-struggling Devils, and Laughton scored his first NHL goal in a 5-1 blasting of cellar-dwelling Carolina. But the goals dried up again in a 3-1 loss to Tampa and then, as Lecavalier was reinstated into the lineup, a 2-1 loss to Florida was Philadelphia's 10th straight in a shootout over two seasons.

On December 19, Mason suffered an upper body injury at practice, necessitating the recall of Rob Zepp, a 33-year-old who had been signed in the summer of 2014 after seven years in the German League.

At Toronto, the Flyers suddenly exploded for seven goals in Emery's 7-4 victory that opened an eight-game road trip—Voracek's four assists putting him back into the NHL scoring lead with 42 points in 32 games. "He can play better," cracked Giroux, who also had four points.

The following night in Winnipeg, Lecavalier scored twice in the third period to bring Philadelphia from behind, enabling Voracek to strip Dustin Byfuglien and score 10 seconds into overtime. The Flyers won, 4-3, and Zepp made history as the oldest goaltender since 1926 to win his NHL debut.

"Thirty-three is the new 83," Zepp joked. "It's been a long road. I always believed I could do it, just needed an opportunity."

Del Zotto had been a healthy scratch in eight of the last 10 games. "Honestly, I don't know what to think. I really don't," he said.

The winning streak went to three games in Minnesota, where Lecavalier scored again, tipping in a MacDonald shot on the way to a 5-2 win.

Before the Flyers boarded their flight home for the league's mandated three-day Christmas holiday, Berube mentioned how he wasn't looking forward to having time off—after the last big break, the team recorded only one win in 10 games.

"Do you want to skip Christmas?" the coach said, laughing. "I don't mind."

Actually, the players volunteered to give up some of it. The CBA mandated December 24-26 off, including practice and travel. But rather than rising early on the 27th to get in a needed skate for a game that night in Nashville, Giroux and his teammates asked to leave the night before. Hextall agreed and the charter left at 8:24 p.m. When the NHL became aware of the transgression, the Flyers were fined an undisclosed amount of money.

"It's pretty hard not to allow [the players] the best possible chance to win the game, given the fact they want to do something they feel is best for the hockey club," Hextall said. "In the end, yeah, we were willing to accept the consequences."

"We were aware of the rule and certainly accept the league's decision."

A good night's sleep did nothing for the team's beleaguered penalty killers. Philadelphia gave up three powerplay goals in a 4-1 loss to Peter Laviolette's Predators.

The Flyers had enjoyed the seventh-best penalty-killing percentage in the NHL during the 2013-14 season. But Timonen's absence was proving acute and one key penalty killer, Adam Hall, had not been re-signed. Emery had slowed—his lack of lateral mobility particularly showing in shorthanded situations. Mason also had not made as many clutch saves as a year earlier. The woes reflected a lack of confidence, too. The kill percentage at home remained respectable, but on the road it was dead last in the NHL.

After missing four games, Mason returned on December 29 in Arizona, but fell behind 3-0. Although Umberger scored twice just three minutes apart, that was as close as Philadelphia would get in the 4-2 loss.

On New Year's Eve in Colorado, Berube's team rallied for third-period goals on a one-timer by Lecavalier and a breakaway by Giroux to go ahead 3-2. But Coburn took a tripping penalty and Jarome Iginla beat Mason on the short side with 7:12 remaining to tie the game. Ryan O'Reilly scored through a screen with 20 seconds remaining in overtime and another good effort was wasted in a disheartening 4-3 defeat.

"It was not a good penalty," the coach said. "We're playing pretty good hockey and finding ways to lose."

At Carolina, Mason was strong, but VandeVelde had the only goal in a 2-1 defeat. The following day in Newark, Emery was pulled after allowing three goals on just 10 shots as Philadelphia lost again, 5-2. So after starting the trip with three wins, the team had earned just one point in the next five contests, four of which had come against bottom-feeders. The Flyers were 5-13-4 on the road.

At least the club was going home. Simmonds scored in the third period, then again after the overtime, to give Philadelphia its first shootout win in 10 tries, 2-1 over Ottawa. In the next game, Umberger tied the Capitals 2-2, in the third period, and then Voracek beat them in overtime. But on January 10, Mason suffered a right knee injury eight minutes into the first period of a home game with Boston, and Emery gave up three goals on only 13 shots in the 3-1 loss. Zepp had to be recalled again.

The offense suddenly broke out and scored three times on the powerplay, all in a five-goal second period, for a 7-3 win over the Lightning on January 12. Coburn, however, was lost for four weeks on another shot to the same foot that was hit at the beginning of the season. Injuries were piling up. Nicklas Grossmann, his shoulder slammed into the boards by Tom Wilson during a 1-0 Washington win at the Verizon Center, would be gone for a month while Laughton was concussed on a hit by the Capitals' Matt Niskanen.

Colaiacovo, who hadn't played since November 19, and Del Zotto were established pros capable of stepping into the regular defensive rotation, but there was no such depth in scoring. Too many forwards continued to struggle. Matt Read had only three goals after playing on a sprained ankle for more than two months, and Brayden Schenn had scored only four times in a 28-game stretch.

Rob Zepp won his first NHL game at age 33, becoming the oldest goalie to win his NHL debut in 88 years.

In Mason's absence, the goaltending was problematic, too. Emery was pulled after allowing three goals on 12 shots in a 4-0 loss to Vancouver, the Flyers' second-straight defeat by shutout.

The league-worst Sabres helped get Philadelphia's offense going in Zepp's 4-3 win at Buffalo. But neither he, nor Emery, stopped much of anything as the Flyers lost their last-ever game at the Nassau Coliseum, 7-4, closing their all-time record in Uniondale at 54-55-15-3, plus 4-7 in the playoffs. The Islanders were moving to Brooklyn's Barclays Center for the 2015-16 season.

Philadelphia was a much more engaged team at the Wells Fargo Center, albeit to a fault—Rinaldo left his feet to crush Pittsburgh's Kris Letang into the boards during the first period, a January 20 hit that would result in an eight-game suspension. From that hostile start grew four second-period bouts, including Bellemare's first in the NHL, before Giroux won the game in overtime, 3-2.

"Everybody just fought for each other, literally," Bellemare said. "It was awesome; the fans were loving it."

Giroux and Voracek represented the Flyers in the All-Star Game at Columbus, where the fans and the league named the players, but Captains Jonathan Toews and Nick Foligno picked the sides. Toews apparently chose best when he took Voracek, whose six points tied a record during Team Toews 17-12 win over Giroux's Team Foligno. Like practically everybody, Giroux had a goal. But Voracek, who started his career with the Blue Jackets, probably had the best time.

Apparently a 17-12 hockey game—and his 56 points that still led the league—turned Voracek onto higher mathematics. As the regular-season resumed, he said Philadelphia, at 19-22-7, would need to win 25 of their last 34 games to make the playoffs.

Raffl was suffering from pneumonia, so the Flyers recalled White, who had been at Lehigh Valley for 11 games since recovering from a torn pectoral muscle. With Mason pronounced healed, but not yet having had a full practice, Emery got the start against Arizona. He lasted just four shots, giving up two goals before being replaced. Mason stopped 22 of 23, and then three Coyote shooters in a 4-3 shootout win, quite a first game back.

He stayed strong, stopping 36 shots in a 5-2 home victory over Winnipeg, shutting out Toronto 1-0 on a goal by Del Zotto, and keeping Philadelphia in a 3-2 shootout loss to the Islanders. Although back to 22-22-8, the Flyers were still nine points shy of the Capitals for the second wild-card spot.

Timonen had not given up on being able to help in a stretch run. Or, maybe, being traded to a contender for one last attempt at getting a Cup. After a CT scan indicated his clotting problem had been reduced to just one in his leg, the defenseman was cleared to do a solo skate on February 9. One month before his 40th birthday, he was a five-year-old at Christmas.

"I was so excited, I really couldn't sleep all night," he said. "I was kind of a little nervous that hopefully I wouldn't fall down right away."

Said Hextall, who watched the workout, "He's as stubborn as a mule, which is a good thing.

"Last summer, I wasn't very optimistic and Kimmo was. It took a lot to get me comfortable. The doctors all being on same page steered us in the direction that this is a reasonable risk."

Laughton returned to the lineup against Washington, sought revenge against Niskanen, and got pounded. But a greater loss happened midway through the second period, when Mason limped off with a knee injury. A third-period goal by Simmonds, then Voracek's into the empty net, gave Emery a 3-2 victory.

Mason needed arthroscopic surgery and was expected to return, but Philadelphia required a lot of points fast if they were going to get into the race. Zepp had gotten hurt at Lehigh Valley, so the backup became Anthony Stolarz, the second-round Flyer pick in 2012. But it was Emery's show now, and this time he responded, stopping 39 of 41 shots in a 2-1 overtime loss at Montreal.

He couldn't hold a 3-1 lead in a 4-3 overtime defeat at Columbus, but did win in Buffalo, 2-1, when Raffl returned to score in the third period.

A 6-0-3 stretch ended with a 44-shot effort wasted in a 5-2 loss to Columbus. The Bruins were sliding, however, and Philadelphia was only six points from the final playoff spot as Timonen returned to practice. He was greeted with a stick-tapping salute by his teammates.

Another top-five defenseman in Flyer history was back in the house on February 19—Eric Desjardins became the 23rd inductee into the Flyer Hall of Fame—before the game against Buffalo. "It was 20 years ago when I received the call that I was going to be a Flyer, and I remember as if it were yesterday," he told the crowd after being introduced by Chris Therien, his long-time partner on defense. "I never thought it would lead to a night like this."

Pierre-Edouard Bellemare, seen hear talking to his linemate, played 12 seasons in France and Sweden before joining the Flyers. He played 81 games in 2014-15.

Buffalo goalie Michal Neuvirth out-dueled Emery in a 3-2 Sabre shootout win. So with Zepp ready again, Berube went back to the greybeard rookie. Zepp defeated Nashville's Pekka Rinne, 3-2, in a shootout, and then beat Washington, 3-2, when Del Zotto jumped off the bench, took a pass from Voracek, and beat Braden Holtby in the final four minutes. With the 3-2 win, Philadelphia was within four points of Boston.

Lecavalier had not been producing on the fourth line with Bellemare and VandeVelde. Some nights the veteran was not even dressing. White gave the unit more energy and a little scoring punch, but second- and third-line production still was absent. Since the New Year, Giroux and Voracek had not been scoring at even strength, so Berube figured breaking them up might help spread the wealth and get some other guys going.

"Broken up?" Giroux laughed after practice. "It sounds pretty sad."

"Chief wanted to change it up a little bit and maybe spread it out," Voracek said. "I'm all for it. You have to try anything to make the playoffs."

One of the ways to do that was beating inferior teams. But after giving up two powerplay goals and losing 4-1 at Carolina on February 24, the Flyers had secured just four wins in the 13 road games they had played against non-playoff teams.

"We have to figure out a way to play consistently regardless of the opponent," said Simmonds.

The team had much more energy in Toronto, but Zepp allowed a Phil Kessel snipe and a Tyler Bozek breakaway goal on eight shots to put Philadelphia in a 2-0 hole. Mason, who was cleared by the doctor but had not practiced, came in to give up a powerplay goal by Dion Phaneuf, which, after Giroux and Brayden Schenn scored in the third period, turned out to decide the game. The Leafs had won, 3-2, despite being outshot 49-17, another hugely painful loss by Berube's team in a season filled with them.

"We gave everything we had tonight and came up short," said Streit. "It sucks. There's no other way to put it."

The Bruins had lost eight of ten, keeping the Flyers only four points back, although Boston had two games in hand. Philadelphia still had a chance and Hextall didn't think he would sabotage it by moving two veteran defensemen with trade value.

Del Zotto had come on significantly, and Shultz had been signed to a two-year extension ($2.25 million cap hit). With Gostisbehere, plus the 2013 and 2014 first-round picks—Sam Morin and Travis Sanheim—on the way, the GM was operating from a position of depth on defense.

On February 27, Timonen was traded to the Blackhawks for a second-round pick in the 2015 draft and a conditional fourth-rounder in 2016, ending the service of one of the most reliable performers in Flyer history.

The conditional draft pick would become a third-round selection if the Blackhawks won two playoff rounds and Timonen played half of the games, and a second-rounder if he played 50 percent of the games over three rounds.

The defensive anchor of Philadelphia's semifinalist club in 2008 and a deluxe No. 2 after Chris Pronger's arrival for the 2009-10 Stanley Cup Final team, Timonen had proven to be worth every penny of the $37.8 million over six years that Holmgren had invested in the defenseman as a key to the fast rebuild in 2007. Now he was going to get a chance to conclude his career with a Stanley Cup contender.

"He was the defenseman we really wanted," said Blackhawk GM Stan Bowman. "Setting aside that he hasn't played, once we get him up to speed, he's a great player. He's been an elite defenseman for a lot of years."

Even though the Flyers lost Grossmann to a concussion two days later in a 4-2 win over the Rangers, Hextall had a good deal on the table with Tampa Bay for the 29-year-old Coburn, and the GM wasn't going to pass it up.

"[GM Steve Yzerman] wanted Coby all along," recalls Hextall. "He knew Coby could play a lot of minutes against big players and fast players."

Yzerman was willing to move one of his two first-round picks in the 2015 draft, making him a perfect trading partner for Hextall, who wanted to lose Coburn's $4.5 million in cap space. But for a 29-year-old defenseman who was signed through the 2015-16 season, the Philadelphia GM wanted more than just the one pick. He asked about 24-year-old defenseman Radko Gudas.

"We wanted young players and assets, not necessarily a defenseman back," recalls Hextall. "The Kings had Radko at our L.A. development camp in 2009 (one year before Tampa drafted him in the third round). I liked him then. Our scouts here liked him. He was a fit.

"We didn't look at him as a throw-in at all. We liked the competitive element he'd bring, the physical element he has.

"You have a lot of people these days who think everything is just about speed and skill, speed and skill. That's all well and good, but, to this very day, will beats skill every time. You can't just put a bunch of fast, skilled players together and think you are going to win.

"Radko is hard to play against. And he's a right-handed shot."

Gudas also was out for the rest of the season after undergoing surgery in January to repair torn knee cartilage, one more reason Yzerman wanted to add Coburn to a team with Cup aspirations.

After midnight on the March 2 morning of the trade deadline, Hextall and Yzerman agreed on a deal that would bring Philadelphia first- and third-round picks in the 2015 draft, plus Gudas, for Coburn.

"I didn't want Coby to wake up in the morning and find out he'd been traded," Hextall said. "So I took the chance of calling him after midnight and, of course, it went to voicemail. I don't like it happening like that, but circumstances dictated."

At 6:30 a.m. Coburn's wife, Nadine, awoke with their 17-month-old son and saw many messages on Coburn's phone. After recording the ninth most regular-season games of any defenseman in team history (567), he no longer was a Flyer.

"It's tough to leave Philly, because this has been my home," Coburn told reporters when he went to the Skate Zone that day to pack up. "I really love it here. My family loves it here. Both my kids were born in Philadelphia, and I'm really proud of that.

"At least I was able to tell them that we're going to be a lot closer to Disney World."

While Coburn had never again matched the 36 points he scored in his first full Flyer season (2006-07) after arriving from Atlanta in a trade for 34-year-old blueliner Alexi Zhitnik, mobility had made the 6-5 defenseman one of the better one-on-one defenders in team history. His pairing with Timonen, who would arrive that summer, proved to be one of the franchise's more enduring and effective combinations.

Nevertheless, Hextall had acquired a high pick, cleared significant cap room, and gained five years in the Coburn-Gudas exchange, all fits for the GM's long-range vision.

"My plan and my thoughts with this franchise moving forward are no different from what they were last summer," he told reporters. "We're on the same path and we're going to continue to go down that path.

"If we win 10 games in a row, we're certainly not going to trade young players for older players to try and get incrementally better right now."

MacDonald, who had sat out four of the last 10 games, and Colaiacovo now had regular jobs on the defense. So did Bellemare on the fourth line. Hextall extended his contract for two more years, giving him a total of $1.425 million.

Couturier and Streit scored third-period goals to salvage a point in a 3-2 overtime home loss to Calgary. Two nights later, Philadelphia was down again in the third period, this time to Ken Hitchcock's Blues, when Del Zotto and Simmonds scored less than two minutes apart and Raffl hit the empty net to complete a 3-1 win.

The Flyers continued to be uncannily better against the good teams, a reflection of the goaltending they were getting since Mason's return. So it was a dumbfounding surprise when Hextall announced on the morning of March 6 that the organization had "mutually" parted ways with goaltending coach Jeff Reese after five-plus seasons.

"This is something that has come out of left field," Mason said after practice. "I don't want to comment on it too much. I will say that with Reeser, he was a huge part of getting me to the point where I am in my career now. I owe a ton to him.

"Sometimes, things happen that are hard to understand in the game of hockey. I think, like Hexy said, it was a mutual thing from the organization's standpoint and Reeser's standpoint. I don't want to [delve] too much into it."

Hextall would not give an explanation, only vehemently denied a subsequent report by *Philadelphia Daily News* beat reporter Frank Seravalli that Reese had been upset when Mason was rushed back into service to relieve Zepp in the February 26 game at Toronto. Today, neither the GM nor Reese will comment on the matter.

"He believed in Mase, and I thought he did a great job with him," Berube recalls, shedding further light on the subject. "I think Reeser had a lot to do with him getting a new contract, resurrecting his career, doing a lot of good things."

Mason had to put it aside immediately for the most important game of the season. The Flyers went to Boston the next day, still just four points behind the Bruins.

With White in the penalty box for hooking Gregory Campbell, Zdeno Chara's first-period point drive deflected through traffic and past Mason to give Boston a 1-0 lead. Midway through the second period, Matt Bartkowski tripped White. On the powerplay, Giroux's left-circle drive hit Brayden Schenn's foot and caromed over to Voracek, who fired a 25-footer past Tuukka Rask to make it 1-1.

The play was as even as it could be while the clock ran down on regulation, until Bellemare won an offensive zone draw from Campbell and got the puck back to Schultz. The first drive was blocked, but Brayden Schenn retrieved and Schultz tried again from almost on the blueline. VandeVelde got a piece of the shot and it trickled past Rask's right pad to put Philadelphia ahead, 2-1, with 4:30 to go.

The Bruins mustered minimal attack for the next two minutes, until Simmonds took a neutral-zone penalty for tripping Daniel Paille. Coach Claude Julien immediately pulled Rask to set up a six-on-four and a frantic final 2:03 in the Flyer end.

Del Zotto twice blocked shots by Torey Krug, and Mason found attempts by Krug and Dougie Hamilton through traffic, holding the puck on the last one for a faceoff with 19 seconds remaining. Patrice Bergeron won it from Giroux, Loui Eriksson fed the point, and Hamilton's shot beat a hopelessly screened Mason with 14 seconds left on the clock to tie the score, 2-2.

In the overtime, Streit, followed by Schultz, forced a Boston turnover just inside the Philadelphia line and Voracek broke away with the game on his stick. He cut to the middle and fired across his body, but Rask got a piece of the shot and the puck dribbled wide.

Forty seconds later, Couturier, looking to make a play as he approached the Bruin line, was stripped by Ryan Spooner and Boston broke the other way. Max Talbot fed Brad Marchand, one-on-one with Del Zotto, who sprawled as Marchand cut to the slot. The shot went off the defenseman and caromed over Mason's glove to win the game 3-2.

The Flyers had lost a point to fall five behind with 16 games remaining. The players looked like they had squandered their life savings.

"We put everything on the line for that game and it just didn't happen for us," recalls Rinaldo. "I think the guys' confidence levels went down, and as soon as that happens it's hard to pick it back up."

Four minutes into a game the following afternoon at Newark, Streit gave away the puck in back of the goal, then again in front as Adam Henrique put New Jersey ahead, 1-0. White tied it in the second period, but Jacob Josefson put in a rebound on a three-on-two and the Devils led again, 2-1.

Eric Gelinas scored through a screen to put New Jersey up 3-1, before Streit had a setup off a faceoff poked away from him for a two-man breakaway goal by Henrique. Just after Raffl cut the lead to 4-2 and Couturier missed an empty net on his backhand, Stephen Gionta got behind Streit and scored on another breakaway. The Devils won 5-2.

"I had a terrible game," said Streit, but his was only the most visible failure of a spiritless team effort. Whatever energy was shown by Philadelphia came from its fourth line. When the Bruins beat Detroit that night, the Flyers, who just a day earlier had been 14 seconds away from being two points out, now trailed by seven.

"Even though we didn't take care of what was needed and lost (to Boston) in overtime, the game in New Jersey bothered me more," recalls Berube. "I didn't see [the effort] I needed to see.

"Watching that, you kind of knew there was something wrong with this team."

Remembers Hextall, "We did fight in Boston, and then we went into Jersey with the wind sucked right out of us. That was a little bit bothersome."

Against Dallas at home two nights later, Philadelphia scored just 73 seconds into the game only to be outshot 32-11 in a 2-1 loss that had Voracek smashing his stick against the boards at the final buzzer.

"There was no desperation," Mason told the media. "It's tough to come in the room after games like that. We need to have a much better effort and it just wasn't there. I'm embarrassed and I hope everyone else is embarrassed, too."

Bluntness from a goalie about what was going on in front of him did not go over well with teammates. But the truth he spoke was undeniable. Two days later in St. Louis, Mason stopped all 35 shots he faced through regulation and overtime, but the Flyers still couldn't win, both Blues' shooters beating the goalie and sending him down to his second 1-0 shootout loss of the season.

With Brayden Schenn, who had scored only twice in his last 20 games, awakening with two goals, Philadelphia caught the Red Wings slumping and won 7-2 at the Wells Fargo Center. But six of the next eight were on the road, where Berube's team carried heavy baggage. The Flyers collapsed in the third period of consecutive 4-1 losses in Vancouver and Calgary. When Mason felt ill during the warm-up in Edmonton, a 3-1 first-period lead handed to Emery dissolved into a 5-4 loss.

Unable to make much of a contribution all season, Umberger went ahead with surgery on his hip and abdominal muscles. Philadelphia looked beyond help anyway. A 4-1 win over Timonen's visiting Blackhawks—the fans chanted "Kimmo! Kimmo!" after a video tribute—was only the second Flyer victory in 10 games. Any joy dissipated when MacDonald (concussion) and Simmonds (broken leg) were both lost for the season's seven remaining games.

Simmonds, who had 28 goals, was being denied a chance to reach 30 for the first time. MacDonald had started poorly, knew he wasn't living up to being a $6 million-a-year player, and allowed guilt and pressure to get to him.

"I was coming off a league-minimum deal, going to the one that I signed," he recalls. "I think it just came down to wanting to live up to those expectations."

It figured that the only Philadelphia road win in the last 11 tries would be in Pittsburgh, where it was also the seventh-straight Flyer victory at CONSOL Energy Center. Mason followed up that 4-1 win by again beating the Penguins 4-1 four days later at the Wells Fargo Center.

Berube's team blew a two-goal lead in the final two minutes against the Islanders only to win 5-4 when goalie Jaroslav Halak muffed an easy shot by Brayden Schenn with two seconds remaining.

Voracek, who finished with 81 points, six behind NHL scoring leader Jamie Benn of Dallas, was presented his second Bobby Clarke Trophy as the Flyer MVP before the final game, a 3-1 loss to Ottawa. Streit, who led all NHL defensemen in powerplay scoring, won his first Barry Ashbee Trophy as best defenseman.

Philadelphia (33-31-18) finished the year with 84 points, 14 back of Pittsburgh, which held off Boston for the last playoff spot in the East. The Flyers had their lowest goals-per-game average (2.56) since 1969-70, and their 10 road wins (10-20-11) were the franchise's fewest since 1972.

In stating at the beginning of the season that the team was at a level down from the top contenders, Hextall's expectations had been realistic. But the inconsistency especially troubled him. The club had gone 12-2-4 in its final 18 games against teams that had made the playoffs while losing 12 straight against those that didn't.

The limited moves by the new GM the previous summer had not worked out. Umberger had not replaced Hartnell's 20 goals and Emery, brought back for a second season, had not played well, a factor since Mason was able to start in only 51 games. Nevertheless, young core players Couturier, and especially, Brayden Schenn and Read, had not progressed, which had to impact the GM's deliberations about going forward with a coach he had inherited. Berube had a year remaining on his contract.

Snider's only instruction to Hextall was, "Do what you think is best."

In meetings immediately following the season's end, the GM and Berube talked about the team's needs going forward, but the coach was not promised he would be around to see them met.

"[Hextall] said to me, 'I've got to go through the process and look at everything,'" Berube recalls. "I wasn't sure what to think. If I were the GM, I would already know what I was going to do."

On the night of April 16, five days after the team's last game, Hextall called Berube and asked him to come into the office in the morning. "Then, I knew," recalls Berube.

The meeting was brief. Told he was being relieved of his duties, Berube left almost immediately. "What's there to say?" he recalls. "[Hextall] didn't know why he fired me. He never told me."

The GM also didn't explain much to reporters, with whom he was deliberately vague about his decision and the time it took to make it.

"It's just a process I went through," the GM said in a conference call. "In the end, I didn't feel like he got enough out of our group. If you don't think it's the right head coach, you've got to move on.

"If it wasn't a tough decision, it would have been done on Sunday (the day following the season's end). I believe Craig is an NHL coach and will go on to be an NHL coach."

Today, Hextall elaborates only a little.

"I think Craig is a good coach," the GM says. "I think he's a terrific guy. I've got all the respect in the world for him and it was a difficult day for me, partly because I consider him a friend, partly because we were once teammates.

"He represented everything we believe in as a franchise. He'd go to war for you, protect anyone on the team. But my job was to decide if he was the right guy moving forward. A lot of it comes down to your gut because as you delve into things, you can find the good and bad with anybody.

"Are you getting the most out of the team over the course of the season? Are you bringing the group together?

"I think he squeezed the most out of those guys the previous year. But I think it's different when you come in and the season is underway. It gets harder that second year."

Berube, who was 75-58-28 as the head coach, agrees that Year Two was more difficult, but that was at least partly because the club had not been improved.

"I think the team was what it was," recalls Berube, now coach of the Chicago Wolves, the Blues' farm team. "In my opinion, it lacked confidence, meaning whether the players thought we were good enough. I think Giroux struggled with that a lot.

"The organization really didn't do anything to make us better. I don't resent [taking the fall for] that. I don't resent anything about the Flyers. This organization has been great to me as a player (for two stretches), and then, in giving me a chance to coach when I retired. You always know that if you don't make the playoffs, you could be fired.

"It's hard to build something in two years. I wish I could have continued to coach them. It was awesome getting the chance."

BAUER
28
C
24

Chapter 17 • 2015-16

Good Night, Good Hockey, Good Life

In hiring a coach to replace Craig Berube, general manager Ron Hextall did due diligence on all the big names available.

Mike Babcock and John Tortorella had won Stanley Cups with Detroit and Tampa Bay, respectively, and Todd McLellan recorded three seasons of 50-plus wins in San Jose. The GM asked Chairman Ed Snider if there were any financial parameters to be heeded in the search and was told no, a green light to go after Babcock, who was leaving the Red Wings in part for financial reasons and was expected to get as much as $8 million a year. But hiring a marquee coach to appease a Philadelphia fan base frustrated by a non-playoff season in 2014-15 was not Hextall's priority. NHL head-coaching experience was not even near the top of his qualifications list.

During visits to the University of North Dakota to watch his son Brett play from 2008 to 2011, Hextall had been hugely impressed with coach Dave Hakstol. The GM-in-waiting knew if he were ever to be in a coach-hiring position, Hakstol would be high on the interview list.

Hakstol, who at UND had developed NHL players such as Jonathan Toews, Travis Zajac, Drew Stafford, T.J. Oshie, Matt Greene, and Flyer forward Chris VandeVelde, had coached a phenomenal six Frozen Four teams in his last 10 seasons. To Hextall, those results seemed like a manifestation of what he had witnessed on trips to Grand Forks.

"I liked the structure of Dave's teams, liked the consistency with which he coached them, the way he carried himself," recalls Hextall. "I always felt, 'that's an NHL coach!'

"I had talked to him a couple of times in passing, but didn't really know the person. Of all the guys I spoke to as I narrowed down my list, he was the one I needed the most to get to know. I had a picture in my mind of what I thought he was, but you have to make sure that the reality is in line with what you picture.

"I will say he was the most intriguing guy right from the start."

After two telephone conversations, Hakstol, 46, flew to Philadelphia to meet with Hextall, nobody else.

"There was a checklist of things I was looking for, and Dave hit all the checks on down the line," recalls the GM. "The only one missing was NHL experience and that mattered the least. I wasn't only thinking about right now for our team, but about being the right guy moving forward.

"Meeting as many days as we did, I felt comfortable that he was exactly who I thought he was. I liked his focus. If there was one single thing to narrow down that I liked, it was his leadership qualities.

"He also needed to know about me, about the organization and how we do things, where we were looking to go, and what coaching in this league would entail.

"He had a lot of success at North Dakota and was as secure in a situation as you're going to find in this business. He's also a very loyal guy and a family man (children then ages nine and seven), so that weighed into the process. There was a lot of risk for him.

"There were other guys on the narrowed-down list who I still liked if things with Dave didn't work out. I was prepared to go through the process with other candidates. One had no NHL experience, just like Dave.

"I'm not a guy to exclude someone because they haven't been in the NHL before. Everyone had no experience at one point, right? A lot of times the [veteran] hire is the right hire, but not in every case. Experience can be gained, the intangibles can't. Same thing with a player. Will you never put a rookie player in the lineup because he has no NHL experience? You can't think that way."

Hextall and Hakstol were two methodical guys, grinding their way through a process. On his second visit, Hakstol met with Snider and other Flyer staffers.

"There was no attempt on either side to fast-forward the process," recalls Hakstol. "It started with just talking hockey, without the specter of there being an offer.

"Not only was I very secure at North Dakota, it was in a place that I loved, a place where, to a certain degree, I'd grown up (as a student-athlete). I felt like I was still challenged at a high level there on a daily basis. And I had a goal of [an NCAA title] that was unfinished.

"The only reason you do something is if you can be all in and things are in place to ultimately have success.

"The NHL never had been my singular goal. But not lost on me was the opportunity to coach at the highest level of your profession.

"There really was no one thing I wanted to hear [from Hextall and the Flyers]. But given the time to learn more about what's going on here, it was intriguing. The realization slowly came to the forefront that this is a pathway to success at the NHL level. Over two, three, four weeks, that sunk in. There was a clear and apparent direction.

"(Wife) Erin said, 'I'm in.' Believe me, she's much more normally involved and in tune than just saying, 'You make the decision.' But that was her take on it. And that's not to say that there wasn't some stress for her, because I'm sure there was."

Hakstol agreed to a five-year contract, two to three years longer than the normal term of an NHL coach, let alone a first-timer. But the dollars were reasonable and Hextall was convinced he was hiring a coach built to last. "If he was going to commit to us, we needed to commit to him," recalls the GM. "Given what he was giving up [at North Dakota], it was fair."

The Hakstols had planned to break the news to their daughter Avery and son Brenden after Avery concluded her participation in a hockey tournament in Minneapolis. But her team made the finals and Erin and Dave had to catch a flight for the press conference the next day. Mom and Dad delivered the news via FaceTime from Philadelphia, the night before Hakstol's May 18 introduction at a Wells Fargo Center press conference.

Because Hakstol's name had not surfaced in one piece of media speculation, the name of the 19th head coach in Flyer history was a stunner, greeted with considerable skepticism because of the limited number of college coaches who had received opportunities in the NHL.

Herb Brooks, University of Minnesota and Olympic mastermind, had beaten the Flyers in two playoffs as coach of the Rangers, failing only in three hard-fought series to get past the Islander dynasty. The University of Wisconsin's Bob Johnson had coached the Flames to a Final in 1986 and the Penguins to the Stanley Cup in 1991. No college coach had gone directly to the NHL since then, so the unusual nature of the Philadelphia hire dominated the introductory press conference.

"It's a gamble," Hextall admitted. "But one thing I know about Dave is that he has all the intangibles to be a very good NHL coach. I'm extremely comfortable with that."

So was Snider. "We have had coaches without NHL experience," he told reporters. "Fred Shero and Mike Keenan both were successful for us. I think everyone is an unknown [entity] until they get here."

Hakstol talked with both of his assistant coaches at North Dakota about joining him on his Philadelphia staff, but Brad Berry was promoted to head coach and Dane Jackson to associate head coach. After speaking at length with incumbent Flyer assistants Ian Laperriere, Gord Murphy and Joe Mullen, the new bench boss decided he couldn't do any better.

"It became pretty clear to me the quality of people that we had here," recalls Hakstol. "Their depth of experience was extremely important. All those guys played and coached at this level.

"They had a lot of things I didn't have—different personalities than me, different talents, areas of focus as coaches. That experience level was extremely important."

The odd man out was Terry Murray, who had told Hextall he wanted to return for a second term (the first was 2004-08) as a Flyer assistant rather than continue as head coach at Lehigh Valley. He took a position under Dan Bylsma, the new coach of the Sabres, who were managed by Tim Murray, Terry's nephew.

"I think Terry is a phenomenal coach and an unbelievable human being," recalls Hakstol. "You just can't have everybody on your staff."

Without Murray, Philadelphia had no one with NHL head-coaching experience, which seemed counter-intuitive since Hakstol had no exposure to the league. But Hextall thought other considerations were more important.

"Dave knew how to run a team," the GM recalls. "I felt knowing the (other) teams and players, knowing some systems, were as, or more, important than having head-coaching experience."

Scott Gordon, an Islander head coach from 2008-10 and three years an assistant with the Maple Leafs, replaced Murray as the Phantom coach. Hextall chose Kim Dillabaugh, eight years in a netminding-development position with Los Angeles, as goalie coach, replacing Jeff Reese, who had abruptly been let go in March. Brady Robinson, nine years a coach with the Victoria Royals of the Western Hockey League and a former associate of Dillabaugh's, was hired for the newly-created position of goaltending-development coach.

Hakstol visited personally, or spoke by telephone, to everybody on the team, traveling to Ottawa to see Giroux, and even flying to Prague just for a two-hour dinner with Jake Voracek. The new coach watched video of the 2014-15 Flyers, but put much more value in getting to know each as a person rather than a player.

"There's minimal information you can gather from video," said Hakstol. "It is not first-hand. My most valuable information came from short meetings and phone conversations. There's lots of time to for hockey specifics as we get into late summer and the fall."

Hextall added mobility to his defense with the signing of Evgeni Medvedev, a three-time all-star in the KHL, to a one-year, $3 million contract. The 32-year-old Russian became the ninth veteran on the Flyer defense, but the GM told reporters on a conference call that he projected Medvedev in the top four. "Good size, skates well, moves the puck well," said Hextall. "He's a real solid, two-way defenseman who can play either side of the ice. He was on the radar for at least a couple years, probably with a lot of teams.

Medvedev had put off his ambitions to give the NHL a try until after the 2014 Sochi Olympics. "In my mind, it was easier to get ready for that while playing in the KHL," he said.

Hextall cleared space on the defense, and $3.5 million to help squeeze in Medvedev, by trading Nicklas Grossmann to Phoenix for center-winger Sam Gagner and a fourth-round draft choice. Gagner had been the 2007 sixth-overall pick.

The Coyotes also took the remaining two years of Chris Pronger's contract, at $575,000 for each season, because the $4.9 million cap hit (an average of the salary over the course of the contact) would help Phoenix reach the required salary floor. Pronger, who hadn't played in four years because of post-concussion symptoms, was working for the NHL in the Department of Player Safety.

Philadelphia had taken defensemen Sam Morin and Travis Sanheim in the first round of the last two drafts, and two more significant blueline prospects—Shayne Gostisbehere, their third-round pick in 2012, and Robert Hagg, the second choice in 2013—were at Lehigh Valley. The organization was not nearly as blessed in future forwards.

But the disappointing 2014-15 season, and the seventh-overall pick that resulted, had given the Flyers an opportunity to land a blue-chip prospect at any position, not just select for need.

A strong top to the 2015 draft included two more defensemen—Boston College's Noah Hanifin and the Brandon Wheat Kings' Ivan Provorov—who were further advanced prospects at age 18 than anybody Philadelphia had taken in the last three Junes. A true Stanley Cup contender needed an anchor defenseman. The more talented D-men the Flyers selected, the greater the odds one of them would turn out to be elite.

The chance of Hanifin, who was ranked the third-best North American prospect by Central Scouting, falling to No. 7 was unlikely, but the Russian-born Provorov was rated seventh, perhaps putting him in obtainable range. Assuming that center Connor McDavid, considered the most gifted prospect since Sidney Crosby, and center Jack Eichel of Boston University were going No. 1 and No. 2 to Edmonton and Buffalo, respectively, Provorov was the top player on director of scouting Chris Pryor's list. He and other members of the Philadelphia organization had interviewed Provorov three times.

Hextall attempted to trade up, but the prices for doing so reflected the quality of the players near the top of this draft. "We tried to do a lot of things," the GM recalls. "We tried to get a high pick outright (not including the seventh selection in a deal). There was nothing reasonable."

Ivan Provorov was pleased to have been selected seventh overall by the Flyers at the 2015 NHL Draft. A physical defenseman for the Brandon Wheat Kings, he led all WHL rookies with 61 points.

So on June 26, the Flyers sat at their table at the BB&T Center in Sunrise, FL and waited as the Oilers took McDavid and Eichel went to the Sabres. Dylan Strome of the Erie Otters, also to nobody's surprise, was selected third by Phoenix. Instead of drafting Hanifin, the Maple Leafs, going fourth, selected center-right wing Mitch Marner of the London Knights, leaving both defensemen still on the board with only two picks remaining until Philadelphia's turn. The chance to select Provorov had just improved significantly.

Hanifin went fifth to Carolina, leaving just the Devils, picking sixth, to announce their selection. "You hear Jersey is going to take (6-3 center Pavel) Zacha (of the Sarnia Sting), but how do you know?" recalls Hextall. "Some teams put it out there so you will hear it. You never know until the pick comes."

Indeed, Zacha was taken by New Jersey. The Flyers had their guy and Provorov his wish. "I was hoping Philadelphia would take me," he said after taking the big walk up to the stage and shaking hands with the brass that included Snider.

"We believe you build from the back end out," Hextall told reporters. "We're really excited to have Ivan. He is a 200-foot player with elite hockey sense and is a real good competitor."

Provorov, 6-0, 191, and born in Yaroslavl, Russia, had arrived in North America at age 13 to prepare for a career in the NHL, joining the Wilkes-Barre/Scranton Knights in the Atlantic Youth Hockey League, for whom former Flyer defenseman Kerry Huffman was director of player development. "For me to grow as a player, I felt I needed to come here, learn the game," he told reporters. "It's faster here, more physical, and you have to make quick decisions."

During his second year at Wilkes Barre/Scranton, Provorov led his team to the Under-16 National Championship, and was then drafted by the Wheat Kings, for whom he scored 61 points in 60 games and showed a capability seemingly beyond his years for controlling play in the defensive zone.

With the 29th pick in the first round, obtained in the trade of Braydon Coburn, the Flyers were determined to go for a forward. There were two prospects—Ottawa center Travis Konecny and Kelowna right wing Nick Merkley—they hoped would fall into their range. Hextall let it be known that the 61st pick, which Philadelphia had received from Chicago for Kimmo Timonen, was in play in case any team was interested in trading down to 29 and picking up an extra selection.

"We were looking to move up, or possibly, if the two guys we really, really wanted were gone, maybe move back," said Hextall. "Toronto (selecting 21st) called. I think it was a reasonable offer, so we discussed it and jumped on it."

The Flyers selected Konecny, undeterred by his 5-10 frame that likely had downgraded him to become a late first-rounder. "Speed, skill, competitiveness," said Hextall. "He is the captain of his team at 17."

The prospect credited his size for helping him grow as a player. "I use that as motivation," he told interviewers. "I know I can compete with anybody as long as I keep working hard, getting stronger, and developing skills.

"It's a dream come true when a team wants you so much they trade up to get you."

The next day, Konecny was named the inaugural winner of the E.J. McGuire Award of Excellence, to be given annually to the "NHL Draft prospect who best exemplifies commitment to excellence through

Hustling center Travis Konecny of the Ottawa 67s was drafted 29th in 2015. He was the first winner of the E.J. McGuire Award of Excellence.

strength of character, competitiveness and athleticism." The award honors the memory of McGuire, the former Flyer assistant coach and director of the NHL's Central Scouting Bureau from 2005 until his death in April 2011.

As free agency began on July 1, Hextall had limited cap room and just one priority—a backup goaltender.

Ray Emery, whose career had been derailed in Ottawa by behavior issues, had proven himself to be a model Flyer in two stretches with the team interrupted by a nearly miraculous recovery from a serious hip condition (avascular necrosis). But at 32, he had not been the same goaltender in his second year backing up Steve Mason, so Hextall decided not to renew Emery's contract.

"Ray was a pro," recalls Hextall. "He helped Mase a lot, was a good team player. He obviously wouldn't have come back from that [hip graft] without a remarkable will. But we felt we had to upgrade.

"We made our list and (free agent) Michal Neuvirth was at the top of it. When I was in L.A., our (Manchester, NH) farm club played Hershey (Washington's affiliate) in the semifinals. That's when I started to really like Neuvy (the second-round Capital pick in 2006). We sat down with our [scouts] and it was a consensus that he was the guy we should target."

Neuvirth won consecutive AHL titles at Hershey and, for a time, held the No. 1 job with the Caps before losing that opportunity due to injuries, inconsistency, and the emergence of Braden Holtby. Traded to Buffalo in the summer of 2014, then, at the trading deadline to the Islanders, Neuvirth served as backup to Jaroslav Halak. Because Neuvirth's only issue was durability, the Flyers had competition for the 27-year-old goaltender, necessitating a two-year, $3.25 million deal.

"He was in [the Czech Republic] with Jake Voracek when he signed with us," recalls Hextall. "Jake had been talking to him about the organization. That may have been in our favor."

Voracek, who had one year remaining on his contract at $4.5 million, was locked up for another eight at $66 million, the maximum allowed under the Collective Bargaining Agreement. "The Jake Voraceks of the world are few and far between," said Hextall.

Sean Couturier, also entering the last year (at $1.5 million) of a pact, was extended for an additional six years and $26 million.

Philadelphia avoided arbitration with defenseman Michael Del Zotto, signing him to a two-year deal worth $7.75 million. They also kept VandeVelde for two-seasons at a combined $1.425 million and brought back Ryan White for another year at $800,000. Zac Rinaldo was traded to the Bruins for a 2017 third-round choice.

Gostisbehere, coming off an ACL tear that limited his AHL season to five games, had three goals in three exhibition contests. "I call him 'Gots To Be Here,'" laughed Snider. But Hextall, determined not to rush any prospect, had no intention of keeping the young defenseman. Medvedev had been signed and Del Zotto retained to provide an upgrade in mobility on the back line, giving the team eight blueliners.

Because Hextall didn't want to expose 25-year-old Brandon Manning to claim, the GM instead waived Andrew MacDonald, knowing no other club would take on a contract with five years and $25.75 million to go. MacDonald cleared and was sent to Lehigh Valley at a cap savings of only $950,000, but every little bit of relief helped.

"We did what we had to do to protect the asset," recalls Hextall. "We had cap, roster and waiver situations, and then there was the (poor) season [MacDonald] had the year before.

"But we were not going to leave him in the minors any longer than we had to. He's a good player."

The GM was trying to find a taker for Vincent Lecavalier, who had three years and $10.5 million left on his deal and did not figure to have a place in the opening day lineup. "It hasn't worked for him, and it hasn't worked for us," Hextall said.

Hakstol thought the players reported to camp in good shape and liked the competition level. Making significant changes in the neutral-zone coverage, he wasn't expecting miracles, so the coach graded the camp a C, which was pretty much what the 2015-16 Flyers were receiving from prognosticators. The additions of Radko Gudas—good to go after knee surgery—Medvedev, Gagner, and rookies Scott Laughton and Manning, were not enough to inspire predictions that the team would make up the 14 points by which it had failed to qualify for the playoffs the previous year.

Hakstol, still in the information-gathering stage, was unsure of his club's potential, but certainly wasn't going to set the bar low. "I had the expectation of being in the postseason, yes," he recalls. "Ultimately, I wouldn't know any other way to approach it."

As usual, Giroux wasn't afraid to exude optimism. "We think we're a playoff team," said the captain, who could have inspired some confidence in the first period of the opener at Tampa Bay by converting a penalty shot. But he missed, as did Laughton, who also was awarded one in overtime, as the NHL debuted its new three-on-three format. Nevertheless, Philadelphia, 3-2 losers in Hakstol's regular-season inaugural, had played close to even against the Lightning, a defending conference finalist, thanks to Mason.

Two nights later at Sunrise, he gave up four goals in the first 6:46 and was pulled from a 7-1 rout. "When your starting goaltender performs like that, it puts everybody behind the eight-ball right away," said Mason. "I take full responsibility."

Having committed nine penalties, his teammates thought they should share the blame, calling a players-only meeting after the second game of the season, never a good sign. "It wasn't necessarily about the score, it was about how we played," Voracek said. Certainly the subject of the powwow was not Mason. The team understood he was going through a sad and sudden personal situation, which the Flyers did not disclose to the media.

In the rematch with Florida, Neuvirth got the start and, thanks to a first-period goal by Brayden Schenn, a 1-0 shutout. Hakstol's first victory also was the first home opener Ed Snider ever missed.

"After finding out (in December 2014) that his cancer had metastasized, he had stayed pretty active," recalls Jay Snider, Ed's son and the former Flyer president. "He was subdued, a little withdrawn, not optimistic like when he was originally diagnosed (in January 2014), but still playing tennis.

"Over the summer, he had been complaining more. All of sudden, he couldn't do things."

The team released a statement saying the Chairman was "resting and recharging after recent medical therapy" at his home in Montecito, CA. Snider was watching his team on television, of course, and remained in contact with Hextall two or three times a week.

"He was excited about our first game," reported the GM. I said, 'I've never heard you happy after a loss.'"

When Chicago followed Florida to the Wells Fargo Center, the Flyers conducted a short ceremony on the ice to honor the retired Kimmo Timonen for the Stanley Cup he had won five months earlier with the Blackhawks. Timonen wanted his parents, who had been at the United Center for the Blackhawk ring ceremony one week earlier, to feel Philadelphia's love, too, so he brought them along.

"I really feel honored the Flyers are doing this for me," said Timonen, who was maintaining his home in Haddonfield, NJ. Before dropping the first puck, he received a huge ovation from the fans, most of whom had been rooting for the Blackhawks because of him. "Kimmo was the only reason I was watching the Final," said Wayne Simmonds.

Chicago remained winless in Philadelphia since clinching the Stanley Cup there in 2010, thanks to Neuvirth's second consecutive shutout, 3-0. Nevertheless, Hakstol went back to Mason for the next game, a 2-1 loss to Dallas. With the first line of Giroux, Voracek and Michael Raffl still goalless, the Flyers weren't scoring much for either netminder. "We're not the kind of team that can blow people away right now," the coach said. "So we have to do all the little things right."

The following night in Boston, Neuvirth was concussed when accidentally struck in the facemask by the stick of Patrice Bergeron, and replaced by Mason. Philadelphia also lost Couturier on a high hit by Rinaldo that earned a five-minute charging penalty. The Bruins scored twice in the second period to take a 4-2 lead, but Mason made a spectacular glove save on David Pasternak and the Flyers rallied on goals by Giroux and Simmonds to force overtime. Giroux's one-timer from the face-off dot on the powerplay won the game, 5-4, his team's first victory in its last seven attempts against Boston.

"No place for it," said Hakstol about the hit by Rinaldo, who was not suspended by the NHL.

The concussed Couturier was going to miss some time. When Raffl, who ran into an elbow by Jarret Stoll when the Rangers visited, collapsed on the bench and had to be helped to the locker room, it appeared he had suffered head trauma, too. On an overtime breakaway, Gagner shot over top after appearing to have Henrik Lundqvist beaten, but redeemed himself with a shootout goal in Mason's 3-2 win.

Doctors couldn't find anything wrong with Raffl. The Hakstol era was off to a 4-2-1 start. "The detail to our game wasn't there, but we were playing hard," recalls the coach.

Like Timonen, Danny Briere had retired (in his case from the Avalanche) in the off-season, albeit without a storybook ending. But Philadelphia fans didn't need one to bestow their love when the Flyers had Briere drop the puck before the October 27 game against his old team, Buffalo. "It was a blast playing here," he said. "This is home

(Haddonfield, NJ) for me now. It's pretty cool to find out the fans love you so."

Brayden Schenn scored his second goal of the third period for a 3-3 tie. But Philadelphia not only lost the game in overtime, 4-3, on a breakaway five-hole score on Mason by Zemgus Girgensons, but also Pierre-Edouard Bellemare to a right leg injury. The team was down to two regular centers, putting Lecavalier in the lineup after sitting for the first seven contests.

Hakstol tried to take the heat for a 4-1 home loss to the Devils in which the Flyers took two penalties for too many men on the ice. "I have to do a better job of communicating," the coach said. But he was minus two centers—Couturier and Bellemare—and Voracek had misplaced his hands when the team needed everybody on deck. Nine games into the season, he had yet to score.

The following night in Buffalo, Neuvirth returned and Philadelphia, beginning a five-game trip, started well until the Sabres scored in the final minute of the first period. Concentration then ebbed in a 3-1 loss, a worrisome reminder of what had happened repeatedly during the Flyers' 10-win road season in 2014-15.

"We tore ourselves apart with (five) penalties in the second period, didn't have the [capability] to stay with our game," recalls Hakstol. "That was an indicator of where we were as a team."

In Vancouver, Giroux had the only goal of a dismal 4-1 loss. At Edmonton, Mason was a last-minute scratch with an illness and Philadelphia, outshot 49-22, generated nothing but bad feelings. Connor McDavid—the Oilers' prized first pick in the draft—lost his edge in trying to get wide of Manning, hit the boards, and suffered a shoulder dislocation, which looked like an accident to everyone but *Hockey Night in Canada*'s Don Cherry. He railed on about an attempt to injure.

The Flyers stood better accused of playing terribly. "We're throwing too many pucks away," White said. "We are winning battles and almost giving the puck right back to them. When you are not winning, you get a bit fragile. We need to calm down."

They did in Calgary, where Couturier returned after six games, and Raffl's goal earned a point in a 2-1 overtime loss. Nevertheless, the team had lost six straight and managed only nine goals in the process. Finally, in Winnipeg, Brayden Schenn scored a first period powerplay goal, Simmonds added another midway in the third, and Neuvirth's third shutout of the season gave Philadelphia a 3-0 victory.

"I thought it was our first high-level team performance of the season," recalls Hakstol. "After some tough nights and some tough discussions, we showed progress at the back end of a tough trip. I think that says it all about the leadership inside the room."

On November 9, Chris Pronger, one of the Flyers' all-time best guys in the room, was inducted into the Hockey Hall of Fame, an indication that he also was dominant on the ice during a five-team career that ended prematurely with a concussion in Philadelphia.

"Paul Holmgren, from those first days in Hartford until my final days in Philly, you were always there to support and look out for me," said the defenseman in his acceptance speech. "You had my back, Homer, and I am very grateful to the Philadelphia Flyers and Mr. Snider for all they did for me while I was battling to recover from my latest injury."

Having passed one test of their professionalism—buckling down in the final game of a long road trip—the Flyers promptly flunked their follow-up exam, losing the often-treacherous first game back at home, 4-0 to Colorado. When a 5-2 home loss to Washington followed, Hakstol ran what he called a grueling "head-clearing" practice the next morning that threatened to be breakfast clearing as well.

"We got away from the level of competition needed to be successful," recalls the coach. Voracek's efforts were above reproach, but 16 games into the season, he still was searching for his first goal.

"In practice today, he was only hitting the post and I started laughing," said Giroux. "I'm like, 'Jake, it's going to start going in, don't worry.'"

Not getting better any time soon was a groin issue turning Mark Streit's 20-plus minutes per game into agony. "He was really struggling and in pain," recalls Hextall. "Something had to be done." Streit's pubic plate had become detached, necessitating surgery that was expected to leave the defenseman out for six weeks.

Philadelphia needed a powerplay point man. As the team flew to Carolina, Hextall went to Allentown to watch Gostisbehere.

"Shayne had not had a great training camp," the GM recalls. "He was skating fine (coming off the ACL repair), just didn't look ready to play in the NHL.

"In my mind—although I didn't tell anybody this—he would be promoted around Christmas, after he got some legs and confidence. He started slow in Lehigh, then started to get a little bit better. I kind of felt the momentum was building when Mark got hurt. Still, if Ghost didn't play well that night, he wasn't going to come up. But he was very good."

The next evening in Raleigh, the Flyers—who had Bellemare back from a seven-game absence—were trailing 2-1 late in the third period when Gostisbehere took a cross-ice pass from Manning, spun away from Chris Terry, and fired a wrist shot from just inside the top of the circle that glanced off Simmonds' knee and past goalie Cam Ward to tie the score.

In overtime, Voracek, redirecting a Del Zotto drive, won the game, 3-2, with his first goal of the season. "I almost forgot how that feels," the winger said.

Hextall hadn't changed his feelings about Gostisbehere. The first game he struggled, the 22-year old was going back to the AHL. Instead, 3:41 into the next contest, he one-timed his first NHL goal off a feed from Giroux, past Kings goaltender Jonathan Quick. As Philadelphia, with Snider in the house, lost 3-2 to L.A., and then 1-0 to the Sharks, both in overtime, it was hard to take consolation in single points. The Flyers had only won two of their last 12 games.

Asked what his team could do, Hakstol said, "We're just going to keep doing the things we're doing. We went through a tough period where we just didn't play well. We're doing all the right things now, so we just have to stick with it."

They did in Ottawa for 38 shots, only to stay stuck in the mud in a 4-0 loss. Through 20 games, Philadelphia's 34 goals were the fewest in the league. "We had some Grade A looks," said Hakstol. "We have to find a way to finish."

The Flyers came into a November 23 home game against Carolina—and Rod Brind'Amour's Flyer Hall of Fame induction—looking punchless. It was reminiscent of the honoree's early days in Philadelphia, when he was the first brick laid in a major rebuild. The fans loved him even then, which hadn't changed in the years following his trade to Carolina in 2000 for Keith Primeau.

"It's been almost 16 years since I put on a Flyers jersey, and I didn't know if you would remember me," Brind'Amour, still serving the Hurricanes as an assistant coach, said after a long ovation. "But I shouldn't be surprised because this is Philadelphia and Flyers fans never forget."

Brind'Amour thanked Paul Holmgren, his first Philadelphia coach, "for instilling in me what was expected as a Flyer." The new Hall-of-Famer praised Snider as "one of the greatest owners in sports." The Chairman, who had hoped to attend, instead spoke to Brind'Amour before and after the ceremony.

In the game, Giroux set up Brayden Schenn's powerplay goal and then scored shorthanded to stake Philadelphia to a 2-0 lead before the Flyers twice lost coverage on rebounds, enabling the Hurricanes to tie it, 2-2, in the third. But 11 seconds into overtime, Couturier drew a penalty and, on the powerplay, Gostisbehere ripped a give-and-go pass from Giroux by goalie Eddie Lack to save Philadelphia, the 3-2 winner, from another squandered point. "I'm still pinching myself a little bit to get such a big goal," Gostisbehere said.

Preaching to the converted: Rod Brind'Amour was inducted into the Flyers Hall or Fame, Novemebr 23, 2015

It didn't seem real to be playing the Islanders anywhere but at the Nassau Coliseum. But the old rivals had moved to Brooklyn's new Barclays Center, where Giroux scored three minutes into Philadelphia's first-ever visit. The promising start faded into just 10 Flyer shots combined in the second and third periods of a 3-1 loss. Hakstol's team had won just seven of its first 22 games, and were one point above last place in the conference.

Injuries to White (shoulder) and Gagner (concussion) caused the call-up of 31-year-old right wing Colin McDonald, whose third-period goal had Philadelphia just 20 seconds away from a Black Friday win over Nashville. Again, the Flyers couldn't close out a game. Mike Fisher's goal with 20 seconds remaining forced overtime. But with the Predators penalized early in the extra session for too many men on the ice, Giroux drew up a play at the bench on the grease board and then fed another Gostisbehere overtime winner, through a Simmonds screen of Pekka Rinne, producing a 3-2 victory.

"It's a fun ride right now, and I don't have any plans of getting off it," said Gostisbehere, who had five points in the seven games since his promotion.

"His impact was immediate, significant, and a real jolt of energy for our team at the right time," Hakstol recalls.

The following day at Madison Square Garden, Simmonds scored in the second-period and Couturier for the first time in the 12 games since returning to the lineup. This time, Philadelphia finished the job when Simmonds scored again into the empty net. The Flyers broke a 10-game regular-season losing streak in New York with Mason's 3-0 shutout.

"There are moments of real good hockey and then moments we fall back, but I thought [Friday] afternoon, and especially today, we were the hungrier team," the goalie said. "The boys weren't giving them any time and space. That's the effort level we need to have. You get rewarded for it."

At Ottawa, Gostisbehere got his team an early lead and Simmonds broke a 2-2 third-period tie, seeding some more confidence in a 4-2 victory. Bellemare scored midway through the third period at New Jersey and was about to be the hero until he took a late penalty enabling Michael Cammalleri to tie the game on a powerplay. But Philadelphia was accustomed to being caught from behind in third periods by now. Matt Read's first goal in 12 games, in overtime off a two-on-one with Couturier, gave the team a 4-3 victory and a four-game winning streak.

The following night at home, the Flyers had White back in the lineup. But old friends Scott Hartnell (goal and two assists) and Sergei Bobrovsky (27 saves) keyed a too-easy 4-1 win by Columbus. Down 3-1 at the Wells Fargo Center to the Islanders, Hakstol yanked Mason and Philadelphia rallied on goals by White and Giroux, but Jaroslav Halak outdueled Neuvirth in the shootout of a 4-3 loss.

Maybe the Flyers just needed another road game. Raffl, Read and Giroux rattled off second-period goals and Neuvirth allowed only a score by David Backes through a big third-period push by Ken Hitchcock's Blues, enabling Philadelphia to hang on to win, 3-2. "[St. Louis] is a good team and we don't have an easier game (in Dallas) tomorrow, so it's good to get this one," said Giroux.

Indeed, the victory seemed exhausting. Hakstol's team was outshot 44 to 20 and Gostisbehere's goal was the only one in a penalty-filled 3-1 loss to the Western Conference leading Stars.

Voracek, still having scored only one goal, was moved to the left side with Couturier and Simmonds. The switch seemed to work. Jake redirected a point shot by Simmonds for a 1-0 lead over the Hurricanes and then set up Gostisbehere's third overtime winner in the 11

games since his call-up. The Flyers again beat Carolina, 4-3, at the Wells Fargo Center.

"Three-on-three is built for him," Voracek said of the rookie. "He's a great skater with a great shot and is smart as well, so he knows when to jump in and what to do with the puck when he's got it."

Mason received his first start in four games and nursed Raffl's first-period goal until Couturier supplied late insurance in a 2-0 win over Vancouver. Behind 2-0 at Columbus in the third period, Laughton's first goal in 17 games and Voracek's third of the season brought Philadelphia back to a tie, but only Simmonds scored during a six-round shootout that became Mason's 3-2 loss and the team's ninth in 10 games to the Blue Jackets.

The Flyers were an improved 7-2-2 in their last 11 games, however, making it a good time for Hextall to visit Snider.

The Chairman was never without family, and there was no shortage of good friends—including music icon David Foster, comedian Dennis Miller, former NHL team owner Howard Baldwin, and mall magnate Herb Simon—happy to drop by as Snider's levels of pain and energy permitted. But if they wanted to watch the Flyers with him, all the better.

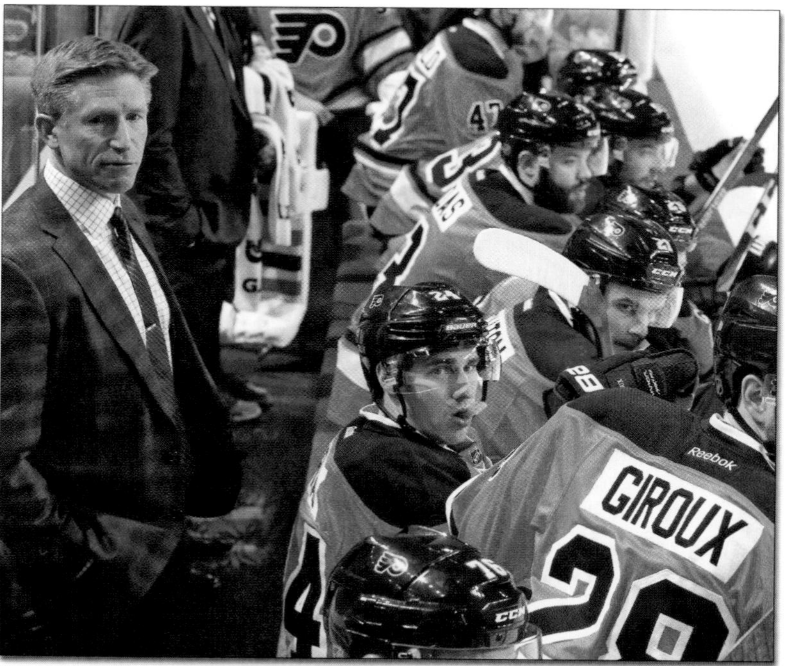

Coach Dave Hakstol made the jump to the NHL after an extremely successful collegiate coaching career at the University of North Dakota.

When Snider's daughter Lindy asked Hextall if he could visit, the GM said of course. "When I told him I was coming out on December 21 to watch a game with him, he got all excited," recalls Hextall. "He said, 'I'll make all the arrangements.' I said, 'I can do that.' He said, 'No, no.' He had his driver pick me up at the (Santa Barbara) airport."

Hextall got the tour of the house with the great room views of the ocean on one side and his fountain fronting the mountains on the other. "Nice place," Hextall said, and got Snider's standard, "Thanks, but you should see Oprah's place next door."

In the 20-seat basement home theatre, they put on the Flyers and Blues telecast from the Wells Fargo Center. Five seconds after St. Louis had gone up 3-0 in the second period, Giroux took a penalty.

"This isn't the way we planned it," Snider said.

"No, it really isn't," Hextall agreed.

Chris VandeVelde put in his own rebound shorthanded. Snider reached over and gave Hextall a high five. Simmonds made it 3-2 before the end of the second, and then scored on the powerplay in the third to tie it. Medvedev's goal with 3:13 to play put Philadelphia ahead.

"With all the pain he was in, he got out of his seat when we scored that fourth goal to give me a hug," recalls Hextall. "It made me think about what this hockey club meant to him. Pretty neat."

The Flyers hung on to win, 4-3, exactly the way Snider and Hextall had planned it. Snider insisted Ron stay for dinner and the night. The next morning, the GM was having coffee when the boss came to breakfast dressed in an orange and black sweat suit.

The big Flyer banner on the flagpole in the window behind Snider forever framed Hextall's memory of the scene. "Sitting and laughing with this Flyer paraphernalia all over him," he says. "I just wish I had taken a picture."

Philadelphia's annual holiday-week Western swing opened in Anaheim, where Raffl's second-period goal gave the team a 2-1 lead for less than two minutes, until Corey Perry beat Mason between the legs on a rebound. The Ducks went on to win 4-2.

Streit returned three nights later at San Jose, but Gostisbehere obviously was not going back to the Phantoms. The "emergency recall" had produced six goals and eight assists in the 18 games since his promotion, and besides, Del Zotto was day-to-day with a wrist injury suffered during the win against the Blues. Instead, Gagner, recovered from his concussion, cleared waivers and was sent to Lehigh Valley.

Against the Sharks, Simmonds stole the puck from Brett Burns and scored on a breakaway to put the Flyers ahead 2-1, getting them to within 16 minutes of only the second win in their last 19 tries against San Jose. But 45 seconds later, R.J. Umberger took a penalty, Burns redeemed himself by scoring on the powerplay, and Joe Pavelski's goal sent the Sharks on to a 4-2 victory.

The next day, New Years Eve, the Flyers practiced at Ice in Paradise, a rink in Montecito that Snider helped to build, and then went to his home for lunch.

"We talked a little bit about hockey, but not that much," said Giroux. "It was more about life. We looked at everything he had in there. There's a lot of cool stuff."

The players stayed less than three hours but gained a sobering sense of Snider's plight and a deeper understanding of how much the Flyers meant to him.

"After our visit, there was naturally more of an investment on the part of our team into what he was going through," Hakstol said.

Said Mason, "I think the guys are trying to make the season special for him."

Two days later at the Staples Center, with Del Zotto back in the lineup, the Kings scored off a Gudas giveaway and then added another goal with Gostisbehere in the box to jump to a 2-0 first-period lead. Brayden Schenn scored as part of a 16-shot final-20 minutes, but the Flyers fell short in a 2-1 loss that completed an 0-3 trip, putting the team back to .500 at 15-15-7.

Without the partnership of a play-making center, Simmonds' production at even strength had suffered for several seasons. Hakstol found just the guy—Giroux—a move that had become feasible with Voracek, the captain's usual right wing, adapting to his switch to the left side. This way, the coach was loading his three best offensive players on one unit while looking for some chemistry on a second one. He seemed to find it. Brayden Schenn, on right wing with Couturier and Raffl, had a goal and two assists in a 4-3 home win over Montreal. "We need that more often out of us," Schenn said.

It was almost as great a necessity to end an uncomfortable situation with Lecavalier, who hadn't dressed since November 12. Hextall also had to thin an overgrown corps of eight defensemen. After six weeks of talks with his former Kings' boss Dean Lombardi, the Philadelphia GM was able to solve both problems with a January 6 deal, acquiring center Jordan Weal and a third-round pick for Lecavalier and Luke Schenn.

The Flyers retained half the salary-cap responsibility for both players going to Los Angeles, but the trade still freed up $4.1 million in space and allowed Lecavalier to escape from his limbo. "[When] Peter Laviolette got let go, the mentality kind of changed and I wasn't really part of their plans," said Lecavalier, 35, after reporting to the Kings. "Very frustrating, but I'm happy I'm here now."

He left behind the highest level of respect from Philadelphia's management, players, and coaches for the way he handled a depressing situation near the end of a likely Hall-of-Fame career.

"(Lecavalier) will go down as one of the great players in the game and one of its most classy, first-class gentlemen," Hakstol recalls. "Being out of the lineup on a daily basis was really hard on him. And I believe in some ways, it was really hard on our players, especially the leadership."

L.A. had lost Matt Greene to season-ending surgery, and wanted Luke Schenn as a third-pair defenseman. A shortage of foot speed and puck-moving instincts had dropped the once fifth-overall pick (by Toronto in 2008) from top-four rotation status with the Flyers, giving them a disappointing return for James van Riemsdyk, the 25-goal scorer Holmgren had traded to the Leafs to obtain Schenn.

In the end, Hextall was happy to get the cap room, the blueline down to a more workable seven defensemen, and Luke Schenn—one of the GM's personal favorites—into a regular role with a contending team. Luke left behind in Philadelphia a younger brother who was thankful he got to play with his sibling for two-and-a-half seasons.

"To have your brother and best buddy for drives to the games and to talk about them on the ride home was pretty cool," recalls Brayden. "But this is a business and we never took it for granted. Hopefully, we will have a chance to do it again one day."

Brayden had two assists in his first game following the deal, a 4-3 win in Minnesota on Del Zotto's overtime goal. Perhaps the trade had cleared his mind from his brother's struggle for playing time.

With the help of three points by Read, Mason shut out the visiting Islanders, 4-0, for a third-straight Flyer win. Philadelphia was down 2-1 to Boston in the third period—no way to mark Nick Schultz's 1,000th NHL game—when Simmonds put in his own rebound on a two-on-one. Streit then scored on a Giroux setup 1:22 later, and the Flyers pulled out a stirring 3-2 victory that pulled them within two points of the Bruins for the final playoff spot.

The new lines were jelling. Schenn and Simmonds scored again against the Rangers, and Philadelphia came back for a second-straight contest to force overtime. But only Mats Zuccarello scored during the shootout, so the extra point got away from Mason and the Flyers in a 3-2 loss.

The following night, against the rested Red Wings at Joe Louis Arena, Philadelphia was held in the contest for two periods mostly by Neuvirth. But they found the legs to come on. Giroux tied the score 1-1 early in the third period, and Gostisbehere's goal with less than two seconds on the clock appeared to win the game until Simmonds was called for making slight contact with goaltender Petr Mrazek as the puck whizzed by. Regardless, shootout goals by Giroux and Voracek produced a resilient 2-1 victory. "All night long, we moved onto the next play," praised Hakstol.

The next play, however, didn't always go the Flyers' way. Gostisbehere's third-period goal seemed to save at least a point against Toronto until Gudas unnecessarily iced the puck and Matt Hunwick scored on a deflection with 7.5 seconds remaining in an excruciating 3-2 loss.

With Couturier struggling with a foot issue, Gagner was recalled from Lehigh Valley. Powerplay goals by Schenn and Voracek seemed to start their team to its standard win at Pittsburgh's CONSOL Energy Center, but the Penguins dominated the second period and withstood a late third-period Philadelphia charge in a 4-3 victory. Against Boston, two more goals by Simmonds went to waste, and another point seemingly in the bag got away when Brett Connolly's deflection beat Mason with just 1:54 to play, giving the Bruins a 3-2 Wells Fargo Center victory.

Two days later, against the league-leading Capitals at Washington, the Flyers won in the end for a change, 4-3, when Voracek walked out from behind the goal on the first shift of overtime and roofed one past Holtby. "The last three games, we had found a way to lose," Voracek said. "We've just got to make sure we don't get too high or too low."

Gudas earned a five-minute clipping penalty by going low on Montreal's Lucas Lessio, shortly after Simmonds' second goal of the game had produced a 3-2 lead. But Mason stopped four Canadien shots on the powerplay and Read hit the empty net to wrap up a 4-2 victory.

Giroux and Simmonds continued to click, each scoring twice in a 6-3 win on February 4 at Nashville. Likely helping the production of the first line was increased opposition attention to the second. But that became problematic when Couturier, who had scored 15 points in 15 games to go with his usual shutdown defensive work, re-injured his foot against the Predators. He was expected to be out four weeks. Philadelphia called up center Nick Cousins, a 2011 third-round pick, who had scored 56 points in 54 games with the Phantoms.

When the Rangers came to town, Gostisbehere's ninth goal staked his team to a 1-0 lead. Three minutes later, Ryan McDonagh tried to protect himself from a Simmonds hit with a crosscheck to the back of the Flyer's helmet, then followed up with a slash. The angry Simmonds surprised McDonagh with a gloved punch, dropping him to the ice and earning a five-minute major and match penalty.

A fan favorite quickly nicknamed "Ghost," Shayne Gostisbehere was the top-scoring rookie defenseman in the NHL in 2015-16.

The top Ranger defenseman was concussed and done for the game. So was Philadelphia after playing decently for 30 minutes. White's goal came on the only Flyer shot of the third period, which still almost was enough to get Mason a win. But Keith Yandle's seeing-eye goal, through three layers of traffic with just 12 seconds remaining, got the game to overtime, and ultimately, into Lundqvist's hands. In the shootout, neither Giroux nor Gagne scored, while Zuccarello and Derek Stepan beat Mason in a tough 3-2 loss. For the third time in seven games, Philadelphia had been scored upon in the final seconds to cost the team a valuable point.

Gostisbehere, stretching a point streak to eight consecutive games, scored to stake the Flyers to another early lead, 1-0 in Washington. After Alex Ovechkin reached 30 goals for the 11th consecutive year, and Dmitri Orlov put the Capitals ahead 2-1, Schultz scored early in the third period to deadlock the game. But neither Del Zotto nor Gostisbehere closed on Matt Niskanen as he skated right to the net for the 3-2 winner.

February 9, 2016 marked 50 years to the day the Flyers were awarded their franchise. So before the game with Anaheim, they dropped the puck on their anniversary celebration with a pregame ceremony featuring Flyer greats and charter season-ticket holders Joe Sahina and Edgar Weinrott. The franchise had enjoyed more than a thousand better nights, fortunately. The Ducks were in control almost throughout their 4-1 victory.

To Umberger, it only seemed like 50 years since he had scored a goal. A 50-game streak was long enough, however, as the winger broke his drought and Cousins scored his first in the NHL, enabling Philadelphia to end its three-game losing streak with a 5-1 home win over Buffalo.

Gostisbehere stretched a point streak to 11—setting a new NHL mark for a rookie defenseman—by tying the Devils with a third-period goal, but Voracek took a penalty in overtime and the Flyers were defeated, 2-1, on a score by Adam Henrique. Worse, they lost Del Zotto, who had been playing for six weeks with reduced strength in his wrist, to ligament surgery, leaving them without him and his 23 minutes a game for the remainder of the season. Hextall recalled MacDonald from the Phantoms.

"When Mac went down (to Lehigh Valley), there was no question in my mind that he was going to come back and play good hockey for us," recalls the GM. "He went with a great attitude, played terrific, and was a leader.

"When Ghost came up (in November), I explained to Mac that with Mark (Streit) out, we needed a different kind of player, a powerplay guy. There was no slight intended. I said, 'Just keep doing what you're doing here.'

"Mac had played for (Phantom coach) Scott Gordon (with the Islanders). That might have helped because he understood Andrew's game and the person. Scott noticed a few things, like he had to move his feet better, which helped rebuild his game. But I think it probably would have been rebuilt here, too. The guy's a total pro."

On Valentine's Day, the Rangers had no flowers for Simmonds after his sucker-punch to McDonagh in their last meeting. The New York captain still was out with a concussion, so Dylan McIlrath called out the Philadelphia winger for a bout 39 seconds into the Madison Square Garden contest. That seemed to settle the grudge, but Hakstol's team lost for a fifth time in six games, 3-1. "We didn't get enough scoring chances tonight," the coach said.

They did the next game. Simmonds had a goal and an assist and Gostisbehere extended his streak to 13 games as the Flyers, after being tied by Jordan Tootoo with 10 minutes remaining, scored four times the rest of the way to pull away from the Devils, 6-3, in Newark. Whenever it appeared Philadelphia's playoff chances were going south, the club came up with a key road win.

"It's cool the way we responded, shows what direction this team is headed," said Gostisbehere. As for himself, the kid kept downplaying how much of a sensation he had become, while his amazing run continued.

In Montreal, he went to the net calling for the puck from Laughton, and then relayed to Raffl for a tap-in that put the Flyers up 2-1 early in the third period. But Max Pacioretty cashed in a Giroux hooking penalty and Neuvirth lost the shootout, 3-2, in a game Philadelphia had dominated. As if the team had not suffered enough, Giroux showed concussion symptoms after taking a shoulder to the head from P.K. Subban well after delivering a shot; the captain would be out indefinitely.

At Toronto, Mason's leg cramped up as Shawn Mathias was scoring the opening goal, forcing Neuvirth into the game. When Mason rehydrated quickly and asked to go back in, Hakstol stayed with Neuvirth as a 3-1 Flyer lead dissolved into a 4-3 third-period deficit before the club rallied. Read, off a pass-out from Raffl, tied the game; Cousins—the next man up for more ice time with Giroux injured—made a chip pass that sprung Voracek and Gostisbehere for a two-on-one in overtime. Gostisbehere went to the net to take a perfect feed and put in the 5-4 winner, becoming the first NHL defenseman to have a 15-game scoring streak since Chris Chelios in 1995-96. It was the rookie's fourth overtime winner of the season.

"It's absolutely incredible what he's doing right now," said Schenn. Philadephia, 5-8-3 without Gostisbehere, was 21-13-8 since his recall. Snider, who had questioned his GMs—only sometimes rhetorically—as to why the Flyers had not drafted and developed an impact defenseman since Jimmy Watson in the seventies, finally was seeing it happen from Montecito, where he had been since early December.

"Dad was so excited about Ghost," recalls Jay Snider. "He was really impressed with Hextall and his disciplined thinking. He also saw a team he didn't expect to make the playoffs coming on under this new coach.

"He expressed to me many times, 'Boy, I'm just not going to get to see this.' It was sad.

"He knew he was dying, expressed his fears about it. He asked me, 'How do you die?' We brought in the oncologist to talk to us. He said, 'Ed, you get to where your pain is so much that you have to increase the morphine to the point you're basically not conscious.'

"So he understood that well. He knew that getting out of pain meant increasing the medication where he'd slip away out of consciousness and then eventually he'd fade. So he resisted doing that, I think, because he wanted to live to see the team. He clearly wasn't ready to not be alive.

"Some people are comfortable with, 'OK, I'm gonna meet my maker,' but he wasn't a spiritual guy. He was 83 but, like a 50-year-old, had too much he still wanted to do.

"He was happy when we won, but I wouldn't say the last few months he was ever joyous, at least from what I saw."

When the Flyers doubled the shots on Carolina, but fell, 3-1, to goalie Cam Ward in Raleigh, Gostisbehere's streak ended at 15 games. "It was a fun thing," he said. "I'm personally happy it's over and we don't have to talk about it anymore."

On to the next topic: Michal Neuvirth. With Minnesota's Charlie Coyle facing an empty net and Philadephia about to suffer another last-second meltdown—this one with less than three seconds to play—the goalie fully extended his stick into the air while diving and knocked the puck to the ice, where he covered and preserved a 3-2 win. Every Wild player had his stick up, but with astonishing athleticism, Neuvirth had cancelled the celebration.

"I've made saves like that sometimes," he told reporters. "In practice."

"The Play-of-the-Year for us, in my mind," Hakstol recalls. When the Flyers hearts started up again, they were only three points behind Boston for the final wildcard playoff spot.

Voracek went out with a knee issue, but Giroux was back after missing three games and took little time to warm up, snapping in a first period powerplay goal in a 4-2 Wells Fargo Center victory over Phoenix. "He touches every aspect of the game," said Gagner.

Perhaps because Jimmy Watson's career was shortened by back problems, one of the elite defenseman in franchise history was overlooked too long for a Flyers Hall of Fame election. When his induction night finally came on February 29—34 years after his retirement—it was hard to not notice him, especially after he put on an orange sports jacket at the podium.

Even as a player, Watson had cared first about the sport above all else. Now an owner and instructor at Ice Works in Aston, PA, he finished his thank-yous by expressing delight about the grassroots growth of the game in the Delaware Valley.

Schenn appeared to be inspired. His first NHL hat trick—bringing him to seven goals in his last 10 contests—and four assists by Giroux keyed a 5-3 win over Calgary. "I've always believed in myself," said Schenn, who set a new career high of 21 goals. "I know it's a bit slower development than maybe some people thought, but I keep chipping away and try to get better."

Since his brother had been traded, Schenn had 23 points in 23 games.

"Brayden had started playing better before the Luke deal, so we'll never know whether that affected it or not," recalls Hextall. "I can only imagine: if my brother was going through a tough time and was a healthy scratch, it probably would have bothered my game."

Raffl, the subject of trade rumors because his contract was entering its final months, instead received a three-year extension worth $2.35 million annually. The February 29 deadline day passed with only one phone call that moved Hextall. It came after 3 p.m. from Snider.

"He called and asked, "Did we get better?" laughs the GM. "Didn't even say hello."

"I had to tell him I hadn't done anything. There was no way we were going to give up young pieces for short-term help. I know he understood."

What the Chairman wanted most of all was to come home to Philadelphia. His wife Lin was resistant, however.

"Dad wanted to tell everyone in his sphere—and I mean right down to people who worked the concession stands and cleaned up—how much he appreciated them," recalls Snider's daughter Lindy. "He thought he was letting them down not coming back and doing that."

Remembers Jay, "[His wife] felt they had everything set up (in Montecito)—from hospice to the doctor coming in every other day adjusting his medication—and that she couldn't replicate that in Philadelphia.

"He said, 'I made my life there. Philadelphia is my home, not here.' He wanted people to come see him and he wanted to die in Philadelphia. I think, personally, all that stuff could have been replicated. You just have to grind it out and do it.

The doctors who began his care (at Fox Chase Cancer Center) were here. Any of his [children] would have dropped everything to make it happen. He wanted to be here, absolutely."

On March 3, the Oilers scored skilled goals with every good chance they had against Neuvirth, winning 4-0 at a subdued Wells Fargo Center and shoving the Flyers five points out of a playoff spot. "Can't dwell on it; tomorrow is a new day," insisted Simmonds.

The next game was the best Gudas ever had. Without a goal in 63 contests, he had two (plus two assists) in a 6-0 home rout of Columbus, joining Erik Karlsson of Ottawa as the only other defensemen in the league to have a four-point night all season. Mason only had to face 19 shots as he returned to the net for the first time after Neuvirth's five-game run.

There were 18 contests remaining when the Atlantic Division-leading Lightning, winner of eight straight, came to Philadelphia for the start of a home-and-home that threatened to make the playoff push the most difficult of climbs. Tampa Bay received a goal four minutes into the contest from Ondrej Palat and sat on it successfully deep into the second period.

"We weren't frustrated," Gostisbehere would say. "We knew we were playing really good hockey. We had them in the palm of our hands."

Raffl made a power move to the net, enabling Gostisbehere to put in a rebound to tie the game. In the third period, he scored on a powerplay one-timer from Giroux before Schenn added another goal. The Flyers needed only 16 Mason saves in a dominating 4-2 victory.

"We got outplayed, outworked, outcompeted, outclassed, out-everythinged," said Lightning coach Jon Cooper, which suggested his team wasn't going to let this happen again two nights later in Tampa. But Philadelphia received a huge early break when J.T. Brown put the puck in his own net while killing a penalty and the Flyers stunningly were in control again. Read scored on another powerplay in the second period, Schenn added No. 23, and Philadelphia, winning for the first time in nine trips to Amalie Arena, completed the eye-opening sweep, 3-1.

"The guys look like they are just overwhelming the opposition right now, which is great to see," said Mason, who only had to stop 17 Tampa Bay shots. "The effort is outstanding."

Gostisbehere, playing for the first time in a Flyer uniform before friends and family in South Florida, tied the Panthers, 4-4, with 1:55 left in the third period, boosting his point total to 38, tops among rookies. But as neither Gagne nor Cousins scored in Hakstol's revolving effort to improve the organization's worst-in-the-NHL shootout mark—32-69 since their inception—the team lost, 5-4.

The Red Wings, who came to town with a three-point lead on Philadelphia for the final postseason spot, were overwhelmed by a 23-3 first-period shot disadvantage and two goals by Raffl. Detroit crept back three times within a goal and pumped 21 third-period shots at Mason, who surrendered only a late score by Tomas Tatar. The Flyers held on for a critical 4-3 win, and perhaps saved some energy for the Stanley Cup champion Blackhawks the following night in Chicago.

Snider, fighting through greater fatigue than any of his players, was being increasingly selective about his guests. But of course, he had plenty of strength remaining for a visit from his executive assistant, Ann Marie Nasuti, Bob Clarke, Bernie Parent, and Joe Watson, who arrived together to watch the game against the Blackhawks with the Chairman.

"Maybe it's all a matter of expectation, but I couldn't believe how good Mr. Snider was," recalls Clarke. Philadelphia's 9-2-2 surge since early January was part of the cocktail of drugs designed to keep the Flyer patriarch as comfortable as possible.

White erased the 1-0 Blackhawk lead and Schenn tied the score, 2-2. Midway through the third period, Gudas's point shot deflected off Christian Ehrhoff and past goalie Scott Darling to give Philadelphia the lead.

"I make a lot of noise when the Flyers are playing," recalls Watson. "Ed told me, 'they can hear you in Chicago.' I was high-fiving him whenever we scored.

"He was excited, didn't say that much. He had to be in a lot of pain. He had something on his hip that would release the medicine whenever he needed it. He rang that little buzzer and two nurses would come running in."

Philadelphia moved into playoff position with Neuvirth's 3-2 victory. "The whole visit rejuvenated Mr. Snider," recalls Nasuti. "He was up the entire day. It was just wonderful."

The Chairman wasn't able to join Clarke, Parent, Watson, Nasuti and Jay Snider as they went out for dinner, but they had lunch at the house the next day.

"As we were leaving, Ed said, "There are people who have known each other for 50 years, but I can't think of any who have worked together for that long," recalls Watson. "It kind of shook me up.

"When we were out the door, I said to Clarkie and Bernie, 'We're never going to see him again.'"

The Flyer schedule wasn't easing. Voracek was back, but the Penguins—23-14-5 since Mike Sullivan had taken over as head coach in mid-December, and winners of five straight—shut down Philadelphia on just 17 shots in a 4-1 victory on March 19 at the Wells Fargo Center.

At Brooklyn, the steady Manning, who had taken Medvedev's spot in the rotation, broke a 1-1 second-period tie, Gagner scored in the third period and Giroux put away a 4-1 victory over the slumping Islanders. With 11 games remaining and the Flyers one point behind Detroit, each win seemed bigger than the last.

Neuvirth was still suffering from a knee problem since his win in Chicago, so Mason had to go again the following night in Columbus. Against the rested Blue Jackets, Hakstol's team had little push in their legs. But Giroux converted a goalmouth feed by Schenn, White put in a rebound on a third-period powerplay and, thanks to Mason and good puck management, Philadelphia was up 2-0 and had the advantage after Ryan Murray slashed Simmonds with 2:33 to go.

Simmonds, from the half-wall of the Flyer zone, took a shot at the empty net and missed. He giggled at his bad aim, but the face-off would now be to Mason's right. With 1:04 remaining, Boone Jenner chopped down a Seth Jones' point drive past Mason to give Columbus life.

When the penalty expired, an exhausted Philadelphia team was still clinging to its 2-1 lead. Simmonds blocked a Jones drive, but when the Jackets forced another opportunity, Mason couldn't get his glove down to cover. Hartnell dug the puck out of a scramble and slid it to Cam Atkinson, who had plenty of room to go high and tie the score with eight seconds remaining.

In overtime, Bobrovsky stoned Simmonds from point-blank range on the rebound of a Gostisbehere drive, and the Flyers lost on Jenner's goal in the fifth round of the shootout.

"We play like that, we won't go anywhere in the playoffs even if we make them," said Giroux, whose team was outshot 53-33. But that almost seemed beside the point after being in a seemingly insurmountable position with the clock under two minutes. Simmonds had made a gross judgment error that had opened the door for an almost impossible Columbus comeback.

"Brain fart," Simmonds would say. "I screwed up. It hurt me a lot, hurt the guys."

The point Philadelphia had gained was a lot better than none, yet provided little consolation.

"You have a 2-0 lead in a huge game and we not only lose, but lose ugly," recalls Hextall. "I worried more about our emotional state than losing the point in the standings."

The Flyers flew to Colorado to play a team similarly scrambling for a playoff spot. Nick Holden's pinball goal beat Mason's short side early in the second period to put the Avalanche ahead, but Bellemare tipped a MacDonald drive to tie the game, 1-1. Six minutes into the third period, Andreas Martinsen got a setup past MacDonald and John Mitchell had position on Gostisbehere at the post to put Colorado ahead, 2-1.

"There was no waver," Hakstol would say. "We had played real well other than a couple of minutes at the start of the second period when they scored their first goal. Guys just stayed with it and kept doing the same things."

The clock was almost down to five minutes when Gudas one-timed a Couturier feed through a perfect Voracek screen to tie the game, 2-2. On the next shift, Simmonds poked the puck away from Erik Johnson at the blueline and went to the net on a two-on-one with Schenn, who made goalie Semyon Varlamov come across to make an exceptional pad save. Giroux, following up, had neither a good look at the net nor a puck lying flat, so he took two steps to the right and scored to put Philadelphia ahead, 3-2. This time the Flyers were smart to the end, when White, pulled down from behind, was credited with an empty-net goal with five seconds remaining.

This win, 4-2, really was the biggest victory of the year and not only because it was the team's latest, or had moved the club back into a tie with Detroit.

"This team doesn't quit," said Snider in a call to Hextall, and the GM tended to agree.

"I told myself, 'Our team has good characteristics,'" Hextall recalls. "That game in Boston (March 2015 when Philadelphia, four points out of playoff spot, was tied in the final seconds and lost in overtime) took the emotions and all the fight out of our team. A year later, the Columbus game was the closest thing to that, and this time we didn't [waver]."

There was no letup in Arizona, just no goals in 34 shots against netminder Mike Smith, until Gostisbehere broke through with 40 seconds remaining on the clock. The Flyers, who had dominated possession, were defeated 2-1 and feared losing Giroux after he was hit into the boards late in the game by Martin Hanzal.

The captain passed the concussion protocol and, after being excused from the morning skate for the start of a three-game home stand, was in the lineup to face Winnipeg. A little more than a minute after Simmonds provided Philadelphia with an early second-period 2-0 lead, Voracek gave the puck away on a Mark Scheifele breakaway goal. Then, early in the third period, Bellemare missed Blake Wheeler on a pass-out by Scheifele, enabling the Jets to tie the score, 2-2.

Giroux thought he had taken his last shift of the overtime when Winnipeg's Dustin Byfuglien had a chance. "I was about to change and then had to get back," the captain said. "He missed the net and I (on a Gostisbehere feed) had a two-on-one.

"But I was pretty tired, couldn't make the pass (to Gostisbehere)."

Scheifele tipped it and was headed the other way, but Gostisbehere gambled, dove, knocked away the puck, and recovered it. "Lucky play, desperation," he would say. Giroux was alone, 20 feet out, to wrist Ghost's backhand feed. The shot glanced off goalie Ondrej Pavelec's shoulder, high into the net with 14 seconds remaining to give the Flyers a 3-2 win.

Washington, the runaway overall-points leader, came to town on March 30 with increasing expectation that it would be back at the Wells Fargo Center for the postseason. Through two intense, scoreless periods, everyone in the building felt like the playoffs already had started.

Early in the third, Evgeny Kuznetsov threw a perfect seam pass to Ovechkin, who pinpointed a wrist shot over Mason's glove to put the Capitals ahead 1-0. But with seven minutes remaining, Marcus Johansson hooked Gudas and, on the powerplay, Schenn redirected Giroux's slapshot to tie the game.

In the overtime, the Flyers had to kill off a Simmonds penalty and did it so impressively that the buzz from the crowd even lasted into the shootout, which rarely had been the franchise's friend. First up was T.J. Oshie, who had scored four times in six attempts to give the USA a win over the Russians at Sochi (Olympic rules allow one player to shoot repeatedly). Oshie made a forehand-to-backhand deke, but Mason didn't buy it and made the save with his arm.

"[Mason] had composure, had a little cockiness to his game in the shootout," Giroux would say. "It motivated the guys a little bit."

Cousins scored between Holtby's pads to put Philadelphia ahead.

Next, Kuznetsov faked Mason to the ice, but the goaltender was able to lunge forward and glove the attempt. "You saw how slowly they were coming in," Mason would say. "I think the idea there is to make sure the goalie loses his depth. I tried to wait him out, then cover as much surface area as I could."

Gagner, like Cousins, went between Holtby's pads to win the game, 2-1, only the third Flyer shootout victory in 11 attempts that season.

Snider called Hakstol with congratulations. The Chairman was setting an even higher example of perseverance than his players, holding out against further morphine dosage increases that would take away his consciousness.

"If not for the cancer, he would have been robust at least until age 90 because his vitals were so strong," recalls Jay. "Heart, lungs, all those readings were phenomenal.

"He had so much [medication] in his system, he often would fall asleep. But he could focus on the games. I'd say something like, 'Damn, we're coughing the puck up.' And he would say, 'I know, it's awful.' The games would bring him back. That's all he had to live for at that point.

"He didn't really complain until almost the end. Finally he said, 'I can't live like this anymore,' and gave the okay to up the medication.

"The last sentence he ever spoke to me was, 'I can't thank the Flyers enough for everything they've given to me and my family.'"

Snider's six children, and second wife Martha, whom he had asked to come to Montecito for the last weeks, watched with amazement rather than sadness.

"He defied the odds," recalls Lindy. "The doctors, including my husband (Dr. Larry Kaiser, professor of thoracic medicine and surgery, and president and CEO of Temple Health) were in shock. The hospice people were in shock. The nurse who lived at the house and took care of him said how long he lasted was unprecedented.

"Everybody collectively saw that he was not going to go until we were in the playoffs. It was extraordinary. Mystical, no question."

The following day at the Wells Fargo Center, for the first time ever, the team photo was taken without the Chairman. "This is my fifth year in Philadelphia and it's weird not to see Mr. Snider in the picture," said Simmonds.

At home against Ottawa, the Flyers scored three powerplay goals—two by Simmonds—and never trailed in Mason's 3-2 victory before running into a buzz saw the following afternoon in Pittsburgh, losing 6-2 to a Penguin team winning for the 12th time in 13 contests. With four games to go, Philadelphia, in a three-way fight for two spots, was even in points with the Red Wings, one up on slumping Boston, and had a critical game in hand on both clubs.

As the Flyers went into Joe Louis Arena, Detroit had to win and played like it. Darren Helm capitalized on a turnover by Gostisbehere to put the Red Wings ahead, Andreas Athanasiou scored shorthanded, and Kyle Quincy's empty-net goal secured Jimmy Howard's 30-shot, 3-0, victory. "I think that was the most complete game we played all year," said the Detroit's Luke Glendening.

The next night at the Wells Fargo Center, Giroux was presented his fourth Bobby Clarke Trophy as team MVP, and Gostisbehere became the second rookie (after Norm Barnes in 1979-80) to win the Barry Ashbee Trophy as best defenseman. Philadelphia, playing its fourth game in six nights, started horribly against an out-of-contention Maple Leaf club. Streit was stripped on a back-door goal by William Nylander to put Toronto ahead. After Voracek gave away the puck, Gudas slipped and Colin Greening scored on a breakaway putting the Leafs up 2-0.

In the second period, Couturier made a gorgeous blind backhand pass to Schenn, who cut the lead in half. But Simmonds gave away the puck on a Michael Grabner breakaway goal and the Flyers, down 3-1, faced an uphill climb as the third period started.

VandeVelde stole the puck behind the Toronto net, and MacDonald fired inside the post on goalie Jonathan Bernier's short side to cut the lead to one. With 58 seconds to go, Simmonds made a beautiful tip of a Streit drive to tie it, 3-3, and a huge third-period effort had saved Philadelphia a point. But in the overtime, MacDonald sprawled on a toe-drag move by Jake Gardiner and ended up tripping him. On the powerplay, Gardiner's point drive through traffic beat Mason, giving the Leafs, outshot 44-26, a 4-3 win, dropping the Flyers a point back of the Bruins after their win over Detroit.

The point the Flyers had saved with the third-period comeback left their glass half-filled. If they won the two remaining games—against the Penguins at the Wells Fargo Center and at the Islanders—Philadelphia would qualify for the postseason no matter what Boston and Detroit did.

"If you'd told us two months ago we'd be in this position, we'd take it," said Giroux.

It was good not to need any help, but aid was appreciated regardless. With Pittsburgh's playoff spot locked, Penguin coach Mike Sullivan held out Sidney Crosby and the team's best defenseman, Kris Letang. By the time of their 3 o'clock puck drop, the Bruins already had been routed in their final game by Ottawa, 6-1, putting the Flyers' magic number at two points.

When the Flyers went to Lauren Hart and Kate Smith's rendition of "God Bless America" for inspiration, this time it wasn't just for the people in the building, but for the Orange-and-Black's biggest fan in California.

"I was out there in February, and there was some hope he might be able to come home," Lauren would tell reporters. "At some point, I realized that wasn't going to happen, and I just couldn't imagine him never being [in the Wells Fargo Center] again.

"It broke my heart. I wanted to give him one more time what it felt like at the beginning of games."

She sang into her telephone as well as the microphone, while Lindy held hers bedside for her father to see and hear.

"I don't know that he was cognizant at that point," recalls Lindy. "I asked my husband about that and he told me that sometimes the person is unresponsive, but can still hear and process.

"A game earlier, Dad hadn't said anything all day and then two minutes before the faceoff said 'hockey game' before drifting back off. That was unbelievable to me. So I want to believe he knew what was going on."

Simmonds told reporters before the game that the team was dedicating the game to Snider. "We're playing to make the playoffs for him," Simmonds said.

A little more than two minutes into the game, Schenn ran into Penguin goalie Matt Murray, forcing into the game third-stringer Jeff Zatkoff, who had not played since February 20. Giroux rang a backhander off the crossbar, giving Zatkoff time to settle down. When Schultz got caught on a pinch, Joe Bonino converted a two-on-one pass from Carl Hagelin to put Pittsburgh ahead, 1-0. "I think our hands were a little too shaky [in the first period]," Simmonds said. "It was like everyone had two cups of coffee too many."

Maybe Mason stuck to the decaf. Late in the period, Kale Moulleart picked up a loose puck in the goalmouth and fired for the corner, but the Philadelphia goalie, glove over his right pad as he came across, made the catch with a flourish. Soon, Giroux picked off a pass by Brian Domoulin and fed Voracek, who perfectly led Simmonds going to the net. He redirected the puck past Zatkoff with 1:03 to go in the first period to tie the game, 1-1.

Simmonds, pulling his stick in close to his body, impressively tipped a Gostisbehere drive in the second period to put the Flyers up 2-1. The Penguins had only nine shots in the final two periods but were still hanging around. With their goaltender pulled, Bellemare tipped a pass at the blueline and raced ahead to the empty net and a 3-1 victory.

Those last 120 feet had proved the easiest on Philadelphia's path to its 40th playoff berth in 48 seasons. After winning just six of the first 20 games, the Flyers had gone 35-18-9 thereafter, closing 17-6-4 to earn a first-round matchup with the Presidents' Trophy-winning Capitals.

Simmonds, whose tying and winning goals were his sixth and seventh in seven games, had redeemed himself from the mindless icing that had cost his team the Columbus game nine contests earlier. But he said the real hero of the season was in his bed across the country. "It's unfortunate Mr. Snider couldn't be here with us today," Simmonds said. "So we played our hearts out. We owe him a lot.

"We're real proud to put on a sweater that he created."

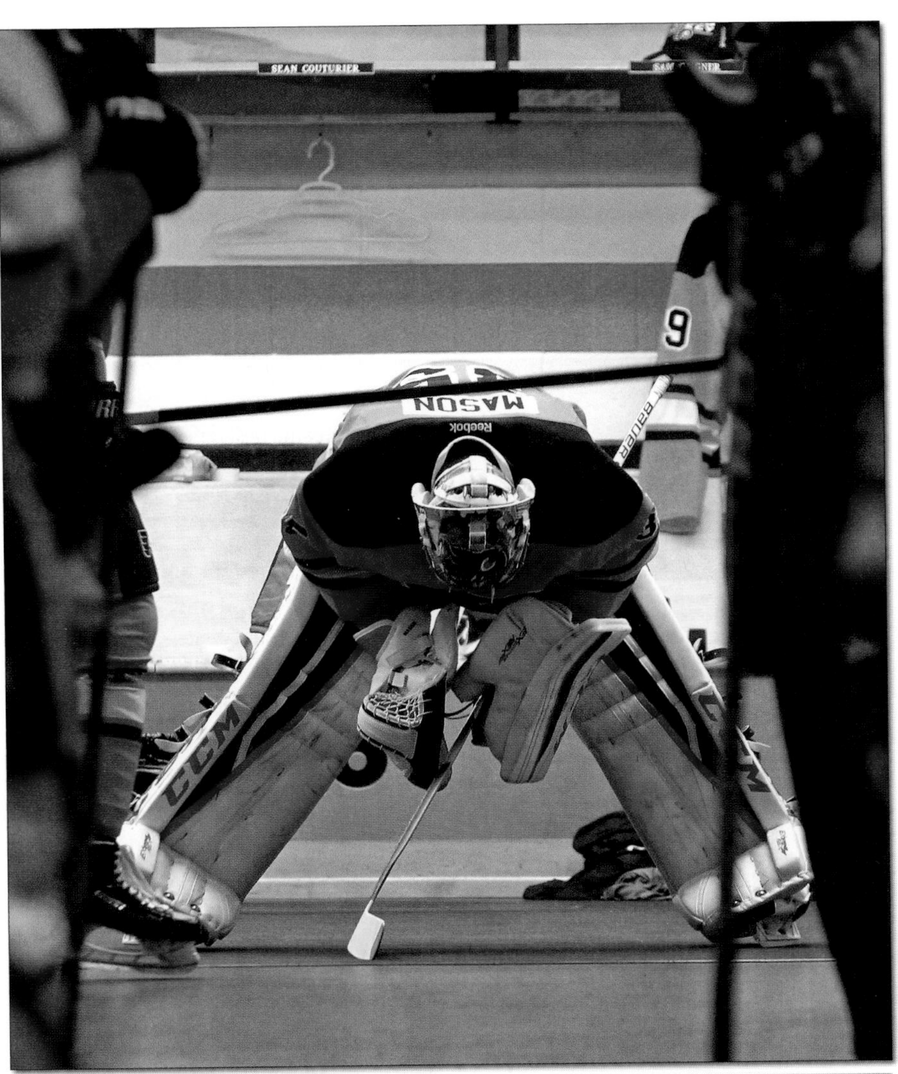

Steve Mason, zoning out before the start of the Flyers' win-or-go-home final regular-season game vs. Pittsburgh.

Thirty-five hours later, just after 2 a.m. PDT on April 11, Ed Snider, founder of the Flyers, a champion of hockey, and the City of Philadelphia, died with his family around him at his home in Montecito. He was 83. Jay waited until after 7 a.m. Philadelphia time to leave phone messages for Clarke and Holmgren, the team president then informing Hextall. These were calls they had understood for a week to be imminent.

"Mr. Snider's passion and drive to be the best has made the Flyer brand one of the most recognizable in sports," said Holmgren. "His spirit and the culture he created will live on with the organization forever."

Said Comcast-Spectacor CEO Dave Scott, "He will be forever remembered for his loyalty. And his impact will endure forever in the hearts of countless players, coaches, team and company employees. His enduring legacy through the Ed Snider Youth Hockey Foundation will live on in generations of young people who will learn his values of integrity and hard work. Ed was a generous philanthropist who cared for people in ways the public never saw."

Said Comcast chairman and CEO Brian Roberts, "Our business partnership lasted more than 20 years, which seemed improbable at the time, and ultimately transcended into a cherished and special friendship. He was completely unique, incredibly passionate, and will be terribly missed."

Expressions of sorrow and respect from outside the organization became as overwhelming as they were appreciated by the Snider family, which found itself too inundated to mourn in private.

"The team around Comcast Corporate was amazing," recalls Jay. "They gave us a chance to review what they were going to do and write a family statement for release. The total outpouring for him surprised me. I knew it would be an event, but I guess I never anticipated the total magnitude of it, maybe because I hadn't thought about it.

"All of that was wonderful. But we had been through a tough time for the last month, watching our father pass away, and now there was stuff that people don't usually have to do when their parents die. I had just lost my best friend—my go-to guy for advice—and my second parent. (Myrna Snider, Ed's first wife, had died, also of cancer, in 2014.) You want some reflection time, and I wasn't getting it that week. So it was good and bad all at once, kind of hard to digest."

Ed Snider had not spent much time in his final months reflecting aloud about his mortality, but was specific in the way he wanted to be memorialized—with a private family ceremony and burial at West Laurel Hill Cemetery in Bala Cynwyd, PA, a reception for his hundreds of business associates and friends (at the Union League), and a public service (later scheduled for April 19) modeled after the one he attended for Ralph Roberts, the Comcast founder who died in 2015. Snider even selected the speakers.

Lindy found all the shared reminiscences helpful. "When Mom passed, my earlier vision of her at her best was replaced by [the struggles] of her final days," she said. "In Dad's case, so many people publicly remembering helped me move past the last days. So the public piece of it was fantastic. But it also was hard because you are feeling so low and have to be on your game to the public.

"Ultimately, I think of him as my friend, more than as the businessman or even my dad. He was a person I could confide in, truly my buddy."

The sport also had lost one of its best friends, the franchise its guardian for five decades, and the team an owner that visibly cared for his players. "What came to the forefront the last couple months is the fact that our players understood the passion and the care that he had for the franchise," Hextall said. "I think that's why we [were winning]."

The Flyers, who finished 41-27-14 after a 5-2 victory against the Islanders at Brooklyn, had honored Snider with one more playoff series. The team would have to play it amid surrounding grief, but Hakstol said he wasn't concerned about sorrow intruding upon his team's motivation.

"Our players have a deep care for Mr. Snider," the coach said. "Certainly, number one right now is having his family in all our thoughts. In terms of preparation (for Washington), if I know our group, this will do nothing but narrow and sharpen our focus."

Said Simmonds, "We'll be playing with heavy hearts. But at the end of the day, I think Mr. Snider wanted us to win a Stanley Cup. Thinking about what he meant to all of Philadelphia kind of puts a little extra pep in your step, because now we have an angel looking down on us. We've got to make him proud."

The players took the ice for Game One at the Verizon Center with a patch reading EMS for Edward Malcolm Snider. The Washington crowd was entirely respectful during a moment of silence observed before the game, which was particularly appropriate. When the Capitals were in financial trouble in the early 1980s, Snider enlisted Flyer players to participate in a television commercial to help save the team.

Mason was not tested much early. Washington was trying to summon emotion after not having played a meaningful game in weeks.

The Capitals took three penalties—John Carlson for hooking Voracek, and two by Brooks Orpik (head hit and interference) against Cousins—but Holtby made a superior save on Voracek, the only good chance on the powerplays. Washington got out of the period scoreless.

In the second, a hard but clean Ovechkin shoulder check in the neutral zone sent Couturier into the boards. He got up and went to the locker room clutching a severely sprained shoulder. Philadelphia started taking penalties; Streit for holding Daniel Winnik, White for charging Dmitry Orlov, and finally, Manning who attempted to bat a puck out of the air and put it over the glass. On the Manning powerplay, the Caps cashed in. Carlson's drive from straight up the slot bounced off Bellemare's arm and hopped up over Mason's glove to put Washington ahead, 1-0, with 3:39 remaining before the second intermission.

Penalties by White, Gagne, Simmonds, Voracek and Gostisbehere in the third period, did not help the catch-up effort. Neither did Voracek's giveaway to Johansson, who fed Jay Beagle's 25-foot wrister from inside the hashmarks over Mason's glove to make the score 2-0. The Flyers had managed only eight shots total in the second and third periods of Holtby's 2-0 Game One victory.

"We had three chances to take control of the game," said Schenn, alluding to the failed first-period powerplays.

Hextall announced Couturier would be out for two weeks. Schenn, having performed at all three forward positions during the season, moved to the middle as Laughton, who had dressed in only two of the last 10 games, went into the lineup for Game Two.

Again, Philadelphia was the more aggressive team in the first period, outshooting Washington 19-5. With Manning in the box for holding Johansson's stick, Carlson blasted away through a Johansson screen, but Mason was looking around the Cap winger to the right as the puck went left. The Capitals led, 1-0, 14 minutes into the game.

In the second period, Mason had just made a tremendous save on Carlson from the slot, when Jason Chimera, wanting a shift change, tipped in from center. Mason tried to steer the most routine of dump-ins to the corner and lifted his stick too soon. The puck went between his legs, and the Caps led, 2-0.

Mason threw back his head in disbelief and self-loathing. "I messed up, put the team in a tough position," he would say. "It's a deflating goal."

Even Holtby found it depressing. "I couldn't watch the replay of it," he said. "I feel for him."

Seven minutes later, Voracek picked up his goalie. The winger pushed forward over the blueline as Schenn took Orpik to the net, and then picked the puck out of the defenseman's skates and snapped it under Holtby's pads as he butterflied. The Flyers were back to within a goal, but not for long. Streit held Nicklas Backstrom and, on the powerplay, Ovechkin one-timed a Backstrom seam pass before Mason could come across to put Washington up, 3-1.

In the third period, Backstrom carried down the wing and beat Mason to the short side over his waffleboard to open up all the breathing room that the smothering Caps, who blocked 28 shots, would need. The Flyers put 42 on Holtby, but Washington, rushing Gostisbehere at the point, had won the battle of the special teams with two powerplay goals in a 4-1 win that put Philadelphia down 2-0 in the series.

Tribute picture banners with "Ed Snider, A Flyer Forever" were draped high on both the North and South walls of the Wells Fargo Center for Game Three. "EMS" was painted on the ice behind both goals. Wristbands were given out to each fan for use during a pregame light show and Lauren Hart wore a Flyer jersey with the number 67 and "SNIDER" on the back, choking back tears as she sang.

"We knew they were going to come out hard," Ovechkin would say. "They have a special moment, a tough moment for them."

Only 57 seconds after the faceoff, Raffl stopped Manning's drive with his skate, held off Orpik, and slid the puck under Holtby for Philadelphia's first lead of the series. The emotion was palpable. But it was fleeting. Simmonds was called for holding Chimera and, on the powerplay, Johansson deflected a Carlson point drive past Mason to tie the score at 1-1 after 4:43.

With Couturier still out, Hakstol felt compelled to play Giroux straight up against Backstrom, not really a matchup conducive to getting his best player—who was playing with an undisclosed hip issue—untracked offensively.

Meanwhile, Ovechkin-duty largely was going to Schultz because of his shot-blocking ability, but there was only so long the Capital star could be contained. Almost nine minutes into the second period, Giroux gave the puck away to Oshie at the Washington line, and Backstrom relayed up the boards to Ovechkin coming off the bench. With the rest of his teammates still changing, he took a shot from well-above the top of the circle and beat Mason inside the far post to put the Caps ahead 2-1.

At the second-period buzzer, Schenn was penalized for a gratuitous slash on Tom Wilson. On the second shift of the third, Justin Williams' wraparound from the right point hit a glass support and caromed crazily into the slot to Kuznetsov, who put the puck under Mason's glove to make the score 3-1.

Seven minutes into the period, with Streit and Oshie off for coincidental minors, Gudas tripped Kuznetsov and Carlson scored a powerplay goal through a Williams screen to boost Washington's lead to 4-1.

The Flyers lost control. Bellemare hit Orlov from behind, drawing a five-minute penalty and, out of multiple confrontations that followed, Gudas and White drew misconducts. When no Washington player was penalized, some fans threw their bracelets on the ice. Told by the referee that Philadelphia would be assessed a delay-of-game penalty unless the pelting stopped, public-address announcer Lou Nolan sternly announced, "Show class. The next one who does it will cause us a minor penalty. Do not do it!"

The fans largely stopped and play continued. But when Ovechkin retrieved his own blocked shot (by Schultz) and fired in the fifth Capital goal over Mason's blocker, more bracelets came down. "Way to go," said Nolan, when a penalty was called as promised.

The Flyers killed that one, but not another after Read slashed Orlov. Beagle, with minimal resistance in front of the net, put in Washington's fifth powerplay goal of the 6-1 rout, putting the Capitals up 3-0 in the series.

Even the fans had gone to the penalty box during one of the more humiliating displays in Flyer playoff history. A memorial had been turned into a mob scene. The team's letdown was also unbecoming, especially since Philadelphia had made the playoffs on an improved focus.

"The way the third goal (carom off the glass) happened took the wind out of our sails, the first time it's happened to us in a while," Hakstol admitted.

The Flyers had only scored two goals in three games. The Capitals were 8-for-17 just on the powerplay. Despite four of those goals generating from Carlson point drives, the Philadelphia coaches decided the bigger poison was Backstrom from the half-wall. The strategy became denying him time to feed Ovechkin one-timers. The other plan was to calm down and take one game at a time—what teams down 0-3 have done since time immemorial.

"We're not going away," Hakstol vowed.

Bellemare was—to the NHL slammer, for one game, having been suspended for the Orlov hit. Hakstol dressed McDonald and moved Schenn to the top line to play left wing alongside Giroux and Simmonds, sliding Voracek down to the left wing with Raffl in the middle.

With little to lose, and not much of a drop-off in ability between his first- and second-string goalies, Hakstol also went to Neuvirth, despite the fact that the only game he had played since March 16 had been the meaningless season finale at Brooklyn (a 5-2 win).

"He's always been pretty clutch, so I'm sure he's going to be fine tonight," said Voracek about his teammate, countryman, and good friend. If Neuvirth needed any additional motivation, the Caps had once traded him and opted to go with Holtby, but vengeance had gotten the Flyers nothing but aggravation and condemnation in Game Three. To keep playing, they had to regain their composure.

It helped that, in Game Four, it was Washington's turn to get in penalty trouble. Taylor Chorney interfered with Cousins in the neutral zone, and Gostisbehere's point drive through a Simmonds screen—Philadephia's first successful powerplay attempt of 13 in the series—gave the Flyers their second early 1-0 lead in two games.

This time, Hakstol's team spent the period unpenalized and even unshaken when Laughton, trying to beat Carlson wide, was taken out, went into the end boards headfirst, and could not get up. Lying on the ice, the winger's legs were moving a little, a good sign, but trainer Jim McCrossin still called for the stretcher. Laughton was taken to Thomas Jefferson University Hospital in Center City Philadelphia for evaluation.

The Flyers still had not been to the box in the game when MacDonald's quick point drive eluded Holtby 3:51 into the second period for a 2-0 lead. Finally Gagner took a penalty, but Backstrom got caught holding MacDonald, thereby shortening the Washington opportunity, at least until Voracek quickly took an offensive-zone penalty. So Philadelphia wound up shorthanded again, but during the Cap advantage, Neuvirth gobbled up a drive by Nate Schmidt and the Flyers took a two-goal cushion into the second intermission.

Early in the third, Oshie pushed Gostisbehere off the puck, then backhanded in a Niskanen rebound to trim Philadelphia's lead to 2-1 with an interminable 17:22 to go. Seven minutes later, Ovechkin had Neuvirth beaten, but whistled the puck an inch wide of the long side. Moments later, Neuvirth made a good leg save on Andre Burakovsky from the bottom of the right circle and kicked out a pad on Wilson from almost point-blank range.

Down the stretch, Gudas got a piece of a dangerous 15-foot drive by Mike Richards, and Manning flawlessly took out Ovechkin as he tried to cut in. With Holtby pulled, MacDonald and Simmonds blocked shots to put away Philadelphia's 2-1 victory.

Asked how long that third period had seemed to a team clinging to its season, Giroux smiled and said, "Not as long as the last game."

The Flyers had avoided the sweep by steering clear of the box. "We didn't take any stupid penalties," said Neuvirth, who finished with 31 saves. "That's the way we've got to play."

Laughton was going to be fine, but not for the rest of the series. Bellemare, his suspension served, was returning for Game Five, when Washington coach Barry Trotz was expecting his team to throw a stronger knockout punch. "I thought we made it a really easy night for [Neuvirth] the first two periods," he said.

Whatever the Caps would bring, Hakstol thought his club could handle it. "Once we won Game Four, I thought we would win the series," he recalls.

Before getting on the train for D.C. the next day, the Flyers were among thousands attending a service at the Wells Fargo Center to celebrate the life of Ed Snider. The season was ongoing, helping to lighten the mood of a ceremony intended to focus on how the Chairman would live on, starting with the Ed Snider Youth Hockey Foundation.

"Crime was a big part of my morning forecast. Neighborhood drug deals (in Kensington) were my basic studies in current events and economics, and the dropout rates were my lessons in statistics," spoke Virlen Reyes, a graduate of the program now employed by Paciolan—the ticket service of Spectra, the arena-management arm of Comcast-Spectacor. "I had few friends and, unfortunately, even fewer caring adults as role models.

"I'd never considered hockey at all, or ice skating. But, in all honesty, I had no other options. Once I heard it was free, I knew it was for me."

The education, health and life skills programs offered by the foundation helped Reyes succeed at Thomas Edison High School. She became the first member of her family to attend college—West Chester University, where she captained the hockey team.

"I'm very proud to say I was the first Snider Hockey kid to go to college," Reyes said. "I'm even prouder to say many have followed."

NHL Commissioner Gary Bettman told the crowd that Snider, despite his highly competitive nature, always put the good of the game and the league first while pulling no punches on behalf of his team's interests.

The Flyer Chairman's fortune, said Bettman, couldn't be measured in dollars, but in the people his philanthropic efforts had reached. "In the course of his 83 years, he had considerable business success," the Commissioner said. "But Snider Hockey, the Snider Foundation, and the Flyers Charities made Ed feel rich."

Philadelphia Mayor Jim Kenney talked about the effect Snider's hockey team had on the city.

"I grew up in South Philly around Fourth and Snyder," Kenney said. "When the Flyers won the first Stanley Cup, our neighborhood exploded. We ran out of our houses, jumped in our cars, and ran to the Spectrum. It was one of the most joyful experiences I've ever had other than the birth of my kids. This sport is my favorite sport, and Ed Snider brought this sport to us.

"My neighborhood was about one-third Jewish and two-thirds Irish Catholic. I learned the Yiddish word *mensch*, for a person of quality, character and integrity. That word describes Ed Snider better than any word I've ever heard. Ed Snider was a *mensch*."

Lindy Snider quoted her father's wish to spend his final days in Philadelphia. "He said. 'they're my people, and they were so good to me.' Whatever he gave to the city and community, he felt could never match what you all gave to him. He loved you for it, and so does [the family]."

Comcast chairman and CEO Brian Roberts spoke of his bond with Snider and the Chairman's relationship with the Delaware Valley.

"From the beginning, Ed was the perfect partner," said Roberts. "Spectacor became Comcast-Spectacor and grew all over the country through his entrepreneurial instincts. As the years passed, Ed and I became close friends, and he became a trusted advisor to my father (Ralph) and me.

"It may surprise a few of you, but Ed was a great listener. He listened to our dreams, encouraged us to grow and to evolve Comcast. He urged us to get more involved with sports nationally, more entertainment. Ultimately, all that led to NBC Universal.

"This truly is an amazing event here today, and I'm not surprised. I have never seen such an outpouring of love and remembrances that we have seen on TV, on radio, and in practically every corner of our city and around the nation.

"All of these farewells and tributes reflect the fact that Ed touched something special, something very profound and very deep, in all of us. For 50 years, he made it possible for us to experience uncountable moments of sheer magic and beauty together, and he did so because he not only shared his team with us, he shared himself.

"Ed, we will always love you and be grateful for you being part of our lives, and most of all, for creating joy and passion in all things Flyers. When I was a kid, every game ended—and Ed, I'm thinking of you now—with the great Gene Hart saying, "Good Night and Good

Hockey." And, if I may add, "Good Life."

Bob Clarke said he considered Snider more than a friend—a second father figure. "Even though we knew Mr. Snider was passing and had time to prepare ourselves, it really hurt. And it's going to hurt for a long time.

"When I pass and we all pass, we don't know where we're going. But for me, I really hope when I get there, I get another chance to play one more game in the orange-and-black under Mr. Snider's Philadelphia Flyers."

Jay Snider probably got the biggest hand of all when he said, "To the Caps: if you're watching this, we're not done."

Washington was hardly finished with Schenn, who had slashed Kuznetsov on the back of his leg in Game Four. "It was a pretty dumb play by me," Schenn had admitted after practice, but the Capitals wanted more than a *mea culpa*. They sent a tape of the incident to the league in an attempt to draw a suspension, and when that failed, Washington tried to take retribution into its own hands. Oshie squared off against Schenn at the opening faceoff of Game Five at the Verizon Center. Schenn won the fight.

One minute into the game, Williams drew Schultz's blood with an accidental high stick, putting Philadelphia on a four-minute powerplay. But on its only real scoring chance, Simmonds was denied by Holtby.

Neuvirth gave away an early opportunity on a bad puck exchange with his defense, but made a save on Beagle, one of 14 stops in a period the Caps dominated despite being shorthanded for six minutes.

In the second period, Ovechkin blew past Schultz, but Neuvirth challenged and made the save. Williams, penalized for the fourth time in the game, had just been freed from the penalty box when White dug a broken-down Streit drive out of a scramble. White couldn't get turned towards the goal, but just as good, banked the puck off the skate of Chorney and past Holtby at 12:08 to give the Flyers a 1-0 lead on their first shot of the period.

Late in the second, Neuvirth made a superior save on a Wilson

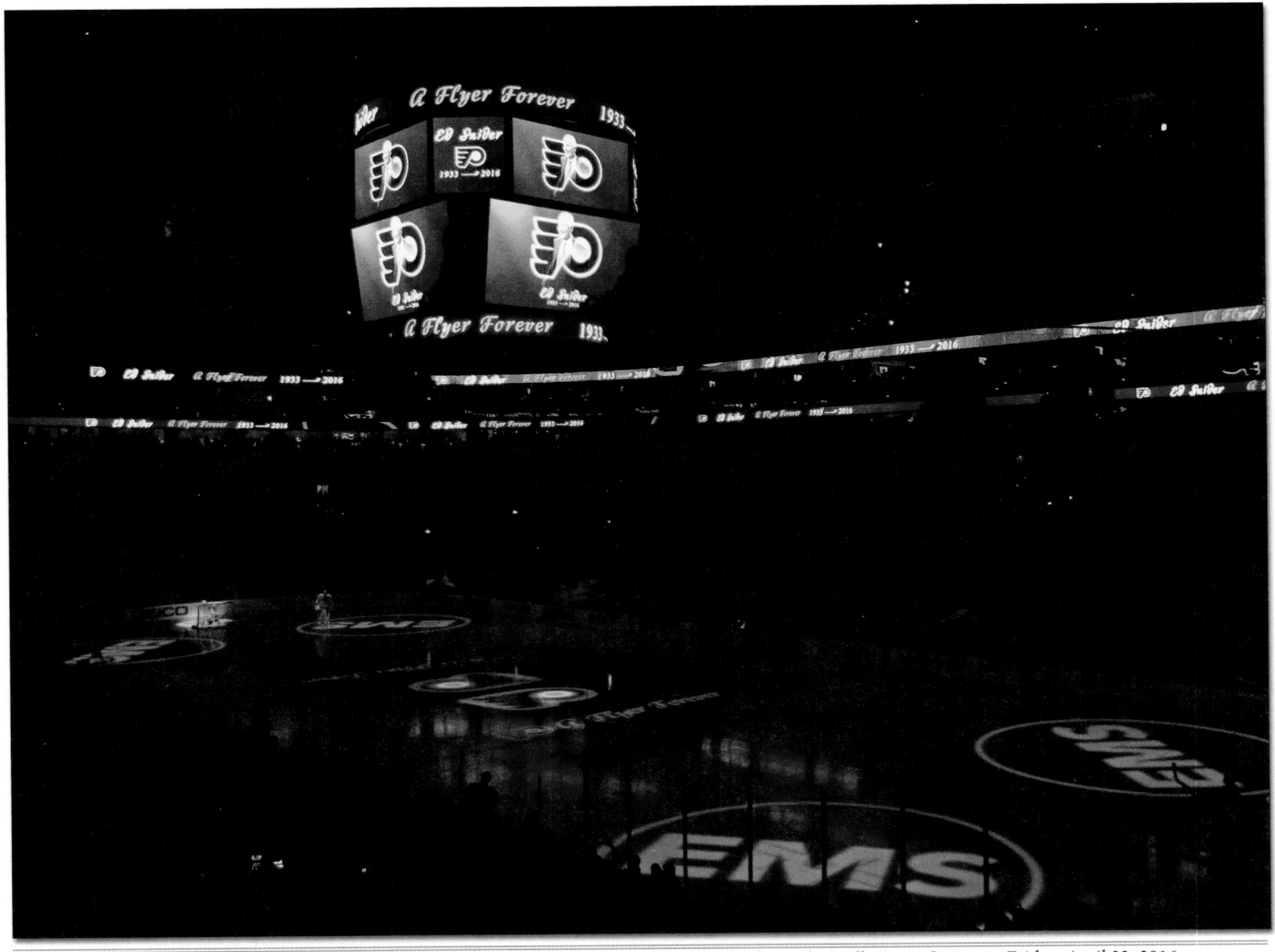

The scoreboard read "A Flyer Forever" as Philadelphians celebrated the life of Ed Snider at the Wells Fargo Center on Friday, April 22, 2016.

turnaround and then on Karl Alzner's rebound. The goalie made consecutive point-blank stops—on Ovechkin, with the left pad, and on Johansson with the right—to get Philadelphia to the final 20 minutes up 1-0, even though it had been outshot by 16-2 in the period.

In the third, Neuvirth stopped Oshie twice and Orlov twice. With 13:09 to go, Chimera blasted Voracek while his back was turned and caused him to bang his head against the glass, drawing a penalty. But the shorthanded Caps had the best chance of the powerplay, when Beagle got away from Giroux to take a centering pass from Johansson. Neuvirth kicked the puck away with his left pad.

Michal Neuvirth shakes hands with John Carlson of the Capitals after the Flyers were defeated 1-0 in Game Six of the First Round of the playoffs.

White went off for unnecessarily interfering with Schmidt with 10:20 remaining, but the Flyer penalty killers did their best work of the series, holding Washington to just one shot from long range by Ovechkin.

The last 10 minutes were Philadelphia's best of the game. With Holtby pulled, Bellemare won a defensive-zone draw from Oshie, and pushed the puck over the blueline to VandeVelde, who soloed to the empty net. Despite just 11 shots, the fewest by a winning team in an NHL playoff game in 18 years, the Flyers had won 2-0, and had cut the Washington series lead to 3-2.

"I like to face a lot of shots," said Neuvirth, who had stopped 44, including eight by Ovechkin, in one of the most memorable goaltending performances in franchise history. "It keeps me in the game.

"Guys did a really good job in front of me (19 blocks). I was seeing the puck well. We didn't take any bad penalties and stuck to our system."

Hakstol glowed, particularly about the poise his team had shown in the final 10 minutes. "Neuvy was our best player, and the guys battled hard in front of him as well," said the coach. "We're playing the game that got us here."

The Caps, who had not advanced past the second round during the Ovechkin-era, had reached only one Stanley Cup Final since their birth in 1974. So the pressure on arguably their best team ever was growing. But having watched his club do everything right in Game Five but score, Trotz wouldn't hear of any reasons to be nervous. "I thought tonight we played excellent," said the coach. "If we play like that next game, we should be fine."

During "God Bless America" before Game Six at the Wells Fargo Center, Anthony Gioia's game presentation crew split the screen on the center-hung scoreboard between Ed Snider and Kate Smith, providing more inspiration for a Flyer attempt to come back from an 0-3 deficit for the second time in six years.

Washington had five of the first six shots. Neuvirth prevented a stuffer by Richards and challenged Ovechkin on a backhander before the trouble grew even greater. Simmonds hooked Alzner and MacDonald high-sticked Johansson 30 seconds apart late in the first period to put Philadelphia down two skaters for the final, frantic 57 seconds of the period. Neuvirth made his best stop yet on a point-blank laser by Williams, Gudas blocked the rebound, and Neuvirth made another save on Carlson before Oshie missed a half-empty net at the buzzer.

The Flyers killed the 13-second carryover of the five-on-three to start the second period. Soon, it was their turn at a grand opportunity. Backstrom went to the penalty box with a double-minor after his high stick opened a gash on White and, just five seconds later, Niskanen hooked Simmonds, giving Philadelphia a two-man advantage for 1:55.

"I was pretty nervous in there," Backstrom would say. But his teammates held the Flyers to three shots, the best one by Giroux, who was stopped from 30 feet out by Holtby. "We watched a lot of their five-on-threes and knew exactly what they were going to do," Alzner said later.

Thirty seconds remained on the advantage when White got whistled for holding Niskanen's stick. Philadelphia had just killed that penalty with a Neuvirth snatch on Johansson when Ovechkin pushed past Gudas at the Flyer blueline. Johansson, coming up the middle, took a pass from Ovechkin and quickly relayed to the other wing. Backstrom, from 18 feet out, fired under the crossbar before Neuvirth could get over. At 8:59 of the second period, the Caps had a 1-0 lead.

"Good pass, unbelievable shot," Neuvirth, beaten for only the second time in 94 shots over three games, said later. "I don't think I could have stopped it."

He could only keep Philadelphia in the game, which he did with a save on Winnik, sent in close by Beagle. But one Washington goal was starting to look like three as the third period began with Flyer chances almost entirely being contained to the outside.

VandeVelde and Manning missed on rebound opportunities. With seven minutes to go, White won an offensive-zone draw from Backstrom, and Streit shot through traffic, but Holtby tracked the puck and made a right pad save, then got his blocker up on another VandeVelde rebound.

Philadelphia forced a faceoff in the Capitals' end with Neuvirth pulled and 1:17 remaining. Giroux won it from Richards, but Holtby knocked down Gostisbehere's point drive and got in front of Voracek's rebound. Alzner blocked a last gasp attempt by Simmonds, and Washington, with a remarkable defensive effort, had finished off the Flyers in six games, 1-0.

The building was silent only for a few seconds before an ovation began. It grew into a "Let's Go Flyers" chant unlike any heard before at the Spectrum or Wells Fargo Center after a first-round loss.

"I'm proud of every single guy in this locker room," Simmonds said. "They pushed it to the limit."

Giroux, who had scored just one point through a hip issue and diligent Washington attention, appreciated the support. But he couldn't find any consolation in the loss of a series close enough for him to have made the difference. "I'm pretty frustrated with myself," he said. "I [should have been able] to find a way."

Philadelphia had only one goal in 24 powerplay opportunities for the series—the biggest reason why they had not won.

"The kills and powerplays create momentum for you," recalls Hextall. "They are pivotal points.

"Are we a better team than Washington? No. They proved over 82 games that they were better than us, but it was still a winnable series. Washington had a lot of pressure to get out of the first round, and I felt like that's something we could have taken advantage of. If we could have won one of the first two games, it would have put a lot of pressure on them."

Under former coach Craig Berube, the 2013-14 Flyers had also made a gallant and successful comeback from a bad start and put up a good fight in a first-round loss, but they went backwards the following season, a reminder that corners are not always easily turned.

"We made small steps in the right direction," Hakstol says. "The harder steps are probably to come.

"But in saying that, we didn't waste any time this year. We took advantage of the opportunities and that's the foundation we have to work from."

The 2015-16 Flyers exceeded expectations, but another year had gone by without the Stanley Cup, still leaving as the organizational standard of excellence the two clubs that won it all in 1974 and 1975.

Forty days after Snider's passing, the Broad Street Bullies lost their most exciting member—Rick MacLeish, at age 66, from meningitis, liver and kidney conditions.

MacLeish's Cup-winning goal in 1974 was one of 53 he scored in the playoffs for the Orange-and-Black. "The Flyers could have a mediocre game, but because of his skills as a player and the athlete he was, he could carry us," said Gary Dornhoefer, the center's former right winger. "He was that gifted.

"I always felt that during the years he played, he never got the recognition he properly deserved."

Philadelphia never had a more explosive player, or one more fun to watch. "Like poetry in motion, so fluid with his skating style and his wrist shot," Bill Barber remembered.

Fans of a certain age recall the Flyers' bid for a third-straight championship being crippled by MacLeish's torn ACL, suffered in February of that season. They also smile remembering his easy, breezy ways, and marveled at his brilliance in big games. When MacLeish was full engaged, his wrist shot, like his patented right-to-left move, was unstoppable.

"Ricky was the most talented player the Flyers had during the 1970s," Bob Clarke said. "Life after hockey wasn't fair to him. He left us far too soon."

So did Bob Dailey, the huge and hugely-talented defensive anchor of the 1980 Final team, who died on September 7, 2016, at age 63, after a six-year battle with cancer. Good friends with MacLeish, and his partner in repeated clutch plays like the ones that brought Philadelphia back from an 0-2 series deficit to Toronto in the 1977 playoffs, the 6-5 Dailey had a big shot and a long reach. He had largely fulfilled GM Keith Allen's projections of dominance until being diminished by injuries. His career ended abruptly with an ankle shattered in a collision with the boards at Buffalo in 1981.

Snider, MacLeish, and Dailey were too much loss for the organization in one year, even with all the apparent gains.

Gostisbehere, whose 17 goals were the most ever by a Flyer rookie defenseman, had revitalized the club with 46 points in 64 contests. Despite missing the first quarter of the season and finishing with a hip issue requiring surgery, Gostisbehere finished third in Calder Trophy balloting.

"Up to his 15th goal of the year, I think every one had won a game or tied it," Hakstol recalls. "That's impact at the right time of a game.

"He arrival was good timing and added an injection of excitement. The fans felt it. No question, he was something we needed."

Gostisbehere was the first arrival in a wave of talented defensive prospects expected over the next few seasons, including Ivan Provorov, named the Western Hockey League's top defenseman for 2015-16, and Travis Sanheim, the WHL's leading scorer among blueliners.

When Schenn signed a four-year contract in July, every core forward—Giroux, Voracek, Simmonds, Couturier and Schenn—was locked up through the 2018-19 season or beyond. Methodically, Hextall is executing his plan. But if Philadelphia emerges as a top contender over the next several seasons, that should also be attributed to Snider's legacy.

"I guess, in true Flyers' sense, he didn't put himself ahead of the organization," said Hextall. "He saw where we were headed and didn't want to hurry the process just because he thought he might not be around.

"I think that was very unselfish of him. It would have been within his right to say, 'Let's speed things up here. Let's take a run this year.'

"He never even mentioned it."

CLAUDE GIROUX

THE NHL'S LEADING SCORER from 2011 to 2016 weighed 155 pounds when he was drafted. So if it is a consolation to any of the 21 teams who whiffed in enabling the Flyers to select Claude Giroux in 2006, appearances can be deceiving.

A player's promise is hard to read. Ten years later, so are Giroux's eyes every time he gets the puck. "I know when he's looking the other way that he's going to pass it to me, so I'm ready for it," said Jake Voracek, Giroux's right wing.

Almost faster than he can dart around the ice, Giroux is rising on the franchise's all-time goals and assists list. And speed is not even the greatest gift that has enabled the captain, who had 367 points in Philadelphia's last 410 games entering the 2016-17 season, to outscore Sidney Crosby, Alexander Ovechkin, Patrick Kane, Evgeni Malkin, and Jamie Benn.

Giroux is an elite player because he sees things, such as teammates open for a tap-in on the other side of a thick forest of legs and sticks. People thought he was hallucinating in publicly insisting the Flyers, off to a 1-7 start in 2013-14, would make the playoffs, but his vision was uncanny that time, too. Giroux peers through all kinds of obstacles with one of the best sets of eyes in the league, to go with arguably its quickest set of hands.

To be fair, Crosby, a two-time Stanley Cup winner almost universally acknowledged as the best player in the game, participated in 70 fewer contests than Giroux between 2011-16. But durability also counts. Since the Philadelphia star has grown to only 5-10 and 185 pounds, the scant nine games he has missed during seven seasons of playing in high-traffic areas is another factor that makes him so remarkable. On the powerplay, which No. 28 ran brilliantly off the halfwall even before Shayne Gostisbehere's dynamic addition at the point during the 2015-16 season, Giroux's 160 points over the before-mentioned five-year period, were 13 more than second-place Ovechkin, and 39 greater than Crosby.

Giroux is consistently one of the league's top face-off men—from 2013-14 through 2015-16, he has the fourth-best percentage (54.7) of the 25 players who have taken the most draws—and, unlike other leading point producers, kills penalties. He might be the most complete player among the NHL's elite scorers.

"His hand-eye coordination and shooting are amazing," says teammate Wayne Simmonds. "But what separates him is his drive. So focused. So motivated. He's just like a little engine out there; he never stops working. That's what accentuates his skills."

To say that Giroux relentlessly keeps coming at the opposition is not to suggest the netminders know exactly what is arriving next. "He hides what he is going to do until the last second, and it catches goalies off-guard," says the Flyers' Steve Mason, who has one of the best jobs in the league because he only has to face Giroux in practice. "He can be showing a pass and end up shooting it, or vice versa.

"He can be stick-handling one second and then the puck is off his stick the other. He's very deceptive. And he doesn't necessarily overpower the puck, just places it so well."

Even if, thankfully for Mason, no one is keeping score in practice, he feels the full gravity of the G-force. "He practices in the same gear with which he plays," says coach Dave Hakstol. "When you talk about Claude's ability, you have to add in how hard he works at his game and how competitive he is."

Giroux does not score empty points at the end of blowouts. The 7-2 game disappeared from the NHL with the 5-9 goalie, making practically every contest close in the third period and the league more competitive than it ever has been. Shot-blocking and back-checking have become obsessions and yet, at age 28, playing in the NHL's lowest-scoring era since the franchise's birth, Giroux is already eighth all-time in Philadelphia assists. With continued good health, he has a good chance of passing everybody except Bobby Clarke and Bill Barber in points. Giroux's 62 points in 63 playoff games is a ratio that trails only Eric Lindros's and Danny Briere's among Flyers with an appreciable number of postseason games.

Giroux played a prominent role in three of the team's top 50 victories chosen for this book. The 2009-10 run to the Stanley Cup Final established him in his first full year as one of Philadelphia's greatest clutch performers.

He scored the shootout goal against New York's Henrik Lundqvist to get the Flyers into the 2010 playoffs on the last day of the season, and then tallied twice in the 3-0 Game Five victory that put away the Devils. Two goals by Giroux in Game Four against Montreal put Philadelphia within one win of the Eastern Conference championship, and his overtime winner in Game Three of the Final versus Chicago put the Flyers back in the series.

In 2012, Giroux's six-point night—three goals and three assists—gave Philadelphia a sweep of the first two games in Pittsburgh. With a once 3-0 series lead down to 3-2, he leveled Crosby and scored a goal, both on the first shift, creating a legendary moment in team history.

The breathtaking goal has become endangered by the five-skater defense played in today's game. But Giroux's winning score with 1:38 to go—on his backhand, from a bad angle, over the shoulder of Columbus goalie Curtis McElhinney while being pushed to the ice by David Savard (December 19, 2013)—was one of the more visually astonishing plays a Flyer ever made, up there in goosebump production with Clarke's wrist shot from his stomach, lifted over Detroit's Ed Giacomin from 25 feet out in 1976.

After Clarke, who was taken 17th-overall in 1969, Giroux was the biggest jackpot Philadelphia ever was smart and lucky enough to hit, if you consider that Bill Barber (seventh in 1972) and Brian Propp (14th in 1979) fell to the Flyers because those drafts were two of the deepest in NHL history. Many more teams screwed up missing Clarke and Giroux.

There is another way that Giroux's story mirrors that of Clarke, the greatest player in franchise history. Just like No. 16's native Flin Flon, Manitoba, you can't go much farther north than No. 28's Hearst, Ontario and still find human beings.

Hearst, a francophone enclave of 5,000, is a nine-hour drive from Toronto and three hours from Timmins, Ontario, the closest town of any size (43,000). The Moose Capital of Canada, as Hearst has named itself, is not only as far north as you can drive a car on a paved road in Ontario, but also a place where Fahrenheit and Celsius often come together at minus-40.

They have power in Hearst. We know that because Giroux's father, Raymond, is an electrician. There is a grocery store, actually a co-op, where Claude's mother, Nicole, worked, and a McDonalds and a Subway. It being Canada, of course there also is a rink, where Giroux's grandmother, Helen, works the concession stand to this day.

"The whole focus in Hearst is basically hockey," says Giroux. "My sister, Isabelle (five years older), played. She was pretty good.

"There are a lot of hard-working, good people in Hearst. I go back every summer to do a golf tournament to benefit the hospital. I still have two grandmas, a grandpa, aunts and cousins there. It feels like the whole city is a big family.

"I was really lucky in minor hockey to have had a lot of adults who put in a lot of time to help the kids. My dad coached me a couple years and so did the dad of one of my friends, Daniel Lapierre. They pushed us hard to get better. We were able to win a lot of tournaments, kids from a little place like Hearst.

"My mom would tell me before each game, in

French, 'Go have fun and [bleep] the rest.' I was lucky not to have parents who pushed me hard. They knew my passion to get better and never told me after a game I had been bad."

When Claude was 14, the family moved to Ottawa, where his sister was attending university. "Dad just brought his business with us," recalls Giroux. "The opportunities for me to play at a higher level were a lot better there, but that wasn't why we went. Well, maybe it was, but I don't think so.

"It was a different culture. My English was pretty sad, actually. But playing midget hockey with English guys helped me a lot. My second year, I got a little more comfortable."

Unselected in the Ontario Hockey League midget draft (of 16-year-olds), and unable to make a Quebec Major Junior Hockey League team—the Gatineau Olympiques—on a tryout, Giroux was invited to join a Junior A team not far away in Cumberland, Ontario. He did well enough that the Olympiques signed him the following season.

Playing on the right wing of center David Krejci, Boston's 2004 second-round pick, Giroux put up 39 goals and 64 assists. He blossomed so dramatically that, by the end of the season, a kid who couldn't even make a major junior team a year earlier, was suddenly rated as a second-round pick—38th on the NHL Central Scouting's list of North American prospects.

"When I saw that, I looked to see who was playing in the NHL after they got drafted in the second round, and there were plenty of guys," recalls Giroux. "So I was like, 'I have a chance!' I became more motivated."

There was an increasing place in the NHL for smaller players, but still reluctance by teams to take them over bigger bodies in the first round. Paul Holmgren, then the Flyer assistant GM who ran the team's draft, was confident Giroux, who had a huge advocate in Quebec scout Simon Nolet, would slip to 21. GM Clarke, who never saw Giroux play, forgot his name in announcing the pick, making the day memorable before it proved momentous.

At his first Philadelphia camp, Giroux got lapped on the mile fitness run, a sign he had to learn how to become a pro, but on the ice, he instantly was showing things that can't be taught. "That first training camp, he had some shootout moves that were like, 'Oh my God!,'" recalls assistant coach Joe Mullen. "We said, 'Yeah, this kid's got something special.'

"He had to get out of some junior habits like pacing himself through a game. They develop that when their coaches play them so much."

The next year, more confident than ever after representing Canada in a summer series against the Russian juniors, Giroux caught a red eye from Moscow to Flyer camp and, 24 hours later, lapped a good portion of the team in the run. He then pulled up a chair next to Holmgren, who was watching from the infield, and asked, "So Mr. Holmgren, what are your plans for me this year?"

CLAUDE GIROUX
FLYER HERO #16

"That was Claude even then," recalls Holmgren. "Very confident, almost bordering on cocky."

Because he wasn't eligible to play for the Phantoms with junior eligibility remaining, the plan, by default, was for one more year at Gatineau, where he scored 53 points in 19 playoff games. Giroux was not expected to need AHL time until he showed up at 2008 training camp in poor condition following dental surgery. "That really affected him," recalls Holmgren. "We sent him down, and he was devastated."

After a couple weeks, Giroux got over it, scoring 34 points in 33 AHL games, prompting a call-up at Christmas. He debuted in Chicago by giving away a goal on his first shift. Then, three games later, he became concussed on a hit by Anaheim's Corey Perry. After resting for two weeks, Giroux was back and scored 27 points in 42 games, and then another five in six playoff contests during a first-round loss to Pittsburgh.

Two seasons later, Mike Richards got traded, in part, because Giroux was ready to become the No. 1 center. When Chris Pronger's career ended prematurely, the team's best player became its captain at age 25. Holmgren and coach Peter Laviolette felt that oratory was down the list of required qualifications for one of the proudest positions in sports—official leader of the Philadelphia Flyers.

"G works really hard in practices and always leaves everything out there," says Voracek. "He's pretty hard on himself, what makes him a better player than everybody else.

"When we don't do well, he takes it personally. I wouldn't say he is that much more verbal than when he first became captain, but he will say something when it has to be said. Mostly, there is a difference in the way he carries himself."

Production and work ethic give Giroux all the cachet he appears to need.

"The biggest thing with a leader is he has to show up every day ready to work," says GM Ron Hextall. "You can't do it, if you don't lead by example.

"That's G. He tries hard every day. He cares about the team and his teammates. I'd say he's a lead-by-example kind of captain, but it's not like he never speaks up.

"Where captains are concerned, everyone's standard in this organization is Clarkie. But we may never see another one like him. Every captain who has come after has been compared to him, and that's not fair. There just aren't a lot of guys like that around."

There aren't many who would want to even try living up to standards set by the franchise icon, but Giroux is not intimidated. "There's a lot of tradition and pressure here, but it's an honor to wear the logo," he says, embracing the Flyer culture and even defining it while leading the team into his prime years.

C
28

CHAPTER 18 • 2016–

The Next 50 Years–Onward and Upward

THE FIRST REASSURANCE THAT THE FLYERS WILL CONTINUE to be the Flyers comes from the organization's executives who believe that Ed Snider is watching every move.

"I think that every day," smiles Shawn Tilger, the club's chief operating officer. "As I did when he was still with us, I ask myself, 'WWED—What would Ed do?'

"His M.O. was hiring good people and giving them the resources to do their jobs. And that's still what's happening. For me, it's been pretty simple. Mr. Snider had a plan when he put Dave Scott in place."

It is not on the agenda of Scott, the Comcast-Spectacor president and CEO, to become the new Snider. "Nobody could replace him," says Scott. But he had more than two years of working with the Flyer founder and Chairman, before Snider's death on April 11, 2016, to appreciate and adopt his values.

Scott emerged from a brief retirement after spending 13 years as field division president and eight years as CFO/EVP of finance for Comcast Cable, following the December 2013 resignation of Peter Luukko. The new boss was hand-picked and mentored by Snider, the revered old boss. Nothing will change, assures Scott, now that Comcast's share of both the team and the Wells Fargo Center has gone from 76 to 100 percent.

"The last thing I want to do is screw this up," says Scott. "It's my job to continue building what Ed started.

"He was a winner. The passion he had not just for the game, but for life itself, was contagious. It is certainly an end of an era, but we want to keep the winning culture that he started, and I think we have the leadership to do it."

Brian Roberts, Comcast chairman and chief executive officer, describes Scott as a "fast study." Roberts took that course—Professor Snider's 'Winning 401'—and aced it in 1995, when Comcast bought out Snider's majority share of the team and its under-construction arena.

By then, Snider had built his empire, so in deciding to give up ownership control and signing a five-year contract to manage Comcast-Spectacor, he had some trepidation.

Twenty-one years later, only death ended what became a beautiful relationship. Because of Roberts' business philosophy and respect for Snider, the Comcast boss kept hands-off, except to periodically shake on a pact between them that no longer needed to be in writing. More than understanding that he didn't need to fix what wasn't broken, Roberts quickly came to be awed by the atmosphere Snider had created.

"There is a family feeling at the Flyers," says Roberts. "Every player is respected and matters. There's a passion to be great."

So if you are worried about Snider being gone and your treasured team being turned into a line on the ledger sheet of a corporate giant, fret not. Consider the Flyers good-to-go for continued Stanley Cup chasing.

"After more than 20 years of partnership, the foundation is so strong and the culture so good that we don't intend to come in and say, "Here's the Comcast way,"' says Roberts. "We never do that.

"It is incumbent on me, in particular, to create a culture that allows individual leadership to flourish without a lot of corporate bureaucracy. In the case of the Flyers, the Wells Fargo Center and Comcast-Spectator, that's exactly how we're structured to operate. Period. Take the best of what a big company can offer—the financial ability to be able to withstand the highs and lows that are sports—and yet not make decisions by committee, which is not as effective without the passion of a leader.

"With Dave Scott now being head of Comcast-Spectacor, and with the help of (Flyer president) Paul Holmgren and (GM) Ron Hextall, I believe it is infused within the organization to be great. That includes striving to win, caring about the community, the fans, the players and their families.

"We planned together (with Snider) for this inevitable day, obviously sooner than anybody would have liked. Ed trusted Comcast to take his life's work and dreams and make sure they were in the right hands for the future. It is a heavy burden and responsibility on all of us to carry on his legacy."

Under Snider, the Flyers won two Stanley Cups, produced six more finalists and an NHL-high (since 1967) 16 semifinalists. The team's deep connection with its fans has helped it survive inevitable performance sags, not only because the slumps were short, but also because Snider always was trying to win.

So read Brian Roberts' lips, whose words are going right to God's ears, especially now that they are being bent by Snider: Asked if the Flyers will continue their long-standing spending practices on player

Left: General manager Rox Hextall presents Claude Giroux with the Bobby Clarke Trophy as team MVP, April 7, 2016.

The Flyers coaching staff: front row, from left: goaltending coach Kim Dillabaugh, head coach Dave Hakstol, assistant coach Joe Mullen. Back row, from left: video coach Adam Patterson, assistant coaches Ian Laperriere and Gord Murphy.

talent, Roberts said, "We try to do what it takes to win. I don't anticipate any change."

Neither does NHL Commissioner Gary Bettman. "If Comcast was bottom-line oriented, you would have seen this for 20 years," he says. "As probably the most prominent organization in the City of Philadelphia, Comcast views the Flyers as an institution essential to the very fiber and fabric of the community. The Flyers are not something that is going to be turned corporate.

"Listen, we miss Ed terribly. However, the league, the City of Philadelphia and the Flyers organization are fortunate that Comcast is here and continuing its commitment."

The company, ranked 37th on the Fortune 500 list in 2016, recently added DreamWorks Animation to its holdings. High on the list of future coveted acquisitions is the Stanley Cup.

"The message we've gotten is: business as usual—we're going to continue to operate the way we have," Hextall says. "I believe we're going to be a cap team or close to it.

"The conversations are similar to what we had when Mr. Snider was around. We requested a bunch of money for renovations of the (Skate Zone) locker room and got it.

"Everything I've seen so far has been exactly the same."

He means as far as autonomy, maintaining a healthy budget, and the organization's drive to succeed. Otherwise, change is ongoing, and a good thing.

State-of-the-art skating and passing rooms, plus a new weight-training facility, were completed at the Skate Zone in November 2016. The mid-level suites at the Wells Fargo Center, which had to be gutted for the use of the Democratic National Convention, became the first phase of a $75-million renovation that in the summer of 2017 will remodel the main concourse and concession areas, followed by the upper level at the end of the 2017-18 season.

Also evolving, according to Hextall, have been the principles he must follow if Philadelphia is to see another Stanley Cup parade.

"I think the last five years of the salary cap have been different than the first five," the GM says. "A lot of teams are spending close to the cap, so there's a lot less flexibility in terms of moving players.

"There are very few clubs that can take a big cap hit now in a trade, which means looking ahead three or four years to make sure you don't put yourself in a tough situation. My biggest fear is being forced to trade a young player because we're unable to move the contract of an older one we brought in whose best days are behind him.

"It's no longer the days when you could spend whatever your owner allows you to spend. You didn't think about money (in deals) because the salaries coming in and going out weren't that much different. Also, if a guy was 25 or 26, he was still five or six years from becoming a free agent. Now he's one or two years away; if you want to keep him, you're going to have to pay him so much.

"All the dynamics have changed. You can't build quickly. It just doesn't happen. The Blackhawks and Kings (three and two Stanley Cups, respectively, in this decade) built slowly, methodically, the only way to do it in the cap world. You have to identify your core players and get them locked in, then [surround] them with less expensive players. It forces tough decisions.

"You are going to overpay in the free-agent market for core players. And if they are available, usually there's a reason. You can't trade or sign free agents to build a team anymore, in my opinion. You have to draft and develop one. And that includes the attitude about the organization by the key players.

"There's a certain pride when a player gets drafted by the Flyers. It's his first team, like his first girlfriend. It's special. Those players take ownership more so than a guy coming from 10 years on other teams. There's something in your blood and heart about the team you came up with. I still have that for this franchise and it's never going to go away. There's a bond there. The teams that are successful build that up over years.

"You don't develop it by allowing any sense of entitlement. I don't care how well-grounded some of these kids are, you hurt them by putting them on the team before they have earned it. We don't just want to hand out jobs."

Hextall inherited a tough cap situation when he became GM three seasons ago. He also was bequeathed, by predecessor Holmgren, a legitimate star in Claude Giroux and a core of young players, most of whom took steps forward last season. The Flyers recovered from winning only six of their first 20 games under new coach Dave Hakstol to go 35-18-9 the rest of the way and take the overall-points leader—the Capitals—to six games in the first round.

"I feel really good about where the organization is in terms of infrastructure, players on the team, and those we have coming," says Hextall. "I'm confident we're going in the direction to be a top team.

Under Holmgren, the front office increasingly employed analytics and sports science in measuring performance. Hextall is taking that to another level, although he won't provide details in order to maintain an edge on the competition.

The Flyers always have been receptive to change. The NFL started to use computers as a drafting aid in the late sixties. Snider brought that with him from the Eagles. He hired the first non-playing assistant coach—Mike Nykoluk in 1973—and put the Flyers in long pants for two years because they were supposedly aerodynamically superior.

Onward and upward. As Tilger says, "The 50th anniversary season is as much about moving forward as a celebration of the last fifty. The best is yet to come."

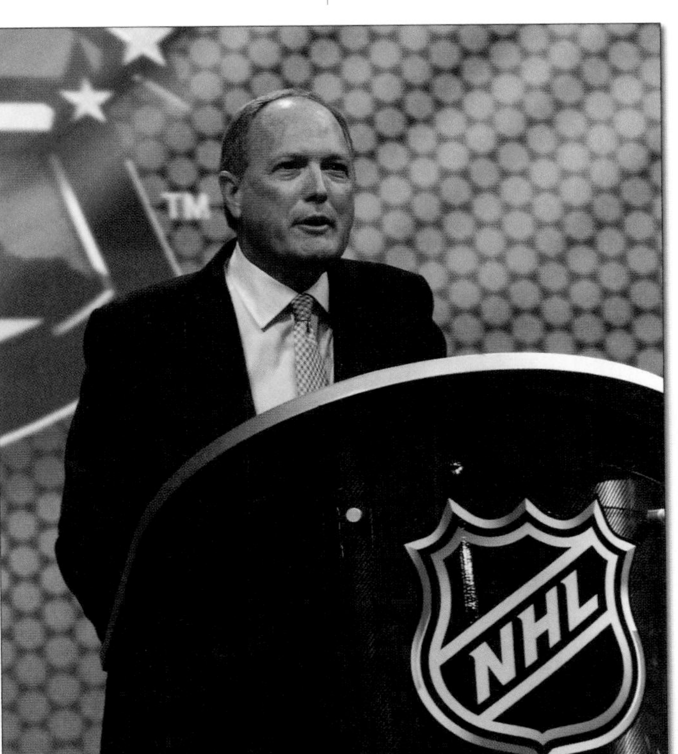

Dave Scott, president & COO, Comcast-Spectacor: "We're going to go for the win every year, like we've always done."

Wanting to devote more of his attention to the Flyers, Scott is hiring a CEO for Spectra—the venue management, food service, and ticketing division of Comcast Spectacor. "We've consolidated a lot of Spectra; it's really running well," he says. "But frankly, the Flyers are a blast, and how I want to spend my time.

"I see Paul being the face of the team, more so than he has been in the past. But I'll clearly play more of a role. I expect to be informed and be used as a sounding board. I don't know everything about hockey, but I'll tell you what I know and think; I'll challenge Paul and Ron because everybody needs to be challenged. But I'm not a micromanager, like Ed wasn't a micromanager.

"Shawn has been with us forever and is a great marketer. Paul and Ron are really running the team. I feel so fortunate Ed put good people in place."

It was Holmgren's idea to bring back Hextall from Los Angeles as the assistant GM and then, in 2014, to bump him up to run the hockey operation. From the president's chair, Holmgren remains a friend, advisor and, more than ever with Snider gone, a key liaison. "Paul understands the tradition and how we think," says Hextall.

During his two years as president, Holmgren has worked at bringing the hockey and business ends of the operation, housed in two different buildings, together. "I feel like we're working as a team and understand each other now," he says. "I don't feel there is a mistrust anymore between the two sides.

"I've known Hexy, (assistant GMs) Barry Hanrahan and Chris Pryor for a long time. But three years ago, I didn't really know Shawn. Now that I do, I realize he has the Flyers' best interests at heart. I think other people from the business end now have a comfort around the hockey people, and more of that will come in time.

"Dave is very smart, wants to learn. He's willing to talk to all of us who have been around hockey for a long time and share his knowledge from other areas."

Before Snider's cancer progressed, Scott had a full year to work with, and understand, him.

"One of the things I learned is Ed was one of the best listeners," Scott says. "I also loved the fact that you would get a candid response from him.

"He had a way of cutting right to the heart of an issue and moving things along. Every day I keep in mind that he was never one to look back."

Flyer fans, excited about the team's progress last season, believe there is much to look forward to. Season ticket holders renewed at a 95 percent rate, up from 82 percent the previous summer, resulting in 2,000 new subscribers.

The 20-year-old Wells Fargo Center will start to feel new next summer with the concourse renovations. A hotel, retail space, and an open amphitheater for summer concerts are in various stages of planning to join XFINITY Live! on the sports complex grounds.

"I just want everyone to feel good about where we're going," said Scott. "Even though the team is owned by a corporation, that corporation has owned it for 20 years, so I just don't think anybody is going to feel any change about the way we operate.

"We're going to go for the win every year, like we've always done."

Take it from Roberts, the guy in the penthouse of the Comcast Center: the sky is the limit more than ever because, after all, that's where Snider now lives.

"While Ed can never be replaced, that doesn't mean we can't take the Flyers and maintain their greatness," said Roberts. "I'm optimistic and proud of our 21-year relationship.

"As a lifelong fan who remembers those parades, I look forward, in Ed's memory, to having them happen again."

TOP 50 FLYER WINS

#1 May 19, 1974 • Rick MacLeish's first-period goal and the goaltending of Bernie Parent defeat Boston 1-0 in Game Six at the Spectrum, bringing the Stanley Cup to Philadelphia for the first time.

#2 May 27, 1975 • Bob Kelly scores 11 seconds into the third period to break a scoreless tie and Parent records his second Cup-clinching shutout in two years as the Flyers win Game Six at Buffalo, 2-0, to repeat as champions.

#3 May 9, 1974 • Bobby Clarke's goal at 12:01 of overtime in Boston caps a rally from a 2-0 deficit, evens the 1974 Final at a game apiece, and gives underdog Philadelphia the home-ice advantage it uses to go on to claim Cup No. 1.

#4 January 11, 1976 • The two-time reigning NHL champions dismantle the perennial Soviet champion Central Red Army team, 4-1, saving the NHL's honor at a Cold War-charged Spectrum.

#5 May 5, 1974 • The Flyers become the first expansion team to eliminate a pre-1967 club from the playoffs, holding off the Rangers 4-3 in Game Seven at the Spectrum to advance to the Final for the first time.

#6 December 22, 1979 • Philadelphia establishes the longest unbeaten streak in NHL history, 29 games on the way to 35, with a smothering 5-2 victory over the Bruins at Boston Garden.

#7 May 13, 1975 • Gary Dornhoefer scores after only 19 seconds and the Flyers, dominating an Islanders team that had come back from a 3-0 deficit, win Game Seven, 4-1, at the Spectrum to reach the Final for a second consecutive year.

#8 May 14, 1974 • Bill Barber's wrist shot from along the boards explodes over Boston goalie Gilles Gilbert's shoulder with 5:35 remaining, breaking a tie and sending the Flyers on to a 4-2 victory that leaves them one game from their first Cup.

#9 May 16, 1985 • Dave Poulin electrifies the Spectrum by scoring unassisted on a breakaway with the Flyers two men short. Philadelphia suffocates Quebec, 3-0 in Game Six to reach the Final for the first time in five years.

TOP 50 FLYER EVENTS

#1 **February 9, 1966** • *NHL Expansion Committee awards one of six new franchises to Philadelphia group headed by Ed Snider, Jerry Wolman and Bill Putnam, who plan for the team to play in a yet-to-be built, privately-financed, 15,000-seat arena at the corner of Broad and Pattison Streets. Announcement is a surprise considering bid was conducted in virtual secrecy, Philadelphia has no minor-league hockey team, and the new East coast franchise was expected to go to Baltimore.*

#2 **August 26, 1967** • *Snider trades his 40 percent share of the Spectrum for Wolman's 22 percent share of the Flyers, becoming 60 percent majority owner of the team six weeks before its inaugural season. Snider and his brother-in-law, Earl Foreman, will buy the Spectrum out of receivership in 1971.*

#3 **June 11, 1969** • *June 11, 1969. At the vehement insistence of scout Jerry Melnyk, Philadelphia selects a diabetic center, Bobby Clarke, with a second-round pick, 17th overall, in the amateur draft. Clarke will captain two Stanley Cup teams, win three Most Valuable Player awards, and become the Flyers' all-time leading scorer.*

#4 **December 22, 1969** • *Snider fires the team's first general manager, Bud Poile, halfway through Year Three and promotes assistant GM Keith Allen to the head position. Allen will assemble consecutive Cup winners in Years Seven and Eight and produce two more finalists and another three semifinalists in 14 seasons running the team.*

#5 **May 20, 1974** • *An estimated two million people overwhelm the police, who expected several hundred thousand, as the Stanley Cup champions, riding in open convertibles, are yanked upon and celebrated in a ticker-tape parade up Broad Street that ends in a rally at Independence Hall.*

#6 **May 28, 1975.** • *Even more fans – an estimated 2.3 million this time – honor the Flyers' repeat Stanley Cup championship with a better organized parade down Broad Street. Players ride on flatbed trucks on a route that ends with a celebration attended by 100,000 at JFK Stadium.*

#7 **March 19, 1996** • *Comcast completes a $500 million deal to take 66 per cent ownership of the Flyers, the under-construction CoreStates Center, the CoreStates Spectrum, and the 76ers. Ed Snider reduces his share of the Flyers to one-third, but remains as Chairman and chief operating officer of the new Comcast-Spectacor.*

#8 **April 11, 2016** • *Ed Snider, 83, the boss of the Flyers since Day One, dies of bladder cancer at his home in Montecito, California.*

#9 **January 31, 1971** • *In the boldest move that shaped the Cup winners, Keith Allen deals his most popular player and tradable asset, goaltender Bernie Parent, to Toronto in a three-way transaction that principally brings center Rick MacLeish, a former fourth-overall pick by Boston, to Philadelphia. MacLeish, who had unimpressive statistics in the minors, will manage just three goals in trials with Philadelphia over the next year-and-a-half before exploding to 50 goals and 50 assists in 1972-73, the Flyers' first winning season. He will score 53 playoff goals in 108 postseason games for Philadelphia.*

TOP 50 FLYER WINS

#10 May 14, 2010 • Simon Gagne's goal with 7:08 remaining climaxes a rally from a three-goal first period deficit and the Flyers become only the third team in NHL history–and the first in 35 years–to win a series it trailed 3-0, defeating the Bruins, 4-3, in Boston to advance to the Confernce final.

#11 May 28. 1987 • J.J. Daigneault's third-period goal with 5:22 to go climaxes the Flyers' third rally from at least a 2-goal deficit during the Stanley Cup Final, giving them a 3-2 win over Edmonton and forcing Game Seven.

#12 May 14, 1987 • Rookie goalie Ron Hextall slams the door and Rick Tocchet's third-period goal climaxes a rally from a two-goal deficit as the Flyers eliminate the defending champion Canadiens at the Forum in Game Six, 4-3, and earn a second Final berth in three seasons.

#13 May 6, 1976 • Reggie Leach ties an NHL playoff record with five goals as Philadelphia eliminates Boston, 6-3, in Game Five at the Spectrum and advances to the Final for the third consecutive spring.

#14 April 10, 1973 • Gary Dornhoefer's Game Five overtime goal gives the Flyers a 3-2 win over the Minnesota North Stars and the Spectrum its first joyous playoff moment. It inspires the "Score" statue outside the building and puts the six-year-old franchise one win from its first playoff series triumph.

#15 May 4, 2000 • Keith Primeau's goal 12:01 into the fifth overtime at Pittsburgh's Mellon Arena ends the third-longest game in NHL history, 2-1, and ties the quarterfinal series with the Penguins at 2-2 on the way to a six-game triumph.

#16 April 13, 1985 • Tim Kerr's four second-period goals break the NHL record for most in a playoff period as the Flyers end a string of three consecutive first-round defeats with a 6-5 victory at Madison Square Garden and a three-game sweep of the Rangers.

#17 May 24, 2010 • Mike Richards scores shorthanded and Jeff Carter's second goal of the game, into the empty net, seals a 4-1 triumph in Game Five as the Flyers complete a 5-game triumph over Montreal at the Wachovia Center to reach the Cup Final for the first time in 13 seasons.

TOP 50 FLYER EVENTS

***#10 May 15, 1973** • Allen reacquires Parent in a trade that sends a first-round pick and goaltender Doug Favell to Toronto. Parent backstops the Flyers to Cups in the first two seasons of his return, clinching both championships with shutouts.*

***#11 June 2, 1971** • Allen gives Fred Shero, who had won four championships and produced two other finalists in coaching New York Ranger minor-league teams for seven seasons, his first NHL bench. Shero's Flyers will win two Cups and reach at least the semifinals in six of his seven Philadelphia seasons.*

***#12 October 19, 1967** • The Spectrum, built in 15 months at a cost of $12 million, hosts its first Flyers game, a 1-0 win over Pittsburgh, enabled by Doug Favell's 21 saves and a third-period goal by Bill Sutherland. Attendance is 7,812.*

***#13 August 31, 1996** • The 19,511-seat CoreStates Center (now Wells Fargo Center), the Flyers' new $210 million home, opens to a capacity crowd with Team USA's 5-3 victory over Canada in the World Cup of Hockey. The building required seven years from conception to completion. $140 million of its cost had been financed by Snider until its purchase by Comcast in 1995.*

***#14 June 30, 1992** • NHL-appointed arbitrator Larry Bertuzzi rules Quebec Nordiques owner Marcel Aubut made an enforceable deal with the Flyers for the rights to Eric Lindros before changing his mind and trading him to the Rangers, awarding perhaps the most anticipated prospect in the game's history to Philadelphia. Flyers give up six players, two first-round draft picks and $15 million to Quebec in the league's biggest deal ever.*

***#15 June 6, 1967** • The Flyers select four young players in their expansion draft – Parent, Gary Dornhoefer, Ed Van Impe and Joe Watson – who will be mainstays seven and eight years later on the Stanley Cup teams.*

***#16 June 8, 1972** • In the 1972 draft, the Flyers select not only Hockey Hall of Famer Bill Barber (with the seventh-overall pick) but one of their best all-time defensemen in Jimmy Watson, plus another regular blueliner on their Cup teams, Tom Bladon. Their fourth-round pick, winger Al MacAdam, will become the principal piece in the trade that brings Reggie Leach to Philadelphia.*

***#17 February 9, 1995** • The largest quality return on a trade in franchise history nets general manager Bob Clarke eventual three-time, 50-plus goal scorer John LeClair, plus seven-time Barry Ashbee Trophy winner-to-be Eric Desjardins from Montreal for star winger Mark Recchi.*

TOP 50 FLYER WINS

#18 May 25, 1997 • Rod Brind'Amour's two goals and one each by Eric Lindros and John LeClair finish off Wayne Gretzky's and Mark Messier's Rangers, 4-2, in Game Five at the Core States Center, giving the Flyers their first berth in the Stanley Cup Final in 10 years.

#19 April 12, 1973 • Behind the goaltending of Doug Favell and two goals by Ross Lonsberry, Philadelphia wraps up the franchise's first-ever playoff series, winning Game Six, 4-1, over Minnesota at the Metropolitan Sports Center.

#20 April 11, 2010 • Brian Boucher stops Olli Jokinen in the Rangers' final shootout attempt, making goals by Danny Briere and Claude Giroux on Henrik Lundqvist stand up as the Flyers, 2-1 winners, beat the Rangers in a Game 82 showdown at the Wachovia Center for the Eastern Conference's final playoff spot. The Flyers will go on to the Stanley Cup Final.

#21 May 2, 1987 • Dave Poulin puts on a flak jacket and undergoes a nerve block to protect broken ribs that had sidelined him for the first six games of the quarterfinals. With the help of a goal and an assist by Brian Propp, the Flyers earn a 5-1 Spectrum victory in Game Seven over an Islander team that had once trailed the series three games to one.

#22 May 4, 2004 • Jeremy Roenick's second goal of the game at 7:39 of overtime in Game Six at the Air Canada Centre and the stalwart goaltending of Robert Esche propel the Flyers to a 3-2 win over Toronto and a berth in the Eastern Conference final.

#23 April 22, 2012 • Claude Giroux flattens Sidney Crosby and scores 32 seconds into the game, then sets up two other goals as the Flyers eliminate Pittsburgh in Game Six of a first-round series, 5-1, at the Wells Fargo Center.

#24 May 26, 1995 • Karl Dykhuis scores twice and the Flyers, back in the playoffs after a 5-year absence, complete a stunning second-round sweep of the defending champion Rangers, 4-1, at Madison Square Garden.

TOP 50 FLYER EVENTS

#18 August 20, 1982 • *Mark Howe, best defenseman in team history and an anchor on two Cup finalists, becomes a Flyer when Allen trades Ken Linseman, Greg Adams and a No. 1 pick to Hartford.*

#19 December 11, 1969 • *Flyers VP Lou Scheinfeld, noting the crowd's indifference to the playing of "The Star-Spangled Banner" during a time of dissent over the Vietnam war, orders a change of pace: Kate Smith's recording of "God Bless America." When the struggling Flyers defeat Toronto, 6-3, then win again after her song is played two games later, Scheinfeld picks his spots and turns Smith into the team's good luck charm. Over the next three seasons, the Flyers go 19-1-1 after "God Bless America" as opposed to 31-38-28 following the national anthem. Kate will appear live to thunderous Spectrum ovations four times, including the opener of the first Cup season and the clinching Game Six.*

#20 November 10, 1985 • *Reigning Vezina Trophy winner Pelle Lindbergh, just 26 years old and beloved by teammates and fans, dies in a wee hours automobile accident caused by his zeal for speed and a night of drinking with his teammates and friends.*

#21 June 1966 • *While franchise founders are brainstorming during an ice cream stop along the New Jersey Turnpike on the way home from attending a Broadway show, Phyllis Foreman, Snider's sister, suggests the name Flyers. A name-the-team contest is subsequently held entirely for promotional reasons. Nine-year-old Alec Stockard of Narberth, Pa., the winner, filled in "Fliers" on the contest form distributed by Acme Markets and won season tickets for Year One, plus a television set. No one remembers why the decision was made to spell the name with a "y."*

#22 November 15, 1984 • *On Bobby Clarke Night, the franchise's greatest-ever player and new general manager is lavished with gifts and a four-minute standing ovation before his team gives him his most appreciated present of all, a 6-1 crushing of Hartford. "I got everything I could out of this body for 15 years," Clarke tells the crowd. "If I had my choice, I would love to do it all over again."*

#23 April 13, 1968 • *St. Louis defenseman Noel Picard, 6-1, 210, sucker punches Claude Laforge (5-8, 160) in Game Two of the 1968 first round, leaving the Flyer forward unconscious in a pool of blood as a melee erupts around him. The Blues manhandle the smaller Flyers in a four-game sweep, causing Snider and his management to swear their team never will be taken advantage of physically again. Two months later, Clarke is the only selection standing under six-feet-tall in a draft that includes Dave Schultz.*

#24 December 29, 1972 • *A fan reaches over the glass and grabs Don Saleski's hair as he puts a stranglehold on the Canucks' Barry Wilcox, causing the Flyers to go into the Vancouver stands, swinging sticks and fists. Fans gather in front of the visiting clubhouse door booing and calling the Flyers "animals" following the 4-4 tie. Criminal charges are laid against seven Flyers, although the only conviction will be a 30-day suspended sentence for backup goalie Bobby Taylor. And the Broad Street Bullies, as nicknamed by* The Evening Bulletin's *Jack Chevalier, are born.*

TOP 50 FLYER WINS

#25 April 28, 1985 • Pelle Lindbergh shuts out the Islanders, one season removed from their four-year dynasty, 1-0, on Ilkka Sinisalo's goal in Game Five at the Spectrum. The Flyers advance to a conference final for the first time in five years.

#26 April 22, 2008 • Joffrey Lupul's power play goal at 6:06 of Game Seven overtime at the MCI Center gives the Flyers, only one year earlier the worst team in the NHL, a first-round series win at Washington, 3-2.

#27 April 29, 1989 • Ken Wregget steps into Game Seven for the injured Ron Hextall to stop 39 shots. Philadelphia advances to the Eastern Conference final with a 4-1 victory at Pittsburgh.

#28 November 14, 1985 • Four days after the death of goaltender Pelle Lindbergh, Flyers conduct a memorial service for him at the Spectrum, then defeat Stanley Cup champion Edmonton Oilers, 5-3.

#29 April 10, 1985 • Mark Howe's goal at 8:01 of overtime in Game One ruins Ranger rallies from 3-0 and 4-3 deficits and ends a nine-game, three-year, playoff losing streak. The Flyers go on to a three-game first-round sweep by a total margin of four goals and eventually reach the Stanley Cup Final.

#30 April 17, 1977 • Behind 2-1 in the series and 5-2 at Maple Leaf Gardens with 7:16 remaining, the Flyers tie the score with 1:33 to play on Bobby Clarke's goal, then beat Toronto, 6-5, when Reggie Leach scores in overtime. It is the second consecutive game the Flyers have tied with the goalie pulled and enables them to even a series they had trailed 2-0. Philadelphia goes on to win in six games.

#31 May 4, 1980 • Bill Barber scores four goals in Game Three at Minnesota's Metropolitan Sports Center, leading the Flyers to a 5-3 victory that turns the Stanley Cup semifinals Philadelphia's way in an eventual five-game triumph.

TOP 50 FLYER EVENTS

***#25** June 9, 1973* • *After the Flyers record their first winning season and playoff series triumph, their young leader, Clarke, wins the first of his three Hart Trophies. "I'm surprised, it usually goes to the big clubs," says Shero, but Philadelphia has become one of them, thanks largely to the Flyers' burgeoning superstar. Snider throws a black tie gala at the Barclay Hotel to celebrate.*

***#26** June 24, 2006* • *Claude Giroux, a 5-10, 185-pound dynamo from the Gatineau Olympiques of the Quebec Major Junior League, is selected by the Flyers with the 22nd pick of the draft. Their future captain and five-time leading scorer will prove to be the franchise's best pick outside of blue chip position – Bill Barber went seventh – in a draft since Clarke. Giroux leads the NHL in points for this decade.*

***#27** June 9, 2010* • *Flyers closest bid for a Stanley Cup in 13 years ends in confusion, then the sickening realization that a bad angle shot by Chicago's Patrick Kane in overtime had gone under goaltender Michael Leighton and lodged under the padding at the bottom of the net on the opposite side, giving the Blackhawks a 4-3 victory in Game Six and the championship.*

***#28** May 24, 1980* • *Linesman Leon Stickle misses an obvious offsides before an Islander first-period goal and the Flyers, who rally from a 2-goal third-period deficit, have their hearts broken when Bob Nystrom wins the Stanley Cup in overtime of Game Six at the Nassau Coliseum.*

***#29** March 1, 1968* • *High winds tear off a 50-by-150 foot portion of the covering of the Spectrum roof during a performance by the Ice Capades, the second incident of damage to the roof within a month. When it is learned proper occupancy permits were not issued at the facility's opening seven months earlier, the city orders the building shut down, forcing the Flyers to move home games to New York and Toronto before Quebec City becomes the team's home-away-from-home for the remainder of the regular season. Regardless, the Flyers go 3-2-2 in their exiled games and win the first championship of the West Division, consisting of the six new clubs. The Spectrum is re-opened for the playoffs.*

***#30** October 11, 1979* • *Bernie Parent's No. 1 is raised to the Spectrum rafters on the season's opening night while fans chant "Bernie! Bernie! Bernie!" one last time for perhaps the most beloved Flyer of all. Parent, whose career ended because of an eye injury suffered eight months earlier, becomes the second player to have his number retired by the franchise, following Barry Ashbee's No. 4.*

***#31** June 23, 2011* • *Hours apart, GM Paul Holmgren shockingly trades Mike Richards and Jeff Carter, two 26-year-old core players signed to long-term contracts. Both had been key players on Flyer finalist and semifinalist teams in the last four years. Richards is moved to Los Angeles for Wayne Simmonds and Brayden Schenn, and Carter goes to Columbus for Jake Voracek and the eighth overall pick in the next day's draft, which the Flyers use to select Sean Couturier.*

TOP 50 FLYER WINS

#32 April 17, 2004 • Danny Markov's goal with 5:23 remaining breaks a 1-1 tie and the Flyers finish off a first-round elimination of the defending champion Devils, 3-1, in Game Five at the Wachovia Center. It is Philadelphia's first series triumph against New Jersey in three tries.

#33 April 16, 2003 • Mark Recchi's goal at 13:54 of the third overtime gives the Flyers, who had lost Game Three in double overtime, a 3-2 win over Toronto in Game Four at the Air Canada Center to tie the series at 2-2. Philadelphia will go on to a Game Seven win, its first series triumph in three years.

#34 April 22, 2003 • Mark Recchi nets two goals as a scoring burst carries the Flyers to a 6-1 Game Seven quarterfinal elimination of Toronto at the Core States Center, ending only the second series in NHL history with three multiple-overtime games.

#35 April 22, 2010 • Claude Giroux scores twice and assists on Danny Briere's goal as the seventh-seeded Flyers complete a five-game quarterfinal triumph over second-seeded New Jersey, 3-0, behind Brian Boucher's shutout at the Prudential Center.

#36 April 11, 1989 • Ron Hextall becomes the first goalie in NHL history to shoot and score a playoff goal, helping the Flyers to a 3-2 quarterfinal series lead with an 8-5 win over Washington at the Capital Centre.

#37 April 13, 1989 • Rick Tocchet's goal from the corner on Pete Peeters with 3:19 remaining gives the Flyers a see-saw 4-3 Game Six Spectrum victory over the Caps and a first-round upset.

#38 May 23, 1997 • Eric Lindros's power play goal with six seconds remaining, off a John LeClair backhand pass, beats Mike Richter to give the Flyers a 3-2 win over the Rangers at Madison Square Garden and a commanding 3-1 lead in a conference final series that the Flyers would win in five games.

#39 May 20, 2004 • Keith Primeau's game-tying goal with 1:49 remaining and Simon Gagne's overtime winner at 18:18 enable the Flyers to force a semifinal Game Seven against Tampa Bay with a 5-4 home victory.

#40 April 16, 1968 • The Flyers, down to their last 15 seconds in Game Six at St, Louis, tie the score on a goal by Andre Lacroix, then win 2-1 when Don Blackburn scores in double overtime to force Game Seven in the franchise's first-ever playoff series.

TOP 50 FLYER EVENTS

***#32 February 1, 1977** • The first Flyers Wives Carnival, benefitting cancer research at Hahnemann Hospital, draws 8,000 fans to the Spectrum and raises $85,167.35. The annual fundraising event, brainstorm of Flyers public relations director Ed Golden after Snider donates the use of the building for the wives' charitable intentions, has raised more than $29 million for hundreds of causes and has been copied by many other sports organizations.*

***#33 July 6, 1995** • Following a semifinal run that establishes the Flyers as a contender again after a five-season playoff drought, Eric Lindros becomes the second member of the team to win a Hart Trophy.*

***#34 December 8, 1987** • Ron Hextall becomes the first NHL goaltender ever to shoot and score a goal as Philadelphia defeats Boston, 5-2, at the Spectrum.*

***#36 January 2, 2012** • Flyers, hosts for the first time of the Winter Classic, draw 46,967 to Citizens Bank Park for a 3-2 loss to the Rangers, decided when Henrik Lundqvist stops Danny Briere on a late penalty shot. Two days earlier, 45,808 had watched a team of Flyers alumni defeat the Rangers alumni, 3-1.*

***#37 May 26, 2000** • Lindros's participation in his last game as a Flyer, Game Seven of the Eastern Conference final, ends in the first period when he is leveled by a shoulder to the head from the Devils' Scott Stevens, causing the sixth concussion of No. 88's career. The Flyers, who had led the series 3-1, lose the game, 2-1, on Patrik Elias's goal in the final three minutes. Lindros will sit out the next season until he is traded to the Rangers.*

***#38 April 11, 1996** • Flyers, past and present, are paired for a last lap around the Spectrum ice at the conclusion of the final regular-season game, a 3-2 Atlantic Division-clinching victory over Montreal. Lindros skates with Clarke. The team concludes its 29-year run in its original home with a regular-season record of 696-294-141. Twenty-eight days later, Philadelphia will lose its final playoff game in the building, 2-1, to Florida.*

***#39 August 9, 1979** • With two draft classes merged by the lowering of the age limit from 20 to 19, Brian Propp becomes available to Philadelphia with the 14th pick. He will become the team's third all-time point producer behind Clarke and Barber. Flyers also take future Vezina Trophy winner Pelle Lindbergh 35th overall and, afterwards, sign the undrafted Tim Kerr, who will score 50-plus goals in four different seasons.*

***#40 April 2, 1972** • Four seconds away from a point that would have clinched a playoff spot, the Flyers lose in Buffalo, 3-2, when goaltender Doug Favell allows Gerry Meehan's goal from well above the top of the circle. "I'll bet in the entire history of hockey, something like this has never happened before," says the devastated Clarke. It is the second time in three seasons the seemingly star-crossed franchise misses a postseason spot on a long-distance goal in the final game, Parent having lost a third-period lob from center ice by Minnesota's Barry Gibbs in a 1-0 defeat denying Philadelphia in 1970.*

TOP 50 FLYER WINS

#41 May 22, 1987 • Brad McCrimmon scores just 17 seconds after Scott Mellanby ties the game and the Flyers become the first team in 33 years to rally to victory from a three-goal deficit in the Cup Final. The 5-3 win at the Spectrum cuts Edmonton's series lead to 2-1.

#42 May 26, 1987 • Rick Tocchet's early third-period goal, off a fourth assist in the game by Brian Propp, lifts the Flyers, once trailing 3-1, to a 4-3 victory in Edmonton, returning them home to Philadelphia for Game Six of the Final.

#43 January 6, 1980 • Goals by Dennis Ververgaert, Bill Barber and Rick MacLeish spark a rally from a 2-1 late second-period deficit and Phil Myre, in relief of the ill Pete Peeters, beats the Sabres, 4-2 at Memorial Auditorium in Buffalo, stretching the Flyers' record-breaking unbeaten streak to 35 games (25-0-10). (It will end the following night with a 7-1 defeat at Minnesota.)

#44 May 3, 2008 • Scottie Upshall's third-period goal breaks a 4-4 tie and the Flyers, last in the league only one year earlier, advance to the Eastern Conference final with a 6-4 win in Game Five at Montreal's Bell Centre.

#45 April 13, 2012 • Nineteen-year-old Sean Couturier becomes the youngest scorer of a playoff hat trick since Teeder Kennedy in 1945. Claude Giroux also scores three goals (plus three assists) as the Flyers erase four deficits in an 8-5 victory at Pittsburgh, taking a 2-0 lead in a series they will win in six games.

#46 May 15, 1980 • Paul Holmgren becomes the first American-born player to score a hat trick in the Stanley Cup Final as the Flyers rout the Islanders, 8-3, at the Spectrum and tie the series, 1-1.

#47 April 20, 1995 • Ron Hextall makes Mikael Renberg's third-period goal hold up in 2-1 Spectrum victory over the Islanders, the Flyers' eighth straight win, clinching their first playoff spot in five years.

TOP 50 FLYER EVENTS

***#41** June 8, 1983 • Despite having traded away their first-round pick to obtain Howe, the Flyers draft three players – Peter Zezel, Derrick Smith and Rick Tocchet – who a year later will play important roles on the 1985 Stanley Cup Final team. A fourth draftee, Pelle Eklund, joins in 1985-86, before Philadelphia goes to the Final again in 1987.*

***#42** June 9, 1982 • After using the fourth overall pick on center Ron Sutter, who would become a heart-and-soul player on two Stanley Cup finalists and a semifinalist, the Flyers take a sixth-round shot on fiery goaltender Ron Hextall. He will key the 1987 drive to Game Seven of the Final, become the franchise's all-time leader in regular-season victories, and serve today as their general manager.*

***#43** June 18, 2007 • With the Flyers coming off a franchise-worst 54-point season, GM Paul Holmgren trades back to Nashville the pick he acquired four months earlier for Peter Forsberg, obtaining exclusive negotiating rights to defenseman Kimmo Timonen and winger Scott Hartnell before they can become free agents in 13 days. Both sign six-year contracts and, combined with the free-agent signing of Briere 13 days later, key a lightning revival that takes Philadelphia to the Eastern Conference final the next season. Timonen becomes a five-time Barry Ashbee Trophy winner and Hartnell a two-time 30-plus goal scorer.*

***#44** May 16, 1977 • Barry Ashbee—All-Star defenseman before losing an eye to a slapshot during the 1974 semifinals, assistant coach/heir apparent to Shero, and a victim of leukemia a stunning 30 days after he was diagnosed—is eulogized as a "man's man" by Clarke before being laid to rest at age 37 in Toronto. More than 1,000 fans attend a memorial service held at the Spectrum on the same day.*

***#45** July 18, 1999 • More than 2,000 attend a service at the First Union Center for the voice of the Flyers for their first three decades, Gene Hart, who died four days earlier at age 68. Classical and opera performers plus Lauren Hart, Gene's daughter and Flyer anthemist, perform in honor of the arts patron and renaissance man credited with teaching hockey to the people of Philadelphia.*

***#46** September 25, 1984 • Bernie Parent becomes the first of eight Flyers to be inducted into the Hockey Hall of Fame, followed by Bobby Clarke (1987), Ed Snider (1988), Bill Barber (1990), Keith Allen (1992), Mark Howe (2011), Fred Shero (2013) and Eric Lindros (2016).*

***#47** March 7, 1968 • Boston's Eddie Shack and Philadelphia's Larry Zeidel engage in a vicious stick fight during a Flyer home game that was moved to Toronto during the Spectrum roof crisis. Pictures of blood pouring down the face of both players horrify citizens of two nations. Incident is fueled by Zeidel trying to rally his slumping, orphaned, team and anti-Semetic remarks made by Boston players. Shack is suspended for three games and Zeidel, who took the first swing, for four.*

TOP 50 FLYER WINS

#48 April 24, 2011 • Scott Hartnell's third period goal ties the game and Ville Leino scores at 4:43 of overtime as the Flyers, 5-4 Game Six winners at Buffalo's HSBC Arena, send their first-round series back to the Wells Fargo Center for Game Seven, which the Flyers would win, 5-2.

#49 April 4, 2008 • Martin Biron's 3-0 Wachovia Center shutout of New Jersey in Game No. 81, clinches a playoff spot for the Flyers one year after they had compiled the league's worst record. They would go on to the Stanley Cup semifinal.

#50 April 9, 2016 • Lauren Hart serenades Ed Snider with "God Bless America" via FaceTime and the Flyers, who won only six of their first 20 games and were next-to-last in the Metropolitan Division on January 2, clinch a playoff spot in Game 81 with a 3-1 victory over Pittsburgh. "If it weren't for Mr. Snider, not one person in this room would be here," says Wayne Simmonds after scoring twice. "We owe him a lot." The Flyers founder dies of bladder cancer 33 hours later.

TOP 50 FLYER EVENTS

***#48** December 2, 1973* • *Oakland Seals defenseman Barry Cummins, responds to the aggravating stick work of Clarke by bashing the Flyer captain over the head, opening a 24-stitch gash. Cummins is attacked en masse by Clarke's teammates, demonstrating the lengths the Broad Street Bullies would go to support each other. Cummins is suspended for three games.*

***#49** March 4, 2004* • *Suddenly it is 1974 again as the Flyers and Senators brawl endlessly through five late third-period play stoppages to set a new NHL record with 419 penalty minutes. Ottawa had eliminated the Flyers the previous two playoffs and Philadelphia was looking to even a score against Martin Havlat, who had retaliated from a hook by Mark Recchi by high sticking the Flyer in the head eight days earlier. Ottawa coach Jacques Martin has Havlat serve penalties so the Flyers are never able to lay a hand on him, just everybody else. Philadelphia finishes with four players on the bench to the Senators' two.*

***#50** December 11, 1977* • *Tom Bladon's eight points on four goals and four assists in a 10-1 Spectrum rout of Cleveland are not only the highest number of points by any player in a single game in Flyer history but the most ever by a defenseman in NHL history until Paul Coffey ties the record in 1986. Bladon's +10 also remains a Philadelphia mark.*

As many as two million happy Flyer fans turned out in Philadelphia's Center City to celebrate Stanley Cup championships in 1974 and 1975.

ERNIE
#1
FLYERS
WE'RE
#1
WE'RE #1
PSFS

FLYERS FOREVER

Deceased Players, Coaches, Scouts, Executives, Broadcasters, Trainers and Beloved Figures

NAME	POSITION	FLYER YEARS	DIED	AGE	CAUSE
Keith Allen	Coach, G.M., V.P.	1967-2014	2014	90	Chronic obstructive pulmonary disease (COPD)
Barry Ashbee	Defense	1970-74	1977	37	Leukemia
Walter Atanas	Scout	1977-91	1991	69	Heart disease
Jenny Barber	Carnival Organizer, wife of Bill	1973-2001	2001	48	Lung cancer
Bob Boucher	Assistant Coach	1979-81	2004	66	Lung cancer
John Brogan	PR Director, Scouting Director	1973-93	2012	74	Cancer
Mike Byers	Right wing	1968-69	2010	64	Cancer
Rev. John Casey	Unofficial Team Chaplain	1967-2000	2000	88	Heart failure
Eric Coville	Scout	1967-83	2002	69	Stroke
Jim Cunningham	Left wing	1977-78	2011	54	Accident: struck by train
Bob Dailey	Defense	1977-82	2016	63	Cancer
Gary Darling	Assistant G.M.	1983-89	2009	69	Complications from diabetes
Alex Davidson	Chief Scout	1967-79	1987	68	Lung cancer
Bill Delaney	Equipment Manager	1970-87	2002	83	Heart failure
Matt DiPaolo	Physical Therapist	1976-80	2012	77	Cancer
F. Eugene Dixon	Limited Partner	1971-76	2006	82	Cancer
Yanick Dupre	Left wing	1991-96	1997	24	Leukemia
Miroslav Dvorak	Defense	1982-84	2008	56	Throat cancer
Don Earle	Broadcaster	1971-77	1993	64	Unknown illness
Reg Fleming	Defense/Left wing	1969-70	2009	73	Chronic traumatic encephalopy, stroke, heart attack
Wayne Fleming	Assistant Coach	2002-06	2013	57	Brain cancer
Bill Flett	Right wing	1972-74	1999	55	Liver failure
Rick Foley	Defense	1971-72	2015	70	Natural causes
Ray Frost	Scout	1967-77	2014	86	Natural causes
Bruce Gamble	Goaltender	1970-72	1982	44	Heart attack
Jean Gauthier	Defense	1967-68	2013	75	Natural causes
John Hanna	Defense	1967-68	2005	70	Cancer
Pat Hannigan	Left wing	1967-69	2007	71	Intestinal infection
Gene Hart	Broadcaster	1967-95	1999	68	Complications from diabetes
Wayne Hillman	Defense	1969-73	1990	52	Cancer
Ed Hoekstra	Center	1967-68	2011	74	Accident: struck by car riding scooter

NAME	POSITION	FLYER YEARS	DIED	AGE	CAUSE
Dave Hoyda	Left wing	1977-79	2015	57	Complications from burns suffered in house fire
Willie Huber	Defense	1987-88	2010	52	Heart attack
Kathy Kerr	Carnival Chairperson, wife of Tim	1988-90	1990	30	Undetermined; ten days after childbirth
Rick Lapointe	Defense	1976-79	1999	44	Heart attack
Michel Larocque	Goaltender	1982-83	1992	40	Brain cancer
Frank Lewis	Trainer	1967-81	2002	82	Lung cancer
Pelle Lindbergh	Goaltender	1981-86	1986	26	Automobile accident
Andrei Lomakin	Right wing	1991-95	2006	42	Cancer
Ross Lonsberry	Left wing	1972-78	2014	67	Lung cancer
Norm Mackie	Head Trainer	1980-82	2000	64	Parkinson's Disease
Rick MacLeish	Center	1970-81 & 1983-84	2016	66	Kidney and liver failure, meningitis
Ralph MacSweyn	Defense	1967-72	1995	52	Cancer
Brad McCrimmom	Defense	1982-86	2011	52	Airplane crash while coaching Yaroslavl team in Russia
E.J. McGuire	Assistant Coach	1984-88 & 2000-02	2011	58	Leiomyosarcoma
Don McLeod	Goaltender	1971-72	2015	68	Heart attack
Jerry Melnyk	Scout, Head Scout (1984-96)	1968-97	2001	66	Leukemia
Larry Mickey	Right wing	1971-72	1982	38	Suicide
Stu Nahan	Broadcaster	1967-69	2007	81	Lymphoma
Roger Neilson	Coach	1998-2000	2003	69	Skin cancer
Jacques Plante	Goaltender Instructor	1978-82	1986	57	Stomach cancer
Norman (Bud) Poile	General Manager	1967-70	2006	80	Parkinson's Disease
William Putnam	President	1967-71	2002	72	Kidney failure
Pat Quinn	Coach	1979-82	2014	71	Various intestinal issues
Cliff Schmautz	Right wing	1970-71	2002	62	Complications from heart surgery
Joe Scott	Limited Partner	1967-84	2002	93	Natural causes
Fred Shero	Coach	1971-78	1990	65	Stomach cancer
Harlan Singer	Radio-TV Producer	1970-79	1992	60	Cancer
Kate Smith	Anthemist	1969-forever	1986	79	Heart failure, complications from diabetes
Ed Snider	Founder and Chairman	1966-2016	2016	83	Bladder Cancer
Myrna Snider	Matriarch, first wife of Ed Snider	1967-81	2014	78	Cancer
Glen Sonmor	Scout	1989-93	2015	86	Alzheimer's disease
Allan Stanley	Defense	1968-69	2013	87	Natural causes
Wayne Stephenson	Goaltender	1974-79	2010	65	Brain cancer
Dmitri Tertyshny	Defense	1998-99	1999	22	Boating accident
Sylvan Tobin	Limited Partner	1984-96	2013	83	Brain cancer
Larry Zeidel	Defense	1967-68	2014	86	Heart failure
Peter Zezel	Center	1984-88	2009	44	Organ failure caused by Hemolytic Anemia

ACKNOWLEDGEMENTS

ED SNIDER ALWAYS SAW VALUE in having a detailed historical record of his team. From the origins of the Flyers detailed in *Full Spectrum* to the final year of his life, I was permitted to write with detail and candor—one more testament to his honesty, courage and vision.

Mr. Snider's pride in the behemoth he founded will outlive him every time the Flyers take the ice, with every young life changed by the Ed Snider Youth Hockey Foundation, and, I hope, through the publication of this work. Fans not yet born must know what he accomplished and how. It is an honor to have been given that responsibility twice.

Just as Jay Snider did for *Full Spectrum*, Flyer COO Shawn Tilger allowed me the freedom to tell the story objectively. Because the losses make the victories that much more thrilling, it is all here, thanks to the openness of the persons who suffered the setbacks and enjoyed the successes.

At our first meeting, Shawn told me that for this project, the product was more important than any profit. In the course of three years, that never changed. Whatever I needed was available. There was money to travel for longer interviews and access to the highest level of executives at Comcast-Spectacor.

From administrators to hard-working support personnel, the enthusiasm I received about a 50th anniversary Flyer history was as endless as the task of tracking down the 263 persons interviewed. Fewer than two handfuls of calls or emails went unreturned, largely because people loved their time in Philadelphia and were excited to talk about it. In some cases, I only needed 15 minutes, but every appointment that was kept and every second granted on the telephone was deeply appreciated.

Over the course of many months, Bob Clarke, Paul Holmgren and Ron Hextall made themselves available for up to 12 hours each. They were exceedingly honest, forthcoming, and seemingly never annoyed when I asked for more time and information.

Space does not permit me to thank everyone who agreed to be interviewed, but the quotes in the book essentially comprise the list. I especially want to cite those who granted multiple sessions or accommodated me in one sitting of longer than 60 minutes:

Bill Barber, Craig Berube, Brian Boucher, Danny Briere, Rod Brind'Amour, Eric Desjardins, Robert Esche, Todd Fedoruk, Simon Gagne, Brian Hart, Lauren Hart, Sarah Hart, Scott Hartnell, Derian Hatcher, Ken Hitchcock, Keith Jones, Mike Knuble, Ian Laperriere, Peter Laviolette, John LeClair, Eric Lindros, Peter Luukko, Brad Marsh, Jim McCrossin, Terry Murray, Simon Nolet, Dennis Patterson, Dave Poulin, Keith Primeau, Chris Pronger, Chris Pryor, Craig Ramsay, Mark Recchi, Luke Richardson, Jeremy Roenick, Ron Ryan, Dave Scott, Jay Snider, Lindy Snider, Martha Snider, John Stevens, Polina Tertyshny, Chris Therien, Rick Tocchet, and John Vanbiesbrouck.

Mostly because *Full Spectrum*, originally conceived as a 25th anniversary book, was completed for Year 30, Mr. Snider's last words to me two weeks before his death were, "You're going to be done on time, right?" I could never have come close without the help of so many.

In editing this volume, my wife Mona gave up a lot of her life, but never her principles on redundancy. She saved me from myself in multitudes of cases big and small, making the copy read more smoothly. I love her for that passion, and owe her more than I can say. She wouldn't let me express it twice regardless.

As I spent many of the seasons covered in this book working in New York, Bill Meltzer was an essential and bottomless well of knowledge. I don't recall him once having to tell me, "I don't know." He fact-checked most of the chapters, some of the profiles, and saved me both little errors and glaring omissions. He also was a huge help in compiling, and whittling down, the 50 Events list. Bill not only transcribed interviews, but corrected recollections of the subjects. He cared about this work like it was his own.

Publisher Dan Diamond impressively framed a cumbersome amount of words to make this book beautiful, provided praise on some days when I really needed it, never panicked while waiting for me to deliver the copy, and gave me as much time as he possibly could.

It was a natural extension of the pride felt by Flyer staffers in the organization that they wanted nothing but the best for this project. Brian Smith guided me to internet places unknown—and in one case unreachable by a Mac—and searched for most of the pictures. Joe Siville took charge of photo selection in the last months and coordinated interviews with the current players, in a few cases firmly making them understand, "No, Jay really needs a full hour."

Archivist Brian McBride, got the clips, the videos, was a guide around that fascinating little museum just below the roof of the Wells Fargo Center, and always got back to me with whatever information I needed. Zack Hill had phone numbers for alums, a few times gave them an extra nudge on my behalf, coordinated some photography and shared his own recollections going way back.

My most prevailed-upon transcribers, Melissa Becktel-Seidel and Meridith Daniel, were always enthusiastic, thorough and responsive, especially when I needed a quick turn-around. But I am no less appreciative of the persons who struggled through one transcription, or did just a few before having to go back to their real jobs or tend to other matters in their lives. Whatever they could do helped. Because it was for the Flyers, I had lawyers and college professors offering their time, even before I knew I could pay them. The 50th anniversary book project did not discriminate against over-qualified assistants and certainly not lovers of hockey. My thanks to:

Blake Allen, Gabriella Baldassin, Tyler Booker, Gail Cohen, Maddy Cohen, Rick Cohen, Nicki Eisenberg, Joy Epstein, Olivia Gomez, Ella Herbine, Joe Kadlec Jr., Kenny Kang, Evan Kashan, Sara Lamachia, Jenny Marlowe, Nancy Mastrola, Randy Miller, Kristin Moore, Karen Moran, John Morath, Bridget Nolan, Ray Parrillo, Judy Romano, Kimberly Sikora, Mary Lou Townsley, and Victoria Wilkinson.

Just like her father on the blueline, Alexandra Samuelsson was hugely trustworthy in fact-checking three chapters and multiple profiles. As time grew short, Alan Bass, Dave Isaac, Bill Meltzer, Jeff Neiburg, Ray Parrillo, and David Strehle gave me a significant head start on later chapters. Chase Rogers, Keith Allen's grandson, did many transcriptions as well as a day-by-day outline of every season from 2009 on, inestimably helping me and all contributors. Ronnie Shuker jumped in during the last, desperate weeks with editing help, and John Moritsugu tidied some chapters and proofed the entire book.

Bob Waterman at Elias Sports Bureau always quickly and happily had the statistics. My good friend Jordan Sprechman volunteered to give the profiles one more read. Joe Kadlec, a member of the organization since Day One, was helpful throughout, especially so for the In Memorium list. Jonathan Weatherdon, director of communications for the NHL Players' Association, put me in touch with some old Flyers with whom the organization had lost contact, as did agents Kevin Epp, Larry Kelley and Gilles Lupien.

Sarah Baicker, Les Bowen, Bob Brookover, Sam Carchidi, Sam Donnellon, Tim Dwyer, Wayne Fish, Frank Fitzpatrick, Bob Ford, Chuck Gormley, Marcus Hayes, Rich Hofmann, Dave Isaac, Adam Kimmelman, Jack McCaffrey, Bill Meltzer, Randy Miller, Ed Moran, Marc Narducci, Tim Panaccio, Rob Parent, Ray Parrillo, Anthony San Filippo, Frank Seravalli, Phil Sheridan, and John Smallwood did the original reporting on these years. As my co-workers and friends, they were generous with their remembrances. When any of them had exclusives, it was my goal to credit each properly.

The Flyers Media Guide, edited by Brian Smith, was the starting point for my research. The following websites were invaluable: Our own Philadelphiaflyers.com; Pete Anson's wonderful Flyershistory.com; hockeyreference.com; hockeyzoneplus.com, hockeydatabase.com; nhlnumbers.com; dropyourgloves.com; Wikipedia, and YouTube.

I did not unilaterally choose and rank the 50 Heroes, 50 Wins and 50 Events. But after informally polling people from both inside and outside the organization, these were the author's call. Have fun disagreeing–this is why we are assigning numbers–but please understand my criteria.

For the events, I leaned towards those that shaped the organization rather than spectacular one-off occurrences. This is why Al Hill's five-point NHL debut finished in 51st on a list of 50. For wins, the later the playoff round, the greater in my mind was the victory's significance, which is why Keith Primeau's goal in an extraordinary fifth overtime, tying a second-round series at 2-2, was ranked lower than victories that put the Flyers into a Final or clinched a Stanley Cup.

Hardest was picking and ranking the heroes. In judging impact, popularity often was a tie-breaking factor.

It is a reflection of the depth of Flyer heritage when I couldn't make room for: Jeff Carter, who had a 46-goal season; John Stevens, who coached Philadelphia out of a disaster to a conference final the very next year; Jim Jackson and Tim Saunders, the team's excellent television and radio voices for 23 and 19 years; and Simon Nolet and Dennis Patterson, long-time scouts who showed the courage and wisdom of their convictions in coming up with Claude Giroux, Simon Gagne and Mike Richards near the end of first rounds.

This is my transparent way to sneak in an unofficial honorable mention list. Then again, everybody recorded in this book as playing for or contributing to the success of this proud franchise is honorably mentioned. Especially to the 587 persons who have worn the Orange-and-Black, thank you for making this a story worth telling.

Jay Greenberg
flyersat50@gmail.com
September 2016

Photo Credits

Courtesy Ben Alexander, 11, bottom right; Brian Babineau/NHLI via Getty Images: 417; Steve Babineau/NHLI via Getty Images: 25, 62, 471; All Bello/Allsport: 86; Al Bello/Getty Images: 442, 445; Bruce Bennett Studios/Getty Images: 6, 7 right, 72; Bruce Bennett/Getty Images: 29, 33, 34, 35, 41, 43, 48, 50, 65, 94, 214, 245, 259, 291, 294, 300, 305, 321, 334, 339, 347, 352, 375, 393, 425, 428, 436, 439, 527, 547; Paul Bereswill/Getty Images: 511, 523, 531; Denis Brodeur/Getty Images: 39, 60; Jonathan Daniel/Getty Images: 353; Jerome Davis/Getty Images: 314; Dan Diamond: 12 bottom, 580; Elsa/Getty Images: 518, 548; Courtesy Jerome and Gregg Epstein: 11, bottom center; Noah Graham/Getty Images: 409; Jeff Gross/Getty Images: 279, 282; Drew Hallowell/Getty Images: 447, 510; Harry How/Getty Images: 250; Robert Laberge/Allsport: 66, 71, 83, 176; Mitchell Layton/Getty Images: 263, 454; M. David Leeds/NBAE v ia Getty Images; Courtesy Dave Leonardi: 11, top left; Scott Levy/NHLI via Getty Images: 524; Jim Leary/Getty Images: 207; Ronald Martinez/Getty Images: 172, 222, 227; Phillip MacCallum/Getty Images: 383; Chris McGrath/Getty Images: 396; Jim McIsaac/Getty Images: 342, 386, 388, 401, 423, 434; NHL Guide & Record Book Archive; 42; Doug Pensinger/Getty Images: 212, 238, 252, 267; Philadlphia Flyers Archive; 4, 7.8.9.10.12, 21, 22, 24, 31, 44, 47, 51, 53, 55, 57, 59, 74, 89, 102, 107, 111, 114, 119, 122, 127, 128, 133, 141, 144, 149, 152, 157, 161, 164, 167, 169, 174, 178, 182, 187, 191, 199, 202, 35, 594; Len Redkoles/Getty Images: 309, 322, 326, 330, 354, 359, 370, 378, 412, 420; Len Redkoles/NHLI via Getty Images: 460 bottom, 448, 451, 453, 462, 465, 467, 474, 505, 507, 509, 515, 517, 528, 532, 536, 544, 551, 552, 559, 563, 564, 567, 568, 570, 594 bottom left and right, back endpaper; Dave Reginek/NHLI via Getty Images: 459, 460 top, 539; Andre Ringuette/Getty Images: 441, front endpaper; Sean Rudyk/NHLI via Getty Images: 460 bottom, 469, 473; Dave Sandford/Getty Images: 219, 230, 235, 243, 249, 293, 362, 433; Dave Sandford/NHLI via Getty Images: 571; Ezra Shaw/Getty Images: 274; Marta Snider collection: 3, 13, 17, 27; Rick Stewart: 99; Rick Stewart/Allsport: 79, 194; Lance Thomson/NHLI via Getty Images: 539; Courtesy Edgar Weinrott: 11, bottom left; Bill Wippert/Getty Images: 367.

INDEX

•A•

Abbott, Neil, 196
Abel, Sid, 18
Acadie-bathurst Titans, 252
Acme Markets, 574
Acton, Keith, 112
Adams, Craig, 486
Adams, Greg, 21, 574
Adams, Kevyn, 208
Afanasenkov, Dmitry, 281, 360
Afinogenov, Maxim, 193, 230
Air Canada Centre, 125, 232, 235-236, 276-277
Akeson, Jason, 522, 538
Alexander, Ben, 11-12
Alfredsson, Daniel, 209, 264
Allegheny University of The Health Sciences, 73
Allen, Blake, 21
Allen, George, 140
Allen, Joyce, 21
Allen, Keith, 1, 3, 7, 13-14, 20-23, 25, 27, 30-31, 36, 41-42, 44-45, 50, 53, 58-61, 130, 195, 300, 351, 565, 572, 577, 580
Allison, Jason, 71
Amalie Arena, 556
America West Arena, 146
American Airlines Arena, 257
American Hockey League, 51, 70, 97, 109, 329, 501
Amonte, Tony, 229, 265, 277, 303-304
Anaheim Ducks, 101, 183, 204, 219, 255, 395, 397, 405, 410, 481, 501, 552, 554
Anderson, Craig, 398
Anderson, Dr. Robert, 317, 330
Anderson, Glenn, 526
Anderson, Pamela, 102
Andersson, Mikael, 121
Andre Savard, 227
Andreychuk, Dave, 192, 279, 287
Angell, Roger, 37
Angotti, Lou, 46, 362
Angus, Blaine, 258, 308
Anisimov, Artem, 420
Antoski, Shawn, 69
Antropov, Nik, 189, 232
Arizona/Phoenix Coyotes, 61, 75, 126, 146, 174-175, 196-197, 216-217, 223, 226, 229, 260, 293, 298, 350, 366, 449, 475, 481, 546
Armstrong, Colby, 366
Arnott, Jason, 160
Arnott, Wade, 455
Art Ross Trophy, 488
Arvedson, Magnus, 240
Asham, Arron, 311, 390, 412, 456, 488
Ashbee, Barry, 3, 9, 17, 22, 28, 43-45, 53, 56, 58, 64, 77, 131, 140, 191, 231, 301, 318, 331, 373, 398, 421, 464, 485, 487, 502, 521, 528, 543, 558, 573, 575, 577, 580
Ashbee, Danny, 45
Atanas, Walter, 580
Athanasiou, Andreas, 558
Atlanta Thrashers, 130, 140, 149, 188, 202-203, 311, 337, 364, 371, 392, 394, 396, 413, 419, 480, 506
Atlantic City Boardwalk Bullies, 299
Atlantic Division, 79, 96, 123, 209, 226, 313, 367-368, 395, 398, 464, 484, 556, 576
Aubut, Marcel, 5, 96, 573
Aucoin, Adrian, 266, 363
Audette, Donald, 79, 106, 192
Avery, Sean, 371, 399
Axelsson, P.J., 189

•B•

Babcock, Mike, 58, 545
Babych, Dave, 105, 223
Back Injury, 146
Backes, David, 551
Backlund, Johan, 419
Backstrom, Nicklas, 373, 561
Bailey, Ace, 198
Bain Capital, 300
Baizley, Don, 305
Baldwin, Howard, 552
Bank of America, 514
BankAtlantic Center, 317
Banner, Joe, 301-302
Baptist Hospital, 122
Barber, Bill, ii, 3, 5, 8-9, 11-12, 18, 22-23, 25-26, 28, 31-32, 38, 48, 61, 63-64, 70, 72, 76, 89, 97, 109, 119, 133, 138, 171, 175-176, 181, 185-195, 197-213, 215-218, 220, 248, 290-291, 392, 394, 411, 446-447, 464, 485, 508, 537, 565-566, 572-573, 575-577, 580
Barber, Brooks, 26
Barber, Jenny, 198, 200, 202, 213, 580
Barber, Kerry, 26, 198
Barclays Center, 539
Barnaby, Matthew, 79, 106, 121, 154, 184
Barnes, Norm, 53, 558
Barnes, Stu, 150
Barnett, Mike, 217
Baron, Murray, 177
Barrie Colts, 98
Barrie, Len, 392
Barry Ashbee Trophy, 56, 77, 191, 231, 318, 331, 373, 398, 421, 464, 487, 521, 543, 573, 577
Bartkowski, Matt, 542
Bartlett, Steve, 196
Bartulis, Oskars, 411, 458, 498
Bast, Ryan, 130, 227
Bathe, Frank, 53
Batterman, Bob, 300
Baumgartner, Ken, 116
Baumgartner, Nolan, 330
Bavis, Mark, 198
Baxter, Paul, 352
Beagle, Jay, 560
Bednarik, Chuck, 56
Begin, Steve, 381, 426
Belafonte, Harry, 170
Belanger, Francis, 130, 184
Belarus, 103, 205
Belfour, Ed, 216, 231, 235, 273, 277
Bell Centre, 266, 310, 380, 382, 394, 406, 418, 434, 577
Bellamy, Rob, 296
Bellemare, Pierre-Edouard, 534, 540, 550
Bellows, Brian, 61
Benn, Jamie, 519, 543
Benoit, Jeremy, 173
Beranek, Josef, 155
Berard, Bryan, 124, 126
Berezin, Sergei, 124, 189
Berg, Aki, 232, 275
Bergeron, Marc-Andre, 433, 436
Bergeron, Patrice, 252, 364, 396, 426, 549
Bergevin, Marc, 225, 512
Berglund, Patrik, 328
Bernier, Jonathan, 558
Berry, Brad, 546
Bertuzzi, Larry, 90, 573
Bertuzzi, Todd, 256, 296
Berube, Craig, 6, 15, 45, 116, 121, 133, 139, 148, 162, 181, 195, 249, 253, 299, 301-302, 328, 360, 384, 390, 395, 410, 415, 453, 478, 487, 514-515, 517, 519, 521, 525, 535, 540, 545, 565, 569, 572
Bettman, Gary, 15, 75, 96, 180, 221, 253, 298, 302, 338, 366, 444, 478, 499, 516, 562, 570
Betts, Blair, 399, 411, 458, 479
Betty Ford Clinic, 352
Biden, Jill, 462
Biden, Joe, Vice President of the U.S., 462
Bieksa, Kevin, 395
Big Mike Heron, 506
Binghamton Senators, 219
Biron, Anne Marie, 374
Biron, Emily Marie, 374
Biron, Martin, 143, 347, 355, 401, 475, 578
Black, Dr. Kevin, 72
Blackburn, Don, 156, 231, 576
Blackwell, John, 99, 133
Bladon, Tom, 27, 573, 578
Blake, Jason, 367
Blake, Rob, 189, 196, 302, 305, 308
Blueshirts, 482
Board of Governors, 109, 185, 298, 300
Boardwalk Hall, 410, 499
Bobby Clarke Trophy, 77, 191, 318, 373, 464, 502, 521, 530, 558, 569
Bobrovsky, Sergei, 454, 457, 473, 475, 520
Bolland, Dave, 437, 513
Bondra, Peter, 200, 222, 311
Bonk, Radek, 210, 239
Boogaard, Derek, 349
Booth, David, 412, 416, 419
Borghesani, Dr. Everett, 32
Boston Bruins, 5, 9, 24, 28, 30-32, 35-36, 38, 41, 44, 48, 54, 60-61, 63, 71, 75, 95, 101, 123, 144, 148-149, 173, 175, 189, 195, 205, 208, 224, 246, 256, 263, 296, 301, 305, 313, 348, 364, 379, 392, 396, 416-417, 426-432, 452-453, 456, 461, 464, 469-472, 479, 482, 540-542, 548-549, 553, 558, 572-573
Boucher, Brian, 20, 130, 136, 143-144, 179, 212, 216-217, 244, 290, 307, 360, 455, 457, 467, 473, 475, 499, 574, 576
Boucher, Bob, 580
Boucher, Guy, 453
Boucher, Philippe, 357
Boughner, Bob, 154, 290, 448
Bouillon, Francis, 368
Boulerice, Jesse, 130, 362
Bourdon, Marc-andre, 481, 512
Bouwmeester, Jay, 218, 257, 364, 397
Bowen, 73, 87-88, 110, 131, 149-150, 205
Bowen, Les, 110, 131
Bower, Cindy, 175
Bowman, Scotty, 18, 28, 48, 291
Bowman, Stan, 541
Boychuk, Johnny, 426, 470, 520
Boyes, Brad, 466
Boyle, Brian, 522
Boyle, Dan, 199, 279
Boynton, Nick, 440, 465, 475
Bradley, Matt, 375, 415
Bragilevskaya, Natalia, 466
Braman, Norman, 14
Brandon Wheat Kings, 547
Brandywine Raceway, 129
Brash87, 329
Brashear, Donald, 220, 274, 329, 373
Brassard, Derick, 522
Brathwaite, Fred, 257
Breeze, Art, 303
Brendl, Pavel, 91, 190, 197, 221, 330
Bricker, Harry, 319, 339, 434, 498
Bridgman, Mel, 357
Briere, Danny, 3, 5, 9, 216, 318-324, 339, 351-352, 355-356, 358-359, 363-383, 385-387, 389, 391-395, 397-403, 411-416, 418-422, 424-434, 437-444, 448-450, 452-453, 458-459, 461-462, 464-471, 477-485, 487-496, 499-504, 509, 511, 513, 517, 528-529, 549, 566, 574, 576-577
Brigley, Travis, 145
Brind'Amour, Rod, 3, 13, 56, 63, 68, 70, 72, 75-85, 87-88, 91, 94, 96, 100, 102-106, 108, 112-114, 116, 118-120, 122-125, 135-137, 140-142, 149, 171, 176-177, 202, 223-224, 246, 290, 313, 346, 366, 394, 418, 435, 446, 463, 551, 574
Brisebois, Patrice, 380
Brisson, Pat, 358, 409, 511
Broad Street Atrium, 198
Broad Street Bullies, 8, 17, 23, 26, 32, 35, 45, 59-60, 64, 67, 103, 129, 163, 175, 352, 504, 509, 516, 519, 565, 574
Brodeur, Martin, 68, 97, 230, 268, 297
Brodsky, Dr. Isadore, 44, 140
Brodziak, Kyle, 419
Brogan, John, 13, 580
Brookbank, Wade, 313
Brooks, Bob, 410
Brooks, Herb, 53, 154, 204, 215, 512-513, 537, 546
Brooks, Jim, 410
Brouwer, Troy, 516
Brown, Bernie, 13
Brown, Curtis, 150, 192
Brown, Dave, 69, 95, 105, 304, 328, 340, 432
Brown, Dustin, 251
Brown, J.T., 556

Brown, Mike, 500
Brown, Rob, 247
Brylin, Sergei, 143, 161, 268
Bryzgalov, Ilya, 297, 344, 475-476, 479-492, 494-497, 499-503, 505, 511, 513, 517
Bucks County Courier Times, 129, 149, 409
Bucyk, John, 25
Buffalo Sabres, 57, 60, 65, 76, 79-80, 83, 106-108, 114, 124, 137, 150-153, 191-194, 208, 222, 258, 314, 317-324, 334, 342, 348, 350, 358, 367, 394, 413, 451, 458, 464-469, 485, 497, 517, 539, 546-547, 550, 577
Bulis, Jan, 314
Bullard, Mike, 261, 353, 410
Bulletin, 574
Burakovsky, Andre, 562
Bure, Pavel, 118
Bureau, Marc, 110, 145
Burke, Brian, 82, 202, 296, 303, 333, 344, 363, 497
Burke, Dr. John, 76
Burke, Sean, 103, 111, 184, 217, 260-261, 263, 268, 297
Burnaby Express, 357
Burns, Pat, 215, 269, 309
Burridge, Randy, 80
Burt, Adam, 120
Bush, George W., President of the U.S., 198
Busniuk, Mike, 53
Butler, Chris, 448, 466
Byers, Mike, 580
Byfuglien, Dustin, 438, 538, 557
Bylsma, Dan, 386, 399, 487, 546
Byrd, Dr. Robert, 342
Byrd, Dr. Thomas, 418, 458

•C•

Cairns, Eric, 256, 263
Calder Cup, 51, 109, 181, 301, 312, 335, 379
Calder Trophy, 503, 565
Calder, Kyle, 331, 339
Calgary Flames, 37, 50, 59, 63, 84, 109, 130, 140, 222, 252, 363, 410, 418, 497, 546
Callahan, Ryan, 483
Cameron, Lonnie, 121
Cammalleri, Michael, 551
Cammisa, Dr. Frank, 472
Campbell, Brian, 319, 346, 440
Campbell, Clarence, 5
Campbell, Colin, 81, 121, 226, 308, 338, 352, 361, 367, 400, 411, 488
Campbell, Gregory, 470, 542
Campbell, Rob, 143, 150, 215, 253
Canada Cup, 26, 33, 40, 42, 69, 90, 174-175
Canadian Press, 338, 407
cancer, 5-6, 14, 26, 29, 35, 44, 49, 52, 72, 92, 97, 129, 139, 149, 153, 170, 175, 181, 186, 188, 198, 220, 223-224, 252, 273, 351, 375, 410, 464, 506, 534, 538, 549, 556, 558, 560, 565, 571-572, 576, 578, 580-581
Capital Centre, 100, 576
car accident, 1, 18, 26
Carbonneau, Guy, 380
Carchidi, Sam, 417
Carcillo, Daniel, 397, 425, 459
Carkner, Terry, ii, 310
Carle, Matt, 12, 393, 406, 455, 471, 480
Carlson, John, 560, 564
Carmichael, Todd, 170
Carney, Keith, 96
Carnival, Flyers Wives Fight for Life, 10, 12, 45, 73, 202, 369, 576, 580, 581
Carolina Hurricanes, 101-103, 141, 149-150, 177, 228, 246, 290, 310, 342-343, 364, 372, 389, 394, 410, 414-416, 418, 452, 481, 551
Carson, Brett, 395
Carson, Lindsay, 63
Carter, Jeff, 251, 301, 321, 327, 351, 389, 401, 411-412, 444, 449-450, 455, 462, 476, 504, 509, 520, 531, 573, 575
Carton, Craig, 76
Casey, Dr. Michael, 138
Casey, Reverend Ed, 129
Casey, Reverend John, 182
Cashman, Wayne, 60, 95, 113, 133, 185
Casper, Howard, 24
CBA (Collective Bargaining Agreement), 96, 173, 180, 253, 295-296, 298, 302, 304, 307, 395, 496, 498, 511, 538, 548
CBC (Canadian Broadcasting Corporation), 274
Cechmanek, Roman, 178-179, 216, 230, 243, 254, 273, 310, 318, 408
Cecil, Brittanie, 221
Central Division, 345
Central Hockey League, 46, 139, 300
Central Scouting, 251-252, 357, 464, 497, 506, 534, 547-548, 567
Challenge Cup, 69
Chapman, John, 109, 134, 327
Chaput, Michael, 455, 463
Chara, Zdeno, 143, 189, 210, 239, 243, 264, 310, 329, 426, 456, 470, 542
Charles, Ray, 67
Checketts, Dave, 111
Cheechoo, Jonathan, 226
Chelios, Chris, 33, 63, 68, 90, 105, 119, 219, 313, 406, 527, 555
Chernov, Mikhail, 130-131
Chevalier, Jack, 574
Chicago Blackhawks, 9, 19, 40, 46, 62, 71, 95, 105, 110, 121, 139, 169, 205, 228-229, 262-263, 312, 330-331, 338, 347, 357, 367, 419, 435, 437-444, 464, 475, 484, 505, 511, 520, 526, 529, 541, 549, 556, 570, 575
Chicago Wolves, 301, 310, 543
Chimera, Jason, 560
Choate Rosemary Hall, 135
Chorney, Taylor, 561
Chouinard, Eric, 109, 227, 251
Christensen, Erik, 420, 422
Churla, Shane, 77
Ciccone, Sam, 10
Citizens Bank Park, ii, 91, 482, 484, 576
Clark, 62, 116, 122, 310
Clark, Chris, 310
Clark, Wendel, 116, 122
Clarke, Bobby, ii, vi, 3, 5, 7-9, 12-20, 22-23, 25-29, 31-33, 36-38, 40, 42-50, 53-54, 56-65, 69-71, 73, 75-77, 79-80, 82, 84-85, 87-89, 91-93, 95-105, 107-123, 126-127, 129-150, 153, 156, 163-164, 168-171, 173, 175, 177, 179-191, 194-197, 200-202, 204, 206-208, 210, 213, 215-220, 223, 225, 227-229, 239, 242-244, 246, 248-249, 251-255, 257-265, 268, 271-273, 276, 279-280, 282-283, 289-292, 295-308, 312, 314-315, 317-318, 321, 325, 327-338, 340, 348, 350-353, 369, 373, 379, 393, 398, 414, 416, 421, 435, 446-447, 462, 464, 482, 484-485, 487, 498, 502, 504, 516, 521, 526-528, 530, 537, 543, 556, 558-559, 563, 565-567, 569, 572-578
Clarke, Cliff, 131
Clarke, Jody, 181
Clarkson, David, 424, 480, 511
Cleary, Dan, 313
Clement, Bill, 17, 64
Cleveland Lumberjacks, 98
Clymer, Ben, 205
Coates, Steve, 98, 120, 129, 372
Coburn, Braydon, 251, 346, 362, 389, 406, 455, 481, 528, 536
Coffey, Paul, 8, 29, 73-74, 95, 100, 109, 299, 406, 578
Colaiacovo, Carlo, 458, 536
Cole, Bob, 274
Cole, Erik, 463
Colgate University, 310
Coliseum, 65, 71, 88, 99, 118-119, 131, 140, 148, 153, 181, 329, 539, 551, 575
Collective Bargaining Agreement, 96, 173, 180, 253, 295-296, 298, 302, 304, 307, 395, 496, 498, 511, 538, 548
Colorado Avalanche, 44, 75-76, 83, 114-115, 120, 144, 194, 260, 305-306, 313, 369, 409, 413, 458, 537, 557
Colorado College, 330, 509
Colorado Rockies, 41
Columbus Blue Jackets, 219, 249, 340, 389, 411, 418, 476-477, 497, 501, 518, 520, 531, 537, 540, 552, 556
Colville, Eric, 580
Combine, Scouting, 19, 92, 230, 272, 328, 357, 477, 506, 512
Comcast Sportsnet, 112, 390, 475
Comcast-Spectacor, 5-6, 15, 181, 223, 257, 302, 307, 357, 375, 406, 410, 455, 511, 517, 559, 562, 569, 571-572
Comeau, Blake, 420
Comrie, Mike, 257, 296
concussions, 5, 40, 50, 82, 91, 100, 104-106, 109-110, 117, 121, 140, 146-147, 180, 183, 203, 233, 235, 246, 262, 265, 267, 276, 278, 281, 285, 290, 292, 295, 298, 306-307, 310, 312-314, 317, 320, 325, 329-330, 333, 339, 342, 346, 361-362, 364, 368-369, 387, 391, 395, 413, 426, 444, 446, 450-453, 458, 468, 481-482, 484, 486, 498, 500-501, 511-512, 520-522, 541, 543, 546, 550-552, 554-555, 557, 576
Condon, Mike, 151
Conference Final, 2, 5-6, 8, 13, 20, 26, 33, 37, 39, 48, 63, 68, 81, 91-93, 162, 196-197, 249, 254, 275, 277-278, 285-286, 290, 292-293, 297, 303-304, 330, 360, 363, 379, 382-383, 386, 392-393, 399, 405, 408, 414, 422, 431, 433, 436, 446, 449, 452, 455, 482, 485, 499, 501, 521, 574-577
Conference Quarterfinal, 267, 314, 354, 401, 425, 465, 467, 491, 523
Conference Semifinal, 153, 243, 274, 383, 428, 471, 473, 495
Conn Smythe Trophy, 8, 48-49, 77, 526
Connolly, Brett, 553
Connolly, Tim, 319-320, 370, 466
CONSOL Energy Center, 420, 458, 486, 488, 497, 520-521, 536, 543, 553
Continental Airlines Arena, 270
Cooke, Matt, 373, 401, 459, 485
Cookson, Rob, 122, 139
Cooper University Hospital, 76
Cooper, Jon, 556
Corbet, Rene, 154
Corel Centre, 50
CoreStates Center, 67-68, 70, 73, 75, 77-78, 80-81, 83-84, 89, 95, 101, 106, 573
Corkum, Bob, 70
Cornell, 70, 95
Cote, Riley, 332, 366, 390, 456
Courtnall, Russ, 82
Cousins, Nick, 477, 505, 554
Couturier, Sean, 450, 453, 477, 479, 505, 513, 531, 538, 548, 575
Crawford, Corey, 518
Crawford, Marc, 103
Creighton, Fred, 53
Crilley, Pamela, 153
Crisp, Terry, ii, 41, 45, 175
Croce, Pat, 40, 113
Crosby, Sidney, 246, 294, 303, 341, 365, 379, 394, 418, 486, 490-491, 518, 537, 547, 558, 566
Crossman, Doug, 50
CSN Philadelphia, 372, 410, 465, 472
Cullen, Mark, 330
Cullimore, Jassen, 285
Cunneyworth, Randy, 76
Cunningham, Jim, 580
Cup, vi-2, 5-9, 11, 14-36, 38-45, 48-54, 56-59, 61-62, 64-65, 67-70, 73, 75, 81, 83-93, 95-96, 101, 103, 109, 111, 115, 117, 127, 129-130, 133, 136, 143-145, 151, 157, 159-162, 164-166, 168-171, 173-177, 179, 181, 183, 185-186, 194, 196, 199, 202, 204, 206, 208, 212, 215-217, 219, 221-222, 225, 227, 229-231, 234, 236, 239-240, 245-249, 253-255, 257, 259-260, 262-263, 265, 267-268, 270, 272-273, 278, 282-285, 288-293, 297-299, 301, 303-305, 307, 312, 316, 319-320, 327, 329, 331-332, 335-336, 342, 346, 350-353, 360, 362-363, 373, 379, 383-384, 387, 391, 393, 397-398, 403, 405-408, 410-411, 414, 416, 418, 421-422, 431-433, 435-437, 439, 441-447, 450, 452-453, 455-457, 461-463, 471-473, 475, 478-479, 483-484, 487, 496, 498, 500-501, 503-505, 507, 509, 511-512, 514, 518-520, 526-529, 533-538, 540-541, 545-547, 549, 556, 559-560, 562, 564-566, 569-570, 572-575, 577-578, 594
Curran, Rick, 120, 252
Currier, Bob, 45
Czech Extra League, 179
Czech Republic, 49, 68, 103, 179-180, 198, 204, 217, 232, 357, 499, 508, 518-519, 530, 548
Czechoslovakia, 26, 530
Czerkawski, Mariusz, 144

•D•

Daigle, Alexandre, 114, 370
Daigneault, J.J., 9, 285, 573
Dailey, Bob, 22, 32, 489, 565, 580
Daily News, The Philadelphia, 16, 22, 68, 87, 107, 109-110, 117, 124, 131, 138, 149, 182, 205, 213, 220, 231, 237, 244, 335, 387, 422, 542
Dalai Lama, 274
Dallas Black Hawks, 139
Dallas Morning News, The, 216

Dallas Stars, 151, 201, 215, 225-226, 248, 257, 265, 303, 306, 357, 362, 366, 410, 463, 485, 511, 517, 551
Daly, Bill, 96, 299, 435
Daly, John, 175
D'Amico, John, 41, 71, 126, 151
D'Anconna, Tom, 118, 123
Dandenault, Mathieu, 380
Daneyko, Ken, 161-162
Daniels, Scott, 69, 99
D'Aprile, Lisa, 230
D'Aprile, Vinny, 230
Dapuzzo, Pat, 126
Darling, Gary, 580
Darling, Scott, 556
Datsyuk, Pavel, 504, 518
Davidson, Alex, 580
Davis, Lorne, 47
Dawe, Jason, 80
Dawes, Nigel, 371
Del Zotto, Michael, 389, 535-536, 548
Delaney, Bill, 580
Delaware County Times, The, 98
Delmore, Andy, 138, 180, 186, 196
Delmore, Bonnie, 155
Delmore, Carl, 155
Delong, Dr. William, 395
Deluca, Dr. Peter, 226, 298
Demers, Jacques, 173
Demitra, Pavol, 100, 121
Denis, Marc, 138
Desjardins, Eric, ii, 3, 10, 12, 20, 42, 56, 68, 70-73, 75, 78, 80-81, 83-89, 92-93, 97, 99-100, 102-103, 105, 107-108, 113-114, 116-117, 120-127, 132-138, 140, 142, 144-148, 150-152, 154-166, 168, 171, 177, 181, 183, 189, 191-194, 197-201, 203, 206, 208, 210-212, 216, 220, 223-224, 226, 229, 231-236, 239-240, 242, 245, 249, 254, 256, 258-259, 265-267, 271, 278, 283, 285-286, 289, 298, 304-305, 308, 310-312, 315, 317-320, 322-325, 329, 331, 343, 390, 521, 529, 540, 573
Despres, Simon, 492
Detroit Jr. Whalers, 261
Detroit Red Wings, 18, 23, 27-28, 30, 46, 48, 53, 56, 58, 75, 83-87, 95, 98, 102, 105, 110, 121, 144, 173, 175, 226, 247, 259, 263, 290, 303-304, 352, 387, 398, 418, 420, 476, 485, 505-506, 511, 513, 529, 543, 545, 553, 556, 558
Detroit Olympia, 29
Deveaux, Andre, 478
Devorski, Paul, 378
diabetes, 17-18, 20, 23, 45, 129, 195, 220, 351, 572, 580-581
Diamond, Neil, 67
Dillabaugh, Kim, 546, 570
Dillman, Lisa, 505
Dimaio, Rob, 70
Dimitrakos, Niko, 360
Dineen, Bill, 30, 117, 215, 246
Dineen, Kevin, 200, 246
Dingle, Ryan, 406
Dingman, Chris, 279
Dionne, Gilbert, 92, 120
DiPaolo, Matt, 580
DiPietro, Rick, 189, 316
Dixon, F. Eugene, 580
Domi, Tie, 71, 125, 190, 232, 273
Donnellon, Sam, 117, 213, 220, 422
Dopita, Jiri, 195, 244
Dornhoefer, Gary, 3, 23, 28, 31, 35-36, 64, 120, 175, 299, 506, 530, 534, 565, 572-573
Dorsett, Derek, 522
Dorshimer, Dr. Gary, 76, 147, 330
Dowd, Jim, ii, 391
Downie, Ann, 303
Downie, Steve, 303, 361, 391, 516
Draper, Kris, 84
Driver, Bruce, 81
Druce, John, 82, 100
Drury, Chris, 319, 322, 355, 420
Druzhba '78, 70
Dryden, Ken, 32, 111, 126
Dubinsky, Brandon, 399, 420
Dubinsky, Steve, 96
Dubnyk, Devan, 516
Duchesne, Steve, 121, 133
Dudley, Rick, 112
Duke University, 418, 511
Dumont, J.P., 192, 258, 319
Dunham, Mike, 231
Dupont, Andre, 3, 23, 31, 60, 218
Dupre, Huguette, 97
Dupre, Jacques, 72, 97
Dupre, Yanick, 72, 97, 198, 449, 580
Dupuis, Pascal, 392
Dvorak, Miroslav, 49, 580
Dwyer, Tim, 87, 95
Dykhuis, Karl, 70, 96, 133, 574

•E•

E.J. McGuire Award of Excellence, 548
Eager, Ben, 312, 335, 338, 438
Earle, Don, 580
East Coast Hockey League (ECHL), 134, 299, 535
Eastern Conference, 13, 37, 39, 81, 91-92, 106, 150, 160, 174, 197, 242-243, 263, 267, 274-275, 277-279, 354, 379, 383, 393, 396, 398, 402, 405, 425, 428, 433, 436, 449, 452, 462, 464-465, 467, 471, 473, 482, 487, 491, 495, 499, 501, 566, 574-577
Eastern High School, 361
Eastern Hockey League, 59, 169, 220
Eastwood, Mike, 82
Eaton, Mark, 112, 137, 182, 231, 399-400
Eaves, Mike, 252
Eaves, Patrick, 252
ECHL, 134, 299, 535
Ed Snider Youth Hockey Foundation, 499, 559, 562
Edmonton Oilers, 6, 32, 39-40, 47, 50, 53, 105, 118, 190, 197, 222, 257, 261, 298, 304, 358, 363, 463, 526, 534, 547, 550, 556, 575
Ehman, Tex, 47
Ehrhoff, Christian, 556
Eichel, Jack, 547
Eichel, Larry, 254
Ekblad, Aaron, 534
Eklund, Pelle, 34, 577
Elias, Patrik, 140, 160, 205, 267-268, 372, 394, 422, 464, 576
Ellerbe Becket, 67
Ellett, Dave, 101
Ellison, Matt, 20, 332
Emery, Ray, 369, 407, 455, 475, 511, 518, 534, 548
Eminger, Steve, 374, 389
Engelland, Deryk, 459
Ennis, Tyler, 466
Enroth, Jhonas, 469, 502
Entry Draft, 30, 42, 90, 134, 219, 252, 328, 479, 496, 506, 533-534, 547-548
Epstein, Gregg, 11
Epstein, Jerome, 11
Erat, Martin, 340, 419
Eriksson, Anders, 121, 144, 363
Eriksson, Loui, 542
Eriksson, Thomas, 40, 51
Erskine, John, 374
Esche, Robert, 8, 20, 216, 230, 244, 249, 254, 267, 297, 310, 325, 360, 408, 475
ESPN, 79, 151, 158, 199
ESPN Classic, 158
ESPN, The Magazine, 199
Esposito, Anthony, 126
Esposito, Phil, 28, 43, 61, 95-96, 290, 351
Esposito, Tony, 87, 526
Evers, Turk, 72, 79, 155, 262
Expansion Draft, 5, 23, 34, 41, 130, 135, 137, 299

•F•

Fairman, Dr. Ronald, 384
Falcone, Chris, 190
Falloon, Pat, 71, 76, 99, 101, 155, 261
Farwell, Russ, 30, 34, 46-47, 63, 133, 177, 248, 307, 336, 352
Fass, Bennett, 67
Faulkner, Dr. John, 184
Favell, Doug, 22, 24, 573-574, 576
Fayne, Mark, 495
Feaster, Jay, 411
Fedorov, Sergei, 84, 199, 373
Fedoruk, Todd, 9, 217, 220, 240, 256, 299, 304, 340, 360, 394
Fedotenko, Ruslan, 183, 218, 355, 399, 498
Fehr, Eric, 374
Fenway Park, 416-417
Ference, Andrew, 371, 396, 431
Ferrill, Pat, 181
Final, Stanley Cup, 1-2, 5-6, 8, 13-18, 20, 22, 25-26, 28-30, 32-40, 42-45, 48-54, 56-63, 65, 67-71, 80-81, 83-89, 91-93, 96-102, 104, 108, 114, 119-120, 122, 124-125, 129-130, 134, 136, 139, 141, 143, 145, 149-152, 158-166, 168, 170-177, 179, 181, 185, 187, 190, 192, 195-197, 199, 201, 204-205, 210-211, 215-217, 219, 225, 227, 231-232, 234-235, 237-238, 240-241, 246, 248-249, 253-254, 260-261, 264-265, 270-271, 273-279, 283-286, 288-293, 296-298, 300-301, 303-304, 312-313, 315-316, 319, 322-325, 329-330, 332, 336, 341-342, 344, 350-352, 359-361, 363, 366, 368-369, 371-372, 374-376, 379-380, 382-387, 390-394, 396, 399-400, 405, 407-408, 410, 413-414, 418-419, 421-425, 428, 430-433, 435-439, 441-447, 449-450, 452-453, 455-457, 462-464, 468-470, 472-473, 475-476, 482, 484-490, 492, 494-496, 498-499, 501-502, 504-505, 508-509, 511, 513-515, 518-519, 521-522, 524-529, 535-537, 540-543, 546, 549-550, 553-560, 562, 564-566, 572-577
Finland, 68, 105, 134, 205, 217, 297-298, 301, 315-316, 330, 336, 347, 365, 390, 418-419, 512, 519, 529, 535
Finnish Elite League, 301
First Union Center, 113, 116, 126, 129, 133, 138-140, 143, 150, 152, 160, 162, 166, 185, 190, 196, 199, 202-206, 209, 211, 226, 228, 232, 237-238, 241, 254
Fish, Dr. Joel, 131
Fish, Peter, 407
Fish, Wayne, 129, 149, 409
Fisher, Mike, 209, 239, 264
Fitzgerald, Tom, 233, 273
Fitzpatrick, Rory, 322
Fitzpatrick, Ross, 463
Fleet Center, 228, 343
Fleischmann, Tomas, 415
Fleming, Reg, 580
Fleming, Wayne, 215-216, 249, 256, 262, 329, 580
Flett, Bill, 130, 534, 580
Fleury, Marc-Andre, 251, 333, 384, 399, 432
Flexer, Allen, 55
Flockhart, Vern, 41
Florida Panthers, 56-57, 69-70, 73, 96, 104, 113, 115, 195, 200, 252, 311, 335, 369, 372, 396, 398, 411, 416, 459, 461, 486, 492, 521, 537, 556
Floyd, Jennifer, 216
Flyers Hall of Fame, 25-26, 29, 34, 36, 41-42, 56, 91, 120, 171, 191, 555
Flyers Skate Zone, 9, 50, 135, 181, 183, 185, 189, 197, 201, 208, 211, 216, 235, 242, 262, 295-296, 298-299, 301, 307, 327, 330, 361, 411, 414, 513, 519, 535, 541, 570
Flyers Wives Fight for Life Carnival, 10, 12, 45, 73, 202, 369, 576, 580, 581
Foley, Rick, 580
Foligno, Nick, 539
Foote, Adam, 69
Forbes, Colin, 79, 101-102, 105
Ford, Bob, 142
Foreman, Earl, 13, 14, 572
Foreman, Phyllis, 13, 574
Forsberg, Peter, 46, 89, 116, 195, 229, 249, 251, 292, 305-307, 325-326, 330, 345-346, 348, 352, 355, 398, 406, 411, 446, 448, 455, 470, 504, 529, 577
Forum, The Fabulous (L.A.), 119
Forum, The Montreal, 32-33, 36, 111, 119, 278-279, 286, 416, 573
Foster Hewitt Award, 8, 129
Foster, David, 552
Foster, Kurtis, 499
France, 204, 534-535, 540
Francis, Emile, 22, 27
Francis, Ron, 78, 104, 273
Franson, Cody, 345
Franzen, Johan, 518
Fraser, Colin, 252
Fraser, Kerry, 83, 284, 308, 421
Fraser, Mark, 424
Frazier, Joe, 43
Friedland, Lloyd, 110
Friedman, Elliotte, 384
Friesen, Jeff, 270
Froese, Bob, 39, 51
Frost, Ray, 580
Ftorek, Robbie, 160
Fuhr, Grant, 134
Full Spectrum, 55
Furlatt, Eric, 402
Futa, Mike, 506

•G•

Gaborik, Marian, 420, 422
Gagne, Pierre, 109, 446
Gagne, Simon, 3, 9, 46, 109, 121, 128, 134-136, 138-140, 143-144, 146, 148-152, 154-157, 159-162, 166, 168, 180, 184-194, 199, 201-206, 209-211, 216, 219, 221-222, 224-229, 231-237, 240, 242, 244, 248, 251, 255-260, 262-263, 266, 268, 270-276, 280-281, 283-289, 291, 295, 297-298, 308-322, 324-325, 327, 329, 331-332, 334-335, 337, 339, 341, 343-348, 350, 357-358, 362-365, 367-369, 387, 391-392, 394-403, 411-413, 416-419, 421, 423-433, 435, 437-440, 442-444, 446-447, 455-457, 461-462, 500, 509, 512-513, 554, 556, 560, 573, 576
Gagner, Sam, 546
Gaines, Jeffrey, 170
Gainey, Bob, 19, 48, 215, 248
Galley, Garry, 79
Gamble, Bruce, 31, 580
Game One, 4, 30, 32, 39, 61, 63, 68, 77, 79-81, 84-85, 87, 89, 93, 106, 117, 124, 150-151, 153, 160, 192, 209, 232, 267-269, 273, 278, 318-320, 323, 325, 373-375, 380, 384-385, 399, 423, 426-427, 432-433, 437-439, 443, 464-465, 470, 488, 492-494, 496, 522, 527, 531, 560, 575
Game Two, 18, 36, 60-61, 68, 78-82, 84, 86, 93, 107, 124, 130, 151, 154-155, 160-162, 192, 209, 232, 240, 243, 267, 269, 273-274, 279-280, 282, 320, 323, 374, 385, 400, 402, 423-424, 426, 428, 432-433, 438-439, 466, 470, 472, 488, 522-523, 560, 574, 594
Game Three, 17, 26, 36-37, 52, 57, 61, 63, 69, 78, 80, 82, 85, 107, 126, 151, 154-156, 161-162, 192, 232-233, 237, 240, 269, 274, 280, 320-321, 374-375, 381, 385, 400-401, 424-425, 427, 433, 439, 466, 470-471, 489, 494, 504, 522, 561, 566, 575
Game Four, 17, 26, 28, 44, 52, 61, 78, 80, 83, 86, 88, 93, 105, 107-108, 125, 152, 156, 159, 162, 165, 171, 192-193, 196, 210, 233, 235, 239, 241, 267, 270, 275, 279-281, 301, 320, 322, 375, 386-387, 401-402, 424, 427-428, 431-432, 437, 440-441, 466, 471-473, 490, 495, 523, 527, 561-563, 566
Game Five, 17, 39, 52, 60, 62, 65, 78, 80-81, 83, 108, 125, 152, 159, 162, 168, 173, 193, 211, 235, 241, 271-272, 275-276, 281-283, 285, 287-288, 297, 304, 314, 323, 330, 376, 382-384, 386-387, 397, 402, 423, 425, 429, 432, 434, 436, 442-443, 462, 467, 472, 491, 496, 504, 508, 523, 562-563, 566, 573-577
Game Six, 2, 6, 9, 12, 17, 25, 31, 37, 39, 46, 53, 63-65, 78, 84, 91, 125, 139, 151, 156, 159, 164-166, 168-169, 193-194, 230, 236-237, 241, 276, 283, 285, 288, 290-293, 295, 297, 322, 324, 376-377, 379-380, 402-403, 429, 442-445, 453, 455-456, 467-468, 470, 491, 493, 508-509, 524-525, 564, 572-578
Game Seven, 2, 5-6, 9, 32-33, 36, 40, 50, 53, 63, 83, 91, 126, 163, 165-168, 173, 193, 197, 237-238, 241, 246, 249, 259, 276, 285-286, 288-293, 297, 330-331, 352, 354, 373, 377-379, 390, 397, 408, 421, 429-432, 439, 443-444, 446, 449, 451-452, 468-470, 478, 482, 491, 508, 524-527, 572-573, 575-578
Gardiner, Jake, 558
Garman, Dr. Rick, 122
Garon, Mathieu, 418
Garrett, Dr. William, 71, 314
Gatineau Olympiques, 327, 567, 575
Gaustad, Paul, 319, 465
Gauthier, Denis, 317, 322, 339, 362
Gauthier, Jean, 205, 580
Gelinas, Eric, 542
Gelinas, Martin, 115
General Motors Place, 327
Gerbe, Nathan, 465
Gere, Richard, 274
Germany, 97, 103, 170, 205, 221, 254, 418, 499
Gernander, Ken, 82
Getz, Stan, 170
Getzlaf, Ryan, 251, 344, 418, 518
Giacomin, Ed, 19, 36, 566
Gibbs, Barry, 36, 350, 576
Gilbert, Greg, 410
Gill, Dr. Thomas, 343
Gill, Hal, 146, 385, 400, 432, 513
Gilmour, Doug, 152, 192, 231
Ginnell, Patty, 18
Gionta, Brian, 225, 268, 334, 343, 432-433, 513
Gionta, Stephen, 494, 542
Girardi, Dan, 521
Girgensons, Zemgus, 550
Giroux, Claude, 3, 6, 10, 12, 35, 46, 327-328, 353, 357, 361, 369, 387, 391, 395-403, 412, 415-416, 419-435, 437, 439-440, 443-444, 450, 453, 455, 458-459, 461-466, 468-471, 476-477, 479-496, 499-502, 505, 509, 511, 513, 515-525, 530-531, 534-543, 546, 549-559, 561-562, 564-567, 569-570, 574-577, 594
Glendening, Luke, 558
Glens Falls Civic Center, 410
Gluckstern, Steven, 134
"God Bless America," 7, 10, 170, 198-199, 321, 400, 434, 558, 574, 578
Golden, Ed, 10, 576
Goligoski, Alex, 394, 458
Gomez, Scott, 160, 268, 355, 392, 432
Gonchar, Sergei, 385, 399
Goode, Mayor Wilson, 67
Goodenough, Larry, ii, 44
Goodenow, Bob, 299
Goodman, T.R., 219, 506
Gordon, Boyd, 378
Gordon, Larry, 98
Gordon, Scott, 546, 554
Gorence, Tom, 65
Gorges, Josh, 382, 434
Gostisbehere, Shayne, 353, 497, 521, 534, 546, 554
Grabner, Michael, 558
Grabovski, Mikhail, 451
Gragnani, Marc-Andre, 465
Graham, Dr. Thomas, 338, 361, 463
Grahame, John, 279
Granato, Cammi, 323
Granato, Tony, 487
Grand-Pierre, Jean-Luc, 151
Gratton, Chris, 96, 137, 449
Gratton, Josh, 317
Graves, Adam, 68, 81
Green, Mike, 373, 501
Green, Travis, 234
Greenberg, Dr. Scott, 391
Greene, Andy, 424, 493
Greene, Earl, 392
Greene, Matt, 545, 553
Greening, Colin, 558
Gregg, Dr. John, 199
Gregson, Terry, 125, 127, 139
Greig, Mark, 124, 389
Gretzky, Wayne, 5, 18, 32, 51, 53, 63, 68, 81, 89, 171, 174, 177, 205, 216, 290, 300, 363, 379, 526, 574
Grier, Mike, 317, 329, 466, 469
Grimson, Stu, 89
Grosek, Michal, 80
Gross, Lewis, 99, 173, 180, 195
Grossman, Jay, 70, 132, 332
Grossmann, Nicklas, 539, 546
Group Baraphe, 61
Gudas, Radko, 541, 549
Guenin, Nate, 397
Guerin, Bill, 400, 458
Gustafsson, Erik, 463, 479, 518, 534
Gustavsson, Jonas, 408, 486

•H•

Hackett, Jeff, 225
Hagelin, Carl, 522, 559
Hagg, Robert, 512, 534, 546
Hagman, Niklas, 357
Hahnemann Hospital, 44, 72, 140, 576
Hakstol, Dave, 530, 545, 552, 566, 570-571
Halak, Jaroslav, 381, 420, 432, 504, 543, 548, 551
Halifax Mooseheads, 357, 530
Hall, Adam, 333, 501, 539
Hall, Glenn, 24, 156, 392
Haller, Kevin, 72
Halpern, Jeff, 264
Hamhuis, Dan, 455
Hamid, George, 169
Hamilton, Dougie, 542
Hammarby, 51-52
Hammarstrom, Inge, 218
Hammond, Brigadier General Jeff, 313
Hamrlik, Roman, 186, 267, 380, 433
Handzus, Michal, 216, 295, 331
Hanifin, Noah, 547
Hanna, John, 580
Hannan, Scott, 413
Hannigan, Pat, 580
Hanrahan, Barry, 98, 130, 301, 475, 512, 571
Hanrahan, Lisa, 130
Hanzal, Martin, 557
Haralson, Bruce, 247
Harper, Shane, 511
Harrold, Peter, 494
Hart Trophy, 9-10, 20, 32, 89, 91, 95, 98, 130, 140, 150, 166, 170-171, 198, 230, 237, 241, 305, 321, 324, 337, 369, 376, 405, 408, 420, 432, 452, 469, 483, 492, 508, 558, 561, 575-578
Hart, Gene, 3, 8-9, 64, 68, 100, 129, 136, 169, 361, 562, 580
Hart, Lauren, 10, 91, 140, 166, 198, 230, 237, 241, 321, 324, 376, 408, 420, 469, 492, 558, 561, 577-578
Hart, Sarah, 169
Hartford Whalers, 15, 21, 30, 73, 101, 181, 261, 290, 336, 352, 411
Hartnell, Scott, 3, 5, 351-353, 355-359, 361-363, 365-374, 376-383, 385-387, 392, 394-400, 402-403, 411, 416, 419, 421-422, 425-432, 434, 438-440, 442-443, 449-450, 452, 458-459, 461, 464, 466-468, 471, 473, 475, 477-478, 481-493, 495, 498-501, 508-509, 515-517, 519-520, 522-525, 529, 533, 536-537, 543, 551, 557, 577-578
Hartsburg, Craig, 216, 249, 251, 299
Hartzell, Dr. Jeff, 105, 139
Harvard, 55, 449
Hasek, Dominik, 75, 98, 102-103, 150, 152, 179, 183
Hasenfratz, Mike, 384
hat trick, 32, 34, 60, 71, 76, 78, 82, 89, 93, 101, 113, 118, 139, 159, 185, 199, 205, 222, 232, 291, 315, 320, 366, 368, 398, 411, 416, 418, 459, 461, 463-464, 484, 489, 500, 516, 524, 555, 577
Hatcher, Derian, ii, 68, 249, 294, 303, 309, 314, 325, 341, 347, 350, 353, 362, 365, 389, 391, 410, 515
Hatcher, Kevin, 46, 69
Hatulevs, Viktors, 10
Havel, Vaclav, 103
Havlat, Martin, 210, 212, 239-240, 263, 578
Hawerchuk, Dale, 8, 71, 98-99, 101, 171, 406
HBO, 13, 204, 478, 481-482
HC Vsetin, 179, 195
Healey, Paul, 101
Hebert, Guy, 143
Hecht, Jochen, 197, 319, 367, 469
Hedberg, Johan, 337, 462
Heinze, Steve, 192
Heiskala, Earl, 65
Hejduk, Milan, 257
Helm, Darren, 558
Henrique, Adam, 493, 516, 554
Hershey Medical Center, 72
Heward, Jamie, 109
Hextall, Bryan, Jr., 526
Hextall, Bryan, Sr., 526
Hextall, Dennis, 526
Hextall, Diane, 526
Hextall, Fay, 526
Hextall, Grandma Gert, 526
Hextall, Rebecca, 71
Hextall, Ron, ii, 2-3, 5, 7, 20, 29, 39, 46, 52, 56-57, 63, 70-71, 77, 85, 90, 93, 95, 130, 172, 174, 188, 195, 215, 328, 331-332, 335, 353, 363, 368, 437, 475, 507, 512, 526, 528-529, 533, 535, 542, 545, 567, 569, 571, 573, 575-577
Hicks, Tom, 304
Hill, Al, ii, 134
Hill, Shawny, 10, 339, 350
Hill, Zack, 146, 262, 292
Hiller, Jonas, 481
Hillman, Larry, 497
Hillman, Wayne, 580
Hitchcock, Ken, 3, 8, 57, 93, 215-216, 218-225, 229-231, 233, 242, 246-249, 254-256, 259, 261, 265-266, 268, 273, 275, 279, 281, 289, 291-293, 297, 299, 304, 307-309, 311-313, 315, 320, 324, 329, 331-337, 340, 360, 389, 414, 446, 501, 531, 542
Hjalmarsson, Niklas, 437
Hlavac, Jan, 190, 197, 330
Hnidy, Shane, 211, 507
Hobey Baker Award, 393

Hockey Canada, 102
Hockey Hall of Fame, 21, 26, 29, 33, 46, 54, 98, 100, 129, 170, 223, 252, 292, 360, 452, 485, 512, 519, 550, 577
Hockey is for Everyone Campaign, 508
Hockey News, The, 199, 252, 411, 417, 427
Hodge, Dave, 88
Hodge, Ken, 25, 95
Hoekstra, Ed, 580
Hofmann, Rich, 124, 182, 231, 237, 244, 387
Hoglund, Jonas, 188, 234
Holden, Nick, 557
Holik, Bobby, 160, 201, 291
Holland, Ken, 196
Hollweg, Ryan, 317
Holmgren, Paul, 3, 7, 17, 19-20, 22, 26, 28, 36-39, 42, 50, 52-54, 57, 62-64, 69, 95, 113-114, 131-134, 141, 169, 175, 177, 184, 202, 208, 215, 219, 221, 248, 251-252, 260, 295, 297, 303, 305, 307-308, 327-328, 330-332, 334-353, 355-367, 369-371, 379, 384, 387, 389-393, 395-399, 403, 405-420, 422, 426-428, 446-450, 452-453, 455-458, 461-463, 472-473, 475-486, 496-507, 509, 511-514, 516, 518, 520-521, 526, 528-530, 533-534, 537, 541, 550-551, 553, 559, 567, 569-571, 575, 577
Holtby, Braden, 540, 548
Holzinger, Brian, 107
Hoodikoff, Kenny, 457
Hope United Methodist Church, 202
Hôpital Maisonneuve-Rosemont, 72
Horton, Nathan, 251
Hossa, Marcel, 333
Hossa, Marian, 210, 239, 263, 384, 437
Housley, Phil, 61, 231
Howard, Jimmy, 558
Howe, Gordie, 29, 69, 190, 290, 379
Howe, Mark, ii, 3, 5, 8, 15, 21-22, 29-30, 33, 37-40, 42, 49-50, 54, 63-64, 69, 92-93, 176, 190-191, 290, 379, 406, 421, 478, 483, 485-486, 527, 529, 574-575, 577
Howson, Scott, 389, 418, 476
Hoyda, Dave, 581
Hrdina, Jan, 268
HSBC Arena, 191, 319, 367, 578
Hubacek, Petr, 182
Huber, Willie, 581
Huberdeau, Jonathan, 477
Huet, Cristobal, 373, 437
Huffman, Kerry, 547
Hughes, Brent, 21, 61
Hughes, Colonel Christopher, 313
Hughes, John, 70
Hughes, Kent, 511
Hughes, Sarah, 70
Hull, Bobby, 48, 437
Hull, Brett, 189, 199, 205, 216, 226
Hull, Jody, 113, 126, 137, 198, 209
Humphrey, Hubert, Vice President of the U.S., 43
Hunter, Dale, 378
Hunwick, Matt, 426, 553
Hutton, Mike, 506

•I•

Ice In Paradise, 552
Ice Palace, 106
Ice Works In Aston, PA, 555
Iginla, Jarome, 205, 302, 308, 418, 508, 539
Igloo, The (Pittsburgh), 402, 420
Inness, Gary, 44
Inquirer, The Philadelphia, 72, 87, 95, 112, 142, 146, 186, 197, 220, 235, 262, 276, 297-299, 330, 343, 417, 472, 476
International Hockey League (IHL), 56, 98, 109, 148, 300
Irbe, Arturs, 105, 149
Isbister, Brad, 186, 222
Isles, 61, 134, 140
Ito, Rick, 131

•J•

Jack Adams Award, 8, 195
Jackson, Bo, 418
Jackson, Dane, 546
Jackson, Dave, 368
Jackson, Jim, 9, 98, 120, 169, 324
Jagr, Jaromir, 78, 104, 154, 197, 266, 308, 329, 371, 451, 474, 477, 520, 530
Jasner, Phil, 68
Jenner, Boone, 557
Jennings Trophy, 20, 230-231, 244, 518
Jennings, Bill, 13
Joe Louis Arena, 137, 199, 263, 398, 462, 515, 517, 558
Johansen, Ryan, 476
Johansson, Marcus, 486
Johnson, Brent, 490
Johnson, Erik, 418, 557
Johnson, Jack, 480
Johnson, Mike, 125
Johnsson, Kim, 91, 190, 197, 249, 254, 272, 297, 305, 329
Johnston, Dr. Karen, 298
Johnston, Eddie, 247
Jokinen, Jussi, 481
Jokinen, Olli, 297, 369, 422
Jones, Blair, 536
Jones, Keith, 114-115, 120, 135, 183, 259, 391
Jones, Randy, 264, 313-314, 332, 348, 362, 365, 389, 395, 411, 426
Jones, Seth, 512, 557
Jonsson, Hans, 159
Jonsson, Lars, 330
Josefson, Jacob, 542
Joseph, Chris, 113, 132
Joseph, Curtis, 69, 105, 177, 216
Joseph, Faisal, 478
Jovanovski, Ed, 70, 182
Juhlin, Patrik, 68
Julien, Claude, 429, 472, 542

•K•

Kaberle, Tomas, 189, 233, 273, 369
Kadlec, Joe, 98, 140, 253
Kaiser, Dr. Larry, 123, 198, 558
Kaleta, Patrick, 465
Kalinin, Dmitri, 193
Kalinski, Jon, 395, 414, 485
Kallio, Tomi, 226
KalPa Kuopio, 390, 529
Kamensky, Valeri, 183
Kamloops Blazers, 215
Kane, Patrick, 357, 395, 437, 442, 445, 509, 566, 575
Kapanen, Kasperi, 278
Kapanen, Sami, 208, 227, 243, 254, 264, 289-290, 292, 295, 307, 330, 341, 356, 390, 529
Kariya, Paul, 98, 205, 312, 340
Karlsson, Erik, 556
Karmanos, Peter, 138, 141
Karpovtsev, Alexander, 77
Kasparaitis, Darius, 104, 154, 290, 315
Kassian, Matt, 458
Katz, Harold, 14
Kazan, 360
Keenan, Mike, 3, 7-8, 15, 29-30, 32-34, 37-40, 50-52, 56, 62-63, 98, 102, 161, 175, 187, 195, 238, 309, 352, 363, 410, 450, 452-453, 464, 482-483, 546
Keith, Duncan, 437
Kelley, Jim, 79
Kelly, Bob, ii, 3, 7, 9, 27-28, 64-65, 129, 257, 482, 572
Kelly, Chris, 470, 536
Kelly, Dr. Bryan, 407-408
Kelly, Dr. James, 3, 146-147, 149, 153, 156, 160, 369
Kelly, Paul, 366
Kelly, Regan, 182
Kelowna General Hospital, 131
Kennedy, Teeder, 577
Kennedy, Tyler, 399, 411, 458
Kerr, Kathy, 33-34, 182, 581
Kerr, Tim, 2-3, 5, 8, 32-34, 37, 40, 50, 63, 77, 169, 171, 175, 182, 292, 384, 530, 573, 576, 581
Kesler, Ryan, 296, 332, 418, 498
Kessel, Phil, 364, 486, 541
Khabibulin, Nikolai, 119, 279, 282
Kidd, Trevor, 275
Kilger, Chad, 274
Kindrachuk, Orest, ii, 534
King, Kris, 125, 139
Kiprusoff, Miikka, 315, 363, 437, 461
Kirke, Gordon, 112, 153, 180
Kitchener Rangers, 301
Kladno, 477, 530
Klatt, Trent, 70, 102
Klee, Ken, 145, 273
Klein, Kevin, 522
knee injuries, 79, 175, 443, 463, 467, 539-540
Knuble, Mike, 246, 295, 300, 314, 334, 341, 361, 365, 409, 446, 500, 506, 512
Kocur, Joe, 84
Koharski, Don, 154, 234
Koivu, Saku, 297, 310, 380
Komisarek, Mike, 380
Konecny, Travis, 548
Konowalchuk, Steve, 71
Konstantinov, Vladimir, 83
Kopecky, Tomas, 437
Korab, Jerry, 64
Kordic, Dan, 98
Kostitsyn, Andrei, 251, 432
Kostitsyn, Sergei, 383
Kostopoulos, Tom, 380
Kotalik, Ales, 319, 367, 370
Koules, Oren, 392
Kovalchuk, Ilya, 371, 422, 493
Kovalenko, Andrei, 118
Kozak, Rick, 252, 264
Kozlov, Viktor, 268, 375
Kravchuk, Igor, 148
Krejci, David, 416, 426, 470, 504
Kronwall, Niklas, 182, 486
Krug, Torey, 542
Kubina, Pavel, 200, 267, 279, 370, 461, 485
Kukkonen, Lasse, 347, 362, 389
Kunitz, Chris, 344, 400, 487
Kurri, Jari, 53, 529
Kuznetsov, Evgeny, 557

•L•

Lacroix, Andre, 576
Lacroix, Eric, 69, 100, 102
Ladd, Andrew, 437, 480
Lafleur, Guy, 89, 379
Lafontaine, Pat, 68
LaForest, Mark, ii
Laforge, Claude, 574
Laich, Brooks, 373, 520
Lake Placid (1980 Olympics), 51, 69, 154, 204, 418, 513
Lalime, Patrick, 184, 209, 239
Lamoriello, Lou, 186, 265, 329, 422
Lang, Robert, 154
Langenbrunner, Jamie, 267-268, 272, 334, 372
Langkow, Daymond, 133, 164, 187, 218, 251, 363, 446
Lanzi, Dr. Guy, 117, 147
Laperriere, Ian, 8, 409, 449, 458, 498, 514, 546, 570
Laperriere, Jacques, 92
Lapierre, Daniel, 566
Lapierre, Maxim, 380
Lapointe, Claude, 229, 238, 254
Lapointe, Leora, 268
Lapointe, Martin, 85
Lapointe, Rick, 58, 581
Laraque, Georges, 366, 394
Larocque, Michel, 581
Larue, Dennis, 483
Latendresse, Guillaume, 382
Laughton, Scott, 497, 537, 549
Laviolette, Peter, 3, 313, 316, 410, 413-424, 426-435, 437-440, 442-443, 452-453, 457-459, 461-473, 476, 478, 480-489, 491-495, 498, 500-502, 504, 509, 511, 513-516, 539, 553, 567
Lawrence, Mark, 143
LCB Line (Leach, Clarke, Barber), 18, 26
Leach, Jamie, 49
Leach, Reggie, ii, 3, 8, 18-19, 22, 26, 31, 44, 48-49, 53, 64, 130, 172, 203, 446, 489, 530, 573, 575
Lecavalier, Vincent, 278, 353, 456, 511, 536, 549
LeClair, Butch, 173
LeClair, John, ii, 3, 10, 20, 56, 66, 68-69, 71, 73, 75-78, 80-81, 83-93, 97-109, 113-117, 119-127, 130, 132, 134, 136, 138-145, 147, 150-152, 154-168, 171-173, 177, 180-196, 198-206, 208, 210-211, 213, 216-217, 220, 222-225, 227-235, 237-242, 244-245, 253-255, 257, 259, 264-265, 269-271, 273-275, 277-279, 281-284, 286-287, 289, 292, 298-299, 303-304, 309, 331, 357, 446, 456, 509, 537, 573-574, 576
Leetch, Brian, 69, 81-82, 273, 332
Lefebvre, Guillaume, 229
Leger, Gilles, 215
Legion of Doom Line, 80, 84, 92, 116, 145, 171, 456, 507
Lehtonen, Kari, 218, 337, 371

Leighton, Michael, 344, 416, 433, 445, 455, 467, 475, 497, 503
Leino, Ville, 404, 418, 441, 455, 469, 475, 509, 578
Leiweke, Tim, 57, 197
Lemaire, Jacques, 423
Lemelin, Reggie, 136, 260, 364
Lemieux, Claude, 161-162
Lemieux, Mario, 63, 75, 77, 177, 188, 205, 300, 352, 379, 479
Leonardi, Dave ("Signman"), 11
Leopold, Jordan, 467
Leschyshyn, Curtis, 239
Lessio, Lucas, 553
Letang, Kris, 386, 411, 458, 488, 521, 539
Lethbridge Hurricanes, 389
Levitt Report, 298
Levitt, Arthur, 298
Levy, Mike, 296, 389
Levy, Steve, 158
Lewis, Bryan, 126
Lewis, Dr. David, 256
Lewis, Frank, 18, 219, 581
Lewis, Helen, 220
Lidstrom, Nicklas, 102, 316
Light, Herb, 170
Lilja, Andreas, 478
Lillienfield, Gerald, 13
Lindbergh family, 52
Lindbergh, Pelle, 1-3, 5-6, 8-9, 20, 38-39, 46, 51-52, 63, 131, 182, 195, 526, 574-576, 581
Linden, Trevor, 103, 300, 302, 308, 533
Lindros, Bonnie, 90, 179
Lindros, Brett, 90-91, 117
Lindros, Carl, 90, 101, 112, 123, 130, 146, 179, 180, 197
Lindros, Eric, ii, 3, 5-6, 8, 16, 19, 30, 56-57, 67-73, 75-78, 80-93, 95-109, 111-125, 127, 130, 132-134, 136-144, 146-151, 153, 156, 160, 162-168, 171-173, 177, 179-180, 182, 184, 188-190, 194, 196-197, 200, 203, 205, 208, 212, 216, 221, 228, 246-247, 258, 271, 285, 290, 292, 303, 306-307, 309-310, 330, 342, 365-366, 374, 406, 446, 448, 456, 470, 482-484, 486, 509, 526, 537, 566, 573-574, 576-577
Lindstrom, Curt, 51
Linkoping, 300
Linseman, Ken, ii, 20-21, 30, 38, 54, 352, 448, 574
Lithuania, 69, 72
Little Flyers, 135
Little, Neil, ii, 109, 208, 260
Locks of Love, 508
Lomakin, Andrei, 581
Lombardi, Dean, 7, 57, 95, 249, 303, 476, 505-506, 526, 553
London Knights, 357
Long, Bill, 58
Long, Brian, 296
Lonsberry, Ross, 31, 35, 534, 574, 581
Los Angeles Kings, 7, 32, 46, 54, 57-58, 62, 93, 109, 118, 121, 130, 138, 182, 189, 198, 223, 228-229, 255, 293, 306, 328, 372, 390, 395, 397, 409, 413, 447, 476-477, 479-480, 496, 498, 500, 505-507, 512, 520, 525-529, 533-534, 538, 541, 547-548, 550, 553, 570
Los Angeles Times, The, 505
Lovejoy, Ben, 489
Low, Ron, 215
Lowe, Kevin, 302, 357-358
Luce, Don, 143, 340, 348, 358, 449
Lucic, Milan, 427, 469, 520
Ludwig, Craig, 225
Lugano, 390
Lukowich, Brad, 226, 280, 344
Lumme, Jyrki, 235
Lundmark, Jamie, 190
Lundqvist, Henrik, 314, 333, 364, 371, 392, 420, 475, 521, 537, 549, 566, 576
Luongo, Roberto, 480
Lupien, Gilles, 317, 407
Lupul, Joffrey, 354, 358, 390, 405, 450, 499, 504, 520, 575
Luukko, Nick, 455
Luukko, Peter, 77, 302, 328, 342, 352, 406, 455, 511, 517, 533
Lydman, Toni, 319, 321
Lyon, Bill, 112

•M•

MacAdam, Al, 48
MacArthur, Clarke, 369
MacDonald, Andrew, 353, 520, 536, 548
MacInnis, Al, 75
MacKinnon, Nathan, 537
MacLeish, Carolyn, 202
MacLeish, Rick, 1, 3, 17, 22, 24, 27, 31-32, 35, 44, 53, 61, 75, 92, 172, 202, 245, 534, 565, 572, 577, 581
MacSweyn, Ralph, 581
MacTavish, Craig, 89, 98, 188
Madden, John, 268, 372, 437
Madigan, Martha, 67
Madison Square Garden, 34, 44, 68, 71, 82, 111, 113, 143, 183, 194, 197, 226, 256, 291-292, 317, 333, 343, 349, 364, 368, 370-371, 396, 399, 416, 420, 462-463, 481, 500, 520, 522, 537, 551, 576
Maine Mariners, 109
Malakhov, Vladimir, 264, 303
Malhotra, Manny, 516
Malik, Marek, 371
Malkin, Evgeni, 339, 384, 386, 399, 486, 566
Malone, Ryan, 384, 394
Manderville, Kent, 148
Maneluk, Mike, 109, 113
Maniago, Cesare, 36
Manning, Brandon, 536
Maple Leaf Gardens, 59, 76, 100, 575
Marchand, Brad, 470, 479, 542
Marine Midland Arena, 71, 79, 81
Markov, Andrei, 380, 432
Markov, Danny, 189, 258-259, 271-272, 297, 304, 576
Marleau, Patrick, 538
Marouelli, Dan, 152, 236
Marsh, Brad, ii, 3, 9, 37-40, 49-50, 63
Martin, Jacques, 181, 241, 253, 264, 397, 432
Martin, Paul, 268, 372, 425, 458, 489
Martinek, Radek, 372
Martinsen, Andreas, 557
Mason, Ron, 36, 177
Mason, Steve, 481, 501, 503, 512, 548, 559, 566
Massachusetts Eye and Ear Infirmary, 351
Massachusetts General Hospital, 343
Masterton Trophy, 8, 34
Matvichuk, Richard, 216
Maurice, Paul, 141
Maxwell, Kevin, 357
Mayers, Jamal, 143
McAllister, Chris, 182, 221
McAmmond, Dean, 190, 361, 425
McCabe, Bryan, 273-274, 416
McCammon, Bob, 20, 23, 26, 32, 36, 38, 49, 61, 175
McCarthy, Kevin, 28, 415, 514
McCarthy, Sandy, 121, 130, 149
McCarty, Darren, 84
McCauley, Wes, 373
McCleary, Trent, 142
McCormick, Cody, 458, 466
McCreary, Bill, 227, 400, 439
McCrimmon, Brad, 32, 37, 42, 61, 75, 450, 478, 577, 581
McCrossin, Jim, 113, 122, 130-131, 238, 291, 296, 330, 357, 407
McCrossin, Robyn, 130, 132
McDavid, Connor, 547
McDonagh, Ryan, 357, 483, 523, 537, 554
McDonald, Colin, 551
McEachern, Shawn, 139, 211
McElhinney, Curtis, 517, 566
McGillis, Dan, 105, 117, 187, 191, 221, 223, 225, 296
McGinn, Tye, 500, 521, 535
McGinnis, Dr. Gerri, 160, 310
McGrattan, Brian, 361
McGuire, E.J., 38-40, 187, 201, 206, 464, 548, 581
MCI Center, 102, 198, 575
McIlhargey, Jack, 415
McIlrath, Dylan, 554
McKay, Randy, 160
McKay-Leach, Kate, 48
McKee, Jay, 80, 192, 194, 319
McLaren, Kyle, 397
McLellan, Todd, 545
McLeod, Don, 581
McMaster, Sam, 175
McNabb, Dr. Ian, 42
McQuaid, Adam, 427, 461, 470
McSorley, Marty, 93
Meadowlands, 42, 92, 116, 138, 140, 143, 161, 171, 201, 205, 209, 225, 227, 230, 255, 257, 269, 271, 313, 316, 318, 341, 343, 350, 365
Medford Ice Rink, 299
Meehan, Donnie, 96, 110-111, 135, 218, 476, 535, 576
Meehan, Gerry, 576
Megna, Jayson, 521
Mel Richman Inc., 10
Mellanby, Scott, 40, 577
Mellon Arena, 188, 341, 384, 387, 402, 419, 573
Melnyk, Jerry, 3, 45, 47, 51, 117, 140, 195, 218, 527, 572, 581
Memorial Auditorium, 36, 64, 97
Memorial Cup, 18, 30, 236, 247, 260, 273, 504
Messier, Mark, 5, 53, 68, 81, 89, 103, 118, 197, 216, 290-291, 574
Meszaros, Andrej, 480, 518
Met Center, 21
Metallica, 100
Metallurg Magnitogorsk, 40, 132
Metropolit, Glen, 390, 435
Meyer, Freddy, 264, 314, 331
Miami Arena, 106
Michalek, Milan, 251, 369
Michalek, Zbynek, 486
Michigan Tech, 509
Mickey, Larry, 581
Mikita, Stan, 18, 437
Milbury, Mike, 134, 179
Miller, Dennis, 552
Miller, Gord, 186
Miller, J.T., 523
Miller, Ryan, 314, 319, 347, 367, 418, 464-465, 470, 520
Millis, Dr. Michael, 408
Milstein, Howard, 134
Minnesota Fighting Saints, 351
Minnesota Line, 71, 114
Minnesota North Stars, 19, 36, 53, 215, 303, 352, 410, 573
Minnesota Wild, 59, 127, 182, 190, 228, 366, 438, 458, 461, 466, 484, 490, 498, 518, 520-521, 537, 540, 555
Mintzer, Dr. David, 139
Miracle On Ice (1980 Olymoics), 418
Mironov, Boris, 262
Mitchell, John, 557
Modano, Mike, 139, 203, 226, 245, 258
Modell's Sporting Goods, 84
Modin, Fredrik, 279, 297, 316
MoDo, 307, 512
Moen, Travis, 433
Moger, Sandy, 71
Mogilny, Alexander, 163, 232, 273
Molson Centre, 69, 142, 225
Montador, Steve, 369, 466
Montgomery, Jim, 92, 171
Montreal Canadiens, 1, 6, 17-19, 21, 24, 36, 40, 44, 53, 65, 68, 76, 92-93, 109, 112, 120, 142, 171-173, 189, 200, 222, 246, 255, 257, 316, 331, 358, 368, 379-384, 397, 408, 418, 420, 432-436, 480, 512-513, 517-519, 525, 535, 573
Moore, Dominic, 433, 523-525
Moore, Greg, 463
Moore, John, 523-525
Moore, Steve, 296
Moorhouse, Christopher, 478
Moran, Ed, 107, 147, 220, 335
Moran, Ian, 77, 158
Moreau, Ethan, 96
Morel, Denis, 156
Morin, Samuel, 512, 534
Morris, 181, 252, 303, 329, 366, 399, 405-406, 416, 450
Morris, Derek, 399, 416
Morris, Pat, 252, 303, 366, 405, 450
Morrison, Lew, 18, 64
Morrisonn, Shaone, 374
Morrow, Brenden, 265
Moscow Dynamo, 360
Mottau, Mike, 372
Mountain, Steve, 70
Mowers, Mark, 348
Mrazek, Petr, 553
Muckler, John, 80
Mullen, Joe, 8, 360, 413, 507, 514, 528, 546, 567, 570
Mulvenna, Glenn, 247

Muni, Craig, 78
Murphy, Gord, 534, 546, 570
Murphy, Larry, 71
Murray, Bob, 19, 96, 119, 397
Murray, Bryan, 96, 341
Murray, Glen, 263, 295, 309
Murray, Marty, 199, 254
Murray, Matt, 559
Murray, Ryan, 557
Murray, Terry, 3, 56-57, 89, 95, 104, 171, 176, 248-249, 304, 329, 360, 390, 452, 498, 507, 527, 546
Murray, Tim, 546
Murray, Troy, 63
Muskegon Lumberjacks, 179
Mustaine, Dave, 381
Myers, Tyler, 465
Myre, Phil, 31, 577

•N•

Nabokov, Evgeni, 455, 485
Nagano (1998 Olympics), 102, 104, 116, 141, 144, 179, 204-205, 229, 519, 529-530
Narcanon, 256
Nash, Rick, 218, 522
Nashville Predators, 231, 300, 345, 355, 357, 419, 453, 498, 509, 529, 533, 535, 539, 554
Nassau Coliseum, 71, 140, 539, 551, 575
Nathan, Stu, 581
National Car Rental Center, 115
National Sports Consultants, 297
Naval Academy, 332
Nedved, Petr, 77, 122, 231, 262, 314, 333
Neely, Cam, 50
Neil, Chris, 211, 264
Neilson, Roger, 5, 8, 31, 91, 104, 112, 132, 175, 181-182, 188, 198, 209, 219, 247, 252, 273, 446, 581
Nemchinov, Sergei, 165
Neumann University, 292
Neuvirth, Michal, 540, 548, 555, 564
New Haven Coliseum, 329
New Jersey Devils, 27, 29, 48, 57, 70, 76-77, 81, 83-84, 97, 99-100, 103-105, 113-116, 123, 135, 138, 140, 143, 147, 149, 157, 160-169, 171, 173-174, 177, 182, 186-187, 201, 205, 209, 223, 227-228, 230-231, 249, 253-255, 257, 262, 265-273, 288, 296, 304, 308, 312, 317-318, 329-330, 340-341, 344, 348, 359, 364-368, 372, 390-396, 398, 410-411, 418, 420, 422-426, 432, 450, 453, 462, 475, 480-481, 484-486, 492-496, 500-501, 506, 516, 518, 520-521, 536, 538, 542, 547, 550, 554, 566, 576
New York Islanders, 9, 27-28, 30, 32-33, 36-37, 40, 42, 47, 52, 61-63, 72-73, 76, 78, 101, 103-104, 117, 120, 134, 143-146, 179, 185, 189, 195, 200-201, 209, 222, 226, 229, 239, 254, 256, 259, 266-267, 303, 309, 311, 315-316, 327, 339-340, 342, 349-350, 364-365, 368, 370-371, 393-394, 399, 408, 412-413, 415-416, 418-420, 428, 430, 453, 461, 464, 477, 484-485, 500-502, 511, 516-518, 520, 526-527, 538-540, 543, 551, 553, 558, 572, 575, 577
New York Rangers, ii, 5-6, 13, 17, 26, 28-30, 32, 34-40, 42-44, 51-54, 58-61, 63, 65, 71, 77, 81-85, 89-93, 95-96, 98, 101-102, 104-106, 110-113, 118, 121, 123, 134, 137-138, 141, 169, 173, 179, 182-183, 190, 194-195, 197-198, 200, 203, 205, 209, 212, 215, 225-226, 228, 231, 238, 262-263, 266, 291, 296, 301, 303-304, 308, 313-318, 328, 332-333, 341, 343, 358-359, 365, 368, 370-371, 384, 389, 391-393, 396, 398-399, 408-409, 411, 416, 418, 420-423, 453, 457, 461, 463-464, 478-479, 482-488, 496, 500-502, 516, 518-525, 538, 541, 546, 549, 553-554, 572-574, 576
Newell, Dave, 19
NHL Board of Governors, 109, 300
NHL Central Scouting, 251-252, 357, 464, 497, 506, 534, 547-548, 567
NHL Draft, 30, 42, 90, 134, 219, 252, 328, 479, 496, 506, 533-534, 547-548
NHL Entry Draft, 30, 42, 90, 134, 219, 252, 328, 479, 496, 506, 533-534, 547-548
NHL Players' Association, 135, 256, 298-301, 366, 499
NHL Scouting Combine, 357
NHL Substance Abuse And Behavioral Health Program, 256
Nichols, Nancy, 121, 138, 181, 252
Nicholson, Bob, 102
Nicholson, George, 31
Niedermayer, Rob, 255, 424, 466
Niedermayer, Scott, 160, 257, 268, 303, 405
Nielsen, Frans, 459
Niemi, Antti, 437, 439
Nieto, Matt, 538
Nieuwendyk, Joe, 273
Niinimaa, Janne, 68
Niittymaki, Antero, 217, 260, 297, 360, 392, 407
Niskanen, Matt, 303, 366, 489, 539, 554
Nodl, Andreas, 392, 414, 459, 466, 478
Nolan, Lou, 9, 199, 256, 402, 561
Nolan, Owen, 231, 435
Nolan, Ted, 79
Nolet, Simon, 23, 25, 46, 70, 109, 218, 251, 327, 446, 512, 567
Norris Trophy, 29, 73, 92-93, 355, 498, 528
North Shore Raiders, 229
North View Pentecostal Church, 253
Northwestern University, 146
Notre Dame University, 36, 38, 112, 137, 176
Novinky Sport, 244
Numminen, Teppo, 319, 529
Nurse, Darnell, 512
Nutter, Mayor Michael, 365
Nykoluk, Mike, ii, 10, 23, 45, 53, 571

•O•

Oasis, 67
Oates, Adam, 8, 207, 218-219, 327, 406
Obama, Barack, President of the U.S., 529
Odjick, Gino, 185
O'Donnell, Sean, 456
Oduya, Johnny, 372
Ohio State, 252, 296, 389
OHL, 38, 90, 98, 175, 181, 184, 361, 464, 477, 504, 506, 512, 567
Okhotnikov, Mikhail, 133
Okposo, Kyle, 327
Okubo, Takashi, 96
Olausson, Fredrik, 78
Olczyk, Ed, 311
Olde City Philadelphia, 353, 361, 379, 392, 397, 409, 417, 504, 508
Olympics, 51, 54, 141-142, 179, 204-205, 208, 216, 292, 298, 307, 315-316, 330, 333, 353, 410-411, 418, 446, 519, 529-530, 546
Ontario Hockey League (OHL), 38, 90, 98, 175, 181, 184, 361, 464, 477, 504, 506, 512, 567
Opera Company of Philadelphia, 170
Oratario, Anthony "Rock", 183, 223
O'Ree, Willie, 508
Orlov, Dmitry, 560
Orpik, Brooks, 340, 399, 488, 560
Orr, Bobby, 20, 26, 28, 41, 43, 54, 61, 64, 81, 208, 379, 416
Orr, Colton, 349, 360
Orr, Frank, 18
Oshawa Generals, 389, 497
Oshie, T.J., 303, 520, 545
Ottawa Senators, 72, 100, 102, 112, 114, 118-120, 123, 148, 183-184, 200, 203, 209-212, 219, 223, 239-242, 253-254, 263-264, 267, 310, 317, 390, 407, 456, 480, 484, 517, 578
Otto, Joel, 67, 103
Ouellet, Maxime, 394
Our Lady of Lourdes Hospital, 129
Outdoor Life Network, 308
Ovations, 67, 482, 574
Ovechkin, Alex, 406, 461, 554
Overhardt, Kurt, 497
overtime, 2, 5, 9, 18, 25-26, 30, 32, 37, 42, 44, 46, 53, 60-61, 63, 68, 70, 76, 80-81, 93, 104-105, 108, 115-117, 122-123, 125-126, 130, 137, 140, 142-145, 151-152, 155-159, 171, 173, 184, 191-193, 200-201, 203-204, 206, 209, 211-212, 223, 225, 228-229, 233-237, 239-240, 245, 249, 255-258, 263, 267, 276-278, 284-285, 291-293, 303, 309-311, 313-315, 317, 319-320, 324-325, 340, 344, 346, 348, 354, 363-364, 368-371, 373, 375-376, 378-380, 390, 392-394, 396-397, 399-400, 408, 410-411, 416, 418-419, 421, 424-426, 428, 431-433, 439-440, 442, 444, 446, 449, 458, 461-462, 464, 467-470, 480-481, 484-486, 488, 492-494, 500-501, 508-509, 516, 518-521, 531, 536, 538-540, 542, 549-551, 553-555, 557-558, 572-576, 594
Owen Sound Attack, 328
Ozolinsh, Sandis, 209

Pacioretty, Max, 512, 555
Paddock, John, 8, 390, 407, 456, 512, 534
Pahlsson, Samuel, 144
Paiement, Rosaire, 31
Paille, Daniel, 471, 542
Palat, Ondrej, 556
Palffy, Ziggy, 173
Palin, Sarah, 391
Panaccio, Tim, 72, 146, 197, 220, 235, 262, 292, 298, 330, 410, 450, 465, 472
Pandolfo, Jay, 163, 165, 270
Parent, Bernie, ii, 1, 3, 5, 8-9, 21-25, 27-28, 31, 33, 35-36, 40, 44-45, 48, 51-52, 54-55, 58-59, 64, 70, 90, 92, 98, 115, 127, 131, 134, 145, 155, 159, 169, 174, 179-180, 188, 190, 197, 245, 247, 290, 299, 308, 310, 350, 357-358, 360, 369, 387, 461, 464, 482, 485, 497, 504, 506, 508-509, 511-512, 519, 521, 530, 549, 556, 560, 567, 572-573, 575-577, 594
Parent, Rob, 98
Parent, Ryan, 345, 347, 357, 369, 391, 396, 398-399, 401, 403, 411-412, 417, 421, 426, 429, 437-438, 441-442, 455-456
Parise, Zach, 252, 418, 424, 497
Parros, George, 500
Patrick, Craig, 78
Patrick, James, 193-194
Patterson, Adam, 268, 570
Patterson, Dennis, 46, 109, 182, 251, 303, 446, 477
Pavelec, Ondrej, 484, 557
Pavelski, Joe, 369, 552
Peca, Michael, 75, 106-107, 151
Peeters, Pete, 51, 576-577
Pelletier, Jean-Marc, 120, 141, 177
Pelletier, Marcel, 22
Pennett-O'Neil, Dana, 202
Pennsylvania Hospital, 118, 156, 166, 198, 201, 412
Penrose Diner, 159
Perezhogin, Alexander, 310
Perreault, Yanic, 97, 125, 188
Perrick, Ron, 112
Perry, Corey, 251, 344, 395, 418, 552, 567
Petit, Michel, 75
Petrovicky, Ronald, 229
Peverley, Rich, 470
Phaneuf, Dion, 251, 513
Phantoms (AHL), 19, 26, 57-58, 67, 70, 101, 109, 113, 119-120, 124, 130, 132-134, 138, 143-144, 156, 170, 181-185, 188-190, 198, 202, 207-208, 217, 222, 226, 229, 257-258, 260, 264, 273, 289, 297, 299, 301, 308, 310, 312-313, 329, 332, 335-339, 341, 347, 358, 360, 362, 369, 390-392, 395, 397, 408, 410-413, 419, 452, 456-457, 461-464, 478-480, 485, 498, 500, 504, 515-516, 521-522, 535, 537, 552, 554, 567
Philadelphia 76ers, 14-15, 67, 99, 109, 169, 196, 257, 299, 461, 572
Philadelphia Business Journal, The, 16
Philadelphia Daily News, The, 16, 22, 68, 182, 220, 335, 387, 422, 542
Philadelphia Eagles, 13-16, 23, 54-55, 278, 298, 301, 571
Philadelphia Evening Bulletin, The, 13, 574
Philadelphia Firebirds, 70
Philadelphia Flyers, ii, 1-2, 5-65, 67-93, 95-127, 129-130, 132-166, 168-171, 173-177, 179-213, 215-242, 244-249, 251-286, 288-292, 295-325, 327-351, 353-387, 389-403, 405-450, 452-453, 455-473, 475-509, 511-529, 531, 533-543, 545-567, 569-578, 580-581, 584, 586, 588, 590, 592, 594
Philadelphia Inquirer, The, 72, 87, 95, 112, 142, 146, 186, 197, 220, 235, 262, 276, 297-299, 330, 343, 417, 472, 476
Philadelphia International Airport, 342
Philadelphia Orchestra, 129
Philadelphia Phillies, 15, 54, 392, 444-445
Philadelphia Ramblers, 220
Philadelphia Revolution, 292
Philips Arena, 149, 392
Phillips, Chris, 190, 211, 241
Phlex, 70
Phoenix Coyotes, 174, 196
Phoenix Suns, 138
Phoenix/Arizona Coyotes, 61, 75, 126, 146, 174-175, 196-197, 216-217, 223, 226, 229, 260, 293, 298, 350, 366, 449, 475, 481, 546
Picard, Alexandre, 335, 370

Picard, Michel, 190
Pierre-Elliott Trudeau International Airport, 379, 508
Pilar, Karel, 276
Pilon, Rich, 76
Pinder, Herb, 110
Pitkanen, Joni, 218-219, 299, 305, 355, 498
Pittsburgh Penguins, 25, 27, 44, 49, 61, 76-78, 83, 104, 106, 115, 142, 153-154, 156-159, 165, 173-174, 191, 204, 207, 215, 219, 230-231, 245-247, 301, 311, 314, 317, 327, 333, 340, 348, 360, 365-366, 368, 373, 384-387, 392, 395, 398-403, 405, 410-411, 416-417, 419, 435, 455-456, 458-459, 461, 477, 481, 486, 488-493, 501, 504, 512, 520-521, 525, 527, 543, 546, 553, 558-559, 573
Plante, Derek, 80, 139
Plante, Jacques, 24, 392, 429, 581
Plante, Pierre, 21, 61
Players' Association, NHL, 53, 70, 99, 101, 134, 179, 253, 256, 297-298, 366, 499, 505
Players' Emergency Assistance Fund, 316
Pleau, Larry, 30, 104, 190
Plekanec, Tomas, 380
Plymouth Whalers, 181
Podein, Shjon, ii, 70, 79, 91, 101, 114
Poile, Bud, 14, 195, 299, 572
Poile, David, 58, 300, 302, 355, 455, 509, 528
Pollock, Kevin, 276
Pollock, Sam, 122
Pominville, Jason, 319, 369-370, 466
Ponikarovsky, Alexei, 274, 494
Popovic, Peter, 156
Poti, Tom, 197, 373
Potulny, Ryan, 252, 341, 367, 411
Potvin, Felix, 71, 76
Poulin, Dave, ii, 3, 8, 20, 33, 36-40, 51, 61, 63, 169, 290, 410, 435, 504, 527, 572, 574
Pouliot, Benoit, 522
Powe, Darroll, 392, 413, 457, 463, 478
PPL Center, 535
Pratt, Nolan, 280, 369
Presidents' Trophy, 5, 239, 350, 559
Price, Carey, 368, 379, 432, 461
Primeau, Keith, ii, 3, 9, 11-12, 20, 70, 91, 93, 96, 102, 138-144, 146-152, 154-155, 157-163, 165-168, 177, 182-197, 199-214, 216-217, 220-221, 223-224, 226-228, 232-234, 236-242, 244-245, 248-249, 255-258, 261-293, 295-296, 298-299, 302, 304, 307, 310-314, 316-317, 319, 324-325, 329-333, 336-337, 341, 344, 362, 365, 435, 446, 551, 573, 576
Primeau, Lisa, 141, 160, 262, 292
Primeau, Wayne, 80, 106, 363
Prince of Wales Trophy, 83, 435
Princeton University, 299
Proctor Academy, 514
Professional Hockey Writers' Association, 97
Pronger, Chris, 3, 70, 139, 300, 303-304, 352-353, 358, 397, 405-406, 409, 411-429, 431, 433-435, 437-440, 442-444, 450-453, 455-459, 461-465, 467-473, 476, 478-482, 497-498, 500, 502, 505, 511-513, 521, 541, 546, 550, 567
Propp, Brian, ii, 3, 9, 31-33, 37-39, 52, 54, 63, 68, 120, 171, 251, 352, 382, 390, 394, 504, 527, 566, 574, 576-577
Prospal, Vinny, 100, 370, 389
Providence Bruins, 301
Providence Civic Center, 329
Provorov, Ivan, 450, 547, 565
Prudential Center, 350, 365, 423, 464, 494, 576
Prust, Brandon, 420
Pryor, Chris, 134, 251, 328, 340, 357, 406, 497, 547
Pulver, Ian, 300, 359
Puppa, Daren, 179
Putnam, Bill, 5, 13, 23, 47, 55, 169, 572, 581
Pyatt, Taylor, 324
Pyatt, Tom, 433

•Q•

QMJHL, 327-328, 512, 530, 567
Quebec Major Junior Hockey League, 327-328, 512, 530, 567
Quebec Nordiques, 37, 39, 63, 89-90, 109, 381, 383, 573
Quebec Remparts, 109, 227, 446
Quenneville, Joel, 104, 437
Quick, Jonathan, 395, 550
Quinn, Larry, 80
Quinn, Pat, ii, 3, 8-9, 15, 26, 32, 41, 49, 52-54, 56, 58, 61, 65, 80, 124-125, 140, 189, 195, 231-232, 238, 273, 275, 278, 315, 482, 537, 581

•R•

Rachunek, Karel, 239
Radivojevic, Branko, 261, 297, 299
Raduns, Nate, 393
Rafalski, Brian, 135, 160, 205, 334
Raffa, Sal, 413
Raffl, Michael, 353, 515, 537, 549
Ragnarsson, Marcus, 249, 297, 304
Raikin, Dr. Steven, 427
Ramsay, Craig, 26, 91, 93, 112, 133, 153, 181, 185, 187, 245, 253, 280
Rand, Ayn, 14
Ranford, Bill, 71
Ranheim, Paul, 180, 194, 226
Rask, Tuukka, 426, 428, 470, 542
Rasmussen, Erik, 192, 271
Rathje, Mike, 249, 303, 309, 332, 341, 353, 361
Ray, Rob, 183
Read, Matt, 353, 478, 514, 523, 539, 551
Recchi, Mark, ii, 3, 20, 92, 120-127, 130, 132-137, 139-147, 149, 151-152, 155-167, 171, 173, 177, 182-185, 187-193, 199-201, 203, 205-206, 208-211, 213, 216, 220-223, 226-228, 231-235, 238-242, 245-248, 254-257, 260, 263-265, 268-273, 275-277, 279-284, 286-289, 295-297, 309, 331, 416, 426-429, 432, 470, 489, 573, 576, 578
Redden, Wade, 211, 240, 264
Regier, Darcy, 348
Reese, Jeff, 410, 457, 475, 498, 502-503, 515, 542, 546
Reggie Lemelin Arena, 364
Reichel, Robert, 103, 233, 273
Reid, Dave, 146
Reid, Tom, 36
Renberg, Mikael, 68, 96, 133, 171, 174, 232, 446, 484
Rendell, Mayor Ed, 84, 129
Renney, Tom, 349
Rexy's, 504
Reynolds, Don, 138
Ribeiro, Mike, 310
Ricci, Mike, 16, 218, 303
Richard, Henri, 18
Richard, Maurice, 29
Richards, Brad, 278, 314, 483, 522
Richards, Mike, 3, 12, 252, 278-282, 285-288, 301, 303-304, 308, 310-315, 317, 319-321, 323-325, 327, 331-332, 334-335, 337-341, 343, 346, 349-352, 359, 362-367, 369, 371-387, 389-392, 394-403, 406, 411-412, 414-436, 438-440, 442-444, 446, 449-450, 452-453, 455, 457-459, 461-462, 464-473, 476-478, 480, 485, 496-497, 504-507, 523-524, 529, 562, 564-565, 567, 573, 575
Richardson, Luke, 6, 96, 133, 144, 175, 183, 188, 218
Richter, Mike, 89, 93, 106, 205, 576
Riley, John, 497
Rinaldo, Zac, 467, 535, 548
Rinne, Pekka, 540, 551
Ristolainen, Rasmus, 512
Robbie, Joe, 54
Roberts, Brian, 6, 559, 562, 569
Roberts, Gary, 232, 275, 365
Robinson, Brady, 546
Robinson, Larry, 36, 48
Robitaille, Luc, 81, 99
Robitaille, Randy, 330
Roenick, Jeremy, ii, 3, 196, 198-211, 216-217, 222-224, 226-242, 244-246, 250, 254-290, 292-293, 297-298, 300-302, 304-306, 329, 331, 359, 392, 574
Rogers Arena, 363
Rollins, Al, 149
Roloson, Dwayne, 437
Rolston, Brian, 144, 227, 256, 424
Ronan, Ed, 80
Rosehill, Jay, 501, 516, 535
Roseman, Howie, 301
Rosenberg, Dr. Steve, 33
Ross, Jared, 388, 391, 397
Rostick, Gary, 517
Rowan University, 339
Roy, Andre, 279
Roy, David, 122, 130, 133
Roy, Derek, 319, 369
Roy, Patrick, 103, 127, 196, 206, 437
Royal York Hotel, 236
Rozsival, Michal, 156
Ruch, Dr. David, 418, 511
Rucinsky, Martin, 296
Rupp, Mike, 255
Russell, Cam, 531
Russia, 82, 131-132, 134, 297, 304, 316, 407-408, 418, 455, 457, 478, 483, 496, 518, 547, 581
Russian Super League, 132, 360
Rutgers, 299
Rutherford, Jimmy, 526
Ruutu, Jarkko, 372
Ruzicka, Stefan, 252, 335, 367
Ryan, Bobby, 303
Ryan, Ron, 15, 98, 153, 166, 170, 198, 221, 230, 253, 301, 307, 328, 333
Ryder, Michael, 428, 472

Sacco, Joe, 226
Saddledome, 117
St. Jacques, Bruno, 218
St. Louis Arena, 41-42
St. Louis Blues, 41-42, 46, 59-64, 75, 104, 114, 121, 126, 139, 143, 156, 177, 190, 203, 216, 249, 327, 344, 396, 409-410, 413, 450, 458, 480, 506, 542-543, 551-552, 574
St. Louis, Martin, 278, 370, 519, 522
St. Pete Times Forum, 278-279, 286, 416
St. Pierre, Justin, 523
St. Vincent's Hospital, 262, 349
Sakic, Joe, 68, 96, 187, 196, 305, 313, 446
Saleski, Don, 7, 60, 574
Salo, Sami, 211
Salo, Tommy, 205, 210
Salt Lake City (2002 Olympics), 54, 58, 204, 216, 298, 316, 418
Salvador, Bryce, 494
Samsonov, Sergei, 394
Samuelsson, Kjell, ii, 75, 84, 181, 245, 337, 515, 526
Samuelsson, Mikael, 251
Samuelsson, Ulf, 77, 180
San Jose Sharks, 63, 69, 71, 95, 139, 187, 203, 293, 303-304, 328, 369, 392-393, 408, 412, 519, 538, 550, 552
Sanderson, Geoff, 152, 330
Sandstrom, Tomas, 86
Sanguinetti, Bobby, 328
Sanheim, Travis, 450, 534, 565
Sarich, Cory, 280
Saskin, Ted, 300, 302
Satan, Miroslav, 107, 140, 426
Sather, Glen, 68, 118, 190, 215, 264, 328, 422, 479
Sator, Ted, 36, 38, 50
Sault Ste. Marie Greyhounds, 299, 477
Saunders, Tim, 10, 98, 158, 299
Sauve, Bob, 229, 254, 331
Savage, Brian, 102, 137, 307, 316
Savard, David, 566
Savard, Marc, 426
Sawchuk, Terry, 149
Sbisa, Luca, 389, 406, 450
Scanlon Rink, 365
Schaefer, Peter, 241
Scheifele, Mark, 477, 557
Scheinfeld, Lou, 574
Schenn, Brayden, 351, 453, 476, 499-500, 505, 512-518, 522-524, 537-538, 541-543, 549-550, 553, 575
Schenn, Luke, 497, 500, 517-518, 521-522, 537, 553-554
Schmautz, Cliff, 581
Schmidt, Nate, 562
Schneider, Mathieu, 331, 397
Schock, Danny, 31
Schultz, Cathy, 202
Schultz, Dave, 3, 9, 11, 21-22, 33, 59-60, 64, 195, 412, 519, 536, 542, 554, 559, 561, 563, 574
Schultz, Jeff, 374
Schultz, Nick, 534, 553
Schwartz, Bob, 67
Scott, Dave, 6, 517, 559, 569, 571
Scott, Greg, 54
Scott, Joe, 3, 14, 54-56, 219, 581
Scouting Combine, 357
Scuderi, Rob, 384, 399
Seabrook, Brent, 438

Seidenberg, Dennis, 221, 276, 299, 301
Seiling, Rod, 19
Sekera, Andrej, 466
Selanne, Teemu, 183, 245, 411, 458
Selke Trophy, 19, 63, 143, 216
Semin, Alexander, 374, 412, 461
Sestito, Tom, 463, 478
Settlemyre, Dave, ii, 69
Shanahan, Brendan, 68, 83, 86, 102, 290, 302, 393, 396, 495
Shannon, Darryl, 79-80, 107, 140
Shantz, Jeff, 73
Sharp, Patrick, 20, 221, 258, 299, 301, 312, 332, 395, 437
Shaw, Dr. Brian, 256
Sheehy, Neil, 464
Shelley, Jody, 420-421, 456, 478
Sheptak, Dr. Peter, 124
Shero, Fred, 3, 7, 22, 26-29, 35-36, 38, 41, 43, 53, 56, 58-60, 81, 166, 170, 188, 195, 264, 314, 331, 341, 352, 452, 512, 520, 538, 546, 573, 577, 581
Shero, Ray, 28, 455, 512, 516
Shick, Rob, 125, 156, 275
Shields, Steve, 79
Shore, Eddie, 23
shoulder injuries, 44, 281, 395, 413, 488
Signman (Dave Leonardi), 11, 238, 376
Silberstein, Dr. Stephen, 146
Sillinger, Mike, 102, 145
Sim, Jon, 308, 314
Simmonds, Cyril, 506
Simmonds, Wanda, 506
Simmonds, Wayne, 3, 351, 353, 395, 476, 478, 480, 482, 484-487, 489-490, 492-494, 496, 498-502, 505-508, 512-513, 516-522, 524-525, 530, 536, 538-543, 549-554, 556-566, 575, 578
Simon, Herb, 552
Simonick, Rip, 79
Simpson, Todd, 142, 264
Sinatra, Frank, 170
Sinden, Harry, 41, 76, 87
Singer, Harlan, 581
Sinisalo, Ilkka, 76, 175, 457, 575
Sittler, Darryl, 5, 8, 26, 37, 188
Sixers, Philadelphia, 14-15, 67, 99, 109, 169, 196, 257, 299, 461, 572
Sjostrom, Fredrik, 366
Skate Zone, Flyers, 9, 50, 135, 181, 183, 185, 189, 197, 201, 208, 211, 216, 235, 242, 262, 295-296, 298-299, 301, 307, 327, 330, 361, 411, 414, 513, 519, 535, 541, 570
Skogkyrkogarden, 52
Skudra, Peter, 159
Slaney, John, 188, 264, 339
Slansky, Vaclav, 179
Slegr, Jiri, 159
Sloane, David, 399
Slovakia, 68, 221, 297, 299, 315-316, 418-419, 499, 519
Smehlik, Richard, 79, 108, 192
Smith, Bobby, 63, 145, 175
Smith, Claire, 186
Smith, Derrick, 175
Smith, Jason, 358, 362, 381, 389, 499
Smith, Judge Thomas S., 360
Smith, Kate, 7, 36, 166, 170, 230, 241, 321, 324, 376, 420, 469, 558, 574, 581
Smith, Mark, 203
Smith, Mike, 557
Smith, Neil, 96
Smithson, Jerred, 419
Smolinski, Bryan, 68, 264, 380
Smyth, Brad, 70
Snider Hockey, 10, 16, 301, 327, 365, 460, 499, 559, 562
Snider, Ed, ii, v-3, 5-10, 13-16, 19-23, 27-30, 36, 38, 40, 43-45, 47, 52-56, 58, 61, 64-65, 67-68, 70, 76, 80, 82-84, 87-88, 90, 95-96, 98-99, 101, 107-110, 112-113, 115, 117, 121-123, 126-127, 129-130, 136-139, 141, 146-147, 149, 152-153, 156, 159, 164, 166, 169, 174, 177, 179, 182, 185-186, 188-189, 194-198, 202, 210, 212-213, 215-216, 219-220, 222, 230-231, 235, 238, 246, 254, 273, 277, 281, 291-292, 298-302, 305-309, 311, 315, 321, 325, 327, 329, 333-336, 338-339, 342-346, 348-353, 358, 361-362, 364-365, 373, 384, 390-392, 406-407, 410-413, 421-422, 431, 435, 437, 447, 449-450, 453, 460-461, 463-464, 471-472, 475, 479, 484, 498-500, 502, 504-505, 508-509, 512-514, 516-517, 519-520, 525-526, 533-535, 538, 543, 545-552, 555-566, 569-578, 580-581
Snider, Jay, 5, 14-16, 20, 23, 38, 72, 80, 90, 163, 165, 192, 194, 218, 257, 270, 307, 319, 336, 352, 364, 370, 389, 397, 501, 516, 535, 538, 549, 555-556, 558-560, 563
Snider, Lin, 555
Snider, Lindy, 16, 123, 198, 323, 468, 552, 555, 558, 560, 562
Snider, Martha, 14-15, 67-68, 558
Snider, Myrna, 15, 538, 560, 581
Snow, Garth, 71, 86, 98, 140, 184, 226, 342, 511, 527
Sochi (2014 Olympics), 518-519, 546, 557
Soderstrom, Tommy, 527
Somik, Radovan, 221, 254-255, 297, 299
Somnell, Kerstin (nee Pietzsch) 51-52
Somnell, Kurt, 52
Sonmor, Glen, 581
Sopel, Brent, 419, 438
Soviet National Team, 87
Soviet Red Army, 8, 41, 129
Spacek, Jaroslav, 334
Spanhel, Martin, 102
Spectacor Management Group, 329
Spectrum, The, 1, 4-5, 9, 11-15, 19-21, 25, 36-37, 42-45, 49-51, 54-55, 61, 64, 67-68, 70-71, 77, 89, 95, 109-110, 133, 137, 146, 169-170, 172, 200, 272, 285, 301, 329, 352, 390-391, 410, 412, 416, 460-462, 526-527, 562, 565, 572-578
Spezza, Jason, 264
Spooner, Ryan, 542
Spoont, Dr. Stanley, 21
Sporting News, The, 199
Sports Complex, 14, 100, 254, 571
Sports Illustrated, 480
Springsteen, Bruce, 133
Staal, Eric, 251
Staal, Jordan, 343, 357, 385, 399, 485, 488, 516
Staal, Marc, 303, 346, 420, 521
Staffin, Allison, 394
Stafford, Drew, 466, 545
Stamkos, Steven, 461, 519
Stanley Cup, vi-2, 5-7, 9, 14, 20-23, 25-26, 28-29, 31-33, 35-36, 38-44, 48-49, 51-54, 56-59, 61-62, 64-65, 67, 75, 81, 83-88, 90, 92-93, 95-96, 101, 111, 127, 129-130, 133, 143-145, 151, 157, 159-162, 164-165, 168-171, 173-175, 177, 179, 183, 186, 194, 199, 202, 204, 212, 215-217, 219, 221, 225, 227, 230-231, 234, 239-240, 245-249, 253-255, 257, 259-260, 262-263, 265, 267-268, 272-273, 278, 283-285, 289-290, 292, 297, 299, 303, 316, 319, 327, 329, 331-332, 336, 342, 346, 350-351, 353, 360, 363, 383-384, 387, 391, 393, 398, 403, 405-407, 410-411, 416, 418, 421-422, 431-432, 435-437, 439, 441-445, 447, 450, 452, 455, 457, 462-463, 473, 475, 478-479, 483-484, 498, 500, 503-505, 507, 511-512, 514, 518, 520, 526, 528-529, 533-534, 536-538, 541, 545-547, 549, 556, 560, 562, 564-566, 569-570, 572-575, 577-578, 594
Stanley, Allan, 8, 581
Staples Center, 138, 413, 538, 553
Star Charter, 138
Stasiuk, Vic, 21, 27
Steckel, David, 373
Stefan, Patrik, 311
Stein, Phil (General Schultz), 11
Stepan, Derek, 522, 554
Stephenson, Wayne, 25, 581
Stevens, John, 57, 109, 133, 181, 301, 329, 333-335, 337, 348, 355, 360, 374, 390, 393, 408, 452, 473, 508, 528
Stevens, Kevin, 173, 180, 188
Stevens, Scott, 61, 91, 157, 197, 576
Stevenson, Turner, 114, 246, 268, 295, 308, 317
Stewart, Chris, 506
Stewart, Mark, 28
Stewart, Paul, 226
Stickle, Leon, 12, 42, 575
Stillman, Cory, 260, 279
Stock, P.J., 185, 193
Stockard, Alec, 574
Stolarz, Anthony, 497, 540
Stoll, Jarret, 549
Stothers, Mike, 119, 133, 154, 181, 187, 504
Straka, Martin, 154
Stralman, Anton, 521, 524
Streit, Mark, 381, 398, 419, 510-511, 536
Strome, Ryan, 477
Stuart, Mark, 430
Sturm, Marco, 416, 426
Subban, P.K., 433, 555
Substance Abuse And Behavioral Health Program, 256
Suchy, Jiri, 531
Sullivan, Mike, 556
Sullivan, Steve, 312, 419, 487
Summers, Danny, 18
Summit Series (1972 Canada vs. Soviet Union), 17, 87, 95
Sundin, Mats, 124, 232, 258, 273, 316, 370, 393
Suter, Gary, 68
Suter, Ryan, 251, 497
Sutherland, Bill, 573
Sutter, Brent, 61-62
Sutter, Brian, 62, 177
Sutter, Darryl, 57, 62, 95
Sutter, Duane, 61
Sutter, Grace, 61
Sutter, Louis, 62
Sutter, Rich, 61, 497
Sutter, Riley, 62
Sutter, Ron, 3, 32, 40, 61-62, 177
Svehla, Robert, 141-142
Svoboda, Petr, 195, 243, 485, 530
Sweden, 40, 51, 68, 103, 204-205, 215, 297, 299-300, 304-305, 307, 315-316, 335, 345, 356, 485, 499, 512, 519, 534-535, 540
Swedish Elite League, 145, 307
Swedish National Team, 51, 145
Swiss League, 390
Switzerland, 176, 204, 299, 315-316, 519, 529
Sydor, Darryl, 279
Sykora, Michal, 180
Sykora, Petr, 315, 384, 493
Syvret, Danny, 411, 465

•T•

Talbot, Cam, 524, 538
Talbot, Max, 309, 385, 400, 478, 513, 516, 542
Tallinder, Henrik, 319
Tanpa Bay Lightning, 15, 26, 38, 95-96, 98, 100, 105, 116, 145, 187, 218, 226, 231, 249, 257, 263, 278-289, 291, 297, 311, 314, 317, 335, 338, 342, 344, 364, 370, 389, 392-393, 410-411, 416, 418-419, 456, 461, 485, 496, 511, 518-519, 521, 549, 556, 577
Tamer, Chris, 123, 134, 140
Tanabe, David, 190
Tangradi, Eric, 490
Tanguay, Alex, 313
Taras, Dr. John, 267
Tarasov, Anatoli, 27
Tastykakes, 12, 255
Tatar, Tomas, 556
Taxin, Johnny, 55
Taylor, Bobby, 24, 129, 169, 188, 574
Taylor, Chris, 152
Taylor, Tim, 279
TD Garden, 397, 426, 429-430, 471
Team Canada, 17, 42, 68-69, 87, 103-104, 216, 518
Team USA, 42, 68-69, 316, 332, 363, 418, 519, 573
Temple University, 343
Teravainen, Teuvo, 497
Terry, Chris, 550
Tertyshny, Dmitri, 9, 130, 133, 168, 184, 198, 581
Tertyshny, Polina, 91, 131
Tertyshny, Sergei, 132
Thayer Academy, 226, 229, 293
The Pentagon, 198, 313
"The Star-Spangled Banner," 574
Theodore, Jose, 412
Theofanus, Paul, 496
Therien, Chris, ii, 57, 75, 89, 93, 99, 113, 130, 177, 181, 216, 248, 254, 292, 304, 329, 390, 398, 540
Therien, Sarah, 329
Therrien, Michel, 366, 399
Thomas, Steve, 124
Thomas, Tim, 348, 371, 416, 461, 470, 479, 515, 531
Thompson, Nate, 461
Thorburn, Chris, 371
Thoresen, Patrick, 369, 390
Thornton, Shawn, 416, 429
Thun, Anton, 501
Tibbetts, Billy, 207

Tilger, Shawn, 6, 15, 302, 307, 339, 360, 390, 569
Tim Hortons, 236, 253
Timander, Mattias, 299, 304
Timonen, Jussi, 340
Timonen, Kimmo, 3, 5, 42, 92, 315, 340, 351-352, 355-359, 361-363, 365, 367-387, 389-392, 394-395, 397-403, 406, 412, 414, 416, 418-419, 424, 428-430, 433-435, 438, 440, 442, 444, 452, 455, 458, 463-464, 466, 468, 470-472, 475, 478, 483, 485-492, 494-496, 500, 509, 511, 513, 516, 518-523, 528-529, 535-536, 539-541, 543, 548-549, 577
Titov, German, 142
Tkachuk, Keith, 96, 190, 216
Tobin, Fran, 56, 219
Tobin, Sylvan, 56, 219, 581
Tocchet, Rick, ii, 3, 7, 38, 61, 92, 114, 145, 148, 173-174, 177, 181, 245, 259, 303, 360, 410, 413, 446, 506, 530, 573, 576-577
Toews, Jonathan, 418, 437, 518, 539
Tollefsen, Ole-Kristian, 411
Tolpeko, Denis, 362
Tommy Dorsey Orchestra, 220
Tonelli, John, 30, 62
Torino (2006 Olympics), 307, 315, 410, 418, 519
Toronto Maple Leafs, 24-25, 38, 50, 54, 111, 123-126, 139-140, 160, 182, 188-190, 197, 205, 231-239, 242, 249, 258, 263, 266, 273-278, 291, 295, 310, 318, 338, 345, 367, 370-371, 398, 410, 419, 428, 430, 437, 457, 463, 480, 486, 511, 513, 520, 541, 546-547, 553, 558
Torrey, Bill, 21
Tortorella, John, 279, 411, 484, 545
Tose, Leonard, 14
TPS Turku, 260, 408
Traktor, 132-133
Traverse, Patrick, 189
Trenton, 64, 134, 169, 182
Tretiak, Vladislav, 32
Trottier, Bryan, 39, 89
Trotz, Barry, 462, 562
TSN, 38, 186, 301, 413-414
Tsyplakov, Vladimir, 151
Tucker, Darcy, 233, 274, 390
Tugnutt, Ron, 154, 157, 290
Turco, Marty, 455
Turek, Roman, 130
Turris, Kyle, 357
Tursi, Dr. Frank, 344
Tverdovsky, Oleg, 204
Twin Towers Civil Servants Emergency Fund, 198

Ukraine, 204
Ullman, Norm, 46
UMPC Presbyterian Hospital, 159
Under-18 World Championship, 360
United States Hockey League (USHL), 179, 292
University of Alabama-Huntsville, 391
University of Maine, 226, 296
University of North Dakota, 545, 552
University of Pennsylvania, 16, 198, 384
University of Toronto, 38, 274
University of Vermont, 172, 221
Upshall, Scottie, 345, 357, 463, 504, 577
USHL, 134
Utica Comets, 8

Vaananen, Ossi, 390
Valk, Garry, 124
Valley Forge Minuteman, 135
Valtin, Rolf, 112
Van Allen, Shaun, 240, 263
Van Impe, Ed, 3, 23, 28, 43-44, 64-65, 299, 529, 573
Van Massenhoven, Don, 226
van Riemsdyk, James, 357, 409, 452, 462, 470, 485, 495, 531, 553
Vanbiesbrouck, John, 20, 70, 105, 111, 117, 124, 130, 171, 179, 189, 205, 217, 486, 527
Vancouver Canucks, 32, 39-40, 51, 62, 72, 75, 100, 102-103, 113, 116-117, 138, 140, 143, 182, 196, 201-203, 227-228, 252, 256, 296, 299-300, 306, 313, 327, 330, 332, 337, 360, 363, 389, 395, 397, 410, 413-414, 437, 455, 461, 472, 480, 500, 515, 517, 539, 543, 550, 552, 574
Vancouver (2010 Olympics), 411, 418
Vandermeer, Jim, 226, 254, 258, 367
Vandevelde, Chris, 535, 545, 552
Vanek, Thomas, 319, 334, 367, 466
Varada, Vaclav, 151, 192, 239
Varekova, Veronica, 314
Varlamov, Semyon, 557
Verb, Doug, 84
Verizon Center, 313, 373, 377, 379, 417, 539, 560, 563
Vermette, Antoine, 267
Vernon, Mike, 84
Versteeg, Kris, 438, 463, 475
Vezina Trophy, 6, 8, 50-52, 126, 150, 243, 456, 464, 467, 470, 475, 526-527, 574, 576
Vezina, Georges, 392
Victoria's Secret, 314
Vigneault, Alain, 521
Viner, Dr. Edward, 25, 45
Virginia High School, 303
Visnovsky, Lubomir, 188
Vitale, Joe, 487
Vokal, Radek, 244
Vokoun, Tomas, 396, 412
Volchenkov, Anton, 241, 484, 496
Voorhees, 65, 90, 99, 103, 118-119, 131, 133, 135, 138, 142, 148, 176, 181, 201-202, 215, 283, 288, 295, 298, 320, 336, 353, 358, 361, 374, 392-393, 410-411, 457, 504, 535
Voracek, Jake, 3, 10, 351, 353, 357, 453, 476-479, 483, 486-494, 498-502, 505, 513, 516-525, 530-532, 535-540, 542-543, 546, 548-562, 564-566, 575
Voros, Aaron, 399, 420

•W•

Wachovia Center, 201, 255-256, 258, 262-263, 265-266, 275, 280, 284-285, 299-301, 307, 311, 314, 316, 321, 324, 333, 338-340, 346, 350, 365, 368, 370-371, 385-386, 391-392, 394-397, 399, 402, 406, 412-413, 415, 418-419, 421, 424, 431-432, 440, 443, 573-574, 576
Waddell, Don, 302, 346
Walker, Matt, 457
Walsh, Allan, 355
Ward, Aaron, 368, 371
Ward, Cam, 550, 555
Ward, Dixon, 106, 151
Ward, Joel, 516
Warrener, Rhett, 192
Warriner, Todd, 227
Warroad High School, 303
Washington Capitals, 29, 38-39, 56, 58, 71, 75, 143, 181, 223, 300, 327, 373, 375-376, 379, 408, 410, 520, 539-540, 553-554, 557, 559-561, 563-565
Washington Post, The, 375
Watkins, Dr. Robert, 182, 220
Watson, Brad, 373
Watson, Jimmy, ii, 3, 9, 25, 41-43, 65, 92, 195, 497, 529, 555, 573
Watson, Joe, ii, 3, 7, 10, 18, 23, 25, 41-44, 55-56, 64, 129, 299, 313, 373, 447, 464, 497, 529, 555-556, 573
WCAU 1210, 100
Weal, Jordan, 553
Weber, Mike, 466
Weber, Shea, 450, 498, 511, 533
Weight, Doug, 297
Weinberg, Phil, 15, 112, 180
Weinrich, Eric, 189, 222, 236, 254, 289, 293, 299
Weinrott, Edgar, 11, 554
Weinrott, Richard, 11
Weiss, Ron, 72, 97
Wells Fargo Center, 6, 9-10, 14, 25, 30, 42, 45, 59, 177, 458, 465, 467, 470, 481, 484, 486-487, 492-493, 500, 502, 511, 513, 516-517, 519-522, 535-537, 539, 543, 549, 551-552, 555-556, 558, 562-565, 569-571, 573, 578
Wellwood, Eric, 485
Wenzell, John, 70
Wesley, Blake, 346
Wesley, Glen, 231
West Point, 254, 266, 309
Western Conference, 285, 290, 304-305, 362, 405, 551
Western Hockey League (WHL), 23, 215, 247-248, 300, 534, 547, 565
Westfield State College, 453
Wheeler, Blake, 427, 557
Wheeling Nailers, 98, 453
White House, The, 529
White, Colin, 161, 166-167, 269, 424
White, Peter, 117, 144, 151, 163-164, 182, 186
White, Ryan, 548
White, Todd, 144, 211, 240
Whitfield, Trent, 429
Whitney, Ray, 384
Whitney, Ryan, 366, 368
WHL, 23, 215, 247-248, 300, 534, 547, 565
Wideman, Dennis, 426
Widener Law School, 54, 124
Wilkes-Barre/Scranton Penguins, 207, 301
Williams, Jeremy, 371
Williams, Justin, 20, 181, 199, 204, 216, 219, 225, 254, 259, 327, 332, 357, 394, 561
Willis, Shane, 207
Wilm, Clarke, 273
Wilson, Behn, 41, 54
Wilson, Ralph, 14
Wilson, Ron, 68
Wilson, Tom, 516-517, 539, 561
Windsor Spitfires, 303
Winnik, Daniel, 560
Winnipeg Jets, 262, 449, 480-481, 484-485, 557
Winter, Rich, 475, 527
WIP, 70, 76, 106, 299
Wirtz, Rocky, 437
Wise, Mike, 375
Witkin, Mark, 359
Wolf, Dr. John, 17
Wolman, Jerry, 13, 23, 219, 572
Woolley, Jason, 78, 108
World Championships, 51, 116, 211, 215-217, 244, 331-333, 360, 363
World Cup of Hockey, 67-70, 73, 103, 204, 278, 297-298, 353, 573
World Hockey Association, 24, 58, 98, 351
World Junior Championships, 132, 134, 140, 346, 358
World Trade Center, 198
Worley, John, 83, 122, 139, 146-147, 165, 179, 262, 277-278, 296
Woywitka, Jeff, 227, 257, 296
WPSG Channel 57, 112
Wregget, Ken, 77, 575
Wright, Larry, 48
Wright, Tyler, 154
WWED—What Would Ed Do?, 569

Xcel Energy Center, 182

Yandle, Keith, 518
Yanick Dupre Class Guy Award, 98, 449
Yanick Dupre Memorial Award, 97
Yaroslavl, 132, 253, 478, 547, 581
Yingst, Doug, 72
York, Mike, 342
YoungStars Game, 204
Yushkevich, Dmitry, 95
Yzerman, Steve, 105, 185, 191, 205, 518, 541

Zajac, Travis, 367, 372, 423, 493, 545
Zeidel, Larry, 581
Zelepukin, Valeri, 76, 113, 132, 180
Zepp, Rob, 538-539
Zetterberg, Henrik, 226, 518
Zezel, Peter, 38, 175, 410, 577, 581
Zherdev, Nikolai, 457, 475
Zhitnik, Alexei, 79, 106, 151, 192, 342
Zibanejad, Mika, 477
Zidlicky, Marek, 494
Zimin, Evgeny, 131
Zimin, Natasha, 132
Zinsser, Dr. Nathaniel, 266
Zito, Bill, 356
Zolnierczyk, Harry, 463, 479
Zubov, Sergei, 132, 265
Zubrus, Dainius, 69, 133, 182, 229, 246, 372, 423-424, 494, 536
Zuccarello, Mats, 522, 553
Zucker, Jason, 537
Zyuzin, Andrei, 190

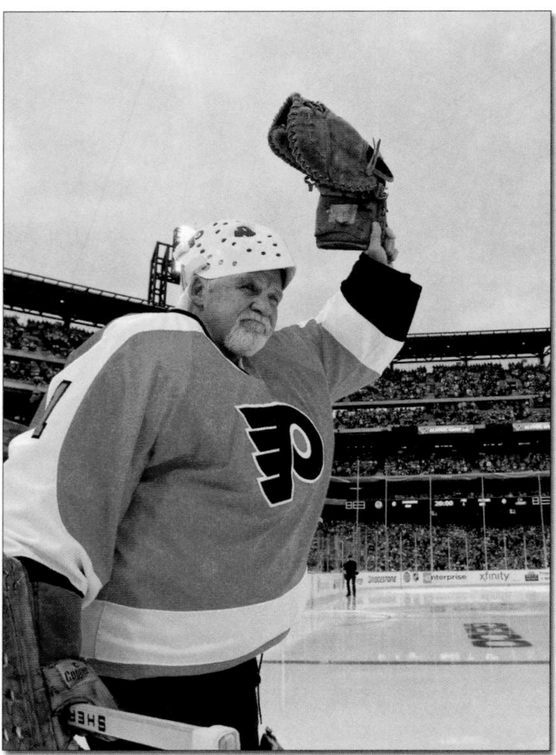

The Philadelphia Flyers at 50, clockwise from top:

Game Two overtime winner en route to the club's first Stanley Cup vs. Boston, 1974; Bernie Parent set to tend goal outdoors at the Legends Game that was part of the the NHL Winter Classic, December 31, 2011 and captain Claude Giroux saluting Flyer fans in 2016.

Bring on the next 50!

7-ELEVEN
7-ELEVEN
BAUER